Readings in

Social Psychology

THIRD EDITION

EDITORIAL COMMITTEE

Eleanor E. Maccoby
Theodore M. Newcomb
Eugene L. Hartley

Prepared for the Committee on the Teaching of Social Psychology of The Society for the Psychological Study of Social Issues

NEW YORK
HOLT, RINEHART AND WINSTON, INC.

Foreword to the Third Edition

TO THE SOCIETY for the Psychological Study of Social Issues *Readings in Social Psychology* has been a continuing source of pride and satisfaction. The publication of a third edition of this widely used and much appreciated volume is for the Society a happy occasion.

Newcomb and Hartley, in their preface to the first edition, spoke of future editions that would keep pace with developments in the field and so meet the needs of teachers and students. They correctly anticipated continuing expansion and development of the field of social psychology. Just as 50 percent of the selections in the second edition consisted of material that did not appear in the first, so does a large proportion of this new version consist of reports of empirical studies that have been carried out since 1952.

The task of surveying the literature of social psychology over a five-year period has become an undertaking of truly staggering proportions. To Eleanor Maccoby, who has carried out with devoted care the greater part of this task, the Society owes an enormous debt of gratitude. We here express to her, to her fellow editors whose wisdom in selecting readings we have come to take for granted, and to the contributors to the volume our heartfelt thanks.

One would like to think that a product of so much effort and care would last a lifetime. But today we have even more reason to be optimistic about the future of social psychology than did Newcomb and Hartley in 1947. There will be future editions of *Readings in Social Psychology.*

NEVITT SANFORD, President
Society for the Psychological
Study of Social Issues.

Preface to First Edition

THE aims of this volume

Teachers of social psychology have for some years been finding that their problems were increasing *pari passu* with the development of their field. They have been forced to take account of recent advances in such diverse fields as ethnology, statistics, clinical psychology, and psychiatry—fields which, a few short student generations ago, would have been thought of as belonging to other disciplines. At the same time, paradoxically enough, they find themselves increasingly self-conscious about having a discipline of their own. New sources of evidence and new tools of research, instead of forcing the social psychologist into a centrifugal whirl, have helped him to bring into clearer focus his own function. It is the peculiar province of the social psychologist to bring to bear upon his study of the behaving organism all relevant factors, from whatever sources and by whatever methods ascertained, which inhere in the fact of association with other members of the species. Most of these factors in the case of human beings have to do in some way with membership in groups.

Our aim in preparing this volume has therefore been to present illustrative selections of the ways in which the influence of social conditions upon psychological processes have been studied. Since we have tried to keep in mind the needs of student and teacher, we have deliberately sacrificed representativeness for what we hope will prove to be usefulness. We make no claim to have "covered the field." Many teachers will find that certain areas have been omitted entirely. We have, for example, included nothing in the field of animal social psychology. There is no section labeled "Personal-

ity," though many readings in other sections deal with social influences upon personality. The topic of delinquency and crime has been omitted altogether. The "great names" in the history of social psychology are not represented; we have not included selections from Tarde, Le-Bon, James, Cooley, McDougall, Ross, or Freud because their writings are elsewhere available, because brief passages from them are rarely satisfying, and because we have preferred to stress reports from the more recent period in which social psychology has come of age. We have also eschewed all discussions of the nature of the field of social psychology.

Editorial responsibility

Matters of policy by which the selection of readings in this volume was determined represent not merely our own predilections. Every major problem of policy and of selection has been referred to the Editorial Committee, and the original outlines have been many times revised at their suggestion. The specific selections included, as well as the policies by which their choice was determined, represent in nearly every case an editorial concensus. The Editorial Committee has performed far more than a nominal function. The original list from which nearly all the finally selected readings were chosen was submitted by them, and most of the proposals for revising and supplementing the early outlines came from them rather than from us. Though we have consulted them at every point except where last-minute decisions had to be made, they have granted us freedom of action whenever we thought we needed it. The general complexion of this volume, in short, reflects the wishes of the Editorial

Committee, but for many of its details the responsibility is ours.

We are happy to include several original contributions, prepared especially for this volume. In some instances these are newly prepared versions of research previously reported; some are anticipatory versions of fuller reports that will be made later. To these authors, whose contributions in terms of time have been very great, we are particularly indebted. We are especially fortunate in having one of the last articles to come from the pen of Kurt Lewin, whose name we have kept on the list of editors in spite of his untimely death just as this volume was going to press.

How to use this book

This book, as "an illustrative selection of empirical studies and of approaches to problems which may supplement systematic presentations and conceptual formulations," does not attempt to provide an over-all theoretical framework for the materials of social psychology. It can be only a supplement to and not a substitute for the continuity and systematization to be found in the standard textbooks, or which may be provided by a series of lectures by a single individual.

Each selection in the volume is reprinted as a unit, and there is practically no "connective tissue" provided by the editors. We have resisted the pressures (and, shall we confess, the temptations) to provide such textual continuity, recognizing that many instructors will wish to adapt the material not only by the deletions suggested above, but also by modifying the context in which single readings or whole topics are considered or by shifting their order. The sequence of the major sections and the ordering of the readings within the sections represents the orientation of the editors, but those who use the book are by no means bound to follow the order as presented. To provide better integration with a particular textbook or lecture sequence, an instructor may choose to recommend readings in almost any order he finds preferable. It may prove desirable to change the order of the major sections or of the assignment of readings within sections. Also, we should like to call attention to the possibility of cross-referencing the readings to reinforce one another or to establish new major units.

We emphasize the flexibility with which the materials of this volume can be used because of our conviction that nearly all teachers of social psychology, no matter how much they may differ in theoretical interpretations, have in common the need for reports of well-designed, objectively conducted, empirical studies. Theoretical controversies and differences of opinion apply to the context in which one chooses to consider the materials and the details of how the findings are to be interpreted. Fundamental theory is of paramount importance, of course, in the planning of research and in interpreting data but in the social sciences it is not true, as so many of the uninitiated insist, "that it is all a matter of opinion." The objective studies and empirical investigations cannot be gainsaid.

In the preparation of the selections for inclusion in this volume, we have taken liberties in the case of many of the readings in omitting some of the lengthier discussions of previous work in the field.

Future editions

We have a lively sense of some of the inadequacies of the following selection of readings. There are doubtless other shortcomings to which we hope our attention will be called by those who use it. We are convinced that substantial improvements in the present volume are possible if the experience of teachers and students with it is properly exploited. We will therefore welcome spontaneous comments and criticisms from those who have used the volume, for we hope to make sure that future editions will not only keep up with current developments but will also meet the changing needs of teachers. We see no reason why social psychologists should fail to apply their own methods to problems which they themselves face as teachers.

T. M. N.
Departments of Sociology
and Psychology
University of Michigan

E. L. H.
Department of Psychology
College of the City of New York

June 1, 1947

Preface to the Third Edition

SINCE the publication of our second edition in 1952 social psychology as a field has undergone a number of changes. The sheer number of articles and books published has been enormous. Certain areas, once taught primarily as subtopics of social psychology, have become specialized fields in their own right. Group dynamics and public opinion, for example, each now have an extensive literature, including books of readings, and are the subjects of specialized courses in many college curricula. New subfields have appeared which were not explicitly represented in previous editions of this book (e.g., perception of persons).

Publications have become more technical. The social psychology journals have seen more use of technical statistics, abstract symbols, specialized terminology, and rigorous experimental design. From the standpoint of the editors this growth is something to applaud, but it does pose certain problems for our new edition which is intended to be useful for general courses in social psychology, where many of the students do not have adequate backgrounds for dealing with the more technical materials.

In consultation with members of the Editorial Board, we have adopted the following principles, which have guided our attempts to solve the above problems and a number of others that arose during our consideration of articles for inclusion or deletion:

1. Fields which have undergone rapid growth and achieved semi-independent status continue to be included in this edition, although, of course, we cannot hope for anything approaching adequate representation of either the writers or the concepts in a particular topical area. The scope of this volume is still intended to be the entire field of social psychology.

2. We have attempted to keep the technical level of most of the selections within the purview of undergraduate students in psychology and sociology who have had only one or two previous courses in these fields. Elementary statistics are used, but we have attempted to eliminate higher-level statistics such as analysis of variance and factor analysis, and a number of articles have been revised by the editors or the authors to this end. Teachers may find they need to give their least-prepared students some help in understanding correlation coefficients and p values.

3. This edition carries even further the empirical principle adopted in the two previous editions. We did not feel we could do justice to both theoretical writing and research reports, and we elected to concentrate heavily upon the latter. We continue to feel (as noted in the Preface to the First Edition) that, while teachers of social psychology may differ widely in their theoretical approach and their interpretation of facts, they share the need for reports of sound empirical research which they can offer to their students as a foundation for theoretical thinking. Although we have not included essays that are exclusively theoretical, we have attempted to choose empirical studies which are relevant to theory, and which include a discussion of the theoretical implications of the research being reported.

4. Where early work has been refined, elaborated, or superseded by recent work, we hoped to be able to show the historical continuity of the work by including both the pioneering articles and the studies which grew out of them. We were able to do

this in a few instances, such as the Lewin "Group Decision" study and the Whorf article on language, but space limitations did not permit our carrying out this plan in a number of other instances in which we would have liked to do so. When faced with a choice between using an earlier "classic" article or more recent related work, we asked ourselves a number of questions: Would students be able to understand the "follow-up" work without having read the original article? Was the follow-up work too detailed, too technical, or simply too great in quantity to permit the student to grasp the main point at issue from one or two selections? The answers to these questions sometimes led us to retain the original article instead of replacing it with newer material, in the expectation that the teacher in lectures would go on from this starting point to present the later developments of concepts and findings.

We feel much more satisfied about the inclusions than about the omissions in this volume. We have every hope that the articles which *are* included will prove readable, provocative, and useful for the understanding of social psychology. Our greater concern is over the many equally good articles that we did not include, either because our coverage of the literature was incomplete or because the need to balance topics and points of view dictated another choice.

The arrangement of articles under topical headings is more eclectic, less systematic, in this edition than in the previous one. The editors examined a number of outlines of courses in social psychology taught at various universities, and it soon became evident that there is no single organizing concept nor theoretical point of view which could be used to arrange the articles in a way that would be satisfactory to all, or even most, teachers. For some teachers, *role* is the central theme around which the course is organized; for others it is *socialization;* for others, *the self*, and for still others *communication* or *interpersonal influence*. In order to make the book as useful as possible to the widest variety of teachers, we have simply grouped articles into familiar categories similar to those used in the first edition, in the expectation that teachers will want to regroup them in reading assignments according to their own ways of organizing the subject matter. We hold no brief for the particular set of categories we chose. We know that "leadership," for example, can be thought of as properly subsumed under "role"; or approached differently, it belongs under "interpersonal influence." We kept it as a separate category so that individual teachers could combine it with other topics in whatever way best suits their course requirements.

This book is the cumulative product of many people's efforts. G. E. Swanson's influence remains strong, since he played a leading role in the preparation of the second edition and much of that material has been carried over directly into the new edition. The Editorial Board, who provided indispensable guidance in selecting articles and deciding upon the over-all composition of the volume, were: R. F. Bales, Herbert Hyman, M. Brewster Smith, and Richard L. Solomon. We would also like to thank Richard Lent for his assistance in compiling the index. Finally, we owe a special debt of gratitude to the authors and publishers who granted permission to reprint their articles in this volume.

E. E. M.
Harvard University

T. M. N.
University of Michigan

E. L. H.
College of the City of New York

March, 1958

Contents

Language and Stereotypes

SCIENCE AND LINGUISTICS   *By Benjamin Lee Whorf*

Every normal person in the world, past infancy in years, can and does talk. By virtue of that fact, every person—civilized or uncivilized—carries through life certain naïve but deeply rooted ideas about talking and its relation to thinking. Because of their firm connection with speech habits that have become unconscious and automatic, these notions tend to be rather intolerant of opposition. They are by no means entirely personal and haphazard; their basis is definitely systematic, so that we are justified in calling them a system of natural logic—a term that seems to me preferable to the term common sense, often used for the same thing.

According to natural logic, the fact that every person has talked fluently since infancy makes every man his own authority on the process by which he formulates and communicates. He has merely to consult a common substratum of logic or reason which he and everyone else are supposed to possess. Natural logic says that talking is merely an incidental process concerned strictly with communication, not with formulation of ideas. Talking, or the use of language, is supposed only to "express" what is essentially already formulated nonlinguistically. Formulation is an independent process, called thought or thinking, and is supposed to be largely indifferent to the nature of particular languages. Languages have grammars, which are assumed to be merely norms of conventional and social correctness, but the use of language is supposed to be guided not so much by them as by correct, rational, or intelligent *thinking*.

Thought, in this view, does not depend on grammar but on laws of logic or reason which are supposed to be the same for all observers of the universe—to represent a rationale in the universe that can be "found" independently by all intelligent observers, whether they speak Chinese or Choctaw. In our own culture, the formulations of mathematics and of formal logic have acquired the reputation of dealing with this order of things, i.e., with the realm and laws of pure thought. Natural logic holds that different languages are essentially parallel methods for expressing this one-and-the-same rationale of thought and, hence, differ really in but minor ways which may seem important only because they are seen at close range. It holds that mathematics, symbolic logic, philosophy, and so on, are systems contrasted with language which deal directly with this realm of thought, not that they are themselves specialized extensions of language. The attitude of natural logic is well shown in an old quip about a German grammarian who devoted his whole life to the

From *Technology Review*, 1940, XLIV, 229–231, 247, 248. Reprinted by permission of the publisher.

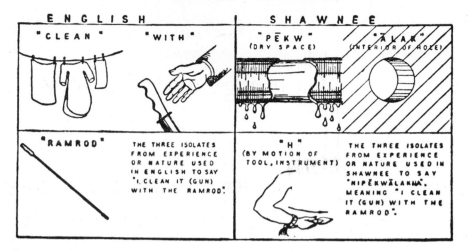

FIG. 1. Languages dissect nature differently. This figure illustrates the different isolates of meaning (thoughts) used by English and Shawnee in reporting the same experience, that of cleaning a gun by running the ramrod through it. The pronouns "I" and "it" are not shown by symbols, as they have the same meaning in each case. In Shawnee "ni-" equals "I"; "-a" equals "it."

study of the dative case. From the point of view of natural logic, the dative case and grammar in general are an extremely minor issue. A different attitude is said to have been held by the ancient Arabians: Two princes, so the story goes, quarreled over the honor of putting on the shoes of the most learned grammarian of the realm; whereupon their father, the caliph, is said to have remarked that it was the glory of his kingdom that great grammarians were honored even above kings.

The familiar saying that the exception proves the rule contains a good deal of wisdom, though from the standpoint of formal logic it became an absurdity as soon as "prove" no longer meant "put on trial." The old saw began to be profound psychology from the time it ceased to have standing in logic. What it might well suggest to us today is that if a rule has absolutely no exceptions, it is not recognized as a rule or as anything else; it is then part of the background of experience of which we tend to remain unconscious. Never having experienced anything in contrast to it, we cannot

isolate it and formulate it as a rule until we so enlarge our experience and expand our base of reference that we encounter an interruption of its regularity. The situation is somewhat analogous to that of not missing the water till the well runs dry, or not realizing that we need air till we are choking.

For instance, if a race of people had the physiological defect of being able to see only the color blue, they would hardly be able to formulate the rule that they saw only blue. The term blue would convey no meaning to them, their language would lack color terms, and their words denoting their various sensations of blue would answer to, and translate, our words light, dark, white, black, and so on, not our word blue. In order to formulate the rule or norm of seeing only blue, they would need exceptional moments in which they saw other colors. The phenomenon of gravitation forms a rule without exceptions; needless to say, the untutored person is utterly unaware of any law of gravitation, for it would never enter his head to conceive of a universe in which bodies behaved otherwise than they do at the earth's surface. Like the color blue with our hypothetical race, the law of gravitation is a part of the untutored individual's background, not something he isolates from that background. The law could not be formulated until bodies that always fell were seen in terms of a wider astronomical world in which bodies moved in orbits or went this way and that.

Similarly, whenever we turn our heads, the image of the scene passes across our retinas exactly as it would if the scene turned around us. But this effect is background, and we do not recognize it; we do not see a room turn around us but are conscious only of having turned our heads in a stationary room. If we observe critically while turning the head or eyes quickly, we shall see no motion, it is true, yet a blurring of the scene between two clear views. Normally we are quite unconscious of this continual blurring but seem to be looking about in an unblurred world. Whenever we walk past a tree or house, its image on the retina changes just as if the tree or house were turning on an axis; yet we do not see trees or houses turn as we travel about at ordinary speeds. Sometimes ill-fitting glasses will reveal queer movements in the scene as we look about, but normally we do not see the relative motion of the environment when we move; our psychic make-up is somehow adjusted to disregard whole realms of phenomena that are so all-pervasive as to be irrelevant to our daily lives and needs.

Natural logic contains two fallacies. First, it does not see that the phenomena of a language are, to its own speakers, largely of a background character and so are outside the critical consciousness and control of the speaker who is expounding natural logic. Hence, when anyone, as a natural logician, is talking about reason, logic, and the laws of correct thinking, he is apt to be simply marching in step with purely grammatical facts that have somewhat of a background character in his

own language or family of languages but are by no means universal in all languages and in no sense a common substratum of reason. Second, natural logic confuses agreement about subject matter, attained through use of language, with knowledge of the linguistic process by which agreement is attained; i.e., with the province of the despised (and to its notion superfluous) grammarian. Two fluent speakers, of English let us say, quickly reach a point of assent about the subject matter of their speech; they agree about what their language refers to. One of them, A, can give directions that will be carried out by the other, B, to A's complete satisfaction. Because they thus understand each other so perfectly, A and B, as natural logicians, suppose they must of course know how it is all done. They think, e.g., that it is simply a matter of choosing words to express thoughts. If you ask A to explain how he got B's agreement so readily, he will simply repeat to you, with more or less elaboration or abbreviation, what he said to B. He has no notion of the process involved. The amazingly complex system of linguistic patterns and classifications which A and B must have in common before they can adjust to each other at all, is all background to A and B.

These background phenomena are the province of the grammarian—or of the linguist, to give him his more modern name as a scientist. The word linguist in common, and especially newspaper, parlance means something entirely different, namely, a person who can quickly attain agreement about subject matter with different people speaking a number of different languages. Such a person is better termed a polyglot or a multilingual. Scientific linguists have long understood that ability to speak a language fluently does not necessarily confer a linguistic knowledge of it—i.e., understanding of its background phenomena and its systematic processes and structure—any more than ability to play a

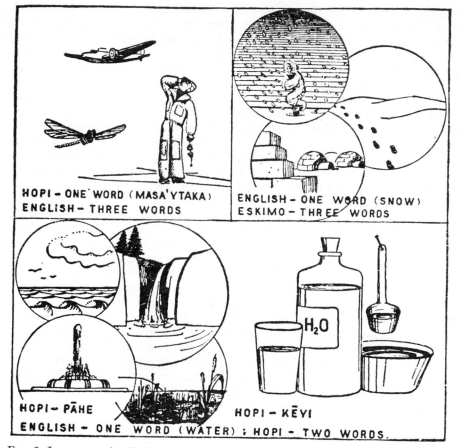

FIG. 2. Languages classify items of experience differently. The class corresponding to one word and one thought in language *A* may be regarded by language *B* as two or more classes corresponding to two or more words and thoughts.

good game of billiards confers or requires any knowledge of the laws of mechanics that operate upon the billiard table.

The situation here is not unlike that in any other field of science. All real scientists have their eyes primarily on background phenomena that cut very little ice, as such, in our daily lives; and yet their studies have a way of bringing out a close relation between these unsuspected realms of fact and such decidedly foreground activities as transporting goods, preparing food, treating the sick, or growing potatoes, which in time may become very much modified simply because of pure scientific investigation in

no way concerned with these brute matters themselves. Linguistics is in quite similar case; the background phenomena with which it deals are involved in all our foreground activities of talking and of reaching agreement, in all reasoning and arguing of cases, in all law, arbitration, conciliation, contracts, treaties, public opinion, weighing of scientific theories, formulation of scientific results. Whenever agreement or assent is arrived at in human affairs, and whether or not mathematics or other specialized symbolisms are made part of the procedure, *this agreement is reached by linguistic processes, or else it is not reached.*

As we have seen, an overt knowledge of the linguistic processes by which agreement is attained is not necessary to reaching some sort of agreement, but it is certainly no bar thereto; the more complicated and difficult the matter, the more such knowledge is a distinct aid, till the point may be reached—I suspect the modern world has about arrived at it—when the knowledge becomes not only an aid but a necessity. The situation may be likened to that of navigation. Every boat that sails is in the lap of planetary forces; yet a boy can pilot his small craft around a harbor without benefit of geography, astronomy, mathematics, or international politics. To the captain of an ocean liner, however, some knowledge of all these subjects is essential.

When linguists became able to examine critically and scientifically a large number of languages of widely different patterns, their base of reference was expanded; they experienced an interruption of phenomena hitherto held universal, and a whole new order of significances came into their ken. It was found that the background linguistic system (in other words, the grammar) of each language is not merely a reproducing instrument for voicing ideas but rather is itself the shaper of ideas, the program and guide for the individual's mental activity, for his analysis of impressions, for his synthesis of his mental stock in trade. Formulation of ideas is not an independent process, strictly rational in the old sense, but is part of a particular grammar and differs, from slightly to greatly, as between different grammars. We dissect nature along lines laid down by our native languages. The categories and types that we isolate from the world of phenomena we do not find there because they stare every observer in the face; on the contrary, the world is presented in a kaleidoscopic flux of impressions which has to be organized by our minds—and this means largely by the linguistic systems in our minds. We cut nature up, organize it into concepts, and ascribe significances as we do, largely because we are parties to an agreement to organize it in this way—an agreement that holds throughout our speech community and is codified in the patterns of our language. The agreement is, of course, an implicit and unstated one, *but its terms are absolutely obligatory;* we cannot talk at all except by subscribing to the organization and classification of data which the agreement decrees.

The fact is very significant for modern science, for it means that no individual is free to describe nature with absolute impartiality but is constrained to certain modes of interpretation even while he thinks himself most free. The person most nearly free in such respects would be a linguist familiar with very many widely different linguistic systems. As yet even no linguist is in any such position. We are thus introduced to a new principle of relativity, which holds that all observers are not led by the same physical evidence to the same picture of the universe, unless their linguistic backgrounds are similar, or can in some way be calibrated.

This rather startling conclusion is not so apparent if we compare only our modern European languages, with perhaps Latin and Greek thrown in for good measure. Among these tongues there is a unanimity of major pattern which at first seems to bear out natural logic. But this unanimity exists only because these tongues are all Indo-European dialects cut to the same basic plan, being historically transmitted from what was long ago one speech community; because the modern dialects have long shared in building up a common culture; and because much of this culture, on the more intellectual side, is derived from the linguistic backgrounds of Latin and Greek. Thus this group of languages satisfies the special case of the clause beginning "unless" in the statement of the linguistic relativity principle at the end of the preceding paragraph. From this condition follows the unanimity of description of the world in the community of modern scientists. But it must be emphasized that "all modern Indo-European-speaking observers" is not the same thing as "all observers." That modern Chinese or Turkish scientists describe the world in the same terms as Western scientists means, of course, only that they have taken over bodily the entire Western system of rationalizations, not that they have corroborated that system from their native posts of observation.

When Semitic, Chinese, Tibetan, or African languages are contrasted with our own, the divergence in analysis of the world becomes more apparent; and when we bring in the native languages of the Americas, where speech communities for many millenniums have gone their ways independently of each other and of the Old World, the fact that languages dissect nature in many different ways becomes patent. The relativity of all conceptual systems, ours included, and their dependence upon language stand revealed. That American Indians speaking only their native tongues are never called upon to act as scientific observers is in no wise to the point. To exclude the evidence which their languages offer as to what the human mind can do is like expecting botanists to study nothing but food plants and hothouse roses and then tell us what the plant world is like!

Let us consider a few examples. In English we divide most of our words into two classes, which have different grammatical and logical properties. Class 1 we call nouns, e.g., "house," "man"; Class 2, verbs, e.g., "hit," "run." Many words of one class can act secondarily as of the other class, e.g., "a hit," "a run," or "to man" the boat, but on the primary level the division between the classes is absolute. Our language thus gives us a bipolar division of nature. But nature herself is not thus polarized. If it be said that strike, turn, run, are verbs because they denote temporary or short-lasting events, i.e., actions, why then is fist a noun? It also is a temporary event. Why are lightning, spark, wave, eddy, pulsation, flame, storm, phase, cycle, spasm, noise, emotion, nouns? They are temporary events. If man and house are nouns because they are long-lasting and stable events, i.e., things, what then are keep, adhere, extend, project, continue, persist, grow, dwell, and so on, doing among the verbs? If it be objected that possess, adhere, are verbs because they are stable relationships rather than stable percepts, why then should equilibrium, pressure, current, peace, group, nation, society, tribe, sister, or any kinship term, be among the nouns? It will be found that an "event" to us means "what our language classes as a verb" or something analogized therefrom. And it will be found that it is not possible to define event, thing, object, relationship, and so on, from nature, but that to define them always involves a circuitous return to the grammatical categories of the definer's language.

In the Hopi language, lightning, wave, flame, meteor, puff of smoke, pulsation, are verbs—events of necessarily brief duration cannot be anything but verbs. Cloud and storm are at about the lower limit of duration for nouns. Hopi, you see, actually has a classification of events (or linguistic isolates) by duration type, something strange to our modes of thought. On the other hand, in Nootka, a language of Vancouver Island, all words seem to us to be verbs, but really there are no Classes 1 and 2; we have, as it were, a monistic view of nature that gives us only one class of word for all kinds of events. "A house occurs" or "it houses" is the way of saying "house," exactly like "a flame occurs" or "it burns." These terms seem to us like verbs because they are inflected for durational and temporal nuances, so that the suffixes of the word for house event make it mean long-lasting house, temporary house, future house, house that used to be, what started out to be a house, and so on.

Hopi has a noun that covers every thing or being that flies, with the exception of birds, which class is denoted by another noun. The former noun may be said to denote the class FC–B, i.e., flying class minus bird. The Hopi actually call insect, airplane, and aviator all by the same word, and feel no difficulty about it. The situation, of course, decides any possible confusion among very disparate members of a broad linguistic class, such as this class FC–B. This class seems to us too large and inclusive, but so would our class "snow" to an Eskimo. We have the same word for falling snow, snow on the ground, snow packed hard like ice, slushy snow, wind-driven flying snow—whatever the situation may be. To an Eskimo, this all-inclusive word would be almost unthinkable; he would say that falling snow, slushy snow, and so on, are sensuously and operationally different, different things to contend with; he uses different words for them and for other kinds of snow. The Aztecs go even farther than we in the opposite direction, with cold, ice, and snow all represented by the same basic word with different terminations; ice is the noun form; cold, the adjectival form; and for snow, "ice mist."

What surprises most is to find that various grand generalizations of the Western world, such as time, velocity, and matter, are not essential to the construction of a consistent picture of the universe. The psychic experiences that we class under these headings are, of course, not destroyed; rather, categories derived from other kinds of experiences take over the rulership of the cosmology and seem to function just as well. Hopi may be called a timeless language. It recognizes psychological time, which is much like Bergson's "duration," but this "time" is quite unlike the mathematical time, T, used by our physicists. Among the peculiar properties of Hopi time are that it varies with each observer, does not permit of simultaneity, and has zero dimensions; i.e., it cannot be given a number greater than one. The Hopi do not say, "I stayed five days," but "I left on the fifth day." A word referring to this kind of time, like the word day, can have no plural. The puzzle picture (Fig. 3) will give mental exercise to anyone who would like to figure out how the Hopi verb gets along without tenses. Actually, the only practical use of our tenses, in one-verb sentences, is to distinguish among five typical situations, which are symbolized in the picture. The timeless Hopi verb does not distinguish between the present, past, and future of the event itself but must always indicate what type of validity the *speaker* intends the statement to have: (*a*) report of an event (situations 1, 2, 3 in the picture); (*b*) expectation of an event (situation 4); (*c*) generalization or law about events (situation 5). Situation 1, where the speaker and listener are in contact with the same objective field, is divided by our language into the two conditions, 1*a* and 1*b*, which it calls present and past, respectively. This division is unnecessary for a language which assures one that the statement is a report.

Hopi grammar, by means of its forms called aspects and modes, also makes it easy to distinguish between momentary, continued, and repeated occurrences, and to indicate the actual sequence of reported events. Thus the universe can be described without recourse to a concept of dimensional time. How would a physics constructed along these lines work, with no T (time) in its equations? Perfectly, as far as I can see, though of course it would require different ideology and perhaps different mathematics. Of course V (velocity) would have to go too. The Hopi language has no word really equivalent to our "speed" or "rapid." What translates these terms is usually a

OBJECTIVE FIELD	SPEAKER (SENDER)	HEARER (RECEIVER)	HANDLING OF TOPIC RUNNING OF THIRD PERSON
SITUATION 1a.			ENGLISH..."HE IS RUNNING". HOPI ... "WARI". (RUNNING. STATEMENT OF FACT.)
SITUATION 1b. OBJECTIVE FIELD BLANK DEVOID OF RUNNING			ENGLISH..."HE RAN". HOPI ... "WARI". (RUNNING, STATEMENT OF FACT.)
SITUATION 2.			ENGLISH HE IS RUNNING HOPI ..."WARI". (RUNNING, STATEMENT OF FACT)
SITUATION 3. OBJECTIVE FIELD BLANK			ENGLISH..."HE RAN". HOPI ... "ERA WARI".(RUNNING, STATEMENT OF FACT FROM MEMORY)
SITUATION 4. OBJECTIVE FIELD BLANK			ENGLISH..."HE WILL RUN". HOPI ... "WARIKNI", (RUNNING, STATEMENT OF EXPECTATION)
SITUATION 5. OBJECTIVE FIELD BLANK			ENGLISH..."HE RUNS". (E.G. ON THE TRACK TEAM.) HOPI ... "WARIKNGWE". (RUNNING, STATEMENT OF LAW.)

FIG. 3. Contrast between a "temporal" language (English) and a "timeless" language (Hopi). What are to English differences of time are to Hopi differences in kind of validity.

word meaning intense or very, accompanying any verb of motion. Here is a clue to the nature of our new physics. We may have to introduce a new term I, intensity. Every thing and event will have an I, whether we regard the thing or event as moving or as just enduring or being. Perhaps the I of an electric charge will turn out to be its voltage, or potential. We shall use clocks to measure some intensities, or, rather, some *relative* intensities, for the absolute intensity of anything will be meaningless. Our old friend acceleration will still be there but doubtless under a new name. We shall perhaps call it V, meaning not velocity but vari-

ation. Perhaps all growths and accumulations will be regarded as V's. We should not have the concept of rate in the temporal sense, since, like velocity, rate introduces a mathematical and linguistic time. Of course we know that all measurements are ratios, but the measurements of intensities made by comparison with the standard intensity of a clock or a planet we do not treat as ratios, any more than we so treat a distance made by comparison with a yardstick.

A scientist from another culture that used time and velocity would have great difficulty in getting us to understand these concepts. We should talk about the intensity of a chemical reaction; he would speak of its velocity or its rate, which words we should at first think were simply words for intensity in his language. Likewise, he at first would think that intensity was simply our own word for velocity. At first we should agree, later we should begin to disagree, and it might dawn upon both sides that different systems of rationalization were being used. He would find it very hard to make us understand what he really meant by velocity of a chemical reaction. We should have no words that would fit. He would try to explain it by likening it to a running horse, to the difference between a good horse and a lazy horse. We should try to show him, with a superior laugh that his analogy also was a matter of different intensities, aside from which there was little similarity between a horse and a chemical reaction in a beaker. We should point out that a running horse is moving relative to the ground, whereas the material in the beaker is at rest.

One significant contribution to science from the linguistic point of view may be the greater development of our sense of perspective. We shall no longer be able to see a few recent dialects of the Indo-European family, and the rationalizing techniques elaborated from their patterns, as the apex of the evolution of the human mind; nor their present wide spread as due to any survival from fitness or to anything but a few events of history—events that could be called fortunate only from the parochial point of view of the favored parties. They, and our own thought processes with them, can no longer be envisioned as spanning the gamut of reason and knowledge but only as one constellation in a galactic expanse. A fair realization of the incredible degree of diversity of linguistic system that ranges over the globe leaves one with an inescapable feeling that the human spirit is inconceivably old; that the few thousand years of history covered by our written records are no more than the thickness of a pencil mark on the scale that measures our past experience on this planet; that the events of these recent millenniums spell nothing in any evolutionary wise, that the race has taken no sudden spurt, achieved no commanding synthesis during recent millenniums, but has only played a little with a few of the linguistic formulations and views of nature bequeathed from an inexpressibly longer past. Yet neither this feeling nor the sense of precarious dependence of all we know upon linguistic tools which themselves are largely unknown need be discouraging to science but should, rather, foster that humility which accompanies the true scientific spirit, and thus forbid that arrogance of the mind which hinders real scientific curiosity and detachment.

STUDIES IN LINGUISTIC RELATIVITY
By Roger W. Brown and Eric H. Lenneberg

Ethnocentrism is that state of mind in which the ways of one's own group seem natural and right for all human beings everywhere. Anthropologists are the natural antagonists of ethnocentrism. Their researches have long since taught us that the values of the American middle class are not dominant everywhere and that it is a kind of parochialism to suppose they ought to be. Nowadays everyone knows that life in Samoa is different from life in Boston, and at least as pleasant.

There is one kind of group practice, the use of a particular language, which we

Prepared for this volume by the authors, using excerpts from previously published articles.

have always thought of as conventional rather than natural. On this matter we have seemed to need no instruction from anthropology. Who is not aware that there are many languages in the world and that one is no more natural to man than any other? However, the particular languages with which we are likely to have any close acquaintance all belong to the same historical family—the Indo-European. English, French, German, Italian, Spanish, Latin, Greek, and Sanskrit are all members of this family, which means they are presumed to have a common linguistic ancestor. Because of their kinship these languages do not display the full range of variation to be found in human languages at large. To get some sense of that range we need to examine the anthropologists' descriptions of the languages of the Far East, of the American Indians, of the many peoples in the Pacific Ocean area. With this perspective Whorf [1] finds the variations among the Indo-European languages to be so unimpressive that he lumps them together as "Standard Average European" and contrasts them as a group with various unrelated languages.

When unrelated languages are compared, cultural relativism takes on a new dimension. The differences between these languages suggest that people speaking different languages must experience the world in different ways.[2] It appears that "culture" includes, in addition to values and technology and religious practices, a particular cognitive structure. Children acquiring their first language learn more than a set of vocal skills; they take on the world view of their group. There are innumerable linguistic contrasts that suggest interesting cognitive differences. We

offer here two examples, a difference of phonology or sound system and a difference of vocabulary. Through experiment and reasoning we have tried to find out what differences like these mean for social psychology.

A DIFFERENCE OF PHONOLOGY

The most obvious way in which one language differs from another is in the sequence of sounds used to convey any particular meaning. We say *city* where the Germans say *Stadt* and the French *ville*. Our first notion of comparative phonology may be that all languages make use of the same set of elementary sounds but make different selections and sequences for any particular meaning. This cannot be the whole story, however, since there are some sounds heard in French and German that never occur in English; e.g., the umlaut vowels and the uvular (*r*). Perhaps then we would do better to imagine a more inclusive repertoire of sounds, extending beyond English or any one language, to include all the sounds heard in all languages. The sounds of one particular language would be a selection from this source having more or less in common with the selection occurring in each other language.

A study of languages more remote than French or German shows that this conception of comparative phonology is inadequate. Not all differences of sound system involve the simple addition or subtraction of a few elementary sounds to an otherwise shared repertoire. There is a more interesting kind of difference in which two languages make use of the same sounds but put a different construction on them. In speaking English, for

---

[1] B. L. Whorf, *Language, Thought, and Reality*, J. B. Carroll (ed.), (New York: John Wiley & Sons, Inc., 1956).

[2] For early statements along this line see Franz Boas (ed.), "Introduction," *Handbook of American Indian Languages*, Part 1 (Washington, D.C.: Government Printing Office, 1911) and Edward Sapir, *Selected Writings of Edward Sapir*, D. G. Mandelbaum (ed.) (Berkeley: University of California Press, 1949). For more recent statements see Clyde Kluckhohn and Dorothy Leighton, *The Navaho* (Cambridge: Harvard University Press, 1946) and Whorf, *op. cit.*

instance, we sometimes sound our vowels for a rather long time and sometimes we cut them short. Speakers of the Navaho language also produce both long and short vowels. However, this variation in speech does not have the same status in the two languages.

The linguistic scientist notices that the length of the vowel in English depends upon the consonant that follows it. The vowel of *bad* is like the vowel of *bat* except that it is longer; similarly with *mode, mote; fade, fate; halve, half*, etc. The rule is that the longer vowel is used before voiced consonants such as *d*, *v*, and *b* while the shorter form is heard before voiceless consonants like *t*, *f*, and *p*. No two words in English are differentiated by vowel length alone. The difference in vowel length is always accompanied by a difference of final consonant. For this reason the linguistic scientist describes the long and short vowels as two forms or varieties of the same basic sound (he would say two *allophones* of a single *phoneme*).

In Navaho the situation is different. The length of the vowel is not predictable from any other feature of the word in which it occurs. Many words of different meaning are exactly alike in form except that the vowel of one is short and the vowel of the other is long. A difference of duration of the vowel is used to signal a difference of meaning. In these circumstances the linguistic scientist classifies the long and short vowels as distinct phonemes. In so doing he says that this change in speech has the same status for the Navaho as a shift from *o* to *i* or from *i* to *a* has for the speaker of English.

All that we have said so far about long and short vowels belongs to descriptive linguistics. We should like to know something about the psychological implications of these phonological differences.

Brown and Horowitz [3] have done a small experiment that clarifies the matter. They worked with a group of native speakers of Navaho and with a group of native speakers of English. The only special materials for the study were eight precision-manufactured color chips. These eight colors were drawn from the Farnsworth-Munsell 100 Hue Test for Color Vision. The 100 Hue Test is made up of chips equally spaced around the hue dimension of the color circle. Saturation and brightness are constant throughout the series. The eight colors used by Brown and Horowitz were drawn from the reddish-violet region of the spectrum. There was the same very small perceptual gap between each adjacent pair of the eight.

Each subject was tested individually. He was first shown the whole series of chips in their proper order and told that the experimenter had a way of classifying the eight colors. It would be the subject's job to discover this classification. The

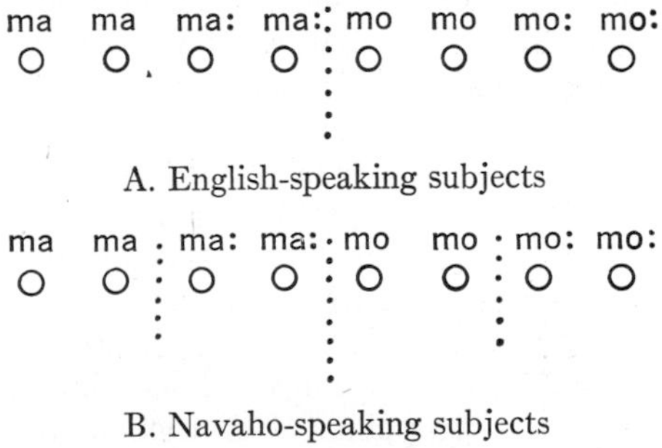

ma   ma   ma: ma: mo   mo   mo: mo:
O   O   O   O   O   O   O   O

A. English-speaking subjects

ma   ma   ma: ma: mo   mo   mo: mo:
O   O   O   O   O   O   O   O

B. Navaho-speaking subjects

FIG. 1. Categorizations of eight color chips by two groups of subjects.

experimenter then moved all the colors out of sight and, afterwards, exposed one at a time (in random order) naming each chip with a monosyllable that is not a color term in either English or Navaho. The subject simply watched this process until all eight had been named. He was

---

[3] This experiment was first reported in Roger W. Brown, "Language and Categories," in Jerome S. Bruner, Jacqueline J. Goodnow, and George A. Austin, *A Study of Thinking* (New York: John Wiley & Sons, Inc., 1956).

then shown the full series once again and asked to group them as the experimenter had grouped them with his use of syllables.

As Figure 1 shows there were four groups of two chips each. The groups were respectively named *ma, ma:, mo,* and *mo:*. The syllables marked with a colon were pronounced with long vowels (as in *mode*) and the syllables without the color were pronounced with short vowels (as in *mote*). The change from *a* to *o* is a change from one vowel phoneme to another for both English and Navaho but the change of length is a change of vowel phoneme for Navaho only.

Fifteen Harvard students whose native language is English, after hearing each color named once, generally divided the colors into two groups of four chips each as in Figure 1. The line of division corresponds to the line of vowel phoneme change. They did not make a division where the vowels changed in length. Since the break into two groups does not correspond to any usual color grouping made in the vocabulary of English we may conclude that it was induced by the change in vowel phoneme.

Fifteen monolingual Navahos given exactly the same problem generally divided the colors into four classes of two colors each as marked by the division line in Figure 1. They made breaks at the points of change in vowel length and these are not points of division in the Navaho color vocabulary. As shown in Table 1 the English-speaking subjects generally persisted in their two-group classification, through four repetitions of the naming procedure, and the Navahos likewise held to their four-group classification.

Were the English-speaking subjects unable to hear the difference in vowel length, the difference to which the Navaho all responded? Brown and Horowitz tried rejecting the two-group classification as erroneous and found, when they did so, that the English-speaking

TABLE 1

The Number of Subjects in Each of Two Groups, by Trial, Who Arranged the Test Colors into Four Categories

Group	Trial				
	1	2	3	4	5 or more
Navaho-speaking subjects (N = 15)	11	1	—	2	1
English-speaking subjects (N = 15)	—	1	—	—	14

subjects started to pay attention to the vowel change. Many of them then remarked that they had noticed the variations of length at the start but had assumed they were accidental. *We could have no better statement of the cognitive status of this speech variation for the speaker of English.* It is not purposeful and significant as is a change from *o* to *a*. It is not expected to signal a change of referent. The Navahos never thought of these variations as accidental. Both groups were perfectly able to hear the difference in question. Apparently, this test does not demonstrate a difference of auditory acuity in two societies but rather a difference in the range of potentially discriminable speech sounds customarily treated as equivalent.

When unrelated languages are compared this sort of phonological difference is ubiquitous. For instance, in English the consonant *p* is sometimes made with a resounding "pop" and is sometimes rather indolently produced. These variations do not change the phoneme; it remains a *p*. In Hopi and many other languages such a change in plosive force is a change of phoneme, like going from *p* to *b* for us. It is clear that different language communities sometimes put a different construction on the same range of experiences. Insofar as these experiences are only the sounds of speech no one but the student of perception or of language learning is likely to be greatly interested. But suppose the phenomena that can be variously construed go beyond speech to the referents named by speech, to the world of colors and textures, of persons and manners and places.

A Difference of Vocabulary

Foreign language textbooks commonly line up words in the new language directly opposite their English equivalents. This arrangement strongly suggests that while English and the new language use different words, they name the same referents. Of course we know that one language sometimes has words that have no equivalents in the other language; e.g., classical Greek has no terms for nectarines and the movies as the speakers of that language had no referents for such terms. This kind of discrepancy in vocabulary should turn up whenever one community is acquainted with a kind of animal or flower or machine unknown to the other community. Insofar, however, as communities are exposed to the same world the familiar European languages suggest that this world imposes itself on the mind with a given structure that is the same for men everywhere.

When we look at more remote languages we find vocabulary differences that suggest another view. Lenneberg and Roberts,[4] for instance, compared the lexicon of color names possessed by native speakers of English with the lexicon of monolingual Zuñi Indians. Groups from the two language communities mapped out on elaborate color charts the semantic ranges of their color terms. A very striking discrepancy occurred in the region that English speakers divide into *yellow* and *orange;* the Zuñi made one category of this whole area and

called it chupc?in:a. Whorf [5] has pointed out that the Eskimo has words for three kinds of snow whereas all of these would be called *snow* in English (see page 7). There are four biologically distinct classes of kin called *aunt* in English; mother's sister, father's sister, mother's brother's wife, and father's brother's wife. Murdock [6] in his study of kinship terminology in 250 societies found great variety in the manner of categorizing these kin, one lexicon having a distinct name for each, others grouping them together in various ways. These language differences are all of the same type. A given region of experience familiar to both societies (colors, snows, kin, etc.) is differently categorized in the vocabularies of different languages.

We shall look closely now at one of these contrasts to determine its psychological significance. Where the Eskimo has words for three kinds of snow, we have just the single word *snow.* Apparently the Eskimo can and does name certain distinctions for which English seems to have no names. Yet Whorf, himself, does name these snows in English. He calls them "snow packed hard like ice," "falling snow," and "snow on the ground." The difference in the two languages is not really one of a name and the lack of a name. It is rather a contrast between short single-word names and longer-phrase names. This is also true of all the other vocabulary contrasts of this kind. Murdock can name the four varieties of aunt, for instance, as *mother's sister, father's sister, mother's brother's wife,* and *father's brother's wife.* Other societies can use single words for one or another of these categories that we name with a phrase.

What psychological conclusions may we draw when a category is named with a short word in one society and with a

[4] Eric H. Lenneberg and John M. Roberts, "The Language of Experience," *Memoir of the International J. Am. Linguistics*, 1956, XXII, No. 13.

[5] B. L. Whorf, "Science and Linguistics." See preceding article.

[6] George P. Murdock, *Social Structure* (New York: The Macmillan Company, 1949).

long phrase in another society? We shall not want to say that the speaker of English is unable to distinguish the three varieties of snow named by the Eskimo. Whorf (a native speaker of English) appears to have grasped the nature of these distinctions and conveys them to us fairly well with simple line drawings. Is there then no difference in the psychological status of these three snows for the speakers of English and of Eskimo? We can make use, at this point, of a relationship discovered by the linguist George Zipf.[7] He has shown that there exists in many languages (all of those studied) a tendency for the length of a word to be negatively correlated with its frequency of occurrence. There are countless familiar examples of English words which have been abbreviated as they increased in frequency. The *automobile* has become the *car; television* is *TV; long-playing records* are *LP*'s. In French the *cinématograph* became the *cinéma* and eventually the *ciné*. The failure of such phrases as *damp soft snow* or *father's brother's wife* to abbreviate to a word suggests that these phrases are not often used, these categories not often named in English. The language that has a word for a category, especially a short word, probably has now or has had in the past frequent occasion to make reference to that category. We will go further and propose that the frequency with which a category is named is an indication of the frequency with which the category is used in perception and thought.

Brown and Lenneberg [8] have expanded the simple difference between a long and a short name into the variable they call *codability*. They suspected that when a category has a single-word name, subjects from the same language community asked to name instances of the category ought to respond quickly, to be in close accord with one another on the name, and to agree with themselves from one occasion to another. Such a category could be said to be highly codable for the community in question. Where a category elicited a longer-phrase name, subjects asked to name instances of the category should respond more slowly, show some disagreement among themselves in their choice of a name, and some disagreement with themselves from one occasion to another. Such a category would have a low codability for the community in question. There should then be numerous indices of codability.

Brown and Lenneberg put this guesswork to test. Their subjects were 24 Harvard and Radcliffe students who spoke English as a native language and who were found to have normal color vision. Subjects were individually tested. They were shown controlled exposures of single Munsell colors (24 colors in all). They were asked to name each color as quickly as possible following its appearance. Five subjects were recalled after a month's time and put through the procedure a second time.

Four measures were drawn from the data: 1. the length of the naming response in syllables; 2. the average reaction time; 3. the degree of agreement among subjects on the naming response; 4. the degree of agreement on two occasions for the same subjects. Table 2 presents the intercorrelations of these four measures. It can be seen that all are related to one another in the anticipated manner. Inconsistency within the group corresponds to inconsistency and hesitation in the individual. It is as though competing social tendencies are competing habits within the individual, a nice example of interiorized social norms. One measure, the amount of agreement between individuals, has higher correlations

[7] George K. Zipf, *The Psycho-biology of Language* (Boston: Houghton Mifflin Co., 1935).

[8] This experiment was first reported in Roger W. Brown and Eric H. Lenneberg, "A Study in Language and Cognition," *J. Abnor. & Soc. Psychol.*, 1954, XLIX, 454–462. Reprinted by permission of the authors and the American Psychological Association, Inc.

TABLE 2

INTERCORRELATIONS OF FOUR INDICES
OF CODABILITY

Measure	1	2	3	4
1. No. of syllables				
2. Reaction time	.387			
3. Interpersonal agreement	− .630 *	− .864 *		
4. Intrapersonal agreement	− .355	− .649 *	.773 *	

* Significantly different from zero with $p < .05$.

than does any of the others. It appears, therefore, to be the best single index of the factor all these measures have in common, the codability factor.

This expansion of the notion of codability into several measures suggests that its usefulness is not limited to cultural comparison. There seem to be three interesting cases to which it applies. There is, first of all, the cross-cultural case in which a particular category is more codable in one language than in another, e.g., *yellows* and *oranges* for English and *chupc?in:a* for Zuñi. In addition there are differences of codability within one language for different categories. Some collections of colors can be named in English with a single word, e.g., *red;* others require a phrase, e.g., *the blue-greens.* Finally, it should be possible to contrast groups and even individuals within one language community for their ability to encode the same category. What the meteorologist calls *cirrus clouds,* we may call *feathery, horsetail clouds;* what we call *schizoid traits,* the meteorologist may call *outlandish, antisocial tendencies.* For the first two cases where groups are being compared, the amount of agreement between individuals is probably the best

index of codability. However, this index cannot be applied to the comparison of individuals. For this purpose we should want to use one of the other indices, probably reaction time (which) shows a very high correlation with the amount of agreement between individuals.

Having English codability scores for 24 colors (this is the second case to which codability applies, scores for different categories in one language) Brown and Lenneberg studied the association between these scores and the ability to recognize colors. From the Munsell collection 120 highly saturated colors were selected, including the 24 for which codability scores had been obtained, and the full set was mounted on a large white board. Subjects were used who had had no part in the earlier experiment, were native speakers of English, and had normal color vision. The basic procedure was to expose simultaneously four of the 24 colors for which codability was known and then ask the subject to point to the four colors he had just seen on the complete chart of 120.

In pretests subjects were asked how they managed to retain the four colors in memory after they had been removed from sight. Most subjects reported that they named the colors to themselves and "stored" the names. When a color elicits a considerable variety of names (low-codability score), the possibility of recovering the color from the name should not be very great. On the other hand colors that are almost always given the same name (high-codability score) ought to be recoverable from the name. This expectation was fulfilled by the experimental results, there was a rank-order correlation of 438 [9] between codability and recognition scores.

Since the reports of the pretest subjects indicated that colors were stored in

---

[9] The ability to recognize a color can also be affected by its inherent discriminability from the colors surrounding it on the large chart. For the correlations reported here discriminability was held constant through statistical control. A full discussion of this problem appears in the original article.

TABLE 3

CORRELATIONS BETWEEN CODABILITY AND RECOGNITION SCORES FOR
FOUR RECOGNITION PROCEDURES

Group		No. of colors originally exposed	Length of interval	Content of interval	Correlation
A	(N = 9)	1	7 seconds	—	.248
B	(N = 9)	4	7 seconds	—	.426 *
C	(N = 16)	4	30 seconds	—	.438 *
D	(N = 9)	4	3 minutes	tasks	.523 *

* Significantly different from zero with $p < .05$.

linguistic code, it seemed plausible that the importance of codability scores would increase as the storage problem was maximized in the recognition situation. If, at one extreme, a single color were exposed, removed, and then identified with minimal delay, subjects might retain some direct trace of the color, conceivably as a mental image. Codability scores should, in these circumstances, have little relation to recognition scores. If, at the other extreme, the number of colors to be recognized were increased to four and a three-minute interval introduced between exposure and recognition during which the subject was occupied with some task, the importance of codability should be increased. Table 3 describes the experimental variations used. Groups *A, B, C, D* were believed to represent an order of increasingly difficult "storage" conditions. Group *C* is the major group for which results have already been described. The tasks which filled the interval for Group *D* were simple but absorbing, e.g., drawing a continuous line connecting in normal order a random array of numbers.

It can be seen in Table 3 that the correlation between recognition and codability scores does increase as the importance of "storage" in the recognition task increases. The particular order obtained would occur by chance only once in 24 times. In the simplest recognition situation the correlation is not large enough

to be regarded as significantly different from zero.

In general, we propose that the more codable category is more frequently used in perception and thought than the less codable category. It is our notion that this principle will hold whether the codability comparison involves different languages, different speakers of one language, or different experiences for the same speakers. The various behavioral consequences of these differences in cognitive structure remain to be worked out, but it appears that performance on a recognition task is among them.

THE USES OF THE NAMED CATEGORY

We have come to similar conclusions concerning a kind of phonological difference and a kind of vocabulary difference. English speakers seem to have the same potentiality for distinguishing vowels by length as do persons born into the Navaho language community. The English speakers are easily able to make the distinction when there is some reason for them to do so. However, they are less prone to make this distinction than are native speakers of Navaho. Probably the two groups do not differ in potential auditory acuity; they do differ in their habitual categorization of audible speech. Similarly, it seems probable that we are as capable as the Eskimo of discriminating varieties of snow but less prone than he to do so. In general it looks as if there is a potential for sensory discrimination characteristic of the whole human species. Language communities do not differ in this potential but rather in their manner of categorizing potentially discriminable experiences.

To treat potentially discriminable experiences as equivalent is to throw away information, and that may seem a surprising thing to do. Why should we call a number of different colors *red*, all sorts of different substances *snow*, all sorts of different people *Americans?* Why not keep track of all the attributes we can register? If we did so, we should experience very few recurrences in the world. What we think of as one person, for instance, proves on close examination to be continually changing—never precisely the same from one instant to another. A close examination of the sounds of speech shows that no two speakers of one language form their vowels and consonants in just the same way. What is more, no two pronunciations of the same speaker appear to be perfectly identical. If we noticed every detail our senses equip us to notice, life would be a stream of unique, never-recurring events.

We categorize because we want to know and need to know how to anticipate the future. It is a principal cognitive concern of every sort of higher animal to form expectancies and the terms of expectancies are categories. It is of no value to remember that on a particular day at a certain hour a change of hue in a light at a certain location was followed by a particular alteration in the pattern of traffic movement. This unique event will never come again. However, red lights (a category) regularly cause the facing traffic to halt (another category). It is of no use remembering that a particular person once said in a deep voice with his own peculiar inflection: "My name is Jed Prouty." That exact saying will never come again. Suppose we correctly categorize the name *Jed*

Prouty, recognizing, for instance, that it does not matter how loudly the *p* is "popped" but it does make a difference if the voice is added to the initial consonant to make *Brouty*. Categorized according to English phonology the name will recur and will stay with the man and can even be used as a surrogate for him. The phonology of a language describes the terms of significant recurrence in speech; the referents of a language are the terms of significant recurrence in the vast world outside speech.

A child spends years learning to make the correct matches between speech categories; learning to recognize dogs and call them *dog*, to recognize knives and call them *knife*, etc. This is an important part of culture transmission and it is prerequisite to a more important part. When one can identify the referents for words he can make use of the expectancies common in his culture. "Knives will cut," "sleeping dogs may bite if kicked," "if it rains before 7, it will be clear before 11," etc. These verbal formulations cannot be used for the guidance of action in the nonlinguistic world until the principal words can be "cashed" into referent categories. No one individual can, from his own experience, arrive at all the useful expectancies formulated by his culture. Furthermore, our language saves us a lot of disagreeable contact with bad-tempered dogs, poison ivy, and toadstools. In this sense, then, language is the repository of culture and the principal vehicle of culture transmission.

How does it happen that in their areas of common experience—vowels, snows, kin, colors, etc.,—the languages of the world have not all hit upon the same categories? With the sounds of speech, variations in categorizing practice probably must be set down as accidental, but with referents this may not be so. Perhaps the case is analogous to differences of vocabulary and referent categories that exist within one community. Consider that important class of referents we call *per-*

sons. A waitress may divide them into *cheap skates* and *good sports*. She is concerned with the prediction of tips and categorizes accordingly. Her categories are not relevant to the purposes of a physician (we trust). He is concerned with disease prognosis and treatment and categorizes patients into *diabetics* and *ulcer* cases and *hypochondriacs*. In our professional roles we focus on particular kinds of recurrences and categorize in the way that reveals these recurrences. Similarly, communities as a whole have their different purposes and, accordingly, their different vocabularies.

Even where purposes are the same, there is reason to expect some variation in categorizing practice. Everyone wants to predict what other people will do but we have no general consensus on the categories that are most useful for discovering general uniformities of behavior. Some people operate with ethnic categories; Negroes are expected to be superstitious and Turks to be cruel. Some people operate with physiognomic categories; nice faces go with nice behavior but look out for the evil eye. The behavioral sciences have not originated the interest in predicting human behavior; they have rather professionalized a prior general concern. The cognitive business of these sciences is essentially continuous with the business of the whole community; to find the categories in terms of which reliable important expectancies may be formed. The vocabularies of these sciences are a promise. If you will learn to categorize people as *marginal*, or as *socially mobile*, or as *compulsive*, you will find new and useful recurrences in the social world. Our predictions of behavior are not as good as we should like them to be and so we continue to recategorize and rename, looking for better expectancies.

The world around us is a human construction susceptible of more than one treatment. Various groups within our society—doctors, psychologists, bus drivers, skiers, philatelists—seize on different aspects of this common reality, aspects relevant to their peculiar purposes. Where our purposes are the same, we may still operate with a variety of categories because no really good set has been found. So long as we cannot predict all the things we should like to predict with the desired precision, the work of categorization is not finished. The languages of the world, like the professional vocabularies within one language, are so many different windows on reality. We should no more wish away the differences among languages than we should wish away the differences among ourselves.

THE FUNCTION OF LANGUAGE CLASSIFICATIONS
IN BEHAVIOR   *By John B. Carroll and Joseph B. Casagrande*

More than fifty years ago George Santayana wrote in his essay *The Sense of Beauty:* "Grammar, philosophically studied, is akin to the deepest metaphysics, because in revealing the constitution of speech, it reveals the constitution of thought and the hierarchy of those categories by which we conceive

Prepared especially for this volume. The two experiments reported here were conducted as a part of the Southwest Project in Comparative Psycholinguistics, sponsored by the Committee on Linguistics and Psychology of the Social Science Research Council under a grant from the Carnegie Corporation of New York. Experiment I was designed and conducted by Carroll; Experiment II, by Casagrande.

the world." [1] The world of experience is characterized by a logic that deals with continua; our experiences present themselves to us in almost limitless variations and shadings; and there are no boundaries between the parts of experience except those which are created by our perceptions.

If a language is to be used for efficient person-to-person communication about the world of experience, it must operate with a logic that deals with discrete entities—a logic of criteriality which distinguishes experiences on certain arbitrary and agreed-upon terms. When we give proper names to individual persons, pet animals, and geographical locations, we are responding to an extreme need for discreteness and specific differentiation, but most of the time we are well satisfied to convey our experiences by means of a relatively small number (a few thousand, say) of general categories into which we learn to fit them. As a first approximation we may regard each word of a language like English as the name of a category of experience: *horse, petunia, he, ecstasy, reprimand, green, very,* and *nevertheless* are all categories of experience. Not all categories of experience are symbolized by discrete words; some are represented by grammatical phenomena such as are indicated in the following contrasts: *horse v. horse's; petunia v. petunias; he v. him; ecstasy v. ecstatic; reprimand; v. reprimanded; green v. greener; the very old man v. the very idea;* and the classic *dog bites man v. man bites dog.*

If we agree that the categories of a language are "arbitrary" in the sense that they could be replaced by other, equally acceptable ways of categorizing experience, we could begin to inquire to what extent the several thousand languages of the world have similar categories. How many languages have a distinct, generic term for *horse?* How many languages have only a term for what we would call *quadruped,* applying it alike to horses, dogs, wolves, giraffes and adding appropriate qualifying terms? Are there languages which have no generic term for *horse* but only terms for particular breeds and conditions of horses? (We are told that Arabic is such a language.) Or let us take a grammatical problem: do all languages distinguish singular and plural? (No, Chinese does not.) Are there languages which have *more* levels of grammatical number than our two? (Yes; some languages have four "numbers," singular, dual, trial, and plural.) Investigations along these lines are not to be undertaken lightly, for they require an immense sophistication in the techniques of linguistic science. We can nevertheless predict the major outlines of the results. There would be many semantic areas of remarkable (though rarely complete) uniformity among languages, while other areas would tend to show considerable diversity. The linguist Morris Swadesh has surveyed a wide variety of languages in an effort to arrive at a list of concepts for which one would be fairly sure to find a distinct word or word-like form in every language. His final list [2] of 100 such concepts includes things like: personal pronouns: *I, thou, we, he, ye, they;* position and movement: *come, sit, give, fly, stand, hold, fall, swim;* natural objects and phenomena: *ice, salt, star, sun, wind;* descriptives: *old, dry, good, new, warm, rotten, cold;* miscellaneous: *name, other, not, burn, blow, freeze, swell, road, kill.* But even in observing this apparent uniformity, we must not be misled into thinking that there are exact semantic correspondences between languages. English *horse,* French *cheval,* and German *Pferd* may have different ranges of application and different semantic overtones; the meas-

---

[1] George Santayana, *The Sense of Beauty* (Boston: Charles Scribner's Sons, 1896), p. 169.

[2] Morris Swadesh, "Towards Greater Accuracy in Lexicostatistic Dating," *Internat. J. Am. Linguistics,* 1955, XXI, 121–137.

urement of such differences is a problem beyond the scope of this paper.[3] Further, we can find rather obvious lacks of correspondence when we look at the different ranges of meaning covered by the English *proceed v.* French *procéder* ("to proceed" but also "to behave or conduct oneself"), or English *experience v.* French *expérience* ("experience" but also "experiment"). It would appear that the categories of one language are sometimes "untranslatable" into another language; even if we ignore such problems as finding the difference between the English and the Russian concepts of democracy, there remain such cases as German *Gemütlichkeit* and French *acharnement* which are presumably incapable of exact rendering in English.[4] Even such a simple concept as that represented by the word *too* is extremely clumsy to express in Amharic, the official language of Ethiopia. In the realm of grammar, Edward Sapir's classic work *Language*[5] will suggest the extent to which languages differ among themselves in grammatical concepts. Although Sapir felt that "no language wholly fails to distinguish noun and verb," his writings suggest that there are few basic concepts which universally find expression in the grammatical structures of languages. This is not to say that there are grammatical concepts which *cannot* be expressed in all languages; in general, any grammatical concept found in one language can be expressed somehow in every language, even if the expression is a little awkward or periphrastic. Languages do differ remarkably, however, in the grammatical concepts which are mandatory: for example, the use of the singular-plural distinction is said to be mandatory in English but completely optional in Chinese. If someone says "I'm going out to hunt bear," he is dispensing with the singular-plural distinction and talking in the pattern of Chinese —which happens to be convenient because he does not know whether he will bag one bear or more than one.

The real question for the social psychologist is this: Is the behavior of a person (aside from his language behavior) a function of the language he happens to speak? Granted that languages differ in the ways we have described, what effects will these differences have on the way a person thinks, the way he deals with other people, or the way he deals with his environment?

The notion that language makes an important difference in behavior has a long history, beginning with the writings of the German philologist W. von Humboldt more than a century ago. In more recent times, the linguist Benjamin Lee Whorf has been the chief exponent of what he termed "linguistic relativity":

". . . the background linguistic system (in other words, the grammar) of each language is not merely a reproducing instrument for voicing ideas but rather is itself the shaper of ideas, the program and guide for the individual's mental activity, for his analysis of impressions, for his synthesis of his mental stock in trade. Formulation of ideas is not an independent process, strictly rational in the old sense, but is part of a particular grammar and differs, from slightly to greatly, between different grammars."[6]

The linguistic relativity hypothesis is a special case of the culture-personality theory. Substituting terms in Smith, Bruner, and White's précis of culture-

[3] The "semantic differential" technique devised by Osgood may be particularly useful here. See C. E. Osgood, G. J. Suci, and P. H. Tannenbaum, *The Measurement of Meaning* (Urbana: Univ. of Illinois Press, 1957).

[4] The success of translation depends partly on the purpose of translation. See J. B Casagrande, "The Ends of Translation," *Internat. J. Am. Linguistics*, 1954, XX, 335–340.

[5] Edward Sapir, *Language* (New York: Harcourt, Brace & Co., 1921), Ch. V.

[6] B. L. Whorf, *Language, Thought and Reality*, J. B. Carroll (ed.), (New York: John Wiley & Sons, Inc., 1956), pp. 212f.

personality theory,[7] we may express it this way: Each language creates a special plight to which the individual must adjust. The human plight is in no sense universal save in this fact: that however different the language may be, it has certain common problems with which to deal—time, space, quantity, action, state, etc. But each language handles these problems differently and develops special ways of communicating. These ways of communicating create special needs, special responses, and lead to the development of special modes of thinking.

The alternative to the linguistic relativity hypothesis would be a statement that the behavior of a person is not a function of the language he happens to speak or be speaking, that his modes of categorizing experience and dealing with his world operate independently of language, that language is simply a way of communicating something which is in every way prior to its codification in language.

This paper reports two experiments designed to explore, in a preliminary way, to what extent and under what conditions the linguistic relativity hypothesis can be accepted.

In order to find evidence to support the linguistic relativity hypothesis it is not sufficient merely to point to differences between languages and assume that users of those languages have correspondingly different mental experiences; if we are not to be guilty of circular inference, it is necessary to show some correspondence between the presence or absence of a certain linguistic phenomenon and the presence or absence of a certain kind of "nonlinguistic" response. This being the case, we must be clear as to what we mean by a nonlinguistic response. Unfortunately, it is extremely difficult to define this rigorously. We might be tempted to do so by saying that a nonlinguistic response is one which can be elicited without the intervention of any symbolic system, but as soon as we realize that the bells, buzzers, lights, levers, and food pellets through which we elicit the behavior of dogs and rats may be regarded as symbolic systems, this definition would serve to exclude large classes of responses which we would still like to call "nonlinguistic." When we come to examine the actual behaviors used in our experiments, we will find that their "nonlinguistic" character resides in the fact that they are neutral, as it were, with respect to the *special* symbolic systems against which they are being tested. For example, in the second experiment to be presented, a child is asked to tell whether a blue rope "goes best with" a blue stick or a yellow rope. Now, by appropriate reinforcement techniques, we could teach the child always to choose on the basis of form or always to choose on the basis of color, and we could do this without using English or Navaho or any other special symbolic systems. Suppose, again, we were studying differences in the arithmetical abilities of children who had learned the decimal system and of children who had learned only the system of Roman numerals. The arithmetical behavior being studied is analogous to our "nonlinguistic" behavior because it is *neutral* to any one special system of arithmetical symbolism in the sense that it is *possible* to operate in either system, though not necessarily with the same efficiency.

As Brown and Lenneberg have suggested,[8] two approaches present themselves for the testing of the linguistic relativity hypothesis. Brown and Lenneberg used the first of these—an *intralinguistic* approach which, capitalizing on

---

[7] M. B. Smith, J. S. Bruner, and R. W. White, *Opinions and Personality* (New York: John Wiley & Sons, Inc., 1956), p. 25.

[8] R. W. Brown and E. H. Lenneberg, "A Study in Language and Cognition," *J. Abnorm. & Soc. Psychol.*, 1954, XLIX, 454–462.

the fact that the speakers of a given language manifest differences in their knowledge and use of that language, attempts to show that these differences are correlated with certain other behaviors. In both experiments reported here, we have used the second approach—an *interlinguistic* design in which nonlinguistic behaviors of speakers of two different languages are compared. Use of this second approach entails an advantage and a danger: it may become possible to select linguistic features in two languages which are strikingly and fundamentally different, but it becomes difficult to assure oneself that any observed behavioral correlates are *not* due to irrelevant factors such as dissimilar cultural backgrounds and experiences.

EXPERIMENT I

In the Hopi language, still spoken in the pueblos of northeastern Arizona, the semantic domains of verbs for various kinds of physical activities have structures quite different from the corresponding domains in English. In speaking of *breaking*, the Hopi must use verbs depending upon whether there is one fission or many fissions (a distinction not unlike that between "break" and "shatter"). He uses the same verb for *spilling* and for *pouring*, but must use a different verb depending upon whether the material being spilled or poured is liquid or nonliquid. He can use the same verb in speaking of denting an object like a fender and in speaking of pressing a doorbell. The question posed in this experiment was whether these linguistic features would show corresponding features of nonlinguistic behavior in speakers of Hopi when contrasted with speakers of English. The "nonlinguistic" behavior chosen for study was that of sorting or classifying pictures of the actions represented by verbs of breaking, spilling, pressing, and similar physical activities.

Method. Line drawings were prepared,

representing various physical actions such as falling, breaking, dropping, etc. These drawings were then assembled in sets of three, or triads, in such a way that, on the basis of comparative linguistic analysis, it could be hypothesized that in each triad native speakers of Hopi would tend to put a different pair of pictures together as contrasted with native speakers of English.

The test was administered individually to 14 Hopi adults (age range 24 to over 66) who were known to be fluent speakers of Hopi. All could speak English with varying degrees of competence, but regarded themselves as more fluent in Hopi. The test was also administered to 28 "Anglos" (as they are called in the Southwest) consisting of 12 adults of comparable degree of education in a rural New England community and 16 graduate students at Harvard University.

The test was introduced as an experiment in "how we think" and started with six pretest items, of which the first is shown as Figure 1. The three pictures were presented as physically separated photographs which could be shuffled and arranged at the will of the subject, who was asked simply to decide which two of the three pictures went together. The subjects had no difficulty in seeing that the two pictures of *falling* objects went together. The remaining five pretest items were designed to reveal whether the subjects understood the task and to make it clear that they were to respond on the basis of the action or type of action represented rather than incidental features of any objects depicted. The test proper consisted of 17 "critical" items and five "control" items about which no linguistic hypothesis was formulated. (We shall omit further discussion of the control items because they showed no interesting differences between Hopis and Anglos.)

The subjects were also asked to tell why their choices went together. No suggestion was given that the experiment

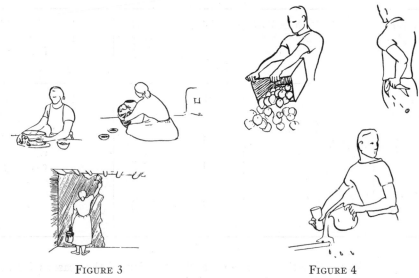

FIGURE 1   FIGURE 2

FIGURE 3   FIGURE 4

Sample Items from Experiment I

had anything to do with language, and most of the Hopis responded in English. Occasionally, however, subjects volunteered that it seemed to "work better" to "think in Hopi," and gave their verbalizations in Hopi. The results, therefore, consist not only of the choices made by the subjects but also (except for three or four cases) the stated reasons for the choices.

Results. The nature of the results and some of the problems in their interpretation may be first illustrated by presenting data for one of the "critical"

items in detail. The pictures for Item 20 are presented in Figure 2.

The linguistic basis for this item resides in the fact that in Hopi there is a verb *'u'ta* which means "to close an opening," and this is the verb normally used for placing covers on open boxes, closing lids, closing holes in tubes or walls, etc.; in contrast, placing a cover on something for protection against dust or damage is represented by the verbs *na:kwapna* or *nönöma*. In English, however, we tend to use *cover* regardless of whether we are covering an opening or not, and we tend

TABLE 1

CHOICES AND REASONS FOR CHOICES FOR THE ITEM OF FIGURE 2

Group	"Hopi" response: A & C combined	"English" response: B & C combined	Neutral: A & B combined
14 Hopi adults	3 Both *'u'ta* 1 Neither is *na:kwapna* 1 Both are boxes 1 Both holding the lid 2 (Not given) (N = 8)	2 Both covering 2 (Not given) (N = 4)	1 Both will be tightly covered 1 Both being covered (N = 2)
12 Rural Anglos	4 Both are boxes 2 Both covering with lids (N = 6)	4 Both covering, v. closing or shutting (N = 4)	1 Both covering 1 Both more familiar (N = 2)
16 Grad. students	1 Putting on a *flat* cover 3 (Not given) (N = 4)	8 Both covering, v. closing or shutting 1 Both putting on top 1 Both "dealing with entire structure" 1 (Not given) (N = 11)	1 Both (customarily) "used and covered" v. one-time covering (N = 1)

to reserve *close* for the situation where an opening can be more or less exactly fitted with a lid or other special stoppage (also for special cases like *closing a book*). On this basis it was hypothesized that Hopis would tend to put together pictures A and C, while Anglos would tend to put together pictures B and C.

In presenting this item to Anglo subjects, it was necessary to explain (without mentioning or suggesting the verbs "cover" or "close") that in picture C a woman was placing a wicker plaque over a box of food (the traditional Hopi "*piki*" corn bread).

Table 1 shows the number of subjects in various classifications making each of three possible groupings, together with

a classification of the reasons for these choices.

The small numbers of cases make statistical significance testing difficult if not impossible, but even if we are to make a statistical test, it must be recognized that a given response may mean different things. Thus, at least three Hopis put pictures A and C together on the ground that both show *'u'ta* "closing an opening," but to at least four Anglos pictures A and C go together because they show boxes. The most striking result here is the fact that Hopis tend *not* to put pictures B and C together, while Anglos, particularly educated ones, show a strong tendency to do so. Only four out of 14 Hopis put pictures B and C together, while 11 out of 16 college-educated Anglos did so.[9] We can look at the reasons for the choices more closely. Only four out of the 14 Hopis mentioned any kind of "covering" in giving their reasons (whatever their choice), while 17 out of 28 Anglos did—a result significant below the 10-percent level.

Although limited, these results suggest that speakers of Hopi tend to organize their perceptions of situations such as those pictured in Figure 1 in terms of "closing openings" instead of "putting covers on things."

There were several other critical items showing results tending to favor our hypothesis. For the pictures of Figure 3, it was expected that Hopis would tend to pair A and C because both represent the action called *leluwi*, "to apply or spread over a surface," while Anglos would pair B and C because they both show "painting." (Hopi has a word for painting, but its use is restricted to cases where one paints a picture or a design, as distinct from covering a surface with paint.) Six of the 14 Hopis paired A and C, while only four of all 28 Anglos did so; of these four, two paired on the basis of the fact that both showed the use of a tool versus the use of one's hands; the significance of this result is at just below the 5-percent level by Fisher's test. Actually, a more striking result was unanticipated: Anglos had a strong tendency to pair either B and C or A and B because they felt both members of these pairs represented "decorating" versus mere painting or covering. "Artistic creation" was also mentioned as a basis for these choices.

Another item showing interesting results is shown in Figure 4. As has been mentioned, "spilling" (accidentally) and "pouring" (intentionally) are not distinguished in Hopi; there is a way of translating the idea of "accidentally"

but this is handled as a separate expression instead of being built into the verb, as in English. Hopi uses slightly different forms for pouring: *wehekna*, "to pour liquid," and *wa:hokna*, "to pour sand, gravel, or other nonliquid loose things," but the form for dropping something is entirely different: *po:sna*. We found that eight out of 14 Hopis (57 percent) paired pictures A and C, consonant with the linguistic forms; these figures contrast with the finding that only seven out of 28 Anglos, or 25 percent, made this pairing. The probability of chance occurrence of a result as extreme as this, determined by the χ^2 test with continuity-correction, is less than 10 percent. At least 16 of the 20 Anglos who paired pictures B and C explained that there was unintentional, accidental action in both of them, while only two Hopis drew attention to this accidental character of the action. Instead, Hopis rarely seemed concerned about whether the man in picture A *meant* to pour out the peaches, while Anglos frequently queried the experimenter about this.

Admitting the results from all 17 "critical" items as evidence, we present in Table 2 a summary to show the extent to which our hypotheses were favored by the data. There is probably not a truly significant difference between the 29 percent representing the tendency of the Hopi subjects to make the expected "Hopi" response of pairing pictures A and C and the 22.6 percent and 24.0 percent, values for the two Anglo groups, but the trend is at least one of those tantalizingly modest ones which can be characterized only as being "in the predicted direction."

Upon re-examination of the purely linguistic data and consideration of certain unanticipated difficulties which had arisen in the subjects' interpretations of the drawings, it was possible to weed out

---

[9] This result is significant at the 5 percent level or higher in a look at significance in a 2×2 contingency table.

TABLE 2

TOTAL FREQUENCY OF PAIRING

		"Hopi" response: A & C		"Anglo" response: B & C		neutral: A & B		Total
17 "critical items"	14 Hopi	69	(29.0%)	126	(52.9%)	43	(18.1%)	238
	12 Rural Anglos	46	(22.6)	119	(58.3)	39	(19.1)	204
	16 Educated Anglos	65	(24.0)	156	(57.5)	50	(18.5)	271
12 "critical items" with "good hypotheses"	14 Hopi	57	(34.0)	80	(47.6)	31	(18.4)	168
	12 Rural Anglos	31	(21.5)	85	(59.0)	28	(19.5)	144
	16 Educated Anglos	36	(18.8)	122	(63.9)	33	(17.3)	191

five items which had gone sour, so to speak, leaving 12 critical items for which the results are presented in the lower part of Table 2. Here we see a sturdier trend in favor of our general hypothesis, although the results are still far from striking. It is not really legitimate to treat Table 2 as a contingency table and apply a χ^2 test, because the events represented there are not necessarily independent; were we to assume that all the choices are independent, however, and were we then to apply a χ^2 test to the lower part of Table 2, we would find that the probability of this χ^2 being exceeded by chance would be less than .01.

The results encourage us to think that not only do we have a promising technique for studying the linguistic relativity hypothesis, but we also have an indication that in further and more extensive trials of this method we may obtain greater assurances that language

categories influence at least one variety of nonlinguistic behavior. Several suggestions towards improvement of the experimental methodology may be offered: (1) drawings should be given extensive pretests to insure that they are interpreted similarly by all subjects; (2) the experiment should utilize contrasting groups of monolinguals (rather than bilinguals as we had to use here); and (3) subjects should be asked to choose which of two pictures, A or B, go best with a fixed third picture, C. (This procedure is used in Experiment II).

EXPERIMENT II

This second experiment was an attempt to show that behavior can be influenced by a grammatical phenomenon as well as a purely lexical or semantic phenomenon.

It is obligatory in the Navaho language, when using verbs of *handling*, to employ a particular one of a set of verbal forms according to the shape or some other essential attribute of the object about which one is speaking. Thus, if I ask you in Navaho to hand me an object, I must use the appropriate verb stem depending on the nature of the object. If it is a long flexible object such as a piece of string, I must say *šaňléh;* if it is a long rigid object such as a stick, I must say *šaňíłĝh;* if it is a flat flexible material such as a paper or cloth, I must say *šaňitcóós,* and so on.

The groups of words in Navaho which together regularly take one or another of these verb stems, say the family of words for all long, rigid objects, carry no linguistic marker of their class membership. They comprise what Whorf [10] has called a *covert class*, as distinguished from an *overt class* such as gender in Latin with the familiar *–us, –i, –a, –ae* case and number suffixes. Nor, in the absence of native grammarians, are there any terms in Navaho for these categories themselves. This like many another grammatical rule operates well below the level of conscious awareness. Although most Navaho-speaking children, even at the age of three or four, used these forms unerringly, they were unable to tell why they used a particular form with any particular object. Even though a child could not name an object, or may not have seen one like it before, in most cases he used the correct verb form according to the nature of the object.

Because of this obligatory categorization of objects in Navaho, it seemed reasonable that Navaho-speaking children would learn to discriminate the "form" attributes of objects at an earlier age than their English-speaking compeers. The finding of American [11] and European [12] psychologists that children tend

first to distinguish objects on the basis of size and color might—at least at the level of verbal facility in dealing with these variables—be partly an artifact of the particular language they use. The hypothesis was, then, that this feature of the Navaho language would affect the relative potency, or order of emergence of such concepts as color, size, shape or form, and number in the Navaho-speaking child, as compared with English-speaking Navaho children of the same age, and that Navaho-speaking children would be more inclined than the latter to perceive formal similarities between objects.

This hypothesis was tested using a variety of experimental materials and several different procedures, of which only one will be reported here. Although the test was expressly adapted to Navaho, the design as well as the basic hypothesis could be extended to other languages since nearly all languages have obligatory categories.

The procedure whose results we will report here was called Ambiguous Sets and was actually interposed between several other procedures well after the child had become accustomed to the experimental situation.

Method. Ten pairs of objects (colored wooden blocks, sticks, and pieces of rope) were used, each of which differed significantly in two respects, e.g., color and size, color and shape, size and shape, or shape and Navaho verb-form classification. These pairs of objects were arranged before the child, one pair at a time. After being presented with a pair of objects, the child was shown a third object similar to each member of the pair in only one of the two relevant characteristics, but of course matching neither, and was asked to tell the experimenter which of the pair went best with

---

[10] Whorf, *op. cit.*, pp. 87–101.

[11] Clara R. Brian and Florence L. Goodenough, "The Relative Potency of Color and Form perception at Various Ages," *J. Exper. Psychol.*, 1929, XII, 197–213.

[12] Alice Descœudres, "Couleur, forme, ou nombre." *Arch. de Psychol.*, 1914, XIV, 305–341.

the object shown to him. For example, one of the pairs consisted of a yellow stick and a piece of blue rope of comparable size. The child was then shown a yellow rope, and the basis of his choice could be either color or the Navaho verb-form classification—since different verbal forms are used for a length of rope and a stick. The ten sets of objects were presented in the alphabetical order of the letters shown in Table 3, with the exception that the first set presented was set O, and the last was set P.

The subjects were 135 Navaho children ranging from three to about ten years of age, drawn from the vicinity of Fort Defiance and Window Rock, Arizona, on the Navaho reservation. On the basis of a bilingualism test and other criteria of language dominance, the 135 subjects were divided into five groups: monolingual in Navaho, Navaho-predominant, balanced bilingual, English-predominant, and English monolingual. For purposes of statistical analysis Navaho monolinguals and Navaho-predominants were grouped together (59 subjects), as were the English monolinguals and English-predominants (43). The remaining 33 subjects were classed as "balanced bilinguals" and this group included a number of individuals whose language status was dubious.

The experiment was conducted in Navaho or, with appropriate modifications in the instructions, in English, as indicated. An interpreter was used with Navaho-speaking children, although the experimenter was able to give instructions in Navaho for some of the procedures used. Most of the testing was done in the children's homes—usually Navaho hogans of the traditional sort—and in the presence of parents, grandparents, siblings, and other interested and very curious onlookers.

Although the establishment of con-trasting groups of Navaho children on the basis of language dominance was regarded as providing adequate control, a supplementary control group was obtained by testing 47 white American middle-class children in the Boston metropolitan area, with an age range roughly comparable to that of the Navaho children.[13]

Results. The children were not at all baffled by the ambiguity inherent in the task; their choices were invariably made with little or no hesitation.

The data were analyzed both item by item and by age. In considering the results, shown in Table 3, it must be remembered that it was our hypothesis that Navaho-dominant children would be more likely to make their choices on the basis of similarity in shape and verb-stem classification than on the basis of size or color. Thus, for the first seven sets listed in Table 3, we would expect the Navaho-dominant children to choose the object listed under (a), the "Navaho choice." This prediction is borne out by the data, for the differences between the two groups of Navaho children are all in the expected direction, and five are significant (by a two-tailed χ^2 test) at better than the 5-percent level. The most striking differences come for those sets of objects that involve a contrast embodied in the Navaho system of verbal categories: sets O and P where the contrast is between color and material and verb stem, and sets H and N where the contrast is between color and verb stem, material being the same, comparing objects of the long-rigid class, and of the so-called "round object" class. The less striking differences involve contrasts which are not formally recognized in Navaho grammar since the same verb stem is used in talking about the cubes and pyramids of set K.

In sets G, J, and M our hypothesis

[13] This testing was performed by Miss Nancy Deupres of the Buckingham School in Cambridge, under the supervision of Carroll.

TABLE 3

RESULTS OF THE "AMBIGUOUS SETS" EXPERIMENT

Set	Attributes contrasted	Objects in set			Percent of "a" choices			
		Comparison model	Alternative choices (a)	(b)	Navaho-dominant Navahos (N = 59)	English-dominant Navahos (N = 43)	P *	White American children (N = 47)
Q	Verb stem, color	blue rope	yellow rope	blue stick	70.7	39.5	<.01	83.0
P	"	yellow rope	blue rope	yellow stick	70.7	39.5	<.01	80.7
H	"	blue stick	yellow stick	blue cylinder	71.2	44.2	<.01	76.6
N	"	blue stick	yellow stick	blue oblong block	72.4	44.2	<.01	82.9
I	shape, size	small blue cube	medium blue cube	small blue sphere	79.7	60.5	<.05	72.4
L	" "	small blue cylinder	large blue cylinder	small blue oblong	59.4	44.2	>.10	82.9
K	shape, color	medium blue cube	medium white cube	medium blue pyramid	45.7	39.5	>.10	70.2
G	size, color	medium blue cube	medium yellow cube	small blue cube	21.0	23.2	>.10	74.4
J	" "	medium blue cube	medium white cube	large blue cube	15.2	14.0	>.10	55.3
M	" "	medium blue cube	medium black cube	small blue cube	59.3	30.2	<.01	74.4

* This is the probability that χ^2 as obtained in a 2 × 2 table comparing the two groups of Navahos would be equalled or exceeded under the hypothesis of no difference.

would not lead us to predict any difference between the groups; they may be regarded as control items. Both groups of children show a marked preference for color rather than size in sets G and J. Set M shows a significant difference between the two Navaho groups, possibly explicable on the basis of the greater po

tency of color for the English-dominant children, the contrast of the blue and yellow of set G and the blue and white of set J being more marked than that between the black and dark blue of set M.

Table 4 shows that there are important and consistent developmental trends for the seven critical sets involv-

TABLE 4

PERCENT OF "a" CHOICES IN THE FIRST SEVEN SETS, BY AGE LEVEL

Age	Navaho-dominant Navahos		English-dominant Navahos		White American children	
	N *	per-cent	N *	per-cent	N *	per-cent
3 4	14	64	7	33	8 10	45 69
5	13	57	9	38	10	91
6	12	64	5	34	8	93
7	9	71	9	36	4	100
8	6	74	5	49	5	83
9–10	5	81	8	75	2	93

* Note that this N is the number of cases yielding data; each case contributes seven responses, and the percentages are computed on the basis of the total number of responses.

ing the contrast between shape or verb form and color—a trend which gives added significance to the differences between the Navaho-dominant and English-dominant groups noted above, since the Navaho-dominant children averaged almost a year younger. In both the Navaho groups (the data for white Americans will be discussed below) the trend is toward the increasing perceptual saliency of shape or form, as compared with color, with increasing age. The curve starts lower and remains lower for English-dominant Navaho children, although it rises rather rapidly after the age of seven. Navaho children stay ahead of their English-speaking age mates, although the two curves tend to converge as age increases.

Thus far discussion has been restricted to the results for two contrasting groups of *Navaho* children. These groups had been established in the hope that maximum possible control would be gained over the variables of race, culture, and environment which might affect the results. All the children tested

were from the same rather small area on the Navaho reservation; the parents of nearly every child were both Navaho, except for the few cases in which one of the parents was a member of some other American Indian tribe. To be sure, the cultural variable could be only imperfectly controlled—the English-dominant children were almost inevitably more acculturated to the local variant of white American culture than were the Navaho-dominant children, but certainly the culture contrast is not as great as between Navaho-speaking children and English-speaking white children, say, from the Eastern United States. However, we may well ask how the performance of these Navaho children compares with that of children speaking English or another language on the same or a comparable test. In an experiment closely similar in materials and procedures to the one reported here, Clara Brian and Florence Goodenough [14] found a marked preference for color over form for American children aged three to six. At age three years six months, 33.6 percent of choices were for

---

[14] Brian and Goodenough, *op. cit.*

form over color; at age four, 24.7 percent for form over color; and at age four years six months, 36 percent (as compared with 64 percent for Navaho-dominant children in this age group and 33 percent for English-dominant children of the same age group). The Brian and Goodenough results are also in substantial agreement with those of Alice Descœudres[15] working with French-speaking children more than 40 years ago.

When we compare our Navaho results with those obtained for 47 white American children in the Boston area, we find that the responses of the white American children are more similar to those for the Navaho-dominant children than for the English-dominant children; as we may see from the last column of Table 3, they consistently tend to choose object "a" on the basis of form or shape in preference to color and size. The white children today, however, can hardly be considered a fair control group for the Indian children, for their cultural background of experiences with forms and colors is enormously different. Early and continued practice with toys of the form-board variety is likely to impress the white American child with the importance of form and size as contrasted with a "secondary" quality like color. Further, social class is known to be correlated with tendency to choose form over color,[16] and our white American children tended to be from the upper middle class. Nevertheless, it is interesting to observe in Table 4 that the white American children show the same developmental trend as either group of Navaho children. As a matter of fact, at the earliest age level,

the three- and four-year-old Navaho-dominant children outstrip their white American age mates in preferring form to color.

If we consider only the two groups over which we have exercised the maximum control over the variables we presume to be relevant, the Navaho-dominant and English-dominant Navaho children, we have shown that language patterning seems to be correlated with a tendency to match objects on the basis of form rather than color or size. When we also consider the data from white American children, as well as the age trends, we may amend our hypothesis in possibly the following form: The tendency of a child to match objects on the basis of form or material rather than size or color increases with age and may be enhanced by either of two kinds of experiences; (a) learning to speak a language, like Navaho, which because of the central role played by form and material in its grammatical structure, requires the learner to make certain discriminations of form and material in the earlier stages of language learning in order to make himself understood at all; or (b) practice with toys and other objects involving the fitting of forms and shapes, and the resultant greater reinforcement received from form-matching. If our results are accepted as supporting this revised hypothesis, they indicate, we believe, that the potential influence of linguistic patterning on cognitive functioning and on the conceptual development of the child, as he is inducted by his language into the world of experience, is a fruitful area for further study.

---

[15] Descœudres, *op. cit.*

[16] Sylvia Honkavaara, "A Critical Re-evaluation of the Color or Form Reaction and Disproving of the Hypotheses Connected with It," *J. Psychol.*, 1958, XLV, 25–36.

THE CONTROL OF THE CONTENT OF CONVERSATION: REINFORCEMENT OF STATEMENTS OF OPINION
By William S. Verplanck

Some kinds of human behavior have seemed to be resistant to experimental investigation because of both their complexity and their apparent variability. One such class includes the commonplace activities of people—for example, whatever the reader was doing just before he picked up this book. Perhaps he was talking to someone.

This paper describes the successful experimental application of some principles of operant [1] conditioning in this area: specifically to conversation between two people. The experimental procedure is based on two assumptions. [2] (1) Apparently heterogeneous human verbal behavior falls into comparatively simple operant-response classes; hence, any one class is susceptible to conditioning. The class of verbal behavior chosen in this study is the *stating of opinions*. (2) It is possible to isolate classes of environmental events that have the property of altering any behavior on which their occurrence has depended, i.e., some events are reinforcing stimuli. Specifically, under our conditions, statements of *agreement* or *paraphrase* are hypothesized to be reinforcing stimuli for the verbal behavior of a speaker. According to these assumptions, if someone agrees with every opinion of a speaker, the speaker should show a sharp increase in his rate of stating opinions. The *stating of opinions* has been conditioned.

Since it is both interesting and important to obtain changes in behavior using conditioning procedures when the subject is not aware that he is "being conditioned" (or, indeed, that his behavior is being manipulated in any way), the present experiments were conducted under conditions in which the occurrence of such "insight" was extremely unlikely.

METHOD

General Plan of the Experiment. The experiment was carried out in a series of ordinary conversations between two people: S, the subject, who was not informed in any way that he was taking part in an experiment, and E, the experimenter. The conversations lasted at least a half hour, divided into three ten-minute periods.

During the first ten-minute period (once the conversation is underway) for four groups of subjects (OAE, OPE, OAD, OPD), E did not reinforce any statement made by S, but determined his basic level of "stating opinions" by ticking off the total number of statements and the number of opinion-statements made by S, in successive one-min-

Condensed from article by the same title in *Journal of Abnormal and Social Psychology*, LI, 668–676. Reprinted by permission of the author and the American Psychological Assn., Inc. The first experiments on this subject were carried out by Mr. Ronald M. Dworkin, as an experimental project in an undergraduate course. His exploratory results were indispensable in setting up the procedures followed in this experiment.

---

[1] An "operant response" is defined as a part of behavior (1) that is recurrently identifiable and hence can be enumerated, and (2) whose rate of occurrence can be determined as a systematic function of certain classes of environmental events.

[2] B. F. Skinner, "The Generic Nature of the Concepts of Stimulus and Response," *J. Gen. Psychol.*, 1935, XII, 40–65; and W. S. Verplanck, "The operant conditioning of human motor behavior," *Psychol. Bull.*, (in press).

ute intervals. This basic level of "opinion-stating" will henceforth be called the "operant level," and the letter O is used to designate the experimental condition under which the operant level is measured.

In the second ten minutes, every opinion statement S made was recorded by E and reinforced. For two groups (OAE and OAD), E agreed with every opinion statement by saying "Yes, you're right," "That's so," or the like, or by nodding and smiling affirmation if he could not interrupt. For two other groups (OPE and OPD), E reinforced by repeating back to S in paraphrase each opinion statement that S made.

In the third ten-minute period, Es attempted to extinguish the opinion statements of two groups (OPE and OAE) by withholding *all* reinforcement, that is, by failing to respond in any way to S's speech, and of two other groups (OPD and OAD) by disagreeing with each opinion stated.

In a fifth, control group (A_1EA_2), run to insure that any changes in S's rate of stating opinions could not be attributed to the passage of time during the experiment, E reinforced by agreement S's opinion statements in the first and third ten-minute periods and withdrew all reinforcement during the second period.

During the first (O) period for the first four groups, and the E period for the fifth group, E asked a "neutral" question ("What did you say?") if S's rate of speaking showed signs of declining. Few such questions were necessary.

Experimental Situation. The experimenters performed the experiment when and where they could, restricted by only three criteria: (a) that only two persons be present, (b) that there be a clock, and

the paper and pencil required for recording, and (c) that enough time be available to both S and E for them to talk for at least a half hour. Es did not suggest to Ss at any time that an experiment was being carried on, and in the rare cases in which an S showed signs of suspicion that this was not an ordinary conversation, the experiment was terminated (although the conversation was carried on).

Seventeen Ss were run in student living quarters, two in restaurants, two in private homes, and one each in a hospital ward, in a public lounge, and over the telephone. In one experiment, contrary to instructions, a third (but uninformed) person was present.

The topics of conversation ranged from the trivial to the "intellectual" and included dates, vacations, Marxism, theory of music, man's need for religion, architecture, and Liberace.

Experimenters. Seventeen members of a course [3] in the "Psychology of Learning" acted as the experimenters. Twelve were Harvard undergraduates, two were Radcliffe undergraduates, and three (two women and one man) were students in the Harvard Graduate School of Education. All the experimenters had had extensive experience in the techniques of conditioning bar-pressing in the rat and of conditioning chin-tapping in the human.[4] Of the seventeen students who undertook the experiment, all were able to collect one or two sets of data as the design demanded.

Subjects and Experimental Groups. Twenty men and four women were used as subjects. Thirteen were described by the Es as friends, seven as roommates, one a date, one an uncle, and one a total stranger. In all but four conversations, S and E were of the same sex. All but six

---

[3] An experiment of this sort very probably could not be successfully performed *de novo* in a laboratory situation suitably equipped for tape-recording and concealed observation. The present strategy was dictated by the need to determine whether positive results could be obtained in conversations on a variety of topics, carried on in a wide variety of situations, and especially in a situation in which it was most unlikely that S would suspect that an experiment was being carried on.

[4] Verplanck, *op. cit.*

*S*s were of college age; of the remaining six, four were in their thirties, and two were 55 and 60, respectively.

These subjects were distributed over the four experimental groups as follows: *OAD*, 5; *OPD*, 6; *OPE*, 2; *OAE*, 4; and A_1EA_2, 7. It will be noted that the designations indicate the experimental treatment for each of the three ten-minute periods. The experimental groups are summarized in Table 1.

There were 20 students in the class, and the design called for *N*s of five and ten, but three students reported that they were unable to undertake the experiment, and of the 17 experimenters, one placed himself in the wrong group.

The Response Conditioned. The response selected for reinforcement was the uttering by *S* of a statement or "sentence" beginning: "I think . . .," "I believe . . .," "It seems to me," "I feel," and the like. *E*s were instructed to be conservative in classifying a statement as an opinion, and to do so only if one or another such qualifying phrase began the statement. No attempt was made to define what constituted a statement or a "sentence" except that *E* should not expect grammatical sentences (1). These instructions proved adequate; no *E* had difficulty in counting such units of verbal behavior, although doubtless many speech units counted would not parse.

Reinforcing Stimuli. Two classes of reinforcing stimuli were used by the *E*s. The first was *agreement* (*A*) defined as the experimenter saying, "You're right," "I agree," "That's so," or the like, nodding the head, smiling (where *E* did not want to interrupt). The second was repeating back to *S* in *paraphrase* (*P*) what he had just said. No further attempt was made to specify paraphrasing. *Extinction* was carried out in one of two ways. In some groups *E* simply refrained from responding in any way to a statement by *S* (*E*) and in others, he disagreed (*D*) with each opinion statement.

*E*s did not speak, except to reinforce,

to disagree, or to "prime" *S* with a question during operant-level determination. They contributed nothing new to the conversation.

Recording. A clock, or watch with sweep-second hand, a pencil, and something to write on were necessary for the recording. One *E* was able to record the whole conversation on a tape-recorder. *E*s ticked off each statement occurring in successive one-minute intervals by making a series of doodles incorporating marks, or by making marks on the margin or text of a book or magazine. Different marks were used for opinions and other statements. Recording proved inconspicuous, and in only one or two cases did an *E* have to terminate an experiment because *S* seemed to notice his recording.

Although problems arose occasionally, *E*s by and large had no difficulty in arriving at and maintaining a criterion for a "sentence" or "statement," i.e., for the unit of speech that they counted, and for the subclass, statement of opinion.

The criteria varied from experimenter to experimenter, in that the rates of speaking of two subjects reported by the same *E*s are correlated (rank-order correlation .65, $N = 14$). The reported rates are a function not only of the subject's rate of speaking and of *E*'s rate of speaking in reinforcing, but also of the criterion for "statements" adopted by *E*.

Execution. In a few cases, the experiment was begun and then terminated by phone calls, third persons entering the room, or because *E* feared that *S* had noticed that he was recording. All the experiments completed are reported in this paper, except one from group A_1EA_2, whose data could not be accurately transcribed.

Two *E*s carried out operant-level determination for only nine minutes, and one went overtime. Four went overtime during reinforcement. The greatest variability appeared during extinction; seven *S*s failed to continue talking for

TABLE 1

Procedures Followed by Experimenters

N	First *Ten minutes*	Second *Ten minutes*	Third *Ten minutes*
5	O—Measure operant level	A—Reinforce each opinion statement by agreement	D—Extinguish by disagreeing with each opinion-statement
2	O—Measure operant level	A—Reinforce each opinion statement by agreement	E—Extinguish by failing to respond to any statement of S (silence)
6	O—Measure operant level	P—Reinforce each opinion statement by paraphrase	D—Extinguish by disagreeing with each opinion-statement
4	O—Measure operant level	P—Reinforce each opinion statement by paraphrase	E—Extinguish by failing to respond to any statement of S (silence)
7	A_1—Reinforce each opinion statement by agreement	E—Extinguish by failing to respond to any statement of S (silence)	A_2—Reinforce each opinion-statement by agreement

ten minutes following the beginning of disagreement, or of nonreinforcement, either leaving the room or falling into silence. Eight Es carried on the conversation past the ten-minute minimum-extinction period. Since Es were not consistent in continuing to record or to converse past this time, data are reported only on the first ten minutes.

In summary, the experiment is designed to determine whether a person, in conversation with another person, can manipulate the second person's conversation by agreeing or disagreeing, or by paraphrasing.

Results

Awareness. *No subject ever gave any evidence that he was "aware"* that he was serving as a subject in an experiment, that his behavior was being deliberately manipulated and recorded, or that he recognized that there was anything peculiar about the conversation. The only qualification that must be made is this: during extinction, some Ss got angry at Es and commented on their disagreeableness, or noted their "lack of in-

terest," and during reconditioning one member of group A_1EA_2 gave E "queer, searching glances," perhaps because of the opinions that E was now agreeing with. These changes of behavior are consistent with those found in other situations when S is undergoing extinction.[5]

Conditioning is demonstrated if the appropriate changes appear in the rate of enunciating opinions (as a function of the conditions of reinforcement). When reinforcement is given, the rate must increase; when it is withdrawn, the rate must decrease.

Distributions were made of the number of opinion statements (N_opin) and of all statements (N_all), and the cumulative values (CN_opin and CN_all) for each minute of the three experimental periods. From the latter, mean rates of statement-making were computed. Relative frequencies of opinions

$$RF_\text{opin} = CN_\text{opin}/CN_\text{all}$$

were determined for each subject for each period.

Rates. The rates of making statements (CN_all/t) showed no significant changes as a function of reinforcement. Data on the distribution of these rates for each

---

[5] *Ibid.*

TABLE 2

MEDIANS AND RANGES FOR EACH TEN-MINUTE PERIOD

	Ten-Minute Period	Groups OAE, OAD, OPE, OPD combined			Group A_1EA_2		
		Procedure	Median	Range	Procedure	Median	Range
Rate	1st	op	5.3	2.2–12.8	cond	7.1	2.4–14.0
(Statements/minute)	2d	cond	5.7	3.2–17.1	ext	6.3	1.9–11.0
	3d	ext	5.2	1.4–12.8	recond	5.8	2.9–14.5
Relative frequency	1st	op	0.32	.01–.65	cond	0.57	.208–.65
of	2d	cond	0.56	.07–.70	ext	0.30	.094–.53
opinion statements	3d	ext	0.33	.05–.64	recond	0.60	.267–.70

interval are given in the upper portion of Table 2. Several tests for significance of difference were made, and none showed a significant difference. The "priming" of S by means of the question, "What did you say?" seems to maintain the rates in the operant periods and in the extinction period of group A_1EA_2, although decreases in rate may be obscured by the fact that E is saying little during these times.

Relative Frequency of Opinions. Table 2 (lower portion) presents the medians and ranges of the distributions of the "opinion rate" for each period. Each of the 24 subjects showed an increase in his relative frequency of opinion during the reinforcement period over his operant level, or (for group A_1EA_2) over his preceding extinction period. The probability that this result would have been obtained if there had been no effect of the experimental variable is $(\frac{1}{2})^{24}$. Twenty-one of the 24 showed a *reduced* opinion rate in the extinction or disagreement period below that of the preceding period of reinforcement. The probability that 21 or

more Ss would change in the absence of an effect of the experimental variable is 1.1 $(\frac{1}{2})$ [13]. Signed rank tests [6] of the significance of the differences yield ps well below the 1-percent level.

We plotted cumulatively the number of opinion statements for each successive minute in each of the three experimental periods. The resulting curves are typical of the conditioning and extinction curves ordinarily obtained in learning experiments with both animal and human subjects.[7]

There is a tendency for paraphrasing to be more effective than agreement in increasing the opinion rate, although the difference is not significant (p between .05 and .10). Paraphrasing and agreement, although both effective, are not equivalent as reinforcing stimuli; paraphrasing is much more variable in its effectiveness (or perhaps the variety of statements made as paraphrases exceeded those called agreements).

The method of extinction also yielded a significant difference in variability, with disagreement producing more var-

[6] F. Wilcoxon, *Some Rapid Approximate Statistical Procedures* (New York: American Cyanimid Co., 1949).

[7] For examples of individual curves, as well as group cumulative curves, see the original publication of this study, *op. cit.*

iability in performance than simple non-reinforcement.

In summary, during the period when opinion statements were being reinforced by paraphrase or agreement, the rate of opinion enunciation changed in accordance with the assumptions made. All Ss increased their rate of stating opinions, regardless of the topic of conversation, its setting, or S's particular relationship with the experimenter. The order of magnitude of the effect depended upon the kind of reinforcement employed.

DISCUSSION

Individual differences in the rates of speech and of giving opinions are most striking and highly significant. We have already noted that they are the joint outcome of S's rate of speech, the length of his sentences, of E's discrimination of his speech, and of E's own speech rate. Of the two Ss who had the lowest rate of making statements, one was a Finn who was able to speak English only with difficulty; the other was a young woman who talked very fast and in very long sentences (and she also scored the highest rate of giving opinions).

Since the experiment was performed, Fries' [8] work has become available, and a study of it suggests the basis of our Es' criteria. The statements that the Es counted during the period of reinforcement are evidently identical with Fries' "utterance units",[9] i.e., stretches of speech bounded by a change of speaker. During reinforcement and during extinction by disagreement, each stretch of S's speech was bounded by E's delivery of successive reinforcements or disagreements. The cues in S's speech that determined E's delivery of a reinforcement probably cannot yet be specified. However, the facts that the rate of uttering

"statements" is stable, and that the rates reported by the same E are correlated with each other suggest that the "statements" or "sentences" counted during the operant level and during extinction (although these are, by definition, not Fries' "utterances," since E says nothing) were stretches of speech such that E was *stimulated* to respond.[10] He did so, not by speaking, but rather by marking his record. If this analysis is correct, then our S's statements were what Fries also terms statements, i.e., "sentences that are regularly directed to eliciting attention to continuous discourse."

Magnitude of the Effect. These data do not permit us to draw conclusions about the magnitude of the effect, although it is clearly some function of the values of reinforcement variables. If S rarely states an opinion, it is difficult for the number of reinforcements to become very great, and the effect is necessarily small.

Acquisition Effects. The not-quite-significant superiority of paraphrasing over simple agreement and the significantly greater variance with paraphrasing are interesting. Probably many different kinds of paraphrases were employed; the differential effectiveness of these as reinforcing stimuli needs investigation. Both the smallest and the greatest changes in the rate of stating opinions were produced by paraphrasing.

Extinction Effects. During extinction by disagreement, some Ss "marshalled the facts," others changed the topic. Some subjects who were extinguished by either treatment became "disturbed" or angry. There is more than a suggestion that when S undergoes complete nonreinforcement, his speech tends to extinguish and, indeed, he tends to leave the experimental situation earlier ("for study," "to go to dinner," and the like), but the

---

[8] C. C. Fries, *The Structure of English* (New York: Harcourt, Brace & Co., 1952).
[9] *Ibid.*, p. 36.
[10] *Ibid.*, p. 49.

ten-minute extinction period is too brief, and the variation among Es in continuing to record is too great to permit evaluation of this tendency.

General Remarks. Certain problems, soluble by further research, set limitations on the generality of the present results.

A variety of specific utterances by E were employed as reinforcing stimuli; a study of the variability in the effectiveness of various kinds of statements by E would be most useful.

The present results do not permit us to state how important is the particular social relationship between S and E. Would agreement by an E whom S disliked reinforce his verbal behavior? These conversations were relatively short, with the result that extinction was carried out to its asymptote in only a few Ss, and, hence, differences between the effect of disagreement and of complete nonreinforcement, although suggested, cannot be tested. Similarly, neither "satiation" effects of continuous and repeated reinforcement nor complete "talking-out" of S on a topic could occur. (It should be recalled that our procedure does not allow E to contribute anything new to the conversation.)

The topics of conversation were, in only a few cases, such that S might be "ego-involved" in their outcome. Perhaps if S were subjected to these procedures when the conversation centered on a subject about which he "felt deeply," the results might differ, e.g., acquisition might be greater and extinction far slower. Orderly *changes* in the topic of conversation should also be observable.

Finally, it should be remembered that our Es were all well-trained in conditioning before undertaking this experiment, and this experience may prove necessary for the successful completion of the experiment.

Despite these limitations, this experiment shows that if, in what is ostensibly an ordinary conversation, one agrees with opinions expressed by a speaker, the speaker will give still more opinions and that returning the speaker's words in paraphrase has the same effect. It also shows that disagreement reduces the number of opinions given, as does ignoring the speaker's statement. The verbal behavior of a speaker, apparently without regard to its content or setting, is under the control not only of the speaker himself but also of the person with whom he is conversing.

These results are in accord with the two hypotheses made. But one may ask, is this operant conditioning? By any empirical, nontheoretical definition of conditioning, the changes in behavior found conform with those of conditioning, and the present results may be classified as conditioning. What are some of the alternatives?

One possibility is that the data depend upon the experimenters' behavior, rather than that of the subjects. That is, knowing that an increase in the frequency of opinions was to be expected under reinforcement conditions, the experimenters may have been more attentive to opinion statements and counted more of them during the reinforcement period. If this were so, it would, in itself, be a finding of interest. The writer is inclined to doubt very much that this occurred to any extent, in view of the phenomenon of "negative suggestibility," and because some experimenters were frankly skeptical about the experiment's outcome before the data were collected and tabulated. Repetition of the experiment, with tape recordings of the verbal behavior of both S and E would permit ready evaluation of these possibilities.

The results of this experiment make psychological and scientific sense and seem to follow common-sense descriptions of conversation ("People like to talk to people who are interested in what they are saying"; "if you ignore him, he'll go away") and, indeed, of other social and political behaviors. The data suggest that, once the appropriate simplifying assumptions are made, a very high degree of order can be revealed in "complex" situations and that a still higher degree of order can be introduced into them.

The simplifying hypotheses made here are derived from the concepts of *response* and of *conditioning*, and they have proved experimentally fruitful in the present instance. This complex behavior is available to direct experimental investigation, and the orderliness and lawfulness of the behavior exhibits itself when irrelevant details are ignored. The heuristic advantages of much of present stimulus-response theory, when it is applied in the field of verbal behavior in a social context, are clear.

If our interpretation is correct, experimental work on a wider variety of human social behavior is possible. The isolation in conversation of independent variables susceptible to direct manipulation and of dependent variables showing orderly change should give a much wider and more significant scope to experimental investigation. The experiments now possible provide new techniques for the investigation of client-therapist relationships and of therapeutic techniques in clinical psychology. They may be applied to the study of the behavior of small groups and of personality.[11]

They suggest how cooperation may be ensured. They lead to questions such as "Can one, by pairing oneself with a reinforcing stimulus, come to control effectively the behavior of a total stranger?" That is to say, if a person agrees with everything said by someone whom he has not previously known, will he then have a means of reinforcing, or of exerting other types of control over, the stranger's behavior? The possibilities are interesting.

SUMMARY AND CONCLUSIONS

Seventeen experimenters carried on conversations with 24 different subjects.

Two assumptions are made: (1) that "stating an opinion" is a class of behavior that acts as a response, and (2) that statements of agreement with, or paraphrases of, such statements of a speaker act as reinforcing stimuli. From these it is inferred that the rate at which a speaker states opinions varies with the administration of agreement or of paraphrase by the person with whom he is conversing. The experimental conversations were carried out on a wide variety of topics of conversation, in a wide variety of places, and in a group of subjects, most of whom were college students. The expected results appeared. Every subject increased in his rate of verbalizing opinions with reinforcement by paraphrase or agreement. Twenty-one subjects decreased in rate with nonreinforcement. Over-all rates of speaking did not change significantly.

In no case was the subject aware that he was the subject of an experiment or that the conversation was an unusual one.

---

[11] Ed. note: The work is also relevant for an evaluation of methods of interviewing in public opinion studies. The "nondirective" interview has relied heavily upon paraphrasing as a device for getting fuller (or more understandable) opinion statements from respondents. The effects of paraphrasing have been assumed to be quite different from those of agreement with a respondent. For further research on verbal reinforcement, the reader is referred to J. Greenspoon, "The Reinforcing Effect of Two Spoken Sounds on the Frequency of Two Responses," *Amer. J. Psychol.*, 1955, LXVIII, 409–416; and George Mandler and W. K. Kaplan "Subjective Evaluation and Reinforcing Effect of a Verbal Stimulus," *Science*, 1956, CXXIV, 582–583.

VERBAL STEREOTYPES AND RACIAL PREJUDICE
By Daniel Katz and Kenneth W. Braly

One outstanding result of investigations of racial prejudice is the uniformity in the patterns of discrimination against various races* shown by Americans throughout the United States. People in widely separated parts of the country show a high degree of agreement in their expressions of relative liking or disliking of different "foreign" groups.

In an early study Bogardus asked 110 businessmen and schoolteachers about the degrees of social intimacy to which they were willing to admit certain ethnic groups. The degrees of social distance employed were: to close kinship through marriage, to my club as personal chums, to my street as neighbors, to employment in my occupation, to citizenship in my country, to my country as visitors only, and exclusion from my country. By weighting these seven classifications Bogardus obtained the following preferential rating of 23 ethnic groups:

Canadians	22.51
English	22.35
Scotch	20.91
Irish	19.38
French	18.67
Swedes	16.20
Germans	14.95
Spanish	14.02
Italians	8.87
Indians	7.30
Poles	6.65
Russians	6.40
Armenians	6.16
German-Jews	5.45
Greeks	5.23
Russian-Jews	4.94
Mexicans	4.57
Chinese	4.12
Japanese	4.08
Negroes	3.84
Mulattoes	3.62
Hindus	3.08
Turks	2.91

The Bogardus study was carried out on the Pacific Coast but studies made in other parts of the United States indicate the same pattern of preferences for the various groups. In the Middle West, for example, Thurstone constructed a scale on the basis of the likes and dislikes of 239 students. The resulting rank order and scale values for 21 ethnic groups follow:

American	0.00
English	−1.34
Scotch	−2.09
Irish	−2.18
French	−2.46
German	−2.55
Swede	−2.90
South American	−3.64
Italian	−3.66
Spanish	−3.79
Jew	−3.92
Russian	−4.10
Pole	−4.41
Greek	−4.62
Armenian	−4.68
Japanese	−4.93
Mexican	−5.10
Chinese	−5.30
Hindu	−5.35
Turk	−5.82
Negro	−5.86

How is the agreement about "foreign" groups to be interpreted? The first possibility is that the foreign groups possess

Adapted by the authors from "Racial Stereotypes of 100 College Students," *Journal of Abnormal and Social Psychology*, 1933, XXVIII, 280–290, and "Racial Prejudice and Racial Stereotypes," *ibid.*, 1935, XXX, 175–193, with permission of the American Psychological Association, Inc.

* The term *race* is here used in the popular, not the scientific, sense, and covers reference to racial, religious, and national groupings.

varying degrees of undesirable qualities upon which most Americans base their preferential ratings. But it is obvious that there are wide individual differences within any nationality group—that is, not all Englishmen are alike, nor are all Frenchmen, nor are all Russians. It is also obvious that few Americans have had much opportunity to know a large number of people from the many nationalities they dislike. It is also highly probable that if we were basing our judgments wholly upon what we know from actual contact with individual Spaniards, we would have differing impressions of what Spaniards are really like, because we would not all have met the same type of Spaniard. Hence a more valid interpretation of the agreement of Americans about foreign groups is that it represents the prejudgments or prejudices, absorbed from the stereotypes of our culture.

Thus the preferential disliking reported by Bogardus and Thurstone may reflect attitudes toward race names and may not arise from animosity toward the specific qualities inherent in the real human beings bearing a given racial label. We have learned responses of varying degrees of aversion or acceptance to racial names and where these tags can be readily applied to individuals, as they can in the case of the Negro because of his skin color, we respond to him not as a human being but as a personification of the symbol we have learned to look down upon. Walter Lippmann has called this type of belief a stereotype—by which is meant a fixed impression which conforms very little to the facts it pretends to represent and results from our defining first and observing second.

THE PRESENT STUDY †

To explore the nature of racial and national stereotypes more fully, the following procedures were employed:

(1) Twenty-five students were asked to list as many specific characteristics or traits as were thought typical of the following ten groups: Germans, Italians, Irish, English, Negroes, Jews, Americans, Chinese, Japanese, Turks. No traits were suggested to the students. This list was then supplemented by characteristics commonly reported in the literature. The result was a final check-list of 84 descriptive adjectives.

(2) One hundred Princeton undergraduates were then asked to select the traits from this prepared list of 84 adjectives to characterize the ten racial and national groups. Specific directions used in the experiment follow in part:

Read through the list of words on page one and select those which seem to you to be typical of the Germans. Write as many of these words in the following spaces as you think are necessary to characterize these people adequately. If you do not find proper words on page one for all the typical German characteristics, you may add those which you think necessary for an adequate description.

This procedure was then repeated for other national and racial groups. When the student had finished this he was asked to go back over the ten lists of words which he had chosen and to mark the five words of each list which seemed most typical of the group in question.

(3) Another group of students was asked to rate the list of adjectives on the basis of the desirability of these traits in friends and associates. The students making this judgment had no knowledge that the characteristics were supposed to describe racial groups. The traits or adjectives were rated from 1 to 10 on the basis of their desirability.

(4) Still another group of students was asked to put in rank order the ten racial and national groups on the basis of preference for association with their

---

† This study was made in 1932.

members. The group which the subject most preferred to associate with was placed first and the group with which he preferred to associate least was placed tenth or last.

RESULTS

Stereotyped Conceptions of Ten Ethnic Groups. Table 1 presents the twelve characteristics most frequently assigned to the ten races by the 100 students. This table summarizes the traits which students rechecked as the five most typical characteristics of each race.

The traits most frequently assigned to the Germans seem consistent with the popular stereotype to be found in newspapers and magazines. Their science, industry, ponderous and methodical manner, and intelligence were pointed out by over one fourth of the students. Scientifically-minded was the most frequently assigned characteristic, as many as 78 percent of the group ascribing this trait to the Germans.

Italians received the common characterization of the hot-blooded Latin peoples: artistic, impulsive, quick-tempered, passionate, musical, and imaginative. The greatest agreement was shown on the artistic qualities of the Italians with 53 percent of the students concurring in this belief.

The characteristics ascribed to the Negroes are somewhat similar to the picture of the Negro as furnished by the *Saturday Evening Post*: highly superstitious, lazy, happy-go-lucky, ignorant, musical, and ostentatious. The greatest degree of agreement for a single trait for any racial group was reached when 84 percent of the students voted the Negroes superstitious. Laziness was given as a typical characteristic by three fourths of the students, but the other traits mentioned above had much lower frequencies of endorsement. It may be noted in passing that for a northern college, Princeton draws heavily upon the South for her enrollment so that this characterization

of Negroes is not exclusively a Northern description.

In the case of the Irish no single trait of the 84 presented could be agreed upon as a typical Irish characteristic by half the students. Forty-five percent, however, thought pugnacity typical and 39 percent agreed upon quick-tempered. Witty, honest, very religious, industrious, and extremely nationalistic were the other adjectives selected by a fifth or more of the students.

The characterization of the English savors more of the English "gentleman" than of the general stereotype of John Bull. The leading characteristic is sportsmanship with an endorsement from 53 percent of the students. Forty-six percent of the students favored intelligence as typical of the English, 34 percent conventionality, 31 percent love of traditions, and 30 percent conservatism. Other adjectives were reserved, sophisticated, courteous, and honest.

The qualities of the competitive business world are used to describe the Jews. They are pictured as shrewd, mercenary, industrious, grasping, ambitious, and sly. Fifteen percent of the students did include Jewish loyalty to family ties. The greatest agreement (79 percent) was shown for shrewdness.

The traits ascribed to Americans show a certain objectivity on the part of the students in describing themselves, for the description given is not greatly at variance with the stereotype held by non-Americans. Americans are described as industrious, intelligent, materialistic, ambitious, progressive, and pleasure-loving. As in the case of the Irish the degree of agreement on these traits is relatively low. Almost one half did assign industry and intelligence to Americans, and a third gave materialistic and ambitious as the most descriptive adjectives.

Apparently the general stereotype for the Chinese among eastern college students is fairly indefinite, for the agreement on typical Chinese characteristics

TABLE 1

THE TWELVE TRAITS MOST FREQUENTLY ASSIGNED TO EACH OF VARIOUS RACIAL AND NATIONAL GROUPS BY 100 PRINCETON STUDENTS

Traits checked, rank order	No.	Percent	Traits checked, rank order	No.	Percent
GERMANS			**NEGROES**		
Scientifically-minded	78	78	Superstitious	84	84
Industrious	65	65	Lazy	75	75
Stolid	44	44	Happy-go-lucky	38	38
Intelligent	32	32	Ignorant	38	38
Methodical	31	31	Musical	26	26
Extremely nationalistic	24	24	Ostentatious	26	26
Progressive	16	16	Very religious	24	24
Efficient	16	16	Stupid	22	22
Jovial	15	15	Physically dirty	17	17
Musical	13	13	Naïve	14	14
Persistent	11	11	Slovenly	13	13
Practical	11	11	Unreliable	12	12
ITALIANS			**IRISH**		
Artistic	53	53	Pugnacious	45	45
Impulsive	44	44	Quick-tempered	39	39
Passionate	37	37	Witty	38	38
Quick-tempered	35	35	Honest	32	32
Musical	32	32	Very religious	29	29
Imaginative	30	30	Industrious	21	21
Very religious	21	21	Extremely nationalistic	21	21
Talkative	21	21	Superstitious	18	18
Revengeful	17	17	Quarrelsome	14	14
Physically dirty	13	13	Imaginative	13	13
Lazy	12	12	Aggressive	13	13
Unreliable	11	11	Stubborn	13	13
ENGLISH			**CHINESE**		
Sportsmanlike	53	53	Superstitious	34	35
Intelligent	46	46	Sly	29	30
Conventional	34	34	Conservative	29	30
Tradition-loving	31	31	Tradition-loving	26	27
Conservative	30	30	Loyal to family ties	22	23
Reserved	29	29	Industrious	18	19
Sophisticated	27	27	Meditative	18	19
Courteous	21	21	Reserved	17	17
Honest	20	20	Very religious	15	15
Industrious	18	18	Ignorant	15	15
Extremely nationalistic	18	18	Deceitful	14	14
Humorless	17	17	Quiet	13	13
JEWS			**JAPANESE**		
Shrewd	79	79	Intelligent	45	48
Mercenary	49	49	Industrious	43	46
Industrious	48	48	Progressive	24	25
Grasping	34	34	Shrewd	22	23
Intelligent	29	29	Sly	20	21
Ambitious	21	21	Quiet	19	20
Sly	20	20	Imitative	17	18
Loyal to family ties	15	15	Alert	16	17
Persistent	13	13	Suave	16	17
Talkative	13	13	Neat	16	17
Aggressive	12	12	Treacherous	13	14
Very religious	12	12	Aggressive	13	14
AMERICANS			**TURKS**		
Industrious	48	48	Cruel	47	54
Intelligent	47	47	Very religious	26	30
Materialistic	33	33	Treacherous	21	24
Ambitious	33	33	Sensual	20	23
Progressive	27	27	Ignorant	15	17
Pleasure-loving	26	26	Physically dirty	15	17
Alert	23	23	Deceitful	13	15
Efficient	21	21	Sly	12	14
Aggressive	20	20	Quarrelsome	12	14
Straightforward	19	19	Revengeful	12	14
Practical	19	19	Conservative	12	14
Sportsmanlike	19	19	Superstitious	11	13

TABLE 2

AVERAGE RANK ORDER OF TEN RACIAL
GROUPS: PREFERENTIAL RANKING

Nationality	Average rank order
Americans	1.15
English	2.27
Germans	3.42
Irish	3.87
Italians	5.64
Japanese	5.78
Jews	7.10
Chinese	7.94
Turks	8.52
Negroes	9.35

TABLE 3

THE RANKING OF TEN RACES ON THE BASIS
OF THE RATING OF THEIR ALLEGED TYPICAL
TRAITS BY 65 STUDENTS

Nationality	Average value of assigned traits
Americans	6.77
English	6.26
Germans	6.02
Japanese	5.89
Irish	5.42
Jews	4.96
Chinese	4.52
Italians	4.40
Negroes	3.55
Turks	3.05

is not great. Three of the 100 students could give no characteristics for the Chinese. Of the 97 who did respond 35 percent thought the Chinese superstitious, 30 percent thought them sly, 30 percent regarded them as conservative. The next most frequently ascribed traits were love of tradition, loyalty to family ties, industry, and meditation.

The picture of the Japanese seems more clear-cut with some recognition of the westernization of Japan. Emphasis was placed upon intelligence, industry,

progressiveness, shrewdness, slyness, and quietness. The Japanese are the only group in which intelligence leads the list as the most frequently assigned characteristic. Forty-eight percent of the students filling in this part of the questionnaire gave intelligence as a typical Japanese trait.

Thirteen students could select no characteristics for the Turks. Fifty-four percent of those responding gave cruelty. Other traits selected described the Turks as very religious, treacherous, sensual, ignorant, physically dirty, deceitful, and sly.

Preferential Ranking of the Ten Groups. The adjectives used to describe the ten groups are a rough index of the esteem in which they are held. More precise measures were furnished (1) by the direct ranking of the ten racial and national names in order of preference (Table 2), and (2) by the desirability of the typical traits attributed to the ten groups (Table 3).

The scores in Table 3 are the average total value of the traits assigned to the various races, computed as follows: For every race the average rating of a trait was multiplied by the number of times it was assigned to that race. The ratings of all the traits assigned to one race were added and divided by the total number of assignments of traits to that race. This division would have been unnecessary if all the 100 students in the original group assigning traits had assigned five traits to every race. In some cases, however, a student made less than five assignments.

When we compare the ranking of the ten groups on the basis of preference for association with their members with their standing based on the desirability of traits attributed to them, we find a few changes in relative placement. The Italians drop from fifth to eighth place; the Irish drop two places, while the Japanese move up two places; and the Jews, Chinese, and Negroes move up one place. In other words, the Italians are regarded more highly and the Japanese are held in lower esteem than the qualities imputed to them would justify.

It also is true that the ethnic groups are bunched much more closely together on the scores based on assigned traits than on the preference ranking. The preference ranking accorded to Americans is five times as desirable as that accorded to the Japanese, but the difference in rating Americans and Japanese on the basis of imputed characteristics is nowhere nearly as great. In part this is an artifact of our method, but in part it is due to the fact that prejudice exceeds the rationalization of undesirable racial characteristics. Nonetheless there is marked similarity between the relative ranking on the basis of preference for group names and the average scores representing an evaluation of typical traits.

Thus racial prejudice is part of a general set of stereotypes of a high degree of consistency and is more than a single specific reaction to a race name. The student is prejudiced against the label Negro because to him it means a superstitious, ignorant, shiftless person of low social status. The whole attitude is more than a simple conditioned response to the race name: it is a pattern of rationalizations organized around the racial label.

This does not mean that the rationalized complex is justified by objective reality—that is, that Negroes really are the type of people described by the stereotype. In fact the clearness or vagueness of the stereotyped conception bear little relation to the degree of prejudice expressed against a group as determined by its preferential ranking.

Relative Clearness and Consistency of Pattern of Stereotypes. Table 4 shows the clearness of the stereotypes about the ten groups in terms of the degree of agreement in assigning typical characteristics to them.

Table 4 lists the least number of traits which have to be included to find 50 per-

TABLE 4

THE LEAST NUMBER OF TRAITS WHICH MUST BE TAKEN TO INCLUDE 50 PERCENT OF THE POSSIBLE ASSIGNMENTS FOR EACH RACE

Races, rank order	Number of traits required
Negroes	4.6
Germans	5.0
Jews	5.5
Italians	6.9
English	7.0
Irish	8.5
Americans	8.8
Japanese	10.9
Chinese	12.0
Turks	15.9

cent of the 500 possible votes cast by the 100 students in the case of every racial and national group. It will be remembered that each student was allowed to select 5 of the 84 traits presented and that there were 100 students. If there were perfect agreement, 2.5 traits would have received 50 percent of the votes. Perfect disagreement or chance would mean that 42 traits would be necessary to give half of the votes. Table 4 shows that in the case of Negroes we can find 50 percent of the votes or selections of traits in 4.6 traits. The agreement here is very high and even in the case of the Turks where 15.9 traits must be included to give 50 percent of the possible 500 assignments or selections the voting is far from a chance selection.

Thus in Table 4 we have a comparison of the definiteness of the ten racial stereotypes. The most definite picture is that of the Negroes. The Germans and the Jews also give consistent patterns of response, while the Chinese, Japanese, and Turks furnish the least clear cut stereotypes.

Though the belief in the undesirable qualities of a national group bolsters the prejudice against the group, it is not necessary to have a well worked out set of such rationalizations to obtain expressions of extreme prejudice. In fact Table 4 shows little relation between degree of disliking and the definiteness of the stereotyped picture. Negroes and Turks both are held in the lowest esteem, yet they represent opposite extremes in sharpness of stereotype. Students agreed among themselves most closely in characterizing Negroes and disagreed most in characterizing Turks. But they were in agreement in putting both groups at the bottom of the list as least desirable as companions or friends.

SUMMARY

1. Ten ethnic groups were placed in rank order by Princeton students on the basis of preference for association with their members. The preferential ranking was similar in its main outline to the results reported by investigators in all parts of the United States. Minor exceptions occurred in the case of the Jews and Japanese, who were placed somewhat lower and higher, respectively, than in other studies.

2. Students not only agreed in their preferential ranking of ethnic groups, but they also agreed in the types of characteristics attributed to these groups. In fact the conception of "foreign" groups is so stereotyped that it cannot be based upon actual contact with or direct knowledge of the groups in question.

3. The clearness or definiteness of the stereotyped picture is not related to the degree of prejudice. The greatest prejudice is expressed against Negroes and Turks. The stereotyped picture of the Negro is very clear-cut while that of the Turk is the vaguest of any of the ten groups included in the study.

4. A list of 84 traits given as the typical characteristics of the ten nationalities by a group of students was rated by another group of students on the basis of their desirability in associates. From these ratings scores were assigned to the ten nationalities, the relative weight of which agreed closely with the preferential ranking. Racial prejudice is thus a generalized set of stereotypes of a high degree of consistency which includes emotional responses to race names, a belief in typical characteristics associated with race names, and an evaluation of such typical traits.

2

Perception, Memory, and Motivation

SOCIAL FACTORS IN RECALL   *By Frederic Charles Bartlett*

EXPERIMENTS ON REMEMBERING: THE
METHOD OF REPEATED REPRODUCTION

I have selected for special consideration a story which was adapted from a translation by Dr. Franz Boas [1] of a North American folk-tale. Several reasons prompted the use of this story.

First, the story as presented belonged to a level of culture and a social environment exceedingly different from those of my subjects. Hence it seemed likely to afford good material for persistent transformation. I had also in mind the general problem of what actually happens when a popular story travels about from one social group to another, and thought that possibly the use of this story might throw some light upon the general conditions of transformation under such circumstances. It may fairly be said that this hope was at least to some extent realized.

Secondly, the incidents described in some of the cases had no very manifest interconnection, and I wished particularly to see how educated and rather

sophisticated subjects would deal with this lack of obvious rational order.

Thirdly, the dramatic character of some of the events recorded seemed likely to arouse fairly vivid visual imagery in suitable subjects, and I thought perhaps further light might be thrown on some of the suggestions regarding the conditions and functions of imaging arising from the use of *The Method of Description.* *

Fourthly, the conclusion of the story might easily be regarded as introducing a supernatural element, and I desired to see how this would be dealt with.

The original story was as follows:

THE WAR OF THE GHOSTS

One night two young men from Egulac went down to the river to hunt seals, and while they were there it became foggy and calm. Then they heard war-cries, and they thought: "Maybe this is a war-party." They escaped to the shore, and hid behind a log. Now canoes came up, and they heard the noise of paddles, and saw one canoe coming

From F. C. Bartlett, *Remembering* (Cambridge, England: Cambridge University Press, 1932). Reprinted by permission of the author and the publisher.

[1] F. Boas, "Kathlamet Texts," *Bulletin 26, Bureau of American Ethnology* (Washington, 1901), pp. 182–184.

* A method used earlier in the book, and not excerpted here.

up to them. There were five men in the canoe, and they said:

"What do you think? We wish to take you along. We are going up the river to make war on the people."

One of the young men said: "I have no arrows."

"Arrows are in the canoe," they said.

"I will not go along. I might be killed. My relatives do not know where I have gone. But you," he said, turning to the other, "may go with them."

So one of the young men went, but the other returned home.

And the warriors went on up the river to a town on the other side of Kalama. The people came down to the water, and they began to fight, and many were killed. But presently the young man heard one of the warriors say: "Quick, let us go home: that Indian has been hit." Now he thought: "Oh, they are ghosts." He did not feel sick, but they said he had been shot.

So the canoes went back to Egulac, and the young man went ashore to his house, and made a fire. And he told everybody and said: "Behold I accompanied the ghosts, and we went to fight. Many of our fellows were killed, and many of those who attacked us were killed. They said I was hit, and I did not feel sick."

He told it all, and then he became quiet. When the sun rose he fell down. Something black came out of his mouth. His face became contorted. The people jumped up and cried.

He was dead.

Each subject read the story through to himself twice, at his normal reading rate. Except in the case which will be indicated later, the first reproduction was made 15 minutes after this reading. Other reproductions were effected at intervals as opportunity offered. No attempt was made to secure uniformity in the length of interval for all subjects; obviously equalizing intervals of any length in no way equalizes the effective conditions of reproduction in the case of different subjects. No subject knew the aim of the experiment. All who were interested in this were allowed to think

that the test was merely one for accuracy of recall.

I shall analyze the results obtained in three ways:

First, a number of reproductions will be given in full, together with some comments;

Secondly, special details of interest in this particular story will be considered;

Thirdly, certain general or common tendencies in the successive remembering of the story will be stated and discussed more fully.

Some Complete Reproductions Together with Comments

After an interval of 20 hours subject H produced the following first reproduction:

The War of the Ghosts

Two men from Edulac went fishing. While thus occupied by the river they heard a noise in the distance.

"It sounds like a cry," said one, and presently there appeared some men in canoes who invited them to join the party on their adventure. One of the young men refused to go, on the ground of family ties, but the other offered to go.

"But there are no arrows," he said.

"The arrows are in the boat," was the reply.

He thereupon took his place, while his friend returned home. The party paddled up the river to Kaloma, and began to land on the banks of the river. The enemy came rushing upon them, and some sharp fighting ensued. Presently someone was injured, and the cry was raised that the enemy were ghosts.

The party returned down the stream, and the young man arrived home feeling none the worse for his experience. The next morning at dawn he endeavoured to recount his adventures. While he was talking something black issued from his mouth. Suddenly he uttered a cry and fell down. His friends gathered round him.

But he was dead.

In general form (1) the story is considerably shortened, mainly by omissions; (2) the phraseology becomes more modern, more "journalistic," e.g., "refused, on the ground of family ties"; "sharp fighting ensued"; "feeling none the worse for his adventures"; "something black issued from his mouth"; (3) the story has already become somewhat more coherent and consequential than in its original form.

In matter there are numerous omissions and some transformations. The more familiar "boat" once replaces "canoe": hunting seals becomes merely "fishing"; Egulac becomes Edulac, while Kalama changes to Kaloma. The main point about the ghosts is entirely misunderstood. The two excuses made by the man who did not wish to join the war-party change places; that "he refused on the ground of family ties" becomes the only excuse explicitly offered.

Eight days later this subject remembered the story as follows:

THE WAR OF THE GHOSTS

Two young men from Edulac went fishing. While thus engaged they heard a noise in the distance. "That sounds like a war-cry," said one, "there is going to be some fighting." Presently there appeared some warriors who invited them to join an expedition up the river.

One of the young men excused himself on the ground of family ties. "I cannot come," he said, "as I might get killed." So he returned home. The other man, however, joined the party, and they proceeded in canoes up the river. While landing on the banks the enemy appeared and were running down to meet them. Soon someone was wounded, and the party discovered that they were fighting against ghosts. The young man and his companion returned to the boats, and went back to their homes.

The next morning at dawn he was describing his adventures to his friends, who had gathered round him. Suddenly something black issued from his mouth, and he fell down uttering a cry. His friends closed around him, but found that he was dead.

All the tendencies to change manifested in the first reproduction now seem to be more marked. The story has become still more concise, still more coherent. The proper name Kaloma has disappeared, and the lack of arrows, put into the second place a week earlier, has now dropped out completely. On the other hand a part of the other excuse: "I might get killed," now comes back into the story, though it found no place in the first version. It is perhaps odd that the friend, after having returned home, seems suddenly to come back into the story again when the young man is wounded. But this kind of confusion of connected incidents is a common characteristic of remembering.

EXPERIMENTS ON REMEMBERING: THE METHOD OF SERIAL REPRODUCTION

Methods for studying remembering often deal with factors influencing individual observers. They help to show what occurs when a person makes use of some new material which he meets, assimilating it and later reproducing it in his own characteristic manner. Already it is clear, however, that several of the factors influencing the individual observer are social in origin and character. For example, many of the transformations which took place as a result of the repeated reproduction of prose passages were directly due to the influence of social conventions and beliefs current in the group to which the individual subject belonged. In the actual remembering of daily life the importance of these social factors is greatly intensified. The form which a rumor, or a story, or a decorative design, finally assumes within a given social group is the work of many different successive social reactions. Elements of culture, or cultural complexes, pass from person to person within a group, or from group to group, and, eventually reaching a thoroughly conventionalized form, may take an established place in the general mass of culture possessed by a specific group. Whether we deal with an institution, a mode of conduct, a story, or an art-form, the conventionalized product varies from group to group, so that it may come to be the very characteristic we use when we wish most sharply to differentiate one social group from another. In this way, cultural characters which have a common origin may come to have apparently the most diverse forms.

The experiments now to be described were designed to study the effects of the combination of changes brought about by many different individuals. The results produced are not entirely beyond the range of experimental research, as I shall show, and the main method which I have used is best called *The Method of Serial Reproduction*.

In its material form this method is simply a reduplication of *The Method of Repeated Reproduction*. The only difference is that A's reproduction is now itself reproduced by B, whose version is subsequently dealt with by C, and so on. In this way chains of reproduction were obtained: (1) of folk-stories, (2) of descriptive and argumentative prose passages and (3) of picture material. The folk-stories were used, as before, because they are predominantly a type of material which passes very rapidly from one social group to another; because most subjects regard them as interesting in themselves; because stories can easily be chosen which were fashioned in a social environment very different from that of any social group that is likely to yield subjects for a given experiment; and because, both as to form and as to content, they undergo much change in the course of transmission. The descriptive and argumentative passages were used because they represent a type of material with which all the subjects of these experiments were already familiar, so that they would provide some kind of check, or control, upon the results with the folk-tales. The picture material was used, because the transmission of picture forms has constantly occurred in the development of decorative and realistic art, and

in order to see whether the same principles of change would operate in spite of the difference of medium dealt with.

In the case of the verbal passages, each subject read the material twice through, to himself, at his normal reading pace. Reproduction was effected after a filled interval of 15–30 minutes. In the case of the picture forms, a subject was allowed adequate time for observation, and he effected his reproduction after a similar interval.

So far as the two chains of reproduction already considered go, it appears that, under the conditions of the experiment, the following are the main types of transformation likely to occur:

1. There will be much general simplification, due to the omission of material that appears irrelevant, to the construction gradually of a more coherent whole, and to the changing of the unfamiliar into some more familiar counterpart.

2. There will be persistent rationalization, both of a whole story and of its details, until a form is reached which can be readily dealt with by all the subjects belonging to the special social group concerned. This may result in considerable elaboration.

3. There will be a tendency for certain incidents to become dominant, so that all the others are grouped about them.

It also seems probable that a cumulative form of story favors the retention of the general series of incidents with little change, and that whatever causes amusement is likely to be remembered and preserved. It may be to this last factor that the preservation of the novel in a commonplace setting is largely due.

SOCIAL PSYCHOLOGY AND THE MATTER OF RECALL

First, then, I propose to consider a few typical cases in which memory appears to be directly influenced by social facts. I shall discuss the psychological explanation of these instances, and, following this, I shall draw certain tentative conclusions bearing upon the psychological significance of social organization, so far as remembering is concerned.

Some years ago the Paramount Chief of the Swazi people, accompanied by several of his leading men, visited England for the purpose of attempting to obtain a final settlement of a long-standing land dispute. When the party returned, there was naturally some curiosity among the British settlers in Swaziland concerning what were the main points of recall by the native group of their visit to England. The one thing that remained most firmly and vividly fixed in the recollection of the Swazi chiefs was their picture of the English policeman, regulating the road traffic with uplifted hand.

Why should this simple action have made so profound an impression? Certainly not merely because it was taken as a symbol of power. Many other illustrations of power, far more striking to the European mind, had been seen and, for all practical purposes, forgotten. The Swazi greets his fellow, or his visitor, with uplifted hand. Here was the familiar gesture, warm with friendliness in a foreign country, and at the same time arresting in its consequences. It was one of the few things they saw that fitted immediately into their own well-established social framework, and so it produced a quick impression and a lasting effect.

I take another case from the same community. Even acute observers often assert of the Swazi the same kind of observation that has been made of the Bantu in general: "The Bantu mind is endowed with a wonderful memory." [2] Yet this sort of statement never seems to have been submitted to any careful experimental test. [3] If such tests were carried out, it would most certainly be found that individual differences are about as pronounced as they are in a European community, and, a fact more to our present purpose, that the lines of accurate and full recall are very largely indeed, just as they are with us, a matter of social organization, with its accepted scales of value.

I myself, having listened to numerous stories about the marvelous word-perfect memory of the Swazi from his childhood up, and having been credibly informed that I could test these stories, with complete certainty of confirmation, upon any person I liked, arranged a simple experiment. Choosing at random a boy of eleven or twelve years of age, a native interpreter and myself concocted a brief message of about twenty-five words which the boy was to take from one end to another of a village. The journey took him about two minutes. The message was given to him very carefully twice over, and he did not know that he was being kept under observation. He was given a lively inducement to be accurate. He delivered the message with three important omissions, doing certainly no better than an English boy of the same age might do. Several times also I tried, with natives of varied ages and both sexes, common observation and description tests, something like the ones I have already recorded in this book, but with modifications so as to make them of greater intrinsic interest to a native observer. The results were much the same as they would have been for similar tests in a typical European group, neither better nor worse.

---

[2] Henri A. Junod, *The Life of a South African Tribe* (London, 1927), Vol. II, p. 619.

[3] It seems very curious that, while a mass of excellent experimental observation has been carried out upon the special sense reactions of relatively primitive people (see, e.g., *Report of the Cambridge expedition to the Torres Straits*, Cambridge, 1903), little controlled investigation has been made upon their higher mental processes. Yet the latter would almost certainly reveal many extremely interesting results, and might go far to correct current views with regard to profound differences of mental life between civilized and uncivilized peoples.

Nevertheless, it is not difficult to show that the common belief has some ground. For example, once, when I was talking with a prominent Scottish settler in Swaziland who has an extensive and sound knowledge of the native, he repeated the usual stories of exceedingly accurate and detailed memory. I told him of my own tests, and he at once agreed that his assertions held good only provided the native were taken in his own preferred fields of interest. Now most Swazi culture revolves around the possession and care of cattle. Cattle are the center of many of the most persistent and important social customs. The settler himself suggested a test case. He guaranteed that his herdsman would give me a prompt and absolutely literal description of all the cattle which he, the owner, had bought a year earlier. The herdsman had been with him while the transactions were completed, and had then driven the beasts back to the main farm. Immediately after the purchase, the cattle had been dispersed to different places and the herdsman had seen them no more. The settler himself had his own written records of the deals, and naturally could not himself remember the details without looking them up. It was arranged that he should not himself look at his records, or interview the herdsman. At the moment, the native was found to be at a "beer-drink," and inaccessible in more ways than one. The next day, however, the man was sent to me. He walked some twenty miles and brought with him the sealed book of accounts, which, in any case, he was not able to read. He knew nothing whatever of the reason for his journey. I asked him for a list of the cattle bought by his employer the year previously, together with whatever detail he cared to give. Squatting on the ground, apparently wholly unmoved, he rapidly recited the list. This was as follows:

From Magama Sikindsa, one black ox for £4;

From Mloyeni Sifundra, one young black ox for £2;

From Mbimbi Maseko, one young black ox, with a white brush to its tail, for £2;

From Gampoka Likindsa, one young white bull, with small red spots, for £1;

From Mapsini Ngomane and Mpohlonde Maseko, one red cow, one black heifer, one very young black bull for £3 in all;

From Makanda, one young grey ox, about two years old, for £3;

From Lolalela, one spotted five year old cow, white and black, for £3, which was made up of two bags of grain and £1;

From Mampini Mavalane, one black polly cow, with gray on the throat, for £3;

From Ndoda Kadeli, one young red heifer, the calf of a red cow, and with a white belly, for £1.

My notes, made at the time, say that the herdsman, a native of something over forty years, "showed no hesitation, no apparent interest, and certainly no excitement. He seemed to be reciting a well-known exercise and in no way reconstructing the deals on the basis of a few definitely remembered details."

The list was correct in every detail but two. The price of the second black ox mentioned was £1. 10s., and the "black" heifer from Mpohlonde Maseko was described in the book as "red." Against these trifling errors, it must be remembered that the herdsman had himself no say in the price of the beasts, and had merely overheard the bargains made by his master; and further that native color names are apt to be rather widely ambiguous.

It seems certain that this was in no way an isolated and remarkable case. The Swazi herdsman has generally an accurate and prodigiously retentive capacity to recall the individual characteristics of his beasts. An animal may stray and get mixed up with other herds. It may be away for a very long time. However long the interval, if the owner comes with a description of the missing beast, his word is almost never questioned, and he is peaceably allowed to drive the animal back. It is true, that, in spite of this, cattle were formerly all earmarked —a custom that appears to have fallen into disuse except in the case of the Royal herds—but altogether apart from these special marks, by common consent, the native herdsman always remembers his beasts individually.

And why should he not? Just as the policeman's uplifted hand was note worthy because of the familiar social background, so the individual peculiarities of the cattle can be recalled freshly and vividly, because herds, and all dealings with them, are of tremendous social importance.

We can now see the general psychology underlying the way in which social conditions settle the matter of individual recall. Every social group is organized and held together by some specific psychological tendency or group of tendencies, which give the group a bias in its dealings with external circumstances. The bias constructs the special persistent features of group culture, its technical and religious practices, its material art, its traditions and institutions, and these again, once they are established, become themselves direct stimuli to individual response within the group. Perhaps, in some so far unexplained way, the social bias of the group may work its way, by actual inheritance, into at least some of the individual members; perhaps all that happens is that it appears in the individual through the pervasive influence of one of the many forms of social suggestion. In any case, it does immediately settle what the individual will observe in his environment, and what he will connect from his past life with this direct response. It does this markedly in two ways. First, by providing that setting of interest, excitement and emotion which favors the development of specific images, and secondly, by providing a persistent framework of institutions and customs which acts as a schematic basis for constructive memory.

SOCIAL PSYCHOLOGY AND THE MANNER OF RECALL

I shall state briefly three principles. I do this with great hesitation. Others could perhaps be derived from the general discussion. In an uncharted realm like the present one, any tentative expression of laws can do no more than form a basis for a further exploration of the relevant facts. The principles, such as they are, must stand or fall as more facts become known. What is beyond dispute is that remembering, in a group, is influenced, as to its manner, directly by the preferred persistent tendencies of that group.

1. In whatever field, where social organization has no specifically directed organizing tendencies, but only a group of interests, all about equally dominant, recall is apt to be of the rote recapitulatory type. This very often is the case over a wide field of daily happenings in the primitive group.

2. Whenever there are strong, preferred, persistent, specific, social tendencies, remembering is apt to appear direct, and as if it were a way of reading off from a copy, and there is a minimum of irrelevance. It may perhaps be that this is due to the adoption of a direct image type of recall, supplemented by the help of prevailing social "schemata" which take the form of persistent customs.

3. Whenever strong, preferred, persistent, social tendencies are subjected to any form of forcible social control (e.g., are disapproved by an incoming superior people, or are opposed to the general immediate trend of social development in the group), social remembering is very apt to take on a constructive and inventive character, either wittingly or unwittingly. Its manner then tends to become assertive, rather dogmatic and confident, and recall will probably be accompanied by excitement and emotion.

Each of these principles has found illustration in the preceding discussion. Obviously they all stand in need of further differentiation before, some day, the whole story of the social control of remembering can be written.

THE BASIC PSYCHOLOGY OF RUMOR
By Gordon W. Allport and Leo J. Postman

RUMORS IN WARTIME

During the year 1942, rumor became a national problem of considerable urgency. Its first dangerous manifestation was felt soon after the initial shock of Pearl Harbor. This traumatic event dislocated our normal channels of communication by bringing into existence an unfamiliar and unwelcome, if at the same time a relatively mild censorship of news, and it simultaneously dislocated the lives of millions of citizens whose futures abruptly became hostages to fortune.

This combination of circumstances created the most fertile of all possible soils for the propagation of rumor. We now know that *rumors concerning a given subject-matter will circulate within a group in proportion to the importance and the ambiguity of this subject-matter in the lives of individual members of the group.*

The affair of Pearl Harbor was fraught with both importance and ambiguity to nearly every citizen. The affair was important because of the potential danger it represented to all of us, and because its aftermath of mobilization affected every life. It was ambiguous because no one seemed quite certain of the extent of, reasons for, or consequences of the attack. Since the two conditions of rumor —importance and ambiguity—were at a maximum, we had an unprecedented

flood of what became known as "Pearl Harbor rumors." It was said that our fleet was "wiped out," that Washington didn't dare to tell the extent of the damage, that Hawaii was in the hands of the Japanese. So widespread and so demoralizing were these tales that, on February 23, 1942, President Roosevelt broadcast a speech devoted entirely to denying the harmful rumors and to reiterating the official report on the losses.

Did the solemn assurance of the Commander in Chief restore the confidence of the people and eliminate the tales of suspicion and fear? It so happens that a bit of objective evidence on this question became available to us almost by accident. On the twentieth of February, before the President's speech, we had asked approximately 200 college students whether they thought our losses at Pearl Harbor were "greater," "much greater," or "no greater" than the official Knox report had stated. Among these students, 68 percent had believed the demoralizing rumors in preference to the official report, and insisted that the losses were "greater" or "much greater" than Washington admitted. Then came the President's speech. On February 25 an equivalent group of college students were asked the same question. Among those who had not heard or read the speech

From *Transactions of The New York Academy of Sciences, Series II*, 1945, VIII, 61–81. Reprinted by permission of the authors and the publisher.

the proportion of rumor-believers was still about two thirds. But among those who were acquainted with the President's speech, the number of rumor-believers fell by 24 percent. It is important to note that, in spite of the utmost efforts of the highest authority to allay anxiety, approximately 44 percent of the college population studied were too profoundly affected by the event and by the resulting rumors to accept the reassurance.

The year 1942 was characterized by floods of similar fear-inspired tales. Shipping losses were fantastically exaggerated. Knapp records one instance where a collier was sunk through accident near the Cape Cod Canal. So great was the anxiety of the New England public that this incident became a fantastic tale of an American ship being torpedoed with the loss of thousands of nurses who were aboard her.[1]

Such wild stories, as we have said, are due to the grave importance of the subject for the average citizen and to the ambiguity to him of the objective situation. This ambiguity may result from the failure of communications, or from a total lack of authentic news, a condition that often prevailed in war-torn countries or among isolated bands of troops who had few reliable sources of news. Again, the ambiguity may be due to the receipt of conflicting news stories, no one more credible than another; or it may be due (as in the case of the Pearl Harbor rumors) to the distrust of many people in the candor of the Administration and in the operation of wartime censorship. As the war progressed, a higher degree of confidence in our news services was rapidly achieved, and rumors concurrently subsided.

In addition to the fear-rumors of 1942,

which persisted until the tide of victory commenced to turn, there was a still more numerous crop of hostility-rumors whose theme dealt always with the shortcomings, disloyalty, or inefficiency of some special group of cobelligerents. The Army, the Navy, the Administration, our allies, or American minority groups were the most frequent scape goats in these rumors. We were told that the Army wasted whole sides of beef, that the Russians greased their guns with lend-lease butter, that Negroes were saving icepicks for a revolt, and that Jews were evading the draft.

These hostility rumors were the most numerous of all. An analysis of 1,000 rumors collected from all parts of the country in 1942[2] revealed that they could be classified fairly readily as:

Hostility (wedge-driving)
    rumors   = 66 percent
Fear (bogey) rumors   = 25 percent
Wish (pipe-dream) rumors = 2 percent
Unclassifiable rumors   = 7 percent

To be sure, the proportion of fear and wish rumors soon altered. As victory approached, especially on the eve of V–E and V–J day, the whirlwind of rumors was almost wholly concerned with the cessation of hostilities, reflecting a goal-gradient phenomenon whereby rumor under special conditions hastens the completion of a desired event. But, throughout the war and continuing to the present, it is probably true that the majority of all rumors are of a more or less slanderous nature, expressing hostility against this group or that.

The principal reason why rumor circulates can be briefly stated. It circulates because it *serves the twin function of explaining and relieving emotional tensions felt by individuals*.[3]

---

[1] R. H. Knapp, "A Psychology of Rumor," *Pub. Op. Quart.*, 1944, VIII, 22–37.

[2] R. H. Knapp, *ibid.*, 25.

[3] This brief formula leaves out of account only the relatively few rumors which serve to serve the purpose of "phatic communication"—a form of idle conversation to facilitate social intercourse. When a lull occurs in a conversation, an individual may "fill in" with the latest bit of gossip that

The Pearl Harbor rumors, for example, helped to *explain* to the teller why he felt such distressing anxiety. Would his jitters not be justified if it were true that our protecting fleet was "wiped out" at Pearl Harbor? Something serious must have happened to account for his anxiety. Families deprived of sons, husbands, or fathers vaguely cast around for someone to blame for their privation. Well, the Jews, who were said to be evading the draft, were "obviously" not doing their share and thus the heavy burden falling on "good citizens" was explained. True, this draft-evasion charge did not last very long, owing, no doubt, to the inescapable evidence of heavy enlistments among Jews and of their heroic conduct in the war. But when shortages were felt, the traditional Jewish scapegoat was again trotted out as a convenient explanation of the privations suffered. Their operation of the black market "explained" our annoying experiences in the futile pursuit of an evening lamb chop.

To blame others verbally is not only a mode of explanation for one's emotional distress, but is at the same time a mode of *relief*. Everyone knows the reduction of tension that comes after administering a tongue lashing. It matters little whether the victim of the tongue lashing is guilty or not. Dressing down *anyone* to his face or behind his back has the strange property of temporarily reducing hatred felt against this person or, what is more remarkable, of reducing hatred felt against any person or thing. If you wish to deflate a taut inner tube you can unscrew the valve or you can make a puncture. Unscrewing the valve corresponds to directing our hostility toward the Nazis or Japanese, who were the cause of our suffering. Making a puncture corresponds to displacing the hostility upon innocent victims or scapegoats. In either case, the air will escape and relaxation follow. To blame Jews, Negroes, the Administration, brass hats, the OPA, or the politicians is to bring a certain relief from accumulated feelings of hostility, whatever their true cause. Relief, odd as it may seem, comes also from "bogey" rumors. To tell my neighbor that the Cape Cod Canal is choked with corpses is an easy manner of projecting into the outer world my own choking anxieties concerning my son or my friends in combat service. Having shared my anxiety with my friend by telling him exaggerated tales of losses or of atrocities, I no longer feel so much alone and helpless. Through my rumor-spreading, others, too, are put "on the alert." I therefore feel reassured.

EXPERIMENTAL APPROACH

Leaving now the broader social setting of the problem, we ask ourselves what processes in the human mind account for the spectacular distortions and exaggerations that enter into the rumor-process, and lead to so much damage to the public intelligence and public conscience.

Since it is very difficult to trace in detail the course of a rumor in everyday life, we have endeavored by an experimental technique to study as many of the basic phenomena as possible under relatively well controlled laboratory conditions.

Our method is simple. A slide is thrown upon a screen. Ordinarily, a semidramatic picture is used containing a large number of related details. Six or seven subjects, who have not seen the picture,

comes to mind, without being motivated by the deeper tensions that underlie the great bulk of rumor-mongering.

In this paper we cannot enter into a fuller discussion of the reasons why people believe some rumors and not others. This question is carefully studied by F. H. Allport and M. Lepkin, "Wartime Rumors of Waste and Special Privilege: Why Some People Believe Them," *J. Abnorm. & Soc. Psychol.*, 1945, XL, 3–36.

FIG. 1. A sample of pictorial material employed in the experiments. Here is a typical terminal report (the last in a chain of reproductions): "This is a subway train in New York headed for Portland Street. There is a Jewish woman and a Negro who has a razor in his hand. The woman has a baby or a dog. The train is going to Deyer Street, and nothing much happened."

wait in an adjacent room. One of them enters and takes a position where he cannot see the screen. Someone in the audience (or the experimenter) describes the picture, giving about twenty details in the account. A second subject enters the room and stands beside the first subject who proceeds to tell him all he can about the picture. (All subjects are under instruction to report as "accurately as possible what you have heard.") The first subject then takes his seat, and a third enters to hear the story from the second subject. Each succeeding subject hears and repeats the story in the same way. Thus, the audience is able to watch the deterioration of the rumor by comparing the successive versions with the stimulus-picture which remains on the screen throughout the experiment.

This procedure has been used with over forty groups of subjects, including college undergraduates, Army trainees in ASTP, members of community forums,

patients in an Army hospital, members of a Teachers' Round Table, and police officials in a training course. In addition to these adult subjects, children in a private school were used, in grades from the fourth through the ninth. In some experiments, Negro subjects took part along with whites, a fact which, as we shall see, had important consequences when the test-pictures depicted scenes with a "racial angle."

All of these experiments took place before an audience (20–300 spectators). By using volunteer subjects, one eliminates the danger of stage fright. There was, however, a social influence in all the audience situations. The magnitude of this influence was studied in a control group of experiments where no one was present in the room excepting the subject and the experimenter.

At the outset, it is necessary to admit that in five respects this experimental situation fails to reproduce accurately the conditions of rumor-spreading in everyday life. (1) The effect of an audience is considerable, tending to create caution and to shorten the report. Without an audience subjects gave on the average twice as many details as with an audience. (2) The effect of the instructions is to maximize accuracy and induce caution. In ordinary rumor-spreading, there is no critical experimenter on hand to see whether the tale is rightly repeated. (3) There is no opportunity for subjects to ask questions of his informer. In ordinary rumor-spreading, the listener can chat with his informer and, if he wishes, cross-examine him. (4) The lapse of time between hearing and telling in the experimental situation is very slight. In ordinary rumor spreading, it is much greater. (5) Most important of all, the conditions of motivation are quite different. In the experiment, the subject is striving for *accuracy*. His own fears, hates, wishes are not likely to be aroused under the experimental conditions. In short, he is not the spontaneous rumor-agent that he is in ordinary life. His stake in spreading the experimental rumor is neither personal nor deeply motivated.

It should be noted that all of these conditions, excepting the third, may be expected to enhance the accuracy of the report in the experimental situation, and to yield far less distortion and projection than in real-life rumor-spreading.

In spite of the fact that our experiment does not completely reproduce the normal conditions for rumor, still we believe that all essential changes and distortions are represented in our results. "Indoor" rumors may not be as lively, as emotionally toned, or as extreme as "outdoor" rumors, and yet the same basic phenomena are demonstrable in both.

What happens in both real-life and laboratory rumors is a complex course of distortion in which three interrelated tendencies are clearly distinguishable.

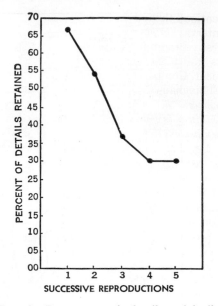

FIG. 2. Percentage of details originally given which are retained in each successive reproduction.

LEVELING

As rumor travels, it tends to grow shorter, more concise, more easily grasped and told. In successive versions, fewer words are used and fewer details are mentioned.

The number of details *retained* declines most sharply at the beginning of the series of reproductions. The number continues to decline, more slowly, throughout the experiment. Figure 2 shows the percentage of the details initially given which are retained in each successive reproduction.

The number of items enumerated in the description from the screen constitutes the 100 percent level, and all subsequent percentages are calculated from that base. The curve, based on 11 experiments, shows that about 70 percent of the details are eliminated in the course of five or six mouth-to-mouth transmissions, even when virtually no time lapse intervenes.

The curve is like the famous Ebbinghaus curve for decline in individual retention, though in his experiments the interval between initial learning and successive reproductions was not as short as under the conditions of our experiment. Comparing the present curve with Ebbinghaus's, we conclude that *social memory accomplishes as much leveling within a few minutes as individual memory accomplishes in weeks of time.*

Leveling (in our experiments) never proceeds to the point of total obliteration. The stabilization of the last part of the curve is a finding of some consequence. It indicates (1) that a short concise statement is likely to be faithfully reproduced; (2) that when the report has become short and concise, the subject has very little detail to select from and the possibilities of further distortion grow fewer; (3) that the assignment becomes so easy that a virtually rote memory serves to hold the material in mind. In all cases, the terminal and the anteterminal reports are more similar than any two preceding reports.

The reliance on rote is probably more conspicuous in our experiments than in ordinary rumor-spreading, where accuracy is not the aim, where time interval interferes with rote retention, and where strong interests prevent literal memory. There are, however, conditions where rote memory plays a part in ordinary rumor-spreading. If the individual is motivated by no stronger desire than to make conversation, he may find himself idly repeating what he has recently heard in the form in which he heard it. If a rumor has become so crisp and brief, so sloganized, that it requires no effort to retain it in the literal form in which it was heard, rote memory seems to be involved. For example:

The Jews are evading the draft;
The CIO is communist controlled;
The Russians are nationalizing their women.

We conclude that whenever verbal material is transmitted among a group of people whether as rumor, legend, or history, change will be in the direction of greater brevity and conciseness. Leveling, however, is not a random phenomenon. Our protocols show again and again that items which are of particular interest to the subjects, facts which confirm their expectations and help them to structure the story, are the last to be leveled out and often are retained to the final reproduction.

SHARPENING

We may define sharpening as the selective perception, retention, and reporting of a limited number of details from a larger context. Sharpening is inevitably the reciprocal of leveling. The one cannot exist without the other, for what little remains to a rumor after leveling has taken place is by contrast unavoidably featured.

Although sharpening occurs in every protocol, the same items are not always emphasized. Sometimes, a trifling detail such as a subway advertising card becomes the focus of attention and report. Around it the whole rumor becomes structured. But, in most experiments, this same detail drops out promptly, and is never heard of after the first reproduction.

One way in which sharpening seems to be determined is through the retention of odd, or attention-getting words which, having appeared early in the series, catch the attention of each successive listener and are often passed on in preference to other details intrinsically more important to the story. An instance of this effect is seen in a series of protocols where the statement, "there is a boy stealing and a man remonstrating with him" is transmitted throughout the entire series. The unusual word "remonstrate" somehow caught the attention of each successive listener and was passed on without change.

Sharpening may also take a *numerical* turn, as in the experiments where emphasized items become reduplicated in the telling. For example, in reports of a picture containing the figure of a Negro, whose size and unusual appearance invite emphasis, we find that the number of Negroes reported in the picture jumps from one to "four" or "several."

There is also *temporal* sharpening manifested in the tendency to describe events as occurring in the immediate present. What happens *here* and *now* is of greatest interest and importance to the perceiver. In most instances, to be sure, the story is started in the present tense, but even when the initial description is couched in the past tense, immediate reversal occurs and the scene is contemporized by the listener. Obviously, this effect cannot occur in rumors which deal specifically with some alleged past (or future) event. One cannot contemporize the rumor that "the *Queen Mary* sailed this morning (or will sail tomorrow) with 10,000 troops aboard." Yet it not infrequently happens that stories gain in sharpening by tying them to present conditions. For example, a statement that Mr. X bought a chicken in the black market last week and paid $1.50 a pound for it may be (and usually is) rendered, "I hear they *are* charging $1.50 a pound on the black market for chicken." People are more interested in today than in last week, and the temptation, therefore, is to adapt (assimilate) the time of occurrence, when possible, to this interest.

Sharpening often takes place when there is a clear implication of *movement*. The flying of airplanes and the bursting of bombs are frequently stressed in the telling. Similarly, the falling flower pot in one picture is often retained and accented. Indeed, the "falling motif" may be extended to other objects such as the cigar which a man in the picture is smoking. In one rumor, it is said to be falling (like the flower pot), though in reality it is quite securely held between his teeth.

Sometimes sharpening is achieved by ascribing movement to objects which are really stationary. Thus, a subway train, clearly at a standstill at a subway station, is frequently described as moving.

Relative size is also a primary determinant of attention. Objects that are prominent because of their size tend to be retained and sharpened. The first reporter calls attention to their prominence and each successive listener receives an impression of their largeness. He then proceeds to sharpen this impression in his memory. The large Negro may, in the telling, become "four Negroes," or may become "a gigantic statue of a Negro."

There are verbal as well as physical determinants of attention. Thus, there is a pronounced tendency for *labels* to persist, especially if they serve to set the stage for the story. One picture is usually introduced by some version of the statement, "This is a battle scene," and this label persists throughout the series of reproductions. Another story usually opens with the statement, "This is a picture of a race riot."

To explain this type of sharpening, we may invoke the desire of the subject to achieve some spatial and temporal schema for the story to come. Such orientation is essential in ordinary life and appears to constitute a strong need even when imaginal material is dealt with.

An additional factor making for preferential retention of spatial and temporal labels is the *primacy* effect. An item that comes first in a series is likely to be better remembered than subsequent items. Usually, the "label" indicating place and time comes at the beginning of a report and thus benefits by the primacy effect.

Sharpening also occurs in relation to familiar symbols. In one series of reports, a church and a cross are among the most frequently reported items, although they are relatively minor details in the original picture. These well-known symbols "pack" meaning and are familiar to all. The subject feels secure in reporting them because they have an accustomed concreteness that the other details in the picture lack. Retention of familiar symbols advances the process of conventionalization that is so prominent an aspect of rumor-embedding. In two of our pictures are a night stick, symbol of police authority, and a razor, stereotyped symbol of Negro violence. These symbols are always retained and sharpened.

Explanations added by the reporter to the description transmitted to him comprise a final form of sharpening. They represent a tendency to put "closure" upon a story which is felt to be otherwise incomplete. They illustrate the "effort after meaning" which customarily haunts the subject who finds himself in an unstructured situation. Such need for sharpening by explanation becomes especially strong when the story has been badly distorted and the report contains implausible and incompatible items. As an example, one subject who received a badly confused description of the subway scene (Fig. 1) inferred that there must have been "an accident." This explanation seemed plausible enough to successive listeners and so was not only accepted by them but sharpened in the telling.

In everyday rumors, sharpening through the introduction of specious explanations, is very apparent. Indeed, as we have said, one of the principal functions of a rumor is to explain personal tensions. To accept tales of Army waste or special privilege among OPA officials could "explain" food shortages and discomfort. Such stories, therefore, find wide credence.

Here, perhaps, is the place to take issue with the popular notion that rumors tend to expand like snowballs, become overelaborate, and verbose. Actually, the course of rumor is toward brevity, whether in the laboratory or in everyday life. Such exaggeration as exists is nearly always a sharpening of some feature resident in the original stimulus situation. The distortion caused by sharpening is,

of course, enormous in extent; but we do not find that we need the category of "elaboration" to account for the changes we observe.

ASSIMILATION

It is apparent that both leveling and sharpening are selective processes. But what is it that leads to the obliteration of some details and the pointing-up of others; and what accounts for all transpositions, importations, and other falsifications that mark the course of rumor? The answer is to be found in the process of *assimilation*, which has to do with the powerful attractive force exerted upon rumor by habits, interests, and sentiments existing in the listener's mind.

Assimilation to Principal Theme. It generally happens that items become sharpened or leveled to fit the leading motif of the story, and they become consistent with this motif in such a way as to make the resulting story more coherent, plausible, and well-rounded. Thus, in one series of rumors, the war theme is preserved and emphasized in all reports. In some experiments using the same picture, a chaplain is introduced, or people (in the plural) are reported as being killed; the ambulance becomes a Red Cross station; demolished buildings are multiplied in the telling; the extent of devastation is exaggerated. All these reports, false though they are, fit the principal theme—a battle incident. If the reported details were actually present in the picture, they would make a "better" *Gestalt*. Objects wholly extraneous to the theme are never introduced—no apple pies, no ballet dancers, no baseball players.

Besides importations, we find other falsifications in the interest of supporting the principal theme. The original picture shows that the Red Cross truck is loaded with explosives, but it is ordinarily reported as carrying medical supplies which is, of course, the way it "ought" to be.

The Negro in this same picture is nearly always described as a soldier, although his clothes might indicate that he is a civilian partisan. It is a "better" configuration to have a soldier in action on the battlefield than to have a civilian among regular soldiers.

Good Continuation. Other falsifications result from the attempt to complete incompleted pictures or to fill in gaps which exist in the stimulus field. The effort is again to make the resulting whole coherent, and meaningful. Thus, the sign, "Loew's Pa . . .," over a moving picture theater is invariably read and reproduced as "Loew's Palace" and Gene *Antry* becomes Gene *Autry*. "Lucky Rakes" are reported as "Lucky Strikes."

All these, and many instances like them, are examples of what has been called, in *Gestalt* terms, "closures." Falsifications of perception and memory they are, but they occur in the interests of bringing about a more coherent, consistent mental configuration. Every detail is assimilated to the principal theme, and "good continuation" is sought, in order to round out meaning where it is lacking or incomplete.

Assimilation by Condensation. It sometimes seems as though memory tries to burden itself as little as possible. For instance, instead of remembering two items, it is more economical to fuse them into one. Instead of a series of subway cards, each of which has its own identity, reports sometimes refer only to "a billboard," or perhaps to a "lot of advertising" (Fig. 1). In another picture, it is more convenient to refer to "all kinds of fruit," rather than to enumerate all the different items on the vendor's cart. Again, the occupants of the car come to be described by some such summary phrase as "several people sitting and standing in the car." Their individuality is lost.

Assimilation to Expectation. Just as details are changed or imported to bear out the simplified theme that the listener has in mind, so also many items take a form that supports the agent's habits of thought. Things are perceived and remembered the way they *usually* are. Thus a drugstore, in one stimulus-picture, is situated in the middle of a block; but, in the telling, it moves up to the corner of the two streets and becomes the familiar "corner drugstore." A Red Cross ambulance is said to carry medical supplies rather than explosives, because it "ought" to be carrying medical supplies. The kilometers on the signposts are changed into miles, since Americans are accustomed to having distances indicated in miles.

The most spectacular of all our assimilative distortions is the finding that, in more than half of our experiments, a razor moves (in the telling) from a white man's hand to a Negro's hand (Fig. 1). This result is a clear instance of assimilation to stereotyped expectancy. Black men are "supposed" to carry razors, white men not.

Assimilation to Linguistic Habits. Expectancy is often merely a matter of fitting perceived and remembered material to preexisting verbal clichés, which exert a powerful influence in the conventionalization of rumors. Words often arouse compelling familiar images in the listener's mind and fix for him the categories in which he must think of the event and the value that he must attach to it. A "zoot-suit sharpie" packs much more meaning and carries more affect than more objective words, such as, "a colored man with pegged trousers, wide-brimmed hat, etc." (Fig. 1). Rumors are commonly told in verbal stereotypes which imply prejudicial judgment, such as "draft dodger," "Japanese spy," "brass hat," "dumb Swede," "long-haired professor," and the like.

MORE HIGHLY MOTIVATED ASSIMILATION

Although the conditions of our experiment do not give full play to emotional tendencies underlying gossip, rumor, and scandal, such tendencies are so insistent that they express themselves even under laboratory conditions.

Assimilation to Interest. It sometimes happens that a picture containing women's dresses, as a trifling detail in the original scene, becomes, in the telling, a story exclusively about dresses. This sharpening occurs when the rumor is told by groups of women, but never when told by men.

A picture involving police was employed with a group of police officers as subjects. In the resulting protocol, the entire reproduction centered around the police officer (with whom the subjects undoubtedly felt keen sympathy or "identification"). Furthermore, the nightstick, a symbol of his power, is greatly sharpened and becomes the main object of the controversy. The tale as a whole is protective of, and partial to, the policeman.

Assimilation to Prejudice. Hard as it is in an experimental situation to obtain distortions that arise from hatred, yet we have in our material a certain opportunity to trace the hostile complex of racial attitudes.

We have spoken of the picture which contained a white man holding a razor while arguing with a Negro. In over half of the experiments with this picture, the final report indicated that the Negro (instead of the white man) held the razor in his hand, and several times he was reported as "brandishing it widely" or as "threatening" the white man with it (Fig. 1).

Whether this ominous distortion reflects hatred and fear of Negroes we cannot definitely say. In some cases, these deeper emotions may be the assimilative factor at work. And yet the distortion may occur even in subjects who have no anti-Negro bias. It is an unthinking cultural stereotype that the Negro is hot tempered and addicted to the use of razors as weapons. The rumor, though

mischievous, may reflect chiefly an assimilation of the story to verbal-clichés and conventional expectation. Distortion in this case may not mean assimilation to hostility. Much so-called prejudice is, of course, a mere matter of conforming to current folkways by accepting prevalent beliefs about an out-group.

Whether or not this razor-shift reflects deep hatred and fear on the part of white subjects, it is certain that the reports of our Negro subjects betray a motivated type of distortion. Because it was to their interest as members of the race to de-emphasize the racial caricature, Negro subjects almost invariably avoided mention of color. One of them hearing a rumor containing the phrase, "a Negro zoot-suiter," reported "There is a man wearing a zoot suit, *possibly* a Negro."

For one picture, a Negro reporter said that the colored man in the center of the picture "is being maltreated." Though this interpretation may be correct, it is likewise possible that he is a rioter about to be arrested by the police officer. White and Negro subjects are very likely to perceive, remember, and interpret this particular situation in quite opposite ways.

Thus, even under laboratory conditions, we find assimilation in terms of deep-lying emotional predispositions. Our rumors, like those of everyday life, tend to fit into, and support, the occupational interests, class or racial memberships, or personal prejudices of the reporter.

CONCLUSION: THE EMBEDDING PROCESS

Leveling, sharpening, and assimilation are not independent mechanisms. They function simultaneously, and reflect a singular subjectifying process that results in the autism and falsification which are so characteristic of rumor. If we were to attempt to summarize what happens in a few words we might say:

Whenever a stimulus field is of potential importance to an individual, but at the same time unclear, or susceptible of divergent interpretations, a subjective structuring process is started. Although the process is complex (involving, as it does, leveling, sharpening, and assimilation), its essential nature can be characterized as an effort to reduce the stimulus to a simple and meaningful structure that has adaptive significance for the individual in terms of his own interests and experience. The process begins at the moment the ambiguous situation is perceived, but the effects are greatest if memory intervenes. The longer the time that elapses after the stimulus is perceived the greater the threefold change is likely to be. Also, the more people involved in a serial report, the greater the change is likely to be, until the rumor has reached an aphoristic brevity, and is repeated by rote.

Now, this three-pronged process turns out to be characteristic not only of rumor but of the individual memory function as well. It has been uncovered and described in the experiments on individual retention conducted by Wulf, Gibson, Allport,[4] and, in Bartlett's memory experiments carried out both on individuals and on groups.[5]

Up to now, however, there has been no agreement on precisely the terminology to use, nor upon the adequacy of the three functions we here describe. We believe that our conceptualization of the three-fold course of change and decay is sufficient to account, not only for our own experimental findings and for the experiments of others in this area, but also for the distortions that everyday rumors undergo.

For lack of a better designation, we speak of the three-fold change as the *embedding* process. What seems to occur in all our experiments and in all related studies is that each subject finds the outer stimulus-world far too hard to grasp and retain in its objective character. For his own personal uses, it must be recast to fit not only his span of comprehension and his span of retention, but, likewise, his own personal needs and interests. What was outer becomes inner; what was objective becomes subjective. In telling a rumor, the kernel of objective information that he received has become so embedded into his own dynamic mental life that the product is chiefly one of projection. Into the rumor, he projects the deficiencies of his retentive processes, as well as his own effort to engender meaning upon an ambiguous field, and the product reveals much of his own emotional needs, including his anxieties, hates, and wishes. When several rumor-agents have been involved in this embedding process, the net result of the serial reproduction reflects the lowest common denominator of cultural interest, of memory span, and of group sentiment and prejudice.

One may ask whether a rumor must always be false. We answer that, in virtually every case, the embedding process is so extensive that no credibility whatever should be ascribed to the product. If a report does turn out to be trustworthy, we usually find that secure standards of evidence have somehow been present to which successive agents could refer for purposes of validation. Perhaps the morning newspaper or the radio have held the rumor under control, but when such secure standards of verification are available, it is questionable whether we should speak of rumor at all.

There are, of course, border-line cases where we may not be able to say whether a given tidbit should or should not be called a rumor. But if we define rumor (and we herewith propose that we should), as *a proposition for belief of topical reference, without secure standards of evidence being present*—then it follows from the facts we have presented that

[4] Conveniently summarized in K. Koffka, *Principles of Gestalt Psychology* (New York: Harcourt Brace and Co., 1935).

[5] F. C. Bartlett, *Remembering* (Cambridge, England: Cambridge University Press, 1932).

rumor will suffer such serious distortion through the embedding process, that *it* *is never under any circumstances a valid guide for belief or conduct.*

THE EFFECT OF AN AUDIENCE UPON WHAT IS REMEMBERED
By Claire Zimmerman and Raymond A. Bauer

Perhaps we should explain how we got started on this problem. We were studying mechanisms whereby foreign travel might affect the attitudes of an American traveler. That led us to a general consideration of the role of the audience in the communications process.

It seemed quite possible that a returning traveler often did not formulate his impressions of his experiences abroad until a friend asked him for these impressions or until he was asked to give a speech. While abroad, he had been absorbed in the business of living. He had feelings about specific men he saw, individual meals, trains, or what not, but little or no impression of the foreign country or countries as a whole. His overall impression, we suspected, he would produce for the first time when confronted (in fact or in thought) with an audience back home for whom he had to make a synthesis. If that were so, the audience, as much as the experience, might prove decisive for what the travel experience meant. If the first speech about the trip were to the League of Women Voters, he might formulate his impressions quite differently than if the speech

were made to the Chamber of Commerce. Faced with an audience of whose wishes, expectations, and values he had a definite image, he would organize his speech in some way as a function of his image of that audience, regardless of whether his intention was to persuade them to his point of view or to gain their approval.

It might well be that an audience, by influencing the way in which an individual organizes the presentation that he makes to it, would in effect cause him to play a role. This might influence his subsequent attitudes and recollection of the subject matter on which he was speaking. Indeed, recent research on communications has shown that role playing can affect an individual's attitudes.[1]

This notion quickly led us further. It is likely that a good deal of a person's mental activity consists, in whole or part, of imagined communication to audiences imagined or real, and that this may have a considerable effect on what he remembers and believes at any one point in time, and in turn on what he is likely to say or do in a given situation. Among the kinds of audience with which he may hold imaginary conversations are

From *The Public Opinion Quarterly*, 1956, XX, 238–248. Reprinted by permission of the authors and the publisher. The experiment was conducted and the results analyzed by Miss Zimmerman. The germinal idea originated with Ithiel de Sola Pool. During the year 1954–55 a study group which included, besides the authors, Jerome S. Bruner and Mr. Pool, met a number of times to explore the ramifications of the role of the audience in the communications process. This experiment was designed in the course of these discussions. A memorandum by Mr. Bauer on "The Role of Audiences in the Communications Process" may be obtained from the Center for International Studies, Massachusetts Institute of Technology.

[1] I. Janis and B. King, "The Influence of Role Playing on Opinion Change," pages 472–482 of this volume.

reference groups and significant internalized figures, as well as his prospective real audiences.

If all this speculation is correct, then it is possible that the groups which a person "carries around in his head" as potential prospective audiences may be a significant factor in the way in which he perceives, organizes, and uses new information. This should, in turn, have important implications for the study of communications, of the processes whereby groups influence the attitudes and behavior of their members, etc.

While all these ideas seemed plausible, our confidence in their significance would be vastly increased if it were possible to test in a controlled situation one of our basic propositions, that the imagined attitudes of prospective audiences can affect what a person will remember of new incoming information. The major specific hypothesis to be tested was that material which was incongruent with the imagined attitudes of a prospective audience would be remembered less well than material which was congruent with these imagined attitudes.

In addition to the main hypothesis, we were interested in testing a second hypothesis, that certain groups of people were more "sensitive" than others. The "sensitive" groups should, according to this hypothesis, show more "audience effect" than the less sensitive groups. There are a number of factors which might differentiate more and less "sensitive" persons. One of them might be traits of personality which would be exhibited in "inner" and "other directedness." Or, the individuals' attitudes toward the content of the communication and/or the particular audiences might prove important. For this first experiment we selected our contrasting groups on the basis of their professional orientation. We selected for half our subjects graduate students in journalism as examples of a group which was likely, because of choice of profession and training,

to be relatively sensitive to audience characteristics. We chose as a contrasting group students in teachers' colleges as persons possibly less sensitive to audience response in general. Furthermore, since the subject matter of the information which was used in the experiment was the topic of teachers' pay, they would be personally concerned with it and perhaps therefore less subject to audience influence. Through our choice of topic and teacher group we were attempting to minimize for these subjects the audience effect. The specific prediction, then, was that if our first hypothesis was supported by the findings of the experiment, the effect should be greater for the experimental subjects from the schools of journalism than for the subjects from the schools of education.

Two sets of arguments were composed about the issue of teachers' salaries. One set presented points in favor of raising teachers' salaries and the other set presented points opposed to raising teachers' salaries. The two sets of materials were of approximately equal length and difficulty, as pretested by the length of time required to learn.

We invented two fictitious audiences: The National Council of Teachers, and The American Taxpayers Economy League. The National Council of Teachers was described to subjects as "a group interested in the welfare of American teachers and the promotion of their interests"; The American Taxpayers Economy League was described to subjects as "a group interested in the welfare of the American taxpayer and in reducing the heavy burdens upon him." Both the names and the descriptions of the audiences were composed to suggest to the subjects that The National Council of Teachers would agree with arguments in favor of raising teachers' salaries and The American Taxpayers Economy League would, presumably, agree with arguments against raising teachers' salaries.

The experimental design involved four groups of subjects allowing for all combinations of kinds of arguments and kinds of audience:

Argument	Audience	
	Nat'l Council of Teachers	Amer. Taxpayers Economy League
Raise salaries	1	2
Do not raise salaries	3	4

We can label groups 1 and 4 "congruent" in the sense that the audience and the arguments are presumed to be in agreement; we can label groups 2 and 3 "incongruent" in the sense that the audience and the arguments are presumed to be in disagreement.

Since we replicated this design with teachers and journalists, the final experiment provided for eight groups of subjects. The major predictions were: (1) incongruent groups will be less accurate in their memory for arguments than congruent groups; and (2) journalism students will show more audience effects than teaching students.

THE PROCEDURE

We selected two schools of journalism, roughly equated in size, locality, and socio-economic background of students. We also selected two state teachers' colleges, equated in the same way. There were 18 subjects in each group.

The experimenter, a woman, was introduced to each class as a representative of the appropriate audience. For example, if she was addressing journalism students whose audience was The National Council of Teachers and whose arguments were to be in favor of raising teachers' salaries, she gave the following information as informally as possible:

The National Council of Teachers has asked me to have some journalism students come talk to them at their next meeting on the topic of teacher salary. The National Coun-

cil of Teachers is a group interested in the welfare of American teachers and the promotion of their interests. The National Council of Teachers will choose these journalism students on the basis of some informal talks that I am going to ask you to write. The talks will be very short—three to five minutes. I'll ask you to write these talks about teacher salary for the Council next week, not today. If your talk should be chosen by the Council and you decide you don't want to go talk with them, that's O.K., too. The Council is interested in your ideas about teacher salary, whether or not you decide to attend their meeting. Only representatives of The National Council of Teachers will see the talk you write, no one here at the college. Today the Council would like you to listen to some statements about teacher salaries. The National Council of Teachers did *not* prepare the statements I'm about to read to you; they have been condensed from an article in a national magazine. Please pay careful attention to these statements since I'll be able to read them only twice and they may help you get some ideas for the talk which you write next week.

The experimenter read the statements in favor of raising teachers' salaries twice in immediate succession and then asked the class to write down all they could remember: "Try to get it verbatim, to give the National Council of Teachers an idea of how many statements like those people can remember when they're read aloud instead of actually seen on paper. This will also help you get the ideas firmly in mind." In order to keep each subject's attention focussed on the audience, he was asked to use "paper furnished by the Council," paper with The National Council of Teachers printed across the top.

Subjects were allowed 15 minutes for writing the material; after five minutes had elapsed, they were urged again to be as accurate as possible. This memory test is referred to below as the first recall test.

The experimenter then reminded the subjects that they would be asked to write a short talk the next week and asked them not to talk or read about the

TABLE 1

Mean Numbers of Points Correct on First Recall Trial
for All Groups

	Tax Audience		Teacher Audience	
	Incongruent Raise salary arguments	*Congruent* Do not raise salary arguments	*Incongruent* Do not raise salary arguments	*Congruent* Raise salary arguments
Students of Journalism	15.2	15.3	17.6	17.7
Teaching	14.9	15.4	15.7	14.4

N = 18 for each group

material and not to prepare their talks during the intervening week; "The Council can get experts to write polished essays, but it wants your own spontaneous views about teachers' salaries."

A week later the experimenter returned and asked the students to write down as much as they remembered of the material read the week before, "so The National Council of Teachers can find out how well people can remember this kind of material after a week's time." Again, paper with audience title was distributed, and again the subjects were urged to be as accurate as possible. Subjects were allowed 15 minutes for writing. This memory test is referred to below as the second recall test.

Following the recall test, subjects were asked to write their short talks, listing the major points they would make. Then they answered a series of questions designed to get information about the geographic origin and socio-economic characteristics of the subjects, the degree to which they agreed with the arguments presented, and their perceptions of the audience as agreeing or disagreeing with these arguments.

The Results

The two sets of arguments, one in favor of raising teachers' salaries, and the other opposed to the raising of teachers' salaries, had each been divided into 25 separate points or units. The number of points which each subject remembered correctly on the first trial immediately after having heard the passage read to him, and then on the second trial a week later, was recorded. The mean numbers of points which were recalled correctly by the members of each group on the first trial are presented in Table 1; those for the second trial are presented in Table 2.

If we look first at Table 2 we see that both of our hypotheses seem to be supported. Apropos of the first hypothesis the mean number of points recalled correctly is in every instance greater when the arguments were congruent with the anticipated attitudes of the audience. When there was incongruence between the argument and the audience, less was remembered. Our second hypothesis is also supported. While there seems to be no difference in the accuracy of recall of journalism students and students in teachers' colleges when the argument and the audience are congruent, journalism students recall fewer points on the average when the audience and argument are incongruent.

There is nothing in the pattern of recall on the first trial, as summarized in

TABLE 2

MEAN NUMBER OF POINTS CORRECT ON SECOND RECALL TRIAL
FOR ALL GROUPS

	Tax Audience		Teacher Audience	
	Incongruent Raise salary arguments	*Congruent* Do not raise salary arguments	*Incongruent* Do not raise salary arguments	*Congruent* Raise salary arguments
Students of Journalism	4.9	11.3	6.1	13.7
Teaching	8.6	11.5	8.8	11.3

N = 18 for each group

Table 1, to suggest that the differences we have just been discussing were a result of the subjects' perception of the passages read to them or of their initial memorizing of the passages. When recalling the passages immediately after having heard them, both groups of students recalled both congruent and incongruent passages with equal accuracy. Furthermore, in each situation the journalism students did at least as well as did the students in the teachers' colleges. Therefore, the differences observed on the second trial seem to have been the result of processes at work in the intervening week or at the point of recall, whether the processes be regarded as "forgetting" or "repression," or some other mechanism.

Although the differences between group means on the first recall trial were insignificant, there was considerable individual variation. Therefore, for computation of the statistical significance of the changes between the first and second trials we used the percentage loss of accurate recall for each individual subject.

An analysis of variance was performed to test the significance of these differences.[2] Three differences were significant beyond the .01 level of confidence: variation due to difference between kinds of students, interaction between audiences and arguments, and interaction between audiences and arguments and students. In other words, all of the differences which bear on our two hypotheses are statistically significant at the .01 level of confidence. Four other interrelations—between audiences, between arguments, between audiences and kinds of students, and between arguments and kinds of students—proved to be of minor significance. None of this latter group of interrelationships bear on our hypotheses.

IMPLICATIONS OF THE FINDINGS

There seems little doubt that we have been able to demonstrate, in a controlled situation, that the anticipation of communicating to an audience of which one has a definite image can affect what an individual will remember of new information to which he is exposed. When the audience is seen as agreeing with the new information or arguments presented, recall of that information is more accurate than when the audience is perceived as

_____

[2] For the analysis of variance tables, see our original publication, *op. cit.*

disagreeing with the information or arguments. Not only was this finding "statistically significant," but the differences were of sufficient magnitude as to be of real practical importance. In the instance of journalism students, they were able to remember accurately only about half as many items in a situation of incongruence as they were able to remember in a situation of congruence between the content of the new information and their image of the anticipated audience.

The fulfillment of our second prediction, that the image of the audience would have more effect on the journalism students than on the students in the teachers' colleges, substantiates the notion that there are predictable differences between individuals with respect to their "audience sensitivity." In this instance, as we have indicated, the prediction was made on a sociological basis. The journalism students were selected because we felt that by virtue of their training and/or self-selection they would be a group strongly sensitive to the characteristics of audiences to which they were supposed to communicate. The teachers' college students, on the other hand, we regarded as sufficiently involved in the issue of teachers' pay that their own values and interests would tend to blunt somewhat their sensitivity to the wishes and expectations of the prospective audiences. The verification of this prediction, and that of the first hypothesis, are significant as an indication of the possible practical importance of the phenomena with which we are concerned. These verifications, however, are not without theoretical ambiguity. We deliberately selected what we considered to be groups which might fall at extremes of a continuum with respect to audience sensitivity. Clarification of the factors which affect "audience sensitivity" demands experimentation in which relationships between subjects and audience and between subjects and subject matter are controlled more precisely. Addition-

ally, personality differences which may affect audience sensitivity should be investigated. Finally, the motivational set of the subjects must either be controlled or studied systematically. It is quite possible that the journalism students were oriented primarily toward pleasing their audiences while the teachers' college students were concentrating on changing the opinions of their audiences, or perhaps they viewed the audiences in different ways.

The intent of this particular experiment was not primarily to investigate the mechanism whereby the audience exerted its influence, but rather to test whether or not our hypothecated "audience effect" was a phenomenon of any importance, and—if so—whether it could be induced in an experimental situation. Nevertheless, certain portions of our analysis and some of the additional data which we gathered suggest some of the processes which may be at work here and thereby indicate fruitful directions for future research. In all instances we have done some form of quantitative analysis. However, because in most cases the number of respondents who answered certain follow-up questions was small or because some stages of quantitative analysis have not been carried to completion, we have to regard such statistical findings extremely tentatively. For fear that their presentation would convey a greater sense of precision than we feel is warranted, we discuss them qualitatively as indications for future research.

When queried about their images of the audiences at the close of the experiment, the journalism students seemed to have retained a more accurate picture of the attitudes of the incongruent audiences as that picture was drawn in the experimenter's description of these audiences in the first experimental setting. The journalism students tended to see the incongruent audiences as hostile to the message, whereas the teachers' college students were more likely to see them as neutral. On a phenotypic level this finding, as slim as the data on which it is based may be, conforms well with our general notion of what was taking place in the course of this experiment. The journalists, being more aware of the conflict between the content of the passage which they had heard read to them and the attitudes of the audience to which they were supposed to address themselves, recalled this material less accurately; the teachers being less aware of the conflict recalled more accurately.

Further analysis of these slim data produced an additional finding pointing in the same direction. Among the teachers' college students, those who perceived the incongruity between the audience and the argument presented them recalled the material less well than did those teachers' college students who saw the audience as neutral. While these findings support our more general and well-established hypothesis of the interrelationship between the subjects' image of the audience and their retention of information, they are somewhat ambiguous as to the direction of influence. If we are willing to argue that the perception of incongruence between information and the audience could affect an individual's remembering of the information, we must also be willing to entertain the possibility that a person strongly committed to the subject matter of the issue (students in teachers' colleges, for instance) might distort his image of the audience in order to make it more congruent with the information. Only further investigation can indicate which influence is in effect in which situations.

We have not yet talked about the cognitive processes involved in the differential accuracy of recall that was affected by our subjects' images of the anticipated audiences. Accuracy may decrease because of complete forgetting (omissions), because of distortions of the information, or because both processes are at work. Preliminary analysis of the groups in the incongruent situations indicates not only that distortions—as contrasted to complete forgetting—do appear but also that these distortions are of a systematic nature. As one might expect, the distortions tend to occur in a direction that makes the information more acceptable to the expected audiences. For example, subjects anticipating a talk to the American Taxpayers' Economy League and trying to recall the argument in favor of raising teachers' salaries, often reduced the discrepancy between the teachers' and the sanitation workers' salaries which were given to them in the original text. Further experimentation, probably with a more difficult body of material, would provide us with more knowledge of the relative role of distortion and complete forgetting.

The replication of this experiment with the use of more complicated passages would perhaps also give us a better notion of why there was no "audience effect" exhibited in the first recall trial. If the process of memory begins, as we believe, with the initial perception of new information, then we would also expect the processes at work to show their effects from the beginning. The passages employed in the present experiment appear to have been sufficiently simple so that they did not invite initial perceptual distortion or short-run selective remembering. With more complicated passages we might expect at least some traces of "audience effect" in the first recall trial.

If we have in fact demonstrated that psychological set to communicate to an audience of specified characteristics can affect what one will remember of new information, what may we assume about the influence of the audience on the attitudes of persons exposed to such a situation? On a *prima facie* basis one might well feel confident that, if one can affect memory by such a device, he ought easily to be able to affect attitudes. However, memory and attitudes are conceptually distinguishable in the context of this situation, and it would be well worthwhile to test the influence of "audience effect" on the attitudes of subjects in the comparable experimental situation.

Finally, there is need to explicate just what is involved in the effect of an audience on "what is remembered." The second recall was tested in a situation designed to bring out the "audience effect." The subjects were asked to recall the content of the passage at a time immediately preceding their writing of the anticipated "speech." Under these circumstances the subjects may have been sufficiently intensely set for the writing of the anticipated speech that their repression or distortion of incongruous information may

well have been accentuated, but not beyond the level frequently found in real life situations. For theoretical purposes it would be crucial to discover how much of the "repressed" or "distorted" information was irrevocably "forgotten." A future experiment could test this by one or both of two changes of design. Preceding the second recall half the subjects could either be informed of the true purpose of the experiment—thus releasing them from the influence of the anticipated audience—or the "audiences" could be reversed. The employment of one or both of these devices would give us a clue to how much of the "forgotten" or "distorted" material was truly lost.

POLITICAL PERCEPTION
By Bernard Berelson, Paul Lazarsfeld, and William N. McPhee

The modern political party in a town like Elmira has an effective existence more in the minds of the partisans than in the local community's formal political organizations. And this existence is primarily expressed through differences in attitudes toward political issues of the day.

But this is not the only way in which the partisans differentiate themselves. There is also the fact of political perception—how the voter *sees* events in the political world. Specifically, we are concerned here with how voters in 1948 saw the issues of the campaign and what difference that made in their political behavior.

Now this is not simply a nice psychological problem with little relevance for the political situation. The process of

political perception can operate to increase cleavage or consensus within the community. It undoubtedly contributes directly to a "real" definition of the differences between the parties, in terms of what might be called their "political norms."

For political beliefs and perceptions have a strongly "normative" quality. They not only state that "this is the way things are," but they also imply that "this is their customary or natural state" and therefore what they "ought" to be. The parties are not only what their leaders do or say; the parties are also what their followers believe they are, expect them to be, and therefore think they should be.

Once again we encounter a brief glimpse of the spiral of cause and effect

From Bernard Berelson, Paul F. Lazarsfeld, and William N. McPhee, *Voting* (Chicago: University of Chicago Press, 1954). Copyright 1954 by University of Chicago, all rights reserved. *Voting* reports a study conducted in Elmira, N. Y., dealing with the presidential election campaign of 1948.

that constitutes political history—in this case the history of political issues: What the parties do affects what the voters think they are and what the voters think they are affects what they subsequently do. Out of this interaction between subjective perception and objective reality, mutually affecting one another over decades, emerges not only our definition but the reality of a political party's role. The popular image of "what Republicans (or Democrats) are like" helps to define and determine what they "really" are. Today's subjective unreality in the voters' minds affects tomorrow's objective reality in the political arena.

About thirty years ago an analyst of public opinion gained lasting distinction by elaborating the differences between "the world outside and the pictures in our heads." Walter Lippmann discussed what many theorists—philosophers, psychologists, sociologists, political scientists, anthropologists—have noted and documented before and since: subjective perception does not always reflect objective reality accurately. Selective perception—sampling the real world—must be taken into account. The mirror that the mind holds up to nature is often distorted in accordance with the subject's predispositions. The "trickle of messages from the outside is affected by the stored-up images, the preconceptions, and the prejudices which interpret, fill them out, and in their turn powerfully direct the play of our attention, and our vision itself. . . . In the individual person, the limited messages from outside, formed into a pattern of stereotypes, are identified with his own interests as he feels and conceives them." [1] Another student of public opinion put it similarly: "Each looks at, and looks for, the facts and reasons to which his attention points,

perceiving little, if at all, those to which his mind is not directed. As a rule, men see what they look for, and observe the things they expect to see." [2]

THE STUDY: THE 1948 PRESIDENTIAL ELECTIONS

The world of political reality, even as it involves a presidential campaign and election, is by no means simple or narrow. Nor is it crystal-clear. Over a period of six months, and intensively for six weeks, the electorate is subjected to a wide variety of campaign events. Even if all the political events were unambiguous, there would still be a problem of political perception; but, as it is, the campaign is composed (often deliberately) of ambiguous as well as clear elements.

Just how clear was the objective field to be perceived in 1948? Some propagandists, and some students of propaganda, believe that ambiguity often promotes effectiveness, since each subject is then free to define the matter in terms satisfactory to himself. While a sharply clear statement may win some friends by its very decisiveness, it may also lose some people for the same reason. Now Truman and Dewey had both been public figures for some time and had taken public stands on many political matters; yet their positions on the issues in the campaign were not equally clear.

In 1948 Truman took a more straightforward and more aggressive position on these issues than Dewey (Table 1). The latter spoke to a large extent on the need for unity, peace, and freedom, while Truman specified his position *for* price control and public housing and *against* the Taft-Hartley Law. And Truman used quite vigorous language in stating his position, whereas Dewey employed a

---

[1] Walter Lippmann, *Public Opinion*, (New York: The MacMillan Company, 1922), p. 31.
[2] A. Lawrence Lowell, *Public Opinion in War and Peace* (Cambridge, Mass.: Harvard University Press, 1923), p. 22.

TABLE 1

POSITIONS TAKEN BY DEWEY AND TRUMAN ON FOUR ISSUES DURING THE CAMPAIGN

	Dewey	Truman
Price control	Causes of high prices were war, foreign aid, the administration's discouragement of production, governmental mismanagement Remedies: cut government spending, reduce national debt, increase production No reference to imposition of controls Only one major reference	Republicans would not act against inflation in Eightieth Congress or special session; they rejected the administration's program Called for price controls or anti-inflation measures on several occasions
Taft-Hartley Law	Referred to it as "Labor-Management Relations Act of 1947," never as "Taft-Hartley Law" Made abstract remarks about "labor's freedoms" which would be "zealously guarded and extended" Approved the law in general ("will not retreat from advances made") but left door open for improvements ("where laws affecting labor can be made a better instrument for labor relations . . .")	Made the "shameful" and "vicious" law a major issue; recalled that Republicans passed it over his veto: "It ought to be repealed" Took this position in at least ten major campaign speeches during October
Policy toward USSR	Took a strong anticommunism position; linked communism to administration Made this a major issue in about seven campaign speeches	Took an anticommunism position; major references twice
Public housing	Only minor references to need for more housing (Republican platform called for housing financed by private enterprise, with federal "encouragement" when private industry and local government were unable to fill need)	Republicans "killed" Taft-Ellender-Wagner Bill Called for public housing sponsored by government in at least ten major campaign speeches

more lofty rhetoric. Except perhaps for the Russian issue (which became involved with the spy and domestic Communist issue), there can be no question but that, objectively, Dewey's position was more amenable to misperception than Truman's.

And this is reflected in the extent of nonperception of the candidates' stands.[3]

On the four issues the proportion of respondents who do not know the candidates' stands average about 10 percent for Truman and about 25 percent for Dewey. (This also reflects the fact that Truman's official position brought him before the public on such issues on numerous occasions; but a counterconsideration is that Dewey's position as gover-

---

[3] The questions followed this form: "From what you know, is Truman (Dewey) for the Taft-Hartley Law or against it?" The respondent could say "Don't know" or state that the candidate had not taken any stand on the issue. The perception questions were asked in August, before the campaign proper; replies may have been different in October.

TABLE 2

PARTY PREFERENCE DOES NOT PARTICULARLY AFFECT THE VOTER'S PERCEPTION
OF WHERE THE CANDIDATES STAND ON SOME CAMPAIGN ISSUES

	Dewey's Stand Percentage of		Truman's Stand Percentage of	
	Republicans	Democrats	Republicans	Democrats
Price controls:				
Put back controls	25	25	85	93
Leave off controls	38	45	8	3
No stand (by candidate)	6	5	0	0
Don't know	31	25	7	4
Taft-Hartley Law:				
For it	48	55	27	21
Against it	9	7	54	65
No stand	5	3	1	1
Don't know	38	35	18	13
Government sponsorship of public housing:				
For it	77	60	67	90
Against it	4	17	13	2
No stand	2	5	2	0
Don't know	17	18	18	8
	(N = 421–501)	(N = 171–204)	(N = 421–501)	(N = 171–204)

nor of New York made him especially familiar to Elmirans.)

Perception and Party Preference. More importantly, the voter's perception of where the candidates stand on the issues is not uniformly affected by partisan preference—only selectively so (Table 2). It is not marked on the central issues of price control and the Taft-Hartley Law. Republicans and Democrats agree that Truman is for price control and against the Taft-Hartley Law and that Dewey is for the Taft-Hartley Law and against price control (although on this last there is by no means a clear perception of where Dewey stood). On public housing (and on the Russian problem) the difference between the parties was greater.

Why should the partisans agree in perception on some issues and disagree on others? For one thing, of course, perception varies with the ambiguity of the situation. The less ambiguous the objective situation (e.g., Truman's position on price control), the less disagreement. But, for another, perception seems to vary with the degree of controversiality of the issues in the community. On price control and the Taft-Hartley Law the respondents with opinions divided about 60–40; on the other two issues (including firmness toward Russia), in Elmira the split is about 90–10. in the latter case, then, there is virtual agreement within the community—which means that one side of the issue is considered "right" and the other side "wrong." Hence there is, so to speak, a standard to guide misperception—and each side pulls its own candidate toward the "correct position" and pushes the opponent away from it. On the two central issues, however, the controversy is too visible to allow a designation of "rightness" for one or the other side, and as a result there

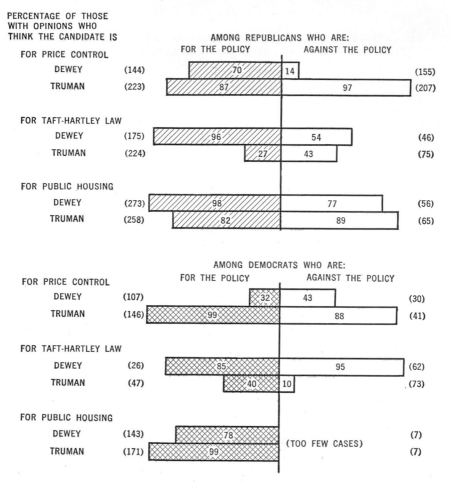

FIG. 1. The voters' own stands on the issues affect their perception of the candidates' stands. For simplification and clarity, the "no stand" and the "don't know" responses have been omitted from this chart. Numbers in parentheses indicate the number of cases on which the percentages are based.

is less motive for or gain in misperception. If the voter gets nothing for his misperception (e.g., being "right"), there is less reason for him to engage in it. Deviation or misperception requires a certain degree of ambiguity in the objective situation being perceived, but it also requires a psychic indulgence for the misperceiver. Where this opportunity is not present, perception is likely to be more accurate.

Perception and Own Stand. This suggests that perception of the candidates'

stands on issues may be affected by the respondents' own stands on them. The voters can thus manage to increase the consistency within their own political position, or at least the apparent consistency. And this is clearly the case. In almost every instance respondents perceive their candidate's stand on these issues as similar to their own and the opponent's stand as dissimilar—whatever their own position (Fig. 1). For example, those Republicans who favor price control perceive Dewey as favoring price con-

PERCENTAGE WHO "DON'T KNOW" THEIR OWN CANDIDATE'S STAND

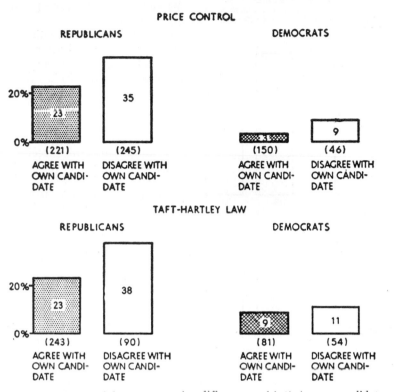

FIG. 2. Partisans tend not to perceive differences with their own candidate
or similarities to the opposition candidate.

trol (70 percent), and those who oppose price control perceive Dewey as opposing controls (86 percent). And the Republicans who are against controls perceive Truman as favoring them somewhat more than the Republicans who are for them. As with their perception of group support, so with their perception of the issues: the partisans manage to "pull" their own candidate and "push" the opposing candidate with considerable consistency. Overlaying the base of objective observation is the distortion effect— distortion in harmony with political predispositions. As Schumpeter says, "Information and arguments in political

matters will 'register' only if they link up with the citizen's preconceived ideas."[4]

At the same time, some voters maintain or increase their perceptual defense on political issues by refusing to acknowledge differences with one's own candidate or similarities to the opposition candidate. Such denial of reality, a defense utilized against uncongenial aspects of the environment, is well documented by case studies and laboratory experiments in the psychological literature of neurosis. Here we have evidence on its operation in the midst of a political campaign where motivation is less strong.

Take the two major issues of price con-

---

[4] Joseph Schumpeter, *Capitalism, Socialism, and Democracy* (New York: Harper & Brothers, 1942) p. 263.

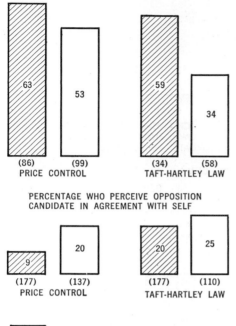

AMONG THOSE OBJECTIVELY IN DISAGREEMENT WITH THE GIVEN CANDIDATE

PERCENTAGE WHO PERCEIVE OWN CANDIDATE IN AGREEMENT WITH SELF

63 53 (86) (99) PRICE CONTROL

59 34 (34) (58) TAFT-HARTLEY LAW

PERCENTAGE WHO PERCEIVE OPPOSITION CANDIDATE IN AGREEMENT WITH SELF

9 20 (177) (137) PRICE CONTROL

20 25 (177) (110) TAFT-HARTLEY LAW

FEEL STRONGLY ABOUT CANDIDATE CHOICE

DO NOT FEEL STRONGLY

FIG. 3. The stronger the political affiliation, the greater the tendency to perceive issues favorably to one's self. This same tendency appears in the case of perception of the support given the candidates by various socioeconomic and ethnic groups. In almost every case strong partisans "pull" approved groups more than weak partisans.

trol and the Taft-Hartley Law, on which the candidates took relatively clear positions. Objectively, an observer would say that Truman was for and Dewey against price control and that Truman was against and Dewey for the Taft-Hartley Law. Yet, when our respondents are asked where the candidates stand, a certain proportion of them do not know or profess not to know. But—and this is the point—the "Don't knows" are more frequent among partisans who them-

selves take a different position from their own candidate or the same position as the opponent (Fig. 2).

Perception and Strength of Feeling. This tendency to "misperceive" issues in a favorable direction does not operate in a uniform fashion within the electorate. The degree of affect attached to the election, in the form of intensity of one's vote intention, also influences perception. Those voters who feel strongly about their vote intention perceive political issues differently from those who do not feel so strongly about the matter (Fig. 3). With remarkable consistency within each party, the intensely involved "pull" their own candidate and "push" the opponent more than the less involved. (Incidentally, it is probably not too much to suggest that this "pull" and "push" are equivalent to the psychological defense mechanisms of generalization and exclusion.)

For example, when objectively they are *not* in agreement with their own party, *strong* Republicans and Democrats perceive their candidate's stand on the issues as more in harmony with their own stand than do weak Republicans and Democrats in the same situation. But, by no means is this a general tendency to see everyone in agreement with themselves. When they objectively disagree with the *opposition* candidate, the strong partisans are quickest to perceive that disagreement. The stronger the partisanship, the *greater* the (mis)perception of agreement with one's own side and the *less* the (mis)perception of agreement with the opposition. Presumably, misperception makes for partisanship, and the reverse. Thus, the people strongest for a candidate—the ones most interested in and active for his election, the ones who make up the core of the party support— are the ones who take the least equivocal position on what their party stands for. And, at the same time, those who favor the party position as they see it are more likely to support the candidate strongly.

PERCENTAGE REPUBLICAN OF TWO-PARTY VOTE

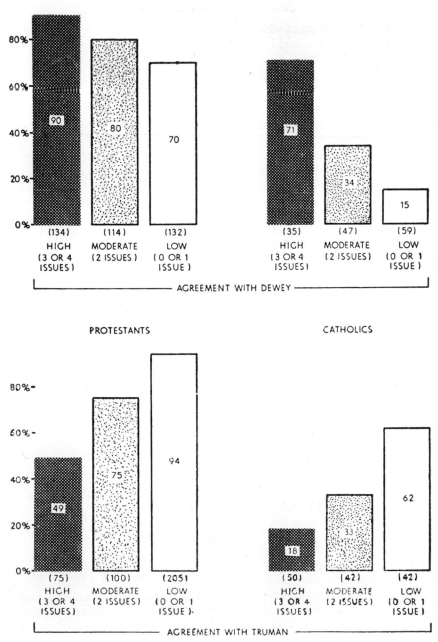

FIG. 4. Social differences in voting remain regardless of perceived agreement with candidates.

TABLE 3

PERCENTAGE VOTING FOR "OWN-GROUP'S" CANDIDATE:
PROTESTANTS AND CATHOLICS

Perceived agreement with candidates of:				
"Own" group	High	Low	High	Low
"Opposite" group	Low	Low	High	High
Percentage voting for "own-group's" candidate	90	70	52	21

In the course of the campaign, then, strength of party support influences the perception of political issues. The more intensely one holds a vote position, the more likely he is to see the political environment as favorable to himself, as conforming to his own beliefs. He is less likely to perceive uncongenial and contradictory events or points of view and hence presumably less likely to revise his own original position. In this manner perception can play a major role in the spiraling effect of political reinforcement.

Necessarily, such partisanly motivated perception increases the recognized or believed differences between the parties. Strong Republicans and Democrats are farther apart in perception of political issues than weak Republicans and Democrats; they disagree more sharply in their perception of campaign events. Among the strongly partisan, then, the process of perception operates to make the opponent into more of an "enemy" and thus to magnify the potential for political cleavage.

But all this should not be taken to exaggerate the effect of perception (or issues). Regardless of their perception of the issues, important social groups still follow their own voting tradition.[5] An index of agreement was constructed between the position of each respondent and the position he perceived each candidate to be taking. Here again Catholics vote more strongly Democratic regardless of the degree of their ideological agreement with Truman or Dewey (Fig. 4). But why does agreement with Dewey make more difference for Catholics, and agreement with Truman for Protestants?

Now when these two indexes of agreement are combined into one, this curious effect of perceived agreement sharpens. If Protestants and Catholics agree with "their own group's" candidate and disagree with the opponent, then the vote is overwhelmingly for one's own candidate; and, if the situation is reversed, so is the vote—though not so strongly. But what of those people who agree with both candidates, as perceived, or with neither? The answer is that voters who *disagree* with both candidates' stands on the issues, as they perceive them, end by supporting their group's "proper" candidate (more strongly than those who agree with both). If they disagree with both, they seem to have no alternative. So they remain loyal, "at home." If they *agree* with both, however, they are more likely to try the other side. When the grass is green in *both* yards, it seems a little greener in the other fellow's!

ACCURACY OF PERCEPTION

The question of "correct" and "incorrect" perception has been implicit in our discussion thus far, since differentia-

[5] Nor was perception related to *changes* in voting. We hypothesized that voters might maintain stability by means of misperception, but there were no differences in the data on voting changes subsequent to the asking of perception questions. If perception questions had been repeated, then one would expect perception to adjust to vote more often than the reverse.

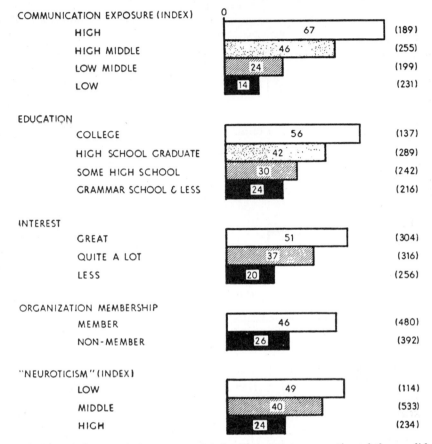

PERCENTAGE WITH 3 OR 4 CORRECT
PERCEPTIONS OUT OF 4 POSSIBLE

COMMUNICATION EXPOSURE (INDEX)   0
HIGH   67   (189)
HIGH MIDDLE   46   (255)
LOW MIDDLE   24   (199)
LOW   14   (231)

EDUCATION
COLLEGE   56   (137)
HIGH SCHOOL GRADUATE   42   (289)
SOME HIGH SCHOOL   30   (242)
GRAMMAR SCHOOL & LESS   24   (216)

INTEREST
GREAT   51   (304)
QUITE A LOT   37   (316)
LESS   20   (256)

ORGANIZATION MEMBERSHIP
MEMBER   46   (480)
NON-MEMBER   26   (392)

"NEUROTICISM" (INDEX)
LOW   49   (114)
MIDDLE   40   (533)
HIGH   24   (234)

FIG. 5. Several characteristics are associated with accurate perception of the candidates' stands on issues. (Each characteristic works independently of the others.)

tion in perception requires a degree of misperception on the part of some perceivers (assuming a definition of objective reality). But the question has not been given explicit consideration. Without retracing our steps, let us now summarize from this vantage point.

Analysis of the perception that occurs during a presidential campaign requires a definition of what is "correct" perception. In the case of political issues, perceiving the candidates' stands as they predominantly appear in the campaign speeches should serve. Since some stands are ambiguous, or at least contain an element of propagandistic vagueness, we use here two stands of Truman and Dewey that are reasonably straightforward and clear—those on the Taft-Hartley Law (with Truman against and Dewey for) and on price control (with Truman for and Dewey against). The index of correct perception on the issues is based upon the number of correct responses given out of the four possible.

In the first place, the amount of correct perception in the community is limited. Only 16 percent of the respondents know

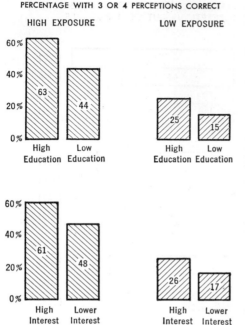

PERCENTAGE WITH 3 OR 4 PERCEPTIONS CORRECT

FIG. 6. Voter perception of the candidates' stands.

the correct stands of both candidates on both issues, and another 21 percent know them on three of the four. Over a third of the respondents know only one stand correctly or none at all. And these are crucial issues in the campaign, much discussed in the communication media. Thus, a good deal less than half the political perception in the community is reasonably accurate, by such definitions.[6]

But any such arbitrary measure is less useful for its absolute than for its relative value. Who are the people more and less likely to perceive political issues correctly? For example, what of attention to the campaign in the press and radio? Do the people who read and listen about politics more than others perceive more correctly, or does selective perception get in the way? It seems that communica-

tion exposure clarifies perception probably more than any other factor (Fig. 5). This is an important consideration: the more reading and listening people do on campaign matters, the more likely they are to come to recognize the positions the candidates take on major issues. It is as though the weight of the media is sufficient to "impose" a certain amount of correct perception, regardless of the barrier presented by the voter's party preference (and despite the fact that those who do most of the reading and listening also feel most strongly for their candidate and are hence more amenable to selective perception). The more that people are *exposed* to political material, the more gets through.

Other characteristics also make for accurate perception. The intellectual training received in the classroom enables the voter to make clearer discriminations in the political arena. And, despite greater affect toward campaign affairs, the interested people manage to maintain a clearer view of the issues (see Fig. 6). In addition, accuracy of perception is a function of cross-pressures. Voters cross-pressured on class and religion are less accurate than those not so cross-pressured (34 percent high to 41 percent); and voters cross-pressured (inconsistent) on price control and Taft-Hartley are less accurate than those not so cross-pressured (42 to 65 percent). But, of all these factors, the strongest is communication exposure. It is more effectively related to accurate perception of where the candidates stand than either education or interest. Reading and listening must make a difference.

INFERENCES: PSYCHOLOGICAL AND POLITICAL

What are the implications of this perceptual situation? Broadly speaking,

---

[6] To repeat: these figures apply to the early campaign period of August. Similar data for October, at the end of the campaign, would almost certainly raise these estimates.

there are two sets of conclusions which can be drawn.

The first deals with the psychology of political perception. For perceptual selection must serve a definite psychological function for the individual voter. As in other spheres of activity, so in the political: one function must be to avoid potential stress. The voter must do this, even though unconsciously, by using his perceptual opportunities as a defense or protection against the complexities, contradictions, and problems of the campaign. Indeed, the extent and nature of misperception suggests that the voter may even be aware of the attitudinal cross-pressures to which the campaign subjects him and from which he gains escape through perceptual processes. For the greater his affect toward the election (in terms of strength of feeling toward the candidates), the greater the degree of psychic protection. The voter tends to oversee or to invent what is favorable to himself and to distort or to deny much of what is unfavorable. This must leave him fewer internal conflicts to resolve—with, so to speak, a favorable balance of perception. In any event, the voters manage to use the materials of politics, even of a presidential campaign, for their own psychological protection—for the avoidance of some inconsistencies in their beliefs that otherwise would be manifest.

Then there are certain political implications of the patterning of perception. First, there are in a sense two political campaigns. One is the objective campaign that is carried on in the "real" world, and the other is the campaign that exists in the voter's mind, that is, the "real" campaign as perceived. There is no one-to-one correspondence between them. Given the chance, some voters transform the objective campaign into a subjective one more satisfying to them. The campaign waged by the candidates —even when deliberately unambiguous —is not the one perceived by all the voters, but this does not make it any less

"real" for the voters themselves. "If men define situations as real, they are real in their consequences."

Second, there is the meaning of perception for rational political judgment. Here its role must make the voter's political judgment *seem* more rational to him because it maximizes agreement with his own side and maximizes disagreement with the opposition. In other words, perception often operates to make the differences between the parties *appear* greater than they actually may be—and thus to make the voter's decision *appear* more rational (in one sense) than it actually is. In this way, paradoxical though it may seem, misperception contributes to a seeming "rationality" in politics.

Third, perception must reduce or even eliminate certain political cross-pressures before they come to the level of visibility—before they start pressing. If the voter finds himself holding opinions championed by opposing parties, it has been thought that he could do one of two things: remain in this "inconsistent" position (which is, of course, altogether legitimate) or remove the "inconsistency" by changing one opinion to fit the other. But he has another out: he can perceptually select, out of the somewhat ambiguous propaganda of the campaign, those political cues which remove the problem by defining it away. He can "see" that the candidates do not disagree on the issue at hand or that his candidate really agrees with him or that the opponent really disagrees or that he cannot tell where his candidate stands. Just as the process may reduce the voter's level of psychological tension, so may it reduce his political inconsistency.

Finally, this serves to introduce the major political implications of our perceptual material—its implications for the problem of cleavage and consensus in the democratic community. The over-all effect of political perception is to increase the amount of political consensus *within* the parties and to increase the amount of political cleavage *between* the parties—once again, homogeneity within and polarization between. Both are achieved by something like the mechanisms of generalization, exclusion, and denial—through the perceptual enlargement of the area of agreement with one's own candidate (generalization) through the misperceived rejection of the opponent's position (exclusion); and through the professed lack of knowledge of one's candidate's stand where disagreement is likely (denial).

Let us close this account by comparing it briefly with our findings on the perception of groups.[7] In each case the perceptions are likely to help voters to maintain their own position, without being too much concerned by contradiction. In the social case it is harmony with people; in the present case it is a harmony with ideas. With groups the matter was fairly simple: each respondent is surrounded by a primary group in which the large majority thinks like himself. No wonder, then, that he infers that "everyone" will vote as he does. (Of course, this tendency is tempered by a strong sense of reality; misperception is only superimposed upon it.) In the case of the candidates' stand, the voter gets his information from reading, listening, and discussion. This is subject to *selective* gathering of information, forgetting of disturbing elements, reinterpretation of what the candidate "really" means—all mechanisms familiar in social psychology. Probably, even, social selection reinforces the selective collection of information, as a result of discussion between like-minded people.

In a way, both phenomena can be subsumed under one heading. Voters cannot have contact with the whole world of people and ideas; they must *sample* them. And the sampling is biased. People pick the people and the ideas to suit their personal equilibrium and then project that

sample upon the universe. First, selective perception, then misperception, then the strengthening of opinion, and then, in turn, more selective perception. Fortunately, there are realities, competing concerns, and corrosion of existing beliefs that, under normal circumstances, do not permit this process to get far out of bounds.

In sum, then, the actual operation of political perception during a presidential campaign decreases tension in the individual and increases tension in the community—one might almost say, *by* increasing tension in the community. The voters, each in the solitude of his own mind, wish to see the campaign in a favorable way, and they use their perception of where the candidates stand to this end. "Democracy in its original form never seriously faced the problem which arises because the pictures inside people's heads do not automatically correspond with the world outside."[8]

SUMMARY

Perception and Voting

1. Party preference does not particularly affect the voter's perception of where the candidates stand on the issues.

2. The less ambiguous the objective situation, the more agreement in perception between the two sides.

3. Partisans tend to perceive the candidate's stand on the issues as favorable to their own stand. (1) They perceive their candidate's stand as similar to their own and the opponent's stand as dissimilar. (2) They tend *not* to perceive differences with their own candidate or similarities to the opposition candidate.

4. Voters who feel strongly about their choice are more likely to misperceive the candidates' stands on the issues as favorable to their own positions.

5. Social differences in voting are

---

[7] Reported in Ch. 5 of Berelson, Lazarsfeld, and McPhee, *op. cit.*
[8] Lippmann, *op. cit.*

largely maintained regardless of perceived agreement with the candidates.

6. Voters who disagree with both candidates' stands, as perceived, support their own candidate more strongly than those who agree with both.

Accuracy of Perception

7. Only about one-third of the voters are highly accurate in their perception of where the candidates stand on the issues.

8. Accuracy of perception is affected by communication exposure, education, interest, and cross-pressures—with communication exposure probably the strongest influence.

SOCIAL PSYCHOLOGY AND PERCEPTION
By Jerome S. Bruner

Contemporary social psychology, one finds in looking through the contents of its professional journals, is much concerned, indeed even preoccupied, with problems of perception. There is constant reference to the manner in which subjects in experiments "perceive the situation." The term "social perception" has come widely into use to describe the manner in which one person perceives or infers the traits and intentions of another, and there is a steady flow of experimental studies on the manner in which social factors induce types of selectivity in what a person perceives and how he interprets it. Social attitudes are defined as a readiness to experience events in certain consistent and selective ways, and the most recent writings on the psychology of language, inspired by Benjamin Lee Whorf, urge that the structure of a language and its lexical units determine or at least influence what one habitually notices in the world about one. Without appropriate attitudes and an appropriate linguistic structure, one does not readily register upon certain events in the environment that another person, appropriately armed with attitudes and a language, would notice as salient.

While this point of view about the central importance of perception has always to some measure been a feature of social psychology—McDougall in his classic textbook of 1912, for example, was sharply aware of the role of social sentiments in biasing the selectivity of attention, and Thomas and Znaniecki made "the definition of the situation" a key concept in their pioneering acculturation study of *The Polish Peasant*—it is only within the last ten or 15 years that the role of perception and "selective registration" has come to be dominant in social psychological theory. In the pages that follow, we shall examine the backgrounds of this emphasis, some of the reasons why perceptual concepts are indispensable to the social psychologist, and the nature of these concepts as they have emerged in the last decade or so.

To the uninitiated, one with a background neither in psychology nor in classical philosophy, perceiving may pose no problems. The simple view, sometimes called naïve realism, would hold that there are objects and events in the external world and that somehow representations of these, called *Eidola* by the pre-Socratic philosophers, emanate from

Prepared especially for this volume.

the things in the world and find their way into the nervous system and eventually into consciousness. Such, however, is not the case save in the most metaphoric sense; rather, the problem is how we integrate into a unitary percept the myriad of sensory stimuli that come from our specialized sense organs. In most instances, there are more things to be noticed than one can possibly register upon simultaneously—as when one walks into a room full of people with several conversations going on at once—and even when the stimulus input is fairly simple, there are various ways in which it can be "looked at" or organized. A tree can be perceived from the point of view of the soundness of its wood, the seasonal status of its foliage, its species, its shade-giving quality, and so on. Perhaps we can notice four or five or six of these features at once, but rarely do we register on more of them. For the abiding fact about the process of knowing, of which perceiving is one aspect, is that organisms have a highly limited span of attention and a highly limited span of immediate memory. Selectivity is forced upon us by the nature of these limitations, and indeed, even if we should operate at maximum capacity (estimated to be an ability to notice and keep in mind about seven independent things simultaneously), the cost in cognitive strain would be considerable.

In the interests of economizing effort we do three things. On the one hand, we narrow the selectivity of attention more or less to those things that are somehow essential to the enterprises in which we are engaged. In social situations, we register on the color of people's skins, but not on the texture. Moreover, we simplify even here and may register solely on whether they are white or colored. Secondly, we "recode" into simpler form the diversity of events that we encounter so that our limited attention and memory span can be protected. Instead of trying to remember how far falling bodies fall, we simply commit to memory the formula $S = \frac{gt^2}{2}$, which preserves the necessary information and allows us to recreate any specific information about distance we want. Sometimes these recodings of information serve their economical function but lead to a serious loss of information, as when we recode information in terms of what Walter Lippmann long ago called a "stereotype." We see a Negro sitting on a park bench, a Jew or Texan changing a check at a bank window, a German dressing down a taxicab driver, and allocate each experience to an established and well-memorized stereotype: lazy Negro, mercenary Jew, rich Texan, bullying German. The behavior is perceived according to the formula, the person saved from having to do much perceptual work aside from picking up a few cues. Not only is information lost, but misinformation is added: the person "sees" the stereotyped individuals he has created—"Why, I saw a big healthy Negro sitting there idle in the park doing nothing the other day," and the behavior is perceived as lazy rather than, perhaps, that the Negro worked the swing shift and was enjoying his hours off in the park. Finally, we deal with the overload of information provided by the environment, the overload relative to our limited capacities for noticing and registering and remembering, by the use of technological aids, aids that are designed to lengthen the noticing process. A simple example of such an aid is pencil and paper: trying to list all that is before us from every point of view. Or we use a camera in the hope of being able to go back over the picture and extract the last ounce of meaning from an event. All of these methods help. None of them can succeed fully, for as Robert Oppenheimer has noted about the cognitive processes, in order to know anything we must somehow give up the aspiration of knowing everything about a particular situation.

All of the ways in which we deal with environmental complexity at the perceptual level are deeply tinged with the hues of the society in which we live. That we notice skin color and not skin texture results from the nature of social customs. Yet, it is curious that closely below the level of habitual awareness there is also a kind of "noticing" of socially less relevant things. Morphologists tell us, for example, that human skin texture can be divided roughly and metaphorically into three types: apple skins, onion skins, and orange skins, the first associated with round pyknic physiques, the second with thin or "scrawny" types, the last with athletic builds. The moment this is mentioned, you have what Herman Melville once called a "shock of recognition"— you somehow knew these types but did not quite recognize them explicitly. So it is, too, with recoding information: new methods of organizing experience, once one can break through the old methods, are "obvious." A mother has been seeing her obstreperous child as "naughty" or "rebellious." A psychologist explains to her that it is five o'clock and that the child is principally tired. If this new way of organizing the welter of movements and expressions that constitute a child's behavior can be accepted by the mother, likely as not she will say, "Of course, but I should have thought of that." The alternative ways of organizing a percept seem somehow to be there in nascent form. So, too, with technological aids like languages and cameras and lists. A photographic plate is immensely limited: the noises that make a Roman street so memorable do not register, no matter how fine-grained the film. But, as in the other two modes of dealing with stimulation overload, technological aids also produce a surplus beyond what is immediately "used" consciously.

I have mentioned the "nascent surplus" of information one obtains in encounters with the environment even though one has been highly selective in noticing things, because it is important from the point of view of creativity and social change and innovation. If it is true that people are selective, must be selective to match their limited cognitive capacities to the complexities of the social and physical environment, it is also true that they are not completely trapped in this selectivity, that the conditions for producing a change in perceiving and thinking about events are there.

The reader will properly ask at this point, "But *is* selectivity forced on a person by the nature of his cognitive apparatus? Can he not take his time and perceive more carefully and comprehensively and get a better sense of what things really mean around him?" The question is a good one, indeed a deep one, and can be answered in several ways. First, there are great individual differences between people in the degree to which they "gamble" in their selectivity, some seemingly content with noticing only a few relevant-to-them things about events they encounter, others being much more deliberate and aware about alternatives and subtleties. Elsewhere in this volume, for example, the reader will find discussions of the authoritarian personality, one of whose notable characteristics is a proneness to seeing things very selectively, in black and white unrelieved by gray. It is also worth remembering that a constant regimen of close inspection of events, a devotion to the alternative ways in which events can be perceived, may conflict with requirements for action. We are forced to decide whether a man is honest or not, whether a group is friendly toward us. If we are to adjust to problems of segregation and desegregation, we must notice whether skins are white or colored. We cannot, like Hamlet, remain long in the state of being "sicklied o'er with the pale cast of thought"—not if we are to act. Finally, there are times when the world is too much like one of Rorschach's ink blots, with ambiguity prevailing. The cues we are forced to use are highly random and probabilistic. We must often decide whether a man is friendly or not on the basis of a cue no more trustworthy than whether or not he is smiling, and are thus forced to fall back on what may be a groundless stereotype. In such situations, perceptual inference may reflect little more than the social conventions or the particular strategy a person uses for coping with his difficulties. It is characteristic, for example, that people are inaccurate, indeed only a bit better than chance, in being able to recognize those members of a group who dislike them— far less good at it than in telling whether others like them.[1] The masking of cues by politesse—we are subtle about showing dislike—plus the protective need of avoiding the sense of being disliked lead perception into all sorts of traps. We end up by seeing those people as disliking us whom we ourselves dislike.

The "New Look" in Perception

Perhaps the immediate impetus to contemporary concern with the role of perceptual processes in social behavior came from a series of experiments on determinants of perceptual organization—determinants that could be called "behavioral" which relate to such influences as need, social values, attitudes, stress, cultural background, etc., in contrast to "autochthonous" which refers to stimulus factors. These experiments, taken as a sequence, came, rather waggishly, to be called the "New Look" in perception. A sampling of some of the principal studies carried out will serve to highlight

some of the critical problems that have faced the theorist concerned with formulating a model of the perceptual process that has some relevance to the understanding of social behavior. In the final section we shall return to the nature of such a theoretical model.[2]

The early studies were principally concerned with showing the nature of "distortion" in perception and the sources of perceptual inaccuracy and were, in the main, influenced by thinking imported from clinical psychiatry where such doctrines as "autistic thinking," "defense," "primary process" (hypothesized infantile wishful hallucination) had become dominant as a result of Freud's pioneering work. The studies of Gardner Murphy and his colleagues are a case in point. Levine, Chein, and Murphy[3] showed their subjects a set of food pictures behind a ground-glass screen that obscured them to the point of ambiguity. The subjects were then asked to give the first association that the obscured pictures brought to mind. They found that associations connected with food and eating increased as the hours of food deprivation of the subjects increased, reaching a maximum around ten to 12 hours of starvation. After this, the number of food associations declined. The authors attempted to explain the finding in terms of the pleasure principle operating under conditions of mild drive, being supplanted by the reality principle when hunger became severe. Like many pioneering experiments, there was much wrong with the design of this study—the kind of associational response employed, the fact that the subjects knew they would be fed after the requisite number

---

[1] See pps. 110ff.

[2] Since there have appeared several hundred experimental investigations of motivational and social determinants of perception, it is indeed difficult and certainly arbitrary to select a few for special mention. The choice of the experiments is based partly on their importance, partly upon the degree to which they illustrate basic theoretical issues, and partly on expository convenience—in about that order.

[3] R. Levine, I. Chein, and G. Murphy, "The Relation of the Intensity of a Need to the Amount of Perceptual Distortion, a Preliminary Report," *J. Psychol.*, 1942, XIII, 283–293.

of hours of being without food, etc. But it stimulated many follow-up studies. We now know that the results of Levine, Chein, and Murphy are a special case of a more general one whose nature is not yet clear.

McClelland and Atkinson,[4] for example, worked with subjects who were unaware of the relation between their hunger and the perceptual test they were being given. The subjects, sailors at a submarine base, were asked to "recognize" "barely perceptible" objects on a screen. Actually the screen was blank. The men showed an increase in instrumental food response—seeing eating utensils and the like—but no increase with hours of deprivation in the number of consummatory food objects seen.

Yet, in another study, under conditions of prolonged and chronic semistarvation, conscientious objectors show no increase at all in the number or quality of food associations or readiness to perceive food objects (see the wartime work of Brosek and his colleagues [5]). Here the question may well have been one of pride: these dedicated young men were doing their service by serving as subjects in an experiment. Giving in to hunger may have been something to avoid as almost a matter of honor. With respect to chronically food-deprived prisoners of war and concentration camp victims that I have interviewed shortly after release, one finds that there is repeated mention of two extreme types: those preoccupied with food and those who avoid the topic as much as possible. One can cite other studies that add further subtleties to the complex pattern that seems to emerge, but there is now enough evidence before us to suggest that not the *amount* of need but the *way* in which a person learns to

handle his needs determines the manner in which motivation and cognitive selectivity will interact. Autism or wishful thinking are scarcely universal modes of coping with one's needs. It is conceivable that in a culture or in a family setting where emphasis is placed upon asceticism and denial of needs, autism would be the exception. On the whole, then, selectivity reflects the nature of the person's mode of striving for goals rather than the amount of need which he seems to be undergoing.

Closely related to this line of investigation are studies on the role of interest, value, and attitude, and this work brings up several additional subtleties. The experimental work of Postman, Bruner, and McGinnies [6] indicated that the speed and ease with which words were recognized when briefly presented in a fast-exposure apparatus (tachistoscope) was a function of the value areas these words represented and of the interest the subjects in the experiment evinced in these various value areas as measured by the Allport-Vernon Study of Values which tests for the relative dominance of religious, esthetic, political, social, theoretical, and economic interests. The general finding was that the greater the dominance of a value in the person, the more rapidly he would recognize words representing that area. The authors found that the hypotheses offered by subjects prior to correct recognition were particularly revealing, suggesting that in the presence of low-value words there was some form of defensive avoidance—the perceiving of blanks, scrambled letters, or even derogatory words which the authors called "contravaluant hypotheses." With high-value words, on the contrary, subjects tended in excess of

---

[4] D. C. McClelland and J. W. Atkinson, "The Projective Expression of Needs: I. The effect of different Intensities of the Hunger Drive on Perception," *J. Psychol.*, 1948, XXV, 205–222.

[5] J. Brozek, H. Guetzkow, and M. G. Baldwin, "A Quantitative Study of Perception and Association in Experimental Semi-starvation," *J. Pers.*, 1951, XIX, 245–261.

[6] L. Postman, J. S. Bruner, and E. McGinnies, "Personal Values as Selective Factors in Perception," *J. Abnorm. Soc. Psychol.*, 1948, XXXIII, 148–153.

chance to propose guesses that were in the value area of the stimulus word prior to correct recognition, in keeping with a subsequent finding of Bricker and Chapanis[7] that subjects can obtain partial information from words when they are presented below threshold. Later studies by Bruner and Postman[8] on blocks in perceiving personally threatening words and by McGinnies[9] on the raising of identification thresholds for taboo words led to the development of the concept of "perceptual defense," a kind of blocking of recognition for classes of materials that were personally and/or culturally unacceptable to the perceiver, a "proscribed list" at the entry port so to speak.

It was argued by Solomon and Howes[10] that the findings on the effect of values could be accounted for by a factor of frequency—that the person interested in religion was more likely to have selective exposure to religious words and symbols. Howes[11] then went on to show that the amount of time required to recognize a word in the English language could be expressed rather precisely as a function of the logarithm of the frequency with which the word appeared in printed English as recorded in the useful Thorndike-Lorge frequency count.[12] But since economic words are likely to be more frequently encountered in printed English than theoretical words, the general frequency of words in English would not be sufficient grounds to explain why some individuals, high in theoretical interests, recognize theoretical words more quickly than economic words such as "money" or "price." We must invoke a notion of "idiosyncratic frequency," an individual's frequency of encounter without regard to frequency in English. Indeed, Postman and Schneider[13] showed that for very common words drawn from the six value-areas of the Allport-Vernon test, the relative position of the values for the subject made little difference. With rarer words it did, with the more valued ones being recognized more easily.

The upshot of this debate, it would appear, is twofold and of considerable significance. Perceptual readiness, the ease with which items are recognized under less than optimal viewing conditions, seems to reflect not only the needs and modes of striving of an organism but also to reflect the requirement that surprise be minimized—that perceptual readiness be predictive in the sense of being tuned to what is likely to be present in the environment as well as what is needed for the pursuit of our enterprises. The predictive nature of perceptual readiness, however, reflects more than the frequency with which things occur. Rather, it is best thought of as the matching of perceptual readiness to the probable *sequences* of events in the environment. We come to learn what goes with what. We *hear* the approaching whistle of a train and are readied to *see* the train. We learn, if you will, the probabilistic texture of the

[7] P. D. Bricker and A. Chapanis, "Do Incorrectly Perceived Tachistoscopic Stimuli Convey Some Information?," *Psychol. Rev.*, 1953, LX, 181–188.

[8] J. S. Bruner and L. Postman, "Emotional Selectivity in Perception and Reaction," *J. Pers.*, 1947, XVI, 69–77.

[9] E. McGinnies, "Emotionality and Perceptual Defense," *Psychol. Rev.*, 1949, LVI, 244–251.

[10] R. L. Solomon and D. W. Howes, "Word Frequency, Personal Values, and Visual Deviation Thresholds," *Psychol. Rev.*, 1951, LVIII, 256–270.

[11] D. Howes, "On the Interpretation of Word Frequency as a Variable Affecting Speed of Recognition," *J. Exp. Psychol.*, 1954, XLVIII, 106–122.

[12] E. L. Thorndike and I. Lorge, *The Teacher's Word Book of 30,000 Words* (New York: Teachers College, Columbia University, 1944).

[13] L. Postman and B. Schneider, "Personal Values, Visual Recognition, and Recall," *Psychol. Rev.*, 1951, LVIII, 271–284.

world, conserve this learning, use it as a guide to tuning our perceptual readiness to what is most likely next. It is this that permits us to "go beyond the information given." That there is danger in using such a guide is illustrated in a study by Bruner and Postman on the perception of incongruity.[14] If playing cards with suit and color reversed—a red four of clubs, say are presented to subjects for brief intervals of a few milliseconds, what occurs is perceptual completion according to high probability linkages we have already learned; the subject "sees" a red four of hearts or a black four of clubs. Thresholds of identification increase grossly: when subjects are presented with these incongruous stimuli, it takes them an inordinately long exposure time to "see" what is actually there. But human organisms unlearn and learn quickly: having seen the incongruity finally, later instances are much more rapidly identified correctly.

It is characteristic of perceptual identification of things that the larger the number of alternatives the person is expecting, the more difficult it is to recognize any single one of the alternatives that does occur. In an experiment by Bruner, Miller, and Zimmerman[15] it was found that it is much easier to recognize a word when it is one of four that may occur than when it is one of eight or 16 or 32 that may occur. This suggests that where speed is required in perception—as under stress conditions or under conditions of exigent motivation—that the likelihood of erroneous perception increases. That is to say, to gain speed, we limit the alternative hypotheses that we are willing to entertain. In the event of ambiguous stimulation, as in social per-

ception generally, such speed-producing monopolistic hypotheses are likely to be confirmed. We expect, for example, a hostile action from a disliked person; he does something equivocal; we "see" it as a hostile act and thus confirm our expectation. It is the case, moreover, that under conditions where alternative expectancies must be limited, we will be more likely to adopt socially conventional expectancies or ones that reflect our more basic needs. It is in this sense that stress and social pressure serve to reduce the subtlety of the registration process.

One final matter must be mentioned before turning briefly to theory. It has to do with the perception of magnitude, a subject which does not at first seem closely related to social psychology. An early study by Bruner and Goodman[16] opened the issue. The study was simply conceived—in both a good and a bad sense. Children, ages 10 to 11, divided into those from fairly prosperous homes and those from a slum settlement house, were given the task of adjusting a variable patch of light to the sizes of pennies, nickels, dimes, quarters, and half dollars. Half the subjects worked with coins in hand, half from memory. Control groups adjusted the light patch to cardboard discs of the same sizes. The findings, in general, were that the sizes of the more valuable coins were overestimated, of less valuable coins underestimated. The effects were greater for the memory condition than for the condition with coin present. No significant effect was found for paper discs. In general, the economically well-to-do children showed less of the value-distortion effect than the poor children.

The study has been repeated several

[14] J. S. Bruner and L. Postman, "On the Perception of Incongruity: A Paradigm," *J. Pers.*, 1949, XVIII, 206–223.

[15] J. S. Bruner, G. A. Miller, and C. Zimmerman, "Discriminative Skill and Discriminative Matching in Perceptual Recognition," *J. Exp. Psychol.*, 1955, XLIX, 187–192.

[16] J. S. Bruner and C. C. Goodman, "Value and Need as Organizing Factors in Perception," *J. Abnorm. & Soc. Psychol.*, 1947, XLII, 33–44.

times, and as McCurdy [17] and Tajfel [18] point out, the same effect found more often than not under a variety of conditions. One experiment by Carter and Schooler [19] found somewhat contrary results. The same trends were observed, but they fell short of statistical significance save for the condition where size was estimated from memory, where significant results were observed. A later study by Bruner and Rodrigues [20] pointed up one faulty assumption of the earlier studies mentioned. Overestimation and underestimation of size is always stated with respect to the measured sizes of the coins, the "physically accurate" size. This is a psychologically naïve way of describing what goes on in judgement of magnitude. Rather, one should ask about the *relative* subjective sizes of coins of different value. The study by Bruner and Rodrigues had as its principal object to show that there was a *greater separation* in subjective size between a nickel and a quarter than there was for comparable-sized white metal discs. Tajfel [21] has developed this point in an interesting theoretical paper, pointing out that it is one of the functions of perceptual judgement to accentuate the apparent difference in magnitudes between objects that differ in value, provided that the difference in magnitude is associated with the difference in value—as if, so to speak, the two attributes, value and magnitude, are confounded in a way to point up and accentuate value difference. In short, even in the estimation of mag-

nitude, judgmental processes reflect the social conventions that establish values for various elements of the environment.[22]

ON THEORETICAL MODELS OF PERCEPTION

Given the operation of behavioral factors in perceiving and cognizing generally, including the operation of social factors, what can be said about a theoretical model of perception that would be of relevance to the social psychologist? It is quite clear at the outset that the psychologist principally concerned with perception cannot work with one kind of theory and the social psychologist, interested in the effects of perceptual selectivity on social behavior and in the cultural patterning of perception as well, work with yet another theory of perception. Let me briefly outline, in conclusion, some of the features that I believe a theory of perception must have in order to do justice to the concerns of both kinds of psychologists. For a fuller account of the points to be made, the reader is referred to Bruner.[23]

The first, and perhaps most self-evident point upon reflection, is that perceiving or registering on an object or an event in the environment involves an act of categorization. We "place" things in categories. That is a "man" and he is "honest" and he is now "walking" in a manner that is "leisurely" with the "intention" of "getting some relaxation."

---

[17] H. G. McCurdy, "Coin Perception Studies and the Concept of Schemata," *Psychol. Rev.*, 1956, LXIII, 160–168.

[18] H. Tajfel, "Value and the Perceptual Judgment of Magnitude," *Psychol. Rev.*, 1957, LXIV, 192–204.

[19] L. F. Carter and K. Schooler, "Value, Need and Other Factors in Perception," *Psychol. Rev.*, 1949, LVI, 200–207.

[20] J. S. Bruner and J. S. Rodrigues, "Some Determinants of Apparent Size," *J. Abnorm. & Soc. Psychol.*, 1953, XLVIII, 17–24.

[21] Tajfel, *op. cit.*

[22] So brief a summary of a field of research as complicated as magnitude estimation and the role of value factors in it is bound to be oversimplified. For a fuller account, the reader is referred to the excellent papers of Tajfel, *op. cit.*, and McCurdy, *op. cit.*

[23] J. S. Bruner, "On Perceptual Readiness," *Psychol. Rev.*, 1957, LXIV, 123–152.

Each of the words in quotation marks involves a sorting or placement of stimulus input on the basis of certain cues that we learn how to use. Now it is of great importance to bear in mind that most of the categories into which we sort for identification are learned on the basis of experience, by virtue of our membership in a culture and a linguistic community, and by the nature of the needs we must fulfill in order to exist beyond some degraded level. Not only are the categories learned, but we learn to estimate the likelihood that placement of an event into a category on the basis of a few cues will be "accurate"—by which we mean, *predictive* in the sense that a closer look will bear it out or that it will be consensually validated when other perceivers come on the scene or it will be confirmed by technological inspection.

We may take it as self-evident that some categories we employ are more amenable to check by prediction. The cues we use for judging an object "distant" or a surface "impenetrable" are checked a thousand times a day in getting about: walking, driving, reaching. Others are less readily checked. Whether, on the basis of a few signs, we can judge whether a man is "honorable," given the difficulty of establishing a quick and adequate criterion, is questionable. The category, established by a culture in response to its social needs, resists validation. It is perhaps the case that modes of categorizing that are amenable to firm and immediate validation with respect to predictiveness are the ones that are more universal to the human race, more easily diffused and learned. The less readily a form of categorizing is able to be predictively validated, the more will it reflect the idiosyncrasies of a culture. It is not surprising that the famous Cambridge expedition to the Torres Straits [24] at the opening of this century found so few differences in the perception of distance, size, etc. in comparing primitive Pacific Islanders and English undergraduates.

It is also apparent that the categories of events with which we become accustomed to dealing are organized into systems or structures, bound together in various ways: by virtue of the fact that one class of events is likely to follow another or because classes of events are closely bound by some other principle than mere association as, for example, that several are required in order for certain objectives to be reached. Thus, displacement of a dot from one position to another is categorized as "a dot moving" and not as "first a dot at position A, then another dot at position B." As we have noted before, recoding into systems serves to keep mental life from becoming burdened with a diversity of unrelated particulars. Highly practiced perception is a case in point. A practiced baseball spectator joins and meshes a highly complex set of categorized events into a structure called a "double play."

In addition to the problem of categories and category systems and how they are formed, there is also a question of the accessibility of such categories for use by a perceiver. It is often the case that we fail to identify an event properly although we are knowledgeable about the class of events which it exemplifies; fail to do so even though the cues are clear. And as the work cited earlier in this paper has shown, certain categories manifest their accessability by permitting rapid identification of relevant objects under conditions of very brief or very "fuzzy" exposure. What makes certain kinds of categorizing responses sometimes available and sometimes not? What can be said in general is that category accessibility reflects two sets of factors. Need and interest states, as we have

---

[24] W. H. R. Rivers, "Vision," *Reports of the Cambridge Anthropological Expedition to Torres Straits*, 1901, II, 1–132.

implied, increase accessibility of those categories of objects that relate to their fulfillment or furthering—not necessarily in a wish-fulfilling or autistic way, as noted before, but in a manner consonant with achieving realistically a desired goal. The second set of factors governing category accessibility has to do with the predictive requirements of perception and the need to avoid disruptive mistakes. These requirements tune the readiness of the perceiver to match the likelihood of events in the environment. When we are hungry, we tend to be alerted to signs of restaurants, if we usually assuage hunger in restaurants. We notice ones we have never noticed before. Our "restaurant" category has become highly "available." But we look for and expect restaurants at the street level and not in the sky or atop trees. It is this balancing of need-induced alertness and event-matching expectancy that makes it possible for perception to act in the service of needs and interests and, at the same time, with due regard for reality.

In conclusion, perceptual readiness reflects the dual requirements of coping with an environment—directedness with respect to goals and efficiency with respect to the means by which the goals can be attained. It is no matter of idle in-terest that a religious man picks up perceptually things that are relevant to his interest more easily and more quickly than other things, and at the same time, this efficiency continues to reflect what is likely to occur in his surroundings. What it suggests is that once a society has patterned a man's interests and trained him to expect what is likely in that society, it has gained a great measure of control not only on his thought processes, but also on the very material on which thought works—the experienced data of perception. It is not surprising, then, that the social psychologist has shown a renewed interest in the process of perceiving. To understand the manner in which man responds to and copes with his social environment we must know what that environment is *to him*. The physicist provides a description of the nature of stimulation in such terms as wave lengths, radiant energy, chemical compounds. Nobody confuses these descriptions with what we experience—colors, brightnesses, tastes. The student of society, like the physicist, provides descriptions of the "external environment" in terms of stratification, totemic clans, moities. The question is how people perceive or register upon these features of the social environment. That is what is crucial in determining how we respond.

THE LEARNING AND FORGETTING OF CONTRO-VERSIAL MATERIAL   *By Jerome M. Levine and Gardner Murphy*

With the recognition that such functions as perception and learning are not determined by cognitive factors alone and that the individual enters into a perceiving or learning situation as a complete individual with his own needs, desires, values, with his own frame of reference, it became necessary to transcend the methods of Ebbinghaus in order to develop a valid social psychology.

The concept of "frame of reference," as discussed by Sherif implies no "inde-

From *Journal of Abnormal and Social Psychology*, 1943, XXXVIII, 507–517. Reprinted by permission of the authors and the American Psychological Association, Inc.

pendent agent intruding into every psychological process as an outsider."[1] He shows that the frame of reference expresses the functional relationships, the functional interdependence, of many describable factors appearing in a concrete situation. The concept, then, introduces us to the field relationships of perceiving and learning.

That such a frame does have an appreciable effect in dominating or modifying a person's experience has been amply demonstrated qualitatively by Bartlett, who has indicated the relationships between the autisms of an individual and those factors in a given situation selected for perception and recall and demonstrated that meaningful prose material could be used to study these processes.[2] Few of the later studies of the effect of frame of reference on learning and recall have been concerned with the process of learning when that learning involves more than a single fixation; and, though such studies have been interested in immediate recall and delayed recall, rarely have more than two points been taken in the definition of a forgetting curve. An investigation by K. B. Clark did, however, analyze the forgetting curve more adequately.[3] Clark presented to high-school students of both sexes a passage representing a male-female conflict, in which the female was represented as superior; he found, throughout the curve of forgetting over a four-week period, differences in the quantity and quality of recall in favor of the female group which could not be attributed to the superiority of verbal memory usually found in females. "In general it may be stated that set (frame of reference) at

the time of perception has a significant effect upon the gross quantitative aspects of the recall of the same meaningful prose material."

Similarly, W. S. Watson and G. W. Hartmann studied the ability of theistic and atheistic students to recall material which supported or denied the validity of their position.[4] Although most of the differences were not statistically significant, the authors state that their results "consistently buttress these conclusions, i.e., that material which supported the subjects' attitudinal frame was retained better than material which opposed it."

A. L. Edwards has reported corroborative data which prove even more interesting.[5] A ten-minute speech was read to a group of college students, one third of whom were pro-New Deal, one third neutral, and one third anti-New Deal. His results tended to suggest that the hypothesis of autistic perception was valid. After 21 days there was a "consistent but statistically unreliable tendency for the relative amount forgotten to be related to the degree of conflict between the material and the frame of reference."

THE PRESENT PROBLEM

Our investigation was approached with emphasis on quantitative conceptions. We were interested in extending the learning period, as well as the curve of forgetting, over several weeks to note the form of the learning curve under conditions of attitudinal bias. Is material congruent with our social attitudes assimilated in such fashion as to yield a different shape of curve from that which appears when the material conflicts with

[1] M. Sherif, *The Psychology of Social Norms* (New York: Harper & Brothers, 1936).
[2] F. C. Bartlett, *Remembering* (Cambridge, England: Cambridge University Press, 1932).
[3] K. B. Clark, "Some Factors Influencing the Remembering of Prose Material," *Arch. Psychol.*, No. 253, 1940.
[4] W. S. Watson and G. W. Hartmann, "The Rigidity of a Basic Attitudinal Frame," *J. Abnor. & Soc. Psychol.*, 1939, XXXIV, 314–335.
[5] A. L. Edwards, "Political Frames of Reference as a Factor Influencing Recognition," *J. Abnor. & Soc. Psychol.*, 1941, XXXVI, 34–61.

one's bias? If the effect of bias appears at the beginning, is the same relative degree of superiority maintained between the groups during the learning period, or does the superiority increase, or decrease? Similarly, we wished to extend the forgetting period, and ask the same questions. Is there a point in the learning process when, despite opposite frames, the amount learned will be the same? What are the time-dynamics of the learning and forgetting process in a situation such as we are testing? These are the questions we sought to answer.

THE EXPERIMENT

The learning material selected for investigation dealt with the Soviet Union. It was felt that, despite the fact that the USSR is now (1941) allied with Britain and the United States, the Soviet Union provided a topic which was vital and which had meaning at the present time. Further, attitude toward the USSR had achieved a certain degree of stability; military affairs would not seriously change the situation during the course of the experiment. Such relative stability was lacking in other vital topics.

Subjects. Two small homogeneous groups of City College students were used, five in each group. One group was pro-Communist, the other anti-Communist. Both groups felt strongly about their beliefs. The subjects were chosen on the basis of their reputations. At least, the pro-Communist group was the type to which one gives a questionnaire to validate communist-differentiating items. The experimenter was personally acquainted with each subject before the experiment was planned, or made his acquaintance before the subject knew he was to be asked to serve in the study. The age range of each group was from 19 to 22.

Both groups were first tested on a neutral passage. As far as memory is concerned the ten subjects turned out to be very much alike. The variation within the two groups was very slight and the differences between the groups insignificant.

Material. Two prose passages were chosen. One was excitedly anti-Communist, the other more moderately pro-Communist (see Appendix). Since the relative difficulty of the paragraphs differed and since the affective tone differed in degree, results on the two paragraphs cannot be meaningfully compared.

Procedure. All sessions were private, with only the subject and the experimenter present. The subjects were given these instructions: "Read over the paragraph twice at your normal reading rate." After the paragraph was read, 15 minutes passed before the first recall. During the 15 minutes the experimenter and the subject chatted about topics not concerned with the experiment. Then the subject was told: "Reproduce as accurately as possible the paragraph which was presented to you. Make an effort to have your reproduction as accurate and as nearly identical with the original paragraph as you possibly can. Be sure to have your reproduction not only accurate but as complete as the original paragraph."

After several minutes this entire procedure was repeated with the second paragraph. Three members of each group had the pro-Communist selection first, while the other two had the anti-Communist selection first. This was to minimize effects due to position.

This procedure was followed at weekly intervals for four weeks. Then, at weekly intervals for five weeks, memory of the selection was tested without submitting the paragraph to the subject. The first part is termed the "learning period," the second, the "forgetting period."

No effort was made to conceal the nature of the experiment, though it was never explicitly stated by either experimenter or subject.

Analysis. The paragraph was analyzed by the same method used by Clark. The

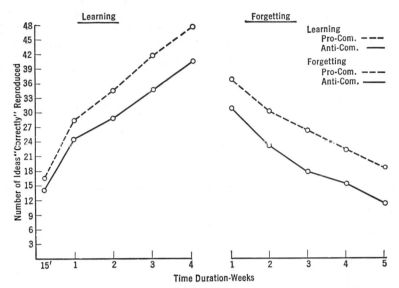

FIG. 1. Learning and forgetting curves for "correct" responses for pro-Communist and anti-Communist groups of the pro-Soviet Union selection.

TABLE 1

AVERAGE NUMBER OF IDEAS "CORRECTLY" REPRODUCED ON THE PRO-SOVIET UNION SELECTION FOR BOTH GROUPS

Group	Learning					Forgetting				
	15'	1 Wk.	2 Wk.	3 Wk.	4 Wk.	1 Wk.	2 Wk.	3 Wk.	4 Wk.	5 Wk.
Pro-Communist	16.8	28.4	34.8	42.0	48.0	37	30.6	26.4	22.6	18.8
Anti-Communist	14.2	24.4	29.0	35.0	41.0	31	23.4	18.0	15.4	11.4
Diff.		2.6	4.0	5.8	7.0	7.0	6	7.2	8.4	7.2	7.4
CR		2.8	2.84	2.9	3.3	3.3	3.2	3.31	3.54	3.5	3.53

paragraphs were divided into idea-groups. The subjects' recall papers were rated in this manner:

1. Those idea-groups which were reproduced in the exact words. or in almost the exact words, of the selection, were graded "correct."

2. Those whose ideas remained the same, but whose words were different, were graded "changed."

3. Those definitely in error were graded "incorrect."

4. Ideas were classified "omitted" if no less than four of one group and no more than one of the other recalled them.

RESULTS

The results will be given (a) for the pro-Soviet selection, (b) for the anti-Soviet selection, (c) for the two selections combined. Student's t for small samples was used to determine statistical significance of the critical ratios.

$$t = \frac{M_1 - M_2}{\sigma_{M_1 - M_2}}.$$

Degrees of freedom $(df \text{ or } n) = n_1 + n_2 - 2$

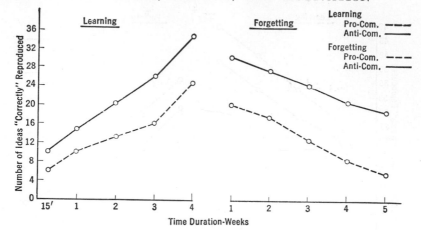

FIG. 2. Learning and forgetting curves for "correct" responses for pro-Communist and anti-Communist groups of the anti-Soviet Union selection.

TABLE 2

AVERAGE NUMBER OF IDEAS "CORRECTLY" REPRODUCED ON THE ANTI-SOVIET UNION SELECTION FOR BOTH GROUPS

Group	Learning					Forgetting				
	15′	1 Wk.	2 Wk.	3 Wk.	4 Wk.	1 Wk.	2 Wk.	3 Wk.	4 Wk.	5 Wk.
Pro-Communist	6.2	10.0	13.2	16.0	24.6	20	17.6	12.8	8.6	5.8
Anti-Communist	10.0	14.8	20.2	26.0	34.4	30	27.2	24.0	20.6	18.6
Diff.	3.8	4.8	7.0	10.0	9.8	10	9.6	11.2	12.0	12.8
CR	3.1	3.3	3.5	3.6	3.9	4.0	3.8	4.2	4.6	4.62

Thus, according to Fisher's table of t values (p. 177), for $df = 8$:[6]

t	Probability of Occurring by Chance
1.860	1
2.306	05
2.896	02
3.355	01

(a) Table 1 and Figure 1 indicate, as we should expect, the superiority of the pro-Communist group on the pro-Soviet selection. Using .01 as the criterion for statistical significance, we see that during the "learning period" the differences more and more approach such signifi-

cance, never actually reaching it, however. In the "forgetting period" the differences become significant at the end of the third week and remain so at the fourth and fifth weeks. The fact that the other differences are not significant at the .01 level may be due to at least two causes: the very small groups may make for a relatively large sigma; and, as suggested by Edwards, the degree of conflict between material and attitude is vital. This may have been material that did not force a sharp enough differentiation between the groups. Table 1 shows, however, that the differences between the means increase throughout the "learn-

[6] R. A. Fisher, *Statistical Methods for Research Workers* (London: Oliver & Boyd, 1938).

ing period," indicating not only that early superiority is maintained, but that the superiority is being increased. In the "forgetting period" the same tendency appears. The increasing superiority in the learning period may in fact be due to selective forgetting. We assume that at the beginning of the first session both groups are equal in having no knowledge of the selection. At the end of this session the pro-Communistic group has the advantage. Since the anti-Communistic group, forgets more than does the pro-group this advantage is continually being built up, being greater at the beginning of each new session.

(b) Table 2 and Figure 2 indicate the marked superiority of the anti-Communist group on the anti-Soviet selection. All t's except that of the first learning session are significant at the .01 level. The tendencies noted in connection with the previous selection are more marked here. The material here is such that it forces the cleavage which we anticipated in setting up our groups.

There appears to be more active agreement and disagreement with this paragraph than with the preceding one. Again the differences between the two groups are seen to increase in the learning period. The explanation, as the writers see it, remains the same. In the forgetting period, the increase in the differences is more marked than in the case of the preceding selection.

How do the curves for the two selections compare?

Learning. In the first selection we find greatest gain taking place during the first week, in the second during the last week. In general, we might characterize the curves of learning in Figure 1 as negatively accelerated, those in Figure 2 as positively accelerated. If any general statements can be made from the results of such small groups, we can say that we see the effect of difference in material. We do find, however, the same tendency of the two curves to spread farther apart.

Forgetting. The trend to separate appears in both graphs. The greatest single loss takes place in the first week, with the exception of that shown by the pro-Communist group on the anti-Soviet selection. Here the greatest drop took place during the third week.

DISCUSSION

Have we secured curves of general validity for all learning and forgetting of controversial material? If field theory is sound, and the writers believe it is essentially so, we should not expect the curves developed in this study to hold for all subjects and all materials. The particular attitude being studied; the number and kind of subjects; their motivation; the difficulty of the material; its affective tone; the degree of conflict between the material and the attitude; the external testing situation, which includes the relations of the experimenter and the subjects; changes in the broader field from which the attitude stems—these are some of the variables that would seem to affect the way in which material which supports or contradicts our social attitudes would be learned and forgotten. Indeed, under the same testing conditions, with the same subjects, we got somewhat different curves on the two selections.

Must we suppose, then, that we can get no general curves which an hypothesis such as ours might seek, that we shall confront completely new conditions for each situation? The question cannot be answered simply, yes or no. If the basic situation is the same, we should expect basically the same general type of curve. But all the factors which we have mentioned above, and which possibly influence our results, cannot be the same in each different situation. Changes then would depend on the structure of the conditions. We cannot expect all people to behave as a group of college students behaved here. What if the individuals involved were not selected in the same manner? And is it sufficient to speak of "controversial" material? Suppose the material to be in one instance merely disagreeable, but in another instance of such a kind as to threaten our whole conception of ourselves and of our world, so that there is deep ego involvement. We noted above how our different paragraphs brought different results.

What, then, on the basis of this study (leaving aside for the moment its inadequacies), are we prepared to say concerning the questions we asked earlier in the paper? Under the conditions of this experiment we noted that there were significant differences in the amount learned, and in the amount forgotten by our different groups. What is the next step? If the question as we have raised it is of importance, then other studies, with other subjects, with other material, with other conditions, must be undertaken. It may be that the problem needs to be attacked in a different manner, not merely making corrections in the technique used herein, but adopting a different conception of the role of time. It may be necessary to have subjects taking questionnaires, or some other form of attitude schedule, throughout the learning and forgetting periods—questionnaires which will seek the same information each time, but so worded that it retains interest and meaning for the subjects. For "time" alone does not cause the forgetting—and postulating a stable frame of reference during the entire experiment may not be appropriate.

A more important question is to ask what the individual will do with material which does not so obviously conflict with his autisms, yet nevertheless cannot be reconciled with them—when the attack is more subtle, when the ego is less aware of the threat. (Cf. the discussion of such issues by Gilbert [7] and Wallen.[8])

SUMMARY AND CONCLUSIONS

Previous studies have indicated the phenomenon of selective perception and recall; an individual notes and remembers material which supports his social attitudes better than material which conflicts with these attitudes. The problem for investigation here was to extend the study of the learning and forgetting processes and to develop curves for these processes.

Attitude toward the Soviet Union was adopted for study. Two paragraphs, one mildly pro-Soviet, the other more bitterly anti-Soviet, were used. The subjects were two groups of college students, one pro-Communist, the other anti-Communist, with five in each group. Learning was studied for four weeks, forgetting for five. K. B. Clark's idea-group method of analysis was used to score the recalled material.

For the pro-Soviet selection, the differences were not statistically significant during the learning period, but became so in the latter part of the forgetting period. The pro-Soviet group showed a tendency to increase in superiority in both periods. The curves were not markedly different except for the points noted in the text. For the anti-Soviet paragraph, differences between the curves were significant throughout.

Some factors for differences and the extent of possible generalization were discussed.

APPENDIX

ANTI–SOVIET UNION SELECTION

From "Stalin" by Souvarine

Russia, | bled white | by Stalin, | leaves the field free | for German dynamism, | and holds itself on the defensive | like the old decadent western nations. | In Russia of today | the appropriation of profit | has an

---

[7] G. M. Gilbert, "New Status of Experimental Studies on the Relationship of Feeling to Memory," *Psychol. Bull.*, 1938, XXXV, 26–35.

[8] D. Wallen, "Ego Involvement as a Determinant of Selective Forgetting," *J. Abnor. & Soc. Psychol.*, 1942, XXXVII, 20–39.

unquestionably | private character. | Private profit is apparent | in the growing social inequality, | which is more revolting | in its arrant injustice | than in the capitalist countries | where it is diminishing, | more intolerable in the terminology of hypocritical equalitarianism. | No society, | it is true, | has ever existed without hierarchy, | without authority. | But the socialist dream | of founding one in Russia | has turned into a nightmare. | The "expropriation of the ex propriators" | has led to a sore of bureaucratic | feudalism | under which the proletariat | and the peasantry, | debased | by the officialdom | and the mandarinate, | have been reduced to a kind of serfdom. | If the methods of production are not entirely capitalistic | it is only because, | for the majority of the Soviet pariahs, | the system deserves rather the name of slavery. | It is a regime of privilege | because one of exploitation, | a regime of police | because one of oppression. | It is a mixed structure without architecture, | without principles, | without solidity, | without roots, | heterogeneous | and full of contradictions. | Liberty of the press | and the right of assembly | exist only in memory. |

The spirit of the liquidation of the kulaks | in the late twenties | still exists in toto. | No contemporaneous records | have been able to keep up | with all the mass arrests | and executions, | the assassinations | which collectivization dragged in its wake. | The secrets of the barbarous deportations | of millions of human beings, | transplanted to Arctic regions | and the Urals | are not revealed. | An American correspondent | extremely favorable to Stalin's interests | estimated at 2 million | the approximate number | banished and exiled in 1929–1930. |

PRO–SOVIET UNION SELECTION

From "Soviet Russia Today"

An American correspondent | for the Christian Science Monitor in Russia, | viewing the transformation | in the Western Ukraine | following Soviet occupation | in 1939, | reports:

"Only a few days have passed | since the provisional government set to work on its new tasks, | but the fruits of its labors | are already in evidence. | Power stations | and other enterprises | are functioning normally. | Departments of education | are being formed, | departments of commerce | and food supplies, | of health | and communal service | and local industries. | Students will be provided with text books | and instruction | in their native language. | A plan is drawn up for the reconstruction of bridges, | roads, | and houses. | The provisional government was elected | by the people of the villages | at the first real election the people of that area have had. |

A group of the peasants went into Russia as the guests of a collective farm. | The farmers took them to see their bright clean cottages, | showed them the cattle enclosures, | and all their rich | modern equipment. | The wonder of the trip was a tractor. | It was the first time the group had seen one. |

*   *   *   *   *   *   *

The popular assembly | of Western Ukraine | passed the following resolution: | "At assemblies and meetings | the people expressed their desire | to merge with the Soviet Union. | For only in the Soviet Union | has the exploitation of man | been abolished. | Hundreds | of powerful factories | and industrial plants | have been built | where a working class is employed | that knows nothing of exploitation. | The Ukrainian peasantry has become economically | strong, | possessing the entire land | and cultivating it with the latest technique. | The people feel that only through the Soviet Union | could they freely | participate in the administration of the state, | in the building of a free | and happy life for themselves." |

Though the peasants are not aware of the world politics, | they seem to have experienced | the abolition of all national oppression, | and the feeling of the unity of peoples, | since the Soviet occupation. |

3

Perception of Persons

CHANGES IN SOCIAL PERCEPTION AS A FUNCTION OF THE PERSONAL RELEVANCE OF BEHAVIOR

By Edward E. Jones and Richard deCharms

The present investigation is an outgrowth of an earlier stated conception of social perception [1] which stressed some conditions under which different inferences will be drawn from the same behavior of another. If the behavior of a stimulus person has clearly defined consequences for the value-maintenance or the goal attainment of the perceiver, the perception of the other's stable characteristics will proceed from a different premise than if the behavior has no such relevant consequences. We may refer to such premises as *inferential sets* and assume that in the former case, when another's behavior has consequences for the perceiver, a *value-maintenance* set has been aroused. The consequent perceptions of the other's characteristics will then vary greatly as a function of whether the other's behavior promotes or interferes with goal attainment or the maintenance of values. If the other's behavior has no such relevant consequences even though

he behaves in an objectively identical way, he will be perceived and evaluated in a different, more neutral, fashion.

Before stating the propositions which follow from these considerations, it is necessary to describe briefly the experimental procedure common to both experiments to be reported below. Groups of five to six subjects worked in parallel on a series of problem-solving tasks. A criterion of over-all success or failure was stated at the outset, and one member of the group (by prearrangement) failed to meet this criterion. For half the groups, the failure of this single member meant that he alone did not receive the promised reward. For the remaining groups, his failure meant that no one in the group received the reward. Trait ratings of this critical member were obtained before and after the tasks. The general proposition to be tested may now be stated as follows: since the value-maintenance set

From *Sociometry*, 1957, XX. Reprinted by permission of the authors and the publisher. This study was conducted in the program of the Organization Research Group of the Institute for Research in Social Science at the University of North Carolina. The ORG is supported jointly by the Ford Foundation and the Office of Naval Research [Nonr-855(04)]. This research was partially financed by a grant to the senior author from the Duke University Research Council.

[1] E. E. Jones, "Inferential Sets in Social Perception," paper read at the meeting of the American Psychological Association, San Francisco, 1955.

will be promoted to a greater extent when the failure of one affects the reward attainment of all, more negative characteristics will be ascribed to the failing person when his failure implies group failure than when it does not. More specific predictions will be stated after the procedure of Experiment I is described in greater detail.

Experiment I

Procedure. Groups of five or six subjects, with one exception, volunteers from the Introductory Psychology Course at North Carolina, met for an experiment on "group prob.em solving." The one exception in each group was a role-playing confederate who was carefully instructed to behave in a neutral fashion and to fail a standard pattern of tasks. In an introductory period prior to the main part of the experiment, procedures (including a "quiz-program" task) and instructions were introduced which attempted: (*a*) to arouse the motivation of the subjects to do their best on the tasks required, (*b*) to encourage enough interaction so that subjects would have some basis for their initial ratings, and (*c*) to give the confederate a chance to establish himself initially as quite intelligent.

The subjects were told that the group problem-solving tasks were well-established measures of individual intelligence. Following the orientation procedures, the *before measure* (trait ratings) was introduced as a measure of intelligence in "that most neglected area, social sensitivity." Rating sheets were passed out containing 21 trait pairs such as friendly-unfriendly, lazy-energetic, etc., separated by a row of eight enclosed boxes, representing the scale points to be checked by each subject. Each subject rated the crucial member (the failing confederate) and one other naïve subject without knowing that all others were also rating the confederate.

After the initial ratings had been completed, the experimenter told the subjects that the criterion of individual success and failure on the four tasks would be based on norms established at a rival college. The experimental groups were told that in order for the group to be successful and for any of the members to receive a monetary reward ($1.00), *all* would have to attain the stated criterion of "passing" three of the four tasks. If one failed, all failed, and no one received the reward. The control groups were told that any individual in the group who attained the (same) criterion would receive the reward, regardless of how well or poorly the other subjects did.

The four tasks involved various verbal, arithmetical, and spatial skills all of which had a plausible relation to intelligence. In every group, the confederate was the only member to fail two of the four tasks. Special deception procedures were devised to allay the suspicions of the naïve subjects, and the genuineness of the confederate's failure was uniformly accepted. There were generally observable differences between experimental and control groups in the extent to which the suspense mounted as the last task neared completion. Sometimes, in the "common-fate" treatment, a subject or two would act as cheer leaders, urging the confederate through the items in hopes that their encouragement would bring success to the subject and hence to the group.

After the tasks were completed, the experimenter announced either that the group (experimental condition) or one member (control condition) would not receive the reward, and subjects were asked to rerate the same two members that they had previously rated.

The Motivation Variable. An attempt was made to vary the importance of "goal attainment" by preselecting subjects in terms of their achievement motivation following procedures described

TABLE 1

EXPERIMENT I. MEAN CHANGE SCORES FOR EACH TRAIT CLUSTER BY CONDITIONS †

	Experimental group ("*common fate*")		Control group ("*individual fate*")	
	High n Ach	Low n Ach	High n Ach	Low n Ach
Competence cluster (Competent, intelligent, quick-witted and well-organized)	1.60 *	1.65 *	.88 *	.60 *
Motivation cluster (Competitive, hard-driving, conscientious, energetic, does his best)	1.02 *	.96 *	.98 *	.38 *
Likeability (Friendly, very likeable, modest, sympathetic toward others, pleasant, considerate)	.10	.52 *	.12	.28
Dependable	2.10 *	1.80 *	1.20 *	1.00 *

† The higher the score, the greater the mean change toward negative evaluation.
* $p < .05$ (significantly greater than zero).

by McClelland *et al.*[2] Experimental and control groups were each composed of ten "highs" and ten "lows" (falling above and below the general class median respectively). Thus the experimental design was essentially a two-by-two design with ten subjects in each of four cells.

Hypotheses and Results. The main hypothesis of this first experiment is that the evaluation of the confederate will change more in a negative direction under experimental than control conditions, since his behavior prevents the subjects' goal attainment under the former and not the latter conditions.

A second hypothesis, which might be stated as a corollary of the first, is that the higher the need for achievement, the greater the difference between experimental and control conditions.

It is now important to consider the nature of the dependent variable, the rating scale. Twenty-one trait pairs were chosen to represent three *a priori* clusters: *perceived competence, perceived motivation,* and *likeability.* In addition to traits judged to fall into each of these clusters, there were several "beta traits"[3] used as fillers to inhibit an evaluative response set. The critical trait, *dependable,* was included to be evaluated on its own. Table 1 shows the extent to which the average change on each cluster (plus *dependable*) differ reliably from zero.

It is apparent from a glance at the table that the average subject, regardless of experimental conditions, sees the confederate as less competent and less highly motivated after he has failed the tasks. While there are no differences between the conditions with regard to perceived motivation, there is a significantly

---

[2] D. C. McClelland, J. W. Atkinson, and E. L. Lowell, *The Achievement Motive* (New York: Appleton-Century-Crofts, Inc., 1953).

[3] T. B. Lemann and R. L. Solomon, "Group Characteristics as Revealed in Sociometric Patterns and Personality Ratings," *Sociometry,* 1952, XV, 7–90.

greater decline in perceived competence for the experimental groups than for the control groups ($p < .05$). This specific difference was unexpected and was not replicated in the second experiment to be described below. It is difficult to interpret this finding unless the competence-cluster data are viewed as an expression of evaluative change through the set of ratings judged by the subject to be most appropriate to the situation.

The most direct test of the main hypothesis involves the *likeability cluster*. The hypothesis is not supported by the data, since there is not a significant difference between experimental and control groups. Moreover, the data actually contradict the hypothesis with regard to the variable of achievement motivation. Subjects who are low in achievement motivation show a greater negative change on likeability items than those high in achievement motivation. It appears that subjects with high-achievement motivation inhibit negative evaluations of the confederate, possibly because his failure serves to emphasize their own success by contrast.

Since previous research has shown that "dependability" is a trait which is especially sensitive to changes in interpersonal perception,[4] it was hypothesized that the confederate will be seen as declining in dependability more under the experimental than the control situation. It was further predicted that this change would be greater for those subjects high in achievement motivation. The first part of this hypothesis was clearly supported ($p < .02$), but again the achievement-motivation variable failed to discriminate.

Thus, while the confederate's failure under conditions of common group fate does not result in his being rated down on the likeability cluster, he is seen to be significantly less dependable than the same person behaving in the same way under conditions of individual-reward attainment.

As a final over-all index of evaluative change, an a priori *halo cluster* was constructed by combining the 14 most clearly evaluative traits. It was possible to test the main hypothesis (of greater change under experimental conditions) in terms of global evaluation. The hypothesis was confirmed at the .05 level. Again the difference between highs and lows on need achievement was negligible.

Discussion of Experiment I. If one compares the reactions to a role-playing confederate under the experimental and control conditions of the first experiment, the results indicate that when the confederate's behavior is relevant to (i.e., prevents) the goal attainment of the perceiver, he is seen as relatively less competent, less dependable, and the over-all evaluation of him is more negative in tone. However, a group of traits specifically chosen to reflect likeability did not discriminate between subjects in the different experimental conditions.

There are several possible reasons for the failure of this particular prediction. It may be that a general reluctance to commit oneself to a "negative-likeability" judgment is a powerful obscurant in the present situation, and that the culturally grounded inhibitions behind this reluctance operate less in other areas of interpersonal evaluation. This would help explain the significant results with regard to the competence and halo clusters which may serve, in a sense, as surrogates for a likeability judgment.

Of somewhat greater theoretical interest is the possibility that the primary hypothesis needs to be qualified to take into account certain perceptual preconditions. It is quite conceivable that the perceived *reason* for the confederate's failure plays an important role in any

---

[4] E. E. Jones, "Authoritarianism as a Determinant of First-Impression Formation," *J. Pers.*, 1954, XXIII, 107–127.

concurrent evaluation of him. Thus, a lowered estimate of the confederate's competence would lead to a different evaluative outcome than a similar reappraisal of the confederate's motivation. While we had hoped to promote the latter judgment by having the confederate initially appear quite intelligent, the results clearly show a decline on both attributes, for the change scores of the competence and motivation clusters are correlated to a significant extent (r for the experimental groups being $+.73$, for the control groups being $+.47$).

But, if the confederate is perceived to fail as a function of inadequate ability, there should be less of a tendency to dislike him than if his failure is due to his not trying hard enough. Competence, by and large, is an attribute cluster over which the individual has little control —the sources of competence are in a sense external to the sphere of individual autonomy and responsibility. Motivation, on the other hand, is an attribute cluster likely to be perceived as self-caused or internally controlled by the behaver in question. Such considerations stem quite directly from the recent experiments of Thibaut and Riecken,[5] which in turn explored various implications of the work of Heider[6] and Michotte.[7]

Examination of the correlation between perceived change in motivation and perceived change in likeability provides some support for this interpretation. While this correlation is negligible ($r = +.02$) for the control subjects, as we would expect, the correlation rises to $+.36$ for the experimental subjects ($p = .10$). Thus, it appears that there *is* some change in direct "likeability" evaluation under conditions of common-

group fate, when the confederate is seen as less motivated in the after than in the before ratings.

Since this relationship is a tenuous one, a second experiment was designed in an attempt to obtain greater control over the subject's attribution of motivational versus competence change. It was also considered highly desirable to provide a direct replication of the positive findings of the first experiment.

Experiment II

In planning the second experiment, an attempt was made to preserve the general procedure outlined above unless there were sound reasons for modification. The major change involved differential instructions designed to induce a perceived decline either in the confederate's motivation or his competence. For half the groups the instructions repeatedly stressed the fact that the tasks were designed to measure motivation ("how hard you're willing to work for an incentive") and that they had been shown in previous work to be unrelated to intelligence or aptitude. In the remaining groups, the high relationship with standard intelligence tests was stressed. A number of minor variations were also introduced.

a. The experiment was conducted by a different experimenter, with a different confederate, and with subjects from a different school.

b. A coding task was substituted for one which made more clear-cut intellectual demands on the subjects.

c. Achievement motivation was not a measured variable in Experiment II.

d. Each subject was asked to rate all other subjects on the before and after

---

[5] J. W. Thibaut and H. W. Riecken, "Some Determinants and Consequences of the Perception of Social Causality," pp. 117–130.

[6] F. Heider, "Social Perception and Phenomenal Causality," *Psychol. Rev.*, 1944, LI, 358–374.

[7] A. Michotte, *La Perception de la Causalité* (Institut supérieur de Philosophie, Univ. de Louvain: Vrin, 1946).

TABLE 2

EXPERIMENT II: MEAN CHANGE SCORE FOR EACH TRAIT CLUSTER BY CONDITIONS †

	Experimental group ("common fate")		Control group ("individual fate")	
	Motivation instructions	Competence instructions	Motivation instructions	Competence instructions
Competence cluster (Competent, intelligent, quick-witted)	2.05 *	1.90 *	1.13 *	2.00 *
Motivation Cluster (Conscientious, does his best)	2.00 *	1.30 *	1.15 *	1.95 *
Likeability cluster (Very likeable, considerate of others, pleasant, modest)	.23	.00	−.15	−.13
Dependable	3.00 *	1.20 *	.20	1.10 *

† The higher the score, the greater the mean change toward negative evaluation.
* $p < .05$ (significantly greater than zero).

ratings. In order to reduce the tedium of repeated ratings, ten of the original 21 traits were selected to represent the same trait clusters as in Experiment I. "Dependability" was also included.

In summary, the experiment was much like the first except that half the groups were told that the tasks definitely measured intelligence, the other half that they definitely did not measure intelligence. The design again compares group reward with individual reward, and each of these treatments is subdivided into two groups, one receiving "Motivation" and the other "Competence" instructions. There were ten subjects in each cell.

Results. *Effectiveness of Experimental Manipulation.* The first relevant question concerns the extent to which the instructions were successful in inducing subjects to perceive failure as attributable to low motivation *or* lack of competence. When asked at the close of the experiment to rate the effectiveness of the tasks in tapping (a) motivation and (b) competence, the subjects generally responded in terms of the treatment to which their

group had been assigned. Furthermore, subjects in the competence condition actually *perform* significantly better on the tasks than subjects in the motivation condition. As Table 2 shows, the motivation versus competence instructions did not systematically affect the subjects' ratings of the confederates' motivation and competence to a significant degree. In other words, while the subjects perceived the tasks as measures of motivation or competence in line with the instructions, this had little effect on whether the confederate was seen as failing for reasons of motivation or ability.

Changes in Evaluation of the Confederate. While we were not entirely successful in creating the conditions for a crucial test of the revised hypothesis, it is still meaningful to examine the changes in evaluation which did take place. Turning to the *likeability cluster*, Table 2 indicates that the results are in the right direction, but fall short of significance.

An a priori *halo cluster* was again constructed to give a test of general positive evaluative change. This type of measure yielded a significant difference between

TABLE 3

EXPERIMENT II: MEANS AND STANDARD DEVIATIONS, HALO CLUSTER

	Experimental group		Control group	
	Motivation instructions	Competence instructions	Motivation instructions	Competence instructions
Mean *	23.0	17.3	14.4	18.9
Standard deviation	10.68	6.27	2.12	9.53

* The greater the mean change, the more negative the "after" evaluation.

experimental and control conditions in Experiment I. It was here predicted that there would be more negative halo in the motivation-experimental condition than in any other combined condition. The means and standard deviations are presented in Table 3. It is clear that the motivation-experimental subgroup has the largest mean, but there is wide variability among the individual scores composing this mean. While some subjects in the motivation-experimental subgroup changed markedly in a negative direction, a few changed very slightly. In the motivation-control subgroup, however, the change was uniform and moderate.

In Experiment I, subjects in the experimental groups saw the confederate as declining more in *dependability* than did subjects in the control groups. In line with the revised hypothesis of Experiment II, this decline should be greater when the reason for failure is perceived to be motivational than when it is perceived to be a matter of competence. Table 2 shows that this is indeed the case, the difference being highly reliable. Thus, despite the fact that the two sets of instructions did not create differential perceptions of the confederate's motivation, they did have the predicted effect on the ratings of dependability.

The main (revised) hypothesis of the present experiment assumes that there will be a greater decline in positive eval-

uation under experimental than under control conditions *if* the confederate's failure is attributed to lack of motivation. Therefore, we would expect the person with low perceived motivation to be liked less under experimental than under control conditions. A comparison of the correlations between perceived motivation and likeability under experimental versus control conditions indicates that this is true in both experiments, but in neither are the differences quite significant statistically.

GENERAL DISCUSSION

There is evidence from both experiments that a person who behaves in a certain way will be perceived differently as a function of the relevance of his behavior to the value maintenance of the perceiver. Specifically, in both experiments, the failing confederate is perceived to be less dependable when his failure prevents others from reward attainment. Furthermore, when the tasks are presented as measures of motivation in Experiment II, this decline in perceived dependability is clearly greater than when the tasks are presented as an intelligence test. By inference, the degree to which the confederate is seen as responsible for behavior which causes the group to fail is a definite factor in evaluating his dependability. The correlational data bear this out in a more tentative way with regard to his "like-ability." Objectively, this contingency between change in perceived motivation and change in evaluation is not entirely reasonable because an incompetent but highly motivated person can be equally obstructive as far as goal attainment is concerned. Subjectively, however, when the locus of phenomenal causality is perceived as internal to the agent of frustration, negative evaluation is more severe.

These related experiments may be seen as a demonstration of the effects of set on the perception of the characteristics of others. Different inferences will be drawn from the same behavior, as a function of the set promoted by the structure of the social situation. The behavior of others does not appear to have a constant meaning, and the attribution of stable characteristics to the behaver is dependent on the significance of his behavior for the perceiver's own value-maintenance or goal attainment.

SUMMARY

Two experiments were conducted in an effort to demonstrate that different inferences will be drawn from the same behavior when this behavior does or does not have personal relevance for the perceiver. A common experimental procedure was adopted for both experiments which involved the ultimate failure of a confederate to meet the announced norms on a series of tasks. The personal relevance of this failure was varied by initially announcing that the attainment of a monetary reward would either be on a group or "common-fate" basis (experimental groups) or on an individual-achievement basis (control groups). In the first experiment, subjects were preselected in terms of their general-achievement motivation, in an attempt to vary the importance of attaining the reward. In the second experiment,

achievement motivation was not a measured variable, but the tasks were presented as either measures of motivation or intelligence. The main hypotheses and results of both experiments may be summarized as follows:

1. When the reward attainment of each subject depends on the successful performance of all subjects, rather than being determined on an individual basis, (a) a failing subject will be seen as relatively less likeable, (b) across all evaluative traits there will be a greater negative halo, and (c) the failing subject will be seen as less dependable in the former than in the latter condition. The results show that (a) is not supported by either experiment, (b) is supported by Experiment I, and as predicted in Experiment II under "motivation instructions" (although heterogeneity of variance precludes a rigorous test), and (c) is supported by both experiments. It is important to note that both negative-halo increase and dependability decline are greater when the tasks are presented as measures of motivation in the second experiment—i.e., when the locus of causality is internal to the subject who fails.

2. There will be a higher correlation between perceived-motivation decline and likeability decline under experimental than control conditions. The results show that, while the correlations in neither experiment differ significantly from each other, they are both in the predicted direction.

While the results of the present investigations are generally in line with theoretical expectations, it is clear that there are many difficulties in controlling social-stimulus cues to yield uniform and consistent patterns of inference. Nevertheless, the results of the present research seem to encourage the belief that progress in understanding the processes of social perception can be served by such experimental attempts

ON THE RELATION BETWEEN FEELINGS AND PERCEPTION OF FEELINGS AMONG MEMBERS OF SMALL GROUPS

By Renato Tagiuri, Jerome S. Bruner, and Robert R. Blake

Are members of a group able to perceive their feelings for each other more accurately than might be predicted by chance? Are their perceptions of how others feel toward them related to their own feelings for others? Is the mutuality of feelings in a small group higher than would be expected by chance? How do these phenomena of accuracy, "congruency," and mutuality relate to each other and affect group functioning? These questions are the concern of this paper.

If the members of a small group are asked to express their likes and dislikes for each other and to express also their "guesses" as to who likes and dislikes them,[1] their responses provide the following relevant data for each member of the group: (a) his preferences and aversions for others in the group, (b) the feelings other group members actually have for him, and (c) how he sees the feelings of others in the group—in short, his guesses about others' preferences or aversions toward him.

Subjects and Procedure. The paper is based on data gathered from 47 groups, ranging in size from six to 32 members, varying in the average age of members from eight to 40 years. The groups, composed mostly of men, were of many kinds: naval crews, summer campers, seminars, semitherapeutic groups—all in existence prior to and independent of our research. Members were asked to indicate, without restriction on number, those in the group they "liked best" and those they "liked least," and to guess which members they thought "liked them best" and least.

Accuracy of Perceiving Affect. The term *accuracy* denotes an instance in which a subject's perception of another's feeling for him is correct. Does accuracy exceed chance level?

In order to test this question it is necessary to determine what accuracy levels might be expected to occur by chance in a group. One can do this by constructing mathematically groups of robots according to the following specifications.[2] For each member of a human group a robot is constructed. Each robot is matched with his human counterpart in terms of number of choices and number of guesses, a necessary specification since the human Ss were permitted to make an unrestricted number of entries in each case. The robot is of course "forbidden" to respond to himself or to the same member twice and is not permitted both to choose

This paper is a quite complete revision and extension of an earlier paper by R. Tagiuri, R. R. Blake, and J. S. Bruner, "Some Determinants of the Perception of Positive and Negative Feelings in Others," *J. Abnorm. Soc. Psychol.*, 1953, XLVIII, 585–592, employing new data and revising the interpretation presented in that discussion. The project was sponsored in part by the United States Navy under ONR Contract No. N5 ori-07646 and in part by the United States Air Force under Contract No. AF 33 (038-12782) monitored by the Human Resources Research Institute.

[1] R. Tagiuri, "Relational Analysis; an Extension of Sociometric Method with Emphasis upon Social Perception," *Sociometry*, 1952, XV, 91–104.

[2] Details of how this is done are given in R. D. Luce, J. Macy, and R. Tagiuri, "A Statistical Model for Relational Analysis," *Psychometrika*, 1955, XX, 319–327; and in R. Tagiuri, J. S. Bruner, and N. Kogan, "Estimating the Chance Expectancies of Dyadic Relationships within a Group," *Psychol. Bull.*, 1955, LII, 122–131.

TABLE 1

Observed and Expected Accuracy, Congruency, and Mutuality for 47 Groups Combined

	Observed		Expected		Chi²*	p
	Sum f	Av. percent	Sum f	Av. percent		
Accuracy (over-all)	3135	46.5	2538	37.6	248.9	.001
choice	1054	43.8	698	29.0	262.7	.001
rejection	437	27.5	315	19.9	100.6	.001
Congruency (over-all)	4725	70.0	2538	37.6	3009.5	.001
choice	1502	62.4	698	29.0	1271.6	.001
rejection	981	62.8	315	19.9	1430.6	.001
Mutuality (over-all)	3010	44.7	2471	36.6	252.2	.001
choice	1238	52.3	916	38.1	201.0	.001
rejection	520	32.7	389	24.4	75.6	.001

* Based on 47 $d.f.$'s.

and reject the same person or to specify another as both choosing and rejecting him.

Table 1 gives the observed and expected data for all the 47 groups combined. We see that 43.8 percent of the guesses individuals made about which other members of the group liked them were accurate—that is, those other individuals actually *did* like them, according to their own report. Our robots, guessing purely by chance, were accurate only 29 percent of the time about the choices of others. Similarly, our subjects were more accurate than chance in guessing which other members of the group *disliked* them. The chi-square test is used to assess the significance of the discrepancy between observed human accuracy and the chance accuracy of our mathematical robots. Significance tests were performed separately on each of the 47 groups and then summed. Our human groups showed a level of accuracy significantly in excess of chance expectancy, a level of accuracy obtainable by chance at the one-in-a-thousand level.

Are our subjects equally accurate in perceiving those who like them and those

who reject them? Statistically, the question is a difficult one to answer for reasons that need not concern us here. But what we have found is that individual groups of subjects are more frequently better than chance in perceiving accurately the choices of others than they are in perceiving rejections—a matter to which we shall presently return.

In sum, while the general perceptual accuracy of our Ss is significantly better than that of matched robots, the major contributing factor in this performance derives from the superiority of humans in perceiving acceptance or choice by others.

Congruency of Feeling and Perception. Do Ss interpret others' feelings in terms of their own feelings toward them? That is to say, if an S likes another, will this lead him to see the other as liking him? This matching of choice and guess we shall refer to as *perceptual-affective congruency,* or more simply, *congruency.*

If congruency prevails, one would expect to find a higher than chance incidence of Ss who both like another and feel chosen by him, and of Ss who dislike another and feel rejected by him. To test this hypothesis the human groups are again compared with their robot counterparts.

The combined chi square of this comparison (Table 1) has a p value of less than .001. Clearly, then, our human Ss tend to perceive the feelings of others in accordance with their own feeling for them. Congruency occurs far in excess of chance.

Is this tendency toward congruency a general one or is it specific to choosing or rejecting? Congruency for both choice and rejection reach highly significant levels, pooled chi squares indicating that such deviations would be obtained by chance less than once in a thousand times. In sum, for both accepting and rejecting, congruency is the rule: one rejects another and sees the other as rejecting one, or one chooses another and sees one's choice reciprocated.[3]

Mutuality of Feelings. Is the incidence of mutual feelings between members—reciprocal choice or omission or rejection—in excess of the chance level set by matched robot groups? A chi-square test shows that mutuality does exceed chance, a pooled chi square yielding a confidence level of less than .001.

Closer examination of the data for individual groups shows, however, that this result is contributed mostly by the larger groups and that mutuality does not greatly exceed chance in absolute terms. Also, as in the case of accuracy the excess over chance is greater for mutuality of choice than for mutuality of rejection.

Interrelation of Accuracy, Congruency, and Mutuality. It is simplest to begin with the relationship between two members of a dyad, A and B. Let us suppose that A chooses B and that, as may well occur, the feeling is reciprocated and B chooses

A. We represent this in the pattern below, noting choice by "$+$" and concentrating on how A will perceive B's feelings for him.

A's feeling for B:	$+$
A's perception of B's feeling:	x
B's feeling for A:	$+$

Now, if it should turn out to be the case (and it is very likely that it will be) that A's choice of B is accompanied by the feeling of being chosen in return by B, then this congruency effect will lead to x being a plus. It would then automatically follow, of course, that A would also be accurate in identifying B as choosing him. Thus, the coexistence of mutuality in excess of chance and of congruency in excess of chance—both known to occur—automatically produces accuracy without any acumen whatsoever on the part of A.

A more general way of putting the matter is to note that

1. if congruency and mutuality are present, then accuracy must occur,
2. if congruency and accuracy are present, then mutuality must be present, and
3. if mutuality and accuracy are present, then congruency must be present.

It follows from this that it is impossible to examine the nature of self-referent accuracy in a dyad without taking into account the concurrent existence of mutuality and congruency. For either *none* of the three may be present or *one* of the three may be present alone, but beyond that the presence of *any two* determines the presence of the *third*.

As a first step toward unravelling this

---

[3] The reader should bear in mind that this discussion of congruency makes no assumptions about whether or not the perceptual side of the affect-perception link is accurate. We are dealing with perceptions in the present instance *as if* all perceptions were responses made in the presence of a blank stimulus. At a later place in the paper, the question of accuracy and congruency will be treated.

skein, we inquire about the relationship of accuracy and congruency. Are perceptions of another's choice more or less accurate when they are accompanied by a corresponding choice? That is, if A feels chosen by B, is he more likely to be right if he also chooses B or not? In our group, we find that the difference between the two perceptual conditions is negligible. We are about as accurate in perceiving the presence of choice, rejection, or omission when we have feelings congruent with these preferences as when we do not —48 percent as compared with 42 percent. In both cases, the performance is in excess of what one would expect from chance robots. Thus, our subjects' accuracy in estimating whether others liked or disliked them was not simply a reflection of the fact that they believed their own choices and rejections were reciprocated.

We may now ask the parallel question about accuracy and mutuality, that is, whether you recognize the feelings of another more easily when you have the same feelings for him as he does for you. This time we find a huge difference. When you feel toward another the same way as he feels toward you, you will be correct in recognizing his feelings 76 percent of the time. But should you feel differently toward him than he feels toward you, you will only be correct in your perception of his feelings 23 percent of the time. Moreover, your correct perception in the presence of mutuality will be notably *in excess* of chance, while the level of accuracy you attain where no mutuality is present will be significantly *below* chance. In a word, if you and another person share common feelings for each other, each of you is very likely indeed to know the feelings the other holds for him—in roughly three out of four cases. If, on the other hand, the two of you feel differently toward each other, each of you is likely to be mistaken about the other's feeling some three in four times.

Before we interpret this interesting finding, we must explore several possible ways in which the phenomenon could have come about. Consider the enormously effective performance of human beings in recognizing the feelings of those with whom there is a mutual bond. It can be produced in two ways. Given mutuality, the correspondence between the feeling "received" and its perception could be the result either of congruency or of real accuracy. If mutual feelings are present and one recognizes them for what they are, the result is an "overproduction" in excess of chance of three types of relationships:

A's feeling for B	A's perception of B's feeling	B's feeling for A
$+$	$+$	$+$
0	0	0
$-$	$-$	$-$

In the present case, the two outside columns are fixed—i.e., mutuality prevails —and the question is whether the middle column is determined by matching the right hand one (accuracy) or the left hand one (congruency). We cannot tell in instances of the above kind. The first thing that can be said is that both in terms of frequency and in terms of the degree to which it exceeds chance, congruency is a significantly more powerful and ubiquitous phenomenon than accuracy (see Table 1). This suggests that the matching of perception to mutuality is more likely to be produced by the tendency to feel chosen by another in a manner congruent with how one feels toward him. But there is a second, direct approach to the problem.

The test is provided by the way in which perception operates under conditions of nonmutuality. Perceptual accuracy where nonmutuality of feeling prevails is significantly *below* chance. Why is this so? Concretely, is this poor performance attributable to congruency or to a lack of perceptual skill? There are six kinds of relationship between two people that may be classified as nonmutual:

A's feeling for B	A's perception of B's feeling	B's feeling for A
+	x_1	0
+	x_2	−
0	x_3	+
0	x_4	−
−	x_5	+
−	x_6	0

We inquire now whether $x_1 \ldots x_6$ correspond to the left-hand column or the right. If they correspond to the left, then we are dealing with congruency, if to the right, then with genuine accuracy. We know already that there is a *below chance* correspondence between $x_1 \ldots x_6$ and the right-hand column: perceptual accuracy is below chance in such nonmutual dyads. We also know that the relation between the middle column and the left one is *above chance*—that is to say, whether accurate or not, one's perceptions are in line with one's own choices and rejections. For this crucial test case, then, we must conclude that perceptual performance (in this case a very poor performance indeed) is attributable to the operation of congruency.

It would be convenient if we could argue from this that the excellent perceptual performance of the members of mutual dyads could be accounted for in the same way. Indeed, such an argument can be made. But it does not follow by necessity that if inaccuracy is attributable to the effects of congruency, therefore accuracy can be thus accounted for in the same way. In truth, the question must be left indeterminate. What we *can* and *must* say, however, is that the happy circumstance that leads people to feel mutually toward each other in excess of chance, and the all too human tendency to see others as feeling toward us in much the same way as we feel toward them—this fortunate concatenation produces a state in which people perforce "know" how the other feels. Even if the origin of this "knowing" is indeterminate, we can at least count our blessings!

SUMMARY AND DISCUSSION

How do human Ss differ from "chance robots" in choosing and rejecting each other and in perceiving these choices and rejections? The Ss were asked to indicate those fellow group members they liked best and those they liked least and those they thought liked them the best and least. No restriction was placed on the number to be chosen or guessed.

There are three principal dimensions in terms of which our results may be examined. The first is *perceptual accuracy:* the extent to which human Ss deviate from robots in recognizing how group members feel toward them. Perceptual-affective *congruency* constitutes the second: the degree to which Ss see the feelings of others as corresponding to their own feelings for others. The final dimension is *mutuality:* the extent to which mutual preferences between Ss prevail.

The *accuracy* with which Ss are able to recognize the feelings they evoke in group members is in excess of chance. This deviation from chance is, however, accounted for in major part by the superiority of human Ss in recognizing correctly those who like them best. Accuracy in recognizing rejection is not as markedly above robot chance, though it is significantly so.

The recognition of affect in others is, like any other form of perceptual recognition, dependent both upon the cues available and upon the degree to which an observer is set to utilize these cues. What is special about the kind of cues we are dealing with here is that they are emitted by human beings rather than by objects and that human beings, given elaborate training in comportment, learn to suppress or mask certain cues in accordance with their cultural dictates.

A facile generalization based on a doctrine of the defense of self-esteem might say that people would more readily recognize cues of acceptance by others than cues of rejection or indifference. Such is one bare finding of our study. But disciplined common sense and clinical observation warn us away from such a conclusion. Concern over rejection—or, more generally, affiliative anxiety—should lead to high accuracy in spotting rejection by others. Why do the findings contradict such conclusions? There are three possible hypotheses: (a) cues of rejection are masked by politeness, (b) cues of rejection are perceptually denied as an act of ego defense, or (c) inadequate training in recognizing cues of rejection. In short, is the failure one of intrinsic difficulty, of defense, or of skill? Let us say at the outset that we do not know which view is the more reasonable or whether any is more reasonable than the others. It is true that rejection and hostility are masked in our culture, and the Ss in these experiments were no exception to the rule. They reported, for example, difficulty and reluctance in making rejections and, indeed, made fewer rejections than choices. With regard to ego-defensive activity, a rich clinical literature speaks directly to the likelihood of such maneuvers. The evidence of strong tendencies to congruency between feeling and perception to which we turn shortly would lend support to the "defensive hypothesis." Finally, such is the embarrassment over rejection in our society that it seems likely that the opportunity for testing cues of rejection through "acting out" is rather markedly reduced—at least in the middle-class culture from which our Ss were drawn—and thus the opportunity for learning is hindered. Also, liking leads to continued interaction that permits learning about its cues, while rejection leads to separation, with a markedly impoverished chance for learning about its manifestations.

A second finding is that human Ss exceed the robots in congruency, that is, in the extent to which the feeling they hold for a person is identical to the feeling they perceive this person to have for them.

The deviation was accounted for by the tendency both to choose another and to see him as accepting, and to reject another and to see him as rejecting.

The psychological dynamics of congruency are not well understood and there is little in our data to shed further light on the subject. Several reasonable hypotheses may be put forward. For example, when one chooses another as one he "likes best," perceiving him as choosing in return, "protects" one from a feeling of rejection. Equally reasonable is the proposition that one responds to a person who is seen as liking one by reciprocating the perceived choice of the other. Either or both of these may operate in a given case. There is neither an a priori nor an empirical basis for choosing between the two. Again, with respect to the congruency of rejection, two equally likely hypotheses suggest themselves. One forms a dislike for another and, in order to relieve guilt over one's hostility toward an "innocent," one then sees the other as disliking one in turn. The process has been described by Murray [4] as complementary projection. The obverse sequence supposes that one sees another as rejecting and rejects in return.

A third finding is that *mutuality* also exceeds chance level significantly.

Consider now the conditions with which *accuracy* is associated. It is not associated with congruency: Ss showed equal accuracy whether their perceptions were congruent with their feelings or not. Accuracy is strikingly in excess of chance under conditions where individuals have mutual feelings for each other, below chance if they happen not to have mutual feelings. Where A and B like each other and A, out of a known tendency to be congruent, thinks B likes him, his perception will necessarily be accurate. If, on the other hand, A likes B who dislikes him in return, A's congruency—thinking B likes him—necessarily leads

---

[4] H. A. Murray, "The Effect of Fear upon Estimates of the Maliciousness of Other Personalities," *J. Soc. Psychol.*, 1933, IV, 310–329.

to inaccuracy. Perceptual skill seems to have relatively little to do with the matter when one considers the genesis of accuracy and inaccuracy in mutual and nonmutual pairs.

The psychological implications of such a finding are provocative. Consider the interaction of A and B under conditions where mutuality plus congruency induce "accuracy." Given these conditions, they will behave toward each other appropriately, the responses of each being consonant both with his own feelings and with the feelings of the other. The ensuing activity is likely to be of such a nature as to reinforce the state of actual and perceived mutuality. Should mutuality be absent, however, the matter is quite different. Given the known tendency toward congruency, perceptions will agree with feelings and inaccuracy will be the consequence. Let A have a positive feeling for B, while B feels negatively toward A. Congruency prevailing, their perceptions of each other will, for a while at least, be in agreement with the feelings they hold for one another. In short order they risk being at cross-purposes: one liking and feeling liked by the other, the second disliking and feeling disliked by the first. Contrary to the case of mutual feelings first discussed, here the tendency toward congruency brings about behavior that differs markedly from what would occur were each participant perceiving correctly the feelings of the other. Not that such a precarious interpersonal situation will necessarily last. Nor, indeed, need we assume that the quasi-autistic accuracy of the mutual case will lead to a stable interaction.

What we wish to point out, and we feel it is of the most central import, is that in both the instance of mutuality-and-accuracy and of nonmutuality-and-inaccuracy, autistic processes are at work: in one case leading to a good preliminary adjustment, in the other to a most unstable one.

In sum, the interpersonal perceptions of individuals in a small face-to-face group appear to be dependent to a large extent upon the operation of a congruency between how a member feels toward another and how the other is seen as feeling toward him. If two individuals have mutual feelings toward each other, their impressions of each other are likely, thereby, to be "accurate." If mutuality of feeling happens to be absent they may be at cross-purposes with each other—a situation relieved by the practice of politeness and reserve designed to mask feelings whose recognition might prove disruptive. In any case, accuracy of perception in interpersonal relations seems as much a product of other factors as a skill in its own right.

Next steps in research require longitudinal studies of groups and the dyads composing them. What form of data is needed for such analysis? We believe they must be of two kinds. First, careful clinical interviews with Ss on the nature of their choices and guesses and on the cues utilized by them in perceiving the feelings of others for them. Second, "longitudinal" data are required: the same kind of data utilized in the present study, but gathered periodically over the lifetime of a group from first acquaintance to some final stable state. Comparable robot computations would, of course, be needed at each stage of a group's existence.[5]

---

[5] The study of the accuracy of interpersonal perception is beset with many methodological pitfalls, only a few of which have been discussed in these pages. For a proper cautionary approach, the reader is referred to the following three papers as a guide: L. J. Cronbach, "Processes Affecting Scores on 'Understanding of Others' and 'Assumed Similarity'," *Psychol. Bull.*, 1955, LII, 177-193; L. J. Cronbach, "Proposals Leading to Analytic Treatment of Social-perception Scores," in R. Tagiuri and L. Petrullo (eds.), *Person Perception* (Stanford, Calif.: Stanford University Press, 1958). R. Tagiuri, "Social Preference and its Perception," in *ibid.*

SOME DETERMINANTS AND CONSEQUENCES OF THE PERCEPTION OF SOCIAL CAUSALITY

By John W. Thibaut and Henry W. Riecken

It is a generally accepted finding of research on group cohesiveness that increased social interaction in a setting of reward or success leads to heightened interpersonal acceptance [1]. It is not entirely clear, however, in just what ways social interaction is responsible for increasing liking between individuals. We shall describe below two experiments in which we have attempted to isolate some simple determinants of the ways in which interaction may be perceived, and to study the consequences of such perceptions for changes in interpersonal acceptance.

A basic determinant of acceptance is the perception that one's instrumental communications (e.g., attempts to influence another) have controlled the recipient. This statement is based on our assumption that veridical perception of such control signalizes goalward locomotion and good predictability of the social environment. Thus, if person X sends influence attempts of equal strength to persons Y and Z, and if Y is perceived to comply while Z is perceived as not complying, then X will tend to accept Y and to reject Z. The authors have reported a preliminary experiment [2] in which it was arranged that X would perceive Y as complying and Z as not complying in the influence attempt. The predicted relative acceptance of Y and rejection of Z were obtained. This relationship between perceived control and acceptance can also be formulated in terms of the perception of social causality. X perceives that his influence attempt (instrumental communication) "causes" a compliant change in behavior or attitude in Y, and not in Z. X accepts Y and rejects Z.

The foregoing statement is restricted to situations where X perceives that his communication has caused compliance from one person but failed to produce it from another. When we consider the case in which two or more persons respond favorably following a communication from X, a new range of problems is introduced, for X may not necessarily perceive his communication as causing the compliance in each case. A comment by Heider [3] notes this possibility. "When we see a moving object A, we can attribute the movement either to A itself or to another object B. In the first case we see the movement as a spontaneous act of A, in the second as passive movement induced by B". [4] In his studies of the per-

From *Journal of Personality*, 1955, XXIV, 113–133 with slight abridgement. Reprinted by permission of the authors and publisher. One experiment was supported by the Institute for Research in Social Science at the University of North Carolina. The data for the other experiment were collected at the Laboratory of Social Relations, Harvard University. The Harvard research was sponsored in part by the United States Air Force under Contract No. AF 33(038-12782).

[1] L. Festinger and H. H. Kelley, *Changing Attitudes through Social Contact* (Ann Arbor: University of Michigan, Research Center for Group Dynamics Institute for Social Research, 1951); J. C. Gilchrist, "The Formation of Social Groups under Conditions of Success and Failure," *J. Abnorm. & Soc. Psychol.*, 1952, XLVII, 174–187; G. C. Homans, *The Human Group* (New York: Harcourt, Brace & Co., 1950); H. W. Riecken and G. C. Homans, "Psychological Aspects of Social Structure," in G. Lindzey (ed.), *Handbook of Social Psychology* (Cambridge, Mass.: Addison-Wesley Co., Inc., 1954), pp. 786–832.

[2] J. W. Thibaut and H. W. Riecken, "Authoritarianism, Status, and the Communication of Aggression," *Hum. Rel.*, 1955, VIII, 95–120.

[3] F. Heider, "Social Perception and Phenomenal Causality," *Psychol. Rev.*, 1944, LI, 358–374.

[4] *Ibid*, p. 358.

ception of mechanical causality, Michotte[5] has described the experimental conditions under which two phenomena quite similar to those noted by Heider can be observed. In "l'effet Lancement ... les observateurs voient l'objet A donner un choc à l'objet B et le chasser, le lancer en avant, le projeter, lui donner une impulsion."[6] Although this "launching" of B is not the same as perceiving B's movement as self-caused, it begins to approximate the perception that B's movement was merely "occasioned" by A. Michotte's "l'effet Entraînement" corresponds very closely to the perception that B is passive and inert, being "carried along" by A. In terms of the perception of social causality, any change in Y's behavior or attitude in a direction conforming to X's instrumental communication may be perceived by X to have been caused by Y himself or by X (or his communication). In this case Y's "compliance" is perceived to be either spontaneous and self-caused or coerced by X. This corresponds to the Lewinian distinction between "own force" and "induced force": X may perceive Y's "compliance" as motivated either by Y's "own force" or by an "induced force" from X.

We suggest that the main factors determining the two types of perceptual attribution are the *power* relations between X and Y and between X and Z. Suppose that: (1) X perceives that Y has relatively high power[7] and that Z has relatively low power, (2) X sends the same (or equally "strong") instrumental communications to Y and Z, (3) X perceives that both Y and Z comply with the communication, and (4) in complying, Y and Z are not behaving as they would have been in the absence of the influence attempt. If the foregoing conditions are met, X will tend to perceive the cause of Y's compliance as located "inside" Y (self-caused) and the cause of Z's compliance as located "outside" Z (i.e., a consequence of coercion by the induced force of X).

The results of these differences in attributions of power and causality are that X will credit Y with motives of friendliness and succorance, whereas Z will be regarded as merely responding passively to coercive power. X will tend to say of Y, "He likes me" or "He's a nice guy"; and of Z, "He had to do it" or "I forced him." Hence, as a result of this experience, X will tend to accept Y more than he does Z.

It should be noted that the predictions immediately above may seem to contradict the earlier statement relating perceived control to acceptance. We began by saying that X prefers Y to Z when X's communication is perceived to cause Y's compliance. We concluded by saying that X prefers Y to Z when X's communication is perceived *not* to cause Y's compliance. A moment's reflection, however, will show that the contradiction is only apparent. When an individual is confronted by a controllable and an uncontrollable other, he will tend to accept or prefer the controllable other, because of the relevance of control to goalward locomotion. On the other hand, when both (or all) others show compliance, discriminations in acceptance will be made on some basis other than the instrumental capacities of the other for satisfying the individual's needs. Since this point may not be immediately obvious, we should like to discuss it in broader outline here.

[5] A Michotte, *La Perception de la Causalité*, Institut Supérieur de Philosophie, Univ. de Louvain: Vrin, 1946.

[6] *Ibid*, pp. 17–18.

[7] Power is used here in the special sense of ability to resist social influence. It is believed, however, that the generalization applies to power from all sources (authority, personal competence, physical strength, etc.) except where the basis is itself liking or admiration as, e.g., where X perceives that Z's low strength to resist is based on Z's cathexis of him.

An individual ordinarily wants to control his social environment in order to gratify his needs. Complete intractability on the part of another increases the chances of deprivation and consequently leads to rejection or dislike of the other. In order to insure a tractable social environment it may behoove an individual to take steps to increase his social power. As his power position improves, his social environment becomes more manageable, but at the same time the individual begins to lose a type of information. What he tends to lose is perceptual evidence concerning the degree to which the compliance of his subordinates is motivated by spontaneous good will and loyalty. We may assume that the perception of autonomous affection for oneself is *per se* gratifying to most individuals, but perhaps of equal importance are the consequences of spontaneous affection and loyalty for improved social prediction. Any controllable person is predictable, but only when compliance is perceived to be caused by spontaneous good will is prediction possible in the absence of the application of power. If compliant behavior is perceived to be contingent on continuous surveillance and coercion, an upward spiraling might be expected in which the absence of any evidence of loyalty and reliability leads to more vigorous applications of power, which in turn reduces the monitor's ability to perceive any spontaneity in the acquiescence. This may be a common affliction of tyrannical governments.

We shall now restate the hypotheses being tested in the present experiments. From the foregoing discussion it is clear that we are supposing a situation in which the individual is confronted with stimulus persons having relatively high and relatively low power and that, in response to the individual's communica-tions, the stimulus persons will indicate compliance by altering their behavior. Our discussion has suggested two closely related hypotheses.

Hypothesis 1: The individual will perceive the causal locus for compliance as "internal" to the high-power stimulus person and as "external" to the low-power stimulus person.

Hypothesis 2: When an individual rates a person before and after a successful influence attempt, there will be a greater positive (or smaller negative) change in ratings of acceptance of the high-power stimulus person than of the low-power stimulus person.

Measurement Techniques

The measurement techniques were virtually identical to those used in an earlier study,[8] which contains a list of the rating-scale items, a statement of the scoring procedures, and the subscale reliabilities. The "opinion survey" administered to all Ss attempts to measure "authoritarianism" and is constituted of the 30-item California F-Scale (forms 40 and 45)[9] and 11 additional items.

A 19-item rating scale was administered to all Ss before the experiment proper had begun and again at the close of the experiment. This scale contains items of two types. Thirteen of the items are designed to measure the degree to which another person is liked, admired, cathected, accepted. In this part of the rating scale, called the "acceptance scale," the items were evaluatively toned questions about a variety of personal attributes, such as: "Is he good-natured or irritable?" Each question was followed by six alternatives from which S chose "the one that best describes" the ratee. These alternatives offered three degrees of "favorable" and three of "unfavor-

[8] Thibaut and Riecken, *op. cit.*

[9] T. W. Adorno, Else Frenkel-Brunswik, D. J. Levinson, and R. N. Sanford, *The Authoritarian Personality* (New York: Harper & Brothers, 1950).

able" judgment. This "acceptance scale" is the same as that used in the earlier study except for the addition of two new items.

The remaining six items in the rating scale are called the "resistance scale." They attempted to measure the degree to which another person is perceived as being able to resist social influence. The same format as above was used in the "resistance scale," which contained three items in which the "strong" end of the continuum was "favorably" connoted ("forceful," "firm," and "strong-minded") and three items in which the "strong" end was "unfavorably" connoted ("stubborn," "obstinate," and "resistant"). This "resistance scale" is the same as that used in the earlier study except for the inclusion of two new items.

Postexperimental interviews were also conducted, but since the form of these differed slightly in the two experiments, these will be described separately in presenting the experimental findings.

EXPERIMENTAL PROCEDURE

The two experiments to be reported are of the same general form. The S meets two stimulus persons (confederates of E) one of whom is of considerably higher status than the other. This manipulation of status is intended to produce perceived differences in the power of the stimulus persons. Immediately after meeting them, S makes an initial evaluation of them on the "acceptance" and "resistance" scales. During the experiment S repeatedly attempts to influence the behavior of the two confederates. Eventually both confederates comply. S again evaluates the two confederates on the "acceptance" and "resistance" scales and is interviewed. This is the basic form of the two experiments, but since the two sets of procedures and manipulations were different, we will describe the experiments separately.

The North Carolina Experiment. The

Ss were 20 male "volunteers" from the introductory course in psychology at the University of North Carolina. Ss were scheduled to arrive singly at the experimental room, their arrival coinciding with that of two experimental confederates who were instructed to behave as though they were also "naïve" Ss. When S and the two confederates were assembled, E asked them to fill out an "opinion survey" (F-Scale plus related items).

The confederates had been rehearsed in advance to insure that they would conduct themselves in standard fashion. After E had briefly introduced himself and the three "subjects" to one another, E casually questioned each of the three about his background and present status. By prearrangement, one of the confederates said that he had just received the Ph.D. degree and was now a member of the instructional staff. This "high-status confederate" (HSC) was neatly dressed and always wore both coat and tie. The other confederate was in shirtsleeves, without tie, and said that he had just finished his freshman year of undergraduate study. The two confederates exchanged statuses with every new S. That is, for half of the Ss confederate A was the HSC; for the other half of the Ss confederate B was the HSC. To make plausible the evident similarity of the confederates' ages, this "low-status confederate" (LSC) also said that he was an Army veteran.

E then described the task that the three were to perform. One of the three would be selected to serve as the communicator and the other two as audience. The communicator would attempt to influence the audience to donate blood for a Red Cross blood drive. The role of communicator was filled by drawing lots and it was contrived that S would invariably draw this assignment. Once the roles had been assigned, the confederates (audience) were asked to wait in an adjoining room for further detailed instructions which they would receive as soon as the communicator had been instructed. In his role as communicator, S was told that he would be evaluated on his ability to plan and execute a strategy of persuasion. The materials with which he must work were 38 previously prepared messages, from which he must select and send the ten that he thought would be most effective in persuading the audience to donate blood. The 38 messages varied considerably in forcefulness. Three examples are: "Please consider this request very carefully"; "I sincerely believe that you ought to participate in this drive"; and "I am in no mood to trifle with any refusals."

In order to give some apparent substance to the task, S was told that he would be evaluated on the "quality of the ten messages he selected," the sequence in which he sent the messages, and the pattern of temporal intervals between messages. Rules governing the communication procedure were that, although the audience would be located in the same room with S, all messages must be written, that E would deliver the messages on a signal from S, and that S must send the *same* message at the same time to both members of the audience. Finally S was told that the audience would be permitted no feed-back communication to him until he had finished sending the ten messages, at which point the members of the audience would individually indicate whether or not they had decided to donate blood.

When S had received his instruction, E explained that to evaluate S's strategy of persuasion it would be necessary to find out what kinds of people S perceived his audience to be. This pretext served to introduce the "acceptance" and "resistance" scales, which were then administered to S. In filling out these scales, S was required to discriminate between the two members of the audience on each item, i.e., for any given item the two members of the audience must be located at different points on the six-point scale.

When S commenced this initial rating, E left the room on the pretext that he must instruct the members of the audience. As soon as S had finished making his ratings, E and the confederates returned to the experimental room and the message-sending began. At the conclusion of the message-sending period, both confederates indicated that they had been effectively influenced. Shortly thereafter they were thanked and dismissed. S then filled out the same "acceptance" and "resistance" scales as before, except that the order of the items was scrambled. Finally S was interviewed. Before S left the room, the purpose of the experiment was explained to him, all deceptions were described, and any questions he had were answered.

The Harvard Experiment. The Ss were 21 sophomore and junior male undergraduates at Harvard University, hired through the student employment service and paid at an hourly rate. Each S reported for a preliminary interview with E one or two days before the actual experimental session. He was given the F-Scale and interviewed on the subjects of family background, education, extracurricular activities, and "experience in groups and in positions of leadership." The resulting information was not used, but this interview served to make plausible to the S the occurrence of similar interviews between E and two confederates which S "accidentally" overheard at the beginning of the actual experimental session. The experiment was explained somewhat vaguely as a study of comparative productivity of individuals and groups in which individuals of different ability worked together. An incidental feature of the experiment, S was told, was that E was interested in using "first-impression" ratings as measures of how well individuals could size each other up as work partners. Therefore, E had arranged matters so S would meet two other men at the experiment who would probably be strangers to him and about whom he would later be asked to give his judgment or rating on certain traits. Thus forewarned, S was dismissed until the experimental session.

When he returned for the experimental session, S was ushered into the experimental room, where he apparently interrupted an interview between E and the high-status confederate (HSC). E apologized for being behind schedule, introduced HSC as one of S's partners in the experiment, and resumed the "interview" in the full hearing of S. The HSC's responses to E's questions revealed that he had attended a well-known private school, an Ivy League University where he had been editor of the daily newspaper, had had command responsibilities in naval combat service, and was currently a Harvard Law School student. The HSC was dressed in a manner appropriate to the stereotype of his background and was poised and confident.

This interview concluded, E left the room momentarily. While he was gone, HSC addressed a standard question and a standard remark to S indicating that he (HSC) expected to find the experiment interesting. This was the only direct interaction S had with HSC. Before the conversation could develop, E returned with the low-status confederate (LSC), whom he introduced and then interviewed. It turned out that LSC was a freshman at a nearby institution of considerably lower prestige (by S's presumed standards), had graduated from a little-known high school in a drab mill town, had never participated in extracurricular activities, and had, as his only "leadership experience," been secretary of his high-school camera club. His socioeconomic status seemed to be "lower," he was rather untastefully dressed, and appeared to be nervous, apologetic about his "background," and self-effacing.

The HSC and LSC were always introduced to S in this manner and in this order, but the two laboratory assistants who played the parts alternated roles so

that half of the Ss confronted one person in the HSC role, the other half a second person. The interviews were carefully rehearsed and were as standard as possible; the "facts" purveyed to S were carefully chosen to accord with stereotypes of high and low prestige individuals that are current in the undergraduate population from which the Ss came.

Following the interviews, E explained that the trio's task was to construct crossword puzzles; today each would work alone, in order to determine their skill as individuals, and later they would be brought together to work as a group, whose leader would be the man who constructed the best puzzle alone. Further incentives were offered, and detailed instructions given. The three "subjects" were told they would work in separate rooms but could communicate by written notes that E would deliver. Finally, E displayed two copies of a "crossword-puzzle dictionary," talked about how helpful it was in the task, and concluded by saying: "There are only two copies of this special dictionary. I'm sorry there aren't more, but you can pass them around if you want to. You do not have to trade off if you do not want to and you might even enjoy working without the dictionary for a while. But you will find it a tremendous help." With that E gave one copy of the dictionary to each of the confederates. After answering any questions, E led the two confederates out, ostensibly to their separate rooms.

When E returned a few minutes later, he conducted a brief, open-ended interview on S's "first impressions" of his "partners." Following the interview, S rated the two confederates on the "acceptance" and "resistance" scales that have already been described. Rating procedure was identical to that in the North Carolina experiment. When the ratings had been completed, S began work on the crossword-puzzle construction.

At the end of about ten minutes E interrupted him. Pointing out that one of the purposes of the experiment was to study how well individuals learned to work together as a group, E said he was especially interested in the cooperativeness of HSC and LSC, as demonstrated by their willingness to share the dictionary with S. Since 15 or 20 minutes had gone by without any spontaneous demonstration of cooperativeness from the other two, E now wanted S to send messages to the others trying to persuade them to share the dictionary. To that end, E had prepared an array of standard messages (in order to "standardize conditions" from group to group) from which S could choose what he wished to send. The only requirement was that S had to send the same message to both other men. E spread the 28 messages out on the table and asked S to choose one and to make two copies of it. As in the previous experiment, these messages varied in forcefulness. Three examples are: "If you are not using the dictionary now, may I please have it?"; "I hope you are going to be cooperative about sharing the dictionary"; and "You have had your share of time with the dictionary. Give it to me."

E took these notes and left the room presumably to deliver them to the confederates. He returned in three or four minutes without a reply, saying that the confederates had made no acknowledgment. He instructed S to continue work on the puzzle and to send another message in five minutes. In reply to the second message, E brought back two standard notes, the authorship of which was assigned randomly to each confederate. One of these read: "I am still using it"; the other, "I need it now." S usually produced interesting material in reacting to these notes; and E, after chatting with him for a few minutes, then pointed out that the experiment was more than half over, and asked him to send another message. Upon his return from this trip, E brought back two dictionaries, evidence that both confederates had complied.

After getting S's comments, E suggested that he might want to return one of the dictionaries, and to whom did he want to return it?

Before setting out on this trip, E asked S to rate his two "partners" again, now that he had further information about their personalities and behavior. The same rating scales, with items scrambled in order, were represented to S, and he was again instructed to employ the forced-choice technique. Finally, S was reinterviewed at length regarding his interpretation of the refusals and the ultimate compliance of HSC and LSC.

When the formal procedure of the experiment had been concluded, the purposes and the methods of the various deceptions were explained to the S and all his questions answered. No S left with curiosity unsatisfied and none seemed displeased at having been deceived. All promised not to reveal the workings of the procedure and seem to have kept their word.

RESULTS

Effectiveness of the Manipulation. Since the primary purpose of introducing the role-playing confederates was to create a perception of difference between the two confederates in their power to resist influence, our first concern is whether or not our procedure was effective. Table 1 provides data on this point from both experiments. The data are shown for each confederate separately in each role, since there were evident differences in the ability of the two confederates in each experiment to play the two roles. The entries in Table 1 were obtained by subtracting the sum of the rating on the six-item "resistance" scale accorded the LSC from that given to the HSC on S's initial rating of the two confederates.

On the whole the manipulation was effective in both experiments (although less impressively so in the North Carolina experiment); and, as a group, Ss found

TABLE 1

DIFFERENCES BETWEEN DEGREES OF POWER TO RESIST EXTERNAL INFLUENCE
ATTRIBUTED INITIALLY TO HIGH- AND LOW-STATUS CONFEDERATES

Status of confederates	North Carolina			Harvard		
	A High B Low (N = 10)	B High A Low (N = 10)	Combined (N = 20)	C High D Low (N = 11)	D Low C Low (N = 10)	Combined (N = 21)
Mean difference *	+3.40	+3.60	+3.50	+10.00	+8.20	+9.14
S. D.	6.50	7.59	6.89	4.92	4.57	4.73
t	1.65	1.50	2.27	6.71	5.66	8.87
p†	.07	.08	<.02	<.001	<.001	<.001

* The plus sign indicates that the high-status confederate was perceived as better able to resist than the low-status confederate.
† One-tailed test.

themselves in the intended situation—facing a relatively strong and a relatively weak person, while sending the same persuasive messages to both.

We will return later on to a discussion of initial differences in the ratings of HSC and LSC on the "acceptance" scale. Right now we would like to move directly into a discussion of the results bearing on the main hypothesis of the study.

Perceived Locus of Causality. Our major hypothesis is simply stated in two parts. The first proposition states: When an individual is attempting to persuade two others, of unequal (perceived) power (to resist influence), the communicator will attribute "internal" reasons for compliance to the person of higher power and "external" reasons to the person of lower power. The second proposition is: When compliance has occurred, the communicator's liking for the others will increase more (or decrease less) if the other is seen as complying for "internal" reasons than if he is seen as complying for "external" reasons.

In this section we will report the data relevant to the first part of the hypothesis. Since in both experiments the status of the confederate appeared to create the appropriate differences in attributed

power, our first proposition can be restated as follows: Ss will perceive the locus of causality for compliance as "internal" to HSC and "external" to LSC.

Perceived locus of causality was inferred in both experiments from responses to a question in the postexperimental interview. In the North Carolina experiment the question was as follows: "Suppose you had to decide that one of the members of the audience said 'yes' (i.e. complied) because you forced him to (that is, put pressure on him) and the other said 'yes' because he just naturally wanted to anyway. Which one would you say you forced and which one just wanted to anyway?" This forced discrimination yielded answers consistent with the hypothesis. Table 2 shows that of the 19 Ss that were able to make the decision, 18 reported that HSC was the one who "just wanted to anyway" (internal causality) and that LSC was the one who was "forced" (external causality).

In the Harvard experiment, perceived causality for compliance was inferred from responses to an interview question that was similar to the one above, except that a discrimination between the confederates was not forced. Instead, the S

TABLE 2

LOCUS OF CAUSALITY FOR COMPLIANCE ATTRIBUTED TO HIGH- AND LOW-STATUS
CONFEDERATES

Status of confederates	HSC Internal LSC External	HSC External LSC Internal	HSC Internal LSC Internal	HSC External LSC External
North Carolina				
A High B Low (N = 10)	10	0		
B High A Low (N = 9 *)	8	1		
Harvard				
C High D Low (N = 11)	8	1	1	1
D High C Low (N = 10)	4	3	1	2

* One S was unable to make a decision.

was allowed to decide separately for each confederate, when he was asked: "Do you think that (HSC) gave you the dictionary because he is a nice guy and just wanted to help you, or did he give it to you because you put pressure on him?" The question was then repeated for the other confederate, with the order of confederates and of alternatives being varied from S to S. Table 2 again shows the results from the interview responses. It will be seen, in the first place, that a little more than one half of the Ss behaved in exactly the predicted way, four Ss behaved in a fashion exactly contradictory to the hypothesis, and the remaining five Ss failed to distinguish a difference in locus of causality.

These last Ss create some difficulties in interpretation. They do not support our first proposition, but it is not clear that they refute it, since the proposition assumes that Ss will make a discrimination in locus of causality between the two confederates. These five Ss who failed to perceive such a difference cannot be used to test our prediction; their behavior does not meet the conditions required by the proposition. We have been unable to dis-

cover anything in the behavior of these Ss that would help account for their failure to perceive differences in causality. It may be that they did not understand the question or that they are not accustomed to thinking in terms of "internal" versus "external" causes of behavior. Or possibly they perceived no difference in the overt behavior of the two confederates.

This sample of four Ss who perceived the locus of causality in exactly the opposite fashion from that hypothesized is equally interesting. These four Ss also perceived HSC as considerably stronger in power to resist influence than LSC, but apparently did not associate the compliance of strong individuals with "internal" motivation.

With the foregoing qualifications in mind we can test our first proposition against the 16 cases in which the Ss' behavior met the requirements of our first proposition (i.e., there was a perceived difference in power in one direction or the other). The binomial expansion provides us with the information that the likelihood of obtaining 12 confirmatory cases out of 16, by chance, is .04. With the

PERCEPTION OF PERSONS

TABLE 3

DIFFERENCES BETWEEN DEGREES OF INITIAL ACCEPTANCE OF HIGH- AND
LOW-STATUS CONFEDERATES

Status of Confederates	North Carolina		Harvard	
	A High B Low (N = 10)	B High A Low (N = 10)	C High D Low (N = 11)	D High C Low (N = 10)
Mean Difference *	+6.10	−2.80	+0.09	+8.80
S.D.	6.94	10.83	7.30	9.68
t	2.79	0.82	0.04	2.88
p †	<.05	....	....	<.02

* The plus sign indicates that the high-status confederate was preferred to the low-status confederate.
† Two-tailed tests.

limitations previously stated, we can consider our first proposition satisfactorily demonstrated.

We must comment, however, on the striking effect of differences in the personal characteristics of the two confederates, and their relative success in inducing the expected perception of their motivation for compliance. Table 1 showed that when Confederate C played the high-status role, the attributed differences in strength to resist influence (initial rating) between HSC and LSC was slightly greater than when Confederate D played this role. Correspondingly, we must note that Confederate C gave an impression of greater formality and sternness of manner, whereas D was comparatively warm and relaxed, being given significantly higher (initial) acceptance ratings in the HSC role than C received. Thus, when C took the role of HSC the difference between the HSC and LSC was exaggerated, but when D played the same role it was minimized. The complicating effect of these "person-carried" characteristics is clearly demonstrated in Table 2, where it can be seen that Confederate C was considerably more successful at inducing the perception that he

had complied for "internal" reasons than Confederate D was.

Before going on to the second part of the hypothesis it may be advisable to pause to consider whether the results relevant to perceived locus of causality may not be explained with equal plausibility by another mechanism. The data appear to confirm the hypothesized relationship between differential power of

TABLE 4

DIFFERENTIAL CHANGE IN ACCEPTANCE
FROM INITIAL TO FINAL RATINGS
(Change in Acceptance of HSC minus
Change in Acceptance of LSC;
North Carolina Data Only)

Status of confederates	Mean difference in change	S.D.	t	p *
A High, B Low (N = 10)	+3.30	5.38	1.94	<.05
B High, A Low (N = 10)	+1.60	3.69	1.37	.10
Combined (N = 20)	+2.45	4.57	2.40	<.02

* One-tailed test.

stimulus persons and the locus of causality for their compliance. But it could be asked: Might the data not equally well support the hypothesis that S initially will prefer HSC to LSC, that this preference will lead S to see HSC as liking him (S), and that in consequence S will perceive HSC's compliance as "internally" caused?

There are two pieces of evidence against this alternative hypothesis. Table 3 shows that only when Confederates A and D played the high-status role was there a clear initial preference for HSC. Yet in the North Carolina experiment, "internal" causality for compliance was attributed in a highly uniform way not only to Confederate A as HSC but also to Confederate B as HSC (see Table 2). In the Harvard experiment, for the 16 cases where Ss discriminated locus of causality, there was no significant difference in initial acceptance between the confederate perceived as complying for "internal" reasons and the one seen as "externally" motivated. Differences are at chance levels (with p values ranging from .85 to .25) for the two confederates considered separately and combined. In 11 of these 16 cases the S showed higher acceptance initially for the confederate to whom he subsequently

attributed "external" reasons for compliance.

Causality and Change in Acceptance. While the first proposition in our hypothesis was concerned with the attribution of "inner" and "outer" reasons for compliance to individuals of different status, the second proposition dealt with the consequences of such attribution— i.e., with the change in acceptability of, or liking for, the compliant person. Specifically, we predicted that an individual's acceptability would increase more (or decrease less) if he was perceived as complying for "internal" reasons.

In the North Carolina experiment for virtually all cases HSC was perceived as complying for "internal" reasons, and LSC as complying for "external" reasons. Hence, the hypothesis leads to the prediction that the increase from initial to final rating in S's prediction of HSC will be greater than the increase in acceptance of LSC. Table 4 presents the data relevant to this prediction. Although when Confederate B is HSC the predicted relationships merely approach statistical significance, the results for confederate A as HSC and for the combined data appear to be satisfactory. On the whole, the hypothesis appears to be confirmed in this experiment.

TABLE 5

DIFFERENTIAL CHANGE IN ACCEPTANCE FROM INITIAL TO FINAL RATINGS
(Change in Acceptance of HSC minus Change in Acceptance
of LSC; Harvard Data Only)

	HSC Internal LSC External (N = 12)	HSC External LSC Internal (N = 4)	HSC Internal LSC Internal (N = 2)	HSC External LSC External (N = 3)
Mean difference in change	+3.42	−11.50	−5.00	−5.33
S.D.	0.94	2.22	2.00	2.35
t	3.64	5.18		
p^*	<.01	<.02		

* One-tailed test.

Table 5 presents the data on change in acceptance (between initial rating and final rating) in the Harvard experiment. The mean change in acceptance is tabulated separately for those Ss who made the predicted discrimination, who made the opposite discrimination, and who made no discrimination at all in locus of causality. For the total group of 21 Ss, the mean level of acceptance of the confederates declined between initial and final rating. The 12 Ss who made the predicted discrimination, however, show a significant *increase* in liking for HSC compared to LSC, while the four Ss who reversed the hypothesized discrimination show an even greater *decrease* in liking for HSC. Since these latter four attribute "external" motivation for compliance to HSC and "internal" to LSC, it is reasonable to reverse the sign of the changes in their acceptance ratings. We thus consider the total of 16 cases in which the confederate was seen as complying for "internal" reasons (regardless of the

status he occupied in the experimental manipulation). Change in acceptance (in the predicted direction) is significant at the .01 level for the group of 12 and at the .02 level for the group of four separately. Combined, the change is significant in the predicted direction at the .001 level (see Table 6, bottom row).

Here again personal differences in the two confederates seem to affect the differential amount of change in acceptance accorded by the Ss. If we consider only the 16 Ss who perceived a difference between the two confederates in their reasons for compliance and reorder the data, we obtain Table 6. The entries in this table were obtained by subtracting the change in acceptance score of the confederate perceived as having complied for "internal" reasons from the change score of his opposite number (who, in these cases, was seen as complying because of "external" pressure). Ss' acceptance of the former confederate tends to increase (or to decrease less), thus adding support to our second proposition, and the observed difference is significant at the .001 level for both confederates combined.

Other Results. We might extend to the present Harvard-North Carolina study an earlier interpretation [10] that as the S's authoritarianism (F-Scale score) increases his sensitivity to the power of a stimulus person will also increase when the power cues originate in "external" sources such as status. From this we would predict a positive relationship between F-Scale score and perceived initial difference in power to resist and would also expect high authoritarians to perceive locus of causality for compliance in the predicted direction more consistently than low authoritarians. Finally, we would expect a positive relationship between F-Scale score and differential change in acceptance of confed-

TABLE 6

CHANGE IN ACCEPTANCE OF "INTERNALLY COMPLYING" CONFEDERATE MINUS "EXTERNALLY COMPLYING" CONFEDERATE
(When S Discriminated Reasons for Compliance; Harvard Data Only)

Status of confederate	Mean difference in change of acceptance	S.T.	t	p*
C High, D Low (N = 11)	+6.18	5.29	3.86	<.01
D High, C Low (N = 5)	+3.80	4.21	2.02	<.10
Combined (N = 16)	+5.44	4.96	4.38	<.001

* One-tailed test.

[10] E. E. Jones, "Authoritarianism as a Determinant of First-impression Formation," *J. Pers.*, 1954, XXIII, 107–127, and Thibaut and Riecken, *op. cit.*

erates. The results in both experiments show none of these expected relationships in any consistent fashion. A possible explanation of these generally negative findings may be that our manipulation of status produced not only "external" cues (to which high authoritarians may be more sensitive) but also numerous correlated "internal" person-produced cues such as differences in ability, personal competence, and the like (to which, if the earlier interpretation is correct, low authoritarians are more sensitive).

DISCUSSION

Differences between the Two Experiments. Besides the superficially different nature of the task confronting the Ss in these two experiments, there is probably a more influential difference in the relationship between the S and the two confederates. There was a clear tendency of Ss in the North Carolina experiment to increase their acceptance of both confederates between initial and final rating, and an equally clear trend for Ss in the Harvard experiment to decrease their acceptance. These contradictory tendencies probably can be traced to differences in the Ss' expectations about getting compliance, and to the effect of refusals to comply. In the North Carolina experiment, Ss do not expect to know whether the confederates will comply until after all of the messages have been sent; in effect, they make a single, sustained attempt to persuade two others and are successful. The only feedback they receive is compliance. On the other hand, Ss in the Harvard experiment are led to expect at least the possibility of compliance after each of the three messages they send, but they receive two refusals followed by compliance on the third round. To the extent that frustration in an influence attempt leads to annoyance, this difference in the experimental procedures satisfactorily accounts

for the over-all differences in acceptance-rejection.

Hence, it may be that these two refusals, encountered by the Harvard Ss, introduce a kind of error or variability into our results. To the extent that Ss expect HSC to comply quickly with their request because they consider him intelligent, able, and better educated, they will tend to resent his noncompliance and to rate him down, while forgiving LSC for noncompliance because they feel he has a greater genuine need for the dictionary. There is some evidence that such a view of the situation was common among the Ss. After they had received both dictionaries, following the third message, they were asked: "Since you don't need two dictionaries, would you like to return one of them? To whom?" Twelve of the 21 Ss chose to return a dictionary to LSC "because he needs it more." These 12 tended to show greater negative change in their acceptance ratings of HSC than of LSC—about 2.5 scale points, on the average. This interpretation of the situation of two confederates and their reasons for noncompliance tends to work against our hypothesis that HSC will be more accepted than LSC.

On the other hand, to the extent that Ss view LSC as a presumptuous nonentity who has no chance in the crossword-puzzle contest and ought to yield at once to their request, one would expect Ss to rate him down (show differentially less acceptance) more than they would HSC. Again, the fragmentary data support this interpretation. Six of our Ss chose to return the surplus dictionary to HSC, usually giving their reason that "He will do a better puzzle," or that he would make more effective use of the dictionary. Compared to the 12 Ss who chose the opposite course, these six tend to show a slight differential in acceptance in favor of HSC. This tendency, of course, works in favor of our major hypothesis, but it should be emphasized that it occurs in many fewer cases than does the contrary trend.

The striking fact is that in spite of the variability introduced by the tendency to perceive LSC's situation sympathetically and thus attenuate the predicted tendency to dislike him (or like him less), the weight of the data supports our hypothesis regarding differential acceptance.

One final difference between the experiments must be noted. In the North Carolina experiment, the influence attempts were made in the name of altruism; the giver-receiver relationship was not immediately present and not identified directly with the interests of the S, who was attempting the influence. On the contrary, in the Harvard experiment, the S was in direct competition with the confederates for a scarce resource. Their refusal to comply labeled them not only resistant, but selfish—and, most important, selfish toward the influencer (and rater). Thus, to the failure to be influenced by two messages is added the strong implication that the confederates are hostile, or at least indifferent, to the welfare of the S. It is not surprising that he would tend to rate them down on "acceptance" items following such a display of coldness toward him.

SUMMARY

Two experiments were designed to test an hypothesis concerning the relationships among the amount of power attributed to a stimulus person, the perceived locus of causality for his complying following an influence attempt, and the consequent relative acceptance of him. In both experiments individual Ss were confronted with two stimulus persons (paid confederates) who played roles having different degrees of status or prestige. In a series of communications S attempted to influence the behavior of the two confederates. Eventually and simultaneously both confederates indicated their compliance. The data relevant to the hypothesis were obtained from a final interview and from the S's initial and final ratings of the two confederates on two scales: a "strength of resistance" scale and an "acceptance" scale.

In general the hypothesis was confirmed in both experiments, although in one of them the test of the hypothesis was not straight-forward. The main findings may be stated in terms of the two parts of the hypothesis:

1. S perceives the causal locus for compliance as "internal" to the high-status stimulus person and as "external" to the low-status stimulus person.
2. The increase from initial to final rating in S's acceptance of the high-status stimulus person is greater than the increase in acceptance of the low-status stimulus person.

4

Communication and Opinion Change

RESISTANCE TO "COUNTERPROPAGANDA" PRO-
DUCED BY ONE–SIDED AND TWO–SIDED "PROPA–
GANDA" PRESENTATIONS
By Arthur A. Lumsdaine and Irving L. Janis

In speculative discussions concerning propaganda effects, the question has often been raised as to whether a persuasive communication is more effective when it concentrates exclusively on the arguments supporting the communicator's position or when it includes some discussion (and/or refutation) of the opposing arguments. Various propaganda strategists have put forth the claim that, in appealing for acceptance of any specific belief or policy, no opposing arguments should be discussed because mentioning rival ideas invites comparison, hesitation and doubt. But experimental evidence reported by Hovland, Lumsdaine and Sheffield indicates that this generalization is not likely to hold true when the audience initially disagrees with the views advocated by the communicator.[1] Their results clearly indicated that among members of the audience who were initially *opposed* to the communicator's position, a two-sided presentation (including mention of opposing as well as supporting arguments)

was much more effective in producing opinion changes in the desired direction than was a one-sided presentation (which mentioned only arguments supporting the communicator's position). The one-sided presentation proved to be more effective only with those members of the audience who were already favorably disposed toward the communicator's position.

In the experiment reported by Hovland, Lumsdaine and Sheffield, the effects of the communications were measured only in terms of *immediate* changes in opinion; it was not possible to compare the effects of one-sided and two-sided communications in terms of "resistance" to the effect of subsequently presented counterarguments or "counterpropaganda." Accordingly, the present experiment was designed to extend the evidence by comparing the effectiveness of the two forms of presentation after part of the audience had been exposed to a second, counterpropaganda communication.[2]

From *Public Opinion Quarterly*, 1953, XVII, 311–318. Reprinted by permission of the authors and the publishers.

[1] C. I. Hovland, A. A. Lumsdaine, and F. D. Sheffield, *Experiments on Mass Communication* (Princeton: Princeton University Press, 1949), pp. 201–227.

[2] This study was conducted at the Institute of Human Relations, Yale University, as part of a

DESIGN OF THE EXPERIMENT

The present experiment was conducted several months before President Truman announced that Russia had produced its first atomic explosion and was designed to compare the effects of two forms of a persuasive communication. Both forms consisted of a transcribed "radio program" in which the same communicator took the position that Russia would be unable to produce large numbers of atomic bombs for at least the next five years.

Program I, the one-sided presentation, contained only the arguments that supported this conclusion, such as the following: Russian scientists have not yet discovered some of the crucial secrets; they cannot learn all the "know-how" through espionage; even after they succeed in making their first A-bomb the Russians will be unable to mass produce the bombs because of insufficient uranium supplies.[3]

Program II, the two-sided presentation, contained the very same arguments presented in identical fashion, but also presented and discussed arguments for the other side of the picture. (These arguments were, for example: Russia has many first-rate atomic scientists; Russian industries have made a phenomenal recovery since the war; Russia has some uranium mines in Siberia.) The opposing arguments were interwoven into the relevant sections of the communication and in some instances no attempt was made to refute them.

The total content of both programs was designed to lead unambiguously to the conclusion that Soviet Russia would be unable to produce A-bombs in quantity for at least five years. Except for the presence of the opposing arguments, the two communications were identical: Program II was recorded first and Program I was constructed by simply deleting the opposing arguments from the tape recording.[4]

Four main experimental groups were used, each composed of several classrooms of high-school students in social-science courses. Classrooms were assigned at random to the different experimental treatments. In order to determine initial level of opinion, all groups were given an initial questionnaire as part of an independent "opinion survey" that was conducted several weeks before the experimental communications were presented. Two groups were then given the one-sided communication (Program I) and the other two groups were given the two-sided communication (Program II). The effects of the communications were measured by a second questionnaire given about a week after the presentation of these communications. Just before the administration of the second questionnaire, however, two of the groups (one having received Program I

coordinated program of research on communication and opinion change, financed by a grant from the Rockefeller Foundation. The communication research program is under the direction of Professor Carl I. Hovland, to whom the authors are indebted for valuable suggestions and criticisms. The authors also wish to express their appreciation to Joseph A. Foran, Superintendent of Schools at Milford, Connecticut, and to the faculty of the Milford High School.

Many of the technical details concerning the way the present experiment was conducted have been described in an earlier publication which made use of data bearing on a different research problem. (Cf. I. L. Janis, A. A. Lumsdaine, and A. I. Gladstone, "Effects of Preparatory Communications on Reactions to a Subsequent News Event," *Pub. Op. Quart.*, 1951, XV, 487–518.)

[3] For a more detailed description of the content of the communications used in this experiment see the earlier publication by Janis, Lumsdaine, and Gladstone, *op. cit.*, p. 494.

[4] Programs I and II contained approximately 2,200 and 2,800 words respectively, the difference of 600 words being due solely to the addition of the opposing arguments in the two-sided presentation. The opposing arguments were selected partly on the basis of spontaneous arguments given in pretest interviews of high school students.

TABLE 1

Experimental Treatments

Sequence of Events (spring 1949)

Groups	Mid-May	Early June	June, one week later
A. *Not* exposed to counterpropaganda			
I. (N = 36)	Initial questionnaire	Program I	Final questionnaire
II. (N = 52)	Initial questionnaire	Program II	Final questionnaire
B. *Exposed* to counterpropaganda			
I. (N = 60)	Initial questionnaire	Program I	Counterpropaganda	Final questionnaire
II. (N = 49)	Initial questionnaire	Program II	Counterpropaganda	Final questionnaire

and the other Program II) were exposed to a second transcribed radio program that was designed to function as "counterpropaganda." In this second communication (about 1300 words in length), the same issue was discussed by a different commentator who took the opposite position. He argued that Russia had probably already developed the A-bomb and within two years would be producing it in large quantities. Most of this communication consisted of playing up and elaborating the opposing arguments that had been mentioned earlier in Program II, but some new material was also introduced, including a description of four plants in Russia alleged to be producing A-bombs. This "counterpropaganda" communication was largely a one-sided presentation but contained a few sentences in which arguments stressed by the earlier communication were mentioned and then refuted.

The treatments administered to the four major experimental groups are summarized in Table 1. The initial and final questionnaires were also administered to a fifth group which received neither the original communication nor the counterpropaganda. This group was included as a control on amount of opinion change

that could be attributed to outside causes which might have been operating during the interval between the two questionnaires. At the time when the other groups were being presented with Program I or II, this control group was given an irrelevant radio program on a completely different topic (social changes in postwar Italy).

Results of the Experiment

The main question designed to measure the effects of the communications was as follows: "About how long from now do you think it will be before the Russians are really producing *large numbers* of atomic bombs?" This "key" question was asked in both the initial questionnaire and the final questionnaire.

The *net change* for each group was calculated as the excess in percentage of subjects increasing their estimates over the percentage decreasing their estimates. The *net effect* of each program (or combination of programs) was taken as the net change for each experimental group minus the corresponding net change for the control group.

As in the previous experiment by Hov-

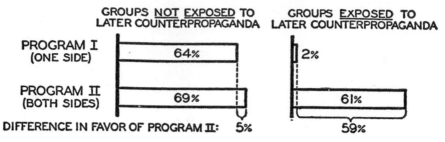

FIG. 1. Comparison of the effectiveness of programs I and II; changes in opinions concerning the length of time before Russia produces large numbers of A-bombs. (New change in the positive direction.*)

* "Positive" changes refer to changes (from initial to final questionnaire) in the direction advocated by the communicator in Programs I and II—i.e., in the case of the key question, an increase in estimated number of years before Russia would produce large numbers of A-bombs. The probability values indicating the reliability of differences in Figure 1 and elsewhere in this article are based on the method described by Hovland, Lumsdaine and Sheffield (*ibid.*, p. 321). They are expressed in terms of one tail of the probability distribution.

The 2 percent net change for the group which received Program I and the later counterpropaganda was slightly smaller than the (nonsignificant) net change of 15 percent found in the control group, which had not been exposed to any of the communications. But the net-change value for each of the other three experimental groups shown in Figure 1 was reliably greater (at beyond the one-percent confidence level) than the corresponding value for the unexposed controls and hence for these groups the net effect was "significant" in terms of the statistical tests used.

When the measures of net change were calculated independently for each classroom, the results on the key question were found to be highly consistent among the different classroom groups that had been randomly assigned to the experimental treatments. The percentage of net change was close to zero for each of the individual classrooms in the group which received the one-sided presentation followed by subsequent counterpropaganda. There was no overlap between these net change values and the ones obtained from classrooms which received any of the other three experimental treatments. The probability of this outcome is less than one in a hundred, so that the general pattern of the results in Figure 1 can be considered reliable even in terms of a stringent test that counts each classroom group as a single observation.

land, Lumsdaine and Sheffield, there was little over-all difference in the effectiveness of the two programs for those groups that were *not* exposed to counterpropaganda.[5] The main interest here is, however, attached to the results for the groups that were exposed to subsequent counterpropaganda, and to the comparison between these groups and those which received no counterpropaganda. The pattern of results is quite clear-cut: for the subjects who were exposed to counterpropaganda, the two-sided presentation was decidedly superior to the one-sided presentation. The results for the key question are presented in Figure 1. After exposure to the counterpropaganda, the second-order difference be-

[5] It will be recalled that in the previous experiment the one-sided communication was superior for those initially in favor of the commentator's position while the two-sided version was superior for those initially opposed; for the over-all results these two opposing effects virtually cancelled out, leaving little net difference in the *average* effectiveness of the two programs. For groups not receiving counterpropaganda in the present experiment, this same pattern of results was observed. However, the differences among subgroups with different initial points of view was not large enough to be reliable. This might be attributed to the fact that initial opinions were not as strongly held as those concerning the issue used in the earlier experiment. Alternatively, it may be supposed that the difference might have been significant in the second experiment had a larger number of cases been available for the small subgroups with different initial opinions.

TABLE 2

COMPARISON OF THE EFFECTIVENESS OF PROGRAMS I AND II FOR GROUPS
EXPOSED TO SUBSEQUENT COUNTERPROPAGANDA *

Supplementary Questions	Net Change in Positive Direction			
	Program I: "One side" (N 60)	Program II: "Both sides" (N 19)	Difference in favor of Program II	p value †
No. of A-bombs Russia will have in 5 years	3%	16%	13%	.22
No. of years before Russia produces its first A-bomb	20%	51%	31%	.02

* Based on opinion changes shown on two supplementary questions.

† The control group, which had not been given any relevant propaganda during the interval between the initial and final questionnaire, showed practically no opinion change on the first and second supplementary questions (net change of 2 percent and 1 percent, respectively). The experimental groups which had received Programs I and II, did not, after exposure to the counterpropaganda, differ reliably from the control group on the first supplementary question (p values = .37 and .13 respectively) but showed sizeable differences on the second supplementary question (p values = .07 and <.01).

tween the net change for the two-sided presentation (61 percent) and that for the one-sided presentation (2 percent) is 59 percent and is statistically reliable at beyond the one-percent level of confidence.[6] The third-order difference between this 59 percent difference and the corresponding difference of only 5 percent for the groups not exposed to counterpropaganda is also reliable at beyond the 1-percent level.

Two supplementary questions were also included in the initial and final questionnaires: (1) "About how many atomic bombs would you guess Russia will have made by five years from now?"; (2) "About how long from now do you think it will be before Russia has made its *first* atomic bomb?" Unlike the key question, neither of these supplementary questions dealt directly with the main conclusion advocated by Programs I and II. Although the first supplementary question was worded so as to be pertinent to the

main conclusion, it specified only a single-time point and relied upon each student's own conception of what figure would constitute a "large number" of A-bombs. (It should be noted that the programs did not refer to any specific number of A-bombs.) The second supplementary question did not deal with the main conclusion but covered an important subconclusion which was heavily emphasized by Programs I and II and which was subsequently opposed by the counterpropaganda.

Data derived from analysis of individual opinion changes on the two supplementary questions for the two groups which were exposed to the subsequent counterpropaganda are shown in Table 2. The results from both supplementary questions are in the same direction as those derived from the key question (see Figure 1). In the case of the first supplementary question the difference is not large enough to be statistically signifi-

[6] For the two groups who were not exposed to subsequent propaganda, the results showed the same pattern as Figure 1: the differences between Programs I and II, although showing a slightly greater effect from Program II, are small and nonsignificant.

cant, but the findings for the second supplementary question again show that Program II was significantly more effective than Program I.

DISCUSSION

The evidence from this experiment supports the following general conclusion: Under conditions where the audience is subsequently exposed to counterpropaganda arguing in favor of the opposing position, a persuasive communication which advocates a definite position on a controversial issue is more effective in the long run if it presents and discusses the opposing arguments than if it presents only the arguments that support the communicator's conclusion.

The rationale leading to the expectation of superior effectiveness for the two-sided over the one-sided communication differs somewhat as between the present experiment and the earlier experiment reported by Hovland, Lumsdaine, and Sheffield. In the earlier experiment which was concerned with immediate effects, the explanation is essentially as follows: If a member of the audience has a strongly held "negative" opinion and is familiar with arguments supporting this opinion, presentation of a one-sided communication supporting the "positive" point of view will encounter a comparatively high degree of resistance. The listener's tendency to think of his own arguments will interfere with acceptance of (or even attention to) the arguments that the communicator is presenting. If, however, the communicator explicitly discusses the listener's own negative arguments, this source of interference is reduced. Moreover, the listener may be more impressed by the communication and less inclined to distrust the arguments as coming from a biased source if the communicator makes it clear that he has taken the negative arguments into account.

To explain the findings of the present experiment, which show differences in resistance to subsequent counterpropaganda, there is no need to introduce any assumptions about the audience's initially negative point of view. Our tentative explanation is as follows. Regardless of initial position, a convincing one-sided communication presenting only positive arguments will tend to sway many members of the audience farther in the direction advocated by the communicator. However, when these persons subsequently hear the opposite point of view, also supported by cogent-sounding arguments, their opinions tend to be swayed back in the negative direction, especially if the new arguments appear to offset the previous positive arguments. But if the initial communication is, instead, a two-sided one, it will already have taken into account both the positive and negative arguments and still have reached the positive conclusion. When the listener is then subsequently exposed to the presentation of opposing arguments in the counterpropaganda, he is less likely to be influenced by them. He is not only familiar with the opposing point of view but has been led to the positive conclusion in a context in which the negative arguments were in evidence. In effect, he has been given an advance basis for ignoring or discounting the opposing communication and, thus "inoculated," he will tend to retain the positive conclusion.

In the preceding statement of the rationale for the superiority of the two-sided communication under the specified conditions, no explicit account has been taken of the manner and extent to which the opposing arguments should be introduced into the communication. In both the present study and the preceding one the opposing arguments were presented in a way that appeared most likely to achieve clear-cut effects, with no attempt at experimental variation of their content and arrangement within the communication. It is apparent, however, that a complete account of the factors determining the effectiveness of two-sided communications would have to deal systematically with the relative number and cogency of opposing arguments, the context in which they are introduced into the discussion, the extent to which they are explicitly refuted or merely overridden by implication, and so on. Experimental analysis of the effects of such factors remains an extensive area for future work.

THE ROLE OF PRIMACY AND RECENCY IN PERSUASIVE COMMUNICATION
By Carl I. Hovland

An important factor influencing the impact of communications upon an audience is the order in which the material is presented. When a controversial issue is being debated, is the side of the issue which the individual hears first likely to have a greater effect than the other side given subsequently? Some writers have argued that it is highly advantageous to present one's position first, before the opposition has had an opportunity to reach the audience, while others have contended that it is better to have "the last say" in a controversy. When the first position turns out to have greater impact, the result is described as a *primacy effect;* when the second side is more persuasive, the term *recency effect* is applied. What circumstances bring about a primacy effect and what ones a recency effect?

At present scientific principles in the field of communication are not sufficiently developed to provide clear-cut answers to such questions.

Answering questions of this sort at present is much more of an art than a science, but the underlying factors upon which the effects of alternative ways of organizing a message depend are ones which are of considerable concern to the scientist interested in communication.

The theoretical factors underlying the choice of alternative organizations do not constitute a closely integrated system, but require reference to a large number of principles of attention, perception, motivation, and learning. . . . [These problems] are theoretically complex and only a small beginning has been made in unraveling the numerous factors involved.[1]

Interest in the problem of presentation order in the type of communication situation where both sides of a controversial issue are presented goes back to the publication in 1925 of a study by Lund.[2] On the basis of his research he enunciated a Law of Primacy in Persuasion, stating that the side of an issue presented first will have greater effectiveness than the side presented subsequently. He had given his classes of college students a mimeographed communication in support of one side of a controversial issue (e.g., "a protective tariff is a wise policy for the United States") and had then presented a second

This article is rewritten from material presented in Carl I. Hovland (ed.) *Studies in Attitude and Communication*, Vol. 1, *The Order of Presentation in Persuasion* (New Haven, Conn.: Yale University Press, 1957). The research was carried out by members of the Yale Communication Research Program under a grant from the Rockefeller Foundation. The research cited in the present article was conducted by Timothy Brock, Enid H. Campbell, Abraham S. Luchins, Wallace Mandell and the writer. The editorial suggestions of Rosalind L. Feierabend in this book are gratefully acknowledged.

---

[1] I. Hovland, I. L. Janis, and H. H. Kelley, *Communication and Persuasion* (New Haven: Yale University Press, 1953), p. 99.
[2] F. H. Lund, "The Psychology of Belief: IV. The Law of Primacy in Persuasion," *J. Abnorm. & Soc. Psychol.*, 1925, XX, 183–91.

communication advocating a diametrically opposed stand on the same issue. He discovered that the communication coming first (whether pro or con) influenced the students significantly more then the one coming second.

Subsequent experiments, however, have not always obtained this outcome. Cromwell,[3] for example, performed a study in which affirmative and negative speeches on socialized medicine and labor arbitration were presented to groups of students whose opinions were measured before and after the talks. A significantly greater change was produced in the direction of that side of the issue presented last. Thus, this investigator obtained a *recency effect* rather than a *primacy effect*.

The problem of order of presentation in communication is of more than academic interest. Should primacy obtain to any significant extent there would be important practical implications for a variety of situations. Doob, for example, postulates the operation of primacy in propaganda:

The propagandist scores an initial advantage whenever his propaganda reaches people before that of his rivals . . . readers or listeners are then biased to comprehend, forever after, the event as it has been initially portrayed to them. If they are told in a headline or a flash that the battle has been won, the criminal has been caught, or the bill is certain to pass the legislature, they will usually expect subsequent information to substantiate this first impression. When later facts prove otherwise, they may be loath to abandon what they believe to be true until, perhaps, the evidence becomes overwhelming.[4]

Another propaganda device which assumes primacy is that used by politicians in "smearing" an opponent. Their expectation is that even if the evidence

subsequently refutes the allegation, the initial charge will still have inflicted considerable damage. Political beliefs have been attributed in part to primacy effects:

Whether we are democrats or republicans, Protestants or Catholics, is frequently observed to be a consequence of paternal or ancestral affiliation. However, it is doubtful whether family ties or family considerations are nearly as important determinants as the fact that we *first* become familiar with the beliefs and the defences of the beliefs of our family.[5]

The primacy effect could also be a factor in determining the outcome of opinion changes following debates. In such situations the conditions for the operation of primacy are closely approximated, since one side first presents its position and then the second side offers a view in direct opposition to that of the first. Elaborate precautions to counterbalance the order effects would be required in order to equalize the persuasive potentiality of the two sides.

Of even greater concern would be conditions for equitable administration of justice. In the presentation of court cases it is generally the rule that the prosecution presents its case and the defense follows. If the law of primacy is operative, we would find a constant bias in favor of the prosecution's position, since it always has the advantage of first position.

While the lawyer of the plaintiff is reviewing his case and making his appeal, the belief of the jurors is already in the process of formation, and they are not to be dissuaded from their position by an equal amount of evidence or persuasive appeal on the part of the defendant's lawyer, according to the law of primacy.[6]

---

[3] H. Cromwell, "The Relative Effect on Audience Attitude of the First versus the Second Argumentative Speech of a Series," *Speech Monogr.*, 1950, XVII, 105–22.

[4] L. W. Doob, *Public Opinion and Propaganda* (New York: Henry Holt & Co., Inc., 1948), pp. 421–22.

[5] Lund, *op. cit.*, p. 191.

[6] *Ibid.*

While there are practical implications derivable from many of the studies described below, the "applied" utility of the research is secondary. The factor motivating the present studies has been the opportunity afforded by research in this area to examine some of the basic theoretical problems involved in the process of influence and persuasion.

In the experiment by Lund mentioned above, written arguments were presented successively for and against an issue, with the affirmative arguments presented first for half of the subjects and the negative first for the remaining subjects. Opinion questionnaires were filled out by the subjects before the presentations and again following the first and the second communications. The change resulting from the first communication was greater than the change brought about by the second communication, and Lund described this outcome as the Law of Primacy in Persuasion. Directly opposed results were reported in a later study by Cromwell,[7] in which speeches presented in second position had a greater influence on the attitude of the listeners than those presented first.

One possible explanation for the disparity in the results from the two studies may lie in the different evaluation procedures they employed. In the Cromwell study the effects of the two communications were evaluated after both sides had been presented. In the Lund study, on the other hand, one of the questionnaires was administered immediately after the first side had been presented. This may have had the effect of requiring the subjects to review the arguments, formulate their own conclusions, and put their position "on record" after reading only one side of the issue. Thus, the measurement process might have had the effect of

"freezing" opinion and of causing individuals to be less likely to change their opinions once they had committed themselves on a questionnaire. Lund mentions this possibility: "the students, *having committed themselves* after the reading of the first discussion, *will remember this rating* and will tend to be influenced by their desire to be consistent when asked to make another rating after reading the opposed discussion." [8] Since commitment on the questionnaire is extraneous to primacy itself, if it were an explanatory factor Lund's results might thus really be attributable to the effect of the measurement process rather than to sequence effects.

The first experiment we will describe [9] had as its original purpose the evaluation of "formulation-commitment" as a factor responsible for the appearance of primacy in Lund's experiment and its absence in Cromwell's. Lund's experiment was repeated but with an additional group in which the subjects were not asked for their opinion until after both sides had been presented. A second objective, which turned out to be of greater interest, was to determine the generality of the results obtained by Lund.

Experiment I

Procedure. Every effort was made to follow Lund's procedures as closely as possible. The questionnaire, of the same type that Lund used, was administered by the instructor two days in advance of the communications.

The list of propositions, such as "Should all men have equal political rights?", was presented accompanied by a scale of belief which ran from +10 (belief allowing for no doubt) to −10 (disbelief allowing for no doubt). Subjects

---

[7] Cromwell, *op. cit.*

[8] Italics ours. From Lund, *op. cit.*, p. 190.

[9] C. I. Hovland and W. Mandell, "Is There a 'Law of Primacy' in Persuasion," Ch. 2 in Hovland (ed.), *op. cit.*

TABLE 1

EXPERIMENT I: MEAN BELIEF RATINGS BEFORE AND AFTER COMMUNICATIONS

	Lund replication		No intervening questionnaire	
	Affirmative first	Negative first	Affirmative first	Negative first
Topic I. "Equal rights"	(N = 26)	(N = 27)	(N = 21)	(N = 16)
Before communications	(a) 5.12	(d) 4.18	(a) 5.24	(d) 4.94
After first side	(b) 6.65	(e) 4.75		
After both sides	(c) 5.92	(f) 5.17	(c) 3.29	(f) 1.88
Effect *	−0.19 (Recency)		+1.11 (Primacy)	
	$p = .77$		$p = .28$	
Topic II. "Protective tariff"				
First replication	(N = 14)	(N = 16)	(N = 28)	(N = 27)
Before communication	(a) 2.00	(d) 0.69	(a) 1.85	(d) 1.70
After first side	(b) 4.71	(e) 1.00		
After both sides	(c) 2.64	(f) 1.50	(c) 3.37	(f) 3.30
Effect	−0.17 (Recency)		−0.08 (Recency)	
	$p = .85$		$p = .89$	
Second replication	(N = 47)	(N = 51)	(N = 33)	(N = 41)
Before communications	(a) −0.26	(d) 0.71	(a) 1.52	(d) 0.41
After first side	(b) 2.23	(e) −0.86		
After both sides	(c) 0.17	(f) 0.04	(c) 2.18	(f) 0.41
Effect	+1.10 (Primacy)		+0.66 (Primacy)	
	$p < .01$		$p = .21$	

* Advantage of first position $= (c - a) - (f - d)$. If value is positive, data show primacy; if negative, recency. The complete formula for advantage of first position is $[(b - a) + (d - e)] - [(b - c) + (f - e)]$ but b's and e's are common terms and hence cancel.

were instructed to check the number corresponding to the extent to which they felt inclined to affirm or deny the validity of the proposition. Two of the topics found to be most effective by Lund were used for the communications: "Should all men have equal political rights?" and "Is the protective tariff a wise policy for the United States?" His material was mimeographed and presented to the subjects to read. Ten minutes were allowed for the reading of each side.

Counterbalancing was employed, so that half of the subjects began with the affirmative version and half with the negative. The "Lund repetition" group was given the rating scale for belief after the first side had been read, while this step was omitted for the other group. Both groups were given the belief scales after the two versions had been read.

This experiment was performed at Hofstra College and Columbia University in a series of undergraduate psychology classes. Twelve classes were employed in this experiment, ranging in size from 14 to 51 students. One class was used for each of the four main conditions on the "equal rights" issue, while the remaining subjects were used for two replications of the "tariff" issue. A total of 357 students participated.

Results. The results from Experiment I are presented in Table 1.

The mean ratings for belief derived from Lund's scales are shown for the repetitions of Lund's experiment and for the additional groups which were not given the belief scale between the first and second communication. Under the conditions originally used by Lund only one of the groups shows primacy ($p < .01$), the other two showing insignificant recency effects. When the opinion questionnaire is omitted after the first side is presented, two of the groups show primacy and one recency. These effects are small and nonsignificant. The omission of the intervening questionnaire does not have any consistent effect; it increases the amount of primacy for one topic and decreases it for the other. But in neither case is the difference statistically significant. The absence of consistent primacy effects of the type obtained by Lund overshadows the problem of the effect of the intervening questionnaire which is significant only when related to an explanation of primacy effects.

Experiment II

In view of the absence of clear-cut primacy effects in the first experiment it was thought desirable to obtain more data on a straight repetition of the Lund condition, using topics of possibly greater current interest. Hence, a second experiment was conducted.

Procedure. In this experiment new communication materials dealing with the issues "Antihistamines should be sold without a prescription" and "An atomic submarine is feasible at the present time"[10] were mimeographed. Two days before the communications

were presented, the instructors administered an opinion questionnaire concerning these issues. A seven-point rating scale for degree of belief was employed. The communications were administered so that one issue was used for each class. In order to counterbalance within each class half the subjects read the positive argument first, while half read the negative first. In addition to the before and after questionnaires, half of the classes took the same questionnaire between the two communications. The time for reading and instructions was the same as in the first experiment.

This experiment was performed at New York University in a series of ten psychology classes. On the first topic the groups totaled 56 and 60 subjects, while for the second there were 37 and 38 students. Thus, the total number of subjects was 191.

Results. The data from this experiment were analyzed in a manner analogous to that of Lund and of the first experiment by determining the mean degree of belief in the propositions discussed in the communications. The data are presented in Table 2. Again we find an absence of evidence for primacy under our conditions. Three of the groups exhibit recency effects, one at a statistically significant level ($p < .01$). Only one of the four groups showed evidence of primacy and this was only significant at the .08 level.

The present findings raise serious doubts as to the generality of the results obtained by Lund. For only two of the seven groups run under his conditions did we find primacy effect and only one of these was statistically significant. The remaining five groups showed a greater effectiveness of the second communication, although only one of the differences was of sufficient size to be statistically significant ($p < .01$). While Lund's own results support the operation of primacy,

---

[10] The study was done in 1949, when this was a much-debated topic.

TABLE 2

EXPERIMENT II: MEAN BELIEF RATINGS BEFORE AND AFTER COMMUNICATIONS

	Affirmative first	Negative first
Topic III. Atomic submarines		
First replication	(N = 39)	(N = 41)
Before communications	(a) 4.87	(d) 5.12
After first side	(b) 4.62	(e) 4.88
After both sides	(c) 4.12	(f) 5.00
Effect	−0.63 (Recency)	
	$p < .01$	
Second replication	(N = 17)	(N = 19)
Before communications	(a) 4.53	(d) 3.96
After first side	(b) 4.48	(e) 3.11
After both sides	(c) 3.83	(f) 3.42
Effect	−0.41 (Recency)	
	$p = .10$	
Topic IV. Antihistamines		
First replication	(N = 18)	(N = 17)
Before communications	(a) 3.77	(d) 2.94
After first side	(b) 4.66	(e) 3.23
After both sides	(c) 4.16	(f) 3.53
Effect	−0.20 (Recency)	
	$p = .67$	
Second replication	(N = 20)	(N = 20)
Before communications	(a) 2.95	(d) 3.00
After first side	(b) 4.85	(e) 3.05
After both sides	(c) 4.25	(f) 3.45
Effect	+0.85 (Primacy)	
	$p > .08$	

he does not give tests of significance to indicate the extent of reliability of his difference. If his variability was of the same order of magnitude as ours, it is unlikely that more than one of his three groups would show a statistically significant effect (his typical group contained approximately 20 subjects).

If there is a significant difference in outcome between our experiment and that of Lund, what variation in condi-tions may have been responsible? In terms of the analysis presented in *Communication and Persuasion* we would seek differences either in the conditions of *learning* or of *acceptance*. With respect to the former, the most likely difference between the two experiments would be in the subjects' motivation to learn. In the Lund study the experimenter was presumably the subjects' regular class-room instructor. Under these conditions one would expect that the motivation to learn the first-presented communications would be derived from previous classroom experiences in which the material presented by the teacher had to be learned, later formed the basis for a test, etc. This would provide strong motivation for learning the first communication. When the teacher then proceeded to reverse his stand, the subjects may have wondered what was happening. They may have suspected that they were being used as guinea pigs in an experiment. As a result of the changed conditions, motivation to learn the second communication might have dropped and thus less attention may have been paid to this second communication. Such conditions would produce a primacy effect (i.e., a greater impact exerted by the first communication than by the second).

This same set of conditions may also have influenced *acceptance* of the communication. Lund's students may have accepted the first communication as being implicitly "sponsored" by the instructor. The subsequent advocacy of an opposed point of view could have aroused their suspicion and reduced their confidence in the communication. Since they were unaware of being experimental subjects at the time that they filled out the first questionnaire, their opinions may have been influenced by the first communication. The adverse effects would become apparent on the second questionnaire and result in reduced effectiveness for the second communication.

In our study the experimenter was not the teacher but rather someone from the outside of the school presenting rival views on the issue. It is our belief that these conditions are more typical of situations to which research findings are likely to be applied than are those of Lund. Thus, in communications involving debates, rival political candidates, or

courtroom alternation of prosecution and defense, the presentations are clearly labeled as opposing points of view and do not secure acceptance of the first material on the basis of classroom conditions of motivation and acceptance. An interesting study in which different orders of presentation of prosecution and defense arguments are compared is reported by Weld and Roff.[11] Our calculations, based on their data, indicate recency effects.

DISCUSSION

The difference in outcome between our experiment and Lund's, and the variations between subgroups within our experiment, make it appear to us premature at present to postulate a general Law of Primacy. Rather we believe an attempt should be made to determine the conditions which operate to make the first side more effective under some circumstances, the second under others, and both sides equally effective under still others. Accordingly, a series of further experiments was conducted to assess the influence of certain variables on the relative prevalence of primacy or recency effects in persuasive communications. Procedures were introduced which would be expected on theoretical grounds to have the effect of either increasing or of decreasing the extent of primacy effects. Space does not permit a full description here of these experiments and their outcomes. The reader is referred to our book on *Order of Presentation in Communication* for a complete report on these and other related experiments. The topics investigated and some of the findings are summarized briefly below:

1. *The effect of public "commitment" to a position after hearing only one side.* One frequent situation which may contribute to the greater effectiveness of the

---

[11] H. P. Weld and M. Roff, "A Study in the Formation of Opinion Based upon Legal Evidence," *Am. J. Psychol.*, 1938, LI, 609–28.

first presentation is that in which the individual takes an action on the basis of hearing only the first side. Hearing the "other side" may then require undoing the action and the inconvenience of this may cause one to persist in the opinion formed after the first communication. The type of action investigated was one in which the individual publicly committed himself to a position after hearing only the first side of a debatable issue.

Hovland, Campbell, and Brock [12] presented one side of a controversial issue to one group of subjects and then asked them to write their opinion on the issue for publication in a magazine read by their peers. Control subjects wrote out their opinions but these were anonymous and no mention was made of possible publication. Subsequently, without prior announcement, the other side of the issue was presented to both groups and opinion measures again secured. The authors found that the public expression of opinion tended to "freeze" the subject's views and to make them resistant to influence by the second side of the issue.

In everyday life the greater effectiveness of the first side of an issue may sometimes be attributable to this mechanism, since an individual often makes decisions after hearing only one side of an issue and then carries out a series of acts on the basis of his decisions. Under these circumstances it may be difficult to produce a reversal of position through presentation of the opposing argument.

The experimenters discussed how the effect may be mediated through social rewards and the need for social approval experienced by the subjects. Having placed his views on record for others to see, the recipient may rehearse his position in anticipation of the social interaction which publication will bring. Knowledge of the social approval

granted to consistency and honesty will prevent him from altering his views. Perhaps, also, rehearsal of his own position prevents him from listening attentively to subsequent contradictory information.

2. *The effect of private commitment after hearing only one side.* Does private commitment operate in a manner analogous to public commitment? Private commitment to a position is involved where one gives his opinion anonymously on a questionnaire after hearing the first side of an argument. In the study of Hovland and Mandell (described above) a comparison was made of the relative effectiveness of the first and second sides of an issue when questionnaires were interpolated between the first and second communications. Control subjects were given the first and second sides without an intervening questionnaire. The study employed the same topics as were used by Lund. It was thought that the intervening expression of opinion required of the experimental subjects might have the effect of forcing them to review the arguments, to formulate their own conclusions, and to crystallize their opinion after reading only one side of the issue. This would be expected to make these subjects more resistant to a subsequent change of opinion. No such effect was found, apparently because no feeling of "commitment" was experienced under these conditions. (An incidental implication of this outcome is that the measurement process is unlikely to produce artifacts due to any commitment factor under anonymous conditions.)

3. *Primacy-recency in forming impressions of personality from a single communication giving contradictory information.* Luchins [13] utilized case-history materials concerning an individual's personal characteristics and behavior to study the role of primacy and recency. Two different blocks of information were prepared con-

---

[12] C. I. Hovland, Enid H. Campbell, and T. Brock, "The Effects of 'Commitment' on Opinion Change Following Communication," Ch. 3 in Hovland (ed.), *op. cit.*

[13] A. S. Luchins, "Primacy-recency in Impression Formation," Ch. 4 in Hovland (ed.), *op. cit.*

cerning the personality characteristics of a person not known to the subjects. One contained principally items characteristic of an extrovertive type of person and the other, items characteristic of an introvertive individual. These blocks of information were given to some subjects in extrovertive-introvertive order and to others in introvertive-extrovertive order. Control groups were given only the extrovertive or the introvertive blocks. Subjects were then asked to select adjectives indicating their impression of the individual in question. In a second experiment they were also asked to write brief personality descriptions and in the third to make predictions about the later behavior and interpersonal relations of the person about whom they had read. It was found that the material presented first was considerably more influential than that presented second in determining what were thought to be the principal personality characteristics of the individual described. This is in accord with Asch's findings using simple adjective lists.[14] It was remarkable how many of Luchins' subjects received incompatible information without realizing that there was any conflict of interpretation involved (over a third of a sample interviewed stated they had not been aware of any contradictions or inconsistencies).

4. *Methods of reducing the extent of primacy-effect by instructions and interpolated activity.* In a subsequent experiment Luchins [15] studied ways of overcoming the disproportionate influence of the first-presented material by various methods, such as discussion of the fallacy of "first impressions." One group of subjects was run under the "standard" conditions utilized in the experiment described above. A second group was explicitly warned about possible "first-impression" fallacies before any information was presented. Group three had the warning interpolated between the first and second blocks of information, while the fourth group had an arithmetic task interpolated between the two blocks of information. Sixty high-school students were used in each of the four groups. At the end of the second communication questionnaires concerning the personality characteristics of the person described were administered and their results revealed that the greater impact of the first block of information existed only for the first (control) group. For the three other groups the second block of information tended to exert a greater influence than the first on their final impressions of the personality of the hypothetical individual. The amount of "recency effect" shown for the latter groups increased progressively from group two to group four. Interpolation of the number task resulted in the greatest amount of recency effect.

IMPLICATIONS FOR FURTHER RESEARCH

The preceding results raise a host of problems for further research. One which has been little investigated involves systematic exploration of the relationship between primacy effects and the degree to which the individual is already familiar with the issue. In most of the experiments herein reported, as well as in the study by Lund, it is probable that the subjects had some prior knowledge about the topic under discussion. As we have seen, a law of primacy under these conditions does not seem to be a valid general principle. It may be that when no prior knowledge of the topic is involved, a law of primacy does operate. The factor of familiarity was actually invoked by Lund to explain one of his groups

---

[14] S. E. Asch, "Forming Impressions of Personality," *J. Abnorm. & Soc. Psychol.*, 1946, XLI, 258–90.
[15] A. S. Luchins, "Experimental Attempts to Minimize the Impact of First Impressions," Ch. 5 in Hovland (ed.), *op. cit.*

which failed to show much influence: "Propositions upon which one has already had ample opportunity to form an opinion should be much less subject to persuasive influence." [16]

This problem suggests that further attention must be given to the appropriate specification of conditions for the operation of a law of primacy. Should primacy be defined as the very first presentation of unknown material to an audience, or is it simply the first portion of any communicated material regardless of the recipient's familiarity with the issue? Rarely is the communicator in a position to be the first to address his audience on a particular subject. Some degree of prior familiarity with almost any topic must be assumed both in experimental and in real-life situations. What, then, is the practical definition of primacy in experimental studies? Since it cannot claim to represent the first material ever presented on the issue, it is generally limited to the first portion of the material in question.

The results of the present series of studies seem to suggest that the nearer one comes to achieving primacy in the sense of the first presentation of unfamiliar material, the more apt one is to obtain primacy effects. Undoubtedly, the material least familiar to the recipient is found in Luchins' studies on forming impressions of personality. In this case the subject was asked to form an impression of an unknown person based upon information which was presented for the first time. But research bearing directly on the relationship between prior familiarity with the topic under discussion and the relative effectiveness of the side of the issue presented first is needed.

One of the effects of familiarity with an issue is to alert one to the fact that there are conflicting points of view involved. This factor is closely related to the results of Luchins which show that

lack of awareness of conflict is associated with the appearance of primacy effects. In his experiment two blocks of contradictory information about an individual were presented. A third of the subjects he interviewed afterwards stated that they were not aware that the material contained conflicting or contradictory statements and over two thirds were not bothered by whatever contradictions they noticed. When experimental variations were introduced which called attention to the possibility of a disparity between the two sets of information, the primacy effect was greatly reduced or eliminated.

Another factor which may serve to reduce or augment awareness of incompatibility involves the presentation of contradictory material by either two communicators or a single communicator. This is an important research problem which has not yet been attacked. Present results are compatible with the hypothesis that primacy is less when the two sides of an issue are presented by different communicators. It will be recalled that only a single communicator was involved in the Lund study, and the same was true in the Luchins studies reported above. On the other hand, different communicators presented the alternate sides of the argument in the Hovland and Mandell experiment and in the control condition of the Hovland, Campbell, and Brock study, and in neither of these were primacy effects obtained. What is needed, however, is systematic experimentation in which topics, subjects, and other factors are held constant while the results obtained from a single communicator versus those from two opposed communicators are compared. Only studies set up specifically to test these hypotheses can establish the validity of the generalizations suggested on the basis of naturalistic variations which occurred in the studies herein reported.

[16] Lund, *op. cit.*, p. 189.

A closely related research problem concerns the expectation of the recipient that a second side will be presented subsequently. Where there is an awareness that there are two sides of the issue to be presented, there may be a tendency not to make up one's mind on the basis of the side which comes first but to wait until both sides have been presented. On the other hand, when the recipient expects that only one side will be presented, he may make up his mind on the basis of the side presented first and even take actions which commit him to the position he initially adopts. In the studies by Hovland and Mandell and by Hovland, Campbell, and Brock using alternate presentations of the two sides, no mention was made at the time of commitment that a second communication giving the other side would follow. An interesting experiment is suggested in which there would be systematic variation of the factor of expectation of refutation, informing half the subjects that the other side would be presented later and giving no such information to the other half. If the subjects anticipate counterargument, it is possible that they will avoid immediate acceptance of the first position in order to avoid the conflict that comes from indecision.

Another factor which probably plays an important role in determining the extent of primacy effects in real-life communications is the degree of exposure to the two positions on an issue. In the experiments reported in this volume we were dealing with classroom situations where we could guarantee some exposure to both sides of the issue under study. In many situations we do not have any control of exposure. Under these circumstances it is highly probable that one of the effects of primacy is to reduce the likelihood of self-exposure to the second side. In real life primacy is often important because the individual who has once

acquired information, a mode of perception, and a new attitude does not permit himself thereafter to be exposed to contradictory information. While experiments dealing with naturalistic situations are notoriously difficult, we have suggested elsewhere [17] a line of research in which results obtained in experiments with captive audiences are compared with those obtained where self-exposure is involved.

Finally, the effects of various types of committing action in "freezing" opinion after a communication need considerable further investigation. In the present study significantly fewer subjects changed their position when exposed to a second communication after they had expressed their opinion publicly. When the expression of opinion was anonymous, no decrease was obtained. These results might be interpreted by some as indicating greater effectiveness of public as compared with private commitment. But actually, in neither of the present studies was an attempt made to have the subjects regard their expression of opinion as a commitment. Would such an attempt have increased the "fixation" of opinion after the first side was presented, and would there have been a difference between public and private commitment in this respect? These are important questions for future research.

Summary and Implications

The general picture which emerges from the experiments in which both sides of an issue are presented successively is that the danger of first impressions becoming lasting impressions is probably exaggerated, at least for situations where representatives of both sides have an opportunity to present their views. The public is not necessarily permanently swayed by the view to which it first lends

---

[17] C. I. Hovland, "Effects of the Mass Media of Communication," in G. Lindzey (ed.), *Handbook of Social Psychology* (Cambridge, Mass.: Addison-Wesley Co., Inc., 1954), pp. 1062–1103.

an ear or biased by the man who first captures its attention.

The present group of experiments indicate the conditions under which the danger that the first presentation will prevail is likely to be pronounced and they also permit some specification of procedures which minimize such a danger. The combined findings from all of the different studies reported suggest that the side of an issue presented first is likely to have a disproportionate influence on opinion under the following conditions: (1) when cues as to the incompatibility of different items of information are absent, (2) when the contradictory information is presented by the same communicator, (3) when committing actions are taken after only one side of the issue has been presented, (4) when the issue is an unfamiliar one, and (5) when the recipient has only a superficial interest in the issue. When one deals with situations in which exposure to both sides cannot be assumed, but where the recipient himself controls whether or not he will expose himself to the second side after hearing the first, additional factors favoring primacy become involved.

For important social situations in which primacy effects have been considered a danger, for example, legal trials, election campaigns and political debates, the issue is usually clearly defined as controversial, the partisanship of the communicator is established, and different communicators present the opposing sides. These factors would give rise to relatively little primacy effect. Our concern then might be concentrated on preventing premature commitment on the basis of the first presentation alone and on developing interest and responsibility on the part of the citizen to insure objectivity and a genuine desire to reach the heart of the issue.

There are other situations, however, in which the dangers of primacy effect are very real. The deliberate use of primacy for propagandistic effect has already been mentioned. It is frequently effective under conditions where the controversial nature of the issue is not mentioned, where early commitment is sought, and where exposure to other points of view is minimized, either through self-selection of exposure or through monopoly control of information. Totalitarian regimes deliberately utilize commitment effects to prevent the "other side" from having its influence, by requiring persons attending political meetings to make public expression of their views as well as to listen to the views of others. In free countries, on the other hand, effort is made to prevent individuals who are being exposed to controversial material from taking any action before the other side is presented. Wise advisors frequently tell the individual "Don't say 'Yes' or 'No' now but think it over" so that both pro and con considerations can be taken into account.

Primacy may frequently operate also in forming impressions of personality, where the present results are consonant with the popular belief about first impressions. Here, bits of information about personality and behavior accumulate slowly over time. When there is no initial indication that the data may be incompatible, considerable primacy prevails. This situation is one in which the educational process must play a role in warning individuals against the fallacy of deciding on the basis of only limited evidence. Such procedures are shown to be quite effective. Presumably other methods of eliminating "halo effects" in judgment might also be applicable.

Undue influence of early observations may sometimes create difficulties in scientific work. Typically the researcher extracts items of information from nature through experimentation and observation. Some of these are consonant with one theory and others with another. The impression formed by early observations and protocols may persist even when no longer compatible with new evidence, in the absence of clear-cut cues as to the incompatibility of the different findings.

Commitment may also be a factor of concern in the example of the scientist just described. It was found that when subjects indicated publicly their position on an issue after only a single side had been presented, they were less apt to take the other side into account when it was subsequently discussed. If the scientific investigator quickly fits his early findings into a theoretical framework on the basis of some hunch, he may be reluctant to relinquish his view in the face of nonconfirming instances. This act of theory construction might be considered analogous

to public commitment. The scientist, having committed himself, albeit privately, is apt to regard all subsequent data from within his adopted theoretical framework as definitive, often discounting later facts which come to his attention. Bias in scientific inquiry thus produced may impede rational theory construction. An important part of scientific training consists of learning to suspend judgment until all the facts have come to light, to be particularly on the look-out for incompatible evidence, and to avoid emotional involvement in the maintenance of one's own theories.

THE EFFECT OF INDUCED AGGRESSIVENESS ON OPINION CHANGE   By *Walter Weiss and Bernard J. Fine*

Previous research by Weiss and Fine [1] has indicated that subjects evidencing high aggressiveness, as measured by the Thematic Apperception Test and the Rosenzweig Picture-frustration Test, were influenced more by a communication designed to provoke punitive opinions than were those evidencing low-fantasy aggressiveness. This finding supported the data of earlier correlational research which related personality variables to opinions at one time, but not to *changes* in opinions. [2] The general research hypothesis for the authors' previous study presented a compound independent variable involving aggressiveness and exposure to a communication. Only the latter aspect was experimentally

controlled. The theoretical advantage of verifying an hypothesis by complete experimental methodology was the primary motive for the present research. While personality factors, such as aggressiveness, cannot readily be influenced, temporary states analogous to them can be induced. This was the method adopted for the current investigation.

The broad theoretical statement underlying the research asserts that communication effectiveness is facilitated when congruency exists between response predispositions of the communicatees and the communication appeals. To elaborate this interactive relationship, the effect of a communication designed to induce lenient opinions on a topic should be

From the *Journal of Abnormal and Social Psychology*, 1956, LII, slightly abridged. Reprinted by permission of the authors and the American Psychological Association. The research reported in this paper was done under Contract NONR-492(04) between Boston University and the Office of Naval Research.

[1] W. Weiss and B. J. Fine, "Opinion Change as a Function of Some Intrapersonal Attributes of the Communicatees," *J. Abnorm. & Soc. Psychol.*, 1955, LI, 246–253.
[2] T. W. Adorno, Else Frenkel-Brunswick, D. J. Levinson and R. N. Sanford, *The Authoritarian Personality* (New York: Harper & Brothers, 1950); G. W. Allport and B. M. Kramer, "Some Roots of Prejudice," *J. Psychol.*, 1946, XXII, 9–39.

examined. The prediction would then be that high aggressives would be less influenced by such a communication than would low aggressives. The verification of this prediction was the second purpose of the current research. It was also considered advisable in view of the assumption of congruency to attempt the development of an ego-satisfying experience, so that aggression arousal may be contrasted with ego satisfaction rather than simply no aggression arousal. As a minimum, this second type of induction should aid the production of two clearly separable groups along the dimension of aggressiveness.

METHOD

General Design. A before-after design was employed. A before-questionnaire on opinions on juvenile delinquency and on the relations of the United States with her allies was taken by the subjects (Ss) in one of their classes. The Rosenzweig P-F Study was also completed at the same time. Approximately two weeks later, Ss were involved individually in either a frustrating, aggression-arousing situation or in an ego-satisfying situation. As part of the experimental session, they read an article on delinquency or on the relations of our allies with Communist China. Immediately afterwards, they responded to a questionnaire seeking their reactions to the article they had read and their opinions on a variety of topics.

Subjects. Ninety-six students from courses in journalism, radio programing, and introductory psychology at Boston University, who volunteered for the individual sessions, comprise the sample employed. The Ss were paid for the experimental hour.

Before-measures. During a meeting of their respective courses, the students filled out an opinion questionnaire containing four items on juvenile delinquency and four on America's relations with her allies. All eight items sought responses on policy; e.g., should delin-

quents be treated leniently or punitively, or should America continue aid to allies who do not follow our lead vis-à-vis communist China. The questionnaire was presented as part of a survey of opinions of college students being conducted by the Division of Research of Boston University. Following this, the students completed the adult form of the Rosenzweig P-F Study, which was ostensibly being tested by the Division as a measure of "creative imagination." Then paid volunteers were requested for an individual session to determine the value of several other tests of creative imagination.

Experimental Session. Forty-eight of these Ss were exposed to the frustrating, aggression-arousing conditions, and 48 to the ego-satisfying treatment; then half of each group read the communication on delinquency and half the communication on the relations of our allies with Communist China. A replication of the basic two-by-two design was completed every time a set of four Ss was tested. Within each replication, Ss were assigned at random to one of the four treatment combinations. A different random assignment was employed for each replication.

At the beginning of an experimental session, Ss were informed that, although they had been designed primarily to measure creative imagination, the tests did provide indirectly an indication of intellectual capacity. The students were also informed that half of the Ss would be asked to return at a later time to take other tests and that the criterion for selection of Ss would be general cooperativeness with the E during the first hour. The instructions were then given for the Arthur Stencil Design Test I. As part of the instructions, the Ss were told that time norms for completion of the designs were available for college students; thus they would be informed by E at the completion of each problem of the adequacy of their performance in comparison with the norm. Furthermore, a maximum of one minute would be allowed for completing each of the designs; this they were told was more than sufficient time for the vast majority of college students. Only eight design problems from the available set of 20 were presented to the Ss. The first three were the same for all Ss. They were relatively easy and were completed within a minute by all. The remaining five designs for the Ss involved in the ego-satisfying situation were somewhat more complex than the first three but still sufficiently simple so that over 90 percent of these Ss were able to complete them. They were also advised that their times for completion were better than the average. Furthermore, E made personally complimentary and encouraging remarks to them. The frustrated, aggression-aroused Ss were given five designs of greater complexity, whose average time for completion was determined by pretest to be beyond one minute. Most of these Ss failed at least three out of five of the complex designs; they were told that the time scores, for those they were able to complete, were beyond the norm. Also E made uncomplimentary and somewhat insulting comments about their performance and abilities, which increased in intensity at the end of the Stencil Design Test. The content and intensity of the insulting remarks varied slightly from S to S depending on their observed effect and on the known academic aspirations of the student.

Following the Design Test, Ss were asked to write stories for two TAT cards, 18GF and 3BM. These were selected as potential discriminators between aggressive and nonaggressive Ss on the basis of previous research. The abbreviated TAT was presented as a second test of creative imagination. The Ss were allowed five minutes to write each story on a page of a prepared booklet. The E examined and commented upon each story immediately after it was completed. Complimentary remarks were made about the stories of the nonfrustrated Ss. The intensity of the derogatory, insulting comments was increased for the other Ss.

At the completion of the TAT, E told the Ss that for the final test they would be asked to read carefully an article and then to respond to some questions about their reactions to it. He advised the nonfrustrated Ss to continue to do well and the frustrated Ss to improve their performance, for it was the over-all impression on all three tests of creative imagination that was important. All Ss were then informed that a second E would administer this last measure.[3]

The article was presented as one received for publication by the editors of a national magazine. We, as well as the editors, were interested in determining if college students and professional editors could arrive at the same judgments of an article by an unnamed author. The Ss were informed that ten minutes would be allowed for reading the article, after which they would be asked questions about their reactions to it. Depending on which treatment combination to which the S had been assigned, he read either the article on delinquency or the one on the relations of our allies with Communist China. The former argued strongly for adopting punitive measures to curb juvenile offenses in contrast to practices of leniency and guidance. The latter urged Americans to consider the special economic, geographic, and military circumstances of other nations which incline them to adopt policies toward China on such matters as trade and diplomatic recognition which differ from our own; also the impracticality of diplomatic threat and withdrawal of aid as a method to compel free nations to follow our lead was emphasized.

Immediately after the article was read,

---

[3] Weiss acted as the first E for all Ss and Fine as the second E. Only one E was in the room with the Ss at any time.

the Ss filled out a questionnaire in which they were asked to indicate their judgments of fairness of presentation and propagandistic intent of the author, their own opinions on the topic of the article, their knowledge of the content of the article as tested by a set of multiple-choice items, and finally their opinions on the topic of the other article and on five issues not dealt with by either article. The before-opinion items on the topics covered by the communications were repeated in the after-questionnaire.

Following this, the E asked the S to express his judgment of the worthwhileness of the tests, whether there was anything he particularly liked or disliked about the experimental session, and if he would be interested in returning for another session at a later time. The first E returned then and informed the S of the nature of the experimental situation. Several interview questions were asked concerning S's reactions to his "failures" on the first two tests and to the disparaging remarks made by E, his ability to concentrate adequately on the article, and the possibility that he thought about Es' opinions on the topic of the article and the influence such thoughts might have had on him.

Scoring. The scoring of the Rosenzweig P-F Study and the opinion responses was the same as that employed by Weiss and Fine. Each picture of the former was scored zero or one depending on the presence or absence of an extrapunitive response; thus, the theoretical range was zero to 24. The opinion responses were scored −1 for an expression of leniency, zero for uncertainty, and +1 for punitiveness; the theoretical range was −4 to +4. Each TAT story was assessed on a five-point basis, zero to four, with zero being assigned for absence of aggression and four for violent aggression.

RESULTS

Before examining the effects of the communications on opinions, it is necessary to determine if the experimental procedures were successful in producing a separation of the groups on the dimension of aggression arousal. The interview material indicated that two thirds of the Ss subjected to the aggression-arousal treatment reported experiencing feelings of hostility toward E, and almost all felt frustrated in their attempts to perform well. The protocols frequently contain such comments as "very angry," "burnt up," "wanted to tell you to shut up," "wondered what value college was going to be to me," "very upset at poor performance," "never experienced such ego deflation so quickly." Only Ss from this group said they would not volunteer for another session, more of these questioned the value of the tests than did those of the other group, and only members of this group said they disliked features of the general experimental situation. The significant difference between the groups on the second TAT story, as indicated in Table 1, supports the interview results.[4] Many of the aggression-aroused Ss said that they viewed the TAT as a second chance to show creativity and were hopeful of improving their performances. But E's derogatory comments after the first story were a severe setback and aggravated feelings of anger and hostility. Most of them still exhibited hostility and

TABLE 1

MEANS FOR TAT STORIES OF
EXPERIMENTAL GROUPS

Card	Aggressive	Non-aggressive	p(one tail)
18GF	2.20	2.24	—
3BM	1.81	1.35	.06
Total	4.02	3.60	> .15

---

[4] In all the tables, comparisons between the total aggressive and nonaggressive groups are based on N's of 48 for each. Comparisons between treatment-article subgroups are based on N's of 24 for each.

concern when the first E returned to the room and expressed great relief at being informed of the nature of the experiment. On the contrary, the other group of Ss reported pleased, satisfied sentiments with their performances; such comments as "felt pleased with myself," "very happy I did well," "good to know you have some creative imagination" were frequently made. It seems evident then that the desired effects of the experimental treatments were adequately realized.

Before proceeding to the main findings of the research, two other items of relevant information should be mentioned. None of the Ss in either group reported in the interviews that they had been concerned at all with assumptions about E's opinion on the topic of the article read, either while reading the article or answering the questionnaire. Also, the distributions of extrapunitive scores, based on the Rosenzweig measure, for the four treatment groups were not reliably different from each other.

Table 2 indicates the effects of the articles on opinions. There were no reliable differences among the groups in before-opinions on either issue. On the topic of delinquency, all groups were decidedly on the lenient side of the attitude dimension; the means for the other topic however were close to zero.[5] Both articles affected opinions significantly on their respective issues. The difference between the aggressive and the nonaggressive groups who read the article on delinquency is significant at the .02 level (one tail); and for the other topic, the difference has a p value of .08 (one tail). The induced affects alone did not produce reliably different changes in opinions on the topics, if the relevant article had not been read.[6]

TABLE 2

MEAN BEFORE-OPINIONS AND CHANGES IN OPINIONS ON TOPICS OF ARTICLES
(Based on Four Items)

Opinions on	Experimental group		Before-opinion	Change score *
Delinquency	Read article	Aggressive	−2.88	+1.83
		Nonaggressive	−2.25	+0.38
	Did not read article	Aggressive	−2.04	−0.21
		Nonaggressive	−2.88	−0.04
America's relations with Allies	Read article	Aggressive	−0.04	−0.54
		Nonaggressive	−0.46	−1.29
	Did not read article	Aggressive	+0.42	+0.04
		Nonaggressive	−0.38	+0.08

* A plus sign signifies change toward punitiveness; a minus sign indicates change toward leniency.

[5] A small, pre-experimental sample of Ss provided a somewhat punitive opinion mean on policy toward America's allies. If it had been known that the mean for the over-all experimental groups would be close to zero, this topic alone could have been used for all treatments. One communication would have urged leniency and the other punitiveness. Methodologically, this would have been a more precise procedure. However, additional control groups would have been needed to determine the effect on opinions of the experimental inductions alone.

[6] The second-order difference on the topic of delinquency is significant at the .03 level, one tail; and the difference on the other topic does not approach significance. These differences are obtained

Acquisition of the content of the communications was examined by a set of multiple-choice items containing four alternative responses for each. The data in Table 3 reveal that, as measured, there were no reliable differences between the relevant groups in learning the communication content.

TABLE 3

MEAN SCORES ON FACT-QUIZ TESTS

Group	Article	
	Delinquency (6 items)	Allies (5 items)
Aggressive	4.21	4.42
Nonaggressive	4.58	4.54
p value (two tails)	$> .30$	$> .60$

Two questions eliciting Ss' judgments of the possible propagandistic intent and fairness of presentation of the communications were included in the after-questionnaires. The aggressively aroused subjects did not differ from their "ego-supported" counterparts in their judgment of the "fairness" of the articles, nor of their propagandistic intent. The article on delinquency was less frequently judged as "fair" and more frequently judged as "a piece of propaganda" than was the article on the relations of our Allies with Communist China. A separate analysis of the relation between judgments and opinion change indicated that those judging the delinquency article as "fair" were reliably more influenced than were those judging it as "one-sided"; judgments of this article on the dimension of propagandistic intent were not however related reliably to communication effectiveness. The effect of judgments on the opinion influence of the other article could not be adequately analyzed be-

cause of the small numbers of Ss considering it as "propaganda" or "one-sided."

DISCUSSION

The data support the main hypotheses that aggression-aroused Ss will be more influenced by a punitively oriented communication and less influenced by a leniency-oriented one than will Ss who are not aggressively aroused. The smaller differential effect of the article on America's relations with her Allies may be due to the relatively nonspecific nature of the persuasion; that is, the expressed viewpoint argued more for viewing the problem of relations with China through the eyes of other nations than for specific policy recommendations, which represented the focus of the opinion items. Previous research indicates that opinions which are the focus of specific communication appeals are influenced more than opinions that are indirectly related to the appeals.[7] Also, the possible difference in the changeability of opinions on the two topics should be considered.

The term nonaggressive rather than ego-satisfied has been used to designate one group of Ss, despite evidence from the interview material that some degree of ego satisfaction was achieved. To maintain a theoretical and experimental distinction between nonaggressiveness and ego satisfaction requires evidence that they differentially affect communication acceptance. The nonaggressive control group needed to determine this was unfortunately not included in the study.

The results are consonant with a frustration-aggression-displacement interpretation. The "failure" technique prevented achievement of a desired goal, and this reflected strongly on the per-

by reducing the difference between the aggressive and nonaggressive groups that read the article by the difference between the groups not reading the article.

[7] C. I. Hovland, A. A. Lumsdaine, and F. D. Sheffield, *Experiments on Mass Communications* (Princeton, N.J.: Princeton University Press, 1949).

son's self-image and self-esteem.[8] The accompanying insults facilitated the arousal of an externally directed aggression, which could not be expressed against the higher-status and more "powerful" instigator. This response predisposition aided the acceptance of a punitively oriented communication, which functioned as an outlet for the expression of aggression with little fear of punishment. Whether this displacement served to reduce the facilitating predisposition to be influenced by following aggressively oriented communications is not known. Previous theory [9] and research [10] suggest the possibility of such a consequence. If this did occur, a socially relevant, cathartic use of mass media can be conceived. Another implication is that the effectiveness of communications ordered on a leniency-aggressiveness dimension may be influenced by the immediately prior and consequent communication context.[11]

Some analysts of the genesis and maintenance of social prejudices have adopted in part an approach based on a frustration-aggression thesis.[12] The current findings are clearly relevant to such interpretations. However, the over-all influence of the communications regardless of experimental inductions should be kept in mind as a cautionary note. The presence of individual differences in response to the treatment-communication combinations must also be considered; with a larger sample, the extrapunitive score could have been used to produce adequate subgroups for reliable examination of the contribution of this response tendency to individual differences. Finally, the evidence is not available in this study for determining the effect of prior reduction in aggressive needs on response to communications.

Aggression arousal was not sufficient by itself to effect changes in opinions. This finding is not consonant with the data of Miller and Bugelski.[13] The different response methodology which they employed may be a factor contributing to the discrepant results. In their study, an increase in displaced aggression following a frustrating experience was evidenced by the assignment of favorable and unfavorable traits to certain nationality groups. This technique may be a more sensitive method than the elicitation of specific opinion responses on policy. Also, opinions on issues which have been in the focus of public attention or to which some prior thought has been given may be less susceptible to fluctuation without some communication pressure than those on topics without such characteristics. Given this qualification, our position is that aggression arousal predisposes a person to certain opinion

[8] A. H. Maslow, "Deprivation, Threat and Frustration," *Psychol. Rev.*, 1941, XLVIII, 337–352.
[9] J. Dollard, L. W. Doob, N. E. Miller, O. H. Mowrer, and R. R. Sears, *Frustration and Aggression* (New Haven, Conn.: Yale University Press, 1939).
[10] S. Feshbach, "The Drive-reducing Function of Fantasy Behavior," *J. Abnorm. & Soc. Psychol.*, 1955, L, 3–11; J. W. Thibaut and J. Coules, "The Role of Communication in the Reduction of Interpersonal Hostility," *J. Abnorm. & Soc. Psychol.*, 1952, XLVII, 770–777.
[11] S. H. Flowerman, "Mass Propaganda in the War against Bigotry," *J. Abnorm. & Soc. Psychol.*, 1947, XLII, 429–439.
[12] G. W. Allport, *The Nature of Prejudice* (Cambridge, Mass.: Addison-Wesley Co., Inc., 1954); B. Bettelheim and M. Janowitz, *Dynamics of Prejudice* (New York: Harper & Brothers, 1950); Dollard, Doob, Miller, Mowrer, and Sears, *op. cit.*; O. Fenichel, "Elements of a Psychoanalytic Theory of Anti-semitism," in E. Simmel (ed.), *Antisemitism: A Social Disease* (New York: International Universities Press, Inc., 1946), pp. 11–32; E. L. Horowitz, "Race Attitudes," in O. Klineberg (ed.), *Characteristics of the American Negro* (New York: Harper & Brothers, 1944), pp. 139–252.
[13] N. E. Miller and R. Bugelski, "Minor Studies in Aggression: The Influence of Frustration Imposed by the In-group on Attitudes Expressed toward Out-groups," *J. Psychol.*, 1948, XXV, 437–442.

changes; but for the predisposition to achieve significant specific effects, communication appeal is needed.

SUMMARY

The research was designed to test the hypotheses that aggressively aroused persons are influenced more by a punitively oriented communication and less by a leniency-oriented one than are persons not so aroused. A before-after design was employed. One main group was exposed to a failure-insult procedure to evoke aggressive tendencies, and the other group to an ego-satisfying experience. Then, one half of each group read a communication urging punitiveness toward delinquents and the other half read a communication suggesting leniency and consideration in America's relations with her allies. An immediate-after opinion questionnaire followed. After being informed of the nature of the experiment, the Ss were interviewed to determine their reactions to the procedures.

The data support the research hypotheses. Also, it was found that an instigation to aggression alone does not seem to affect opinions on leniency-punitive issues which are not dealt with by the communication read.

WHEN PROPHECY FAILS
By Leon Festinger, Henry W. Riecken, and Stanley Schachter

A man with a conviction is a hard man to change. Tell him you disagree and he turns away. Show him facts or figures and he questions your sources. Appeal to logic and he fails to see your point. We are familiar with the variety of ingenious defenses with which people protect their convictions, managing to keep them unscathed through the most devastating attacks.

But man's resourcefulness goes beyond simply protecting a belief. Suppose an individual believes something with his whole heart; suppose further that he has a commitment to this belief and that he has taken irrevocable actions because of it; finally, suppose that he is presented with evidence, unequivocal and undeniable evidence, that his belief is wrong: what will happen? The individual will frequently emerge, not only unshaken, but even more convinced of the truth of his beliefs than ever before. Indeed, he may even show a new fervor for convincing and converting other people to his view.

How and why does such a response to contradictory evidence come about? Let us begin by stating the conditions under which we would expect to observe increased fervor following the disconfirmation of a belief. There are five such conditions.

1. A belief must be held with deep conviction and it must have some relevance to action, that is, to what the believer does or how he behaves.

2. The person holding the belief must have committed himself to it; that is, for the sake of his belief, he must have taken some important action that is difficult to undo. In general, the more im-

Adapted and condensed from Leon Festinger, Henry W. Riecken, Jr., and Stanley Schachter; *When Prophecy Fails* (Minneapolis: University of Minnesota Press, 1956). The research reported here was supported by the Laboratory for Research in Social Relations at the University of Minnesota and by a grant-in-aid from the Ford Foundation. All the persons and places mentioned have been given fictitious names.

portant such actions and the more difficult they are to undo, the greater is the
individual's commitment to the belief.

3. The belief must be sufficiently specific and sufficiently concerned with the
real world so that events may unequivocally refute the belief.

4. Such undeniable disconfirmatory
evidence must occur and must be recognized by the individual holding the belief.

The first two of these conditions specify
the circumstances that will make the belief resistant to change. The third and
fourth conditions, on the other hand,
point to factors that would exert powerful pressure on a believer to discard his
belief. It is, of course, possible that an individual, even though deeply convinced
of a belief, may discard it in the face of
unequivocal disconfirmation. We must,
therefore, state a fifth condition specifying the circumstances under which it will
be maintained with new fervor.

5. The individual believer must have
social support. It is unlikely that one isolated believer could withstand the kind
of disconfirming evidence we have specified. If, however, the believer is a member of a group of convinced persons who
can support one another, we would expect the belief to be maintained and the
believers to attempt to proselytize or to
persuade nonmembers that the belief is
correct.

These five conditions specify the circumstances under which increased proselytizing would be expected to follow disconfirmation. Given this set of hypotheses, our immediate concern is to locate
data that will allow a test of the prediction of increased proselytizing. Fortunately, throughout history there have
been recurring instances of social movements which satisfy the conditions adequately. These are the millennial or messianic movements, a contemporary instance of which forms the basis for the
present study. Let us see just how such
movements do satisfy the five conditions
we have specified.

Typically, millennial or messianic
movements are organized around the
prediction of some future events. Our
conditions are satisfied, however, only
by those movements that specify a date
or an interval of time within which the
predicted events will occur as well as de-
tailing exactly what is to happen. Sometimes the predicted event is the second
coming of Christ and the beginning of
Christ's reign on earth; sometimes it is
the destruction of the world through a
cataclysm (usually with some select
group slated for rescue from the disaster); or sometimes the prediction is concerned with particular occurrences that
the messiah or a miracle worker will
bring about. Whatever the event predicted, the fact that its nature and the
time of its happening are specified satisfies the third point on our list of conditions.

The second condition specifies strong
behavioral commitment to the belief.
This usually follows almost as a consequence of the situation. If one really believes a prediction (the first condition),
for example, that on a given date the
world will be destroyed by fire, that the
sinners will die and the good be saved, he
does things about it and makes certain
preparations as a matter of course. These
actions may range all the way from
simple public declarations to the neglect
of worldly things and the disposal of
earthly possessions. Through such actions and through the mocking and scoff-
ing of nonbelievers, the believers usually
establish a heavy commitment. What
they do by way of preparation is difficult
to undo, and the jeering of nonbelievers
simply makes it far more difficult for the
adherents to withdraw from the movement and admit that they were wrong.

Our fourth specification has invariably
been provided. The predicted events
have not occurred. There is usually no
mistaking the fact that they did not
occur and the believers know that. In
other words, the unequivocal disconfir-

mation does materialize and makes its impact on the believers.

Finally, our fifth condition is ordinarily satisfied—such movements do attract adherents and disciples, sometimes only a handful, occasionally hundreds of thousands. The reasons why people join such movements are outside the scope of our present discussion, but the fact remains that there are usually one or more groups of believers who can support one another.

History has recorded many such movements. Ever since the crucifixion of Jesus, many Christians have hoped for the second coming of Christ and movements predicting specific dates for this event have not been rare. However, most of the very early ones were not recorded in such a fashion that we can be sure of the reactions of believers to the disconfirmations they may have experienced. Occasionally historians make passing reference to such reactions as does Hughes in his description of the Montanists:

Montanus, who appeared in the second half of the second century, does not appear as an innovator in matters of belief. His one personal contribution to the life of the time was the fixed conviction that the second coming of Our Lord was at hand. The event was to take place at Pepuza—near the modern Angora—and thither all true followers of Our Lord should make their way. His authority for the statement was an alleged private inspiration, and the new prophet's personality and eloquence won him a host of disciples, who flocked in such numbers to the appointed spot that a new town sprang up to house them. *Nor did the delay of the second advent put an end to the movement. On the contrary, it gave it new life and form* as a kind of Christianity of the elite, whom no other authority guided in their new life but the Holy Spirit working directly upon them. . . . [Italics ours.]

In this brief statement are all the essential elements of the typical messianic movement. There are convinced fol-lowers; they commit themselves by uprooting their lives and going to a new place where they build a new town; the Second Advent does not occur. And, we note, far from halting the movement, this disconfirmation gives it new life.

Why does increased proselytizing follow the disconfirmation of a prediction? How can we explain it, and what are the factors that will determine whether or not it will occur? For our explanation, we shall introduce the concepts of consonance and dissonance.

Dissonance and consonance are relations among cognitions—that is, among opinions, beliefs, knowledge of the environment, and knowledge of one's own actions and feelings. Two opinions, or beliefs, or items of knowledge are dissonant with each other if they do not fit together—that is, if they are inconsistent, or if, considering only the particular two items, one does not follow from the other. For example, a cigarette smoker who believes that smoking is bad for his health has an opinion that is dissonant with the knowledge that he is continuing to smoke.

Dissonance produces discomfort and, correspondingly, there will arise attempts to reduce dissonance. Such attempts may take any or all of three forms. The person may try to change one or more of the beliefs, opinions, or behaviors involved in the dissonance; to acquire new information or beliefs that will increase the existing consonance and thus cause the total dissonance to be reduced; or to forget or reduce the importance of those cognitions that are in a dissonant relationship.

If any of these attempts is to be successful, it must be met with support from either the physical or the social environment. In the absence of such support, the most determined efforts to reduce dissonance may be unsuccessful.

Theoretically, then, what is the situation of the individual believer at the pre-disconfirmation stage of a messianic movement? He has a strongly held belief in a prediction—for example, that Christ will return—a belief that is supported by the other members of the movement. By way of preparation for the predicted event, he has engaged in many activities that are entirely consistent with his belief. In other words, most of the relations among relevant cognitions are, at this point, consonant.

Now what is the effect of the disconfirmation, of the unequivocal fact that the prediction was wrong, upon the believer? The disconfirmation introduces an important and painful dissonance. The fact that the predicted events did not occur is dissonant with continuing to believe both the prediction and the remainder of the ideology of which the prediction was the central item. The failure of the prediction is also dissonant with all the actions that the believer took in preparation for its fulfillment. The magnitude of the dissonance will, of course, depend on the importance of the belief to the individual and on the magnitude of his preparatory activity.

In the type of movement we have discussed, the central belief and its accompanying ideology are usually of crucial importance in the believers' lives and hence the dissonance is very strong—and very painful to tolerate. Accordingly, we should expect to observe believers making determined efforts to eliminate the dissonance or, at least, to reduce its magnitude. How may they accomplish this end? The dissonance would be largely eliminated if they discarded the belief that had been disconfirmed, ceased the behavior which had been initiated in preparation for the fulfillment of the prediction, and returned to a more usual existence. Indeed, this pattern sometimes occurs. But frequently the behavioral commitment to the belief system is so strong that almost any other course of action is preferable. It may even be less painful to tolerate the dissonance than to discard the belief and admit one had been wrong. When that is the case, dis-

sonance cannot be eliminated by abandoning the belief.

Alternatively, the dissonance would be reduced or eliminated if the members of a movement effectively blind themselves to the fact that the prediction has not been fulfilled. But most people, including members of such movements, are in touch with reality and simply cannot blot out of their cognition such an unequivocal and undeniable fact. They can try to ignore it, however, and they usually do try. They may convince themselves that the date was wrong but that the prediction will, after all, be shortly confirmed; or they may even set another date. Believers may try to find reasonable explanations, very often ingenious ones, for the failure of their prediction. Rationalization can reduce dissonance somewhat, but for rationalization to be fully effective, support from others is needed to make the explanation or the revision seem correct. Fortunately, the disappointed believer can usually turn to others in the same movement, who have the same dissonance and the same pressures to reduce it. Support for the new explanation is, hence, forthcoming and the members of the movement can recover somewhat from the shock of the disconfirmation.

Whatever the explanation, it is still by itself not sufficient. The dissonance is too important and though they may try to hide it, even from themselves, the believers still know that the prediction was false and all their preparations were in vain. The dissonance cannot be eliminated completely by denying or rationalizing the disconfirmation. There is, however, a way in which the remaining dissonance can be reduced. *If more and more people can be persuaded that the system of belief is correct, then clearly it must after all, be correct.* It is for this reason that we observe the increase in proselytizing following disconfirmation. If the proselytizing proves successful, then by gathering more adherents and effectively surrounding himself with supporters the believer reduces dissonance to the point where he can live with it.

In the light of this explanation of the phenomenon that proselyting increases as a result of a disconfirmation, we sought a modern instance of disconfirmation, an instance which could be observed closely enough so that our explanation could be put to an empirical test.

One day at the end of September the Lake City *Herald* carried a two-column story, on a back page, headlined: PROPHECY FROM PLANET. CLARION CALL TO CITY: FLEE THAT FLOOD. IT'LL SWAMP US ON DEC. 21, OUTER SPACE TELLS SUBURBANITE. The body of the story expanded somewhat on these bare facts:

Lake City will be destroyed by a flood from Great Lake just before dawn, Dec. 21, according to a suburban housewife. Mrs. Marian Keech, of 847 West School street, says the prophecy is not her own. It is the purport of many messages she has received by automatic writing, she says. . . . The messages, according to Mrs. Keech, are sent to her by superior beings from a planet called "Clarion." These beings have been visiting the earth, she says, in what we call flying saucers. During their visits, she says, they have observed fault lines in the earth's crust that foretoken the deluge. Mrs. Keech reports she was told the flood will spread to form an inland sea stretching from the Arctic Circle to the Gulf of Mexico. At the same time, she says, a cataclysm will submerge the West Coast from Seattle, Wash., to Chile in South America.

Since Mrs. Keech's pronouncement made a specific prediction of a specific event, since she, at least, was publicly committed to belief in it, and since she was apparently interested to some extent in informing a wider public about it, this seemed to be an opportunity to conduct a "field" test of the theoretical ideas to which the reader has been introduced. Therefore, the authors joined Mrs. Keech's group in early October and re-mained in constant touch with it throughout the events to be narrated here.

About nine months before the newspaper story appeared, Marian Keech had begun to receive messages in "automatic writing" from beings who said they existed in outer space and were instructing her to act as their representative to warn the people of earth of the coming cataclysm. Mrs. Keech told many of her friends and acquaintances of her messages, and by September had attracted a small following of believers. Among them was Dr. Thomas Armstrong, a physician who lived in a college town in a nearby state. Dr. Armstrong spread the word among a group of students ("The Seekers") who met at his home regularly to discuss spiritual problems and cosmology. Dr. Armstrong and his wife also visited Lake City frequently to attend meetings of Mrs. Keech's group there.

Throughout the fall months the groups in Lake City and Collegeville held a series of meetings to discuss the lessons from outer space and to prepare themselves for salvation from cataclysm. As December 21 drew near some members gave up their jobs, others gave away their possessions, and nearly all made public declarations of their conviction. In September, Dr. Armstrong had prepared two "news releases" about the prediction of flood, although Mrs. Keech had not sought any publicity herself and had given only the one interview to the Lake City reporter who called on her after he had seen one of Dr. Armstrong's news releases. Except for that interview, Mrs. Keech had confined her proselyting to friends and acquaintances, and Dr. Armstrong had virtually limited his activities to "The Seekers." During October and November, a policy of increasingly strict secrecy about the beliefs and activities of the believers had been developing in both Collegeville and Lake City.

In December, Dr. Armstrong was dismissed from his hospital post, and the ac tion brought him nation-wide publicity. Had the group been interested in carrying their message to the world and securing new converts, they would have been presented with a priceless opportunity on December 16 when representatives of the nation's major news-reporting services converged on the Keech home, hungry for a story to follow up the news break on Dr. Armstrong's dismissal from the college. But the press received a cold, almost hostile reception, and their most persistent efforts were resisted. In two days of constant vigil, the newspapermen succeeded in winning only one brief broadcast tape and one interview with Dr. Armstrong and Mrs. Keech—and that only after a reporter had virtually threatened to print his own version of their beliefs. A cameraman who surreptitiously violated the believers' prohibition against taking photographs was threatened with a lawsuit. Between December 16 and the early morning of December 21, the Keech home was the object of a barrage of telephone calls and a steady stream of visitors who came seeking enlightenment or even offering themselves for conversion. The telephone calls from reporters were answered by a flat, unqualified "No comment." The visitors, mostly potential converts, were paid the most casual attention and the believers made only sporadic attempts to explain their views to these inquirers.

By the late afternoon of December 20 —the eve of the predicted cataclysm— the hullaballoo in the house had died down somewhat, and the believers began making their final preparations for salvation. Late that morning, Mrs. Keech had received a message instructing the group to be ready to receive a visitor who would arrive at midnight and escort them to a parked flying saucer that would whisk them away from the flood to a place of safety, presumably in outer space. Early in the evening, the ten believers from Lake City and Collegeville had begun rehearsing for their departure.

First, they went through the ritual to be followed when their escort arrived at midnight. Dr. Armstrong was to act as sentry and, having made sure of the caller's identity, admit him. The group drilled carefully on the ritual responses they would make to the specific challenges of their unearthly visitor, and the passwords they would have to give in boarding the saucer. Next, the believers removed all metal from their persons. The messages from outer space left no doubt in anyone's mind that it would be extremely dangerous to travel in a saucer while wearing or carrying anything metallic, and all of the group complied painstakingly with this order—excepting only the fillings in their teeth.

The last ten minutes before midnight were tense ones for the group assembled in Mrs. Keech's living room. They had nothing to do but sit and wait, their coats in their laps. In the silence two clocks ticked loudly, one about ten minutes faster than the other. When the faster clock pointed to 12:05, someone remarked about the time aloud. A chorus of people replied that midnight had not yet come. One member affirmed that the slower clock was correct; he had set it himself only that afternoon. It showed only four minutes before midnight.

Those four minutes passed in complete silence except for a single utterance. When the (slower) clock on the mantel showed only one minute remaining before the guide to the saucer was due, Mrs. Keech exclaimed in a strained, high-pitched voice: "And not a plan has gone astray!" The clock chimed twelve, each stroke painfully clear in the expectant hush. The believers sat motionless.

One might have expected some visible reaction, as the minutes passed. Midnight had come and gone, and nothing had happened. The cataclysm itself was less than seven hours away. But there was little to see in the reactions of the people in that room. There was no talking, nor sound of any sort. People sat stock still, their faces seemingly frozen and expressionless.

Gradually, painfully, an atmosphere of despair and confusion settled over the group. They re-examined the prediction and the accompanying messages. Dr. Armstrong and Mrs. Keech reiterated their faith. The believers mulled over their predicament and discarded explanation after explanation as unsatisfactory. At one point, toward 4 A.M., Mrs. Keech broke down and cried bitterly. She knew, she sobbed, that there were some who were beginning to doubt but that the group must beam light to those who needed it most, and that the group must hold together. The rest of the believers were losing their composure, too. They were all visibly shaken and many were close to tears. It was now almost 4:30 A.M. and still no way of handling the disconfirmation had been found. By now, too, most of the group were talking openly about the failure of the escort to come at midnight. The group seemed near dissolution.

But this atmosphere did not continue long. At about 4:45 A.M. Mrs. Keech summoned everyone to attention, announcing that she had just received a message. She then read aloud these momentous words: "For this day it is established that there is but one God of Earth and He is in thy midst, and from his hand thou hast written these words. And mighty is the word of God—and by his word have ye been saved—for from the mouth of death have ye been delivered and at no time has there been such a force loosed upon the Earth. Not since the beginning of time upon this Earth has there been such a force of Good and light as now floods this room and that which has been loosed within this room now floods the entire Earth. As thy God has spoken through the two who sit within these walls has he manifested that which he had given thee to do."

This message was received with enthusiasm. It was an adequate, even an ele-

gant, explanation of the disconfirmation. The cataclysm had been called off. The little group, sitting all night long, had spread so much light that God had saved the world from destruction.

The atmosphere in the group changed abruptly and so did their behavior. Within minutes after she had read the message explaining the disconfirmation, Mrs. Keech received another message instructing her to publicize the explanation. She reached for the telephone and began dialing the number of a newspaper. While she was waiting to be connected, someone asked: "Marian, is this the first time you have called the newspaper yourself?" Her reply was immediate: "Oh, yes, this is the first time I have ever called them. I have never had anything to tell them before, but now I feel it is urgent." The whole group could have echoed her feelings, for they all felt a sense of urgency. As soon as Marian had finished her call, the other members took turns telephoning newspapers, wire services, radio stations, and national magazines to spread the explanation of the failure of the flood. In their desire to spread the word quickly and resoundingly, the believers now opened for public attention matters that had been thus far utterly secret. Where only hours earlier they had shunned newspaper reporters and felt that the attention they were getting in the press was painful, they now became avid seekers of publicity. During the rest of December 21, the believers thrust themselves willingly before microphones, talked freely to reporters, and enthusiastically proselytized the visitors and inquirers who called at the house. In the ensuing days they made new bids for attention. Mrs. Keech made further predictions of visits by spacemen and invited newspapermen to witness the event. Like the millennial groups of history, this one, too, reacted to disconfirmation by standing firm in their beliefs and doubling their efforts to win converts. The believers in Lake City clearly displayed the reaction to disconfirmation that our theory predicted.

Among the members of the Collegeville group who had not gone to Lake City for the flood, matters took quite a different turn. Most of them were students who had gone to their homes for Christmas vacation. All but two of them spent December 20 and 21 in isolation from each other, surrounded by unbelievers. These isolates reacted to the disconfirmation in a very different fashion from their fellows in Lake City. Instead of recovering from the initial shock of disconfirmation, they either gave up their beliefs completely or found their conviction seriously weakened. There was no upsurge of proselytizing among the stay-at-homes in "The Seekers" even after they had been informed of the message rationalizing the disconfirmation. Indeed, the reverse seems to have occurred in two cases where the individuals attempted to conceal their membership in "The Seekers." Thus, most of the Collegeville group reduced the dissonance created by disconfirmation by giving up all their beliefs, whereas in Lake City the members held fast and tried to create a supportive circle of believers.

The comparison of the two situations —Lake City and Collegeville—permits at least a crude test of the importance of one element of the theory proposed to explain the proselyting reaction to disconfirmation: namely, the element of social support. In Lake City, most of the members were in the constant presence of fellow believers during the period immediately following disconfirmation. They had social support; they were able to accept the rationalization; and they regained confidence in their beliefs. On the other hand, all of the members of the Collegeville group, with the exception of one pair, faced the morning of December 21 and the following days either with people who neither agreed nor disagreed or with people who were openly opposed to the views of "The Seekers." It would seem that the presence of supporting cobelievers is an indispensable requirement for recovery from disconfirmation.

At the beginning of this article, we specified the conditions under which disconfirmation would lead to increased proselytizing and, for most of the members of the Lake City group, these specifications were satisfied. Most of them believed in Mrs. Keech's prediction and were heavily committed to this belief. Disconfirmation was unequivocal, and the attempted rationalization by itself was never completely successful in dispelling dissonance. Finally, the members of the group faced disconfirmation and its aftermath together. The members responded with strong, persistent attempts at proselytizing. Among "The Seekers," all the conditions were the same except that the supportive group of cobelievers was missing. Among these isolates there was no increase in proselyting, no attempt to seek publicity, but rather their characteristic response was to give up their belief and even to conceal their earlier membership.

SOME REASONS WHY INFORMATION CAMPAIGNS FAIL
By Herbert H. Hyman and Paul B. Sheatsley

To assume a perfect correspondence between the nature and amount of material presented in an information campaign and its absorption by the public, is to take a naïve view, for the very nature and degree of public exposure to the material is determined to a large extent by certain psychological characteristics of the people themselves.[1] A number of these psychological characteristics are discussed below under the following topics:

The Chronic "Know-Nothings" in Relation to Information Campaigns
The Role of Interest in Increasing Exposure
Selective Exposure Produced by Prior Attitudes
Selective Interpretation Following Exposure
Differential Changes in Attitudes after Exposure

THERE EXISTS A HARD CORE OF CHRONIC "KNOW-NOTHINGS"

All persons do not offer equal targets for information campaigns. Surveys consistently find that a certain proportion of the population is not familiar with any particular event. Offhand, it might be thought that information concerning that event was not distributed broadly enough to reach them, but that this group would still have an equal chance of exposure to other information. Yet, when the knowledge of this same group is measured with respect to a second event, they tend also to have little information in that area. And similarly, they will have little or no information concerning a third event.

If all persons provided equal targets for exposure, and the sole determinant of public knowledge were the magnitude of the given information, there would be no reason for the same individuals always to show a relative lack of knowledge. *Instead, there is something about the uninformed which makes them harder to reach, no matter what the level or nature of the information.*

Thus, in May 1946, National Opinion Research Center (NORC) asked a question to determine public knowledge of the report of the Anglo-American Committee on Palestine which recommended the admission of 100,000 Jewish immigrants to that country. Only 28 percent of the national sample expressed any awareness of this report. It might be assumed that the remaining 72 percent were ready and willing to be exposed, but that there had been too little information about the report. Yet Table 1 shows that this unaware group consistently tended to have less awareness of other information about the international scene which had been much more widely reported.

The size of this generally uninformed group in the population may be indicated by computing an index of general knowledge based on all five information questions in the field of foreign affairs, which were asked on that particular survey. The five subjects covered by these questions were:

1. The Palestine report spoken of above [1][2]

From *The Public Opinion Quarterly,* 1947, XI, 413–423. Reprinted by permission of the authors and Princeton University Press.

[1] For a theoretical discussion of the problem, see Daniel Katz, "Psychological Barriers to Communication," *The Annals,* March 1947.

[2] Figures in brackets refer to actual question-wordings which are reported in the note at the end of this article.

TABLE 1

Group	Percent aware of		
	Acheson report	Foreign ministers' meeting, Paris 1946	Proposed loan to England
Not aware of Palestine report (N − 931)	32	39	73
Aware of Palestine report (N = 358)	64	85	96

2. The Acheson-Lilienthal report on atomic energy [2]
3. The Paris meeting of the Big Four foreign ministers, then in progress [3]
4. The proposed loan to England, then being debated in Congress [4]
5. The political status of Palestine, the fact that she is ruled by England [5]

TABLE 2

Aware of	Percent of national sample
No items	14
One item	18
Two items	20
Three items	17
Four items	19
Five items	12
Total sample (N = 1,292) .	100

Table 2 shows how the population divided in its awareness of these five items. As may be seen, roughly one person out of seven reported no awareness of *any* of the five items, and approximately one person in three had knowledge of no more than *one* of them. This generally uninformed group, therefore, is of considerable magnitude.[3] It is possible, of course, that the existence of this group may be related to external factors of accessibility to information media, and that if the information were somehow channeled into their vicinity, they would soon become exposed. For example, information on foreign affairs is probably less easily available to small-town residents than it is to city-dwellers, and we find a relationship, as shown in Table 3, between size of community and awareness of our five items. These differences, however, are relatively small, in comparison with the psychological differences to be shown later in Table 4 and elsewhere. The next section discusses the effect of certain psychological factors on level of knowledge.

TABLE 3

Size of community	Mean score on knowledge index numbers of items known
Metropolitan districts over 1,000,000	2.81
Metropolitan districts under 1,000,000	2.45
Cities 2,500 to 50,000 . . .	2.38
Towns under 2,500	2.28
Farm	2.03

[3] If anything, the size of the group is underrepresented, for two reasons: (1) the respondent's claim to awareness was accepted at face value, without any check on his actual knowledge; (2) polls consistently tend to oversample the more literate, higher socio-economic groups in the population.

INTERESTED PEOPLE ACQUIRE THE MOST INFORMATION

The importance of *motivation* in a-chievement or learning, or in assimilating knowledge, has been consistently shown in academic studies. Yet this important factor is often ignored in information campaigns, amid all the talk of "increasing the flow of information." The widest possible dissemination of material may be ineffective if it is not geared to the public's interests.

It is well known that opinion polls can measure areas of knowledge and ignorance, but the complementary areas of apathy and interest have been more often overlooked. Yet they can be just as readily measured, and they are highly significant in understanding the factors behind a given level of knowledge.

NORC, in a poll taken in May 1946, measured the public's interest in eight different issues in the field of foreign affairs [6]. These issues were:

1. Our relations with Russia
2. The atomic bomb
3. Our policy toward Germany
4. The United Nations organization
5. The British loan
6. The meeting of foreign ministers in Paris
7. Our relations with Franco Spain
8. Our policy toward Palestine

Public interest varied widely in these eight issues, ranging from 77 percent of the national sample which reported "considerable" or "great" interest in our relations with Russia to 28 percent which reported "considerable" or "great" interest in our policy toward Palestine. Thus, it is clear that each specific information campaign does not start with the same handicap in terms of public apathy. Motivation is high on some issues, low on others.

Nevertheless, there is consistent evidence that interest in foreign affairs tends to be *generalized*. Some people are inter-

TABLE 4

Degree of interest	Percent of total sample expressing degree of interest
High	37
All eight issues . .	11
Seven issues . . .	11
Six issues	15
Medium	40
Five issues	15
Four issues . . .	14
Three issues . . .	11
Low	23
Two issues	7
One issue	5
None	11
Total sample (N = 1,292) . . .	100

ested in many or all of the issues; another large group is apathetic toward most or all of them. Intercorrelations (based on approximately 1290 cases) between interest in one issue and interest in each of the other seven, definitely establish this point. The 28 tetrachoric correlation coefficients range from .40 to .82, with a median r of .58. Table 4 shows how the population divides in its interest in these eight issues.

It will be noticed that 11 percent of the sample expressed little or no interest in any of the eight issues, and that another 12 percent were interested in only one or two of them. Almost one quarter of the population, therefore, reported interest in no more than two of the eight issues—a state of apathy all the more significant when it is remembered that the list included such overpowering subjects as the atomic bomb and our relations with Germany and Russia, and that the respondent's own estimate of his degree of interest, doubtless subject to prestige considerations, was accepted without question.

The close relationship between apathy on the one hand, and ignorance of infor-

TABLE 5

Respondents with	Percent who have heard of	
	Acheson report on atomic energy	Anglo-American report on Palestine
Great or considerable interest in atomic bomb (N = 953)	48	
Little or no interest in atomic bomb (N = 337)	20	
Great or considerable interest in Palestine policy (N = 365)		51
Little or no interest in Palestine policy (N = 921)		19

mation materials on the other, is shown in Table 5. It is a likely assumption that both the contrasted groups in the table had equal *opportunity* to learn about the two reports. Yet the information reached approximately half of the interested group, and only about one fifth of the disinterested.[4]

The relationship between interest and knowledge can be demonstrated in a different way, if we compare the scores of each of our interest groups on our knowledge index. As seen in Table 6, at

TABLE 6

Interested in	Mean score on knowledge index
No items	.85
One item	1.42
Two items.	1.12
Three items	1.89
Four items	2.37
Five items	2.64
Six items	3.15
Seven items	3.50
Eight items	3.81

each stage of increasing interest, knowledge rises correspondingly.

It can be argued, of course, that the exposed people became interested after they had been exposed to the information, and that the disinterested persons were apathetic only because they were not exposed. It is probable that the two factors *are* interdependent; as people learn more, their interest increases, and as their interest increases, they are impelled to learn more. Nevertheless, from the point of view of initiating a *specific* campaign at some point in time, it remains true that in the case even of outstanding public issues, large groups in the population admit "little or no interest" in the problem.

This fact cannot be ignored by those in charge of information campaigns. Such groups constitute a special problem which cannot be solved simply by "increasing the flow of information." *Scientific surveys are needed to determine who these people are, why they lack interest, and what approach can best succeed in reaching them.*

PEOPLE SEEK INFORMATION
CONGENIAL TO PRIOR ATTITUDES

Information campaigns, while they involve the presentation of *facts*, never-

[4] Lazarsfeld reports a similar finding on the relationship of interest to exposure to political information. See Lazarsfeld, Berelson, and Gaudet, *The People's Choice* (New York: Duell, Sloan & Pearce, 1944), p. 79.

TABLE 7

Respondents with	Percent of those with opinions who favor	
	U.S. aid in keeping order in Palestine	Breaking relations with Franco
Previous knowledge of committee report (N = 339)	36	
No previous knowledge (N = 805) . . .	30	
Previous knowledge of three-power statement (N = 657)		32
No previous knowledge (N = 268) . . .		21

theless present materials which may or may not be congenial with the attitudes of any given individual. Lazarsfeld,[5] in describing the exposure of a sample panel to political campaign propaganda, concludes that "People selected political material in accord with their own taste and bias. Even those who had not yet made a decision (on their vote) exposed themselves to propaganda which fit their not-yet-conscious political predispositions."

Our evidence from polling national samples in other information areas supports the view that people tend to expose themselves to information which is congenial with their prior attitudes, and to avoid exposure to information which is not congenial. Although it was not possible to administer before-and-after tests of attitudes, the following technique offers indirect evidence to support the argument of selective exposure.

National samples were asked if they had heard or read anything about a given piece of information. The entire sample was then given the gist of the information in one or two sentences. (In the case of those who had admitted familiarity with the material, the description was prefaced by some small phrase as, "Well, as you

remember . . . .") Immediately following the description of the information, the entire sample was then asked some relevant attitude question.

We found in every case that the group who reported prior exposure to the information had a different attitudinal reaction from those without prior exposure. One could assume that this difference reflected the influence of the information on those previously exposed, except that, as described above, *both groups*, before being asked the attitude question, had been supplied with identical descriptions of the information in question.

Thus, in June 1946, a national sample of the adult population was asked whether they had heard or read about the Anglo-American Committee report on Palestine [1]. Every respondent was then either told or reminded of the essential provisions of the report, and was asked whether he favored United States assistance in keeping order in Palestine if 100,000 additional Jews were admitted to that country [7]. As seen in Table 7, those with prior knowledge of the report were inclined to be more favorable toward such assistance.

Similarly, in April 1946, a national sample was asked whether they had

[5] Lazarsfeld, Berelson, and Gaudet, *op. cit.*, p. 80.

heard or read about the recent joint statement by England, France, and the United States which denounced the Franco government of Spain [8]. Included in the question was the gist of the statement: "the hope that General Franco's government in Spain would soon be followed by a more democratic one." The entire sample was then asked its attitude toward this country's Spanish policy [9]. Again, those who had prior knowledge of the three-power statement were significantly more hostile in their attitudes toward Franco. See Table 7.

It is true that those who learned about the report or statement for the first time during the interview were more inclined to offer no opinion when questioned on their attitudes, but the above table excludes the "No opinion" group, and comparisons are based only on those with definite opinions.

The differences reported, which are in all likelihood not due to chance, suggest the phenomenon of "selective exposure" to information. In both cases, every respondent was aware of the contents of the statement or report when he answered the question on policy. Yet in each case, those with *prior* knowledge of the information had significantly different attitudes. It would appear, therefore, that persons reached by the Palestine report were those who were more likely in the first place to favor United States assistance there, rather than that they favored U.S. assistance because they were familiar with the information contained in the report. Similarly, it would seem that the group which had prior knowledge of the statement on Spain was already more anti-Franco in their attitudes, rather than that they became more anti-Franco by virtue of exposure.

The fact that people tend to become exposed to information which is congenial with their prior attitudes is another factor which must be considered by those in charge of information campaigns. Merely "increasing the flow" is not enough, if the information continues to "flow" in the direction of those already on your side!

PEOPLE INTERPRET THE SAME INFORMATION DIFFERENTLY

It has just been shown that it is false to assume a perfect correspondence between public exposure to information and the amount of material distributed. It is equally false to assume that exposure, once achieved, results in a uniform interpretation and retention of the material.

In a series of experimental studies beginning with the work of Bartlett,[6] and carried on by a host of other investigators such as Margolies,[7] Clark,[8] Nadel,[9] and Murphy,[10] it has been consistently demonstrated that a person's perception and memory of materials shown to him are often distorted by his wishes, motives, and attitudes. One demonstration of these general psychological findings in the area of international affairs is available in a recent NORC survey.

In September 1946, a national sample was asked whether they thought that the newspapers *they read* made Russia out to look better than she really is, worse than she really is, or whether they

---

[6] F. C. Bartlett, *Remembering* (New York: Macmillan Co., 1932).

[7] B. Margolies (unpublished M.A. thesis, Columbia University, New York City).

[8] K. Clark, "Some Factors Influencing the Remembering of Prose Material," *Archives of Psychology*, 1940, No. 253.

[9] S. F. Nadel, "A Field Experiment in Racial.Psychology," *British Journal of Psychology*, 1937, XXVIII, 195–211.

[10] G. Murphy and J. M. Levine, "The Learning and Forgetting of Controversial Material," *Journal of Abnormal and Social Psychology*, 1943, XXXVIII, 507–518.

TABLE 8

Respondents who	Percent who say their newspapers make Russia look worse than she really is
Blame Russia entirely for Russian-American disagreements (N = 458)	41
Blame United States entirely or blame both countries (N = 168)	54

presented accurate information about Russia [10]. The same survey also asked a question to determine where the respondent put the blame for Russian-American disagreements [11]. When the sample was classified into two groups—those who blamed Russia entirely and those who put the responsibility on both countries or on the United States alone—there were revealed striking differences in beliefs as to whether Russia was being presented fairly or unfairly in the newspapers they read (see Table 8). It is clear from this finding that people selectively discount the information they are exposed to, in the light of their prior attitudes.

The finding is all the more striking when one considers the fact that people tend to read the particular newspapers which are congenial to their own attitudes and beliefs. Thus, one would expect the anti-Russian group to be reading newspapers which, if studied by means of objective content analysis, would be found to slant their editorial content against Russia. Similarly, one would expect the pro-Russian group to read newspapers which, if measured objectively, would be found to emphasize favorable news about Russia. Despite this, the anti-Russian group is *less* likely to say *their* newspapers present Russia unfavorably, while the pro-Russian group is *more* likely to say *their* newspapers present Russia unfavorably.

Here, then, is another pyschological problem that faces those responsible for information campaigns. Exposure in itself is not always sufficient. People will interpret the information in different ways, according to their prior attitudes.

INFORMATION DOES NOT NECESSARILY CHANGE ATTITUDES

The principle behind all information campaigns is that the disseminated information will alter attitudes or conduct. There is abundant evidence in all fields, of course, that informed people actually do react differently to a problem than uninformed people do. But it is naïve to suppose that information always affects attitudes, or that it affects all attitudes equally. The general principle needs serious qualification.

There is evidence, based on investigations made with academic samples, that individuals, once they are exposed to information, change their views *differentially*, each in the light of his own *prior* attitude. Data gathered by NORC in recent national surveys show that these academic findings are equally applicable to the entire adult population.

In a continuing study of attitudes toward the proposed British loan, conducted between December 1945 and February 1946, it was found that a significant factor influencing attitudes toward the loan was the belief that this country would or would not get something out of it economically [12]. As shown by Table 9, those who were of the opinion that the loan held advantages

TABLE 9

Respondents who feel	Percent who approve loan to England
We will get advantages from the loan (N = 265)	66
Don't know if advantages (N = 291)	29
We will not get advantages (N = 294)	20

to this country were strongly in favor, while those of a contrary opinion, or doubtful, were overwhelmingly opposed to the loan.

Furthermore, 39 percent of those who expressed approval of the loan mentioned some economic advantage as their reason, while 75 percent of those opposed listed an economic argument. Under these circumstances, it was logical to suppose that attitudes could be changed toward approval of the loan, by informing the public of its economic advantages to the United States. It was not possible to conduct a before-and-after test of this thesis, but some interesting findings were revealed by a study of two equivalent samples which were polled simultaneously.

One of these samples was given the appropriate information before being questioned on their attitude. They were told that England had agreed to pay the money back with interest over a period of years, and that England had further agreed to take definite steps to remove restrictions on her trade with us and to join us in promoting world trade in general.[11] They were then asked whether they approved or disapproved of lending England the specified amount [13]. This was the experimental sample. The control sample was simply asked whether they approved or disapproved of the proposed loan, on the basis of what they had heard about it, with no additional information supplied them [4].

The experiment proved that the given information did materially change attitudes toward the loan. The experimental sample registered a 14 percent higher "Approve" vote than did the equivalent control sample which was not given the information. But this over-all comparison obscured the *differential* effect of the information.

For example, there was no difference between the two samples in the proportion of "Disapprovers" who gave an economic argument for their disapproval. Fifty-one percent of those in the control group who were opposed gave as their reason that "England won't pay us back," and 50 percent of those in the experimental group who were opposed offered the same argument—in spite of the fact that they had been specifically informed of England's agreement to return the money with interest. It was apparent that a large group of those opposed to the loan were rooted to their belief that the money would not be repaid, and the mere information that England had *agreed* to repay the loan was of no effect in changing their attitudes.

Table 10 shows another significant differential effect of the information. Among those who were already favorably disposed toward England, the information given to the experimental group was sufficient to sway a large proportion toward approval of the loan [14]. Less than half of this group friendly to England favored the loan in the control

---

[11] This sample was also informed that President Truman had asked Congress to approve the loan, an additional prestige factor probably having some persuasive effect.

TABLE 10

Group	Percent approving loan among those who	
	Trust England to cooperate with us	Do not trust England to cooperate with us
Control sample not exposed to information (N = 619)	45 (N = 619)	17 (N = 231)
Experimental sample exposed to information	70 (N = 242)	18 (N = 133)

sample, but in the experimental sample, which was given the information, the proportion rises to 70 percent. But among those with hostile or suspicious attitudes toward England, the information had *no effect whatever*. This group was overwhelmingly opposed to the loan without the information, and they remained overwhelmingly opposed to it even when they were exposed to the information.

CONCLUSIONS

The above findings indicate clearly that those responsible for information campaigns cannot rely simply on "increasing the flow" to spread their information effectively. The psychological barriers we have pointed out create real problems for those charged with the task of informing the public, and in many cases public-opinion surveys offer the only means by which these problems can be recognized, and thereby overcome.

Surveys are already widely used to provide the information director with scientific knowledge of the quantitative distribution of his material. They can tell him how many people have been reached by his information and, more important, which particular groups have not been reached. Surveys, too, can quite easily measure public interest in information materials and areas, thus providing him with accurate knowledge of the handicaps

his program faces within various population groups.

But on a different and higher level, surveys can inform the information director of the whole structure of attitudes on any public issue. They can tell him the major factors affecting public opinion on the issue, and the relative influence of these various factors in determining attitudes. They can tell to what extent information has reached the public and how far it has changed existing opinions. They can also tell what information is still needed and what aspects of it must be stressed in order to reach the unexposed or unsympathetic groups.

Psychological barriers to information campaigns are readily admitted by those who stop to consider the point, but they seem often to be overlooked in the general eagerness simply to distribute *more* information. The data we have cited in this paper are merely those which happen to be available from recent NORC surveys, but the kinds of barriers we have mentioned apply eternally to all types of public information. By documenting the very real effects that these psychological barriers have on public exposure to and interpretation of information materials, we hope we will encourage a proportionately greater attention to these intangible factors on the part of those who plan and carry out programs involving mass communication.

NOTE—QUESTIONS REFERRED TO
IN TEXT OF ARTICLE

1. Did you hear or read anything about the recent report by the Anglo-American Committee on Palestine?
2. Did you hear or read anything about the report on the control of atomic energy, which was published by the State Department a few weeks ago? It's sometimes called the Acheson report.
3. Have you heard or read anything about the recent meeting in Paris where Secretary of State Byrnes has been talking with the foreign ministers of England, France, and Russia?
4. Have you heard about the recent proposals for a United States loan to England, and for other economic and financial agreements between the two countries? (If "Yes") In general, do you approve or disapprove of these proposals?
5. As far as you know, is Palestine an independent country, or is she ruled by someone else? (If "Someone else") Do you happen to know what country does rule her?
6. We'd like to know how much interest the public takes in some of these questions. For instance, how much interest do you take in news about (each item below)—a great deal of interest, a considerable amount, only a little, or none at all? (The United Nations, Our policy toward Palestine, The proposed loan to England, Our policy toward Germany, Our relations with Franco Spain, The atomic bomb, The recent meeting of foreign ministers in Paris, Our relations with Russia.)
7. (As you remember) The report recommends that 100,000 more Jewish refugees be admitted to Palestine in spite of protests by the Arabs there. President Truman has said he thinks this ought to be done. Now England says that the United States ought to help her keep order in Palestine if trouble breaks out between the Jews and the Arabs. Do you think we *should* help keep order there, or should we keep out of it?

8. Now about Spain. Have you heard about the recent statement, in which the United States joined with England and France to express the hope that General Franco's government in Spain would soon be followed by a more democratic one?
9. Which one of these three statements comes closest to *your* opinion about our government's policy toward Spain?

(Card handed to respondent)

A. We should go even further in opposing Franco, and should break diplomatic relations with his government.
B. It was a good thing to speak out against Franco, but we have gone far enough for the present.
C. We have already gone too far in working against Franco, and are interfering in Spain's internal affairs.

10. Do you think the newspapers you read generally make Russia look better or worse than she really is?
11. In the disagreements between Russia and the United States, do you think one of the countries is entirely to blame, or do you think both countries have something to do with the misunderstanding?
12. Aside from getting paid interest on the loan, do you know whether the United States would be getting anything else out of the deal—that is, would *we* be getting any advantages or concessions? (If "Yes") What?
13. Under these proposals, we would lend England nearly four billion dollars, which they have agreed to pay back with interest during the next fifty years. England has also agreed to take definite steps to remove restrictions on our trade with them, and to join us in promoting world trade in general. President Truman has now asked Congress to approve this plan. Do you think Congress should or should not approve it? (*Unless "Don't know"*) Why do you think so?
14. In general, do you think England can be trusted to cooperate with us in the future, or don't you think so?

5

Interpersonal Influence

EFFECTS OF GROUP PRESSURE UPON THE MODI-FICATION AND DISTORTION OF JUDGMENTS
By S. E. Asch

We shall here describe in summary form the conception and first findings of a program of investigation into the conditions of independence and submission to group pressure.[1]

Our immediate object was to study the social and personal conditions that induce individuals to resist or to yield to group pressures when the latter are perceived to be *contrary to fact*. The issues which this problem raises are of obvious consequence for society; it can be of decisive importance whether or not a group will, under certain conditions, submit to existing pressures. Equally direct are the consequences for individuals and our understanding of them, since it is a decisive fact about a person whether he possesses the freedom to act independently, or whether he characteristically submits to group pressures.

The problem under investigation requires the direct observation of certain basic processes in the interaction between individuals, and between individuals and groups. To clarify these seems necessary if we are to make fundamental advances in the understanding of the formation and reorganization of attitudes, of the functioning of public opinion, and of the operation of propaganda. Today we do not possess an adequate theory of these central psycho-social processes. Empirical investigation has been predominantly controlled by general propositions concerning group influence which have as a rule been assumed but not tested. With few exceptions investigation has relied upon descriptive formulations concerning the operation of suggestion and prestige, the inadequacy of which is becoming increasingly obvious, and upon schematic applications of stimulus-response theory.

Basic to the current approach has been the axiom that group pressures characteristically induce psychological changes *arbitrarily*, in far-reaching disregard of the material properties of the given conditions. This mode of thinking has almost exclusively stressed the slavish submis-

Prepared by the author from data previously reported in: S. E. Asch, "Effects of Group Pressure upon the Modification and Distortion of Judgments," in Harold Guetzkow (ed.), *Groups, Leadership and Men* (Pittsburgh: Carnegie Press, 1951). Some portions reprinted by permission of Carnegie Press.

---

[1] The earlier experiments out of which the present work developed and the theoretical issues which prompted it are discussed in S. E. Asch, *Social Psychology* (New York: Prentice-Hall, Inc., 1952), Ch. 16.

A full account of the procedures and data on which the present report is based will be published shortly.

sion of individuals to group forces, has neglected to inquire into their possibilities for independence and for productive relations with the human environment, and has virtually denied the capacity of men under certain conditions to rise above group passion and prejudice. It was our aim to contribute to a clarification of these questions, important both for theory and for their human implications, by means of direct observation of the effects of groups upon the decisions and evaluations of individuals.

THE EXPERIMENT AND FIRST RESULTS

To this end we developed an experimental technique which has served as the basis for the present series of studies. We employed the procedure of placing an individual in a relation of radical conflict with all the other members of a group, of measuring its effect upon him in quantitative terms, and of describing its psychological consequences. A group of eight individuals was instructed to judge a series of simple, clearly structured perceptual relations—to match the length of a given line with one of three unequal lines. Each member of the group announced his judgments publicly. In the midst of this monotonous "test" one individual found himself suddenly contradicted by the entire group, and this contradiction was repeated again and again in the course of the experiment. The group in question had, with the exception of one member, previously met with the experimenter and received instructions to respond at certain points with wrong—and unanimous—judgments. The errors of the majority were large (ranging between $\frac{1}{2}''$ and $1\frac{3}{4}''$) and of an order not encountered under control conditions. The outstanding person —the critical subject—whom we had placed in the position of a *minority of one* in the midst of a *unanimous majority*— was the object of investigation. He faced, possibly for the first time in his life, a situation in which a group unanimously contradicted the evidence of his senses.

This procedure was the starting point of the investigation and the point of departure for the study of further problems. Its main features were the following: (1) The critical subject was submitted to two contradictory and irreconcilable forces—the evidence of his own experience of a clearly perceived relation, and the unanimous evidence of a group of equals. (2) Both forces were part of the immediate situation; the majority was concretely present, surrounding the subject physically. (3) The critical subject, who was requested together with all others to state his judgments publicly, was obliged to declare himself and to take a definite stand *vis-à-vis* the group. (4) The situation possessed a self-contained character. The critical subject could not avoid or evade the dilemma by reference to conditions external to the experimental situation. (It may be mentioned at this point that the forces generated by the given conditions acted so quickly upon the critical subjects that instances of suspicion were infrequent.)

The technique employed permitted a simple quantitative measure of the "majority effect" in terms of the frequency of errors in the direction of the distorted estimates of the majority. At the same time we were concerned to obtain evidence of the ways in which the subjects perceived the group, to establish whether they became doubtful, whether they were tempted to join the majority. Most important, it was our object to establish the grounds of the subject's independence or yielding—whether, for example, the yielding subject was aware of the effect of the majority upon him, whether he abandoned his judgment deliberately or compulsively. To this end we constructed a comprehensive set of questions which served as the basis of an individual interview immediately following the experimental period. Toward the conclusion of

TABLE 1

Lengths of Standard and Comparison Lines

Trial	Length of standard line (in inches)	Comparison lines (in inches)			Correct response	Group response	Majority error (in inches)
		1	2	3			
1	10	$8\frac{3}{4}$	10	8	2	2	—
2	2	2	1	$1\frac{1}{2}$	1	1	—
3	3	$3\frac{3}{4}$	$4\frac{1}{4}$	3	3	1 *	$+\frac{3}{4}$
4	5	5	4	$6\frac{1}{2}$	1	2 *	-1.0
5	4	3	5	4	3	3	—
6	3	$3\frac{3}{4}$	$4\frac{1}{4}$	3	3	2 *	$+1\frac{1}{4}$
7	8	$6\frac{1}{4}$	8	$6\frac{3}{4}$	2	3 *	$-1\frac{1}{4}$
8	5	5	4	$6\frac{1}{2}$	1	3 *	$+1\frac{1}{2}$
9	8	$6\frac{1}{4}$	8	$6\frac{3}{4}$	2	1 *	$-1\frac{3}{4}$
10	10	$8\frac{3}{4}$	10	8	2	2	—
11	2	2	1	$1\frac{1}{2}$	1	1	—
12	3	$3\frac{3}{4}$	$4\frac{1}{4}$	3	3	1 *	$+\frac{3}{4}$
13	5	5	4	$6\frac{1}{2}$	1	2 *	-1.0
14	4	3	5	4	3	3	—
15	3	$3\frac{3}{4}$	$4\frac{1}{4}$	3	3	2 *	$+1\frac{1}{4}$
16	8	$6\frac{1}{4}$	8	$6\frac{3}{4}$	2	3 *	$-1\frac{1}{4}$
17	5	5	4	$6\frac{1}{2}$	1	3 *	$+1\frac{1}{2}$
18	8	$6\frac{1}{4}$	8	$6\frac{3}{4}$	2	1 *	$-1\frac{3}{4}$

* Starred figures designate the erroneous estimates by the majority.

the interview each subject was informed fully of the purpose of the experiment, of his role and of that of the majority. The reactions to the disclosure of the purpose of the experiment became in fact an integral part of the procedure. The information derived from the interview became an indispensable source of evidence and insight into the psychological structure of the experimental situation, and in particular, of the nature of the individual differences. It should be added that it is not justified or advisable to allow the subject to leave without giving him a full explanation of the experimental conditions. The experimenter has a responsibility to the subject to clarify his doubts and to state the reasons for placing him in the experimental situation. When this is done most subjects react with interest,

and some express gratification at having lived through a striking situation which has some bearing on them personally and on wider human issues.

Both the members of the majority and the critical subjects were male college students. We shall report the results for a total of fifty critical subjects in this experiment. In Table 1 we summarize the successive comparison trials and the majority estimates. The reader will note that on certain trials the majority responded correctly; these were the "neutral" trials. There were twelve critical trials on which the responses of the majority responded incorrectly.

The quantitative results are clear and unambiguous.

1 There was a marked movement toward the majority. One third of all the

estimates in the critical group were errors identical with or in the direction of the distorted estimates of the majority. The significance of this finding becomes clear in the light of the virtual absence of errors in the control group, the members of which recorded their estimates in writing. The relevant data of the critical and control groups are summarized in Table 2.

2. At the same time the effect of the majority was far from complete. The preponderance of estimates in the critical group (68 percent) was correct despite the pressure of the majority.

3. We found evidence of extreme individual differences. There were in the critical group subjects who remained independent without exception, and there were those who went nearly all the time with the majority. (The maximum possible number of errors was 12, while the actual range of errors was 0–11.) One fourth of the critical subjects was completely independent; at the other extreme, one third of the group displaced the estimates toward the majority in one half or more of the trials.

The differences between the critical subjects in their reactions to the given conditions were equally striking. There were subjects who remained completely confident throughout. At the other extreme were those who became disoriented, doubt-ridden, and experienced a powerful impulse not to appear different from the majority.

For purposes of illustration we include a brief description of one independent and one yielding subject.

Independent. After a few trials he appeared puzzled, hesitant. He announced all disagreeing answers in the form of "Three, sir; two, sir"; not so with the unanimous answers on the neutral trials. At Trial 4 he answered immediately after the first member of the group, shook his head, blinked, and whispered to his neighbor: "Can't help it, that's one."

His later answers came in a whispered voice, accompanied by a deprecating smile. At one point he grinned embarrassedly, and whispered explosively to his neighbor: "I always disagree—darn it!" During the questioning, this subject's constant refrain was: "I called them as I saw them, sir." He insisted that his estimates were right without, however, committing himself as to whether the others were wrong, remarking that "that's the way I see them and that's the way they see them." If he had to make a practical decision under similar circumstances, he declared, "I would follow my own view, though part of my reason would tell me that I might be wrong." Immediately following the experiment the majority engaged this sub-

TABLE 2

DISTRIBUTION OF ERRORS IN EXPERIMENTAL AND CONTROL GROUPS

Number of critical errors	Critical group * (N = 50)	Control group (N = 37)
	F	F
0	13	35
1	4	1
2	5	1
3	6	
4	3	
5	4	
6	1	
7	2	
8	5	
9	3	
10	3	
11	1	
12	0	
Total	50	37
Mean	3.84	0.08

* All errors in the critical group were in the direction of the majority estimates.

ject in a brief discussion. When they pressed him to say whether the entire group was wrong and he alone right, he turned upon them defiantly, exclaiming: "You're *probably* right, but you *may* be wrong!" To the disclosure of the experiment this subject reacted with the statement that he felt "exultant and relieved," adding, "I do not deny that at times I had the feeling: 'to heck with it, I'll go along with the rest.'"

Yielding. This subject went with the majority in 11 out of 12 trials. He appeared nervous and somewhat confused, but he did not attempt to evade discussion; on the contrary, he was helpful and tried to answer to the best of his ability. He opened the discussion with the statement: "If I'd been first I probably would have responded differently"; this was his way of stating that he had adopted the majority estimates. The primary factor in his case was loss of confidence. He perceived the majority as a decided group, acting without hesitation: "If they had been doubtful I probably would have changed, but they answered with such confidence." Certain of his errors, he explained, were due to the doubtful nature of the comparisons; in such instances he went with the majority. When the object of the experiment was explained, the subject volunteered: "I suspected about the middle—but tried to push it out of my mind." It is of interest that his suspicion did not restore his confidence or diminish the power of the majority. Equally striking is his report that he assumed the experiment to involve an "illusion" to which the others, but not he, were subject. This assumption too did not help to free him; on the contrary, he acted as if his divergence from the majority was a sign of defect. The principal impression this subject produced was of one so caught up by immediate difficulties that he lost clear reasons for his actions, and could make no reasonable decisions.

A First Analysis of Individual Differences

On the basis of the interview data described earlier, we undertook to differentiate and describe the major forms of reaction to the experimental situation, which we shall now briefly summarize.

Among the *independent* subjects we distinguished the following main categories:

(1) Independence based on *confidence* in one's perception and experience. The most striking characteristic of these subjects is the vigor with which they withstand the group opposition. Though they are sensitive to the group, and experience the conflict, they show a resilience in coping with it, which is expressed in their continuing reliance on their perception and the effectiveness with which they shake off the oppressive group opposition.

(2) Quite different are those subjects who are independent and *withdrawn*. These do not react in a spontaneously emotional way, but rather on the basis of explicit principles concerning the necessity of being an individual.

(3) A third group of independent subjects manifests considerable tension and doubt, but adhere to their judgment on the basis of a felt necessity to deal adequately with the task.

The following were the main categories of reaction among the *yielding* subjects, or those who went with the majority during one half or more of the trials.

(1) *Distortion of perception* under the stress of group pressure. In this category belong a very few subjects who yield completely, but are not aware that their estimates have been displaced or distorted by the majority. These subjects report that they came to perceive the majority estimates as correct.

(2) *Distortion of judgment.* Most submitting subjects belong to this category. The factor of greatest importance in this group is a decision the subjects reach that

their perceptions are inaccurate, and that those of the majority are correct. These subjects suffer from primary doubt and lack of confidence; on this basis they feel a strong tendency to join the majority.

(3) *Distortion of action*. The subjects in this group do not suffer a modification of perception nor do they conclude that they are wrong. They yield because of an overmastering need not to appear different from or inferior to others, because of an inability to tolerate the appearance of defectiveness in the eyes of the group. These subjects suppress their observations and voice the majority position with awareness of what they are doing.

The results are sufficient to establish that independence and yielding are not psychologically homogeneous, that submission to group pressure and freedom from pressure can be the result of different psychological conditions. It should also be noted that the categories described above, being based exclusively on the subjects' reactions to the experimental conditions, are descriptive, not presuming to explain why a given individual responded in one way rather than another. The further exploration of the basis for the individual differences is a separate task.

EXPERIMENTAL VARIATIONS

The results described are clearly a joint function of two broadly different sets of conditions. They are determined first by the specific external conditions, by the particular character of the relation between social evidence and one's own experience. Second, the presence of pronounced individual differences points to the important role of personal factors, or factors connected with the individual's character structure. We reasoned that there are group conditions which would produce independence in all subjects, and that there probably are group conditions which would induce intensified yielding in many, though not in all.

Secondly, we deemed it reasonable to assume that behavior under the experimental social pressure is significantly related to certain characteristics of the individual. The present account will be limited to the effect of the surrounding conditions upon independence and submission. To this end we followed the procedure of experimental variation, systematically altering the quality of social evidence by means of systematic variation of the group conditions and of the task.

The Effect of Nonunanimous Majorities. Evidence obtained from the basic experiment suggested that the condition of being exposed *alone* to the opposition of a "compact majority" may have played a decisive role in determining the course and strength of the effects observed. Accordingly we undertook to investigate in a series of successive variations the effects of *nonunanimous* majorities. The technical problem of altering the uniformity of a majority is, in terms of our procedure, relatively simple. In most instances we merely directed one or more members of the instructed group to deviate from the majority in prescribed ways. It is obvious that we cannot hope to compare the performance of the same individual in two situations on the assumption that they remain independent of one another; at best we can investigate the effect of an earlier upon a later experimental condition. The comparison of different experimental situations therefore requires the use of different but comparable groups of critical subjects. This is the procedure we have followed. In the variations to be described we have maintained the conditions of the basic experiment (e.g., the sex of the subjects, the size of the majority, the content of the task, and so on) save for the specific factor that was varied. The following were some of the variations studied:

1 *The presence of a "true partner."*
(a) In the midst of the majority were *two*

naïve, critical subjects. The subjects were separated spatially, being seated in the fourth and eighth positions, respectively. Each therefore heard his judgments confirmed by one other person (provided the other person remained independent), one prior to, the other after announcing his own judgment. In addition, each experienced a break in the unanimity of the majority. There were six pairs of critical subjects. (b) In a further variation the "partner" to the critical subject was a member of the group who had been instructed to respond correctly throughout. This procedure permits the exact control of the partner's responses. The partner was always seated in the fourth position; he therefore announced his estimates in each case before the critical subject.

The results clearly demonstrate that a disturbance of the unanimity of the majority markedly increased the independence of the critical subjects. The frequency of promajority errors dropped to 10.4 percent of the total number of estimates in variation (a), and to 5.5 percent in variation (b). These results are to be compared with the frequency of yielding to the unanimous majorities in the basic experiment, which was 32 percent of the total number of estimates. It is clear that the presence in the field of *one other* individual who responded correctly was sufficient to deplete the power of the majority, and in some cases to destroy it. This finding is all the more striking in the light of other variations which demonstrate the effect of even small minorities provided they are unanimous. Indeed, we have been able to show that a unanimous majority of 3 is, under the given conditions, far more effective than a majority of 8 containing 1 dissenter. That critical subjects will under these conditions free themselves of a majority of 7 and join forces with one other person in the minority is, we believe, a result significant for theory. It points to a fundamental psychological difference between the condition of being

alone and having a minimum of human support. It further demonstrates that the effects obtained are not the result of a summation of influences proceeding from each member of the group; it is necessary to conceive the results as being relationally determined.

2. *Withdrawal of a "true partner."* What will be the effect of providing the critical subject with a partner who responds correctly and then withdrawing him? The critical subject started with a partner who responded correctly. The partner was a member of the majority who had been instructed to respond correctly and to "desert" to the majority in the middle of the experiment. This procedure permits the observation of the same subject in the course of the transition from one condition to another. The withdrawal of the partner produced a powerful and unexpected result. We had assumed that the critical subject, having gone through the experience of opposing the majority with a minimum of support, would maintain his independence when alone. Contrary to this expectation, we found that the experience of having had and then lost a partner restored the majority effect to its full force, the proportion of errors rising to 28.5 percent of all judgments, in contrast to the preceding level of 5.5 percent. Further experimentation is needed to establish whether the critical subjects were responding to the sheer fact of being alone, or to the fact that the partner abandoned them.

3. *Late arrival of a "true partner."* The critical subject started as a minority of 1 in the midst of a unanimous majority. Toward the conclusion of the experiment one member of the majority "broke" away and began announcing correct estimates. This procedure, which reverses the order of conditions of the preceding experiment, permits the observation of the transition from being alone to being a member of a pair against a majority. It is obvious that those critical subjects

TABLE 3

Errors of Critical Subjects with Unanimous Majorities of Different Size

Size of majority	Control	1	2	3	4	8	10–15
N	37	10	15	10	10	50	12
Mean number of errors . . .	0.08	0.33	1.53	4.0	4.20	3.84	3.75
Range of errors	0–2	0–1	0–5	1–12	0–11	0–11	0–10

who were independent when alone would continue to be so when joined by a partner. The variation is therefore of significance primarily for those subjects who yielded during the first phase of the experiment. The appearance of the late partner exerts a freeing effect, reducing the level of yielding to 8.7 percent. Those who had previously yielded also became markedly more independent, but not completely so, continuing to yield more than previously independent subjects. The reports of the subjects do not cast much light on the factors responsible for the result. It is our impression that some subjects, having once committed themselves to yielding, find it difficult to change their direction completely. To do so is tantamount to a public admission that they had not acted rightly. They therefore follow to an extent the precarious course they had chosen in order to maintain an outward semblance of consistency and conviction.

4. *The presence of a "compromise partner."* The majority was consistently extremist, always matching the standard with the most unequal line. One instructed subject (who, as in the other variations, preceded the critical subject) also responded incorrectly, but his estimates were always intermediate between the truth and the majority position. The critical subject therefore faced an extremist majority whose unanimity was broken by one more moderately erring person. Under these conditions the frequency of errors was reduced but not significantly. However, the lack of unanimity determined in a strikingly consistent way the *direction* of the errors. The preponderance of the errors, 75.7 percent of the total, was moderate, whereas in a parallel experiment in which the majority was unanimously extremist (i.e., with the "compromise" partner excluded), the incidence of moderate errors was 42 percent of the total. As might be expected, in a unanimously moderate majority, the errors of the critical subjects were without exception moderate.

The Role of Majority Size. To gain further understanding of the majority effect, we varied the size of the majority in several different variations. The majorities, which were in each case unanimous, consisted of 2, 3, 4, 8, and 10–15 persons, respectively. In addition, we studied the limiting case in which the critical subject was opposed by one instructed subject. Table 3 contains the mean and the range of errors under each condition.

With the opposition reduced to 1, the majority effect all but disappeared. When the opposition proceeded from a group of 2, it produced a measurable though small distortion, the errors being 12.8 percent of the total number of estimates. The effect appeared in full force with a majority of 3. Larger majorities did not produce effects greater than a majority of 3.

The effect of a majority is often silent, revealing little of its operation to the subject, and often hiding it from the experimenter. To examine the range of effects it is capable of inducing, decisive variations of conditions are necessary. An indication of one effect is furnished by the following variation in which the conditions of the basic experiment were simply reversed. Here the majority, consisting of a group of 16, was naïve; in the midst of it we placed a single individual who responded wrongly according to instructions. Under these conditions the members of the naïve majority reacted to the lone dissenter with amusement. Contagious laughter spread through the group at the droll minority of 1. Of significance is the fact that the members lacked awareness that they drew their strength from the majority, and that their reactions would change radically if they faced the dissenter individually. These observations demonstrate the role of social support as a source of power and stability, in contrast to the preceding investigations which stressed the effects of social opposition. Both aspects must be explicitly considered in a unified formulation of the effects of group conditions on the formation and change of judgments.

The Role of the Stimulus-Situation. It is obviously not possible to divorce the quality and course of the group forces which act upon the individual from the specific stimulus-conditions. Of necessity the structure of the situation molds the group forces and determines their direction as well as their strength. Indeed, this was the reason that we took pains in the investigations described above to center the issue between the individual and the group around an elementary matter of fact. And there can be no doubt that the resulting reactions were directly a function of the contradiction between the observed relations and the majority position. These general considerations are sufficient to establish the need to vary the stimulus-conditions and to observe their effect on the resulting group forces.

Accordingly we have studied the effect of increasing and decreasing the discrepancy between the correct relation and the position of the majority, going beyond the basic experiment which contained discrepancies of a relatively moderate order. Our technique permits the easy variation of this factor, since we can vary at will the deviation of the majority from the correct relation. At this point we can only summarize the trend of the results which is entirely clear. The degree of independence increases with the distance of the majority from correctness. However, even glaring discrepancies (of the order of 3–6″) did not produce independence in all. While independence increases with the magnitude of contradiction, a certain proportion of individuals continues to yield under extreme conditions.

We have also varied systematically the structural clarity of the task, employing judgments based on mental standards. In agreement with other investigators, we find that the majority effect grows stronger as the situation diminishes in clarity. Concurrently, however, the disturbance of the subjects and the conflict-quality of the situation decrease markedly. We consider it of significance that the majority achieves its most pronounced effect when it acts most painlessly.

SUMMARY

We have investigated the effects upon individuals of majority opinions when the latter were seen to be in a direction contrary to fact. By means of a simple technique we produced a radical divergence between a majority and a minority, and observed the ways in which individuals coped with the resulting difficulty. Despite the stress of the given conditions, a substantial proportion of individuals retained their independence throughout. At the same time a substantial minority yielded, modifying their judgments in accordance with the majority. Independence and yielding are a joint function of the following major factors: (1) The character of the stimulus situation. Variations in structural clarity have a decisive effect: with diminishing clarity of the stimulus-conditions the majority effect increases. (2) The character of the group forces. Individuals are highly sensitive to the structural qualities of group opposition. In particular, we demonstrated the great importance of the factor of unanimity. Also, the majority effect is a function of the size of group opposition. (3) The character of the individual. There were wide and, indeed, striking differences among individuals within the same experimental situation.

INFLUENCE THROUGH SOCIAL COMMUNICATION
By Kurt W. Back

INTRODUCTION

The experiment described in this paper investigates a property of groups which has been given various names but will be called here "cohesiveness," following the use in a study by Festinger, Schachter, and Back.[1] Cohesiveness was defined by them as the resultant forces which are acting on the members to stay in a group; in other words, cohesiveness is the attraction of membership in a group for its members. In the study cited, it was found that under certain conditions there will be increased pressure toward uniformity within a group with increase in cohesiveness. In the present experiment, a laboratory situation was created in which the consequences of this relationship could be studied in detail.

From the relationship between the forces to remain in the group and pressure to agree on important topics, some other relationships can be deduced.

1. The increase in pressure toward uniformity should show itself in a discussion between members. Either members will attempt to influence each other more in highly cohesive groups, or they will be more receptive to influence.

2. The basis for participation in a discussion of group members lies partly in individual motives, which may vary among individuals, and pressure arising from the group, which affects all members. Since the factor which is common to all members is larger in highly cohesive groups than in less cohesive groups, we would expect less individual differences in participation in these groups.

3. As the pressure toward uniformity in highly cohesive groups is stronger, the activities of the groups—discussion, for example—should have a greater effect on the members than activities of less cohesive groups.

4. Weak pressures toward uniformity in less cohesive groups can therefore lead only to little changes in individual members. Hence, the preferred outcome should be a compromise solution where all members change their positions slightly and equally. In highly cohesive groups, individual members may change considerably. Agreement can be established at any point with little consideration given the degree to which some individuals may have to change.

Individuals may want to belong to a group because they like the other mem-

From *The Journal of Abnormal and Social Psychology*, 1951, XLVI, 9–23. Reprinted by permission of the American Psychological Association, Inc. For brevity, several of the more detailed technical passages have been omitted. The reader is referred to the original article for this material.

[1] L. Festinger, S. Schachter, and K. Back, *Social Pressure in Informal Groups* (New York: Harper, 1950).

Set A *Set B*

Picture 1

Picture 1

Picture 2

Picture 2

Picture 3

Picture 3

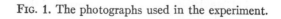

Fig. 1. The photographs used in the experiment.

bers, because being a member of a group may be attractive in itself (for example, it may be an honor to belong to it), or because the group may mediate goals which are important for the members. All these are bases for attractiveness of a group. In the experiment, groups were established on all three bases. The strength of cohesiveness for each basis was varied.

The main purpose of the experiment was to measure the effect of strength of cohesiveness on the pressure toward uniformity within groups and the consequences of this effect. At the same time the effect of different bases of cohesiveness could be studied.

The Method of the Experiment

Introduction. The experiment included the following features:

1. The topic of discussion was the interpretation of a set of pictures. This was an unusual task on which hardly any group standards could have been established outside the experimental situation.

2. The pictures depicted a simple situation which could be discussed in a few minutes. They were so unclear that a change in interpretation was easily possible.

3. Each subject received a set of three pictures, believing that all sets were identical. Actually, there were slight differences among the sets which led to different interpretations. The differences were too slight to be detected in a discussion without seeing the photographs again. This device was successful, and subjects never realized that there were differences (see Figure 1 for the two sets).

4. The experiment was introduced as a cooperative working situation; the eventual outcome, however, consisted of the independent products of each subject. The discussion was introduced as an opportunity to improve their own stories. Necessity for influence was specifically

denied, and both length and manner of the discussion were left to the subjects.

5. In order to trace influence to one person only, the experimental groups consisted of pairs.

6. Although most of the subjects attended the same class (of about 250 students), each member of a pair attended a different discussion section of this class. After the session, each subject was asked whether he had known his partner previously, and if he had, the results of this group were discarded. As the subjects were recruited for a single session of one experiment, they did not expect any prolonged existence of the group.

General Procedure. After the subjects were introduced to each other, each of them was taken to a different room and given the following instructions.

Your task is to write a story from a set of three photographs which depict quite a commonplace incident. This gives you an opportunity to give play to your imagination, although the story should be plausible and supported by features of the pictures. The pictures, being taken from a film strip, form a sequence which you will have to reconstruct. Then you will write a story connecting the pictures. Right now you will write a preliminary story. Then you will talk over your ideas with your partner, and afterward you will write a final story. Remember, you should write a good story, but it is important to make it plausible by the use of the available clues.

In addition, they were given the special instructions appropriate to their experimental conditions, which will be explained later. Then they received the pictures and wrote the preliminary story. There was no time limit.

When they were finished they came together to discuss their stories. At the start of the discussion, the subjects were reminded that its object was to help them to improve their own stories. They were cautioned that it was not necessary to conclude with a common story and that they could stop the discussion at any time that they saw its usefulness at an end. The amount and manner of communication was therefore left to the subjects.

After the discussion, the subjects returned to their separate rooms to write their final stories. They were instructed: *"Write what you now think to be the best story."* They could not see the pictures again; therefore, they could not check information which they had received from their partners.

After the completion of the experiment, the subjects were told the significant features of the set-up, and all their questions were answered truthfully. In conclusion, they were asked not to discuss the experiment and were thanked for their cooperation.

Introduction of the Experimental Variables. The experiment was designed to differentiate the pairs by the attractiveness of the group and on the basis of this attractiveness. Three sources of attractiveness were introduced: (1) attraction to the partner, (2) mediation of other goals (task direction), and (3) prestige of the group itself. Each of these variables was introduced in two different strengths. The combination of strength and type gave six different experimental treatments. A seventh treatment was introduced in which any force toward the group was kept at a minimum. The execution of this design required a technique which started at the time the subjects were recruited.

When the subjects signed up in their classes, they were told only that they were going to participate in a group experiment. The sign-up blank included a few questions which were ostensibly going to help in making up the groups. Some questions asked for self-description and self-ratings. The concluding questions read: "You will be paired with another student of your own sex. As we want people together who are congenial, can you describe the type of person you

want to work with?" and "What would be the most objectionable traits in a person you would work with?"

Personal Attraction. The questionnaire aided in controlling the personal attraction the subjects had for each other when they entered the discussion. In the treatments where attraction was to be the basis of cohesiveness, the experimenter referred to the questionnaire after giving the instructions and reported on the effectiveness of the matching.

To create weak cohesiveness, he said, "You remember the questions you answered when you signed up in class? We tried to find a partner with whom you could work best. Of course, we couldn't find anybody who would fit the description exactly, but we found a fellow who corresponded to the main points, and you probably will like him. You should get along all right."

To create strong cohesiveness, he said, "You remember the questions you answered in class about the people you would like to work with? Of course, we usually cannot match people the way they want, but for you we have found almost exactly the person you described. As a matter of fact, the matching was as close as we had expected to happen once or twice in the study, if at all. You'll like him a lot. What's even more, he described a person very much like you. It's quite a lucky coincidence to find two people who are so congenial, and you should get along extremely well."

Task Direction. In the treatments where the group was to mediate goals, the *outcome of the task was stressed.* The experiment was introduced as a test; the importance of its result for the subject was varied to create different degrees of cohesiveness. The questionnaire was mentioned in passing as an unsuccessful attempt to match partners.

For low cohesiveness: "This is a part of a study of the way people use their imaginations. We developed a somewhat special procedure to test this ability." After the instructions for the task were given, the experimenter continued, "In this way, you will have the best chance to show your ability and get a high score in the test—you know, we had some idea of putting people together who were congenial. But that didn't work because of schedule difficulties; so all we could do was to take into account the objections you stated."

For high cohesiveness, the same introduction to the task was given. After the instructions, the experimenter continued, "Remember, the whole test shows how well you can use your imagination: your product will be judged in comparison with that of other people. We intend, for instance, to compare students from this and other universities, and men and women. The group you are in is a special prize group. There are ten such groups, and the two members who produce the best story get $5 each. You know, we had some idea of putting people together who were congenial, but that didn't work out because of schedule difficulties. All we could do was to take into account the objections you stated."

Group Prestige. Another way in which cohesiveness was produced was by *stressing the value of belonging to the group.* This was done by making selection for this particular group an important achievement. The rarity of this achievement was varied to create different strengths of cohesiveness. Here, too, the idea of being matched by personality was played down.

For low cohesiveness, the experiment was introduced: "This is part of a study in the use of imagination. We are trying to compare good groups and bad groups in this type of work, and your lab section instructor told us you would be particularly good material for a good group. You know, we had some idea of putting people together who were congenial, but that didn't work out because of schedule difficulties. All we could do was to take into account the objections you stated." Then the instructions were given.

For high cohesiveness, the experimenter stated: "This is part of a study in the use of imagination. We select at first the pairs of people to work together by means of the questionnaire you filled out in class (although the part about putting congenial

people together didn't work out because of schedule difficulties; all we could do was to take into account the objections you stated). We try to put people together who should be especially good at this kind of task. We checked on assignments with your lab instructor. From all we could learn, you have all the qualifications which have been set up to be good in this task: you two should be about the best group we have had. So we want to use you as a model group after which we can train other people to be more productive in this task." Then the instructions were given.

Negative Treatment. To minimize all forces to belong to the group, the attraction to the partner, the outcome of task, and the pleasure of the discussion itself were put in a dim light.

After the instructions were given, the experimenter said, "I am sorry, but the idea of putting people together who are congenial didn't work. Especially in your case we had some trouble because of scheduling. So the fellow you are going to work with may irritate you a little, but I hope it will work out all right. The trouble is that the whole thing is quite frustrating and the conversation somewhat strained, so we would have preferred to have you with a person you liked. But anyway, do the best you can."

In addition to the talk by the experimenter, some treatments were stressed by the headings of the paper on which the subjects wrote their stories—for instance, "prize group" for task-directed and "model group" for prestige high-cohesive groups.

Ten groups were used in each treatment. Both members of each pair were of the same sex. In each treatment, seven pairs were male and three female. Assignment of a pair to a treatment was a matter of chance, independent of the answers to the questionnaire. One exception in discarding the questionnaire results had to be made: subjects were assigned to a condition where personal attraction was important, only if they had made a reasonable amount of specification about their partners.

Measurement. *The Measurement of Influence.* Influence could be measured by the change from the preliminary story to the final story. In order to arrive at a numerical measure of the change, the stories were broken down into small units, and the amount of change could be measured by the change of these elements.

The changes were determined only by comparison of the codes without going back to the original stories. Any difference in the coded stories, omissions or additions, were considered changes. These could then be separated into those toward the partner's position and independent changes.

Changes toward the partner were considered those which tended toward the position the partner had shown in either his first or final story. All changes which did not meet these criteria were considered to be independent changes.

The Recording of the Communication. The communication process itself was recorded by two observers, who afterward rated the total discussion.

One observer noted all the communication. His observation blank contained 20 categories, which fell into three groups:

One group contained all the methods which could be used to influence the partner.

The second group contained the reactions to attempted influence. There were five such categories, arranged along an acceptance-rejection dimension. They were given arbitrary weights from 1 to 5; from them a mean level of reaction could be computed.

The categories which were not concerned with influence attempts made up the last group.

The second observer noted only the attempts to influence. From his observations the strength of attempted influence could be measured. He classified the attempts used into 17 categories, such as assertion, hypothetical example, rhe-

torical question, and exhortation. One sentence was scored as a unit.

Weighting factors were assigned to the different categories by having each observer (five observers alternated in this task) rate the influence attempts which he noted on a four-point scale of intensity. The amount of influence attempted by one person during a period of time was computed as the number of units scored weighted by the factors of the categories in which they occurred.

Reliability of this measure was checked in three different groups by having two observers rate the same meeting and then comparing the values they obtained for "number of observations" and "strength of attempted influence" for each partner, minute by minute. For the number of observations the correlations are $+.91$, $+.78$, and $+.64$, and for strength of attempted influence, $+.87$, $+.68$, and $+.61$.

After the meeting both observers attempted to characterize the whole discussion by a pattern of discussion. Although they were permitted to distinguish five patterns for purposes of analysis, these were reduced to two main types, active patterns and withdrawing patterns:

Active patterns implied acceptance of the discussion situation where the main emphasis of the discussion was on discovering the important facts in the pictures, on reaching an agreement, or on arguing for argument's sake.

Withdrawing patterns implied little involvement in the situation. They included discussion which consisted mainly of telling the stories without additional comments or of agreeing that the problem was too indefinite.

A specific type of pattern was assigned to a group when both observers checked the same one. Agreement was reached in sixty-three of the seventy groups.

Inasmuch as the observers administered the instructions, they always knew which type of group they were observing.

They were, however, mainly unaware of the nature of the hypotheses under investigation. Therefore, it is unlikely that they would have biased the results. The principal measure derived from the observation—strength of attempted influence—was derived so indirectly from the actual observations that any bias is excluded for the measure. The categories could only be weighted after all experimental sessions had been concluded.

Other Measures. Additional ratings and questions used will be discussed in the next section.

A sociometric scale was designed to measure the effects of the experimental situation on interpersonal relationships. The scale consisted of seven questions which were known to correspond to different strengths of attraction. The questions were scaled by an abbreviated Thurstone technique.[2] The questions used were selected from a set of forty original questions by a group of judges which consisted of seventeen students in social psychology. Each judge divided the statements into seven groups according to the desire for intimacy expressed. The questions which showed the smallest dispersion and for which medians corresponded to the seven integers, were used in the scale (scale value in parentheses), as follows:

I would like to see him around campus
sometime (1)
I would want to have him in the same
lab section (2)
I would enjoy talking to him (3)
I would enjoy an animated discussion
with him (4)
I would like to discuss serious general
problems with him (5)
I would want him to come to me with
his problems (6)
I would discuss important personal
problems with him (7)

In the course of the experiment it was found that 71 percent of the 140 subjects gave a perfect scale pattern (that is, a "yes" answer to any question implied a "yes" to any question with a lower scale value). An additional 16 percent gave scale patterns which were only one point off. It seemed justified to take the total number of "yes" answers as the score assigned by the scale.

RESULTS

Strength of Cohesiveness. *Effects on Communication.* In a high cohesive group, it is our hypothesis that the members will try to come to an agreement on differences in point of view. Discussion on relevant topics, then, should be sought, and its importance should be accepted.

The patterns of discussion provide a first test of this hypothesis. In the low cohesive groups, the withdrawing patterns predominate. Of twenty-six of these groups, nineteen were rated as having withdrawing patterns. In twenty-seven high cohesive groups only eleven showed withdrawing patterns, while sixteen showed active patterns. (In four low cohesive and three high cohesive groups, no agreement between the observers could be reached.) This difference is significant at the 2-percent level (chi square test). The dominant behavior in the active class—arguing, seeking agreement, and seeking facts—implies a considerable attempt to influence the partner. This over-all measure indicates that low cohesive groups react to realization of difference by withdrawing from the situation, while high cohesive groups tend to eliminate the difference.

On the more molecular level, the importance of the discussion for the partners is indicated by the reaction to the partners' attempts at influence. An average reaction level could be computed

---

[2] L. L. Thurstone and E. J. Chave, *The Measurement of Attitudes* (Chicago. University of Chicago Press, 1929).

TABLE 1

LEVEL OF REACTION

Group	Personal attraction	Task direction	Group prestige	Negative
Low cohesive	2.10	2.22	2.38	
				2.25
High cohesive	2.49	2.85	2.50	

$$F = \frac{V \text{ strength}}{V \text{ within groups}} = 3.91; df = 1 \text{ and } 54; p < .06$$

for the five categories in which the observation of reaction was recorded, as the mean of all the values of these observations.

Table 1 shows that the level of reaction was higher in the more cohesive groups. These groups tend more toward argument and serious consideration of the partner's position than the less cohesive groups. It may seem surprising that the more cohesive groups show more outward signs of resistance, like objecting to the partner's story. From our interpretation of the reaction level, however, it may be suggested that argument against the partner is not a real indicator of resistance; rejecting the group as a reference group would imply polite agreement as a means of avoiding entering the discussion at all. Giving expression to disagreement suggests a more important role for the discussion and offers opportunities for later agreement.

This interpretation derives some support if we consider the extremes of reactions with different strengths of cohesiveness. Taking the mean of the most "accepting" reactions occurring in each group, we find no difference between high and low cohesive groups. The mean value of these "minimum" reactions is 1.47 for low cohesive and 1.43 for high cohesive groups. The difference is pronounced, however, if the mean of the most "objecting" reactions in each group is used. This is 3.83 for high and 3.10 for low cohesive groups. There is

just as much agreement in both types of groups, but in the high cohesive groups it is accompanied by serious argument, while in the low cohesive groups, it seems to mean mere politeness.

Self-ratings on resistance confirm the interpretation that the more argumentative level in the high cohesive groups does not mean greater resistance to the partner's arguments. These ratings show a slight decrease in resistance, not statistically significant, with all three bases of cohesiveness.

Observation has shown that more influence is being exerted in the more cohesive groups. Conversely, the participants feel that more pressure has been exerted on them. In postsession interviews the subjects were asked, "Did you think that your partner tried to influence you?" Less than half (21 of 45) of the members of the low cohesive groups reported that they felt some pressure, while more than two thirds (36 of 51) of the members of the high cohesive groups did so. The remainder did not answer adequately for coding. This difference is significant at the 2-percent level (chi-square test).

Acceptance of the discussion group as a meaningful reference point means more, however, than a stronger effort to come to an agreement with the partner. It should be manifested also by a great acceptance of the partner as a participant in the discussion. In general, we can assume that, because of individual differences, one person will be more interested

TABLE 2

PERCENTAGE OF ATTEMPTED INFLUENCE IN HIGHER INDUCER

Group	Personal attraction	Task direction	Group prestige	Negative
Low cohesive	62.4	64.6	60.2	60.0
High cohesive	58.9	54.9	56.7	

$$F = \frac{V \text{ strength}}{V \text{ within cells}} = 6.98; df = 1 \text{ and } 54; p < .02$$

than another in convincing his partner of the superiority of his story. But if pressures from the group are great, they will affect both members strongly, and the ultimate effect of individual differences will be less pronounced. Further, the partners should try to adjust to each other, and give each other a greater opportunity to press their points. The total effect would be that influence attempts are more evenly distributed in high cohesive than in low cohesive groups.

Table 2 confirms this hypothesis: the mean percentage of attempted influence for the higher "inducer" is above 60 percent in all low cohesive conditions, while it falls to 54–59 percent in the high cohesive groups. In only nine of the thirty high cohesive groups does one partner account for more than 60 percent of

attempted influence, while this occurred in more than half of the low cohesive groups.

In line with the hypothesis that attempted influence is a question of personal preference in low cohesive groups while it is made necessary by the pressures toward uniformity in high cohesive groups, we can expect members of high cohesive groups to accept their partner's greater share of influence attempts. We can test this by comparing the scores on the sociometric scale given to high and low inducers in the different treatments. In Table 3, we see that the lower inducers like their partners less than do the higher inducers in the low cohesive groups, while no such differences are shown in the high cohesive groups.

Until now, we have limited the discus-

TABLE 3

EXTENT TO WHICH HIGH AND LOW INDUCERS LIKE THEIR PARTNERS

Group	Personal attraction		Task direction		Group prestige		Negative	
	High inducer	Low inducer	High inducer	Low inducer	High inducer	Low inducer	High inducer	Low inducer
Low cohesive . . .	4.7	3.8	4.60	3.20	4.55	3.90	4.55	3.90
High cohesive . . .	4.25	4.35	3.90	4.15	4.50	4.40		

Low cohesive groups: $F = \dfrac{V \text{ strength of inducers}}{V \text{ within cells}} = 6.097; df = 1 \text{ and } 54; p < .03$

High cohesive groups: F not significant

TABLE 4

Changes Influenced by the Partner

Group	Personal attraction	Task direction	Group prestige	Negative
Low cohesive	7.9	8.9	6.7	8.5
High cohesive	10.5	11.0	8.3	

$$F = \frac{V \text{ strength}}{V \text{ within cells}} = 3.13; \; df = 1 \text{ and } 54; \; p < .11$$

sion to the six treatments in which some degree of cohesiveness was created. In the negative condition, on the other hand, the forces toward the group were kept at a minimum. Without any forces of this kind, there was no pressure toward uniformity within the group. But acceptance of the experimental situation, interest in the problem itself, and a desire to help the experimenter combined to make the subjects try to make something of the discussion.

The reaction level of the negative groups is 2.25, which is close to the average reaction level (2.33) of the low cohesive groups (Table 1). The high inducers in these groups account for 60 percent of the total attempted influence, just as the percentages in the low cohesive groups were 60 percent or more (Table 2). They agree, too, with the low cohesive groups in that the high inducers were more attracted to partners than were the low inducers (Table 3).

The members of negative groups, however, attempted more influence than those of the low cohesive groups. Six of the 10 discussions in these groups were rated as having "active" patterns. In the same way, nine of 15 subjects in this treatment reported that the partner tried to influence them. This, too, is a similar proportion to that of the high cohesive groups.

The foregoing can be interpreted as indicating that in the negative groups there was little acceptance of the other member of the pair as a partner in the discussion; the subjects do not seem to consider the discussion as a serious step in establishing an idea about the stories. But, on the other hand, they are much freer in expressing their opinions and pushing their own ideas.

Effects on Influence. Table 4 shows the amount of influence which was shown by both partners. There is a definite increase in change toward features of the partners' stories when cohesiveness increases. That this represents influence and not increased motivation, and hence a greater willingness to change and improve the story, can be seen from a comparison with changes which were not in the partner's direction. These changes (which cannot be ascribed to the influence of the partner) increase slightly only in two of three conditions. The mean of the low cohesive groups is 5.3, of the high cohesive groups 5.7; this difference is statistically not significant. It would seem, therefore, that the change in Table 4 does represent influence and not a greater desire to improve the story.

The increase in total change within the group does not give an adequate picture of the manner in which influence changes with an increase in cohesiveness. We have shown before how uneven distribution of change within the group can be taken as a sign of strong pressures toward uniformity. In line with this, Table 5 shows how much the partner who changed more and the partner who

TABLE 5

CHANGE TOWARD THE PARTNER: HIGHER CHANGERS AND LOWER CHANGERS

(a) *Higher Changers*

Group	Personal attraction	Task direction	Group prestige	Negative
Low cohesive	5.0	5.6	4.8	7.0
High cohesive	7.3	7.3	6.1	

(b) *Lower Changers*

Group	Personal attraction	Task direction	Group prestige	Negative
Low cohesive	2.9	3.3	1.9	1.5
High cohesive	3.2	3.7	2.2	

High changers: $F = \dfrac{V \text{ strength}}{V \text{ within cells}} = 4.78$; $df = 1$ and 54; $p < .05$

Low changers: F not significant

changed less were influenced in each treatment. We can see that almost the total increase in influence is the function of one member of the pair. As we expected, the greater pressure toward uniformity in the high cohesive groups results in the possibility that some members can be influenced quite strongly; as long as the agreement is reached at some point, perhaps close to the original position of one of the partners, it does not matter whether some members will show much change and some only a little. In low cohesive groups, however, both partners can merely show small and approximately equal changes.

The negative groups show an average amount of change which is mainly borne by one member of the group. This result seems surprising, as it would make the negative groups very similar to the high cohesive groups. But we shall see later that the meaning of change is different in these groups and that different members of the group are primarily affected.

The data presented in this section show that cohesiveness can indeed be considered as a unitary concept, although the increase in cohesiveness corresponded to very different operations in the various treatments. We could predict the same effect in each case by deriving the consequences of increasing the attraction of the group.

The Basis of Cohesiveness. We shall attempt now to explore further the meaning of the different conditions of attractiveness.

If an individual is attracted to a group because he wants to be with some of the members, he will consider the group activity mainly a means of meeting them. We should expect therefore that he will try to be pleasant and active with less regard to the performance of the group activity as such.

If an individual enters the group to achieve ulterior goals, we can expect him to try to perform the required task as efficiently and as fast as possible. There should be less effort to establish a relationship with the other group members except in so far as it is necessary to perform the work successfully.

If an individual enters a group because membership as such is attractive, we

TABLE 6

TIME OF DISCUSSION

(seconds)

Group	Personal attraction	Task direction	Group prestige	Negative
Low cohesive	412.5	415.5	307	330
High cohesive	449	321.5	362.5	

t not significant	$t = 2.91$	$t = 3.65$	
	$p < .01$	$p < .01$	

can expect that he will be concerned about his behavior in order to stay in the favored position. His behavior toward the other group members will be determined by his perception of them as parts of the environment in which he has to succeed. He should adjust quickly to their attitude toward him; we should expect, therefore, rapid development of complementary personal roles and a conscious effort to show good behavior.

The Effects of Personal Attraction. Several signs in the observations of the personal-attractiveness treatment suggest that the discussion gave more attention to influences as such and was more related to interpersonal relationship than in the other conditions.

From the observations of the discussion we find some evidence of the increased attention to the process of influence. One measurement of this tendency is the number of groups in which the category "asks to be influenced" was coded by the observer who recorded all communications. Statements of this kind occurred quite rarely. But they were noted in ten of the twenty groups in the personal attraction treatment and in only five of the other fifty groups.

The types of attempted influence, which the same observer recorded, give evidence in the same direction The personal attraction groups favor the more direct approach while the most distant method—"stating one's own position"—is less represented than in the other conditions.

A further suggestion on how personal the influence process becomes in this treatment is shown in the analysis of the sociometric scores. With high personal attraction, the high changer likes his partner less than his partner likes him. This difference amounts to two steps on the sociometric scale. This difference is significant at the 1-percent level.

The Effects of Task Direction. The relationship created by setting up a goal which can be reached by the group activity tends to have somewhat opposite effects from those of the personal attraction relationship. Group activity is seen as a necessity which is to be completed as quickly and as efficiently as possible.

The intent toward accomplishment is shown in the average decrease of 95 seconds in the time taken for the discussion when cohesiveness increases (Table 6). This shortening of interaction does not mean any withdrawal from the situation; however, the discussion becomes more intense. This is indicated by the strength of attempted influence per minute. It increases correspondingly to the decrease in time between the low and high conditions. This increase is almost statistically significant (11-percent level). There is no comparable increase in the other conditions. There, attempted influence increases with cohesiveness because the time of discussion

TABLE 7

CHANGES OF ALL KINDS

Group	Personal attraction	Task direction	Group prestige	Negative
Low cohesive	13.2	14.5	11.6	13.4
High cohesive. . . , .	16.5	17.7	12.7	

$$F = \frac{V \text{ types}}{V \text{ within cells}} = 2.33; df = 2 \text{ and } 54; p < .08$$

increases, while in the task-direction condition, the intensity increases.

The Effects of Group Prestige. We have suggested before that cohesiveness based on group prestige will have the following implications: Members will be careful of their own behavior, guiding their actions by some general notions of how they are supposed to act. As they focus their attention on their own proper behavior, the partner becomes the background in this situation, though a very important one. They will therefore adjust quickly to their partners' behavior, and a mutual adjustment of personal roles will result.

We should expect that the feeling of being "on the spot" would result in wariness during the experimental situation. We saw that in these conditions the discussion tended to be short— an average of 335 seconds (Table 6). Further, relatively little change occurred. Table 7 shows the combined changes, both toward the partner and independently, and we see that the prestige groups clung most to the original story. This may be interpreted as an avoidance of the discussion situation.

If the complementary relationship between the partners is established here, it should result in an unequal distribution of influence. We have seen that there is a general tendency in this direction in the high cohesive groups. Evidence is given in Table 8 that, in the prestige groups, this differentiation is a function of the amount of attempted influence by the group members. We see that in groups of this kind, especially with high cohesiveness, the low inducer changes more than the higher inducer. This would suggest that, in this treatment, making the larger change corresponds to a submissive role.

It would be reasonable to suppose that under the stress of the group-prestige situation, a conscious effort was made to let the partner have his say, particularly by the member who felt in control of the situation. If we assume that this effort will be made after the relationship is established, we could expect that the difference in attempted influence in the first part of the discussion would be quite large but would vanish during the later part. Analysis of the difference in attempted influence in the first and second half of the discussions bears out this hypothesis. Of all conditions, only the high prestige group showed an appreciable difference between the first and second half of the discussion. The difference between the partners dropped from 8.3 "attempt units" to virtual equality between the partners (0.9 units). This is the closest the two partners came to equality in any of the treatments. The difference between the two parts of the discussion in these groups is significant at the 5-percent level.

Table 8 shows the negative condition In striking contrast to the high prestige condition. Here the higher inducer changes most. No genuine interaction

TABLE 8

CHANGES OF HIGH AND LOW INDUCERS

Group	Personal attraction		Task direction		Group prestige		Negative	
	High inducer	Low inducer	High inducer	Low inducer	High inducer	Low inducer	High inducer	Low inducer
Low cohesive	4.0	3.9	4.0	4.9	2.4 *	4.3 *	6.6 ‡	1.9 ‡
High cohesive. . . .	5.3	5.2	5.9	5.2	2.7 †	5.6 †		

* $t = 1.36, p < .20$ † $t = 2.42, p < .05$ ‡ $t = 3.38, p < .02$
Remaining differences not significant.
Note: Two groups with tied scores of attempted influence excluded.

seems to be involved but, rather, two people acting independently and convincing only themselves that they should change.

CONCLUSIONS

Within this setting the results show that an increase in cohesiveness, independent of its nature, will produce the following consequences:

1. In the high cohesive groups the members made more effort to reach an agreement. Both the ratings of the total discussion and direct observation showed more serious effort to enter the discussion in highly cohesive groups. The subjects' own statements also confirmed the high pressures in these groups.

2. Behavior in the highly cohesive groups was more affected by the situation than in the low cohesive groups. The amount of attempted influences measured in highly cohesive groups showed less individual differences, and those differences which did exist were not considered on a personal level.

3. In the highly cohesive groups the discussion was more effective in that it produced influence—that is, group members changed more toward the partners' positions than they did in the less cohesive groups.

4. In the highly cohesive groups the change was quite unevenly distributed between the members, while in the less cohesive groups the changes were more evenly distributed. On the average, one member of the highly cohesive groups changed more than either member of the less cohesive groups; and the other member of the highly cohesive group was nearly the same as one member of the less cohesive groups.

The four points summarize the effects of the forces to belong to the group, of cohesiveness considered as a unitary concept. The differences among the ways in which cohesiveness was produced led to the following interpretations about patterns of communication and influence:

1. If cohesiveness was based on personal attraction, group members wanted to transform the discussion into a longish, pleasant conversation. The discussion was taken as a personal effort, and rejection of persuasion tended to be resented.

2. If cohesiveness was based on the performance of a task, group members wanted to complete the activity quickly and efficiently; they spent just the time necessary for performance of the task, and they tried to use this time for the performance of the task only. They tended to participate in the discussion only as much as they thought it valuable to achieve their purposes.

3. If cohesiveness was based on group prestige, group members tried to risk as little as possible to endanger their status: they acted cautiously, concentrated on their own actions, and adjusted to their partners as the social environment. One partner would easily assume a dominant role, and the submissive member was influenced more, without their actually trying to establish this relationship.

Finally, with cohesiveness at a minimum, the members of the pair acted independently and with little consideration for each other. As the subjects did not try to adjust to the other member of the pair, each member was concerned only with his own discussion. Influence, accordingly, did not depend on the action of the partner but on the interest of the member himself in entering the group activity.

GROUP DECISION AND SOCIAL CHANGE
By Kurt Lewin

The following experiments on group decision have been conducted during the last four years. They are not in a state that permits definite conclusions. But they show the nature of the problems and the main factors concerned. They also indicate the type of concepts to which the attempt to integrate cultural anthropology, psychology, and sociology into one social science may lead.

Scientifically the question of group decision lies at the intersection of many basic problems of group life and individual psychology. It concerns the relation of motivation to action and the effect of a group setting on the individual's readiness to change or to keep certain standards. It is related to one of the fundamental problems of action-research, namely, how to change group conduct so that it would not slide back to the old level within a short time. It is in this wider setting of social processes and social management that group decision should be viewed as one means of social change.

SOCIAL CHANNELS AND SOCIAL PERCEPTION

The meaning and the over-all effect of a group decision depends upon the nature of the process itself, and upon the

position of the group, within the total social field. In regard to these broader questions we will consider two aspects of social steering, namely, steering through gatekeepers and the function which reality perception should have.

Channels, Gates, and Gatekeepers.— *Food Habits and Food Channels.* The first experiment on group decision was part of a larger study on food habits. Its main objective was a comparison of different ethnic and economic groups in a midwestern town. The favorite family food was studied, what food was considered essential, what main frame of reference and values guided the thinking of these groups about foods, and what authorities were seen as standing behind these standards and values. Children at different ages were included to indicate the process of acculturation of the individual in regard to food. Since this study was part of a larger problem of changing food habits in line with war needs, we were interested in including an attempt to bring about some of the desired changes at least on a small scale.

The data acquired give considerable insight into the existing attitudes and practices of the various groups. However, in this, as in many other cases, such data

Prepared especially for this volume by the author shortly before his death.

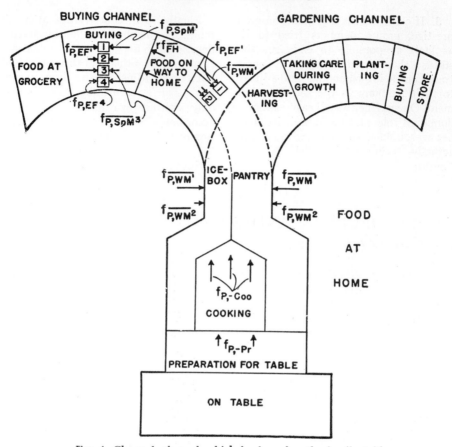

FIG. 1. Channels through which food reaches the family table.

about a present state of affairs do not permit many conclusions in regard to how to proceed best to bring about a change. Should one use radio, posters, lectures, or what other means and methods for changing efficiently group ideology and group action? Should one approach the total population of men, women, and children who are to change their food habits, or would it suffice and perhaps be more effective to concentrate on a strategic part of the population? Obviously the housewife plays some particular role in food habits. What are the underlying assumptions?

Food which comes to the family table

is likely to be eaten by someone in the family since little is thrown away. If this is correct, to consider methods of changing family food habits we have first to ask: how does food come to the table?

Food comes to the table through different channels, such as the Buying Channel or the Gardening Channel.[1] After the food has been bought, it might be placed in the icebox or put in the pantry to be either cooked later or prepared directly for the table (Fig. 1). Similarly, the food moves through the garden channel in a step-by-step fashion.

To understand what comes on the table we have to know the forces which

[1] For quantitative data, see K. Lewin, "Forces Behind Food Habits and Methods of Change," *Bull. Nat. Res. Coun.*, 1943, CVIII, 35–65.

determine what food enters a channel. Whether food enters the channel to the family table or not is determined in the buying situation. The buying situation can be characterized as a conflict situation. Food 1 (Fig. 1) might be attractive, that is, the force $(f_{P,EF})$ toward eating is large but at the same time the food might be very expensive and therefore the opposing force $(f_{P,SpM})$ against spending money is large too. Food 2 might be unattractive but cheap. In this case the conflict would be small. The force toward buying might be composed of a number of components, such as the buyer's liking for the food, his knowledge of his family likes and dislikes, or his ideas about what food is "essential."

The opposing forces might be due to the lack of readiness to spend a certain amount of money, a dislike of lengthy or disagreeable form of preparation, unattractive taste, lack of fitness for the occasion, etc. Food is bought if the total force toward buying becomes greater than the opposing forces (Food 3) until the food basket is filled. Food of type 1 can be called conflict food.

It is culturally significant that the average conflict rating is considerably higher in the middle group (7.44) than in the high (4.35) or the low economic group (5.62). This conflict is probably the result of the greater discrepancy between the standards this group would like to keep up and their ability to do so in a situation of rising prices.

In comparing the conflict rating of different foods for the same group, one finds that meat stands highest for the low group, whereas it is second for the middle and third for the high economic group. That probably means that the conflict between "like" and "expense" in the low group is most outspoken for meat. The high conflict rating of vegetables for the high and middle economic group is probably an expression of the fact that vegetables are desirable as health food but not well liked and not easily prepared. The ratos are.

Food	High group	Middle group	Low group
Vegetables . .	.89	1.44	.57
Milk	.70	.89	.33
Meat	.65	1.28	.95
Butter	.30	.94	.67
Fruits	.43	.94	.62
Potatoes . . .	. . .	.33	.76

The Gate. It is important to know that once food is bought some forces change its direction. Let us assume the housewife has finally decided to buy the high conflict Food 1. The force against spending money, instead of keeping the food out of the channel, will then make the housewife doubly eager not to waste it. In other words, the force $(f_{P,WM})$ against wasting money will have the same direction as the force toward eating this food or will have the character of a force against leaving the channel.

This example indicates that a certain area within a channel might function as a "gate": The constellation of the forces before and after the gate region are decisively different in such a way that the passing or not passing of a unit through the whole channel depends to a high degree upon what happens in the gate region. This holds not only for food channels but also for the traveling of a news item through certain communication channels in a group, for movements of goods, and the social locomotion of individuals in many organizations. A university, for instance, might be quite strict in its admission policy and might set up strong forces against the passing of weak candidates. Once a student is admitted, however, the university frequently tries to do everything in its power to help everyone along. Many business organizations follow a similar policy. Organizations which discriminate against members of a minority group frequently use the argument that they are not ready to accept individuals whom

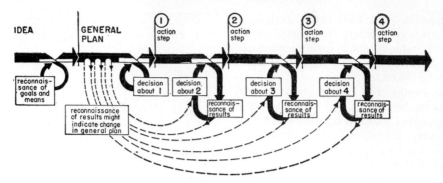

FIG. 2. Planning, fact-finding, and execution.

they would be unable to promote sufficiently.

The Gatekeeper. In case a channel has a gate, the dominant question regarding the movements of materials or persons through the channel is: who is the gatekeeper and what is his psychology?

The study of the high, middle, and low groups, as well as of a group of Czechs and of Negroes in a midwestern town, revealed that all channels except gardening were definitely controlled by the housewife.

We can conclude from this that changes of food habits in the family finally depend on changes of the psychology of the housewife in the buying situation. Changes of the attitudes and desires of children and husbands will affect actual food habits only to the degree they affect the housewife.

Similar considerations hold for any social constellation which has the character of a channel, a gate, and gatekeepers. Discrimination against minorities will not be changed as long as the forces are not changed which determine the decisions of the gatekeeper. Their decision depends partly on their ideology, that is, the system of values and beliefs which determines what they consider to be "good" or "bad," partly on the way they perceive the particular situation. This latter point will be considered more closely by discussing problems of planning.

Planning, Fact-finding, and Execution.
Planning usually starts with something like a general idea. For one reason or another it seems desirable to reach a certain objective. Exactly how to circumscribe this objective and how to reach it is frequently not too clear. The first step, then, is to examine the idea carefully in the light of the means available. Frequently more fact-finding about the situation is required. If this first period of planning is successful, two items emerge: an "over-all plan" of how to reach the objective and a decision in regard to the first step of action. Usually this planning has also somewhat modified the original idea.

The next period is devoted to executing the first step of the over-all plan. In highly developed fields of social management, such as modern factory management or the execution of a war, this second step is followed by certain fact-findings. For example, in the bombing of Germany a certain factory may have been chosen as the first target after careful consideration of various priorities and of the best means and ways of dealing with this target. The attack is pressed home and immediately a reconnaissance plane follows with the one objective of determining as accurately and objectively as possible the new situation (Fig. 2).

This reconnaissance or fact-finding has four functions: It should evaluate the action by showing whether what has been achieved is above or below expectation. It should serve as a basis for correctly planning the next step. It should serve as a basis for modifying the "over-all plan." Finally, it gives the planners a chance to learn, that is, to gather new general insight, for instance, regarding the strength and weakness of certain weapons or techniques of action.

The next step again is composed of a circle of planning, executing, and reconnaissance or fact-finding for the purpose of evaluating the results of the second step, for preparing the rational basis for planning the third step, and for perhaps modifying again the over-all plan.

Rational social management, therefore, proceeds in a spiral of steps each of which is composed of a circle of planning, action, and fact-finding about the result of the action.

In most social areas of management and self-management of groups, such as conducting a conference and committee meeting, family life, or the improvement of intergroup relations within and between nations, we are still lacking objective standards of achievement. This has two severe effects: (1) People responsible for social management are frequently deprived of their legitimate desire for reconnaissance on a realistic basis. Under these circumstances, satisfaction or dissatisfaction with achievement becomes mainly a question of temperament. (2) In a field that lacks objective standards of achievement, no learning can take place. If we cannot judge whether an action has led forward or backward, if we have no criteria for evaluating the relation between effort and achievement, there is nothing to prevent us from coming to the wrong conclusions and encouraging the wrong work habits. Realistic fact-finding and evaluation is a prerequisite for any learning.

Social Channels, Social Perception, and Decision. The relation between social channels, social perception and decisions is methodologically and practically of considerable significance.

The theory of channels and gatekeepers helps to define in a more precise way how certain "objective" sociological problems of locomotion of goods and persons intersect with certain "subjective" psychological and cultural problems. It points to sociologically characterized places, such as gates in social channels, where attitudes and decisions have a particularly great effect.

The relation between group decision and pre- and post-action diagnosis is two-fold: (1) group decision depends partly upon how the group views the situation and therefore can be influenced by a change in this perception. (2) A correct perception of the result of social action is essential for the decision of the next step. The measurement of the effect of group decisions is in line with the need for objective evaluation as a prerequisite for making progress in social management and self management of groups.

GROUP DECISION

Lecture Compared with Group Decision (Red Cross Groups). A preliminary experiment in changing food habits [2] was conducted with six Red Cross groups of volunteers organized for home nursing. Groups ranged in size from 13 to 17 members. The objective was to increase the use of beef hearts, sweetbreads, and kidneys. If one considers the psychological forces which kept housewives from using these intestinals, one is tempted to think of rather deep-seated aversions requiring something like psychoanalytical treatment. Doubtless a change in this respect is a much more difficult task than, for instance, the introduction

---

[2] The studies on nutrition discussed in this article were conducted at the Child Welfare Research Station of the State University of Iowa for the Food Habits Committee of the National Research Council (Executive Secretary, Margaret Mead).

of a new vegetable such as escarole. There were, however, only 45 minutes available.

In three of the groups attractive lectures were given which linked the problem of nutrition with the war effort, emphasized the vitamin and mineral value of the three meats, giving detailed explanations with the aid of charts. Both the health and economic aspects were stressed. The preparation of these meats was discussed in detail as well as techniques for avoiding those characteristics to which aversions were oriented (odor, texture, appearance, etc.). Mimeographed recipes were distributed. The lecturer was able to arouse the interest of the groups by giving hints of her own methods for preparing these "delicious dishes," and her success with her own family.

For the other three groups Mr. Alex Bavelas developed the following procedure of group decision. Again the problem of nutrition was linked with that of the war effort and general health. After a few minutes, a discussion was started to see whether housewives could be induced to participate in a program of change without attempting any high-pressure salesmanship. The group discussion about "housewives like themselves" led to an elaboration of the obstacles which a change in general and particularly change toward sweetbreads, beef hearts, and kidneys would encounter, such as the dislike of the husband, the smell during cooking, etc. The nutrition expert offered the same remedies and recipes for preparation which were presented in the lectures to the other groups. But in these groups preparation techniques were offered after the groups had become sufficiently involved to be interested in knowing whether certain obstacles could be removed.

In the earlier part of the meeting a census was taken on how many women had served any of these foods in the past. At the end of the meeting, the women

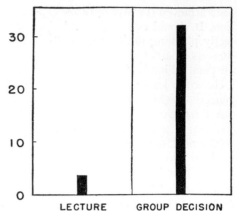

FIG. 3. Percentage of individuals serving type of food never served before, after lecture and after group decision.

were asked by a showing of hands who was willing to try one of these meats within the next week.

A follow-up showed that only 3 percent of the women who heard the lectures served one of the meats never served before, whereas after group decision 32 percent served one of them (Fig. 3).

If one is to understand the basis of this striking difference, several factors may have to be considered.

1. *Degree of Involvement.* Lecturing is a procedure in which the audience is chiefly passive. The discussion, if conducted correctly, is likely to lead to a much higher degree of involvement. The procedure of group decision in this experiment follows a step-by-step method designed (a) to secure high involvement and (b) not to impede freedom of decision. The problem of food changes was discussed in regard to "housewives like yourselves" rather than in regard to themselves. This minimized resistance to considering the problems and possibilities in an objective, unprejudiced manner, in much the same way as such resistance has been minimized in interviews which use projective techniques, or in a sociodrama which uses an assumed situation of role playing rather than a real situation.

2. *Motivation and Decision.* The prevalent theory in psychology assumes action to be the direct result of motivation. I am inclined to think that we will have to modify this theory. We will have to study the particular conditions under which a motivating constellation leads or does not lead to a decision or to an equivalent process through which a state of "considerations" (indecisiveness) is changed into a state where the individual has "made up his mind" and is ready for action, although he may not act at that moment.

The act of decision is one of those transitions. A change from a situation of undecided conflict to decision does not mean merely that the forces toward one alternative become stronger than those toward the other alternative. If this were the case, the resultant force should frequently be extremely small. A decision rather means that the potency of one alternative has become zero or is so decidedly diminished that the other alternative and the corresponding forces dominate the situation. This alternative itself might be a compromise. After the decision people may feel sorry and change their decision. We cannot speak of a real decision, however, before one alternative has become dominant so far as action is concerned. If the opposing forces in a conflict merely change so that the forces in one direction become slightly greater than in the other direction, a state of blockage or extremely inhibited action results rather than that clear one-sided action which follows a real decision.

Lecturing may lead to a high degree of interest. It may affect the motivation of the listener. But it seldom brings about a definite decision on the part of the listener to take a certain action at a specific time. A lecture is not often conducive to decision.

Evidence from everyday experience and from some preliminary experiments by Bavelas in a factory indicate that even group discussions, although usually leading to a higher degree of involvement, as a rule do not lead to a decision. It is very important to emphasize this point. Although group discussion is in many respects different from lectures, it shows no fundamental difference on this point.

Of course, there is a great difference in asking for a decision after a lecture or after a discussion. Since discussion involves active participation of the audience and a chance to express motivations corresponding to different alternatives, the audience might be more ready "to make up its mind," that is, to make a decision after a group discussion than after a lecture. A group discussion gives the leader a better indication of where the audience stands and what particular obstacles have to be overcome.

In the experiment on hand, we are dealing with a group decision after discussion. The decision, itself, takes but a minute or two. (It was done through raising of hands as an answer to the question: Who would like to serve kidney, sweetbreads, beef hearts next week?) The act of decision, however, should be viewed as a very important process of giving dominance to one of the alternatives, serving or not serving. It has an effect of freezing this motivational constellation for action. We will return to this point later.

3. *Individual versus Group.* The experiment does not try to bring about a change of food habits by an approach to the individual, as such. Nor does it use the "mass approach" characteristic of radio and newspaper propaganda. Closer scrutiny shows that both the mass approach and the individual approach place the individual in a quasi-private, psychologically isolated situation with himself and his own ideas. Although he may, physically, be part of a group listening to a lecture, for example, he finds himself, psychologically speaking, in an "individual situation."

The present experiment approaches the individual as a member of a face-to-face group. We know, for instance, from experiments in level of aspiration [3] that goal setting is strongly dependent on group standards. Experience in leadership training and in many areas of re-education, such as re-education regarding alcoholism or delinquency,[4] indicates that it is easier to change the ideology and social practice of a small group handled together than of single individuals. One of the reasons why "group carried changes" are more readily brought about seems to be the unwillingness of the individual to depart too far from group standards; he is likely to change only if the group changes. We will return to this problem.

One may try to link the greater effectiveness of group decision procedures to the fact that the lecture reaches the individual in a more individualistic fashion than group discussion. If a change of sentiment of the group becomes apparent during the discussion, the individual will be more ready to come along.

It should be stressed that in our case the decision which follows the group discussion does not have the character of a decision in regard to a group goal; it is rather a decision about individual goals in a group setting.

4. *Expectation.* The difference between the results of the lectures and the group decision may be due to the fact that only after group decision did the discussion leader mention that an inquiry would be made later as to whether a new food was introduced into the family diet.

5. *Leader Personality.* The difference in effectiveness may be due to differences in leader personality. The nutritionist and the housewife who did the lecturing were persons of recognized ability, experience, and success. Still, Mr. Bavelas, who led the discussion and subsequent decision, is an experienced group worker and doubtless of unusual ability in this field.

To determine which of these or other factors are important, a number of systematic variations have to be carried out. To determine, for instance, the role of the decision as such, one can compare the effect of group discussion with and without decision. To study the role of group involvement and the possibility of sensing the changing group sentiment, one could introduce decisions after both, lecture and discussion, and compare their effects.

The following experiments represent partly analytical variations, partly repetitions with somewhat different material.

Lecture versus Group Decision (Neighborhood Groups). Dana Klisurich, under the direction of Marian Radke, conducted experiments with 6 groups of housewives composed of 6–9 members per group. She compared the effect of a lecture with that of group decision. The topic for these groups was increasing home consumption of milk, in the form of fresh or evaporated milk or both.[5]

The procedure followed closely that described above. Again there was no attempt at high-pressure salesmanship. The group discussion proceeded in a step-by-step way, starting again with "what housewives in general might do" and only then leading to the individuals present. The lecture was kept as interesting as possible. The knowledge transmitted was the same for lecture and group decision.

A check-up was made after two weeks and after four weeks. As in the previous experiments, group decision showed considerably greater effectiveness, both after two weeks and after four weeks and for both fresh and evaporated milk (Figs.

---

[3] K. Lewin, "Behavior and Development as a Function of the Total Situation" in L. Carmichael (ed.), *Manual of Child Psychology* (New York: John Wiley, 1946), pp. 791–844.

[4] K. Lewin and P. Grabbe (eds.), "Problems of Re-education," *J. Soc. Issues*, (August) 1945, I, No. 3.

[5] M. Radke and D. Klisurich, Experiments in Changing Food Habits. Unpublished manuscript.

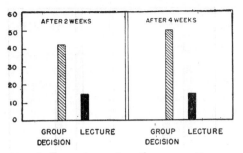

Fig. 4. Percentage of mothers reporting an increase in the consumption of fresh milk.

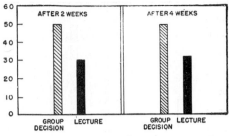

Fig. 5. Percentage of mothers reporting an increase in the consumption of evaporated milk.

4 and 5). This experiment permits the following conclusions:

1. It shows that the greater effectiveness of the group decision in the first experiment is not merely the result of the personality or training of the leader. The leader was a lively person, interested in people, but she did not have particular training in group work. She had been carefully advised and had had a try-out in the group decision procedure. As mentioned above, the leader in lecture and group decision was the same person.

2. The experiment shows that the different effectiveness of the two procedures is not limited to the foods considered in the first experiment.

3. It is interesting that the greater effectiveness of group decision was observable not only after one week but after two and four weeks. Consumption after group decision kept constant during that period. After the lecture it showed an insignificant increase from the second to the fourth week. The degree of permanency is obviously a very important aspect of any changes in group life. We will come back to this point.

4. As in the first experiment, the subjects were informed about a future check-up after group decision but not after the lecture. After the second week, however, both groups knew that a check-up had been made and neither of them was informed that a second check-up would follow.

5. It is important to know whether group decision is effective only with tightly knit groups. It should be noticed that in the second experiment the groups were composed of housewives who either lived in the same neighborhood or visited the nutrition information service of the community center. They were not members of a club meeting regularly as were the Red Cross groups in the first experiment. On the other hand, a good proportion of these housewives knew each other. This indicates that decision in a group setting seems to be effective even if the group is not a permanent organization.

Individual Instruction versus Group Decision. For a number of years, the state hospital in Iowa City has given advice to mothers on feeding of their babies. Under this program, farm mothers who have their first child at the hospital meet with a nutritionist for from 20–25 minutes before discharge from the hospital to discuss feeding. The mother receives printed advice on the composition of the formula and is instructed in the importance of orange juice and cod liver oil.

There had been indication that the effect of this nutrition program was not very satisfactory. An experiment was carried out by Dana Klisurich under the direction of Marian Radke to compare the effectiveness of this procedure with that of group decision.[6]

With some mothers individual instruction was used as before. Others were

[6] M. Radke and D. Klisurich, Experiments in Changing Food Habits. Unpublished manuscript.

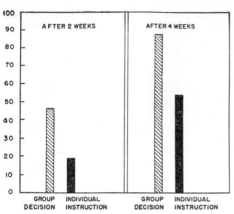

FIG. 6. Percentage of mothers following completely group decision or individual instruction in giving cod liver oil.

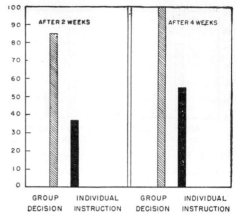

FIG. 7. Percentage of mothers following completely group decision or individual instruction in giving orange juice.

divided into groups of six for instruction on and discussion of baby feeding. The manner of reaching a decision at the end of this group meeting was similar to that used in the previous experiments. The time for the six mothers together was the same as for one individual, about 25 minutes.

After two weeks and after four weeks, a check was made on the degree to which each mother followed the advice on cod liver oil and orange juice. Figures 6 and 7 show the percentage of individuals who completely followed the advice. The group decision method proved far superior to the individual instruction. After four weeks every mother who participated in group decision followed exactly the prescribed diet in regard to orange juice.

The following specific results might be mentioned:

1. The greater effect of group decision in this experiment is particularly interesting. Individual instruction is a setting in which the individual gets more attention from the instructor. Therefore, one might expect the individual to become more deeply involved and the instruction to be fitted more adequately to the need and sentiment of each individual. After all, the instructor devotes the same

amount of time to one individual as he does to six in group decision. The result can be interpreted to mean either that the amount of individual involvement is greater in group decision or that the decision in the group setting is itself the decisive factor.

2. Most of the mothers were not acquainted with each other. They returned to farms which were widely separated. Most of them had no contact with each other during the following four weeks. The previous experiment had already indicated that the effectiveness of group decision did not seem to be limited to well-established groups. In this experiment the absence of social relations among the mothers before and after the group meeting is even more clearcut.

3. The data thus far do not permit reliable quantitative, over-all comparisons. However, they point to certain interesting problems and possibilities. In comparing the various experiments concerning the data two weeks after group decision, one finds that the percentage of housewives who served kidneys, beef hearts or sweetbreads is relatively similar to the percentage of housewives who increased the consumption of fresh milk or evaporated milk or of mothers who followed completely the

diet of cod liver oil with their babies. The percentages lie between 32 and 50. The percentage in regard to orange juice for the baby is clearly higher, namely, 85 percent. These results are surprising in several respects. Mothers are usually eager to do all they can for their babies. This may explain why a group decision in regard to orange juice had such a strong effect. Why, however, was this effect not equally strong on cod liver oil? Perhaps, giving the baby cod liver oil is hampered by the mothers' own dislike of this food. Kidneys, beef hearts, and sweetbreads are foods for which the dislike seems to be particularly deep-seated. If the amount of dislike is the main resistance to change, one would expect probably a greater difference between these foods and, for instance, a change in regard to fresh milk. Of course, these meats are particularly cheap and the group decision leader was particularly qualified.

4. The change after lectures is in all cases smaller than after group decision. However, the rank order of the percentage of change after lectures follows the rank order after group decision, namely (from low to high), glandular meat, fresh milk, cod liver oil for the baby, evaporated milk for the family, orange juice for the baby.

The constancy of this rank order may be interpreted to mean that one can ascribe to each of these foods—under the given circumstances and for these particular populations—a specific degree of "resistance to change." The "force toward change" resulting from group decision is greater than the force resulting from lecture. This leads to a difference in the amount (or frequency) of change for the same food without changing the rank order of the various foods. The rank order is determined by the relative strength of their resistance to change.

5. Comparing the second and the fourth week, we notice that the level of

consumption remains the same or increases insignificantly after group decision and lecture regarding evaporated or fresh milk. A pronounced increase occurs after group decision and after individual instruction on cod liver oil and orange juice, that is, in all cases regarding infant feeding. This seems to be a perplexing phenomenon if one considers that no additional instruction or group decision was introduced. On the whole, one may be inclined to expect weakening effect of group decision with time and therefore a decrease rather than an increase of the curve. To understand the problems involved, it is essential to formulate the question of condition of social change on a more theoretical level.

Quasi-stationary Social Equilibria and the Problem of Permanent Change. 1. *The Objective of Change.* The objective of social change might concern the nutritional standard of consumption, the economic standard of living, the type of group relation, the output of a factory, the productivity of an educational team. It is important that a social standard to be changed does not have the nature of a "thing" but of a "process." A certain standard of consumption, for instance, means that a certain action—such as making certain decisions, buying, preparing, and canning certain food in a family—occurs with a certain frequency within a given period. Similarly, a certain type of group relations means that within a given period certain friendly and hostile actions and reactions of a certain degree of severity occur between the members of two groups. Changing group relations or changing consumption means changing the level at which these multitude of events proceed. In other words, the "level" of consumption, of friendliness, or of productivity is to be characterized as the aspect of an ongoing social process.

Any planned social change will have to consider a multitude of factors characteristic for the particular case. The change may require a more or less unique

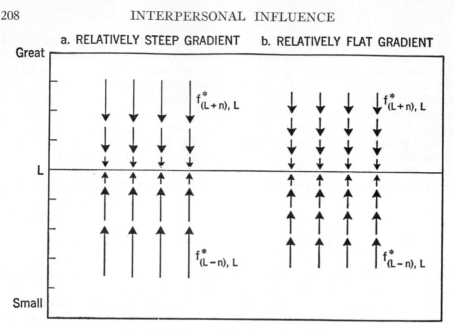

FIG. 8. Gradients of resultant forces (f*).

combination of educational and organizational measures; it may depend upon quite different treatments or ideology, expectation and organization. Still, certain general formal principles always have to be considered.

2. *The Conditions of a Stable Quasi-stationary Equilibrium.* The study of the conditions for change begins appropriately with an analysis of the conditions for "no change," that is, for the state of equilibrium.

From what has been just discussed, it is clear that by a state of "no social change" we do not refer to a stationary but to a quasi-stationary equilibrium; that is, to a state comparable to that of a river which flows with a given velocity in a given direction during a certain time interval. A social change is comparable to a change in the velocity or direction of that river.

A number of statements can be made in regard to the conditions of quasi-stationary equilibrium. (These conditions are treated more elaborately elsewhere.[7])

(A) The strength of forces which tend to lower that standard of social life should be equal and opposite to the strength of forces which tend to raise its level. The resultant of forces on the line of equilibrium should therefore be zero.

(B) Since we have to assume that the strength of social forces always shows variations, a quasi-stationary equilibrium presupposes that the forces against raising the standard increase with the amount of raising and that the forces against lowering increase (or remain constant) with the amount of lowering. This type of gradient which is characteristic for a "positive central force field"[8] has to hold at least in the neighborhood of the present level (Fig. 8).

(C) It is possible to change the strength of the opposing forces without changing the level of social conduct. In this case the tension (degree of conflict) increases.

[7] K. Lewin, "Frontiers in Group Dynamics: Concept, Method and Reality in Social Science; Social Equilibria and Social Change," *Human Relations*, I, 1, June, 1947, pp. 5–42.
[8] *Ibid*.

3. *Two Basic Methods of Changing Levels of Conduct.* For any type of social management, it is of great practical importance that levels of quasi-stationary equilibria can be changed in either of two ways: by adding forces in the desired direction, or by diminishing opposing forces. If a change from the level L_1 to L_2 is brought about by increasing the forces toward L_2, the secondary effects should be different from the case where the same change of level is brought about by diminishing the opposing forces.

In both cases the equilibrium might change to the same new level. The secondary effect should, however, be quite different. In the first case, the process on the new level would be accompanied by a state of relatively high tension; in the second case, by a state of relatively low tension. Since increase of tension above a certain degree is likely to be paralleled by higher aggressiveness, higher emotionality, and lower constructiveness, it is clear that as a rule the second method will be preferable to the high pressure method.

The group decision procedure which is used here attempts to avoid high pressure methods and is sensitive to resistance to change. In the experiment by Bavelas on changing production in factory work (as noted below), for instance, no attempt was made to set the new production goal by majority vote because a majority vote forces some group members to produce more than they consider appropriate. These individuals are likely to have some inner resistance. Instead a procedure was followed by which a goal was chosen on which everyone could agree fully.

It is possible that the success of group decision and particularly the permanency of the effect is, in part, due to the attempt to bring about a favorable decision by removing counterforces within the individuals rather than by applying outside pressure.

The surprising increase from the second to the fourth week in the number of mothers giving cod liver oil and orange juice to the baby can probably be explained by such a decrease of counterforces. Mothers are likely to handle their first baby during the first weeks of life somewhat cautiously and become more ready for action as the child grows stronger.

4. *Social Habits and Group Standards.* Viewing a social stationary process as the result of a quasi-stationary equilibrium, one may expect that any added force will change the level of the process. The idea of "social habit" seems to imply that, in spite of the application of a force, the level of the social process will not change because of some type of "inner resistance" to change. To overcome this inner resistance, an additional force seems to be required, a force sufficient to "break the habit," to "unfreeze" the custom.

Many social habits are anchored in the relation between the individuals and certain group standards. An individual P may differ in his personal level of conduct (L_P) from the level which represents group standards (L_{Gr}) by a certain amount. If the individual should try to diverge "too much" from group standards, he would find himself in increasing difficulties. He would be ridiculed, treated severely and finally ousted from the group. Most individuals, therefore, stay pretty close to the standard of the groups they belong to or wish to belong to. In other words, the group level itself acquires value. It becomes a positive valence corresponding to a central force field with the force $f_{P,L}$ keeping the individual in line with the standards of the group.

5. *Individual Procedures and Group Procedures of Changing Social Conduct.* If the resistance to change depends partly on the value which the group standard has for the individual, the resistance to change should diminish if one diminishes the strength of the value of the group

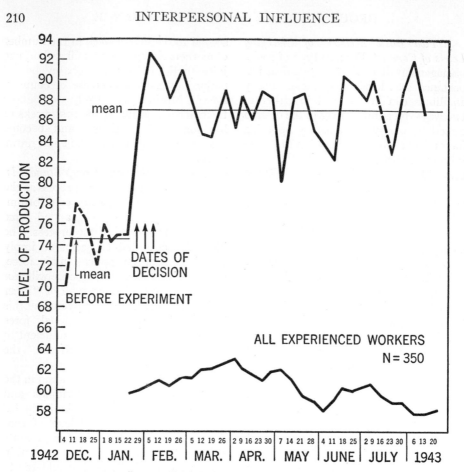

FIG. 9. Effect of group decision on sewing-machine operators.

standard or changes the level perceived by the individual as having social value.

This second point is one of the reasons for the effectiveness of "group carried" changes[9] resulting from procedures which approach the individuals as part of face-to-face groups. Perhaps one might expect single individuals to be more pliable than groups of like-minded individuals. However, experience in leadership training, in changing of food habits, work production, criminality, alcoholism, prejudices, all indicate that it is usually easier to change individuals formed into a group than to change any one of them separately.[10] As long as group standards are unchanged, the individual will resist changes more strongly the farther he is to depart from group standards. If the group standard itself is changed, the resistance which is due to the relation between individual and group standard is eliminated.

6. *Changing as a Three-step Procedure: Unfreezing, Moving, and Freezing of a Level.* A change toward a higher level of group performance is frequently short lived: after a "shot in the arm," group life soon returns to the previous level. This indicates that it does not suffice to define the objective of a planned change in group performance as the reaching of a

[9] N. R. F. Maier, *Psychology in Industry* (Boston: Houghton Mifflin Co., 1946).
[10] K. Lewin and P. Grabbe (eds.) *op. cit.*

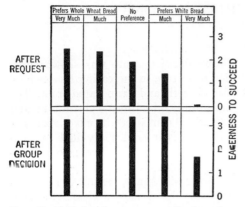

FIG. 10. Relation between own food preferences and eagerness to succeed.

different level. Permanency of the new level, or permanency for a desired period, should be included in the objective. A successful change includes therefore three aspects: unfreezing (if necessary) the present level L_1, moving to the new level L_2, and freezing group life on the new level. Since any level is determined by a force field, permanency implies that the new force field is made relatively secure against change.

The "unfreezing" of the present level may involve quite different problems in different cases. Allport[11] has described the "catharsis" which seems to be necessary before prejudices can be removed. To break open the shell of complacency and self-righteousness, it is sometimes necessary to bring about deliberately an emotional stir-up.

Figure 9 presents an example of the effect of three group decisions of a team in a factory reported by Bavelas[12] which illustrates an unusually good case of permanency of change measured over nine months.

The experiments on group decision reported here cover but a few of the necessary variations. Although in some

cases the procedure is relatively easily executed, in others it requires skill and presupposes certain general conditions. Managers rushing into a factory to raise production by group decisions are likely to encounter failure. In social management as in medicine there are no patent medicines and each case demands careful diagnosis.

One reason why group decision facilitates change is illustrated by Willerman.[13] Figure 10 shows the degree of eagerness to have the members of a students' eating cooperative change from the consumption of white bread to whole wheat. When the change was simply requested the degree of eagerness varied greatly with the degree of personal preference for whole wheat. In case of group decision the eagerness seems to be relatively independent of personal preference; the individual seems to act mainly as a "group member."

SUMMARY

Group decision is a process of social management or self management of groups. It is related to social channels, gates and gatekeepers; to the problem of social perception and planning; and to the relation between motivation and action, and between the individual and the group.

Experiments are reported in which certain methods of group decision prove to be superior to lecturing and individual treatment as means of changing social conduct.

The effect of group decision can probably be best understood by relating it to a theory of quasi-stationary social equilibria, to social habits and resistance to change, and to the various problems of unfreezing, changing and freezing social levels.

---

[11] G. W. Allport, "Catharsis and the Reduction of Prejudice" in K. Lewin and P. Grabbe (eds.), op. cit., 3–10.

[12] N. R. F. Maier, op. cit,

[13] V. Lewin "Forces behind Food Habits . . .," op. cit.

SOME FACTORS IN "GROUP DECISION"
By Edith Bennett Pelz

The major historical antecedents of this experiment were three studies reported by Kurt Lewin [1] and performed under his direction in the 1940's, comparing the effectiveness of a procedure Lewin named "group decision" with that of another method used to induce a change in food habits.

By "group decision" Lewin meant a group discussion about the desirability of a particular action to be taken by members of the group *as individuals*. The discussion always ended with the leader's request for individual decisions regarding intended action. This experiment also focused upon individuals under inducement to reach a personal decision in a group setting. This use of the term should be clearly differentiated from one involving collective solutions of group problems in which action decisions have implications for the discussion participants as group members rather than as individuals.

The first of the Lewinian studies, performed by Bavelas, Festinger, Woodward, and Zander [2] found that a method of group decision was vastly superior to the lecture method in persuading housewives to serve intestinal meats. The second experiment, by Radke and Klisurich,[3] again compared group decision to lecture, improving on the previous design by holding the factor of leader personality constant over both methods.

Group decision again was shown superior to lecture in increasing housewives' use of fresh and evaporated milk. The third study, cited by Lewin, Radke and Klisurich [4] compared the effectiveness of group decision and individual instruction in persuading mothers to supplement infant diets with orange juice and cod-liver oil. Again, results were favorable to the group decision method, though differences this time were not as striking as in the previous studies. Neal Miller succinctly summarized both the significance and the limitations of the Lewinian researches:

The investigators found that a group of housewives who participated in a discussion, made a public decision by raising their hands, and were told that there would be a follow-up study to check on what they did were much more likely to serve the nonpreferred meat than another group who listened to a lecture without making a public decision and without being told to expect a follow-up study. In this pioneer stage these investigators have tended to lump together a number of factors such as hearing the views of other group members, having a chance to express one's objections, being required to make some immediate public or private decision, etc.[5]

The present experiment was designed to analyze further the operation of group decision as used by Lewin and his coworkers by breaking it down into several

Condensed by the author from E. B. Bennett, "Discussion, Decision, Commitment and Consensus in 'Group Decision'," *Hum. Rel.*, 1955, VIII, 251–274.

---

[1] See K. Lewin, preceding article.

[2] A. Bavelas, L. Festinger, P. Woodward, and A. Zander, "The Relative Effectiveness of a Lecture Method and a Method of Group Decision for Changing Food Habits," *Bulletin of the Committee on Food Habits* (National Research Council).

[3] M. Radke and D. Klisurich "Experiments in Changing Food Habits," *J. Amer. Dietetic Assn.*, 1947, XXIV, 403–409.

[4] *Ibid.*

[5] N. E. Miller, "Learnable Drives and Rewards," in S. S. Stevens (ed.), *Handbook of Experimental Psychology* (New York: John Wiley & Sons, Inc., 1951), p. 468.

separate factors which could be individually assessed.

Group decision, in the Lewinian experiments, consisted of group discussions concluding with a request for decision. These discussions yielded 100-percent positive decisions which were made publicly. In addition, they always included a specifically stated time period within which the requisite action was to be taken (and after which experimental effects were measured), as well as the information that a follow-up would be made. The contrasted approaches, lecture and individual instruction, were similar *only* in so far as the same information was conveyed. On every other variable they differed.

A specific time limit and knowledge of follow-up were entirely eliminated from the present experiment. Four factors were thus isolated for study in the research reported here:

1. *Group discussion* as a means of conveying information;
2. *Decision* to perform a specific action;
3. *Commitment*—the degree to which the decision is indicated publicly;
4. *Degree of consensus* by the group in reaching the requested decision.

In addition to the separation of these four factors, an important improvement over previous designs was the provision of an *objective action criterion*.

HYPOTHESES

For each of the four major variables a hypothesis, testable without reference to the effectiveness of the remaining factors, was formulated.

Hypothesis I: Group discussion, as an influence technique, is a more effective inducement to action than is the lecture method or no persuasion attempt at all.

Hypothesis II: The process of coming to a decision regarding future action raises the probability of the execution of the action.

Hypothesis III: Where a decision is made, a more public commitment or indication of the decision is more effective in assuring the execution of such action than is a less public one.

Hypothesis IV: A high degree of group consensus on intention to act raises the probability that individual members of the group will execute the action above the probability of action by members of groups in which there was a low degree of consensus.

EXPERIMENTAL PROCEDURES

The experimental manipulations attempted to raise the willingness of University of Michigan students in a beginning psychology course to volunteer as subjects in behavioral-science experiments.

Three types of "influence-attempt" and four "decision and commitment" variations were combined to create twelve experimental treatments:

The four variations along the vertical axis represent two of the experimental variables relevant to the testing of two of the hypotheses: (1) The "no-decision" variation is differentiated from all of the other three with reference to the factor of reaching a decision; (2) decision levels II, III, and IV differ with reference to the degree of anonymity with which decisions were indicated.

Thirty-six groups of eight to 16 students were assembled and three groups were assigned to each of the 12 experimental variations. Three male graduate students with teaching experience were trained in practice discussions with subjects comparable to the experimental population. On the basis of the practice discussion, they prepared common lecture outlines and discussion objectives. Leader personality was held constant by assigning each man to lead one of the three groups in each of the experimental variations.

In the discussion groups all possible ex-

TABLE 1

Twelve Experimental Variations
(with total number of Ss participating in each)

Commitment level	Influence attempt			
	Discussion	Lecture	Control	Total
I. No decision	39	44	52	135
II. Anonymous decision	40	35	37	112
III. Partially anonymous decision	46	32	35	113
IV. Public commitment	40	33	40	113
Total	165	144	164	473

pectations about participating in experiments were elicited and discussed—fears and distrust as well as individual and social gains. Lectures covered the same topics. The control groups heard no arguments pro or con.

Decision-level I groups were dismissed after influence attempts. Control groups at decision-level I were not contacted at this stage of the experiment. In Type II groups students wrote anonymous statements about their willingness to volunteer, if asked. In Type III groups those who thought they would volunteer in the future raised their hands. The most public commitment, Type IV, involved raising hands and publicly giving names to the leader, who openly recorded them.

Several days after the completion of experimental sessions, a letter was sent to all subjects announcing the establishment of a "central file" of prospective volunteers by the "Committee for Recruiting Experimental Subjects." They were invited to appear at a specified place during a limited-time period, to make their names, telephone numbers, etc. available to experimenters. Subjects who came to sign up fulfilled the criterion of having "taken action." A week after

TABLE 2

Number and Proportion of Subjects Exposed to Each of the Influence Attempts Who Fulfilled the Action Criterion

	Total no.	No. acting	Percentage acting
Discussion	165	34	21
Lecture	144	31	22
Control	164	31	19

$$\chi^2 = .374 \quad p = .84 *$$

* Probabilities reported throughout this paper are two-tailed chance probabilities. However, where a hypothesis correctly predicts the *direction* of deviation from expected frequencies, the probability of chance occurrence of results is smaller than that read from the table of chi square; e.g., one half as great for a two-by-two analysis (See A. M. Mood and W. J. Dixon, "A Method for Obtaining and Analyzing Sensitivity Data," *J. Am. Stat. Assn.*, 1948, XLIII, 109–126). Such cases arise later in this paper.

the volunteering period a questionnaire was administered during class session, yielding further information on the reported commitments (Did you decide to volunteer?), perceived consensus (How many from your group would you estimate signed up?), and reported action (Did you actually go to sign up?).[6]

[6] The interested reader is referred to E. B. Bennett, *op. cit.*, and E. B. Bennett, *The Relationship of Group Discussion, Decision, Commitment and Consensus to Individual Action*, published Ph.D. thesis (Ann Arbor: University of Michigan Press, 1952). These sources give fuller descriptions of procedures in equating groups, training leaders, and experimental manipulations.

TABLE 3

NUMBER AND PROPORTION OF SUBJECTS EXPOSED TO EACH
OF THE INFLUENCE ATTEMPTS WHO..

	When asked to reach a decision made a positive one			Responded *yes* to later question, *Did you decide to volunteer?*			Percentage difference
	Total	N	Percent	Total	N	Percent	
Discussion	126	95	75	104	45	44	31
Lecture	92 *	70	76	83	46	55	21
Control	112	80	71	90	54	60	11
	$\chi^2 = .604$; $p = .73$			$\chi^2 = 5.853$; $p = .06$			

* This datum was lost for eight subjects in the lecture-III variation. The reduced totals for questionnaire data were caused by normal absenteeism in beginning psychology courses.

RESULTS

I. Group Discussion as a Factor. Hypothesis I stated that group discussion, as an influence technique, would have a significantly greater effect upon action than would the lecture method or no influence attempt at all. This prediction was not satisfied by results on the objective-action criterion. Table 2 shows no difference between the influence variations in the proportion of subjects who signed up with the "central file."

One of the postexperimental questionnaire measures, however, does show a striking difference in the influence-attempt groups: In all treatments fewer subjects reported having made a positive decision than had actually done so during the experimental sessions. But, while there had been no differences in the proportion of positive decisions (experimental commitment) in the discussion, lecture and control groups, the reported commitment data show the greatest divergence between the two figures for discussion subjects, the smallest for control subjects. A distortion phenomenon which is especially strong among participants in a group discussion has clearly emerged here.

II. Decision as a Factor. Hypothesis II stated that the process of coming to a decision on future action would raise the probability that such a decision would be executed. This hypothesis was tested in two ways.

The Lewinian experiments demonstrated the greater likelihood of action on the part of subjects who had been asked to reach a decision than on the part of those who had not been exposed to a decision request. This approach to the hypothesis is taken in Table 4 in which subjects who were not asked to come to a decision (decision-level I) are compared with those from all other decision variations. The results are in the predicted direction and of respectable magnitude (cf. footnote to Table 2).

The second interpretation of the decision hypothesis was not testable in the pioneer "group-decision" experiments, in which 100 percent positive decisions were always the goal and the outcome. In the present experiment some subjects who were asked to make a decision did *not* decide to volunteer as research subjects. This fact makes possible a comparison of action by positive and negative deciders (regardless of experimental variation). Here, not a single subject who

TABLE 4

NUMBER AND PROPORTION OF "ACTORS"
AMONG SUBJECTS WHO WERE AND
WERE NOT ASKED TO REACH A
DECISION

	Total no.	No. acting	Percentage acting
No Decision	135	20	15
Decision	338	76	22

$$\chi^2 = 3.509 \quad p = .07$$

had responded negatively to a request for decision took the action step.

If failure to indicate a positive decision can be interpreted as a decision *not* to act, Table 5 reveals that such negative decisions were consistently executed. The hypothesis identifying decision as an effective factor in "group decision" has been substantially confirmed, with reference to both positive and negative deciders.

III. Public Commitment as a Factor. Hypothesis III stated that a more public commitment to an action decision would be more effective in assuring the execution of the action than a less public one. This hypothesis was tested by comparing results with the three different manners of indicating decisions.

It had been predicted that the number who actually carried out their decision at each commitment level would be in the order: level IV greater than III greater than II, on the basis of the proposition that giving one's name to the leader is a more public commitment than raising one's hand. Nevertheless, results showing either of the "decision-plus" variations to be more effective than "pure decision" could be accepted as evidence tending to confirm the commitment hypothesis.

The obtained results, however, directly contradict even the less stringent interpretation of Hypothesis III.

The commitment hypothesis, thus, was not supported by the data.

IV. Group Consensus as a Factor. Hypothesis IV stated that a high degree of consensus in a group regarding intention to act would raise the probability of action by individual group members.

A. Objective Consensus. Analyses reported here consider the action data in terms of individual group sessions (three in each experimental cell) rather than in terms of experimental variations. A new classification, "high" and "low" positive decision, is introduced here.

For this analysis, the nine groups (level I) who were not asked to make a decision are omitted. In the other 27 groups, subjects were asked to make a decision, and groups varied considerably in the proportion of members who made a positive decision. The group proportions ranged from 100 percent to 41 percent with a mean of 72.5 percent.

Groups with above- and below-average proportions of positive decisions were separated; 13 "high" and 14 "low" groups were thus identified.[7] "High" as well as "low" categories represented subjects exposed to all three sets of treatments on the influence attempt and commitment axes. In this analysis, experimental treatment—the manner in which given levels of consensus were stimu-

TABLE 5

FREQUENCY OF POSITIVE AND NEGATIVE
DECISIONS AMONG THOSE WHO DID AND
DID NOT FULFILL THE ACTION
CRITERION

	Positive decision	Negative decision	Total
Actors	76	0	76
Nonactors	169	85	254
Total	245	85	330

$$\chi^2 = 34.322 \qquad p < .001$$

---

[7] These were rechecked for their pre experimental comparability with each other and the nine "no-decision" groups. No original differences were found. See E. D. Bennett, *op. cit.*

TABLE 6

NUMBER AND PROPORTION OF SUBJECTS IN EACH COMMITMENT VARIATION WHO FULFILLED THE ACTION CRITERION

	Total no.	No. acting	Percentage acting
II. Anonymous Decision	112	32	29
III. Partially Anonymous Decision	113	22	19
IV. Public Commitment	113	22	19

$$\chi^2 = 3.542 \qquad p = .18$$

TABLE 7

NUMBER AND PROPORTION OF SUBJECTS IN "HIGH" AND "LOW" CONSENSUS GROUPS WHO SUBSEQUENTLY ACTED *

	No. committed	No. acting	Percentage acting
High	131	45	34
Low	112	31	28

$$\chi^2 = 1.233 \qquad p = .27$$

* This table includes only those who made a positive decision.

lated—may be considered to have been held constant.

In view of the finding (Table 5) that negative deciders did not act and the fact that by definition there are more committed subjects in the "high" than in the "low" groups, Hypothesis IV had to be tested by a comparison of action and nonaction among committed subjects only (that is, among those who decided to act). Differences in Table 7 lie in the predicted direction but do not support the hypothesis with a very high degree of confidence.

B. Perception of Consensus. The dichotomy employed above was based on the objectively measured reactions of subjects to the decision request. Another approach to the hypothesis involves considering group members' perception of these reactions and their belief that action would follow the commitments.

The postexperimental questionnaire item, "How many from your group would you estimate signed up with the central file?" was used to check the assumption that seeing others make a commitment is equivalent to believing that they will act. A comparison between objective consensus and answers to this question corroborated this assumption with a relationship significant at the .01 level of confidence.

Perceived consensus could then be tested for its effect on a group member's tendency to act. A separate comparison was made of actors' and nonactors' estimates of the action of others in the "high" consensus, "low" consensus and "no-decision" groups. The 13 individual group sessions within the "high" classification (in each of which consensus was, of course, *objectively* identical for all participants) were then inspected for actors' and nonactors' estimates of the action of others. In ten of these 13 sessions, people who actually did go to sign up with the central file assumed that more of their fellow group members had also done so than was the case for the nonactors.

C. Consensus and Reported Action. At this point it was interesting to look at reports of action (postexperimental questionnaire item: "Did you go to sign up?") There were only ten subjects who had not actually met the action criterion but reported having done so.

A disproportionate number of those came from the groups in which there was high consensus ($p = .14$, and cf. footnote to Table 2).

Hypothesis IV, then, received a measure of support. Where a decision request yielded a high proportion of positive decisions and where members of the group perceived this high degree of consensus, the data showed some probability that members would (a) carry out the action themselves, or (b) report having done so, more often than members of groups with smaller proportions of positive decisions.

V. A Redefinition of "Group Decision." The preceding sections have reported results that rejected Hypotheses I and III and gave support to II and IV. That is, group discussion *per se* was not found to be a variable heightening the probability of action nor was public commitment found to be an effective variable.

The factor of decision, on the other hand, was found to account for significant differences in action. A high degree of actual and perceived consensus regarding intention to carry out an action also showed some relation to action and reported action.

In the Lewinian experiments, it will be remembered, "group decisions" were invariably obtained with 100 percent unanimity. Action (or reported action) from such groups was, in all cases, compared with that of subjects who had been exposed to no request for decision. Populations from our study might now be selected in such a manner as most closely to approximate the populations in the three Lewinian experiments with respect to only those variables that were, here, demonstrated to have an effect on action.

Subjects most like Lewin's "group-decision" participants were those who had been asked to make a decision and themselves decided to volunteer in the setting of groups in which a high proportion of positive decisions had been indicated. There are 131 cases fitting these criteria (cf. Table 7).

Subjects most like Lewin's contrasted groups, in terms of the two effective variables, were, of course, the 135 students who had been exposed to no decision request at all (cf. Table 4).

A comparison of the number who fulfilled the action criterion finds 34 percent in the former group and only 15 percent in the latter, a difference at the significance level $p = < .001$.

Of course, this highly significant result represents a combination of two effects previously established and not an independent confirmation of a virgin hypothesis. Nevertheless, the impressive differences obtained between two experimental conditions in the Lewinian experiments could be said, in this manner, to have been reproduced. This reproduction permits a much clearer identification of the variables to which their large differences can be attributed.

The line of argument followed here indicates that results that have been associated with "group decision" do not need the group-discussion technique. The factors of decision and objective or perceived group consensus alone have been shown to be as effective in increasing the probability of action as "group decision" in the Lewinian experiments.

CONCLUSIONS

The purpose of this experiment was the assessment of the contribution of four variables to previously demonstrated effects of a set of experimental conditions termed "group decision." Two of the factors—group discussion as an influence technique and public commitment—were found not to be essential to the reproduction of previously obtained results.

It was further shown that the combination of the two other variables—the process of making a decision and the degree to which group consensus is obtained and perceived—was alone capable of generating differences as large as those reported in the classic experiments of Lewin's co-workers.

The reports of both the Lewinian studies and the present one have referred to "group discussion" and "lecture" as simple, self-evident operations. Yet, there undoubtedly exist tremendous qualitative variations in both. Variables such as leadership technique, salience of subject matter, group cohesiveness, etc., would certainly be expected to affect the influence of the manipulations on subsequent action by participants.

The results of this experiment, then, need not imply a blanket rejection of the usefulness of group discussion and public commitment. The experiment was designed, rather, to test the overgeneralizations that have, at times, been drawn from the dramatic results of the Lewinian studies.

The label "group decision" is, actually, still consistent with the procedures here demonstrated to be effective in influencing behavior of group members. The use of the term, however, is now likely to create more confusion than it has in the past. The same term is widely used in the

field of human relations to refer to a genuine group solution of problems involving commonly perceived obstacles to group goals. Since the publication of the results of the Lewinian experiments in the immediate area of decision about individual goals in a group setting, the term "group decision" has also become associated with a procedural requirement of conducting a group discussion before the introduction of a stimulus for decision.

In the light of the findings here reported, therefore, "group decision" might profitably be redefined as "decision about individual goals in a setting of shared norms regarding such goals."

GROUP INFLUENCES UPON THE FORMATION OF NORMS AND ATTITUDES   *By Muzafer Sherif*

HYPOTHESIS TO BE TESTED

We have seen that if a reference point is lacking in the external field of stimulation, it is established internally as the temporal sequence of presentation of stimuli goes on. Accordingly we raise the problem: What will an individual do when he is placed in an objectively unstable situation in which all basis of comparison, as far as the external field of stimulation is concerned, is absent? In other words, what will he do when the external frame of reference is eliminated, in so far as the aspect in which we are interested is concerned? Will he give a

hodgepodge of erratic judgments? Or will he establish a point of reference of his own? *Consistent* results in this situation may be taken as the index of a subjectively evolved frame of reference.

We must first study the tendency of the individual. We must begin with the individual in order to do away with the dualism between "individual psychology" and "social psychology." In this way we can find the differences between individual responses in the individual situation and in the group situation.

Coming to the social level we can push our problem further. What will a group of people do in the same unstable

From Muzafer Sherif, *The Psychology of Social Norms* (New York: Harper & Brothers, 1936), and from M. Sherif, "An Experimental Approach to the Study of Attitudes," *Sociometry*, 1937, I, 90-98, with the permission of the authors and the publishers.

situation? Will the different individuals in the group give a hodgepodge of judgments? Or will they establish a collective frame of reference? If so, of what sort? If every person establishes a norm, will it be his own norm and different from the norms of others in the group? Or will there be established a common norm peculiar to the particular group situation and depending upon the presence of these individuals together and their influence upon one another? If they in time come to perceive the uncertain and unstable situation which they face in common in such a way as to give it some sort of order, perceiving it as ordered by a frame of reference developed among them in the course of the experiment, and if this frame of reference is peculiar to the group, then we may say that we have at least the prototype of the psychological process involved in the formation of a norm in a group.

The Autokinetic Effect: Its Possibilities for Our Problem

With these considerations clearly in mind, our first task has been to find objectively unstable situations that would permit themselves to be structured in several ways, depending on the character of the subjectively established reference points. From among other possible experimental situations that could be used to test our hypothesis, we chose to use the situation that is suitable to produce autokinetic effects, as meeting the requirements demanded by our hypothesis.

The conditions that produce the autokinetic effect afford an excellent experimental situation to test our hypothesis. We can easily get the autokinetic effect. In complete darkness, such as is found in a closed room that is not illuminated, or on a cloudy night in the open when there are no other lights visible, a single small light seems to move, and it may appear to move erratically in all directions. If you present the point of light repeatedly to a person, he may see the light appearing at different places in the room each time, especially if he does not know the distance between himself and the light. The experimental production of the autokinetic effect is very easy and works without any exception, provided, of course, that the person does not use special devices to destroy the effect. For in a completely dark room a single point of light *cannot* be localized definitely, because there is nothing in reference to which you can locate it. The effect takes place even when the person looking at the light knows perfectly well that the light is not moving. These are facts which are not subject to controversy; any one can easily test them for himself. In this situation not only does the stimulating light appear erratic and irregular to the subject, but at times the person himself feels insecure about his spatial bearing. This comes out in an especially striking way if he is seated in a chair without a back and is unfamiliar with the position of the experimental room in the building. Under these conditions some subjects report that they are not only confused about the location of the light; they are even confused about the stability of their own position.

The autokinetic effect is not a new artificial phenomenon invented by the psychologists. It is older than experimental psychology. Since it sometimes appears in the observation of the heavenly bodies, the astronomers [1] had already noticed it and offered theories to explain it.

---

[1] For a concise history of the autokinetic effect as a scientific problem, see H. F. Adams, "Autokinetic Sensations," *Psychol. Monog.,* 1912, No. 59, 32–44. Several theories have also been advanced by psychologists to explain the nature of the autokinetic effect. These are immaterial for our present problem. The important fact for us to remember is that the autokinetic effect is produced whenever a visual stimulus object lacks a spatial frame of reference.

We have studied the influence of such social factors as *suggestion* and the *group situation* on the extent and direction of the experimental movement. The study of the extent of the experienced movement permits a quantitative study for the approach to the formation of norms. We shall therefore report on the extent of movement.

PROCEDURE

We have studied the extent of the movement experienced in two situations: (1) when alone, except for the experimenter (in order to get the reaction of the individual unaffected by other experimentally introduced social factors, and thus to gain a basic notion about the perceptual process under the circumstances); and (2) when the individual is in a group situation (in order to discover modifications brought about by membership in the group).

The subject was introduced into the group situation in two ways: (1) He was brought into a group situation after being experimented upon when alone. This was done to find out the influence of the group situation after he had an opportunity to react to the situation first in accordance with his own tendencies and had ordered it subjectively in his own way. (2) He was first introduced to the situation in the group, having no previous familiarity with the situation at all, and afterwards experimented upon individually. This was done to find out whether the perceptual order or norm that might be established in the group situation would continue to determine his reaction to the same situation when he faced it alone. This last point is crucial for our problem. The others lead up to it and clarify its implications.

The subjects, apparatus, and procedures used will be only briefly outlined here. They are reported in full elsewhere.[2] The experiments were carried on in dark rooms in the Columbia University psychological laboratory. The subjects were graduate and undergraduate male students at Columbia University and New York University. They were not majoring in psychology. They did not know anything about the physical stimulus setup, or the purpose of the experiment. There were 19 subjects in the individual experiments; 40 subjects took part in the group experiments.

INDIVIDUAL EXPERIMENTS

The stimulus light was a tiny point of light seen through a small hole in a metal box. The light was exposed to the subject by the opening of a small shutter controlled by the experimenter. The distance between the subject and the light was five meters. The observer was seated at a table on which was a telegraph key. The following instructions were given in written form: "When the room is completely dark, I shall give you the signal *Ready*, and then show you a point of light. After a short time the light will start to move. As soon as you see it move, press the key. A few seconds later the light will disappear. Then tell me the distance it moved. Try to make your estimates as accurate as possible."

These instructions summarize the general procedure of the experiment. A short time after the light was exposed following the *Ready* signal, the subject pressed the key; this produced a faint but audible ticking in the timing apparatus indicating that the subject had perceived the (autokinetic) movement. The exposure time, after the subject pressed the key to indicate that he had begun to experience the movement, was two seconds in all cases. The light was physically stationary during the entire time and was not moved at all during any of the experiments.

After the light had disappeared, the subject reported orally the distance

---

[2] M. Sherif, "A Study of Some Social Factors in Perception," *Arch. Psychol.*, 1935, No. 187.

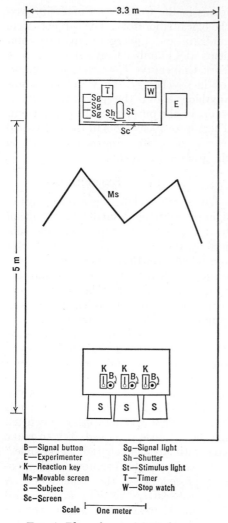

B—Signal button   Sg—Signal light
E—Experimenter   Sh—Shutter
K—Reaction key   St—Stimulus light
Ms—Movable screen   T—Timer
S—Subject   W—Stop watch
Sc—Screen

Scale |——— One meter ———|

FIG. 1. Plan of experimental room.

through which it had moved as he experienced it. The experimenter recorded each judgment as soon as it was spoken by the subject, writing each one on a separate sheet of a small paper pad. One hundred judgments were obtained from each subject. The subjects reported their estimates in inches (or fractions of inches).

The quantitative results are reported elsewhere.[3] Here we shall present only

the conclusions reached on the basis of these quantitative results, and give some important introspections that clarify these conclusions further.

The results unequivocally indicate that when individuals perceive movements which lack any other standard of comparison, *they subjectively establish a range of extent and a point (a standard or norm) within that range which is peculiar to the individual,* that may differ from the range and point (standard or norm) established by other individuals. In other words, when individuals repeatedly perceive movement which offers no objective basis for gauging the extent of movement, there develops within them, in the course of a succession of presentations, a standard (norm or reference point). This subjectively established standard or norm serves as a reference point with which each successive experienced movement is compared and judged to be short, long, or medium—within the range peculiar to the subject.

To express the point more generally, we conclude that in the absence of an objective range or scale of stimuli and an externally given reference point or standard, each individual builds up a range of his own and an internal (subjective) reference point within that range, and each successive judgment is given within that range and in relation to that reference point. The range and reference point established by each individual are peculiar to himself when he is experimented upon alone.

In the second series of the individual experiments, it was found that once a *range,* and a point of reference within that range, is established by an individual, there is a tendency to preserve these in the experiments on subsequent days. A second and third series of 100 judgments each show a median score for a given subject which is very similar to

[3] M. Sherif, "A Study of Some Social Factors in Perception," *Arch. Psychol.,* 1935, No. 187.

that found in the first series, but with a reduced variability.

The written introspective reports obtained from every observer at the end of the experiment further corroborate these conclusions based upon the quantitative results. Introspections of the following sort, which are typical, show that the subjects first found it hard to estimate distance because of the lack of externally given reference points or standards:

"Darkness left no guide for distance."

"It was difficult to estimate the distance the light moved, because of the lack of visible neighboring objects."

"There was no fixed point from which to judge distance."

Introspections of the following sort indicate that the subjects developed standards of their own in the absence of objective ones:

"Compared with previous distance."

"Used first estimate as standard."

This reveals once more the general psychological tendency to experience things in relation to some frame of reference. What we did in the group experiments was to carry this finding of experimental psychology into social psychology and note how it operates when the individual is in a group situation.

GROUP EXPERIMENTS

On the basis of the results given, the problem which we must study in the group situation becomes self-evident. The individual experiences the external field of stimulation in relation to a frame of reference. When a frame of reference is given in the objective situation, this will usually determine in an important way the structural relationships of the experience; in such cases all other parts will be organized as determined or modified by it. But at times such an objective frame of reference is lacking the field of stimulation is unstable, vague, and not well structured. In this case the individual perceives the situation as shaped by his own internally evolved frame of reference. The questions that arise for the experiment in the group situation, then, are the following:

How will an individual who is found in the group situation perceive the stimulus field? Will there evolve in him again a range and a standard (norm) within that range that will be peculiar to him, as was the case when individuals were experimented on alone? Or will group influences prevent him from establishing any well-defined range and reference point within that range, and thus spoil his capacity to perceive the uncertain situation in any sort of order? Or will the individuals in the group act together to establish a range, and a reference point within that range, which are peculiar to the group? If such a range and reference point are established, what will be the influence of such a group product on the individual member when he subsequently faces the same stimulus situation alone?

The questions outlined above represent more or less pure cases. There are, of course, other possibilities that lie between these pure cases.

With these questions, we face directly the psychological basis of social norms. We must admit that we have reduced the process to a very simple form. But the first fundamental psychological problem is the way an individual perceives a stimulus situation. The behavior follows upon this perception rather than upon the bald physical presence of the stimulus. There is no simple and direct correlation between the stimulus and the subsequent behavior, especially on the level of behavior with which we are dealing. A simple perceptual situation is the first requirement for experimental analysis of the problem.

We purposely chose a stimulus situation in which the external factors are unstable enough, within limits, to allow the internal factors to furnish the dominating role in establishing the main characteristics of organization. This enables us to say that any consistent product in the experience of the individual members of the group, differing from their experience as isolated individuals, is a function of their interaction in the group.

We do not face stimulus situations involving other people, or even the world of nature around us, in an indifferent way; we are charged with certain modes of readiness, certain established norms, which enter to modify our reactions. This important consideration shaped the planning of the group experiments. We studied the differences between the reactions (a) when the individuals first faced our stimulus situation in the group, and (b) when they faced the group situation after first establishing their individual ranges and norms in the individual situation. Accordingly, twenty of the subjects began with the individual situation and were then put into groups in subsequent experimental sessions; the other twenty started with group sessions and ended with individual sessions.

This rotation technique enabled us to draw conclusions regarding the following important questions: How much does the individual carry over from his individually established way of reacting to a later situation when facing the same stimulus in the group? How much will he be influenced by his membership in the group after once his range and norm have been established individually when alone? How will he experience the situation when alone, after a common range and norm have been established peculiar to the group of which he is a member? In short, will the common product developed in the group serve as a determining factor when he subsequently faces the same situation *alone?*

The experimental setting was in general the same as in previous experiments. Of course, additional techniques were necessary to handle two or more members of a group at the same time. One major addition was the use of signal lights. As the subjects were new to the experimenter, he could not tell from the voice alone who was giving a judgment. So as each subject gave his judgment aloud, he pressed a push button connected with a dim signal light of a particular color by which the experimenter might know who the speaker was.

There were eight groups of two subjects each and eight groups of three subjects each. Four groups in each of the two categories started with the individual situation (one whole session for each individual), and then functioned as groups. Four groups in each category started in group situations for the first three sessions on three different days (all subjects of each group being present), and were then broken up and studied in the individual situation.

In order to make the relation of individual members to one another as natural as possible, within the limits of the experimental setting, the subjects were left free as to the order in which they would give their judgments. In fact, they were told at the start to give their judgments in random order as they pleased. Whether the judgments of the person who utters his first have more influence than the others becomes a study in leadership, which is a further interesting problem. Perhaps such studies will give us an insight into the effect of polarization on the production of norms in a group situation. But from the examination of our results, we can say that the reporting of the judgments has a gradual cumulative effect; aside from whatever influence the first judgment may have on the second or third at a given moment, the judgments of the third individual at a given presentation are not without effect on the subsequent judgments of the first subject in the round of presentations following. Thus the production of an established group influence is largely a temporal affair and not the outcome of this or that single presentation. We shall refer to this point again later.

Besides the quantitative judgments obtained during the experiments, the subjects were asked at the end of each experimental session to write down their introspections. Questions were asked which aimed at finding whether they became conscious of the range and norm they were establishing subjectively. These questions were: "Between what maximum and minimum did the distances vary?" "What was the most frequent distance that the light moved?"

Certain facts stand out clearly from our results. We may summarize these facts in a few paragraphs.

When an individual faces this stimulus situation, which is unstable and not structured in itself, he establishes a range and norm (a reference point) within that range. The range and norm that are developed in each individual are peculiar to that individual. They may vary from the ranges and norms developed in other individuals in different degrees, revealing consistent and stable individual differences. The causes of these individual differences are difficult problems in themselves, the understanding of which may prove to be basic to a satisfactory understanding of our problem. But for the time being it may be worth while to work on our main theme.

When the individual, in whom a range and a norm within that range are first developed in the individual situation, is put into a group situation, together with other individuals who also come into the situation with their own ranges and norms established in their own individual sessions, the ranges and norms tend to converge. But the convergence is not so close as when they first work in the group situation, having less opportunity to set up stable individual norms. (See left-hand graphs, Figures 2 and 3.)

When individuals face the same unstable, unstructured situation as members of a group for the first time, a range and a norm (standard) within that range are established, which are peculiar to the group. If, for the group, there is a rise or fall in the norms established in successive sessions, it is a group effect; the norms of the individual members rise and fall toward a common norm in each session. To this the objection may be raised that one subject may lead, and be uninfluenced by other members of the group; the group norm is simply the leader's norm. To this the only possible empirical reply is that in our experiments the leaders were constantly observed to be influenced by their followers—if not at the moment, then later in the series and in subsequent series. Even if the objection has occasional force, the statement regarding group norms is in general true. Even if the group norm gravitates toward a dominating person, the leader represents a polarization in the situation, having a definite relationship toward others which he cannot change at will. If the leader changes his norm after the group norm is *settled* he may *cease thereupon to be followed*, as occurred several times strikingly in our experiments. In general, such cases of complete polarization are, however, exceptional. (See right-hand graphs, Figures 2 and 3.)

The fact that the norm thus established is peculiar to the group suggests that there is a factual psychological basis in the contentions of social psychologists and sociologists who maintain that new and supra-individual qualities arise in the group situations. This is in harmony with the facts developed elsewhere in the psychology of perception.

When a member of a group faces the same situation subsequently *alone*, after once the range and norm of his group have been established, he perceives the situation in terms of the range and norm that he brings from the group situation. This psychological fact is important in

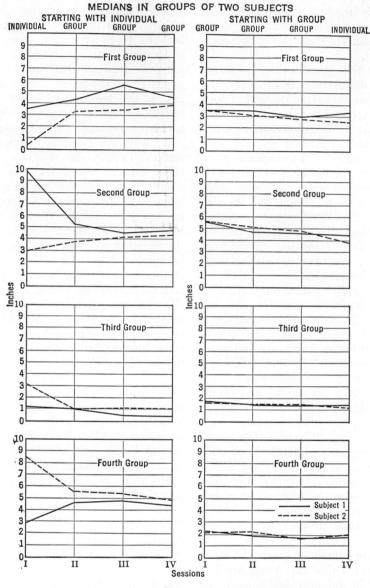

FIGURE 2

that it gives a psychological approach to the understanding of the "social products" that weigh so heavily in the problem of the stimulus situation.

DISCUSSION OF RESULTS

The experiments, then, constitute a study of the formation of a norm in a simple laboratory situation. They show in a simple way the basic psychological process involved in the establishment of social norms. They are an extension into the social field of a general psychological phenomenon that is found in perception and in many other psychological fields, namely, that our experience is organized

MEDIANS IN GROUPS OF THREE SUBJECTS

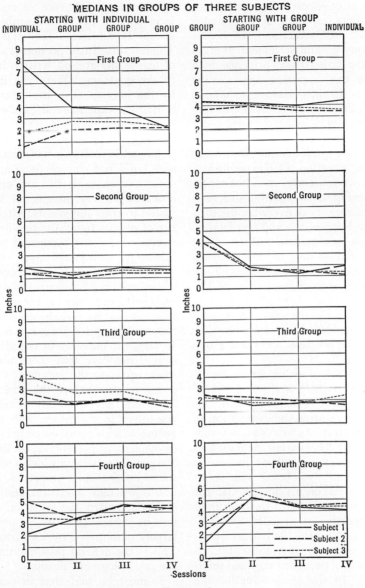

FIGURE 3

around or modified by frames of reference participating as factors in any given stimulus situation.

On the basis of this general principle considered in relation to our experimental results, we shall venture to generalize. The psychological basis of the established social norms, such as stereo-

types, fashions, conventions, customs and values, is the formation of common frames of reference as a product of the contact of individuals. Once such frames of reference are established and incorporated in the individual, they enter as important factors to determine or modify his reactions to the situations that he will face later—social, and even non-social at times, especially if the stimulus field is not well structured. Of course this is a very general statement. It gives us only the broad basic principle with which we can approach any specific social norm. In each instance we have to take into consideration particular factors that participate in its production.

Our experiments merely show the formation of a specific frame of reference in a group situation. Our experimental situation, we must say, does not represent a pressing social situation such as is found in the reality of everyday life with its intense hunger, sex and ego factors. It is simply one unstable, unstructured situation that is new for the subjects participating in the experiments. They have no set norms of reaction to it. The situation, therefore, is plastic enough to be structured by the effect of experimentally introduced social factors such as suggestion, prestige, and other group influences.

In this situation, within certain limits, there is no "right" or "wrong" judgment. One subject demonstrated this spontaneously during the experiment, in spite of the fact that he was not supposed to talk: "If you tell me once how much I am mistaken, all my judgments will be better." Not being sure about the correctness of his judgments, the subject feels uneasy. This we know from the introspective reports. In the individual situation, the individual structures the unstructured situation by furnishing his own peculiar range and reference point. In the group situation the members of the group tend to structure the situation by converging toward a common norm in their judgments. If in the beginning of the experimental situation they start with divergent judgments, in the course of the experiment they come together, the divergent one feeling uncertain and even insecure in the deviating position of his judgments. This convergence is not brought about instantly

by the direct influence of one or two judgments of the other members of the group. It exhibits a temporal pattern. The following introspection of a member of one of the groups, written in answer to the question, "Were you influenced by the judgments of the other persons during the experiments?" illustrates our point clearly. This subject wrote, "Yes, but not on the same observation. My judgment in each case was already made, and I did not change to whatever the other person said. But on subsequent observations my judgments were adjusted to their judgments. After a number of observations, the previous agreement or lack of it influenced me in adjusting my own perspective."

Despite the above case, every individual need not be aware of the fact that he is being influenced in the group situation, or that he and the other members are converging toward a common norm. In fact, the majority of the subjects reported not only that their minds were made up as to the judgment they were going to give before the others spoke, but that they were not influenced by the others in the group. This fact is in harmony with many observations in the psychology of perception; we know that the general setting in which a stimulus is found influences its properties, and that unless we take a critical and analytic attitude toward the situation we need not be aware that its properties are largely determined by its surroundings. This is the general principle underlying the psychology of "illusions."

It must be said that in our experimental setting the subjects are not moved by a common interest or drive such as is found in a group that faces a common danger, such as starvation or the cruel authority of a tyrant. In these vital situations there is a certain gap that has to be filled. Until this gap is properly filled, the instability of the situation continues. If the norms and slogans that arise under the stress of a tense and uncertain situation that requires a solution do not meet the situation adequately, the instability is not removed, and new norms and new slogans are likely to arise until the tension is removed. For example, in a hungry mass of people searching for food, a leader or a small party may standardize certain norms or slogans as guides to an outlook upon the situation and as guides to action. If these norms do not lead to the satisfaction of hunger, other leaders or interested parties may spring up and standardize other norms or slogans. This (dialectic) dynamic process moves on and on until the appropriate norms or slogans are reached that meet the situation best. For example, many in America who were enthusiastically motivated into action during the First World War by the slogan, "A war to end war!" are totally deaf to such a slogan after seeing the results of that war.

In spite of laboratory simplicity and lack of vital motivational factors, our experimental setting possesses certain important characteristics of actual group situations.

AN EXPERIMENTAL APPROACH TO THE STUDY OF ATTITUDES

From the foregoing experiments we conclude that when an individual perceives autokinetic movement which lacks an objective standard of comparison, and is asked during repeated stimulation to report in terms of the extent of movement, he subjectively establishes a range of extent and a point (a standard or norm) within that range which is peculiar to himself, differing from the range and the point (standard or norm) established by other individuals. When individuals face the same unstable, unstructured situation as members of a group *for the first time*, a range and a norm (standard) within that range are established which are peculiar to the group. When a member of the group faces the same situation subsequently *alone*, after

once the range and norm of his group have been established, he perceives the situation in terms of the range and norm that he brings from the group situation. The ranges and norms established are not prescribed arbitrarily by the experimenter or by any other agent. They are formed in the course of the experimental period and may vary from individual to individual, or from group to group, within certain limits.

Our concern being the study of social influence, we may go further and put the question: can we experimentally make the subject adopt a prescribed range and norm directed by specific social influences?

Different kinds of social influences may be experimentally utilized to define certain prescribed ranges and norms. Among many possible ones we took the following: (a) The influence of group situations on the individual as a member of the group. We have already mentioned the main conclusion of this previous work. (b) The influence of the direct suggestion of the experimenter in raising or lowering the reported extents of movement. (c) The influence of a fellow member with prestige (cooperating with the experimenter) on another ("naïve") member of the group. (d) The influence of one naïve member on the judgment of another. In this last case there is no prestige effect, because the subjects have not met each other prior to the experiment.

We shall say only a few words about the experiments under (b). If the subject is distributing his judgments, say, about three inches, without any socially introduced influence, the remark of the experimenter, "You are underestimating the distances" tends to raise the point round which the judgments are distributed to about five or six inches.

The following experiment under (c) shows how the autokinetic phenomenon can be utilized as a sensitive index of the prestige effect of one person on another

Here we report verbatim the account of an experiment with prestige:

"Miss X and I (Assistant in Psychology, Columbia University) were subjects for Dr. Sherif. I was well acquainted with the experiment but Miss X knew nothing whatsoever about it. Since she was a close friend of mine, and I carried some prestige with her, Dr. Sherif suggested that it would be interesting to see if we could predetermine her judgments. It was agreed beforehand that I was to give no judgments until she had set her own standard. After a few stimulations it was quite clear that her judgments were going to vary around five inches. At the next appropriate stimulation, I made a judgment of twelve inches. Miss X's next judgment was eight inches. I varied my judgments around twelve inches and she did the same. Then I changed my judgment to three inches, suggesting to Dr. Sherif that he had changed it. She gradually came down to my standard, but not without some apparent resistance. When it was clear that she had accepted this new standard, Dr. Sherif suggested that I make no more judgments lest I might influence hers. He then informed her on a subsequent stimulation that she was underestimating the distance which the point moved. Immediately her judgments were made larger and she established a new standard. However, she was a little uneasy with it all, and before the experiment had progressed much farther, whispered to me, 'Get me out of here.'

"When we were again in my office, I told her that the point had not moved at all during the experiment. She seemed quite disturbed about it, and was very much embarrassed to know that we had been deceiving her. Noting her perturbation, I turned the conversation to other matters. However, several times during our conversation she came back to the subject, saying, 'I don't like that man' (referring to Dr. Sherif) and similar statements indicating her displeasure

with the experience. It was not until some weeks later when she was again in my office that I discovered the full extent of her aversion. I asked her to serve as a subject for me in an experiment and immediately she exclaimed, 'Not down in *that* room,' pointing to Dr. Sherif's experimental room."

The experiment which will be given presently deals with the influence of a fellow member in the adoption of a prescribed norm. There were seven groups in this experiment, each group consisting of two members. In every group one subject cooperated with the experimenter, i.e., deliberately distributed his judgments within the range and around the norm assigned to him by the experimenter beforehand. The other subject was unaware of this predetermination. The degree of this "naïve" subject's conformity to the norm and range of the cooperating subject may be taken as the index of the social influence. In all the groups the subject who was cooperating with the experimenter was the same person. This was done in order to keep the influencing member constant in all groups.

The range and norm prescribed for every group were different. For the first group, the prescribed range was 1–3 inches, 2 inches being the prescribed norm. For the second group, the prescribed range was 2–4, and 3 inches the norm, and so on to the eighth group for which the range and norm were 7–9 and 8, respectively. It will be observed that the prescribed range was rather narrow; consequently in the course of the experimental period the cooperating subject gave no judgments which deviated from the norm by more than one inch in either direction.

In the first experimental session, both subjects (the cooperating and the "naïve") took part. After each exposure of the point of light for two seconds, the subjects spoke their judgments aloud one at a time and the experimenter recorded

TABLE 1

DATA FROM GROUP 1, EXPERIMENTALLY OBTAINED FROM "NAÏVE" S

Prescribed	Session I (in group)	Session II (alone)
Range 1–3 inches	1–5 inches	1–4 inches
Norm 2 inches	3.36 inches	2.62 inches
No. of the 50 judgments falling within the prescribed range	41	47

these on separate sheets of different colored pads. In order not to stress the factor of primacy, the cooperating subject was instructed to let the other subject utter his judgment first, at least half the time. The social influence in our previous experiments with the autokinetic effect was found to be not so much a function of this and that separate judgments as of the temporal sequence of judgments. Fifty judgments were taken from each subject.

In the second session only the naïve subject was present, so that we might see how much of the prescribed range and norm he carried from the first group session. In this individual session also, fifty judgments were taken. As the norm formation in the autokinetic effect is a fragile and, in a sense, artificial formation, such an arbitrary prescription may break down easily beyond a certain number of judgments. Our whole point is that the autokinetic effect can be utilized to show a general psychological tendency and not to reveal the concrete properties of norm-formation in actual life situations.

In the presentation of results we give the prescribed range and norm, and the number of judgments of the "naïve" subject falling within the prescribed range, and his norms (as represented by the median of the distribution of his judgments) in the first (group) and second (individual) sessions. The means and medians of the distributions of the judgments given by the cooperating subject in the group sessions are not exactly identical with the prescribed norms, though the modes and ranges are the same. We did not think it necessary for him to memorize a perfectly normal distribution. Our aim is chiefly to show a fundamental psychological tendency related to norm-formation.

At the end of the second (individual) session the subject was asked to answer in writing four questions related to the problem. The answers to two of the questions further verify our former results. We shall therefore confine ourselves to the introspections given to the other two questions which are important for our present concern. These questions were: (1) What was the distance that the light most frequently moved? (this was formulated to find out whether the subjects became conscious of the norm formed in the course of the experiment); (2) Were you influenced by the judgments of the other person who was present during the first session? (this question was formulated in order to find out whether the subjects were conscious of the fact that they were being influenced by the cooperating subject).

The introspections of the subject in Group 1 are important for any theory of suggestion and norm formation:

1. "Most frequent distance was 2 inches. Seemed to be more consistently 2 inches second day than on first day.

2. "Yes, they were despite my efforts to be impartial. Probably many of my judgments were inordinately large be-

cause of small distances given by other subject. I think this was an attempt at avoiding suggestion and in so doing going to the other extreme. I do not think I was influenced by first day's judgments on the second day. I tried to be impartial in my judgments the first day. I felt resentment toward the other subject the first day because of the successive equal judgments by him. I tried to be objective toward this feeling: that is to banish the thought. But I feel that this resentment caused my judgments to differ from his by a greater amount than they would have if the judgments had been kept separate; that is if I had not heard his judgments. The second day I felt more independence in my judgments and I believe that these judgments were therefore more accurate."

*   *   *

From these results we may conclude that the subjects may be influenced to perceive an indefinite stimulus field in terms of an experimentally introduced norm. The degree of the influence may be different in different subjects, ranging from a large to a negligible amount. Even in the latter case, an influence on the norm (not in the range) is evident.

The introspections reveal that the subjects become conscious of the norm which develops in the course of the experiment. However, they need not be conscious of the fact that they are being influenced toward that norm by the other member of the group. In connection with this point, it is interesting to note that in some cases, the *conformity* to the prescribed range and norm when the *influencing* person is no longer present (Session II) is closer than the *conformity* produced by his actual presence.

It seems to us that the psychological process embodied in these facts may be basic to the daily phenomena of suggestion, especially to the role of suggestion in the formation of attitudes. It is not a rare occurrence in everyday life to react negatively or hesitatingly to suggestion on some topic raised by an acquaintance while in his presence, but to respond positively after leaving him (perhaps there is a disinclination to accept suggestions readily unless there is some strong prestige or pressing demand; to appear easily yielding is not so pleasant for an "ego").

Attitudes, whatever else they may be, imply *characteristic modes of readiness in reacting* to definite objects, situations and persons. Our experiment has demonstrated in a simple way how a *characteristic* kind of readiness may be experimentally obtained in relation to an indefinite stimulus field. Perhaps this may constitute a step in the direction of the truly psychological investigation of attitudes.

OVERCOMING RESISTANCE TO CHANGE *By Lester Coch and John R. P. French, Jr.*

INTRODUCTION

It has always been characteristic of American industry to change products and methods of doing jobs as often as competitive conditions or engineering progress dictates. One of the most serious production problems faced at the Harwood Manufacturing Corporation has been the resistance of production workers to the necessary changes in methods and jobs. This resistance expressed itself in several ways, such as grievances about the piece rates that went with the new methods, high turnover, very low efficiency, restriction of output, and marked aggression against management.

Efforts were made to solve this serious problem by the use of a special monetary allowance for transfers, by trying to enlist the cooperation and aid of the union, by making necessary layoffs on the basis of efficiency, etc. In all cases, these actions did little or nothing to overcome the resistance to change. On the basis of these data, it was felt that the pressing problem of resistance to change demanded further research for its solution. From the point of view of factory management, there were two purposes to the research: (1) Why do people resist change so strongly? and (2) What can be done to overcome this resistance?

Starting with a series of observations about the behavior of changed groups, the first step in the over-all program was to devise a preliminary theory to account for the resistance to change. Then on the basis of the theory, a field experiment was devised and conducted within the context of the factory situation. Finally, the results of the experiment were interpreted in the light of the preliminary theory and the new data.

BACKGROUND

The main plant of the Harwood Manufacturing Corporation, where the present research was done, is located in the small town of Marion, Virginia. The plant produces pajamas and, like most sewing plants, employs mostly women. The plant's population is about 500 women and 100 men. The workers are recruited from the rural, mountainous areas surrounding the town, and are usually employed without previous industrial experience. The average age of the workers is 23; the average education is eight years of grammar school.

The policies of the company in regard to labor relations are liberal and progressive. A high value has been placed on fair and open dealing with the employees, and they are encouraged to take up any problems or grievances with the management at any time. Every effort is made to help foremen find effective solutions to their problems in human relations, using conferences and role-playing methods. Carefully planned orientation, designed to help overcome the discouragement and frustrations attending entrance upon the new and unfamiliar

From *Human Relations*, 1948, I, 512–532. Reprinted by permission of the authors and Tavistock Publications, Ltd. Grateful acknowledgments are made by the authors to Dr. Alfred J. Marrow, president of the Harwood Manufacturing Corporation, and to the entire Harwood staff for their valuable aid and suggestions in this study. The authors have drawn repeatedly from the works and concepts of Kurt Lewin for both the action and theoretical phases of this study. Many of the leadership techniques used in the experimental group meetings were techniques developed at the first National Training Laboratory for Group Development held at Bethel, Maine, in the summer of 1947. Both authors attended this laboratory.

situation, is used. Plant-wide votes are conducted where possible to resolve problems affecting the whole working population. The company has invested both time and money in employee services, such as industrial music, health services, lunchroom, and recreation programs. As a result of these policies, the company has enjoyed good labor relations since the day it commenced operations.

Harwood employees work on an individual incentive system. Piece rates are set by time study and are expressed in terms of units. One unit is equal to 1 minute of standard work: 60 units per hour equal the standard efficiency rating. Thus, if on a particular operation the piece rate for one dozen is 10 units, the operator would have to produce 6 dozen per hour to achieve the standard efficiency rating of 60 units per hour. The skill required to reach 60 units per hour is great. On some jobs, an average trainee may take thirty-four weeks to reach the skill level necessary to perform at 60 units per hour. Her first few weeks of work may be on an efficiency level of 5 to 20 units per hour.

The amount of pay received is directly proportional to the weekly average efficiency rating achieved. Thus, an operator with an average efficiency rating of 75 units per hour (25 percent more than standard) would receive 25 percent more than base pay. However, there are two minimum wages below which no operator may fall. The first is the plant-wide minimum, the hiring-in wage; the second is a minimum wage based on six months' employment and is 22 percent higher than the plant-wide minimum wage. Both minima are smaller than the base pay for 60 units per hour efficiency rating.

The rating of every piece worker is computed every day, and the results are published in a daily record of production which is shown to every operator. This daily record of production for each production line carries the names of all the operators on that line arranged in rank order of efficiency rating, with the highest rating girl at the top of the list. The supervisors speak to each operator each day about her unit ratings.

When it is necessary to change an operator from one type of work to another, a transfer bonus is given. This bonus is so designed that the changed operator who relearns at an average rate will suffer no loss in earnings after change. Despite this allowance, the general attitudes toward job changes in the factory are markedly negative. Such expressions as, "When you make your units (standard production), they change your job," are all too frequent. Many operators refuse to change, preferring to quit.

THE TRANSFER LEARNING CURVE

An analysis of the after-change relearning curves of several hundred experienced operators rating standard or better prior to change showed that 38 percent of the changed operators recovered to the standard efficiency rating of 60 units per hour. The other 62 percent either became chronically substandard operators or quit during the relearning period.

The average relearning curve for those who recover to standard production on the simplest type job in the plant reaches 60 units per hour after eight weeks and, when smoothed, provides the basis for the transfer bonus. The bonus is the percent difference between this expected efficiency rating and the standard of 60 units per hour. It is interesting to note that this relearning period for an experienced operator is longer than the learning period for a new operator. This is true despite the fact that the majority of transfers—the failures who never recover to standard—are omitted from the curve. However, changed operators rarely complain of "wanting to do it the old way," etc., after the first week or two; and time and motion studies show few false moves after the first week of change. From this evidence it is deduced that proactive inhibition or the interference of previous habits in learning the new skill is either nonexistent or very slight after the first two weeks of change.

An analysis of the relearning curves for forty-one experienced operators who were changed to very difficult jobs, compared the recovery rates for operators making standard or better prior to change with those below standard prior to change. Both classes of operators dropped to a little below 30 units per hour and recovered at a very slow but similar rate. These curves show a general (though by no means universal) phenomenon: that the efficiency rating prior to change does not indicate a faster or slower recovery rate after change.

A PRELIMINARY THEORY OF RESISTANCE TO CHANGE

The fact that relearning after transfer to a new job is so often slower than initial learning on first entering the factory would indicate, on the face of it, that the resistance to change and the slow relearning is primarily a motivational problem. The similar recovery rates of the skilled and unskilled operators tend to confirm the hypothesis that skill is a minor factor and motivation is the major determinant of the rate of recovery. Earlier experiments at Harwood by Alex Bavelas demonstrated this point conclusively. He found that the use of group-decision techniques on operators who had just been transferred resulted in very marked increases in the rate of relearning, even though no skill training was given and there were no other changes in working conditions.[1]

Interviews with operators who have been transferred to a new job reveal a common pattern of feelings and attitudes which are distinctly different from those of successful nontransfers. In addition to resentment against the management for transferring them, the employees typi-cally show feelings of frustration, loss of hope of ever regaining their former level of production and status in the factory, feelings of failure, and a very low level of aspiration. In this respect these transferred operators are similar to the chronically slow workers studied previously.

Earlier unpublished research at Harwood has shown that the nontransferred employees generally have an explicit goal of reaching and maintaining an efficiency rating of 60 units per hour. A questionnaire administered to several groups of operators indicated that a large majority of them accept as their goal the management's quota of 60 units per hour. This standard of production is the level of aspiration according to which the operators measure their own success or failure; and those who fall below standard lose status in the eyes of their fellow employees. Relatively few operators set a goal appreciably above 60 units per hour.

The actual production records confirm the effectiveness of this goal of standard production. The distribution of the total population of operators in accordance with their production levels is by no means a normal curve. Instead there is a very large number of operators who rate 60 to 63 units per hour and relatively few operators who rate just above or just below this range. Thus we may conclude that:

(1) There is a force acting on the operator in the direction of achieving a production level of 60 units per hour or more. It is assumed that the strength of this driving force (acting on an operator below standard) increases as she gets nearer the goal—a typical goal gradient.

On the other hand restraining forces operate to hinder or prevent her from reaching this goal. These restraining forces consist among other things of the difficulty of the job in relation to the operator's level of skill. Other things

---

[1] Kurt Lewin, "Frontiers in Group Dynamics," *Human Relations*, 1947, I, 5–41.

being equal, the faster an operator is sewing the more difficult it is to increase her speed by a given amount. Thus we may conclude that:

(2) The strength of the restraining force hindering higher production increases with increasing level of production.

In line with previous studies, it is assumed that the conflict of these two opposing forces—the driving force corresponding to the goal of reaching 60 and the restraining force of the difficulty of the job—produces frustration. In such a conflict situation, the strength of frustration will depend on the strength of these forces. If the restraining force against increasing production is weak, then the frustration will be weak. But if the driving force toward higher production (i.e., the motivation) is weak, then the frustration will also be weak. Probably both of the conflicting forces must be above a certain minimum strength before any frustration is produced; for all goal-directed activity involves some degree of conflict of this type, yet a person is not usually frustrated so long as he is making satisfactory progress toward his goal. Consequently we assume that:

(3) The strength of frustration is a function of the weaker of these two opposing forces, provided that the weaker force is stronger than a certain minimum necessary to produce frustration.[2]

From propositions (1), (2), and (3) we may derive that the strength of frustration: (a) should be greater for operators who are below standard in production than for operators who have already achieved the goal of standard production; (b) should be greater for operators on difficult jobs than for operators on easy jobs; (c) should increase with increasing efficiency rating below standard

production. Previous research would suggest the hypothesis that:

(4) One consequent of frustration is escape from the field.[3]

An analysis of the effects of such frustration in the factory showed that it resulted, among other things, in such forms of escape from the field as high turnover and absenteeism. The rate of turnover for successful operators with efficiency ratings above standard was much lower than for unsuccessful operators. Likewise, operators on the more difficult jobs quit more frequently than those on the easier jobs. Presumably the effect of being transferred is a severe frustration which should result in similar attempts to escape from the field.

In line with this theory of frustration, and the finding that job turnover is one resultant of frustration, an analysis was made of the turnover rate of transferred operators as compared with the rate among operators who had not been transferred recently. For the year September 1946 to September 1947 there were 198 operators who had not been transferred recently—that is, within the thirty-four-week period allowed for relearning after transfer. There was a second group of 85 operators who had been transferred recently—that is, within the time allowed for relearning the new job. Each of these two groups was divided into seven classifications according to their unit rating at the time of quitting. For each classification the percent turnover per month, based on the total number of employees in that classification, was computed.

The results are given in Figure 1. Both the levels of turnover and the form of the curves are strikingly different for the two groups. Among operators who have not been transferred recently the average

[2] John R. P. French, Jr., "The Behavior of Organized and Unorganized Groups under Conditions of Frustration and Fear, Studies in Topological and Vector Psychology, III," *University of Iowa Studies in Child Welfare,* 1944, XX, 229–308.

[3] *Ibid.*

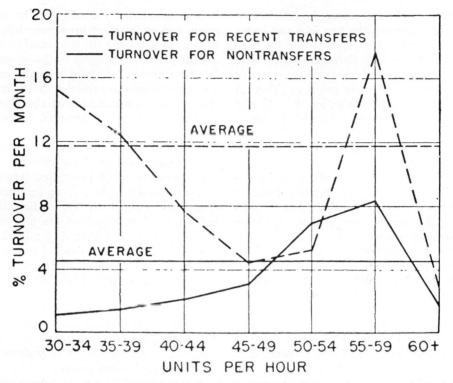

Fig. 1. The rate of turnover at various levels of production for transfers as compared with nontransfers.

turnover per month is about $4\frac{1}{2}$ percent; among recent transfers the monthly turnover is nearly 12 percent. Consistent with the previous studies, both groups show the predicted very marked drop in the turnover curve after an operator becomes a success by reaching 60 units per hour or standard production. However, the form of the curves at lower unit ratings is markedly different for the two groups. As predicted the nontransferred operators show a gradually increasing rate of turnover up to a rating of 55 to 59 units per hour. The transferred operators, on the other hand, show a high peak at the lowest unit rating of 30 to 34 units per hour, decreasing sharply to a low point at 45 to 49 units per hour. Since most changed operators drop to a unit rating of around 30 units per hour when changed and then drop no further,

it is obvious that the rate of turnover was highest for these operators just after they were changed and again much later just before they reached standard. Why?

It is assumed that the strength of frustration for an operator who has *not* been transferred gradually increases because both the driving force toward the goal of reaching 60 and the restraining force of the difficulty of the job increase with increasing unit rating. This is in line with hypotheses (1), (2), and (3) above. For the transferred operator, on the other hand, the frustration is greatest immediately after transfer when the contrast of her present status with her former status is most evident. At this point the strength of the restraining forces is at a maximum because the difficulty is unusually great due to proactive inhibition.

Then as she overcomes the interference effects between the two jobs and learns the new job, the difficulty and the frustration gradually decrease and the rate of turnover declines until the operator reaches 45–49 units per hour. Then at higher levels of production the difficulty starts to increase again, and the transferred operator shows the same peak in frustration and turnover at 55–59 units per hour.

Though our theory of frustration explains the forms of the two turnover curves in Figure 1, it hardly seems adequate to account for the markedly higher level of turnover for transfers as compared to nontransfers. On the basis of the difficulty of the job, it is especially difficult to explain the higher rate of turnover at 55–59 units per hour for transfers. Evidently additional forces are operating.

Another factor which seems to affect recovery rates of changed operators is the cohesiveness of the work group. Observations seem to indicate that a strong psychological subgroup with negative attitudes toward management will display the strongest resistance to change. On the other hand, changed groups with high cohesiveness and positive cooperative attitudes are the best relearners. Collections of individuals with little or no cohesiveness display some resistance to change but not so much as the groups with high cohesiveness and negative attitudes toward management.

An analysis of turnover records for changed operators with high cohesiveness showed a 4-percent turnover rate per month at 30 to 34 units per hour, not significantly higher than in unchanged operators but significantly lower than in changed operators with little or no cohesiveness. However, the acts of aggression are far more numerous among operators with high than among operators with low cohesiveness. Since both types of operators experience the same frustration as individuals but react to it so differently,

it is assumed that the effect of the in-group feeling is to set up a restraining force against leaving the group and driving forces toward staying in the group. In these circumstances, one would expect some alternative reaction to frustration rather than escape from the field. This alternative is aggression. Strong cohesiveness provides strength so that members dare to express aggression which would otherwise be suppressed.

One common result in a cohesive subgroup is the setting of a group standard concerning production. Where the attitudes toward management are antagonistic, this group standard may take the form of a definite restriction of production to a given level. This phenomenon of restriction is particularly likely to happen in a group that has been transferred to a job where a new piece rate has been set; for they have some hope that if production never approaches the standard, the management may change the piece rate in their favor.

A group standard can exert extremely strong forces on an individual member of a small subgroup. That these forces can have a powerful effect on production is indicated in the production record of one presser during a period of forty days.

In the group	
Days	*Efficiency rating*
1–3	46
4–6	52
7–9	53
10–12	56

Scapegoating begins	
13–16	55
17–20	48

Becomes a single worker	
21–24	83
25–28	92
29–32	92
33–36	91
37–40	92

For the first twenty days she was working in a group of other pressers who were producing at the rate of about 50 units per hour. Starting on the thirteenth day, when she reached standard production and exceeded the production of the other members, she became a scapegoat of the group. During this time her production decreased toward the level of the remaining members of the group. After twenty days the group had to be broken up, and all the other members were transferred to other jobs leaving only the scapegoat operator. With the removal of the group, the group standard was no longer operative; and the production of the one remaining operator shot up from the level of about 45 to 96 units per hour in a period of four days. Her production stabilized at a level of about 92 and stayed there for the remainder of the twenty days. Thus it is clear that the motivational forces induced in the individual by a strong subgroup may be more powerful than those induced by management.

THE EXPERIMENT

On the basis of the preliminary theory that resistance to change is a combination of an individual reaction to frustration with strong group-induced forces, it seemed that the most appropriate methods for overcoming the resistance to change would be group methods. Consequently an experiment was designed employing three degrees of participation in handling groups to be transferred. The first variation involved *no participation* by employees in planning the changes, though an explanation was given to them. The second variation involved *participation through representation* of the workers in designing the changes to be made in the jobs. The third variation consisted of *total participation* by all members of the group in designing the changes. Two experimental groups received the total participation treatment. The four experimental groups were roughly matched

with respect to: (1) the efficiency ratings of the groups before transfer; (2) the degree of change involved in the transfer; (3) the amount of cohesiveness observed in the groups.

In no case was more than a minor change in the work routines and time allowances made. The no-participation group, the eighteen hand pressers, had formerly stacked their work in one-half-dozen lots on a flat piece of cardboard the size of the finished product. The new job called for stacking their work in one-half-dozen lots in a box the size of the finished product. The box was located in the same place the cardboard had been. An additional two minutes per dozen was allowed (by the time study) for this new part of the job. This represented a total job change of 8.8 percent.

The group treated with participation through representation, the thirteen pajama folders, had formerly folded coats with prefolded pants. The new job called for the folding of coats with unfolded pants. An additional 1.8 minutes per dozen was allowed (by time study) for this new part of the job. This represented a total job change of 9.4 percent.

The two total participation groups, consisting of eight and seven pajama examiners respectively, had formerly clipped threads from the entire garment and examined every seam. The new job called for pulling only certain threads off and examining every seam. An average of 1.2 minutes per dozen was subtracted (by time study) from the total time on these two jobs. This represented a total job change of 8 percent.

The no-participation group of hand pressers went through the usual factory routine when they were changed. The production department modified the job, and a new piece rate was set. A group meeting was then held in which the control group was told that the change was necessary because of competitive conditions, and that a new piece rate had been set. The new piece rate was thoroughly explained by the time-study man, questions were answered, and the meeting dismissed.

The group which participated through representatives was changed in a different manner. Before any changes took place, a group meeting was held with all the operators to be changed. The need for the change was presented as dramatically as possible, showing two identical garments produced in the factory; one was produced in 1946 and had sold for 100 percent more than its fellow in 1947. The group was asked to identify the cheaper one and could not do it. This demonstration effectively shared with the group the entire problem of the necessity of cost reduction. A general agreement was reached that a savings could be effected by removing the "frills" and "fancy" work from the garment without affecting the folders' opportunity to achieve a high efficiency rating. Management then presented a plan to set the new job and piece rate:

(1) Make a check study of the job as it was being done.

(2) Eliminate all unnecessary work.

(3) Train several representative operators in the correct methods.

(4) Set the piece rate by time studies on these specially trained operators.

(5) Explain the new job and rate to all the operators.

(6) Train all operators in the new method so they can reach a high rate of production within a short time.

The group approved this plan (though no formal group decision was reached), and chose the operators to be specially trained. A submeeting with the "special" operators was held immediately following the meeting with the entire group. They displayed a cooperative and interested attitude and immediately presented many good suggestions. This attitude carried over into the working out of the details of the new job, and when the new job and piece rates were set, the "special" operators referred to the resultants as "our job," "our rate," etc. The new job and piece rates were presented at a second group meeting to all the operators involved. The "special" operators served to train the other operators on the new job.

The total participation groups went through much the same kind of meetings. The groups were smaller, and a more intimate atmosphere was established. The need for a change was once again made dramatically clear; the same general plan was presented by management. However, since the groups were small, all operators were chosen as "special" operators—that is, all operators were to participate directly in the designing of the new jobs, and all operators would be studied by the time-study man. It is interesting to note that in the meetings with these two groups, suggestions were immediately made in such quantity that the stenographer had great difficulty in recording them. The group approved of the plans, but again no formal group decision was reached.

Results. The results of the experiment are summarized in graphic form in Figure 2. The gaps in the production curves occur because these groups were paid on a time-work basis for a day or two. The no-participation group improved little beyond their early efficiency ratings. Resistance developed almost immediately after the change occurred. Marked expressions of aggression against management occurred, such as conflict with the methods engineer, expression of hostility against the supervisor, deliberate restriction of production, and lack of cooperation with the supervisor. There were 17 percent quits in the first forty days. Grievances were filed about the piece rate, but when the rate was checked, it was found to be a little "loose."

The group treated with participation through representation showed an unusually good relearning curve. At the end of fourteen days, the group averaged 61 units per hour. During the fourteen

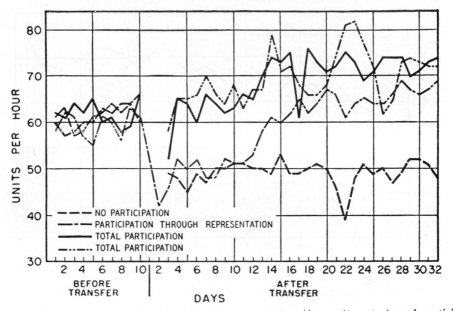

FIG. 2. The effects of participation through representation (Group I) and of total participation (Groups II and III) on recovery after an easy transfer.

days, the attitude was cooperative and permissive. They worked well with the methods engineer, the training staff, and the supervisor. (The supervisor was the same person in the cases of the first two groups.) There were no quits in this group in the first forty days. This group might have presented a better learning record if materials had not been scarce during the first seven days. There was one act of aggression against the supervisor recorded in the first forty days. It is interesting to note that the three special representative operators recovered at about the same rate as the rest of their group.

Overcoming Resistance to Change. The total participation groups recovered faster than the other experimental groups. After a slight drop on the first day of change, the efficiency ratings returned to a prechange level and showed sustained progress thereafter to a level about 14 percent higher than the prechange level. No additional training was provided them after the second day.

They worked well with their supervisors, and no indications of aggression were observed from these groups. There were no quits in either of these groups in the first forty days.

A fifth experimental group, composed of only two sewing operators, was transferred by the total-participation technique. Their new job was one of the most difficult jobs in the factory, in contrast to the easy jobs for the four other experimental groups. As expected, the total participation technique again resulted in an unusually fast recovery rate and a final level of production well above the level before transfer.

In the first experiment, the no-participation group made no progress after transfer for a period of thirty-two days. At the end of this period the group was broken up, and the individuals were reassigned to new jobs scattered throughout the factory. Two and a half months after their dispersal, the thirteen remaining members of the original group, having regained standard production, were again

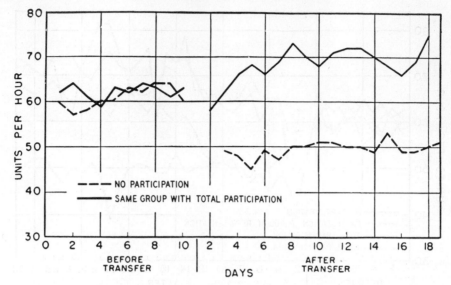

FIG. 3. A comparison of the effect of no participation with the different participation procedures on the same group.

brought together as a group for a second experiment.

This second experiment consisted of transferring the group to a new job, using the total participation technique. The new job was a pressing job of comparable difficulty to the new job in the first experiment. On the average it involved about the same degree of change. In the meetings no reference was made to the previous behavior of the group on being transferred.

The results of the second experiment were in sharp contrast to the first (see Figure 3). With the total-participation technique, the same group now recovered rapidly to their previous efficiency rating, and, like the other groups under this treatment, continued on beyond it to a new high level of production. There was no aggression or turnover in the group for nineteen days after change, a marked modification of their previous behavior after transfer. Some anxiety concerning their seniority status was expressed, but this was resolved in a meeting of their elected delegate, the union business agent, and a management representative.

INTERPRETATION

The purpose of this section is to explain the drop in production resulting from transfer, the differential recovery rates of the three experimental treatments, the increases beyond their former levels of production by the participating groups, and the differential rates of turnover and aggression.

The first experiment showed that the rate of recovery is directly proportional to the amount of participation, and that the rates of turnover and aggression are inversely proportional to the amount of participation. The second experiment demonstrated more conclusively that the results obtained depended on the experimental treatment rather than on personality factors like skill or aggressiveness, for identical individuals yielded markedly different results in the no-participation treatment as contrasted with the total-participation treatment.

Apparently total participation has the same type of effect as participation through representation, but the former has a stronger influence. In regard to recovery rates, this difference is not unequivocal because the experiment was unfortunately confounded. Right after transfer, the latter group had insufficient material to work on for a period of seven days. Hence their slower recovery during this period is at least in part due to insufficient work. In succeeding days, however, there was an adequate supply of work, and the differential recovery rate still persisted. Therefore, we are inclined to believe that participation through representation results in slower recovery than does total participation.

Before discussing the details of why participation produces high morale, we will consider the nature of production levels. In examining the production records of hundreds of individuals and groups in this factory, one is struck by the constancy of the level of production. Though differences among individuals in efficiency rating are very large, nearly every experienced operator maintains a fairly steady level of production, given constant physical conditions. Frequently the given level will be maintained despite rather large changes in technical working conditions.

As Lewin has pointed out, this type of production can be viewed as a quasi-stationary process—in the ongoing work the operator is forever sewing new garments, yet the level of the process remains relatively stationary.[4] Thus there are constant characteristics of the production process permitting the establishment of general laws.

In studying production as a quasi-stationary equilibrium, we are concerned with two types of forces: (1) forces on production in a downward direction, (2) forces on production in an upward direction. In this situation we are dealing with a variety of both upward forces

tending to increase the level of production and downward forces tending to decrease the level of production. However, in the present experiment we have no method of measuring independently all of the component forces either downward or upward. These various component forces upward are combined into one resultant force upward. Likewise the several downward component forces combine into one resultant force downward. We can infer a good deal about the relative strengths of these resultant forces.

Where we are dealing with a quasi-stationary equilibrium, the resultant forces upward and the forces downward are opposite in direction and equal in strength at the equilibrium level. Of course, either resultant forces may fluctuate over a short period of time, so that the forces may not be equally balanced at a given moment. However, over a longer period of time and on the average the forces balance out. Fluctuations from the average occur, but there is a tendency to return to the average level.

Just before being transferred, all the groups in both experiments had reached a stable equilibrium level at just above the standard production of 60 units per hour. This level was equal to the average efficiency rating for the entire factory during the period of the experiments. Since this production level remained constant, neither increasing nor decreasing, we may be sure that the strength of the resultant force upward was equal to the strength of the resultant force downward. This equilibrium of forces was maintained over the period of time when production was stationary at this level.[5] But the forces changed markedly after transfer, and these new constellations of forces were distinctly different for the various experimental groups.

For the no-participation group the period after transfer is a quasi-stationary

4 Kurt Lewin, *op. cit.*
5 *Ibid.*, p. 29.

equilibrium at a lower level, and the forces do not change during the period of thirty days. The resultant force upward remains equal to the resultant force downward and the level of production remains constant. The force field for this group is represented schematically in Figure 4. Only the resultant forces are shown. The length of the vector represents the strength of the force; and the point of the arrow represents the point of application of the force—that is, the production level and the time at which the force applies. Thus the forces are equal and opposite only at the level of 50 units per hour. At higher levels of production the forces downward are greater than the forces upward; and at lower levels of production the forces upward are stronger than the forces downward. Thus there is a tendency for the equilibrium to be maintained at an efficiency rating of 50.

The situation for the other experimental groups after transfer can be viewed as a quasi-stationary equilibrium of a different type. Figure 5 gives a schematic diagram of the resultant forces for all the participation groups. At any given level of production, such as 50 units per hour or 60 units per hour, both the resultant forces upward and the resultant forces downward change over the period of thirty days. During this time the point of equilibrium, which starts at 50 units per hour, gradually rises until it reaches a level of over 70 units per hour after thirty days. Yet here again the equilibrium level has the character of a "central force field" where at any point in the total field the resultant of the upward and the downward forces is in the direction of the equilibrium level.

To understand how the differences among the experimental treatments produced the differences in force fields represented in Figures 4 and 5, it is not sufficient to consider only the resultant forces. We must also look at the component forces for each resultant force.

There are three main component forces influencing production in a downward direction: (1) the difficulty of the job; (2) a force corresponding to avoidance of strain; (3) a force corresponding to a group standard to restrict production to a given level. The resultant force upward in the direction of greater production is composed of three additional component forces: (1) the force corresponding to the goal of standard production; (2) a force corresponding to pressures induced by the management through supervision; (3) a force corresponding to a group standard of competition. Let us examine each of these six component forces.

1. Job Difficulty. For all operators the difficulty of the job is one of the forces downward on production. The difficulty of the job, of course, is relative to the skill of the operator. The given job may be very difficult for an unskilled operator but relatively easy for a highly skilled one. In the case of a transfer a new element of difficulty enters. For some time the new job is much more difficult, for the operator is unskilled at that particular job. In addition to the difficulty experienced by any learner, the transfer often encounters the added difficulty of proactive inhibition. Where the new job is similar to the old job there will be a period of interference between the two similar but different skills required. For this reason a very efficient operator whose skills have become almost unconscious may suffer just as great a drop as a much less efficient operator. Except for Group V, the difficulty of these easy jobs does not explain the differential recovery rates because both the initial difficulty and the amount of change were equated for these groups. The two operators in Group V probably dropped further and recovered more slowly than any of the other three groups under total participation because of the greater difficulty of the job.

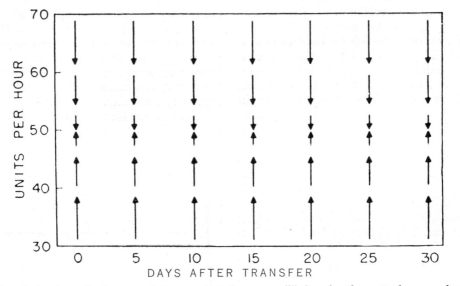

FIG. 4. A schematic diagram of the quasi-stationary equilibrium for the control group after transfer.

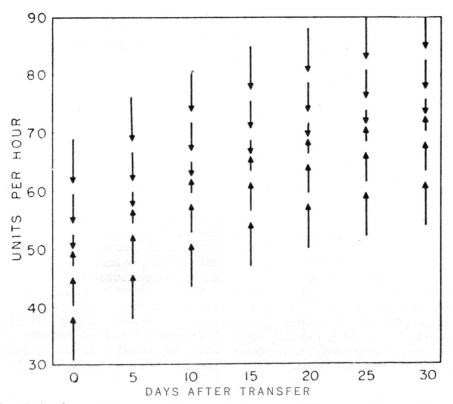

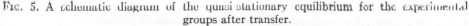

FIG. 5. A schematic diagram of the quasi stationary equilibrium for the experimental groups after transfer.

2. Strain Avoidance. The force toward lower production corresponding to the difficulty of the job (or the lack of skill of the person) has the character of a restraining force—that is, it acts to prevent locomotion rather than as a driving force causing locomotion. However, in all production there is a closely related driving force toward lower production, namely "strain avoidance." We assume that working too hard and working too fast is an unpleasant strain; and corresponding to this negative valence there is a driving force in the opposite direction, namely towards taking it easy or working slower. The higher the level of production the greater will be the strain and, other things being equal, the stronger will be the downward force of strain avoidance. Likewise, the greater the difficulty of the job the stronger will be the force corresponding to strain avoidance. But the greater the operator's skill the smaller will be the strain and the strength of the force of strain avoidance. Therefore:

(5) The strength of the force of strain avoidance =

$$\frac{\text{job difficulty} \times \text{production level}}{\text{skill of operator}}$$

The differential recovery rates of the three experimental groups in Experiment I cannot be explained by strain avoidance because job difficulty, production level, and operator skill were matched at the time immediately following transfer. Later, however, when the participation treatments had produced a much higher level of production, these groups were subjected to an increased downward force of strain avoidance which was stronger than in the no-participation group in Experiment I. Evidently other forces were strong enough to overcome this force of strain avoidance.

3. The Goal of Standard Production. In considering the negative attitudes toward transfer and the resistance to being transferred, there are several important aspects of the complex goal of reaching and maintaining a level of 60 units per hour. For an operator producing below standard, this goal is attractive because it means success, high status in the eyes of her fellow employees, better pay, and job security. On the other hand, there is a strong force against remaining below standard because this lower level means failure, low status, low pay, and the danger of being fired. Thus it is clear that the upward force corresponding to the goal of standard production will indeed be strong for the transfer who has dropped below standard.

It is equally clear why any operator shows such strong resistance to being changed. She sees herself as becoming a failure and losing status, pay, and perhaps the job itself. The result is a lowered level of aspiration and a weakened force toward the goal of standard production.

Just such a weakening of the force toward 60 units per hour seems to have occurred in the no-participation group in Experiment I. The participation treatments, on the other hand, seem to have involved the operators in designing the new job and setting the new piece rates in such a way that they did not lose hope of regaining the goal of standard production. Thus the participation resulted in a stronger force toward higher production. However, this force alone can hardly account for the large differences in recovery rate between the no-participation group and the other experimental groups; certainly it does not explain why the latter increased to a level so high above standard.

4. Management Pressure. On all operators below standard the management exerts a pressure for higher production. This pressure is no harsh and autocratic treatment involving threats. Rather it takes the form of persuasion and encouragement by the supervisors. They attempt to induce the low-rating operator to improve her performance and to attain standard production.

Such an attempt to induce a psychological force on another person may have several results. In the first place the person may ignore the attempt of the inducing agent, in which case there is no induced force acting on the person. On the other hand, the attempt may succeed so that an induced force on the person exists. Other things being equal, whenever there is an induced force acting on a person, the person will locomote in the direction of the force. An induced force, which depends on the power field of an inducing agent—some other individual or group—will cease to exist when the inducing power field is withdrawn. In this respect it is different from an "own" force which stems from a person's own needs and goals.

The reaction of a person to an effective induced force will vary depending, among other things, on the person's relation to the inducing agent. A force induced by a friend may be accepted in such a way that it acts more like an "own" force. An effective force induced by an enemy may be resisted and rejected so that the person complies unwillingly and shows signs of conflict and tension. Thus in addition to what might be called a "neutral" induced force, we also distinguish an *accepted* induced force and a *rejected* induced force. Naturally the acceptance and the rejection of an induced force can vary in degree from zero (i.e., a neutral induced force) to very strong acceptance or rejection. To account for the difference in character between the acceptance and rejection of an induced force, we make the following assumptions:

(6) The acceptance of an induced force sets up additional "own" forces in the same direction.

(7) The rejection of an induced force sets up additional "own" forces in the opposite direction.

The grievances, aggression, and tension in the no-participation group in

Experiment I indicate that they rejected the force toward higher production induced by the management. The group accepted the stereotype that transfer is a calamity, but the no-participation procedure did not convince them that the change was necessary, and they viewed the new job and the new piece rates set by management as arbitrary and unreasonable. The other experimental groups, on the contrary, participated in designing the changes and setting the piece rates so that they spoke of the new job as "our job" and the new piece rates as "our rates." Thus they accepted the new situation and accepted the management-induced force toward higher production.

From the acceptance by the participation groups and the rejection by the no-participation group of the management-induced forces, we may derive [by (6) and (7) above] that the former had additional "own" forces toward higher production whereas the latter had additional "own" forces toward lower production. This difference helps to explain the better recovery rate of the participation groups and the fact that they exceeded their original level of production.

5. Group Standards. Probably the most important force affecting the recovery under the no-participation procedure was a group standard, set by the group, restricting the level of production to 50 units per hour. Evidently this explicit agreement to restrict production is related to the group's rejection of the change and of the new job as arbitrary and unreasonable. Perhaps they had faint hopes of demonstrating that standard production could not be attained and thereby obtain a more favorable piece rate. In any case there was a definite group phenomenon which affected all the members of the group.

We have already noted the striking example of the presser whose production was restricted in the group situation to about half the level she attained as an individual. In the no-participation group, too, we would expect the group to induce strong forces on the members. The more a member deviates above the standard, the stronger would be the group-induced force to conform to the standard, for such deviations both negate any possibility of management's increasing the piece rate and at the same time expose the other members to increased pressure from management. Thus individual differences in levels of production should be sharply curtailed in this group after transfer.

An analysis was made for all groups of the individual differences within the group in levels of production. In Experiment I the forty days before change were compared with the thirty days after change; in Experiment II the ten days before change were compared to the seventeen days after change. As a measure of variability, the standard deviation was calculated each day for each group. The average daily standard deviations *before* and *after* change were as follows:

Group	Variability	
	Before change	After change
Experiment I		
No participation . .	9.8	1.9
Participation through		
representation . .	9.7	3.8
Total participation .	10.3	2.7
Total participation .	9.9	2.4
Experiment II		
Total participation .	12.7	2.9

There is indeed a marked decrease in individual differences within the no-participation group after this trial transfer. In fact the restriction of production

resulted in a lower variability than in any other group. Thus we may conclude that the group standard at 50 units per hour set up strong group-induced forces which were important components in the central-force field shown in Figure 4. It is now evident that for this group the quasi-stationary equilibrium after transfer has a steep gradient around the equilibrium level of 50 units per hour—the strength of the forces increases rapidly above and below this level. It is also clear that the group standard to restrict production is a major reason for the lack of recovery in the no-participation group.

The table of variability also shows that the experimental treatments markedly reduced variability in the other four groups after transfer. In participation by representation this smallest reduction of variability was produced by a group standard of individual competition for improvement in efficiency rating. Competition among members of the group was reported by the supervisor soon after transfer. This competition was a force toward higher production which resulted in good recovery to standard and continued progress beyond standard.

The total participation groups showed a greater reduction in variability following transfer. These two groups in Experiment I under total participation were transferred on the same day. Each group tried to set a better record for improvement than the other group. This group competition, which evidently resulted in stronger forces on the members than did the individual competition, was an effective group standard. The standard gradually moved to higher and higher levels of production with the result that the groups not only reached but far exceeded their previous levels of production.

Probably a major determinant of the strength of these group standards in the cohesiveness of the group.[6] Whether this power of the group over the members was used to increase or to decrease productivity seemed to depend on the use of participation.[7]

Turnover and Aggression. Returning now to our preliminary theory of frustration, we can see several revisions. The difficulty of the job and its relation to skill and strain avoidance has been clarified in proposition (5). It is now clear that the driving force toward 60 is a complex affair; it is partly a negative driving force corresponding to the negative valence of low pay, low status, failure, and job insecurity. Turnover results not only from the frustration produced by the conflict of these two forces but also as a direct attempt to escape from the region of these negative valences. For the members of the no-participation group, the group standard to restrict production prevented escape by increasing production, so that quitting their jobs was the only remaining escape. In the participation groups, on the contrary, both the group standards and the additional own forces resulting from the acceptance of management-induced forces combined to make increasing production the distinguished path of escape from this region of negative valence.

In considering turnover as a form of escape from the field, it is not enough to look only at the psychological present; one must also consider the psychological future. The employee's decision to quit the job is rarely made exclusively on the basis of a momentary frustration or an undesirable present situation; she usually quits when she also sees the future as equally hopeless. The operator transferred by the usual factory procedure (including the no-participation group) has in fact a realistic view of the proba-

bility of continued failure because, as we have already noted, 62 percent of transfers do in fact fail to recover to standard production. Thus the higher rate of quitting for transfers as compared to nontransfers results from a more pessimistic view of the future.

The no-participation procedure had the effect for the members of setting up management as a hostile power field. They rejected the forces induced by this hostile power field, and group standards to restrict production developed within the group in opposition to management. In this conflict between the power field of management and the power field of the group, the group attempted to reduce the strength of the hostile power field relative to the strength of their own power field. This change was accomplished in three ways: (1) the group increased its own power by developing a more cohesive and well-disciplined group, (2) they secured "allies" by getting the backing of the union in filing a formal grievance about the new piece rate, (3) they attacked the hostile power field directly in the form of aggression against the supervisor, the time-study engineer, and the higher management. Thus the aggression was derived not only from individual frustration but also from the conflict between two groups. Furthermore, this situation of group conflict both helped to define management as the frustrating agent and gave the members strength to express any aggressive impulses produced by frustration.

CONCLUSIONS

It is possible for management to modify greatly or to remove completely group resistance to changes in methods of work and the ensuing piece rates.

[6] L. Festinger, K. Back, S. Schachter, H. Kelley, and J. Thibaut, *Theory and Experiment in Social Communication* (Ann Arbor: Edwards Bros., 1950).

[7] S. Schachter, N. Ellertson, D. McBride, and D. Gregory, "An Experimental Study of Cohesiveness and Productivity," *Hum. Rel.*, 1951, IV, No. 3.

This change can be accomplished by the use of group meetings in which management effectively communicates the need for change and stimulates group participation in planning the changes.

Such participation results in higher production, higher morale, and better labor-management relations.

Harwood's management has long felt that such field experiments are the key to better labor-management relations. It is only by discovering the basic principles and applying them to the true causes of conflict that an intelligent, effective effort can be made to correct the undesirable effects of the conflict. In addition to these practical values, therefore, this experiment also contributes to our theories of group productivity, group processes, and intergroup relations.

A CROSS-CULTURAL REPLICATION

This experiment was replicated in a similar Norwegian factory in 1956, although necessarily using somewhat different operational definitions.[8] Nine 4-man groups were changed to producing new products with a new piece rate. The four control groups had low participation in planning the changes, but the five experimental groups were given more participation through a series of meetings which were similar to the "total participation" procedures in the previous experiment. However, this treatment probably produced somewhat weaker psychological participation (defined as the amount of influence which the person perceives that he exerts on a jointly made decision which affects all participants).

The effects of participation on several dimensions of labor-management relations and on job satisfaction were measured by a questionnaire. It was predicted that these effects would increase with increasing legitimacy of participation and with decreasing resistance to the methods of introducing the change.

Compared to the control groups, the experimental groups showed trends in the direction of greater job satisfaction and more favorable attitudes toward management. As predicted these effects became significant when we controlled for the legitimacy of participation and for the amount of resistance to change as measured by the questionnaire. Thus participation produces improved morale only to the extent that it is legitimate (i.e., the workers feel they have as much influence as they should have). Likewise participation produces improved morale only to the extent that there is no strong resistance to the methods of introducing change.

There was no difference between the experimental and the control groups in the level of production, probably because the participation was less relevant and because there were stronger group standards restricting production.

The revised theory, specifying the conditioning variables, accounts for the results of both experiments and also for individual differences in reactions to participation.

---

[8] J. R. P. French, Jr., J. Israel, and D. Aos, "An Experiment on Participation in a Norwegian Factory," *Hum. Relat.*, 1958 (in press).

THE DYNAMICS OF POWER: A FIELD STUDY OF SOCIAL INFLUENCE IN GROUPS OF CHILDREN

By Ronald Lippitt, Norman Polansky, Fritz Redl, and Sidney Rosen

INTRODUCTION

This is one in a series of reports on a program of research into the process of social influence in groups of children. Our initial curiosity focused on the phenomenon of behavioral contagion described and clinically conceptualized by Redl [1] in an analysis of some of the operational problems of group therapy. We defined behavioral contagion as the spontaneous pick up or imitation by other children of a behavior initiated by one member of the group, where the initiator did not display any intention of getting the others to do what he did. This is distinguished from direct influence in which the actor initiates behavior which has the manifest objective of affecting the behavior of another member of the group. We decided to study the hypothesis that the initiation of, and receptivity to, such social influence was related to the position of the actor in the social structure of the group.

Our first study, in 1948, collected data on the processes of contagion and direct influence in two camps for disturbed children, a boys' camp and a girls' camp.[2] In 1950 we decided it would be methodologically desirable to replicate the study in the same boys' camp (hereinafter referred to as M-camp). We selected the same age group as in 1948 (10–13 years old) and, as before, studied four cabins during each of the two four-week camp sessions.

The first study included sixteen groups of lower socio-economic background, emotionally disturbed, children. For the 1950 study we decided to find a contrasting camp population of middle-class, adjusted boys, as well as to replicate the study in the original boys' camp. We were fortunate to obtain the full collaboration of such a camp (hereinafter referred to as W-camp) which matched the other camp in size of cabin groups, age range, length of camp period, adult-child ration, and type of program philosophy.[3]

Prepared especially for this volume. The reader will find more complete details of this study in a forthcoming article in *Human Relations*.

This research program has been supported by a grant from the National Institute of Mental Health of the U.S. Public Health Service. Fritz Redl and Ronald Lippitt have functioned as coprincipal investigators. Norman Polansky and Sidney Rosen have served as project directors. Members of the field teams for this study were: Joseph Masling, Sidney Rosen, Will Kyselka, Robert Tropp, Alan M. Walker, and Robert J. Wolff.

Previous reports have been: Norman Polansky *et al.*, "Problems of Interpersonal Relations in Research on Groups," *Human Relations*, 1949, II, 281–292; N. Polansky, R. Lippitt, and F. Redl, "An Investigation of Behavioral Contagion in Groups," *Human Relations*, 1950, III, 319–348; N. Polansky, R. Lippitt, and F. Redl, "The Use of Near-Sociometric Data in Research on Group Treatment Processes," *Sociometry*, 1950, XIII, 39–62; D. Grosser, N. Polansky, and R. Lippitt, "A Laboratory Study of Behavioral Contagion," *Human Relations*, 1951, IV, 115–142.

[1] F. Redl, "The Phenomenon of Contagion and Shock Effect in Group Therapy," in *Searchlights on Delinquency* (New York: International Universities Press, 1949), pp. 315–328.

[2] N. Polansky, R. Lippitt, and F. Redl, "An Investigation of Behavioral Contagion in Groups," *op. cit.*

[3] We wish to express deep appreciation to William Morse, director of the University of Michigan Fresh Air Camp, and to Elmer Ott, director of Camp Manito-wish in Wisconsin, for their understanding support, without which this project would not have been possible.

This report summarizes the comparative findings on behavioral contagion and direct influence processes in the M- and W-camps, and also reports the 1948 data so that the replication of findings in M-camp can be evaluated, as well as the degree of generalization of the findings to the new type of population in W-camp.

Two research teams of three persons each were trained together in the use of the same instruments and then spent the summer separated, collecting data in the two camps. One member of the research team assigned to the W-camp spent a final week in M-camp to get an estimate of intercamp observation reliability.

After a number of exploratory excursions it has seemed to us most fruitful to formulate our theorizing as contributing to a systematic theory of social power in the face-to-face group. Theorizing about the dynamics of power in larger social structures has proved stimulating (e.g., the contributions of Max Weber [4] and Goldhamer and Shils [5]). Goldhamer and Shils have suggested that power may be measured by the number of successful power acts divided by the number of attempts made. This idea is very similar to one of the indices used in our two studies (percent of success of direct influence attempts). Another springboard for our theorizing has been the work of Festinger and his coworkers.[6] They have followed Lewin [7] in defining power as potentiality to exert influence. As we see it, the dimensions of the concept of social power can be differentiated as units in the following definition:

Social power is: (1) the potentiality (2) for inducing forces (3) in other persons (4) toward acting or changing in a given direction.

Obviously there can be no direct operational definition of this concept because so many situations and interactions would have to be explored to discover the exact boundaries of "potential" power. In our study we have made two attempts to approximate a measurement of power.

By getting the judgments of all members on the degree of ability of each member to influence "the other fellow," we have computed an *index of attributed power*. This index is, of course, an inadequate direct measure of power for several reasons. For example, the power of one or several members may be untested by the events of group life. There may be a bias of being unwilling to recognize the power of a member to whom one does not willingly submit. But the stability of the index over time, the amount of intermember agreement in making the judgments, and the consistent predicted relationships to other variables suggest this index represents a good approach to one aspect of the power syndrome.

The second measure is an index of the degree of behavioral success the member has in attempting to influence others. We might call this an *index of manifest power*. This also is only an indirect approximation of power, because a person with high power may not attempt to exert that power, or may exercise it only in very limited degrees and situations.

It is within this general theoretical framework that we have attempted to

---

[4] H. H. Gerth and C. W. Mills, editors, *From Max Weber: Essays in Sociology* (New York: Harper & Bros., 1950).

[5] H. Goldhamer and E. Shils, "Types of Power and Status," *American Journal of Sociology*, XLV (1939), 171–182.

[6] L. Festinger, S. Schachter, and K. Back, *Social Pressures in Informal Groups* (New York: Harper & Bros., 1950).

[7] Kurt Lewin, *Field Theory and Social Science* (New York: Harper & Bros., 1951).

organize our findings, and we shall return to this framework for interpretive insights in the final section.

METHODS OF DATA COLLECTION AND ANALYSIS

A. The Measurement of Attributed Power. In the first study the children sorted the pictures of the other members of the group into colored boxes on a number of dimensions which were combined into a prestige- or attributed-power index. This was an individual interview situation.[8] The combined attributed-power index correlated highly with the scores on the single "group-influence question" ("Who is best at getting the other fellows to do what he wants them to do?"). So in the 1950 study the attributed-power index for each boy was derived from the group judgments on the single question of "Who has influence," on which each boy ranked every other boy in his cabin by hanging the photographs in rank order on a row of nails on a board.

We decided to use this single "purer" measure of attributed power rather than the combined index, because it seemed likely to us that, if the two camps were as widely different as we predicted, the various questions about physical strength, sex sophistication, etc., would have quite different meanings and relations to attributed power in the two camps. Therefore in our report of findings our improved direct measurement of perceived influence has been compared with the combined attributed-power index of the 1948 study. As in that study, these sociometric interviews were conducted during the first and last weeks of the four-week camp session.

B. Measurement of Liking and Identification. In 1948 and 1950, each child ranked the other members of his cabin group on the criterion of "Like to be with." In the 1950 study, we added another question which asked each boy to select the one other boy in the cabin he "Would most like to be." We hoped this latter question would sharpen our understanding of the relationship between interpersonal feelings and the exerting of social influence.

C. Measurement of Perceived Characteristics of Each Member. Using the picture-ranking technique, each child ranked the other group members on: goodness in sports, fighting ability (added in the 1950 study), sex sophistication, and knowledge of campcraft.

Each counselor ranked each child in his group four times during the period on scales of: adult relatedness, impulsiveness, group-belongingness need, feeling of acceptance by the group, conformity to group pressures, warmth of relations with peers, social sensitivity, and activity level. The counselors also did the same rank-ordering task as the boys on the sociometric items.

D. The Measurement of Self-perception. The big addition to the measurement program of the second study was asking each child to place his own picture in the rank order for the dimensions of fighting ability, independence of adults, being liked, and influence in the group. A pilot study had indicated the children were ready and able to do this without any discoverable problems of anxiety or other aftereffects in the group.

E. The Measurement of Behavioral Contagion and Direct Influence. A precategorized observation schedule was used by a team of field observers to record influence behavior on a sampling basis as outlined in the typical time schedule below. As in the first study, an incident of *behavioral contagion* was defined as "an event in which a person's behavior is changed to resemble that of

---

[8] N. Polansky, R. Lippitt, and F. Redl, "The Use of Near-Sociometric Data in Research on Group Treatment Processes." *op. cit.*

another person. This change occurs in a social-interaction situation in which the person acting as the 'initiator' has not communicated intent to evoke such a change in the other." Each child who picked up the behavior was recorded as a recipient of the particular contagion. A *direct-influence attempt* was defined as "a social interaction in which one child consciously and deliberately tries to get another child to do something, in such a way that the research observer is aware of the intent." The manner of the influence attempt was coded as directive (ordering, commanding) or nondirective (suggesting, requesting). All three observers checked their reliability periodically by observing the same group at the same time. Intercamp reliability was computed by one observer participating in reliability tests in both camps.

F. The Measurement of Total Activity. On a periodic sampling basis, as indicated by the time schedule below, the observer focused on a single child in the group and recorded all of his activity, coding it in the two categories of social activity and nonsocial activity. Social acts had other persons as their target and referred to the realm of social interaction. Nonsocial acts were directed toward objects or were focused on individual activity and autistic verbalizations and expressive movements.

G. Measurement of Other Characteristics of Social Interaction. In addition to the recording of influence, and total activity, the observers coded a number of "other behavioral indicators" designed to test hypotheses about behavioral aspects of status. These categories were: (1) implies superior knowledge or skill in the other; (2) asks permission of the other; (3) sympathetic or solicitous behavior; (4) affection-seeking behavior; (5) negative or hostile behavior. All observations, in all categories, were recorded in terms of the initiator and the recipient of the act.

H. The Behavior Sampling Procedure. The observer, following the group throughout the day, recorded data whenever at least three children of the particular cabin group were together. The three observers were rotated systematically among the four cabins being studied. A typical sampling sequence went like this:

1. Observation of contagion and direct influence . . . . . 15 mins.
2. Rest period for observer . . 5 mins.
3. Observation of contagion and behavior indicators . . . . 10 mins.
4. Rest period for observer . . 1 min.
5. Observation of total activity of one child . . . . 2 mins.
6. Rest period for observer . . 1 min.
7. Observation of total activity of second child . . . . . 2 mins.

Then the total cycle began again and picked up the other children individually for total activity observation. During the total camp period, certain children were, of course, observed together more than others. This was an interesting item of data. But to compare the children on such things as behavioral influence all the data were corrected to equate for the amount of time each pair of children spent together. The behavior totals used in the study are drawn from the following cumulated time samples:

1. Average time each child was under observation for behavioral contagion
   M-camp, 15 hrs.
   W-camp, 11 hrs.
2. Average time each child was under observation for direct influence
   M-camp, 9 hrs.
   W-camp, $6\frac{1}{2}$ hrs.
3. Average time each child was under observation for behavioral indicators
   M-camp, 6 hrs.
   W-camp, $4\frac{1}{2}$ hrs.
4. Average time each child was under observation of individual activity
   M-camp, 30 mins.
   W-camp, 13 mins.

I. Interobserver and Intercamp Reliability of Observations of Behavior. Periodic interobserver reliability checks were made in each camp by having two observers record a sample of cabin behavior simultaneously. The observations of each observer were systematically paired with each other observer's records. The reliability was computed as a rank-order correlation of the data of the two observers for each time sample. The results are indicated in Table 1. The cor-

TABLE 1

INTEROBSERVER RELIABILITY IN
1950 STUDY

Behavior observed	M-Camp Ave. rho	W-Camp Ave. rho
Contagion initiation	.79	.90
Contagion pick-up .	.76	.70
Direct attempt to influence	.91	.76
Recipient of influence attempt	.87	.59
Initiator of behavior indicators . . .	.89	.87
Recipient of behavior indicators . . .	.77	.82
Total activity level	.87	.87
Percent social behavior	77	87

relations seem uniformly high enough to give us confidence in relating our various items of data, and in comparing data from the two camps. Intercamp reliability was of the same order.

Although all these figures were not computed in a comparable manner in the first study, we do have a comparable average reliability correlation of .87 for contagion initiation and .76 for contagion pick-up in M-camp.

J. Securing Other Objective Indices on Each Camper. In addition to the observation data, counselor rating data, and camper rank-order judgments, we

obtained the following information for each camper: (1) age, (2) height, (3) weight, (4) last school grade completed, (5) socio-economic status of parent as estimated by classification of father's occupation, and (6) I.Q. estimate from the vocabulary section of the Stanford-Binet (Form L, 1937).

THE FINDINGS

The results of our two studies are summarized in four sections which focus on answering the following questions: (1) To what extent is behavior toward power figures consistent with verbalized attribution of power? (2) To what extent is there a self-perception of own power? Does it seem to "guide" behavior output? (3) How is the behavior of recipients of high attributed power different from that of recipients of low attributed power? (4) What evidence is there concerning the determinants of how power is acquired in the group?

I. The Attributor's Behavior toward His High-power Choice. *A. The group member is more likely to "contage" from the behavior of a high-power member.* This central hypothesis is supported by the data from the M-camp in 1948 and 1950, and the generalization is extended by the similar findings from the new population of normal middle-class boys. Table 2 indicates that in all four populations studied, a total of thirty-two groups, group members tend to imitate the behavior of those members to whom they have attributed power to influence the group.

An inadequacy of the 1948 study was that we were unable to handle the possibility that the greater volume of behavioral contagion from acts initiated by high-power children might be due to a generally higher behavior output by such children. In the second study an independent measure of total behavior output was made, as described on page 626.

TABLE 2

RELATIONSHIP OF ATTRIBUTED POWER TO CONTAGION INITIATION

Population	N	1948 study Ave. rho	Sig.	N	1950 study Ave. rho	Sig.	Ave. rho corrected for total activity 1950 study
Mich. boys . .	8 groups 64 boys	.52	.001	8 groups 63 boys	.58	.001	.52
Girls	8 groups 40 girls	.71	.001				
Wis. boys . . .				8 groups 65 boys	.58	.001	.52

The frequency of contagion initiation for each child was then divided by his total activity index, and this weighted frequency was correlated with the attributed-power ranking of each child. As indicated in the right-hand column of Table 3, there was no significant drop in the relationship between attributed power and contagion pick-up when this correction factor for total activity level was introduced. Our initial interpretation that perception of power, rather than sheer activity output, is a major determinant of contagion pick-up seems to be confirmed.

B. *The group member is more likely to accept direct attempts to influence him which are initiated by a high-power member.* The 1948 study discovered a relationship between success of direct induction attempts and attributed power as well as between contagion pick-up and attributed power. Table 3 indicates that this relationship is confirmed by the replication study and can be generalized to the new population. In the population of M boys the second study found an average cabin correlation (rho) of .61 as compared with a correlation of .56 in the first study. The new population of groups of W boys

TABLE 3

RELATIONSHIP OF ATTRIBUTED POWER TO FREQUENCY OF SUCCESSFUL INFLUENCE ATTEMPTS

Population	N	1948 study Ave. rho	Sig.	N	1950 study Ave. rho	Sig.	Ave. rho corrected for total activity 1950 study
Mich. boys . .	8 groups 64 boys	.56	.001	8 groups 63 boys	.61	.001	.60
Girls . .	8 groups 40 girls	.54	.001				
Wis. boys . .				8 groups 65 boys	.48	.001	.45

yields an average correlation of .48. All of these relationships are statistically significant.

Again we were able to check in the second study on the extent to which total behavior output might be a factor in determining the frequency of successful influence. The right-hand column of Table 3 indicates that a correction for total activity of each child does not change the relationship appreciably.

A second and even more important question may be asked: Is the member with high attributed power really more likely to succeed with each of his influence attempts or does he just make more influence attempts? To check this question we computed the percentage of all influence attempts made by each child that were successful and correlated the rank order of these percentage indices with the rank order of prestige in each cabin. The average correlation for the 16 groups in 1950 is .42 which is statistically significant ($p = .001$). The average correlation is identical in both camps. In general, then, the higher a member's attributed power, the more likely it is that each of his influence attempts will be successful.

C. A check on the actual relative attributed-power positions of the actor and the recipient for each "recipient" of contagion initiation and of successful direct-influence attempts. The statistical analyses reported above have shown that, in general, the boys who receive the most verbal choices as power figures in the group are the most frequent sources of behavioral contagion and are most successful in their direct-influence attempts. But this does not demonstrate that the behavior of a particular actor is consistent with his particular attribution of power to others. Perhaps this relationship works in general but is not a very consistent psychological phenomenon from member to member. To check on this possibility a more refined analysis was made in the second

study. The data for each boy were analyzed to check the average amount of his contagion pick-up and acceptance of direct influence from members whom he ranked high (upper half of group) or low (lower half of group) on the dimension of group influence. Because of our interest in the development of social stratification, we made separate analyses for the first and second half of the four-week camp sessions. These data are presented in Table 4.

The upper half of the table indicates that in both camps, during the early and later parts of the periods, the average camper picked up more behavioral contagion from the boys he rated high on power than from those he rated in the bottom half of the cabin group. But in the lower half of the table we note that in the M-groups of boys, during the early part of their life together, the average member did not accept a significantly larger proportion of the direct-influence attempts directed toward him by his high-power choices than of such attempts directed by his low-power choices. A more consistent relationship between perception of power and influence acceptance seems to have developed by the second half of the camp period. In the W-groups behavior seems to be more consistently in line with power perception from the very beginning.

D. Attempts to influence high-power figures are more likely to be nondirective in manner. The 1948 study found that when the average group member attempted to influence high-power members he tended to be deferential in his manner of induction. The distinction made by the observers was between the directive and nondirective manner of influence attempts. This relationship was confirmed again in the 1950 M-groups, but did not hold in the W-groups. This is one of a number of clues pointing to differences in "style of social influence" in the two camp cultures.

TABLE 4

RELATION OF OWN POWER CHOICES TO BEHAVIOR

A

Contagion Pick-up from High- as Compared to Low-power Choices

	W-groups			M-groups		
	N *	M. diff. †	Sig. ‡	N	M. diff.	Sig.
First half session . . .	64	+.42	.001	61	+.60	.001
Second half session . . .	65	+.76	.001	57	+.81	.001

B

Percentage of Direct-Influence Attempts Accepted from High- as Compared to Low-power Choices

	W-groups			M-groups		
	Number showing greater percentage acceptance from		Chi-square test	Number showing greater percentage acceptance from		Chi-square test
	High	Low	Sig.	High	Low	Sig.
First half session	41	19	.01	31	30	not sig.
Second half session . . .	40	25	.10	38	19	.02
Combined halves . . .	45	19	.01	31	25	not sig.

* The number of campers changes slightly from first to second half of the session because of new boys entering groups or insufficient data on several children.

† M. diff. equals mean pick-up of contagion from high-power choices minus mean pick-up of contagion from low-power choices.

‡ P-value was based on a *t* test of the difference between related means.

E. Behavior directed toward high-power figures tends to be deferential and approval-seeking. It seems probable that there are many behavioral cues by which one member of this group communicates his degree of respect and deference for another member. Some individuals and groups will be clearer in this communication than others. Some individuals will be more sensitive in reading the cues. As described in the section on methodology, the observers in this study systematically recorded behaviors which had the meaning of "implying superior skill," "implying superior knowledge," and "asking for permission." In the 1948 study such data from a sample of four groups in each camp were analyzed. It was found that the upper half of the power hierarchy received significantly more of these behaviors than the lower half (by a *t*-test, $p = .01$ level in boys' camp, .10 in girls' camp). In 1950, this finding was confirmed by a more complete correlational study of all groups in the M- and W-camps.

II. The Perception of Own Power Position in the Group. On the basis of the 1948 study we inferred that, from the types of interaction reported above, each member would receive cues which would tell him that he was being looked "up to" or "down at" by his fellow members. We inferred that these behavioral messages would usually effect the self-perception of own power or lack of power in the group, and that this self-perception would tend to steer one's influence attempts in the group. Certainly there would be many distortions in these self-perceptions arising from past experience in other groups and from wishful thinking in the present situation, but we postulated that a specific self-percept about position in the present group was being formed and was exercising some control over behavior output. In the first study we lacked the data to check directly on this inference. We had evidence that members behaved deferentially toward those to whom they attributed various degrees of power, that the members behaved as though they were aware of this information in their attempts to exert influence. But we lacked a measure of the inferred intervening of self-perception of power. In the second study each boy ranked himself on amount of power in the group.

An analysis of the degree of correspondence of self-rankings and attributed rankings of power in the group reveals a significant positive relationship ($p =$ .001) in both camps. In general, the boys who had power attributed to them perceived that they had it. The deviates who overrated or underrated their own power are the special subjects of another study.

The second part of this analysis reveals that in M-camp the boys who perceived themselves as having high power made more frequent influence attempts, were more directive in making these attempts, and were more resistant to accepting influence from others than were boys who perceived themselves as having less power in the group. In the W-groups the boys who saw themselves as powerful in the group were not more directive in their behavior, nor were they more resistant to influence from others than were boys who perceived themselves as less powerful. But they did make more frequent influence attempts and were more active in general. It does seem clear that self-perception of own power was dynamically related to the efforts the boys made to utilize their power in the group. But differences in group standards about appropriate types of behavior also seem to play an active part in the two camp cultures.

III. **The Behavior of the Recipient of Attributed Power in the Group.** Now we will turn to the data bearing on the relationship between attributed power and the behavior of the recipients of the attributions.

A. The recipient of attributed power will make more frequent attempts to influence the behavior of others, and will be more successful in these attempts. As we have seen above, those members to whom high power has been attributed tend to be correct in perceiving this attribution. They tend to use this perceived status as a basis for making more influence attempts than do less powerful members. From this linkage we would expect to find a positive relationship between attributed position and volume of influence attempts. Table 5 confirms this inference.

We have already noted in Table 3 that these influence attempts tend to be more successful when initiated by recipients of high power ratings. Although these relationships are all significant, they are low enough to remind us that important forces are not taken into account. As the 1948 study pointed out, some children who are not high in attributed power act as though they were, in terms of influence attempts, and other children who do have high prestige positions do not use their power to wield influence in the group.

B. The recipient of attributed power will be more directive in his influence attempts.

TABLE 5

RELATIONSHIP OF ATTRIBUTED POWER TO FREQUENCY OF INFLUENCE ATTEMPTS

Population	N	1948 study Ave. rho	Sig.	N	1950 study Ave. rho	Sig.
Mich. boys	8 groups 64 boys	.43	.01	8 groups 63 boys	.49	.001
Girls	8 groups 40 girls	.66	.01			
Wis. boys				8 groups 65 boys	.35	.02

We have noted previously that both of our M-camp studies show that members with high attributed power in the group of boys tend to be approached more non-directively in the influence attempts that are directed toward them. This did not seem to be the case in the groups of W boys. Now we ask the question, do members with the power to make successful inductions tend to be more directive in their manner? We find that high-power boys in M-groups are significantly more directive (average rho of .49 in 1948, and .39 in 1950; $p = .01$ in both cases) in their influence attempts. This relationship was positive but did not reach significance in W-camp. This confirms the 1948 findings in the M-camp, and confirms the picture of a different influence style in W-camp.

IV. Characteristics Associated with Being a Recipient of Attributed Power. Although the focus of the study was on the process of influence rather than on the determinants of influence positions, we have a variety of clues about the latter which can be summarized at this point.

A. High-power boys tend to be different in the amount and pattern of their total activity output. The reader will remember that independent samples of total activity were taken which were broken down into social or person-oriented behavior and nonsocial (i.e., object and

activity-oriented behavior). A chi-square test of the difference in volume of social behavior of children in the upper half of the power rankings versus the volume of such behavior by campers in the lower half indicated positive relationships (M, $p = .10$; W, $p = .003$). The relationships of attributed power with nonsocial activity were not significant. In making the analysis it was noted that boys in the W-camp who were very low or very high in object-oriented behavior seemed to have less attributed power than those boys who showed an average amount. A chi-square of the middle half against the combined upper and lower quarters on attributed power showed a significant relationship ($p = .05$). This suggests that the high-power boy tends to be one who, among other characteristics, is high in his social-relations output and who shows an average amount of object-related and program-activity-related behavior. Boys who are lowest in power are low in social activity and are either very high or very low in nonsocial activity.

B. High-power boys have physical superiority. On the basis of clinical observations we postulated that the group standards of the M and W cabin groups would place a positive value on physical prowess as a basis for attributing influence position in the group. This idea is confirmed by the highly significant rho of .81 found in each camp between at tributed power and perceived fighting ability.

When we explore the meaning of this relationship further we find that neither height nor weight is significantly related to attributed power, but in the W-camp height, weight, and age are significantly related to perceived fighting ability (by chi-square, the respective p's are 0.1, .001 und .001). In the M-camp, however, none of these variables relates to perceived fighting ability. Observations in the two camps suggest that in the W-camp, where fighting hardly ever occurs, the perception of fighting ability is really a perception of potential fighting ability and is based on the most obvious cues of physical size, but in the M-camp, where a good deal of fighting actually takes place, the perception is based on performance, which probably does not correlate very highly with physical size or age in such a relatively homogeneous age population.

C. *High-power boys are superior in campcraft.* We also thought it was probably in these groups that some prestige value would be attached to skill in performing the variety of campcraft activities which the adult leadership provides as part of camp life. This hypothesis is also confirmed. In the M-camp, the rho between skill in campcraft as perceived by cabinmates and ratings of power made by the same boys was .74; in the W-camp, the rho was .68. Both are significant at the .001 level.

D. *High-power boys are liked better and identified with more than other group members.* Certainly we are not able, in this type of analysis, to demonstrate whether boys who achieve high-power positions become liked because of their positions or whether boys who are liked have power attributed to them. Such an analysis calls for a developmental or experimental study. It will be recalled that each boy did rank all other members of the group on a dimension of personal liking,

and also selected the boy in the group they would most like to be. The M and W rhos between campers' rankings of the order in which they like cabinmates and the order in which they see cabinmates as being influential are .63 and .76. The respective camp rhos between attributed power and ranking according to the order in which campers identify with cabinmates are .68 and .82. Again, all are significant at the .001 level.

The intercorrelations between liking, perceived fighting ability, and perceived campcraft skills are appreciably lower than the correlation of each of these factors with attributed power. Probably the various attributes contribute to varying degrees in attributing influence to the power figures in the group.

E. *Other clues on determinants of attributed power.* We were able to compute an estimate of intelligence (I.Q.) in each camp from scores on a vocabulary test. As would be expected, the mean I.Q. estimate was significantly higher in the W-camp (121 as compared to 103), but the total dispersion of scores was greater in the M-camp. In the M-camp there was no significant relationship of I.Q. level to attributed power, although the boys in the middle range on I.Q. tended to have more attributed power than those boys at the top or bottom of the scale. In the W-camp there was a significant positive relationship ($p = .01$) between I.Q. and attributed power.

Another measure which was of considerable theoretical interest to us as the result of our findings in the first study was the counselor rating of impulse control. In the 1948 study we found no relationship between rated level of impulsiveness and influence in the *general run* of camp situations. This negative finding was confirmed in the 1950 study in both camps. But we would like to recall the additional insight we gained in the first study on the relation of impulsiveness to behavioral contagion. Our hypothesis was

TABLE 6

DETERMINANTS OF CONTAGION INITIATION IN GENERAL
AND IN A SITUATION OF GROUP FRUSTRATION

	In general camp situation		Experimental situation	
	F	P	F	P
Attributed power $\times$ contagion initiation . .	8.666	.01	2.601	Not sig·
Impulsiveness $\times$ contagion initiation . . .	.160	Not sig.	4.040	.05

N = 32

that, although impulsive children did not have high attributed power and did not serve as contagion triggers in the general run of group situations, we would expect them to be high contagion initiators in situations of high group frustration where adult controls were irritating. We set up a special experimental situation with four cabin groups in M-camp.

The children were brought into a room, knew that they were going to be asked to go through a group interview with the aid of a projective picture. However, as the situation was staged, the picture was to be brought by some outside person who had not arrived as yet with it. His orders to us were that the treats—which were in full and obvious view and enticingly referred to—could not be had until the picture arrived. As had been expected, this situation was adequate for producing frustration, if various sorts of aggression toward each other and toward us may be taken as any index. For the four groups, the average waiting period until we felt that further frustration would be totally disruptive was 18 minutes. Contagion (initiations) as well as running protocol material were recorded during these sessions.

The children in these groups may be divided according to whether they had been above or below the median in attributed power, and above or below the median in impulsiveness in terms of the counselors' ratings. In Table 6 is given the relationship between these two factors for the children in general throughout the four-week period, and in this

specific situation (as based on analysis of variance into four components).

Although the relationship between contagion-initiation ability and attributed power for these children throughout the four-week period of observation was significant at beyond the 1-percent level, the relationship between these two factors during the experimental situation does not approach significance. On the other hand, although throughout the four weeks of observation the relationship between contagion-initiation ability and impulsiveness was not significant, it is significant at just below the 5-percent point during these experiments.

In relation to the question of who is most susceptible to the kinds of contagion which occur in such situations, results are in the same direction—that is, there was no relationship found throughout the camp period between the level of impulsiveness and contagion susceptibility. In this particular experimental situation, however, we find that the general susceptibility to both contagion *and* impulsiveness is significantly related to the numbers of contagions "received" at beyond the .01 level. Of the two, "general susceptibility" plays the greater role (ratio of the variances being about 2 : 1). It would seem, then, that the child who was generally susceptible to contagious influence continued to be so in these situations, although the character of the actors and acts imitated

THE DYNAMICS OF POWER   263

as well as of his typical cocontagers had altered.

The results of this small series of experiments indicate that, *under a situation of stress in which there is a dominant group mood, the usual determinant of influence in these groups broke down, and the impulsive child came into his own as an initiator of behavioral contagion, and as a ready follower thereof.*

SUMMARY AND CONCLUSIONS

In our introduction we stated three objectives of the study reported in this paper. It seems appropriate to summarize in terms of these aims:

Replication of Previous Field Study. Our repetition of essentially the same study design in the same camp (of disturbed lower socio-economic-class children) revealed the same relationship between the variables of attributed power, contagion initiation, successful direct influence, contagion pick-up, and acceptance of influence. The following relationships were confirmed:

1. The group member is more likely to imitate the behavior of those members to whom he attributes high power in the group.

2. The group member is more likely to accept the induction attempts of members with high attributed power.

3. Attempts to influence members with high attributed power are more nondirective in manner than those attempts directed toward low-power choices.

4. Members with high attributed power receive more deference behavior from other members than do low-power choices.

5. Members with high attributed power initiate more social influence attempts than do low-power choices, and are more successful.

6. Members with high attributed power are more directive in the manner of their influence attempts than the low-power members.

7. Members with high attributed power voluntarily pick up behavioral contagion more frequently than do low-power choices, and tend to resist direct influence attempts more frequently than do low-power choices.

8. It was again found that attributed-power choices were highly related to the children's judgments of physical prowess and personal liking.

9. There was no relationship between ratings of behavioral impulsiveness and attributed power in the over-all camp situation. The cabin experiment on impulse control in the 1948 study showed a significant relationship between impulsiveness and group influence under special conditions of group frustration.

This confirmation of all the major findings of the first study seems to us to be a rather impressive check on the type of behavior sampling and categorization techniques used, as well as lending weight to the validity of the data as representing a true picture of the social influence dynamics of this type of population of groups.

Checking Additional Hypotheses. 1. In the theoretical interpretation of the findings of the first study we postulated the existence of a self-perception of own power which we inferred would develop from the behavioral feedback of deferential behavior from fellow members. We inferred that this self-percept would act as one determinant of behavior output. By extending our methodology to the measurement of perception of own power in the second study we were able to confirm that:

a. Perception of own power position in the group is positively related to actual attributed position.

b. Perception of own power is related to social behavior produced. Those with a self-perception of high power make more frequent, more successful, and more directive-influence attempts, and are more resistant to inductions from others. They also are more active in voluntarily picking up behavior patterns initiated by others (behavioral contagion).

2. A second missing link in our first study was the lack of information on the variable of total activity level. It was impossible to check on the possible interpretation that high-power children might be more frequent sources of contagion because of a higher total activity level than low-power children. Our independent measurement of activity level in the second study makes it possible for us to conclude that:

a. Activity level is not an independent determinant of frequency of contagion initiation or of successful induction.

b. Members with high attributed power do tend to be more socially active than low-power choices. This is not true for frequency of nonsocial behavior.

3. In our attempt to explore further some of the determinants of attributed power in M-camp we discovered that:

a. Old campers do not have significantly more attributed power.

b. Intelligence level is not significantly related to attributed power.

Generalization to a Different Type of Population. Our third objective was to explore the generalization of our findings to a contrasting population of normal middle-class children in a different summer camp setting. As indicated in our presentation of results, most of the basic relations between attributed power, perception of own power, and behavioral influence were found to hold for this different population of groups. But differences were also discovered which have provided clues to further comparative analysis which will be reported elsewhere. Camp differences noted in this paper are:

1. In the W-camp low-power members are not significantly more nondirective in attempting to influence high-power members.

2. High-power members are not more directive in their attempts to influence low-power members.

3. In the W-camp the boys with high attributed power were not more spontaneously active in picking up the behavior of others (contagion pick-up) than were low-power boys.

4. In the W-camp the boys who perceived themselves as having high power were not more directive than low-power boys.

5. Nor were these boys more resistant to influence attempts than the low-power choices.

6. In the W-camp there was a significant relationship between intelligence and attributed power, and between height and weight and attributed fighting ability. None of these relationships held in M-camp.

These differences seem to suggest a difference in the style and reciprocity of social influence in the two camps, and also differences in certain sources of power, e.g., intelligence, physical size, and conformity.

6

Reference Groups

ATTITUDE DEVELOPMENT AS A FUNCTION OF REFERENCE GROUPS: THE BENNINGTON STUDY
By Theodore M. Newcomb

Membership in established groups usually involves the taking on of whole patterns of interrelated behavior and attitudes. This was one of the hypotheses pursued in the study which is reported here in part. The group selected for study consisted of the entire student body at Bennington College—more than 600 individuals—between the years 1935 and 1939. One of the problems to be investigated was that of the manner in which the patterning of behavior and attitudes varied with different degrees of assimilation into the community.

Not all of the attitudes and behaviors that are likely to be taken on by new members, as they become absorbed into a community, can be investigated in a single study. A single, though rather inclusive, area of adaptation to the college community was therefore selected for special study, namely, *attitudes toward public affairs*. There were two reasons for this selection: (1) methods of attitude measurement were readily available; and

(2) there was an unusually high degree of concern, in this community at this time, over a rather wide range of public issues. This latter fact resulted partly from the fact that the college opened its doors during the darkest days of the depression of the 1930's, and its formative period occurred in the period of social change characterized by the phrase "the New Deal." This was also the period of gathering war clouds in Europe. Underlying both of these circumstances, however, was the conviction on the part of the faculty that one of the foremost duties of the college was to acquaint its somewhat oversheltered students with the nature of their contemporary social world.

In a membership group in which certain attitudes are approved (i.e., held by majorities, and conspicuously so by leaders), individuals acquire the approved attitudes to the extent that the membership group (particularly as symbolized by leaders and dominant subgroups) serves as a positive point of reference. The findings of the Bennington study seem to be better understood in terms of this thesis than any other. The distinction between membership group and reference group is a crucial one, in fact, although the original report did not make explicit use of it.

The above statement does not imply that no reference groups other than the membership group are involved in attitude formation; as we shall see, this is distinctly not the case. Neither does it imply that the use of the membership group as reference group necessarily results in adoption of the approved attitudes. It may also result in their rejection; hence the word *positive* in the initial statement. It is precisely these variations in degree and manner of relationship between reference group and membership group which must be known in order to explain individual variations in attitude formation, as reported in this study.

The essential facts about the Bennington membership group are as follows: (1) It was small enough (about 250 women students) so that data could be obtained from every member. (2) It was in most respects self-sufficient; college facilities provided not only the necessities of living and studying, but also a cooperative store, post office and Western Union office, beauty parlor, gasoline station, and a wide range of recreational opportunities. The average student visited the four-mile-distant village once a week and spent one week end a month away from the college. (3) It was self-conscious and enthusiastic, in large part because it was new (the study was begun during the first year in which there was a senior class) and because of the novelty and attractiveness of the college's educational plan. (4) It was unusually active and concerned about public issues, largely because the faculty felt that its educational duties included the familiarizing of an oversheltered student body with the implications of a depression-torn America and a war-threatened world.

(5) It was relatively homogeneous in respect to home background; tuition was very high, and the large majority of students came from urban, economically privileged families whose social attitudes were conservative.

Most individuals in this total membership group went through rather marked changes in attitudes toward public issues, as noted below. In most cases the total membership group served as the reference group for the changing attitudes. But some individuals changed little or not at all in attitudes during the four years of the study; attitude persistence was in some of these cases a function of the membership group as reference group and in some cases it was not. Among those who did change, moreover, the total membership group sometimes served as reference group but sometimes it did not. An oversimple theory of "assimilation into the community" thus leaves out of account some of those whose attitudes did and some of those whose attitudes did not change; they remain unexplained exceptions. A theory which traces the impact of other reference groups as well as the effect of the membership group seems to account for all cases without exception.

The general trend of attitude change for the total group is from freshman conservatism to senior nonconservatism (as the term was commonly applied to the issues toward which attitudes were measured). During the 1936 presidential election, for example, 62 percent of the freshmen and only 14 percent of the juniors and seniors "voted" for the Republican candidate, 29 percent of freshmen and 54 percent of juniors and seniors for Roosevelt, and 9 percent of freshmen as compared with 30 percent of juniors and seniors for the Socialist or Communist candidates. Attitudes toward nine specific issues were measured during the four years of the study, and seniors were less conservative in all of them than freshmen; six of the nine differences are statistically reliable. These differences are best shown by a Likert-type scale labeled Political and Economic Progressivism (PEP) which dealt with such issues as unemployment, public relief, and the rights of organized labor, which were made prominent by the New Deal. Its odd-even reliability was about .9, and it was given once or more during each of the four years of the study to virtually all students. The critical ratios of the differences between freshmen and juniors-seniors in four successive years ranged between 3.9 and 6.5; the difference between the average freshman and senior scores of 44 individuals (the entire class that graduated in 1939) gives a critical ratio of 4.3.

As might be anticipated in such a community, *individual prestige was associated with nonconservatism*. Frequency of choice as one of five students "most worthy to represent the College" at an intercollegiate gathering was used as a measure of prestige. Nominations were submitted in sealed envelopes by 99 percent of all students in two successive years, with almost identical results. The nonconservatism of those with high prestige is not merely the result of the fact that juniors and seniors are characterized by both high prestige and nonconservatism; in each class those who have most prestige are least conservative. For example, ten freshmen receiving 2 to 4 choices had an average PEP score of 64.6 as compared with 72.8 for freshmen not chosen at all (high scores are conservative); eight sophomores chosen 12 or more times had an average score of 63.6 as compared with 71.3 for those not chosen; the mean PEP score of five juniors and seniors chosen 40 or more times was 50.4 and of the fifteen chosen 12 to 39 times, 57.6, as compared with 69.0 for those not chosen. In each class, those intermediate in prestige are also intermediate in average PEP score.

Such were the attitudinal characteristics of the total membership group,

expressed in terms of average scores. Some individuals, however, showed these characteristics in heightened form and others failed to show them at all. An examination of the various reference groups in relation to which attitude change did or did not occur, and of the ways in which they were brought to bear, will account for a large part of such attitude variance.

Information concerning reference groups was obtained both directly, from the subjects themselves, and indirectly, from other students and from teachers. Chief among the indirect procedures was the obtaining of indexes of "community citizenship" by a guess-who technique. Each of twenty-four students, carefully selected to represent every cross section and grouping of importance within the community, named three individuals from each of three classes who were reputedly most extreme in each of twenty-eight characteristics related to community citizenship. The relationship between reputation for community identification and nonconservatism is a close one, in spite of the fact that no reference was made to the latter characteristic when the judges made their ratings. A reputation index was computed, based upon the frequency with which individuals were named in five items dealing with identification with the community, minus the number of times they were named in five other items dealing with negative community attitude. Examples of the former items are: "absorbed in college community affairs," and "influenced by community expectations regarding codes, standards, etc."; examples of the latter are: "indifferent to activities of student committees," and "resistant to community expectations regarding codes, standards, etc." The mean senior PEP score of fifteen individuals whose index was +15 or more was 54.4; of sixty-three whose index was +4 to −4, 65.3; and of ten whose index was −15 or less, 68.2.

To have the reputation of identifying oneself with the community is not the same thing, however, as to identify the community as a reference group for a specific purpose—e.g., in this case, as a point of reference for attitudes toward public issues. In short, the reputation index is informative as to degree and direction of tendency to use the total membership group as a *general* reference group, but not necessarily as a group to which social attitudes are referred. For this purpose information was obtained directly from students.

Informal investigation had shown that whereas most students were aware of the marked freshman-to-senior trend away from conservatism, a few (particularly among the conservatives) had little or no awareness of it. Obviously, those not aware of the dominant community trend could not be using the community as a reference group for an attitude. (It does not follow, of course, that all those who are aware of it are necessarily using the community as reference group.) A simple measure of awareness was therefore devised. Subjects were asked to respond in two ways to a number of attitude statements taken from the PEP scale: first, to indicate agreement or disagreement (for example, with the statement: "The budget should be balanced before the government spends any money on social security"); and second, to estimate what percentage of freshmen, juniors and seniors, and faculty would agree with the statement. From these responses was computed an index of divergence (of own attitude) from the estimated majority of juniors and seniors. Thus a positive index on the part of a senior indicates the degree to which her own responses are more conservative than those of her classmates, and a negative index the degree to which they are less conservative. Those seniors whose divergence index more or less faithfully reflects the true difference between own and class attitude may (or may not) be using the

class as an attitude reference group; those whose divergence indexes represent an exaggerated or minimized version of the true relationship between own and class attitude are clearly not using the class as an attitude reference group, or if so, only in a fictitious sense. (For present purposes the junior-senior group may be taken as representative of the entire student body, since it is the group which "sets the tone" of the total membership group.)

These data were supplemented by direct information obtained in interviews with seniors in three consecutive classes, just prior to graduation. Questions were asked about resemblance between own attitudes and those of class majorities and leaders, about parents' attitudes and own resemblance to them, about any alleged "social pressure to become liberal," about probable reaction if the dominant college influence had been conservative instead of liberal, etc. Abundant information was also available from the college personnel office and from the college psychiatrist. It was not possible to combine all of these sources of information into intensive studies of each individual, but complete data were assembled for (roughly) the most conservative and least conservative sixths of three consecutive graduating classes. The twenty-four nonconservative and nineteen conservative seniors thus selected for intensive study were classified according to their indexes of conservative divergence and of community reputation. Thus eight sets of seniors were identified, all individuals within each set having in common similar attitude scores, similar reputations for community identification, and similar degrees of awareness (based upon divergence index) of own attitude position relative to classmates. The following descriptions of these eight sets of seniors will show that there was a characteristic pattern of relationship between membership group and reference group within each of the sets.

1. *Conservatives, reputedly negativistic, aware of their own relative conservatism.* Four of the five are considered stubborn or resistant by teachers (all five, by student judges). Three have prestige scores of 0, scores of the other two being about average for their class. Four of the five are considered by teachers or psychiatrist, or by both, to be overdependent upon one or both parents. All of the four who were interviewed described *their major hopes*, on entering college, *in terms of social rather than academic prestige;* all four felt that they had been defeated in this aim. The following verbatim quotations are illustrative:

E2: "Probably the feeling that (my instructors) didn't accept me led me to reject their opinions." (She estimates classmates as being only moderately less conservative than herself, but faculty as much less so.)

G32: "I wouldn't care to be intimate with those so-called 'liberal' student leaders." (*She claims to be satisfied with a small group of friends.* She is chosen as friend, in a sociometric questionnaire responded to by all students, only twice, and reciprocates both choices; both are conservative students.)

F22: "I wanted to disagree with all the noisy liberals, but I was afraid and I couldn't. *So I built up a wall inside me against what they said. I found I couldn't compete, so I decided to stick to my father's ideas. For at least two years I've been insulated against all college influences.*" (She is chosen but once as a friend, and does not reciprocate that choice.)

Q10: (who rather early concluded that she had no chance of social success in college) "It hurt me at first, but now I don't give a damn. *The things I really care about are mostly outside the college.* I think radicalism symbolizes the college for me more than anything else." (Needless to say, she has no use for radicals.)

For these four individuals (and probably for the fifth also) the community serves as reference group in a *negative* sense, and the home-and-family group in a positive sense. Thus their conservatism is dually reinforced.

2. *Conservatives, reputedly negativistic, unaware of their own relative conservatism.* All five are described by teachers, as well as by guess-who judges, to be stubborn or resistant. Four have prestige scores of 0, and the fifth a less than average score. Each reciprocated just one friendship choice. Four are considered insecure in social relationships, and all five are regarded as extremely dependent upon parents. In interviews four describe with considerable intensity, and the fifth with more moderation, precollege experiences of rebuff, ostracism, or isolation, and all describe their hopes, on entering college, in terms of making friends or avoiding rebuff rather than in terms of seeking prestige. All five felt that their (rather modest) aims had met with good success. Each of the five denies building up any resistance to the acceptance of liberal opinions (but two add that they would have resented any such pressure, if felt). Three believe that only small, special groups in the college have such opinions, while the other two describe themselves as just going their own way, *paying no attention to anything but their own little circles and their college work.* Typical quotations follow:

Q47: "I'm a perfect middle-of-the-roader, neither enthusiast nor critic. I'd accept anything if they just let me alone. . . . I've made all the friends I want." (Only one of her friendship choices is reciprocated.)

Q19: "*In high school I was always thought of as my parents' daughter.* I never felt really accepted for myself. . . . I wanted to make my own way here, socially, but independence from my family has never asserted itself in other ways." (According to guess-who ratings, she is highly resistant to faculty authority.)

L12: "What I most wanted was to get over being a scared bunny. . . . I always resent doing the respectable thing just because it's the thing to do, but I didn't realize I was so different, politically, from my classmates. At least I agree with the few people I ever talk to about such matters." (Sociometric responses place her in a small, conservative group.)

Q81: "I hated practically all my school life before coming here. I had the perfect inferiority complex, and I pulled out of school social life—out of fear. I didn't intend to repeat that mistake here. . . . I've just begun to be successful in winning friendships, and I've been blissfully happy here." (She is described by teachers as "pathologically belligerent"; she receives more than the average number of friendship choices, but reciprocates only one of them.)

For these five individuals, who are negativistic in the sense of being near-isolates rather than rebels, the community does not serve as reference group for public attitudes. To some extent, their small friendship groups serve in this capacity, but in the main they still refer such areas of their lives to the home-and-family group. They are too absorbed in their own pursuits to use the total membership group as a reference group for most other purposes, too.

3. *Conservatives, not reputedly negativistic, aware of their own relative conservatism.* Three of the five are described by teachers as "cooperative" and "eager," and none as stubborn or resistant. Four are above average in prestige. Four are considered by teachers or by guess-who raters, or both, to retain very close parental ties. All four who were interviewed had more or less definite ambitions for leadership on coming to college, and all felt that they had been relatively successful—though, in the words of one of them, none ever attained the "really top-notch positions." All four are aware of conflict between parents and college community in respect to public attitudes,

and all quite consciously decided to "string along" with parents, feeling self-confident of holding their own in college in spite of being atypical in this respect. Sample quotations follow:

Q73: "*I'm all my mother has in the world. It's considered intellectually superior here to be liberal or radical. This puts me on the defensive,* as I refuse to consider my mother beneath me intellectually, as so many other students do. Apart from this, I have loved every aspect of college life." (A popular girl, many of whose friends are among the nonconservative college leaders.)

Q78: "*I've come to realize how much my mother's happiness depends on me, and the best way I can help her is to do things with her at home as often as I can.* This has resulted in my not getting the feel of the college in certain ways, and I know my general conservatism is one of those ways. But it has not been important enough to me to make me feel particularly left out. If you're genuine and inoffensive about your opinions, no one really minds here if you remain conservative." (Another popular girl, whose friends were found among many groups.)

F32: "*Family against faculty has been my struggle here.* As soon as I felt really secure here I decided not to let the college atmosphere affect me too much. Every time I've tried to rebel against my family I've found out how terribly wrong I am, and so I've naturally kept to my parents' attitudes." (While not particularly popular, she shows no bitterness and considerable satisfaction over her college experience.)

Q35: "I've been aware of a protective shell against radical ideas. When I found several of my best friends getting that way, I either had to go along or just shut out that area entirely. I couldn't respect myself if I had changed my opinions just for that reason, and so I almost deliberately lost interest— really, *it was out of fear of losing my friends.*" (A very popular girl, with no trace of bitterness, who is not considered too dependent upon parents.)

For these five the total membership group does not serve as reference group in respect to public attitudes, but does so serve for most other purposes. At some stage in their college careers the conflict between college community and home and family as reference group for public attitudes was resolved in favor of the latter.

4. *Conservatives, not reputedly negativistic, not aware of their own relative conservatism.* All four are consistently described by teachers as conscientious and cooperative; three are considered overdocile and uncritical of authority. All are characterized by feelings of inferiority. All are low in prestige, two receiving scores of 0; all are low in friendship choices, but reciprocate most of these few choices. Two are described as in conflict about parental authority, and two as dependent and contented. All four recall considerable anxiety as to whether they would fit into the college community; all feel that they have succeeded better than they had expected. Sample statements from interviews follow:

D22: "I'd like to think like the college leaders, but I'm not bold enough and I don't know enough. So the college trend means little to me; I didn't even realize how much more conservative I am than the others. *I guess my family influence has been strong enough to counterbalance the college influence.*" (This girl was given to severe emotional upsets, and according to personnel records, felt "alone and helpless except when with her parents.")

M12: "It isn't that I've been resisting any pressure to become liberal. The influences here didn't matter enough to resist, I guess. *All that's really important that has happened to me occurred outside of college,* and so I never became very susceptible to college influences." (*Following her engagement to be married, in her second year, she had "practically retired" from community life.*)

Q68: "If I'd had more time here I'd probably have caught on to the liberal drift here. But I've been horribly busy making money and trying to keep my college work up. *Politics and that sort of thing I've always associated with home instead of with the college.*" (A "town girl" of working-class parentage.)

Q70: "Most juniors and seniors, if they really *get excited about their work, forget about such community enthusiasms as sending telegrams to Congressmen.* It was so important to me to be accepted, I mean intellectually, *that I naturally came to identify myself in every way with the group which gave me this sort of intellectual satisfaction.*" (One of a small group of science majors, nearly all conservative, who professed no interests other than science and who were highly self-sufficient socially.)

For none of the four was the total membership group a reference group for public attitudes. Unlike the nonnegativistic conservatives who are aware of their relative conservatism, they refer to the total membership group for few if any other purposes. Like the negativistic conservatives who are unaware of their relative conservatism, their reference groups for public attitudes are almost exclusively those related to home and family.

5. *Nonconservatives, reputedly community-identified, aware of their relative nonconservatism.* Each of the seven is considered highly independent by teachers, particularly in intellectual activities; all but one are referred to as meticulous, perfectionist, or overconscientious. Four are very high in prestige, two high, and one average; all are "good group members," and all but one a "leader." None is considered overdependent upon parents. All have come to an understanding with parents concerning their "liberal" views; five have "agreed to differ," and the other two describe one or both parents as "very liberal." All take their public attitudes seriously, in most cases expressing the feeling that they have

bled and died to achieve them. Interview excerpts follow:

B72: "*I bend in the direction of community expectation*—almost more than I want to. I constantly have to check myself to be sure it's real self-conviction and not just social respect." (An outstanding and deeply respected leader.)

M42: "My family has always been liberal, but the influences here made me go further, and for a while I was pretty far left. Now I'm pretty much in agreement with my family again, but it's my own and it means a lot. It wouldn't be easy for me to have friends who are very conservative." (Her friendship choices are exclusively given to nonconservatives.)

E72: "I had been allowed so much independence by my parents that I needed desperately to identify myself with an institution with which I could conform conscientiously. Bennington was perfect. I drank up everything the college had to offer, including social attitudes, though not uncritically. I've become active in radical groups and constructively critical of them." (Both during and after college she worked with C.I.O. unions.)

H32: "I accepted liberal attitudes here because *I had always secretly felt that my family was narrow and intolerant, and because such attitudes had prestige value.* It was all part of my generally expanding personality—*I had never really been part of anything before.* I don't accept things without examining things, however, and I was sure I meant it before I changed." (One of those who has "agreed to differ" with parents.)

Q43: "It didn't take me long to see that liberal attitudes had prestige value. But all the time I felt inwardly superior to persons who want public acclaim. Once I had arrived at a feeling of personal security, I could ꜱᴇᴇ ᴛʜᴀᴛ it wasn't important—it wasn't enough. *So many people have no security at all. I became liberal at first because of its prestige value. I re-*

main so because the problems around which my liberalism centers are important. What I want now is to be effective in solving the problems." (Another conspicuous leader, active in and out of college in liberal movements.)

The total membership clearly serves as reference group for these individuals' changing attitudes, but by no means as the only one. For those whose parents are conservative, parents represent a negative reference group, from whom emancipation was gained via liberal attitudes. And for several of them the college community served as a bridge to outside liberal groups as points of reference.

6. *Nonconservatives, reputedly community-identified, not aware of their own relative nonconservatism.* The word *enthusiastic* appears constantly in the records of each of these six. All are considered eager, ambitious, hard-working, and anxious to please. Four are very high in prestige, the other two about average. None is considered overdependent upon parents, and only two are known to have suffered any particular conflict in achieving emancipation. Each one came to college with ambitions for leadership, and each professes extreme satisfaction with her college experience. Sample quotations follow:

Qx: "Every influence I felt tended to push me in the liberal direction: my underdog complex, *my need to be independent of my parents, and my anxiousness to be a leader here.*"

Q61: "I met a whole body of new information here; I took a deep breath and plunged. When I talked about it at home my family began to treat me as if I had an adult mind. *Then too, my new opinions gave me the reputation here of being open-minded and capable of change.* I think I could have got really radical but I found it wasn't the way ᴛᴏ ɢᴇᴛ ᴘʀᴇꜱᴛɪɢᴇ ʜᴇʀᴇ." (She judges most of her classmates to be as nonconservative as herself.)

Q72: "I take everything hard, and so of course I reacted hard to all the attitudes I found here. I'm 100-percent enthusiastic about Bennington, and that includes liberalism (but not radicalism, though I used to think so). Now I know that you can't be an *extremist if you're really devoted to an institution,* whether it's a labor union or a college." (A conspicuous leader who, like most of the others in this set of six, *judges classmates to be only slightly more conservative than herself.*)

Q63: "*I came to college to get away from my family,* who never had any respect for my mind. Becoming a radical meant thinking for myself and, figuratively, thumbing my nose at my family. *It also meant intellectual identification with the faculty and students that I most wanted to be like.*" (She has always felt oppressed by parental respectability and sibling achievements.)

Q57: "It's very simple. *I was so anxious to be accepted that I accepted the political complexion of the community here.* I just couldn't stand out against the crowd unless I had many friends and strong support." (Not a leader, but many close friends among leaders and nonconservatives.)

For these six, like the preceding seven, the membership group serves as reference group for public affairs. They differ from the preceding seven chiefly in that they are less sure of themselves and are careful "not to go too far." Hence they tend to repudiate "radicalism," and to judge classmates as only slightly less conservative than themselves.

7. *Nonconservatives, not reputedly community-identified, aware of own relative nonconservatism.* Each of the six is described as highly independent and critical-minded. Four are consistently reported as intellectually outstanding, and the other two occasionally so. All describe their ambitions on coming to college in intellectual rather than in social terms. Four of the five who were interviewed stated that in a conservative

college they would be "even more radical than here." Two are slightly above average in prestige, two below average, and two have 0 scores. Three have gone through rather severe battles in the process of casting off what they regard as parental shackles; none is considered overdependent upon parents. Sample interview excerpts follow:

Q7: "*All my life I've resented the protection of governesses and parents.* What I most wanted here was the intellectual approval of teachers and the more advanced students. Then I found you can't be reactionary and be intellectually respectable." (Her traits of independence became more marked as she achieved academic distinction.)

Q21: "I simply got filled with new ideas here, and the only possible formulation of all of them was to adopt a radical approach. *I can't see my own position in the world in any other terms. The easy superficiality with which so many prestige-hounds here get 'liberal' only forced me to think it out more intensely.*" (A highly gifted girl, considered rather aloof.)

C32: "*I started rebelling against my pretty stuffy family before I came to college.* I felt apart from freshmen here, because I was older. Then I caught on to faculty attempts to undermine prejudice. I took sides with the faculty immediately, against the immature freshmen. I crusaded about it. *It provided just what I needed by way of family rebellion,* and bolstered up my self-confidence, too." (A very bright girl, regarded as sharp tongued and a bit haughty.)

J24: "*I'm easily influenced by people whom I respect,* and the people who rescued me when I was down and out, intellectually, gave me a radical intellectual approach; they included both teachers and advanced students. *I'm not rebelling against anything.* I'm just doing what I had to do to stand on my own feet intellectually." (Her academic work was poor as a freshman, but gradually became outstanding.)

For these six students it is not the total membership group, but dominant sub-groups (faculty, advanced students) which at first served as positive reference groups, and for many of them the home group served as a negative point of reference. Later, they developed extracollege reference groups (left-wing writers, etc.). In a secondary sense, however, the total membership group served as a negative point of reference—i.e., they regarded their nonconservatism as a mark of personal superiority.

8. *Nonconservatives, not reputedly community-identified, not aware of own relative nonconservatism.* Each of the five is considered hard-working, eager, and enthusiastic but (especially during the first year or two) unsure of herself and too dependent upon instructors. They are "good citizens," but in a distinctly retiring way. Two are above average in prestige, and the other three much below average. None of the five is considered overdependent upon parents; two are known to have experienced a good deal of conflict in emancipating themselves. All regard themselves as "pretty average persons," with strong desire to conform; they describe their ambitions in terms of social acceptance instead of social or intellectual prestige. Sample excerpts follow:

E22: "*Social security is the focus of it all with me.* I became steadily less conservative as long as I was *needing to gain in personal security, both with students and with faculty.* I developed some resentment against a few extreme radicals who don't really represent the college viewpoint, and that's why I changed my attitudes so far and no further." (A girl with a small personal following, otherwise not especially popular.)

D52: "*Of course there's social pressure here to give up your conservatism.* I'm glad of it, because for me this became the vehicle for achieving independence from my family. So changing my attitudes

has gone hand in hand with two *very important things: establishing my own independence and at the same time becoming a part of the college organism.*" (She attributes the fact that her social attitudes changed, while those of her younger sister, also at the college, did not, to the fact that she had greater need both of family independence and of group support.)

Q6: "I was ripe for developing liberal or even radical opinions because so many of my friends at home were doing the same thing. So it was really wonderful that I could agree with all the people I respected here and the same time move in the direction that my home friends were going." (A girl characterized by considerable personal instability at first, but showing marked improvement.)

Qy: "I think my change of opinions has given me *intellectual and social self-respect at the same time.* I used to be too timid for words, and I never had an idea of my own. As I gradually became more successful in my work and made more friends, I came to feel that it didn't matter so much whether I agreed with my parents. It's all part of the feeling that I really belong here." (Much other evidence confirms this; she was lonely and pathetic at first, but really belonged later.)

These five provide the example *par excellence* of individuals who came to identify themselves with "the community" and whose attitudes change *pari passu* with the growing sense of identity. Home-and-family groups served as supplementary points of reference, either positive or negative. To varying degrees, subgroups within the community served as focal points of reference. But, because of *their need to be accepted, it was primarily the membership group as such which served as reference group for these five.*

SUMMARY

In this community, as presumably in most others, all individuals belong to the total membership group, but such membership is not necessarily a point of reference for every form of social adaptation, e.g., for acquiring attitudes toward public issues. *Such attitudes, however, are not acquired in a social vacuum. Their acquisition is a function of relating oneself to some group or groups, positively or negatively.* In many cases (perhaps in all) the referring of social attitudes to one group negatively leads to referring them to another group positively, or vice versa, so that the attitudes are dually reinforced.

An individual is, of course, "typical" in respect to attitudes if the total membership group serves as a positive point of reference for that purpose, but "typicality" may also result from the use of other reference groups. It does not follow from the fact that an individual is "atypical" that the membership group does not serve for reference purposes; it may serve as negative reference group. Even if the membership group does not serve as reference group at all (as in the case of conservatives in this community who are unaware of the general freshman-to-senior trend), it cannot be concluded that attitude development is not a function of belonging to the total membership group. The unawareness of such individuals is itself a resultant adaptation of particular individuals to a particular membership group. The fact that such individuals continue to refer attitudes toward public issues primarily to home-and-family groups is, in part at least, a result of the kind of community in which they have membership.

In short, the Bennington findings seem to support the thesis that, in a community characterized by certain approved attitudes, the individual's attitude development is a function of the way in which he relates himself both to the total membership group and to one or more reference groups.

SOME ATTITUDINAL EFFECTS OF EXPERIMENTALLY INCREASED SALIENCE OF A MEMBERSHIP GROUP

By W. W. Charters, Jr., and Theodore M. Newcomb

A commonplace subscribed to by the man-in-the-street as well as by the social scientist is the proposition that many of the attitudes of an individual are greatly influenced by the norms of groups to which he belongs. Most individuals, however, are members of more than one group, and consequently may face a particular problem when these different groups prescribe opposing attitudes toward the same object. It seems reasonable to hypothesize that an individual's resolution of this problem will be a function of the relative potencies of his various group memberships. If the potency of one of the groups is extremely high in relation to the others, he may adopt the attitude prescribed by this particular group; if the potencies of the groups are of equal strength, he may either reach a compromise between the conflicting norms, or he may yield to the attitudinal position prescribed by the group the potency of which is highest at the moment.

We have attempted a simple test of the proposition that attitudinal response is a function of the relative strengths of momentary forces toward or away from membership in groups with conflicting norms. By increasing the potency of one of an individual's membership groups, we would expect to find that his expressed attitudes would resemble more closely the attitudes prescribed by the norms of that group. There are many ways by which the potency of group membership may be varied experimentally for an individual, but we shall limit ourselves to the one H. H. Kelley has called "salience." Operationally, this means simply heightening the individual's awareness of his membership in the specified group by vivid reminders of this membership.

Prepared especially for this volume.

EXPERIMENTAL PROCEDURE

From a large class of introductory psychology students we selected those who we knew were also members of one of three strong religious organizations whose norms with respect to attitudes on religious matters differed from the norms associated with membership in the university community at large. We chose as subjects students who had indicated during college registration their religions as Roman Catholic, Jewish, or Protestant. Among the Protestants, we used as subjects only those students who indicated membership in a church we judged to be "evangelical"; these students were primarily Lutheran.

We randomly divided members of the Jewish and evangelical Protestant groups into control and experimental groups; Catholics were separated into one experimental and two control groups. Students assigned to experimental groups were instructed to meet in small rooms with the other members of their religious groups, while the control subjects (except for one of the Catholic control group subjects) received no instructions and reported along with other class members to the auditorium at which they ordinarily attended a psychology-class lecture.

The control selectees had no knowledge that they had been singled out among the other psychology students as participants in the experiment. Members of one of the Catholic control groups were assigned to a small room in a manner identical with that of the experimental subjects, but the experimental procedure of arousing awareness of their group membership was omitted. (We shall refer to this Catholic control group as the "alone" controls and to the Catholic control group that met in the lecture hall as the "auditorium" controls.)

In the experimental groups, the group leaders (each of whom was a member of the same religious group as the students in his group) attempted to establish an unambiguous awareness of common religious membership. The leaders explained that all in the room were Catholics (or Jews or Protestants) brought together to help construct a questionnaire on religious beliefs.

Following the statement of alleged purpose, in which considerable emphasis was put on the common group membership of all in the room, the leaders conducted uncontroversial discussions on the "basic assumptions which *underlie* the opinions of all Catholics (or Jews or Protestants)," carefully avoiding expressions of what loyal Catholics (or Jews or Protestants) *should* believe and expressions of opinions on specific issues. The leaders continued the discussions until they judged that the students were quite conscious of their common religious affiliations and then distributed a set of "preliminary questions" to which students were asked to respond with their *own personal opinions*. Judging from the frequency of "dissident" replies, there were few if any subjects who answered consistently as "good Catholics (or Jews or Protestants) are supposed to answer" instead of giving their own opinions. They were assured anonymity and told that only by responding with their own opinions would their contributions be of any value in constructing the final questionnaire. In order to keep their religious affiliations before them as they filled out the questionnaires, the leader asked them to check statements they believed to be especially important to their religious groups.

In the auditorium, the regular lecturer asked all the students (including the control subjects) to respond to a self-explanatory questionnaire. The lecturer explained that several different groups meeting elsewhere also were taking part in an experiment which had to do "with certain attitudes and values concerning which students differ." No intimation was given to the students of the religious bearing of the experiment prior to answering the questionnaire. The Catholic "alone" controls were instructed the same way as the auditorium group. In both experimental and control groups, leaders explained candidly and in detail the purpose of the experiment after all questionnaires had been returned.

We evaluated our success in equalizing control and experimental groups through random assignment by comparing the distributions of age, sex, and political preference. (Members of each group provided these data at the end of the questionnaire.) The proportions of subjects in the control and experimental groups with respect to these personal characteristics were sufficiently similar to indicate they were from the same population.[1]

The questionnaires, consisting of 72 Likert type statements, were identical for all groups. There were nine statements eliciting opinions of a generally religious nature, twenty-three statements directed specifically to the three religious groups—seven each for Catholics and Protestants and nine for Jews, twenty-four items adapted from Thurstone and Chave's scale of attitudes toward the Church, seven items from Kirkpatrick's feminism scale, and nine other statements from Newcomb's political and economic progressivism scale considered to be irrelevant to the norms of any of the three religious groups. Feminist statements were included as part of a parallel investigation of the potency of sex-group membership, but the equivocal results will not be reported here. Irrelevant statements were included for two reasons: one, to ascertain, if control-experimental differences were found, whether they were due to the effects of the proper

---

[1] No Chi-square tests of control-experimental differences exceeded the .05 level of significance.

group norms, in which case responses to statements irrelevant to the religious group norms would not show differences; and, two, to disguise the religious nature of the questionnaire in order not to arouse awareness of religious-group membership among the controls. Subjects were asked to respond to each statement by circling the appropriate letters from "strongly agree" to "strongly disagree," as in the following illustration:

Every person should have faith in some supernatural power to which he willingly subordinates himself.

SA   A   ?   D   SD

We expected all experimental group members to reply in greater agreement than persons in control groups to this general religious question in our illustration. (Illustration of other types of statements are found in the appendix to this article.)

We undertook two kinds of analyses of the data. We evaluated the probability of control-experimental differences in distributions of responses to each item by means of the Chi-square test and then estimated the probability of finding consistent differences over a series of items by a formula for combined probabilities.[2] In addition, scores were assigned to each individual on the basis of his responses to a series of items, and differences in mean scores of control and of experimental subjects were evaluated by means of "t" tests. Items were weighted 1, 2, 3, 4, or 5, according to whether an individual's response was SA, A, ?, D, SD, respectively, so that a low score indicated conformity to the norms of the religious group. (About half the statements were reversed in such a way that disagreement indicated conformity,

in which cases the scoring was correspondingly reversed.) Scores were computed similarly for the nonreligious items, and for the feminism and progressivism scales, on the basis of Kirkpatrick's and Newcomb's published methods, respectively.[3]

CATHOLIC RESULTS

Our initial hypothesis was clearly confirmed for the Catholic religious group. Catholic subjects in the experimental group for whom the potency of religious-group membership was deliberately increased more closely approximated the orthodox Catholic position than control subjects whose awareness of membership was not increased. Table 1 shows that for all three groups of relevant items the control-experimental differences in mean scores are significant at the .01 level or less. (The two Catholic control groups are combined for this demonstration.) Results for the Jewish and Protestant groups were ambiguous and will be discussed in the next section.

Significant differences between control and experimental subjects did not appear in attitudes toward matters irrelevant to the Catholic religion—attitudes toward political, feminist, Jewish, and Protestant matters. This fact supports the contention that the differences which *were* demonstrated resulted from the increased potency of the religious-group membership.

As we have suggested, the expression of an individual's attitudes is influenced by the norms associated with the various groups of which he is a member. We hypothesized that the attitudes of our Catholic students would be influenced, on the one hand, by their membership in the Catholic religious group and, on the

---

[2] To discover if the combined probabilities of any series of tests are so great as to exceed chance, even though the individual probabilities do not reach significance, we have used the method described in E. F. Lindquist, *Statistical Analysis in Educational Research* (Boston: Houghton Mifflin Company, 1940), p. 46f.

[3] See Clifford Kirkpatrick, "The Construction of a Belief-Pattern Scale for Measuring Attitudes toward Feminism," *J. Soc. Psychol.*, 1936, VII, 421–437, and T. M. Newcomb, *Personality and Social Change* (New York: Dryden Press, 1943).

TABLE 1

Mean Scores of Catholic Subjects,
Classified by Type of Item

Type of item	Theoretical orthodoxy	Experimental group	Both control groups	University norms (residual group)
Catholic	1.00	2.09 *	2.36	2.73 *
General religious . . .	1.00	2.04 *	2.41	2.77 *
Church	1.00	1.50 *	1.80	2.15 *
Protestant	1.00	2.56	2.67	2.60
Jewish	1.00	2.36	2.38	2.23
Feminist	1.00	1.76	1.78	1.65
Political	1.00	1.95	2.07	2.17

* Difference between mean scores of control subjects and experimental or residual subjects is at or beyond the .01 level of significance.

other hand, by their membership in the university community. At this point, therefore, we must establish the polar positions of the university community and of the theoretically orthodox Catholic group.

We may take the mean scores of the group of 338 students who did not participate either as experimentals or controls, composed largely of non-"evangelical" Protestants and students with no religious affiliation, to represent roughly the dominant norms of the university community. These scores are reported in Table 1. In addition, we may consider the orthodox Catholic pole of the continuum with regard to the general religious, Catholic, and church items to be represented by consistently favorable responses (or unfavorable responses, in the case of reversed items), which would yield a theoretical mean score over all relevant items of 1.00.

The scores of both the combined Catholic control and the Catholic experimental groups fall between the extreme poles of the continuum, indicating that subjects in both groups are subject to other than Catholic or university community influences. Inasmuch as the mean scores of Catholic experimental subjects

on items relevant to Catholic group norms are more nearly in accord with the orthodox Catholic pole than are the mean scores of the control subjects, we have evidence that their membership in the Catholic group had relatively greater potency for them than for control subjects. Controls, on the other hand, were less affected by the Catholic influence and more affected by the influence of the university community.

Thus far in our analysis we have treated the two Catholic control groups as one. How justified are we in assuming that the mere difference in conditions under which the groups met (in groups of 35 to 60 for the experimentals, but as part of a group of 500 for the controls) do not account for our findings? A comparison of the responses of Catholics in the "alone" and in the "auditorium" control situations assures us that the different conditions did not influence subjects' attitudes. (The condition under which the "alone" controls replied to the questionnaire was precisely the same as the condition under which experimentals responded, except for the deliberate arousal of their awareness of religious membership.) No differences between "alone" and "auditorium" control subjects' responses were significant beyond the .05 level on the general religious and Catholic items.[4] We therefore have some justification for considering the "auditorium" group an adequate control in our consideration of Jewish and Protestant results.

RESULTS FOR JEWS AND PROTESTANTS

The findings for Jews and evangelical Protestants do not confirm our initial hypothesis. On only one statement out of the eighteen general religious and specific statements for the Jews and on one out of the sixteen for the Protestants were their control-experimental differences significant beyond the .10 level. Although on fourteen of the eighteen statements differences between the Jewish groups were in the expected direction, the combined probabilities reveal that this distribution of probabilities would occur by chance about 50 times out of 100. Less than half the Protestant control-experimental differences were in the expected, "more religious" direction. Neither Jewish nor Protestant experimental subjects responded significantly more favorably than their controls with respect to attitudes toward the church.

We hesitate to reject our hypothesis on the basis of these results in view of the supporting evidence among the Catholic subjects. We shall therefore propose some reasonable explanations to account for the negative results for Jews and evangelical Protestants. We hasten to emphasize that *post factum* explanations cannot be accepted without further investigations designed explicitly to test them.

There is some indication that the norms associated with evangelical Protestantism had a less powerful influence upon the Protestant college population which we studied than the influence of Catholic norms on the Catholic students. Inspection of our data reveals that the attitudes of Protestant control subjects were quite similar to those of the residual group, but that attitudes of Catholic controls were considerably "more religious." If this is the case, then salience of religious membership would be less effective in inducing attitude change among Protestants than among Catholics. This cannot be a sufficient explanation, because Jewish controls also manifested attitudes quite dissimilar to attitudes among the residual group.

We do not overlook the possibility that some Jews and evangelical Protestants may react negatively to a recognition of their religious membership—that is, their group may serve them as a negative reference group.[5] If this were the situation, these subjects would respond antithetically under the experimental condition while the remainder would respond according to our expectations. This would cancel differences which might otherwise appear. There is some evidence in our data to support this explanation, but because of the small number of subjects involved, we cannot evaluate its importance. If we compare the proportions of subjects in each control and experimental group who deviated from the modal response of their fellows on a relatively large number of items, we find that there are slightly more deviants among the experimentals. *Fewer* Catholic experimental subjects gave deviant responses as compared with Catholic controls. Table 2 shows these comparisons.

There is, then, some equivocal evidence that the lack of confirmation of our initial hypothesis is due, in the case of evangelical Protestants, to the relatively small influence upon them of religious

---

[4] Chi-square analysis of responses to individual items of the church scale are not available, but analysis of the mean scores revealed no significant differences between "alone" and "auditorium" controls.

[5] See Theodore M. Newcomb, *Social Psychology* (New York: Dryden Press, 1950), especially pp. 225–232.

TABLE 2

PERCENTAGE OF SUBJECTS IN EACH GROUP
WITH HIGH DEVIATION SCORES *

Religious group	Control	Experi-mental
Catholic	24	8
Jewish	3	6
Protestant	9	16

* Figures entered in this table represent the proportion of subjects in the respective categories with high deviation scores. Total number of subjects in each category is:

Catholic "auditorium" control	58
Catholic experimental	46
Jewish control	92
Jewish experimental	58
Protestant control	45
Protestant experimental	33

group norms; and in the case of both Protestants and Jews, to some persons who reacted negatively to awareness of their religious affiliation. These limiting conditions must be substantiated by further experimentation. The data from the Catholic groups strongly suggest that an individual's expression of atti-tudes is a function of the relative momentary potency of his relevant group memberships.

APPENDIX: SAMPLE QUESTIONNAIRE ITEMS

General religious:
    One of the things wrong with this country is that so many Americans have ceased to have any strong sense of right and wrong.

Catholic:
    All American children should receive at least part of their education in public (state-supported) schools.
    Birth-control information should be provided to all married individuals who desire it.

Jewish:
    Our government should take a more active part in attempts to solve the problems of European DPs (displaced persons).
    Under no conditions is there any justi-fication for quotas limiting admission to schools and colleges on a racial or religious basis.

Evangelical Protestant:
    If one is deeply convinced of one's values, one should do everything one can to dem-onstrate their supreme importance to others.
    Religious experience of the kind which occurs at revivals is purely the result of crowd excitement.

A SOCIAL DETERMINANT OF THE LEVEL OF ASPIRA-TION   *By Dwight W. Chapman and John Volkmann*

The conditions which govern the setting of a level of aspiration (*Anspruchsni-veau*), in the sense of an estimate of one's future performance in a given task, may be regarded as a special case of the effect upon a judgment of the frame of refer-ence within which it is executed. Sherif has recently drawn attention to the gen-eral fact that all judgmental activities take place within such referential frame-

From *Journal of Abnormal and Social Psychology,* 1939, XXXIV, 225–238. Reprinted by permission of the authors and the American Psychological Association, Inc.

works.[1] The lability of the judgment, for example, varies inversely with the determinateness of the frame of reference. McGregor, too, has shown that predictive judgments similarly are influenced by the definiteness of structure of the system of knowledge relative to which they are made.[2]

Hitherto research on the level of aspiration has considered only those determinants which result from individual experiences of success and failure, as in the general law that success tends to raise the level, failure to lower it. But there are presumably important features in the frame of reference surrounding the setting of the aspiration-level which come from the social environment. Indeed, as Sherif indicates, the importance of the concept of a frame of reference lies in large part in the fact that it is the paradigm for the individual's interiorization of the norms, values, and standards of his culture.

One way in which the social environment might determine the level of aspiration of a given individual would be through his knowledge of the achievement of groups whose status or ability, relative to his own, he could assess. In actual life, men do not usually approach tasks in a vacuum of ignorance about the achievements of others. Whether their knowledge is accurate or false, the task is understood as something easy or difficult by social standards; and the frame of reference in such a case is richer than that produced merely by individual experience or conjecture.

The first of the experiments which we report here concerns the level of aspiration of subjects who have had no experience with the particular task in hand, but who are furnished information about the performance on that task of groups inferior, superior, or similar to their own group. The second experiment treats the

same situation, with the exception that here the subjects are permitted to acquire considerable first-hand experience with the task to be performed. It seems possible, from the results, to make some generalization about the relative effects of personal experience and knowledge of the performance of other groups, when these two determinants are brought into competition.

The experiments correspond to the socially important case in which exhortation toward a level of aspiration (e.g., an ambition, an intention to act) makes use of the example of the accomplishments of other groups, in the face of more or less personal experience which would tend to keep the level stable. Thus, for example, the labor leader faces the problem of creating the confident belief that a union can be formed in some industry —sometimes in an industry where such action is a new idea to the rank and file workers, sometimes in an industry in which a history of organizational failures has led to discouragement. One device is obviously that of pointing to concrete examples of achievement in some other field. The auto worker may be encouraged to a sit-down strike by a knowledge that the rubber workers have successfully conducted one. Whatever change in aspiration-level is induced by a change in the frame of reference may have enormous social consequences: the new judgment may serve as a catalyst for major social changes in which whole groups abruptly revise their ambitions and perhaps their status. It would seem, then, of importance to know under what circumstances the socially-determined features of the frame of reference may modify the individually determined ones.

Experiment I: Procedure

Since in Experiment I the subjects stated their levels of aspiration before

[1] M. Sherif, *The Psychology of Social Norms* (New York: Harper & Brothers, 1936), Ch. 3.

[2] D. M. McGregor, "The Major Determinants of the Prediction of Social Events," *J. Abnor. & Soc. Psychol.*, 1938, XXXIII, 179–204.

having had any experience with the task, the term *level of aspiration* no longer fitted the definition given by J. D. Frank: ". . . the level of future performance in a familiar task which an individual, knowing his level of past performance in that task, explicitly undertakes to reach." [3] As the results of our experiment show, however, the level of aspiration estimated in advance of performance is estimated neither at random nor without reference to the ability to perform the task. The subject has some information upon which he can base his estimate, although knowledge of his actual performance would give him a great deal more.[4]

The actual content of the task used in Experiment I is of little importance, since the performance of the task followed the estimate of the level of aspiration. It consisted of a test of literary acquaintance, assembled solely for the limited purposes of the experiment. The test contained 50 items in multiple-choice form, and permitted work without a time-limit. The instructions, quoted below, showed two sample items. The subjects were students in extension courses in elementary psychology, and undergraduate students in intermediate courses in psychology—86 in number. Four experimental groups, A, B, C, and D, were formed by selecting students at random, and each group received a different set of instructions. The process of random selection was as follows: in a given classroom the first student in a row received instruction A, the second student instruction B, the third instruction C, the fourth instruction D, the fifth instruction A, and so on around the room. No student knew, however, that the instructions received by the other students were not the same as his.

Group A received no special instruc-tions; the students in this group were not told how any other group had performed on the test. Group B were told that a group of authors and literary critics had made an average score of 37.2; group B would be likely to regard this other group as *superior* in respect of literary ability. Group C were told that a group of students in psychology had made an average score of 37.2; this was information about the performance of a *similar* group. Group D were told that a group of unselected WPA workers had made an average of 37.2; this was information about the performance of a group likely to be regarded by Group D as *inferior* in respect of literary ability. All groups were told the maximum score possible (50) and the approximate score to be obtained by chance alone (17). The score on the test was the number of questions correctly answered.

All groups received the following general instructions:

On the following pages is a test of acquaintance with literature. It consists of 50 questions like the following:
Example 1. *David Copperfield* was written by
  (1) Thackeray, (2) Dickens, (3) Thomas Hardy.   1   2   3
Example 2. The Blind Harp Player is a character in
  (1) *Werther*,   (2) *Faust*,   (3) *Wilhelm Meister*.   1   2   3
Each question is to be answered by encircling one of the numbers which follows it. If you do not know the correct answer, make your best possible guess.

Your score on the test will be the number of questions which you answer correctly. You cannot, therefore, obtain a score higher than 50. And since there are three possible choices for each question, you would probably obtain a score of about 17 by simply guessing.

Before turning the page, indicate on the line below the score which you expect to make on this test.

---

[3] J. D. Frank, "Individual Differences in Certain Aspects of the Level of Aspiration," *Am. J. Psychol.*, 1935, XLVII, 119–128.

[4] We hold, therefore, that the definition of *level of aspiration* might well be enlarged to include all such estimates, regardless of past experience.

TABLE 1

STATISTICAL CONSTANTS FOR THE ASPIRATION-LEVELS OF GROUPS IN EXPERIMENT I

Statistical constant	Group A No suggestion	Group B vs. experts	Group C vs. own average	Group D vs. inferiors
Number of subjects . .	22	22	22	20
Mean aspiration-level . .	26.95	23.09	31.09	33.05
σ of aspiration-levels . .	6.33	3.46	8.95	8.57
σ_{mean}	1.35	.74	1.91	1.92

TABLE 2

PROBABILITY OF TRUE DIFFERENCE BETWEEN MEAN ASPIRATION-LEVELS OF GROUPS IN EXPERIMENT I

Group	Group A	Group B	Group C	Group D
A	.....	.994	.962	.996
B	.....	.....	.999	.999
C	.....	.....	.....	.767

Group A received no further instructions. The instructions given to group B contained the following, inserted as the sentence next before the last one:

This test has been tried on a group of authors and literary critics, who made an average score of 37.2.

Group C received these additional instructions:

This test has been tried on a group of students in psychology, who made an average score of 37.2.

Group D received these additional instructions:

This test has been tried on a group of unselected WPA workers, who made an average score of 37.2.

EXPERIMENT I: RESULTS

Table 1 shows for each of the groups A–D the number of subjects in the group, the mean aspiration-level, the standard-deviation of the aspiration level, and the standard error of the mean. Table 2 shows the probability that the differences between the mean aspiration-levels are true differences. For purposes of discussion, let the mean aspiration-level of group A, 26.95, serve as a reference point; this group received no additional instructions, and is accordingly a control group. Group B, confronted with the ostensible performance of a *superior* group, sets its mean aspiration-level lower. Group C sets its mean to approach the performance of a group *similar* to it. Group D sets its aspiration-level even higher, showing a tendency to approach or exceed the performance of an *inferior* group. None of the mean estimates actually reached the suggested figure 37.2, however. All of the differences are highly reliable, with the exception of the difference between the means of groups C and D. In advance of actual performance of the task, the suggested achievements of other groups can change the level of aspiration.

EXPERIMENT II: PROCEDURE

The task of Experiment II consisted of four forms of 32 items each taken from the Otis Self-Administering Tests of Mental Ability, Higher Examination, Forms A and B. The four forms were balanced for type of item. The subjects were students in the elementary course in psychology in the Summer Session who had not yet studied the topic of intelligence. They took the four forms on four successive days, one form per day. The instructions imposed a time-limit of six minutes. The test was called a "test of the ability to solve problems," rather than a test of intelligence.

First day. All subjects received the same instructions, which ran as follows:

This is a test of the ability to solve problems. It contains questions of different kinds. Here is a sample question already answered correctly. Notice how the question is answered: Which one of the five words below tells what an apple is?

1 flower, 2 tree, 3 vegetable, 4 fruit, 5 animal .... (4). The right answer, of course, is "fruit"; so the word "fruit" is underlined. And the word "fruit" is No. 4; so a figure 4 is placed in the parentheses at the end of the dotted line. This is the way you are to answer the questions.

If the answer to any question is a number or a letter, put the number or letter in the parentheses without underlining anything. Make all letters like printed capitals.

The test contains 32 questions. You are not expected to be able to answer all of them, but do the best you can. You will be allowed 6 min. after the examiner tells you to begin. Try to get as many right as possible. Be careful not to go so fast that you make mistakes. Do not spend too much time on any one question. No questions about the test will be answered by the examiner after the test begins. Lay your pencil down.

Do not turn this page until you are told to begin.

Second day. All subjects were told their first day's score; they then stated an aspiration-level, and took the test. The instructions read:

This is a test of the same kind as the test which you took yesterday. It likewise con-

tains 32 questions, and you will be allowed the same time (6 minutes).

Your score on yesterday's test was ____.

Please write on the line below the score you think you will make on to-day's test. (The score is the number of questions correctly answered.) ____

Third day. The subjects were divided into two approximately equal groups, A and B, matched in respect of performance on the second day's test. The analysis of the results in Table 3 will show that the matching was adequate. Both groups were told their scores of the previous two days, in a general instruction which was similar to the second day's instruction, shown above. In addition, group A was told the following:

These tests, with the same time-allowance, were originally tried on a group of unselected WPA workers, who made an average score of 0.9 points (*above*, *below*) your score of yesterday.

Half of the subjects in group A were told "0.9 points above" and half "0.9 points below." The purpose of so doing was to suggest, *on the average,* a level of performance equal to the subject's level without arousing the subject's suspicion. The blanks were filled in with writing in ink, to conceal the fact that other subjects were receiving precisely the same suggestion. The subjects of group A were told, in effect, that a group likely to be regarded by them as being in some way inferior, had done as well as they.

Group B received a suggestion similar in form, but referring to a group likely to be regarded as superior:

These tests, with the same time-allowance, were originally tried on a group of New York members of the National Academy of Sciences, who made an average score of 0.9 points (*above*, *below*) your score of yesterday.

Fourth day. The general instructions followed the pattern of the second day's instructions; all three of the subject's previous scores were stated. The special

TABLE 3

Statistical Constants for the Two Groups of Experiment II
on Successive Days

Statistical constant	First day	Second day		Third day		Fourth day	
	Score	A–L	Score	A–L	Score	A–L	Score
Group A: WPA							
Number of subjects . .	24	24	24	23	24	23	23
Mean aspiration-level . .	13.42	16.17	17.46	19.52	19.58	21.30	18.26
σ of aspiration-levels . .	4.09	5.37	5.08	5.40	4.97	5.62	4.26
σ_{mean}	.....	.....	1.03	1.13	.....	1.17	.....
Group B: NAS							
Number of subjects . .	25	24	25	23	24	23	23
Mean aspiration-level . .	12.96	16.58	17.40	20.09	20.33	21.39	19.65
σ of aspiration-levels . .	4.06	5.02	4.97	4.09	5.27	5.65	4.67
σ_{mean}	.....	.....	.99	.85	.....	1.18	.....
Probability of true difference	.....	.....	.516	.655	.....	.520	.....

instructions attempted to change the
level of aspiration by representing the
average performance of the group as being
considerably below, or above, the performance of the individual subject.
Groups A and B are the same groups as
those of the third day. Group A was told:

The average score of the class to date is
5.2 points *below* your average score to date.

Group B was told:

The average score of the class to date is
5.2 points *above* your average score to date.

The figure "5.2" was used for every
subject.

Experiment II: Results

Table 3 shows for group A and group B
the number of subjects in the group,
the mean scores and mean aspiration-
levels, the standard-deviations and the
standard errors of the mean. The last
line of the table shows for the crucial
data the probability that the difference
between means is a true difference. The
first figure in this line, .516, indicates
that groups A and B were adequately
matched on the basis of the second day's
score; if the matching had been perfect,
the figure would have been .500. The
next two figures, .655 and .520, show
that neither the information given on the
third day nor that on the fourth day
produced a reliable difference in the mean
aspiration-levels. Under the conditions of
this experiment, which included prior
performance and knowledge of this performance, the level of aspiration was *not*
changed by knowledge of the achievements of other groups.

Discussion

The interpretation of the foregoing
results requires an analysis of the frames
of reference that apparently determined
the levels of aspiration. Prominent features of these frames were their *anchoring
points:* points which determine the position of a scale of judgment, and, in consequence, the particular judgments ren-
dered in terms of this scale. Various
agents can produce anchoring: specially
designated stimuli; features of a perceptual frame of reference, such as the
horizontal in visual space; points which
the subject himself selects in the absence
of stimulation and merely "holds in

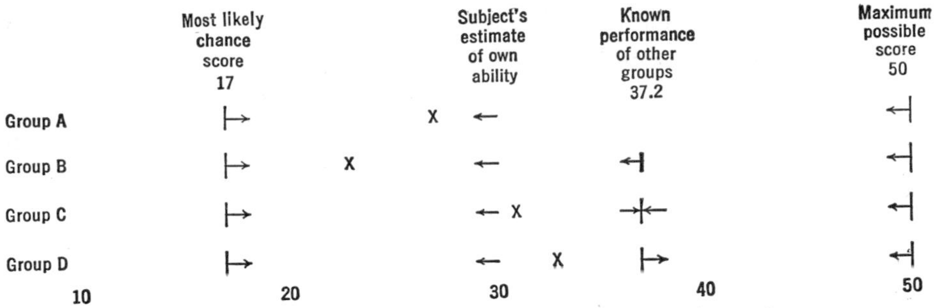

	Most likely chance score 17		Subject's estimate of own ability	Known performance of other groups 37.2	Maximum possible score 50
Group A	$\vdash$		X ←		⊢∣
Group B	$\vdash$	X	←	◄∣	⊢∣
Group C	$\vdash$		← X	→∣←	⊢∣
Group D	$\vdash$		← X	⊢	◄∣
10	20		30	40	50

FIG. 1. An analysis of the frame of reference in experiment 1.

mind." [5] Anchoring can play an important role in the frame of reference of the affective judgment.[6]

Figure 1 presents an analysis of the frames of reference that were effective in Experiment I. The headings designate the anchoring points: the approximate score to be attained by chance alone (17), the subject's average estimate of his own ability, the suggested score (37.2), and the maximum score possible (50). Groups A–D are treated separately, in successive lines of the figure. The scale at the bottom is the 50-point scale of the literary acquaintance test. The mean aspiration-level is represented in each line by an X. Anchoring effects may have characteristic directions; these are shown by arrows.

In all groups the score 17 exerted an upward or positive anchoring effect, for even a small degree of literary acquaintance would lead the subject to expect a score higher than the mean chance-score. Similarly, the maximum score 50 exerted a downward or negative effect, because the likelihood of making even a few mistakes would lead him to expect a score below 50.

The mean aspiration-level of group A (26.95) implies that the subjects in this group, and by inference those in the other groups also, had low estimates of their own abilities; accordingly, a nega-

tive (i.e., downward) anchoring effect is shown for all four groups. The subjects in group A did tend to estimate their abilities correctly; the correlation between aspiration-level and test-score in this group was $+.523 \pm .105$. This correlation is fairly high, considering the fact that both the test and the statement of aspiration-level are probably unreliable, and that the correlation is in consequence reduced. Further, the mean score of group A was in fact low (23.77). These evidences of insight show that the subject's estimate of his ability could operate in determining his aspiration-level, and could even operate to place this level in approximately the correct position.

Acting in combination, the three anchoring effects shown in the figure place the mean aspiration-level for group A somewhat below the middle of the whole range of scores, 17–50. Group B was subject to these anchoring effects and another one in addition: the negative effect created by the suggestion that a *superior* group (of authors and literary critics) had made a certain average score (37.2). The subjects in group B very probably felt that their scores would lie below those of this group of experts. The result of an additional negative anchoring effect is a mean aspiration-level still lower than that of group A. The sugges-

[5] J. Volkmann, "The Anchoring of Absolute Scales" (abstract), *Psychol. Bull.*, 1936, XXXIII, 742 f.

[6] W. A. Hunt and J. Volkmann, "The Anchoring of an Affective Scale," *Am. J. Psychol.*, 1937, XLIX, 88–92.

tion of the average score of a *similar* group (students in psychology) probably tends to increase aspiration-levels which are considerably below this average score, and to decrease those which are considerably above it; hence the representation of two opposed anchoring effects for the suggested score (37.2) in the case of group C. The subjects who have low aspiration-levels may wonder whether they cannot approach the suggested average more closely; those who have high aspiration-levels may question whether they should so far exceed the average. The combination of the five effects, two positive and three negative, gives group C a mean aspiration-level slightly below the center of the range 17–50. Group D find in their suggestion a positive effect; they are likely to feel that they can do better than the (supposedly) inferior WPA group. The combination of two positive and two negative effects gives a mean aspiration-level near the center of the range 17–50.

It is entirely reasonable that anchoring effects should act in combination, since single anchoring points exert only a partial influence. It is not reasonable to suppose, however, that the various anchoring effects mentioned above are equally strong; nothing is known of the strengths of the anchoring effects considered separately, nor whether they combine in strict additive fashion or otherwise.

The standard-deviation of the aspiration-level is greatest for groups C and D, less for group A, and least for group B. The end-points 17 and 50 probably tend to reduce variability, and the means of groups C and D are farthest from these points. In addition, the means of C and D lie in the vicinity of anchoring effects of opposite tendency, positive and negative, a fact which may explain the greater variability of these groups.

In Experiment II the anchoring effects were apparently quite different. There were still the minimum and maximum scores (0 and 32), and probably a subjective estimate of ability, but the suggested scores of other groups had no appreciable effect. The subject's own previous scores provided the most effective anchoring. Why should they have done so? In the first place, what the subject has himself accomplished with labor is likely to have "ego-value"; it means more to him than does the verbally reported accomplishment of someone else. The subject accepts his own work with satisfaction if it seems to be of high grade; he may still accept it, under the protection of some rationalization, if it seems to be of low grade. In the second place, the subject's previous scores provide the most objective basis for predicting his future ones, and the subject will use this basis if he values objectivity. He will extrapolate from his information in order to make a prediction, as many of McGregor's subjects did.[7]

Sherif's experiments with autokinesis illustrate the difference between an *indeterminate* frame of reference and a *determinate* one.[8] In complete darkness the visual frame of reference is relatively indeterminate; the point of light is then free to wander, and its localization is open to the influence of suggestion. In a lighted room, however, the walls, floor, and solid objects provide a highly determinate frame of reference, within which stationary stimuli are regularly perceived as stationary. In our Experiment I, the frame of reference was relatively indeterminate; new information could exert a new anchoring effect. In Experiment II, the subject's knowledge of his scores made the frame much more determinate; new information was ineffective in establishing anchoring points.[9]

[7] D. M. McGregor, *op. cit.*, 200.

[8] M. Sherif, *op. cit.*, Ch. 6.

[9] The determination of a judgment seems to us to be analyzable into two phases. There is first the

There should be mentioned certain differences in procedure between Experiment I and Experiment II. The tasks were different; Experiment I required no special task, while Experiment II required 4 forms approximately equated and of some reliability. The test of "ability to solve problems" may have seemed more important to the subjects of Experiment II than the degree of "literary acquaintance" did to the subjects of Experiment I. This difference in subjective importance could hardly have produced the difference in results, however, for McGregor concluded that increased importance is conducive to increased ambiguity (indeterminacy).[10] There were also differences between the two experiments in respect of the form in which the added information was offered: for example, the subjects of groups B–D, Experiment I, were told that a certain group had made a certain absolute score; the subjects of Experiment II were told that a certain group had made a certain score relative to the subject's own score. It is difficult to evaluate this and like differences in procedure, but it is not probable that they account for the clearly contrasting results of the two experiments.

FURTHER PROBLEMS

The present experiments, representing a limited investigation of the social components in the frame of reference surrounding the aspiration-level, leave unanswered many interesting questions. We are led to conclude, for instance, that

before the level of aspiration has become too dependent upon direct experience with a task, knowledge of the performance of other groups may raise or lower it. But is the amount of the raising or lowering a function of the perceived difference in ability between the individual and these other groups? Our research leaves this point in question; for while we have dealt with groups which the subjects clearly regard as different from themselves, we have not attempted to measure the degree of this difference, nor to vary it. Again, is the effect of group-differences a phenomenon more prominent in our competitive culture than in noncompetitive ones? Would it be absent or greatly diminished in a society in which ego-values were otherwise developed? Further, would the effect be stronger if the individual had knowledge of the performance of another group which he felt to be not merely different from him (as in our experiment) but actually in strong competition with him? There is suggestive evidence from athletic contests, for example, that sheer rivalry with another group—whether or not that group is rated as inferior or superior—may exert a strong upward force on the level of aspiration.

It must be remembered also that this experiment tests only one of presumably many social influences bearing upon the individual's aspiration-level. The fact that, in Experiment II, knowledge about other groups was impotent in the face of detailed acquaintance with the task must not be interpreted to mean that

question as to what stimuli are effective in producing anchoring points in the frame of reference; here the familiar laws of attention and attitudinal selection play a major role. Secondly, there is the question, once the anchoring points exist, as to how labile they are and consequently how rigidly they confine the judgment. Can the judgment vary from moment to moment? Can a new anchoring point be easily intruded upon the frame of reference?

Sherif has used the terms "structured and unstructured stimulus situations." It seems to us, however, that structuredness applies not to stimulus situations but to the subjective frames of reference which they produce. Better is McGregor's term, "ambiguous and unambiguous stimulus situations." In the present paper we use such adjectives as "determinate" and "indeterminate" to apply to frames of reference whose anchoring points determine judgments with greater or less rigidity.

[10] D. M. McGregor, *op. cit.*, 192 f.

this would be true of all social influences. We cannot say what might have happened to the aspiration-level had the subjects suddenly been introduced to some device and informed that by means of this device other groups had been able to raise their performance. ("Hundreds have taken ten strokes off their golf scores by using my natural method of driving." . . . "This isn't going to be an ordinary strike; it's going to be a sit-down.") Nor do we know whether a sudden experience of success might not free the whole referential framework from over-determination by experience and open it to determination by suggestion. ("Nothing succeeds like success.") Finally, it ought to be determined whether, when a familiar task is perceptually reconstructed (e.g., insightfully or by new verbal identification) it may not act for the aspiration-level as if it were a new task with a labile frame of reference. The laws of identity in both perception and social observation suggest that this may

be a feasible device for freeing aspiration-levels from constraint.

We believe that research on these and other similar problems will show the richness of the socially determined framework within which the individual commonly adjusts his aspirations.

SUMMARY

This investigation concerned the effect upon level of aspiration of one social determinant, knowledge of the performance of other groups. In the first experiment, such knowledge was furnished the subjects before they had formed a first-hand acquaintance with the task; under these conditions the aspiration-level was changed. In the second experiment knowledge of the performance of other groups was furnished only after considerable experience with the task; under these conditions, the aspiration-level was not changed. The difference in results is discussed in terms of the concept of frame of reference.

7

Behavior under Situational Stress

THE INVASION FROM MARS   *By Hadley Cantril*

On the evening of October 30, 1938, thousands of Americans became panic-stricken by a broadcast purported to describe an invasion of Martians which threatened our whole civilization. Probably never before have so many people in all walks of life and in all parts of the country become so suddenly and so intensely disturbed as they did on this night.

Such rare occurrences provide opportunities for the social scientist to study mass behavior. They must be exploited when they come. Although the social scientist unfortunately cannot usually predict such situations and have his tools of investigation ready to analyze the phenomenon while it is still on the wing, he can begin his work before the effects of the crisis are over and memories are blurred. The situation created by the broadcast was one which shows us how the common man reacts in a time of stress and strain. It gives us insights into his intelligence, his anxieties, and his needs, which we could never get by tests or strictly experimental studies. The panic situation we have investigated had all the flavor of everyday life and, at the same time, provided a semi-experimental condition for research. In spite of the unique conditions giving rise to this particular panic, the writer has attempted to indicate throughout the study the pattern of the circumstances which, from a psychological point of view, might make this the prototype of any panic.

The fact that this panic was created as a result of a radio broadcast is today no mere circumstance. The importance of radio's role in current national and international affairs is too well known to be recounted here. By its very nature radio is the medium *par excellence* for informing all segments of a population of current happenings, for arousing in them a common sense of fear or joy, and for exciting them to similar reactions directed toward a single objective.

Because the social phenomenon in question was so complex, several methods were employed to seek out different answers and to compare results obtained by one method with those obtained by another. Much of our information was derived from detailed interviews of 135 persons. Over 100 of these persons were selected because they were known to have been upset by the broadcast.

Long before the broadcast had ended, people all over the United States were praying, crying, fleeing frantically to escape death from the Martians. Some ran to rescue loved ones. Others telephoned farewells or warnings, hurried to inform neighbors, sought information from newspapers or radio stations, summoned ambulances and police cars. At

A partial summary by Cantril of Hadley Cantril, Hazel Gaudet, and Herta Hertzog *The Invasion from Mars* (Princeton, N. J.: Princeton University Press, 1940). Reprinted by permission of the authors and the publisher.

[10] O. Klineberg, *Social Psychology* (New York: Holt, 1940, p. 338).

least six million people heard the broadcast. At least a million of them were frightened or disturbed.

For weeks after the broadcast, newspapers carried human-interest stories relating the shock and terror of local citizens. Men and women throughout the country could have described their feelings and reactions on that fateful evening. Our own interviewers and correspondents gathered hundreds of accounts. A few of these selected almost at random will give us a glimpse of the excitement. Let the people speak for themselves.

"I knew it was something terrible and I was frightened," said Mrs. Ferguson, a northern New Jersey housewife, to the inquiring interviewer. "But I didn't know just what it was. I couldn't make myself believe it was the end of the world. I've always heard that when the world would come to an end, it would come so fast nobody would know—so why should God get in touch with this announcer? When they told us what road to take and get up over the hills and the children began to cry, the family decided to go out. We took blankets and my granddaughter wanted to take the cat and the canary. We were outside the garage when the neighbor's boy came back and told us it was a play."

From a small midwestern town came Joseph Hendley's report. "That Hallowe'en Boo sure had our family on its knees before the program was half over. God knows how we prayed to Him last Sunday. It was a lesson in more than one thing to us. My mother went out and looked for Mars. Dad was hard to convince or skeptical or sumpin', but he even got to believing it. Brother Joe, as usual, got more excited than he could show. Brother George wasn't home. Aunt Grace, a good Catholic, began to pray with Uncle Henry. Lily got sick to her stomach. I don't know what I did exactly but I know I prayed harder and more earnestly than ever before. Just

as soon as we were convinced that this thing was real, how pretty all things on earth seemed; how soon we put our trust in God."

Archie Burbank, a filling-station operator in Newark, described his reactions. "My girl friend and I stayed in the car for awhile, just driving around. Then we followed the lead of a friend. All of us ran into a grocery store and asked the man if we could go into his cellar. He said, 'What's the matter? Are you trying to ruin my business?' So he chased us out. A crowd collected. We rushed to an apartment house and asked the man in the apartment to let us in his cellar. He said, 'I don't have any cellar! Get away!' Then people started to rush out of the apartment house all undressed. We got into the car and listened some more. Suddenly, the announcer was gassed, the station went dead so we tried another station but nothing would come on. Then we went to a gas station and filled up our tank in preparation for just riding as far as we could. The gas station man didn't know anything about it. Then one friend, male, decided he would call up the *Newark Evening News*. He found out it was a play. We listened to the rest of the play and then went dancing."

Mrs. Joslin, who lives in a poor section of a large eastern city and whose husband is a day laborer, said, "I was terribly frightened. I wanted to pack and take my child in my arms, gather up my friends, and get in the car and just go north as far as we could. But what I did was just set by one window, prayin', listenin', and scared stiff and my husband by the other snifflin' and lookin' out to see if people were runnin'. Then when the announcer said 'evacuate the city,' I ran and called my boarder and started with my child to rush down the stairs, not waitin' to ketch my hat or anything. When I got to the foot of the stairs I just couldn't get out, I don't know why. Meantime my husband he tried other stations and found them still runnin'. He couldn't smell any gas or see people runnin', so he called me back and told me it was just a play. So I set down, still ready to go at any minute till I heard Orson Welles say, 'Folks, I hope we ain't alarmed you. This is just a play!' Then, I just set!"

If we are to explain the reaction, then, we must answer two basic questions: Why did this broadcast frighten some people when other fantastic broadcasts do not? And why did this broadcast frighten some people but not others? An answer to the first question must be sought in the characteristics of this particular program which aroused false standards of judgment in so many listeners.

No one reading the script can deny that the broadcast was so realistic for the first few minutes that it was almost credible to even relatively sophisticated and well-informed listeners. The sheer dramatic excellence of the broadcast must not be overlooked. This unusual realism of the performance may be attributed to the fact that the early parts of the broadcast fell within the existing standards of judgment of the listeners.

A large proportion of listeners, particularly those in the lower income and educational brackets, have grown to rely more on the radio than on the newspapers for their news. Almost all of the listeners, who had been frightened and who were interviewed, mentioned somewhere during the course of their retrospections the confidence they had in radio and their expectation that it would be used for such important announcements. A few of their comments indicate their attitudes:

"We have so much *faith in broadcasting*. In a crisis it has to reach all people. That's what radio is here for."

"The announcer would not say if it was not true. *They always quote if something is a play*."

As in many situations where events and ideas are so complicated or far removed from one's own immediate everyday experience that only the expert can really understand them, here, too, the layman was forced to rely on the expert for his interpretation.

The logical "expert" in this instance was the astronomer. Those mentioned (all fictitious) were Professor Farrell of the Mount Jennings Observatory of Chicago, Professor Pierson of the Princeton Observatory, Professor Morse of MacMillan University in Toronto, Professor Indellkoffer of the California Astronomical Society and "astronomers and scientific bodies" in England, France, and Germany. Professor Richard Pierson (Orson Welles) was the chief character in the drama.

When the situation called for organized defense and action the expert was once more brought in. General Montgomery Smith, commander of the State Militia at Trenton, Mr. Harry McDonald, vice-president of the Red Cross, Captain Lansing of the Signal Corps, and finally the Secretary of the Interior described the situation, gave orders for evacuation and attack, or urged every man to do his duty.

This dramatic technique had its effect.

"I believed the broadcast *as soon as I heard the professor from Princeton* and the officials in Washington."

"I knew it was an awfully dangerous situation *when all those military men were there and the Secretary of State spoke*."

The realistic nature of the broadcast was further enhanced by descriptions of particular occurrences that listeners could readily imagine. Liberal use was made of the colloquial expressions to be expected on such an occasion. The gas was "a sort of yellowish-green"; the cop warned, "One side, there. Keep back, I tell you"; a voice shouts, "The darn thing's unscrewing." An example of the specificity of detail is the announcement of Brigadier General Montgomery Smith: "I have been requested by the Governor of New Jersey to place the counties of Mercer and Middlesex as far west as Princeton, and east to Jamesburg, under martial law. No one will be permitted to enter this area except by special pass issued by state or military authorities. Four companies of State Militia are proceeding from Trenton to Grovers Mill and will aid in the evacuation of homes within the range of military operations."

The events reported proceeded from the relatively credible to the highly incredible. The first announcements were more or less believable, although unusual to be sure. First there is an "atmospheric disturbance," then "explosions of incandescent gas." A scientist then reports that his seismograph has registered a shock of earthquake intensity. This is followed by the discovery of a meteorite that has splintered nearby trees in its fall. So far so good.

But as the less credible bits of the story begin to enter, the clever dramatist also indicates that he, too, has difficulty in believing what he sees. When we learn that the object is no meteorite but a metal casing, we are also told that the whole picture is "a strange scene like something out of a modern Arabian Nights," "fantastic," that the "more daring souls are venturing near." Before we are informed that the end of the casing is beginning to unscrew, we experience the announcer's own astonishment: "Ladies and gentlemen, this is terrific!" When the top is off he says, "This is the most terrifying thing I have ever witnessed. . . . This is the most extraordinary experience. I can't find words. . . ."

The bewilderment of the listener is shared by the eye-witness. When the scientist is himself puzzled, the layman recognizes the extraordinary intelligence of the strange creatures. No explanation of the event can be provided. The resignation and hopelessness of the Secretary of the Interior, counseling us to "place our faith in God," provides no effective guide for action.

In spite of the realism of the broadcast, it would seem highly unlikely that any listener would take it seriously had he heard the announcements that were clearly made at the beginning of the hour. He might then have been excited, even frightened. But it would be an excitement based on the dramatic realism of the program. There would not be the intense feeling of personal involvement. He would know that the events were happening "out there" in the studio, not "right here" in his own state or his own county. In one instance a "correct" (esthetically detached or dramatic) standard of judgment would be used by the listener to interpret events, in another instance a "false" (realistic or news) standard of judgment would be employed. Tuning in late was a very essential condition for the arousal of a false standard of judgment. To be sure, many people recognized the broadcast as a play even though they tuned in late. It is important to raise and to answer the question of how anyone who tuned in at the beginning could have mistaken the clearly introduced play for a news broadcast. Analysis of these cases reveals two main reasons why such a misinterpretation arose. In the first place, many people who tuned in to hear a play by the Mercury Theatre thought the regular dramatic program had been interrupted to give special news bulletins. The technique was not a new one after their experience with radio reporting of the war crisis in September 1938. The other major reason for the misunderstanding is the widespread habit of not paying attention to the first announcements of a program. Some people do not listen attentively to their radios until they are aware that something of particular interest is being broadcast.

Tuning in late was very decisive in determining whether or not the listener would follow the program as a play or as a news report. For the story of the Martian invasion was so realistic that misinterpretation was apt to arise without proper warning signals.

In spite of the fact that many persons tuned in late to hear this very realistic broadcast, by no means all of them believed it was news. And not all of those who thought the invasion was upon them behaved the same way in the face of danger. Before we can understand the reasons for the varying behavior, the reactions must be arranged in some significant grouping. Otherwise no fruitful conceptualization is possible.

CLASSIFYING THE LISTENERS

1. **Those Who Checked the Internal Evidence of the Broadcast.** The persons in this category were those who did not remain frightened throughout the whole broadcast because they were able to discern that the program was fictitious. Some realized that the reports must be false because they sounded so much like certain fiction literature they were accustomed to.

"At first I was very interested in the fall of the meteor. It isn't often that they find a big one just when it falls. But *when it started to unscrew and monsters came out, I said to myself, 'They've taken one of those Amazing Stories and are acting it out.'* It just couldn't be real. It was just like some of the stories I read in *Amazing Stories* but it was even more exciting."

2. **Those Who Checked the Broadcast against Other Information and Learned That It Was a Play.** These listeners tried to orient themselves for the same reasons as those in the first group—they were suspicious of the "news" they were getting. Some simply thought the reports were too fantastic to believe; others detected the incredible speeds revealed; while a few listeners checked the program just because it seemed the reasonable thing to do. Their method of verifying their hunches was to compare the news

on the program to some other information.

"I tuned in and heard that a meteor had fallen. Then when they talked about monsters, I thought something was wrong. *So I looked in the newspaper* to see what program was supposed to be on and discovered it was only a play."

3. **Those Who Tried to Check the Program Against Other Information but Who, for Various Reasons, Continued to Believe the Broadcast Was an Authentic News Report.** Two characteristic differences separated the people in this group from those who made successful checks. In the first place, it was difficult to determine from the interviews just why these people wanted to check anyway. They did not seem to be seeking evidence to test the authenticity of the reports. They appeared, rather, to be frightened souls trying to find out whether or not they were yet in any personal danger. In the second place, the type of checking behavior they used was singularly ineffective and unreliable. The most frequent method employed by almost two thirds of this group, was to look out the window or go outdoors. Several of them telephoned their friends or ran to consult their neighbors.

There are several reasons why the checks made by these persons were ineffectual. For some of them, the new information obtained only verified the interpretation which their already fixed standard of judgment provided.

"I looked out of the window and everything looked the same as usual *so I thought it hadn't reached our section yet.*"

"We looked out of the window and Wyoming Avenue was black with cars. *People were rushing away, I figured.*"

"No cars came down my street. '*Traffic is jammed on account of the roads being destroyed,*' I thought."

4. **Those Who Made No Attempt to Check the Broadcast or the Event.** It is usually more difficult to discover why a

person did *not* do something than why he did. Consequently it is more difficult for us to explain why people in this group did not attempt to verify the news or look for signs of the Martians in their vicinity than it was to determine why those who attempted unsuccessful checks displayed their aimless behavior. Over half of the people in this group were so frightened that they either stopped listening, ran around in a frenzy, or exhibited behavior that can only be described as paralyzed.

Some of them reported that they were so frightened they never thought of checking.

"We were so intent upon listening that we didn't have enough sense to try other hook-ups—*we were just so frightened.*"

Others adopted an attitude of complete resignation. For them any attempt to check up, like any other behavior, appeared senseless.

"I was writing a history theme. The girl from upstairs came and made me go up to her place. Everybody was so excited I felt as if I was going crazy and kept on saying, 'what can we do, *what difference does it make* whether we die sooner or later?' We were holding each other. Everything seemed unimportant in the face of death. I was afraid to die, just kept on listening."

Some felt that in view of the crisis situation, action was demanded. A few prepared immediately for their escape or for death.

"I couldn't stand it so I turned it off. I don't remember when, but everything was coming closer. My husband wanted to put it back on but I told him *we'd better do something instead of just listen*, so we started to pack."

Some listeners interpreted the situation in such a way that they were not interested in making a check-up. In a few instances the individual tuned in so late that he missed the most incredible parts of the program and was only aware

of the fact that some kind of conflict was being waged.

"I was in my drugstore and my brother phoned and said, 'Turn the radio on, a meteor has just fallen.' We did and heard gas was coming up South Street. There were a few customers and *we all began wondering where it could come from.* I was worried about the gas, it was spreading so rapidly but I was puzzled as to what was actually happening, when I heard airplanes I thought another country was attacking us."

WHY THE PANIC?

A variety of influences and conditions are related to the panic resulting from this particular broadcast. We have found no single observable variable consistently related to the reaction, although a lack of critical ability seemed particularly conducive to fear in a large proportion of the population. Personality characteristics made some people especially susceptible to belief and fright; the influence of others in the immediate environment caused a few listeners to react inappropriately. The psychological pattern revealed by these and other influences must be shown if we are to understand the situation as a whole and not have to resort exclusively to the understanding of single, isolated cases.

WHY THE SUGGESTION WAS OR WAS NOT BELIEVED

What is most inconceivable and therefore especially interesting psychologically is why so many people did not do something to verify the information they were receiving from their loudspeakers. The failure to do this accounts for the persistence of the fright. To understand any panic—whether the cause is a legitimate one or not—it is necessary to see precisely what happens to an individual's mental processes that prevents him from making an adequate check-up.

The persons who were frightened by the broadcast were, for this occasion at least, highly suggestible, that is, they believed what they heard without making sufficient checks to prove to themselves that the broadcast was only a story. Those who were not frightened and those who believed the broadcast for only a short time were not suggestible—they were able to display what psychologists once called a "critical faculty." The problem is, then, to determine why some people are suggestible, or to state the problem differently, why some people lack critical ability.

There are essentially four psychological conditions that create in an individual the particular state of mind we know as suggestibility. All these may be described in terms of the concept of standard of judgment.

In the first place, individuals may refer a given stimulus to a standard or to several standards of judgment which they think are relevant for interpretation. The mental context into which the stimulus enters in this case is of such a character that it is welcomed as thoroughly consistent and without contradiction. A person with standards of judgment that enable him to "place" or "give meaning to" a stimulus in an almost automatic way finds nothing incongruous about such acceptance; his standards have led him to "expect" the possibility of such an occurrence.

We have found that many of the persons who did not even try to check the broadcast had preexisting mental sets that made the stimulus so understandable to them that they immediately accepted it as true. Highly religious people who believed that God willed and controlled the destinies of man were already furnished with a particular standard of judgment that would make an invasion of our planet and a destruction of its members merely an "act of God." This was particularly true if the religious frame of reference was of the eschatological variety providing the individual with definite attitudes or beliefs regarding the end of the world. Other people we found had been so influenced by the recent war scare that they believed an attack by a foreign power was imminent and an invasion—whether it was due to the Japanese, Hitler, or Martians—was not unlikely. Some persons had built up such fanciful notions of the possibilities of science that they could easily believe the powers of strange superscientists were being turned against them, perhaps merely for experimental purposes.

Whatever the cause for the genesis of the standards of judgment providing ready acceptance of the event, the fact remains that many persons already possessed a context within which they immediately placed the stimulus. None of their other existing standards of judgment was sufficiently relevant to engender disbelief. We found this to be particularly true of persons whose lack of opportunities or abilities to acquire information or training had insufficiently fortified them with pertinent standards of judgment that would make the interpretation of the broadcast as a play seem plausible. More highly educated people, we found, were better able to relate a given event to a standard of judgment they *knew* was an *appropriate* referent. In such instances, the knowledge itself was used as a standard of judgment to discount the information received in the broadcast. These listeners, then, had the ability to refer to relevant standards of judgment which they could rely on for checking purposes and therefore had no need of further orientation.

A second condition of suggestibility exists when an individual is not sure of the interpretation he should place on a given stimulus and when he lacks adequate standards of judgment to make a reliable check on his interpretation. In this situation the individual attempts to check on his information but fails for one of three reasons: (1) He may check his original information against unreliable data which may themselves be affected by the situation he is checking. We found that persons who checked unsuccessfully tended to check against information obtained from friends or neighbors. Obviously, such people were apt themselves to be tinged with doubt and hesitation which would only confirm early suspicions. (2) A person may rationalize his checking information according to the original hypothesis he is checking and which he thinks he has only tentatively accepted. Many listeners made hasty mental or behavioral checks but the false standard of judgment they had already accepted was so pervasive that their check-ups were rationalized as confirmatory evidence. For example, one woman said that the announcer's charred body was found too quickly but she "figured the announcer was excited and had made a mistake." A man noticed the incredible speeds but thought "they were relaying reports or something." Others turned to different stations but thought the broadcasters were deliberately trying to calm the people. A woman looked out of her window and saw a greenish eerie light which she thought was from the Martians. (3) In contrast to those who believe almost any check they make are the people who earnestly try to verify their information but do not have sufficiently well-grounded standards of judgment to determine whether or not their new sources of information are reliable.

A third and perhaps more general condition of suggestibility exists when an individual is confronted with a stimulus which he must interpret or which he would like to interpret and when *none* of his existing standards of judgment is adequate to the task. On such occasions the individual's mental context is unstructured, the stimulus does not fit any of his established categories and he seeks a standard that will suffice him. The less well structured is his mental context, the fewer meanings he is able to call forth,

the less able will he be to understand the relationship between himself and the stimulus, and the greater will become his anxiety. And the more desperate his need for interpretation, the more likely will he be to accept the first interpretation given him. Many conditions existed to create in the individuals who listened to the invasion from Mars a chaotic mental universe that contained no stable standards of judgment by means of which the strange event reported could be evaluated. A lack of information and formal educational training had left many persons without any generalized standards of judgment applicable to this novel situation. And even if they did have a few such standards these were vague and tenuously held because they had not proved sufficient in the past to interpret other phenomena. This was especially true of those persons who had been most adversely affected by the conditions of the times.

The prolonged economic unrest and the consequent insecurity felt by many of the listeners was another cause for bewilderment. The depression had already lasted nearly ten years. People were still out of work. Why didn't somebody do something about it? Why didn't the experts find a solution? What was the cause of it anyway? Again, what would happen, no one could tell. Again, a mysterious invasion fitted the pattern of the mysterious events of the decade. The lack of a sophisticated, relatively stable economic or political frame of reference created in many persons a psychological disequilibrium which made them seek a standard of judgment for this particular event. It was another phenomenon in the outside world beyond their control and comprehension. Other people possessed certain economic security and social status but wondered how long this would last with "things in such a turmoil." They, too, sought a stable interpretation, one that would at least give this new occurrence meaning.

The war scare had left many persons in a state of complete bewilderment. They did not know what the trouble was all about or why the United States should be so concerned. The complex ideological, class, and national antagonisms responsible for the crisis were by no means fully comprehended. The situation was painfully serious and distressingly confused. What would happen, nobody could foresee. The Martian invasion was just another event reported over the radio. It was even more personally dangerous and no more enigmatic. No existing standards were available to judge its meaning or significance. But there was quick need for judgment and it was provided by the announcers, scientists, and authorities.

Persons with higher education, on the other hand, we found had acquired more generalized standards of judgment which they could put their faith in. The result was that many of them "knew" that the phenomenal speeds with which the announcers and soldiers moved was impossible even in this day and age. The greater the possibility of checking against a variety of reliable standards of judgment, the less suggestible will a person be. We found that some persons who in more normal circumstances might have had critical ability were so overwhelmed by their particular listening situation that their better judgment was suspended. This indicates that a highly consistent structuration of the external stimulus world may, at times, be experienced with sufficient intensity because of its personal implications to inhibit the operation of usually applicable internal structurations or standards of judgment. Other persons who may normally have exhibited critical ability were unable to do so in this situation because their own emotional insecurities and anxieties made them susceptible to suggestion when confronted with a personally dangerous circumstance. In such instances, the behavioral consequence is

the same as for a person who has no standards of judgment to begin with, but the psychological processes underlying the behavior are different.

A fourth condition of suggestibility results when an individual not only lacks standards of judgment by means of which he may orient himself, but lacks even the realization that any interpretations are possible other than the one originally presented. He accepts as truth whatever he hears or reads without even thinking to compare it to other information.

WHY SUCH EXTREME BEHAVIOR?

Granted that some people believed the broadcast to be true, why did they become so hysterical? Why did they pray, telephone relatives, drive at dangerous speeds, cry, awaken sleeping children, and flee? Of all the possible modes of reaction they may have followed, why did these particular patterns emerge? The obvious answer is that this was a serious affair. As in all other panics, the individual believed his well-being, his safety, or his life was at stake. The situation was a real threat to him. Just what constitutes a personal threat to an individual must be briefly examined.

When an individual believes that a situation threatens him he means that it threatens not only his physical self but all of those things and people which he somehow regards as a part of him. This Ego of an individual is essentially composed of the many social and personal values *he* has accepted. *He* feels threatened if his investments are threatened, *he* feels insulted if his children or parents are insulted, *he* feels elated if his alma mater wins the sectional football cup. The particular pattern of values that have been introcepted by an individual will give him, then, a particular Ego. For some individuals this is expanded to include broad ideals and ambitions. *They* will be disturbed if a particular race is persecuted in a distant country because that persecution runs counter to their ideal of human justice and democracy; *they* will be flattered if someone admires an idea of theirs or a painting they have completed.

A panic occurs when some highly cherished, rather commonly accepted value is threatened and when no certain elimination of the threat is in sight. The individual feels that he will be ruined, physically, financially, or socially. The invasion of the Martians was a direct threat to life, to other lives that one loved, as well as to all other cherished values. The Martians were destroying practically everything. The situation was, then, indeed a serious affair. Frustration resulted when no directed behavior seemed possible. One was faced with the alternative of resigning oneself and all of one's values to complete annihilation or of making a desperate effort to escape from the field of danger, or of appealing to some higher power or stronger person whom one vaguely thought could destroy the oncoming enemy.

If one assumed that destruction was inevitable, then certain limited behavior was possible: one could cry, make peace with one's Maker, gather one's loved ones around and perish. If one attempted escape, one could run to the house of friends, speed away in a car or train, or hide in some gas-proof, bomb-proof, out-of-the-way shelter. If one still believed that something or someone might

repulse the enemy, one could appeal to God or seek protection from those who had protected one in the past. Objectively none of these modes of behavior was a direct attack on the problem at hand, nothing was done to remove the cause of the crisis. The behavior in a panic is characteristically undirected and, from the point of view of the situation at hand, functionally useless.

In short, the extreme behavior evoked by the broadcast was due to the enormous felt ego-involvement the situation created and to the complete inability of the individual to alleviate or control the consequences of the invasion. The coming of the Martians did not present a situation where the individual could preserve one value if he sacrificed another. It was not a matter of saving one's country by giving one's life, of helping to usher in a new religion by self-denial, of risking the thief's bullet to save the family silver. In this situation the individual stood to lose *all* his values at once. Nothing could be done to save *any* of them. Panic was inescapable. The false standard of judgment used by the individual to interpret the broadcast was not itself the motivational cause of the behavior but it was absolutely essential in arousing the needs and values which may be regarded as the sources of the actions exhibited. A false standard of judgment aroused by the broadcast and causing the individual to be disturbed had its roots in values which were a part of the Ego.

INDIVIDUAL AND MASS BEHAVIOR IN EXTREME SITUATIONS   *By Bruno Bettelheim*

The author spent the year 1938–39 in the two German concentration camps at Dachau and at Buchenwald. In these camps the prisoners were deliberately tortured; they suffered from extreme malnutrition but had to perform hard

Prepared by the author from material more fully reported in *Journal of Abnormal and Social Psychology*, 1943, XXXVIII, 417–452.

labor. Every single moment of their lives was strictly regulated and supervised. The prisoners did not know why they were imprisoned nor for how long. This may explain why the prisoners were persons finding themselves in an "extreme" situation.

The acts of terror committed in these camps aroused in the minds of civilized persons justified emotions which led them to overlook that terror was used by the Gestapo only as a means for attaining certain ends. The results which the Gestapo tried to obtain by means of the camps were varied. Among them were: *to break the prisoners as individuals* and to change them into docile masses from which no individual or group act of resistance could arise; *to spread terror among the rest of the population* by using the prisoners as hostages and by demonstrating what happens to those who oppose the Nazi rulers; *to provide the Gestapo members with a training ground* in which they were educated to lose all human emotions; *to provide the Gestapo with an experimental laboratory* in which to study the effective means for breaking civilian resistance, the minimum food requirements needed to keep prisoners able to perform hard labor when the threat of punishment takes the place of other incentives, and the influence on performance if the prisoners are separated from their families.

In this short paper, an effort is made to deal with *the concentration camp as a means of producing changes in the prisoners which will make them more useful subjects of the Nazi state.*

These changes were produced by exposing the prisoners to extreme situations which forced them to adapt themselves entirely and with the greatest speed. This adaptation produced interesting types of private, individual, and mass behavior. "Private" behavior originates in a subject's particular background and personality, rather than in

the experiences to which the Gestapo exposed him, although they were instrumental in bringing it about. "Individual" behavior is developed by individuals independently of one another, although it is the result of experiences common to all prisoners. "Mass" behavior were those phenomena which could be observed *only* in a group of prisoners when functioning as a mass. Although these three types of behavior were overlapping, the subdivision seems advisable. The discussion is restricted mainly to individual and mass behavior. One example of private behavior is discussed below.

The purpose of changing the prisoners into useful subjects of the Nazi state was attained by exposing them to extreme situations. During this process different stages could be recognized. The first of them centered around *the initial shock of finding oneself unlawfully imprisoned.* The main event of the second stage was *the transportation into the camp and the first experiences in it.* Next was a slow process of change in the prisoner's life and personality; *the adaptation to the camp situation.* The final stage was reached when *the prisoner had adapted himself to the camp;* it was characterized by a definitely changed attitude to, and evaluation of, the Gestapo.

WHY THE MATERIAL WAS COLLECTED

Before discussing these stages of a prisoner's development a few remarks on *why the material was collected* seems advisable. This study was a mechanism developed by the author *ad hoc* in order to retain some intellectual interests and thus be better equipped to endure life in the camp. His observing and collecting of data was a particular type of defense, individually developed, not enforced by the Gestapo, and based on his training and interests. It was developed to protect him against a disintegration of his personality. It is an example of private behavior. Private behaviors follow characteristically the individual's former life interests.

Since it is the only example of a *private behavior* presented in the paper, how it developed deserves mention. During the first days in the camp, the writer realized that he behaved differently from the way he used to. He observed, for instance, the split in his person into one who observes and one to whom things happen, a typical psychopathological phenomenon. He also observed that his fellow prisoners, who had been normal persons, now behaved like pathological liars, were unable to restrain themselves and to make objective evaluations. Thus the question arose, "How can I protect myself against disintegration?" The answer was: to find out what changes occurred in the prisoners and why they took place. By occupying myself with interviewing prisoners, by pondering my findings while forced to perform exhausting labor, I succeeded in killing the time in a way which seemed constructive. As time went on, the enhancement of my self-respect due to my ability to continue to do meaningful work despite the contrary efforts of the Gestapo became even more important than the pastime.

THE INITIAL SHOCK

The initial psychological shock of being unlawfully locked into a prison may be separated from the shock originating in the torture to which the prisoners were exposed. The prisoners' reactions on being brought into prison can best be analyzed on the basis of two categories: their socio-economic class and their political education. These categories can be separated only for the purposes of presentation.

The *politically educated prisoners* sought support for their self-esteem in the fact that the Gestapo had singled them out as important enough to take revenge on. In their imprisonment they saw a demonstration of how dangerous for Nazis their former activities had been.

The *nonpolitical middle-class prisoners* were a small minority among the prisoners. They were least able to withstand the initial shock. They found themselves utterly unable to comprehend what happened to them. In their behavior became apparent the dilemma of the politically uneducated German middle classes when confronted with the phenomenon of National Socialism. They had no consistent philosophy which would protect their integrity as human beings. They had obeyed the law handed down by the ruling classes without questioning its wisdom. And now the law-enforcing agencies turned against them, who always had been their stanchest supporters. They could not question the wisdom of law and police. Therefore what was wrong was that *they* were made objects of a persecution which in itself *must* be right, since it was carried out by the authorities. Thus they were convinced that it must be a "mistake."

These prisoners resented most to be treated "like ordinary criminals." After some time they could not help realizing their actual situation. Then they disintegrated. Suicides were practically confined to this group. Later on, they were the ones who behaved in an antisocial way; they cheated their fellow prisoners; a few turned spies. They lost their middle-class sense of propriety and their self-respect; they became shiftless and disintegrated as autonomous persons.

Members of *the upper classes* segregated themselves as much as possible. They seemed unable to accept what was happening to them. They expressed their conviction that they would be released within the shortest time because of their importance. This conviction was absent among the middle-class prisoners. Upper-class prisoners remained aloof even from the upper classes. They looked down on all other prisoners nearly as much as they despised the Gestapo. In order to endure life in the camp they developed such a feeling of superiority that nothing could touch them.

The *political prisoners* used another psychological mechanism at a later time, which might already have played some part in the initial development. It seems that many political leaders had some guilt-feeling that they had fallen down on the job of preventing the rise of Nazi power. This guilt-feeling was relieved to a considerable degree by the fact that the Nazis found them important enough to bother with. It might be that prisoners managed to endure living in the camp because their punishment freed them from their guilt-feeling. Indications are found in remarks with which prisoners responded when reprimanded for undesirable behavior. They asserted that one cannot behave normally when living under such circumstances and that after liberation they would again act in civilized ways.

Thus it seems that most prisoners tried to protect themselves against the initial shock by mustering forces helpful in supporting their badly shaken self-esteem. Those groups which found in their past life some basis for the erection of such a buttress to their endangered egos seemed to succeed.

THE TRANSPORTATION INTO THE CAMP AND THE FIRST EXPERIENCES IN IT

During the transportation into the camp, the prisoners were exposed to constant tortures. Corporal punishment intermingled with shooting and wounding with the bayonet alternated with tortures the goal of which was extreme exhaustion. For instance, the prisoners were forced to stare into glaring lights or to kneel for hours. Several were killed; the injured were not permitted to take care of their wounds. The guards also forced the prisoners to hit one another, and to defile their most cherished values. They were forced to curse their God, to

accuse themselves of vile actions and their wives of prostitution. This continued for many hours. The purpose of the tortures was to break the resistance of the prisoners, and to assure the guards that they were superior.

It is difficult to ascertain what happened in the minds of the prisoners while they were exposed to this treatment. Most of them became so exhausted that they were only partly conscious of what happened. In general, prisoners did not like to talk about what they had felt and thought during the time of torture. The few who volunteered information made vague statements which sounded like devious rationalizations, invented for justifying that they had endured treatment injurious to their self-respect without trying to fight back. The few who had tried to fight back could not be interviewed; they were dead.

The writer recalls his extreme weariness, resulting from a bayonet wound and a heavy blow on the head. He recalls, nevertheless, his thoughts and emotions. He wondered that man can endure so much without committing suicide or going insane; that the guards tortured prisoners in the way it had been described in books on the concentration camps; that the Gestapo was so simple-minded as to enjoy forcing prisoners to defile themselves. It seems that he gained emotional strength from the following facts: that things happened according to expectation; that, therefore, his future in the camp was at least partly predictable from what he already was experiencing and from what he had read; and that the Gestapo was more stupid than he had expected. He felt pleased that the tortures did not change his ability to think or his general point of view. In retrospect these considerations seem futile, but they ought to be mentioned because, if asked to sum up what was his main problem during the time he spent in the camp, he would say: *to safeguard his ego in such a way, that, if he should regain liberty, he would be approximately the same person he was when deprived of liberty.*

The writer feels that he was able to endure the transportation and what followed, because he convinced himself that these horrible and degrading experiences somehow did not happen to "him" as a subject, but only to "him" as an object. The importance of this attitude was corroborated by statements of other prisoners. They couched their feelings usually in such terms as, "The main problem is to remain alive and unchanged." What should remain unchanged was individually different and roughly covered the person's general attitudes and values.

The author's thoughts and emotions during the transportation were extremely detached. It was as if he watched things happening in which he only vaguely participated. Later he learned that many prisoners developed this same feeling of detachment, as if what happened really did not matter to oneself. It was strangely mixed with a conviction that "this cannot be true, such things do not happen." Not only during the transportation but all through the time spent in camp, the prisoners had to convince themselves that this was real and not just a nightmare. They were never wholly successful. The feeling of detachment which rejected the reality of the situation might be considered a mechanism safeguarding the integrity of the prisoners' personalities. They behaved in the camp as if their life there could have no connection with their "real" life. Their evaluation of their own and other persons' behavior differed from what it would have been outside of camp. The separation of behavior patterns and schemes of values inside and outside of camp was so strong that it could hardly be touched in conversation; it was one of the many "taboos" not to be discussed. The prisoners felt that what they were doing at camp and what happened to them there did not count;

everything was permissible as long as it contributed to helping them to survive.

During the transportation no prisoner fainted. To faint meant to get killed. In this particular situation fainting was not protective against intolerable pain; it endangered a prisoner's existence because anyone unable to follow orders was killed.

THE ADAPTATION TO THE CAMP SITUATION

Differences in the Response to Extreme and to Suffering Experiences. It seems that camp experiences which remained within the normal frame of reference of a prisoner's life experience were mastered by normal psychological mechanisms. For mastering experience which transcended this frame of reference, new psychological mechanisms were needed. The transportation was only one of the experiences transcending the normal frame of reference and the reaction to it may be described as "unforgettable, but unreal."

Attitudes similar to those developed toward the transportation could be observed in other extreme situations. On a terribly cold winter night, all prisoners were forced to stand at attention without overcoats for hours. They were threatened with having to stand all through the night. After about 20 prisoners had died from exposure the threats of the guards became ineffective. To be exposed to the weather was a terrible torture; to see one's friends die without being able to help, and to stand a good chance of dying, created a situation similar to the transportation. Open resistance was impossible. A feeling of utter indifference swept the prisoners. They did not care whether the guards shot them; they were indifferent to acts of torture committed by the guards. It was as if what happened did not "really" happen to oneself. There was again the split between the "me" to whom it happened, and the "me" who really did not care and was a detached observer.

After more than 80 prisoners had died, and several hundred had their extremities so badly frozen that they had later to be amputated, the prisoners were permitted to return to the barracks. They were completely exhausted, but did not experience the feeling of happiness which some had expected. They felt relieved that the torture was over, but felt at the same time that they no longer were free from fear.

The psychological reactions to events which were within the sphere of the normally comprehensible were different from those to extreme events. Prisoners dealt with less extreme events in the same way as if they had happened outside of the camp. A slap in one's face was embarrassing, and not to be discussed. One hated the individual guards who kicked, slapped, or abused much more than the guard who wounded one seriously. In the latter case one hated the Gestapo as such, but not the individual inflicting the punishment. This differentiation was unreasonable, but inescapable. One felt deeper and more violent aggressions against particular Gestapo members who had committed minor vile acts than one felt against those who had acted in a more terrible fashion. Thus it seems that experiences which might have happened during the prisoner's "normal" life history provoked a "normal" reaction. Prisoners seemed particularly sensitive to punishments similar to those which a parent might inflict on his child. To punish a child was within their "normal" frame of reference, but that they should be the object of punishment destroyed their adult frame of reference. So they reacted to it not in an adult, but in a childish way—with shame and violent, impotent, unmanageable emotions directed, not against the system, but against the person inflicting the punishment. It seems that if a prisoner was cursed, slapped, pushed

around "like a child" and if he was, like a child, unable to defend himself, this revived in him behavior patterns and psychological mechanisms which he had developed in childhood. He was unable to see his treatment in its general context. He swore that he was going "to get even," well knowing that this was impossible. He could not develop an objective evaluation which would have led him to consider his suffering as minor when compared with other experiences. The prisoners as a group developed the same attitude to minor sufferings; they did not offer help and blamed the prisoner for not having made the right reply, for letting himself get caught, in short, accused him of behaving like a child. So the degradation of the prisoner took place not only in his mind, but also in the minds of his fellow prisoners. This attitude extended to details. A prisoner did not resent being cursed by the guards during an extreme experience, but was ashamed of it when it occurred during some minor mistreatment. As time went on the difference in the reaction to minor and major sufferings slowly disappeared. This change in reaction was only one of many differences between old and new prisoners.

Differences in the Psychological Attitudes of Old and New Prisoners. In the following discussion the term "new prisoners" designates those who had not spent more than one year in the camp; "old" prisoners are those who have spent at least three years in the camp.

All the emotional efforts of the new prisoners seemed to be directed toward returning to the outer world as the same persons who had left it. Old prisoners seemed mainly concerned with the problem of how to live well within the camp. Once they had reached this attitude, everything that happened to them, even the worst atrocity, was "real" to them. No longer was there a split between one to whom things happened and the one who observed them. When they reached this stage the prisoners were afraid of returning to the outer world. Moreover, they then hardly believed they would ever return to it. They seemed aware that they had adapted themselves to the life in the camp and that this process was coexistent with a basic change in their personality. There was considerable variation among individuals in the time it took them to make their peace with the idea of having to spend the rest of their lives in the camp. How long it took a prisoner to cease to consider life outside the camp as real depended to a great extent on the strength of his emotional ties to his family and friends. Some of the indications for the changed attitude were: scheming to find a better place in the camp rather than trying to contact the outer world, avoiding speculation about one's family or world affairs, concentrating all interest on events taking place inside of the camp. Some of the old prisoners admitted that they no longer could visualize themselves living outside the camp, making free decisions, taking care of themselves and their families. Other differences between old and new prisoners could be recognized in their hopes for their future lives, in the degree to which they regressed to infantile behavior, and in many other ways.

Changes in Attitudes toward One's Family and Friends. The new prisoners received most signs of attention. Their families were trying everything to free them. Nevertheless, they accused them of not doing enough, of betraying them. They would weep over a letter telling of the efforts to liberate them, but curse in the next moment when learning that some of their property had been sold without their permission. Even the smallest change in their former private world attained tremendous importance. This ambivalence seemed due to their desire to return exactly the person who had left. Therefore they feared any change, however trifling, in their former

situation. Their worldly possessions should be secure and untouched, although they were of no use to them at this moment.

It is difficult to say whether the desire that everything remain unchanged was due to their realization of how difficult it might be to adjust to an entirely changed home situation or to some sort of magical thinking running along the following lines: If nothing changes in the world in which I used to live, then I shall not change, either. In this way they might have tried to counteract their feeling that they were changing. The violent reaction against changes in their families was then the counterpart of the realization that they were changing. What enraged them was probably not only the fact of the change, but also the change in their status within the family which it implied. Their families had been dependent on them for decisions, now they were dependent. The only chance they saw for becoming again the head of the family was that the family structure remain untouched despite their absence. The question arises as to how they could blame their families for changes which occurred in them, and whose cause they were. It might be that the prisoners took so much punishment that they could not accept any blame. They felt that they had atoned for any past shortcomings in their relations to their families and friends, and for any changes which might occur in them. Thus they felt free to hate other people, even their own families, for their defects.

The feeling of having atoned for all guilt had some real foundation. When the concentration camps were established the Nazis detained in them their more prominent foes. Soon there were no more prominent enemies left. Still, an institution was needed to threaten the opponents of the system. Many Germans were dissatisfied with the system. To imprison all of them would have interrupted the functioning of the industrial production. Therefore, if a group of the population got fed up with the Nazi regime, a selected few members of the group were brought into the concentration camp. If lawyers, for instance, became restless, a few hundred lawyers were sent to the camp. The Gestapo called such group punishments "actions." During the first of them only the leaders of the opposing group were punished. That led to the feeling that to belong to a rebellious group as a member only was not dangerous. Soon the Gestapo revised its system and punished a cross section of the different strata of the group. This procedure had not only the advantage of spreading terror among all members of the group, but made it possible to destroy the group without necessarily touching the leader if that was for some reason inopportune. Though prisoners were never told why they were imprisoned, those imprisoned as representatives of a group came to know it. Prisoners were interviewed by the Gestapo to gain information about their friends. During these interviews prisoners were told that if their fate did not teach the group to behave better they would get a chance to meet them in the camp. So the prisoners rightly felt that they were atoning for the rest of the group.

Old prisoners did not like to be reminded of their families and former friends. When they spoke about them, it was in a very detached way. A contributing factor was the prisoners' hatred of all those living outside of the camp, who "enjoyed life as if we were not rotting away." The outside world which continued to live as if nothing had happened was in the minds of the prisoners represented by those whom they used to know, namely, by their relatives and friends. But even this hatred was subdued in the old prisoners. It seemed that, as much as they had forgotten to love their kin, they had lost the ability to hate them. *They had learned to direct a great amount of aggression against themselves so as not to get into too many conflicts with the Gestapo, while the new prisoners still directed their aggressions against the outer world, and—when not supervised—against the Gestapo.* Since the old prisoners did not show much emotion either way, they were unable to feel strongly about anybody.

Old prisoners did not like to mention their former social status; new prisoners were rather boastful about it. New prisoners seemed to back their self-esteem by letting others know how important they had been. Old prisoners seemed to have accepted their state of dejection, and to compare it with their former splendor was probably too depressing.

Hopes about Life after Liberation. Closely connected with the prisoners' attitudes toward their families were their hopes concerning their life after release from camp. Here they embarked a great deal on individual and group daydreams. To indulge in them was one of the favorite pastimes if the general emotional climate in the camp was not too depressed. There was a marked difference between the daydreams of the new and the old prisoners. *The longer the time a prisoner had spent in camp, the less true to reality were his daydreams;* so much so that the hopes and expectations of the old prisoners often took the form of eschatological or messianic hopes. They were convinced that out of the coming world war and world revolution they would emerge as the future leaders of Germany at least, if not of the world. This was the least to which their sufferings entitled them. These grandiose expectations were coexistent with great vagueness as to their future private lives. In their daydreams they were certain to emerge as the future secretaries of state, but they were less certain whether they would continue to live with their wives and children. Part of these daydreams may be explained by the fact that they seemed to feel that only a high public position could help them to regain their standing within their families.

The hopes and expectations of the new prisoners were truer to reality. Despite their open ambivalence about their families, they never doubted that they were going to continue to live with them. They hoped to continue their public and professional lives in the same way as they used to.

Regression into Infantile Behavior. Most of the adaptations to the camp situation mentioned so far were more or less individual behaviors. The regression to infantile behavior was a mass phenomenon. It would not have taken place if it had not happened in all prisoners. The prisoners did not interfere with another's daydreams or his attitudes to his family, but they asserted their power as a group over those who objected to deviations from normal adult behavior. Those who did not develop a childlike dependency on the guards were accused of threatening the security of the group, an accusation which was not without foundation, since the Gestapo punished the group for the misbehavior of the individual. The regression into childlike behavior was more inescapable than other types of behavior imposed on the individual by the impact of the conditions in the camp.

The prisoners developed types of behavior characteristic of infancy or early youth. Some of them have been discussed, such as ambivalence to one's family, despondency, finding satisfaction in daydreaming rather than in action. During the transportation the prisoners were tortured in a way in which a cruel and domineering father might torture a helpless child; at the camp they were also debased by techniques which went much further into childhood situations. They were forced to soil themselves. Their defecation was strictly regulated. Prisoners who needed to eliminate had to obtain the permission of the guard. It seemed as if the educa-

tion to cleanliness would be once more repeated. It gave pleasure to the guards to hold the power of granting or withholding the permission to visit the latrines. This pleasure found its counterpart in the pleasure the prisoners derived from visiting them, because there they could rest for a moment, secure from the whips of the overseers.

The prisoners were forced to say "thou" to one another, which in Germany is indiscriminately used only among small children. They were not permitted to address one another with the many titles to which middle- and upper-class Germans are accustomed. On the other hand, they had to address the guards in the most deferential manner, giving them all their titles.

The prisoners lived, like children, only in the immediate present; they lost the feeling for the sequence of time; they became unable to plan for the future or to give up immediate pleasure satisfactions to gain greater ones in the near future. They were unable to establish durable object-relations. Friendships developed as quickly as they broke up. Prisoners would, like adolescents, fight one another tooth and nail, only to become close friends within a few minutes. They were boastful, telling tales about what they had accomplished in their former lives, or how they succeeded in cheating guards. Like children they felt not at all set back or ashamed when it became known that they had lied about their prowess.

Another factor contributing to the regression into childhood behavior was the work the prisoners were forced to perform. Prisoners were forced to perform nonsensical tasks, such as carrying heavy rocks from one place to another, and back to the place where they had picked them up. They were forced to dig holes in the ground with their bare hands, although tools were available. They felt debased when forced to perform "childish" and stupid labor, and preferred even harder work when it produced something that might be considered useful. There seems to be no doubt that the tasks they performed, as well as the mistreatment by the Gestapo which they had to endure, contributed to their disintegration as adult persons.

THE FINAL ADJUSTMENT TO THE LIFE IN THE CAMP

A prisoner had reached the final stage of adjustment to the camp situation when he changed his personality so as to accept as his own the values of the Gestapo. A few examples may illustrate this.

The prisoners suffered from the steady interference with their privacy on the part of the guards and other prisoners. So a great amount of aggression accumulated. In new prisoners it vented itself in the way it might have done in the world outside the camp. But slowly prisoners accepted, as expression of their verbal aggressions, terms which definitely were taken over from the vocabulary of the Gestapo. From copying the verbal aggressions of the Gestapo to copying their form of bodily aggressions was one more step, but it took several years to make it. Old prisoners, when in charge of others, often behaved worse than the Gestapo because they considered this the best way to behave toward prisoners in the camp.

Most old prisoners took over the Gestapo's attitude toward the so-called unfit prisoners. Newcomers presented difficult problems. Their complaints about life in camp added new strain to the life in the barracks; so did their inability to adjust to it. Bad behavior in the labor gang endangered the whole group. Thus newcomers who did not stand up well under the strain tended to become a liability for the other prisoners. Moreover, weaklings were those most apt eventually to turn traitors. Therefore old prisoners were sometimes instrumental in getting rid of the unfit, thus shaping their own behavior in the image of Gestapo ideology. This was only one of the many situations in which old prisoners molded their way of treating other prisoners according to the example set by the Gestapo. Another was the treatment of traitors. Self-protection asked for their destruction, but the way in which they were tortured for days and slowly killed was copied from the Gestapo.

Old prisoners tended to identify with the Gestapo not only in respect to aggressive behavior. They tried to arrogate to themselves old pieces of Gestapo uniforms. If that was not possible, they tried to sew and mend their uniforms so that they would resemble those of the guards. When asked why they did it they admitted that they loved to look like one of the guards.

The satisfaction with which old prisoners boasted that, during the twice daily counting of the prisoners, they had stood well at attention can be explained only by their having accepted as their own the values of the Gestapo. Prisoners prided themselves on being as tough as the Gestapo members. This identification with their torturers went so far as copying their leisure-time activities. One of the games played by the guards was to find out who could stand to be hit longest without uttering a complaint. This game was copied by old prisoners.

Often the Gestapo would enforce nonsensical rules, originating in the whims of one of the guards. They were usually forgotten as soon as formulated, but there were always some old prisoners who would continue to follow these rules and try to enforce them on others long after the Gestapo had forgotten about them. These prisoners firmly believed that the rules set down by the Gestapo were desirable standards of human behavior, at least in the camp situation. Other areas in which prisoners made their peace with the values of the Gestapo included the race problem, although race discrimination had been alien to their previous scheme of values.

Among the old prisoners one could observe other developments which indicated their desire to accept the Gestapo along lines which definitely could not originate in propaganda. It seems that, since they returned to a childlike attitude toward the Gestapo, they had a desire that at least some of those whom they accepted as all-powerful father-images should be just and kind. They divided their positive and negative feelings—strange as it may be, they had positive feelings—toward the Gestapo in such a way that all positive emotions were concentrated on a few officers who were high up in the hierarchy of camp administrators, but hardly ever on the governor of the camp. They insisted that these officers hid behind their rough surfaces a feeling of justice and propriety; they were supposed to be genuinely interested in the prisoners and even trying, in a small way, to help them. Since these supposed feelings never became apparent, it was explained that they hid them effectively because otherwise they would not be able to help the prisoners. For instance, a whole legend was woven around the fact that of two officers inspecting a barrack one had cleaned his shoes before entering. He probably did it automatically, but it was interpreted as a rebuff to the other officer and a clear demonstration of how he felt about the concentration camp.

After so much has been said about the old prisoners' tendency to identify with the Gestapo, it ought to be stressed that this was only part of the picture. Old prisoners who identified with the Gestapo at other moments also defied it, demonstrating extraordinary courage in doing so.

SUMMARY

The concentration camp had an importance reaching far beyond its being a place where the Gestapo took revenge on its enemies. It was the training ground for young Gestapo soldiers who were planning to rule Germany and all conquered nations; it was the Gestapo's laboratory for developing methods for changing free citizens into serfs who in many respects accept their masters' values while they still thought that they were following their own life goals and values. The system was too strong for an individual to break its hold over his emotional life, particularly if he found himself within a group which had more or less accepted the Nazi system. It seemed easier to resist the pressure of the Gestapo if one functioned as an individual; the Gestapo knew it and therefore insisted on forcing all individuals into groups which they supervised. The Gestapo's main goal was to produce in the subjects childlike attitudes and childlike dependency on the will of the leaders.

THE CHINESE INDOCTRINATION PROGRAM FOR PRISONERS OF WAR: A STUDY OF ATTEMPTED "BRAINWASHING" *By Edgar H. Schein*

In this paper I shall try to present an account of the "typical" experiences of United Nations prisoners of war in Chinese Communist hands and to interpret these experiences in a social-psychological framework. Before the return of United Nations prisoners, the "confessions" of such prominent men as Cardinal Mindszenty and William Oatis had already aroused considerable interest in so-called brainwashing. This interest was heightened by the widespread rumors of collaboration among United Nations prisoners of war in Korea. Following their repatriation in August 1953, a rash of testimonial articles appeared in weekly magazines, some attempting to show that the Chinese Communist techniques were so terrifying that no one could withstand them, others roundly condemning the collaborative activities of the so-called "progressives" [1] as having been selfishly motivated under conditions in which resistance was possible. These various accounts fall short because they are too emotionally charged to be objective, and because they fail to have any generality, since they are usually based on the personal experiences of only one man.

The data upon which this paper is based were gathered in an attempt to form a generalized picture of what happened to the average man from the time he was captured until the time he was repatriated. The data were collected during August 1953 at Inchon, Korea, where the repatriates were being processed, and on board the U.S.N.S. *General Black* in transit to the United States from September 1 to September 16.

The data were collected, in the main, during intensive interviews conducted in Inchon.[2] The intensive interviewing was felt to be appropriate for gathering the data presented here, because the material to be obtained was highly novel and because the men had been through a highly traumatic situation which might have made the eliciting of *any* information very difficult. It was also recognized that the men might find it difficult to remember, might be reluctant to relate certain of their experiences, and might retrospectively falsify many events.

Of approximately 20 repatriates selected at random at different stages of the repatriation, each was asked to tell in chronological order and in as great detail as possible what had happened to him during his captivity. Emphasis was placed on what the Chinese or North Koreans *did* in their handling of the prisoners and how the men reacted. The men were particularly encouraged to relate the reactions of *others*, in order to avoid arousing anxiety or guilt over their own behavior and thereby blocking the flow of memories. The interviews varied in length from two to four hours.

The picture presented is not to be viewed as the experience of any single person nor as the experience of all the

From *Psychiatry*, 1956, XIX, 149–172. A few deletions and minor changes have been made for the sake of brevity. Reprinted by permission of the author and the publisher. Copyright held by William Alanson White Psychiatric Foundation.

---

[1] Commonly called *pro's* by their fellow prisoners.

[2] As part of the processing procedure, psychiatric interviews were initiated at Inchon during the two or three days that the men were there. The procedure of processing has been described in detail by Henry A. Segal in "Initial Psychiatric Findings of Recently Repatriated Prisoners of War," *Am. T Psychiat.*, 1954, CXI, 358-363.

men. Rather, it represents a composite or typical account which, in all its details, may or may not have been true for any one prisoner.

THE PRISONER-OF-WAR EXPERIENCE

Capture, the March, and Temporary Camps. United Nations soldiers were captured by the Chinese and North Koreans at all stages of the Korean conflict, although particularly large groups were captured during November and December 1950. The conditions under which men were captured varied widely. Some men were captured when their positions were overrun or surrounded; others ran into road blocks and were cut off; still others fought for many days on a shifting front before they succumbed. The situation in the front lines was highly fluid and there was a good deal of confusion on both sides. When a position was overrun, the men often scattered and became disorganized.

The initial treatment of prisoners by the North Koreans was typically harsh and brutal—they often took the prisoner's clothing, gave him little if any food, and met any resistance with immediate severe punishment or death. The Chinese, on the other hand, often tried to create an atmosphere of friendliness and leniency. Some men reported that their Chinese captors approached them with outstretched hands, saying, "Congratulations! You've been liberated." It was made clear to the man that he could now join forces with other "fighters for peace." This Chinese tactic was part of their "*lenient policy,*" which was explained to groups of prisoners shortly after capture in these terms: Because the UN had entered the war illegally and was an aggressor, all UN military personnel were in fact "war criminals" and could be shot summarily. But the average soldier was, after all, only carrying out orders for his leaders who were the real criminals. Therefore, the Chinese would consider the POW a "student" and would teach him the "truth" about the war. Anyone who did not cooperate by going to school and by learning voluntarily could be reverted to his "war-criminal" status and shot, particularly if a confession could be obtained from him.

Often the Chinese soldiers pointed out to their captives how lucky they were not to have been captured by the North Koreans. Some men reported incidents of Chinese beating off North Koreans who were "trying to hurt" American prisoners or of punishing their own guards for being too rough or inconsiderate. The men were usually allowed to keep their clothing, and some consideration was given to the sick and wounded. However, the food and medical attention were only slightly better than that provided by the North Koreans.

For the first six to 24 hours after capture, a man was usually in a state of dazed shock, unable to take any kind of integrated action and, later, unable to report any kind of feeling he had had during this period. Following this, he expected death or torture at the hands of his captors, for rumors that this would happen had been widely circulated in the front lines, often based on stories of men who had fallen into North Korean hands. These fears were, however, quickly dispelled by the friendly attitude of the Chinese soldiers; and this friendly attitude and the emphasis on "peace" was the first and perhaps most significant step in making the prisoner receptive to the more formal indoctrination which was to come later.

In the next weeks or months the prisoner was exposed to great physical hardship and to a series of psychological pressures which amounted to a cyclical reactivation of fears and their relief by actual events or by extravagant promises. Implicit in most of what the Chinese said and did was the suggestion that these stresses could be brought to an end by the adoption of a "cooperative" attitude by the prisoner, although at first it was not clear just what this meant.

The men were collected behind the lines and were marched north in groups of varying sizes. The men marched only at night, averaging about 20 miles, and were kept under strict cover in the daytime. Conditions on the march were very hard. Most men reported having great difficulty eating strange and badly prepared foods; however, they were often reminded, whether true or not, that they were getting essentially the same rations as the average Chinese footsoldier. Medical care was almost nonexistent, but this too was depicted as being equally true for Chinese soldiers because of supply shortages. Almost all the men had diarrhea, many had dysentery, and most of them suffered from exposure. Every day would find a few more dead.

Although the columns were not well guarded, few escapes were attempted because the men were too weak, did not know the terrain, were on the whole poorly organized, and were afraid of the North Koreans. The few who did escape were almost always returned to the group within a short time.

During these one- to two-week marches the men became increasingly disorganized and apathetic. They developed a slow plodding gait, called by one man a "prisoner's shuffle." Lines of authority tended to break down and the prevailing attitude was "every man for himself." Open competition for food, clothing, and shelter made the maintenance of group ties almost impossible. Everything that happened tended to be frustrating and depriving, yet there was no ready outlet for hostility and no opportunity for constructive resistance. The only *realistic* goal was to get to prison camp where, it was hoped, conditions would be better.[3]

Uppermost in the men's minds were fantasies of food—memories of all the good meals they had had in the past, or plans for elaborate menus in the future. The only competing fantasies concerned loved ones at home, or cars, which seemed symbolically to represent the return to their homes and to freedom.

Arrival at one of the temporary camps was usually a severe disappointment. Many men reported that the only thing that had kept them going on the march was the hope of improved conditions in the camp; but they found the food as bad as ever, living conditions more crowded than before, and a continued lack of consideration for the sick and wounded. Moreover, there was now nothing to do but sit and wait. The news given the men was mostly false, playing up Communist military victories, and was, of course, particularly demoralizing. Many of the men became extremely apathetic and withdrawn, and according to some reports these apathy states sometimes became so severe as to result in death.[4]

The Chinese continually promised improvements in conditions or early repatriation, and failures of these promises to materialize were blamed on obstructions created by United Nations air activity or lack of "cooperation" among the prisoners. It was always made clear that only certain prisoners could hope to get a break: those who "did well," "cooperated," "learned the truth," and so on.

[3] Not all of the men participated in such severe marches. Those captured in 1951 and 1952 were sometimes taken north by truck or under less severe conditions. The sick and wounded were given somewhat more consideration, although never much in the way of medical aid. Numerous incidents were reported of Chinese guards helping men, occasionally even carrying them. It should also be mentioned that the North Korean civilians seemed ambivalent toward the prisoners. Many of them were sadistic, but many others helped the Americans by hiding them or giving them food and clothing.

[4] For a more complete description of these apathy reactions, see H. D. Strassman, Margaret Thaler, and E. H. Schein "A Prisoner of War Syndrome: Apathy as a Reaction to Severe Stress," *Am. J. Psychiat.*, 1956, CXII, 998–1003.

The Chinese distributed propaganda leaflets and required the men to sing Communist songs. Apparently, even guards were sensitized to finding potential collaborators among the prisoners by observing their reactions to such activities. Outright indoctrination was not attempted on the marches and in the temporary camps, but those men who finally reached one of the permanent camps were ill-prepared physically and psychologically for the indoctrination pressures they were about to face.

Life in the Permanent Prisoner-of-war Camp. Most of the permanent camps were parts of small Korean villages, often split into several compounds in different parts of the village. The camps were sometimes surrounded by a fence, by barbed wire, or by natural barriers, although sometimes not enclosed at all. While guards were posted at key places, they were not sufficiently plentiful to prevent escapes or excursions to other parts of the village. The camp usually consisted of a series of mud huts in which the men slept on the floor or on straw matting, and a schoolhouse or other permanent building which was used as administrative headquarters, for lectures, and for recreation. The various Chinese officer and enlisted billets were usually scattered through the village. Mess and latrine facilities were very inadequate and conditions were crowded, but far better than in the temporary camps.

In camp the men were segregated by race, nationality, and rank and were organized into companies, platoons, and squads. The squads varied in size from ten to 15 men, who usually shared the same living area. No formal organization was permitted among the prisoners. The Chinese put their own personnel in charge of the platoons and companies and appointed certain prisoners as squad leaders without consideration of rank.

Although the daily routine in camp varied, the average prisoner arose at dawn, was required to do calisthenics for an hour or more, was assigned to various details—such as gathering wood, carrying water, cooking, repairing roads, burying other prisoners, and general maintenance of the camp—and then was given a breakfast of potato soup or some form of cereal at around eight o'clock. The rest of the morning and afternoon was usually spent on indoctrination or work details. Whether there was a midday meal depended on the attitude of the prisoner, the supply of food, and the general state of the political situation. The main meal was served around five o'clock and usually consisted of vegetables, grains, rice, and occasional bits of pork fat or fish. For men on such a meager diet, details involving many miles of walking or very hard work were especially exhausting.

Recreation varied with the camp and with the political situation. During the first year or so, a heavy emphasis was placed on indoctrination, and recreation was restricted to reading Communist literature, seeing propaganda films, and playing such games as checkers and chess. As the truce talks progressed and repatriation became a possibility, conditions in the camps improved generally. Less emphasis was placed on indoctrination and more leeway was given to the prisoners to engage in recreation of their own choice. The improvement in living conditions made physical recreation more feasible and the men were permitted to devise athletic fields and equipment. Intercamp "Olympics" conducted by the Chinese—and used by them for their own propaganda purposes—drew wide participation among the more athletically inclined, regardless of their political sentiments.

There are few data available concerning the sexual activities of the prisoners. There were Korean women available in the villages, but men seldom visited them. Reports of homosexuality were very infrequent.

The Indoctrination Program

All of these conditions in the permanent camp were, in actual practice, interlocked with the indoctrination program. This program should not be viewed as a collection of specific techniques routinely applied, but rather as the creation of a whole set of social conditions within which certain techniques operated. Whether the Chinese manipulation of the social setting to create certain effects was intentional can only be conjectured; intentional or not, it was an important factor in such success as the indoctrination program achieved.

Removal of Belief, Attitude, and Value Supports. On matters of opinion, people tend to rely primarily on the opinions of others for determination of whether they themselves are "right" or "wrong"—whether these opinions of others are obtained through mass media of communication or through personal interaction. All of the prisoners' accustomed sources of information concerning daily events on a local, national, or international level were cut off by the Chinese, who substituted their own, usually heavily biased, newspapers, radio broadcasts, and magazines. *The Daily Worker* from various cities was available in the camp libraries, as were numerous magazines and journals from China, Poland, Russia, and Czechoslovakia. Radio news broadcasts usually originated in China. The camp headquarters had no scruples concerning accuracy in the news announcements made over the camp public-address system.

The delivery of mail from home was systematically manipulated; the evidence indicates that all mail which contained information about the war or the truce talks, or which contained favorable personal news, was withheld, while letters containing no general information, or bad personal news, were usually delivered.

Personal contact with visitors from outside the camps was very limited, mainly restricted to Communist news correspondents. For most prisoners, there was simply no way to find out accurately what was going on in the world.

The Chinese also attempted to weaken the means of consensual validation by undermining personal contacts among the men. First of all, the men were segregated by race, apparently in order to put special indoctrination pressure on members of certain minorities, especially Negroes. The men were also segregated by rank, in what appeared to be a systematic attempt to undermine the internal structure of the group by removing its leaders. Thus, the noncommissioned officers, who were at first in the enlisted camps, were put into a special camp when the Chinese found out that they were quite effective in keeping the other men from various kinds of collaboration. It was reported that this segregation was often followed by a considerable increase in collaboration, particularly among the younger enlisted men.

The Chinese emphasized that rank was no longer of any significance; the entire group was now part of a wider "brotherhood"—the earlier mentioned "fighters for peace"—in which, under communism, everyone was to be equal. The Chinese sometimes put particularly young or inept prisoners in command of the squads to remind the men that former bases of organization no longer counted. While such a procedure aroused only resistance and hostility in most of the prisoners, a few malcontents welcomed the opportunity to gain occupancy of the favored positions that had never been available to them before.

There was also persistent emphasis on undermining all friendships, emotional bonds, and group activities. For instance, the Chinese prohibited all forms of religious expression and ruthlessly persecuted the few chaplains or others who tried to organize or conduct religious services. Bonds to loved ones at home were weakened by the withholding of mail, as the Chinese frequently pointed out to the men that the lack of mail meant that their friends and relatives no longer cared for them.

The systematic use of Chinese spies and also informers from prisoner ranks made it possible for the Chinese to obtain detailed information about almost all activities going on in camp. The men reported that the Chinese were forever sneaking around their quarters and listening to conversations or observing activities from hidden posts, and they also knew that some of their number were acting as informers. These circumstances helped to create a feeling of general distrust, and the only fully safe course was to withdraw from all intimate interaction with other prisoners.

When any semblance of effective organization appeared spontaneously among the men, the Chinese would immediately remove and segregate the leaders or key figures. Informal groups which might have supported resistance activities were also systematically broken up. The few that were not broken up either were not effective or died because of lack of internal support, thus indicating that this system of social control was highly effective. Usually groups were formed for one of three purposes—to plan for and aid in escapes, to prevent men from collaborating, or for social reasons. According to most reports, the groups organized around escape were highly ineffective. Usually such groups were quickly liquidated by being physically broken up. A few poorly planned escapes were attempted, but the marginal diet, the strangeness of the surrounding terrain, and the carefully built-up fear of the North Koreans all served to minimize escapes. When an escape did occur, the Chinese usually recovered the man easily by offering a bag of rice to anyone turning him in. The groups organized to keep men from collaborating, or to retaliate against them if they did, were usually

composed of some of the more outspoken and violent resisters. One such group, labelled the "Ku Klux Klan" by the Chinese because of its militant policy, appeared to be composed mainly of men who had served some time in prison for various infractions of camp rules. They threatened potential collaborators through anonymous notes, but the number of incidents in which they followed through was relatively small. Usually the Chinese discovered their plans and whenever they became dangerous disrupted their activities. The third type of group consisted of prisoners who were solely interested in each other's company; one such group, made up primarily of older prisoners, was called "The Old Soldiers' Home."

A few groups remained intact even though the Chinese knew about them, perhaps because the Chinese did not consider them very dangerous, or because their leaders, as spokesmen for the prisoners, provided a valuable sounding board whenever the Chinese wanted to know how the group would react to certain changes in policy.

Various other groupings of men existed, some, such as the squad, for administrative reasons, others to support various Chinese enterprises. Soon after capture, the Chinese made a concerted effort to recruit men for a number of "peace committees" whose purpose it was to aid in the indoctrination by conducting personal interviews with resistant prisoners and to deter any resistance activity. They also were charged with such propaganda missions as the preparation of leaflets, peace petitions, and scripts for radio broadcasts—all under the guise of running such innocuous camp activities as recreation. An intercamp peace organization was also formed to draw up peace appeals and petitions to be submitted to the United Nations, carrying, of course, the endorsement of a large number of prisoners.

The members of the camp peace committees and the delegates to intercamp peace rallies were usually selected by a pseudodemocratic method. However, the men who ended up in the key positions were usually those the Chinese wanted, or, in any case, approved of—that is, men who were willing to cooperate with the Chinese and who had sincerely or falsely convinced their captors that they were sympathetic to the communist cause. Sometimes the election was held over and over again until the right man was chosen. At other times the men resigned themselves to the fact that all would go more smoothly if they selected at the beginning the man the Chinese wanted, for the group could be dissolved at will anyway.

Each camp also had a number of other committees operating under the peace committee. They were responsible for the daily routine affairs of the camp, such as sanitation, food, recreation, study, and entertainment. The number of noncollaborators who were allowed to be members appeared to depend on the mood of the Chinese and the degree to which they wanted to keep in touch with prisoner opinions. It is likely that with the general improvement in camp conditions in 1952 and 1953, the membership of the various committees became more representative. The peace committees were, by then, largely defunct; they had been exploited as much as possible by the Chinese and no longer served any function in their propaganda campaigns.

Various social groups formed by pro's were left intact—perhaps as a reminder to other prisoners that one way to enter into meaningful relationships with others was through common political activities for the Communists.

One of the most significant facts about the few types of groups that did exist in camp is that they were highly unstable from an internal point of view because of the possible presence of informers and spies. Mutual distrust existed especially in the peace committees and in groups sanctioned by the Chinese, because no member was ever sure whether any other member was really a pro or was just pretending to "go along." If a man was pretending, he had to hide this carefully lest a real pro turn him in to the Chinese. Yet a man who sincerely believed in the Chinese peace effort had to hide this fact from others who might be pretenders, for fear they might harm him directly or blacklist him for the future, at the same time convincing other pro's that he really was sincere.

The members of resistance groups and social groups also had to be wary of each other, because they never knew whether the group had been infiltrated by spies and informers. Furthermore, the fact that the group might be broken up at any time tended to keep any member from becoming too dependent on, or close to, another.[5]

From the point of view of this analysis, the most important effect of the social isolation which existed was the consequent emotional isolation which prevented a man from validating any of his beliefs, attitudes, and values through meaningful interaction with other men at a time when these were under heavy attack from many sources and when no accurate information was available.

Direct Attacks on Beliefs, Attitudes, and Values. The chief method of direct indoctrination was a series of lectures that all prisoners had to attend at some time during their imprisonment. These lectures were given daily and lasted from two to three hours. Each camp had one or more political instructors who read the lectures from a prepared text. Often one instructor read while another seemed to follow a second copy of the text, as if to make sure that the right material was being presented. The lectures were direct, simple, black-and-white propaganda,

---

[5] Segal, *op. cit.*, has aptly described such prisoner groups as "groups of isolates."

They attacked the United Nations and particularly the United States on various political, social, and economic issues, at the same time glorifying the achievements of the Communist countries, and making strong appeals for "peace."

Most men reported that the anti-American material was naïve and seldom based on adequate or correct information about the United States. Even the pro-Communist arguments were sometimes weak and susceptible to attack. Occasionally a well educated prisoner debated points on communism successfully with instructors who had little knowledge of the classical works of communism. Usually the instructors presented the neo-Communist views of writers such as Mao Tse-tung and were unable to counter the arguments of prisoners who knew Marx and Lenin. The number of prisoners with sufficient education to engage in such arguments was, however, extremely small.

The constant hammering at certain points, combined with all the other techniques used—and in a situation where the prisoners had no access to other information—made it likely that many of the Chinese arguments did filter through enough to make many of the men question some of their former points of view. It is also likely that any appeal for "peace," no matter how false, found a receptive audience among combat-weary troops, especially when it was pointed out that they were fighting on foreign soil and were intervening in a civil war which was "none of their business." Both lectures and didactic "interrogations" emphasized detailed predictions of what would happen to the prisoners upon repatriation, some of which turned out to be accurate.[6] The Chinese implied that certain problems which would arise would be the result of the "weakness" or "unfairness" of the democratic ideology.

Another direct technique was the distribution of propaganda leaflets and the showing of Communist films glorifying the accomplishments of the Communist regime in Russia and China, and pointing out how much more had been done by communism for the peasant and laborer than by the capitalist system. While such films might have been highly ineffectual under ordinary circumstances, they assumed considerable importance because of the sheer lack of any other audio-visual material.

Perhaps the most effective attack on existing values, beliefs, and attitudes was the use of testimonials from prisoners who were ostensibly supporting Communist enterprises. These included peace petitions, radio appeals, speeches, and confessions. The use of such testimonials had a double effect in that it further weakened group ties while presenting pro-Communist arguments. As long as the men unanimously rejected the propaganda, each of them could firmly hold to the position that his beliefs must be right, even if he could not defend them logically. However, *if even one other man became convinced, it was no longer possible to hold this position.* Each man was then required to begin examining his beliefs and was vulnerable to the highly one-sided arguments that were repeatedly presented.

Of particular importance were the germ-warfare confessions which were extracted from a number of Air Force officers and enlisted men. The Chinese made a movie of one or two of the officers giving their testimony to the "international" commission which they had set up to investigate the problem and showed this movie in all the camps. Furthermore, one or two of the officers personally went

---

[6] The various problems that faced repatriates have been discussed by Segal, *op. cit.*, and by Robert J. Lifton in "Home by Ship: Reaction Patterns of American Prisoners of War Repatriated from North Korea," *Am. J. Psychiat.*, 1954, CX, 732–739.

from camp to camp and explained how United Nations forces had used these bombs; this made a powerful impression on many men who had, until then, dismissed the whole matter as a Chinese propaganda project. The great detail of the accounts, the sincerity of the officers, the fact that they were freely going from camp to camp and did not look as if they were then or had previously been under any duress made it difficult for some men to believe that the accounts could be anything but true.

The Chinese also used Koreans to give testimonials concerning the barbarity of the United Nations; in one instance women and children told one of the peace committees how United Nations planes had dropped toys which exploded when children tried to pick them up. It is difficult to evaluate the effects of such propaganda, but it is not likely that many prisoners believed stories of such extremity.

Indirect Attacks on Beliefs, Attitudes, and Values. In the direct attacks which I have been discussing, the source of propaganda was external. In the indirect attacks, a set of conditions was created in which each prisoner of war was encouraged to participate in a way that would make it more possible for him to accept some of the new points of view. One attempt to accomplish this was by means of group discussions following lectures.

Most lectures ended with a series of conclusions—for example, "The South Koreans started the war by invading North Korea," or "The aim of the capitalist nations is world domination." The men were then required to break up into squads, go to their quarters, and discuss the material for periods of two hours or more. At the end of the discussion each squad had to provide written answers to questions handed out during the lecture —the answers, obviously, which had already been provided in the lecture. To "discuss" the lecture thus meant, in effect, to rationalize the predetermined conclusions.[7]

A monitor was assigned to each squad to "aid" the men in the discussion, to make sure that they stayed on the proper topic, and to collect the answers and make sure that they were the "right" ones. Initially, the monitor for most squads was an English-speaking Chinese, but whenever possible the Chinese turned the job over to one of the squad members, usually the one who was most cooperative or sympathetic to the Communist point of view. If one or more members of the squad turned in "wrong" answers— for example, saying that the North Koreans had invaded South Korea—the entire squad had to listen to the lecture again and repeat the group discussion. This procedure might go on for days. The Chinese never tired of repeating the procedure over and over again, apparently believing that group discussion had a better chance of success in converting men to their point of view than individual indoctrination.

The success of such discussions often depended on the degree of supervision. If the monitor was lax, the groups would talk about anything but the required material. But a prisoner-of-war monitor who was actively pro-Communist or a Chinese who had a good understanding of English idiom might obtain considerable discussion. Supervised discussion did not necessarily lead a man to question his own beliefs; in many cases it permitted POW's to strengthen their former beliefs by giving them an opportunity for consensual validation.

A second means of indirect attack was

---

[7] During the last year or so of imprisonment, many of the features of indoctrination which earlier had been compulsory were put on a voluntary basis. Any prisoners who were interested in learning more about communism could attend special lectures and group discussions. The men who participated in such voluntary programs were known as "self-study pro's" and were given many privileges not accorded to other prisoners.

interrogation. Interrogations were carried on during all stages of internment, but their apparent function and the techniques utilized varied from time to time. Almost all men went through lengthy and repetitive military interrogations. Failure to answer questions seldom led to severe physical punishment. Instead, various psychological pressures were applied. For instance, all information was cross-checked against earlier interrogations and against the information from other men. If an answer did not tally with other information, the respondent had to explain the discrepancy. Continuous pressure to resolve contrary answers often forced a man to tell the truth.

The Chinese tried to create the impression that they could obtain *any* information from *anyone* by the following interrogation technique: If a man continued to refuse to answer a question, despite great fatigue and continued repetition of the question, the interrogator would suddenly pull out a notebook and point out to the man the complete answer to the question, sometimes in astonishingly accurate detail. The interrogation would then move on to a new topic and the same procedure would be repeated, until the man could not assess whether there was indeed *anything* that the Chinese did *not* know. In most cases the man was told that others had already given information or "confessed," so why should he hold back and suffer? [8]

A further technique was to have the man write out the question and then the answer. If he refused to write it voluntarily, he was asked to copy it from the notebooks, which must have seemed like a harmless enough concession. But the information which he had copied could then be shown to another man as evidence that he had given information of his own volition. Furthermore, it could be used to blackmail him, because he would have a hard time proving that he had merely copied the material.

Another type of interrogation to which almost all men were subjected involved primarily nonmilitary information. The Chinese were very curious about all aspects of life in the Western world and asked many questions about it, often in great detail. They also endeavored, by means of printed forms, to obtain a complete personal history from each prisoner, with particular emphasis on his social-cultural background, his class status, his and his parents' occupational histories, and so on. The purpose was apparently to determine which prisoners' histories might predispose them toward the Communist philosophy and thus make them apt subjects for special indoctrination.

Most men did not give accurate information. Usually the prisoner filled out the form in terms of fictitious characters. But later he would be required to repeat the entire procedure and would usually be unable to remember his earlier answers. He would then be confronted with the discrepancies and would be forced into the fatiguing activity of having to invent justification after justification to resolve them.

If and when the Chinese felt that they had obtained a relatively true account, it was used in discussion between the interrogator and the prisoner to undermine the prisoner's beliefs and values. Various points in the life history were used to show a man the "errors" of his past life— for example, that he or his parents had been ruthless capitalists exploiting workers, yet had really received only meager benefits from such exploitation. The Chinese were particularly interested in any inconsistencies in the life histories and would focus discussion on them in order to bring to light the motivations involved. Whenever possible, any setbacks that a man had experienced economically or so-

---

[8] Many men reported that they felt the Chinese were boasting when they told what they knew that they were very proud of their ability as interrogators and felt a need to show off to their captors.

cially were searchingly analyzed, and the blame was laid on the capitalistic system.

The fact that many men were unclear about why they were fighting in Korea was a good lever for such discussions. The interrogator or instructor could point out the basic injustices of foreign intervention in a civil war, and simultaneously could arouse longings for home and the wish that the United Nations had never taken up the fight in the first place. It was not difficult to convince some men that being in Korea was unfair to the Koreans, to themselves, and to their families who wanted them home.

Interrogations might last for hours, days, or even weeks. In some cases the interrogator lived with his subject and tried to create an atmosphere of warmth and friendliness. The main point seemed to be to get the prisoner talking, no matter what he was talking about. The discussions sometimes became effective didactic sessions because of the friendly relationship which the interrogator built up. If there were any weaknesses or inconsistencies in a man's belief systems, once he lowered his guard and began to examine them critically, he was in danger of being overwhelmed by the arguments of the instructor. This did not, of course, occur typically. For many men such critical self-evaluation served as a reinforcement to their own beliefs and actually enabled them to expose weaknesses in the Communist arguments.

Another effective technique for getting the men to question their own beliefs and values was to make them confess publicly to wrongdoings and to "criticize" themselves. Throughout the time that the men were in camp they were required to go through these rituals over and over again, no matter how trivial the offense. These offenses usually were infractions of camp rules. Soon after the men had arrived in permanent camp they were given copies of the camp rules and were required to sign a statement that they would abide by them. Most of the men were far too

hungry and cold to read several pages of script covering every aspect of camp life in such minute detail that it was practically impossible not to break one of the rules from time to time. For example, an elaborate set of rules governed where in camp a man was allowed to expectorate.

Sooner or later a minor or major infraction of the rules would occur. The man would be immediately brought up before the camp commander, where his offense would be condemned as a serious crime—one for which he, the commander would point out, could be severely punished, if it were not for the lenient Chinese policy. In line with the great show which the Chinese made of treating the prisoner as a responsible person, the fact that he had agreed in writing to abide by the rules would be emphasized. The prisoner could not now say that he had not read the rules, for this would expose him to further embarrassment. The camp commander would then ask whether the man would admit that he had broken the rule, whether he was sorry that he had done so, and whether he would promise not to behave in such a "criminal" manner in the future. If the offender agreed, which seemed at the time to be harmless enough and an easy way to get off, he would be asked to write out a confession.

Sometimes this ended the matter. But frequently the man was required to read his confession to a group of prisoners and to follow it by "self-criticism," which meant that the description of the wrong deed had to be analyzed in terms of the wrong *idea* that lay behind it, that the self had to be "deeply and sincerely" criticized in terms of a number of reasons why the idea and deed were "wrong," and that an elaborate set of promises about future conduct had to be made, along with apologies for the past. Such public self-effacement was a humiliating and degrading experience, and set a bad precedent for other men who had been attempting to resist getting caught in this net.

Writing out confessions, reading them, and criticizing oneself for minor misconduct in camp did not seem too great a concession at first when viewed against the possibility of physical punishment, torture, or imprisonment. However, these techniques could become a psychological torture once the initial concession had been made. A man who had broken a rule and had gone through the whole ritual of criticism would shortly afterward break another rule, which would arouse increased hostility on the part of the Chinese and lead to correspondingly greater demands for confession and self-criticism. Men who had confessed at first to trivial offenses soon found themselves having to answer for relatively major ones.[9]

It should be pointed out, however, that the prisoners found numerous ways to obey the letter but not the spirit of the Chinese demands. For example, during public self-criticism sessions they would often emphasize the wrong words in the sentence, thus making the whole ritual ridiculous: "I am sorry I called Comrade Wong *a no-good son-of-a-bitch.*" Another favorite device was to promise never to "get caught" committing a certain crime in the future. Such devices were effective because even those Chinese who knew English were not sufficiently acquainted with idiom and slang to detect subtle ridicule.

There is also some evidence that the Chinese used enforced idleness or solitary confinement to encourage prisoners to consider the Communist point of view. One of the few activities available, in such circumstances, was to read Communist literature and books by Western authors who directly or indirectly attacked capitalism. The camp libraries were wholly made up of such literature. Those who

did not have the strength or inclination to go on physically taxing details found themselves with no alternative but to spend their time reading pro-Communist material. In addition, some read because they felt so emotionally isolated from other prisoners that they could enjoy only solitary activities.

The Eliciting of Collaboration by Rewards and Punishments. For a number of propaganda purposes the Chinese seemed to want certain men to cooperate in specific ways, without caring whether they accepted communism or not. These men did not seem to enjoy as much status as other pro's and were cast off by the Chinese as soon as they had ceased to be useful. Such collaboration was elicited directly by a system of rewards and incentives on the one hand, and threats and punishments on the other. It was made clear to all prisoners, from the time of their capture on that cooperation with the Chinese would produce a more comfortable state of affairs, while noncooperation or open resistance would produce a continuing marginal existence. Which rewards were of primary importance to the men varied with their current condition. On the marches and in the temporary camps physical conditions were so bad that more food, any medication, any clothing or fuel, better and less crowded living conditions, and the like constituted a powerful reward. Promises of early repatriation, or at least of marked improvement of conditions in the permanent camps, were powerful incentives which were chronically exploited.

In the permanent camps there was some improvement in the physical conditions, so that basic necessities became less effective incentives. The promise of early repatriation continued to be a great

---

[9] It can be seen that such a technique of "training" a man to confess can ultimately lead to the demand that he confess not only to misdeeds and the "wrong" ideas which lay behind them, but also to "wrong" thoughts and feelings which had not even resulted in action. In conjunction with public self-appraisal, prisoners were also often encouraged to keep diaries of their activities and thoughts. Usually only those prisoners who seriously studied communism kept diaries.

incentive, however, despite the fact that it had been promised many times before without result. Communicating with the outside world now became a major concern. To let those at home know they were alive, some prisoners began to collaborate by making slanted radio broadcasts or filling their letters with propaganda or peace appeals in order to make sure that they were sent.

As conditions continued to improve, some of the luxury items and smaller accessories to living assumed greater significance. Cigarettes, combs, soap, candy, small items of clothing, a cup of hot tea, a drink of liquor, fresh fruit, and other items of this kind were sought avidly by some men.[10] Obtaining such items from the Chinese was inextricably linked with the degree to which the prisoner was willing to "cooperate." Any tendency toward "cooperation" was quickly followed by an increase in material rewards and promises for the future.

In some cases rewards were cleverly linked with participation in the indoctrination. For example, highly valued prizes such as cigarettes or fresh fruit were offered for essays dealing with certain aspects of world politics. The winning entries were published in the camp newspaper or magazine. Usually the winning entry was selected on the basis of its agreement with a Communist point of view, and the winner was usually someone well on the road to collaboration anyway, but the whole competition succeeded in getting the men to participate —to consider the various sides of an issue and to examine their previous views critically.

The Chinese also used rewards and punishments to undermine group organization. For example, shortly after capture, a number of men were led to believe that if they made radio broadcasts to the United Nations lines they would be repatriated early. The content of the broadcasts was not specified, but the men agreed to make them in the hope of letting their relatives know that they were alive. These men were then conspicuously assembled in front of other prisoners and were taken to a special location some distance away, where the broadcasts were to be made. In the meantime, other prisoners were encouraged to believe that these men were obtaining special privileges because they were "cooperating" in bringing "peace" to Korea.

The actual content of the radio messages turned out to be a peace appeal which tacitly condemned the United Nations, and a statement that the prisoners were being well treated by the Chinese. When the men saw the messages that they were to read, some of them refused to make the broadcast, despite threats of severe punishment. Other men agreed to make the broadcast but tried to code a message into the prescribed text, and still others hoped that the recipients of the broadcasts would somehow know that they were under duress. At least their families would know that they were alive if they broadcasted something.

When these men rejoined the other prisoners, they found that they had aroused the suspicion and hostility of many, especially since the Chinese showed their "appreciation" by ostentatiously bestowing favors on them. In order to retain these special privileges— and having in any case incurred the hostility or even ostracism of their own group—some of these men continued to collaborate, rationalizing that they were not really harming the United Nations cause. They became self-appointed secret agents and attempted to infiltrate the

---

[10] A number of men reported that black-market activities flourished among the prisoners. Those items of value which men did not wish to use themselves were bartered or sold to other men. Even valuable medicines could sometimes be obtained only by bartering with pro's who had obtained them from the Chinese.

Chinese hierarchy to gather "intelligence information," in which capacity they felt that they could actually aid the United Nations cause.

Among the most effective rewards used by the Chinese were special privileges and certain symbolic rewards, such as rank and status in the prison hierarchy. Perhaps the most important of the privileges was freedom of movement; the pro's had free access to the Chinese headquarters and could go into town or wherever they wished at any time of the day or night. They were given certain preferred jobs, such as writing for the camp newspaper, and were excused from the more unpleasant chores around the camp. They were often consulted by the Chinese in various policy matters. They received as a status symbol a little peace dove to be worn in the lapel or a Mao Tse-tung button which served as an identification badge. And many rewards were promised them for the future; they were told that they were playing a vital role in the world-wide movement for "peace," and that they could enjoy positions of high rank in this movement if they stayed and continued to work for it.

If one asks why men "fell" for this kind of line—why they were able to believe this kind of promise—one must look to the circumstances described earlier. These men had no sources of contrary information to rely on, and once they had collaborated even a little they were ostracized by their buddies, thus losing the support of the group which might have kept them from collaborating further.

Just as the probability of collaborative behavior could be increased through the use of rewards, the probability of resistance could be decreased through negative or painful stimulation. Usually threats of punishment were used when prisoners refused to "cooperate," and actual punishment was meted out for more aggressive resistance. Threats of death, nonrepatriation, torture, reprisals against families, reduction in food and medication, and imprisonment were all used. While the only one of these threats which was carried out with any degree of consistency was imprisonment, which sometimes involved long periods of solitary confinement, the other threats were nevertheless very effective and the possibility that they might be carried out seemed very real. Especially frightening was the prospect of nonrepatriation, which seemed a likely possibility before the prisoner lists were exchanged at Panmunjom. The threat of death was also effective, for the men knew that they could be killed and listed officially as having died of heart failure or the like.[11] With regard to food and medication, the men could not determine whether they were actually being punished by having these withheld, or whether the meager supply was merely being reserved for "deserving" prisoners.

An effective threat with officers was that of punishing the whole group for which the officer was responsible if he personally did not "cooperate." The incidence of such group punishment was not revealed in the accounts, but it is clear that if an officer did "cooperate" with the Chinese, he was able both to relieve his own fears and to rationalize his cooperation as being the only means of saving the men for whom he was responsible.

Reinforcing all these threats was the vague but powerful fear of the unknown; the men did not know what they were up

---

[11] There is evidence that the Chinese sometimes staged "executions" in order to elicit cooperation. A prisoner might be marched out into a field, an empty gun placed to his head, and the trigger actually pulled. This procedure first created a state of high anxiety and then a state of grateful relief when it was discovered by the prisoner that he would not be executed after all.

against in dealing with the Chinese and could not predict the reactions of their captors with any degree of reliability. The only course that led to a consistent reduction in such tension was participation in Chinese enterprises.

Overt punishment varied with the offense, with the political situation, and with the person administering it. Shortly after capture there were numerous incidents of brutality, most of them committed by North Koreans. During early interrogations the Chinese frequently resorted to minor physical punishment such as face-slapping or kicking when answers were not forthcoming, but a prisoner who continued to be silent was usually dismissed without further physical punishment.

Physical punishments in permanent camps had the effect of weakening rather than injuring the men. They varied from severe work details to such ordeals as standing at attention for long periods; being exposed to bright lights or excessive cold; standing on tiptoe with a noose around the neck; being confined in the "cage," a room too small to allow standing, sitting, or lying down, being thrown in the "hole," a particularly uncomfortable form of solitary confinement; or being kept in filthy surroundings and denied certain essentials for keeping clean. Those who were *chronically* uncooperative were permanently segregated from the rest of the group and put into special camps where more severe forms of discipline backed by harsher punishments were in effect. Basically, the "lenient policy" applied only to those men whom the Chinese hoped they could use.

More common forms of punishment for minor infractions were social in character, intended to degrade or embarrass the prisoner in front of his fellows. Public confessions and self-criticisms were the outstanding forms of such punishment, with blackmail being frequently used if a prisoner had once collaborated

to any extent. There is *no* evidence that the Chinese used any drugs or hypnotic methods, or offered sexual objects to elicit information, confessions, or collaborative behavior. Some cases of severe physical torture were reported, but their incidence is difficult to estimate.

General Principles in All Techniques. Several general principles underlay the various phases of the Chinese indoctrination, which may be worth summing up at this point. The first of these was *repetition*. One of the chief characteristics of the Chinese was their immense patience in whatever they were doing; whether they were conducting an interrogation, giving a lecture, chiding a prisoner, or trying to obtain a confession, they were always willing to make their demand or assertion over and over again. Many men pointed out that most of the techniques used gained their effectiveness by being used in this repetitive way until the prisoner could no longer sustain his resistance. A second characteristic was the *pacing of demands*. In the various kinds of responses that were demanded of the prisoners, the Chinese always started with trivial, innocuous ones and, as the habit of responding became established, gradually worked up to more important ones. Thus after a prisoner had once been "trained" to speak or write out trivia, statements on more important issues were demanded of him. This was particularly effective in eliciting confessions, self-criticism, and information during interrogation.

Closely connected with the principle of pacing was the principle of constant *participation* from the prisoner. It was never enough for the prisoner to listen and absorb; some kind of verbal or written response was always demanded. Thus, if a man would not give original material in question-and-answer sessions, he was asked to copy something. Likewise, group discussions, autobiographical statements, self-criticisms, and public confessions all demanded as active participation by the prisoner.[12]

In their propaganda campaign the Chinese made a considerable effort *to insert their new ideas into old and meaningful contexts.* In general this was not very successful, but it did work for certain prisoners who were in some way not content with their lot in the United States. The obtaining of autobiographies enabled each interrogator to determine what would be a significant context for the particular person he was dealing with, and any misfortune or setback that the person had suffered served as an ideal starting place for undermining democratic attitudes and instilling communistic ones.

No matter which technique the Chinese were using, they always structured the situation in such a way that the correct response was followed by some form of *reward*, while an incorrect response was immediately followed by *threats* or *punishment.* The fact that the Chinese had complete control over material resources and had a monopoly of power made it possible for them to manipulate hunger and some other motives at will, thereby giving rewards and punishments their meaning.

Among the various propaganda techniques employed by the Chinese, their use of *prestige suggestion* was outstanding. The average prisoner had no way of disputing the germ-warfare confessions and testimonials of Air Force officers, or the conclusions of an investigation of the germ-warfare charges by ostensibly impartial scientists from many nations.

Among the positive propaganda appeals made, the most effective was probably the *plea for peace.* The Chinese presented an antiwar and laissez-faire ideology which strongly appealed to the war-weary combat soldier.

In addition, the Chinese used a number of *manipulative tricks*, which were usually successful only if the prisoner was not alert because of fatigue or hunger. One such trick was to require signatures, photographs, or personal information for a purpose which sounded legitimate, then using them for another purpose. Some prisoners reported that they were asked to sign "camp rosters" when they first arrived in camp and later found that they had actually signed a peace petition.

In essence, the prisoner-of-war experience in camp can be viewed as a series of problems which each man had to solve in order to remain alive and well integrated. Foremost was the problem of physical privation, which powerfully motivated each man to improve his living conditions. A second problem was to overcome the fears of nonrepatriation, death, torture, or reprisals. A third problem was to maintain some kind of cognitive integration, a consistent outlook on life, under a set of conditions where basic values and beliefs were strongly undermined and where systematic confusion about each man's role in life was created. A fourth problem was to maintain a valid position in a group, to maintain friendship ties and concern for others under conditions of mutual distrust, lack of leadership, and systematically created social disorganization. The Chinese had created a set of conditions in which collaboration and the acceptance of communism led to a resolution of conflicts in all these areas.

---

[12] The Chinese apparently believed that if they could once get a man to participate, he was likely to continue and that eventually he would accept the attitudes which the participation expressed. However, it may have also been true that the interrogators, for instance, were in danger of losing face with their own group if they could not produce concrete evidence that they had obtained some information; at times they seemed to want any kind of answers, so long as they had something to show in headquarters as proof that they had done their job. Similarly, the material obtained at the end of the group discussions was perhaps used as evidence that the instructors were doing their jobs properly. Thus, it is possible that part of the aim was a check by the Chinese on each other.

REACTIONS TO THE INDOCTRINATION

In discussing the reactions of the POW's to these pressures it is necessary to distinguish between collaboration and ideological change, for neither of these necessarily implies the other. *Collaboration* may be considered as any kind of behavior which helped the enemy: signing peace petitions, soliciting signatures for peace petitions, making radio appeals, writing radio scripts, writing false information home concerning conditions in the camps (or recording statements to this effect), writing essays on communism or working for the Communist-controlled newspaper, allowing oneself to be photographed in "rigged" situations, participating in peace rallies or on peace committees, being friendly with the enemy, asking others to cooperate with the enemy, running errands for the enemy, accepting special privileges or favors, making false confessions or pro-enemy speeches, informing on fellow prisoners, divulging military information, and so on.

Nothing about ideological conversion is implied in this definition. A man who engaged in any of these collaborative behaviors because he wanted an extra cigarette was just as much a collaborator as one who did so because he wanted to further the Communist cause. Moreover, the definition does not take into account the temporal pattern of such behavior. Many men collaborated at one time during their imprisonment when one set of conditions existed but did not collaborate at other times under other conditions. The man who moved from collaboration to resistance was obviously different from the man who moved from resistance to collaboration. Perhaps most important of all, this definition says nothing about the particular pattern of motivations or circumstances that drove a man to the first collaborative act and subsequently into a situation in which it was difficult to stop collaborating.

Ideological change may be defined as a reorganization of political beliefs, which could vary from acquiring mild doubts concerning some aspects of the democratic ideology to the complete abandonment of this ideology and a total embracing of communism. The latter I shall label *conversion*. The problem of measuring the *degree* of ideological change is complicated by the lack of good behavioral criteria. One might be tempted to say that anyone could be termed a convert who actively attempted to convince others of the worth of communism, who took all the advanced courses in camp, and who was able to demonstrate in his overt behavior a disregard for democratic values. But such behavior might also characterize a relatively intelligent man who had begun to read Communist literature out of boredom, only to find that both his friends and the Chinese took this as evidence of his genuine interest in communism. He might then be ostracized by his friends and pressed into collaboration by the Chinese, who, it was rumored, severely punished anyone who deceived them.

Of all the prisoners, 21 refused repatriation; one might assume that these represent the total number of converts, but such a criterion is inadequate on at least two grounds. On the one hand, some converts would undoubtedly have been sent back to the United States to spread communism and form a potential fifth column. On the other hand, some collaborators who had not changed ideologically might have been afraid to return, knowing that court-martial proceedings and personal degradation probably awaited them.

Thus, it is more difficult to determine how the prisoners responded to indoctrination techniques ideologically than it is to determine what overt collaboration occurred. What the prisoners *did* is, relatively speaking, a matter of fact; why they did it is a matter of conjecture. In presenting a classification of types of reactions and the motivation patterns or situations that elicited them, one must rely primarily on the *consensus* of the accounts of the repatriates and must recognize the possible biases that can arise in such an analysis after the fact. I am not implying that each prisoner could be placed into one of the categories to be presented below; it is more likely that each man fell into several categories at any given time, and, moreover, that his motivation-situation complex shifted as different sets of circumstances presented themselves.

The "Get-alongers." The predominant reaction of prisoners was to establish a complex compromise between the demands of the Chinese and the demands of their own ideology. This kind of behavior was labeled "playing it cool" by the men and consisted primarily in a physical and emotional withdrawal from all situations which might arouse basic conflict. Men who reacted in this way were unwilling to do anything that did not have to be done and learned after some months to "suspend" their feelings about most events, no matter how provoking they might be. This was not an easy adjustment to maintain, since the prisoner had to make some concessions to the Chinese to avoid the more severe physical or psychological pressures, at the same time avoiding cooperating to such an extent as to arouse the suspicion and hostility of his fellow prisoners. The safest course was to withdraw emotionally both from the Chinese and from the rest of the prisoner group; this withdrawal was made easier by the apathy and physical weakness induced by life under marginal conditions.[13]

Most of the men who achieved this kind of compromise successfully without too great a toll on their personality were well integrated and retained secure and stable group identifications from before their prisoner-of-war experience. Their judgment concerning the extent to which they could collaborate safely had to be relatively unimpaired, and they had to be able to evaluate objectively and dispassionately threats made by the Chinese.

The Resisters. A number of men developed chronic resistance as their main mode of behavior in camp, refusing to go along with even the most trivial of Chinese requests. This lack of cooperation varied from passive resistance to active, organized obstructionism. Such men were a great trial to the Chinese, who labeled them "reactionaries" and either imprisoned them, if they felt they had some justification, or segregated them in special camps. According to the dynamics involved, these men seem to have fallen into four somewhat separate classes.

The obstructionist. These men were characterized by a life-long pattern of indiscriminate resistance to all forms of authority,[14] and had histories of inability to get along in the United Nations Army just as they were unable to get along with the Chinese. They openly defied any attempt to get them to conform, and performed deeds which other prisoners considered heroic, such as withstanding severe torture. Usually these men spent a major part of their internment in the camp prison, in solitary confinement, or in the "hole."

The idealist or martyr. These men had unusually powerful identifications with

---

[13] For Puerto Ricans and other foreign nationals whose knowledge of English was very shaky, the problem was easily solved. These men conveniently forgot what little English they knew, and because the Chinese did not have instructors who could speak their languages, they were permitted to withdraw to a relatively comfortable existence of doing details or routine chores. A few others successfully convinced the Chinese that they were illiterate or in some other way incapacitated for study. Some men resolved the conflict by volunteering for all the heavy or unpleasant details, but obviously such a solution was available only to the physically strong and healthy.

[14] This pattern has been well described by Lifton, *op. cit.*

groups whose ideology demanded that they actively resist all forms of pressure from the Chinese. The best example would be the man who was deeply religious and whose faith demanded absolute noncooperation with a "Godless enterprise" of the type the Chinese represented.

The anxious guilt-ridden person. This was the man who was afraid of his own inclination to be tempted by the positive rewards that the Chinese offered for collaboration and who could handle these impulses only by denying them and overreacting in the other direction. He was chronically guilt-ridden over his unpatriotic and antisocial impulses and absolved himself by indulging in exaggerated forms of resistance.

The well-integrated resistance leader. Probably the majority of resisters fell into this class, although there is no way to estimate their number. Because of extensive experience in difficult situations and a thorough understanding of the military, they were able systematically to organize other men and to set important precedents for resistance. The chief characteristic of these men seemed to be their ability to make valid judgments concerning possible courses of action in a situation in which there was little information on which to base such judgments. They had to be able to guess what Chinese reactions would be, what United Nations reactions would be, and most important, how to handle the other prisoners.

The Cooperators. This group is the most difficult to delineate, since I am attempting to include not only those whom the Chinese considered progressives but all those who collaborated to any significant extent. The accounts of prisoners concerning men who collaborated make possible the discrimination of six somewhat separate patterns of motivation for such behaviors.

The weakling. This was the man who was chronically unable to resist any form

of authority and who was unable to withstand any degree of physical or psychological discomfort. Such men probably became collaborators very soon after their internment, with a minimum of ideological involvement, because it was the easiest way. They often found that the more they collaborated, the more collaboration was demanded of them. They were highly susceptible to threats of blackmail by the Chinese, who could exhibit the evidence of their collaboration to the other prisoners or the United Nations authorities. From the point of view of these men, collaboration was an acceptable adjustment under the physical strains of internment, and they developed elaborate rationalizations to justify their behavior and to convince themselves that they would not suffer for it in the future.

The opportunist. These men exploited the role of pro for all its material benefits, again without any ideological involvement, and with little consideration for the future welfare of themselves or others. They were characterized chiefly by their lack of stable group identifications either inside or outside the Army. They met all situations as they arose and tried to make the most out of them for themselves.

The misguided leader. A minority of commissioned and noncommissioned officers engaged in various types of collaborative activities under the firm impression that they were furthering the United Nations cause and resisting the enemy. Their primary error was one of judgment. They reasoned that the best way to resist indoctrination was to go along with it, to find out what the Chinese were up to, to get into the inner circle so as to better plan resistance. In most cases, they managed merely to set a bad precedent for other prisoners, who felt that if their superiors were getting special privileges they should be getting them as well. These officers, like others, found that once they had begun to collaborate it was difficult to stop. Some of these men were probably weakling types who personally preferred the path of least resistance, but who, because of their responsible positions, had to develop adequate rationalizations. They could not see that their course of action was highly inappropriate; they saw only a justification which met their own needs.

The bored or curious intellectual. Of the very small number of men who had superior education, some turned to Communist literature out of boredom or curiosity, and then found that they had aroused both the hostility of their own group and the expectations of the Chinese that they would collaborate. Only a few managed to interest themselves in the Communist literature without falling into this dilemma. More often, material rewards for the intellectual's interest resulted in his ostracism from his own group and drove him in the direction of collaboration. Some of these men were fooled by the promise of early repatriation in return for collaboration, and they felt that their collaboration would be sufficiently minor not to damage their own futures. These men, like those previously described, seldom became ideologically confused or converted. Essentially they used bad judgment in an ambiguous situation.

The "low-status" person. The man who was most vulnerable *ideologically* was one who had never enjoyed any kind of secure or rewarding status position either in his home community or in the Army. This type included the younger and less intelligent, the malcontent, and the man whose social reference groups made the attainment of status difficult—that is, the member of various racial, religious, national, or economic minority groups. These men had little realization of the benefits of democracy because they had

never experienced them in a meaningful way. They felt that the society was more to blame for their failures than they were. Such men were ready to give serious consideration to an ideology that offered remedies for their misfortunes. As pro's within the Communist hierarchy they could, for the first time, enjoy some measure of status and privilege, and the Chinese wisely promised them important roles in the future of the "peace movement." Some of these men were probably among those who declined repatriation—perhaps out of fear, when they realized how seriously they had jeopardized their position in the Army and at home, perhaps in order to stay with the cause which had for the first time allowed them to be important. It is difficult to determine whether such men underwent a complete ideological conversion, but there is no doubt that they gave serious consideration to the Communist cause, at least to the limit of their intellectual capacity.[15]

The accounts of the repatriates were unclear regarding the reactions of members of the various minority groups, especially the Negroes. The Communist technique of segregating the Negroes and giving them special indoctrination was probably a tactical error. Many Negroes felt that if they were going to be segregated, they might as well be segregated in the United States—that there was nothing new or better about communism in this respect. Moreover, the propaganda given them was too extreme; even the very low-status Negro knew that his circumstances in the United States were not as bad as the Communists painted them.

However, because of the low-status category of most of the Negroes, the positive appeals made to them must have

---

[15] The men who were most vulnerable to ideological appeals were not necessarily the ones the Chinese encouraged to become pro's. There is considerable evidence that the Chinese were quite selective in giving important jobs to prisoners and that they favored more mature and stable ones. Thus, the younger, less intelligent, and less stable person was exploited by the Chinese in the same manner as he had probably been exploited before. The Chinese made what use they could of such men and then rejected them when they ceased to be useful.

struck responsive chords in some. They had an opportunity to be leaders and to enjoy fully equal status if they became pro's, and they could rationalize that they would be able to improve the position of their race by participating in Communist peace movements which advocated equality. It is not possible to determine to what extent these positive appeals outweighed the deterrents, and thus to estimate the degree to which ideological change occurred among the Negroes. In any case, the Chinese probably could have persuaded more Negroes to collaborate and to embrace communism had they not made the fundamental errors of segregation and poor propaganda.

The Communist sympathizer. This was the man who, even before he had joined the Army, was sympathetic to the Communist cause and who, therefore, felt no conflict about his course of action in the prisoner-of-war camp. However, if there were loyal Communists in the camps, it is unlikely that the Chinese divulged their identity by calling them pro's, since they would be of far more use as undercover agents.

Attitudes toward Progressives. The reaction of most men toward the pro's was one of perplexity, fear, and hostility. They could not understand how anyone could "swallow the junk" the Chinese were presenting, yet they were afraid that they, too, might be swayed, for among the pro's were many men like themselves. If the pro was a "weak-minded guy" or a man who did not have the stamina to resist the physical pressures, other men felt some sympathy for him, but at the same time they resented the extra privileges that his weakness gained for him. If the pro was perceived to be an opportunist, he was hated and threatened with retaliation during internment or following repatriation. If the pro was a person who had status or rank, the men felt perplexed and afraid; they could not decide what they themselves should do, especially if such a pro tried to con

vince them that it was acceptable to collaborate.

The pro's were made conspicuous in camp by their identification symbols, by their special privileges—which they did not hesitate to flaunt—and by the fact that they usually congregated around camp headquarters. This made them ideal scapegoats and targets for hostility.

They were ostracized by the other prisoners who often refused even to carry on conversations with each other when a pro was present, forcing the pro's into interaction with each other. Thus they tended to form tightly knit groups, which continued even after the end of their internment. The men accused the pro's of informing, imputed to them many motives about which they themselves felt guilty, and attributed any punishment they suffered to some report by a pro. They threatened the pro's with physical violence, but were usually prevented by the Chinese from carrying out such threats. Later, on board ship, the men frequently said that they would now "get even," but the low rate of incidents suggests that no realistic plans underlay the threats. Perhaps most men felt too guilty about their own actual or fantasied collaboration to be comfortable about retaliating against those who had succumbed to the temptations.

The attitudes of the pro's varied with their motivations. Those who had been tricked or "seduced" into collaborating before they could fully realize the consequences remained aloof from other prisoners because they felt guilty and afraid. The opportunists or low-status prisoners felt their collaboration to be entirely justified by the prison-camp situation and viewed noncollaborators as "fools who don't know a good thing when they see it." They tried to persuade others to collaborate—in some cases because they sincerely believed part of the Chinese propaganda and in other cases because they knew that the Chinese would reward them still further if they succeeded. Many pro's tried hard to remain liked both by the Chinese and by the other prisoners, but few succeeded. Since the Chinese presented themselves as benevolent captors, the pro's were the only group in camp who could consistently be used as an outlet for all the hostility engendered by the prison-camp situation.

THE EFFECTIVENESS OF THE INDOCTRINATION TECHNIQUES

By disrupting social organization and by the systematic use of reward and punishment, the Chinese were able to elicit a considerable amount of collaboration. This is not surprising when one considers the tremendous effort the Chinese made to discover the weak points in individual prisoners and the unscrupulousness with which they manipulated the environment. Only a few men were able to avoid collaboration altogether— those who adopted a completely negativistic position from the moment of capture without considering the consequences for themselves or their fellow prisoners. At the same time the number of men who collaborated to a sufficient extent to be detrimental to the United Nations cause was also very small. The majority collaborated at one time or another by doing things which seemed to them trivial, but which the Chinese were able to turn to their own advantage. Such behavior did not necessarily reflect any defection from democratic values or ideology nor did it necessarily imply that these men were opportunists or neurotics. Often it merely represented poor judgment in evaluating a situation about which they had little information and poor foresight regarding the reactions of the Chinese, other prisoners, and people back home.

The extent to which the Chinese succeeded in converting prisoners of war to the Communist ideology is difficult to evaluate because of the previously mentioned hazards in measuring ideological change and because of the impossibility of determining the *latent* effects of the indoctrination. In terms of *overt* criteria of conversion or ideological change, one can only conclude that, considering the effort devoted to it, the Chinese program was a failure. Only a small number of men decided to refuse repatriation—possibly for reasons other than ideological change [16]—and it was the almost unanimous opinion of the prisoners that most of the pro's were opportunists or weaklings. One can only conjecture, of course, the extent to which prisoners who began to believe in communism managed to conceal their sympathies from their fellows and the degree to which repatriates are now, as a result of their experience, predisposed to find fault with a democratic society if they cannot make a go of it.

It is difficult to determine whether to attribute this relative failure of the Chinese program to the inadequacy of their principles of indoctrination, to their technical inefficiency in running the program, or to both these factors. In actual practice the direct techniques used were usually ineffective because many of the Chinese instructors were deficient in their knowledge of Western culture and the English language. Many of their facts about America were false, making it impossible for them to obtain a sympathetic audience, and many of their attempts to teach by means of group discussion failed because they were not sensitive to the subtle ways in which prisoners managed to ridicule them by sarcasm or other language devices. The various intensive

[16] A discussion of some background factors in the lives of these men is presented by Virginia Pasley in *21 Stayed* (New York: Farrar, Strauss & Cudahy, Inc., 1955). Unfortunately her study is inconclusive because she did not investigate the background factors in a control group of men who decided to be repatriated.

pressures brought to bear on single prisoners and the fostering of close personal relationships between prisoner and instructor were far more effective in producing ideological change, but the Chinese did not have nearly enough trained personnel to indoctrinate more than a handful of men in this intensive manner.

The technique of breaking up both formal and spontaneous organization was effective in creating feelings of social and emotional isolation, but it was never sufficiently extended to make the prisoners completely dependent on the Chinese. As long as the men lived and "studied" together, there remained opportunities for consensual validation and thus for resisting indoctrination. However, as a means of social control this technique was highly effective, in that it was virtually impossible for the prisoners to develop any program of organized resistance or to engineer successful communication with the outside by means of escapes or clandestine sending out of information.

The most powerful argument against the intellectual appeal of communism was the low standard of living which the men observed in the Korean villages in which they lived. The repatriates reported that they were unable to believe in a system of values which sounded attractive on paper but which was not practiced, and they were not impressed by the excuse that such conditions were only temporary.

Most men returned from prison camp expressing strong anti-Communist feelings.

In summary, it can be said that the Chinese were successful in eliciting and controlling certain kinds of behavior in the prisoner population. They were less successful in changing the beliefs of the prisoners. Yet this lack of success might have been due to the inefficiency of a program of indoctrination which could have been highly effective had it been better supported by adequate information and adequately trained personnel.

Collaboration with the enemy occurs to a greater or lesser extent in any captive population. It occurred in the Japanese and German prisoner-of-war camps during World War II. But never before have captured American soldiers faced a *systematic effort* to make them collaborate and to convert them to an alien political ideology. The only precedent in recent history was the handling of political prisoners by the Nazis, described by Bettelheim.[17] By means of extreme and degrading physical and psychological torture the Nazis attempted to reduce the prison population to an "infantile" state in which the jailer would be viewed with the same awe as the child views his father. Under these conditions, the prisoners tended, in time, to identify with the punitive authority figures and to incorporate many of the values they held, especially with respect to proper behavior in camp. They would curry the favor of the guards, would imitate their style of dress and speech, and would attempt to make other prisoners follow camp rules strictly.

It is possible that such a mechanism also operated in the Chinese prison camps. However, the Nazis attempted, by brutal measures, to reduce their prisoners to docile slave laborers, while the Chinese attempted, by using a "lenient policy" and by treating the prisoners as men in need of "education," to obtain converts who would actively support the Communist point of view. Only those prisoners who showed themselves to be "backward" or "reactionary" by their inability to see the fundamental "truths" of communism were treated punitively.

The essence of this novel approach is to gain complete control over those parts of the physical and social environment which sustain attitudes, beliefs, and values, breaking down interactions and emotional bonds which support the old

---

[17] Bruno Bettelheim, see preceding article.

beliefs and values, and building up new interactions which will increase the probability of the adoption of new beliefs and values. If the only contacts a person is permitted are with persons who *unanimously* have beliefs different from his own, it is very likely that he will find at least some among them with whom, because of growing emotional bonds, he will identify and whose beliefs he will subsequently adopt.

Is the eliciting of collaborative behavior in itself sufficient to initiate the process of ideological change? One might assume that a person who had committed acts consonant with a new ideology might be forced to adopt this ideology in order to rationalize his behavior. This might happen especially if the number of possible rationalizations were limited. The situation in the prison camps, however, allowed the men to develop rationalizations which did not necessarily involve Communist premises. Furthermore, it is likely that whatever rationalizations are adopted, they will not acquire the permanence of beliefs unless supported by social reinforcements. When the prisoners re-entered the democratic setting, most of them gave up whatever Communist premises they might have been using to rationalize their collaboration and found new rationalizations that attempted to explain, from the standpoint of democratic premises, why they had collaborated. Apart from the technical difficulties the Chinese experienced in running their indoctrination program, they were never able to control social interactions to a sufficient extent to reinforce in meaningful social relationships the Communist rationalizations for collaboration.

Taken singly, there is nothing new or terrifying about the specific techniques used by the Chinese; they invented no mysterious devices for dealing with people. Their method of controlling information by controlling the mass media of communication has been a well-known technique of totalitarian governments throughout history. Their system of propagandizing by means of lectures, movies, reading materials, and testimonials has its counterparts in education and in advertising. Group discussions and other methods requiring participation have their counterparts in education and in psychiatry. The possibility that group discussion may be fundamentally superior to lectures in obtaining stable decisions by participants has been the subject of extensive research in American social psychology. The Chinese methods of interrogation have been widely used in other armies, by the police, by newspaper reporters, and by others interested in aggressively eliciting information. Forced confessions and self-criticism have been widely used techniques in religious movements as a basis for conversion or as a device to perpetuate a given faith. The control of behavior by the manipulation of reward and punishment is obviously the least novel of all the techniques, for men have controlled each other in this way since the beginning of history.

Thus, the only novelty in the Chinese methods was the attempt *to use a combination of all these techniques and to apply them simultaneously* in order to gain complete control over significant portions of the physical and social environment of a group of people.

8

The Socialization of the Child

THE MAMMAL AND HIS ENVIRONMENT
By D. O. Hebb

The original intention in this paper was to discuss the significance of neurophysiological theory for psychiatry and psychology and to show, by citing the work done by some of my colleagues, that the attempt to get at the neural mechanisms of behavior can stimulate and clarify purely behavioral—that is, psychiatric and psychological—thinking. The research to be described has, I think, a clear relevance to clinical problems; but its origin lay in efforts to learn how the functioning of individual neurons and synapses relates to the functions of the whole brain and to understand the physiological nature of learning, emotion, thinking, or intelligence.

In the end, however, my paper has simply become a review of the research referred to, dealing with the relation of the mammal to his environment. The question concerns the normal variability of the sensory environment and this has been studied from two points of view. First, one may ask what the significance of perceptual activity is during growth; for this purpose one can rear an animal with a considerable degree of restriction, and see what effects there are upon mental development. Secondly, in normal animals whose development is complete, one can remove a good deal of the supporting action of the normal environment, to discover how far the animal continues to be dependent on it even after maturity.

THE ROLE OF THE ENVIRONMENT DURING GROWTH

The immediate background of our present research on the intelligence and personality of the dog is the work of Hymovitch [1] on the intelligence of rats. He reared laboratory rats in two ways: (1) in a psychologically restricted environment, a small cage, with food and water always at hand and plenty of opportunity for exercise (in an activity wheel) but with no problems to solve, no need of getting on with others, no pain; and (2) in a "free" environment, a large box with obstacles to pass, blind alleys to avoid, other rats to get on with, and thus ample opportunity for problem-solving and great need for learning during growth. Result: the rats brought up in a psychologically restricted (but biologically adequate) environment have a lasting inferiority in problem-solving. This does not

From the *American Journal of Psychiatry*, 1955, CXI, 826–831. Reprinted by permission of the author and the publisher.

[1] B. Hymovitch, in *J. Comp. Physiol. Psychol.*, 1952, XLV, 313.

mean, of course, that environment is everything, heredity nothing: here heredity was held constant, which prevents it from affecting the results. When the reverse experiment is done, we find problem-solving varying with heredity instead. The *same* capacity for problem-solving is fully dependent on both variables for its development.

To take this further, Thompson and others have been applying similar methods to dogs.[2] The same intellectual effect of an impoverished environment is found again, perhaps more marked in the higher species. But another kind of effect can be seen in dogs, which have clearly marked personalities. Personality—by which I mean complex individual differences of emotion and motivation—is again strongly affected by the infant environment. These effects, however, are hard to analyze and I cannot at present give any rounded picture of them.

First, observations during the rearing itself are significant. A Scottish terrier is reared in a small cage, in isolation from other Scotties and from the human staff. Our animal man, William Ponman, is a dog lover and undertook the experiment with misgivings, which quickly disappeared. In a cage 30 by 30 inches, the dogs are "happy as larks," eat more than normally reared dogs, grow well, are physically vigorous: as Ponman says, "I never saw such healthy dogs—they're like bulls." If you put a normally-reared dog into such a cage, shut off from everything, his misery is unmistakable, and we have not been able to bring ourselves to continue such experiments. Not so the dog that has known nothing else. Ponman showed some of these at a dog show of national standing, winning first-prize ribbons with them.

Observations by Dr. Ronald Melzack on pain are extremely interesting. He reared two dogs, after early weaning, in complete isolation, taking care that there was little opportunity for experience of pain (unless the dog bit himself). At maturity, when the dogs were first taken out for study, they were extraordinarily excited, with random, rapid movement. As a result they got their tails or paws stepped on repeatedly—but paid no attention to an event that would elicit howls from a normally reared dog. After a few days, when their movements were calmer, they were tested with an object that gave electric shock and paid little attention to it. Through five testing periods, the dog repeatedly thrust his nose into a lighted match and, months later, did the same thing several times with a lighted cigar.

A year and a half after coming out of restriction they are still hyperactive. Clipping and trimming one of them is a two-man job; if the normal dog does not stand still, a cuff on the ear will remind him of his duty; but cuffing the experimental dog "has as much effect as if you patted him—except he pays no attention to it." It seems certain, especially in view of the related results reported by Nissen, Chow, and Semmes [3] for a chimpanzee, that the adult's perception of pain is essentially a function of pain experience during growth—and that what we call pain is not a single sensory quale but a complex mixture of a particular kind of synthesis with past learning and emotional disturbance.

Nothing bores the dogs reared in restriction. At an "open house," we put two restricted dogs in one enclosure, two normal ones in another, and asked the public to tell us which were the normal. Without exception, they picked out the two alert, lively, interested animals— not the lackadaisical pair lying in the corner, paying no attention to the visitors. The alert pair, actually, were the restricted; the normal dogs had seen all

[2] W. R. Thompson and W. Heron, *Canad. J. Psychol.*, 1954, VIII, 17, 1954.
[3] H. W. Nissen, R. L. Chow, and Josephine Semmes, *Am. J. Psychol.*, 1951, LXIV, 485.

they wanted to see of the crowd in the first two minutes and then went to sleep, thoroughly bored. The restricted dogs, so to speak, do not have the brains to be bored.

Emotionally, the dogs are "immature," but not in the human or clinical sense. They are little bothered by imaginative fears. Dogs suffer from irrational fears, like horses, porpoises, elephants, chimpanzees, and man; but it appears that this is a product of intellectual development characteristic of the brighter, not the duller, animal. Our dogs in restriction are not smart enough to fear strange objects. Things that cause fear in normal dogs produce only a generalized, undirected excitement in the restricted. If both normal and restricted dogs are exposed to the same noninjurious but exciting stimulus repeatedly, fear gradually develops in the restricted; but the normals, at first afraid, have by this time gone on to show a playful aggression instead. On the street, the restricted dogs "lead well," not bothered by what goes on around them, while those reared normally vary greatly in this respect. Analysis has a long way to go in these cases, but we can say now that dogs reared in isolation are not like ordinary dogs. They are both stupid and peculiar.

Such results clearly support the clinical evidence, and the animal experiments of others,[4] showing that early environment has a lasting effect on the form of adjustment at maturity. We do not have a great body of evidence yet and before we generalize too much, it will be particularly important to repeat these observations with animals of different heredity. But I have been very surprised, personally, by the lack of evidence of emotional instability, neurotic tendency, or the like, when the dogs are suddenly plunged into a normal world. There is,

in fact, just the opposite effect. This suggests caution in interpreting data with human children, such as those of Spitz[5] or Bowlby.[6] Perceptual restriction in infancy certainly produces a low level of intelligence, but it may not, by itself, produce emotional disorder. The observed results seem to mean, not that the stimulus of another attentive organism (the mother) is necessary from the first, but that it may become necessary only as psychological *dependence* on the mother develops. However, our limited data certainly cannot prove anything for man, though they may suggest other interpretations besides those that have been made.

THE ENVIRONMENT AT MATURITY

Another approach to the relation between the mammal and his environment is possible: that is, one can take the normally reared mammal and cut him off at maturity from his usual contact with the world. It seems clear that thought and personality characteristics develop as a function of the environment. Once developed, are they independent of it? This experiment is too cruel to do with animals but not with college students. The first stage of the work was done by Bexton, Heron, and Scott.[7] It follows up some work by Mackworth on the effects of monotony, in which he found extraordinary lapses of attention. Heron and his co-workers set out to make the monotony more prolonged and more complete.

The subject is paid to do nothing 24 hours a day. He lies on a comfortable bed in a small closed cubicle, is fed on request, goes to the toilet on request. Otherwise he does nothing. He wears frosted glass goggles that admit light but do not allow pattern vision. His ears are covered by a sponge-rubber pillow in which are em-

[4] F. A. Beach and J. Jaynes, *Psychol. Bull.*, 1954, LI, 239.

[5] R. A. Spitz, "Hospitalization," in *Psychoanalytic Study of the Child*, 1946, II, 113.

[6] J. Bowlby, *Maternal Care and Mental Health* (Geneva: WHO Monogr. #2, 1951).

[7] W. H. Bexton, W. Heron, and T. H. Scott, *Canad. J. Psychol.*, 1954, VIII, 70.

bedded small speakers by which he can be communicated with, and a microphone hangs near to enable him to answer. His hands are covered with gloves and cardboard cuffs extend from the upper forearm beyond his fingertips, permitting free joint movement but with little tactual perception.

The results are dramatic. During the stay in the cubicle, the experimental subject shows extensive loss, statistically significant, in solving simple problems. He complains subjectively that he cannot concentrate; his boredom is such that he looks forward eagerly to the next problem, but when it is presented he finds himself unwilling to make the effort to solve it.

On emergence from the cubicle the subject is given the same kind of intelligence tests as before entering and shows significant loss. There is disturbance of motor control. Visual perception is changed in a way difficult to describe; it is as if the object looked at was exceptionally vivid, but impaired in its relation to other objects and the background —a disturbance perhaps of the larger organization of perception. This condition may last up to 12 or 24 hours.

Subjects reported some remarkable hallucinatory activity, some which resembled the effects of mescal or the results produced by Grey Walter with flickering light. These hallucinations were primarily visual, perhaps only because the experimenters were able to control visual perception most effectively; however, some auditory and somesthetic hallucinations have been observed as well.

The nature of these phenomena is best conveyed by quoting one subject who reported over the microphone that he had just been asleep and had a very vivid dream and although he was awake, the dream was continuing. The study of dreams has a long history and is clearly important theoretically, but is hampered by the impossibility of knowing how much the subject's report is distorted by memory. In many ways the hallucinatory activity of the present experiments is indistinguishable from what we know about dreams; if it is in essence the same process but going on while the subject can describe it (not merely hot but still on the griddle), we have a new source of information, a means of direct attack, on the nature of the dream.

In its early stages the activity as it occurs in the experiment is probably not dream-like. The course of development is fairly consistent. First, when the eyes are closed the visual field is light rather than dark. Next there are reports of dots of light, lines, or simple geometrical patterns, so vivid that they are described as being a new experience. Nearly all experimental subjects reported such activity. (Many, of course, could not tolerate the experimental conditions very long and left before the full course of development was seen.) The next stage is the occurrence of repetitive patterns, like a wallpaper design, reported by three-quarters of the subjects; next, the appearance of isolated objects, without background, seen by half the subjects; and finally, integrated scenes, involving action, usually containing dream-like distortions and apparently with all the vividness of an animated cartoon, seen by about a quarter of the subjects. In general, these amused the subject, relieving his boredom, as he watched to see what the movie program would produce next. The subjects reported that the scenes seemed to be out in front of them A few could, apparently, "look at" different parts of the scene in central vision, as one could with a movie, and up to a point could change its content by "trying." It was not, however, well under control. Usually, it would disappear if the subject were given an interesting task, but not when the subject described it nor if he did physical exercises. Its persistence and vividness interfered with sleep for some subjects and at this stage was irritating.

In their later stages the hallucinations were elaborated into everything from a peaceful rural scene to naked women diving and swimming in a woodland pool to prehistoric animals plunging through tropical forests. One man saw a pair of spectacles, which were then joined by a dozen more, without wearers, fixed intently on him; faces sometimes appeared behind the glasses, but with no eyes visible. The glasses sometimes moved in unison, as if marching in procession. Another man saw a field onto which a bathtub rolled: it moved slowly on rubber-tired wheels, with chrome hub caps. In it was seated an old man wearing a battle helmet. Another subject was highly entertained at seeing a row of squirrels marching single file across a snowy field, wearing snowshoes and carrying little bags over their shoulders.

Some of the scenes were in three dimensions, most in two (that is, as if projected on a screen). A most interesting feature was that some of the images were persistently tilted from the vertical and a few reports were given of inverted scenes, completely upside down.

There were a few reports of auditory phenomena—one subject heard the people in his hallucination talking. There was also some somesthetic imagery, as when one saw a doorknob before him, and as he touched it felt an electric shock; or when another saw a miniature rocket ship maneuvering around him and discharging pellets that he felt hitting his arm. But the most interesting of these phenomena the subject, apparently, lacked words to describe adequately. There were references to a feeling of "otherness," or bodily "strangeness." One said that his mind was like a ball of cotton wool floating in the air above him. Two independently reported that they perceived a second body, or second person, in the cubicle. One subject reported that he could not tell which of the two

bodies was his own and described the two bodies as overlapping in space—not like Siamese twins, but two complete bodies with an arm, shoulder, and side of each occupying the same space.

THEORETICAL SIGNIFICANCE

The theoretical interest of these results for us extends in two directions. On the one hand, they interlock with work using more physiological methods of brain stimulation and recording and, especially, much of the recent work on the relation of the brain stem to cortical "arousal." Points of correspondence between behavioral theory and knowledge of neural function are increasing, and each new point of correspondence provides both a corrective for theory and a stimulation for further research. A theory of thought and of consciousness in physiologically intelligible terms need no longer be completely fantastic.

On the other hand, the psychological data cast new light on the relation of man to his environment, including his social environment, and it is this that I should like to discuss a little further. To do so I must go back for a moment to some earlier experiments on chimpanzee emotion. They indicate that the higher mammal may be psychologically at the mercy of his environment to a much greater degree than we have been accustomed to think.

Studies in our laboratory of the role of the environment during infancy and a large body of work reviewed recently by Beach and Jaynes [8] make it clear that psychological development is fully dependent on stimulation from the environment. Without it, intelligence does not develop normally and the personality is grossly atypical. The experiment with college students shows that a short period—even a day or so—of deprivation of a normal sensory input produces

---

[8] Beach and Jaynes, *op. cit.*

personality changes and a clear loss of capacity to solve problems. Even at maturity, then, the organism is still essentially dependent on a normal sensory environment for the maintenance of its psychological integrity.

The following data show yet another way in which the organism appears psychologically vulnerable. It has long been known that the chimpanzee may be frightened by representations of animals, such as a small toy donkey. An accidental observation of my own extended this to include representations of the chimpanzee himself, of man, and of parts of the chimpanzee or human body. A model of a chimpanzee head, in clay, produced terror in the colony of the Yerkes Laboratories, as did a lifelike representation of a human head, and a number of related objects such as an actual chimpanzee head, preserved in formalin, or a colored representation of a human eye and eyebrow. A deeply anesthetized chimpanzee, "dead" as far as the others were concerned, aroused fear in some animals and vicious attacks by others.[9]

I shall not deal with this theoretically. What matters for our present purposes is the conclusion, rather well supported by the animal evidence, that the greater the development of intelligence the greater the vulnerability to emotional breakdown. The price of high intelligence is susceptibility to imaginative fears and unreasoning suspicion and other emotional weaknesses. The conclusion is not only supported by the animal data but also agrees with the course of development in children, growing intelligence being accompanied by increased frequency and strength of emotional problems—up to the age of five years.

Then, apparently, the trend is reversed. Adult man, more intelligent than chimpanzee or five-year-old child, seems not more subject to emotional disturbances but less. Does this then disprove the conclusion? It seemed a pity to abandon a principle that made sense of so many data that had not made sense before, and the kind of theory I was working with—neurophysiologically oriented—also pointed in the same direction. The question then was, is it possible that something is concealing the adult human being's emotional weaknesses?

From this point of view it became evident that the concealing agency is man's culture which acts as a protective cocoon. There are many indications that our emotional stability depends more on our successful avoidance of emotional provocation than on our essential characteristics: that urbanity depends on an urbane social and physical environment. Dr. Thompson and I [10] reviewed the evidence and came to the conclusion that the development of what is called "civilization" is the progressive elimination of sources of acute fear, disgust, and anger, and that civilized man may not be less, but more, susceptible to such disturbance because of his success in protecting himself from disturbing situations so much of the time.

We may fool ourselves thoroughly in this matter. We are surprised that children are afraid of the dark or afraid of being left alone and congratulate ourselves on having got over such weakness. Ask anyone you know whether he is afraid of the dark and he will either laugh at you or be insulted. This attitude is easy to maintain in a well-lighted, well-behaved suburb. But try being alone in complete darkness in the streets of a strange city or alone at night in the deep woods and see if you still feel the same way.

We read incredulously of the taboo rules of primitive societies; we laugh at

---

[9] D. O. Hebb, "On the Nature of Fear," *Psychol. Rev.*, 1946, LIII, 259.

[10] D. O. Hebb and W. R. Thompson, "The Social Significance of Animal Studies," in G. Lindzey (ed.), *Handbook of Social Psychology* (Cambridge, Mass.: Addison-Wesley Co., Inc., 1954).

the superstitious fear of the dead in primitive people. What is there about a dead body to produce disturbance? Sensible, educated people are not so affected. One can easily show that they are, however, and that we have developed an extraordinarily complete taboo system—not just moral prohibition, but full-fledged ambivalent taboo—to deal with the dead body. I took a poll of an undergraduate class of 198 persons, including some nurses and veterans, to see how many had encountered a dead body. Thirty-seven had never seen a dead body in any circumstances, and 91 had seen one only after an undertaker had prepared it for burial; making a total of 65 percent who had never seen a dead body in, so to speak, its natural state. It is quite clear that for some reason we protect society against sight of, contact with, the dead body. Why?

Again, the effect of moral education, and training in the rules of courtesy, and the compulsion to dress, talk and act as others do, adds up to ensuring that the individual member of society will not act in a way that is a provocation to others—will not, that is, be a source of strong emotional disturbance, except in highly ritualized circumstances approved by society. The social behavior of a group of civilized persons, then, makes up that protective cocoon which allows us to think of ourselves as being less emotional than the explosive four-year-old or the equally explosive chimpanzee.

The well-adjusted adult, therefore, is not intrinsically less subject to emotional disturbance: he is well-adjusted, relatively unemotional, as long as he is in his cocoon. The problem of moral education, from this point of view, is not simply to produce a stable individual but to produce an individual that will (1) be stable in the existing social environment and (2) contribute to its protective uniformity. We think of some persons as being emotionally dependent, others not; but it looks as though we are all completely dependent on the environment in a way and to a degree that we have not suspected.

ADOLESCENCE IN PRIMITIVE AND IN MODERN SOCIETY   *By Margaret Mead*

To many thinkers the *primitive* as opposed to the civilized or sophisticated means one who is close to nature, close to the raw materials of life. Such a *primitive* man is supposed to recognize the vital importance of life crises with a wealth of ceremonial. These points of significance to the individual are believed to be muffled by elaborate forms which enable the individual as a member of the social group to make terms with life and death. It is true that from the mass of recorded practice of primitive peoples it is possible to find many illustrations of such rituals. Yet some primitive peoples are as arbitrary as ourselves in the construction of patterns which ignore the more obvious facts of life and

Abridged by the author from "Adolescence in Primitive and Modern Society" in V. F. Calverton and S. D. Schmalhausen, eds., *The New Generation* (New York: Macauley, 1930). Reprinted by permission of the author and the Citadel Press.

death, and superimpose man-made definitions of the life cycle. So among the Todas of India, where one woman is taken to wife by a group of brothers, paternity is established by a ceremony, performed usually by the oldest brother. This ceremony determines the paternity of all subsequent children until a new aspirant to social fatherhood performs the same ceremony in his turn. Children are sometimes considered as the offspring of a man who has been dead ten years. A similar overlay of physical facts, which, though known, go socially unacknowledged, is found in many societies which practice infanticide. The child is not regarded as a member of the social group, simply because it is delivered from its mother's womb. Rather it must wait upon a social recognition of its existence; until that is given, to kill it is not murder. Among the Wotjobaluk tribe of southeast Australia a newborn child was often killed to give strength to an older sibling. The older child was a human being, a member of the group, the newborn baby, material of which alternative disposition might be made. At the other pole are the Manus who give an early miscarriage all the honors accorded an adult. The foetus is named, mourned, and an elaborate economic machinery is set in motion.

As with birth, so with death. In Fiji an old chief whose death has been determined upon is spoken of as dead. His wives and concubines are strangled in his presence and as he sits by, awaiting interment.

If social conventions can so distort the recognition of paternity, of birth, and of death, it is not surprising that the same distortion applies to the period of puberty. About puberty it is possible to center a number of cultural ideas: attitudes of fear and dread towards menstruation, education either social or individual, practices for the attainment of beauty and charm, magical preparation for life, or mere acceptance into the tribal life. Some societies stress one at the expense of all the others; some stress none. In general, it may be said that when the social emphasis lies upon the fact of menstruation itself rather than upon such derivative points as the girl's entry into tribal society or her marriage, the correspondence between first menses and ceremonial observance is closest. But although the observance of the girl's first menstruation was the principal tribal event among many California Indians, even here we find tribes, like the Luiseno, where the event had become socialized to such an extent that a whole group of girls were treated at once; only one of these was at the actual physiological period.

Whenever the emphasis shifts from menstruation to the more general point of maturity, correspondence between ceremonies and puberty becomes less or may vanish altogether. Among the Dobuans where the sex life of girls begins long before puberty, there is no initiation into tribal life and there is no cultural fear of menstruation. Among these people adolescence goes unremarked.

Among the peoples who do recognize puberty there is great diversity of emphases. Northern California tribal attitudes stressed particularly the danger which the girl could do to the community. Her glance could dry up a spring or banish the deer. But among the Yuki in North Central California, the whole focus of the ritual was to influence the food supply of the people for good. The word for adolescence contains an element meaning *to lie*. The quieter the girl lay, the better would the sun be pleased and the more plentiful would be the crops. The girl herself was important because of her potency for either good or evil. The society gathers up all its resources for its own sake rather than to tide a weak new member over a crisis.

In strong contrast to this formalization is a type also found in California but especially pronounced among the Thompson Indians of British Columbia. Here adolescence was regarded as a magical preparation for the girl's later life. The girl was separated from other people and lived by herself for four months in a special hut of fir branches and bark. During this time she practiced a series of acts of magical potency. She ran long races that she might be fleet of foot; she split fir trees that she might be strong of body. She dug trenches to shorten the duration of her monthly periods. She let pebbles fall from beneath her dress that she might bear children easily.

In these ceremonies the whole stress is upon the girl: she is at the threshold of her career, her observance of taboo and performance of symbolic acts will ensure her a happy and useful life.

Girls in the Gilbert Islands of the Western Pacific were also subjected to a long period of confinement, but the motivation was different. The actual arrival of puberty was an anxious time for parents for the Gilbertese believed that the girl was now especially sensitive to enemy magic. To protect her from this evil she was made to sit perfectly still facing the west, without moving more than was absolutely necessary, eating no cooked food. Afterwards she was usually confined to a special house called a *ko*, where she lived in an inner cubicle in a dense gloom. Here she lived sometimes for a year or eighteen months that her skin might be whitened and her beauty enhanced. She was attended by her grandmother, who massaged her skin and molded her breasts and arms. She lived in idleness, as it was too dark for handiwork. But her grandmother taught her all the spells that she knew.

These scattered examples are sufficient to show that physiological puberty, when it is recognized, may be recognized in many different ways.

In Samoa there are no important taboos relating to menstruation. Women are neither segregated, avoided, nor forbidden to prepare food. The girl at her first menstruation shares in this general lack of interest. The public eye is not upon her. Nor must she hide this new state from her friends: boys and girls can tell accurately the stage of physiological development of every girl in the village. As she has been familiar with all the facts of procreation since early childhood, no new revelations come at this time. She is not regarded as immediately marriageable, nor even as ready for an amorous career. The whole tradition of Samoa is against hurry, against forcing any aspect of life. So a Samoan girl is seen to have passed puberty, but no new way of life is thrust suddenly upon her. Some time in the next two or three years will come her formal entrance into the group of girls who surround the high chief's daughter. Here she associates with girls whom she has known intimately all her life and she will continue as a member of this loose, hardly defined group, until the husband whom she will marry presently, assumes a title, when she automatically becomes a titled man's wife. This will not happen until she is many years older, if at all. Meanwhile, two or three years after puberty her casual unimportant love life begins. Her favors are distributed among so many youths, all adepts in amorous technique, that she seldom becomes deeply involved. Pregnancy is rare: illegitimate children are greeted kindly if they do appear. Heavier industrial tasks are assumed when warranted by the girl's growth: this may precede or follow the attainment of puberty. Painlessly, quietly, she slips from childhood into womanhood, loitering by the way, doing her share of the family work, but guarding herself against a reputation for too great proficiency which might lead to early marriage.

Adolescence becomes not the most difficult, most stressful period of life, but perhaps the pleasantest time the Samoan girl will ever know. In the Samoan household of some fifteen or twenty individuals small girls have much work and little leisure. But the sixteen-year-old girl is near the center of pressure, with as many younger children to command as there are elders to command her. She is relieved of the duties of baby-tending and errand-running and instead performs definite longer tasks. By common consent the nights belong to the youth for dancing, courting and love making. So the young girl has freedom but slight responsibility, assurance that she will marry but no pressure to marry quickly.

The sea-dwelling people of the Admiralties put puberty in quite a different setting. Here the whole interest of the society is centered about the exchange of property. Children are often betrothed very young and from the time of the formal betrothal, they are regarded as married. The little girl is shrouded in a long mat whenever she goes abroad where she is likely to meet either her future husband or any of his male relatives. The line of demarcation between the growing girls in the village is not between those who have passed puberty and those who have not attained it, but between the betrothed and the unbetrothed. The occasional unbetrothed girl past puberty goes about freely with uncovered head and eyes which have no need to be alert against forbidden encounters. But the ten-year-old in whose name large numbers of cooking pots and grass skirts, pigs, sacks of sago and jars of oil have been given away, sits demurely veiled and speaks of "we married women." Engaged girls should not run about too much with younger children, should not play with boys, should stay at home and make bead work for their dowries.

The fact of physical puberty is fitted into this context. Every household must make some display when a girl child has her first menses; only if she is "married" is the burden onerous. When a father sees that his daughter is at the point of puberty he collects a large number of coconuts. The day that her menses

appear these are all thrown into the sea and the neighbors' children dive in and rescue them. The whole village now knows that the girl has attained puberty. A little room is made for her in the center of the house where she must sit for five days without washing. If she is engaged, pots of sago and coconut milk are delivered steaming to her future husband's family. His relatives bring fish. Every night most of the unmarried girls in the village over nine or ten years old go to sleep with the girl. At the end of five days large pieces of raw sago are prepared and torches are made of thin bamboo. All the girls gather in the house, to which comes the girl's paternal aunt or her paternal grandmother. The torches are heaped in the fireplace until the house is ablaze with light. Then the officiating older woman seizes a torch and chases the girl up and down the house. The chase ended, she pronounces an incantation over her, appealing to all the ancestral spirits of her father's line to bless her, give her strength, give her wealth to finance the marriages of many boys and many girls, and grant that she may become a substantially wealthy woman.

The incantation ended, the visiting girls carry the torches and lumps of sago out to a canoe and punt through the village shouting, to place a torch and a lump of sago on the veranda of every relative. The girl is now free to move about the house but she may not leave it except to bathe after dark. Her kin are busy working sago to make a big exchange with her betrothed's family. When all is in readiness, and all her relatives from afar have come over the sea to bring their contributions, the final ceremonies are held. Specially prepared sago balls are placed in shallow bowls in the family canoes. The female population repairs to a shallow part of the lagoon. The girl is ceremonially ducked and splashed by all the smaller girls, after which they swim about and pass the sago refreshments. The paternal aunt pours oil over the girl's head and again recites an incantation. The canoes then return to the girl's house where she is decked in strings of dogs' teeth and shell money. Her hair is dyed red; her cheeks are painted. Heavy earrings distend her ears. About her waist are fastened two heavy aprons of shell money. All her slender charm is blotted out as she is made into a peg upon which to hang property. The other girls are clothed in a part of this same finery, and they board a large canoe and solemnly parade through the village. A few days later canoes laden with oil and pigs and sago are rowed proudly through the village to the bridegroom's family. The procession passes an island where the skeletons of all the fish the girl has eaten during her confinement are thrown away with an invocation.

The ceremonies (many details of which I have omitted) are at an end. Her relations to her fellows are unchanged. The tasks prescribed for her — bringing wood and water, a little fishing, a little bead-work, lending an occasional hand with the sago making—these are unchanged also.

But the girl has made one discovery: namely, that a woman menstruates every month and that she must exercise the most unfailing vigilance in concealing her condition at such times.

For through the great antagonism and lack of confidence between the sexes in Manus, coupled with shame and extreme prudery in regard to all the natural functions of the body, women conceal from men the truth about menstruation. Everyone knows of first menstruation—it is heralded through the village—but no man knows, nor will believe if told by an outsider, that a girl menstruates between puberty and marriage. The menstruation of married women is attributed by men to intercourse; conception is the result of the combination of menstrual blood and semen. This conspiracy of silence is only half-conscious. Unmarried

girls presume that married men know the truth; married women are not very clear about the limits of their secret, but simply jealously guard all knowledge of menstruation and birth from all males, including their husbands.

The little girl who is the center of all this ceremonial is shy and solemn and behaves very much as she does when she has her ears pierced, that is, with an air of self-importance tempered by embarrassment. Older girls when questioned about their puberty ceremonials invariably stress two points: how many of their friends came to sleep with them every night and how much property was given away at the final feast.

So here we have elaborate puberty ceremonial involving taboo, confinement, magical incantations, ceremonial washing and anointing with oil, offerings and invocations to the family dead. Immense amounts of property are displayed and exchanged. The ceremony for one engaged adolescent girl may occupy the entire community for weeks. This is equally true of the big economic ceremonies surrounding betrothal, marriage, or birth. It is upon these ceremonious financial exchanges that the attention of actors and spectators is focussed.

But with all this stress and fuss and institutionalization of adolescence, it is of very little psychological importance to the girl herself. She does nothing to prepare herself for life; she is confronted with no dangers. She cannot seize this moment to realize her dreams of personal beauty. She is a pawn in an elaborate social scheme and is as much and as little interested as any pawn ever is. The real moments of crises and strain in her life are quite different. If she was engaged as a very small child, she is already set apart from her freer age mates and as she grows older sees one after another join her state. The growing up of the girls is marked by less and less fellowship between them. They have no happy secrets to share with one another. They are marrying boys they have never seen, whose very names they are not allowed to utter. The Manus language has no word for love, no word for affection or caress. The slightest bit of sex life outside legal marriage, except a little kin-determined joking, is punished by the spirits. The few young people who do become involved in a hasty, unromantic sex experiment, are reviled by their elders, shunned by their companions. Moonlight falls whitely on the village but there is no sound of singing on the water; the daughters of the house are safely within doors.

The adolescent years, sometimes the early years of womanhood, sometimes all the years of childhood, are spoiled by the omnipresent demands of society upon the engaged girl, demands enforced by that subtlest instrument of torture, shame. Whatever age the veil descends upon her is the beginning of psychological maturity which will not leave her until as the mother of children, the manager of financial transactions in the community, she becomes a person of importance and resumes her childhood freedom. Her married life is one of prudish respectability, and often outspoken hostility toward her husband.

It is noteworthy that the strain in a Manus girl's life is distributed with so little reference to puberty—and this in a society which gives puberty such thoroughgoing cultural recognition. The whole weighty ritual slips over the girl's head and leaves her far less moved than she is by the first occasion when she must go shrouded about the village where formerly she has run free as a boy. Nor is the period of adolescence that of greatest rebellion in Manus. This comes rather in the early years of marriage, especially when there have been no children or the children have all died.

So it is possible to leave puberty unstressed or to stress it; nor is the deciding factor whether or not the adolescent years will be the storm center in the girl's life. The pattern of social institutions alone is not sufficient to produce or eradicate conflict; it is rather in the far less tangible balancing of cultural forces that the seeds of conflict lie. In Samoa there is no conflict, because the adolescent girl is faced by neither revelation, restriction, nor choice, and because the society expects her to grow up slowly and quietly like a well-behaved flower. In Manus the insistence upon the shamefulness of sex, the repression of all freedom of action that the taboos of betrothal may be observed, the low standard of relations between the sexes, all serve to produce conflict irrespective of the period of adolescence or its elaborate ceremonial.

We have kept a large enough amount of Victorian prudery so that menstruation seems salacious to men and shameful to girls. We still have many girls who do not know of menstruation until they attain puberty. Our attitude remains such that we could not seize upon first menstruation and institutionalize it even if we wished to do so. The physical facts have been relegated to the backstairs, and our girls are taught the need for lying and circumlocution to account for their backaches and headaches and refusals to play tennis. Menstruation among ourselves is a problem of hygiene, not a focus for social ceremonial. Yet we confront the adolescent girl with a state of mind which demands a far more complex response from her than is demanded by a ritual of sitting still and scratching her head with a scratching stick and observing similar taboos. The California Indians, the Thompson River Indians, the Gilbert Islanders, prescribed a ritual, a series of definite, easily comprehended acts, often exacting, often boring, but not baffling.

We prescribe no ritual; the girl continues on a round of school or work, but she is constantly confronted by a mysterious apprehensiveness in her parents and guardians. Her society—if it be a self-conscious one—has all the tensity of a roomful of people who expect the latest arrival to throw a bomb. This is our puberty ceremonial, uninstitutionalized in its broader aspects, gaining some explicitness in girls' clubwork, social secretaries, personnel workers, etc. Such an attitude begets its own offspring— self-conscious nervous unrest in the adolescent.

Yet Samoa and Dobu both suggest that adolescence is not necessarily a period of stress and strain, that these familiar and unlovely symptoms flow from cultural anxieties. But our present attitude consists not so much in examining the cultural set which produces these conditions as in regarding the result of these conditions as inevitable and rooted in human nature.

A consideration of primitive society will also throw some light upon the degree to which culture may schematize the conflicts which face adolescents.

Despite wide cultural and individual variations, the development of heterosexual interest and activity at puberty does serve to distinguish this period from the periods preceding it and from maturity, in which in most societies heterosexual patterns of behavior have been established.

The growing individual is presented with at least one new problem to solve. This is undoubtedly less of a problem if she has, like the Dobuan or Trobriand girl, engaged in sex play during childhood; it is less of a problem if she has learned something of the mechanism of her own body from manipulation and also has pretty full data about the activities of her elders as in Samoa. It is even less of a problem for the country girl than for the city girl in our own culture: the country girl can hardly escape a minimum of physiological knowledge which a city girl often lacks. But all these different educational factors simply vary the intensity with which the girl confronts the need for heterosexual adjustment. Culture can artificially dis-

tort the age at which these problems must be met, but there will still be a period at which adjustment must be made which seems to fall in the years following physical puberty in both primitive and modern societies. Students who draw freely on primitive material are likely to assert either that primitive society seizes this period as the most impressionable in a girl's life or that it constructs a gracious *rite de passage* to tide her over a period pregnant with difficulty.

Yet primitive material does not support either point of view. At whatever point the society decides to stress a particular adjustment, it will be at this point that adjustment becomes acute to the individual. This is true within the limits indicated above, even of sex. It is preeminently true of adjustment to cultural values less directly oriented to physiology. The period at which religious problems become acute to the individual is the period which social usage declares suitable. Among the Winnebago Indians young children are sent out into the wilderness to fast and see visions. In societies like that of some of the Plains Indians, where all men are expected to see visions, religious experience becomes a far more pressing matter than among the California Indians where such experience is reserved for those who wish to become shamans. In Manus the only people who are expected to have any direct contact with the spiritual world are women who have lost male children. Only the mature woman with a dead child, who has paid an older medium to train her and still finds herself unable to understand the talk of the spirits, is faced by a definitely spiritual problem. The society can define the age and range and sex to which religious experience is presented as a problem to be solved.

Even more subject to cultural definition is the question of the assumption of social responsibility. The Cheyenne treated a tiny bird caught by a child hunter as seriously as the buffalo shot by a grown man. Very young boys were permitted to join war parties and were tenderly guarded by the older men lest thoughtless youth should ridicule their presence. Here social participation was made so gradual and gentle a business that the irksomeness of a sudden accession of responsibilities was lacking. In contrast to this is the Manus system by which young boys are free as birds, owing no obligations to their elders until marriage, which reduces them to an ignominious position of acute economic dependence and which makes large demands on their time and energy. Samoa follows a third system in pushing the period when real responsibility is assumed up into the thirties: until that time a man and woman, although married, are insignificant members of a larger household directed by someone else. Perhaps the most drastic deferring of responsibility yet reported is found in the island of Mentawie where some men do not publicly acknowledge their wives nor assume the responsibilities of the head of a household until their own children are h~' ~rown men and old enough to w   them.

As it i   to find societies which can assi   solution of these problems to different ages or omit their solution entirely, it is not reasonable to regard them as inherently part of the adolescent period of development. If we are faced with adolescents trying to solve all these difficulties at once, this is an aspect of American civilization, not of human adolescence.

The American girl does not grow up in a coherent society as does the Manus girl and the Samoan girl. Instead she must enter a world filled with conflicting standards, contrasting philosophies, angry propaganda. Choices—of religion or doubt, of kind of work, of type of love —face the girl from the moment she reaches a thinking age. She can choose not only whom she will love, but whether

she will love in or out of wedlock, one or many. She can choose love without marriage, marriage without children; she may be tempted occasionally to choose children without marriage. And every girl who consciously makes one of these choices sets small patterns for scores of weaker, less articulate comrades.

The average American girl is asked to leave school, become a wage earner, meet the new demands of living, economically independent but socially dependent in the home where she was hitherto entirely dependent, and to subject her home and its religious and ethical standards to the ordeal of contrast with other standards. All of this is thrust upon her suddenly, in addition to the problem of sex adjustment. Thus a number of relatively unrelated forces have combined to make the adolescent in America stand at the point of highest pressure and difficulty, just as another set of forces place her at the lowest point of pressure in Samoa.

Most of the factors which complicate the lives of the adolescent: changing sex mores, the present economic system, the heterogeneity of American society, are hardly subject to manipulation by the most earnest social legislator or purveyor of panaceas. We cannot make the choices of our adolescents easy, nor can we postpone them. Probably the most we can do is to devise a new ritual of expectation.

The attitudes of the adult world are by and large the more malleable material for manipulation. The Gilbert Islander kindles a fire on his son's shaven head and expects the boy to bear it without flinching. If he denied the presence of the fire on the one hand and with the other nervously grasped a pail of water to quench the flames if they spread too far, the ordeal would be far harder for the boy.

In comparing primitive and modern societies, one other marked contrast between their adolescents is most notable. If we lay aside the purely physical definition of maturity and consider adolescence as the period following childhood during which the individual becomes placed in his society, we are struck at once by the enormous difference in range. Our material on individual adjustments in primitive society is slight, but such as it is it suggests that the unplaced person who has as yet come to no terms with his society is comparatively rare. Even marked potentialities for maladjustment, such as definite inversion, are very frequently fitted into a social pattern.

Any complex modern society presents a contrast to this. Although a civilization like America may set a definite premium upon a career which deals with things, either as an engineer or a financier, there are groups which regard the career of the artist, the writer, the evangelist as of far higher value. Whether or not any one girl can actually make her own the one of these many choices which is most congenial to her, does not change the effect upon youth's adjustment. With a range of possibilities equal to the range of temperaments, or at least fitted to many temperaments, though most unequally possible of achievement, adolescence as a period of adjustment is inevitably prolonged.

This aspect of complex societies has affected men for generations. It is just beginning to affect women in our society. To her the choice of a sex pattern is more pressing than to her brother; she has now also the possibilities of choice among careers, among ways of life which answer needs not met by any pattern of personal relations or physiological function. Because sex complicates a woman's life more conspicuously than a man's, the adolescent unplaced woman is perhaps an even more frequent phenomenon in urban life than is the unplaced man.

The contrast between primitive and modern society is increased when we consider adolescence as the growth period of personality, as a function of the complexity of society, not merely of the human life cycle. It is conceivable that in societies more complex than ours this type of adolescence will encroach even more on the years of maturity and that, while the primitive boy or girl is ready to assume the burden of his or her tradition at twenty and carry it unquestioningly to the grave, many of our most potentially gifted individuals will die adolescent, unplaced, and without realizing any of the promise of their genius. Among the Thompson Indians the gifted and the ungifted pass through a definite ritual to take their ordained places in their society. But for the adolescence of the spirit there is no puberty ceremonial.

THE SOCIALIZATION OF AGGRESSION
By Robert R. Sears, Eleanor E. Maccoby, and Harry Levin

Aggression, as the term is commonly used, means behavior that is intended to hurt or injure someone. Most human adults have quite a repertory of acts that fit this definition. Some of these are bold and violent, others sly and attenuated. Some are accompanied by rage or annoyance; others are done coldly and seemingly, to the perpetrator, without emotion. The complexity and subtlety of adult aggression is the end product of two of three decades of socialization by the individual's parents and peers, however, and bears little resemblance to the primitive quality of the infant's action patterns, from which it is developed.

To understand the problem of aggression in child rearing, one does well to remind himself firmly that man is a mammal and that there are certain kinds of behavior which characterize all mammals. The two that are most relevant to the problem of aggression are fighting and the *expression of rage.*

From the lowest quadruped to the highest biped, physical attack is used for defense. Techniques vary, depending on the sharpness of hooves, the strength of jaws, and the presence of specialized weapons like antlers. Man, being the most intelligent and inventive of all, makes use of many of the other species' techniques and adds a host of new ones that, happily, no other animal has ever dreamed of.

Physical fighting is not the commonest form of human aggression. *Injury* is a broad term, and the socialization process develops many motives that can be thwarted. Interference with any of these motives causes pain or anguish and if this was the intention, the interfering act was truly aggressive.

Defensive fighting is usually accompanied by expressions of rage. The older child or adult, who can report his feelings, may recognize his desire to hurt and be very aware of his angry emotion. But this quality of aggression is attenuated, too, in the process of socialization, and there are many forms of hurt that an adult inflicts with little emotional arousal.

In a civilized society adults are rarely beaten or knifed or lashed. More often, they are hurt by attacks on their pride or status, their desire for social approval, or their feelings of affection for their families and friends. These kinds of hurt can be far more serious and more prolonged than most physical hurts. The withholding of affection by a loved spouse, for example, can have the meaning of pain that goes far beyond that from broken legs or crushed fingers. Nor do injuries that come through sheer accident, the vagaries of nature, hurt like injuries to self-esteem.

Not all injuries are so great as these, of course. There are the little obstinacies in one's friends and the noncooperative indifferences of one's working associates. There are the irritants of family living— a tired and sassy child, a grumpy and complaining husband, a daughter who dawdles. Since all these cause discomfort, they *can* be forms of aggression. Whether they are in fact, however, depends on whether the discomfort they engender was *designed* by the perpetrator to hurt someone else.

Not all acts that hurt are intended to

This article is composed of excerpts from Chapter 7, Sears, Maccoby, and Levin, *Patterns of Child Rearing* (Evanston, Ill.: Row, Peterson & Co., 1957). The material reported here is derived from interviews with 379 mothers in the greater-Boston metropolitan area, each of whom had a five-year-old child in kindergarten. For details concerning the selection of the sample and the methods employed in the research, see Ch. 1 of *ibid.*

do so. Even sophisticated and sensitive adults sometimes fail to anticipate the effects of what they do. The unanswered letter can seem a slight; the unasked question can be interpreted as indifference. With children, the problem is especially noticeable in the manipulation of physical forces. A child's innocently swinging stick only too easily turns into a painful club, the experimental bombing into a brother's broken toys.

Since these hurts are obviously unintentional, they do not qualify as *aggression* in the technical sense of the word. There are certain borderline examples, however, that are hard to be sure about. There are acts that sometimes are and sometimes are not aggressive. Most mothers consider obedience of some importance, for they use much verbal guidance in instructing and controlling their children. The children know their mothers want compliance with directions and, hence, willful disobedience is widely recognized as a form of aggression. Now if a child has been told to pick up his clothes a dozen times and if he has remembered to do this the last half-dozen times, his mother may look suspiciously at his motives if he forgets the thirteenth time. Did he just forget? Or was he angry and disobedient? People differ considerably in the degree to which they perceive an aggressive intent in the behavior of others and what one mother calls carelessness another will call disobedience.

If we disregard borderline cases and accidents, however, there is still a great deal of human behavior that is designed to hurt. Such activity develops early in life and is a disrupting influence on family living. Later it becomes a problem for the peer group.

CONTROL OF AGGRESSION

All human societies, even all colony-living subhuman primates, have rules to limit the kinds and direction of aggression that may be expressed. The most fundamental of these is the high degree of prohibition on in-group fighting. The closer together people live, the more interdependent they are, the less they dare be aggressive toward one another. Free fighting and antagonism within the household—whether it be a nomad's hut or a suburbanite's four-bedrooms-and-two-baths—could only lead to wreckage of the family unit. Hence, all societies require that only very attenuated forms of aggression be expressed among family members and that, within the parent-child relationship, aggression be expressed only downward. One mother described this principle with great clarity [1]:

I. How do you handle it (if he strikes you)?
M. I don't allow it. I slap him and punish him for it, and explained that he was never to raise his hand to anyone older than himself, that he must respect older people—his mother and father especially. Never! But they do attempt it, of course; but I do think it should be checked right away.
I. How did you handle this?
M. I would just put him right in his room. Just take hold of him right at the moment and put him right in his room, and say "You mustn't do that! You never should hit your mother and father, ever; they're always right." I always make a big issue out of it.
I. That your mother and father are always right?
M. Always right; "You must never raise your hand to your mother or father."

Not all mothers felt as strongly as this one did, and different societies have different degrees of tolerance for in-family aggression, but the prohibition exists in some degree in all known societies.

Outside the family, limitations are less severe in most societies. The mothers in this present study were less concerned—more permissive—about fighting be-

---

[1] In these excerpts from interviews, *I* designates the questions put by the interviewer and *M* the replies of the mother.

tween their own children and neighbor youngsters than about sibling quarrels. There were a number of instances in which mothers felt children must be encouraged to fight, to protect their own interests. Even so, there is still a good deal of necessary restriction on the more severe forms of aggression, no mattter toward whom they are directed.

To insure the firm establishment of these rules many mothers feel they must begin the control of aggression very early in the child's life. A newborn infant is not particularly dangerous, even to himself, but he represents a potential threat nevertheless. The family, indeed the whole society, has a delicate balance; the forces of aggression are being kept in check, and cooperation and love outweigh noncooperation and hate. The baby is an alien who does not know the rules. He must be taught them if he is to be an acceptable member of society.

METHODS OF CONTROL

Aggression, being a frustration to its object, has a strong tendency to evoke counteraggression or punishment. This built-in relationship between the aggressor and his victim has an important consequence. It means that every child grows up with the experience of being punished in some degree for his aggressive behavior. The extent and severity of such punishment differs greatly from one child to another, of course, depending on the tolerance of his parents and siblings. It is our impression, however, that the average child in our sample received more actual *punishment* (as distinguished from *nonreward*) for aggressive behavior than for any other kind of change-worthy action.

One significant effect of punishment is the production of anxiety. If the punishment is repeated many, many times through early childhood, situations that provoke aggressive feelings gradually come to arouse anxiety, too anxiety

over the danger of being punished for aggression. Eventually, the aggression itself or the accompanying feeling of being angry becomes sufficient to arouse anxiety. In such cases the anxiety may properly be called aggression-anxiety.

The formation of such a reaction has two kinds of consequences that are relevant to the socialization process. One is the uneasiness and discomfort that become connected with the arousal of aggressive impulses. By and large, adults in our culture do not tolerate aggression comfortably, neither their own nor that displayed by others. It evokes too much anxiety; this may be reflected in feelings of worry, dislike, avoidance, guilt, or moral disapproval. They cannot feel fully comfortable when they are angry. They are in conflict—ambivalent—about their own impulses. The carrying through of an aggressive act is often followed not simply by the catharsis or satisfaction that one would expect from a successful action (assuming the action accomplished the intended results), but also by feelings that arise from the undercurrent anxiety. These may be shame, embarrassment, guilt, regret, self-deprecation, or even just plain fear of retaliation. A mother's uneasiness and conflict often make difficult a calm use of reason in deciding how to handle a child's aggressive actions.

A second consequence of punishment and its ensuing anxiety is the development, by the child, of techniques for avoiding punishment. The child who is consistently punished for swearing is likely to cease the practice in his parents' presence. This does not necessarily mean he will stop swearing, for punishment seems usually to have a rather localized inhibiting effect. The impulse to be aggressive is not reduced but only the overt aggressive act that was punished. The total impulse to aggression is made stronger than ever, for the punishment is itself an additional frustration.

MEASURES OF MOTHERS' BEHAVIOR

We can turn now to the findings from our interviews. We will describe first the ways in which the mothers handled aggression, with respect to both permissiveness and punishment. Then we will examine the relation between these child-rearing practices and the mothers' own reports of their children's aggressiveness to discover what procedures seemed to influence such behavior.

In the discussion so far we have talked of aggression as a change-worthy form of behavior, particularly that directed toward the parents. This is a generalization, however, that hides a multitude of individual differences among the mothers. As might easily be predicted from what has been said of aggression-anxiety, parents differ greatly from one another in the amount of aggression they can tolerate. Some set great store by a completely nonaggressive child; others accept the inevitability of a certain amount of aggression even as late as age five; a few believe aggression is such a natural quality of early childhood behavior that they simply ignore all but the most violent episodes.

In our interviews, the mothers described the ways in which children got on adult nerves, found ingenious devices for expressing annoyance or getting revenge, and in general created the social and emotional havoc that goes with anger. They also expressed their own attitudes toward their children's aggression and gave descriptions of how this change-worthy behavior was handled. With respect to aggression of children toward their parents, the mothers were asked:

Sometimes a child will get angry at his parents and hit them and kick them or shout angry things at them. How much of this sort of think do you think parents ought to allow in a child of (his, her) age? How do you handle it when (child's name) acts like this?

Following are examples of the kinds of statements parents made in answer to these questions.

Case A

M. I think he's at the age right now where you're apt to get quite a lot of it. I think as they get a little bit older, you can stop and reason with them, but right now I think that they get pretty angry at times and they do say things. And afterwards they're sorry for it, so I let him say it and it's over with, and afterwards I might say, "You weren't very nice to Mummy," and he'll generally admit it.

Case B

I. In what ways do you get on each other's nerves?
M. I think our mutual tempers, as much as anything, as he has one, and so have I. I attempt to control it, so for instance I can understand things that he does. He gets very angry and he goes upstairs and throws things, and I can understand that perfectly. I don't know whether I was ever allowed to or whether I ever did throw things, but I wanted to, so that heaving things into the closet, I can easily understand; so that kind of thing doesn't aggravate me the way it would somebody else, and the same way with getting very angry at me. I never mind that as much, because I also get angry at him, and if I am going to, he has got to be allowed that privilege also.

Case C

M. Well, she'll say, "I don't like you." She seldom says, "I hate you." or "I don't like you anymore," or something like that. I have let her go up to now because I feel she's just getting it out of her system. If it isn't too loud, or if she isn't too angry about it, I just let it go. If it's something that I can't turn my back on, if it's something that she's so angry about that she won't stop, then I speak to her. Otherwise she'll say, "Well, I don't like you." And I say, "Well, that's all right," or something like that. I don't pay too much attention to it because I know that she doesn't actually mean it. She means it because she isn't getting what she wants, and she doesn't mean it actually.

If she kicked me or if she slapped me, I'd

slap her back. I just told her that it doesn't feel good to get slapped. If she didn't want to get slapped herself, not to slap other people. The reaction would be the same in anyone that got slapped—they wouldn't like it.

Case D

M. They never should allow him to hit them back. If he hits them, they should hit him right back. If you let him get away with it once he will always want to get away with it.
I. How do you handle it when he acts like this?
M. If he hits me I hit him back twice as hard, and if he does it again, I just get my paddle I have, and I give it to him again, and then he stops.
I. How do you handle it if he is deliberately disobedient?
M. I take off his clothes and he's in for the day and he's not to play with anything—not even his toys or anything that belongs to him—he's not to touch anything—he's to leave things alone and stay in bed.

Case E

M. That is something I will not tolerate—my child has never done it. I mean, they have done it once in a while, both of them, but I would absolutely not tolerate it.
I. How did you teach them not to do this?
M. I don't know—I guess I just told them once, in no uncertain terms, that it was something that was never done, and I have never had any trouble with it; and if I did, I don't know just how I would cope with it, because I wouldn't stand for it.
I. How much of this sort of thing do you think a parent ought to allow?
M. I don't think they should allow it at all. I think a child should be allowed to express himself, and all that, but I don't think there is ever an exception for a child to hit his parents.

Responses of these kinds, together with much other relevant material elsewhere in the interview, enabled us to rate each mother on two dimensions: (1) her *permissiveness* for aggression directed by the child toward herself and (2) the amount (and severity) of *punishment* she had administered to the child

for such aggression. Under the heading of permissiveness we included not only the mother's stated values as to whether aggression should be allowed but also her behavior toward the child, i.e., whether she actually *did* allow it or whether she always tried to take measures to prevent or stop it.

As might be expected, the two scales were correlated. That is, the mothers who were permissive about aggression, tended to use little punishment, while the nonpermissive mothers used quite a bit. But the correlation was only $-.46$, a low enough value to warrant considering the two dimensions separately. The two scales did not correlate more closely because there were a number of mothers who did not permit aggression from their children, but stopped it by other means than punishment. Surprisingly, there were also a number whom we rated both quite permissive and highly punishing. In this latter group were some mothers who felt they *should* allow their children to display aggression; but they could restrain their own impulses to suppress the child's aggression only so long, and then they would blow up. When the punishment came, it was likely to be severe.

In this sample of 379 normal mothers, we found that a majority were most accurately rated at the *nonpermissive* end of our permissiveness scale. The social norm prevailing in these families was one of little tolerance about parent-directed aggression from children, although there was considerable variation in the severity with which this value was enforced.

It is of some interest to note that parents allowed somewhat more aggression from their sons than from their daughters, and that working-class parents were less permissive about aggression than parents at the middle-class level.

EFFECTS ON CHILDREN'S AGGRESSION

We turn now to a consideration of the child's aggressiveness, and will then address ourselves to the question: Does the amount of overt aggression a child displays at home have any relation to the values parents hold about aggression and the techniques they have employed in dealing with the child's aggression?

Measure of Aggression. Among these youngsters, there were a few whose mothers could recall almost no angry behavior around home, but this was not the case for most of them. In spite of the general aura of prohibition, the majority of the youngsters had displayed many varieties and combinations of angry emotional response. Some children were more aggressive toward one parent than the other, some quarreled mainly with siblings and were pleasant toward the parents, some expressed themselves openly, and some relied chiefly on non-cooperation for their expression.

Nearly all the mothers gave fairly detailed reports of the typical forms of aggression their children displayed. It was thus possible to make a rating of *amount of aggression exhibited in the home* (excluding that toward siblings).

These ratings can be compared with the mothers' reports of child-rearing practices to discover what characteristics of the latter were associated with high or low degree of reported aggression by the child.

The measures of the mothers' practices and the children's reactions were not independent. Both came from the mother herself. We cannot be certain in any particular case, therefore, that we have secured an unbiased report of the child's actual behavior. It is possible that some quality in a given mother—for instance, a sense of despair about her effectiveness as a child rearer—might lead her to give an exaggerated report about her child's aggressiveness. If we find, as we do, that mothers who felt little confidence in themselves had more (reportedly) aggressive children, we cannot tell whether this finding results from

exaggerated reports by these mothers, or whether there was actually something about their behavior toward children that evoked more child aggressiveness. It would not be surprising if both were true, for the same qualities of her personality that influence her perception of the child may also induce a characteristic set of responses in him.

Permissiveness and Punishment. There is a constant tug of war in a child's behavior between the instigation and the inhibition of aggression. On the one hand there are frustrations, threats, or other stimulating situations that tend to evoke aggressive action; on the other, there are warnings that inhibit aggression and there are instigators to competing responses that the mother finds more desirable than aggression. One of the major research problems in the investigation of the socialization process is the discovery of just what kinds of maternal behavior fall into these classifications. What does the mother do that excites aggression in her child? What does she do that inhibits it?

The two scales of *permissiveness for aggression* and *severity of punishment for aggression* are obviously relevant dimensions to examine. What should we expect of their relation to the reported amount of aggression the child shows in the home? Permissiveness, by definition, is an expression of the mother's willingness to have the child perform such acts. A simple and straightforward prediction is that children with permissive mothers will be more aggressive than children with nonpermissive mothers. Similarly with punishment: if we assume that this method of discipline establishes in the child a fear of behaving aggressively, then the more punitive the mother is, the more the child should avoid being aggressive. These two predictions fit together nicely. As we noted above the scales for *permissiveness* and *punishment* are correlated −.46; that is, to some degree the more permissive mothers

TABLE 1

PERCENTAGE OF HIGHLY AGGRESSIVE CHILDREN IN SUBGROUPS *

| Subgroup | Highly aggressive † | | | |
| | Boys | | Girls | |
	Percent	N	Percent	N
Low permissiveness, low punishment	3.7	27	13.3	30
Low permissiveness, high punishment	20.4	51	19.1	47
High permissiveness, low punishment	25.3	81	20.6	63
High permissiveness, high punishment	41.7	36	38.1	22

* Divided according to whether mother was in upper or lower half of the distribution on permissiveness and severity of punishment for aggression toward parents.

† By "highly aggressive" is meant that the child was rated in one of the two highest levels of aggression on a 5-point rating scale.

tended to be less severe in their punishment.

In point of fact, however, one of the predictions is right and the other is wrong. It is true that high *permissiveness* is associated with high aggression. The correlation is +.23. But *punishment* works just the other way: the more severe the punishment, the more aggression the child showed. The correlation is +.16. Both these correlations are small, but they are significant and they are artificially reduced by the negative correlation between the permissiveness and punitiveness scales. Their true importance is substantially greater as may be seen in Table 1.

We interpret these findings in this way. When a mother adopts a permissive point of view about aggression, she is saying to her child, in effect, "Go ahead and express your angry emotions; don't worry about me." She gives few signals in advance that would lead the child to fear to be aggressive. On the contrary, her attitude is one of expectancy that he *will* be and that such behavior is acceptable. It is scarcely surprising that the child tends to fulfill her expectations. The nonpermissive mother, however, does something quite different. She has an attitude that aggression is wrong, that it is not to be tolerated, and an expectancy (often very subtly expressed) that the child will not behave in such undesirable ways. When

he is aggressive, she does something to try to stop it—sometimes by punishment, sometimes by other means. He, also, fulfills his mother's expectations. This dimension of permissiveness, then, is a measure of the extent to which the mother prevents or stops aggression, the nonpermissive extreme being the most common.

Punishment is apparently a somewhat different matter. It is a kind of maternal behavior that occurs *after* the child's aggression has been displayed. The child has already enjoyed the satisfaction of hurting or of expressing anger—and so has had a reinforcement for aggressive action. But then he gets hurt in turn. He suffers further frustration. This should, and on the average does, incite him to more aggression. If the punishment is very severe, he may gradually learn to fear the consequences of his own actions and the particular acts that get most repeatedly punished may be inhibited. But the total frustration is increased and hence the total amount of aggression displayed in the home is higher. The dimension called *severity of punishment for aggression toward parents*, then, is one measure of the amount of painful frustration that is imposed on the child without direct guidance as to what would be a more acceptable form of behavior.

It is evident from this analysis that the mothers who were most permissive but also most severely punitive would have the most aggressive children; those who were most nonpermissive but least punitive would have the least aggressive ones. As may be seen in Table 1, this was the case for both sexes. The children of mothers in the other two groups were in between.

These findings are similar to those of an earlier study [2] in one respect. In that research, 40 children were observed in nursery school. The amount of aggression they showed there was compared with their mothers' reports of the severity of punishment for aggression that they suffered at home. In that study, too, high aggression was found to be associated with severe punishment, especially in the boys. There was some indication that the *most* severely punished girls had become quite passive and inhibited. They displayed little activity of any kind, including aggression. When activity level was taken into consideration, they tended to be more like the boys, i.e., the more severely punished girls were *relatively* more aggressive than the less severely punished. It is interesting to note the similarity between the present findings and the earlier study, because in that research the measure of child aggression was entirely independent of the measures of child-rearing practices.

A word of caution must be said here about the interpretation of our results. We have shown that the mothers who punished their children most severely for aggression tended to report that their children displayed more than the average amount of aggression toward their parents. We have implied in our discussion that the maternal behavior *caused* the child behavior. It is entirely possible, of course, that the correlation could be explained as a parental response to the child's pre-existing temperament. That

is, some children may have been born with a higher level of aggressive impulses than others, and the more aggressive the child naturally was, the more his parents may have been forced to punish him for aggression. We have chosen to interpret the matter the other way around: that punishment by the mother bred counter-aggression in the child. Our reason is that permissiveness was also associated with aggression and we cannot see why aggression in the child should elicit permissiveness in the mother.

Our interpretation must be tentative, however, for the other explanation of the results cannot be ruled out without further research. It is quite possible, of course, that a circular process develops: the parent's punishment makes the child aggressive, this aggression leads to further punishment, and so on. Which came first, to set the whole thing in motion, is a problem we cannot solve with our existing information.

Our findings suggest that the way for parents to produce a nonaggressive child is to make abundantly clear that aggression is frowned upon and to stop aggression when it occurs, but to avoid punishing the child for his aggression. Punishment seems to have complex effects. While undoubtedly it often stops a particular form of aggression, at least momentarily, it appears to generate more hostility in the child and lead to further aggressive outbursts at some other time or place. Furthermore, when the parents punish—particularly when they employ physical punishment—they are providing a living example of the use of aggression at the very moment they are trying to teach the child not to be aggressive. The child, who copies his parents in many ways, is likely to learn as much from this example of successful aggression on his parents' part as he is from the pain of punishment. Thus, the most peaceful

---

[2] R. R. Sears, J. W. M. Whiting, V. Nowlis, and P. S. Sears, "Some Child-rearing Antecedents of Aggression and Dependency in Young Children," *Genet. Psychol. Monogr.*, 1953, XLVII, 135–234.

home is one in which the mother believes aggression is not desirable and under no circumstances is ever to be expressed toward her, but who relies mainly on non-punitive forms of control. The homes where the children show angry, aggressive outbursts frequently are likely to be homes in which the mother has a relatively tolerant (or careless!) attitude toward such behavior, or where she administers severe punishment for it, or both.

These conclusions will certainly not astonish anyone who has worked professionally with children and their parents, but they will not find ready acceptance by many other people. There are two reasons.

First, *punishment is satisfying* to the parent. When a child aggresses toward his mother, he angers her, interferes with what she is doing, with her peace of mind, with her dignity and self-respect. Aggression hurts. It is meant to. And it produces in the mother the appropriate stimulation to retaliate in kind. Combined with her sense of obligation to rear her child properly, this retaliation comes out in a way she thinks of as "punishment"—that is, a form of aggression designed to have a good *training* effect on its recipient. Many mothers have developed strong beliefs that punishment is a helpful method of control. (Sometimes it is, too.) These beliefs are essential to the peace of mind of such mothers. Without the conviction that "punishment is *good* for my child," these mothers would be forced to view their own behavior as retaliatory, aggressive, childish —in short, contemptible. This would not long provide a tolerable self-image. It is to be expected, then, that our demonstration of the deleterious effect of severe punishment of aggression will not be an easy finding for many people to swallow.

A second matter has to do with permissiveness. The difficulty grows out of the problem of punishment. During the

last three decades there has developed, among the more literate and sensitive part of the American people, an uneasy recognition that punishment sometimes eliminates a few specific responses but leaves a strongly hostile drive bottled up within the child. There is evidence to support this belief. With this consideration in mind and an urgent desire to provide better mental hygiene for their children, not a few parents have developed what almost amounts to a cult of being permissive about aggression. They seem to have assumed (we think wrongly) that if they are to avoid punishing their children for aggression, they must allow the children's aggression to go unchecked. Their aim is to avoid repression, to permit the child easier and freer expression of his impulses, and thus to prevent the development of aggression-anxiety, with its accompanying displacements, projections, and sometimes uncontrollable fantasies.

This aim is good, both for the children and the society they will compose, but whether it can be achieved by a high degree of permissiveness for expression of aggression toward the parents is a question. Does a permissive attitude, with the consequent freer expression of aggression help the child to "get his aggression out of his system" and thus decrease the strength of projective fantasies? There is no indication in our own data that it does. Each of the children in the present study was tested with two 20-minute sessions of doll play. The children of the more nonpermissive half of the group of mothers showed little if any more fantasy aggression under these circumstances than the children of the more permissive half. It seems, therefore, that the parents' refusal to permit aggression had not produced a "bottled-up" aggressive force in the children that sought expression in fantasy. This finding is in sharp contrast to that with respect to punishment; the children of the more severely punishing mothers displayed quite significantly more fantasy aggression than the children of the less severely punishing ones.[3]

Permissiveness does not seem to decrease fantasy indications of aggressive impulses. Permissiveness *does* increase the amount of aggression in the home, however, and it is worth considering what this does to the child himself. An angry child is not usually a happy child nor is he one who receives affection and willing companionship from others. He is a source of discomfort to family and peers and probably receives a certain amount of retaliation. He upsets his siblings, raises the level of frustration imposed on his parents, and inevitably has an increase, to some extent, of his own aggression-anxiety. There seems little advantage in all this, either to the child himself or to his parents.

One cautionary point: we are not suggesting that parents should band together in omnipotent suppression of every justifiable angry response the child makes. The right to be angry without fear or guilt is as inalienable as any other, and more important than some. But since anger interferes with constructive action in the face of many, if not most, problem situations that the child and his family face, parents are understandably anxious to keep it within reasonable bounds; and our interest has been in showing what parental actions are likely to have the desired effects and what actions are likely to have undesired side-effects.

THE FUNCTION OF MALE INITIATION CEREMONIES AT PUBERTY
By John W. M. Whiting, Richard Kluckhohn, and Albert Anthony

Our society gives little formal recognition of the physiological and social changes a boy undergoes at puberty. He may be teased a little when his voice changes or when he shaves for the first time. Changes in his social status from childhood to adulthood are marked by a number of minor events rather than by any single dramatic ceremonial observance. Graduation from grammar school and subsequently from high school are steps to adulthood, but neither can be considered as a *rite de passage*. Nor may the accomplishment of having obtained a driver's license, which for many boys is the most important indication of having grown up, be classed as one. Legally the twenty-first birthday is the time at which a boy becomes a man; but, except for a somewhat more elaborate birthday party this occasion is not ceremonially, marked and, therefore, cannot be thought of as a *rite de passage*. Neither physiologically, socially, nor legally is there a clear demarcation between boyhood and manhood in our society.

Such a gradual transition from boyhood to manhood is by no means univer-

Prepared especially for this volume. A cross-cultural study of the function of male-initiation rites involving some of the variables of this study as well as a number of others was the basis of the doctoral dissertation of Albert S. Anthony, *A Cross-Cultural Study of the Function of Initiation Rites at Puberty*, unpublished Ed.D. thesis, Graduate School of Education, Harvard University, 1956. A version of this paper was read at the meetings of the American Anthropological Association in December, 1956.

[3] H. Levin and R. R. Sears, "Identification with Parents as a Determinant of Doll Play Aggression," *Child Devel.*, 1956, XXVII, 135–153.

sal. Among the Thonga, a tribe in South Africa, every boy must go through a very elaborate ceremony in order to become a man.[1] When a boy is somewhere between ten and 16 years of age, he is sent by his parents to a "circumcision school" which is held every four or five years. Here in company with his age-mates he undergoes severe hazing by the adult males of the society. The initiation begins when each boy runs the gauntlet between two rows of men who beat him with clubs. At the end of this experience he is stripped of his clothes and his hair is cut. He is next met by a man covered with lion manes and is seated upon a stone facing this "lion man." Someone then strikes him from behind and when he turns his head to see who has struck him, his foreskin is seized and in two movements cut off by the "lion man." Afterwards he is secluded for three months in the "yards of mysteries," where he can be seen only by the initiated. It is especially taboo for a woman to approach these boys during their seclusion, and if a woman should glance at the leaves with which the circumcised covers his wound and which form his only clothing, she must be killed.

During the course of his initiation, the boy undergoes six major trials: beatings, exposure to cold, thirst, eating of unsavory foods, punishment, and the threat of death. On the slightest pretext he may be severely beaten by one of the newly initiated men who is assigned to the task by the older men of the tribe. He sleeps without covering and suffers bitterly from the winter cold. He is for-

bidden to drink a drop of water during the whole three months. Meals are often made nauseating by the half-digested grass from the stomach of an antelope which is poured over his food. If he is caught breaking any important rule governing the ceremony, he is severely punished. For example, in one of these punishments, sticks are placed between the fingers of the offender, then a strong man closes his hand around that of the novice practically crushing his fingers. He is frightened into submission by being told that in former times boys who had tried to escape or who revealed the secrets to women or to the uninitiated were hanged and their bodies burnt to ashes.

Although the Thonga are extreme in the severity of this sort of initiation, many other societies have rites which have one or more of the main features of the Thonga ceremony. Of a sample of 55 societies [2] chosen for this study, 18 have one or more of the four salient features of the Thonga ceremony, e.g., painful hazing by adult males, genital operations, seclusion from women, and tests of endurance and manliness, the remaining 37 societies either have no ceremony at all or one which does not have any of the above features.[3]

HYPOTHESES

It is the purpose of this paper to develop a set of hypotheses concerning the function of male initiation rites which accounts for the presence of these rites in some societies and the absence of them in others. The theory that we have

---

[1] The following account is taken from Henri A. Junod, *The Life of a South African Tribe* (London: Macmillan & Co., Ltd., 1927), pp. 74–95.

[2] The method of sample selection is discussed below.

[3] Seven of these societies have a minor ceremony which generally takes place during adolescence. In these societies the boy's change in status is announced by investing him with some symbol of manhood such as the donning of long pants which played such a role in our society in former years. Specifically these are tatooing—Maori and Ontong Javanese; tooth filling—Alorese, Balinese and Lakher; donning the "sacred thread"—Hindu (Khalapur Radjput). The Kwakuitl fall in a similar category. Their ceremony consists of a potlach given for the boy by his father. The ceremonies in these societies are so different in sociopsychological import from those to be described below that they will be classed hereafter with those societies which lack puberty ceremonies.

chosen to test has been suggested by previous explanations for the rites, particularly those of psychoanalytic origin.[4] These explanations were modified to fit the problem of this research in two respects. First, certain of the concepts and hypotheses were restated or redefined so as to be coherent with the growing general behavioral theory of personality development,[5] and second, they were restated in such a way as to be amenable to cross-cultural test, i.e., cultural indices were specified for each variable.

We assume that boys tend to be initiated at puberty in those societies in which they are particularly hostile toward their fathers and dependent upon their mothers. The hazing of the candidates, as well as the genital operations, suggests that one function of the rites is to prevent open and violent revolt against parental authority at a time when physical maturity would make such revolt dangerous and socially disruptive. Isolation from women and tests of manliness suggest that another function of the rites is to break an excessively strong dependence upon the mother and to ensure identification with adult males and acceptance of the male role.

It is to be noted here that the educational and disciplinary functions of the initiation are not limited in time to the actual period of initiation. The boy knows all during childhood and latency about the initiation which he will face at puberty. While he is overtly not supposed to know any of the secrets of the rite, he actually knows almost everything that will happen to him. He is both afraid of what he knows will happen and also envious of the kudos and added status which his older friends have ac-

quired through having successfully gone through this rite. Thus, through the boy's whole life the initiation ceremony serves as a conditioner of his behavior and his attitudes towards male authority, while at the same time emphasizing the advantages of becoming a member of the male group through initiation.

We assume that a long and exclusive relationship between mother and son provides the conditions which should lead to an exceptionally strong dependence upon the mother. Also, we assume that if the father terminates this relationship and replaces his son, there should be strong envy and hostility engendered in the boy which, although held in check during childhood, may dangerously manifest itself with the onset of puberty, unless measures are taken to prevent it.

As we indicated above, the hypothesis is derived from psychoanalytic theory. However, it should be noted that there are some modifications which may be important. First, no assumption is being made that the envy is exclusively sexual in character. We are making the more general assumption that if the mother for a prolonged period devotes herself to the satisfaction of all the child's needs—including hunger, warmth, safety, freedom from pain, as well as sex—he will become strongly dependent upon her. In accordance with this we believe rivalry may be based upon a competition for the fulfillment of any of these needs. Second, we do not propose, as most psychoanalysts do, that Oedipal rivalry is a universal, but rather we claim it is a variable which may be strong or weak depending upon specific relationships between father, mother, and son. Thus, we assume father-son rivalry may range from a

---

[4] See, e.g., Sigmund Freud, *Moses and Monotheism* (New York: Alfred A. Knopf, Inc., 1939); Bruno Bettelheim, *Symbolic Wounds* (Glencoe, Ill.: Free Press, 1954); Margaret Mead, *Male and Female* (New York: William Morrow & Co., Inc., 1949).

[5] See, e.g., J. W. M. Whiting and Irwin L. Child, *Child Training and Personality* (New Haven: Yale University Press, 1953); Robert R. Sears, Eleanor E. Maccoby, and Harry Levin, *Patterns of Child Rearing* (Evanston, Ill.: Row, Peterson & Co., 1957); and John Dollard and Neal E. Miller, *Personality and Psychotherapy* (New York: McGraw-Hill Book Co., 1950).

value of zero to such high intensities that the whole society may be required to adjust to it.

An illustration of cultural conditions which should intensify the dependency of a boy on his mother and rivalry with his father is found in the following case.

Kwoma Dependency. The Kwoma,[6] a tribe living about 200 miles up the Sepik River in New Guinea, have initiation rites similar to those of the Thonga. Examination of the differences in the relationship of a mother to her infant during the first years of his life reveals some strong contrasts between the Kwoma and our own society. While in our society an infant sleeps in his own crib and the mother shares her bed with the father, the Kwoma infant sleeps cuddled in his mother's arms until he is old enough to be weaned, which is generally when he is two or three years old. The father, in the meantime, sleeps apart on his own bark slab bed. Furthermore during this period, the Kwoma mother abstains from sexual intercourse with her husband in order to avoid having to care for two dependent children at the same time. Since the Kwoma are polygynous and discreet extramarital philandering is permitted, this taboo is not too hard on the husband. In addition, it is possible that the mother obtains some substitute sexual gratification from nursing and caring for her infant.[7] If this be the case, it is not unlikely that she should show more warmth and affection toward her infant than if she were obtaining sexual gratification from her husband. Whether or not the custom can be attributed to this sex taboo, the Kwoma mother, while her co-wife does the housework, not only sleeps

with her infant all night but holds it in her lap all day without apparent frustration. Such a close relationship between a mother and child in our society would seem not only unbearably difficult to the mother, but also somewhat improper.

When the Kwoma child is weaned, a number of drastic things happen all at once. He is suddenly moved from his mother's bed to one of his own. His father resumes sexual relations with his mother. Although the couple wait until their children are asleep, the intercourse takes place in the same room. Thus, the child may truly become aware of his replacement. He is now told that he can no longer have his mother's milk because some supernatural being needs it. This is vividly communicated to him by his mother when she puts a slug on her breasts and daubs the blood-colored sap of the breadfruit tree over her nipples. Finally he is no longer permitted to sit on his mother's lap. She resumes her work and goes to the garden to weed or to the swamp to gather sago flour leaving him behind for the first time in his life. That these events are traumatic to the child is not surprising. He varies between sadness and anger, weeping and violent temper tantrums.

It is our hypothesis that it is this series of events that makes it necessary, when the boy reaches adolescence, for the society to have an initiation rite of the type we have already described. It is necessary to put a final stop to (1) his wish to return to his mother's arms and lap, (2) to prevent an open revolt against his father who has displaced him from his mother's bed, and (3) to ensure identification with the adult males of the society.

---

[6] For a description of the Kwoma child-rearing reported here see J. W. M. Whiting, *Becoming a Kwoma* (New Haven: Yale University Press, 1941), pp. 24–64.

[7] This is, of course, difficult to determine and is a presumption based upon the following factors: (1) Kwoma informants reported that mothers had no desire for sexual intercourse as long as they were nursing the infant and (2) clinical evidence from women in our own society suggests that nursing is sexually gratifying to some women at least. See Therese Benedek, "Mother-child, the Primary Psychomatic Unit," *Am. J. Ortho-Psychiatry,* 1949, XIX; Helene Deutsch, *The Psychology of Women* (New York: Grune & Stratton, Inc., 1944–45), Vols. I and II; Sears, Maccoby, and Levin, *op. cit.*

In other words, Kwoma infancy so magnifies the conditions which should produce Oedipus rivalry that the special cultural adjustment of ceremonial hazing, isolation from women, and symbolic castration, etc., must be made to resolve it.

If our analysis of the psychodynamics in Kwoma society is correct, societies with initiation rites should have similar child-rearing practices, whereas societies lacking the rite should also lack the exclusive mother-son sleeping arrangements and *post-partum* sexual taboo of the Kwoma.

TESTING THE HYPOTHESIS

To test this hypothesis a sample of 56 societies was selected. First, the ethnographic material on more than 150 societies was checked to determine whether or not there was an adequate description of our variables e.g., sleeping arrangements, *post-partum* sex taboo, and initiation rites at puberty. Only half of the societies reviewed fulfilled these conditions. Although we had initially endeavored to select our cases so as to have maximum distribution throughout the world, we found that some areas were represented by several societies, while others were not represented by any. To correct for any bias that might result from this sample, we made a further search of the ethnographic literature in order to fill in the gaps, and we thereby added several societies from areas previously not represented. Finally, to maximize diversity and to minimize duplication through selection of closely related societies, whenever there were two or more societies from any one culture area which had the same values on all our variables, we chose only one of them. Using these criteria, our final sample consisted of 56 societies representing 45 of the 60 culture areas designated by Murdock.[8]

The societies comprising our final sample range in size and type from small, simple, tribal groups to segments of large, complex civilizations such as the United States or Japan. In the latter case, our information has been drawn from ethnographic reports on a single delineated community.

When this sample had finally been chosen, the material relevant to our variables was first abstracted, and then judgments were made for each society as to the nature of the transition from boyhood to manhood, the sleeping arrangements, and the duration of the *post-partum* sex taboo. To prevent contamination, the judgments on each variable were made at different times and the name of the society disguised by a code. All judgments were made by at least two persons and in every case where there was a disagreement (less than 15 percent of the cases for any given variable), the data were checked by one of the authors, whose judgment was accepted as final. Our findings with respect to initiation rites have been tabulated in Table 1 below.

We discovered that only five societies out of the total number had sleeping arrangements similar to our own, that is, where the father and mother share a bed and the baby sleeps alone. In only three societies did the mother, the father, and the baby each have his or her own bed. In the remaining 48, the baby slept with his mother until he was at least a year old and generally until he was weaned. In 24 of the latter, however, the father also shared the bed, the baby generally sleeping between the mother and father. The remaining 24 societies had sleeping arrangements like the Kwoma in which the mother and child sleep in one bed and the father in another. Often the father's bed was not even in the same house. He either slept in a men's club house or in the hut of one of his other wives leaving mother and infant not only alone in

[8] G. P. Murdock, "World Ethnographic Sample," *Am. Anthropol.*, 1957, LIX, 664–687.

the same bed but alone in the sleeping room.

Similarly, the societies of our sample were split on the rules regulating the resumption of sexual intercourse following parturition. Twenty-nine, like our own, have a brief taboo of a few weeks to permit the mother to recover from her delivery. In the remaining 27, the mother did not resume sexual intercourse for at least nine months after the birth of her child, and in one instance, the Cheyenne, the ideal period adhered to was reported as ten years. The duration of the taboo generally corresponded to the nursing period and in many cases was reinforced by the belief that sexual intercourse curdles or sours the mother's milk, thus making it harmful for the infant. In other societies, like the Kwoma, the taboo is explicitly for the purpose of ensuring a desired interval between children where adequate means of contraception are lacking. In these societies the taboo is terminated when the infant reaches some maturational stage, e.g., "until the child can crawl," "until the child can walk," or "until he can take care of himself." For the 27 societies that have this taboo, more than a few weeks long, the average duration is slightly more than two years.

RESULTS AT THE CULTURAL LEVEL

Our hypothesis may now be restated in cultural terms as follows: *Societies which have sleeping arrangements in which the mother and baby share the same bed for at least a year to the exclusion of the father and societies which have a taboo restricting the mother's sexual behavior for at least a year after childbirth will be more likely to have a*

ceremony of transition from boyhood to manhood than those societies where these conditions do not occur (or occur for briefer periods). For the purposes of this hypothesis, transition ceremonies include only those ceremonies characterized by at least one of the following events: painful hazing of the initiates, isolation from females, tests of manliness, and genital operations.

The test of this hypothesis is presented in Table 1. It will be observed from this table that of the 20 societies where both antecedent variables are present, 14 have initiation ceremonies and only six do not. Where both antecedent variables are absent only two of the 25 societies have the ceremonies. Thus, over 80 percent of the 45 pure cases correspond with the prediction.[9] Though our hypothesis was not designed for predicting the mixed cases, that is, where only one of the antecedent variables is present, it seems that they tended not to have the transition ceremonies.

Although the eight cases which are exceptional to our theory, the six in the upper left-hand column and the two in the lower right-hand column may be simply misclassified through error of measurement, re-examination uncovers some other unanticipated factor which may account for their placement.[10] This analysis turns out to be enlightening.

Reviewing, first the six cases in the upper left-hand column, that is, the societies which have both exclusive mother-son sleeping arrangements and a *postpartum* sex taboo but no initiation, we found that four of them (Khalapur, Trobrianders, Nyakusa, and Yapese) have an adjustment at adolescence which may serve as a psychological substitute

[9] Even though we made every effort to ensure at least a reasonable degree of independence for our cases, there are many instances of known historical connections among them. A statistical test of significance is therefore difficult to interpret. If the cases were independent, the probabilities are less than one in one thousand that this relationship could be obtained by chance ($\chi^2 > 18$).

[10] This procedure was suggested by G. G. Homans and D. M. Schneider, *Marriage, Authority, and Final Causes; A Study of Unilateral Cross-Cousin Marriage* (Glencoe, Ill.: Free Press, 1955). It was used most effectively in their cross-cultural study of authority patterns and cross-cousin marriage.

TABLE 1

THE RELATIONSHIP BETWEEN EXCLUSIVE MOTHER-SON SLEEPING ARRANGEMENTS
AND A *Post-partum* SEX TABOO * AND THE OCCURRENCE
OF INITIATION CEREMONIES AT PUBERTY

Customs in infancy		Customs at adolescent initiation ceremonies		
Exclusive mother-son sleeping arrangements	*Post-partum* sex taboo	Absent	Present	
Long	Long		Azande	*hgs* †
			Camayura	*hs*
			Chagga	*hgs*
			Cheyenne	*ht*
			Chiricahua	*ht*
			Dahomeans	*hgs*
			Fijians	*gs*
			Jivaro	*ht*
		Ganda	Kwoma	*hgs*
		Khalapur (Rajput)	Lesu	*gs*
		Nyakyusa	Nuer	*hs*
		Tepoztlan	Samoans	*g*
		Trobrianders	Thonga	*hgs*
		Yapese	Tiv	*hgs*
	Short	Ashanti		
		Malaita	Cagaba	*ht*
		Siriono		
Short	Long	Araucanians	Kwakiutl	*s*
		Pilaga	Ojibwa	*t*
		Pondo	Ooldea	*hgs*
		Tallensi		
	Short	Alorese	Hopi	*hs*
		Balinese	Timbira	*hst*
		Druz		
		Egyptians (Silwa)		
		Eskimos (Copper)		
		French		
		Igorot (Bontoc)		
		Japanese (Suye Mura)		
		Koryak (Maritime)		
		Lakher		
		Lamba		
		Lapps		
		Lepcha		
		Maori		
		Mixtecans		
		Navaho		
		Ontong Javanese		
		Papago		
		Serbs		
		Tanala (Menabe)		
		Trukese		
		United States (Homestead)		
		Yagua		

* Both of a year or more duration.
† The letters following the tribal designations in the right-hand column indicate the nature of the ceremony—*h* = painful hazing, *g* = genital operations, *s* = seclusion from women, and *t* = tests of manliness.

for the initiation ceremony. The boys at this time leave the parental home and move to a men's house or a boys' village where they live until they are married. Malinowski [11] observed this type of adjustment amongst the Trobrianders in 1927. He wrote:

But the most important change, and the one which interests us most is the partial break-up of the family at the time when the adolescent boys and girls cease to be permanent inmates of the parental home ... a special institution ... special houses inhabited by groups of adolescent boys and girls. A boy as he reaches puberty will join such a house. . . . Thus the parent home is drained completely of its adolescent males, though until the boy's marriage he will always come back for food, and will also continue to work for his household to some extent. . . .[12]

At this stage, however, when the adolescent has to learn his duties, to be instructed in traditions and to study his magic, his arts and crafts, his interest in his mother's brother, who is his teacher and tutor, is greatest and their relations are at their best.[13]

This account suggests that this change of residence serves the same functions that we have posited for initiation ceremonies, for example, by establishing male authority, breaking the bond with the mother, and ensuring acceptance of the male role. It is important for our hypothesis, also, that there are only two other societies in our sample where such a change of residence occurs. One of these is the Malaita which has one but not both of our antecedent variables; the other is the Ashanti where the boy may move to the village of his mother's brother at or before puberty, but this is not mandatory and only half the boys do so. Thus, if we were to revise our hypothesis such that a change of residence was considered to be equivalent to intitiation, the four societies mentioned should be moved over to the right-hand column and the exceptional cases would be reduced from eight to four.

Some comment should be made on the two remaining cases in the upper left-hand column. The Ganda are reported to have an interesting method of child rearing which may or may not be relevant to our theory. For the first three years of his life, a Ganda child sleeps exclusively with his mother and she is subject to a sexual taboo. At this point the boy is reported to be weaned and transferred to the household of his father's brother by whom he is brought up from then on. It might be assumed that this event would obviate the need for later ceremonial initiation into manhood. Since several other societies that do have initiation also have a change of residence at weaning, however, this simple explanation cannot be accepted and the Ganda must remain an unexplained exception. Finally Lewis [14] reports for the Tepoztlan that there was some disagreement among his informants as to the length of the taboo and exclusive sleeping arrangements. Since again there were other equally equivocal cases, we shall have to accept the verdict of our judges and let this case also remain an exception.

A reconsideration of the two exceptions in the lower right-hand column, the Hopi and the Timbira, which have the type of initiation into manhood required by our theory but have neither exclusive sleeping arrangements nor a prolonged *post partum* sex taboo, also turns out to be fruitful. In neither of these societies does the father have authority over the

[11] B. Malinowski, *Sex and Repression in Savage Society* (New York: Harcourt, Brace & Co., 1927).
[12] *Ibid.*, p. 67.
[13] *Ibid.*, p. 69.
[14] O. Lewis, *Life in a Mexican Village: Tepoztlan Restudied* (Urbana: University of Illinois Press, 1951).

children.[15] This is vested in the mother's brother who lives in another household.[16] That these societies should have an initiation rite, again, does not seem to contradict our general theory, even though it does contradict our specific hypothesis. From clinical studies in our own society it is clear that even with the lack of exclusive sleeping arrangements and a minimal *post partum* sex taboo, an appreciable degree of dependence upon the mother and rivalry with the father is generated. The cases here suggest that, although these motives are not strong enough to require ceremonial initiation into manhood if the father is present in the household and has authority over the child, this may be required if he lacks such authority.

But what of the cases which have but one of the antecedent variables? Taking into account the societies with exclusive sleeping arrangements but no *post-partum* sex taboo, our theory predicts that these conditions should produce dependency and rivalry. However, since the mother is receiving sexual satisfaction from her husband, she has less need to obtain substitute gratification from nurturing her infant, so that the dependency she produces in her child would be less intense and the need for initiation should be attenuated. Three of the four cases with exclusive sleeping arrangements but no taboo appear to fulfill these conditions. As we have reported above, the Ashanti and the Malaita practice a change of residence which, it could be argued, is somewhat less drastic than initiation. In any case this is permissive and not required for the Ashanti. When the Cagaba boy reaches adolescence, he is given instruction in sexual intercourse by a priest and then sent to practise these instructions with a widow who lives with him temporarily in a specially built small hut. The boy is not allowed to leave this hut until he succeeds in having sexual intercourse with her. This trial is reported to be terrifying to the boy and it is often several days before he does succeed. This type of initiation, however, does not seem to compare with other societies which like the Thonga have a full-fledged ceremony. The Siriono, on the other hand, do not have any ceremonial recognition of the shift from boyhood to manhood and they must be regarded as an exception to our theory.

The final group of cases to consider are those that have a long *post-partum* sex taboo but not exclusive mother-son sleeping arrangements. For these, our theory would also predict an attenuated need for initiation ceremonies. Although the mothers of this group are presumed to gain substitute sexual gratification from being especially nurturant and loving toward their infants, they have less opportunity to do so than with those of societies where there are also exclusive sleeping arrangements.

As in the previous group of societies the ceremonies are, except for the Ooldea which will be discussed below, mild. The Kwakiutl have a ceremony which consists of a potlach given by the father for the son. There the boys undergo no hazing or genital operations but are secluded and expected to perform a dance. For the Ojibwa, the boy is expected to obtain a guardian spirit in a vision before he reaches maturity. Thus, generally when he is 11 or 12 years old, he goes alone into the forest where he stays often for several days without food, water, and generally without sleep until he either has a vision or returns home to recuperate before trying again. Again neither hazing or genital operations are involved.

The Ooldea, a tribe situated in south-

---

[15] A consideration of the influence of authority patterns was suggested by the work of Homans and Schneider, *op. cit.*

[16] This is also true of the Trobrianders discussed above, but of no other society in our sample about which we have information on authority patterns.

western Australia do, however, have a full-fledged initiation rite with hazing, isolation, and a very painful genital operation. This apparently runs counter to our assumption that the rites should be mild if only one determinant is present.

Radcliffe-Brown, however, reports that in many Australian tribes

... the discipline of very young children is left to the mother and the other women of the horde. A father does not punish and may not even scold his infant children, but if they misbehave he will scold the mother and perhaps give her a blow with a stick. He regards the mother as responsible for misbehavior by very young children. When they are a little older, the father undertakes the education of the boys but leaves the education of the girls to the mother and the women of the horde. But the father behaves affectionately and is very little of a disciplinarian. Discipline for a boy begins when he approaches puberty and is exercised by the men of the horde. The big change comes with the initiation ceremonies when, in some tribes, the father, by a ceremonial (symbolic) action, hands over his son to the men who will carry out the initiation rites. During the initiation period of several years the boy is subjected to rigid and frequently painful discipline by men other than his father.[17]

If the Ooldea be one of those Australian tribes described above, they fall, along with the Trobrianders, Hopi, and Timbira, into the class of societies where the function of initiation is to make up for the lack of discipline exercised by a father over the boy during childhood.

A study of those societies without exclusive sleeping arrangements and with a long *post-partum* sex taboo which do not have the rites is interesting. In the first place both the Pondo and the Araucanians are reported to have had initiation ceremonies in the recent past, indicating that they are perhaps near the threshold of needing them. The Tallensi also are interesting. An observer notes that the

Tallensi should have invented the Oedipus-conflict theory since they are quite open and conscious of the strong rivalry and hostility between father and son, a conflict which remains strong and dangerous, guarded only by ritualized forms of etiquette, until the father dies and the son takes his place. Furthermore, family fissions are reported to occur frequently and the oldest son often leaves the family to establish a new lineage of his own.

Thus, the presence of a *post-partum* sex taboo alone seems to produce tension, which these societies commonly seek to resolve through initiation ceremonies. Societies in this group which do not have ceremonies either had them recently or show evidence of unresolved tension.

Summary. The cross-cultural evidence indicates that:

1. A close relationship is established between mother and son during infancy as a consequence of either (a) their sleeping together for at least a year to the exclusion of the father or (b) the mother being prohibited from sexual intercourse for at least a year after the birth of her child or (c) both of these together have measurable consequences which are manifested in cultural adjustments at adolescence.

2. The cultural adjustments to the presence of the above factors are made when the boy approaches or reaches sexual maturity. These adjustments are either (a) a ceremony of initiation into manhood involving at least one and generally several of the following factors; painful *hazing* by the adult males of the society, tests of endurance and manliness, seclusion from women, and genital operations, or (b) a change of residence which involves separation of the boy from his mother and sisters and may also include some formal means for establishing male authority such as receiving instructions from and being required to be respectful

---

[17] Cited from a letter by A. R. Radcliffe-Brown to these authors in Homans and Schneider, *op. cit.*, p. 41.

TABLE 2

THE RELATIONSHIP OF INFANCY FACTORS TO CULTURAL ADJUSTMENTS
AT ADOLSCENCE.

Customs in infancy and childhood			*Cultural adjustment at adolescence*		
Authority of father over son	Exclusive mother-son sleeping arrangement	Post-partum sex taboo	None	Change of residence	Initiation ceremony
Present	Long	Long	2	3	14
		Short	1	2	1
	Short	Long	4	0	2
		Short	23	0	0
Absent			0	1	3

to the mother's brother or the members of the men's house.

3. If both the factors specified in (1) are present, the consequences at adolescence tend to be more elaborate and severe than if only one is present.

4. The cultural adjustments specified in (2) also occur in societies where the father does not have the right to discipline his son, whether or not the conditions specified in (1) are present.

The evidence for these statements is summarized in Table 2.

THE SOCIOPSYCHOLOGICAL IMPLICATIONS

So much for the manifest results at the cultural level. But what is the most reasonable sociopsychological interpretation of these relationships? What are the psychodynamics involved? We are not concerned with the bizarre rites of the Thonga or the peculiar life of a Kwoma infant, for their own sakes, but rather in discovering some general truths about human nature. We, therefore, wish to state what we believe to be the underlying processes that are involved. These are processes that we have not directly observed and which must be accepted or rejected on the grounds of their plausibility or, more important, on the basis of further research implied by our theory.

We believe that six sociopsychological assumptions are supported by our findings:

1. The more exclusive the relationship between a son and his mother during the first years of his life, the greater will be his emotional dependence upon her.

2. The more intensely a mother nurtures (loves) an infant during the early years of his life, the more emotionally dependent he will be upon her.

3. The greater the emotional dependence of a child upon a mother, the more hostile and envious he will be toward anyone whom he perceives as replacing him in her affection.[18]

4. If a child develops a strong emotional dependence upon his mother during infancy, and hostility toward and envy of his father in early childhood at the time of weaning and the onset of in-

---

[18] If, however, the mother herself is perceived by the child as the one responsible for terminating the early intense relationship, this should lead the boy to both envy her and identify with her. This should produce conflict with respect to his sex role identity, which initiation rites would serve to resolve.

dependence training, these feelings (although latent during childhood) will manifest themselves when he reaches physiological maturity in (a) open rivalry with his father and (b) incestuous approaches to his mother, unless measures are taken to prevent such manifestations.

5. Painful hazing, enforced isolation from women, trials of endurance or manliness, genital operations, and change of residence are effective means for preventing the dangerous manifestation of rivalry and incest.

6. Even a moderate or weak amount of emotional dependence upon the mother and rivalry with the father will be dangerous at adolescence if the father has no right to (or does not in fact) exercise authority over his son during childhood.

If these sociopsychological hypotheses are true, they have some interesting implications for individual differences in our own society.[19] It has long been known that there is an association between certain types of juvenile delinquency and broken homes.[20] We would predict that the probability of a boy becoming delinquent in such instances would be highest where the separation of the mother and father occurred during the early infancy of the boy and where she remarried when he was two or three years old.

We would further predict that insofar as there has been an increase in juvenile delinquency in our society, it probably has been accompanied by an increase in the exclusiveness of mother-child relationships and/or a decrease in the authority of the father. It is not unreasonable that industrialization and urbanization have done just this, but, of course, this matter should be investigated before such an interpretation is accepted.

Finally, if further research shows that juvenile delinquency in our society is in part a function of the early childhood factors that have been described in this paper, then it can be countered either by decreasing the exclusiveness of the early mother-child relationship, increasing the authority of the father during childhood, or instituting a formal means of coping with adolescent boys functionally equivalent to those described in this paper. Change of residence would seem more compatible with the values of our society than an initiation ceremony. The Civilian Conservation Corps camps of the 1930's were an experiment which should provide useful data in this regard. The present institution of selective service would perhaps serve this purpose were the boys to be drafted at an earlier age and exposed to the authority of responsible adult males.

---

[19] In a study of infant training William Sewell reports that "the children who slept with their mothers during infancy made significantly poorer showings on the self-adjustment, personal freedom, and family relations components of the California Test of Personality and suffered more sleep disturbances than did those who slept alone." W. H. Sewell, "Infant Training and the Personality of the Child," *Am. J. Sociol.*, 1953, LVIII, 157.

[20] Cf. for example, E. Glueck and S. Glueck, *Unravelling Juvenile Delinquency* (New York: Commonwealth Fund, 1950); W. W. Waltenberg and J. J. Balistrieri, "Gang Membership and Juvenile Misconduct," *Am. Sociol. Rev.*, December 1950, XV, 744–752.

9

Social Stratification

THE CLASS SYSTEM OF THE WHITE CASTE — *By Allison Davis, Burleigh B. Gardner, and Mary R. Gardner*

The "caste line" defines a social gulf across which Negroes may not pass either through marriage or those other intimacies which Old City calls "social equality." A ritual reminder is omnipresent in all relationships that there are two separate castes—a superordinate white group and a subordinate Negro group. Within each of these separate social worlds there are other divisions: families, religious groups, associations, and a system of social classes.[1]

The most fundamental of these divisions within each caste is that of social class; and the researchers, both white and Negro, were initiated into the intricacies of class behavior at the same time that they were being taught how to act toward persons of the opposite caste. Whether it was a matter of accepting an invitation to a party, deciding to visit a family, or planning to attend a church, the participant-observers, who had been "adopted" by people of relatively high social status within their respective castes, were advised upon the important matter of "who" and "where." Certain people were to be approached, not as

equals, but as subordinates. There were places where one "could not afford to be seen" having a "good time," or even worshipping, without loss of status unless it was for purposes of research.

There were many clews to assist in the "placing" of people within broad limits, some easily observable, such as peculiarities of speech, type of clothing worn, the manner of drinking and "carrying" liquor, or occupation. (Among Negroes there was the added factor of color evaluation.) Other criteria were far more subtle—genealogies and inner thoughts—which were ascertainable only after prolonged acquaintance with the society. "Stratifying" the inhabitants of Old City was, thus, one of the major research problems, that is, finding out the values cherished by people of varying circumstances, checking their behavior against their beliefs about status, and finding a systematic way of describing the class structure of the society.

SOCIAL STRATIFICATION

As one becomes acquainted with the white people of Old City, he soon realizes

[1] As here used, a "social class" is to be thought of as the largest group of people whose members have intimate access to one another. A class is composed of families and social cliques. The interrelationships between these families and cliques, in such informal activities as visiting, dances, receptions, teas, and larger informal affairs, constitute the structure of a social class. A person is a member of that social class with which most of his participations, of this intimate kind, occur.

that they are continually classifying themselves and others. There are "Negroes" and "whites"—the caste groups —a relatively simple dichotomy. There are also "leading families," "fine old families," "the four hundred," "the society crowd," "plain people," "nice, respectable people," "good people, but nobody," "po' whites," "red necks," etc.—all terms used to refer to different groups within the white caste. Not only do the whites frequently refer to these subdivisions within their own caste group, but they do so in such a manner as to indicate that they think in terms of a social hierarchy with some people at the "top," some at the "bottom"; with some people "equal" to themselves, and others "above" or "below" them. There are recurrent expressions such as: "He isn't our social equal," "She isn't our kind," "They are just nobody," "Those folk are the way-high-ups," "They're nothing but white trash!" "Oh, they're plain people like us." These expressions refer not only to individuals but also to groups, so that one may speak of superordinate and subordinate groups within the white society. And, most important of all, people tend to act in conformity with these conceptions of their "place" and the social position of others in the society.

When the individuals and groups so designated are studied, striking differences between them with regard to family relations, recreational behavior, standards of living, occupation and income, education, and other traits are immediately apparent. On the basis of these differences, it is possible to define the social classes within the white society and to describe them in detail. It was soon evident that people at all levels were thinking in terms of, and often referring to, three broad social classes— "upper," "middle," and "lower"—although, when designating particular individuals, there were divergences of opinion as to their social position. There was some difference of opinion, too, as to

the things that made one upper, middle, or lower; but an analysis of the relative social positions of the informants showed that these variations in conceptions of class status were, themselves, related to the social position of the informant. Thus, a "po' white," as defined by persons of the higher classes, conceived of the total structure in a somewhat different manner from an upper-class planter. In other words, the social perspective varied with the social position of the individual. People in the same social positions agreed, in the main, however, on the traits which characterized the classes, although the class traits did not apply to everyone within a class in absolute fashion. Thus, a member of a group defined by consensus as "superior" might have a few characteristics in common with a person of an "inferior" group; but when each group was considered as a whole, the differences were large and significant. Thus, "the society crowd," as a group, owns more property than the "po' whites," although some "society folks" own none at all; the "poor, but respectable" people, in the aggregate, are more church-minded than "trash," though some are not affiliated with churches.

The researchers were able to describe the structure of the society by interviewing a large number of informants drawn from various occupational, associational, and other status groups who "placed" individuals and stated their conceptions of class criteria. The observers were also alert to "off-the-record" remarks and to behavior in public places and in crisis situations, in order to ascertain the bearers of prestige, the wielders of power, and the persons who associated together on various occasions. The resulting picture of the society is that of a class system in operation, with a description of the way it appears to the people within it.

While generalized conceptions of the class structure were readily obtainable from interviewing, a detailed study of class characteristics depended upon a method of determining the social position of specific individuals. The first step was to establish a series of individuals distributed from the "top" of the society to the "bottom." This was done through interviewing, since almost any member of the society could point to some other individuals or groups whom he considered at the very top, at the very bottom, or "in between." Interviewing and observing the people who were thus placed resulted in the identification of a group of individuals who considered themselves either superordinate, subordinate, or equal in relationship to one another. Continuous interviewing of these informants made possible a detailed study of their ideology and behavior. Wide discrepancies in placement were studied as special cases, with the purpose of relating them to the system of relationships which was gradually emerging, and of accounting for the differing opinions of their social position. Thus, over a period of eighteen months, interviewing, coupled with observation of overt behavior, permitted the researchers to establish with certainty a sample of the personnel of the different social classes.

After identifying these individuals within the classes, it was possible to study their relationships and characteristics in detail and to correlate traits such as income, property, education, and church and associational memberships with social position and general behavior. An additional check was provided by interviewing for the "values" which people attributed to various types of behavior and class traits when they talked about them. It was thus possible to relate ideology to social class.

Because of the limitations of time, it was impossible to stratify every individual in the society by the interview-observation technique; but once the characteristics of the known individuals had been determined, criteria were available for placing any individual about whom some important facts were available.

Thus, when a person's participation could not be checked, if some pertinent facts about his job, his family, his education, and his children were known, one could state the participation potentialities which his social personality bore.

On the basis of the attitudes of many informants of various social positions, together with observations of many kinds of social behavior, the researchers concluded that the three main class divisions recognized by the society could be objectively described. Each of these was characterized by its particular behavior pattern and by a distinctive ideology. Closer study revealed the existence of subclasses within each of these three larger groups, and these are referred to in this study as the "upper-upper class," "lower-upper class," "upper-middle class," "lower-middle class," "upper-lower class," and the "lower-lower class." We shall examine, first, the conceptions of class which each of these groups holds, for the very way in which people conceive of the class divisions varies with their social position.

CLASS PERSPECTIVE AND THE CLASS STRUCTURE

The Upper-upper Class. It was evident from the outset that certain persons were at the very top of the social hierarchy. They were accorded deference in nearly all types of relationships; people were anxious to associate with them; they belonged to the exclusive churches; their names were sought for patron's lists; they lived in imposing mansions inherited from Old City's "antebellum past" (or at least their parents did); and, on ritual occasions of high import, they dominated the scene and tended to organize community behavior. They were, without doubt, in almost everyone's eyes, members of the "upper-upper class." Neither whites nor Negroes questioned their position even when they resented it; and resentment, itself, tended to dissolve when they were functioning as symbols of the total community on such occasions as the annual Historical Week, when visitors from the entire nation came to Old City. It was this upper-upper class which made the finest distinctions when ranking or "stratifying" other people.

Members of this highest status group recognize five class divisions in the society (see Fig. 1). They visualize themselves at the top of the society, an "*old* aristocracy" whose superordination has its origin and stability in "time." They consider themselves the highest group in the society by inheritance, because, as they phrase it: "Our families have always been the best people." Immediately below them on the social scale the members of this class point out another group, which has been designated the "lower-upper class." These are people with whom the "old aristocracy" is willing to participate in informal relationships, whom they know intimately and recognize as fundamentally no different from themselves in income, consumption standards, education, intellectual interests, and general behavior pattern. But they are not "*old* aristocracy"; they haven't been upper class long enough. An analysis of these two upper groups indicates that the division between them is reflected hardly at all by differences in overt behavior or other characteristics. It is a subjective division which finds objective expression only in certain very intimate situations when antagonisms between the two groups are verbalized.

Beneath the lower uppers, the upper uppers see the "nice, respectable people" (the upper-middle class) who have "never been prominent at all." They know these people by name, speak to them on the street, and may converse with them at church or associational meetings; but they do not participate with them at social affairs of the more intimate kinds.

The upper-middle class is contrasted with the "good people" who are "just nobody" (the lower-middle class). With the lower-middle class, the upper uppers have only formal and definitely limited relations, usually economic in nature, such as those of employer-to-employee or merchant-to-customer. The type of behavior in such relationships is explicitly delimited; and, in general, upper-upper individuals resent the social mobility of lower-middle-class persons, probably because such a movement involves a change in these relatively impersonal economic relationships and the corresponding traditional behavior pattern.

Finally, at the very bottom of the society are the people whom the upper uppers call the "working class," "the poorer class," or just "po' white." They have little contact with this group, tending to ignore their existence. They make no distinction between tenant-farmers, fishermen, factory workers, as these people, themselves, do. Nor do they distinguish between other variant behavior patterns within this lower-class world.

The Lower-upper Class. The lower uppers, whom the upper uppers call "aristocracy, but not *old*," make the same general distinctions between social groups. They do not emphasize the distinction between themselves and the upper uppers so much as the upper uppers do, however. This may be attributed to the fact that most of the members of this group have, during their lifetime, been socially mobile, and they have moved into the upper class from the upper-middle group. Consequently, while they recognize themselves as a group apart from, and below, the upper uppers, they tend to ally themselves with this group and to minimize the value of family background. Their actual status is evident, however, in their individual relations and in their verbally expressed antagonisms toward the upper uppers on

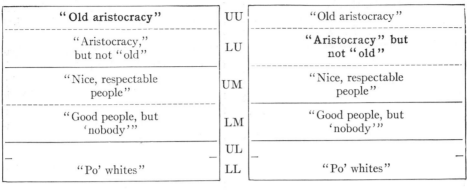

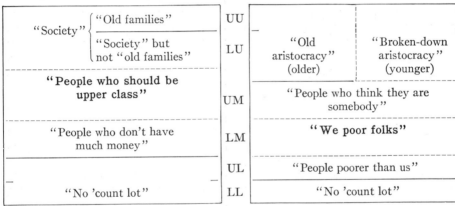

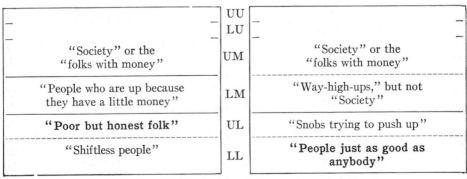

Fig. 1. The social perspectives of the social classes

certain occasions. In several cases, lower uppers resisted subordination by upper-upper individuals through face-to-face criticisms of their ancestry; Thus, Mrs. Bowley, upper upper and proud of her family, was both hurt and indignant at lower-upper Mrs. Duncan's remarks about her ancestry:

I said something to Mrs. Duncan about being related to the Montgomerys. She said; "Well, that is nothing to be proud of. I wouldn't brag about it!" I said I didn't see why not; my father had always taught me to be proud of the Montgomery blood in my veins. Then she said that the first Montgomery was nothing but a gambler, and that that was nothing to be proud of. Well, that isn't true! He wasn't *really* a gambler. . . .

Similarly, the lower uppers' definition of the upper-middle class, as a group, is both vague and reluctant. Directly questioned, they frequently deny that persons stratified as upper middle are really below them on the social scale, or they will attempt an evasion. (Their overt behavior, however, belies their words.) They will say, for instance: "I don't mean that Mrs. Atkins and people like that aren't nice and all that. She is. She is very nice and well-thought-of here. We just don't happen to know her very well, and *she doesn't enjoy the same things we do.*" This hesitancy about actually identifying persons as upper-middle class is probably related to the fact that they, themselves, have rather recently moved out of the upper-middle stratum, and many of them still have kinsmen in this social position. (Equally logical, perhaps, are attempts by some persons to overestimate the social distance between themselves and the class from which they came.)

The lower-middle class, on the other hand, is clearly defined by these ascending uppers. In general, they have the same limited contact with the lower-middle class as the upper uppers have; but they seem less inclined to resent the rise of lower middles into the upper-middle class, or their economic improvement. This is, perhaps, due to the fact that specific limited relations with these persons, and a corresponding behavior pattern, are less well established and less fixed by tradition than in the case of upper-upper relations with the lower middles.

Toward the lower class, as a whole, lower uppers present the same indifference and lack of precise definition that their upper-upper associates display.

The Upper-middle Class. Stratification of the society by persons immediately below the upper class (here designated the "upper-middle class") is frequently associated with an expression of moral attitudes and with definite conceptions of the positive value and important role of wealth. These persons are often unable to reconcile the existing social hierarchy with a hierarchy that "should be." In their thinking, their own class group "should be" the highest group in the society, since it is the wealthiest group and the one whose behavior reflects most precisely the traditional teachings of the Protestant church. In spite of this condemnatory attitude, however, they conceive of the upper class as a group separate from themselves. Its superordination in the existing scheme of things is generally acknowledged, albeit somewhat reluctantly. Occasionally, certain persons whom upper uppers place as lower uppers are not included in this group by the upper-middle class. But the "*old* aristocracy" is quite definitely assigned its place at the top; its ascendancy is resented; and the group is condemned for its "immoral behavior."

Upper-middle class individuals who are attempting to rise in the social scale point out beneath them the "lower middles" as a separate class group and almost invariably attempt to exaggerate their social distance from it. Behavior and attitudes of these mobile middle-class individuals toward the subordinate lower middles are similar to those of the upper class, and their relationships with this group tend to be formal and economic. Stable upper middles, however, know many lower middles and sometimes participate with them informally, especially in the younger age ranges. In general, they attribute this differentiation more to the lower economic position of these people than to other traits. They do not try to maintain great social distance between lower middles and themselves.

Like members of the upper-class groups, upper middles make no distinctions within the lower-class group, although they seem somewhat more aware of the presence of this group at the bottom of the white society. While they do have somewhat more frequent contact with them than uppers, especially in employer-employee relationships, all of the lower class is thought of as "just the working class," the "poorer class."

The Lower-middle Class. "We poor folks" and the "other poor people like us" make up the lower-middle class. But, "it shouldn't be that way," they think. "The people who are up are there mainly because they have money," they insist. Persons in this group have rather strong class feelings. Above them they see the upper middles, people like themselves, but with more money. Above the upper middles, they recognize an "aristocracy." Within this "aristocracy" (upper upper and lower upper together) they distinguish between the older persons who have established their superiority through the possession of great wealth in the past and younger individuals, on the other hand, who are not now wealthy or who never have been. These latter have no claim to the position of "upper class," they say; yet they are there. They are just a "broken-down aristocracy." Lower middles think in terms of "younger" and "older" aristocrats, rather than in terms of an upper-upper and lower-upper class, with all age ranges within each group.

Toward the upper middles they level a frequent taunt, "They think they *are* somebody"; and, as a group, lower middles prefer not to recognize the social distance between themselves and such people. They resent all attempts by this class to express any social distance. In

general, too, they seem to resent mobility from the upper-middle class into the upper class more than they do mobility from their own ranks into the upper-middle class.

Here, for the first time, a group subdivides the lower class. There is one group, immediately below them, for whom the lower middles have pity but whom they do not condemn or scorn. These are people "even poorer than us," the upper lowers, who are definitely distinguished from the "po' whites," the "no-count," and the "worthless"—the lower lowers.

The Upper-lower Class. Members of the upper-lower class have a sense of solidarity and speak often of "people like us" as distinct both from the lower-middle class above them and the lower lowers below them. Like the middle classes, they think of social stratification in Old City as an absolute hierarchy of wealth. (They are less accurately informed of the actual economic status of individuals above them, however, than one would infer from their conversation.) Their interpretation of class differences is less often tinged with moral concepts than in the case of the middle class.

At the top of the social world, as they see it, is "Society," composed of nearly all those persons who are upper upper, lower upper, and upper middle. All these people are said to be "wealthy." Their high social position is thus recognized and accepted as a fact. Beneath "Society," the upper-lower class recognizes the members of the lower-middle class, whose assumption of social superiority they resent. They are sure that these people occupy a superordinate position simply because they have more wealth.

Between themselves and the lower-lower class, upper lowers make a very careful distinction in their verbalizations, although in actual overt behavior little social distance is maintained. They visit and borrow, exchange domestic services, and converse on the street and in the stores, although such relations are not so frequent as with members of their own group. Thus, while they participate as equals with lower lowers in many one-to-one, face-to-face relations, they do not, as a group, wish to be identified with those whom they consider inferior, unkempt, and improvident.

The Lower-lower Class. The lower lowers, like the upper lowers, also see "Society" at the top, a vague category for persons above the lower-middle position. Lower-lower-class women occasionally refer to the "very wealthy ladies" in this group. Sometimes, even a few lower-middle-class individuals are included in "Society"; more often, however, lower-middle-class individuals are recognized as a separate group with "some money, but not Society." The small shopkeepers with whom they trade, some policemen, artisans with whom they have some contact, and other members of the lower-middle class are spoken of as "way high up" but distinct from "Society." Lower lowers resent the position of the upper-lower class, the members of which are thought to be socially ambitious and snobbish. Their attempts at refinement are generally ridiculed. The upper lowers' claim to a higher social position is thought to be unjustified and to be based entirely on their economic superiority, their better jobs, and more adequate housing.

Summary. Members of any one class thus think of themselves as a group and have a certain unity of outlook. This is indicated by their frequent reference to "people like us" and to persons "not our kind." Expressions of this group solidarity are particularly prevalent when individuals are discussing groups immediately above and below them. When expressing resentment at exclusion from the class above and antagonism toward mobility from the class below, social classes betray unconsciously their sense of solidarity and "we-ness." It will be seen subsequently, too, that members

of these classes and subclasses have a further unity through a common set of beliefs, a common pattern of overt behavior, and other traits which function as symbols of status.

While members of all class groups recognize classes above and below them, or both, the greater the social distance from the other classes the less clearly are fine distinctions made. Although an individual recognizes most clearly the existence of groups immediately above and below his own, he is usually not aware of the social distance actually maintained between his own and these adjacent groups. Thus, in all cases except that of members of the upper-lower class the individual sees only a minimum of social distance between his class and the adjacent classes. This is illustrated by the dotted lines in Figure 1. Almost all other class divisions, however, are visualized as definite lines of cleavage in the society with a large amount of social distance between them.

In general, too, individuals visualize class groups above them less clearly than those below them; they tend to minimize the social differentiations between themselves and those above. This difference in perspective is partly explained by the fact that class lines in the society are not permanent and rigid and that upward mobility is fairly frequent. It is, further, due to the natural tendency in such a status system to identify with "superiors." In view of this situation it is not surprising that individuals in the two upper strata make the finest gradations in the stratification of the whole society and that class distinctions are made with decreasing precision as social position becomes lower.

Not only does the perspective on social stratification vary for different class levels, but the very bases of class distinction in the society are variously interpreted by the different groups. People tend to agree as to where people are but not upon why they are there.

Upper-class individuals, especially upper uppers, think of class divisions largely in terms of time—one has a particular social position because his family has "always had" that position. Members of the middle class interpret their position in terms of wealth and time and tend to make moral evaluations of what "should be." Both middle-class groups accept the time element as an important factor in the superordinate position of the "old aristocracy," but for the rest of the society they consider only individual wealth and moral behavior as differentiating factors. Lower-class people, on the other hand, view the whole stratification of the society as a hierarchy of wealth. The lower lowers think that all those above them on the social scale are progressively wealthy and that their own subordination is dependent upon this economic factor alone. While upper lowers have a similar idea of those above them, they frequently add a moral note in explaining the subordinate position of lower lowers.

The identity of a social class does not depend on uniformity in any one or two, or a dozen, specific kinds of behavior but on a complex pattern or network of interrelated characteristics and attitudes.

Among the members of any one class, there is no strict uniformity in any specific type of behavior but rather a range and a "modal average." One finds a range in income, occupation, educational level, and types of social participation. The "ideal type" may be defined, however, for any given class—the class configuration—from which any given individual may vary in one or more particulars. Also, two individuals may belong to the same association, fall in the same occupational category, belong to the same church, or have the same ideas about local politics; but identity in any one or two such particulars does not necessarily indicate that both individuals belong to the same social class. Class position is determined rather by the configuration of traits which an individual possesses.

An important aspect of this configuration is "ideology"—the set of concepts and the complex of attitudes toward individuals and institutions which individuals exhibit. The members of any one class or subclass share the same general attitudes and beliefs—that is, the same ideology. The conceptions of class which have been described in this section represent one aspect of the class ideologies.

SOCIAL STATUS IN JURY DELIBERATIONS
By Fred L. Strodtbeck, Rita M. James, and Charles Hawkins

Occupational specialization has two distinguishable effects. First, it increases productivity and, second, it provides the basis for a status hierarchy. Perhaps it is less commonplace to think that role differentiation in face-to-face groups arises

from a similar economic process and results in similar status differences. For groups to define and achieve their goals, however, they must control the use of their primary-group resource—their common time together. Only one or, at most,

Prepared especially for this volume. A report of one phase of the experimental jury investigations conducted as part of the Law and Behavioral Science Project with funds granted by the Ford Foundation at the Law School, the University of Chicago. Lee H. Hook and Kathleen Beaufait, current staff members, and Margaret R. McDonald, Leo Lynch, and Noreen Haygood, former staff members, are appreciatively acknowledged for their contribution toward the accumulation of the data on which this report is based.

a few persons can talk at any given instant and be understood. Who talks and how much he talks is, within limits, determined by the reactions of the group to the speaker. Acts that are perceived as relevant to the solution of the group's problems are generally favorably received and the responsible speaker is encouraged to continue. In the long run participation tends to become differentiated, and a small fraction of the group's members will account for most of the participation.

For the purposes of the present study which inquires into the relationships between occupation and selected aspects of role differentiation, it is desirable that the focus of the small-group discussion is not too narrowly circumscribed by status prerogatives. For example, a group of officers and enlisted men discussing military problems or a group of doctors and nurses discussing a medical problem would not provide the circumstance we require. A greater presumption of equality is desired.

In the jury situation not only does the widespread norm assume that group members should act toward one another as equals, but the presumption of equality is reinforced by the requirement that the verdict be unanimous. Equal and responsible participation in the deliberation, therefore, is an institutionalized expectation. If evidence indicates that the status differences of the larger community become manifest during the deliberation, then it may be expected that a similar generalization of status will be found in other situations of interaction where hierarchical considerations are more prominent.

It is essential for our study that wide background differences be present within the juror population. This is assured in metropolitan areas such as Chicago, St. Louis, and Minneapolis where our experimental jury research has been conducted since jurors are selected here by a random process from voting-registration lists. The resultant jury-pool population compares closely with the expected population computed from census reports, although there are several known sources of bias. Lawyers, doctors, teachers, policemen, and other local and federal employees, including elected officials, are excused from jury service. Aliens, foreign visitors, recent migrants, and persons under 21 who are not eligible to vote do not appear on the jury lists. Finally, men who operate "one-man" businesses and prospective jurors with pressing personal problems can ordinarily have their jury service deferred or cancelled. The net effect is that the professions and very low education and occupation groups are slightly underrepresented.

Occupations are classified in four groups: proprietor, clerical, skilled, and labor. "Proprietor" includes the census category [1] of proprietors, managers and officials as well as professionals such as architects, accountants, and engineers who are not excluded from service. "Clerical" and "skilled" categories correspond to the census categories and "labor" subsumes the census categories of semiskilled workers, nonfarm laborers, and servants. Farm owners and laborers are absent from our populations, and retired persons have been classified by their occupations prior to retirement. Women are classified by their stated occupations, except that housewives are classified by their husbands' occupations.

Previous studies indicate that power and participation in face-to-face situations are related to status. Caudill [2] observed the daily exchange of information

---

[1] Alba M. Edwards, *Bureau of the Census Alphabetical Index of Occupations by Industries and Social-Economic Groups* (Washington, D.C.: Department of Commerce, 1937).

[2] William Caudill, *The Psychiatric Hospital as a Small Society* (Cambridge, Mass.: Harvard University Press, 1957).

at administrative conferences among the staff of a small psychiatric hospital and found that the relative participation by the director of the service, the residents, the head nurse, the nurses, and the occupational therapist were ordered by their statuses in the hospital, even though the lower-status persons ordinarily spend more time with the patients. Torrance [3] used nonmilitary problems but found that pilots, navigators, and gunners recognized a power hierarchy in the contrived situation which paralleled that ordinarily in effect in airship operation. Strodtbeck [4] demonstrated that the greater economic and religious power of Navaho in contrast with Mormon women was reflected in their greater power in husband-wife decision-making. More pertinent, perhaps, is a study [5] relating to the continuation in jury deliberations of a strong emphasis by women on expressive and integrative acts. The components that had been found descriptive of women's roles in family-interaction situations were found to characterize women's roles in jury deliberations.

It is important to stress that while the related studies are consistent insofar as they suggest a parallel between generalized status and status in face-to-face systems, they do not provide a firm basis for generalizing to the situation at hand, at least in terms of the measure of correspondence. In Torrance's experiment the pilots probably dominated to a lesser degree in the experimental situation than they would have when the airship was in operation. While the ordering was preserved, it was undoubtedly attenuated. In the present case, what differences are to be expected? The relation between roles like pilot and gunner or clerical

worker and laborer is not equally clear in the interaction differences they imply. There is no compelling reason to believe that clerical workers and laborers will have had sufficient experience together to evolve a stable pecking order. Furthermore, once the jurors have completed their deliberations, they do not expect a continued relationship that would provide an opportunity for external status differences to become manifest. If status differences are present in the jury room, it is almost certain that they arise in part because the varied requirements of the deliberation re-create within the jury the need for the differential experiences associated with status. Whether or not the differences which stem from the external system are great enough to become apparent in a one- to two-hour deliberation is the empirical question we seek to answer.

SOURCE OF DATA

Mock jury deliberations were conducted in which the participants were jurors drawn by lot from the regular jury pools of the Chicago and St. Louis courts. The jurors listened to a recorded trial, deliberated, and returned their verdict—all under the customary discipline of bailiffs of the court. The jury deliberations were recorded, fully transcribed, and scored in terms of interaction-process categories.

This paper is based primarily upon 49 deliberations for which interaction-process analysis has been carried out. Although further work is in process on more than 100 additional deliberations which have been collected by the project during the past three years, the present report is final since further interaction-

[3] E. P. Torrance, *Some Consequences of Power Differences on Decision Making in Permanent and Temporary Three-Man Groups*, "Research Studies," XXII (Pullman: State College of Washington, 1954), pp. 130–140.

[4] F. L. Strodtbeck, "Husband-Wife Interaction over Revealed Differences," *Am. Sociol. Rev.*, 1951, XVI, 141–145.

[5] F. L. Strodtbeck and R. D. Mann, "Sex Role Differentiation in Jury Deliberations," *Sociometry*, 1956, XIX, 3–11.

process analysis of the type reported here is not contemplated. Two civil trials were used as the basis for the deliberations. In the first (29 deliberations) the plaintiff, a secretary, sought compensation for injuries incurred in a two-car collision. In the second (20 deliberations) a young child sought compensation for facial disfigurement incurred in a fire alleged to have been caused by a defective vaporizer. A total of 49 by 12, or 588, different jurors were involved. Data on 14 additional vaporizer cases and 28 recent experimental trials are utilized in other portions of the paper. In total data from 91 juries are used in the examination of different status effects.

PROCEDURES

Selecting a Foreman. After the jury listened to the case, they were told to select their foreman and begin their deliberation. In more than half of the deliberations, the foreman was nominated by one member and then quickly accepted by the remainder of the group. In about a third of the deliberations the man who opened the discussion and sought either to nominate another, or to focus the group's attention on their responsibility in selecting a foreman, was himself selected foreman. However, in all instances the selection of a foreman was quickly and apparently casually accomplished. There was no instance in which mention of any socioeconomic criteria was made, but this is not to say that socioeconomic criteria were not involved. For example, Table 1 shows that some foremen were selected from all strata, but the incidence was three and a half times as great among proprietors as among laborers. In addition, although the details are not given in the table, tabulations show that only one fifth as many women were chosen as foreman as would be expected by chance.

Relative Participation. The deliberations were recorded with two micro-

TABLE 1

OCCUPATIONAL STATUS OF
49 JURY FOREMEN

Occupation	Expected *	Observed	Index
Proprietor	9.73	18	185
Clerical	15.03	15	100
Skilled	9.56	8	84
Labor	14.68	8	54

* Computed under assumption that foremen will be proportional to portion of sample in the given occupation.

phones to facilitate binaural identification of individual participants. The protocols were fully transcribed, and from the protocol each speaker's contributions were separated into units of discrete action, each of which is roughly the equivalent of a simple declarative sentence. Identification of the speaker was checked with the original observer's notes, and an assistant tabulated the scores with the aid of the recording plus indications of nonverbal gestures made by the original observer.

Since there were 12 persons in the jury, one twelfth of the total acts is the pro-rata percentage for each juror's acts. This provides the base line against which the effects of external status may be appraised. The higher the average participation of an occupational group, the greater their relative share of the common resource of time. It may be seen in Table 2 that in all occupations males talked more than females and the amount of participation was sharply differentiated between higher than expected values for proprietors and clerical workers, and lower than expected values for skilled and unskilled laborers.

While the moderately differing values in Table 2 are averages based upon the scores of more than 500 persons, within any particular deliberation there was a very steep differentiation between the most- and least-verbal jurors. For example, in 82 percent of the juries the top three participators accounted for one

TABLE 2

PERCENTAGE RATES OF PARTICIPATION IN JURY DELIBERATION
BY OCCUPATION AND SEX OF JUROR

Sex	Occupation				Combined
	Proprietor	Clerical	Skilled	Laborer	
Male	12.9	10.8	7.9	7.5	9.6
	(N = 81) *	(N = 81)	(N = 80)	(N = 107)	(N = 349)
Female	9.1	7.8	4.8	4.0	6.0
	(N = 31)	(N = 92)	(N = 28)	(N = 62)	(N = 213)
Combined	11.8	9.2	7.1	6.4	8.5
	(N = 112)	(N = 173)	(N = 108)	(N = 169)	(N = 562) †

* Numbers of jurors are shown in parentheses.
† Twenty-six of 588 jurors from the 49 juries used were not satisfactorily classified by occupation and are omitted.

half or more of the total acts, while the remaining acts were distributed among the other nine members. It is to be emphasized that the averages of Table 2 describe the relative participation of occupation and sex groups; they do not reflect the wide variation within any one jury.

One source of differences in participation within a jury may be attributed to the election of one member to play the role of foreman. The foreman was responsible for approximately one fourth of the total acts and as shown in Table 1 was more frequently selected from the higher-status groups. When foreman scores were eliminated the average-participation values were:

proprietor	8.9
clerical	7.0
skilled	6.3
labor	5.9

The gap between clerical and skilled workers is narrower but the rank order is unchanged.[6]

The latent premise in the study of participation is that high participation indicates greater ability to influence others. Earlier research supports such an interpretation for *ad hoc* problem-solving groups and for families. Further evidence is available from the present research. Jurors were asked before the deliberation what, if anything, they would award the plaintiff. A detailed examination of individual predeliberation decisions with the subsequent group awards in 29 deliberations reveals that the more active jurors shifted their predeliberation position less often than less active jurors in the process of reaching a unanimous group verdict.[7] This interpretation of the relation between participation and influence by status level may be documented by comparing the average pre-

[6] A further check was made on the effects of jury participation when another person of one's own occupation group was also present. For juries in which at least two of each occupational group are present, the values are quite similar to Table 2, and while there is some tendency for higher-status persons to talk more when they are alone, or in a marked minority, further corrections have minor effects.

[7] Allen Barton, *Persuasion and Compromise in Damage Awards*, December, 1956, unpublished manuscript

TABLE 3

Average Votes Received as Helpful Juror
by Occupation and Sex

Sex	Occupation				Combined
	Proprietor	Clerical	Skilled	Laborer	
Male	6.8	4.2	3.9	2.7	4.3
	(N = 113)	(N = 108)	(N = 115)	(N = 143)	(N = 479)
Female	3.2	2.7	2.0	1.5	2.3
	(N = 34)	(N = 116)	(N = 36)	(N = 76)	(N = 262)
Combined	6.0	3.4	3.5	2.3	3.6
	(N = 147)	(N = 224)	(N = 151)	(N = 219)	(N = 741) *

* This number includes 14 additional juries for which interaction process scores are not available.

deliberation award (listed according to occupational group) with the jury verdict. The correlations are:

proprietor	.50
clerical	.11
skilled	.29
labor	.02

$(p < .05)$

Members from the same occupational group sometimes initially favored different verdicts, and in this case not all the members of this group achieved their desired outcome. Nonetheless, the correlation between the proprietors' average and the jury verdicts is significant. This result corresponds to the participation values after they have been corrected by eliminating the foreman. Since our content analyses clearly show that foremen were more neutral than other actively participating jurors during the discussion of monetary awards, the corrected participation values are probably a more satisfactory measure of influence in the damage-award deliberation.

The meaning of participation levels may be viewed from still another perspective. After the deliberation, the jurors were asked to answer a battery of questions concerning their personal satisfaction with the quality of the delibera

tion and the tone of interpersonal relations. The level of an individual's satisfaction was positively correlated with the level of his own participation ($r = .52$, $p < .05$). The involvement that high participation represented in the jury is not unlike the involvement of higher-status people in the affairs of the larger community; both are instruments for group-derived satisfactions.

In addition, responses to the post-deliberation question, "Who do you believe contributed most to helping your group reach its decision?" were tabulated by occupation of the target person. The average number of helpfulness votes received by occupation groups (see Table 3) closely parallels the participation by occupation groups (see Table 2). The correlation between votes received and participation is about .69 when sets of individual values are correlated. Male clerical workers get slightly fewer votes than their participation would appear to warrant and male skilled workers get slightly more, but the overwhelming impression is that the number of such votes received, like participation, influence, and satisfaction, parallels status differentiation in society at large.

Perceived Fitness as Jurors. Where is the quality of justice to be found? The

TABLE 4

CHOICE OF JUROR IF MEMBER OF RESPONDENT'S FAMILY WERE ON TRIAL,
BASED UPON OCCUPATION STEREOTYPES
(Pro rata expected is 100) *

Respondent's occupation		Preferred occupation			
		Proprietor	Clerical	Skilled	Laborer
Proprietor	(N = 63)	241	95	51	13
Clerical	(N = 107)	206	112	71	11
Skilled	(N = 72)	172	55	139	33
Laborer	(N = 76)	126	42	147	84

* These data were collected from jurors in our 28 most recent experimental juries.

Courts Martial reform, which permitted enlisted men to request other enlisted men for their trial panels, was largely nullified by their preference to leave their cases in the hands of officers. How do jurors react? A departure from random selection might have two possible effects. Given a choice, jurors might tend to overselect people in the higher occupations just as they had in distributing their helpfulness ballots. Or, taking the class theory as the basis of our prediction, we might assume that the chooser might select more jurors from his own occupation group. How these counter tendencies might be balanced is a question for which we have no theoretical answer and, therefore, must investigate empirically.

In an effort to probe deeper for evidence of class identifications, the following question was asked of 28 juries.

The jury pool is made up of people from all walks of life. However, if a member of your family were on trial and you had your choice, which of the following kinds of people would you prefer to make up the majority of the jurors who would hear your case?

—— business and professional people
—— clerical and white collar workers
—— skilled workers
unskilled workers

The expected values, determined by assuming that equal preference will be shown for each status group, have been divided into the observed values, and the resultant ratio was multiplied by 100 to give the index numbers shown in Table 4. All groups, except laborers, would prefer to have a member of their family tried before a jury the majority of whose members were proprietors. Like other groups, laborers were also upwardly oriented in their preferences but their first choice was skilled workers, then proprietors. Clerical and skilled workers chose persons from their own occupation group as their second choice. All groups except laborers ranked laborers last. Laborers placed themselves third and clerks last. It is to be stressed that Table 4 represents the choice of jurors in terms of occupational stereotypes. It is what a member of one occupational group perceives in terms of his generalized conception of his own and other occupational groups.

We also asked jurors to choose "four of your fellow jurors whom you would best like to have serve on a jury if you were on trial." This question asks jurors not for generalized conceptions of other occupational groups but for evaluations of particular persons. We wished to know if the selections made on the basis of face-to-face contact were similar or different

TABLE 5

CHOICE OF JUROR IF RESPONDENT WERE ON TRIAL,
BASED UPON DELIBERATION EXPERIENCE
(Pro rata expected is 100) *

Respondent's occupation		Preferred occupation			
		Proprietor	Clerical	Skilled	Laborer
Proprietor	(N = 78)	169	110	119	39
Clerical	(N = 129)	145	100	101	75
Skilled	(N = 74)	147	104	84	73
Laborer	(N = 130)	162	100	112	74

* The expected values used to form the index numbers have been determined by assuming that each person distributes his four choices simultaneously under conditions that give an equal chance of each of the 11 fellow juror's being chosen. For example, for two proprietor, four clerical, two skilled and four labor the expected distribution of the eight proprietor votes would be 2/11(8), 8/11(8), 4/11(8) and 8/11(8). It is assumed that no fellow juror can be chosen twice by the same subject. The expected and observed choices for individuals on one jury are combined by status groups and accumulated for the different juries. Only six randomly selected jurors in the 20 vaporizer cases were asked this form of the question, so the 411 responses come from a potential population of (29 × 12) + (20 × 6), or 468.

from stereotype choices.[8] If a prototype of a social system had grown during deliberation, jurors might come to regard one another more in terms of performance in the task at hand than in terms of general social status. It was also possible for the deliberation to reveal status-based ideologies that would open latent schisms. The data suggest that differences were ordinarily not magnified by the deliberation and the jurors came to be convinced that a just job had been done. The special thrust of the question "if a member of your family were on trial" could have sensitized jurors to think in terms of personal interests rather than abstract principles such as competence or justice. Possibly these respondents became so sensitive to their personal interests that they turned away from those jurors who had been the arbiters of consensus in their own deliberations.

Table 5 shows a preference for pro-

prietors but at a somewhat lower level. More detailed effects of the face-to-face experience in contrast with the response to occupational categories may best be illustrated by subtracting Table 4 from Table 5. It is to be noted that while Tables 4 and 5 are based on different populations, the respondents in both cases are random samples from the population available in successive weeks in the jury pool. When Table 4 is subtracted from Table 5 (see Table 6) a positive value in the matrix represents an increase in index value associated with the face-to-face experience.

The main diagonal shows that "own group" choices were lower at each occupation level, particularly among proprietors and skilled laborers. That is, choices after the deliberation experience are not determined by a narrow "interest group." In addition, all values above the main diagonal are positive. That is, face-

[8] The stereotype-juror preference question was not asked of the juries in Table 5. The 28 juries of Table 4 are an entirely different set, so that the possible bias of face-to-face choices by the prior administration of the stereotype choices is avoided.

TABLE 6

CHANGE IN INDEX VALUE ASSOCIATED WITH DELIBERATION EXPERIENCE
(Value of Table 4 subtracted from Table 5)

Respondent's occupation	Preferred occupation			
	Proprietor	Clerical	Skilled	Laborer
Proprietor	−72	15	68	26
Clerical	−61	−12	30	64
Skilled	−35	49	−55	40
Laborer	36	58	−35	−10

to-face experience caused lower-status persons to be evaluated more highly! As shown below the main diagonal, proprietors were reduced in the evaluation of clerical and skilled workers and increased in the evaluation of laborers; clerical workers were rated more highly by both skilled workers and laborers; and laborers decreased their former preference for skilled workers. The lower range of index values in the face-to-face situation arose in part from the effects of forcing the distribution of four votes among the 11 jurors who were members of the respondent's particular jury. Notwithstanding this flattening effect, it still appears that the face-to-face experience (1) results in fewer proprietor and skilled worker "own group" choices; and (2) brings the choice gradients into smoother conformity with the observed contribution of each status group to the deliberation.

DISCUSSION

Jury deliberations have been used to examine the intersection of occupational status and sex with the typically small-group measures of participation, influence, satisfaction, and perceived competence. The assumption that there is no relation between these modes of classification can be safely rejected. Men, in contrast with women, and persons of higher status, in contrast with lower-status, occupations have higher participation, influence, satisfaction, and perceived competence for the jury task.

The present study does little to explain the cause of this differentiation. Insofar as selection of the foreman may be taken as a guide to more general expectations concerning desirable attributes for the jury task, it appears that the foreman is expected to be a male, preferably a male of higher occupational status. Although we know of no empirical studies, we assume that the business discipline and related experiences of higher-status occupations involve both substantive knowledge and interactional skills that may be used during the deliberation. Hence, in the competition for the available deliberation time, higher-status males may rise to prominence because their comments are perceived to have greater value. On the other hand, since the cues of status—dress, speech, and casual references to experiences—are easily read, the differentiation may in part be explained by these expectations instead of actual performance.

Jurors who spoke at greater length were perceived by respondents to be the jurors desired if they were on trial. This finding suggests that whatever the criteria used by the groups to regulate the contributions of their members, these criteria were broadly held. The differ ent distribution of speaking time was achieved without serious violation of developing group norms. Further, choices made after face-to-face experience, in contrast with those based on occupational stereotypes, tended to smooth into a gradient which paralleled both activity rates and status. These findings and others reported above constitute a preliminary clarification of the small-group process during a jury deliberation.

While our data do little to illuminate *how* differentiation arises, they show that status gradients emerge clearly in as brief a time as the one- or two-hour discussions under study. Although careful study will be required to determine the degree to which one may generalize from status in the larger social system to a particular interaction context, this demonstration of status continuity should be noted in any theory concerned with describing the process of status affirmation and maintenance.

THE SHIFTING ROLE OF CLASS IN POLITICAL ATTITUDES AND BEHAVIOR   *By Philip E. Converse*

The first studies of social class to use the new techniques of large-scale sampling documented a number of relationships between status and politico-economic attitudes. Such empirical demonstration was a valuable, if not always surprising, contribution. We learned, for example, that people lodged in different strata of the social system have tended to hold somewhat different attitudes regarding the benevolence of the existing social order, much as interest-group theory and classical views on stratification had postulated. We became familiar, furthermore, with the finding that different status groups may implement these beliefs in differential voting behavior. Thus, over the last 25 years, high-status persons in the United States have favored the Republican party while the less fortunately placed have subscribed instead to the Democratic party.

Although some particulars of these findings have been subject to controversy, their broad outlines have been so completely absorbed into the basic lore of attitude research as to become commonplace. We have come to consider them, implicitly at least, as relationships of roughly constant magnitude and, hence, diminishing fascination. However, the passage of time now permits us to evaluate the extent to which changes can occur in the role played by social class in political opinions and behavior.

It is only such observation of stability and change over a lengthening period of our national history that can provide an empirical test for some of the more important hypotheses as to the significance of social class in a modern society. The first round of survey studies in this area served for the most part to document only a static description of class differences. There was found to be indeed a visible divergence of opinion on matters of economic interest between members of different class levels. But the grand dynamic models of the classic-stratification theorists received little empirical support or challenge in these materials. Marx, for example, had taken the existence of social strata with divergent interests as a postulate, self-evident beyond need for proof, and proceeded to spin a theory concerning the social and economic conditions under which class consciousness might be expected to vary

Prepared especially for this volume.

as modern industrial society developed. However obsolete his speculations may appear today, it can be fairly said that we have yet to exploit modern research vehicles toward a more adequate understanding of the dynamic role which status plays in the political life of a modern state as it passes through depression, war, and prosperity.

It is our theses that in the United States the strength of relationships between status and political variables is subject to more short-term variation than is generally recognized. Yet we hold that this instability need not be a source of dismay to the student of social class; if we accept the strength of these relationships as a critical variable in its own right and seek its determinants in the major events which impinge upon the social system, we shall have taken a first step toward putting a dynamic view of social class and its political consequences on an empirical footing.

Such analysis requires comparative measurement over time. A national sample survey conducted by the Survey Research Center (SRC) of the University of Michigan during October and November of 1956 permits a detailed comparison of class attitudes in 1956 with those encountered by Richard Centers in his 1945 study.[1] A cross-sectional sample of 1,772 respondents, chosen by strict probability methods from all adult citizens living in private households in the United

States, was interviewed just prior to the 1956 presidential election and again just subsequent to it. Since the 1945 survey involved a sample of 1,097 adult white males, the following comparison is based upon the 728 white male respondents interviewed in the 1956 study.[2]

Centers' detailed description of the assignment of respondents to an occupational status in his pioneering study allowed us to make a matching array within our sample. The second measure of status, the respondent's self-assignment to a social class, was obtained in 1956 through an elaboration of the original question devised for this purpose by Centers.[3] Each person interviewed was asked: "There's quite a bit of talk these days about different social classes. Most people say they belong either to the middle class or to the working class. Do you ever think of yourself as being in one of these classes?" If the response was affirmative, the respondent was simply asked "Which one?" If the response was negative, the ensuing question was "Well, if you had to make a choice, would you call yourself middle class or working class?" In both cases, the respondent was then asked, "Would you say you are about an average (class selected) person or that you are in the upper part of the (class selected)?"

The results of the class identification question are shown in Table 1. Although three rebellious spirits—all women—

---

[1] The 1956 study was carried out at the Survey Research Center under the direction of Angus Campbell and Warren E. Miller. It was supported by a grant from the Rockefeller Foundation. A full report of the study will become available at a later date. The 1945 study by Richard Centers is fully reported in *The Psychology of Social Classes* (Princeton: Princeton University Press, 1949).

[2] It might be noted that the findings to be presented here hold generally for the total cross-sectional sample, however. While certain factors such as the relative indeterminacy of the occupation status of many women act to reduce slightly the clarity of some of the relationships reported, our data for females look substantially like those for males. On the other hand, inclusion of nonwhite respondents would, if anything, serve to sharpen relationships, as such racial groups fall at an extreme of the status continuum and manifest opinions and political behavior appropriate to this extreme. Nevertheless, our interest in the specific magnitude of relationships over time legislated against treatment here of any elements of the sample not directly comparable with the 1945 data.

[3] This question was phrased: "If you were asked to use one of these four names for your social class, which would you say you belonged in: the middle class, lower class, working class, or upper class?"

TABLE 1

SUBJECTIVE CLASS IDENTIFICATION OF WHITE MALES

	SRC 1956				SRC 1952	Centers 1945
	Aware of social class	Unaware of social class	Total		Total	Total
Average working class	50%	42%	47%	(Lower class)	2%	1%
Upper working class	11	+10	11	(Working class)	59	51
Working-class total	61	52	58		61	52
Average middle class	33	34	33	(Middle class)	35	43
Upper middle class	6	5	5	(Upper class)	1	3
Middle-class total	39	39	38		36	46
Reject idea of class		5	2		1	1
Don't know, not ascertained	*	4	2		2	1
	(N = 456)	(N = 272)	(N = 728)		(N = 666)	(N = 1097)

* Less than one half of one percent.

assigned themselves to the "upper class" despite the wording of the question, it will be noted that we have sacrificed the differentiation of the handful of people who chose "upper" or "lower" class in the 1945 study to subdivide each major class into an "average" or "upper" segment more susceptible to detailed analysis. If, however, we restrict our attention to gross comparisons between frequencies in the two major classes, we find a sizeable shift from choice of middle class to choice of working class, by comparison with the 1945 distribution.

It is impossible to judge whether these differences are a result of a shift in underlying parameters in the interim, or whether more mechanical discrepancies are involved. The quota sample design used in the Princeton study may have been vulnerable to a systematic upward shift in economic status of respondents

chosen. It seems fairly safe to say, however, that the differences in distribution of class identification are not a result of the change in question wording, since we see that the Centers question repeated verbatim from a 1952 SRC study produced a distribution which coincides almost exactly with that found by the SRC using the revised wording in 1956 (Table 1).

As a final point of comparison, we find that the subjective choice of class affiliation as obtained with the 1956 question related to status as objectively determined by occupation in much the same fashion as it did within the 1945 data. Among the nonfarm portion of the sample, we find some tendency for higher-status respondents in 1956 to place themselves more frequently in the working class. Nonetheless, the correlation between the two modes of status measure-

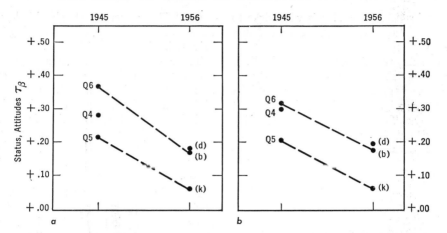

FIG. 1. Status and attitudes,* 1945 and 1956, showing (*a*) the relationships between attitudes and occupation status, and (*b*) the relationships between attitudes and subjective class. (Letters and numbers in parentheses refer to attitude items on the 1945 and 1956 questionaires.†)

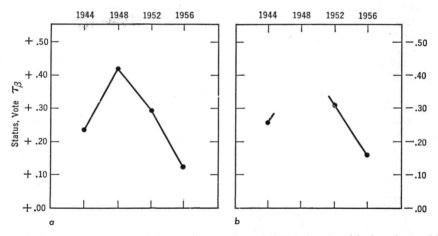

FIG. 2. Status and presidential vote,* 1944 through 1956, showing (*a*) the relationships between vote and occupational status, and (*b*) the relationships between vote and subjective class.

* We have followed the usage of the 1945 study in removing farm occupations from the basic occupation-status array. For purposes of comparability, therefore, all coefficients in Figures 1 and 2 are based on a subsample of white males reporting nonfarm occupations. The 1945 coefficients in Figure 1 represent an N ranging from 758 to 835, while the N for the 1956 coefficient varies between 525 and 574. In Figure 2, elimination of nonvoters reduces the N in 1945 to about 700, to 141 in 1948, 455 in 1952, and 480 in 1956. In all cases, the addition of white females to the Survey Research Center data would more than double the number of cases without any substantial effect on the coefficients involved.

† Question 4 in the 1945 study was "Would you agree that everybody would be happier, more secure, and more prosperous if the working people were given more power and influence in government, or would you say we would all be better off if the working people had no more power than they have now?" For questions 5 and 6, see footnote 5.

ment in 1956 ($\tau_\beta = .46$) is very close to that represented in the earlier study ($\tau_\beta = .49$).[4]

In sum, then, there seems to be little question about the comparability of measurement between the two studies with regard to the primary independent variables. Therefore, it seems reasonable to assume that any notable differences which we may find in relationships between these status measures and political variables after the lapse of a decade are due to actual changes in the American scene.

Social Class and Political Attitudes in 1956

Politico-economic attitudes constituted a major type of dependent variable for the 1945 study. From a large battery of questions concerning governmental policy asked in the 1956 SRC study we have chosen three which appear most closely related in content to the items employed by Centers in forming his scale of "conservatism-radicalism." These agree-disagree items are as follows:

(b) "The government in Washington ought to see to it that everyone who wants to work can find a job;"

(d) "The government ought to help people get doctors and hospital care at low cost;"

(k) "The government should leave things like electric power and housing for private businessmen to handle."

These questions have as a common core the distinction between what Centers referred to in 1949 as "two opposed philosophies of government—an individualistic one and a collectivistic one." Centers considers this "the central issue of all today's politico-economic strife" and the locus of the largest differences in class attitude.[5]

It would be dangerous to make comparisons of absolute response distributions for questions similar in spirit though not in letter. However, if the empirical situation is like that which Centers encountered, we would have a right to expect these basic politico-economic orientations to relate clearly to status variables much as they did in 1945. Instead, we find a general decline in the strength of these relationships (see Figure 1).

Each of our three questions shows a lower order of relationship with both subjective class and occupational status than Centers' data show for 1945. If we draw a trend line between the questions from the two studies which are most closely matched in content the contrasts are striking.[6] Assuming an equivalence between the questions, we find the em-

---

[4] The tau-beta statistic due to Kendall will be used throughout this analysis to fulfill the need for a measure of degree of association between variables. Such coefficients have been computed from the bivariate distributions published by Centers as well as for our own data. This statistic is derived from a rank-order correlation technique which handles any number of ranked categories or ties. The tau-beta tends to produce coefficients which are lower in magnitude than corresponding Pearson-product-moment coefficients computed from the same data. Therefore, the absolute magnitude of the coefficients may appear somewhat conservative to the reader accustomed to the Pearson r, and considerably more conservative than the tetrachoric r originally used by Centers.

[5] See Guy E. Swanson, Theodore M. Newcomb, and Eugene L. Hartley (eds.), *Readings in Social Psychology* (New York: Henry Holt & Co., Inc., 1952), p. 301.

[6] This matching equates our question (b) with Centers' question (6): "Which one of these statements do you most agree with? (1) The most important job for the government is to make it certain that there are good opportunities for each person to get ahead on his own. (2) The most important job for the government is to guarantee every person a decent and steady job and standard of living." The 1956 item (k) is likewise paired with question (5) in the Princeton study: "As you know, during this war, many private businesses and industries have been taken over by the government. Do you think wages and salaries would be fairer, jobs more steady, and that we would have fewer people out of work if the government took over and ran our mines and industries in the future, or do you think things would be better under private ownership?"

ployment-guarantee issue more highly related to both subjective and objective status than the free-enterprise issue in 1956, exactly as it was in 1945. But by 1956 both relationships have receded and the respective slopes of their decline are very close to parallel.

We cannot conclude that politico-economic attitudes are no longer significantly associated with statuses and self-perceptions in the economic order. Indeed, when we introduce more refined measurement, such as the distinction between the "average" and "upper part" of the two major subjective classes, we find that we can restore at least a part of the old strength of relationship which Centers treats. But if we can assume that the two gross classes and the politico-economic attitudes as measured in 1956 may be legitimately compared with those of Centers in 1945, it is beyond dispute that a sizable decline in the association between them has occurred in the interim.

SOCIAL CLASS AND POLITICAL BEHAVIOR IN 1956

A prime behavioral outlet for class consciousness is the act of voting. Centers acknowledges the relevance of the vote by employing it as a validity criterion for his scale of conservatism-radicalism and by describing its familiar relationships to various definitions of status.[7] The relationship between status and vote allows a more extensive test of the assertion that status differentials fluctuate considerably in their degree of impact on mass political behavior. The series of presidential election studies at the Survey Research Center provides

material for status-trend lines similar to those we have used for attitudes, yet with more frequent data.[8] By prefixing computations from Centers' tables on status and the vote, we can thus observe a span of four presidential elections.

Figure 2 reveals a striking range of variation in the strength of the status-vote relationship since the last Roosevelt election in 1944. The degree to which people of self-designated middle- or working-class status have given their votes to the presidential candidates of the Republican and Democratic parties respectively has fluctuated widely over little more than a decade.

In the face of this variation, two regularities which emerge from the data become most noteworthy. The first is the degree of coincidence between the objective and subjective variants of the status-vote relationship over time. As we have seen, class identification, while strongly related to occupation status, still enjoys considerable variation independent of it.[9] One form of the relationship could, for example, lag behind the other in its temporal cycles, or vary within narrower limits. Instead, we find psychological and social status, despite their differing division of the sample, producing almost identical relationships with the vote over three elections.

The second regularity is apparent if we compare Figures 1 and 2. The decline in the status-attitude relationships between 1945 and 1956 matches the two terminal points of the status-vote trend in provocative fashion. Unfortunately, we lack comparable attitudinal material for the intervening period with which to fill out Figure 1. We have, of course, no

---

[7] Centers, *op. cit.*, pp. 45–47, p. 115.

[8] Moreover, while the comparability of attitudinal items used in the two studies is not perfect, the act of voting provides nearly identical behaviors for comparison.

[9] For example, if we were to make the arbitrary assumption that people of nonmanual occupation were a "true" middle class, with the manual occupations constituting the working class, we would find roughly equivalent portions of the sample, amounting to more than a quarter of the total, indulging in "misclassification" upward or downward. Given such slippage between the two definitions of status, we might expect more differential variation between each of them and the vote

guarantee that status-vote relationships need follow the fluctuation of relationships between status and certain relevant politico-economic attitudes. We shall have occasion to comment below on some of the factors which may disrupt direct translation of crystallized economic interest into voting behavior. Nevertheless, the congruence between the status-vote and status-attitude trends lends strong support to the conclusion that we are dealing with variation in an important property of a social system.

We suggest, therefore, that the *strength of relationship* between status and relevant politico-economic variables may be taken as a fairly reliable measure of such a system property at a point in time. For easy reference, we shall label this relational concept *status polarization*.[10]

By definition, status polarization is a group-level concept. It should indicate the degree to which groups at opposing ends of the status continuum have taken up mutually antagonistic value positions in the politico-economic sphere. We may imagine that as polarization increases it is likely to become manifest in values less immediately bound up with economic self-interest and public policy, so that a more salient and generalized antagonism exists between class groups. Its limiting case is class war.

The counterpart of status polarization at the individual level would be, therefore, the familiar concept of class consciousness. The fit is not perfect. We can imagine a mild divergence of beliefs between various class subcultures without any of the visible loyalty to a class group or hostility toward another class which we associate with full-fledged class consciousness. But in a rough way, the po-

larization of a social system is taken to reflect the extent and intensity of class consciousness measured over a representative portion of its members.

Richard Centers was concerned with the measurement of class consciousness and his demonstration of the psychological reality of class is a move in this direction. However, his implication that "self-affiliation" alone is sufficient to distinguish the "internally cohesive . . . social groupings" which we tend to associate with class consciousness is not entirely convincing.[11] The claim is compounded by the use of the label "class identification" for the self-affiliation procedure. We can take "identification" to refer to a sense of belongingness with a group, a usage which accords fairly well with the concept of class consciousness. Or—and this is closer to the Centers procedure—we can take it to refer merely to the nominal assignment of an object to a category.

The interview question with which we prefaced our requests for self-assignment to a class was less an attempt to sort out respondents who were class-conscious in the old militant sense than to improve upon the Centers technique by distinguishing a group for whom the notion of class was most salient and self-allocation most nearly habitual. With this limited objective in mind, we shall speak of "class awareness" rather than "class consciousness." However, it seems reasonable to suppose that we have to some degree "tightened the ring" on a small group of people who may be sufficiently class-conscious to merit the term: we would expect the two thirds of our sample who admitted class awareness to contain most of them. Therefore, we may take our measure of awareness as a serv-

_____

[10] It should be emphasized that it is difficult to attach any unequivocal meaning at this point to the *absolute magnitude* of coefficients of the relationship between status and attitudes or the vote. Given its operational definition, status polarization can show a hypothetical variation between .00 and 1.00. However, it is clear that the absolute magnitude of any coefficient is a function of the dependent variables employed.

[11] Centers, *op. cit.*, p. 28. See also pp. 74–76.

TABLE 2

STATUS-VOTE AND STATUS-ATTITUDE RELATIONSHIPS FOR WHITE MALES
ACCORDING TO AWARENESS OF SOCIAL CLASS *

	Attitudes, 1956			
	1956 presidential vote	Item (b) Government guarantee of employment	Item (d) Government medical aid	Item (k) Government vs. private industry
Aware of social class	.20 (N = 358)	.17 (N = 430)	.22 (N = 416)	.08 (N = 388)
Unaware of social class	.07 (N = 207)	.09 (N = 228)	.12 (N = 227)	−.01 (N = 203)

* The cell entry indicates the τ_β for the relationship between subjective status and vote or attitudes; the number of cases is included for each coefficient.

iceable individual measure relating to status polarization.

We lack the data from earlier samples requisite to test the hypothesis that fluctuation in our measure of status polarization would be directly reflected in variation in class awareness over a period of time. But with minimal inference we may substitute a cross-sectional test for a longitudinal one. If our measure of awareness is reliable and our concept of status polarization meaningful, we should expect higher status-attitude and status-vote relationships within the group of people who are aware of class than within the group who are unaware.

Table 2 provides some support for this proposition. While the low general level of relationships between status and our dependent variables coupled with the large proportion of the sample who reported being "aware" imposes a ceiling on variation, there is indication that lack of awareness of class reduces the likelihood that the respondent will hold beliefs and will vote along lines most "appropriate" for his subjective class group. A more differentiated measure of awareness might show bigger differences in re-

lationships between these groups. However, it seems reasonable to suppose that status polarization in a society will reflect, over time, the varying extent and intensity of awareness of social class among its members.

SOME DETERMINANTS OF
STATUS POLARIZATION

We turn now to the consideration of some of the factors that may account for variations in status polarization. Without a more adequate accumulation of data, we cannot pursue the argument closely at an empirical level. However, initial and cursory speculation will serve to mark out directions for investigation.

We assume that status polarization in a society reflects concern about the allocation of rewards and deprivations across the status continuum. In modern western democracies this concern has been primarily economic, directed at the distribution of wealth. Under prevailing expectations the inequity represented by a bimodal distribution of wealth would undoubtedly be accompanied by status polarization as well. Conversely, in the

United States the expansion of a middle class engaged in service occupations which fail to fit the old ownership-proletariat cleavage may currently be functioning to set upper limits on the polarization potential of the society.

In the shorter term, given a fairly constant pattern of wealth distribution, we would predict that polarization would increase in time of depression and decrease in periods of prosperity. The net decline of status polarization which we have seen in relevant attitudes between 1945 and 1956 lends credence to such a proposition, if we consider the general increase in prosperity which has characterized the period since the depression of the 1930's.

However, the sharp crest attained by status-vote relationships in 1948 suggests that this decline in attitude polarization may not have been monotonic during the intervening period. On the other hand, the mild levelling of the economy in the reconversion period between the end of the war boom and the recession of 1949 would hardly seem sufficient, in itself, to generate the rapid increase in polarization suggested by our data. We conclude that a single-factor theory is oversimplified and that we must cope with a more complex explanatory burden.

Consideration of the effects which war may have on status polarization is an obvious first step toward explanation of our data and consequent modification of our theory. Even an overseas war, it must be conceded, has a major impact on any population involved; yet this impact, in contrast to that of a depression, is less clearly distributed along status lines. Pressing questions of foreign policy eclipse those concerns of domestic economics which lead so directly to cleavage among status-interest groups. Therefore, we would propose that war and the preeminence of foreign policy considerations may act to reduce status polarization temporarily. For the case in point we would suggest that polarization tendencies carrying over from the depression

were dampened by the national crisis imposed by World War II but rebounded toward their prewar level after that conflict was concluded.

The temporary evaporation of the most burdensome foreign problems, along with the sudden unleashing of pent-up class-relevant actions, particularly the great postwar strikes in major industries, the struggle in Congress to place legislative controls on the activities of labor unions, and the development of first anxieties concerning an "inevitable" postwar depression, all must have contributed to a rise in the relative salience of domestic economic issues which had remained dormant during the war. After the 1948 peak of status polarization, we may speculate that the renewal of the threat of global war along with the outbreak of hostilities in Korea ought to have acted, in concert with increasing prosperity, to depress the level of status polarization once again.

If war and the consequent prominence of foreign-policy concerns do in fact work toward a reduction of polarization, we should be able to find traces of this effect in our 1956 sample, who were interviewed at a time when many voters were still apprehensive about war. It would follow from our argument that respondents showing marked concern over foreign policy could not be expected to vote in accordance with their subjective class position, whether or not they were aware of that position. On the other hand, respondents who were aware of their self-assigned status and for whom domestic policy controversies were more salient than foreign affairs and the possibility of war should show a higher status-vote relationship than that found in the total sample.

In the 1956 interview a series of open-ended questions which enabled the respondent to volunteer comments on aspects of the current political scene which were important for him permitted us to test this proposition. Table 3 bears out

TABLE 3

STATUS–VOTE RELATIONSHIPS FOR
WHITE MALES ACCORDING TO
RELATIVE CONCERN OVER DOMESTIC
OR FOREIGN ISSUES *

	Higher domestic issue concern	Equivalent concern	Higher foreign issue concern
Aware of social class	.25 (N = 191)	.20 (N = 105)	.00 (N = 62)
Unaware of social class	.04 (N = 99)	.14 (N = 74)	−.02 (N = 34)

* The cell entry indicates the τ_β for the relationship between subjective status and vote or attitudes; the number of cases is included for each coefficient.

our speculations rather well. While it represents once again a cross-sectional rather than a longitudinal test, we can infer that, other things equal, status polarization will vary inversely with the salience of war over a period of time.

Other political factors in addition to the intrusion of foreign policy may affect the level of polarization or act to disturb the correspondence between attitudinal polarization and the status-vote relationship. For example, rapid changes in degree of attitudinal polarization may be reflected only imperfectly in voting behavior due to loyalties which have grown up between the voter and a particular political party. Thus, theories of voting behavior which imply, by suggesting that status can affect the vote only

as an expression of economic self-interest, that the level of attitudinal polarization is an upper limit for a status-vote relationship, are not entirely adequate; we can imagine conditions under which party identifications born in time of polarization could conserve a status-vote relationship after relevant status attitudes had faded.

Other prominent elements in the election situation may tend to mitigate the simple expression of economic interest. A magnetic presidential candidate can have a broad public appeal which defies status lines. It is at least suggestive that three of the four elections recorded in Figure 2 were dominated by such personalities, while it is the remaining election in 1948 which produced the high-water point of the status-vote trend line. Once again we may turn to our 1956 data for evidence concerning the degree to which the personal characteristics of the candidates may draw the attention of the voters away from domestic economic concerns and thereby weaken status voting. Table 4, constructed on the basis of volunteered comments similar to those in Table 3, offers some support for this proposition, although the differences generated are less sharp than in the case where the intruding factor is concern over foreign affairs.[12]

Another type of political factor which must serve to set varying limits on the status-vote relationship over time is the convergence and divergence of the domestic-policy positions of the two major parties. However high the level of attitudinal polarization in the society, the impact of status on vote decision is de-

[12] It is interesting to note that further combination of political orientations of this sort can produce a "purified" group for whom the status-vote relationship is extremely high. Another category of volunteered response not subsumed under the domestic-issue comments treated above covers those cases in which a party or a candidate is seen to support or discriminate against—in economic terms—some group in the society such as the "working man," the "aged," etc. If we isolate an extreme group of 60 "aware" voters who gave the most frequent group references and domestic-issue comments, while giving a minimum of responses concerning foreign issues or the candidates, we find a τ_β of .49 between subjective status and vote, in contrast with the coefficient of .16 for white male voters over the total sample in 1956.

TABLE 4*

STATUS-VOTE RELATIONSHIPS FOR WHITE MALES
ACCORDING TO RELATIVE CONCERN OVER
DOMESTIC ISSUES AS OPPOSED TO INTEREST IN THE CANDIDATES

	High domestic issue concern	Balanced candidate interest & domestic issue concern	High candidate interest
Aware of social class	.30	.21	.17
	(N = 87)	(N = 103)	(N = 159)
Unaware of social class	.06	.10	.04
	(N = 47)	(N = 76)	(N = 81)

* The cell entry indicates the τ_β for the relationship between subjective status and vote or attitudes; the number of cases is included for each coefficient.

pendent on the degree to which the political parties proffer clear and equally polarized policy alternatives. Where party differences with regard to economic philosophy are not perceived by the electorate, political translations from attitude to vote will lose any discernible status significance.

It is likely that differences between the parties on status-relevant economic issues had by 1956 reached a decade's low. However, since our respondents were asked for each of our three questions on economic policy whether or not they saw differences in the way in which the two parties would handle the problem, we can inquire whether the status-vote relationship is not highest among people in the sample who still perceive these differences between the parties.

If we include the variable of class awareness as a precondition for meaningful status voting, we find the coefficients

in Table 5 which clearly support the general argument.[13] Of course, discrimination between the two parties with regard to domestic policy may accompany high salience of domestic issues, both at the objective policy level and in the reflection of these differences in perceptions of an interested segment of the electorate. Therefore, Table 5 is, in conjunction with Tables 3 and 4, part of a larger whole. If the salience of domestic issues rests at a constant level over a period of time, any tendency for the two parties to climb on the same domestic-policy bandwagon in appealing for public support must act as a force reducing status polarization of the vote.

By reflecting on some of the factors which must influence status polarization, we have been able to sort out of our 1956 sample a group for whom status remains a significant determinant of vote, despite the general decline of predictive efficacy

[13] Similar differences are evident in data from the Survey Research Center study of the 1952 election, although we lack in this case the variable of class awareness with which to sharpen the findings. Among people who saw differences between the two parties on general policy with regard to the degree of government welfare activity, the status-vote relationship was .41(τ_β) as opposed to .19 among those who failed to discriminate between the parties at this point.

TABLE 5*

STATUS-VOTE RELATIONSHIPS FOR WHITE MALES
ACCORDING TO PERCEPTION OF DIFFERENCES BETWEEN THE
PARTIES ON THREE DOMESTIC ISSUES

	Perceived no differences	Perceived differences on one or more issues
Aware of social class	.04 (N = 94)	.20 (N = 263)
Unaware of social class	.08 (N = 75)	.03 (N = 131)

* The cell entry indicates the τ_β for the relationship between subjective status and vote or attitudes; the number of cases is included for each coefficient.

of status over the total sample. Some of these factors, such as the intrusion of war, are likely to reduce the general level of polarization in the society as a whole. Others which we have discussed may intervene to disturb the direct translation of economic attitudes into political action. Both types of factors must be examined in detail if we are to piece together an understanding of the varying role of status differences in public life over time.

SUMMARY

By replicating, after the lapse of a decade, the Richard Centers study of relationships between objective and psychological status on the one hand and certain attitudes and the vote on the other, we have demonstrated considerable variability in the strength of these relationships. We have proposed that such variability be exploited as a tool by investigators who wish to bring some empirical "reality testing" to dynamic theories of class and status. Toward this end, we have tried to show the clear relationships between this "status polarization" as a property of a social system and the concept of individual class consciousness prominent in such dynamic theory.

Finally, we have taken recent variation in status polarization as the basis for a preliminary discussion of some of the factors which seem to determine its level, as measured by either status-attitudes or status-vote relationships at any point in time. We assume that investigation proceeding along such lines may increase our general understanding of the long-term effect of status position on political attitudes and behavior.

SOCIALIZATION AND SOCIAL CLASS THROUGH TIME AND SPACE   By Urie Bronfenbrenner

I. BACKGROUND AND RESOURCES

During the past dozen years, a class struggle has been taking place in American social psychology—a struggle, fortunately, not *between* but *about* social classes. In the best social revolutionary tradition the issue was joined with a manifesto challenging the assumed superiority of the upper and middle classes and extolling the neglected virtues of the working class. There followed a successful revolution with an overthrow of the established order in favor of the victorious proletariat, which then reigned supreme—at least for a time. These dramatic changes had, as always, their prophets and precursors, but they reached a climax in 1946 with the publication of Davis and Havighurst's influential paper on "Social Class and Color Differences in Child Rearing." [1] The paper cited impressive statistical evidence in support of the thesis that middle-class parents "place their children under a stricter regimen, with more frustration of their impulses than do lower-class parents." For the next eight years, the Davis-Havighurst conclusion was taken as the definitive statement of class

differences in socialization. Then, in 1954, came the counterrevolution; Maccoby and Gibbs published the first report [2] of a study of child-rearing practices in the Boston area which, by and large, contradicted the Chicago findings: in general, middle-class parents were found to be "more permissive" than those in the lower class.

In response, one year later, Havighurst and Davis [3] presented a reanalysis of their data for a subsample more comparable in age to the subjects of the Boston study. On the basis of a careful comparison of the two sets of results, they concluded that "the disagreements between the findings of the two studies are substantial and large" and speculated that these differences might be attributable either to genuine changes in child-rearing practices over time or to technical difficulties of sampling and item equivalence.

A somewhat different view, however, was taken by Sears, Maccoby, and Levin [4] in their final report of the Boston study. They argued that Davis and Havighurst's interpretation of the Chicago data as reflecting greater permissiveness for the working-class parent was

This article was prepared especially for this volume. It was made possible only by the work of others; for, in effect, it is a synthesis of the contribution of a score of investigators over a score of years. The author is particularly grateful to Nancy Bayley, Melvin L. Kohn, Richard A. Littman, Daniel R. Miller, Fred L. Strodtbeck, Guy E. Swanson, and Martha S. White, who made available copies of their research reports prior to publication. For their invaluable suggestions, he is also indebted to John E. Anderson, Wesley Allinsmith, Alfred L. Baldwin, John A. Clausen, Robert J. Havighurst, Harry Levin, Eleanor E. Maccoby, and Theodore M. Newcomb.

---

[1] A. Davis and R. J. Havighurst, "Social Class and Color Differences in Child Rearing," *Am. Sociol. Rev.*, 1948, XI, 698–710.

[2] E. E. Maccoby, P. K. Gibbs, and the staff of the Laboratory of Human Development at Harvard University, "Methods of Child Rearing in Two Social Classes," in W. E. Martin and C. B. Standler (eds.), *Readings in Child Development* (New York: Harcourt, Brace & Co., 1954).

[3] Havighurst and Davis, "A comparison of the Chicago and Harvard Studies of Social Class Differences in Child Rearing," *Am. Sociol. Rev.*, 1955, XX, 438–442.

[4] R. R. Sears, Maccoby, and H. Levin, *Patterns of Child Rearing* (Evanston, Ill.: Row, Peterson & Co., 1957).

unwarranted on two counts. First, they cited the somewhat contrasting results of still another research—that of Klatskin [5] in support of the view that class differences in feeding, weaning, scheduling, and toilet training "are not very stable or customary." Second, they contended that the Chicago findings of greater freedom of movement for the lower-class child were more properly interpreted not as "permissiveness" but as "a reflection of rejection, a pushing of the child out of the way." Such considerations led the Boston investigators to conclude:

This re-examination of the Chicago findings suggests quite clearly the same conclusion that must be reached from Klatskin's study and from our own: the middle-class mothers were generally more permissive and less punitive toward their young children than were working-class mothers. Unfortunately, the opposite interpretation, as presented by Davis and Havighurst, has been widely accepted in education circles during the past decade. This notion of working-class permissiveness has been attractive for various reasons. It has provided an easy explanation of why working-class children have lower academic achievement motivation than do middle-class children—their mothers place less restrictive pressure on them. It has also provided a kind of compensatory comfort for those educators who have been working hard toward the goal of improving educational experiences for the noncollege-oriented part of the school population. In effect, one could say, lower-class children may lack the so highly desirable academic motivation, but the lack stems from a "good" reason—the children were permissively reared.[6]

It would appear that there are a number of unresolved issues between the protagonists of the principal points of view—issues both as to the facts and their interpretation. At such times it is not unusual for some third party to attempt a reappraisal of events in a broader historical perspective with the aid of documents and information previously not available. It is this which the present writer hopes to do. He is fortunate in having at his disposal materials not only from the past and present, but also seven manuscripts unpublished at the time of this writing, which report class differences in child-rearing practices at four different places and five points in time. To begin with, Bayley and Schaefer [7] have reanalyzed data from the Berkeley Growth Study to provide information on class differences in maternal-behavior ratings made from 1928 to 1932, when the children in the study were under three years old, and again from 1939 to 1942, when most of them were about ten years old. Information on maternal behavior in this same locale as of 1953 comes from a recent report by Martha Sturm White [8] of class differences in child-rearing practices for a sample of preschoolers in Palo Alto and environs. Miller and Swanson have made available relevant data from their two comprehensive studies of families in Detroit, one based on a stratified sample of families with children up to 19 years of age,[9] the other a specially selected sample of boys, ages 12 to 14 years.[10] Limited information on another

---

[5] E. H. Klatskin, "Shifts in Child Care Practices in Three Social Classes under an Infant Care Program of Flexible Methodology," *Am. J. Orthopsychiat.*, 1952, XXII, 52–61.

[6] Sears, Maccoby, and Levin, *op. cit.*, pp. 446–447.

[7] N. Bayley and E. S. Schaefer, "Relationships between Socioeconomic Variables and the Behavior of Mothers toward Young Children," unpublished manuscript, 1957.

[8] M. S. White, "Social Class, Child Rearing Practices, and Child Behavior," *Am. Sociol. Rev.* 1957, XXII, 704–712.

[9] D. R. Miller and G. E. Swanson, *The Changing American Parent* (New York: John Wiley & Sons., Inc., in press).

[10] Miller and Swanson, *Inner Conflict and Defense* (New York: Henry Holt & Co., Inc., to be published in 1959).

TABLE 1

DESCRIPTION OF SAMPLES

Sample	Principal investigator source	Date of field work	Age	No. of cases			Description of sample
				Total	Middle class	Working class	
National Cross Section,* I II III IV	Anderson	1932	0–1 1–5 6–12 1–12	494 2420 865 3285	217 1131 391 1522	277 1289 474 1763	National sample of white families "having child between 1 and 5 years of age" and "representing each major geographic area, each size of community and socioeconomic class in the United States." About equal number of males and females. SES (seven classes) based on Minnesota Scale for Occupational Classification.
Berkeley, Cal., I–II	Bayley and Schaefer	1928–32 1939–42	1–3 9–11	31 31	Information not available		Subjects of both sexes from Berkeley Growth Study, "primarily middle class but range from unskilled laborer, relief, and three-years education to professional, $10,000 income and doctoral degrees." SES measures include education, occupation (Taussig Scale), income, home and neighborhood rating, and composite scale.
Yellow Springs, Ohio	Baldwin	1940	3–12	124	Information not available		Families enrolled in Fels Research Institute Home Visiting Program. "Above average" in socioeconomic status but include "a number of uneducated parents and from the lower economic levels." No SES index computed but graphs show relationships by education and income.
Chicago, Ill., I*	Davis and Havighurst	1943	5 (approx.)	100	48	52	Middle-class sample "mainly" from mothers of nursery-school children; lower class from "areas of poor housing." All mothers native born. Two-level classification SES following Warner based on occupation, education, residential area, type of home, etc.
Chicago, Ill., II	Duvall	1943–44	5 (approx.)	433	230	203	Negro and white (Jewish and non-Jewish) mothers. Data collected at "regular meetings of mothers' groups." SES classification (four levels) following Warner.

Location	Investigator	Date	Age				Description
New Haven, Conn., I*	Klatskin	1949–50	1 (approx.)	222	114	108	Mothers in Yale Rooming-in Project returning for evaluation of baby at one year of age. SES classification (three levels) by Hollingshead, following Warner.
Boston, Mass.*	Sears, et al.	1951–52	4–6	372	198	174	Kindergarten children in two suburbs. Parents American born, living together. Twins, adoptions, handicapped children, and other special cases eliminated. Two-level SES classification follows Warner.
New Haven, Conn., II	Strodtbeck	1951–53	14–17	48	24	24	Third-generation Jewish and Italian boys representing extremes of under- and over-achievement in school. Classified into three SES levels on basis of occupation.
Detroit, Mich., I*	Miller and Swanson	1953	12–14	112	59	53	Boys in grades 7–8 above borderline intelligence within one year of age for grade, all at least third-generation Americans, Christian, from unbroken, nonmobile families of Northwest European stock. SES (four levels) assigned on basis of education and occupation.
Detroit, Mich., II*	Miller and Swanson	1953	0–18	479	Information not available		Random sample of white mothers with child under 19 and living with husband. Step-children and adoptions eliminated. SES (four levels) based primarily on U.S. census occupation categories.
Palo Alto, Cal.,*	White	1953	2½–5½	74	36	38	Native-born mothers of only one child, the majority expecting another. Unbroken homes in suburban area. SES (two levels) rated on Warner scale.
Urban Connecticut	McClelland et al.	1953–54	6–18	152	Information not available		Parents between 30–60 having at least one child between six and eighteen and representing four religious groups. "Rough check on class status", obtained from educational level achieved by parent.
Upstate New York	Boek, et al.	1955–56	3–7 months	1,432	595	837	Representative sample of N.Y. state mothers of newborn children, exclusive of unmarried mothers. SES classification (five levels) as given on Warner scale.
Eugene, Oregon,*	Littman, et al.	1955–56	0–14	206	86	120	Random sample of children from preschool classes and school rolls. Two SES levels assigned on same basis as in Boston study.
Washington, D.C.	Kohn and Clausen	1956–57	10–11	339	174	165	Representative samples of working- and middle-class mothers classified by Hollingshead's index of social position.

* Denotes studies used as principal bases for the analysis.

sample of adolescent boys comes from Strodtbeck's investigation of "Family Interaction, Values, and Achievement".[11] Also, Littman, Moore, and Pierce-Jones [12] have recently completed a survey of child-rearing practices in Eugene, Oregon for a random sample of parents with children from two weeks to 14 years of age. Finally, Kohn [13] reports a comparison of child-training values among working and middle-class mothers in Washington, D.C.

In addition to these unpublished sources, the writer has made use of nine published researches.[14] In some instances —notably for the monumental and regrettably neglected Anderson report— data were reanalyzed and significance tests computed in order to permit closer comparison with the results of other investigations. A full list and summary description of all the studies utilized in the present review appear in Table 1. Starred items designate the researches which, because they contain reasonably comparable data, are used as the principal bases for analysis.

II. ESTABLISHING COMPARABLE SOCIAL-CLASS GROUPINGS

Although in most of the studies under consideration the investigators have based their classification of socioeconomic status (SES) explicitly or implicitly on the criteria proposed by Warner,[15] there was considerable variation in the number of social class categories employed. Thus, in the Anderson report data were analyzed in terms of seven SES levels, the New York survey distinguished five, the second Chicago and the two Detroit studies each had four, and Klatskin used three. The majority, however, following the precedent of Havighurst and Davis, differentiated two levels only—middle vs. lower or working class. Moreover, all of these last studies have been reanalyzed or deliberately designed to facilitate comparison with each other. We have already mentioned Havighurst and Davis' efforts in this regard, to which the Boston group contributed by recalculating their data in terms of medians rather than means.[16] Both White and Littman et al. were interested in clarifying the contradictions posed by the Chicago and Boston studies and hence have employed many of the same indices. As a result, both necessity and wisdom call for dropping to the lowest common denominator and reanalyzing the results of the remaining researches in terms of a two-level classification of socioeconomic status.

[11] F. L. Strodtbeck, "Family Interaction, Values, and Achievement," in A. L. Baldwin, Bronfenbrenner, D C. McClelland, and F. L. Strodtbeck, Talent and Society (Princeton, N. J.: D. Van Nostrand Co., 1958).

[12] R. A. Littman, R. A. Moore, and J. Pierce-Jones, "Social Class Differences in Child Rearing: A Third Community for Comparison with Chicago and Newton, Massachusetts," Am. Sociol. Rev., 1957, XXII, 694–704.

[13] M. L. Kohn, "Social Class and Parental Values," paper read at the Annual Meeting of the American Sociological Society, Washington, D.C., August, 27–29, 1957.

[14] H. E. Anderson (Chrmn.), The Young Child in the Home, report of the Committee on the Infant and Preschool Child, White House Conference on Child Health and Protection (New York: D. Appleton-Century, 1936); A. L. Baldwin, J. Kalhorn, and F. H. Breese, Patterns of Parent Behavior, Psychol. Monogr., 1945, LVIII, No. 3 (Whole No. 268): W. E. Boek, E. D. Lawson, A. Yankhauer, and M. B. Sussman, Social Class, Maternal Health, and Child Care (Albany: New York State Department of Health, 1957); Davis and Havighurst, op. cit.; E. M. Duvall, "Conceptions of Parenthood," Am. J. Sociol., 1946–1947, LII, 190–192; Klatskin, op. cit.; E. E. Maccoby and P. K. Gibbs, op. cit.; D. C. McClelland, A. Rindlisbacher, and R. DeCharms, "Religious and Other Sources of Parental Attitudes toward Independence Training," in McClelland (ed.), Studies in Motivation (New York: Appleton-Century-Crofts, Inc., 1955); Sears, Maccoby, and Levin, op. cit.

[15] W. L. Warner, M. Meeker, and others, Social Class in America (Chicago: Science Research Associates, 1949).

[16] Sears, Maccoby, and Levin, op. cit., p. 427.

In most instances, the delicate question of where to establish the cutting point was readily resolved. The crux of the distinction between middle and working class in all four of the studies employing this dichotomous break lies in the separation between white- and blue-collar workers. Fortunately, this same differentiation was made at some point along the scale in each of the other researches included in the basic analysis. Thus, for the several studies [17] using four levels of classification (upper and lower middle, upper and lower lower), the split occurred, as might be expected, between the two middle categories. For the New York State sample an examination of the occupations occurring at each of the five class levels used pointed to a cutting point between Classes III and IV. Klatskin, in comparing the social-class groupings of the New Haven study with the middle and lower classes of the original Chicago research, proposed a division between the first and second of her three SES levels, and we have followed her recommendation. Finally, for the seven-step scale of the Anderson report, the break was made between Classes III and IV, placing major clerical workers, skilled mechanics and retail business men in the middle class, and farmers, minor clerical positions, and semiskilled occupations in the working class.

In all of the above instances it was, of course, necessary to compute anew percentages and average scores for the two class levels and to calculate tests of significance (almost invariably X^2, two-tailed test, with Fisher-Yates correction for continuity). These computations, the results of which appear in the tables to follow, were performed for the following samples: National I–IV, New Haven I, Detroit I and II, and Upstate New York. All other figures and significance tests cited are taken from the original reports.

The effort to make the division between middle and working class at similar points for the basic samples, however successful it may have been, does not eliminate many other important sources of difference among the several researches. We now turn briefly to a consideration of these.

III. PROBLEMS OF COMPARABILITY

The difficulties involved in comparing the results of more than a dozen studies conducted at different times and places for somewhat different purposes are at once formidable, delicate, and perilous. First of all, even when similar areas are explored in the interview, there is the problem of variation in the wording of questions. Indeed, however marked the changes may be in child-rearing practices over time, they are not likely to be any more dramatic than the contrasts in the content and, above all, connotation of the queries put to mothers by social scientists from one decade to the next. Thus, the comprehensive report from the first White House Conference which covered the gamut from the number of children having rattles and changing their underwear to the number of toothbrushes by age, and the times the child was frightened by storms (analyzed by seven SES levels), says not a murmur about masturbation or sex play. Ten years later, in Chicago, six questions were devoted to this topic, including such items as: "How did you frighten them out of the habit?" and "What physical methods did you use (such as tight diaper, whipping them, tying their hands, and so forth)?" In the next decade the interviewer in the Boston study (perhaps only a proper Bostonian) was more restrained, or simply less interested. He asked only two questions: first, whether the mother noticed the child

---

[17] Duvall, *op. cit.*, Miller and Swanson, *Inner Conflict and Defense* and *The Changing American Parent*, *op. cit.*

playing with himself; then, "How important do you feel it is to prevent this in a child?" Nor is the difficulty completely eliminated in those all-too-few instances when a similar wording is employed in two or more studies, for there is the very real possibility that in different contexts the same words have different meanings.

Serious problems arise from the lack of comparability not only in the questions asked but also in the character of the samples employed. Havighurst and Davis, for example, point out that the Chicago and Boston samples had different proportions of cases in the two bottom categories of the Warner scale of occupations. According to the investigators' reports, the Palo Alto and Eugene studies deviated even further in both directions, with the former containing few families from the lowest occupational categories, and the Oregon group exceeding previous studies in representation from these same bottom levels. The authors of several studies also call attention to the potential importance of existing differences in ethnicity, religious background, suburban vs. urban residence, and strength of mobility strivings.

A source of variation perhaps not sufficiently emphasized in these and other reports is the manner in which cases were selected. As Davis and Havighurst properly pointed out in their original publication, their sample was subject to possible bias "in the direction of getting a middle-class group which had been subjected to the kind of teaching about child rearing which is prevalent among the middle-class people who send their children to nursery schools." Equally important may be the relatively high proportion in the Chicago lower-class sample of mothers coming from East European and Irish background, or the four-year discrepancy in the average ages of the mothers at the two-class levels. The first New Haven sample consisted entirely of mothers enrolled in the Yale

Rooming-in Project who were sufficiently interested to bring the baby back for a check-up a year after mother and child had left the hospital. As Klatskin recognized, this selectivity probably resulted in a "sample composed of the families most sympathetic to rooming-in ideology," a fact which, as she noted, was reflected in her research results. White's Palo Alto group consisted solely of mothers of only one child, most of whom were expecting a second offspring; cases were recruited from a variety of sources including friends, neighbors, personnel managers, nursery school teachers, Public Health nurses, and maternal prenatal exercises classes. In short, virtually every sample had its special eccentricities. For some of these, one could guess at the extent and direction of bias; in others, the importance or effect of the selective features remains a mystery. Our difficulties, then, derive as much from ignorance as from knowledge—a fact which is underscored by the absence, for many of the samples, of such basic demographic information as the distribution of subjects by age and sex.

It is clear that many factors, some known and many more unknown, may operate to produce differences in results from one sample to the next. It is hardly likely, however, that these manifold influences will operate in a consistent direction over time or space. The possibility of obtaining interpretable findings, therefore, rests on the long chance that major trends, if they exist, will be sufficiently marked to override the effects of bias arising from variations in sampling and method. This is a rash and optimistic hope, but—somewhat to our own surprise—it seems to have been realized, at least in part, in the analyses that follow.

IV. Social Class Differences in Infant Care, 1930–1955

In interpreting reports of child-rearing practices it is essential to distinguish between the date at which the information was obtained and the actual period to which the information refers. This caution is particularly relevant in dealing with descriptions of infant care for children who (as in the Eugene or Detroit studies) may be as old as 12, 14, or 18 at the time of the interview. In such instances it is possible only to guess at the probable time at which the practice occurred by making due allowances for the age of the child. The problem is further complicated by the fact that none of the studies reports SES differences by age. The best one can do, therefore, is to estimate the median age of the group and from this approximate the period at which the practice may have taken place. For example, the second Detroit sample, which ranged in age from birth to 18 years, would have a median age of about nine. Since the field work was done in 1953, we estimate the date of feeding and weaning practices as about 1944.[18] It should be recognized, however, that the practices reported range over a considerable period extending from as far back as 1935 to the time of the interview in 1953. Any marked variation in child-rearing practices over this period could produce an average figure which would in point of fact be atypical for the middle year 1944. We shall have occasion to point to the possible operation of this effect in some of the data to follow.

If dates of practices are estimated by the method outlined above, we find that the available data describe social-class differences in feeding, weaning, and toilet training for a period from about 1930 to 1955. The relevant information appears in Tables 2 through 4.

It is reasonable to suppose that a mother's reports of whether or not she employed a particular practice would be somewhat more reliable than her estimate of when she began or discontinued that practice. This expectation is borne out by the larger number of statistically significant differences in tables presenting data on prevalence (Tables 2 and 3) rather than on the timing of a particular practice (Tables 4–6). On the plausible assumption that the former data are more reliable, we shall begin our discussion by considering the results on frequency of breast feeding and scheduled feeding, which appear in Tables 2 and 3.

General Trends. We may begin by looking at general trends over time irrespective of social-class level. These appear in column 6 of Tables 2 and 3. The data for breast feeding are highly irregular, but there is some suggestion of decrease in this practice over the years.[19] In contrast, self-demand feeding is becoming more common. In both instances the trend is more marked (column 8) in the middle class; in other words, it is they especially who are doing the changing. This fact is reflected even more sharply in column 9 which highlights a noteworthy shift. Here we see that in the earlier period—roughly before the end of World War II—both breast feeding and demand feeding were less common among the middle class than among the working class. In the later period, however, the direction is reversed; it is now the middle-class mother who more often gives her child the breast and feeds him on demand.

The data on duration of breast feeding (Table 4) and on the timing of weaning and bowel training (Tables 5 and 6) simply confirm, somewhat less reliably,

---

[18] It is true that because of the rising birth rate after World War II the sample probably included more younger than older children, but without knowledge of the actual distribution by age we have hesitated to make further speculative adjustments.

[19] As indicated below, we believe that these irregularities are largely attributable to the highly selective character of a number of the samples (notably, New Haven I and Palo Alto) and that the downward trend in frequency and duration of breast feeding is probably more reliable than is reflected in the data of Tables 2 and 4.

SOCIAL STRATIFICATION

TABLE 2

FREQUENCY OF BREAST FEEDING

1. Sample	2. Approx. date of practice	No. of cases reporting			Percentage breast fed			
		3. Total sample	4. Middle class	5. Working class	6. Total sample	7. Middle class	8. Working class	9. Difference *
National I	1930	1856	842	1014	80	78	82	−4 †
National II	1932	445	201	244	40	29	49	−20 †
Chicago I	1939	100	48	52	83	83	83	0
Detroit I	1941	112	59	53	62	54	70	−16
Detroit II	1944	200	70	130	Percentages not given			+
Eugene	1946–47	206	84	122	46	40	50	−10
Boston	1947–48	372	198	174	40	43	37	+6
New Haven I	1949–50	222	114	108	80	85	74	+11 †
Palo Alto	1950	74	36	38	66	70	63	+7
Upstate New York	1955	1432	594	838	24	27	21	+6 †

* Minus sign denotes lower incidence for middle class than for working class.
† Denotes difference significant at 5-percent level of confidence or better.

TABLE 3

SCHEDULED VERSUS SELF-DEMAND FEEDING

1. Sample	2. Approx. date of practice	No. of cases reporting			Percentage fed on demand			
		3. Total sample	4. Middle class	5. Working class	6. Total sample	7. Middle class	8. Working class	9. Difference *
National I	1932	470	208	262	16	7	23	−16 †
Chicago I	1939	100	48	52	25	4	44	−40 †
Detroit I	1941	297	52	45	21	12	53	−41 †
Detroit II	1944	205	73	132	55	51	58	−7
Boston	1947–48	372	198	174	Percentages not given			−
New Haven I	1949–50	191	117	74	65	71	54	+17
Palo Alto	1950	74	36	38	59	64	55	+9

* Minus sign denotes lower incidence of self-demand feeding in middle class.
† Denotes difference significant at 5-percent level of confidence or better.

TABLE 4

DURATION OF BREAST FEEDING
(for those breast fed)

Sample	Approx. date of practice	No. of cases ††			Median duration in months			
		Total sample	Middle class	Working class	Total sample	Middle class	Working class	Difference **
National II *	1930	1488	654	834	6.6	6.2	7.5	−1.3 †
Chicago I	1939	83	40	43	3.5	3.4	3.5	−.1
Detroit I *	1941	69	32	37	3.3	2.8	5.3	−2.5
Eugene	1946–47	95	34	61	3.4	3.2	3.5	−.3
Boston	1947–48	149	85	64	2.3	2.4	2.1	+.3
New Haven I *	1949–50	177	97	80	3.6	4.3	3.0	+1.3
Upstate New York	1955	299	145	154	1.2	1.3	1.2	+.1

* Medians not given in original report but estimated from data cited.
† Denotes difference significant at 5-percent level if confidence or better.
** Minus sign denotes shorter duration for middle class than for working class.
†† Number of cases for Chicago, Eugene, Boston, and Upstate New York estimated from percentages cited.

all of the above trends. There is a general tendency in both social classes to wean the child earlier from the breast but, apparently, to allow him to suck from a bottle till a somewhat later age. Since no uniform reference points were used for securing information on toilet training in the several studies (i.e., some investigators report percentage training at six months, others at ten months, still others at 12 or 18 months), Table 6 shows only the direction of the difference between the two social classes. All these figures on timing point to the same generalization. In the earlier period, middle-class mothers were exerting more pressure; they weaned their children from the breast and bottle and carried out bowel and bladder training before their working-class counterparts. But in the last ten years the trend has been reversed—

it is now the middle-class mother who trains later.

These consistent trends take on richer significance in the light of Wolfenstein's impressive analysis [20] of the content of successive editions of the United States Children's Bureau bulletin on *Infant Care*. She describes the period 1929–38 (which corresponds to the earlier time span covered by our data) as characterized by:

... a pervasive emphasis on regularity, doing everything by the clock. Weaning and introduction of solid foods are to be accomplished with great firmness, never yielding for a moment to the baby's resistance. ... bowel training ... must be carried out with great determination as early as possible ... The main danger which the baby presented at this time was that of dominating the parents. Successful child training meant winning out

[20] M. Wolfenstein, "Trends in Infant Care," *Am. J. Orthopsychiat.*, 1953, XXIII, 120–130. Similar conclusions were drawn in an earlier report by Stendler surveying 60 years of child-training practices as advocated in three popular women's magazines. *Cf.* C. B. Stendler, "Sixty Years of Child Training Practices," *J. Pediatrics*, 1950, XXXVI, 122–134.

TABLE 5

AGE AT COMPLETION OF WEANING
(either breast or bottle)

Sample	Approx. date of practice	No. of cases			Median age in months			
		Total sample	Middle class	Working class	Total group	Middle class	Working class	Difference *
Chicago I	1940	100	48	52	11.3	10.3	12.3	−2.0 †
Detroit I	1942	69	32	37	11.2	10.6	12.0	−1.4 †
Detroit II	1945	190	62	128	— Under 12 months —			—
Eugene	1947–48	206	85	121	13.6	13.2	14.1	−.9
Boston	1948–49	372	198	174	12.3	12.0	12.6	−.6
New Haven I	1949–50	222	114	108	— Over 12 months —			—
Palo Alto	1951	68	32	36	13.1	14.4	12.6	+1.8

* Minus sign denotes earlier weaning for middle than for working class.
† Denotes difference significant at 5-percent level of confidence or better.

TABLE 6

TOILET TRAINING

Sample	Approximate date practice begun	No. of cases		Direction of relationship			
		Bowel training	Bladder training	Beginning bowel training	End bowel training	Beginning bladder training	End bladder training
National II	1931	2375	2375		− †		− *
National I	1932	494	494		−	−	
Chicago I	1940	100	220†	− †	−	− †**	+ †
Detroit I	1942	110	102		−	+	−
Detroit II	1945	216	200	+ †	−		
Eugene	1947–48	206	206	+	−	+	+
Boston	1948–49	372			−	+ †	
New Haven I	1950–51	214		+ †			
Palo Alto	1951	73		+ †			

* Minus sign indicates that middle class began or completed training earlier than lower class.
† Denotes difference significant at 5-percent level of confidence or better.
** Based on data from 1946 report.

against the child in the struggle for domination.

In the succeeding period, however,

... all this was changed. The child became remarkably harmless ... His main active aim was to explore his world ... When not engaged in exploratory undertakings, the baby needs care and attention; and giving these when he demands them, far from making him a tyrant, will make him less demanding later on. At this time mildness is advocated in all areas: thumbsucking and masturbation are not to be interfered with; weaning and toilet training are to be accomplished later and more gently.[21]

---

[21] Wolfenstein, *op. cit.*, p. 121.

The parallelism between preachment and practice is apparent also in the use of breast feeding. Up until 1945, "breast feeding was emphatically recommended," with "warnings against early weaning." By 1951, "the long-term intransigence about breast feeding is relaxed." States the bulletin edition of that year: "Mothers who find bottle feeding easier should feel comfortable about doing it that way."

One more link in the chain of information completes the story. There is ample evidence that, both in the early and the later period, middle-class mothers were much more likely than working-class mothers to be exposed to current information on child care. Thus Anderson cites table after table showing that parents from higher SES levels read more books, pamphlets, and magazines, and listen to more radio talks on child care and related subjects. This in 1932. Similarly, in the last five years, White, in California, and Boek, in New York, report that middle-class mothers are much more likely than those in the working class to read Spock's best-seller, *Baby and Child Care* [22] and similar publications.

Our analysis suggests that the mothers not only read these books but take them seriously, and that their treatment of the child is affected accordingly. Moreover, middle-class mothers not only read more but are also more responsive; they alter their behavior earlier and faster than their working-class counterparts.

In view of the remarkably close parallelism in changes over time revealed by Wolfenstein's analysis and our own, we should perhaps not overlook a more recent trend clearly indicated in Wolfenstein's report and vaguely discernible as well in the data we have assembled. Wolfenstein asserts that, since 1950, a conservative note has crept into the child-training literature; "there is an at-

tempt to continue . . . mildness, but not without some conflicts and misgivings . . . May not continued gratification lead to addiction and increasingly intensified demands?" [23] In this connection it is perhaps no mere coincidence that the differences in the last column of Tables 2 to 4 show a slight drop after about 1950; the middle class is still more "relaxed" than the working class, but the differences are not so large as earlier. Once again, practice may be following preachment—now in the direction of introducing more limits and demands—still within a permissive framework. We shall return to a consideration of this possibility in our discussion of class differences in the training of children beyond two years of age.

Taken as a whole, the correspondence between Wolfenstein's data and our own suggests a general hypothesis extending beyond the confines of social class as such: *child-rearing practices are likely to change most quickly in those segments of society which have closest access and are most receptive to the agencies or agents of change (e.g., public media, clinics, physicians, and counselors).* From this point of view, one additional trend suggested by the available data is worthy of note: rural families appear to "lag behind the times" somewhat in their practices of infant care. For example, in Anderson's beautifully detailed report, there is evidence that in 1932 farm families (Class IV in his sample) were still breast feeding their children more frequently but being less flexible in scheduling and toilet training than nonfarm families of roughly comparable socioeconomic status. Similarly, there are indications from Miller and Swanson's second Detroit study that, with SES held constant, mothers with parents of rural background adhere to more rigid techniques of socialization than their urban counterparts.

[22] Benjamin Spock, *Baby and Child Care* (New York: Pocket Books, Inc., 1957).

[23] Wolfenstein, *op. cit.*, p. 121.

Finally, the two samples in our data most likely to contain a relatively high proportion of rural families—Eugene, Oregon and Upstate New York—are also the ones which are slightly out of line in showing smaller differences in favor of middle-class permissiveness.

The above observations call attention to the fact that the major time trends discerned in our data, while impressive, are by no means uniform. There are several marked exceptions to the rule. True, some of these can be "explained" in terms of special features of the samples employed. A case in point is the New Haven study, which—in keeping with the rooming-in ideology and all that this implies—shows the highest frequency and duration of breast feeding for the postwar period, as well as the greatest prevalence of feeding on demand reported in all the surveys examined. Other discrepancies may be accounted for, at least in part, by variations in time span encompassed by the data (National 1930 *vs.* 1932), the demonstrated differential rate in breast feeding for first *vs.* later children (Palo Alto *vs.* National 1930 or Boston), ethnic differences (Boston *vs.* Chicago), contrasting ages of mothers in middle- *vs.* working-class samples (Chicago), etc. All of these explanations, however, are "after the fact" and must therefore be viewed with suspicion.

Summary. Despite our inability to account with any confidence for all departures from the general trend, we feel reasonably secure in our inferences about the nature of this trend. To recapitulate, over the last 25 years, even though breast feeding appears to have become less popular, American mothers—especially in the middle class—are becoming increasingly permissive in their feeding and toilet-training practices during the first two years of the child's life. The question remains whether this tendency is equally apparent in the training of the child as he becomes older. We turn next to a consideration of this issue.

V. Class Differences in the Training of Children beyond the Age of Two

Once we leave the stage of infancy, data from different studies of child training become even more difficult to compare. There are still greater variations in the questions asked from one research to the next, and results are reported in different types of units (e.g., relating scales with varying numbers of steps diversely defined). In some instances (as in the Chicago, Detroit II, and, apparently, Eugene surveys) the questions referred not to past or current practices but to the mother's judgment about what she would do at some later period when her child would be older. Also, when the samples include children of widely varying ages, it is often difficult to determine at what period the behavior described by the mother actually took place. Sometimes a particular age was specified in the interviewer's question and when this occurred, we have made use of that fact in estimating the approximate date of the practice. More often, however, such information was lacking. Accordingly, our time estimates must be regarded as subject to considerable error. Finally, even though we deal with substantially the same researches considered in the analysis of infant care, the total period encompassed by the data is appreciably shorter. This is so because the mothers are no longer being asked to recall how they handled their child in infancy; instead they are reporting behavior which is contemporary, or at least not far removed, from the time of the interview.

All of these considerations combine to restrict severely our ability to identify changes in practices over time. Accordingly, the absence of evidence for such changes in some of the data is perhaps more properly attributed to the limitations of our measures than to the actual course of events.

TABLE 7

Permissiveness toward Impulse Expression

Sample	Approx. date of practice	No. of cases reported	Direction of trend for middle class			
			Oral behavior	Toilet accidents	Sex	Aggression
National I	1932	470			More infants allowed to play on bed unclothed.*	
Chicago	1943	100		Treated by ignoring,* reasoning or talking, rather than slapping,* scolding, or showing disgust.*		More children allowed to "fight so long as they don't hurt each other badly."*
Detroit II	1946	70–88	Less often disciplined for thumb sucking.		Less often disciplined for touching sex organs	
New Haven	1949–50	216	Less often disapproved for thumb sucking, eating habits, mannerisms, etc.*			
Eugene	1950	206		Less often treated by spanking or scolding	More permissive toward child's sexual behavior.*	Fewer children allowed "to fight so long as they don't hurt each other badly." More permissiveness toward general aggression.
Boston	1951–52	372	Less restriction on use of fingers for eating.*	Less severe toilet training.*	Higher sex permissiveness (general index).*	More permissive of aggression toward parents,* children† and siblings. Less punishment of aggression toward parents.*
Palo Alto	1953	73		Less severe toilet training.*		More permissive of aggression toward parents.* Less severe punishment of aggression toward parents.

* Indicates difference between classes significant at the 5-percent level or better.
† The difference between percentages is not significant but the difference between ratings is significant at the 5-percent level or better.

TABLE 8

RESTRICTION ON FREEDOM OF MOVEMENT

Sample	Approx. date of practice	No. of cases reported	Age	Item	Direction of relationship *
National II	1932	2289	1–5	Play restricted to home yard	—
				Play restricted to block	+
				Play restricted to neighborhood	+†
				No restriction on place of play	+†
National III	1932	669	6–12	Child goes to movie with parents	+
				Child goes to movie with other children	+
National IV	1932	2414	1–12	Child goes to bed earlier	+
Chicago	1943	100	5	Age at which child is allowed to go to movie alone or with other children	+†
				Age at which child is allowed to go downtown	—†
				Time at which children are expected in at night	+†
New Haven I	1949–50	211	1	Definite bed time	—†
Boston	1951–52	372	5	Restriction on how far child may go from home	—
				Frequency of checking on child's whereabouts	—**
				Strictness about bed time	—†
				Amount of care taken by persons other than parents	—†
Detroit II	1953	136	0–18	Child supervised closely after 12 years of age	—†
Palo Alto	1953	74	2½–5½	Extent of keeping track of child	0

* Plus sign denotes greater restriction for middle class.
† Denotes difference significant at 5-percent level or better.
** The difference between percentages is not significant but the difference between mean ratings is significant at the 5-percent level or better.

Permissiveness and Restriction on Freedom of Movement. The areas of impulse expression documented in Table 7 reflect a continuity in treatment from babyhood into early childhood. With only one minor, statistically insignificant exception, the results depict the middle-class parent as more permissive in all four spheres of activity: oral behavior, toilet accidents, sex, and aggression. There is no suggestion of a shift over the somewhat truncated time span. The now familiar trend reappears, how-

ever, in the data on restriction of freedom of movement shown in Table 8.

In Table 8 we see a gradual shift over time with the middle class being more restrictive in the 1930's and early 1940's but becoming more permissive during the last decade.

Training for Independence and Achievement. Thus far, the trends that have appeared point predominantly in one direction—increasing leniency on the part of middle-class parents. At the same time, careful consideration of the nature of these data reveals that they are, in a sense, one-sided: they have been concerned almost entirely with the parents' response to the expressed needs and wishes of the child. What about the child's response to the needs and wishes of the parent, and the nature of these parental demands? The results presented in Table 9 are of especial interest since they shed light on all three aspects of the problem. What is more, they signal a dramatic departure from the hitherto unchallenged trend toward permissiveness.

Three types of questions have been asked with respect to independence training. The first is of the kind we have been dealing with thus far; for example, the Boston investigators inquired about the mother's reaction to the child's expression of dependence (hanging on to the mother's skirt, demanding attention, etc.). The results for this sort of query, shown in column 6 of Table 9, are consistent with previous findings for the postwar period; middle-class mothers are more tolerant of the child's expressed needs than are working-class mothers. The second type of question deals with the child's progress in taking care of himself and assuming responsibility (column 7). Here no clear trend is apparent, although there is some suggestion of greater solicitousness on the part of the middle-class mother. For example, in the 1932 material the middle-class child excelled in dressing and feeding himself only "partially," not "completely." In the 1935 Palo Alto study, the middle-class mother viewed her child as more dependent even though he was rated less so by the outside observer. It would appear that middle-class mothers may be on the alert for signs of dependency and anxious lest they push too fast.

Yet, as the data of column 8 clearly indicate, they push nevertheless. By and large, the middle-class mother expects more of her child than her working-class counterpart. All five of the statistically significant differences support this tendency and most of the remaining results point in the same direction. The conclusion is further underscored by the findings on class differences in parental aspirations for the child's academic progress, shown in column 9. The only exception to the highly reliable trend is in itself noteworthy. In the Boston study, more middle-class mothers expected their children to go to college, but they were less likely to say that it was important for their child to do well in school. Are these mothers merely giving what they consider to be the socially acceptable response, or do they really, as Sears and his colleagues suggest, have less cause for concern because their children are living up to expectations?

The preceding question raises an even broader and more significant issue. Our data indicate that middle-class parents are becoming increasingly permissive in response to the child's expressed needs and desires. Yet, these same parents have not relaxed their high levels of expectations for ultimate performance. Do we have here a typical instance of Benedict's "discontinuity in cultural conditioning," [24] with the child first being encouraged in one pattern of response and then expected to perform in a very different fashion? If so, there are days of disappointment ahead for middle-class fathers and mothers. Or, are there other elements in the parent-child relationship of the middle-class family which impel the child to effort despite, or, perhaps, even because of, his early experiences of relatively uninhibited gratification? The data on class differences in techniques of discipline shed some light on this question.

Techniques of Discipline. The most

---

[24] R. Benedict, "Continuities and Discontinuities in Cultural Conditioning," *Psychiat.*, 1938, I, 161-167.

TABLE 9

TRAINING FOR INDEPENDENCE AND ACADEMIC ACHIEVEMENT

1. Sample	2. Approx. date of practice	3. No. of cases reported	4. Age	5. Item	Direction of Relationship			
					6. Parents' response to child's dependency	7. Child's behavior*	8. Parental demands and expectations	9. Academic aspirations for child*
National II	1932	2380	1–5	Dress self not at all		+		
				Dress self partially		+		
				Dress self completely		–		
		2391		Feed self not at all		–		
				Feed self partially		+		
				Feed self completely		–		
National III	1932	2301	6–12	Children read to by parents				+
		865		Runs errands		0		
				Earns money		–		
				Receive outside lessons in music, art, etc.				++†
National IV	1932	2695	1–12	Books in the home				++†
Chicago I	1943	100	5	Age child expected to dress self			0	
				Expected to help at home by age 5			++†	
				Expected to help with younger children			++†	
				Girls expected to begin to cook			++	
				Girls expected to help with dishes				
				Child expected to finish high school only				++†
				Child expected to finish college				++†
				Father teaches and reads to children				++†

TABLE 9 (*Continued*)

Location	Year	N	Age	Item	Class difference
Detroit II	1946	128	0–18	All right to leave three-year-old with sitter.	0
	1947	127		Expected to pick up own toys	+
	1948	126		Expected to dress self by age 5	++†
	1948			Expected to put away clothes by age 5	0
				Children requested to run errands at age 7	
				Agree child should be on his own as early as possible	+
Urban Connecticut	1950	152	6–18	Age of expected mastery (Winterbottom scale)	++†
Eugene	1950	206	0–18	Household rules and chores expected of children	+
Boston	1951–52	372	5	Parent permissive of child dependency	-†
				Punishment, irritation for dependency	-†
				Parents give child regular job around house	
				Importance of child's doing well at school	0
				Expected to go to college	-†
New Haven II	1951–53	48	14–17	Father subscribes to values of independence and mastery	++†
		1151 **	14–17	Expected to go to college	++†
				Family checks over homework	++†
Palo Alto	1953	74	2½–5½	M's report of child's dependency	-
				Amount of attention child wants	+
				Child objects to separation	-
				Judge's rating of dependency	+
Upstate New York	1955	1433	0–1	Mother's educational aspirations for child	+†

* Plus sign denotes greater independence or achievement required for middle-class child.
† Difference between classes significant at the 5-percent level or better.
** This is the entire high-school sample which Strodtbeck surveyed in order to select his experimental and control group.

TABLE 10

Techniques of Discipline

Sample	Approx. date of practice	No. of cases reporting	Age	Direction of relationship *				Nature of Love-oriented technique	Other significant trends for middle class
				Physical punishment	Reasoning	Isolation	Love-oriented technique		
National II	1932	1947	1–5	−†					Infractions more often ignored†
National III	1932	839	6–12			+†			More children deprived of pleasure as punishment
National IV	1932	3130	1–12		+†				
Chicago I	1943	100	5	+		−	+†	Praise for good behavior.	Soiling child more often ignored,† rather than spanked† or shown disgust
Detroit I	1950	115	12–14	−†			+†	Mother expresses disappointment or appeals to guilt	
Detroit II	1950	222	0–19	−			+	Mother uses symbolic rather than direct rewards and punishments	
Eugene	1950	206	0–18	−	0	+†	0		
Boston	1951–52	372	5	−†	+	+	0	No difference in overall use of praise or withdrawal of love	Less use of ridicule,† deprivation of privileges** or praise for no trouble at the table†

＊ Plus sign indicates practice was more common in middle class than in working class.

† Denotes difference between classes significant at 5-percent level or better.

** The difference between percentages is not significant but the difference between mean ratings is significant at the 5-percent level or better.

consistent finding documented in Table 10 is the more frequent use of physical punishment by working-class parents. The middle class, in contrast, resort to reasoning, isolation, and what Sears and his colleagues have referred to as "love-oriented" discipline techniques.[25] These are methods which rely for their effect on the child's fear of loss of love. Miller and Swanson referred to substantially the same class of phenomena by the term "psychological discipline," which for them covers such parental behaviors as appeals to guilt, expressions of disappointment, and the use of symbolic rather than direct rewards and punishments. Table 10 shows all available data on class differences in the use of corporal punishment, reasoning, isolation, and "love-oriented" techniques. Also, in order to avoid the risks, however small, involved in wearing theoretical blinders, we have listed in the last column of the table all other significant class differences in techniques of discipline reported in the studies we have examined.

From one point of view, these results highlight once again the more lenient policies and practices of middle-class families. Such parents are, in the first place, more likely to overlook offenses, and when they do punish, they are less likely to ridicule or inflict physical pain. Instead, they reason with the youngster, isolate him, appeal to guilt, show disappointment,—in short, convey in a variety of ways, on the one hand, the kind of behavior that is expected of the child; on the other, the realization that transgression means the interruption of a mutually valued relationship.

These consistent class differences take on added significance in the light of the finding, arrived at independently both by the Boston and Detroit investigators, that "love-oriented" or "psychological"

techniques are more effective than other methods for bringing about desired behavior. Indeed, both groups of researchers concluded on the basis of their data that physical punishment for aggression tends to increase rather than decrease aggressive behavior. From the point of view of our interest, these findings mean that middle-class parents, though in one sense more lenient in their discipline techniques, are using methods that are actually more compelling. Moreover, the compelling power of these practices, rather than being reduced, is probably enhanced by the more permissive treatment accorded to middle-class children in the early years of life. The successful use of withdrawal of love as a discipline technique implies the prior existence of a gratifying relationship; the more love present in the first instance, the greater the threat implied in its withdrawal.

In sum, to return to the issue posed in the preceding section, our analysis suggests that middle-class parents are in fact using techniques of discipline which are likely to be effective in evoking the behavior desired in the child. Whether the high levels of expectation held by such parents are actually achieved is another matter. At least, there would seem to be some measure of functional continuity in the way in which middle-class parents currently treat their children from infancy through childhood.

Before we leave consideration of the data of Table 10, one additional feature of the results deserves comment. In the most recent study reported, the Boston research, there were three departures from the earlier general trend. First, no class difference was found in the over-all use of praise. Second, working-class parents actually exceeded those of the middle class in praising good behavior at the table. Third, in contrast to earlier

---

[25] These investigators also classify "isolation" as a love-oriented technique, but since this specific method is reported in in several other studies as well, we have tabulated the results separately to facilitate comparison.

findings, the working-class mother more frequently punished by withdrawing privileges. Although Sears *et al.* did not classify "withdrawal of privileges" as a love-oriented technique, the shift does represent a change in the direction of what was previously a method characteristic of the middle-class parent. Finally, there is no clear trend in the differential use of love-oriented techniques by the two social classes. If we view the Boston study as reflecting the most recent trends in methods of discipline, then either middle-class mothers are beginning to make less use of techniques they previously relied upon, or the working class is starting to adopt them. We are inclined toward the latter hypothesis in the belief that the working class, as a function of increasing income and education, is gradually reducing its "cultural lag." Evidence from subsequent studies, of course, would be necessary to confirm this speculative interpretation, since the results cited may merely be a function of features peculiar to the Boston study and not typical of the general trend.

Over-all Character of the Parent-child Relationship. The material considered so far has focused on specific practices employed by the parent. A number of researches document class differences as well in variables of a more molar sort— for example, the emotional quality of the parent-child relationship as a whole. These investigations have the additional advantage of reaching somewhat further back in time, but they also have their shortcomings. First of all, the results are not usually reported in the conventional form of percentages or means for specific social-class levels. In some studies the findings are given in terms of correlation coefficients. In others, social status can only be estimated from educational level. In others still, the data are presented in the form of graphs from which no sig-

nificance tests can be computed. Partly to compensate for this lack of precision and comparability, partly to complete the picture of available data on class differences in child rearing, we cite in Table 11 not only the results from these additional studies of molar variables but also all other statistically significant findings from researches considered previously which might have bearing on the problem at hand. In this way, we hope as well to avoid the bias which occasionally arises from looking only at those variables in which one has a direct theoretical interest.

The data of Table 11 are noteworthy in a number of respects. First, we have clear confirmation that, over the entire 25-year period, middle-class parents have had a more acceptant, equalitarian relationship with their children. In many ways, the contrast is epitomized in Duvall's distinction between the "developmental" and "traditional" conceptions of mother and child. Duvall asked the mothers in her sample to list the "five things that a good mother does" and the "five things that a good child does." Middle-class mothers tended to emphasize such themes as "guiding and understanding," "relating herself lovingly to the child," and making sure that he "is happy and contented," "shares and cooperates with others," and "is eager to learn." In contrast, working-class mothers stressed the importance of keeping house and child "neat and clean," "training the child to regularity," and getting the child "to obey and respect adults."

What is more, this polarity in the value orientation of the two social classes appears to have endured. In data secured as recently as 1957, Kohn [26] reports that working-class mothers differ from those of the middle class in their choice of characteristics most desired in a child; the former emphasize "neatness, clean-

[26] Kohn, *op. cit.*

TABLE 11

OVERALL CHARACTER OF PARENT-CHILD RELATIONSHIP

Sample	Approx. date of practice	No. of cases reported	Age	Middle-class trend	Working-class trend
Berkeley I	1928–32	31	1–3	Grants autonomy Cooperative Equalitarian	Expresses affection Excessive contact Intrusive Irritable Punitive Ignores child
National I	1932	494	0–1		Baby picked up when cries †
National IV	1932	3239	1–12	Higher percentage of children punished †	Nothing done to allay child's fears †
Yellow Springs, Ohio	1940	124	3–12	Acceptant-democratic	Indulgent Active-rejectant
Berkeley II	1939–42	31	9–11	Grants autonomy Cooperative Equalitarian Expresses affection	Excessive contact Intrusive Irritable Punitive Ignores child
Chicago I	1943	100	5		Father plays with child more †
Chicago II	1943–44	433	1–5	"Developmental" conception of "good mother" and "good child." †	"Traditional" conception of "good mother" and "good child." †
New Haven I	1949–50	219	1	More necessary discipline to prevent injury or danger. †	More prohibitive discipline beyond risk of danger or injury.
Boston	1951–52	372	5	Mother warmer toward child † Father warmer toward child * Father exercises more authority * Mother has higher esteem for father † Mother delighted about pregnancy † Both parents more often share authority *	Father demands instant obedience † Child ridiculed † Greater rejection of child † Emphasis on neatness, cleanliness, and order † Parents disagree more on child-rearing policy *
New Haven II	1951–53	48	14–17	Fathers have more power in family decisions † Parents agree in value orientations †	
Palo Alto	1953	73	2½–5½	Baby picked up when cries †	Mother carries through demands rather than dropping the subject †
Eugene	1955–56	206	0–18	Better relationship between father and child †	
Washington, D.C.,	1956–57	400	10–11	Desirable qualities are happiness,* considerateness,* curiosity,* self-control *	Desirable qualities are neatness-cleanliness,* obedience *

* Trend significant at 5-percent level or better.
† The difference between percentages is not significant but the difference between mean ratings is significant at the 5-percent level or better.

liness, and obedience," while the latter stress "happiness, considerateness, and self-control."

Yet, once again, it would be a mistake to conclude that the middle-class parent is exerting less pressure on his children. As the data of Table 11 also show, a higher percentage of middle-class children are punished in some manner, and there is more "necessary" discipline to prevent injury or danger. In addition, though the middle-class father typically has a warmer relationship with the child, he is also likely to have more authority and status in family affairs.

Although shifts over time are difficult to appraise when the data are so variable in specific content, one trend is sufficiently salient to deserve comment. In the early Berkeley data the working-class parent is more expressive of affection than his middle-class counterpart. But in the follow-up study of the same children eight years later the trend is reversed. Perhaps the same mothers behave differently toward younger and older children. Still, the item "Baby picked up when cries" yields a significant difference in favor of the working-class mother in 1932 and a reliable shift in the opposite direction in 1953. *Sic transit gloria Watsoniensis!*

Especially with terms as heavily value laden as those which appear in Table 11, one must be concerned with the possibility that the data in the studies examined document primarily not actual behavior but the middle-class mother's superior knowledge of the socially acceptable response. Undoubtedly, this factor operates to inflate the reported relationships. But there are several reassuring considerations. First, although the items investigated vary widely in the intensity of their value connotations, all show substantially the same trends. Second, four of the studies reported in Table 11 (Berkeley I and II, Yellow Springs, and New Haven II) are based not on the mother's responses to an interview but on observation of actual interaction among family members. It seems highly unlikely, therefore, that the conclusions we have reached apply only to professed opinions and not to real behavior as well.

VI. RETROSPECT AND PROSPECT

It is interesting to compare the results of our analysis with the traditional view of the differences between the middle- and lower-class styles of life, as documented in the classic descriptions of Warner,[27] Davis,[28] Dollard,[29] and the more recent accounts of Spinley,[30] Clausen,[31] and Miller and Swanson.[32] In all these sources the working class is typically characterized as impulsive and uninhibited, the middle class as more rational, controlled, and guided by a broader perspective in time. Thus Clausen writes:

The lower class pattern of life ... puts a high premium on physical gratification, on free expression of aggression, on spending and sharing. Cleanliness, respect for property, sexual control, educational achievement—all are highly valued by middle class Americans—are of less importance to the lower class family or are phrased differently.[33]

[27] W. L. Warner and P. S. Lunt, *The Social Life of a Modern Community* (New Haven: Yale University Press, 1942); Warner, Meeker, and Others, *op. cit.*

[28] A. Davis, B. Gardner, and M. R. Gardner, *Deep South* (Chicago: University of Chicago Press, 1941).

[29] J. Dollard, *Caste and Class in a Southern Town* (New Haven: Yale University Press, 1937).

[30] B. M. Spinley, *The Deprived and the Privileged: Personality Development in English Society* (London: Routledge & Kegan Paul, Ltd., 1953).

[31] J. A. Clausen, "Social and Psychological Factors in Narcotics Addiction," *Law and Contemporary Problems*, 1957, XXII, 34–51.

[32] Miller and Swanson, *The Changing American Parent*, *op. cit.*

[33] Clausen, *op. cit.*, p. 42.

To the extent that our data even approach this picture, it is for the period before World War II rather than for the present day. The modern middle class has, if anything, extended its time perspective so that the tasks of child training are now accomplished on a more leisurely schedule. As for the lower class the fit is far better for the actual behavior of parents rather than for the values they seek to instill in their children. As reflected in the data of Tables 10 and 11, the lower-class parent — though he demands compliance and control in his child — is himself more aggressive, expressive, and impulsive than his middle-class counterpart. Even so, the picture is a far cry from the traditional image of the casual and carefree lower class. Perhaps the classic portrait is yet to be seen along the skid rows and Tobacco Roads of the nation, but these do not lie along the well-trodden paths of the survey researcher. He is busy ringing doorbells, no less, in the main section of the lower-class district, where most of the husbands have steady jobs and, what is more important, the wife is willing to answer the door and the interviewer's questions. In this modern working-class world there may be greater freedom of emotional expression, but there is no laxity or vagueness with respect to goals of child training. Consistently over the past 25 years, the parent in this group has emphasized what are usually regarded as the traditional middle-class virtues of cleanliness, conformity, and control, and although his methods are not so effective as those of his middle-class neighbors, they are perhaps more desperate.

Perhaps this very desperation, enhanced by early exposure to impulse and aggression, leads working-class parents to pursue new goals with old techniques of discipline. While accepting middle-class levels of aspiration he has not yet internalized sufficiently the modes of response which make these standards readily achievable for himself or his children. He has still to learn to wait, to explain, and to give and withhold his affection as the reward and price of performance.

As of 1957, there are suggestions that the cultural gap may be narrowing. Spock has joined the Bible on the working-class shelf. If we wish to see the shape of the future, we can perhaps do no better than to look at the pages of the newly revised edition of this ubiquitous guidebook. Here is a typical example of the new look—a passage not found in the earlier version:

> If the parent can determine in which respects she may be too permissive and can firm up her discipline, she may, if she is on the right track, be delighted to find that her child becomes not only better behaved but much happier. Then she can really love him better, and he in turn responds to this.[34]

Apparently "love" and "limits" are both watchwords for the coming generation of parents. As Mrs. Johnson, down in the flats, puts away the hairbrush and decides to have a talk with her unruly youngster "like the book says," Mrs. Thomas, on the hill, is dutifully striving to overcome her guilt at the thought of giving John the punishment she now admits he deserves. If both ladies are successful, the social scientist may eventually have to look elsewhere in his search for everlarger F's and t's.

Such speculations carry us beyond the territory yet surveyed by the social scientist. Perhaps the most important implication for the future from our present analysis lies in the sphere of method rather than substance. Our attempt to compare the work of a score of investigators over a score of years will have been worth the labor if it but convinces future researchers of the wastefulness of such uncoordinated efforts. Our best hope for an understanding of the differences in

---

[34] Spock, op. cit., p. 326.

child rearing in various segments of our society and the effects of these differences on personality formation lies in the development of a systematic long-range plan for gathering comparable data at regular intervals on large samples of families at different positions in the social structure. We now have survey organizations with the scientific competence and adequate technical facilities to perform the task. With such hopes in mind, the author looks ahead to the day when the present analysis becomes obsolete, in method as well as substance.

VII. Recapitulation and Coda

A comparative analysis of the results of studies of social-class differences in child rearing over a 25-year period points to the following conclusions.

A. Trends in Infant Care

1. Over the past quarter of a century, American mothers at all social-class levels have become more flexible with respect to infant feeding and weaning. Although fewer infants may be breast fed, especially over long periods of time, mothers are increasingly more likely to feed their children on demand and to wean them later from the bottle.

2. Class differences in feeding, weaning, and toilet training show a clear and consistent trend. From about 1930 till the end of World War II, working-class mothers were uniformly more permissive than those of the middle class. They were more likely to breast feed, to follow a self-demand schedule, to wean the child later both from breast and bottle, and to begin and complete both bowel and bladder training at a later age. After World War II, however, there has been a definite reversal in direction; now it is the middle-class mother who is the more permissive in each of the above areas.

3. Shifts in the pattern of infant care —especially on the part of middle-class mothers—show a striking correspondence to the changes in practices advocated in successive editions of U.S. Children's Bureau bulletins and similar sources of expert opinion.

4. In addition to varying with social-class level, methods of infant care appear to differ as a function of cultural background, urban vs. rural upbringing, and exposure to particular ideologies of child rearing.

5. Taken together, the findings on changes in infant care lead to the generalization that socialization practices are most likely to be altered in those segments of society which have most ready access to the agencies or agents of change (e.g., books, pamphlets, physicians, and counselors).

B. Trends in Child Training

6. The data on the training of the young child show middle-class mothers, especially in the postwar period, to be consistently more permissive toward the child's expressed needs and wishes. The generalization applies in such diverse areas as oral behavior, toilet accidents, dependency, sex, aggressiveness, and freedom of movement outside the home.

7. Though more tolerant of expressed impulses and desires, the middle-class parent, throughout the period covered by this survey, has higher expectations for the child. The middle-class youngster is expected to learn to take care of himself earlier, to accept more responsibilities about the home, and—above all— to progress further in school.

8. In matters of discipline, working-class parents are consistently more likely to employ physical punishment, while middle-class families rely more on reasoning, isolation, appeals to guilt, and other methods involving the threat of loss of love. At least two independent lines of evidence suggest that the techniques preferred by middle-class parents are more likely to bring about the development of internalized values and controls. Moreover, the effectiveness of

such methods, should, at least on theoretical grounds, be enhanced by the more acceptant atmosphere experienced by middle-class children in their early years.

9. Over the entire 25-year period studied, parent-child relationships in the middle class are consistently reported as more acceptant and equalitarian, while those in the working class are oriented toward maintaining order and obedience. Within this context, the middle class has shown a shift away from emotional control toward freer expression of affection and greater tolerance of the child's impulses and desires.

In the past few years, there have been indications that the gap between the social classes may be narrowing. Whatever trend the future holds in store, let us hope that the social scientist will no longer be content to look at them piecemeal but will utilize all the technical resources now at his command to obtain a systematic picture of the changes, through still more extended space and time, in the way in which humanity brings up its children.

FACTORS ASSOCIATED WITH PREVALENCE OF MENTAL ILLNESS   By August B. Hollingshead

INTRODUCTION

Mental illness in recent years has been recognized as the most serious unsolved health problem facing our society. A few figures will indicate the number of persons known and believed to be suffering from psychiatric disorders. *First*, there are 750,000 persons currently hospitalized in mental institutions in the United States; these patients occupy some 55 percent of the hospital beds in the nation. *Second*, hundreds of thousands of ambulatory patients are treated in psychiatric clinics and in private practice. *Third*, some 16,000 to 17,000 persons commit suicide each year and there are about 3,800,000 alcoholics in the adult population.[1] In addition, estimates indicate there are from seven to eight million other Americans who could benefit from psychiatric care if it were available.

The problem of mental disturbances is not new. Historical evidence indicates mental illnesses have been known in all civilized societies. Mental aberrations of kings, generals, priests, and other personages have been recorded since ancient times. Even though the problem of mental illness is an old one, the American public is more aware of it today than in earlier years. Moreover, responsible leaders have begun to see possibilities of alleviating it through the application of scientific knowledge.

Determination of the number of mentally ill persons in a defined population is the first requisite to an intelligent approach to the problem before us. Let me first present a few elementary definitions before I begin discussion of the problems involved in obtaining accurate information about the frequency of mental illness.

Based upon a paper read before the Institute for Preventive Psychiatry in 1957. The data included in this paper are discussed at length in A. B. Hollingshead and F. C. Redlich, *Social Class and Mental Illness* (New York: John Wiley and Sons, 1958). The research was supported by a grant from the National Institute of Mental Health of the United States Public Health Service (MH-263) to Yale University under the direction of Dr. F. C. Redlich, Department of Psychiatry, and Professor August B. Hollingshead, Department of Sociology.

[1] Kenneth Appel, "Present Challenge of Psychiatry," *Am. J. Psychiat.*, 1954, III, 1-12.

Prevalence is defined as the number of cases of a specified disease present in a population aggregate during a stated interval of time. The criteria that define a "case" need to be stated fully. The size and characteristics of the population aggregate have to be specified. Finally, the time interval has to be stipulated.

Incidence is the number of *new cases* of a disease developing in a defined population within a specified interval of time. Incidence differs from prevalence in that a prevalence count includes *all* cases of a given disease "active" in the population, whether they are "old" or "new."

Although national censuses in a number of different countries have attempted to gather statistical data on inhabitants who are mentally ill, none of these efforts have been successful. The studies that have been made of incidence and prevalence of mental illnesses in particular populations have not been made carefully, they deal only with clinical cases, or they are not comparable.[2] The net result is this: satisfactory data do not exist on the endemic distribution of mental disorders in the population of any society. All we have are very rough estimates.

The computation of *incidence* and *prevalence rates* in mental illness is extremely difficult for a number of reasons—such as the fear of mental illness in the population and the lack of clarity among psychiatrists as to who is a "case." In spite of various attempts by psychiatrists to draw a clearly demarcated line between the "well" and the "sick," the boundary between mental health and mental illness remains indeterminate.[3] Unfortunately, psychiatry lacks a standard measure of what is "normal" and what

is "abnormal" in emotional and psychological functioning. A standard measure of "normality" and "abnormality" would enable researchers to determine the presence or absence of mental illness in a population. It also might enable them to estimate the proneness of some persons to mental illness. In sum, the lack of criteria for dividing the "sick" from the "well" presents great obstacles to investigators who desire to make studies of incidence and prevalence of mental illness in a population.

The determination of true or endemic prevalence and incidence of mental disorders in a defined population is dependent upon the development of standardized criteria for measuring "normality" and "abnormality" of psychological and emotional functioning. If this could be done, then a researcher might be able to examine either a total population or an adequate probability sample. The next problem would be to obtain enough competently trained psychiatrists or clinical psychologists to make the examinations. The population to be studied would have to be cooperative and subject itself to the necessary examinations and tests. These conditions have not been met by any research team and it is probable that some time will elapse before they are realized by any such group.

With these preliminary remarks as a frame of reference, I shall begin our presentation of empirical data to demonstrate how selected social, biological, and disease phenomena are interrelated in the prevalence of *treated* psychiatric disorders in a defined population. The data presented here are from the continuing, extensive study of mental disorders in the population of the New

---

[2] Paul Lemkau, Christopher Tietze, and Marcia Cooper, *A Summary of Statistical Studies on the Prevalence and Incidence of Mental Disorder in Sample Populations*. Pub. Health Rep., V, No. 53 December 31, 1943.

[3] For a review of the literature pertinent to this point, see Frederick C. Redlich, "The Concept of Health in Psychiatry," in Alexander Leighton, John Clausen, and Robert N. Wilson (eds.), *Explorations in Social Psychiatry* (New York: Basic Books, 1957).

Haven, Connecticut, community.[4] The data were assembled by a team of three psychiatrists,[5] two sociologists,[6] and a clinical psychologist [7] to test postulated assumptions of interdependence between social class and the prevalence of treated psychiatric disorders.

RESEARCH DESIGN

Three technical operations had to be completed before hypothesized relationships [8] between class status and mental illnesses could be tested empirically. These were: (1) the determination of who is a psychiatric "case," (2) selection of a cross-sectional sample of the community's population as a control, and (3) the stratification of both the control and the psychiatric populations.

1. The Psychiatric Census. We determined who was a psychiatric "case" by taking a census of psychiatric patients. The *psychiatric census* was limited to residents of the community who were patients of a psychiatrist, a psychiatric clinic, or were in a psychiatric institution between June 1, 1950 and December 1, 1950. To make reasonably certain that all patients were included in the enumeration, the research team gathered data from all public and private psychiatric institutions and clinics in Connecticut and nearby states, and from private practitioners in Connecticut and the metropolitan New York area. It received the cooperation of all clinics and

institutions and of all practitioners except a small number in New York City. Checks indicate we have data on at least 98 percent of all residents in the community who were receiving psychiatric care on the date of the census.

Forty-four items of information were gathered about each patient and placed on a schedule. The psychiatrists selected material regarding referrals, symptomatology and diagnosis, onset of illness, and the nature, intensity, and duration of treatment. The sociologists obtained information on age, sex, occupation, education, religion, race and ethnicity, family history, marital experiences, and so on.

2. The Control Population. The second research operation was the selection of a *5-percent systematic sample* from the population of the community. Data on age, sex, occupation, education, religion, and income of family members, as well as other items necessary for our purposes, were placed on the interview schedule. This sample, known as our control population, provided a standard of comparison for the psychiatric patient population.

3. Stratification of the Population. The control population and the psychiatric patients were stratified by the use of *Hollingshead's index of social position.* This index utilizes three factors to determine an individual's class: ecological area of residence, occupation, and education.[9] The principal classes may be characterized as follows:

---

[4] The New Haven community includes the City of New Haven, and the towns of West Haven, East Haven, North Haven, and Hamden. The 1950 population of the community was estimated at 240,000.

[5] F. C. Redlich, B. H. Roberts, and L. Z. Freedman.

[6] August B. Hollingshead and Jerome K. Myers.

[7] Harvey A. Robinson.

[8] See A. B. Hollingshead and F. C. Redlich, "Social Stratification and Psychiatric Disorders," *Am. Sociol. Rev.*, 1953, XVIII, 163–169, for a statement of the hypotheses tested in this research.

[9] Ecological area of residence is measured by a six-point scale; occupation and education are each measured by a seven-point scale. To obtain a score on an individual we must know his address, his occupation, and the number of years of school he has completed. Each of these factors is given a scale score, and the scale score is multiplied by a factor weight determined by a standard regression equation. The three factor scores are summed and the resultant score is taken as an index of this individual's position in the community's social-class system. The development of this scale will be described in detail in a forthcoming book by A. B. Hollingshead and F. C. Redlich, *Social Class and Mental Illness, op. cit.*

CLASS I.

This stratum is composed of well-to-do families whose wealth is often inherited and whose heads are leaders in the community's business and professional pursuits. Its members live in residential areas generally regarded as "the best"; the adults are college graduates, usually from famous private institutions. Their social life revolves around private clubs, cliques of families, and exclusive organizations of one kind or another. Almost all gentile families are listed in the local *Social Directory*, but few Jewish families are so listed. Three percent of the population is in Class I.

CLASS II.

Adults in this stratum are almost all college graduates; the males occupy high managerial positions and many are engaged in the lesser ranking professions. These families live well, but there is no substantial inherited or acquired wealth. Its members live in the "better" residential areas. The social life of this stratum tends to revolve around the family and church organizations. Less than 5 percent of the families in this class are listed in the *Social Directory*. Nine percent of the community's population is in Class II.

CLASS III.

This stratum includes the vast majority of small proprietors, white-collar office and sales workers, and a considerable number of skilled manual workers. Adults are predominately high-school graduates, but a considerable percentage have attended business schools and small colleges for a year or two. They live in "good" residential areas. Their social life tends to be concentrated in the family, the less prestigeful churches, and in lodges. Twenty percent of the population is in Class III.

CLASS IV.

This stratum consists predominately of semiskilled factory workers. Its members have finished the elementary grades but the older people have not completed high school. However, adults under 35 have generally graduated from high school. Their residence is scattered over wide areas. Social life is centered in the family, the neighborhood, the labor union, and public places. Its members comprise 30 percent of the community.

CLASS V.

Occupationally, class V adults are overwhelmingly semiskilled factory hands and unskilled laborers; most have not completed the elementary grades. The families are concentrated in the "tenement" and "coldwater flat" areas of New Haven city. Only a small minority belong to organized community institutions. Their social life takes place in the family flat, on the street, or in neighborhood social agencies. Eighteen percent of the population is in this stratum.

Now that we have outlined the research design and sketched the major features of the community's class structure, we will turn to the presentation of data on the prevalence of *treated* mental illnesses. We will confine the discussion to five factors: sex, age, diagnosis, length of time in treatment, and class status, to see how these attributes and variables are related to prevalence.

PREVALENCE RATES AND
SELECTED FACTORS

Age, Sex, and Diagnosis. We began the analysis of the data from the *psychiatric census* and the *5-percent sample* with the assumption that the prevalence of treated mental illnesses would be related to the sex and age structure of the population and to the diagnosis of the patients' disorders. Therefore, the data are presented separately for sex, age, and diagnostic groups. The division by males and females needs no explanation. The age and diagnostic groups we used require a word of clarification.

Age Groups. The patients and the population were divided into six age groups: Under 15 years of age, 15 through 24; 25 through 34; 35 through 44; 45 through 54; and 55 years of age and over. We think these categories reflect changes in social and psychiatric variables associated with age in our society. Individuals under 15 years of age are generally viewed as children. Adolescence and young adulthood is encompassed mainly in the period from 15 through 24 years of age when young people complete school and college. Moreover, most males and females marry in this phase of the life cycle and establish adult behavior patterns. Social and physiological changes are not so marked in the decades from 25 through 44, but they cover years of social and emotional growth, as well as stress for the average person; youth has passed and middle age has begun. The involutional period generally occurs in the decade from 45 through 54; marked endocrinological changes occur in men and women in these years. Socially the family of procreation is dissolved since the children of men and women in this age range mature and leave the home. Economically, the family reaches the peak of its earning power. From a psychiatric viewpoint, the middle fifties are the years when senium disorders make their appearance clinically. Individuals at 55 years of age are on the edge of the decline that eventually leads to the physical impairments of old age and the withdrawal of the individual from active participation in society.

Diagnosis. The psychiatrists on the team adopted the diagnostic scheme developed by the Veteran's Administration [10] during World War II as the best one available at the time the data were gathered.[11] The Veteran's Administration schema enabled the psychiatrists to integrate the diagnostic categories of the several institutions from which we collected data with the diagnostic categories used by analytically oriented clinics and private practitioners. Each patient was diagnosed by the three psychiatrists and the clinical psychologist on the team in terms of his predominant symptomological syndrome. Diagnoses were made on the basis of the notes in the case record and the symptomatology given by the patient's psychiatrist. The specific diagnoses made by the psychiatrists were recorded, and subsequently the decision was reached to condense the many diagnoses into seven categories of neurotic reactions and five types of psychotic disorders. By combining specific diagnoses into larger categories with a similar symptomatic base the data could be more easily handled statistically.

For the purposes of this paper the data will be condensed into the two major diagnostic categories; neurotic reactions and psychotic disorders. We will not have time to discuss the various subdivisions of the neuroses and the psychoses.

Prevalence of Neuroses. *By Sex and Age.*[12] The prevalence of neurotic patients in the population of the New Haven community by sex and age shown in Figure 1 indicates that both sex and age are related to prevalence. The curve for males parallels the one for females at all age levels, but there is a sharper differential in prevalence between males and females at approximately 30 years of age than at any other period in the life cycle. Between 25 and 34 years of age males have a rate per 100,000 approximately 150 higher than females. The next largest differential by age is among boys and girls under 14 years of age. The rate for boys is approximately three times higher than for girls. At all other ages there is little difference between the prevalence of neu-

---

[10] *Psychiatric Disorders and Reactions*, Veterans Administration, Technical Bulletin 10A–78, Washington, October 1947.

[11] After our data were collected the Veterans Administration nomenclature and category system was superceded by an outline developed by the American Psychiatric Association. However, there is strong similarity between the Veterans Administration classification and the outline used currently by the American Psychiatric Association.

[12] Two different ages are used in these analyses. The present age is used for the control population. The age when the patient entered treatment is used for the patient population.

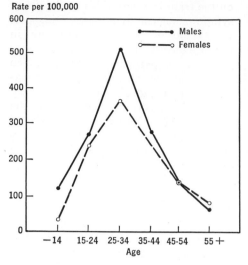

FIG. 1. Prevalence of neurotic patients in the New Haven community by age and sex.

rotic disorders for males and females, but males have higher rates until the involutional period is reached. From 45 through 54 years of age there is no difference between the two sexes; after 55 years of age females have rates that are slightly higher than males.

The salient point about the rate curves in Figure 1 is the sharp peak in the 25-through-34 age period for both males and females. During adolescence and early adult life the rate rises sharply. After 35 years of age it drops just as sharply through the years of late maturity to old age. Clearly there is a close relationship between age and the prevalence of treated neurotic reactions.

Age and Class. When we view the prevalence of treated neurotic disorders from the perspectives of age and social class, with the data adjusted for sex, the peaking phenomena illustrated in Figure 1 is repeated. This may be seen by a glance at Figure 2. However, there are real differences in prevalence in the different classes by age.

In classes I and II the rate is low in the childhood years. It rises almost perpendicularly through the adolescent and

early adult years to a climax in the 25-through-34-year period. The rate drops sharply in the 35-through-44 age bracket and continues to fall without any change in slope through the involutional years. There is a slight shift but still downward from 55 years of age to the end of life.

The curve for class III parallels that of classes I and II until age 25. Then it drops almost in a straight line in each of the successive age periods. The shape of the curve for class IV is similar to that for classes I and II, but the rate per 100,000 is much lower during every age period.

The prevalence curve for class V follows a unique pattern. In the years 14 and under, the rate is 160 per 100,000. It drops to 120 in the adolescent and early adult years and rises to 320 in the years from 25 through 34. Then it drops

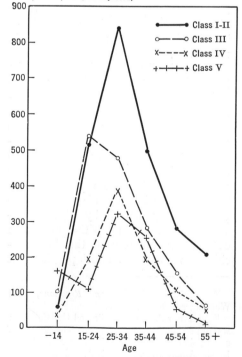

FIG. 2. Prevalence of neurotic patients in the New Haven community by age and class.

Rate per 100,000

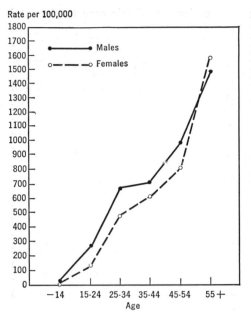

FIG. 3. Prevalence of psychotic disorders in the New Haven community by age and sex.

irregularly in each of the successive age periods. The rates of treated neurotic disorders differ significantly from class to class. The level of significance from one class to another is beyond .001.

Prevalence of Psychoses. *By Sex and Age.* The prevalence of treated psychotic disorders in the community's population by age and sex is depicted in Figure 3. The curve for females increases from almost zero at 14 years of age to 1,600 per 100,000 at 55 years of age and above. Males trace the same pattern except that between 25 and 44 years of age the increase in rate is slight. After 44 years of age the rate increases rapidly and parallels that for females.

The age distribution of psychotic disorders is dramatically different from that of neurotic reactions. Among the neurotic patients the rate for both males and females is highest in the 25-through-34 age group; the rate is 510 for males and 260 for females per 100,000 in these years. During the same age interval the rate for psychotic disorders is 700 for

males and 500 for females. Moreover, these 25-through-34 rates for the prevalence of psychoses are only one third as high as they are for females after 55 years of age; they are less than one half the rate for males 55 years of age and older.

In passing, it is interesting to note that the rates for both neurotic and psychotic females are slightly below those for males at all ages except above 55 years of age when the psychotic rate for females exceeds that of males.

By Age and Class. We will turn now to an examination of the prevalence of psychotic disorders by age and class. The rates, adjusted for sex, are depicted in Figure 4. A perusal of this chart will show there are marked differences among the several classes from one age group to another. In classes I and II the rate rises constantly from adolescence through the early adult years. It falls sharply from 25 through 44; it remains constant through the years of later maturity and rises after 55 years of age. It is worth noting, how-

Rate per 100,000 (sex adjusted)

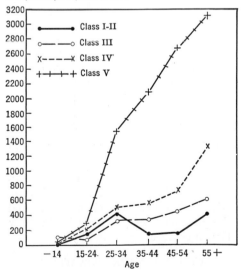

FIG. 4. Prevalence of psychotic disorders in the New Haven community by age and class.

ever, that the rate is only 50 higher per 100,000 after age 55 than it is during the years 25 through 34.

The rate for class III parallels that for classes I and II until 34 years of age, but unlike classes I and II, the rate in class III gradually increases each decade. The rate for class IV parallels the three higher classes until age 34, but it is higher in each age range. It levels off between 35 and 44 years of age just as class III does. It increases somewhat to age 54, then it expands sharply throughout the remainder of the life span.

Class V exhibits a distinctly different curve in comparison with the other classes. The rate is higher than in any other class at all age levels. The rate is low in the childhood years but in the 15-through-24 age range it rises to 303 and to 1,540 in the years between 25 and 34. Above 35 years of age the increase is in a straight line year after year as the population ages. However, we should note that the largest increase comes in the years between 15 and 34.

The widest differences in the prevalence of psychotic disorders from one class to another occur in the adult years. These differences increase with age, especially in classes IV and V. After 55 years of age the prevalence of psychotic disorders by class is as follows:

Class	Rate per 100,000
I–II	434
III	638
IV	1,353
V	3,161

The great differences in prevalence of psychotic disorders above 55 years of age revealed by these rates call for further analysis. There is a definite inverse relationship between class status and the prevalence of psychosis in the New Haven community. But why?

COMPONENTS IN PREVALENCE

For our purposes, prevalence is the ratio of persons in the population who are under psychiatric care to the total population of the community during the months of June through November 1950. In the preceding discussion no differentiation is made between patients who have been in treatment for a week and those who have been under psychiatric care for a number of years. When the data are viewed from the perspective of the differences in the length of time the patients have been in treatment, we find some patients entered treatment recently, others had been in treatment at one time, were discharged and re-entered treatment, while still others have been in continuous treatment for a varying number of years. The question we are now asking is this: Is the time when the patients enumerated in the *psychiatric census* entered treatment related to class status?

The schedule used in the *psychiatric census* was designed to give us an answer to such a question. We collected detailed information on each patient's illness; the date when he entered treatment for the first time, the duration of his first treatment, the date of his discharge, the date or dates of his re-entry into treatment, the date of his discharge a second or third time and so on. The information yielded by these questions enabled us to analyze the data by the length of time the patients had been in treatment.

Patients who were in treatment on May 31, 1950 and continued in treatment until December 1, 1950 are categorized as *continuous* cases. Individuals who entered treatment for the first time between May 31, 1950 and December 1, 1950 are categorized as *new* cases. Individuals who had been psychiatric patients at some previous time and re-entered treatment between May 31, 1950 and December 1, 1950 are counted as *re-entry* cases. The *continuous, new,* and *re-entry* cases make up the aggregate of *total* cases.

The patients were divided into these three time categories; then sex-and-age adjusted rates were computed to determine if class status is linked to the duration of treatment. For our present purposes no differentiation has been made between neurotic and psychotic diagnoses. In sum, we are dealing with all treated mental illnesses. The results of these analyses are summarized in Figure 5.

A glance at the four curves in Figure 5 will reveal sharp differences in their shapes. The curve for *total* cases is similar to that for the *continuous* cases, that is, those in treatment for more than six months, but the distance between the lines is much less in class IV than it is for classes I–II and III. This relationship indicates there are proportionately fewer class IV patients in the *re-entry*-into-treatment and *new*-case categories. The gap between *total* and *continuous* cases is wider in class V than in the other classes. The rates are also some two and one half to three times higher in class V than in class IV. The rates for *total* cases are related even more strongly to class than are those for the *continuous* cases.

The curves for *re-entry*-into-treatment and *new* cases are dramatically different from those for *total* and *continuous* cases. The *new* and *re-entry*-into-treatment curves parallel one another with little variation from class to class except that the rate for *new* cases in class III is almost double the rate for *re-entry* into treatment; 114 per 100,000 versus 69 per 100,000. In class V, by way of comparison, the rate for *new* cases is 139 per 100,000 and for *re-entry*-into-treatment cases, the rate is 123 per 100,000. Although the variations in the *new* and *re-entry* rates from class to class are not as spectacular as the rates for *continuous* cases, the differences are significant beyond the .001 level of probability.

Classes I and II contribute almost exactly the number of *new* cases as we would expect on the basis of their proportions of the community's population.

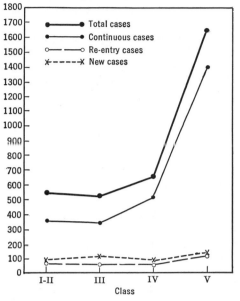

Rate per 100,000 (age & sex adjusted)

●——● Total cases
●——● Continuous cases
○– – –○ Re-entry cases
✕– – – –✕ New cases

FIG. 5. Age and sex adjusted rates for the New Haven community (by class and components in prevalence).

Class IV has a lower number than could be expected proportionately, whereas class V has an excess of 36 percent. Class V is contributing disproportionately to the number of new patients entering treatment for the first time as well as to the accumulation of *continuous* cases. Moreover, class V patients *re-enter* treatment in excessively large numbers. On a proportionate basis there is an excess of 61 percent of class V patients who re-entered treatment in the six months prior to the *psychiatric census*. Class IV, by way of contrast, has a deficiency of 15 percent; classes I and II have the expected number of *re-entry* cases.

When the three components in the curve for *total* cases are viewed both in relation to one another and to class status, the differential in rates between class I–II and class V changes markedly. The rate for *continuous* cases in class V is 3.8 times higher than in class I–II; 1406 per 100,000 against 369 per 100,000.

The differential for *new* cases from class I–II to class V is less (97 cases per 100,000 in class I–II compared to 139 cases per 100,000 in class V or an increase of 43 percent). The difference in rates for *re-entry* into treatment between class I–II and class V is likewise small (88 per 100,000 compared with 123 per 100,000); this is an increase of 39 percent.

The varying magnitudes of these differences produce the gap between the *continuous* and the *re-entry*-into-treatment curves. The gap is slightly less for class III than for class I–II, but the rate of *continuous* cases increases sharply from class III to class IV and dramatically so from class IV to class V. The widening gap between the rates for *continuous* and *re-entry*-into-treatment cases indicates *something is happening in the treatment of patients in the two lower classes which produces this difference.*

The increase in the *total* patient load in classes IV and V cannot be explained on the basis of sharply increased rates for *new* cases and *re-entry* cases. Obviously, there is a build-up of patients in class IV and especially in class V who have been in *continuous* treatment for more than six months. The question of how much longer will be discussed in the next analysis. There we will present data on the number of years patients in the study have been in the care of psychiatrists. Here we are concerned only with the question of how the prevalence of total treated cases is related to class from the perspective of the principal components; of the total case load: *new, continuous,* and *re-entry* cases.

CLASS AND YEARS IN TREATMENT

The mean and median number of years neurotic and psychotic patients have been in their present course of treatment are shown in Figure 6. The data summarized here reveal that the number of years patients have been in

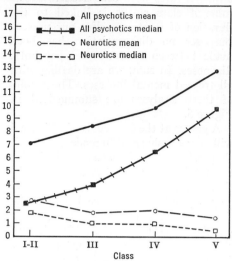

Duration of treatment in years

Fig. 6. The mean and median number of years psychotic and neurotic patients (from the New Haven community) have been in their present course of treatment.

treatment is linked to class status. Among neurotic reactions, the higher the class the longer the patients have been in treatment. Among psychotic reactions, the lower the class the longer the patients have been in treatment. A glance at the curves symbolizing the mean and median number of years the neurotic and psychotic patients have been in continuous psychiatric care will indicate that the effects of class position are starkly real whether the mean or median is used.

In the lower classes, particularly in class V, once a patient is diagnosed as psychotic and is committed to a state hospital he tends to remain there.

Some readers may jump to the easy conclusion that our figures on duration of treatment are no longer valid, because the *psychiatric census* was taken before the era of tranquilizing drugs. Shortly after the *psychiatric census* was completed we selected a random sample of 100 state-hospital patients for follow-up purposes. These patients were followed until March 1, 1956 or for five years and four months after the *census* was taken. Fifty-four of the 100 were still in hospital on March 1, 1956, 30 had died in the hospital, and 16 had been discharged between the date of the *psychiatric census* and the end of the field work. The 54 patients who were still in hospital five years and four months after the *census* date had been there a long time. When the follow-up stopped, the mean number of years these patients had been in continuous psychiatric care was: class I through III, 14; class IV, 18; class V, 22.5. The experiences of these patients during the present years of the "tranquilizing era" do not lead to the conclusion either that the new drugs are "emptying" the state hospitals or that the class differences in duration of treatment are growing shorter with the passage of the years.

The duration of treatment curves for the neurotic patients are not as dramatic as those for the psychotic patients. Nevertheless, the differences in the length of time the neurotics have been under psychiatric care are highly significant. The mean in class I–II is 33 months. It declines rather consistently to 18 months in class V. The median shows greater variation from one class to another; it is 23 months in class I–II but only 6 months in class V. The differences between the mean and the median measure the tendency of patients in the several classes to remain in treatment or to drop out of it. In class I–II the neurotic patients remain in treatment much longer than in classes III and IV. The vast majority of the class I–II neurotic patients are in ambulatory treatment with private psychiatrists. On the other hand, the class V neurotics are either clinic patients or they have been committed to the state hospital. Those treated in the clinics tend to drop out of treatment shortly after they begin, but the neurotics in the state hospital tend to be retained in hospital indefinitely. These counter trends produce the relatively large amount of disparity between the mean and the median figures for neurotic reactions below the class I–II level.

DISCUSSION

If we confine our attention to class differences in the occurrence of mental disease, we have found two major trends. (1) Mental disease diagnosed as neurosis is more common among individuals in the higher social classes, relative to the population in these classes; furthermore, a neurotic individual tends to remain in treatment longer if he is in a higher class. (2) Mental disease diagnosed as psychosis is more common among individuals in the *lower*-class groups, and lower-class psychotics remain in treatment longer than psychotics coming from the higher social classes. What could be responsible for these differences?

A possibility that comes readily to mind is the "drift" hypothesis. Perhaps individuals who are so severely ill as to be diagnosed psychotic cannot function well enough to maintain a position in classes I through III, even if they originated there. They may drift downward in the class structure because of their disability. If this were the case, it would of course result in a high concentration of psychotics in classes IV and V. Our data permit us to reject this hypothesis unequivocally. In another publication [13] we have shown that 91 percent of the schizophrenic patients whom we studied (and whose histories were adequate for determining their class of origin) were in the same class as their parents; and among those patients who were mobile, there were more who

[13] A. B. Hollingshead and F. C. Redlich, "Schizophrenia and Social Structure," *Am. J. Psychiat.*, 1954, CX, 9, 695–701

moved *up* the social scale than who moved down.

Other possible explanations of our findings we cannot evaluate so readily. Is it possible, for example, that one factor lies in the diagnostic process itself? We have already mentioned the difficulties in establishing criteria for what is "abnormal" behavior. There are equally great difficulties in assigning a case to one of the diagnostic categories, and the same mentally ill individual is sometimes called a psychotic by one doctor at one time and place and a neurotic by another doctor at another time and place. Perhaps some doctors are more likely to label mental disease psychotic if it occurs in a lower-class individual than if similar symptoms are observed in an upper-class person. Or perhaps the underlying causes of specific mental illnesses are not more common in one class than another, but the symptoms may vary by class if they depend upon certain life experiences (such as socialization practices) that differ between social classes. Finally, it is possible that there is something about the living conditions of lower-class people that produces (or accentuates) psychotic tendencies, while the setting of upper- and upper-middle-class life is such as to produce or accentuate neurosis. Until more is known about the etiology of mental disease and a more reliable system of classification is available, we cannot choose among these alternative possibilities.

10

Role and Role Conflict

TASK ROLES AND SOCIAL ROLES IN PROBLEM-SOLVING GROUPS   *By Robert F. Bales*

During the last ten years, a number of laboratories for the study of social interaction within small groups and organizations have been started in university research centers, hospitals, clinics, and military installations. The studies and experiments I shall describe were conducted in one of these laboratories, which was established in 1947 at Harvard University.

The laboratory consists of a large, well-lighted room for the group under study and an adjoining room for observers who listen and watch from behind windows with one-way vision. The subjects are told at the beginning that the room has been constructed for the special purpose of studying group discussion, that a complete sound recording will be made, and that there are observers behind the one-way mirrors. The purpose of the separation is not to deceive the subjects but to minimize interaction between them and the observing team.

Over a number of years we have evolved a more or less standard type of group and task which has formed the setting for a number of studies. The data I shall report came from several studies, all done under essentially the same conditions, so that a description of the most recent investigation will serve in substance for the others.

PROCEDURES

The sample which provided data for the most recent investigation consisted of 30 five-man experimental groups. Subjects were 150 Harvard freshmen who were recruited by letters sent to a random sample of the entering class which briefly described the experiment as one concerned with group problem-solving and decision-making. Volunteers were offered a dollar an hour. The groups were randomly composed. Typically the members of a group did not know each other, nor were they introduced to each other. In effect, they were faced with the problem of getting organized as well as with the more obvious problem that was issued to them.

The more obvious problem, which we call the standard task, involved the discussion of a human-relations case, a five-page presentation of facts about a problem facing an administrator in his organization. Members were given separate identical copies of the case to read ahead of time and were told that, although each was given accurate information, we intended to leave them uncertain as to whether they each had exactly the same range of facts. The cases were collected after they had been read by the members individually, to prevent direct compari-

Prepared especially for this volume.

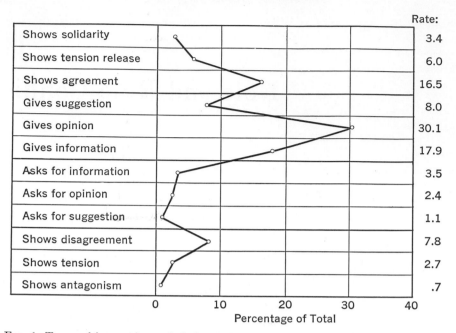

FIG. 1. Types of interaction and their relative frequencies. This profile of rates is the average obtained on the standard task from 24 different groups, four of each size from two to size seven, each group meeting four times, making a total of 96 sessions. The raw number of scores is 71,838. (From Robert F. Bales, "How People Interact in Conferences," *Scientific American*, Vol. 192 [March, 1955].)

son of typed copies, although members were allowed to take notes. The task defined for each group was to assemble the information, to discuss why the people involved were behaving as they did, and to decide what should be recommended as action for the solution to the problem presented. The groups were asked to time themselves for 40 minutes and to dictate the group solution for the sound record in the final one or two minutes of the meeting.

While the group members began to organize themselves and to solve the case problem, the observers got to work in the observation room. They systematically recorded every step of the interaction, including such items as nods and frowns. Each observer had a small machine with a moving paper tape on which he wrote in

code a description of every act—an act being defined essentially as a single statement, question, or gesture. Acts ordinarily occurred at the rate of 15 to 20 per minute. The recorded information on each act included identification of the person speaking and the person spoken to and classification of the act according to predetermined categories. The categories included attempts to solve either the organizational problems of the group or the task problems by the offering of information, opinions, and suggestions.

Questions and several types of positive and negative reactions completed the set of 12 categories (see Figure 1). This method is called "interaction-process analysis." [1] The categories are meant to have a general-purpose usefulness for group research and their use is not con-

[1] Robert F. Bales, *Interaction Process Analysis: A Method for the Study of Small Groups* (Cambridge, Mass.: Addison-Wesley Co., Inc., 1950).

fined in any way to the laboratory conditions described here, although the best norms exist for the standard task and the group type described here.[2]

As Figure 1 shows, on the average about half (56 percent) of the acts during a group session on the standard task fall into the categories of problem-solving attempts; the remaining 44 percent are distributed among positive reactions, negative reactions, and questions. In other words, the process tends to be two-sided, with the reactions serving as a more or less constant feedback on the acceptability of the problem-solving attempts. The following example will illustrate the pattern of interchange.

Member 1: I wonder if we have the same facts about the problem? [Asks for opinion.] Perhaps we should take some time in the beginning to find out. [Gives suggestion.]

Member 2: Yes. [Agrees.] We may be able to fill in some gaps in our information. [Gives opinion.] Let's go around the table and each tell what the report said in his case. [Gives suggestion.]

Member 3: Oh, let's get going. [Shows antagonism.] We've all got the same facts. [Gives opinion.]

Member 2: (Blushes) [Shows tension.]

A number of interesting generalizations can be made about the way in which rates of activity in the various categories tend to differ according to group size, time periods within a meeting, development of a group over a series of meetings, pre-established status characteristics of members, and the like.[3] The present article, however, will be concerned with a particular set of problems in which the interaction data have played an important part—whether there are tendencies for persons to develop different roles during interaction, even though there are no pre-established status differences, and if so, what kind, and why? There are several plausible views about this set of problems. The following account presents four distinguishable views and shows how research led from one view to another in the course of several studies.

THE HYPOTHESIS OF A SINGLE-STATUS ORDER

Perhaps the most ordinary conception of a group is that it consists of a leader and several followers who fall into a kind of status order from highest to lowest. The leader is the best-liked member of the group, participates most actively, and is felt to be the best performer of whatever task activities the group undertakes. No matter which of these criteria the researcher takes, he will come out with the same rank order of members. The expectation that most groups are structured like this and that departures from this simple form of organization may be treated as the result of special circumstances may be called the hypothesis of a "single-status order."

This is a plausible hypothesis. It underlies much research on leadership. It is congruent with the ideological position that for good leadership it is very important that a good leader should be an all-around "great man," and it assumes that there are such men, at least relative to the other members in a given group.[4] This hypothesis assumes role differentiation but essentially only along a single quantitative dimension, leadership status.

[2] For norms, see Robert F. Bales and Edgar F. Borgatta, "Size of Group as a Factor in the Interaction Profile," in A. Paul Hare, Edgar F. Borgatta, and Robert F. Bales, *Small Groups, Studies in Social Interaction* (New York: Alfred A. Knopf, Inc., 1955), pp. 396–413.

[3] For a short review, see Robert F. Bales "Some Uniformities of Behavior in Small Groups" in the previous edition of this book, Guy E. Swanson, Theodore M. Newcomb, and Eugene L. Hartley (eds.), *Readings in Social Psychology* (New York: Henry Holt & Co., Inc., 1952), rev. ed., pp. 146–159.

[4] For some evidence that there are some such men, in relative terms, see Edgar F. Borgatta, Arthur S. Couch, and Robert F. Bales, "Some Findings Relevant to the Great Man Theory of Leadership," *Am. Sociol. Rev.*, 1954, XIX, 755–759.

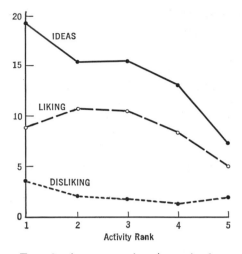

FIG. 2. Average ratings * received on ideas, liking, and disliking by men of each activity rank. (From Robert F. Bales, "The Equilibrium Problem in Small Groups," Ch. IV in Talcott Parsons, Bales, and Edward A. Shils [eds.], *Working Papers in the Theory of Action* [Glencoe, Ill.: Free Press, 1953], p. 146.)

* Each entry at a given activity rank is a mean over 12 sessions for the persons who occupied that rank as of each meeting. (Four separate five-man groups were involved.) The idea index is not actually a rating but an index obtained by adding rankings received (including self-rankings) and subtracting the total from the highest possible, 25. The like and dislike indexes are average ratings received, with the highest possible, 28.

Early in the research we began to ask group members about their likes and dislikes for each other, their opinions of who had the best ideas and who showed the most leadership, and other similar questions. We wanted to know how these questions related to each other and to our observations of interaction. The question as to whether or not there is role differentiation within a group can be reduced in part to whether group members show some consensus that certain members stand higher than others on a given criterion and whether different criteria give different status orders rather than a single-status order.

When I first began to examine data from our experimental groups, I worked under the assumption that there might be some such thing as a "simply organized group," that is, one in which the rank order of members on activity, task ability, and likeability would coincide, and that these groups would in some sense or other be the most successful or best satisfied.[5]

Figure 2 shows the results which raised a most interesting set of questions. The total interaction initiated by one man in the course of a meeting establishes the basis for ranking him relative to the others on activity. If there is a strong tendency toward a single-status order, top men on activity should also rank highest in group-member responses to such questions as "who has the best ideas," and should also receive the highest number of "liking" votes and lowest of "disliking."[6] The second man on activity should, on the average, be second highest on the other criteria of excellence, and so on. The rank order on each criterion should be highly correlated to the rank order on the other criteria.

What does Figure 2 suggest? First, there seems to be a positive correlation between activity rank and idea rank, although the second man seems a little low. But on liking-received rank, there is a marked discrepancy. The top man on activity appears considerably lower than expected on liking received. Both the second and the third men are higher on the average than he. Is the top man doing something to lose likes and provoke dislikes? Here one notes the dislike curve.

[5] Robert F. Bales, "The Equilibrium Problem in Small Groups," Ch. IV in Talcott Parsons, Robert F. Bales, and Edward A. Shils (eds.), *Working Papers in the Theory of Action* (Glencoe, Ill.: Free Press, 1953).

[6] The actual questions used are presented in the source indicated at the foot of Figure 3. They are omitted in the present paper for the sake of brevity.

The differences are small and probably not significant but they suggest that the top man is possibly the highest on dislikes received. Liking seems to be centering on the second and third man in activity, and they both seem to be lower than expected on idea ranking. Can it be that these men are tending to avoid too heavy an emphasis on the task area for fear of being disliked?

On further investigation of this problem it turned out that something happened in groups over a series of four sessions that was equally thought-provoking. In the first sessions, if a given man held top position on the idea ranking by his fellow members, the probability was about 50–50 that he would *also* hold a top position on a likeability ranking. But in the second meeting the probability dropped markedly, and by the fourth meeting was only about one in ten. The percentage of cases in which the same man held the top position on liking and idea rankings at the same time, divided by session, may be charted as follows:

Sessions

1	2	3	4
56.5	12.0	20.0	8.5

Could it be that there was something about arriving in a top-status position, owing to technical contribution to the task problems of the group, that tended to "lose friends and alienate people"? If so, was another man likely to arise who paid more attention to the social-emotional problems of the group and so tended to collect more liking? The idea that this happens with sufficient frequency that it can be viewed as typical

may be called "the hypothesis of two complementary leaders."

THE HYPOTHESIS OF TWO COMPLEMENTARY LEADERS

Why, if at all, should groups tend to have two complementary leaders, one a task specialist, the other a social-emotional specialist? [7] Perhaps it would be helpful to look at the interaction of men highest on idea ranking received but not highest on liking received, and vice versa. It may be that men of these two types behave differently and the differences in behavior may give us some clues as to the reasons for the differences.

Table 1 shows the composite profiles of 44 matched session-pairs [8] of idea men (who were not best liked in their group) and best-liked men (who were not top in idea ranking). Slater, from whose paper the table is taken, comments: "The most salient general difference in Table 1 is the tendency for the Idea man to initiate interaction more heavily in Area B (Problem-Solving Attempts) and the Best-liked man in Area A (Positive Reactions). The Idea man also seems to disagree somewhat more, and show a little more antagonism, while the Best-liked man asks more questions and shows more tension." [9]

On the receiving end, the situation is largely reversed, with the idea man receiving more agreement, questions, and negative reactions, while the best-liked man receives more problem-solving attempts, and more solidarity and tension release. The general picture is thus one of specialization and complementarity, with the idea man concentrating on the task

[7] A theory is advanced in Robert F. Bales and Philip E. Slater, "Role Differentiation in Small Decision-making Groups," Ch. V in Talcott Parsons *et al.* (eds.), *Family, Socialization, and Interaction Process* (Glencoe, Ill.: Free Press, 1955).

[8] Although the number of *sessions* was 44, the number of separate individuals involved was not 88, since each group ran over four sessions, and some individuals were in the same position more than once.

[9] Slater, *op. cit.* in footnote to Table 1. It is not possible to state that all of the detailed differences indicated are significant, because rates in the various categories are interdependent. However, Slater shows that the two types are in general significantly different from each other.

TABLE 1 *

COMPOSITE PROFILES IN PERCENTAGES OF 44 TOP MEN ON IDEA RANKING
AND 44 TOP MEN ON LIKE RANKING FOR THE SAME SESSIONS

	Interaction category	Initiated		Received	
		Idea men	Best-liked men	Idea men	Best-liked men
Area A: Positive reactions	Shows solidarity	3.68	4.41	2.57	3.15
	Shows tension release	5.15	6.98	7.95	9.20
	Shows agreement	14.42	16.83	23.29	18.27
Area B: Problem-solving attempts	Gives suggestion	8.97	6.81	7.01	7.22
	Gives opinion	32.74	28.69	25.52	31.09
	Gives orientation	18.54	17.91	14.06	14.54
Area C: Questions	Asks orientation	3.04	3.71	3.62	2.80
	Asks opinion	1.84	2.94	1.94	1.74
	Asks suggestion	.93	1.33	.85	.84
Area D: Negative reactions	Shows disagreement	8.04	7.60	10.65	9.35
	Shows tension increase	1.92	2.16	1.59	1.35
	Shows antagonism	.73	.63	.95	.45

* From Philip E. Slater, "Role Differentiation in Small Groups," *Am. Sociol. Rev.*, 1955, XX, 305.

and playing a more aggressive role, while the best-liked man concentrates more on social-emotional problems, giving rewards and playing a more passive role.

The kind of complementarity that shows in the behavior, then, is a kind that occurs in short interchanges in conversations where a problem-solving attempt by one person is followed by an agreement or disagreement from some other, or where a pleasant remark or a joke by one is followed by a smile or a laugh from the other. Such a division of labor by type of act is very common and easily recognized. There may or may not be a specialization so that one person continues to produce more of one form of behavior than the other.

But now consider an important fact. Almost exactly the same sort of difference in interaction profile tends to be found between high participators and low participators,[10] even if one ignores the idea and like ratings. High participators tend to specialize in problem-solving attempts, low participators tend to specialize in positive or negative reactions or questions. Moreover, the proportion of problem-solving attempts increases when a man is placed with lower participators and decreases when he is working with higher participators.[11] What do these facts suggest?

For one thing, these facts seem to imply that the qualitative differences in the type of act attributed to a given person may be more or less forced by the tendency of others in the group to talk a little or a great deal, thus giving him an opportunity to make the problem-solving attempts or leaving him only in a position to respond to the quicker or more valuable proposals of others.

Insofar as the ratings a man receives

[10] See Edgar F. Borgatta and Robert F. Bales, "Interaction of Individuals in Reconstituted Groups," *Sociometry*, 1953, XVI, 302–320.

[11] *Op. cit.*

are based on the way he behaves, the ratings others give him will surely be dependent on how much he talks. Let us suppose that a man can receive a high rating on ideas only if he makes many problem-solving attempts. He can do this only by talking a good deal. Then, to receive a high rating on ideas he will have to talk a lot. Or, conversely, let us suppose that a man can receive a high rating on liking only if he rewards others by positive reactions. He can do this only if he permits them to make many problem-solving attempts, which in turn requires that he let the other(s) talk a lot. Then, to receive a high rating on liking he will have to talk less.

This line of reasoning seems to fit with the facts so far presented and, moreover, has a certain plausibility in terms of common organizational arrangements. The husband and wife in many families seem to play complementary roles of the sort described. Many administrators find cases from their experience where organizations in fact have two leaders, one who specializes on the task side, one on the social-emotional side. It is a kind of political maxim that it is almost impossible to elect the person who is technically best suited for an office—he is generally not popular enough. Surely there must be many persons in leadership positions who welcome any theory that explains to them that their lack of popularity is no fault of their own but a result of a specialization that is in the nature of things.

The problem now is that it might be inferred from this ideological version of the theory that there is no essential distinction between sheer activity and rat-ings received on goodness of ideas and, moreover, that there is a negative correlation between these two and liking received. Is it true that leaders must choose between task effectiveness and popularity?

THE HYPOTHESIS OF THREE ORTHOGONAL FACTORS

Fortunately, a number of studies in the literature bear on this question and the results of a number of researchers tend to converge on an answer. When members of small groups are asked to rate and choose each other on a wide variety of descriptive criteria or are assessed by observers, three factors or distinct dimensions generally tend to appear.

Carter [12] indicates the frequency with which these factors are found in reviewing a series of factor analytic studies, such as those of Couch and himself, Sakoda, Wherry, and Clark.[13] A recent study by Wispe [14] may be added to the list.

Carter describes the factors as follows:

Factor I. *Individual prominence and achievement:* behaviors of the individual related to his efforts to stand out from others and individually achieve various personal goals.

Factor II. *Aiding attainment by the group:* behaviors of the individual related to his efforts to assist the group in achieving goals toward which the group is oriented.

Factor III. *Sociability:* behaviors of the individual related to his efforts to establish and maintain cordial and so-

---

[12] Launor F. Carter, "Recording and Evaluating the Performance of Individuals as Members of Small Groups," *Personn. Psychol.*, 1954, VII, 477–484.

[13] Arthur S. Couch and Launor F. Carter, "A Factorial Study of the Rated Behavior of Group Members," Paper read at Eastern Psychological Association, March 1952; J. M. Sakoda, "Factor Analysis of OSS Situational Tests," *J. Abnorm. & Soc. Psychol.*, 1952, XLVII, 843–852; R. J. Wherry, *Factor Analysis of Officer Qualification Form QCL-2B* (Columbus: Ohio State University Research Foundation, 1950); R. A. Clark, "Analyzing the Group Structure of Combat Rifle Squads," *Am. Psychologist*, 1953, VIII, 333.

[14] Lauren G. Wispe, "A Sociometric Analysis of Conflicting Role-Expectations," *Am. J. Sociol.*, LXI (1955), 134–137.

cially satisfying relations with other group members.

These factors seem to represent underlying dimensions in the evaluations persons make of each other, whether as observers or as fellow group members. It may be that the best way of looking at these factors is not as personality traits but as frameworks in which the perceiver responds to personality traits of others.

But the important thing to note is that in these studies the three factors, which I shall call "activity," "task ability," and "likeability," are not, in general, mutually exclusive: a high standing on one does not preclude or interfere with a high standing on the other. Nor are they mutually supportive in general but, rather, they tend to be uncorrelated.

The fact that they are uncorrelated in general does not necessarily mean, of course, that there are no dynamic relationships between the phenomena represented by the factors. It means that there is no simple linear relationship that tends to be found over all populations, so that knowing where a man stands on one does not allow for a prediction of his standing on either or both of the others. If there are dynamic relationships between the factors they must be more complicated, nonlinear, or circumstantial. What suggestions of relationship are there left?

THE HYPOTHESIS OF INDIVIDUAL DIFFERENCES IN OVERTALKING

Although it is not true that simply by talking a great deal does one guarantee a high rating on the quality of his ideas, it is still probably true that in groups of the sort we were studying it is very difficult to make a substantial contribution to the task without talking a great deal, especially in the first meeting, and overtalking may be resented by other members as a threat to their own status and a frustration of their own desire to talk. Results of other experimenters provided some findings that are congruent with this line of thought. Let us look for a moment at some of these results.

Leavitt and Mueller [15] explored the effect of one-way communication in a restricted communication situation where the receiver of the information is given no opportunity to "feed back" acknowledgements, questions, or negative reactions to the sender. They find that an initial reaction of hostility toward the sender tends to appear.

Thibaut and Coules [16] find that receivers who are not permitted to communicate to a person who has sent them an act of hostility show less post experimental friendliness to the sender than those permitted to reply.

A peripheral position in a restricted network approximates in some ways the position of a receiver with no opportunity for feedback. In an experiment where members were allowed to communicate only in written form through set channels on a task of assembling information, Leavitt [17] finds that members in peripheral positions are less well satisfied with their jobs than those in central positions.

These results suggested to us that the relatively low average of likeability preferences received by top participators might be due to the presence of some men in the total population of top men who overtalk, in the sense that they do not allow an appropriate amount of feedback of objections, qualifications, questions, and countersuggestions to occur. Our method of observation allowed us to ex-

[15] H. J. Leavitt and R. A. H. Mueller, "Some Effects of Feedback on Communication," *Hum. Relat.*, 1951, IV, 401–410.

[16] J. W. Thibaut and J. Coules, "The Role of Communication in the Reduction of Interpersonal Hostility," *J. Abnorm. & Soc. Psychol.*, 1952, XLVII, 770–777.

[17] H. J. Leavitt, "Some Effects of Certain Communication Patterns on Group Performance," see pp. 546–563 in this volume.

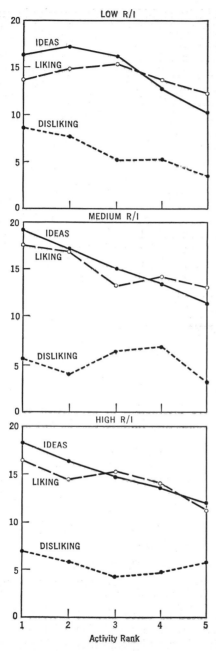

FIG. 3. Average ratings * received on ideas, liking, and disliking by men of each activity rank, according to their feedback ratio (R/I). (Condensed from Robert F. Bales, "Task Status and Likeability as a Function of Talking and Listening in Decision making Groups," in Leonard D. White [ed.], *The State of the Social Sciences*

amine the amount of interaction a given man received in relation to the amount he initiated. We thus arrived at the hypothesis that the ratio of interaction received to that initiated might help distinguish between those top interactors who were proportionately well liked and those who were not.

In general, as has been indicated, activity, task-ability ratings, and liking ratings appear in many studies as orthogonal factors, uncorrelated with each other over the total population assessed. It is important to recognize, however, that subparts of a population, or a different population, may show the variables related in a different way. It is the possibility that subparts of our population may show different relationships of these variables that we now explore.

We first make a basic division of the population according to the rank of each person within his own group on the gross amount of participation he initiated and call this his activity. Five ranks are thus recognized, since the groups were five-man groups.

The second division of the population is made within each rank. All the men of each rank are divided into three subpopulations according to their own ratio of amount of participation received from others to the amount of participation they initiate. This ratio is known as the R/I, or the feedback ratio. Within each rank, then, there are three subpopulations of ten men each, low, medium, and high on the feedback ratio.

Figure 3 shows the average values of ratings or ranking received for each of the subpopulations of ten men on liking, disliking, and ideas. The ratings or rank-

[Chicago: University of Chicago Press, 1956], pp. 148–161.)

* Each entry at a given activity rank is the mean for ten persons. The idea index is not actually a rating, but an index obtained by adding rankings received (including self-rankings) and subtracting the total from the highest possible, 25. The like and dislike indexes are average ratings, with the highest possible, 28.

ings were given to each man by his four fellow group members and have been converted for plotting in such a way that high numbers mean high average rankings received.

The point of greatest interest is the difference in the relations of liking to activity when the feedback ratio is taken into account. Figure 3 indicates that among the third of the population with a low feedback ratio, the top two men seem definitely lower than would be expected if liking received increased linearly in proportion to activity. The correlation between activity and liking received is near zero.

However, both the medium R/I and the high R/I thirds show a positive correlation. From these data it is still plausible to suppose that the top man even in the high R/I third shows a little less liking received than one would expect. But the effect is slight.

The data obtained by asking about dislikes present essentially the same picture. The highest participators among the third of the population with the lowest feedback ratio not only are less well liked but are more disliked than their less active colleagues in the same subpopulation. In this third of the population, the more the person talks, the more he is disliked. But in the opposite third of the population, those who have a high feedback ratio, there is no relation between how much a man talks and how much he is disliked.

With regard to idea rankings received, there is a definite indication that the highest participators in the third of the population with the low feedback ratio tend to suffer on idea rankings received, as they do on liking received, although the effect is not so marked. This effect seems to disappear completely in the medium R/I and high R/I groups.

It is plain, however, that there is an appreciable linear correlation between activity and idea rankings received over the total of the three subpopulations. This finding thus differs from other studies which find these two variables to be generally orthogonal. We attribute the correlation in our groups at least partly to the fact that we are dealing in this study with data from first meetings entirely. Data on groups running over four sessions indicate that this correlation tends to fall over time, especially in groups where the initial consensus as to who has the best ideas is low.[18] The correlation between ideas and liking also tends to fall as indicated above in Table 1. In short, the three factors tend to separate out as independent more clearly in later meetings than in the first.

To summarize briefly: In the groups in this total sample there is only a weak correlation between liking received and activity, providing one makes no breakdown into subpopulations. But for about one third of the population there is a positive and linear correlation between how much a man talks and how well he is liked. This is the third, who receive more interaction in proportion to the amount they initiate, that is, who have a high feedback ratio. The falling-off of liking received among the individuals who talk the most in total population is attributable especially to the other extreme third of the population, who talk proportionately most above the amount they receive. The same may be said for their rankings.

CONCLUSION

It appears that activity, task-ability ratings, and likeability ratings should be treated as three distinct factors, since over a large population of members, meetings, and groups they tend to be uncorrelated with each other. If one accepts this assumption a simple and very useful classification of role types in small groups suggests itself.

[18] Philip E. Slater, "Role Differentiation in Small Groups," Am. Sociol. Rev., 1955, XX, 300–310.

1. A member who is high on all three of the factors corresponds to the traditional conception of the good leader, or the "great man." Such men are found, but, if the factors are uncorrelated, are rare.

2. A member who is high on activity and task-ability ratings but less high on likeability is a familiar type who may be called the "task specialist." This type is not so rare as the first type and may operate effectively in cooperation with the third.

3. A member who is high on likeability but less high on activity and task ability may be called the "social specialist." This type is much less rare than the first type and groups which operate under the dual leadership of a man of this type and of the second type are common.

4. A member who is high on activity but relatively low on task ability and likeability ratings may be called an "overactive deviant." This type is not rare. This is the person who, in the leadership literature, is said to show "domination" rather than "leadership."

5. A member who is low on all three may be called an "underactive deviant" and may indeed be a kind of scapegoat. On the assumption that the factors are uncorrelated this type should be as rare as the first type, but since the lack of correlation traces mainly to discrepancies at the upper end of the scales, this type is not actually so rare as the first type and is, in fact, probably very common.

Logically, of course, one can distinguish many additional types. Those mentioned, however, have a certain intuitive distinctness and for present purposes serve to summarize and harmonize the various views on role differentiation that have been examined in this paper.

ROLE CONFLICT AND ITS RESOLUTION
By Neal Gross, Alexander W. McEachern, and Ward S. Mason

In certain situations an individual may find himself exposed to conflicting expectations: some people expect him to behave in one way, others in another, and these expectations are incompatible. How will individuals behave when faced with such conflicts? This is the problem with which our paper is concerned. Later we shall offer a theory of role-conflict resolution and present a test of its usefulness. Before doing this it is necessary to try, first, to clarify the meaning of role conflict and introduce definitions of the concepts we shall employ; second, to present the methods we used in a study of role

conflicts of school superintendents; and third, to describe their behavior when they perceived their exposure to conflicting expectations.

CONCEPTS

An examination of the literature concerned with "role conflict" reveals that this term has been given different meanings by different social scientists. Some have used it to denote incompatible expectation situations to which an actor is exposed, whether he is aware of the conflict or not. Other social scientists use

Especially prepared for this volume. The article represents a condensed and simplified version of the analysis of role conflict which may be found in Neal Gross, Ward S. Mason, and Alexander McEachern, *Explorations in Role Analysis: Studies of the School Superintendency Role* (New York: John Wiley & Sons, Inc., 1957). For a more detailed treatment of the problems considered in this paper and a critical appraisal of the theory presented, the reader is referred to Chapters XV, XVI, and XVII of *Explorations*.

"role conflict" to mean situations in which the actor *perceives* incompatible expectations. A foreman's subordinates and his boss may hold quite opposite expectations for his behavior but he may or may not be aware of this discrepancy.

Some formulations of role conflict specify that the actor must be exposed to conflicting expectations that derive from the fact that he occupies two or more positions simultaneously. For example, a young man may occupy simultaneously the positions of son and a member of a fraternity, and his father and his fraternity brothers may hold contradictory expectations for his "drinking behavior." Other formulations include in role conflict those contradictory expectations that derive from an actor's occupancy of a single position. A professor may be expected to behave in one way by his students, in another way by his dean.

Some writers limit role conflict to situations in which an actor is exposed to conflicting *legitimate* expectations or "obligations" whereas others do not make this restriction.

In view of these differences it is necessary to specify the way we defined and limited our problem. First, our interest was in role conflicts which were *perceived* by the individuals subject to them. Second, we were concerned with incompatible expectations resulting from an actor's occupancy of single as well as of multiple positions; *intra-role* as well as *inter-role* conflicts were within the focus of inquiry. Third, the analysis was not restricted to incompatible expectations which were perceived as legitimate. Attention was directed to situations involving both legitimate and illegitimate incompatible expectations.

Limiting the problem in this way the following definitions of basic concepts were used. A *role congruency* is a situation in which an actor as the incumbent of one or more positions perceives that the same or highly similar expectations are

held for him. A school superintendent who perceived that his teachers, principals, students, and school board all expected him to handle a discipline problem in the same way would be confronted with a role congruency.

There are situations, however, in which an actor perceives that he is exposed to expectations which are incompatible. A school superintendent may think teachers and parents hold conflicting expectations for his behavior in dealing with a truant child. Any situation in which the incumbent of a position perceives that he is confronted with incompatible expectations will be called a *role conflict*.

The person for whom an expectation is held may consider it to be *legitimate* or *illegitimate*. A legitimate expectation is one which the incumbent of a position feels others have a right to hold. An illegitimate expectation is one which he does not feel others have a right to hold. An expectation which is felt to be legitimate will be called a *perceived obligation*. One which is felt to be illegitimate will be called a *perceived pressure*.

A *sanction* is either a reward or a punishment, conditional on how an individual behaves. For our analysis we will not be concerned with negative sanctions, nor will we be concerned with *actual* sanctions, but rather with an individual's *perceptions* of the sanctions others may apply to him. Whether or not the perceived and actual sanctions are the same in any given situation is an empirical problem which will not be relevant to these analyses.

METHODOLOGY

One hundred and five school superintendents were included in the study. They represented a 48 percent stratified random sample of all school superintendents in Massachusetts in 1952–53. The data to be reported were obtained from each of these superintendents in the course of an eight-hour interview conducted in the staff research offices.

After considerable experimentation with various methods of isolating the role conflicts to which superintendents were exposed, the following procedure was developed. Four situations were presented to the superintendent, each involving problems with which all superintendents must deal and which, on the basis of the pretests, were judged likely to arouse incompatible expectations. They concerned (1) the hiring and promotion of teachers, (2) the superintendent's allocation of his after-office hours, (3) salary increases for teachers, and (4) the priority the superintendent gives financial or educational needs in drawing up the school budget. For each situation we offered three alternative expectations that incumbents of relevant counter-positions might hold. For example, in the situation which is concerned with teachers' salaries these three expectations were described:

A. Expect me to recommend the highest possible salary increases for teachers so that their incomes are commensurate with their professional responsibilities.

B. Expect me to recommend the lowest possible salary increases for teachers.

C. Have no expectations one way or another.

Eighteen potentially relevant groups or individuals were then listed, and each of the superintendents was asked to indicate which of the three statements most nearly represented what each of the groups or individuals expected the superintendent to do in the situation. If he said that one or more individuals held expectation A and one or more held expectation B, then he was reporting incompatible expectations from incumbents of positions counter to his own.

In addition, the superintendents were asked whether or not they felt that the expectations they said others held were "legitimate." Furthermore, if incompatible expectations were perceived by the superintendent, the interviewer probed with open-end questions to discover how much anxiety was thus created, how the conflict was resolved, and what sanctions the superintendent thought would result from selecting one or the other of the incompatible alternatives.

An example of a city superintendent's responses to the role conflict instrument illustrates the exact method of securing the data for this analysis. Table 1 summarizes the responses of this superintendent to the question of which groups or individuals held which expectations for him with respect to salary increases for teachers.

It is clear that he perceived incompatible expectations. He perceived that labor unions, the Parent-Teacher Association (PTA) and parent groups, some teachers, some of his personal friends, some service clubs, some of the school-board members, and his family expect him to recommend the highest possible salary increases. A number of other groups and individuals hold the contrary expectation; these are politicians, religious groups, some parents, some personal friends, taxpayers' association, economic influentials, service clubs, some school-board members, the town finance committee and the press.

In four cases some members of a given category held one expectation, according to the superintendent, while others in the same category held the contrary expectation. School-board members, parents, personal friends, and service clubs were all described by the superintendent in this way.

THE INCIDENCE AND RESOLUTION OF ROLE CONFLICT

In view of space limitations it is necessary to limit consideration of the incidence and resolution of role conflict to

TABLE 1

A SAMPLE QUESTIONNAIRE

THREE ATTITUDES OF VARIOUS GROUPS AND INDIVIDUALS WHICH
ONE SUPERINTENDENT PERCEIVED IN HIS COMMUNITY

	A	B	C		A	B	C
1. Politicians		X		11. Service clubs	X	X	
2. Church or religious groups		X		12. Fraternal organizations			X
3. Farm organizations			X	13. Veterans organizations			X
4. Business or commercial organizations			X	14. Individual school-committee members	X	X	
5. Labor unions	X			15. Town finance committee		X	
6. Parents (PTA)	X	X		16. My wife, family	X		
7. Teachers	X			17. Chamber of commerce			X
8. Personal friends	X	X		18. The press		X	
9. Taxpayers' association		X		19. Other			
10. Individuals influential for economic reasons		X					

DIRECTIONS: For each group or individual listed above please check the box which most nearly represents what they think you should do about this:

A. Expect me to recommend the *highest* salary increases possible for teachers so that their incomes are commensurate with their professional responsibilities.
B. Expect me to recommend the *lowest* possible salary increases for teachers.
C. Have no expectations one way or another.

only one of the four situations studied. The teacher-salary issue will be used. An examination of this potential area of role conflict will serve as a background to the theory of role-conflict resolution and yield part of the data with which one test of it can be made.

That the teacher-salary issue is a fertile source of role conflict is clear from the fact that 88 percent of the superintendents perceived that they were exposed to conflicting expectations in this

area. Table 2 reports the proportions of superintendents who perceived that incumbents of each of the listed counterpositions held: (1) the expectation that he recommend the highest salary increases possible; (2) the expectation that he recommend the lowest salary increases possible; (3) mixed expectations (that is, some held the *A* and others the *B* expectation); (4) no expectations regarding this issue.

Whereas 99 percent of the superintend-

TABLE 2

PERCENTAGE OF SUPERINTENDENTS WHO PERCEIVED PARTICULAR EXPECTATIONS
FROM SPECIFIED GROUPS AND INDIVIDUALS WITH RESPECT TO
THEIR SALARY RECOMMENDATIONS

Group or individual	A. High salary expectation (percent)	B. Low salary expectation (percent)	C. Mixed expectation (percent)	D. No expectation (percent)	N *
1. Politicians	14	51	6	29	105
2. Church or religious groups	34	6	3	57	104
3. Farm organizations	12	17	2	69	62
4. Business or commercial organizations	15	34	4	47	105
5. Labor unions	63	2	2	33	53
6. Parents (PTA)	78	1	9	12	105
7. Teachers	99	0	1	0	105
8. Personal friends	57	1	5	37	105
9. Taxpayers' association	9	77	4	11	61
10. Individuals influential for economic reasons	11	45	7	37	105
11. Service clubs	35	7	7	50	87
12. Fraternal organizations	19	3	3	74	93
13. Veterans' organizations	27	5	4	64	104
14. Individual school-committee members	70	14	14	2	105
15. Town finance committee or city council	18	60	11	10	103
16. My wife, family	71	0	0	29	103
17. Chamber of commerce	20	27	7	47	65
18. The Press	28	25	2	45	88

* When N is less than 105 it is usually because the group or individual did not exist in a number of communities; the "no answers" when the group or individual did exist are also excluded.

ents perceived that their teachers expected them to recommend the highest salary increases possible, 75 percent of those with taxpayers' associations in their communities reported that these associations held the opposite expectation (column 2). Similarly a majority of the superintendents said that their town finance committee or city council and local politicians expected them to minimize salary increases for teachers. In addition to reporting that their teachers expected them to recommend the highest possible salary increases, a majority of the superintendents reported that labor organizations, parents and the PTA, personal friends, individual school-board members, and their wives held the same expectation. Relatively few superintendents, however, are confronted with the "mixed" expectation from members of the same group or category, school-board members obtaining the highest percentage (14 percent in column 3) and town finance-committee members the next highest (12 percent in column 3).

From these data it is possible to conclude not only that superintendents are frequently confronted with role conflicts with respect to their teacher salary recommendations, but also that these conflicts may stem from different groups and individuals or from groups and individuals of the same kind. For the 88 percent of the superintendents who perceived that they were exposed to incompatible expectations, there is clearly a problem which must be resolved. How do superintendents act when they perceive that some groups or individuals expect them to behave in a contradictory manner?

When a superintendent had indicated that he was exposed to incompatible expectations, he was asked how he resolved the dilemma implied by this condition. Of the 92 superintendents (88 percent) who were exposed to role conflict in this situation (13 were not), seven gave insufficient information to permit coding their behavior, 54 conformed to the expectation of recommending the highest possible salary increases (64 percent of the 85 who told us what they did), eight recommended the lowest possible increases (9 percent of 85), and 23 (27 percent of 85) adopted some kind of strategy which did not require them to make an unequivocal choice between the two incompatible alternatives. Before we turn to an effort to predict which people will resolve the conflict in which way, let us examine briefly the different resolution techniques of those 23 superintendents who did not make a definite choice but developed a procedure whereby they could to some degree satisfy (18 or 21 percent) or ignore (5 or 6 percent) both demands.

One of the five superintendents who ignored both demands was not yet on tenure and perceived that his school board members, the town finance committee, the taxpayers' association, and individuals who were economically influential all expected him to recommend the lowest possible salary increases, whereas his teachers held the contrary expectation. He described his situation in this way:

I put it all in the hands of the school committee. It's a hot potato so I let the school committee handle it. The teachers feel I should represent them; the school committee feels I should represent them: I'd hang myself by getting involved. But I go along with the school committee recommendation one hundred percent, whatever they decide.

Four of the 18 superintendents who compromised assumed the position of negotiator when confronted with this dilemma. They apparently worked on the assumption that, although the expectations they face conflict, it is their duty to negotiate "a settlement" that will be most satisfactory to everyone. One superintendent perceived that his teachers, the school board, and the PTA expected him to recommend high salary increases to hold and attract competent personnel, while the town finance committee and taxpayers' association expected him to recommend the lowest increases, because they felt that the town was approaching a financial crisis. This superintendent says: "I use the salesman's technique. I tell the town, 'You don't want cheap teachers if you want a good school system.' I tell the teachers they have to be reasonable, that there has to be a compromise . . . if I completely agreed with the teachers, I'd be out of a job."

Three of the superintendents who compromise rejected both sets of expectations and substituted a new criterion in making their recommendations. They took the position that since they could not fully conform to both sets of expectations they try to develop a defensible rationale for their recommendations which is independent of the incompatible expectations of others. One of the superintendents recommended that the salary increases be contingent on a cost of living index. The others recommended an increase that would keep their school system in a competitive position with those of comparable size and wealth. One superintendent said he tried ". . . to do what's fair in light of what other communities are doing. I don't want my teachers to be at a disadvantage, but neither do I want our system to be a leader in the salaries we pay."

Ten of the 18 superintendents who compromised resolved the salary dilemma by trying to modify the conflicting expectations of one group so that they more nearly approximated the expectations of other groups. This technique differs from that of the superintendents who tried to adopt the position of negotiator, in that no attempt was made by these ten to modify both sets of expectations, and additionally, once one group's expectation had been modified, the superintendents gave their clear support to it. One superintendent told his teachers that if they gave him ". . . a reasonable request, I'll fight for it. If it's unreasonable, I won't. Then I tell them what I think is reasonable according to the town's ability to pay. . . . It's the realistic way to support the profession."

The remaining superintendent who compromised combined several of the previously described strategies. His primary objective was to obtain the maximum salary increases possible. According to his assessment, however, the way to do this was a little at a time. This superintendent said that he worked on this principle: "He who fights and runs away, lives to fight another day." He went on to say that ". . . it's a give and take matter. If your goal isn't damned you haven't lost. I have friends operating for better salaries for teachers who are on the town finance committee. This is the effective way to get results over time, if done consistently. You have to make compromises, and get part of what you want one year and part the next. You can't move too fast. The idea is to make steady progress."

The above excerpts from interviews have illustrated strategies of compromise or avoidence. We saw earlier that while some superintendents compromised, others made a clear choice between the two kinds of behavior expected of them. What determines the choice an indi-

vidual will make in resolving role conflict?

THE THEORY

The starting point for this theory of role-conflict resolution is the actor's definition of the situation. We assume that actors will have perceptions of whether or not the expectations to which they are exposed are legitimate. Furthermore, we assume that they will have perceptions of the sanctions to which they would be exposed if they did not conform to each of the expectations. In addition, we assume that individuals may be differentiated into three types according to whether they are primarily oriented toward legitimacy or sanctions in making decisions.

The first type characterizes the person who, when faced with a role conflict, gives most weight to the legitimacy of expectations. His definition of the situations places stress on *the right* of others to hold their expectations and de-emphasizes the sanctions he thinks will be applied to him for nonconformity to them. We shall say such a person has a *moral* orientation to expectations. He will be predisposed to behave in a role-conflict situation in such a way that he can fulfill legitimate expectations and reject illegitimate ones. If one of the incompatible expectations is viewed as legitimate and the other is not, he will be predisposed to conform to the legitimate expectation, regardless of what sanctions are involved. If both are legitimate he will adopt a compromise behavior in order to conform, at least in part, to both of them. If both are perceived as illegitimate, he will be predisposed to conform to neither of them and will adopt in consequence some type of avoidance behavior. In short, for an individual with a moral orientation to expectations we will ignore his perceptions of the probable sanctions in making predictions about his behavior. From his definition of the legitimacy of the expectations we can make

TABLE 3

PREDICTED AND ACTUAL BEHAVIORS OF MORALISTS IN 16 TYPES OF ROLE CONFLICT

Types of role conflict				Pre-dicted behav-ior *	Number of moral superintendents exposed to each type of conflict	Frequency of actual behavior	Proportion of correct predictions
Superintendent's perception of:							
Expectation A		Expectation B					
Is it legiti-mate?	Sanctions for non-conformity?	Is it legiti-mate?	Sanctions for non-conformity?				
1. Yes	Yes	Yes	Yes	c	2	$c = 2$	2/2
2. Yes	No	Yes	Yes	c	1	$c = 1$	1/1
3. Yes	Yes	Yes	No	c	0	—	—
4. Yes	No	Yes	No	c	0	—	—
5. Yes	Yes	No	Yes	a	4	$a = 3; c = 1$	3/4
6. Yes	No	No	Yes	a	4	$a = 4$	4/4
7. Yes	Yes	No	No	a	7	$a = 7$	7/7
8. Yes	No	No	No	a	1	$a = 1$	1/1
9. No	Yes	Yes	Yes	b	0	—	—
10. No	No	Yes	Yes	b	0	—	—
11. No	Yes	Yes	No	b	0	—	—
12. No	No	Yes	No	b	0	—	—
13. No	Yes	No	Yes	d	0	—	—
14. No	No	No	Yes	d	0	—	—
15. No	Yes	No	No	d	0	—	—
16. No	No	No	No	d	0	—	—
			Total:		19		18/19 (.95)

  * The abbreviations used in this column are as follows: a = conformity to expectation A, b = conformity to expectation B, c = compromise, and d = avoidance.

predictions about his behavior, and in Table 3 these predictions are specified.

The second type of orientation to expectations may be called *expedient*. An individual who has this orientation is one who gives priority to the sanctions others will bring to bear if he does not conform to their expectations. Such a person, we will assume, will act so as to minimize the negative sanctions involved in the role-conflict situation. He will try to provide the best defense for himself in view of the relative severity of the sanctions he feels others will apply to him for nonconformity to their expectations. Whether others have a right to hold certain expectations is irrelevant or of secondary importance to him. When he perceives strong sanctions for nonconformity to one expectation and weaker sanctions for nonconformity to the other, he will conform to the expectation which would result in the stronger sanctions for nonconformity. If he perceives that equally strong sanctions result from both, he will compromise in order to minimize sanctions. If he perceives no sanctions for nonconformity to either of the expectations, then the sanctions dimension will be of no value as a predictor of his behavior. Under this condition the other factor in the model, the legitimacy dimension, would be the only basis for predicting his behavior. In Table 4 the predictions for expedients are specified.

A third type of orientation to expectations will be called *moral-expedient*. A person who has this orientation does not give primacy to either the legitimacy or

TABLE 4

Predicted and Actual Behaviors of Expedients in 16 Types of Role Conflict

Types of role conflict				Pre-dicted behav-ior *	Number of expedient superintendents exposed to each type of conflict	Frequency of actual behavior	Proportion of correct predictions
Superintendent's perception of:							
Expectation A		Expectation B					
Is it legiti-mate?	Sanctions for non-conformity?	Is it legiti-mate?	Sanctions for non-conformity?				
1. Yes	Yes	Yes	Yes	c	3	$c = 1, d = 2$	1/3
2. Yes	No	Yes	Yes	b	2	$b = 2$	2/2
3. Yes	Yes	Yes	No	a	2	$a = 2$	2/2
4. Yes	No	Yes	No	c	0	—	—
5. Yes	Yes	No	Yes	c	3	$c = 3$	3/3
6. Yes	No	No	Yes	b	4	$b = 4$	4/4
7. Yes	Yes	No	No	a	7	$a = 7$	7/7
8. Yes	No	No	No	a	0	—	—
9. No	Yes	Yes	Yes	c	0	—	—
10. No	No	Yes	Yes	b	0	—	—
11. No	Yes	Yes	No	a	0	—	—
12. No	No	Yes	No	b	0	—	—
13. No	Yes	No	Yes	c	1	$c = 1$	1/1
14. No	No	No	Yes	b	0	—	—
15. No	Yes	No	No	a	1	$a = 1$	1/1
16. No	No	No	No	d	0	—	—
				Total:	23		21/23 (.91)

* The abbreviations used in this column are as follows: a = conformity to expectation A, b = conformity to expectation B, c = compromise, and d = avoidance.

sanctions dimensions but takes both relatively equally into account and behaves in accordance with the perceived "net balance." For some role-conflict situations the decisions of an individual with a moral-expedient orientation are relatively simple since both the legitimacy and sanctions elements lead him to the same behavior. If, for example, expectation A is perceived as legitimate and expectation B illegitimate and if he perceives greater sanctions for nonconformity to expectation A than for nonconformity to B, he will conform to expectation A. In general, if the legitimacy dimension leads him to the same behavior indicated by the sanctions dimension, no problem exists for him. Either criterion leads him to the same behavior. By comparing Tables 3 and 4 and ob-

serving which types of role conflict lead moralists and expedients to the same behavior we can easily isolate all the nonproblematic situations for the moral-expedients.

What is required as a basis for predicting his behavior in the remaining types of role conflict? A person with a moral-expedient orientation is one who takes both the legitimacy and sanctions dimensions into account and is predisposed to adopt a behavior that emerges from a balancing of these two dimensions. Thus, if expectations A and B are both viewed as legitimate but he perceives greater negative sanctions for nonconformity to A than to B, he will conform to expectation A. Weighing the two dimensions would result in clear-cut resolutions of the role conflict in types 2, 3, 5, 9, 14, and

15 of Table 5. In each of these instances on the basis of the sanctions and legitimacy dimensions there are two predispositions to one of the behaviors and only one to the other.

How would a moral-expedient behave when the sanctions and legitimacy dimensions lead him to conform to opposite expectations, as in types 6 and 11? In type 6, the legitimacy dimension would require conformity to expectation A, but the sanctions dimension would lead to conformity to expectation B. Since the actor is a moral-expedient he will try to do both or compromise because this seems to be the best balancing of the two dimensions when they lead to opposite behaviors; he is predisposed to do A on the basis of legitimacy and B on the basis of sanctions, and is, therefore, predisposed to both A and B, or to a compromise of the two.

We are left with one additional type in Table 5, type 13. In this case neither of the expectations is viewed as legitimate but nonconformity to both is perceived as leading to strong negative sanctions. The legitimacy dimension leads him to an avoidance behavior and the sanctions dimension suggests a compromise. It seems clear that he will not conform to expectation A or to B. To minimize sanctions he would compromise or try to conform to both A and B, and to emphasize legitimacy he would avoid or fail to conform to both A and B. It is clear that an avoidance reaction does not conform at all to either A or B; but it seems equally clear that a compromise fails to conform in part to both A and B and, therefore, is partially an avoidance. Consequently, the most probable resolution of situations of this kind by moral-expedients would be a compromise, which in part avoids and in part conforms to both expectations.

In Table 5 the predictions made on the basis of legitimacy and sanctions for "moral-expedients" are specified. Tables 3, 4, and 5 together describe all of tho

predictions made on the basis of the theory.

The Data for a Test of the Theory. If the superintendent's responses to the salary instrument revealed that contradictory expectations were held for his behavior, we designated the situation as a role conflict. On the basis of his answers to the interview questions, each of the superintendents was then coded on (1) his perception of the legitimacy or illegitimacy of the expectations, (2) the perceived sanctions for noncompliance with each expectation, and (3) how he resolved the role conflict.

The remaining element of the theory that requires consideration is the superintendent's orientation to expectations, that is, whether he was a moralist, expedient or moral-expedient. The superintendent's responses to another and completely independent instrument provided the data used for this categorization. Each item in this instrument refers to expectations that could be applied to a superintendent. For the 37 items in this instrument, he was asked: "As a school superintendent, what obligation do you feel that you have to do or not to do the following things?" The response categories were: absolutely must; preferably should; may or may not; preferably should not; absolutely must not.

We reasoned that a person who would typically react to expectations in terms of "it depends" is one who possesses an *expedient* orientation to expectations. In operational terms he would respond to the expectation items with the "preferably should," "preferably should not," or "may or may not" response categories.

On the other hand, a person whose typical response is not a contingent one but is in terms of "absolutely must" or "absolutely must not" carry out expectations is one who is primarily oriented toward their rectitude. He does not think in terms of factors in the situation that would lessen his obligations. Such a person would be predisposed "to honor" le-

TABLE 5

PREDICTED AND ACTUAL BEHAVIORS OF MORAL-EXPEDIENTS IN 16 TYPES
OF ROLE CONFLICT

Types of role conflict				Pre-dicted behav-ior *	Number of moral-expedient superintendents exposed to each type of conflict	Frequency of actual behavior	Proportion of correct predictions
Superintendent's perception of:							
Expectation A		Expectation B					
Is it legiti-mate?	Sanctions for non-conformity?	Is it legiti-mate?	Sanctions for non-conformity?				
1. Yes	Yes	Yes	Yes	c	6	c = 5; d = 1	5/6
2. Yes	No	Yes	Yes	b	2	b = 2	2/2
3. Yes	Yes	Yes	No	a	6	a = 6	6/6
4. Yes	No	Yes	No	c	1	c = 0; d = 1	0/1
5. Yes	Yes	No	Yes	a	4	a = 3; c = 1	3/4
6. Yes	No	No	Yes	c	3	c = 2; d = 1	2/3
7. Yes	Yes	No	No	a	20	a = 19; c = 1	19/20
8. Yes	No	No	No	a	1	a = 1	1/1
9. No	Yes	Yes	Yes	b	0	—	—
10. No	No	Yes	Yes	b	0	—	—
11. No	Yes	Yes	No	c	0	—	—
12. No	No	Yes	No	b	0	—	—
13. No	Yes	No	Yes	c	0	—	—
14. No	No	No	Yes	b	0	—	—
15. No	Yes	No	No	a	0	—	—
16. No	No	No	No	d	0	—	—
				Total:	43		38/43 (.88)

* The abbreviations used in this column are as follows: a = conformity to expectation A, b = con-formity to expectation B, c = compromise, and d = avoidance.

gitimate expectations regardless of the sanctions involved in the situation. Such a person would be a moralist.

One who shows no "typical" response to expectations but vacillates between the conditional and mandatory categories in his reactions to expectations would possess the characteristic required for the moral-expedient orientation. This lack of consistency in orientation to expectations suggests that he is the type of person who would tend to take *both* the sanctions and legitimacy dimensions into account in reacting to perceived expectations.

This line of reasoning led to the following procedure. Each superintendent was given a score of 1 for each item in this instrument for which he gave a mandatory response (absolutely must, or absolutely must not). This provided a range of scores from 1 through 30 for the 37 items in the instrument. The estimated reliability of these scores is .884. These scores were then split into the following three categories: 1–9, 10–18, and 19–30. On the reasoning outlined above those superintendents who fell into the low mandatoriness group (1–9) were defined as expedients, those who fell into the high mandatoriness group (19–30) were considered moralists, and those who fell in the middle category (10–18) were categorized as moral-expedients.

A TEST OF THE THEORY

If we accept each of these operational indexes as adequately representing the variables and conditions described by the theory of role conflict resolution, we can use our data to perform an exploratory test of the theory. We have 48 possible "types" of situations. That is, the moralists, expedients, and moral-expedients can each be subdivided into four groups according to their judgments about the legitimacy of the expectations directed toward them (i.e., both expectations legitimate; both illegitimate; A legitimate and B illegitimate, and A illegitimate and B legitimate). Each of the resulting 12 groups can be further subdivided into four categories according to whether the subject believed sanctions would be forthcoming for nonconformity to A, B, both, or neither.

By comparing the behavior predicted on the basis of the theory for each of these 48 types with the actual behavior of the superintendents who fell within these categories, we may say whether or not the theory has led in each case to the correct prediction.

As can be seen in Tables 3, 4, and 5 for 77 (91 percent) of the 85 role-conflict cases the theory led to the correct prediction. In order to test the theory it is necessary to ask whether the proportion of correct predictions obtained could have occurred by chance. To answer this question, the numbers of correct and of incorrect predictions were compared with the numbers expected on the basis of chance. Statistical details are presented elsewhere.[1] The theory led to significantly more correct predictions than would be expected by chance (at the .01 level). We are consequently led to the conclusion that the findings provide significant support for the theory in the teacher-salary role-conflict situation.

A review of the predictions made for moralists, moral-expedients, and expedients will reveal that for many of the types of role conflict the theory leads to exactly the same prediction no matter what the orientation of the individual involved. It is particularly interesting, therefore, to ask how well the theory does in the "difficult" cases. How will the theory do in predicting the behavior in only those cases of role conflict where it makes a difference (according to the theory) what the orientation of the individual is? It would be inappropriate to apply a significance test to only those cases, but it is nevertheless revealing of the power of the theory to consider them separately.

Let us consider those cases for moralists and those for expedients in which the theory makes a prediction which differs from the one made in the case of the moral-expedient orientation. In types 2, 6, 11, 13, 14, and 15 of the moralist orientation and types 5, 6, 9, and 11 of the expedient orientation the theory leads to a prediction which differs from the one to which it leads for the moral-expedients. There were 12 school superintendents with either a moralist or expedient orientation who experienced role conflicts of these types. For how many of these did the theory lead to the correct prediction? For how many would the correct prediction have been made by assuming that their resolution of role conflict would be the same as that of moral-expedients? The answer is that in all 12 cases (as may be verified by reviewing the appropriate types of conflict in Tables 3 and 4) the theory led to the correct prediction, and in none of these cases would the correct prediction have been made on the basis of the assumption that these moral or expedient individuals resolved their conflicts in the same way as do moral-expedients.

In this paper we have not been able to consider a number of questions that the critical reader would ask about the theory. How does this theory differ from

---

[1] See Neal Gross, Ward S. Mason, and Alexander McEachern, *Explorations in Role Analysis: Studies of the School Superintendency Role* (New York: John Wiley & Sons, Inc., 1957).

others? What accounts for the errors in the predictions? Have we ignored certain variables which affect the resolution of certain types of role-conflict situations? We have tried to consider these problems elsewhere.[2]

---

[2] *Ibid.*

THE SIGNIFICANCE OF MULTIPLE–GROUP MEMBERSHIP IN DISASTER   *By Lewis M. Killian*

Although the importance of multiple-group membership as one of the salient features of modern social life is widely recognized by sociologists and psychologists, the task of exploring its many implications has only just been begun. Cooley, a pioneer in the study of the importance of group membership for the individual, recognized the existence of multiple-group memberships, describing the individual in modern society as a point through which numerous arcs, representing different group memberships, pass.[1] Before him, William James declared that a man has "as many social selves . . . as there are distinct groups of persons about whose opinions he cares."[2]

In recent years other students have begun a more systematic exploration of the implications of identification with several different groups for the individual and for the society of which he is a part. The creation of psychological problems for the individual and the development of new strata in the social structure as the result of some types of multiple-group membership are discussed in the work of Robert E. Park,[3] Everett Stonequist,[4] and E. C. Hughes.[5] Hughes has demonstrated that possession of contradictory roles in different groups may create "dilemmas and contradictions of status" for the individual.

Muzafer Sherif, in his elaboration of the concepts of "membership group" and "reference group," has furnished valuable conceptual tools for the analysis of multiple-group identifications and conflicting group loyalties.[6] He suggests, furthermore, that identification with numerous different reference groups and the lack of a unitary ego are the keys to the understanding of inconsistencies in certain types of behavior, such as intergroup relations.[7]

In a study of the reactions of people in four Southwestern communities to physical disasters—explosions and tornadoes—made by the University of Oklahoma Research Institute, it was found that conflicting group loyalties and contradictory roles resulting from multiple-

From the *American Journal of Sociology*, 1952, LVII, 309–314. Reprinted by permission of the author and the publisher.

---

[1] Charles H. Cooley, *Human Nature and the Social Order* (New York: Charles Scribner's Sons, 1900), p. 114.

[2] William James, *Principles of Psychology* (New York: Henry Holland & Co., 1890), Vol. I, p. 294.

[3] Robert E. Park, "Human Migration and the Marginal Man," *Am. J. Sociol.*, 1928, XXXIII, 881–893.

[4] Everett Stonequist, *The Marginal Man* (New York: Charles Scribner's Sons, 1937).

[5] E. C. Hughes, "Dilemmas and the Contradictions of Status," *Am. J. Sociol.*, 1945, L, 353–359.

[6] Muzafer Sherif, *An Outline of Social Psychology* (New York: Harper & Brothers, 1948), pp. 122–125.

[7] Muzafer Sherif, "The Problems of Inconsistency in Intergroup Relations," *J. Soc. Issues*, 1949, V, 32–37

group membership were significant factors affecting individual behavior in critical situations. The dilemmas created by the disasters also brought to light latent contradictions in roles not ordinarily regarded as conflicting.

In spite of the fact that multiple-group memberships do create dilemmas and inconsistencies, the majority of people in modern urban society manage to function efficiently as members of many groups, often being only vaguely aware of contradictions in their various roles. Sherif points out that the individual is often not aware of the derivation of the "cross-pressures" which cause inconsistent behavior.[8] Newcomb declares that many role prescriptions are "relatively nonconflicting" and says:

Most of us, most of the time, manage to take quite different roles, as prescribed by the same or by different groups, without undue conflict. . . . Indeed, it is rather remarkable how many different roles most of us manage to take with a minimum of conflict.[9]

He points out that many roles are "nonoverlapping." A man may play the role of a businessman, acting in terms of the work situation, during most of the day. For a few hours in the evening he may play the role of "the family man," leaving his work at the office. In a small community he may, on certain occasions, act as a functionary of the town government, as a volunteer fireman or as a town councilman. Simultaneously, he has other group memberships which call for certain behavior—in a social-class group, in a racial group, in the community of which he is a citizen, and in "society-at-large."[10]

When catastrophe strikes a community many individuals find that the latent conflict between ordinarily nonconflict-ing group loyalties suddenly becomes apparent and that they are faced with the dilemma of making an immediate choice between various roles. In his classic study of the Halifax disaster, S. H. Prince noted this conflict when he wrote:

But the earliest leadership that could be called social, arising from the public itself, was that on the part of those who had no family ties, much of the earliest work being done by visitors in the city. The others as a rule ran first to their homes to discover if their own families were in danger.[11]

People who had been present in the explosion port of Texas City and in three Oklahoma tornado towns during disasters were asked, among other questions, "What was the first thing you thought of after the disaster struck?" and "What was the first thing you did?" Their answers revealed not only the conflict between loyalties to the family and to the community, described by Prince, but also dilemmas arising from conflicting roles derived from membership in other groups. The individuals concerned were not always conscious of the dilemmas or of the existence of "cross-pressures," but even in such cases the choice of roles which the person made was significant in affecting the total pattern of group reaction to the disaster. In some cases subjects indicated that they recognized *after* the emergency that their reaction had been of critical social importance. On the basis of the experiences of people involved in these four community disasters it is possible to suggest the types of groups between which dilemmas of loyalty may arise in modern communities. Tentative generalization as to how these dilemmas will be resolved and as to their significance for *group* reactions to disaster may also be formulated.

---

[8] *Ibid.*, p. 37.

[9] Theodore Newcomb, *Social Psychology* (New York: Dryden Press, Inc., 1950), p. 449.

[10] *Ibid.*, p. 544.

[11] S. H. Prince, *Catastrophe and Social Change*, Columbia University Studies in History, Economics, and Public Law, Vol. XCIV (New York: Columbia University Press, 1921), p. 61.

The choice required of the greatest number of individuals was the one between the family and other groups, principally the employment group or the community. Especially in Texas City, many men were at work away from their families when disaster struck and presented a threat to both "the plant" and "the home." In all the communities there were individuals, such as policemen, firemen, and public utilities workers, whose loved ones were threatened by the same disaster that demanded their services as "trouble-shooters." Even persons who had no such definite roles to play in time of catastrophe were confronted with the alternatives of seeing after only their own primary groups or of assisting in the rescue and relief of any of the large number of injured persons, regardless of identity. Indeed, only the unattached person in the community was likely to be free of such a conflict.

How these conflicts between loyalty to the family group and loyalty to other membership groups, including the community and "society-at-large," were resolved was of great significance for the reorganization of communities for rescue, relief, and prevention of further disaster. In Texas City, at the time of the first ship explosion, many men were working in oil refineries, where failure to remain on the job until units were shut down could result in additional fires and explosions. In all the communities studied, failure of community functionaries, such as firemen and policemen, to perform the duties appropriate to their positions could result in the absence of expected and badly needed leadership in a disorganized group. This, in turn, could cause costly delay in the reorganization of the community for emergency rescue, traffic control, and fire-fighting activity. Preoccupation of large numbers of able survivors with their own small primary groups could result in the atomization of the community into small, unco-ordinated groups, again delaying reorganiza-

tion into a relatively well-integrated, unified, large group. As Prince indicated in his statement, quoted above, this would increase the dependence of the community on outside sources of leadership.

The great majority of persons interviewed who were involved in such dilemmas resolved them in favor of loyalty to the family or, in some cases, to friendship groups. Much of the initial confusion, disorder, and seemingly complete disorganization reported in the disaster communities was the result of the rush of individuals to find and rejoin their families. Yet in none of the four communities studied did the disastrous consequences contemplated above seem to have materialized. In the first place, there were important exceptions to the tendency to react first in terms of the family. Most of the refinery workers in Texas City did stay on the job until their units were safely shut down, as they had been trained to do. The significance of conflicting group loyalties in a disaster situation is underlined, however, by the importance of the actions taken by a few exceptional individuals in each town who were not confronted with such conflicts. In Texas City the chief of police remained at his post from the moment of the first explosion until seventy-two hours later, never returning to his home during the entire period and playing a vital part in the reorganization of the community. He ascribed his ability to give undivided attention to his official duties to the fact that he knew that his family was safely out of town, visiting relatives, at the time of the explosion. One member of the volunteer fire department of a tornado town told of the thin margin by which his community escaped a disastrous fire following the "twister":

I was at my home, right on the edge of where the storm passed, when it hit. Neither me nor my wife was hurt. The first thing I thought of was fires. I knew there'd be some, so I went to the fire station right away. On the way I could see that there was a fire right in the middle of the wreckage—a butane tank had caught fire. I got out of the truck, drove over there, and fought the fire by myself until the army got there to help me.

All the rest of the firemen had relatives that were hurt, and they stayed with them. Naturally they looked after them. If it hadn't been that my wife was all right, this town probably would have burned up. It's hard to say, but I kind of believe I would have been looking after my family, too.

Devotion to the family as the primary object of loyalty did not always redound to the detriment of aid to other groups, however. Many people who served as rescue workers, assisting injured people whom they did not even know, were drawn to the areas of heavy casualties because of concern for members of their own families whom they believed to be there. Apparently they found their identification with society-at-large and the emphasis of American culture upon the importance of human life too great to permit them to pass an injured stranger without assisting him. Hence, many stayed to assist in the common community task of rescuing the injured in both Texas City and in the tornado towns. In one of the latter a man sensed the approach of the tornado only minutes before it struck. In spite of great personal danger he rushed through the storm to a theater where his children were attending a movie. There he prevented the frightened audience from pouring forth into the storm by holding the doors closed. Later he was acclaimed as a hero whose quick action had saved the lives of many of his fellow citizens. He himself denied that he had any thought of taking the great risk that he took for the sake of the anonymous audience itself; he was thinking only of his own children.

A second, but less common, type of conflict was found in the case of people who were confronted with the alternatives of playing the "heroic" role of rescue worker and of carrying out what were essentially "occupational roles." In terms of group loyalty, they were impelled, on the one hand, to act as sympathetic, loyal members of society-at-large and to give personal aid to injured human beings. On the other hand, they were called to do their duty as it was indicated by their membership in certain occupational groups.

One such person was a minister in Texas City who, upon hearing the explosion, started for the docks with the intention of helping in the rescue work. On the way he became conscious of the choice of roles which confronted him. He said:

After I heard the first explosion my first impulse was to go down to the docks and try to help there. But on the way down I saw two or three folks I knew who had husbands down there. I saw then that my job was with the families—not doing rescue work. I had a job that I was peculiarly suited for, prepared for, and I felt that I should do that.

More important for the reorganization of a tornado-stricken town was the choice made by a state patrolman between his role as a police officer and his role as friend and neighbor to the people of the community in which he was stationed. His story was:

As I drove around town after the tornado had passed I realized that the best thing I could do was to try to make contact with the outside and get help from there. I started out to drive to the next town and try to call from there. As I drove out of town people I knew well would call me by name and ask me to help them find their relatives. Driving by and not stopping to help those people who were looking to me as a friend was one of the hardest things I ever had to do.

As a result of this difficult decision this man became the key figure in the development of organized rescue work, after he recruited and organized a large force of rescue workers in a nearby community.

A similar dilemma faced many public utilities workers who were forced to disregard the plight of the injured if they were to perform their task of restoring normal community services. Unlike the minister and the patrolman, these workers reported no awareness of a conflict of roles, regarding it as a matter of course that they concentrated on their often quite dangerous jobs. Some indicated that preoccupation with the job was so intense that they were scarcely aware of what went on around them. Yet the instances of devotion to prosaic duty cited above were exceptional. Many policemen, firemen, and other functionaries acted heroically but quite outside the framework and discipline of their organizations.

For people whose usual occupational roles bore little or no relationship to the needs created by a disaster, identification with the community as a whole and disregard of their occupational roles came still more easily. Many merchants and clerks rushed from their stores to aid in rescue work, leaving both goods and cash on the counters. The postmaster in one tornado town left the post office completely unguarded, even though the windows were shattered and mail was strewn about the floor. This was, it is true, an extreme case of abandonment of the occupational role.

A third type of conflict of loyalties was that between the loyalty of employees to "the company" as an organization and to fellow employees as friends and human beings. It might seem that the choice, essentially one between life and property, should have been an easy one; but the fact that different choices were made by men with different degrees of identification with other workers reveals that a basic conflict was present. In Texas City many plant officials were also residents of the community and friends of the workers. After the explosions, in which several top executives were killed, some men found themselves suddenly "pro-

moted" to the position of being in charge of their company's damaged property. At the same time men with whom they had worked daily for several years were injured or missing. The most common, almost universal, reaction was to think of the men first and of the plant later. One plant official, active in rescue work in spite of a broken arm and numerous lacerations, described his reaction to the sudden, dramatic conflict between loyalty to the company and loyalty to the workers as follows:

Property! Nobody gave a damn for property! All that was important was life. I've often wondered just how it would be to walk off and let a plant burn up. That was the way it was. We didn't even consider fighting the fire.

In sharp contrast to this reaction, however, was that of a man in charge of a neighboring plant. While he was in Texas City at the time of the first blast, he had never lived in the community and scarcely knew his workers. He described his first reaction in the following words:

I got in my car and drove over to another refinery to find out what had happened. The assistant superintendent told me that their top men had been killed and asked me what I thought he should do. I told him, "You should take charge of the company's property. That's what the president of your company would tell you if he were here. You look after the property. I'm going over to Galveston to call our president, and I'll call yours at the same time."

While this reaction was exceptional, it is significant as suggesting an alternate way of resolving the conflict between loyalty to "the company" and "the men."

Finally, some individuals suddenly discovered, in the face of disaster, that there was a conflict between loyalty to the community and loyalty to certain extra-community groups. At the time of two of the disasters telephone workers in the Southwest were on strike. In both communities the striking workers were allowed to return to duty by union leaders but were ordered to walk out again a few days later. In both cases the union officials considered the emergency to be over sooner than did the townspeople of the stricken communities. In one town the workers obeyed the union's orders only to find themselves subjected to harsh criticism by their fellow townsmen. In the other community the workers resigned from the union rather than forsake their loyalty to their other membership group. It was almost a year before union officials were able to reorganize the local in this town, and some workers never rejoined.

As was pointed out earlier, the individual may, under normal circumstances, carry out roles appropriate to membership in several groups without having to make a choice between basically conflicting group loyalties. He may even do so without seriously impairing his performance of any of his roles. The worker may wish that he could spend more time at home with his family but resigns himself to the fact that he cannot if he is to keep the job he wants. On his way to work he may pass the scene of a fire and be vaguely conscious that, as a citizen, he is indirectly responsible for the protection of life and property; but he assumes that the limit of his direct responsibility for action extends only to notifying the fire department, if it is not already there. The employer may, within certain limits, think of the workers as persons and friends and still not be disloyal to the company's interests. In the crisis induced by disaster, however, these individuals may find that it is impossible to serve two masters, to act in two roles. An immediate choice is demanded, but it may be difficult because the demands of the competing groups may appear equally urgent. The nature of the choice made by the individual, particularly if one of his roles is associated with a key position in the community, may have important consequences for the reorganization of the community. Large-scale reorganization, coordination, and direction of efforts are necessary to speedy rescue work and the restoration of normalcy. Activities carried on in terms of the demands of many diverse, competing groups act as an impediment to this reorganization.

Further research is needed to make possible the prediction of the choices that will be made by individuals in these conflicts. The frequency with which individuals thought and acted first in terms of family and close friends suggests that loyalty to primary groups stands first in the hierarchy of group loyalties, as might be expected. On the other hand, important exceptions in which persons played relatively impersonal roles as leaders or working with matériel, rather than people, indicate that some factors, such as training or feelings of responsibility, may predispose the individual to adhere to secondary-group demands even in a disaster. Knowledge of what these factors are and how they may be induced would contribute to greater understanding of group reactions to disorganization and of methods of facilitating group reorganization.

AN EXPERIMENTAL ANALYSIS OF ROLE BEHAVIOR
By Theodore R. Sarbin and Donal S. Jones

CONCEPTS

Concepts stemming from the coordinate notions of self and role have been extensively employed by social psychologists and personologists in discussing interactional behavior. Among such concepts are role expectations,[1] role-taking ability,[2] role playing,[3] role perception,[4] and role enactment.[5] Following G. H. Mead [6] most of these authors have also dealt with the self both as a cognitive structure and as a phenomenal object. For the most part, the employment of these concepts has been in the *post hoc* analysis of social phenomena, rather than in the empirical testing of specific hypotheses concerning the determinants of interactional behavior. Definitions of these concepts have often been ambiguous, making difficult or impossible the empirical testing of the *post hoc* analyses.

The first part of the present paper will be concerned with definition of the constructs and their operational specifications. The second part will present results from preliminary experimental tests of specific hypotheses derived from assumptions about the interrelationships among the defined constructs. Our attention is focused on the following conceptions: role expectations, role enactment, role-taking aptitude, and the self.

Role Expectations. A role expectation is a cognitive structure inferred, on the stimulus side, from the person's previous commerce with regularities in others' behaviors, and, on the response side, from the person's tendency to group a number of descriptions of actions and qualities together with the name of a specific social position. A *role* is defined as the content common to the role expectations of the members of a social group. We explicitly distinguish between a person's furnishing a verbal description of his expectations for a specific role and his actual performance in the role.

Role expectations may be assessed by an inventory composed chiefly of action sentences [7] or by an instrument which taps qualitative aspects. Since we were more interested in the latter, role expectations were assessed by means of a 200-item adjective check list. The subjects were instructed to check those words which denoted traits appropriate, for example, to the role of daughter in contemporary American society. The measured validity of a person's role expectation is the degree to which the assessed qualitative expectation is conformant with the social role as derived from the pooled expectations of a specified group of persons.

Role Enactment. Observations of role enactment may be of two kinds: the specific actions of a person enacting a role can be recorded, or qualitative descriptions inferred from the entire sequence

From the *Journal of Abnormal and Social Psychology*, 1956, LI, 236–241. Reprinted by permission of the authors and the American Psychological Association.

[1] T. Parsons and E. Shils (eds.), *Toward a General Theory of Action* (Cambridge, Mass.: Harvard University Press, 1951).

[2] N. Cameron, *The Psychology of Behavior Disorders*, (Boston: Houghton Mifflin, 1947); T. M. Newcomb, *Social Psychology* (New York: Dryden Press, Inc., 1950).

[3] H. G. Gough, "A Sociological Theory of Psychopathy," *Am. J. Sociol.*, 1948, LIII, 359–366.

[4] H. Bonner, *Social Psychology, An Interdisciplinary Approach* (New York: World Book Co., 1953).

[5] J. L. Moreno, *Psychodrama*, Vol. I (New York: Beacon House, Inc., 1946).

[6] G. H. Mead, *Mind, Self, and Society* (Chicago: University of Chicago Press, 1934).

[7] Annabelle B. Motz, "The Role Conception Inventory," *Am. Sociol. Rev.*, 1952, XVII, 465–471.

of behaviors may be obtained. An example of the first method would be the protocol statement, "father strikes daughter with a stick." An example of the second would be the statement, "vis-à-vis daughter, father is dominant, cautious, aloof." In the present study, our interest is in observations of the second kind. For the qualitative assessment of role enactment, the same 200-item adjective check list was employed as in the assessment of role expectations. In the experiment, the observers (judges) were instructed to check those words which appeared to characterize the behavior of the person under observation.

Validity of role enactment is the congruence of a *role enactment* as assessed by the group with pooled *expectations* of the members of the evaluating group. If the performance as qualitatively recorded is conformant with the group norm, then the role enactment is said to be valid. The validity of role enactment depends upon at least the following factors [8]:

1. The validity of the performing person's expectations of the role;

2. The nature and degree of his motivation for the specific role enactment;

3. The repertoire of specific verbal and motor skills required for role enactment.

It can be demonstrated that these three preconditions are necessary for socially valid role enactments. However, we assert that they are not sufficient; i.e., if persons were equated on these three determinants consistent individual variation in validity of role enactment would remain. This variation we attribute to the operation of another variable: role-taking aptitude, or the ability to take the role-of-the-other. In the present experiment the three preconditions were controlled, and role-taking aptitude was allowed to vary.

Role-taking Aptitude. The assessment of role-taking aptitude follows from descriptions and observations of G. H. Mead,[9] and from refinements introduced by Cottrell,[10] Cameron,[11] Gough,[12] Sarbin,[13] and others. The central theme in the description of role-taking aptitude is the skill in shifting perspectives from one's own position to that of the other, in vicariously oscillating between self and role. More specifically, it is the ability of the person to behave, with or without observable enactment, *as if* he were in a social position other than the one he is actually occupying. Such behavior may be relatively covert (empathy) or relatively overt (role playing or role enactment).

This role-taking variable may be analyzed along at least two partially independent dimensions: (*a*) degree of dissimilitude and (*b*) organismic involvement. By degree of dissimilitude is meant the extent to which the role-of-the-other is different from one's own role in the specific interaction situation. By organismic involvement is meant the extent to which the relatively covert, diffuse affective aspects of the role are achieved. To put it another way, organismic involvement refers to the degree of involvement of the self in the role. Our test (described below) is heavily weighted for indicators of organismic involvement. Valid role taking is not a function of these two dimensions alone. It depends also upon the veridicality of the person's more-or-less differentiated expectations

---

[8] T. R. Sarbin, "Role Theory," in G. Lindzey (ed.), *Handbook of Social Psychology* (Cambridge, Mass.: Addison-Wesley, Inc., 1954); T. R. Sarbin, "Contributions to Role-taking Theory, I: Hypnotic Behavior," *Psychol. Rev.*, 1950, LVII, 255–260.

[9] Mead, *op. cit.*

[10] L. S. Cottrell, Jr., "Some Neglected Problems in Social Psychology," *Am. Sociol. Rev.*, 1950, XV, 705–712.

[11] Cameron, *op. cit.*

[12] Gough, *op. cit.*

[13] Sarbin, 1954, *op. cit.*; T. R. Sarbin, 1950, *op. cit.*

of the role-of-the-other. His overt or covert role taking is in part a function of his expectations of the real or imagined occupant of the *reciprocal role*. In the experiment described below, the differentiated expectations of the other and the degree of dissimilitude were experimentally controlled, but organismic involvement was allowed to vary.

On *a priori* grounds, the most direct, or at least the most face-valid method for assessing role-taking aptitude is to administer a task which calls for behavior based upon the *as-if* formula.[14] A number of such tasks have been described in the literature. The subject is asked to perform some action such as filling out a questionnaire under the instruction to behave as if he were another person or occupying another social position. Our variant of this procedure was this. Each subject was asked to write answers to the following questions: (1) "How would your life have been different if you had been born a member of the opposite sex?," and (2) "How would your life have been different if you had been born a Russian?" For purposes of exposition, this test is called the *as-if* test. It is our experimental specification of role-taking aptitude. Its empirical justification is described in a later paragraph.

The self. As a phenomenal object, the self is a cognitive product and can be described, at least partially, in terms of qualities or traits.[15] The assessment of the self can be made from statements of the person under instructions to describe himself. In the present study, this assessment was facilitated by the use of a 200-item adjective check list, the same as employed in the assessment of role expectations and role enactment. The subject was instructed simply to check those words which characterized himself.

In addition to self descriptions, we were interested in inferences made by behavior analysts or others about the more enduring dispositions of a person, referred to as ego characteristics. One of our measures is Barron's "ego-strength" scale,[16] which has been derived from test correlates of response to psychotherapy.

HYPOTHESES

Having spelled out briefly the constructs and their experimental specifications, we turn to a statement of predictions concerning the interrelationships among the variables.

While the gross performances involved in a role enactment are specified in a valid set of role expectations, the "fine tuning" which gives the added increment of validity to the enactment is a function of being able accurately to take the role-of-the-other, thus allowing the actor to adjust to the subtleties of the interactional context. If subjects are equated (*a*) for validity of role expectations for a specific role, (*b*) for motivation for role enactment, and (*c*) for having the requisite specific motor and verbal skills, then the validity of their enactment of the experimental role will be primarily determined by the remaining variable, role-taking aptitude (Hypothesis I).

A second hypothesis flows from a restatement of Mead's ideas about the influence of role enactment on the self. Persons who possess the role-taking aptitude to a great extent have the ability to become organismically involved in the interaction situation. If this is so, then the enactment of a specified role should reflect such organismic involvement in shifts in self-conception. Conversely, self-perceptions for persons low on the role-taking aptitude dimension would be

---

[14] H. Vaihinger, *The Philosophy of "As-if"* (London: Kegan Paul, Trench, Trubner & Co., 1924).

[15] T. R. Sarbin and B. G. Rosenberg, "Contributions to Role-taking Theory, IV: A Method for Qualitative Analysis of the Self," *J. Soc. Psychol.*, 1958, XLII, 71–81.

[16] F. Barron, "An Ego-strength Scale Which Predicts Response to Psychotherapy," *J. Consult. Psychol.*, 1953, XVII, 327–333.

relatively constant. Thus, a negative relationship between role-taking aptitude and self-constancy is predicted (Hypothesis IIa). Furthermore, organismic involvement in a role leaves a cognitive residue which has a certain degree of specificity. This cognitive residue (change in self-description) will show the effects of interaction with the *specific other* in the experimental role enactment situation (Hypothesis IIb).

In the application of role theory to psychopathology by Cameron [17] and by Gough,[18] social adjustment is regarded as a function of role-taking aptitude. We would predict a positive correlation between scores on our role-taking aptitude test and adjustment variables. One such variable is that of ego-strength.[19] Our hypothesis is that scores on the *as-if* test and on the ego-strength scale of the MMPI will be positively related (Hypothesis III).

METHOD

The participants in this study were 35 upper-division female college students. Early in the semester, each was given the Personality Word Card—a 200-item adjective check list—and was asked to check those words which characterized herself. In addition, subjects filled out the Minnesota Multiphasic Personality Inventory, Group Form (MMPI). Two weeks later, each student was given two Personality Word Cards and was asked to check those words which characterized the role of daughter in contemporary American society on one card, and words which characterized the role of father on the other card. Following this, the *as-if* test was administered.

From the 35 subjects, six were selected to serve as performers (social objects)

in a role-enactment situation. These six were equated in age and in validity of expectation for the daughter role and for the father role. Validity of expectation was computed by assigning each subject a score on the words which she checked for the role, each word being weighted for its frequency of occurrence in the composite expectation of the entire group. The six subjects were then selected on the basis of divergent *as-if* scores, the ranks of their scores in the group ranging from 2 to 33 ($N = 35$). All six subjects agreed willingly to participate and gave no apparent evidence of differences in motivation for enactment.

The enactment situation was the same for all six subjects. Each subject was given the following instructions: "You have just been informed by the dean that your grade average does not warrant your remaining in the University. You have returned home and are about to tell your father about it. Mr. *P* will take the role of your father."

The role of father was played by a volunteer, age 42, who appeared somewhat older than his years. He had been instructed to ask the same questions and to behave as nearly identically as possible during the six enactments.

Each subject enacted [20] the role for five minutes before the remaining 29 members of the group. After each subject had performed the role, the group filled out Personality Word Cards. After all six subjects had performed, the observers were asked to furnish another index of enactment by ranking the subjects in order of *adequacy of enactment* of the role of daughter. In addition, each of the performers filled out a self-descriptive check list immediately following role enactment.

---

[17] Cameron, *op. cit.*

[18] Gough, *op. cit.*

[19] Barron, *op. cit.*

[20] This is role enactment rather than role playing since all the subjects performing the role of daughter were, in fact, occupants of the social position of daughter.

ANALYSIS AND RESULTS

In attempting to develop a composite measure of *both* dissimilitude and organismic involvement two scoring techniques were developed for the *as-if* test: (a) a simple count of the number of words in the subject's answer which were judged relevant to answering the question and (b) a content-analysis procedure, with weights being assigned to various categories of response. The number-of-relevant-words score showed interrater reliability of .96 for two independent raters. The categories for the content analysis in the second scoring method, pointed toward assessing the organismic involvement dimension, were as follows: (a) describes a real difference in self-concept under the circumstances presented in the question, e.g., "If I were a man, I would not be anxious so much of the time"; (b) describes a difference in role behavior, e.g., "If I were a man, I would be an engineer," and (c) describes a difference in impinging social or physical environment, e.g., "If I had been born a Russian, I would be living among people with different customs." Each subject's answers to the sex question and the Russian question were analyzed separately, and a score computed by weighting each instance of a 3, of b 2, and of c 1, then summing the subject's weighted responses. Interrater reliability for two independent raters was .89.

For the number-of-words score, the correlation between scores on the two questions for our 35 subjects was .74; for the content-analysis scores the correlation was .79. If we consider the two questions as halves of the test, we may correct the correlation between them by the Spearman-Brown formula to obtain the reliability of our total scores. These values are .85 for the number-of-words and .88 for the content score.

A single number-of-words score and a single content score were then computed for each subject, combining her scores on the two questions. The two sets of scores derived by different methods correlate .78 with each other. In view of the values of the split-half reliabilities and of the interrater reliabilities, the magnitude of this correlation suggests that the two scores are equally effective measures. Because of the much greater ease of computation, the number-of-words score was the one used in further analysis.

The following adjectives were found to be characteristic of the qualitative expectations of "the role of daughter in contemporary American society" by at least 40 percent of the group. This list comprises the *group norms* against which conduct is evaluated. The italicized words appear on the composite father role as well.

informal	humorous	*kind*
imaginative	sentimental	*sympathetic*
conventional	sensitive	*understanding*
modest		*fair-minded*
relaxed		*reasonable*
cheerful	*dependable*	*reliable*
pleasure-seeking	*responsible*	honest
well-mannered	*efficient*	sincere
sociable	*ambitious*	self-confident
warm	*broad-minded*	soft-hearted
gentle	*patient*	affectionate
trusting	*pleasant*	lovable
capable	*good natured*	energetic
natural	*friendly*	active
poised	*helpful*	enthusiastic
feminine	*considerate*	generous

Two measures of validity of role enactment were computed: (a) conformance, the correlation between the frequencies with which adjectives were checked about a subject by the observer group and the frequencies with which these words had been checked for expectations of the daughter role, and (b) the mean rank for "adequacy of performance" assigned by the observers after the six enactments were completed. The rankings of subjects on these indices are included in Table 1.

The rank-order correlation of 1.00 between each measure of validity of role

TABLE 1

RANKS ON MEASURES OF VALIDITY OF ROLE ENACTMENT ON TEXT
OF ROLE-TAKING APTITUDE AND ON SELF-CONSTANCY FOLLOWING
A SPECIFIC ROLE ENACTMENT

Subject	Validity of role enactment		Role-taking aptitude	Self-constancy
	Conformance	Adequacy		
A	1	1	1	6
B	2	2	2	5
C	3	3	3	4
D	4	4	4	3
E	5	5	5	2
F	6	6	6	1

enactment and the measure of role-taking aptitude is significant, $(p = .01)$ for N of 6.[21] These are the results predicted from Hypothesis I.

Hypothesis IIa predicted that the self-conceptions of persons low on role-taking aptitude would be most constant, that is, would not be markedly influenced as a result of the role enactment. Persons high on role-taking aptitude would, conversely, show the most marked shifts in self-conceptions as a result of taking the specified role. Our measure of self-constancy was simply the number of adjectives on the Personality Word Cards checked about self after the enactment but not before, plus the number of words checked before but not after. Table 1 shows a perfect inverse rank-difference correlation between role-taking aptitude and this index of self-constancy.

Hypothesis IIb accounts in another way for the degree of organismic involvement in enacting a role. If a subject has the ability to become greatly involved in the interactional role situation, then the *direction* of shift in self-conception as a result of specific role playing can be predicted. Our procedure was to list those adjectives which had been checked for self after the enactment but which had not been checked for self before the enactment. A score was then calculated for each of the six subjects by tallying the number of words on this derived list which also appeared on the subject's role-expectation check lists for *both father and daughter*. This measure indicated the direction of the shift in self-conception, taking into account the role of the other. The product-moment correlation of this measure with score on the *as-if* test (number-of-words score) was .92. This value is significant for $N = 6$, thus supporting Hypothesis IIb.

In order to test Hypothesis III, that our test of role-taking aptitude was related to general ego characteristics, product-moment correlations were computed for all 35 subjects between the score on Barron's ego-strength scale and the two scores from the *as-if* test. These values were .61 for the content-analysis score and .53 for the number-of-words score. These correlations lend support to the interpretation of role-taking aptitude as a correlate of ego strength in the area of interpersonal behavior.

[21] W. J. Dixon and F. J. Massey, *Introduction to Statistical Analysis* (New York: McGraw-Hill Book Co., 1951).

DISCUSSION

Our interest in this experiment was twofold: first, we wished to test in a preliminary way some of the implications of role theory, and second, we sought to explore the use of a relatively simple methodology for getting at complex social interactions. As a rule, when a social psychologist sets out to test hypotheses drawn from a general theory, the relationship of the experimental variable to the rational variable which it is supposed to represent is not always a clear one. It is our conviction that the experimental tasks closely resemble the rational variables. We think it is patent, for example, that role expectations are in large part conceptualized by persons using Indo-European languages as qualities and that qualities can be communicated by means of adjectives. Furthermore, the use of the qualitative form is closer, at least in middle-class American society, to the phenomenology of social interaction than is the action form of expression.[22] Except in formal group structures, such as a bureaucracy, where most behavior is codified in action-sentences, the preferred mode of organizing role behaviors and role expectations is the qualitative one. The use of the adjective check list is a systematic way of recording qualities.

In the same way, our use of the *as-if* formulation is a direct, face-valid approach to the experimental variable—role-taking aptitude. By the use of this simple and face-valid method, we have shown how one of Mead's notions could be put to test: the influence of role enactment on the self. To be sure, in this miniature situation we did not expect nor did we achieve extreme and permanent changes in the self. Nevertheless, we did observe a shift in current self-conceptions following a validly judged role enactment. Further, the direction of the change was related to the degree of role-taking aptitude. (Janis and King [23] using a somewhat different method and operating within another conceptual framework have presented results which are congruent with our own.) From this part of our experiment, we hasten to add, we do not draw the inference that the more valid a role enactment, the more shift in self-perception. Other results are predicted when congruence between self and role expectations or agreement of one's own role expectations with the group norm are not experimentally controlled. The determination of the effects of free variation in the last-named conditions upon role enactment and upon changes in self-description requires another experiment.

Concern with establishing empirical correlates for the *as-if* test led us to so-called ego variables. On *a priori* grounds, the person who can effectively take the role-of-the-other is in a better position to deal with the manifold requirements of complex social life. This is much the same as saying that such a person has a "strong ego." The measure of ego strength that we employed is an empirically established MMPI scale that differentiates response to psychotherapy.[24] Illustrative of the items in the scale are the following:

36. I seldom worry about my health. (True)
217. I frequently find myself worrying about something. (False)
253. I can be friendly with people who do things which I consider wrong. (True)
344. Often I cross the street in order not to meet someone I see. (False)
380. When someone says silly or ignorant things about something I know about, I try to set him right. (True)

---

[22] In the words of the popular song, "It's not what you do, but the way you do it."
[23] I. L. Janis and B. T. King, "Influence of Role-playing on Opinion Change," see article following in this volume.
[24] Barron, *op. cit.*

410. I would certainly enjoy beating a crook at his own game. (True)

430. I am attracted by members of the opposite sex. (True) [25]

In view of the small number of subjects involved, the results are interpreted as lending tentative support to all of the hypotheses investigated. The value of the present experiment lies not only in the relatively successful attempts at establishing the hypotheses but also in the demonstration of the feasibility of investigating quite directly the process of social interaction. It would seem that relatively simple and face-valid techniques may possess considerable value for the study of social-psychological behavior.

SUMMARY

Six subjects, equated for age, conformance of expectation of the role of daughter in contemporary American culture, and congruence of self with daughter role, each engaged in a brief enactment of the role of daughter. The subjects varied systematically in role-taking aptitude, as assessed by a simple face-valid *as-if* procedure. The following hypotheses were subjected to empirical test and supported by the data: role-taking aptitude and validity of role enactment are positively correlated; role-taking aptitude and self-constancy following role enactment are negatively correlated; the shift in self-conception following role enactment is in part a function of the *specific* role enacted; and, finally, role-taking aptitude and a social adjustment variable are positively correlated.

The experiment also demonstrated the utility of face-valid procedures in the investigation of social interaction.

---

[25] These measures of role-taking aptitude and ego strength might reasonably be expected to correlate with measures of general intelligence. Since general intelligence is—if it is anything—a conglomeration of many variables, the constructs ego strength and role-taking aptitude may profitably be regarded as partial aspects of, rather than as dependent upon, general intelligence. The demonstrated existence of nonintellective factors in intelligence, which can be scaled nicely in personality-questionnaire items, supports the notion that the traditional reverent attitude toward intelligence as the master independent variable be re-examined. (An example of a scaled nonintellective factor may be found in H. G. Gough, "A Non-intellectual Intelligence Test," *J. Consult. Psychol.*, 1953, XVII, 242–246.)

THE INFLUENCE OF ROLE PLAYING ON OPINION CHANGE   *By Irving L. Janis and Bert T. King*

In many everyday situations, people are induced to play social roles in which they express ideas that are not necessarily in accord with their private convictions. That certain types of role-playing experiences can facilitate changes in personal opinions has been suggested by various impressionistic observations (e.g., Myers [1]). In recent years, psychodramatic techniques which involve role playing have been developed for use in adult-education programs, leadership

From *Journal of Abnormal and Social Psychology*, 1954, XLIX, 1954, 211–218. Reprinted by permission of the authors and the American Psychological Association.

---

[1] G. C. Myers, "Control of Conduct by Suggestion: An Experiment in Americanization," *J. Appl. Psychol.*, 1921, V, 26–31.

training, employee counseling, and psychotherapy.[2] The usual procedure consists of having persons in a group play specified roles in a simulated life situation. One of the main values of this role-playing device, according to its proponents, is that it has a corrective influence on various beliefs and attitudes which underlie chronic difficulties in human relations (cf. Maier [3]).

As yet little is known about the conditions under which role playing leads to actual changes in personal opinions. The present experiment was designed to investigate the effects of one type of demand that is frequently made upon a person when he is induced to play a social role, namely, the requirement that he overtly verbalize to others various opinions which may not correspond to his inner convictions.

As a preliminary step in exploring the effects of role playing, one of the present authors interviewed a group of collegiate debaters who, as members of an organized team, repeatedly were required to play a role in which they publicly expressed views that did not correspond to their personal opinions. Most of the debaters reported that they frequently ended up by accepting the conclusions which they had been arbitrarily assigned to defend. Myers'[4] impressionistic account of the improvement in morale attitudes produced by participation in an Army public-speaking course points to the same phenomenon and suggests that attitude changes may occur even when role playing is artificially induced. If true, it would appear that "saying is believing"—that overtly expressing an opinion in conformity to social demands will influence the individual's private

opinion. Consequently, it seemed worth while to attempt to investigate the effects of this type of role playing in a more controlled laboratory situation where, if the alleged gain from role playing occurs, it might be possible to isolate the critical factors and to explore systematically the mediating mechanisms.

The role-playing effects described above have not as yet been verified by systematic research. If verified, they would still remain open to a variety of alternative explanations. For instance, inducing the individual to play a role in which he must advocate publicly a given position might guarantee exposure to one set of arguments to the exclusion of others. An alternative possibility, however, is that even when exposed to the same persuasive communications, people who are required to verbalize the content to others will tend to be more influenced than those who are only passively exposed. In order to test this hypothesis, the present experiment was designed so that communication exposure would be held constant by comparing the opinion changes of active participants and passive controls who were exposed to the same communications.

METHOD AND PROCEDURES

An initial questionnaire, which was administered as an opinion survey in a large classroom of male college students, contained a series of questions concerning expectations about the future. Included in this "before" questionnaire were the following key opinion items, which dealt with the subject matter of the three communications to which the experimental groups were subsequently exposed:

---

[2] A. Bavelas, "Role-playing and Management Training," *Sociatry*, 1947, I, 183–191; R. Lippitt, "The Psychodrama in Leadership Training," *Sociometry*, 1943, VI, 286–292; N. R. F. Maier, *Principles of Human Relations* (New York: John Wiley & Sons, Inc., 1952); J. L. Moreno, *Psychodrama*, Vol. 1 (New York: Beacon House, Inc., 1946); A. Zander, and R. Lippitt, "Reality-practice as Educational Method," *Sociometry*, 1944, VII, 129–151.

[3] Maier, *op. cit.*

[4] Myers, *op. cit.*

TABLE 1

SCHEMA OF THE EXPERIMENTAL CONDITIONS

Communication	Group A (N = 31)	Group B (N = 29)	Group C (N = 30)
A: movie theaters	active participants	passive controls	passive controls
B: meat supply	passive controls	active participants	passive controls
C: cold cure	passive controls	passive controls	active participants

Item A: During the past year a number of movie theaters were forced to go out of business as result of television competition and other recent developments. At the present time there are about *18,000* movie theaters remaining. How many commercial movie theaters do you think will be in business three years from now?

Item B: What is your personal estimate about the *total supply of meat that will be available for the civilian population* of the United States during the year 1953? (. . . .— percent of what it is at present.)

Item C: How many years do you think it will be before a *completely effective* cure for the common cold is discovered?

The experimental sessions were held approximately four weeks after the initial questionnaire had been filled out, and were represented as being part of a research project designed to develop a new aptitude test for assessing oral speaking ability. The subjects (Ss) were asked to give an informal talk based on an outline prepared by the experimenters (Es) which stated the conclusion and summarized the main arguments to be presented. The arguments were logically relevant but highly biased in that they played up and interpreted "evidence" supporting only one side of the issue. Each active participant was instructed to play the role of a sincere advocate of the given point of view, while two others, who were present at the same experimental session, listened to his talk and read the prepared outline. Each S delivered one of the communications and was passively exposed to the other two. In order to prevent selective attention effects, the active participant was not told what the topic of his talk would be until his turn came to present it. He was given about three minutes to look over the prepared outline, during which time the others (passive controls) also were requested to study duplicate copies of the same outline so as to be prepared for judging the adequacy of the speaker's performance. After the first talk was over, another S was selected to present the second communication, and then the remaining S presented the third communication, the same procedures being followed in each case.

Immediately after the last talk was finished, Ss were given the "after" questionnaire, much of which was devoted to rating the performance of each speaker. The key opinion items were included among numerous filler items, all of which were introduced as questions designed to provide information about the student's interests and opinions concerning the three topics so as to enable the investigators to select the most appropriate topic for future applications of the oral speaking test.

In all three communications, the conclusion specified an opinion estimate which was numerically *lower* than that given by any of the students on the "before" test. Thus, all active participants

TABLE 2

COMPARISON OF ACTIVE PARTICIPANTS WITH PASSIVE CONTROLS ON
AMOUNT OF CHANGE IN OPINION ESTIMATES

Changes in opinion estimates † (by percentage)	Communication A: movie theaters		Communication B: meat shortage		Communication C: cold cure	
	Active participants (N = 31)	Passive controls (N = 57) *	Active participants (N = 29)	Passive controls (N = 57)	Active participants (N = 30)	Passive controls (N = 53)
Sizable increase	0	2	0	2	7	6
Slight increase	3	9	7	14	10	9
No change	23	20	24	16	13	19
Slight decrease	29	46	27	49	23	15
Sizable decrease	45	23	41	19	47	51
Total	100	100	100	100	100	100
Net change (increase minus decrease)						
Slight or sizable change	−71	−58	−62	−52	−53	−51
Sizable change	−45	−21	−41½	−17	−40	−45
p	.01		.01		> .30	

* The number of cases in each passive control group is slightly smaller than expected from the N's shown in Table 1 because the data from a few cases were inadequate and hence were eliminated from the analysis (e.g., the individual failed to give an answer to the particular question).

† The "net change (slight or sizable)" is defined as the percentage changing in the direction advocated by the communication minus the percentage changing in the opposite direction. The "net sizable change" in the case of Communication A refers to the difference in the percentages who lowered and raised their estimate by 5,000 (movie theaters) or more. For Communication B, a sizable change was 25 (percent) or more; for Communication C it was 5 (years) or more.

were required to argue in favor of an extreme position which differed from their initial beliefs. The influence of each communication could readily be observed by noting the degree to which the students in each group *lowered* their opinion estimates on the "after" test.

The basic schema of the experiment is shown in Table 1. In each row of the table which represents exposure to a given communication, there is one group of active participants and two contrasting groups which, when combined, form the group of passive controls. In effect, the experimental treatments were repeated with different communication contents, providing three separate instances of active versus passive exposure, although the same Ss were used throughout.

In order to obtain some information for checking on selective attention effects, a variation of the passive control condition (not represented in the table) was introduced into the experiment by using a small supplementary group who listened and took notes on all three talks. In addition, base-line data for assessing the effectiveness of the communications were obtained from a comparable group of "pure" controls who were not exposed to any of the communications.

RESULTS AND DISCUSSION

Effects of Active Participation. Initially, on each of the three key items in the precommunication questionnaire, the difference between the active participation group and the passive control group

TABLE 3

Comparison of Active Participants with Passive Controls on Amount of Change in Confidence

Subgroup breakdown according to changes in opinion estimates	Net change in confidence (Percent increase minus percent decrease)					
	Communication *A*		Communication *B*		Communication *C*	
	Active participants	Passive controls	Active participants	Passive controls	Active participants	Passive controls
1. *Uninfluenced:* opinion estimates increased or unchanged	−12 (N = 8)	−5 (N = 18)	0 (N = 9)	+6 (N = 18)	−11 (N = 9)	−11 (N = 18)
2. *Influenced:* opinion estimates slightly or sizably decreased	+9 (N = 23)	−10 (N = 39)	+20 (N = 20)	+5 (N = 39)	+57 (N = 21)	+26 (N = 35)
gain from active participation	+19		+15		+31	
3. *Highly influenced:* opinion estimates sizably decreased	−7 (N = 14)	−38 (N = 13)	+25 (N = 12)	0 (N = 11)	+64.5 (N = 14)	+15 (N = 27)
gain from active participation	+31		+25		+49.5	

was nonsignificant. The opinion changes observed after exposure to the three communications are shown in Table 2.[5] The results indicate that in the case of two of the three communications (*A* and *B*), the active participants were more influenced than the passive controls. For both communications, the differences in net sizable change are statistically reliable, and the differences in net (slight or sizable) change, although nonreliable, are in the expected direction.

In the case of the third communication (*C*), the two groups showed approximately the same amount of opinion change. But additional findings (based on confidence ratings given by each *S* immediately after answering the key opinion questions) indicate that the active participants who presented Communication *C*, like those who presented the other two communications, expressed a higher level of *confidence* in their post-communication estimates than did the corresponding passive controls. Table 3 shows the net changes in confidence rat-

[5] The table does not include the data on the "pure" (unexposed) control group. The net changes for this group were approximately zero in the case of all three key items, and the corresponding net changes for the active participants and the passive controls (shown in the last rows of the table) were significantly greater (p's range from .10 down to > .01). Hence, all three communications had a significant effect on the opinions of those who were either actively or passively exposed to them.

The probability values reported throughout this paper are based on one tail of the theoretical distribution. Whenever intergroup comparisons are made with respect to the net percentage who changed by a given amount, the reliability of the difference was tested by the formula presented in C. I. Hovland, A. A. Lumsdaine, and F. D. Sheffield, *Experiments on Mass Communication* (Princeton, N.J.: Princeton University Press, 1949) p. 321.

ings for each of the three communications in terms of a breakdown that takes account of the direction and magnitude of opinion change. The breakdown was necessary inasmuch as a successful communication would be expected to increase the confidence only of those who changed their opinions in the direction advocated by the communication. The net change in confidence shown for each subgroup is based on a comparison of pre- and post-communication ratings given by each S, and was computed by subtracting the percentage who showed a decrease in confidence from the percentage who showed an increase in confidence. In general, the findings in Table 3 reveal a consistent pattern for all three communications: in every instance, active participation tended to have at least a slight positive effect with respect to increasing the confidence of those whose opinion estimates were influenced by the communication. The results indicate that active participation resulted in a significant gain in confidence, particularly among those students whose opinion estimates were markedly influenced by Communication C.[6] This finding is especially striking in view of the fact that the opinion-change results for Communication C (Table 2) failed to show any gain from active participation.

Insofar as confidence ratings can be regarded as indicators of the degree of conviction with which the new opinions are held, the positive findings based on the opinion change data for Communications A and B are partially confirmed by the confidence change data based on Communication C. Thus, the data based on all three communications contribute evidence that the effectiveness of the communications (as manifested by opinion changes or by confidence changes) tended to be augmented by active participation.

Although Ss were not told what their topic would be until they were about to begin giving the talk, it is possible that the ego-involving task of presenting one of the talks may have given rise to emotional excitement or other interfering reactions which could have had the effect of reducing the S's responsiveness when passively exposed to the other two communications. This possibility appears extremely improbable, however, in the light of supplementary control observations:

1. Some of the passive controls had been exposed to the communications *before* giving their own talk, while others were passively exposed *after* having given their own talk. Nonsignificant differences were found in the amount of opinion change shown under these two conditions.

2. The results from the passive controls were "replicated" by the results from an independent group of 16 students who did not give an oral presentation, but who were asked to follow the prepared outline carefully and to note down the

---

[6] For the entire group of active participants who were exposed to Communication C, there was a net increase in confidence of 37 percent; the corresponding net increase for the entire group of passive controls was only 13.5 percent. This difference was due entirely to the marked gain in confidence manifested by those students in the active group who had changed their opinion estimates in the direction advocated by the communication. The results in the first row of Table 3 indicate that, among the students whose opinion estimates were uninfluenced by Communication C, the active participants showed a small net decrease in confidence which was equal to that shown by the passive controls. The next row of Table 3 indicates that, among those students who decreased their opinion estimates by at least one half or more after exposure to Communication C, the active participants showed a greater net increase in confidence than the passive controls; the difference of 31 percent approaches statistical significance ($p = .07$). Finally, the last row of the table shows than an even greater difference in confidence changes emerges when the comparison is limited to those students who decreased their opinion estimates by five years or more. (The 49.5 percent difference is reliable at beyond the .05 confidence level.) Further analysis of the subgroup data indicated that the differences shown in this table could not be attributed to statistical artifacts arising from initial differences between the various subgroups

main arguments given by each of the three speakers. Despite the fact that their notes were fairly complete and indicated a relatively high degree of attention to the content of all three communications, these supplementary controls displayed approximately the same amount of opinion change as the original group of passive controls.[7]

Observations Pertinent to Explanatory Hypotheses. Many different types of speculative hypotheses could be put forth to account for the facilitating effects of active participation, postulating a gain in attention and learning from overtly rehearsing the communication, or a gain in comprehension from reformulating the arguments in one's own words, or a gain in motivation from playing the role of communicator, etc. Some supplementary observations were made for the purpose of exploring various factors which might provide leads to the key mediating mechanisms. Although far from conclusive, the evidence derived from these observations provides a preliminary basis for selecting explanatory hypotheses which warrant further experimental analysis.

The findings based on the supplementary controls (who were required to take notes on the three talks) suggest that variation in attention level probably was not a crucial factor that could explain the participation effects observed in the present experiment. More promising clues were discovered by taking account of differences in the types of reactions evoked by the three communications. We have seen that in the case of Communications A and B, a clear-cut gain from active participation was manifested by changes in opinion estimates; but, in the case of Communication C, opinion estimates were unaffected, the gain being manifested only in the form of increased confidence. With a view to discovering some differentiating factor, we examined the available evidence bearing on the question of why active participation might be more effective under certain stimulus conditions (represented by Communications A and B) than under other conditions (represented by Communication C).

The first step in this inquiry was to examine E's notes on: (a) the active Ss' behavior while giving their talks and (b) Ss' statements in the informal interviews conducted at the end of each experimental session. These observations provide two suggestive leads:

1. The active participants who presented Communication C seemed to engage in *less improvisation* than those who presented the other two communications. The Communication C group appeared to adhere much more closely to the prepared outline, making little attempt to reformulate the main points, to insert illustrative examples, or to invent additional arguments.

2. Active participants in the Communication C group seemed to experience much more difficulty than the other groups in presenting their talks. During their performance they appeared to be more hesitant and tense. Afterwards, they expressed many more complaints about the task, claiming that their topic was more difficult to present than either of the other two. In general, these subjects seemed *less satisfied* with their performance than those who presented the other two topics.

The first observation suggests that mere repetition of a persuasive commu-

---

[7] It is conceivable, of course, that the activity of taking notes on the talks might have interfered with responsiveness to the persuasive content of the communications. While this possibility cannot be excluded, it seems implausible inasmuch as our Ss were college students who had had considerable practice in taking notes during lectures. Educational research on the effects of note-taking indicates that this form of activity generally has a beneficial rather than a detrimental effect on the student's ability to absorb the content of an oral communication (C. E. Crawford, "Some Experimental Studies of the Results of College Note Taking," *J. Educ. Res.*, 1925, XII, 379 386).

nication may have little or no effect as compared with an improvised restatement. This observation is in line with some suggestive findings from an opinion-change study by Kelman [8] in which seventh-grade students were given a communication, and, immediately afterwards, were offered various incentives to write essays in support of the communicator's position. Kelman observed that the essays written by the group which showed the greatest amount of opinion change tended to be longer, to include more improvisation, and to be of better over-all quality (as rated by several judges) than the essays written by the other experimental groups.

Reformulating and elaborating on the communication might be a critical factor in producing the gain from active participation, perhaps because the communicatee is stimulated to think of the kinds of arguments, illustrations, and motivating appeals that he regards as most convincing. The importance of the improvisation factor in relation to participation effects could not be investigated further with the data at hand from the present experiment, but is currently being studied by the present authors in another experiment that is specifically designed to compare the effects of different types of active participation.

With respect to the second observation, it should be noted that there may have been an objective basis for the greater dissatisfaction experienced on Communication C because of the greater amount of unfamiliar technical material it contained. The "cold-cure" outline referred to a great many technical details concerning the cold virus, antibiotics, allergic reactions, and antihistamines. Many of these details were probably unfamiliar to Ss, and consequently, it may have been difficult for them to "spell out" the implications of the arguments. In con-

trast, the outlines for the other two topics contained very little technical material, relying mainly on arguments that were likely to be quite familiar to college students.

Systematic evidence relevant to Ss' perception of the difficulty of presenting each communication was obtained by making use of the self-rating schedule which each student filled out after exposure to the three communications. Table 4 shows the percentage in each experimental group who rated their own performance as adequate or satisfactory on each of six self-appraisal items.

The most comprehensive question was the following: "What is your over-all rating of the informal talk given by this speaker—how good a job do you think he did in presenting his material? Excellent; Very Good; Satisfactory; Poor; Very Poor."

The percentage who rated themselves as "satisfactory" or better (shown in the first row of the table) was significantly lower for the group who presented Communication C than for the groups who presented Communications A and B ($p = .002$ and $.04$, respectively). On the remaining five items, each of which dealt with a specific aspect of the speaker's performance, the Communication C group also tended to rate themselves lower than did the other two groups. (On the combined rating, based on all six items, the percentage differences are statistically significant at beyond the .05 confidence level.) The findings consistently indicate that the students in the Communication C group felt less satisfied with their oral performance than did those in the other two groups. Since the group differences in self-ratings tend to parallel the group differences in amount of gain from active participation, the results suggest that *satisfaction with one's own performance* may be a critical factor

---

[8] H. C. Kelman, "Attitude Change as a Function of Response Restriction," *Hum. Relat.*, 1953, VI, 185–214.

TABLE 4

SELF-RATINGS OF ACTIVE PARTICIPANTS IN EACH EXPERIMENTAL GROUP

Self-rating response (by percentage)	Experimental groups (active participants)		
	Communica- tion A: movie theaters (N = 31)	Communica- tion B: meat supply (N = 29)	Communica- tion C: cold cure (N = 30)
1. *Over-all performance* was at least "satis- factory"	94	83	63
2. Rarely or never spoke in a *monotonous* tone of voice	64	76	53
3. Rarely or never *incoherent* in presenting arguments	74	83	57
4. No *distortions* or *misinterpretations* of ar- guments in the prepared outline	32	52	13
5. No *omissions* of any of the main argu- ments	74	72	70
6. Succeeded in giving the impression of being "sincere"	52	52	43
Combined rating on all six items: five or more favorable self-ratings	39	52	13

that determines the magnitude of partici- pation effects.

Further evidence which supports this hypothesis was obtained from an analysis of individual opinion changes, comparing active participants with high and low self-ratings for each of the three commu- nications. For example, among the active participants who presented Communica- tion C, there were 18 students whose self- ratings were comparatively "high" (three to six favorable responses) and 12 cases whose self-ratings were predominantly "low" (zero, one, or two favorable re- sponses); 55 percent of the "highs" as against only 17 percent of the "lows" showed a sizable net opinion change in the direction advocated by the commu- nications ($p = .05$). In general, the com- parisons based on all three communica- tions consistently indicate that a greater amount of opinion change occurred among those active participants who rated their oral performance as satisfac-

tory or better. Active participants who felt that they performed poorly, on the other hand, failed to show any more opinion change than the passive controls, and, in the case of Communication C, showed markedly less change than the passive controls ($p = .07$).

During the experimental sessions there were no apparent sources of external social rewards from the environment. Since the others present remained silent, the active participant had no oppor- tunity to know how they were reacting to his talk, except possibly by subtle signs from their facial expressions or from their bodily movements. But even in the absence of any external cues to social approval, it seems probable that *anticipations* concerning such approval would occur if the individual felt that he was performing well, as expressed in his self-ratings. Thus, expectations of favora- ble audience reactions may have occurred less frequently among Ss who were required to perform the relatively difficult task of presenting the unfamiliar technical material in Communication C than among those who were required to perform the less difficult task of presenting Communication A or B. The increase in opinion change produced by role playing might be mediated by the individual's sense of achievement or his elated feelings about the adequacy of his oral performance. One hypothesis that would follow from this assumption is that when a person conforms outwardly to social demands by playing a role which requires him to advocate a given opinion, he will begin to believe what he is saying if he is made to feel that he says it well.

Although the above hypothesis is suggested by the supplementary correlational findings, it will obviously remain open to question until tested by more precise methods. One cannot be certain that the responses used to assess "satisfaction" represent a separate variable which is causally related to opinion changes. Acceptance of the communication might be a common factor which inclines those who are most influenced to perceive themselves as having performed well, in which case the self-ratings might merely reflect the same thing as the measures of opinion change. Moreover, even if the two variables can be varied and measured independently, the possibility remains that the observed relationship may be due to some third variable, such as amount of improvisation.

As was noted earlier, the group of active participants who showed the least amount of opinion change not only expressed a low degree of satisfaction but also displayed a relative absence of improvisation in their oral performances. Either the "satisfaction" factor or the "improvisation" factor might prove to be a critical mediating variable. Before drawing a definite conclusion, it is necessary to investigate each factor experimentally—for instance, by giving the Ss "expert" performance ratings which raise

or lower their feelings of satisfaction and by using instructions which increase or decrease the amount of improvisation. These methods are currently being employed in our further research on the effects of role playing.

There is another important problem which arises from the findings in the present experiment and which also requires systematic investigation: Does social role playing facilitate the internalization of externally imposed value judgments, mores, and taboos? The persuasive communications used in this study dealt with relatively impersonal beliefs about the future, and the main findings show that acceptance of opinions of this sort was markedly increased by experimentally induced role playing. It remains problematical, however, whether active participation also influences the acceptance of opinions and attitudes that are more directly tied up with daily life activities, interpersonal relationships, and emotionally charged dilemmas.

Obviously, it is unsafe to generalize widely from a single exploratory study based on the opinion changes of college students and produced in a somewhat artificial test situation. Nevertheless, the present experiment provides preliminary evidence indicating that verbal conformity elicited by role playing can significantly influence the acceptance of new beliefs. Under certain specifiable conditions which await further investigation, it seems to be true that "saying is believing."

SUMMARY AND CONCLUSIONS

The experiment was designed to determine whether or not overt verbalization, induced by role playing, facilitates opinion change. Male college students were assigned at random to two main experimental groups: (a) active participants, who, with the aid of a prepared outline, played the role of sincere advocates of the given point of view, and (b) passive con-

ROLE AND ROLE CONFLICT

trols, who silently read and listened to the same communication. In the experimental sessions, three different communications were used, each of which argued in favor of a specific conclusion concerning expected future events and was presented by a different active participant. Opinion measures obtained at the end of the session were compared with the "before" measures obtained about one month earlier.

In general, the active participants tended to be more influenced by the communications than were the passive controls. In the case of two of the communications the active participants showed significantly more opinion change than the passive controls. In the case of the third communication, both groups showed approximately the same amount of opinion change, but active participation, nevertheless, tended to increase the level of confidence of those whose opinion estimates were influenced by the communication. The main findings, together with various methodological checks, support the hypothesis that overt verbalization induced by role playing tends to augment the effectiveness of a persuasive communication.

Additional observations were analyzed in order to explore possible mediating factors underlying the gain in opinion change due to active participation. From behavioral records and interviews, two suggestive leads emerged. In those cases where role playing produced a marked increase in opinion change: (1) the individual displayed a relatively great amount of improvisation in his talk, and (2) he felt comparatively well satisfied with his oral performance. The first factor suggests that the gain from role playing may occur primarily because the active participant tends to be impressed by his own cogent arguments, clarifying illustrations, and convincing appeals which he is stimulated to think up in order to do a good job of "selling" the idea to others. The second factor suggests an alternative explanation in terms of the rewarding effects of the individual's sense of achievement or feelings of satisfaction with his performance in the role of active participant. Additional evidence pertinent to the second factor, based on a self-rating questionnaire which the Ss filled out immediately after giving the talk, consistently indicated that the greatest amount of opinion change occurred among those active participants who felt that their oral performance had been satisfactory. Both the "improvisation" factor and the "satisfaction" factor warrant further investigation.

11

Leadership

LEADERSHIP AND SOCIOMETRIC CHOICE
By Helen Hall Jennings

Leadership phenomena "happen" in a human setting where people get into interaction on the basis of feeling, or *tele*. As Moreno demonstrates, the tele process of attraction and repulsion must be considered dependent upon *both* individuals in a relationship (even though the flow of feeling on the part of one individual toward another may be unknown by the second), since its direction is not random but depends upon the second person. The tele is not, therefore, viewed merely as the subjective, independent product of a single person.[1, 2]

The existence of tele relationships may be observed in terms of the expressions of choices on the part of individuals for each other. The choice process in a community occurs in a particularized fashion, along the lines of association for work or for living which are important to its population. These may be called *socio-groups*, since association is founded on a collective criterion. In *psyche-groups*, on the other hand, association, though equally real and important, is strictly a private matter; choices for members of such groups have a private, personalized basis. (I, as Mary Jones, feel toward you, as Sally Smith, thus and so. . . .) Choices within the socio-group have a collective, impersonal basis freer of the uniqueness of private personality aspects of response. (I, an unemployed woman holding membership in this union, feel toward you, as an employed woman also holding membership in this union, thus and so. . . .) The membership of a given psyche-group may also overlap and be a part of a socio-group, but while functioning as socio-group members, the individuals apparently expect to relinquish roles appropriate in psyche-group membership.

By psyche-group is not meant, in sociological terms, the same thing as a face-to-face group or a primary group. There are such groups which never become either totally or in part what is here meant by the term psyche-group. The psyche-group is an interpersonal structure where the uniqueness of the individual as a personality is appreciated and allowed for, with varying degrees of spontaneous indulgence and affection. It is where one counts "altogether" as a person, not merely as an individual or as a member of a socio-group. In indus-

---

Prepared by the author from data more fully reported in *Leadership and Isolation* (2d ed.; New York: Longmans, Green & Co., Inc., 1950).

[1] J. L. Moreno, *Who Shall Survive? A New Approach to the Problem of Human Interrelations* (Washington: Nervous and Mental Disease Monograph Series, No. 58, 1934).

[2] ____ and H. H. Jennings, "Statistics of Social Configurations," *Sociometry*, 1938, 1, 342–374.

try it springs up in the informal grouping that comes to exist as men work side by side. But in such psyche-group formations, as these develop inside socio-groups, the individual must consider his participation separately from his participation as a socio-group member. In a particular socio-group, only certain aspects of personality are appreciated by other members, as only certain aspects are appropriate to the tasks important in the specific socio-group life. Within the socio-group, there may be many members chosen by others as socio-group members who at the same time are rejected or unchosen by these same individuals in the latters' several psyche-groups.

It is the confusion between a socio-group and a psyche-group, or the lack of a clear-cut delineation between them, that has complicated the study of leadership phenomena. It is necessary to ask: Leadership in what respect? For whom? In what sort of group? What kind of psychological position in respect to the given population did the individual showing leadership have at the time he displayed it?

THE NATURE OF THE INVESTIGATION

The laboratory of the research was the New York State Training School for Girls, a closed community comprising over 400 girls committed by the Children's Courts of the state. The population represents a cross section of the socially and economically underprivileged in the state. To be admitted, the girl must be over 12 and under 16 years of age, and of normal intelligence.

The sociometric test, devised by Moreno,[3] discloses the feelings which individuals have toward each other in respect to membership in the groups in which they are at a given moment (ideally, all groups in which they are or could be). It is an *action* test. The criterion for choice must have explicit meaning for the subject, and offer him the specific opportunity to give information for reconstruction or retention of the situations which he is in. The results are put into operation to the optimal satisfaction of *all* subjects.[4, 5] Thus, in respect to the criterion of the group's formation, the psychological position of every member in the composition of the group structure is brought to light. By periodic testing, changes in this structure can be traced, followed, and evaluated.

The following excerpt from the test instructions [6] illustrates the simplicity and directness of the approach used:

You will notice that your paper is divided into eight squares or boxes. In the first Yes box, marked "Live with," write the names of whatever girls there are anywhere on the campus or in your own house whom you would prefer to live with. In the No box marked "Live with," write the names of whatever girls there are anywhere on the campus or in your own house whom you would prefer not to live with. Do the same for the "Work with" boxes. Then, those you would prefer not to work with, place in the No box for work. Next, do your "Recreation or Leisure," and then your "Study or School" boxes, having in mind the same instructions. . . . The No boxes should contain only the names of those, *if any*, whom you definitely *don't* want in your group for the particular function or functions which it happens to be. The Yes boxes should contain only the names of those, *if any*, whom you definitely *do* want in your group for the particular function or functions which it happens to be. . . . Do the boxes in any other order than that suggested, if you prefer.

[3] Moreno, *op. cit.*
[4] *Ibid.*
[5] J. L. Moreno and H. H. Jennings, "Sociometric Control Studies of Grouping and Regrouping," *Sociometry Monographs*, No. 7, 1947.
[6] The complete protocol appears in H. H. Jennings, "A Sociometric Study of Emotional and Social Expansiveness," in R. G. Barker, J. S. Kounin, and H. F. Wright (eds.), *Child Behavior and Development* (New York: McGraw-Hill Book Co., 1943).

As previously employed, the socio-metric test has been found to have an average reliability of .95, based on tests given on four successive weeks with five choices allowed on the criterion of tent-mates in a summer camp.[7] At the college level, using also five choices and one cri-terion (membership in a discussion group), reliability coefficients ranging from .93 to .95 are reported from tests given on successive days.[8] These coeffi-cients are based on the extent to which the subject is chosen by others on two or more occasions; they relate to the choices individuals *receive from others*. The more stringent comparison of the present study, by use of unlimited choices and a much longer retest inter-val, also reveals that even under these conditions there is a fairly high correla-tion. A comparison of the individual's self-consistency on separate occasions (his extent of expenditure of choices), with unlimited choices allowed, reveals that the individual shows a *characteris-tic repertoire* in choice expression for others.

The first tests were given during the last week of December 1937. The test population included all individuals (443) comprising the school population as of that date. Retests were given during the first week of September 1938, to all in-dividuals (457) comprising the popula-tion at that time.

The method of analysis is a compari-son of the number of *different* individuals reacted to positively (chosen) or nega-tively (rejected) by the subjects, with the number of different individuals re-acting positively or negatively to the subjects. The data used in the analysis include all choices and rejections, either on the criterion of living or on the cri-terion of working, given to or received by 133 subjects present for both tests

and occupying the same housing units on both occasions.

The problem of this report is to note the relation between behavior shown in interaction with others and the socio-metric choice status of the individual. In order to examine behavior at different levels of choice status, "under-chosen" is defined as placing one standard devia-tion or more below the mean of the 133 subjects, "over-chosen" as placing one standard deviation or more above the mean, and "average-chosen" as placing approximately at the mean, in number of individuals choosing the sub-ject. The number of under-chosen posi-tions is 41 (19 on Test I and 22 on Test II); the number of over-chosen positions is 43 (22 on Test I and 21 on Test II). For purposes of comparison, 41 other positions placing nearest the mean on either test were selected.

Among other evidence which might be cited, the following is offered to show that high choice status is closely related to leadership in this community. Elec-tions to a House Council were held in the fall of 1937. The individual receiving the highest number of votes automatically became a member of the Community Council. The election was held under the supervision of the Club Director, and the ballots were closed. Four members were elected to the Council from each house. For the purpose of comparing membership in the Councils with rank in positive sociometric choices received from others, only data for the two mem-bers in each living unit receiving the highest and second highest number of votes were used. This comparison reveals that of the 20 such Council members (two from each of the ten housing units of this study), 18 or 90 percent place among the over-chosen, as here defined. The two Council members who do not so

[7] W. I. Newstetter, M. Feldstein, and T. M. Newcomb, *Group Adjustment* (Cleveland: Western Reserve University, 1938).
[8] L. D. Zeleny, "Sociometry of Morale," *Am. Soc. Rev.*, 1938, IV, 799–808.

rank place just below this point. When
allowance is made for the difference between being chosen from a community-
wide base and being elected from the
limited house population, it is evident
that there is practically a one-to-one
relationship between being elected to
represent the house body in matters concerning the group and being chosen by
community members on the sociometric
criteria of living and/or working with
them.

Observation of the personalities of the
over-chosen subjects and study of the
motivations given for choice provide
the following clues to their choice status.
Each over-chosen subject, to a greater
or less extent:

enlarges her social space, for interchange
of ideas and activities;

secures more and more responsibilities
to be held by members in her work
groups, her housing unit, and in the
community as a whole;

takes definite stands on what she considers right, and will "fight for it";

aids the average-chosen individuals to
broaden their conceptions of their
potential capacities; shows faith in
their abilities by taking it for granted
that they can and want to contribute
to their own development and to the
life of the community;

shows ability to establish rapport quickly
and effectively with a wide range of
other personalities and to win their
confidence in varying circumstances;

insists on an impersonal fairness, and succeeds in gaining respect for this level
of interaction between members;

raises the level of conduct of average
members by demanding considerate
behavior towards the less able (in the
sense of less contributing) members;

calls to account individuals who attempt
to exclude participation by the relatively noncontributing or destructively
contributing members; shows towards
them protective behavior;

exhibits anger and censuring almost exclusively towards only those members
whom they consider "should know
better," rather than towards all alike;

controls the destiny of nonadjusting
members (i.e., nonadjusting to the
kind of regime instituted by such behaviors as listed above) by influencing
other members to aid them, by blocking
their possible satisfactions in nonadjusting behaviors, and by obliging
other members to show respect for
them in the community as a whole
(e.g., not to carry unfavorable reports
about them into the "networks" by
telling out-group members of occurrences which would prejudice their
standing in the community);

causes others to feel that she aids them
to meet their problems.

These behavior tendencies are confirmed and further expanded when housemother reports commending or complaining of the individual's behavior are
examined in relation to the individual's
choice-status. To the over-chosen, as
compared with the average-chosen, are
attributed three times as many incidences of initiatory behavior in making
innovations without permission, twice
as many incidences showing planning
and organization, four times as many
occasions showing initiative in starting
new projects, over four times as frequent
behavior exhibiting ingenuity in changing conduct of "problem" members or
fostering understanding between new
members and others, and about twice as
many rebellious behaviors. In these reports, the incidences for the under-
chosen range from none to half as many
as for the average-chosen.

To the under-chosen are attributed
twelve times as many incidences of
actively or passively interfering with the
group's activities, as to the over-chosen,
while such incidences are practically
missing for the average-chosen. For the
over-chosen are reported *almost three
times* as great an incidence of retaliatory
behavior (among other over-chosen) as
for average-chosen, and this behavior is
rare for under-chosen. (Could this reflect
less earnest competition to give occasion

for such behavior among the latter members?)

On the other hand, the most often spontaneously given "praise" of the housemother by the over-chosen is for her listening to and considering the members' opinions in planning; such comment is made only a third as often by the average-chosen and not at all by the under-chosen.

Thus, it appears that the under-chosen show in common many varieties of behaviors the effect of which may tend to separate and draw individuals apart rather than to bring them together. The average-chosen show somewhat less than half as great an incidence of such behaviors, and about twice as great an incidence of behaviors the effect of which may tend to bring individuals into constructive relationship with one another. Further, in the very behaviors in which the average-chosen outrank the under-chosen, the over-chosen in turn are found to exceed the average citizen by approximately twice as great an incidence. And in those behaviors which "make new events happen" or "enlarge the kind and extent of activity" the over-chosen surpass the average citizen by over four times as great an incidence.

Just as isolated-from-choice positions and over-chosen positions are but two ends of one continuum, so behaviors when analyzed in relation to such choice-status of the individual (at the time he has the particular choice-status) appear as forming extremes on another continuum—at one end showing expressions disruptive (or "clogging") to the life of the group, and at the other, expressions conducive to an expanding life for the group. Sociometric choice for the individual thus appears to depend directly upon the nature of the group *in which he is to be functioned with.*

For the citizen who would earn choice, it appears as much a matter of what behaviors she rarely exhibits as of those she frequently shows which will determine what choice status she will hold in a socio-group for working or living. The average citizens of this study are not in any sense average in all constructive behaviors; the incidence of behaviors having a negative import for interpersonal exchange (in common work and living) appears to offset those having a positive import sufficiently, in the case of such individuals, to hold them down to an average-status.

Leadership and isolation appear, from this study, as phenomena which arise out of individual differences in interpersonal capacity for socio-group participation and as phenomena which are *indigenous to the specific milieu of the socio-group* or socio-groups *in which they are produced.*

Individuals who emerge as leaders in one socio-group may or may not emerge in a similar role in another community, or even in another socio-group in the same community. Likewise, individuals who classify as isolates in terms of choice from their associates in one socio-group in a given community may or may not change in choice-status in another socio-group in the same or another community.

Nevertheless, it is a reasonable hypothesis that when certain qualities have become pronounced and integrated in the personality expression of the individual (such a quality as relatively great freedom from self-concern, sufficient to enable him to be concerned with matters affecting many others than himself), these are likely to persist, for they reflect a high level of emotional growth and maturity, and thus may be expected to act favorably upon his future relationships with persons in other socio-groups.

It would also appear, similarly, that certain qualities (such a quality as relative inability to observe and orient one's actions to the elements of a situation and the persons comprising it) may, unless outgrown, continue to act unfavorably upon the individual's future relationships.

The "why" of leadership appears, however, not explainable by any personality quality or constellation of traits. Some individuals are found who are as emotionally mature and as resourceful in ideas as the leader-individuals of this study, yet they were not allowed a role of leadership, nor chosen more than the average citizen in the community. The why of leadership appears to reside in the interpersonal contribution of which the individual becomes capable in a specific setting eliciting such contribution from him. Similarly, isolation appears as but the opposite extreme on this continuum of interpersonal sensitivity between the membership and the individual in the socio-group.

The over-chosen personalities showing certain behaviors in common differ markedly from one another in the "style" of these behaviors and the "style" they show *in contact with* specific other individuals. As persons, they are very unlike. (Similarly, isolates and near-isolates differ greatly from each other.) An analysis of their ways of behaving shows the leadership they exert to be definable as *a manner of interacting with others*—a manner which moves others in directions apparently desired by the latter, even though they may be doing little themselves towards attaining such directions. It is as if these individuals recognize and think more of the needs of others than others think of their own needs. The leader-individuals often take actions in behalf of others whom they do not choose and who do not know of the effort made for them. For example, three times as frequently the over-chosen individual, as compared with the average-chosen subject, made "unasked-for-suggestions to the psychologist for the welfare of others." Further, "visits to the psychology office in behalf of another individual (instead of self)" were made approximately seven times as often by the over-chosen individuals as by the average-chosen, and not at all

by the under-chosen. Such actions by the average individuals almost invariably involve others whom they choose and thus may be inferred to be of more personalized interest to them.

While the varieties of styles of leadership (and of isolation) are many, nevertheless, a number of characteristics of leader-individuals stand out as common attributes. The social milieu is "improved" from the point of view of the membership through the efforts of each leader. Each widens the area of social participation for others (and indirectly his own social space) by his unique contribution to this milieu. Each leader seems to sense spontaneously when to censure and when to praise, apparently is intellectually and emotionally uncomfortable when others are "left out," and acts to foster tolerance on the part of one member towards another. At the same time they may give little quarter to other leaders. (By contrast, the isolates and near-isolates appear relatively "self-bound," behaving in ways which tend to show little capacity to identify with others or to bridge the gap between their own personalities and others as members of the socio-group.)

The leadership thus exhibited in the community by various members appears, in each instance, to reflect a "style" of leadership—a particularized way of behaving, derived from the personality attributes of the individual in an over-chosen position. Actually, however, the success of several "types" of personality in achieving leadership status through their ways of behaving while a member of the population appears to depend, in turn, upon the fact that the population itself is comprised of so great a variety of personalities that no one personality has a constellation of attributes necessary to win an exclusive position in esteem and influence necessary to a role of exclusive leadership. Each leader makes a contribution *to some parts* of the membership which all members do not equally want or need. There may be very little overlap between the individuals who support one leader and those who support another.

Leadership appears as a process in which no one individual has a major role but in which relatively many share. The superior capacity which one individual may have to recognize and respond to the needs of others does not show itself as a generalized capacity which may relate him to all other individuals. It appears in the special sensitivity between the individual and *specific* other persons, resulting in interaction between them.

The psychological structure resulting from choice behavior on the part of the members of the test-community, this research finds, may be most accurately envisioned as *an equilibrium in flux*. The movements which take place continually within it are compensatory movements which do not disturb the total structure viewed as a totality. The total structure tends to retain its characteristics from one time to another *even though the respective positions of its carriers* (the members of the population) alter from time to time. The shifts "upward" and "downward" that are shown in the choice-status of the individuals in the population are, so to speak, bound to occur since interaction cannot be static. The reasons for this stability and this slowness of flux within the structure appear in the behaviors distinguishing choice-status. A social process of interaction *by and towards* the individuals respectively isolated or lifted to leadership is found to form the very basis of the isolation and of the leadership. Personality *per se*, in so far as it is reflected in social structure, is the capacity for interplay with other personalities, for responding to and being responded to, in a reciprocal situation, in which the individual is in common with other individuals.

LEADERSHIP, FOLLOWERSHIP, AND FRIENDSHIP: AN ANALYSIS OF PEER NOMINATIONS
By E. P. Hollander and Wilse B. Webb

From its early conception by Moreno,[1] through the basic work of Jennings and others,[2] sociometry has grown steadily in stature. In more recent years, the value of sociometric techniques to problems of applied research has become increasingly apparent. In at least one sense, evidence of its value is provided by the volume of investigations in applied psychology which have as their core the utilization of some form of sociometric measure. This is particularly true of the so-called peer nomination.

During the past decade several studies of military groups have yielded provocative findings regarding the validity of

From the *Journal of Abnormal and Social Psychology*, 1955, L, 163–167. Reprinted by permission of the authors and the American Psychological Association.

[1] J. L. Moreno, *Who Shall Survive?* (New York: Beacon House, Inc., 1934).

[2] J. H. Criswell, "Sociometric Methods of Measuring Group Preferences," *Sociometry*, 1943, VI, 398–408; J. H. Criswell, "Foundations of Sociometric Measurement," *Sociometry*, 1946, IX, 7–14; H. H. Jennings, *Leadership and Isolation* (New York: Longmans, Green & Co., Inc., 1943); M. L. Northway, "A Method for Depicting Social Relationships Obtained by Sociometric Testing," *Sociometry*, 1940, III, 144–150.

peer nominations on leadership in predicting performance criteria considerably divorced in time from the original point at which nominations were gathered.[3] With a view toward qualifying as well as quantifying the relevant variables underlying this demonstrable validity, concern has developed regarding the precise interpretations which may be drawn from sociometric leadership data. Two problems in particular appear to be fundamental to the maximization of meaning from such data. One of these is the "followership" issue—that is, the interpretation which may be made from leadership-nomination data concerning characteristics of followership. Perhaps the most current implicitly held position considers that individuals nominated "low" or disregarded on leadership nominations constitute a potential followership group. This view rests largely on the assumption that leadership and followership fall at opposite poles of a status continuum. An alternative position, however, which makes no such assumption, might hypothesize this "nonleader" group to be neither desirable as leaders *nor* desirable as followers. Thus, it is probable that within given institutional structures, leadership and followership qualities are interdependent. Then too, it is likely that such differences in interpretation of leadership-followership relations which arise may stem from the particular definition of followership which one adopts; a further explication of our own position on this point is detailed below. It should be noted here, however, that we have confined ourselves to a direct concern with the specific leadership-followership relationship as it is revealed through sociometric nomination techniques. This is done with a recognition of the existence of a still broader problem of the interdependence of various sociometric status continua. Such a broader consideration is typified by the recent paper of Lemann and Solomon.[4]

A second issue with which we are concerned is the lingering doubt that peer nominations represent much more than a "popularity contest." Here, in effect, the critic asks the pragmatic question: Are leadership nominations so much a function of "relevant" factors as they are a consequence of ·sheer popularity, i.e., considerations of friendship? It is worth recalling that the question of the relationship of popularity to leadership is fundamental to much sociometric research and has been given considerable attention. Although the literature in this area cannot be encompassed within this paper, it is well recognized that multiple contributions to this problem have resulted from the work of Jennings,[5] Criswell,[6] Northway,[7] and Lemann and Solomon,[8] among others. Because of its unique comparability to the problem and population of this current study, a particularly pertinent reference here is the work of Wherry and Fryer.[9] Reporting on their research at the Signal Corps Officer Candidate School, they contend that peer ratings on leadership yield su-

---

[3] E. P. Hollander, "Peer Nominations on Leadership as a Predictor of the Pass-fail Criterion in Naval Air Training," *J. Appl. Psychol.*, 1954, XXXVIII, 150–153; R. J. Wherry and D. H. Fryer, "Buddy Ratings: Popularity Contest or Leadership Criterion?" *Personnel Psychol.*, 1949, II, 147–159; S. B. Williams and H. J. Leavitt, "Group Opinion as a Predictor of Military Leadership," *J. Consult. Psychol.*, 1947, XI, 283–291.

[4] T. B. Lemann and R. L. Solomon, "Group Characteristics as Revealed in Sociometric Patterns and Personality Ratings," *Sociometry*, 1952, XV, 7–90.

[5] Jennings, *op. cit.*

[6] Criswell, 1943, *op. cit.;* Criswell, 1946, *op. cit.*

[7] Northway, *op. cit.*

[8] Lemann and Solomon, *op. cit.*

[9] Wherry and Fryer, *op. cit.*

perior predictions of performance and hence constitute something beyond, or divorced from, popularity as such. Their case is substantiated by analyses against criteria external to the ratings, with conclusions drawn inferentially from the obtained relationships. This is sound evidence, but only in one aspect. The fact remains that the qualities of popularity or friendliness determining ratings in one area may well be the common determinant of success in later performance. Complementary data drawn from a more direct approach to this question would appear to be required.

In this approach, we shall treat these problems of followership, leadership, and friendship together for several reasons. First, there is the interest in any differential effect that friendship may play in leadership and followership choices. Second, and perhaps more critically, there is the realization that if a relationship were to be found between leadership and followership, it would be desirable to know the extent to which this was a function of common characteristics rather than merely a choice of friends for common roles. The ultimate aim is to provide a somewhat more complete view of the meaning of peer nominations.

Problem

Simply put, the purpose of the present study is to define more clearly the interrelationships among sociometrically derived measures of leadership, followership, and friendship. Two typical questions of a general nature to be studied are these:

1. In what way and to what degree is followership related to leadership?

2. In what way and to what degree is friendship related to leadership, and how does this compare with the relationship, if any, between friendship and followership?

Method

The sample consisted of 187 naval aviation cadets representing eight sections graduating from a 15-week preflight training course at Pensacola Officer Candidate School (OCS) in the fall of 1953. The characteristic "OCS-type" regimen to which the cadets are exposed tends to bring about strong in-group affiliations within the sections. By the end of the preflight course, it is reasonable to expect that each of the cadets has had an opportunity to observe his section mates under a variety of conditions. With regard to background, it might be noted, too, that all of the cadets had had a minimum of two years of college or its equivalent and have a mean age slightly in excess of 21.

During its last week of training, each section was asked to complete three sociometric nomination forms; the first two of these were on leadership and followership, the third on friendship. In the case of the leadership and followership forms, the cadet was instructed on the sheet to assume that he was assigned to "a special military unit with an undisclosed mission." For leadership, he was asked to nominate in order *three* cadets from his section whom he considered best qualified ("high") to lead this special unit and *three* cadets from his section whom he considered least qualified ("low"). On the followership form, a similar set was presented with the instruction that the cadet assume that he *himself* had been assigned to the leadership of this special unit; he was asked to nominate *three* cadets from among his section mates whom he would want as part of his unit and *three* whom he would not want. Both forms stressed that cadets were to be selected in terms of the abilities which the *nominator* considered to be important for these roles. The third form solicited the names of *three* cadets whom the nominator considered to be his best friends within his section.

Scores on the leadership and follower-ship variables were derived by weighting positive nominations +3, +2, and +1, and negative nominations −1, −2, and −3. An algebraic summation of these weights was then divided by the poten-tial number of nominators in the section for any one man ($N - 1$), thus yielding an index of a cadet's standing from +3 to −3 on both the leadership and fol-lowership continua. While this technique is not totally refined in that it may ob-scure the group's ambivalent evaluation of a given individual, it has been found to be sensitive to the identification and ordering of the higher and lower ends of the distribution. Its reliability, moreover, is quite adequate, as will be seen below. Since it is applied here to the three vari-ables for the derivation of scores to be intercorrelated and studied in relation-ship to one another, it presumably serves well the function of broadly highlighting the relative magnitudes of the r's in-volved. Friendship nominations were treated by a simple summation of a cadet's nominations divided by $N - 1$; in this instance no signs were involved since only positive nominations were ob-tained. The split-half reliabilities secured for the three scores, using odd-even nomi-nators ($N = 104$), were as follows: leader-ship, .94; followership, .91; friendship, .41. The r's reported have been corrected by the Spearman-Brown prophecy for-mula. Because of its idiosyncratic na-ture, the reliability for friendship is not surprisingly low.

ANALYSES AND RESULTS

The findings of correlational analysis are presented in Table 1. The intercorre-lations of the three sociometric variables

TABLE 1

INTERCORRELATIONS AMONG LEADERSHIP, FOLLOWERSHIP, AND FRIENDSHIP SCORES

Correlated variables	r*	p
Leadership vs. followership	.92	<.001
Leadership vs. friendship	.47	<.001
Followership vs. friendship	.55	<.001
(N = 187)		

* A significance of difference beyond the .01 level between all combinations of these coeffi-cients was obtained.

will be seen to reach a significant confi-dence level, with the coefficient between leadership and followership ($r = .92$) at-taining the highest magnitude of the three. The correlation of .47 between leadership and friendship is in accord with relationships of a similar magnitude obtained between leadership and popu-larity in previous studies reviewed by Stogdill [10]. To determine the significance of the difference between the three com-binations of paired correlations, the t test was applied. Computation of the stand-ard error of the difference was accom-plished through a technique suggested by Peatman [11] which allows for dependent samples with one array in common. As indicated, all of these differences are sig-nificant beyond the .01 level, with the ob-tained magnitudes indicating that friend-ship contributes relatively less weight to leadership than it does to followership. A partial r calculated between leadership and followership, with friendship held constant, yields a coefficient of .90. Therefore, the effect of friendship on the basic leadership-followership relationship appears to be negligible.

[10] R. M. Stogdill, "Personal Factors Associated with Leadership: A Survey of the Literature," *J. Psychol.*, 1948, XXV, 59.

[11] J. G. Peatman, *Descriptive and Sampling Statistics* (New York: Harper & Brothers, 1947).

TABLE 2

MEAN FREQUENCY OF DISTRIBUTION OF HIGH- AND LOW-LEADERSHIP
NOMINATIONS ON FOLLOWERSHIP
(N = 187)

Leadership	Followership			Sum of means
	High	Not mentioned	Low	
Nominated high	$M = 1.67$ $\sigma = .75$	$M = 1.31$ $\sigma = .74$	$M = .02$ $\sigma = .16$	3.00
Nominated low	$M = 0$ $\sigma = 0$	$M = 1.06$ $\sigma = .79$	$M = 1.94$ $\sigma = .79$	3.00

Since the nomination scores were group-derived, with weightings introduced which might serve to obscure personal interactions, two additional analyses were completed with direct utilization of individual choice-response patterns. These are summarized simply in Tables 2 and 3. Both of these tables represent the ultimate distillation of full-scale interaction matrices. In Table 2 consideration is given to the disposition of a nominator's three high- and three low-leadership choices, so far as his nominations for followership are concerned. The analysis questions whether a nominator tends to choose his high-leadership nominees as high on followership, and whether the reverse holds true as well. Reading across the top row, the mean in each cell represents the mean number of all the nominators' three high-leadership choices who were chosen high or low or not mentioned on followership. The sum of these means across will equal 3.00. Consider, as an illustration, the first cell; the mean of 1.67 indicates that this number, out of *three* high-leadership nominees, were nominated—on the average— as high on followership. An alternative way of viewing these data is in percentage form. In the first cell, then, 56 percent (1.67/3.00) of nominations are represented. The bottom row presents the

identical analysis for those nominated low on leadership. Here, as might be anticipated, the trend of mean size is reversed, reflecting the high correlation between leadership and followership.

An analysis similar to the previous one is presented in Table 3. The focus of attention here is on the disposition of friends within leadership- and followership-nomination categories. Specifically, consideration has been given to the mean number of the nominators' friends who are nominated, on the average, as high or low or not at all on leadership, in the top row, and on followership, in the bottom row. From the first two top cells it will be noted that, of the three friends, an average of .83 of them are nominated high on leadership whereas 2.11 of them are disregarded in these nominations. This stands in contrast to the adjacent bottom cells where means of 1.33 and 1.63 friends are nominated high on followership or disregarded. These means, of course, may be simply transformed to percentages as indicated for Table 2. This over-all pattern is noteworthy in demonstrating that an average of more than two out of three friends are *disregarded* on leadership nominations; so far as followership nominations are concerned, no such marked tendency evidences itself. Significant *t* values

TABLE 3

MEAN ASSIGNMENT OF LEADERSHIP AND FOLLOWERSHIP
NOMINATIONS FOR THE THREE FRIENDS NOMINATED
(N = 186)

	High	Not mentioned	Low	Sum of means
Leadership nominations of three friends	$M = .83$ $\sigma = .81$	$M = 2.11$ $\sigma = .71$	$M = .06$ $\sigma = .24$	3.00
Followership nominations of three friends	$M = 1.33$ $\sigma = .73$	$M = 1.63$ $\sigma = .73$	$M = .04$ $\sigma = .18$	3.00

($p < .001$) were obtained for the first and second columns.

DISCUSSION

With respect to the fundamental questions underlying this investigation the results indicate first that leadership and followership nominations are intimately related in a positive direction. The implication of this finding is that the more desired followers tend to be at the upper extremes of the leadership distribution; a corollary of this would be that those who are low or disregarded on leadership nominations are not viewed as desirable followers.

The second major finding is that leadership and followership nominations are, to a considerable extent, independent of the friendship choice of the nominators. This finding tends to substantiate the fact that peer nominations are not mere "popularity contests," but represent, at least for the variables of this study, evaluations of the individual's potential for performance largely independent of the dimension of friendship.

In discussion of the relatively high correspondence between leadership and followership, the crux of the matter lies, of course, in our definition of followership. The term may be broadly approached from the viewpoint of the leader or that of the led, i.e., the followers. In other words, the followers may be evaluated on

their capacity as followers or their willingness to be followers. One may adopt either or both views. We have chosen to view followership as it is judged from the leadership standpoint. We have made this choice for two reasons: first, the reality of institutional demands, and, second, the nature of the sociometric process and its established validity. A composite of followership nominations from potential leaders—followership as viewed by all group members acting as a leader—presents a reasonably satisfactory picture of this kind of followership. As it emerges here, then, our definition of followership is the extent to which an individual is desired by potential leaders of a group functioning within a circumscribed institutional context.

In keeping with this line of thinking, an additional analysis was conducted to determine whether individuals chosen high on leadership differed essentially in their choice of followers from individuals chosen low on leadership. By correlating the followership scores derived from nominations made by individuals in the top half of the leadership continuum with followership scores derived from nominations made by individuals in the lower half, it was found that the leadership-status factor made little difference in the selection of followers; the correlation between the followership scores obtained independently from these two nominator groups was .82. Noting that the split-half reliability is a correlation between two sets of followership scores obtained independently of the leadership status of those making nominations, we find this r of .82 accords well with followership's uncorrected reliability of .83.

The finding that good leaders are also judged as good followers makes sense when viewed within an institutional framework like the military establishment. The principle represented applies as well to other institutions, however. With the increasing complexity of our society, the role of the institutional leader demands something more than leaping on a white charger to gallop off in a solely self-determined direction. Typically, he must effectively lead his group in directions which have been assigned to that group. Given this circumstance, the leader must himself be a good follower or his group may find itself destroyed or performing inefficiently in a total organizational mission. This point has been well elucidated in a number of recent studies, among them an industrial study of the first-line supervisor by Pelz.[12]

Granted that this paper is exploratory, it nonetheless raises certain practical points. It seems reasonable from the findings that one cannot make the simple assumption that those individuals not chosen as leaders may be integrated within the group as effective followers. Then, too, re-enforcement has been offered the view that friendship is not necessarily crucial to other forms of group status. As with all such studies, however, generalizations from particular samples should be handled with caution. On the other hand, generalizations to the military institution—from which this sample was drawn—may be reasonably made. Finally, while no pretense has been made here that any broad implications for so-ciometry have been contributed, it is hoped that, within an applied sphere, certain fundamental notions regarding the interrelationship of leadership, followership, and friendship may have been developed.

SUMMARY AND CONCLUSIONS

The relationship between leadership, followership, and friendship peer nominations was studied within eight sections of naval aviation cadets, $N = 187$. Two related problems of some significance to the interpretation of peer-nomination data were specified: (*a*) a consideration of followership status as an element of leadership status; and (*b*) an examination of friendship as a variable underlying leadership and/or followership nominations. The results indicated that leadership and followership nominations were related to a high degree, $r = .92$. Friendship nominations were *not* found to bear appreciably on this relationship, $r_{LF \cdot F} = .90$. Leadership and friendship were found to be correlated at a significantly *lower* level than followership and friendship. An average of more than two out of three friendship nominees were not mentioned at all in the leadership nominations. Finally, the leadership status of nominators, as determined from peer nominations, was found to be unrelated to the followership choices which they made.

From the results it may be concluded that peer nominations on leadership are by no means a total function of friendship ties; quite the contrary, friendship appears to play only a minor role in the emergence of leadership nominations. Furthermore, followership status is not necessarily implied by nonleader status on peer nominations. It appears evident that the popular dichotomy between leadership and followership is in need of

---

[12] D. C. Pelz, "Influence: A Key to Effective Leadership in the First-line Supervisor," *Personnel*, 1952, XXIX, 209–217.

reappraisal. Rather understandably, the nature of our complex, hierarchical institutions demands that the effective leader be equally effective as a follower. It may be considerably more realistic, therefore, to consider characteristics of followership as one functional component of good leadership.

AN EXPERIMENTAL STUDY OF LEADERSHIP AND GROUP LIFE *By Ronald Lippitt and Ralph K. White*

The study here reported, conducted in 1939 and 1940, attempted in an exploratory way to discover the extent to which various aspects of leadership behavior and of total group life could be fruitfully studied by experimental procedures of controlled matching and planned variation in conditions. The study had as its objectives:

1. To study the effects on group and individual behavior of three experimental variations in adult leadership in four clubs of eleven-year-old children. These three styles may be roughly labeled as "democratic," "authoritarian" and "laissez-faire."

2. To study the group and individual reactions to shifts from one type of leadership to another within the same group.

3. To seek relationships between the nature and content of other group memberships, particularly the classroom and family, and the reactions to the experimental social climates.

4. To explore the methodological prob-lems of setting up comparative "group test situations," to develop adequate techniques of group process recording, and to discover the degree to which experimental conditions could be controlled and manipulated within the range of acceptance by the group members.

The major experimental controls may be described briefly as follows:

1. *Personal characteristics of group members.* Because a large group of volunteers were available from which to select each of the small clubs, it was possible to arrange for comparability of group members on such characteristics as intelligence, and on such social behaviors (measured by teachers' ratings) as obedience, amount of social participation, leadership, frequency of quarreling, amount of physical energy, etc.

2. *The interrelationship pattern of each club.* In each group, by the use of a sociometric questionnaire in each classroom, it was possible to select groups which were very closely matched in terms of patterns of rejection, friendship, mutu-

Prepared by the authors from data more fully reported in (1) Kurt Lewin, Ronald Lippitt, and Ralph K. White, "Patterns of Aggressive Behavior in Experimentally Created 'Social Climates,'" *J. Soc. Psychol.*, 1939, X, 271–299; (2) Ronald Lippitt, "An Experimental Study of Authoritarian and Democratic Group Atmospheres" in *Studies in Topological and Vector Psychology, I, University of Iowa Studies in Child Welfare*, No. 16, 1940; (3) Ronald Lippitt, "An Analysis of Group Reactions to Three Types of Experimentally Created Social Climates" (Unpublished doctoral thesis, State University of Iowa, 1940); (4) Ronald Lippitt, "Field Theory and Experiment in Social Psychology: Authoritarian and Democratic Group Atmospheres," *Am. J. Sociol.*, 1939, XLV, 26–49; (5) Ronald Lippitt, "The Morale of Youth Groups," in Goodwin Watson (ed.), *Civilian Morale* (Boston: Published for Reynal & Hitchcock by Houghton Mifflin Co., 1942); and (6) Ronald Lippitt and Ralph K. White, "The 'Social Climate' of Children's Groups," in Roger Barker, Jacob Kounin, and Herbert Wright, *Child Development and Behavior* (New York: McGraw-Hill Book Co., 1943).

	Period 1 (7 weeks)	Period 2 (7 weeks)	Period 3 (7 weeks)
Treatment	Autocracy	Autocracy	Democracy
Club	Sherlock Holmes	Sherlock Holmes	Sherlock Holmes
Leader	I	IV	II
Treatment	Autocracy	Democracy	Autocracy
Club	Dick Tracy	Dick Tracy	Dick Tracy
Leader	II	III	I
Treatment	Democracy	Autocracy	Democracy
Club	Secret Agents	Secret Agents	Secret Agents
Leader	III	II	IV
Treatment	Democracy	Democracy	Autocracy
Club	Charlie Chan	Charlie Chan	Charlie Chan
Leader	IV	I	III

ality of relationship, and leadership position.

3. *Physical setting and equipment.* All clubs met in the same clubroom setting, two at a time in adjacent meeting spaces, with a common equipment box.

4. *Activity interests.* It was important to know the extent to which initial interest in the planned activities might be responsible for differences in degree of involvement in activity during the experiment. Therefore it was ascertained in the beginning that all groups of boys were comparably interested in the range of craft and recreational activities in which they would later be engaged.

5. *Activity content.* It is clear that the structure and content of an activity often exerts a powerful influence on the patterns of interdependence, cooperation, competition, etc. in group life. Therefore, it was important that activity content should be equated in these three types of leadership situations. In order to insure this, the clubs under democratic leadership met first in time during the week, and the activities which were selected by those clubs were automatically assigned to the parallel clubs under authoritarian leadership. In the laissez-faire situation, there were a number of potential activities of the same type as that selected by the "democratic clubs."

6. *The same group under different*

leadership. The experimental design also made it possible to have a perfect matching of club personnel on the same analysis by comparing the same club with itself under three different leaders.

EXPERIMENTAL VARIATIONS

In the beginning the experimenters had planned for only two major variations in adult leader behavior: an authoritarian pattern and a democratic pattern. Later it was decided that it would be more fruitful to add a third variation of "laissez-faire" adult behavior, although with the four available clubs it would make the experimental design less rigorous. The method of systematic rotation can be noted in the above chart, which refers to the earlier experiment (the same method was followed in the later experiment).

The three types of planned variation were as follows:

1. *The sequence of social climates.* A number of the hypotheses focused upon the effect of a particular type of group history in determining the reactions of a group to a present pattern of leadership. The chart indicates the variety of group history sequences which were selected for exploratory study.

2. *"Leader role" and "leader personality."* There was a question as to the extent to which certain basic personal-

ity characteristics of the adult leaders would be important determinants in the individual and group behavior patterns which resulted. To study this variable, four adults with very different personality patterns were selected as leaders and all of them after proper indoctrination took two or three different leadership roles with different groups during the course of the experiment as indicated on the chart. This made it possible to discover whether certain of the leaders induced common reaction patterns which could be traced to their "personality" as contrasted to their "leadership role."

3. *The three planned leadership roles.* The three variations in leader role which were worked through in careful detail by the four club leaders may be summarized as follows:

Plan for authoritarian leadership role. Practically all policies as regards club activities and procedures should be determined by the leader. The techniques and activity steps should be communicated by the authority, one unit at a time, so that future steps are in the dark to a large degree. The adult should take considerable responsibility for assigning the activity tasks and companions of each group member. The dominator should keep his standards of praise and criticism to himself in evaluating individual and group activities. He should also remain fairly aloof from active group participation except in demonstrating.

Plan for the democratic leadership role. Wherever possible, policies should be a matter of group decision and discussion with active encouragement and assistance by the adult leader. The leader should attempt to see that activity perspective emerges during the discussion period with the general steps to the group goal becoming clarified. Wherever technical advice is needed, the leader should try to suggest two or more alternative procedures from which choice can be made by the group members. Everyone should be free to work with whomever he chooses, and the divisions of responsibility should be left up to the group. The leader should attempt to communicate in an objective, fact-minded way the bases for his

praise and criticism of individual and group activities. He should try to be a regular group member in spirit but not do much of the work (so that comparisons of group productivity can be made between the groups).

Plan for laissez-faire leadership role. In this situation, the adult should play a rather passive role in social participation and leave complete freedom for group or individual decisions in relation to activity and group procedure. The leader should make clear the various materials which are available and be sure it is understood that he will supply information and help when asked. He should do a minimum of taking the initiative in making suggestions. He should make no attempt to evaluate negatively or positively the behavior or productions of the individuals or the group as a group, although he should be friendly rather than "stand-offish" at all times.

The data below will indicate the extent to which these planned variations were carried out and the pattern of social stimulation which was represented by the leader behavior in each of the clubs.

THE THREE PATTERNS OF LEADER BEHAVIOR

From the great variety of observations recorded on the behavior of each leader it was possible to compute quantitative profiles of leader performance which could be compared to see the extent to which the three different types of leadership role were different and the degree to which the adults carrying out the same role were comparable in their behavior patterns. Figure 1 illustrates some of the major differences in the patterns of behavior of the three leadership roles. Most of the comparisons on the graph meet the test of statistical significance. The "average leader" comparisons are based on four democratic, four authoritarian, and two laissez-faire leader roles. The first three classifications of behavior, "leader orders," "disrupting commands" and "nonconstructive criticism," may be thought of as representing adult behavior

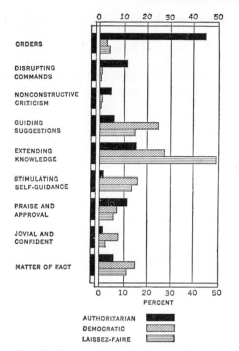

FIG. 1. Comparison of behavior of average authoritarian, democratic, and laissez-faire leader.

which has a limiting effect upon the scope and spontaneity of child activity. About 60 percent of all of the behavior of the average authoritarian leader was of these types as compared to 5 percent for the democratic and laissez-faire leaders. The data show that the authoritarian leader usually initiated individual or group activity with an order, often disrupted on-going activity by an order which started things off in the new direction not spontaneously chosen, and fairly frequently criticized work in a manner which carried the meaning, "It is a bad job because I say it is a bad job" rather than, "It is a poor job because those nails are bent over instead of driven in."

The next three behavior classifications, "guiding suggestions," "extending knowledge," "stimulating self-guidance," may be thought of as extending individual and group freedom and abili-

ties. We note here some of the major differences between the democratic and the laissez-faire leadership role. Whereas the democratic leader took the initiative (where he felt it was needed in making guiding suggestions) much more frequently than the laissez-faire leader, a major proportion of the latter leadership role was giving out information when it was asked for. It is clear, however, that the democratic leader did not take initiative for action away from the group as indicated by the fact that the average democratic leader showed a greater proportion of "stimulating self-guidance" than even the laissez-faire leader. The category of "stimulating self-guidance" was made up of three main items: "leader's requests for child's opinions on individual and group plans," "use of child judgment as criterion," and "taking consensus of opinion." The data indicate that the democratic leaders stimulated child independence eight times as often as the authoritarian leader and about twice as often as the laissez-faire leader, although the latter two types of adults showed about the same proportion of this behavior in their total pattern of activity.

The classification on the graph entitled, "praise and approval" is made up of such behavior items as "praising," "giving credit," "giving O.K.s," etc. It indicates largely the functioning of the adult as a dispenser of social recognition. The authoritarian adult was significantly more active in this regard than either of the other two types of leaders.

The extent to which the adult discussed personal matters unrelated to the club situation (home, school, etc.), and also joked on a friendly basis with the club members, is indicated by the "jovial and confident" classification. The democratic leader had social interactions of this type with the group members about eight times as often as either the authoritarian or laissez-faire leaders. This is perhaps one of the best indices of the extent to which the democratic leaders were "on the same level" as the club members.

The last classification on Figure 1, "matter of fact," indicates one measurement of the extent to which the various social atmospheres were "fact-minded" as compared to "personal-minded" as far as the behavior of the adults was concerned.

The degree to which all the adult leaders, delegated to assume a given leadership role, behaved in a comparable fashion on these major aspects of leadership role is indicated by the fact that, on all comparisons differentiating major characteristics of the three roles, there is no overlapping of the behavior of any representative of one role with any representative of a different role. Thus it is possible to conclude that three clearly different leadership patterns were created with a much smaller range of individual differences in leader behavior within each pattern than between the patterns.

Leadership Role and Personality Style. An examination of the behavior patterns of the different leadership roles by the same individuals (see chart on page 499) reveals that on the items of leader behavior there is no greater similarity between the different performance patterns of the same individual than between those of different individuals. If we turn to the data of the three interviews with each club member in which at each transition stage in their club life they compared their leaders and talked very fully about them, we find again that there is no evidence of any adult personalities being rated favorably or unfavorably independently of their particular leadership role (i.e., authoritarian, democratic, laissez-faire). All leaders stood high as well as low for one group or another and all the comments about their "personalities" were concerned with attributes of their leadership roles which had been measured.

The following excerpts from interviews of club members who had just completed six months of club life which included an authoritarian, a laissez-faire, and a democratic leader (in that sequence) indicate rather clearly the aspects of "leadership personality" which were perceived as important.

"RW (democratic) was the best leader and DA (laissez-faire) was the poorest. RW has good ideas and goes right to the point of everything . . . and always asked us what to do next time the club met, which was very nice. . . . DA gave us no suggestions like RW did, and didn't help us out at all, though he was very nice to us . . . but let us figure things out too much. I liked RL (authoritarian) pretty well for that kind of work."

"RL (authoritarian) was best, and then RW (democratic) and DA (authoritarian). RL was the strictest and I like that a lot. DA and RW let us go ahead and fight, and that isn't good, though RW didn't do it as much as DA did. DA just didn't give us much to do. RW was OK, but he didn't have so many ideas as RL did. RW wanted to do what we did; RL didn't want to go with us lots of times, and he decided what we were to do."

"I liked RW (democratic) best, then DA (laissez-faire) and then RL (authoritarian). RW was a good sport, works along with us and helps us a lot; he thinks of things just like we do and was just one of us—he never did try to be the boss, and wasn't strict at all, but we always had plenty to do (the golden mean). DA didn't do much, just sat and watched; there wasn't much I didn't like about him, but he didn't help us much . . . not like with RW when we had regular meetings and that was very good. RL was all right mostly; he was sort of dictator like, and we had to do what he said pretty nearly; he helped us work but he was sort of bossy."

"I liked RW (democratic) the best and RL (authoritarian) the least. RW was in between DA and RL, I like everything about him. I once said I didn't want to change from DA but I'm glad we changed. We could do what we pleased with DA but he was too easy going, not hard enough nearly, but he's a real nice person. With RL we always had something to do, and we did get a lot of things done, but I didn't like anything about him; he was much too strict. He was not cross, but very direct."

"I'd take RW (democratic) for a club leader, and DA (laissez-faire) was the worst. RW is just the right sort of combination; RL (authoritarian) was just about as good as RW, but he was kind of cross once in a while. RW had interesting things to do, he was just about right in everything. DA was too easy; he didn't know anything about the club—didn't know about its ways. He didn't understand us boys at all. . . . I didn't like him as well as RL because he had too few things for us to do." [1]

Another indirect indication that individual personality characteristics were not of any great significance in influencing group life in this study might be inferred from the finding that the total patterns of group reactions of different clubs to the same atmosphere tend to be remarkably homogeneous in spite of differences in adult leadership.

DATA COLLECTION AND ANALYSIS

Before continuing to summarize the individual and group behaviors which resulted from these three variations in leadership role, we will indicate briefly the types of data collection and analysis in the total study.

Eight types of club records were kept on each group, of which the four most important were kept by four different observers as follows.

1. A quantitative running account of the social interactions of the five children and the leader, in terms of symbols for directive, compliant, and objective (fact-minded) approaches and responses, including a category of purposeful refusal to respond to a social approach.
2. A minute-by-minute group structure analysis giving a record of activity subgroupings, the activity

goal of each subgroup, whether the goal was initiated by the leader or spontaneously formed by the children, and rating on degree of unity of each subgrouping.
3. An interpretive running account of strikingly significant member actions and changes in the atmosphere of the group as a whole.
4. Continuous stenographic records of all conversation.

These data were synchronized at minute intervals so that placed side by side they furnished quite a complete and integrated picture of the on-going life of the group.

Five other types of data covering the lives of the club members were collected, the three most important being:

1. Interviews with each child by a friendly "non-club" person during each transition period from one kind of group atmosphere and leader to another. These interviews elicited comparisons of the various club leaders with one another, with the teacher and with parents as well as other data about how the club could be run better, who were the best and poorest types of club members, what an ideal club leader would be like, etc.
2. Interviews with the parents, concentrating on kinds of discipline used in the home, status of the child in the family group, personality ratings on the same scales used by the teachers, discussion of the child's attitude toward the club, school and other group activities.
3. Talks with the teachers concerning the transfer to the schoolroom of behavior patterns acquired in the club and vice versa.

The reliability of the eleven trained observers ranged from .78 to .95 with an

---

[1] Beside indicating the leadership characteristics perceived as important by the boys, the reader will note that one boy in this club (an army officer's son) preferred his authoritarian leader and that the other four split in that two preferred their authoritarian leader second best and two liked their laissez-faire leader second best.

average reliability of .84. Another reliability computation on the coding of three thousand units of conversation into twenty-three categories of behavior showed a percent agreement of 86. The analyses of what constituted a "group life unit" showed reliabilities ranging from .90 to .98. A number of methodological researches carried on since the date of this study seem to suggest that it is possible to get much more meaningful and reliable observation data than has been generally believed if much more time and effort are spent on a careful "calibration" of psychologically well-trained observers.

Comparative Group Test Situations. The experimenters also postulated that a fruitful way to discover some of the major differences between the three types of group atmosphere would be to arrange comparable "test episodes" in each club. So at regular intervals the following situations occurred:

(1) Leader arrives late.
(2) Leader called away for indeterminate time.
(3) Stranger ("janitor" or "electrician") arrives while leader out and carries on critical attack of work of individual group member, then of group as a whole.

THE FOUR RESULTANT STYLES OF GROUP LIFE

Some of the major findings, summarized from stenographic records and other case material which are elsewhere reproduced, are as follows: Two distinct types of reaction were shown to the same pattern of authoritarian leadership. All of the data, including the documentary films, indicate that three of the clubs responded with a dependent leaning on the adult leader, relatively low levels of frustration tension, and practically no capacity for initiating group action, while the fourth club demonstrated con-

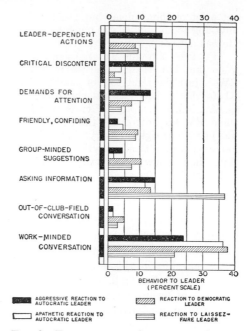

FIG. 2. Four patterns of group reaction to the three different types of leadership.

siderable frustration and some degree of channelized aggression toward the authoritarian leader. (This latter pattern is much more comparable to the behavior of the club under authoritarian leadership in a previous experimental study of two clubs.[2])

Figure 2 indicates the major differences in the relations which developed between the group members and the adult leaders in the four resultant social atmospheres. In both types of authoritarian atmosphere the members were markedly more dependent upon the leader than in either the democratic or laissez-faire situations, dependence being somewhat greater in the more passive clubs. All other clubs showed a somewhat greater feeling of discontent in their relations with the adult leader than did the members of the democratic clubs, members of the "aggressive autocracy" being outstanding in their expression of rebellious feelings. There is evidence

* See (2) of footnote on p. 340.

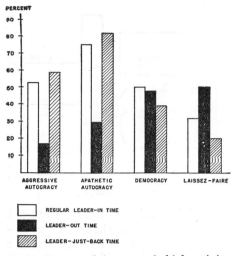

PERCENT

AGGRESSIVE AUTOCRACY   APATHETIC AUTOCRACY   DEMOCRACY   LAISSEZ-FAIRE

☐ REGULAR LEADER-IN TIME

■ LEADER-OUT TIME

▨ LEADER-JUST-BACK TIME

FIG. 3. Percent of time spent in high activity involvement.

from other sources that the actual "felt discontent" in the "apathetic autocracies" was somewhat higher than indicated by the conversation which was considerably more restricted than was that of the democratic and laissez-faire club members.

In both types of authoritarian situations the demands for attention from the adult were greater than in the other atmospheres. It seemed clear that getting the attention of the adult represented one of the few paths to more satisfactory social status in the authoritarian situation where all of the "central functions" of group life were in the hands of the dominator.

The category "friendly, confiding" indicates that the members of the democratic and laissez-faire clubs initiated more "personal" and friendly approaches to their adult leaders, and the data on "out-of-club-field conversation" further indicate the more spontaneous exchanging of confidences about other parts of one's life experience in the democratic club atmosphere.

The data on "group-minded sugges-

tions" to the leader show that the members in the democratic atmosphere felt much freer and more inclined to make suggestions on matters of group policy than in the other three group atmospheres. It is clear from other data that the lower level of suggestions in the laissez-faire situation is not because of any feeling of restricted freedom but because of a lack of a cooperative working relationship between the adult and the other group members.

The much greater responsibility of the members of the laissez-faire clubs to get their own information is shown by the fact that about 37 percent of their behavior toward their leader consisted of asking for information, as compared to about 15 percent in the other three club situations.

The final category in Figure 2, "work-minded conversation," indicates that a considerably larger proportion of the initiated approaches of the club members to their leaders were related to on-going club activity in the democratic and in the apathetic authoritarian situations than in the other two types of social climate.

Resultant Relationships of Club Members. The relationships between the club members also developed along quite different lines in the four social climates. Expressions of irritability and aggressiveness toward fellow members occurred more frequently in both the authoritarian atmospheres and the laissez-faire situation than in the democratic social climates. Unlike the relationships of high interpersonal tension and scapegoating which developed in the previous aggressive autocracy[3] the club in this experiment seemed to focus its aggression sufficiently in other channels (toward the leader and toward the out-group) so that in-group tension did not rise to a dangerously high point.

There were more requests for attention

_____

[3] See (2) of footnote on p. 540.

and approval from fellow club members to each other in the democratic and laissez-faire situations than in the two authoritarian climates. It seems clear that the child members depended upon each other to a great extent for social recognition and were more ready to give recognition to each other in the democratic and laissez-faire situations.

It is interesting to find nearly as high a level of interpersonal friendliness in the authoritarian situations as in the democratic and laissez-faire atmospheres. The underlying spirit of rebellion toward the leader and cooperation in out-group aggression seem to be the "cohesive forces" in aggressive autocracy, while in apathetic autocracy with its much lower level of felt frustration, the shared submissiveness seemed to do away with all incentive to competition for social status.

Intermember suggestions for group action and group policy were significantly lower in both types of autocracy than in the laissez-faire and democratic atmospheres. The dissatisfactions arising from any lack of feeling of real progress in the laissez-faire situation led to a high frequency of expression of ideas about "something we might do." Contrary to the democratic situation, these suggestions seldom became reality because of the lack of the social techniques necessary for group decision and cooperative planning. The group achievement level, as contrasted to the "wish level," was far lower in laissez-faire than in any of the other three atmospheres.

Other Differences. By having the leaders arrive a few minutes late at regular intervals in each club life, it was possible to discover that in the five authoritarian situations no group initiative to start new work or to continue with work already under way developed, as contrasted with the democratic situations where leaders who arrived late found their groups already active in a productive fashion. The groups under the

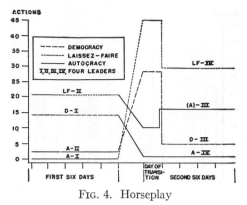

FIG. 4. Horseplay

laissez-faire leaders were active but not productive. Figure 3 shows the percentage of total club time in each of the four social atmospheres which was spent in giving major attention to some planned club project. For each atmosphere there is a comparison between the time when the leader was in the room, the time when the leader had been called out for planned experimental periods, and the unit of time just after the leader returned. The data here give striking evidence of the extent to which work motivation was leader-induced in the two types of authoritarian situation. "Working time" dropped to a minimum with the leader out, and most of what was done was in the minutes just after the leader had left the room. We see that in the democratic atmosphere the absence or presence of the leader had practically no effect. The apparent increase in group productive time with the laissez-faire leader out of the room may or may not be a meaningful result. Two or three times it was noted that when the adult left, one of the boys exerted a more powerful leadership and achieved a more coordinated group activity than when the relatively passive adult was present.

The behavior of the groups under authoritarian domination after their transition to a freer social atmosphere provided a very interesting index of unexpressed group tension. In Figure 4 it can be noted that both of these apathetic

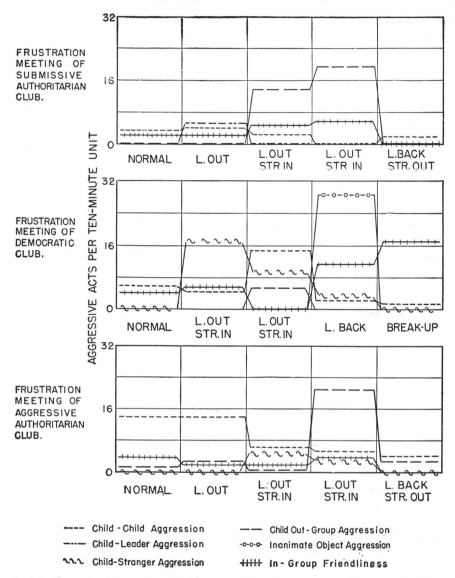

FIG. 5. Channels of group tension release in clubs of eleven-year-old boys under different types of leadership.

authoritarian clubs showed great outbursts of horseplay between the members on the first day of their transitions to a laissez-faire and a democratic group situation. This need to "blow off" disappeared with more meetings in the freer atmosphere.

It will be recalled that in certain situations all groups were subject to the same frustration of hostile criticism by a strange adult (e.g., "janitor") while the adult leader was gone. Under the different types of leaders, the groups handled these frustrations differently. Members of the apathetic authoritarian clubs tended to accept individually and to internalize the unjust criticism or, in one or two cases, they "blow off steam" in aggressive advances toward an out-group (the other club meeting in the adjacent clubroom; see Figure 5). In the aggressive authoritarian situation, the frustration was typically channeled in aggression toward the out-group, although in several cases there was some direct reaction to the source of frustration, the hostile stranger (see Figure 5). In the democratic atmospheres there was evidence of a greater readiness to unite in rejection of the real source of frustration, the stranger, and to resist out-group aggression. Figure 5 shows an interesting case of a democratic club which first expressed its aggression directly against the stranger, then showed a slight rise in intermember tension, followed by an aggressive outburst against a sheet of three-ply wood with hammer and chisels accompanied by a striking rise in ingroup friendliness and a quick return to cooperative harmony. It was particularly interesting to discover that the clubs under democratic leaders resisted scapegoating as a channel of aggressive release.

The data indicate that the democratic type of adult role resulted in the greatest expression of individual differences, and that some type of uniformity-producing forces brought about a slightly lessened individual variability in the laissez-faire situation, and a much reduced range of individuality in the authoritarian clubs. Figure 6 gives an example of this analysis for the same group of individuals under three different leaders.

INDIVIDUAL DIFFERENCES AND THE GROUP ATMOSPHERES

We now come to the question of to what extent it is correct to report the data as though all individuals and all groups under the same type of adult leadership role reacted with a high degree of uniformity to the induced social climate. Before turning to the final section of interpretation of individual differences in reaction to the same social climate, it

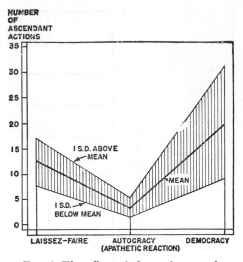

FIG. 6. The effect of changed atmosphere upon the range of individual differences within the same group.

will be interesting to look at the various club lives and see the extent to which the personalities making up each club or the different social atmospheres in which they lived seemed to be the most determining influence in the resulting behavior patterns. Two of the clubs had all three types of leadership. For these two groups it was possible by the techniques of analysis of variance to compare the effects of differences in child personnel and differences in all three experimental treatments. All four clubs were compared in the same way on various items of behavior for the two treatments of autocracy and democracy. It can be reported that in nearly all cases differences in club behavior could be attributed to differences in the induced social climate rather than to constant characteristics of the club personnel. One club showed a consistent variation from the rest through all atmospheres in level of friendliness between members, and one group showed a consistently lower level of social interaction which was not related wholly to their particular club environment.

We have already indicated on pages 500 and 501 that boys in the same club indicated quite different social perceptions of the behavior of the same leader and also made differing comparative judgments about their preferred leaders after having had two or three. Although all but one boy preferred the democratic leader to the other two types, there was quite a split in the population as to whether they preferred as a second choice the laissez-faire or authoritarian type of adult. To get some clews as to the basis for these differences the experimenters made an attempt to study the personality structure of each individual boy as it showed itself in his reactions to the other boys, to his adult leaders, and to his school and home environments. The records taken during the experiments constituted a type of data which is infrequently found in other approaches to personality study. The most commonly used techniques for studying an individual include interviews, questionnaires, Rorschachs, thematic apperception tests, psychoanalytic free association, and the social case history, consisting of interviews with parents and relatives, but not direct observations of social behavior.

It is not felt, of course, that such records are more useful than interviews, social case histories, or other customary techniques, but only that *when combined* with other techniques they are a valuable part of the total picture and are an extremely useful addition to the tool-chest of the clinical psychologist, the educator, the vocational counselor, and others who want to understand and to help a particular individual.

To show this concretely, one condensed case study is summarized below. Like our other case studies, it is based primarily upon club behavior data with much less interview material and home study data than would be found in a first class clinical analysis, but with enough of these data to suggest how the club behavior data can be combined with other sorts in the building up of an integrated personality structure.

The case chosen is one of two extremes, not in a single trait only, but in the large structure of intercorrelated traits, which has been found to be more important than any other trait cluster in our data. This cluster includes such variables as not being aggressive, not demanding attention, high work-mindedness, contentment in the strict but orderly atmosphere of autocracy, discontent in the free but disorderly atmosphere of laissez-faire, consistency of discipline in the home, and warmth of emotional relationship to parents.[4] These variables are statistically correlated to a marked degree; that is, the boys who show one of them usually show most of the others also. The reader can form his own judgment as to an appropriate name for the cluster. The boys who stand low in the cluster as a whole would often be called "bad" by the exasperated adults who have to deal with them, while those who stand high in it would be called "good." Goodness, then, or conscientiousness, might be as good a name as any. It should be noticed, though, that the cluster includes some things, such as liking autocracy better than laissez-faire, which are not included in the ordinary connotations of the word "conscientious." It should be noticed too that the boys who stand low in the cluster—boys like Reilly[5] who is described here—are not necessarily "bad" or antagonistic to adult values and requirements; they may be only heedless and relatively indifferent to those values. In groups such as ours, which contain only healthy "normal" children, with no actual delinquents, it would do violence to common usage to

---

[4] A factor-analysis of the data will be published elsewhere; its technical character makes it unsuitable for this brief report.

[5] Names and other identifying data have been changed here.

call any of the boys "bad." [6] For these and other reasons the rather cumbersome term "adult-value-centeredness" seems more accurate than "conscienticusness" as a name for the cluster.

REILLY

Club Personality. Reilly was the most talkative, the most conspicuous, and the most popular member of the Charlie Chan club. He was also one of the most irritating to those of his adult leaders who found themselves unable to cope with him. It was Reilly, for instance, who gleefully shouted, "Let's make war!" at the beginning of the first big water battle with the Secret Agents; it was Reilly whose vociferousness, as much as Fred's and Leonard's more aggressive horseplay, led to the complete disintegration of the group under laissez-faire leadership; and it was Reilly who led the "sitdown strike" against the autocratic leader, which was the one instance in any of the clubs of more or less organized rebellion against authority.

While he was so heedless of adult values and adult wishes, he was at the same time very popular with the other boys. He was the best-liked boy in his schoolroom, as determined by a sociometric questionnaire, and he had been elected president of his class. Yet he asserted his personality as vigorously in competition with other boys as in competition with adults. His personality contrasts sharply with that of Eddie, who was the best-liked boy in the other schoolroom from which our club members were selected. Where Eddie was conscientious, quiet, unassuming, and genuinely friendly with everyone, Reilly was exuberant, self-advertising, constantly bombarding the eyes and ears of others with his demands for attention, and, as the statistics showed, relatively low in both friendly and group-minded conversation. He was not actually a leader in the sense that he showed any planning or organizing ability; he was too impatient and too lacking in time-perspective for that. He was a leader only in the sense that he was liked, and also, perhaps, in the sense that his headlong, self-centered activity was imitated by others in the group.

It is interesting to find that, unlike the other two boys who stood with him at the bottom of the total group in the trait-cluster of "conscientiousness," he was never sullen, hostile, or maliciously mischievous. His scores in aggression were only about average, and his aggression (i.e., criticisms of other boys and playful collective aggression) was never really hostile in character. Even toward adults he was competitive rather than hostile. He ranked highest among the seventeen boys [7] in the proportion of his adult-contacts which had an attention-demanding character. Characteristically, he would loudly interrupt when the adult was talking to some other club member, and vociferously demand that the adult pay attention to him rather than to the other boy. The absolute frequency of this behavior was also very high, as evidenced by the fact that he also ranked highest, out of 17, in the absolute volume of his verbal contacts with the adult leader, in both autocracy and democracy. (The motivation behind these contacts, to be sure, was probably rather different in the two atmospheres. In autocracy it seems to have been almost entirely an expression of competition for

---

[6] The Freudian concept of the "super-ego" is relevant here; a "weak super-ego" does not necessarily mean active "badness" or antisocial tendencies. It may be noticed also that the cluster found in our data is similar to one which seems to have been discovered independently by a number of other investigators. It closely resembles Webb's (9) "w" factor, which Thurstone renamed "conscientiousness."

[7] All statistics are based on a population of 17 rather than 20, since there were three boys about whom there was not an adequate amount of home background information.

power—perhaps in order to win boy-admiration—while in democracy it was also an expression of genuine man-to-man friendliness.) It would seem, then, that his somewhat paradoxical popularity was not due to the kind of warm liking which drew other boys to the quiet and unassuming Eddie. Rather, it seems to have been due to the fact that he was so successful in getting a rather gullible public to accept him at his own valuation, while at the same time the absence of malice in his self-assertion kept it from arousing hostility in others. In spite of his competitiveness and essential self-centeredness, the group accorded him a sort of hero worship, perhaps largely because each of them would have liked to be the sort of vital and self-confident person—completely uncowed by adults—which he unquestionably was.

The statistical club-behavior data and interview data support this impressionistic picture. In addition to the quantitative data already mentioned, we find that he had unusually high scores in volume of conversation (with boys as well as with the adult leader), and in percent of "out-of-field" conversation, which in his case represented such things as bragging about his father's hardware store, his own chemistry set at home, etc. In the interviews he expressed a preference for his laissez-faire leader as compared with his autocratic leader, indicating, probably, that his need for orderliness was less than his need for free self-assertion. He also showed unusual frankness in his avowed preference for the boy-valued activity of "fighting," as compared with the adult-valued activity of working. In describing his autocratic leader he said, "We didn't have any fun then—we didn't have any fights."

Summarizing his club personality, we can say first that he was not noticeably motivated by any of the adult-sponsored values which were conspicuous in the conscientious boys—obedience, respectfulness, nonaggression, order, self con-

trol, hard work; second, that his primary goal in the club situation was apparently competition, or *superiority* in the eyes of the other boys; and third, that he tended to perceive adults, not as objects of obedience, respect, or hostility, but as equals, with whom he could compete (or be friendly, as he was with his democratic leader) on very much the same basis as with any of the other boys. These more basic characteristics of his present personality-structure, and not the peripheral behavior-traits of talkativeness, attention-demanding, etc., are what must be especially taken into account, whether our interest is the practical interest of the adult group-leader who has to cope with him, or the scientific interest of the clinical investigator who wants to trace the origins of his present personality-structure in his home background and the behavior of his parents.

Home Background. His indifference to adult-sponsored values becomes intelligible when we discover that neither of his parents seems to have given him any incentive—neither fear of punishment nor hope of loving approval—to develop these values. His indulgent father apparently enjoyed his company (in a man-to-man relationship which offers a clew to his warm reaction to his democratic club leader), but his father was extremely busy and apparently accepted little or no responsibility for his training. His mother apparently disliked him, but felt helpless in relation to him; in the constant feud between them, there was neither the warmth which might have made him want to win her love by being "good," nor the firmness which might have made him fear her restrictions when he was "bad." These two attitudes, rejection and a feeling of helplessness, repeatedly came out in the interview with his mother. According to her, he is impudent, he is irresponsible, he is lazy, he is impatient and unable to stay long at one thing, he continually quarrels with his older brother and teases his younger brother. She blurted out these criticisms in a weary but almost defiant way. According to her, "punishment doesn't do him any good. I used to lose my temper and whip him; I was pretty mean, I guess," but he would be just as bad or worse afterward, so that now she doesn't ever punish him. "He sasses me back, and I can't stand a sassy child." Sometimes he argues for hours at a time; "maybe it's because I've given in to him several times," and he knows it's a good way to get things. For a while he had an allowance, but "he'd borrow on the next week's allowance and then expected to get it just the same," so the plan was discontinued. He now gets money for movies at least twice a week; if she tells him he can't go, he often goes to his father and gets the money from him.

Not only his indifference to adult values, but also his desire for superiority and his tendency to perceive adults as equals now seem more intelligible. Since his father does not try to exert much authority, and his mother lets the authority situation become a feud in which he often gets the upper hand, he naturally tends to look upon adults as equals. Since his father's affection is always present and his mother's never is, his life is not geared to the winning of affection; the goal of superiority, first of all in relation to his mother and his brothers, has tended to take its place. And, finally, his exuberant vitality and absence of hostility, which were noted as major reasons for his popularity, now make sense in the light of the fact that his home life contains no major frustrations, and no repressed hostilities. Though his personality-structure may bring him trouble later in life, his existence at the moment is full of affection from his father, triumph over his mother, and exciting, successful competition with other boys.

Interpretive Summary

The foregoing condensed and highly selective research report has attempted to show some of the interdependencies of leadership role, group composition, group history, and membership personality structure in this study of four experimental clubs of preadolescent boys.

The leader-induced social atmosphere of the group, together with the group history (the preceding club atmospheres), established a hierarchy of channels of expression of response to frustration. Whereas the "aggressive autocracy" club was more ready to express its frustrations in interclub wars, the "apathetic autocracies" were more prone to internalize the aggression, and the "democratic" and "laissez-faire" groups to react against the source of frustration.

Passive acceptance by the group of the socially induced frustrations of authoritarian leadership was found in some cases to mean a nonfrustrated acceptance of a dependent relationship, and in other cases to mean a frustrated hopelessness in the face of overwhelming power. When a transition to a freer atmosphere occurred these latter cases gave evidence by their "blow-off" behavior of their previous frustrations.

The adult restrictiveness of the benevolent authoritarian role and the environmental unstructuredness of the laissez-faire situation were both found to inhibit greatly genuine "psychological freedom" as contrasted to "objective freedom."

The adult-leader role was found to be a very strong determiner of the pattern of social interaction and emotional development of the group. Four clear-cut types of social atmosphere emerged, in spite of great member differences in social expectation and reaction tendency due to previous adult-leader (parent, teacher) relationships.

It was clear that previous group history (i.e., preceding social climates) had an important effect in determining the social perception of leader behavior and reaction to it by club members. A club which had passively accepted an authoritarian leader in the beginning of its club history, for example, was much more frustrated and resistive to a second authoritarian leader after it had experienced a democratic leader than a club without such a history. There seem to be some suggestive implications here for educational practice.

It was found in this exploratory study that the process of small-group life could be experimentally manipulated in a satisfactory way for scientific study and could be recorded adequately for meaningful quantitative analysis. There emerged a variety of meaningful clusters of correlations between member case history, member social perception of the group situation, member and group behavior, and leader behavior.

THE EFFECTS OF VARYING COMBINATIONS OF AUTHORITARIAN AND EQUALITARIAN LEADERS AND FOLLOWERS By William Haythorn

Recently attention has been focused on the relationships between the personality characteristics of group members and the nature of the leadership that emerges from the interaction of these individuals with each other and their tasks.[1] The behavior of leaders in groups is determined not only by their own personalities but also by the underlying needs, role expectations, and values of the group members. Conversely, the behavior of group members is partly determined by the personality of the leaders, particularly in its interaction with their own needs and expectations. Of particular interest are groups in which the leaders' and followers' personalities show some consistent similarity or dissimilarity, creating situations where the interaction of different needs, expectations, perceptions, and values can be studied systematically. The present study was de-signed to investigate a specific case of the relation between leader's and followers' personalities in the determination of group behavior.

This paper describes part of the results reached in a study of the behavior of authoritarian and equalitarian personalities in small groups. The California F-scale was used as the principal measure of the authoritarian personality.[2] This scale purports to measure a broad syndrome of attitude toward authority, which constitutes a basic aspect of personality. Individuals high on the F-scale are allegedly prone to accept the existing authority structure in society, comfortably receiving orders from those higher and giving orders to those lower in the hierarchy. High-F, or F-plus, individuals are apt to be religious, politically conservative, socially conforming, sometimes superstitious, and practical

Revised from a paper appearing in the *Journal of Abnormal and Social Psychology*, 1956, LII, 210–219. The portions used are reprinted by permission of the authors and the American Psychological Association. The work reported here was done under a contract between the U.S. Navy, Office of Naval Research, and the University of Rochester. Dr. Launor F. Carter was the responsible investigator for that contract.

[1] L. F. Carter, "Leadership and Small-group Behavior," in M. Sherif and M. W. Wilson (eds.), *Group Relations at the Crossroads* (New York: Harper & Brothers, 1953); and C. A. Gibb, "The Research Background of an Interactional Theory of Leadership," *Aust. J. Psychol.*, 1950, III, 19–42.

[2] T. W. Adorno, Else Frenkel-Brunswick, D. J. Levinson, and R. N. Sanford, *The Authoritarian Personality* (New York: Harper & Brothers, 1950).

(as opposed to idealistic). The F-scale was selected as the principal measuring instrument for this study because it was believed to be related to the interactions of leaders and followers in such a way as to permit reliable predictions of behavior.

A previous paper describing another part of this study [3] reported behavioral differences between groups composed entirely of individuals high on the F-scale and those composed entirely of individuals low on the F-scale. It was found that a more "democratic" group culture prevailed in the low-F groups, and the low-F groups were more effective in dealing with the task problem. Even more marked than the differences in performance between the groups as a whole were the differences between the kinds of leaders who emerged in the two kinds of groups. Emergent leaders in the groups made up of nonauthoritarian personalities were more sensitive to others, more effective leaders, more likely to make their suggestions for action subject to group sanction, and less likely to give direct orders to others.

In the present study these same subjects were assembled again. This time leaders were appointed instead of being allowed to emerge spontaneously as they had before. In half of the groups, appointed leaders had F scores similar to those of the other group members, while in the other half the appointed leaders had scores at the opposite end of the scale. The design is shown in Figure 1. This arrangement permitted us to study several things: (a) the effects of authoritarian vs. nonauthoritarian leadership; (b) the effect of authoritarian vs. nonauthoritarian followers, and (c) the effects of assembling groups with leaders whose personalities were similar to those of other group members, as compared with groups whose leaders' personalities

were unlike those of other members. The major hypotheses examined were as follows:

Hypothesis I. F-plus leaders, regardless of the personalities of their followers (1) engage in less equalitarian behavior than F-minus leaders; (2) are less concerned with group approval for their actions; (3) engage in more autocratic behavior; and (4) show less sensitivity to others than do F-minus leaders.

Hypothesis II. F-plus followers, regardless of the personalities of their leaders, (1) engage in less equalitarian behavior; (2) show less sensitivity to others; (3) are more satisfied with appointed leaders; (4) are less critical of their own group; and (5) are more submissive toward appointed leaders than F-minus followers.

Hypothesis III. Under F-minus leadership followers, regardless of their own personalities, (1) have more influence on group processes; (2) develop a less formal group structure; and (3) express greater differences of opinion than under F-plus leadership.

Hypothesis IV. With F-minus followers leaders, regardless of their own personalities (1) are not likely to engage in as much autocratic behavior and (2) are not as distinct from other group members as are leaders with F-plus followers. In contrast, leaders with F-plus followers are likely, under pressure, to take decisive, directive action in order to get the job done, because of the expectations of F-plus followers regarding an appointed leader's role.

Hypothesis V. In groups composed of leaders and followers with similar F-scale scores (1) followers are more secure; (2) followers are more motivated to achieve the common group goal; (3) followers are more satisfied with the appointed leadership; (4) there is less personality conflict within the group;

[3] W. Haythorn, A. Couch, D. Haefner, P. Langham, and L. F Carter, "The Behavior of Authoritarian and Equalitarian Personalities in Small Groups," *Hum. Relat.*, 1956, IX, 57–74.

(5) there is less conflict between the leader and group members; and (6) there is higher group morale and productivity than in groups composed of leaders and followers with dissimilar F-scale scores.

METHOD

Subjects. The subjects (Ss) for the experiment consisted of (a) 32 male undergraduate students at the University of Rochester who were high on the F-scale, "conservative" as judged by the Cattell Q1 scale (designed to measure a conservatism-radicalism dimension, highly correlated with the F-scale), and relatively normal as judged by the Minnesota Multiphasic Personality Inventory (MMPI); and (b) 32 male undergraduate students who had low F-scale scores, were liberal as judged by the Cattell Q1 scale, and were also normal according to the MMPI. The mean F-scale scores for the two groups were 124.5 and 66.9, respectively, using the 30-item, 7-points-per-item scale described in *The Authoritarian Personality*.[4] The Cattell Q1 scale and the MMPI were used to help screen selection errors made with the F-scale alone. There was no overlap in scores between the two groups on either the F-scale or the Cattell Q1 scale.

The task. The task given the groups was the discussion and composition of a short script involving a human-relations problem. Complete instructions were read to the Ss before they began working, to the effect that they were to help E in developing a test of human-relations skills. They were to be shown a film of a human-relations problem, after which they were to answer a number of questions about how the problem had been handled, how it should have been handled, etc. When they finished answering the questions as individuals, they were to discuss similar questions as a group and arrive at answers to which they all agreed. Following completion of this phase of the task, they were to compose dialogue for similar films. Once their script was completed, they were to record it on a magnetic tape recorder. After reading the instructions, E showed the film and then left the room. He did not return until the group had completed all phases of the procedure outlined in the instructions. A typed copy of the latter was left on the table with the Ss.

Observation Procedures. While Ss worked on the task in the experimental room, observers (Os) watched through one-way vision mirrors from an adjacent room. Four Os (first- and second-year graduate students) recorded their observations in three ways:

1. While observing, two Os simultaneously categorized and "typed out" behavioral units as they occurred, using a Stenotype system of interaction recording described in an earlier paper.[5] The category system was revised, however, to fit the needs of this study. Forty-three categories were used, but in order to simplify the analysis and increase the frequency of acts per category, these were combined into 17 category indices: friendly acts; positive-affect acts; direction-taking acts; self-emphasizing acts; asking for suggestion or sanction; asking for group evaluation; "democratic" acts; directive acts; expressions of confusion or lack of orientation; hostile acts; negative-affect acts; initiating and integrating acts; diagnosing and clarifying acts; general task-participation acts; self-isolating acts; withdrawing and out-of-field activity; and tension release and out-of-field activity. These indices are not independent, in that some categories

---

[4] Adorno, *et al.*, *op. cit.* Further details regarding the selection of subjects in the present study are given in Haythorn *et al.*, *op. cit.*

[5] L. F. Carter, W. Haythorn, Beatrice Meirowitz, and J. Lanzetta, "Note on a New Technique of Interaction Recording," *J. Abnorm. & Soc. Psychol.*, 1951, XLVI, 258 260.

of behavior were included in more than one index. For a more complete description of the categories and indices, the reader is invited to consult the earlier report.[6]

2. At the end of 30 minutes of recording, the pair of Os was relieved by another pair. Immediately after being relieved, Os rated each S on 16 behavioral characteristics, defined in the previous report,[7] as follows: striving for individual prominence, friendliness, security, influence, equalitarianism, striving for group approval, submissiveness, striving for goal achievement, self-isolating behavior, effective intelligence, sensitivity to others, leadership, aggressiveness, autocratic behavior, social ability, and nonadaptability. These ratings had an average interobserver reliability of .75, with a range from .31 to .91. Since the group sessions varied in length from two to four hours, each S was rated by each O at least once, and usually two or more times.

3. At the end of each group session, all four Os and E filled out a Post-meeting Reaction Sheet (PMRS) designed to describe aspects of the group not easily attributed to single individuals. Examples of the items on the PMRS are: (a) This group was not serious enough— there was too much playing around; (b) group effectiveness was interfered with by personality clashes between members. There were 37 such items and the Os indicated the extent of their agreement on each, using a 7-point scale.

4. In addition, Ss were asked to fill out a very similar PMRS and to rate the degree to which they were satisfied with their group, the extent to which they thought the group had been productive, to rank the group members in order of how well they were liked, and to rank group members in terms of their relative contributions to the achievement of group goals.

"Emergent" Group Sessions. The Ss were scheduled to come to the laboratory workroom in groups of four. In their first session—results of which are described in the previous paper [8]—each of the 16 groups were composed of Ss homogeneous with regard to F-scale scores. In this first session, there was no experimental structuring of leadership. The findings based on that session will not be discussed in the present paper.

Appointed-leader Sessions. After the emergent sessions, all individuals were reassembled with three members from their original emergent groups and another member from a different group. The alien member was appointed as leader (by telling him he was to take charge of group activities that day and would be responsible for getting the job done). In half of the groups the leader had an F score similar to that of group members, while in the other half it was dissimilar. Thus, there were four groups with F-plus leaders and F-plus followers, four with F-plus leaders and F-minus followers, four with F-minus leaders and F-plus followers, and four with F-minus leaders and F-minus followers. (See Fig. 1.)

	F + leaders	F − leaders
F + followers	4 groups	4 groups
F − followers	4 groups	4 groups

Fig. 1. Experimental design. (This design was replicated in Sessions II and III of the experiment.)

In Session III, two of the original emergent-group members who had been together in Session II were reassembled

[6] Haythorn, *et al.*, *Hum. Relat.*, *op. cit.*
[7] *Ibid.*
[8] *Ibid.*

with the member who had been withdrawn during Session II. In addition, a new alien member was introduced as the leader for that session. Groups having had an F-plus leader in Session II were given an F-minus leader in Session III, and vice versa.

Characteristics of Appointed Leaders. The experimental design required that 32 of the 64 *S*s be appointed as leaders, 16 in Session II and 16 in Session III. Two were chosen from each of the original emergent groups.

We chose as "authoritarian" leaders the two individuals in each F-plus group who were highest on an average score which took into account (1) the observers' ratings of leadership, (2) the subjects' leadership nominations, and (3) the observers' ratings of autocratic behavior. Our F-minus (nonauthoritarian) leaders were the two individuals from each of the original F-minus groups who were high not only on leadership (as determined by observers' ratings and subjects' nominations) but who had been rated high on equalitarian behavior by the observers. Thus, all our leaders had shown by their actions in Session I that they were capable of assuming leadership. Our authoritarian leaders were shown to be so not only by their high F scores but by their autocratic dealings with other group members in Session I, while our equalitarian leaders had both low F scores and a demonstrated penchant for equalitarian behavior, as revealed in Session I.

Observers were not informed of the composition of the groups during the experiment and were unable to guess the composition pattern with significantly more accuracy than chance. This finding may be attributed to an observer expectation that authoritarian individuals would be more aggressive, argumenta-tive, and generally uncompromising towards others. Instead, in the emergent sessions they were rated as being significantly more concerned with group approval than were the F-minus *S*s. Such concern for group approval in groups having no formal authority structure is theoretically a central facet of the authoritarian personality structure,[9] underlying the tendency to conform to social mores. However, our *O*s apparently tended to identify pleasant social behavior as evidence of equalitarianism and consequently made many errors in attempting to estimate group composition. The fact that analyses generally supported our hypotheses in spite of observer failure to distinguish the groups is presumptive evidence that our results are not a reflection of observer bias.

RESULTS

The Effects of Varying Leader Personality. Table 1 presents the principal results relevant to Hypotheses I and III, concerning the differences between groups led by an authoritarian appointed leader and those led by an equalitarian appointed leader, in (a) leader behavior, (b) follower evaluation of the leaders, and (c) observer evaluation of the groups. In our earlier publication [10] analysis of variance was employed and presented with the appropriate group means and tests of significance. In the present report, for purposes of simplification, we have combined groups and indicated significance levels without the variance estimates. First, we combined all groups with authoritarian leaders, regardless of the F-scale scores of the followers; similarly, all groups with equalitarian leaders were combined regardless of the F-scale score of the followers. For each variable in Table 1, a higher number

---

[9] Gibb, *op. cit.*

[10] W. Haythorn, A. Couch, D. Haefner, P. Langham, and L. F. Carter, "The Effects of Varying Combinations of Leaders and Followers," *J. Abnorm. & Soc. Psychol.*, 1956, LIII, 210 219.

TABLE 1

COMPARISONS OF GROUPS HAVING AN APPOINTED AUTHORITARIAN LEADER
WITH THOSE HAVING AN APPOINTED EQUALITARIAN LEADER

	Session	Authoritarian leaders (mean scores)	Equalitarian leaders (mean scores)
A. Leader's behavior: observer's ratings of behavioral traits.			
Equalitarianism	II	4.16	5.05
	III	3.65	5.18 *
Striving for group approval	II	3.75	4.37 *
	III	3.71	4.33
Autocratic behavior	II	2.81	2.41
	III	2.77	1.92 *
Effective intelligence	II	4.39	5.07 *
	III	4.05	5.19 †
Sensitivity to others	II	3.76	4.68
	III	3.56	5.09 †
B. Follower's evaluation on Group Post-meeting Reaction Sheet.			
Relative efficiency of leadership	II	5.79	4.87 *
	III	4.78	4.48
C. Observer's evaluation on Post-meeting Reaction Sheet.			
Degree of equal participation	II	3.02	3.05
	III	2.78	3.63 *
Striving for equal participation	II	3.14	4.19 *
	III	4.15	5.25 *
Formality of group structure	II	2.80	2.32
	III	2.87	2.15 *
Motivation toward group goal	II	4.27	5.10
	III	4.17	4.97 *
Difference of opinion in group	II	2.87	4.17 *
	III	2.98	3.07

* PL .05
† PL .01

indicates a greater amount of the measure listed. Only those measures are listed for which statistically significant differences were found for at least one session in our analyses of variance.

It is not surprising that our observers rated our authoritarian leaders as more autocratic in their behavior and our equalitarian leaders as more equalitarian. It is gratifying, however, to have this further indication of our reliability in selecting leaders on the basis of their personalities—particularly gratifying in view of the fact that the observers could not distinguish the two kinds of leaders when they consciously tried to do so. More interesting is the fact that our equalitarian leaders appeared more anxious to secure group approval for their activities, more effective in bringing their intelligence to bear upon the problem the group faced, and more sensitive to the feelings and attitudes of their followers than were the authoritarian leaders.

Followers, regardless of their own personalities, rated the authoritarian leaders as more efficient relative to other leaders with whom they had worked. In their Post-meeting Reaction Sheets, observers reported that the groups with authoritarian leaders were significantly more formal in group structure, had a lower degree of equal participation (that is, there was a greater tendency for some members to do most of the work while others did less), had less striving for equal participation, were less highly motivated toward group goals, and had fewer differences of opinion than those groups with equalitarian leaders.

The Effects of Varying Follower Personality. To examine Hypotheses II and IV, measures obtained from groups having authoritarian followers were combined, regardless of leader personality, and compared with combined measures obtained from groups having equalitarian followers. These results are given in Table 2.

As shown in the table, leaders in groups with authoritarian followers were rated as striving for individual prominence more than the equalitarian leaders. They were also significantly more aggressive and more autocratic in their behavior toward other group members. It is important to note here that these behavioral differences occurred even though there was no F scale difference between the two sets of leaders—both contained four authoritarians and four equalitarians.

Equalitarian followers, regardless of their leaders' personalities, were rated as showing more equalitarian behavior, more striving for goal achievement, and greater effective intelligence. In addition, equalitarian followers performed more diagnostic and clarifying acts, and engaged in much less tension release and out-of-field activity. They were clearly more goal-oriented, from the observers' viewpoint, than were the authoritarian followers.

In some respects, followers' evaluations of their own groups revealed a marked contrast to observers' ratings and behavioral indices. For example, the authoritarian followers rated their groups as significantly higher on striving for equal participation, group productivity, and motivation toward the group goal than did equalitarian followers. We have interpreted these differences as reflecting subject-response tendencies rather than actual behavioral differences, since they are so completely contrary to the more objective behavioral-category results and observers' ratings. Also, self-criticism is theoretically more characteristic of equalitarian than of authoritarian personalities.

Authoritarian followers rated their own groups as having more definite leadership, as being more dominated by the appointed leaders, and as being more satisfied with the appointed leaders than

TABLE 2

COMPARISON OF GROUPS HAVING AUTHORITARIAN FOLLOWERS WITH
THOSE HAVING EQUALITARIAN FOLLOWERS

	Session	Groups with authoritarian followers	Groups with equalitarian followers
A. Leaders' behavior: observer ratings.			
Individual prominence	II	4.34	3.67 †
	III	4.39	3.30 *
Aggressiveness		2.45	2.13
		2.45	1.49 *
Autocratic behavior	II	2.92	2.30
	III	2.88	1.81 *
B. Follower behavior: observer ratings.			
Equalitarianism	II	2.89	3.54
	III	2.62	3.46 *
Striving for goal achievement	II	3.49	3.92
	III	3.87	4.27 *
Effective intelligence	II	3.36	3.79
	III	3.43	3.86 *
C. Follower behavior: behavior-category indices.			
Diagnosing and clarifying acts	II	2.66	5.14 †
	III	2.02	3.45
Tension release and out-of-field activity	II	36.49	11.68 †
	III	35.76	25.62
D. Followers' evaluation of group: Post-meeting Reaction Sheet.			
Definiteness of leadership	II	5.26	3.99 †
	III	4.35	3.98 *
Striving for equal participation	II	5.85	4.81 †
	III	5.87	4.98 *
Group productivity	II	7.33	6.33 *
	III	6.97	6.83
Motivation toward group goal	II	5.33	3.91 *
	III	5.45	4.41
Domination by appointed leader	II	3.33	2.48 †
	III	2.75	2.23
Satisfaction with appointed leader	II	5.12	4.00 *
	III	5.23	3.78 *

* PL .05
† PL .01

Table 2 (CONTINUED)

E. Observers' evaluation of group: Post-meeting Reaction Sheet.			
Dissatisfaction with goal progress	II	3.16	2.72
	III	3.52	2.21 *
Degree of personality conflict	II	3.60	2.24
	III	3.73	3.04 *
Definiteness of leadership	II	5.33	4.55 *
	III	4.96	4.59
Competence of members	II	5.27	5.36
	III	4.76	5.89 *
Motivation toward group goal	II	4.40	4.97
	III	3.90	5.25 †
Group productiority	II	6.75	5.72
	III	5.67	7.20 †

* *PL .05*
† *PL .01*

did the equalitarian followers. These ratings, though concerned directly with the group leadership, were determined more by the personalities of the followers than of the leaders.

In groups with authoritarian followers, observers noted more frequent personality conflicts, more definite leadership, less member competence, less motivation toward the group goal, and less productivity than in groups with equalitarian followers. Observers were generally less satisfied with the goal progress of groups with authoritarian followers.

The Effects of Varying the Homogeneity of Leader and Follower Personalities. Finally, Hypothesis V is concerned with the effects of having leader and followers homogeneous with respect to the F-scale. All groups in which leader and followers were either both authoritarian or both equalitarian were combined and compared with all other groups (in which either the leader was authoritarian and followers equalitarian or vice versa). These means and significance levels are shown in Table 3.

Regardless of the personality characteristics of either the leaders or followers, leaders of the homogeneous groups were less submissive, more aggressive, and more autocratic than the leaders of heterogeneous groups. Followers in the homogeneous groups showed more striving for group approval and engaged in more withdrawing and out-of-field activity.

Observers evaluated the morale of homogeneous groups as higher and saw more personality conflict between the leader and group members in heterogeneous groups. Observers were more satisfied with the leadership in homogeneous groups and reported a greater lack of cooperation among members of heterogeneous groups. In summary, the personality differences between leader and followers seem to have created conflicts in the groups, detracting from group morale.

DISCUSSION

The results, then, support most of the hypotheses tested, indicating significant differences for each of the five major comparisons. Two of these—the comparison of F-plus and F-minus leaders and the comparison of F-plus and F-

TABLE 3

Comparison of Homogeneous Groups with Heterogeneous Groups

	Session	Homogeneous groups (leaders and followers similar in personality)	Heterogeneous groups (leader different personality than followers)
A. Leader behavior: observer ratings.			
Submissiveness	II	2.89	3.35
	III	2.82	3.55 *
Aggressiveness	II	2.73	1.85 *
	III	2.14	1.79
Autocratic behavior	II	3.12	2.10 *
	III	2.60	2.09
B. Follower behavior: observer ratings.			
Striving for group approval	II	3.08	2.94
	III	3.47	3.12 *
C. Follower behavior: behavior-category indices.			
Withdrawing and out-of-field activity	II	14.13	6.50 *
	III	11.95	10.02
D. Observers' evaluation of group: Post-meeting Reaction Sheet.			
Satisfaction with leadership	II	4.90	5.32
	III	5.75	4.72 †
Morale	II	4.19	4.59
	III	5.26	4.22 †
Personality conflict between leader and group members	II	2.87	2.74
	III	2.13	3.44 †
Lack of cooperation in group	II	3.90	3.17
	III	2.77	4.00 †

* PL .05
† PL .01

minus followers—are rather conventional types of comparisons. They simply indicate that the behavior of individuals can be predicted, to some extent, from measures of those individuals' attitudes or personality characteristics.

The other three major comparisons, however, are quite different. Each of these suggests that to some extent the behavior of individuals in groups is dependent on the personalities of other group members. We found, for example, that there were differences between leaders with F-plus followers and leaders with F-minus followers. This finding indicates that the behavior of leaders is, to a significant degree, a function of the attitudes or personality characteristics of the followers. Conversely, the behavior of followers is found to be significantly a function of the attitudes or personality characteristics of the leaders. The latter, of course, is almost a *sine qua non* for the concept of leadership, but the former has received less attention theoretically and almost none empirically.

Finally, the differences between F-plus and F-minus leaders are contingent on whether the followers are high or low F, and vice versa. This result supports the so-called interaction theory of leadership [11] even more forcefully than the observations referred to in the preceding paragraph. It directs attention to the mutually dependent, adaptive nature of small-group behavior and appears to facilitate our ability to predict.

It is particularly interesting to note that differences in authoritarian behavior between leaders with authoritarian followers and leaders with equalitarian followers (Table 2) were in exactly the same direction as differences between authoritarian and equalitarian leaders (Table 1), and between the leaders who emerged in authoritarian and equalitarian groups when no leader was appointed.[12] It appears likely that when followers expect their leader to play his role in a particular way, he is very apt to do so.

Previous evidence [13] has indicated that appointing an individual to a position of leadership in laboratory groups results in his behaving differently from other group members. Another study [14] has shown that group characteristics can be predicted from behavioral and personality measures of individual group members. The present study indicates that conclusions drawn from these previous studies must be tempered by considerations of the interaction among group members, and particularly that between leaders and other group members. All of these findings, of course, are probably contingent on such specifics as the kind of task considered, the population studied, and the nature of the leadership appointment.

SUMMARY

Four-man groups were required to perform a task in which Ss discussed specific human-relation problems presented by film, then composed and recorded dialogue for similar problems. One of the four men in each group was appointed as leader. The California F-scale was administered to all Ss and group composition was varied systematically to yield four conditions: (1) high-F leaders with high-F followers; (2) high-F leaders with low-F followers; (3) low-F leaders with high-F followers; and (4) low-F leaders with low-F followers. Observations of behavior were recorded by: (a) ratings of individuals on 16 behavorial characteristics, (b) an interaction recording technique using a classification of behavior acts into 43 categories, and (c) responses by Os and Ss to a Post-meeting Reaction Sheet involving questions about the group.

Five major comparisons were made:

---

[11] Gibb, *op. cit.*

[12] Haythorn, *et al.*, *Hum. Relat.*, *op. cit.*

[13] L. F. Carter, W. Haythorn, Beatrice Shriveer, and J. Lanzetta, "The Behavior of Leaders and Other Group Members," *J. Abnorm. & Soc. Psychol.*, 1951, XLVI, 589–595.

[14] W. Haythorn, "The Influence of Individual Members on the Characteristics of Small Groups," *J. Abnorm. & Soc. Psychol.*, 1953, XLVIII, 276–284.

(1) F-plus leaders with F-minus leaders; (2) F-plus followers with F-minus followers; (3) leaders of F-plus followers with leaders of F-minus followers; (4) followers with F-plus or F-minus leaders; and (5) groups in which leader and followers were homogeneous as compared to groups in which they were heterogeneous with regard to F-scale scores. For each comparison, significant differences were found consistent with a number of hypotheses drawn from the theory of the "authoritarian personality."

Results indicate that F-plus appointed leaders differ behaviorally from F-minus leaders and that F-plus followers differ from F-minus followers. These two comparisons are conventional tests of behavioral differences related to personality characteristics. In addition, the behavior of leaders was a function of whether their followers were F-plus or F-minus, and the behavior of followers depended on the F-scale scores of their leaders. Several significant individual and group differences were found between heterogeneously and homogeneously composed groups.

GROUP LEADERSHIP AND INSTITUTIONALIZATION
By Ferenc Merei

PRELIMINARIES TO THE EXPERIMENT

The problem we set ourselves concerns the relationship between leader and group. To tackle it, we took the following steps.

Children suitable to form a group were selected. Previous observation showed that from the age of 5 upward, in spontaneously formed groups the sexes as a rule do not mix. Hence, the groups had to be homogeneous as to sex. They had to be homogeneous as to age, too, be-

cause, as our observations showed, in spontaneous groupings the age differences seldom exceed two years. Homogeneity was desirable also regarding the ties between members, e.g., children had to be chosen who had no strong likes or dislikes for one another. Finally, for the most pertinent purpose of our experiment, we tried to select children with an average capacity for leadership and social influence.

To rate the individual on these scores, we made some preliminary observations.

From *Human Relations*, 1949, II, 23–39. Reprinted by permission of Tavistock Publications, Ltd. The material contained in this article appeared in a larger Hungarian publication by the author, and with the author's consent was translated and prepared in its present form by Mrs. David Rappaport for *Human Relations*.

We saw the children of two day nurseries for 35 to 40 minutes each day for a period of two weeks. Two people worked simultaneously and afterward unified their notes. The observations were not selective: everything that occurred in the nursery during that period was chronologically and fully recorded. On the basis of these observations we picked out those children whose social qualities were an average for that nursery group and who were *not* leaders. Children were selected in whom the frequency of: (*a*) "following orders" greatly outnumbered "giving orders"; (*b*) imitation outnumbered being imitated; (*c*) participation in group play was an average in number as well as in degree of cooperation; and (*d*) acts of attacking, crying, telling on each other, were about the average of the group. Furthermore, their ties to one another had to be no more solid or lasting than to other members of the nursery.

The children were formed into a group. An assembly was considered a group when it developed a relatedness, with permanent rules, habits, traditions, entirely of its own.

The children chosen were put in a separate room. Their field was permanent: the same set of furniture, toys, and tools every day. In this room they spent 30 to 40 minutes each day. Their actions were fully recorded by two observers who later synchronized and combined their notes. The observers were completely passive.

The group thus met until a tendency to "institutionalization" became noticeable, and their habits and traditions appeared to become lasting. Only such habits were considered traditions as were not found in the day nurseries, but had developed during the experimental period. This gave us an objective criterion of the point at which an assembly constituted a group. To form a tradition from three to six meetings were needed.

The children formed traditions such as permanent seating order (who should sit where); permanent division of objects (who plays with what); group ownership of certain objects, ceremonies connected with their use, expressions of belonging together; returning to certain activities; rituals; sequence of games; forming a group jargon out of expressions accidentally uttered, etc.

A leader was placed in the group so formed. The leader was chosen from the same day nursery. He was a child who the nursery-school teachers—they had spent many days with him—considered to have initiative and directing power, who was older than the members of the group, and who, during the preliminary observation, more often gave than followed orders, more often was imitated than imitating, and more often was the attacker than the attacked.

Thus the leader was chosen because he was older, domineering, imitated, aggressive rather than submissive, and because he had initiative.

After the group had formed fixed traditions we added such a leader. The place, the objects remained the same. Recording went on as before.

What did we expect to learn from the experiment thus set up? Our question was: Do group habits and traditions change with the appearance of a leader? Does the leader introduce new habits, and does the group accept them? Does the group follow the leader, or does it force its traditions upon him? We see the group through its traditions—the objective expressions of the existing relationship. Hence, the vector of forces between the stronger leader and the group of weaker individuals is determined not by *who* gives the orders but by *what* the orders are. The question is not whether they accept leadership, but whether they give up their traditions by accepting what the leader initiates, whether they form new habits, rules, traditions, under his influence.

By carrying out this experiment we hoped to get the answer to our question.

The Experimental Plan

The experimental plan used the method of *varying the situation*. Individuals who scored high on leadership were observed in three situations:

1. In a larger group, where the members had no particular relationship with each other and where the leader's influence was felt by the group as a whole;

2. In a more closely knit group of the presocial stage formed through evolving group traditions; and

3. In a group with strong traditions of its own, facing a leader stronger than any one group member.

To record the entire process, we needed an adequate technique. We evolved a system of 76 symbols, each representing one complex act. The five people taking the notes synchronized them at 5-minute intervals.

Further variation was afforded through the objects in the room. By giving as many toys as there were children, we weakened group activity, since each could find something to do. By giving one object only we strengthened group activity, since all had to congregate around it. Setting a concrete task also strengthened the group. If an object familiar only to the leader was given, he was strengthened and the group weakened.

The choice of objects offers further possible variations which we have not sufficiently explored as yet.

We tried out many objects. Finally, the younger children (4 to 7 years) were given a tin toy house and a box of building blocks, the older ones (8 to 11 years) cardboard, picture magazines, scissors, crayons, paste, and paint brushes, and the instruction, "We want to make an exhibition." Of the latter objects there were fewer than there were children in the group, so that some manner of collaboration was required.

Most groups consisted of three children plus the leader, with some groups of four

and six as well. The number chosen was determined by previous observations which showed that spontaneously formed groups, up to the age of 7, lasted longer when consisting of three to four children, and, between the ages of 7 and 10, of three to six children. Larger groups easily disintegrated.

We worked with twelve groups. In them we tried out the power of penetration of twenty-six children capable of leadership. The ages of all children ranged from 4 to 11 years. The difference within a group never exceeded two years. In every case but one the leader was older than any group member.

The Conquered Conqueror

Let us now see the results of this experiment.

To summarize schematically, the same definite tendencies could be observed in all the experimental units: the group absorbed the leader, forcing its traditions on him. The leader takes over the habits and traditions of children who are younger than himself and who in the day nursery had been his underlings following his guidance. Now he engages in those activities which the group had developed before he entered it. His own undertakings either remain unsuccessful or gain acceptance only in a modified form suiting the traditions of that group.

Examples from our material demonstrate the point.

The table below will be understood from the following definitions:

Modeling is one of the most important types of social behavior. When a child's act or behavior is spontaneously imitated by some others, the child, we say, is *modeling*. When a child, even if unintentionally, imitates another—as members of a group do to take over each other's mode of behavior and thereby form common habits—we say that he is *being modeled*. We avoid the word "imitation" because it has a connotation of intention.

The ratio of *modeling* to *being modeled* is a measure of the social penetrating power of a person.

MODELING : BEING MODELED

Subject no.	In day nursery	In the experimental situation	
		Without leader	With leader
13 . . .	3 : 4	17 : 5	10 : 5
15 . . .	1 : 4	3 : 8	1 : 2
25 . . .	1 : 5	1 : 11	3 : 4
10 . . .	2 : 8	0 : 2	0 : 3
20 (leader)	6 : 3		5 : 11

The table shows the ratio *modeling/being modeled* of four children (Nos. 13, 15, 25, 10). In the day nursery all four tended to follow some model, rather than to serve as a model to others. It was for just this behavior that we selected them.

When they became members of a separate group forming its own traditions, a change occurred: one of the four children (No. 13) took on the modeling role, while the others went on being modeled.

It was after this change had taken place that the leader (No. 20) joined the group. In the day nursery he did the modeling: he served as a model six times, but followed another model only three times, making this ratio of social penetration 6 : 3. (Column 2 "In day nursery" shows an inverse ratio for all the others in this group.)

In the experimental situation—when the leader was confronted with a developed group—his ratio changed: his power of social penetration diminished. Formerly he was *modeling* (6 : 3), but now he was *being modeled* (5 : 11)—that is, the others did not take over his mode of action, but he took over the habits developed by the group. In other words, he followed those who in the day nursery had followed him.

In other groups and with other leaders a similar tendency was observed. The ratio *modeling/being modeled* of an extremely influential and willful leader in the day nursery changed from 9 : 5 to 0 : 8. For another such child the ratio changed from 6 : 2 to 1 : 6.

This portion of our results shows that, in a group possessing traditions, the leader introduced does not become the source of new habits and rules; rather, he will be the one to take over existing group traditions and thus to follow a model. This happens in spite of the fact that in the larger social formation (day nursery) he had served as a model to every member of the group.

Since "forming traditions" was our criterion of social influence, we came to the conclusion that, *confronted by a group having its own traditions, the leader proves weak; this in spite of the fact that when confronting them singly he is stronger than any one member of the group—stronger precisely as to his social penetrating power.*

PLAY OF FORCES

The last paragraph is only a schematic summary of our results. Reality is richer and more varied; what we see in reality is a wide variety of *tendencies*—a pull of the group force facing other pulls in other directions.

What does this mean? Though the group generally assimilates the leader, we find that it does so only on certain conditions and within certain limits. We find that the leading personality, while accepting the traditions and habits of the group, also influences and changes them. Let us then inquire into the modes of this influence, into the conditions which allow the assimilated leader to become that group's leader.

On the twenty-six leaders of the experiment the group force acted in varied ways.

At one extreme is the case where the group entirely assimilated the child who previously showed definite capacity to lead. This occurred in a group that possessed particularly strict traditions, and had well established and meticulously carried out rituals of activity. One such group played with a doll house and two dolls. In the course of three play periods they worked out a ritual of activity of playing around the house and of taking the dolls for a walk. The leader, one and a half years their senior, joining the group at its fourth meeting, tried to introduce something new (fourth and fifth play periods). He suggested a circle game and group singing. He was not followed. When he started singing alone they followed him for a few moments, then returned to their old game. The third time he came (sixth play period), the leader joined in the group's original game. Only for a few moments, here and there, did he start new activities, but he was followed by no one. At the seventh and eighth play periods no sign was left that this child had once (before these same children had developed a group habit) been a leader among them.

At the other extreme is the case of the child who proved to be stronger than the group: he broke its traditions. There was one such case. The leader, a little girl (a year and a half older than the members) completely reorganized the group. She gave orders, she modeled, she decided what to do and how to play. The rules she introduced took the place of those the group had had.

This group's history is important: it was subjected to increasing difficulties, while the leader was given virtual training in leadership. After the group had formed its habits, each day a different leader was introduced. In three days three different leaders tried to foist their initiative upon it and to change its rituals. Against these three leaders the group was able to preserve its customs, rejecting their suggestions, in the face of all the enticing and aggression these leaders tried out on it. However, the struggle exhausted the group and it began to weaken. This weakening showed itself in that the children more often played by themselves, less often played their old organized games, playing instead merely side by side. The traditions were still formally there, but the members of the group tended to observe them singly, by themselves. The group lost much of its coherence.

These are borderline cases. *In the overwhelming majority of our cases the leader was forced to accept the group's traditions —that is, he proved weaker than the group but still managed to play the role of leader.* We observed each leader's ways of doing this.

1. The Order-giver. The group whose data on "modeling" and "being modeled" was given above had fully developed customs when the leader was introduced. The new boy, older, more experienced, and more of a leader than any member of the group, attempted to take over. He gave orders, made suggestions, bossed everybody. The children carefully avoided him, ignored his orders, and carried on in their traditions.

Soon the leader found himself alone. Suddenly his behavior changed, he joined the group in its activities and quickly learned its rituals. He learned their expressions, their habits, their games. During his second play period with them, he again gave orders. Though keeping within the frame of activities he had just learned from them, and according to their rules, he told the children what to do—that is, he ordered them to do exactly what they would have done anyway. He appropriated the leadership without being able to change the group's traditions. The members accepted this situation by following his orders, since this did not change their habitual activities.

The data on the frequency of group activity shows this. The following table contains the proportion of *order-giving* to *order-following*.

ORDER-GIVING : ORDER-FOLLOWING

Experimental subject no.	In day nursery	In experimental situation	
		Without leader	With leader
13 . . .	3 : 5	3 : 6	1 : 4
15 . . .	1 : 2	8 : 1	0 : 2
25 . . .	1 : 4	0 : 2	2 : 5
10 . . .	2 : 3	0 : 3	0 : 3
20 . . .	12 : 2		11 : 3

Four members of the group (Nos. 13, 15, 25, 10) were *order-followers* in the day nursery. After they had formed a separate homogeneous group, one of them (No. 15) became an *order-giver*. When group habits were developed and a leader (No. 20) was added, all followed the leader's orders, as in the day nursery. In the group with a tradition, the leader became just as much of an order-giver (11 : 3) as he was in the day nursery (12 : 2). Regarding order-giving, then, the leader was stronger than the group (he gave orders—they accepted them). At the same time, however, he was the one to copy the others; he took over their ways (his modeling proportion changed from 6 : 3 to 5 : 11).

If a person should observe the group for only a short period of time, for example by the Goodenough 1-minute or 5-minute method, he would see a leader giving orders and a group obeying. A prolonged observation of the group plus its history would, however, soon disclose the inner workings of this *order-giving:* the leader gives such orders as have reference to the group's traditional activities; he expropriates the leadership without changing the group's traditional modes of activity.

The leader is weaker than the group because he takes over its traditions and because his own suggestions do not take root. At the same time he is also stronger because everyone follows his orders.

The gist of the phenomenon lies just in this dichotomy.

The leader is stronger than any one group member. (He gives orders—they obey.) He is weaker than *group traditions* and is forced to accept them. He is stronger than the individual member, weaker than the "plus" which a group is over and above the sum of the individuals in it. He is stronger than the members, weaker than the formation.

In the relationship between group and leader, two factors stand out: (1) the group as a particular order of quality, whose strength is expressed by the change of the leader's modeling proportion (from 6 : 3 to 5 : 11); and (2) the members, whose *weakness* is expressed by the constancy (12 : 2 to 11 : 3) of the leader's ratio of *order-giving/order-following.*

Thus the curious situation obtains where the order-giver imitates, while the models follow the orders of their imitator.

What appears here is the "group plus" —the unique reality of a group—experimentally verified.

2. The Proprietor. A second way in which leadership may express itself is ownership: the leader joining the developed group takes possession of all the objects in the room. They continue being used according to group tradition; the games played with them remain the same. The leader joins in these games, but all the objects "belong" to him. The following table presents the data on this phenomenon, concerning the group discussed before.

FREQUENCY OF OBJECT APPROPRIATION

(Borrows or takes away from another child)

Experimental subject no.	In the experimental situation	
	Without leader	With leader
13	21	1
15	9	0
25	7	1
10	3	1
20		12

The frequency of taking possession of objects sharply falls for group members, and rises for the leader.

Into some groups, after traditions had been formed, outstanding leading personalities were placed—leaders obeyed in the day nursery by everyone, virtual dictators to more than thirty children. Let us follow one of them. If a child's behavior displeased him, he beat up that child; he allowed no opposition, and always had to have his way. The group into which he was put consisted of children younger than himself, children who in the day nursery always obeyed him. The result was unexpected: this structured group virtually swallowed him. (His proportion of modeling changed from 9 : 5 to 0 : 8). He followed the group's every activity, accepted its every custom, while his own suggestions were *never* followed.

However, his exceptional personality still asserted itself with the group. The children gave him every object without his asking, and with that acknowledged his authority. The group had two traditional activities: using blocks they built a train, and using chairs they built a bridge. The leader soon learned these constructions and used the objects acquired to build just these. From time to time the group gathered around him, eloquently praising whatever he did. They praised his beautiful creation, his skill, the wonderful things he made (which he had learned from them), as if to placate some dangerous genie. At the same time they followed him in nothing; on the contrary they drew him into their own activities and caused him to accept their habits. Their play remained unchanged; the same game with the same toys. They talked of the toys as they did before—Johnny's blocks, Tom's box—but occasionally they said; "The blocks belong to Andrew" (Andrew was the leader), or: "Tom's box belongs to Andrew." The owners of the objects became their users, while the right of

ownership was given over, voluntarily or otherwise, to the new leader.

Observation over only a short period would lead to mistaken conclusions. One might see only that one child has all the toys, while the others surround and admire him. Only prolonged observation would show that those are but scenes of ceremonial offerings with which the children purchase, as it were, the leader's continued trust, with which they protect their traditions.

Again we see that apparently the leader is stronger than *the members* of the group (he appropriates their belongings), but weaker than *the group* because he is forced to accept its customs, traditions, and forms of activity.

3. The Diplomat. The third way of asserting leadership, as observed in our experimental situation, is quite devious. The cases belonging here are peculiar. The leader, having a greater force of social penetration than the group members, attempts to force upon them a new mode of activity. He fails. However, the leader, for reasons as yet unclear to us— perhaps through his personality, perhaps because of the tense situation—does not get lost in the group, nor take over its habits, as did those leaders who complied in order to rule or in order to take possession of the toys.

This type of leader takes a roundabout course: he accepts the traditions of the group in order to change them.

Into old forms he pours new contents. What takes place here is a veritably dramatic struggle. We had one group with particularly strong traditions and institutionalization. This group rose to the highest level of spontaneous organization of games: to the level of division of roles.

One of the children, who in the day nursery showed no leadership, in this narrower group developed into a leader: games he suggested were followed, and their various parts became traditional with the group. It was at this point that a new leader was added. He tried to suggest new games but was not accepted. Then he joined their traditional game and slowly took over the leadership. The first day there were only two instances in which he led, the second day there were already nine. However, he was the one being modeled, taking over the group's habits. He accepted those habits but introduced minute changes. For example, he joined in the block game traditional with the group, but he demanded that always the red side of a block be on top. He was being modeled, he imitated, but he also introduced changes; then he became the leader of the traditional activities thus changed.

The third time he was with the group he again suggested new activities. One was "hide and seek." (They had a game involving hiding, and this feature attracted the leader). The group did not accept the suggestion and played instead another traditional game they called "acting with hats."

The leader yielded, joined the "hat game" and instantly began to organize it, in the course of which he made changes so as to combine with it the hide-and-seek game he had suggested. He was *being modeled* to the group, but he also *modeled* the group; he accepted their traditions but changed them.

His roundabout road to leadership is clear here:

1. *He tries to do away with the group traditions and lead it on to new ones.*

2. *He is rejected.*

3. *He accepts the traditions and quickly learns them.*

4. *Within the frame of those traditions he soon assumes leadership, and, though reluctantly, the group follows him because he does a good job.*

5. *He introduces insignificant variations, loosening the tradition.*

6. *He then introduces new elements into the ritual already weakened by variation.*

In this case accepting the traditions is a roundabout way to introducing new

ones. This is a very active process in which the leader plays an important role. Only children with exceptional social influence and a great deal of initiative could act this way.

Thus, between the extremes of total assimilation and total conquest, we find three types of behavior. In the experimental situation the leader either (1) is being modeled—but gives orders; or (2) is being modeled—but obtains possession of the toys; or again (3) is being modeled—but he also models the others.

It has to be emphasized that in all these cases the leader must accept the traditions and can give orders only within their framework. The following is a nice example: into a well-developed group of children, 4 to 5 years old, a leader of $6\frac{1}{2}$ with a strong personality was introduced. The group had traditional ways of using the toys. It was exactly determined who would play with what. Each toy, though they might exchange them for a while, traditionally constituted the possession of a certain child.

The leader was unable to change this rule of ownership. Yet he found himself a place in the system. At the beginning of the play period he distributed the objects, giving each child the one that "belonged to him." The children continued to ask the "owners" for the blocks or boxes when they wanted to play with them; they continued to exchange toys as before. Only now the blocks, house, or boxes were distributed by the leader at the beginning of the period. Thus he found himself a role in an order which was there when he first arrived, though unable essentially to change the existing traditions.

THE FORMING OF TRADITION

We have examined the influence of the group on a new leader. We have seen that the group forces its traditions on the leader; and that with varying circumstances the process involves changes, while the basic tendency remains the same. We have seen that the capitulating leader still makes his superior personality felt. Even though he accepts the group's traditions, he exerts an influence. Even in the case of total assimilation of the leader we find changes in the group's life which can be ascribed to his influence.

For example, one group always built trains out of blocks. The leader followed this activity. He too built trains, only he put a chimney on his locomotive. The others followed suit.

Another group's traditional game was to climb up and hang on to the top edge of a wardrobe and to swing there. The leader—of the type that gives orders but is being modeled—soon joined the game. Only one child at a time could swing on the wardrobe. On each side stood a chair to climb up on. Shortly after the leader joined the group he introduced a "one-way traffic." Everything went on as before with the exception that the children had to climb up one side and down the other. This innovation added color to the game without changing its structure. Such phenomena occurred often. Almost every leader, just as soon as he met the group, reorganized it, introducing direction and order.

In other cases this coloring lent by the leader pertained rather to the contents, as when a fitting little story was introduced. One group that played with a small house said: "This is the mailman's house—in the evening he comes home—in the morning he leaves." In the game itself there was no mailman. The children put nothing into the house. The mailman was not even symbolically represented. The words were merely additional coloring. On this the leader elaborated: "The mailman brings coal—they put it on wagons and trucks, etc." The others took over these little themes and their activity, though undamaged, became more colorful.

Often the leader would step up the pace of activity. This is another way to impose his will on the group. He would dictate a very fast tempo, driving them. A certain type of leader is needed to create this acceleration of pace: a child who is very active, who has many interests, whose attention is divided, and who has a stormy temperament. Such leaders busy themselves with several things at once, join several games at once, and with their "swing" accelerate the group's life.

An interesting influence of the leader is the *widening of the terrain*. The group's accustomed space becomes larger: a group that has worked in one portion of the room will, after the leader appears, expand into the entire room. The way this occurs clearly shows the relationship between a developed group and a new leader.

One group would play around a table in the middle of the room. From time to time they would go to the wardrobe in one corner of the room and try to climb up. Then the new leader appropriated the table, whereupon a migration to the wardrobe took place where they started the game of climbing up. The leader followed them and started organizing that game. Slowly the children shifted back to the table, but the leader was on their trail. The result was a pendulum-like movement between table and wardrobe. Then one child went to a new place and started doing something there. At once the leader extended his pendulum motion to that place. A veritable pilgrimage began. Everywhere the leader was being modeled: he was the one who adjusted to the others' mode of activity.

Another frequent influence of the leader is that he changes the degree of concerted action. The degree of group action is not to be confused with the degree of creative activity of a person. When a presocial formation of four people sit together, one reading a philosophical treatise, the other solving a mathematical problem, the third writing an ode, etc., without having anything in common with each other, the group is of a lower social level than a foursome playing bridge.

During our investigations we observed that in some cases the leader brings a presocial group to a higher degree of concerted action, in other cases to a lower one. If, for example, a group that has merely congregated around a set of toys is organized into one with a division of roles, the group level has been raised. It will be lowered if group activity is reduced to mere side-by-side play. Such raising or lowering of group level depends mostly on the personal qualities of the leader, especially on his capacity to organize. The capacity consists of the bent to remember every custom, to see to it that objects are returned where they belong and that the rituals are observed, even if these were learned from the group. The leader who has this quality raises the group level even if he totally submits to the group's traditions.

The Power of the Group

Our question was: Which is stronger, the group made up of individuals of average social penetration, or the individual of high degree of social penetration but alien to the group?

Our criterion was, not the relationship between the new leader and the individual group members, but that "plus" arising from "groupness" which raises the power of the group above the aggregate strength of its members. This "plus" shows in the habits, customs, rules, and relationships making for institutionalization. Accordingly, the individual is the stronger of the two if he can change those traditions; but the group is the stronger if it assimilates the leader.

Couching our inquiry in these terms lent decisive importance to the ratio *modeling/being modeled*.

Our investigations have shown that the group with a tradition is stronger than the leader (though he is stronger than any one group member).

The play of forces between leader and group resulted in the following graduations:

1. The leader is totally assimilated;
2. The leader is being modeled but gives orders;
3. The leader is being modeled but gains possession of the toys;
4. The leader is being modeled but modifies the traditions;
5. The leader destroys the group's traditions and introduces new ones. It is rare that the leader should become not only the center of the group but also the maker of its rules.

Which of these five situations will obtain depends on:

1. The degree of crystallization of traditions;
2. The extent of collaborative play;
3. The degree of group cohesion (the marginal child included).

These conditions issue from the nature of the group. It is no doubt important what kind of person, what character type the new leader is. It may be that in the child who expropriates the toys in order to set himself up as leader a desire for acquisition asserts itself; it may be that the child who gives orders is driven by narcissism and aggression. However, our investigation did not extend to these motivations.

Even the leader who is forced to accept existing traditions makes his superiority felt: he may lend color to activities, step up the pace, widen the field, or change the group level by influencing cohesion.

In our experiment, individuals of strong social penetrating power seldom became changers of traditions; however, being modeled to the existing traditions, they influenced them.

We were thus able to experience that "plus" which makes the group more than and different from the aggregate of its members: as in cases where the new leader conquered everyone, where each child followed his orders—as long as *what* he ordered was in agreement with the group's traditions.

It is in this peculiar strength of tradition that this group "plus" appears. Its carriers are the individuals constituting the group. By belonging to the group each is "more" and stronger. This became clear when children who in the day nursery were *being modeled* by leaders there, became the models of these leaders in the organized group.

Thus the group "plus" is not some substance hovering above the group: it is the hold their customs and habits have on the members; it is tradition, the carrier of which is the individual, who, in turn, is strengthened by it. Conceivably, the feeling of heightened intensity always evoked by group experience is the experiencing of just this "plus."

Why does the leader accept the group's traditions? Is it because he is weaker than its members, or more suggestible? No. We have seen him in the day nursery, modeling the others. Is it because he is in a new situation where the group members have the advantage of being familiar with the situation? This is contraindicated by the behavior of

leaders who give orders quite without inhibition. The dichotomy is clear: the leader is supraordinated since he gives orders; but he is also subordinated since he is being modeled. He has the upper hand *vis à vis* the members but has to bow to group tradition.

Thus the reaction of the group to the new leader clearly brings into view the power of the group "plus." It is this "plus" that is stronger than the leader, who is stronger than any one group member.

With this we can discard all hypotheses which deny the uniqueness of the group, and which attempt fully to account for the group by assessing its members.

Our experiment refutes the prejudice of metaphysical social psychology that the group, through an evening effect, lowers the level of the individual. We observed exactly the opposite: the strength of the group strengthens its members. Group experience not only pleases, it also strengthens.

SOCIAL RELATIONS AND INNOVATION IN THE MEDICAL PROFESSION: THE EPIDEMIOLOGY OF A NEW DRUG   By Herbert Menzel and Elihu Katz

In the last few years, research on communications and opinion formation has taken more and more account of the various ways in which interpersonal relations may "intervene" in the communication process. Thus, for example, the role played by personal influence in affecting individual decisions has re-

ceived increasing attention. Events in the world outside, be they political acts, technological innovations, or fashion releases, seem to impinge upon the individual not so much through the direct channels of the mass media, as through the mediation of face-to-face contacts with other individuals—some of whom,

From the *Public Opinion Quarterly*, 1955–56, XIX, 337–352. Reprinted by permission of the authors and the publisher. This paper is Publication No. A-190 of the Bureau of Applied Social Research, Columbia University. The study was supported by a grant from Chas. Pfizer & Co., Inc., manufacturers of chemicals and pharmaceuticals. The authors acknowledge the contribution of Dr. Joseph A. Precker, then director of market research, at Pfizer & Co., in initiating the study and in participating in its design. Contributions to various phases of the planning of the study were made by James Coleman, Philip Ennis, Marjorie Fiske, and Rolf Meyersohn, all then of the Bureau of Applied Social Research. See also Katz' review article, "The Two-step Flow of Communication—An Up-to-date Report on an Hypothesis," *Pub. Op. Quart.*, 1957, XXI, 61–78.

in turn, are affected by the mass media.[1] This realization of the role of so-called "opinion leaders" has been accompanied by another awareness: sources of influence which are not inherently relevant to the subject matter at hand must be considered even where expert opinions and specialized sources of information are available. Among the sources which influence a very wide arc of the individual's behavior with very little respect for the boundaries of subject matter are enduring networks of social contacts. Thus, for example, in politics, neither the newspaper editor nor even the ward heeler appear to affect the individual's vote as powerfully as his parents, his spouse, or his ethnic and religious loyalties.[2]

But personal influence is not the only aspect of interpersonal relations which is relevant to an understanding of the flow of mass communications and their effects on individual decisions. The extent of an individual's integration in a group may be an important variable, for example. Thus, one study has shown that children who are relatively well integrated in groups of peers tend to make quite different use of adventure stories on the radio than children who are relatively isolated from such contacts.[3] Or, an earlier study has shown that Allied propaganda to German troops did not take effect until the soldier was cut off from his intimate, interpersonal ties—when his own small unit of peers and noncommissioned officers broke up.[4]

If "belonging or not belonging" is a key variable, so is belonging to one group rather than another. An individual is ordinarily reluctant to depart from the norms of his particular group, unless the departure itself receives some form of group support, and a communication aimed at influencing his thoughts or actions may therefore fail. When changes occur, it is usually only when the individual perceives that his group approves, or that support comes from a dissident subgroup, or from an outside group toward which the individual sees himself moving or whose presumed standards he accepts.[5]

COMMUNICATION IN THE MEDICAL PROFESSION

A current study on the flow of scientific information in the medical profession has provided an opportunity to apply these ideas to a new and substantively different sociological field. By contrast to earlier studies of opinion formation and decision-making, we are dealing here with a relatively closed community of specialists. We are not concerned with topics where everybody

[1] See, e.g., Paul Lazarsfeld, Bernard Berelson, and Hazel Gaudet, The People's Choice, 2d ed., (New York: Columbia University Press, 1948), Ch. XVI, R. K. Merton, "Patterns of Influence," in Paul Lazarsfeld and Frank Stanton (eds.), Communication Research 1948–49 (New York: Harper & Brothers, 1949); and Elihu Katz and Paul Lazarsfeld, Personal Influence (Glencoe, Ill.: Free Press, 1955).

[2] See Bernard Berelson, Paul F. Lazarsfeld, and William McPhee, Voting (Chicago: University of Chicago Press, 1954).

[3] M. W. Riley and J. W. Riley, "A Sociological Approach to Communications Research," Pub. Op. Quart., 1951, XV, 445–460.

[4] E. A. Shils and M. Janowitz, "Cohesion and Disintegration in the Wehrmacht," Pub. Op. Quart., 1948, XII, 280–315.

[5] This thinking is implicit, for example, in Kurt Lewin's approach to "Group Decision and Social Change" (see pp. 197–212) and in subsequent studies in this tradition. An important illustration is H. H. Kelley and E. H. Volkart, "The Resistance to Change of Group-anchored Attitudes," Am. Sociol. Rev., 1952, XVII, 453–465. Of obvious relevance, too, is the tradition of research and theory concerning "reference groups" synthesized in R. K. Merton and A. Kitt, "Contributions to the Theory of Reference Group Behavior," in Merton and Lazarsfeld (eds.), Continuities in Social Research: Studies in the Scope and Method of the American Soldier (Glencoe, Ill.: Free Press, 1950).

is supposed to be entitled to his own opinion but with matters based on scientific findings, where the relevant expert sources are generally recognized, easily identified, and universally available. The hypothesis of the roles of less expert sources and of interpersonal channels as mediators of influences is therefore put to a more crucial test.[6]

The general concern of this project is physicians' reactions to innovations in therapy, particularly with regard to new drugs. Drugs, unlike other matters of medical practice, have standardized names and easily ascertainable release dates, and it is possible to pinpoint the time of first use of a drug by each physician. In this sense, then, the process of diffusion of a new drug can be traced through the social structure of the medical community.

The data we shall draw upon are from a pilot study conducted in May, 1954, in a New England city of approximately 30,000; 33 of the 40 doctors practicing in the community were interviewed. Since the behavior in which we are interested (prescribing of new drugs) can take place only among physicians, we have thus interviewed 83 percent of the relevant members of the community. But because of the small number of cases, the findings must be treated as highly tentative. We present these early results primarily for the purpose of calling attention to the clues implicit here for research in the flow of influence and innovation. The analysis of later interviews with over 200 doctors in the Midwest is reported in later publications (see footnote 7).

In this paper, we will consider the ways in which the doctor's position in the social structure of his local medical fraternity affects his acceptance of new pharmaceutical products. Our procedure differs from that of most previous studies which have sought to trace the role of personal influences in individual decisions. Typically, in these other studies, individuals who have recently made some decision are first identified and whenever their account shows that another person has figured in the decision, they are asked to identify this "opinion leader." The nature of the social relationship between the influential person and the person influenced, as well as the characteristics differentiating the two, are then determined.

In our study, however, we first interviewed *all* the local doctors we could and, by means of three sociometric questions, determined the network of social relations among them without reference to any one particular decision. The channels of information and influence which entered into a recent drug decision were also ascertained in all interviews, and compared with the doctor's position in the social network. Only then did we superimpose on the social network the flow of adoptions of a new practice, as indicated by the precise sequence of dates on which each respondent introduced a certain new medication. This latter information was obtained through an examination of the prescription files of local pharmacies.

SOCIOMETRIC QUESTIONS, STARS, AND ISOLATES

To locate each of the 33 physician-respondents in the structure of his local medical community, three sociometric questions were asked. The first question was, "Could you name the three or four

---

[6] This is not, of course, to say that such communication is "unscientific"; direct communication among colleagues is vital to all sciences. This paper attempts to show how influential such communication is, even on the local level, and in spite of the existence of multitudes of professional journals which—potentially—bring relevant articles by the top authorities in each field directly to the desk of each practicing physician.

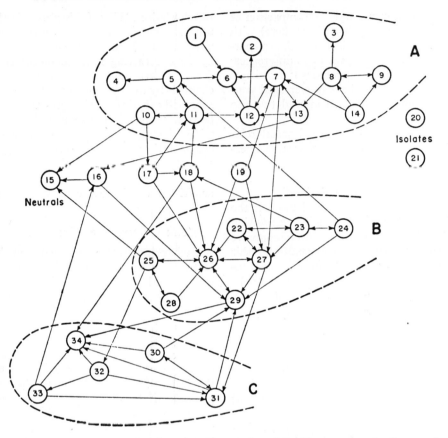

FIG. 1. Sociogram showing answers to the question, "Could you name the three or four physicians whom you meet most frequently on social occasions?" Each circle represents a physician. Out-of-sample and out-of-town choices are omitted, except for Dr. 34 who was not interviewed but is included here because of the large number of choices he is given.

physicians you meet most frequently on social occasions?" The resulting sociogram is shown in Figure 1.[7] Three major networks of choices appear, designated *A*, *B*, and *C*. (*B* and *C* may also be regarded as subgroups of the same network, since their segregation from one another is not as definite as that of either from

A.) There are also two isolated individuals and five "neutrals," who choose into cliques *A* and *B* equally.

A second sociometric question was aimed at a more specialized kind of social contact: "Who are the three or four physicians in your conversations with whom the subject of drug therapy

[7] The sociogram was constructed by a trial-and-error method. Clusters of mutually choosing stars were first identified, and others then grouped around them, so that individuals were nearest that cluster to which they seemed most closely tied, and so that cross-overs were minimized. For the larger study which is reported in the publications listed below, it was necessary to develop more standardized techniques. See Coleman, Katz, and Menzel, "The Diffusion of an Innovation among Physicians," *Sociometry*, 1957, XX, 253–270; Menzel, "Public and Private Conformity under Different Conditions of Acceptance in the Group," *J. Abnorm. & Soc. Psychol.*, 1957, LV, 398–402; Coleman, Katz, and Menzel, *Doctors and New Drugs: A Case Study in the Diffusion of an Innovation* (Glencoe, Ill.: The Free Press, In preparation.)

most often comes up?" A comparison of the resulting map (not shown here) with Figure I shows that the basic pattern holds for both, with two differences: fewer drug-talk companions than friends are named, and there is increased concentration of attention around two top leaders.

A third map of informal social relations was obtained by still another question: "When you need added information or advice about questions of drug therapy, where do you usually turn?" This question was designed to elicit the names of individuals to whom a position of authority is accorded. As might have been anticipated, the responses in this case were even more heavily concencentrated on a small number of stars.

As we have indicated in the introduction, the role of interpersonal relations in individual decisions is not confined to the conveying of information and to the channeling of influence. For example, a doctor who shares an office with another may feel less hesitant about the risk of trying out new drugs in general, and not merely because of anything the other doctor may have said about any particular drug; or, a doctor whose friendship is not reciprocated by other doctors may develop quite a different relationship to other channels of information—he may become more friendly with the pharmaceutical salesman, for example—than the doctor who is well integrated in the medical community. Thus, a doctor's association with other doctors may serve (1) as an important source of information and influence on a particular innovation, and (2) as an important determinant of his response to innovations in general, and to information and influence emanating from other sources.

For this reason, the sociometric data will be related to doctors' behavior in two basically distinct ways. The first of these is the examination of certain characteristics which differentiate individuals who have received many and few socio-

metric choices. What, for instance, is the use made of the diverse channels of communication by the sociometric stars— by those receiving many choices? How does it differ from the use made of these channels by their less popular colleagues? A second use of the sociometric data will be to ask what difference it makes with *which* doctors a given doctor is associated, rather than *how many* name him, say, as a friend. For example, is a doctor more ready to adopt a new drug if he has friends who have already adopted it?

THE CHANNELS OF INFLUENCE

Each respondent was asked how he had learned about two of the drugs he had recently adopted. Table 1 crosstabulates the replies with the popularity of the doctor among his colleagues. An interesting pattern emerges. Journal reading plays a much larger role in the drug adoptions of doctors who receive one or more designations than among the isolates. This conforms to the hypothesis of the "two-step flow of communications," which states, in essence, that messages originating outside of the individual's face-to-face group do not impinge on him directly, but are mediated by a few members of his group, who expose themselves to messages from the outside world more than their confreres.

The source of this hypothesis is in mass-media research, where it has been found that opinion leaders are in closer contact with the mass media than their followers. But doctors can keep in touch with the outside world in other ways than through the printed media—e.g., by attendance at medical meetings in other cities. The two-step flow hypothesis, therefore, leads one to expect that out-of-town meetings as well as journals would be more important in the decisions of the most popular drug-discussion partners than in those of their less popular colleagues. Table 1 bears out this expectation: only those who receive three

TABLE 1

DRUG-TALK CHOICES AND CHANNELS EMPLOYED IN DECISIONS ON TWO
RECENT DRUG ADOPTIONS *

	Drug-talk choices received (by percentage)		
	None	One, two	Three or more
Mail and periodicals from drug houses	30	18	21
Journal articles	10	39	32
Detail men (salesmen)	40	25	21
Colleagues	15	13	16
Meetings	0	0	11
Other channels	5	3	0
(No. of channels)	(20)	(34)	(19)

* The percentages are based on the total number of channels mentioned, which exceeds the number of doctors in each category, since many doctors reported on two decisions, and the average number of channels per decision was 1.88.

choices or more report that what they learned at meetings entered into their decisions. It would seem that the star does indeed serve as a relay: he incorporates what he has learned at the meetings into his own decisions and, it may be assumed, into his conversations with others.

The drug decisions of the sociometric isolate, by contrast, are marked by heavier reliance on commercial sources—direct-mail advertising from the pharmaceutical companies and the "detail man" as the drug house representative is called. These sources, to be sure, also come from out of town. What differentiates them from journals and meetings is that, being commercial sources, they carry less prestige, and that it requires less effort to keep up with them. Evidently the two-step flow hypothesis does not apply to *all* channels from the outside world. Some of the channels *do* impinge on most members of their intended audiences directly and are not disproportionately utilized by the opinion leaders.

Incidentally, the differential importance which the detail man has for the social isolate is not limited to his role as a purveyor of information about new

medicines. Two of the four doctors who received no friendship choices volunteered the information that they very often talked with the detail man on subjects other than drugs: "We'll get off the track sometimes on economics, politics, family affairs," said one. Another relatively isolated doctor commented on the detail men as follows:

They are helpful—they know all the doctors in the communities around here and give you all the dirt and gossip and incidental news about what is going on amongst the doctors in this community.

This pharmaceutical salesman evidently serves as a near-professional companion for men who are relatively cut off from informal contacts with other physicians.

A final observation from Table 1 yields a surprise. The classic model of the two-step flow of communication provides that it is the rank-and-file members who are influenced by the opinion leaders, while the latter are influenced by the mass media. But in Table 1 "colleagues" are mentioned exactly as frequently by opinion leaders as by the rest. The most likely explanation is that the opinion leaders may themselves turn to colleagues of even higher status, and that

TABLE 2

USE OF CHANNELS OF COMMUNICATION IN DECISIONS REGARDING ACUTE AND
CHRONIC CONDITIONS *

	Percent of total channels mentioned	
	Acute conditions	Chronic conditions
Mail and periodicals from drug houses	23	17
Articles in journals	26	27
Detail men	33	27
Colleagues	7	22
Meetings	0	5
Other channels	10	2
(No. of channels)	(30)	(41)

* The percentages are based on the total number of channels mentioned, which exceeds the number of doctors in each category, since many doctors reported on two decisions, and the average number of channels per decision was 1.88.

it may take three or four steps, perhaps rather than two, before a level of leadership is reached where dependence on personal contacts is markedly decreased.[8]

Revision of the model to allow for multistep flow of communications would thus seem in order. A second revision has already been pointed out: messages from the outside world need not come through the printed word or other mass media. In the case of physicians, we have seen that attendance at society meetings may take over this function. As the multistep flow hypothesis is applied to still other publics, it may be found that the opinion leader can keep in touch with relevant parts of the outside world in still other ways. Finally, the model may not apply to channels of low prestige and unusually easy accessibility.

One more finding, still tentative, regarding the channels of information used in recent drug decisions is especially worthy of attention. Medical problems differ widely in the degree to which their answers are well-structured and generally established. Table 1 includes the reports of doctors concerning their adoptions of a variety of different drugs. We can,

however, divide these into two broad classes: one class of drugs is applicable to certain acute conditions which call for immediate action and present a very small number of alternate methods of treatment; success or failure is visible in a day or two. The other class of drugs is applicable to chronic conditions where many dozens of treatments compete, and the effectiveness of therapy is very difficult to gauge. We find that colleagues constitute only seven percent of the channels reported as leading up to the adoption of a drug for the acute conditions but represent 22 percent of channels concerned with the chronic diseases. In other words, the role of colleagues increases substantially in the relatively more ambiguous situation (see Table 2). In a sense, this recalls the studies of suggestion and influence by Sherif and others: the role of personal influence is more important in the relatively more unstructured situation.

THE SOCIAL NETWORK AND THE
DIFFUSION OF DRUG ADOPTIONS

To explore further the workings of person-to-person relations in this realm, we

[8] Regarding the relatively low over-all frequency of mentions of "colleagues" in Table 1, see note 12 below.

TABLE 3

DATE OF FIRST PRESCRIPTION OF A SPECIFIED NEW DRUG BY EACH DOCTOR *

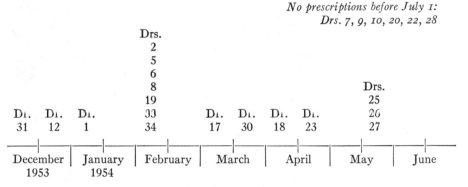

No prescriptions before July 1:
Drs. 7, 9, 10, 20, 22, 28

			Drs. 2 5 6 8 19 33 34					Drs. 25 26 27		
D₁. 31	D₁. 12	D₁. 1		D₁. 17	D₁. 30	D₁. 18	D₁. 23			
December 1953	January 1954	February		March	April		May		June	

* Each doctor is represented by his identifying number. Doctors following specialties not usually prescribing drugs through commercial pharmacies are omitted.

shall now turn from correlates of the number of sociometric designations received to the question, "What difference does it make to *which* clique you belong?" Age, ethnicity, religion, father's occupation, and pursuing a specialty practice were all found to be correlated with clique membership. The existence of these background correlations lends some feel of reality to the division into cliques which the sociometric data indicated.[9] In order to relate the social network to the adoption of a new item of behavior, the local pharmacists were asked to search their files for the first prescription written by each of the interviewed doctors for a certain drug which had come on the market a few months before. Table 3 is a presentation of the chronological order in which doctors in the sample adopted the drug. (Surgeons and other specialists not normally prescribing drugs through pharmacies are excluded from this table.) Intervals on the table correspond roughly to the time intervals involved.

Our original intention was simply to correlate early or late use of the new drug with characteristics of individual doctors. But after Table 3 was drawn up, we were intrigued by the strange alternation of slow periods and spurts which it shows: first, three pioneers adopt the new drug at three-week intervals. Then, suddenly, during a period of only eleven days in February seven doctors start writing prescriptions for the new drug. During the next three months, only four doctors start prescribing the drug, at widely spaced intervals. Then, again, three doctors initiate use of the drug within a period of only five days in mid-May. No further doctors appear on the table after this, although our data are complete for an additional month and a half. There thus remain six doctors who either do not prescribe the drug at all, or do so only at an unknown time very much later than any of their colleagues.[10]

How is this alternation of slow and fast periods to be accounted for? One possibility is, of course, that the fast

[9] Our findings fit very well with Oswald Hall's much more extensive study of interpersonal relations in a New England medical community considerably larger than the one under discussion here. See "The Informal Organization of the Medical Profession," *Canadian J. Eco. & Polit. Sci.*, 1946, XII, No. 1.

[10] Data collected elsewhere subsequent to the termination of this survey make it likely that most of those "diehards" did at least try out the new drug some time during 1951.

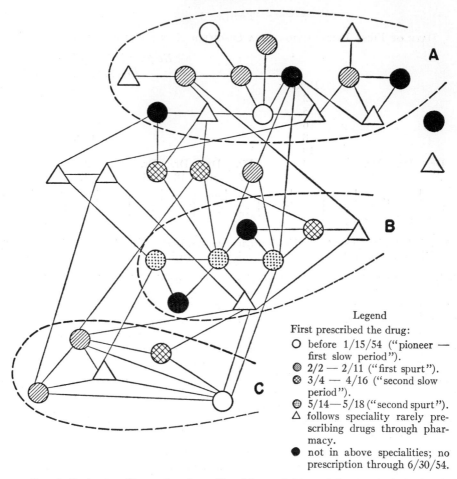

Legend

First prescribed the drug:

○   before 1/15/54 ("pioneer — first slow period").

◍   2/2 — 2/11 ("first spurt").

⊗   3/4 — 4/16 ("second slow period").

⊕   5/14—5/18 ("second spurt").

△   follows speciality rarely prescribing drugs through pharmacy.

●   not in above specialities; no prescription through 6/30/54.

FIG. 2. Sociogram illustrating the epidemiology of doctors' drug prescriptions.

periods are those when there is more need for this particular drug in the community—times of epidemics, for instance. However, the slow and fast periods do not coincide with the known seasonal variations in the incidence of diseases for which this drug is indicated. A second possible explanation for the alternation of slow and fast periods is that the two fast periods correspond to two sales campaigns that may have been carried on by the pharmaceutical companies involved. This may be the case but fails to explain why certain doctors responded to the first campaign, while others did not.

The third possibility is that the alternations can be accounted for by social relations. During the initial slow period a few hardy individuals try out the new product—perhaps watched with interest by their more conservative colleagues. Each spurt then represents the almost simultaneous adoption of the drug by a well-integrated group of physicians. This hypothesis, unlike the other two, would not only explain why spurts occur at all but also why it is the *particular* doctors who participate in each spurt that act in unison—e.g., why Drs. *A, B, C,* and *D* act simultaneously, but not Drs. *D, E,* and *F*.

We therefore decided to bring together the data on first prescription dates with the data on social groupings. The result is the sociogram in Figure 2 which is identical with Figure 1 but adds information on the date of each doctor's first prescription for the new drug. Different shadings denote the time periods during which each doctor first prescribed it. Triangles indicate doctors following specialties not normally prescribing drugs through pharmacies. Solid circles indicate other doctors who did not prescribe the drug at all during the period covered by the survey. Let us now trace the flow of the innovation through this map of friendships among the physicians. Two questions will occupy us as we do so: (a) are doctors who adopt the drug on successive dates in contact with one another? (b) is each spurt of adoptions located within one of the cliques?

1. *Initial Slow Period*. The first three doctors are symbolized by blank circles. Their initial prescriptions took place on December 1, December 22, and January 10.

2. *First Spurt*. Seven physicians represented by single hatched circles adopted the drug between February 1 and 11. Four of them are in direct contact with a pioneer (i.e., a blank circle), and the remaining three have second-order contact with a pioneer.

At the end of this February spurt, three out of four doctors in clique *C* have used the drug; so have six out of eight doctors in clique *A*; but not a single member of clique *B*. (Surgeons and other nonprescribing specialists are excluded.) Even more striking than this contrast between the proportions of each clique who have used the drug by February 11 is another fact. One might think that the remainder of cliques *A* and *C* would follow suit after some lag—perhaps two or three weeks later. But in fact only one of them ever filed a prescription for the new drug with the pharmacies reporting to us throughout the period covered i.e.,

through the end of June. In other words, after the first pioneering period and the February spurt, only real diehards still hold out in cliques *A* and *C*.

3. *Second Slow Period*. Several more doctors (recorded as cross-hatched circles) adopt the drug during the next few weeks; their dates are widely dispersed over a long period of time (March 4, March 29, April 9, and April 16).

4. *Second Spurt*. Then suddenly, between May 14 and 18, three doctors in clique *B*, represented by dotted circles, prescribe the drug leaving only two doctors as nonprescribers in clique *B*. Again, these two are not merely a little behind their colleagues, but they are "diehards," having no prescriptions for the new drug on record throughout the period covered by our survey.

We have now traced the sequence of prescriptions of a new drug through our map of friendships among the doctors in this city, much as doctors themselves do when they trace the "epidemiology" of an infectious disease on the map of a city. What we have seen can be summarized in three propositions:

1. That half or more of the members of each clique who are ever to adopt the drug do so within a few days of one another.

2. That for each of the three cliques, it is possible to state a cut-off date such that those members who have not adopted the drug by that date do not adopt it at all during the survey period. Only one respondent deviates from this generalization.

3. That no one (except the three pioneers) adopts the drug unless he has a direct sociometric contact with a doctor who adopted it before him. Three respondents deviate from this generalization, and it is therefore restated as follows: that drug adoptions on any particular date are more frequent among doctors who are in direct sociometric contact with others who have already adopted the drug, than among doctors who lack such contact.

TABLE 4

Cliques and Spurts * of Drug Adoptions

Clique	Cut-off date	Total adoptions	Adoptions prior to spurt	Adoptions during spurt		Adoptions after cut-off date (deviations)			Non-adoptions
				N	Percent	N	Total adoptions (percent)	Possible deviations (percent)	
A	2/10	6	2	4	67	—	—	—	3
B	5/18	4	1	3	75	—	—	—	2
C	2/11	4	1	2	50	1	25	50	—
All cliques		14	4	9	64	1	7	14	5
Neutrals		3							1
Total		17							6

* "Spurt" is defined as the seven days ending with the cut-off date. Doctors following specialties not normally prescribing drugs through pharmacies are excluded from Table 4.

TABLE 5

Adoptions of the New Drug among Doctors Who, on the Day the Adoption Occurred, Were and Were Not in Direct Sociometric Contact with Another Doctor Who Had already Adopted It *

Date	No. of doctors who, on date indicated, had not yet adopted new drug and:						Grand total
	Were in contact and			Were not in contact and			
	Adopted	Did not adopt	Total	Adopted	Did not adopt	Total	
Feb. 1	0	6	6	1	7	8	14
Feb. 5	2	5	7	0	6	6	13
Feb. 6	1	6	7	0	4	4	11
Feb. 10	1	5	6	1	3	4	10
Feb. 11	1	4	5	0	3	3	8
Mar. 4	0	4	4	1	2	3	7
Mar. 29	1	3	4	0	2	2	6
Apr. 6	1	2	3	0	2	2	5
Apr. 16	1	2	3	0	1	1	4
May 14	1	1	2	0	1	1	3
May 18	2	0	2	0	0	0	2
After	—	—	0	—	—	0	0
	(N = 11)	(N = 31) $p = .22$	(N = 49)	(N = 3)	(N = 31) $p = .09$	(N = 34)	—

* Doctors who never adopted the drug during the period covered by the survey, as well as doctors following specialties not normally prescribing drugs through pharmacies, are excluded from Table 5, as are the three earliest adopters. The results are not substantially altered when the length of the intervals between the dates is taken into account and the three earliest adopters are added.

Tables 4 and 5 constitute quantitative expressions of the empirical deviations from these three propositions. Table 4 shows no deviations from the first proposition. It also shows that the one doctor who actually deviated from the second proposition and prescribed the drug after the cut-off date for his clique constitutes but 14 percent of the deviations that *could* have occurred. Table 5 tabulates the deviations from the third proposition. It was necessary to compute separately for each date on which an adoption occurred the number of eligible doctors who had not already adopted the new drug but were in contact with others who had, and the number of similar doctors lacking such contact. Summing for all the dates, we find 49 contact situations and 34 noncontact situations. Each of these could have led to an adoption on the date involved. Actually, 22 percent of the contact situations and only 9 percent of the noncontact situations eventuated in a drug adoption. The corresponding percentages for the case of complete dependence of contacts and adoptions would be 29 percent and zero percent; for complete independence, 17 percent and 17 percent.[11]

We therefore feel justified in proposing that the spread of this innovation in the medical community flows through social channels, and that each of the spurts of adoptions in middle February and mid-dle May does indeed represent the simultaneous adoption of the drug by a socially close-knit group of physicians. There are a variety of ways in which such simultaneous decisions may be reached: (1) perhaps a decision, once reached by one member of a clique, is easily accepted by his associates who trust his judgment; (2) perhaps members of the same clique share norms of reliability and criteria of judgment to such an extent that whatever is convincing to one member is likely to be equally appealing to the rest; (3) perhaps each group shares exposure to channels, so that they are homogeneous as to stimuli received; (4) perhaps they even look at a case in the hospital together and are apprised on such an occasion of the success of a new treatment. [The occurrence of two sales campaigns for the new drug, which was mentioned as a possibility, would be compatible with items (2) or (3).] Whatever the process by which a group of doctors reaches such a near-simultaneous decision, it would be followed by a slow period of sporadic adoptions by doctors in other groups until some event—perhaps endorsement by a respected leader—triggers off a new spurt of adoptions in one of these other groups. In each group certain "diehards" would be left over, who cannot be convinced of the usefulness of the new drug.[12]

What sort of doctors are the three

---

[11] In the case of Propositions 1 and 2 (Table 4), we have not, so far, been able to determine the chance-expected values for the case of "complete independence." Reflection on what would constitute a "chance" model from which empirical deviations in the direction of satisfying our hypotheses could be measured suggests that these hypotheses imply deviation from "independence" in some or all of at least three different ways: (1) That the community-wide distribution of adoptions over time deviates from the chance-expected distribution over time. (It is an open question what the proper model for the chance-expected distribution should be.) (2) That the clique-specific distribution curves of adoptions over time have their peaks and other characteristic features at different points along the time-continuum. (3) That all the clique-specific curves of adoptions over time have a similar shape, which approximates some one hypothesized characteristic shape (e.g., that corresponding to a "spurt").

[12] Only the first of these four mechanisms by which groups may reach simultaneous decisions requires "personal influence" in the strict sense of the term. In the doctors' own accounts of the channels of information and influence which went into the making of a drug decision, it may be recalled (Table 1), colleagues constitute only 16 percent of the channels mentioned. (They are mentioned in 30 percent of the accounts, but most accounts contain more than one channel.) This is much less often than personal influence is usually mentioned in interviews on marketing or similar

pioneers who prescribed the new drug as early as December and January? Contrary to our expectations, they are neither outstanding specialists, nor outstanding leaders by any available criterion, nor in possession of an unusual degree of access to outside information. By contrast, the outstanding sociometric stars in our sample are predominantly late-comers in the adoption of the drug.

This inverse correlation between early prescription for the new drug and leadership is surprising, and one is tempted to conjecture as to the process that might be at work if the finding is a reliable one. It would almost seem as if each clique had its early experimenters or "advance scouts," who were willing to try out an innovation before any of their local colleagues. In each clique, the sociometric stars are among the last to adopt the drug; but when they finally do, all the other members except the real diehards fall in line immediately. This would account for the sudden final spurts of adoptions which we have observed. We must caution, however, that the reliability of this finding is in doubt. Our later midwestern data show a direct leadership-innovation correlation. We do not know whether this is due to a true regional difference or to error in one of the sets of data. It is noteworthy that the study of the diffusion and acceptance of new farm practices has given rise to equally contradictory findings concerning the extent of overlap between

innovators and influentials. Eugene Wilkening's North Carolina study finds little overlap; Herbert Lionberger's Missouri study finds considerable overlap. A recent study by Marsh and Coleman implies a possible basis for reconciliation: in a "low-adoption" neighborhood —that is, where the neighborhood norm is conservative with respect to farm innovations—the leaders or influentials did not have significantly higher adoption rates than nonleaders; in "high adoption" areas, however, the leaders were far ahead.[13]

In summary, we have found that the bringing together of independently established information on social relationships, on innovating behavior, and on the use of channels of information in decision-making supports the hypotheses of the role played by face-to-face contacts in mediating innovations from the world outside.

We have seen that the notions of the importance of interpersonal relations are applicable to a case of decision-making among specialists concerning matters based on scientific findings where well-recognized expert sources of knowledge exist. This, we noted, is particularly the case when decisions are required for relatively ambiguous situations.

Finally, we have found it necessary to propose amendments for the model of the two-step flow of communications: by considering the possibility of multistep rather than two-step flow; by noting that sources other than printed publica-

---

decisions, and also much less than would seem to correspond to the indications just reported, that the spread of this innovation flows through social channels. Two explanations of the low frequency of mentions of colleagues in the doctors' own accounts are possible: (1) that the doctors' reports understate the extent to which their colleagues actually have a part in their decisions; (2) that personal influence actually is lower in these drug decisions than in ordinary consumer products decisions, and that the congruence of social relations and drug adoptions reported in this section is not achieved by direct personal influence, but through one of the other three mechanisms suggested above.

[13] See E. A. Wilkening, "Informal Leaders and Innovators in Farm Practices," *Rural Sociol.*, 1952, XVII, 272–275; H F. Lionberger, "Some Characteristics of Farm Operators Sought as Sources of Farm Information in a Missouri Community," *Rural Sociol.*, 1953, XVIII, 327–338; C. P. Marsh and A. L. Coleman, "Farmers' Practice Adoption Rates in Relation to Adoption Rates of Leaders," *Rural Sociol.*, 1954, XIX, 180–181. These three studies are excellent representatives of a research tradition of the greatest importance for students of communication.

tions may be the channels to the outside world maintained by the opinion leaders; by noting that the model may not apply to channels of low prestige and unusually easy accessibility; and by differentiating various kinds of leadership, especially by emphasizing the differential roles of the innovator or pioneer on the one hand and the opinion leader or arbiter on the other.

12

Group Structure and Process

SOME EFFECTS OF CERTAIN COMMUNICATION
PATTERNS ON GROUP PERFORMANCE   *By Harold J.
Leavitt*

INTRODUCTION

Cooperative action by a group of individuals having a common objective requires, as a necessary condition, a certain minimum of communication. This does not mean that all the individuals must be able to communicate with one another. It is enough, in some cases, if they are each touched by some part of a network of communication which also touches each of the others at some point. The ways in which the members of a group may be linked together by such a network of communication are numerous; very possibly only a few of the many ways have any usefulness in terms of effective performance. Which of all feasible patterns are "good" patterns from this point of view? Will different patterns give different results in the performance of group tasks?

In a free group, the kind of network that evolves may be determined by a multitude of variables. The job to be done by the group may be a determinant, or the particular abilities or social ranks of the group members or other cultural factors may be involved.

Even in a group in which some parent

organization defines the network of communication, as in most military or industrial situations, the networks themselves may differ along a variety of dimensions. There may be differences in number of connections, in the symmetry of the pattern of connections, in "channel capacity" (how much and what kind of information), and in many other ways.

It was the purpose of this investigation to explore experimentally the relationship between the behavior of small groups and the patterns of communication in which the groups operate. It was our further purpose to consider the psychological conditions that are imposed on group members by various communication patterns, and the effects of these conditions on the organization and the behavior of its members. We tried to do this for small groups of a constant size, using two-way written communication and a task that required the simple collection of information.

Some Characteristics of Communication Structures. The stimulus for this research lies primarily in the work of Bavelas,[1] who considered the problem of defining some of the dimensions of group structures. In his study, the structures

From *The Journal of Abnormal and Social Psychology*, 1951, XLVI, 38–50. Reprinted by permission of the author and of the American Psychological Association, Inc. The stimulus for this research derives from the work and the thinking of Professor Alex Bavelas.

[1] A. Bavelas, "A Mathematical Model for Group Structures," *Appl. Anthrop.*, 1948, VII, 16–30.

analyzed consist of cells connected to one another. If we make persons analogous to "cells" and communication channels analogous to "connections," we find that some of the dimensions that Bavelas defines are directly applicable to the description of communication patterns. Thus, one way in which communication patterns vary can be described by the sum of the neighbors that each individual member has, neighbors being defined as individuals to whom a member has communicative access. So, too, the concept of *centrality*, as defined by Bavelas, is of value in describing differences within and between structures. The most central position in a pattern is the position closest to all other positions. Distance is measured by number of communicative links which must be utilized to get, by the shortest route, from one position to another.

Bavelas also introduced a *sum of neighbors* measure—sum of neighbors being a summation, for the entire pattern, of the number of positions one link away from each position. Similarly, *sum of distances* is the summation, for all positions, of the shortest distances (in links) from every position to every other one.

Unfortunately, these dimensions we have mentioned do not in themselves uniquely define a pattern of communication. What defines a pattern is the *way* the cells are connected, regardless of how they are represented on paper. In essence, our criterion is this: if two patterns cannot be "bent" into the same shape without breaking a link, they are different patterns. A more precise definition of unique patterns would require the use of complex topological concepts.

Some Operational Characteristics of Communication Patterns. Consider the pattern depicted as A in Figure 1. If at each dot or cell (lettered a, b, etc.) we place a person; if each link (line between dots) represents a two-way channel for written communications; and if we assign to the five participants a task requiring

that *every* member get an answer to a problem which can be solved only by pooling segments of information originally held separately by each member, then it is possible a priori to consider the ways in which the problem can be solved.

Pattern flexibility. First we note that the subjects (Ss) need not always use all the channels potentially available to them in order to reach an adequate solution of the problem. Although pattern A (Fig. 1) contains potentially seven links or channels of communication, it can be solved as follows with three of the seven channels ignored:

Step 1: a and e each send their separate items of information to b and d respectively.
Step 2: b and d each send their separate items of information, along with those from a and b respectively, to c.
Step 3: c organizes all the items of information, arrives at an answer, and sends the answer to b and then to d.
Step 4: b and d then send the answer to a and e respectively.

The use of these particular four channels yields pattern C (Fig. 1). The original seven-link pattern (A) can be used as a four-link pattern in various ways. For instance, each of the four Ss diagrammatically labeled c, b, a, and e might send his item of information to d who would organize the items, arrive at the answer, and send it back to each respectively. Use of these particular four channels would yield the pattern B in Figure 1. The problem could also be solved by the Ss using five, six, or all of the seven potential channels.

Operational flexibility. Secondly, with the specification that a given number of links be used, any pattern can be operrated in a variety of ways. Thus the pattern D (Fig. 1), which has no pattern flexibility, can be used as shown in D–1, with information funneled in to C and the answer sent out from C. It is also possible to use it, as in D–2, with E as the key position; or as in D 3. These are

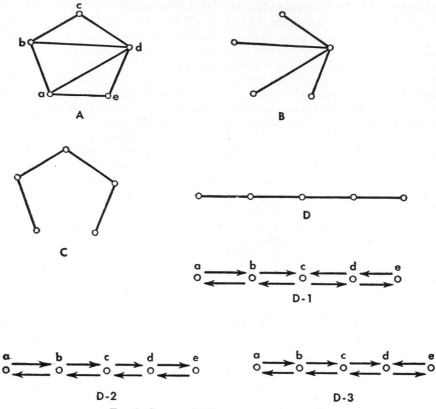

Fɪɢ. 1. Communication patterns (see text).

operational differences that can be characterized in terms of the roles taken by the various positions. Thus in D–1, C is the decision-making position. In D–2, it is E or A. Some patterns can be operated with two or three decision-makers.

The Definition of Maximum Theoretical Efficiency. Before going further it may be helpful to state the task used in this research. To each S, labeled by color (see Fig. 2), was given a card on which there appeared a set of five (out of six possible) symbols. Each $S's$ card was different from all the others in that the symbol lacking, the sixth one, was a different symbol in each case.

Thus, in any set of five cards there was only one symbol in common. The prob-

lem was for every member to find the common symbol. To accomplish this each member was allowed to communicate, by means of written messages, with those other members of the group to whom he had an open channel (a link in our diagrams). Every separate written communication from one S (A) to another (B) was considered one message. An S who had discovered the answer was allowed to pass the answer along.

Minimum number of communications. For any pattern of n Ss, the minimum number of communications, C, is given by C = $2(n - 1)$.

Theoretically, then, with *number of messages as the sole criterion*, any pattern of n Ss is as efficient as any other n-sized pattern.

| | Six Symbols Used:. ○ △ ◇ □ + ✳ | | | | | |

Trial No.	Symbol Missing From:					Common Symbol
	White	Red	Brown	Yellow	Blue	
1	△	◇	✳	○	□	+
2	◇	○	□	△	+	✳
3	+	✳	□	△	◇	○
4	□	◇	△	✳	+	○
5	○	✳	+	△	□	◇
6	△	○	□	✳	◇	+
7	□	+	○	◇	△	✳
8	◇	✳	□	+	○	△
9	✳	◇	□	△	○	+
10	+	○	□	✳	◇	△
11	○	+	△	◇	✳	□
12	✳	○	□	△	+	◇
13	△	○	◇	□	+	✳
14	□	◇	+	✳	△	○
15	+	○	□	◇	✳	△

FIG. 2. Symbol distribution by trial.

The minimum time required for solution. If we assume "standard" *Ss*, all of whom work, think, and write at the same speed, it is possible to calculate the limit set by the communication pattern on the speed with which the problem can be solved. Toward this end, we can arbitrarily define a *time unit* as the time required to complete any message, from its inception by any *S* to its reception by any other.

For any *n* not a power of 2 and *with unrestricted linkage*, when $2^x < n < 2^{x+1}$ and *x* is a power of 2, $x + 1$ equals the minimum possible time units for solution of the problem. Thus, for a five-man group we have $2^x < 5 < 2^{x+1}$ becoming $2^2 < 5 < 2^3$, and $x + 1 = 3$ time units. *No* five-man pattern can be done in less than three time units, although several require more than three time units. When *n* is an even power of 2, the formula $2^x = n$ holds, and $x = $ minimum time.[2]

It will be noted that, although some patterns require fewer time units than others, they may also require more message (*m*) units. This phenomenon, effectively the generalization that it requires increased messages to save time units, holds for all the patterns we have examined. It is, however, true that certain patterns requiring different times can be solved in the same number of message units.

Some Possible Effects of Various Patterns on the Performance of Individuals. There are two general kinds of reasons which dictate against our theoretically perfect performance from real people. The first of these is the obvious one that people are not standardized. There are also the forces set up by the patterns themselves to be considered. The problem becomes one of analyzing the forces operating on an individual in any particular position in a communication pattern and then predicting how the effects of these forces will be translated into behavior.

It is our belief that the primary source of differential forces will be *centrality*. Centrality will be the chief (though perhaps not the sole) determinant of behavioral differences because centrality reflects the extent to which one position is strategically located relative to other positions in the pattern.

Our selection of centrality derives from the belief that availability of information necessary for the solution of the problem will be of prime importance in affecting one's behavior. Centrality is a measure of one's closeness to all other group members and, hence, is a measure of the availability of the information necessary for solving the problem.

Availability of information should affect behavior, in turn, by determining one's role in the group. An individual who can rapidly collect information should see himself and be seen by others in a different way from an individual to whom vital information is not accessible. Such roles should be different in the extent to which they permit independence of action, in the responsibility they entail, and in the monotony they impose. Finally, differences in independence, in responsibility, and in monotony should affect the speed, the accuracy, the aggressiveness, and the flexibility of behavior.

METHOD

The Problem to Be Solved. We have already described the task to be given our *Ss*—a task of discovering the single common symbol from among several symbols. When *all five* men indicated that they knew the common symbol, a

---

[2] This is an empirical generalization derived chiefly from an analysis of a four-man square pattern. In such a pattern, *A* and *B*, and *C* and *D* may swap information in one time unit. Then *A* and *C*, and *B* and *D* may swap in two time units to yield a complete solution. For an eight-man ladder pattern the same simultaneous swapping process yields a minimum time. For the intervening *n*'s, at least "part" of a time unit is required, in addition to the minimum time for the four-man pattern. A detailed account of this analysis may be found in a paper, as yet unpublished, by J. P. Macy, Jr.

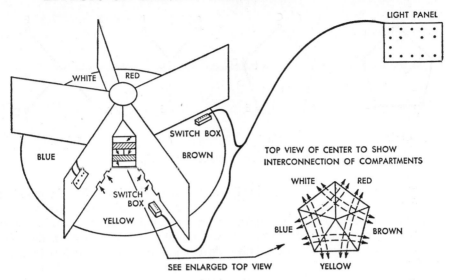

FIG. 3. Apparatus.

trial was ended. Another set of cards, with another common symbol, was then given to the *Ss*, and another trial was begun.

Each group of *Ss* was given 15 consecutive trials. The composition of the standard sets of cards, used for all groups, is indicated in Figure 2, which shows the symbol *not* on each person's card for each trial. By referring this missing symbol to the set of six symbols at the top, the reader may reconstruct the symbols actually on each man's card. The common symbol (the right answer) is also shown in Figure 2.

The Apparatus. The *Ss* were seated around a circular table (Fig. 3) so that each was separated from the next by a vertical partition from the center to six inches beyond the table's edge. The partitions had slots permitting subjects to push written message cards to the men on either side of them.

To allow for communication to the other men in the group, a five-layered pentagonal box was built and placed at the center of the table. The box was placed so that the partitions just touched each of the five points of the pentagon. Each of the five resulting wedge-shaped

work spaces was then painted a different color. The *Ss* were supplied with blank message cards whose colors matched that of their work spaces. Any message sent from a booth had to be on a card of the booth's color. On the left wall of each partition, 16 large symbol cards, representing 16 trials, were hung in loose-leaf fashion. The cards were placed in order with numbered backs to *S*. At the starting signal, *S* could pull down the first card and go to work.

In addition, each work space was provided with a board in which were mounted six switches. Above each switch appeared one of the six symbols. When *S* got an answer to the problem, he was to throw the proper switch, which would turn on an appropriate light on a master board of 30 lights in the observer's room. When five lights (whether or not they were under the correct symbol), representing five different *Ss*, were lit, the observer called a halt to the trial. The observer could tell by a glance at the light panel whether (*a*) five different *Ss* had thrown their switches, (*b*) whether all five had decided on the same answer, and (*c*) whether the answer decided on

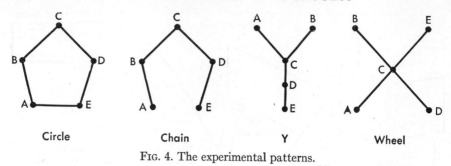

FIG. 4. The experimental patterns.

was right or wrong. The same detailed instructions were given to all *Ss*.

A preliminary series of four problems, in which each *S* was given all the information required for solution, was used. This was done to note the extent of differences among *Ss* in the time required to solve such problems.

The Procedure. One hundred male undergraduates of M.I.T.,[3] drawn from various classes at the Institute, served as *Ss* for these experiments. These 100 were split up into 20 groups of five men each. These 20 groups were then further subdivided so that five groups could be tested on each of four experimental patterns.

Each group was given 15 consecutive trials on *one* pattern, a process which required one session of about fifty minutes. These *Ss* were *not used again*. The order in which we used our patterns

was also randomized. Just in case the color or geographical position of one's work space might affect one's behavior, we shifted positions for each new group. After a group had completed its 15 trials, and before members were permitted to talk with one another, each member was asked to fill out a questionnaire.

The Patterns Selected. The four five-man patterns selected for this research are shown in Figure 4.

These four patterns represented extremes in centrality (as in the circle vs. the wheel), as well as considerable differences in other characteristics (Table 1).

RESULTS

The data which have been accumulated are broken down in the pages that follow into (*a*) a comparison of total patterns and (*b*) a comparison of positions within patterns.

TABLE 1

CHARACTERISTICS OF THE EXPERIMENTAL PATTERNS

Pattern	No. of links	Most central position	Sum of neighbors	Sum of distances	Min. time units	Min. messages
Chain	4	C (6.7)	8	40	5 (8*m*)	8 (5*t*)
Y	4	C (7.2)	8	36	4 (8*m*)	8 (4*t*)
Wheel	4	C (8.0)	8	32	5 (8*m*)	8 (5*t*)
Circle	5	All (5.0)	10	30	3 (14*m*)	8 (5*t*)

[3] Data on female graduate students are being gathered at M.I.T. by Smith and Bavelas, and the indications are that their behavior differs in some ways from the behavior of our male *Ss*.

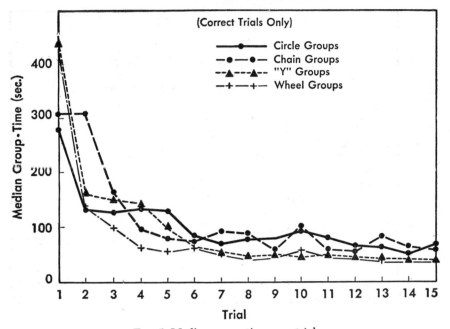

FIG. 5. Median group times per trial.

A. Differences among Patterns

It was possible to reconstruct a picture of the operational methods actually used by means of: (*a*) direct observation, (*b*) postexperimental analysis of messages, and (*c*) postexperimental talks with *Ss*.

The *wheel* operated in the same way in all five cases. The peripheral men funneled information to the center where an answer decision was made and the answer sent out. This organization had usually evolved by the fourth or fifth trial and remained in use throughout.

The Y operated so as to give the most central position, *C* (see Fig. 4 and Table 1), complete decision-making authority. The next-most-central position, *D* (see Fig. 4), served only as a transmitter of information and of answers. In at least one case, *C* transmitted answers first to *A* and *B* and only then to *D*. Organization for the Y evolved a little more slowly than for the wheel, but, once achieved, it was just as stable.

In the *chain* information was usually

funneled in from both ends to *C*, whence the answer was sent out in both directions. There were several cases, however, in which *B* or *D* reached an answer decision and passed it to *C*. The organization was slower in emerging than the Y's or the wheel's, but consistent, once reached.

The *circle* showed no consistent operational organization. Most commonly messages were just sent in both directions until any *S* received an answer or worked one out. In every case, all available links were used at some time during the course of each trial.

Direct Measures of Differences among Patterns. *Time.* The curves in Figure 5 are for *correct* trials only—that is, for trials in which all five switches represented the correct common symbols. In most cases, the medians shown are for distributions of five groups, but in no case do they represent less than three groups.

The variability of the distributions represented by these medians is considerable. In the fifteenth trial, the distribution for the circle has a range of 50–96

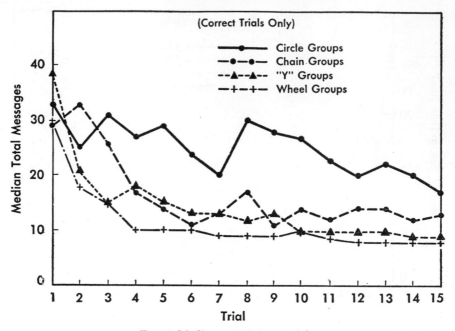

FIG. 6. Median messages per trial.

seconds; for the chain, 28–220 seconds; for the Y, 24–52 seconds; and for the wheel, 21–46 seconds. Moreover, much of the time that went to make up each trial was a constant consisting of writing and passing time. Any differences attributable to pattern would be a small fraction of this large constant and would be easily obscured by accidents of misplacing or dropping of messages.

Despite all these factors, one measure of speed did give statistically significant differences. A measure of the *fastest single trial* of each group indicates that the wheel was considerably faster (at its fastest) than the circle (Table 2.)

Messages. The medians in Figure 6 represent a count of the number of messages sent by each group during a given (correct) trial. It seems clear that the circle pattern used more messages to solve the problem than the others.

TABLE 2

FASTEST SINGLE CORRECT TRIAL

	Circle	Chain	Y	Wheel	Diff.	p *
Mean	50.4	53.2	35.4	32.0	Ci–W	<.01
Median	55.0	57.0	32.0	36.0	Ch–W	<.10
Range	44–59	19–87	22–53	20–41	Ci–Y	<.05
					Ch–Y	<.20

* Significance of differences between means were measured throughout by *t*-tests. The *p*-values are based on distributions of *t* which include both tails of the distribution (see Freeman, H., *Industrial Statistics:* New York: Wiley, 1942). Where differences are between proportions, *p* is derived from the usual measure of significance of differences between proportions. Ci-W means the circle-wheel difference, and so on.

TABLE 3

ERRORS

Pattern	Total errors (15 trials)		Total errors (last 8 trials)		Final errors		Mean no. of trials with at least one final error
	Mean	Range	Mean	Range	Mean	Range	
Circle	16.6	9–33	7.6	1–18	6.4	2–14	3.4
Chain	9.8	3–19	2.8	0–11	6.2	1–19	1.8
Y	2.6	1 8	0	0	1.6	0 5	.8
Wheel	9.8	0–34	0.6	0–2	2.2	0–7	1.2

p Values Ci-Y $< .02$

Errors. An error was defined as the throwing of any incorrect switch by an S during a trial. Errors that were *not* corrected before the end of a trial are labeled "final errors"; the others are referred to as "corrected errors."

It should be pointed out that the error figures for the *wheel* in Table 3 are distorted by the peculiar behavior of one of the five wheel groups. The center man in this group took the messages which he received to be *answers* rather than simple information, and, in addition to throwing his own switch, passed the information on *as an answer*. This difficulty was cleared up after a few trials, and the figures for the last 8 trials are probably more representative than the figures for the full 15 trials.

In addition to the differences in errors, there are differences in the proportion of total errors that were corrected. Although more errors were made in the circle pattern than in any other, a greater proportion of them (61 percent) were corrected than in any other pattern. Too, the frequency of unanimous five-man final errors is lower, both absolutely and percentage-wise, for the circle than for the chain.

Questionnaire Results

1. "*Did your group have a leader? If so, who?*"

Only 13 of 25 people who worked in the circle named a leader, and those named were scattered among all the positions in the circle. For all patterns, the total frequency of people named increased in the order *circle, chain, Y, wheel*. Similarly, the unanimity of opinion increased in the same order so that, for the wheel pattern, all 23 members who recognized any leader agreed that position C was that leader.

2. "*Describe briefly the organization of your group.*"

The word "organization" in this question was ambiguous. Some of the Ss understood the word to mean pattern of communication, while others equated it with their own duties or with status difference.

These differences in interpretation were not random, however. Sixteen people in the wheel groups fully reproduced the wheel structure in answer to this question, while only one circle member reproduced the circle pattern.

3. "*How did you like your job in the group?*"

In this question Ss were asked to place a check on a rating scale marked "disliked it" at one end and "liked it" at the other. For purposes of analysis, the scale was translated into numerical scores from 0 at the dislike end to 100. Each rating was estimated only to the closest decile.

Again, we find the order *circle, chain, Y, wheel*, with circle members enjoying their jobs significantly more than the wheel members.

4. *"See if you can recall how you felt about the job as you went along. Draw the curve below."*

The *Ss* were asked to sketch a curve into a space provided for it. We measured the height of these curves on a 6-point scale at trials 1, 5, 10, and 15. These heights were averaged for each group, and the averages of the group averages were plotted.

Although the differences between groups are not statistically significant, trends of increasing satisfaction in the circle and decreasing satisfaction in the wheel seem to corroborate the findings in the question on satisfaction with one's job. Except for a modest Y-chain reversal, the order is, as usual, from circle to wheel.

5. *"Was there anything, at any time, that kept your group from performing at its best? If so, what?"*

The answers to this question were categorized as far as possible into several classes.

None of the circle members feels that "nothing" was wrong with his group; a fact that is suggestive of an attitude different from that held by members of the other patterns. So, too, is the finding that insufficient knowledge of the pattern does not appear as an obstacle to the circle member but is mentioned at least five times in each of the other patterns.

6. *"Do you think your group could improve its efficiency? If so, how?"*

Circle members place great emphasis on *organizing* their groups, on working out a "system" (mentioned 17 times). Members of the other patterns, if they felt that any improvement at all was possible, emphasized a great variety of possibilities.

7. *"Rate your group on the scale below."*

For purposes of analysis, these ratings (along a straight line) were transposed into numbers from 0, for "poor," to 100.

The same progression of differences that we have already encountered, the progression *circle, chain, Y, wheel*, holds for this question. Once again the circle group thinks less well of itself (Mean = 56) than do the other patterns (M_{ch} = 60; M_y = 70; M_w = 71).

Message Analysis. The messages sent by all *Ss* were collected at the end of each experimental run and their contents coded and categorized. Some of these categories overlapped with others, and hence some messages were counted in more than one category.

The now familiar progression, *circle, chain, Y, wheel*, continues into this area. Circle members send many more informational messages than do members of the other patterns (M_{ci} = 283; M_w = 101). Circle members also send more answers (M_{ci} = 91; M_w = 65).

The same tendency remains in proportion to total errors as well as absolutely. The circle has a mean of 4.8 recognition-of-error messages for a mean of 16.6 errors; the chain has a mean of 1 recognition-of-error messages for a mean of 9.8 errors.

We were concerned, before beginning these experiments, lest *Ss* find short cuts for solving the problem, thus making certain comparisons among patterns difficult. One such short cut we have called "elimination." Instead of taking time to write their five symbols, many *Ss*, after discovering that only six symbols existed in all, wrote just the missing symbol, thus saving considerable time. This method was used by at least one member in two of the circle groups, in all the chain groups, in three of the Y groups, and in four of the wheel groups. In *both* the circle cases, the method was used by *all five members* during final trials. In the chain, though present in every group, elimination was used only once by all five members, twice by three members, and twice by just one member. In the Y, the method was adopted once by four members (the fifth man was *not*

TABLE 4

NUMBER OF MESSAGES SENT BY EACH POSITION

Group		A	B	C	D	E	Diff.	p
Circle	Mean	78.4	90.0	83.6	86.2	81.0	A–B	<.30
	Range	64–101	63–102	60–98	60–122	72–90		
Chain	Mean	24.8	70.8	82.4	71.8	27.6	C–E	<.01
	Range	20–34	43–112	45–113	42–101	22–43		
Y	Mean	28.0	23.8	79.8	63.8	25.6	A–C D–C D–E	<.01 <.20 <.01
	Range	20–44	21–28	65–104	43–78	21–37		
Wheel	Mean	29.4	26.2	102.8	26.6	30.2	C–E	<.01
	Range	19–48	17–40	78–138	17–39	22–43		

the center) and twice by two members. There was at least one case (in the wheel) in which a member who suggested the use of elimination was ordered by another member not to use it.

The questions raised here are two. Is the idea of elimination more likely to occur in some patterns than in others? Is an innovation like elimination likely to be more readily accepted in some patterns than in others? To neither of these questions do we have an adequate answer.

B. A Positional Analysis of the Data

Observation of the experimental patterns indicates that every position in the circle is indistinguishable from every other one. No one has more neighbors, is more central, or is closer to anyone than anyone else. In the wheel, the four peripheral positions are alike, and so on. Despite our inability to differentiate these positions from one another, we have set up the data in the following sections as if all positions in each pattern were actually different from one another.

Direct Observations. *Messages.* The most central positions, it will be seen from Table 4, send the greatest number of messages; the least central ones send the fewest.

Errors. The analysis of total errors made in each position showed nothing of significance.

Questionnaire Results by Position

1. *"How much did you enjoy your job?"*

The most central positions in other patterns enjoy their jobs more than any circle position. Peripheral positions, on the other hand, enjoy the job less than any circle position (Table 5).

2. *"See if you can recall how you felt about the job as you went along. Draw the curve below."*

The data for this question are gathered after all most-peripheral and all most-central positions are combined. Peripheral positions were: positions A and E, in the chain; position E in the Y; and positions A, B, D, and E in the wheel. Central positions were all C positions with the exception of C in the circle. The data thus combined highlight the trend toward higher satisfaction with increasing centrality. The central positions progress from a mean of 2.1 at trial 1 to a mean of 3.9 at trial 15. Peripheral positions decline from 3.9 to 2.3.

Message Analysis by Position. One of the things that immediately stand out from an examination of the messages is

TABLE 5

ENJOYMENT OF THE JOB

Group			A	B	C	D	E	Diff.	p
Circle		Mean	58.0	64.0	70.0	65.0	71.0	A–E	<.70
		Range	0–100	0–100	20–100	40–100	25–100		
Chain		Mean	45.0	82.5	78.0	70.0	24.0	C–E	<.02
		Range	25–55	50–100	50–100	40–100	0–70	C–AE	<.01
Y		Mean	46.0	49.0	95.0	71.0	31.0	C–A	<.02
		Range	0–100	25–100	75–100	30–100	0–75	C–AB	<.01
Wheel		Mean	37.5	20.0	97.0	25.0	42.5	D–E	<.10
								B–C	<.01
		Range	0–50	0–40	85–100	0–75	0–100	C–E	<.02
								ABED–C	<.01

an apparent peculiarity in the *informational message* category. Although the most central man in the chain sends more informational messages (52) than the other positions in that pattern, the same is not true of the most central men in the Y and the wheel. In the Y, it is position *D*, the next-most-central position, that sends most; while in the wheel all positions are about equal. This peculiarity becomes quite understandable if we take into account (*a*) the kind of organization used in each pattern and (*b*) the fact that these figures represent the entire 15 trials, some of which occurred before the group got itself stably organized. In the wheel, the Y, and the chain, the center man really needed to send *no* informational messages, only answers; but in the *early* trials, before his role was clarified, he apparently sent enough to bring his total up to or higher than the level of the rest.

It can also be noted that the number of *organizational messages* (messages which seek to establish some plan of action for future trials) is negatively correlated with positional centrality. The most peripheral men send the greatest numbers of organizational messages, the most central men least.

DISCUSSION

Patternwise, the picture formed by the results is of differences almost always in the order *circle, chain, Y, wheel*.

We may grossly characterize the kinds of differences that occur in this way: the circle, one extreme, is active, leaderless, unorganized, erratic, and yet is enjoyed by its members. The wheel, at the other extreme, is less active, has a distinct leader, is well and stably organized, is less erratic, and yet is unsatisfying to most of its members.

There are two questions raised by these behavioral differences. First, what was wrong with our a priori time-unit analysis? The results measured in clock time do not at all match the time-unit figures. And second, to what extent are behavioral differences matched by centrality differences?

The Time Unit. It was hypothesized earlier that the time taken to solve a problem should be limited at the lower end by the structure of the pattern of communication. If pattern does set such a limitation on speed, the limitation is not in the direction we would have predicted. Our analysis (Table 1), based on a theoretical time unit, led us falsely to expect greatest speed from the circle pattern.

There are three outstanding reasons for the failure of the time-unit analysis to predict clock time. First, the time unit, itself, was too gross a measure. We defined the time unit as the time required for the transmission of one message from its inception to its reception. In actuality, different kinds of messages required very different clock times for transmission. *Ss* could send two messages simultaneously. They could also lay out and write several messages before sending any.

A second reason for the failure of the time-unit analysis was the assumption that *Ss* would gravitate to the theoretically "best"-operating organization. Only the wheel groups used the theoretically "best" method (the minimum time method) consistently.

Finally, it should be pointed out that differences in speed among patterns were subject to major fluctuations for reasons of differences in writing speed, dexterity in passing messages, and other extraneous factors.

The Relation of the Centrality Measure to Behavior. Our second and more important question is: Are the behavioral differences among patterns and among positions related consistently to the centrality index? An examination of Table 1 indicates that the centrality index shows the same progression, *circle, chain, Y, wheel*, as do most of the behavioral differences. On a positional basis, centrality also differentiates members of a pattern in the same order that their behavior does.

Because such a relationship does exist between behavior and centrality, a more detailed consideration of the centrality concept is in order.

The central region of a structure is defined by Bavelas as "the class of all cells with the smallest p to be found in the structure." The quantity, p, in turn, is defined as the largest distance between

one cell and any other cell in the structure. Distance is measured in link units. Thus the distance from A to B in the chain is one link; from A to C the distance is two links. The most central position in a pattern is the position that is closest to all other positions. Quantitatively, an index of the centrality of position A in any pattern can be found by (a) summing the shortest distances from each position to every other one and (b) dividing this summation by the total of the shortest distances from position A to every other position.

Centrality, then, is a function of the size of a pattern as well as of its structure. Thus in a five-man circle, the centrality of each man is 5.0. In a six-man circle, the centrality of each man jumps to 6.0. The two most peripheral men in a five-man chain each have a centrality of 4.0. But in a seven-man chain, the two most peripheral men have centralities of 5.3.

In Figure 7 are given the centralities of each position in each of our four test patterns. The sum of centralities is also given. Both total centrality and distribution of centralities fall in the order *circle, chain, Y, wheel*.

These centrality figures correlate with the behavior we have observed. But it seems unreasonable to assume that the correlation would hold for larger n's. Certainly we would not expect *more* message activity or *more* satisfaction from peripheral positions in a chain of a larger n than from a five-man chain.

To obviate this difficulty, a measure we have called "relative peripherality" may be established. The relative peripherality of any position in a pattern is the difference between the centrality of that position and the centrality of the most central position in that pattern. Thus, for the two end men in a five-man chain, the peripherality index is 2.7 (the difference between their centralities of 4.0 and the centrality of the most central position, 6.7). For a total pattern, the peripherality index may be taken by summating

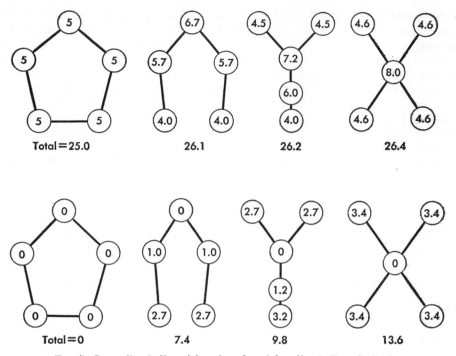

FIG. 7. Centrality indices (above) and peripherality indices (below).

all the peripherality indices in the pattern (Fig. 7).

Examination of the data will show that observed differences in behavior correlate positively with these peripherality measures. *By total pattern*, messages, satisfaction, and errors (except for the wheel) vary consistently with total peripherality index. Similarly, by position, messages and satisfaction vary with peripherality. Errors, however, show no clear relationship with peripherality of position, a finding which is discussed in detail later in this section.

Recognition of a leader also seems to be a function of peripherality, but in a somewhat different way. A review of our leadership findings will show that leadership becomes more clear-cut as the differences in peripherality *within a pattern become greater*. Recognition of a leader seems to be determined by the extent of the difference in centrality between the most central and next-most-central man.

There arises next the question: What is the mechanism by which the peripherality of a pattern or a position affects the behavior of persons occupying that pattern or position?

A reconstruction of the experimental situation leads us to this analysis of the peripherality-behavior relationship:

First, let us assume standard Ss, motivated to try to solve our experimental problem as quickly as possible. Let them be "intelligent" Ss who do not send the same information more than once to any neighbor. Let them also be Ss who, given several neighbors, will send, with equal probability, their first message to any one of those neighbors.

Given such standard Ss, certain specific positions will probably get an answer to the problem before other positions. In the chain, position C will be most likely to get the answer first, but, in the circle, all positions have an equal opportunity.

To illustrate, consider the chain pattern (see Fig. 4): During time unit 1, A may send only to B. B may send either to C or to A. C may send either to B or to D. D may send either to C or to E. E may send only to D. No matter where B, C, and D send their messages, B and D will have, at the end of one time unit, A's and E's information. During the second time unit, if B and/or D have sent to C the first time, they will now send to A and E. If they sent to A and E the first time, they will send to C, and C will have the answer. Even if B and D do not send to C until the third time unit, C will get the answer either before or simultaneously with B and D. In *no* case can any other position beat C to the answer. In the wheel, C cannot even be tied in getting an answer. He will *always* get it first.

Our second concern is with Ss' perceptions of these answer-getting potentials. We suggest that these random differences in answer-getting potentials rapidly structure members' perceptions of their own roles in the group. These differences affect one's independence from, or dependence on, the other members of the group. In the wheel, for example, a peripheral S perceives, at first, only that he gets the answer and information from C and can send only to C. C perceives that he gets information from everyone and must send the answer to everyone. The recognition of roles is easy. The peripheral men are dependent on C. C is autonomous and controls the organization.

In the circle, an S's perception must be very different. He gets information from both sides; sometimes he gets the answer, sometimes he sends it. He has two channels of communication. He is exclusively dependent on no one. His role is not clearly different from anyone else's.

Thirdly, having closed the gap between structural pattern and Ss' perceptions of their roles in the group, the problem reduces to one purely psychological. The question becomes: How do differences in one's perception of one's own dependence or independence bring about specific behavior differences of the sort we have observed?

Differences in satisfaction level are relatively easy to relate to independence. In our culture, in which needs for autonomy, recognition, and achievement are strong, it is to be expected that positions which limit independence of action (peripheral positions) would be unsatisfying.

A fairly direct relationship between centrality (and, hence, independence) and the speed with which a group gets organized is also perceptible. In the wheel, unless Ss act "unintelligently," an organization, with C as center, is forced on the wheel groups by the structural pattern. In the circle, no such differences in role and, hence, in organization are forced on the group.

Message-activity can also be related to centrality by means of the independence-of-action concept. A peripheral person in any pattern can send messages to only one other position. Only one informational message is called for. Extra messages would be repetitious. Central positions, however, are free to send more than one nonrepetitious informational message until an organization evolves. Once the most central man perceives that he is most central, he need send *no* informational messages. But so long as the most central man does not perceive his own position, it is intelligent to send informational messages to whomever he feels may require some information. It is in keeping with this analysis that the circle should yield maximum messages and the wheel minimum messages.

If the behavior of one of the wheel groups can be discounted, then an explanation, in terms of peripherality, is also possible for both differences in tendencies to correct errors and total error differences.

If peripherality determines one's independence of action, it seems very likely that positions most limited in independence should begin to perceive themselves as subordinates whose sole function is to send information and await an answer. That they should then uncritically accept whatever answer they receive is perfectly in keeping with their subordinate, relatively unresponsible positions—hence, very little correction of errors in the patterns in which there are great differences in peripherality.

Total errors, it will be recalled, were correlated with total peripherality indices but showed no clear relationship with the relative peripherality of particular positions. A consideration of our definition of error may shed some light on this apparent anomaly.

The "errors" that we recorded were signals from the S that indicated a wrong answer. But these wrong answers derived from a variety of sources. First, Ss might wrongly interpret the correct information they received. They might also make errors in throwing switches; and they might also *correctly* interpret *wrong* information. In all three cases, "errors" were recorded.

We submit that this broad definition of error should yield a total pattern relationship with peripherality, but no positional relationship. Our reasoning can be illustrated by an example. Suppose that the central man in the wheel wrongly interprets information sent to him, and, hence, throws an incorrect switch. This is a "real" error. He then funnels out the wrong answer to the other members. At least three of these intelligently conclude that the answer sent them is correct and also throw the wrong switches. We then have three "false" errors consequent to our single "real" one. When several independent answer decisions are made (as in the circle), we should expect several real errors, multiplication of these by a factor of about 3, and a larger total of errors. This process should lead to a correlation between total pattern behavior and peripherality

but not to a correlation between positional behavior and peripherality. The process simply multiplies real errors more or less constantly for a whole pattern but obscures positional differences because the "real" and the "false" errors are indistinguishable in our data.

We submit, further, that pattern differences in real errors, if such there be, may be attributable to "overinformation"; too much information to too many members which, under pressure, leads to errors. Central positions or positions which are no less central than others in the pattern should be the ones to yield the greatest number of real errors, while peripheral positions, which require no such rapid collation of information, should be the false error sources. Such a hypothesis would be in keeping with our total pattern findings and might also clarify our positional findings. Only an experiment designed to differentiate real from false errors can answer this question.

It is in keeping with this peripherality-independence analysis, also, that we should find the recognition of a single leader occurring most frequently in the wheel and Y groups. It is also to be expected that we should find circle members emphasizing need for organization and planning and seldom giving a complete picture of their pattern. Perhaps, too, it is reasonable to expect that the whole group should be considered good in the highly organized wheel (and not so good in the unorganized circle) even though one's own job is considered poor.

In summary, then, it is our feeling that centrality determines behavior by limiting independence of action, thus producing differences in activity, accuracy, satisfaction, leadership, recognition of pattern, and other behavioral characteristics.

SUMMARY AND CONCLUSIONS

Within the limits set by the experimental conditions—group size, type of problem, source of Ss—these conclusions seem warranted:

1. The communication patterns within which our groups worked affected their behavior. The major behavioral differences attributable to communication patterns were differences in accuracy, total activity, satisfaction of group members, emergence of a leader, and organization of the group. There may also be differences among patterns in speed of problem-solving, self-correcting tendencies, and durability of the group as a group.

2. The positions which individuals occupied in a communication pattern affected their behavior while occupying those positions. One's position in the group affected the chances of becoming a leader of the group, one's satisfaction with one's job and with the group, the quantity of one's activity, and the extent to which one contributed to the group's functional organization.

3. The characteristic of communication patterns that was most clearly correlated with behavioral differences was *centrality*. Total pattern differences in behavior seemed to be correlated with a measure of centrality we have labeled the *peripherality index*. Positional differences in behavior seemed to be correlated with the positional peripherality indices of the various positions within patterns.

4. It is tentatively suggested that centrality affects behavior via the limits that centrality imposes upon independent action. Independence of action, relative to other members of the group, is, in turn, held to be the primary determinant of the definition of who shall take the leadership role, total activity, satisfaction with one's lot, and other specific behaviors.

More precisely, it is felt that where centrality and, hence, independence are evenly distributed, there will be no leader, many errors, high activity, slow organization, and high satisfaction. Whatever frustration occurs will occur as a result of the inadequacy of the group, not the inadequacy of the environment.

Where one position is low in centrality relative to other members of the group, that position will be a follower position, dependent on the leader, accepting his dictates, falling into a role that allows little opportunity for prestige, activity, or self-expression.

A COMPARISON OF INDIVIDUALS AND SMALL GROUPS IN THE RATIONAL SOLUTION OF COMPLEX PROBLEMS

By Marjorie E. Shaw

The work done before 1920 in the field of group activity as compared with individual activity has been summarized adequately by Allport.[1] Since then other studies have been made, principally by G. B. Watson,[2] Bechterew and Lange,[3] South,[4] and Belaev.[5] Many of these studies deal primarily with groups wherein individuals are interested in the same stimulus but there is little or no direct social intercourse and stimulation. The work of these individuals is contrasted with that done by isolated individuals.

The present study aimed to present individuals with an actual problematic situation which would call for real thinking to arrive at a proper solution. The problems selected (given in detail below) involve a number of steps all of which must be correct in order that the right answer may be found. The problems were to be given to single individuals and to small groups of cooperating individuals, in order that the abilities of these two might be compared. The problems were such as to make it practically impossible for one individual in the group to get a correct answer instantaneously by a sudden insight into the situation. Rather, they allow all to participate in arriving at a solution; they call for interchange of ideas and for acceptance or criticism and rejection of any idea put forth. At least some of the previous studies have dealt more with the performance of certain rather elementary tasks such as word-building, vowel cancellation, multiplication, turning fishing reels, etc., which have allowed but little constructive cooperation wherein ideas may be accepted or rejected either in whole or in part.

The problems used here are still quite far from the usual type of problematic situation met in real life. They are problems admitting of only one answer; there is only one type of best solution. They arouse none, or very little, of the emotional bias with which persons characteristically approach life situations. It can

From *American Journal of Psychology*, 1932, XLIV, 491–504. Reprinted by permission of the author and the American Psychological Association, Inc.

---

[1] F. H. Allport, *Social Psychology* (Boston: Houghton Mifflin Co., 1924), ch. 11.

[2] G. B. Watson, "Do Groups Think More Efficiently than Individuals?", *J. Abnor. & Soc. Psychol.*, 1928, XXIII, 328–336.

[3] W. Bechterew and A. Lange, "Die Ergebnisse des Experiments auf dem Gebiete der kollektiven Reflexologie," *Zeit. f. angew. Psychol.*, 1924, XXIV, 305–344.

[4] E. B. South, "Some Psychological Aspects of Committee Work," *J. Appl. Psychol.*, 1927, XI, 348–368, 437–464.

[5] B. V. Belaev, abstract received from the author, entitled "The Problem of the Collective and Its Internal Structure." Other references are: W. A. Barton, Jr., "Group Activity Versus Individual Activity in Developing Ability to Solve Problems in First-Year Algebra," *J. Educ. Admin. & Supervis.*, 1926, XII, 512–518; H. E. Burtt, "Sex Differences in the Effect of Discussion," *J. Exper. Psychol.*, 1920, III, 390–395; M. P. Follett, *Creative Experience* (New York: Longmans, Green & Co., 1924); K. Gordon, "Group Judgments in the Field of Lifted Weights," *J. Exper. Psychol.*, 1924, VII, 398–400; K. Gordon, "A Study of Esthetic Judgments," *ibid.*, 1923, VI, 36–42; E. C. Lindeman, *Social Discovery* (New York: New Republic, 1924); A. D. Sheffield, *Creative Discussion* (New York: Association Press, 1927); and T. W. Thie, "Testing the Efficiency of the Group Method," *English J.*, 1925, XIV, 134–137

be seen at once, then, that not all of the results obtained are directly applicable to any or all group situations.

METHOD AND PROCEDURE

Subjects. The Ss in this experiment were the students in the class in Social Psychology at Columbia University. This group is a rather highly selected one, in view of the fact that almost all are graduate students, a large percentage of them working for advanced degrees. The experiment was divided into halves; 3 problems were used in the first half and 3 in the second half given 2 weeks later. In the first half there were 2 groups of 4 women each and 3 groups of 4 men each. There were 9 men and 12 women working on the problems individually in the same room. In the second half of the experiment there were 2 groups of 4 men each and 3 groups of 4 women each; and 10 men and 7 women worked as separate individuals in the same room. Thus data were received from an equal number of groups of men and women, i.e., 5 groups of each. It will be seen from the above that a group was never composed of the two sexes, but in all cases of either 4 women or 4 men. It was believed that this arrangement would, in general, make for better cooperation and more smoothly running groups. The grouping was not made for any purpose of sex comparisons; no such comparisons are made in this study.

Problems. (*a*) **First Half of Experiment.** The directions used in the first half of the experiment were as follows:

(1) Materials for this problem are in the envelope marked "Problems I and II." Use disks H1, H2, H3, W1, W2, W3. (For the present disregard the symbols on the reverse side.) Side 1 of the card. On the A-side of a river are three wives (W1, W2, W3) and their husbands (H1, H2, H3). All the men but none of the women can row. Get them across to the B-side of the river by means of a boat carrying only three at one time. No man will allow his wife to be

in the presence of another man unless he is also there.

(2) Materials for this problem are in the envelope marked "Problems I and II." Use disks marked M1, M2, M3, C1, C2, RC. (Reverse side of the disks just used.) Side 1 of the card. Three Missionaries (M1, M2, M3) and three Cannibals (C1, C2, RC) are on the A-side of a river. Get them across to the B-side by means of a boat which holds only two at one time. All the Missionaries and one Cannibal (RC) can row. Never under any circumstances or at any time may the Missionaries be outnumbered by the Cannibals. (Except, of course, when there are no Missionaries present.)

(3) Materials for this problem are in the envelope marked "Problem III." Side 2 of the card. In Circle A arrange the disks in order of size, that is with the largest on the bottom, etc., ending with the smallest on top. Using Circle B as a transfer station, transfer the disks to Circle C so that they will be in the same order in Circle C that they are now in Circle A. Never place a larger disk on a smaller one and move only one disk at a time. (Number the disks for reference if you wish.)

The card referred to in these problems contained on the one side a diagram of a river, for convenience in solving the first two problems, and on the other side a diagram of the three circles necessary to a solution of the third problem.

(*b*) **Second Half of Experiment.** The directions used in the second half of the experiment were as follows:

(1) Materials for the problem are in the envelope marked "Problem I." Put these words, taken from the envelope, together so that they form the last sentence (only one sentence) of the unfinished prose selection.

In New Orleans there is a tree which nobody looks at without curiosity and without wondering how it came there. It reminds one of the warm climes of Africa and Asia. Indeed, with its sharp and thin foliage, sighing mournfully under the blast of one of our November northern winds, it looks as sorrowful as an exile.

(2) Materials for this problem are in the envelope marked "Problem II." These words when put in the proper order form the last

three and one half lines of the unfinished sonnet below. Arrange them as nearly as possible in the proper order.

A boy named Simon sojourned in a dale;
Some said that he was simple, but I'm sure
That he was nothing less than simon pure;
They thought him so because forsooth, a whale
He tried to catch in Mother's water-pail.
Ah! little boy, timid, composed, demure—
He had imagination. Yet endure
Defeat he could, for he of course did fail.
But there are Simons of a larger growth,
Who, too, in shallow waters fish for whales,
And when they fail

(3) A consolidated school is to be built in the rural district shown in the diagram. The capital letters (A, B, C, etc.) indicate points (not towns) where pupils are to be picked up by two school buses. The mileage between each point is indicated on the diagram. The capacity of each bus is 35 pupils and the driver. Find the most desirable location for this school and give the route each bus must take. The buses may start at ANY point and need not necessarily start from the school each morning. Following are the number of pupils to be picked up at each point:

Point	No. Pupils	Point	No. Pupils	Point	No. Pupils
A	6	D	4	G	3
B	13	E	2	H	10
C	17	F	5	I	3

The diagram for problem 3 is given below. It was furnished to each individual who was working alone and was drawn to the scale of 1 inch to the mile. Only one diagram was provided in each group; it was drawn to the scale of 2 inches to the mile.

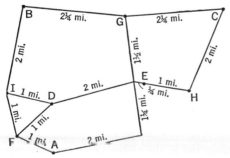

In addition to the specific instructions given above, the following general instructions appeared at the top of each set of problems given the separate individuals working in the same room:

Below are three problems. Work them as quickly and accurately as possible. There is a correct solution to each problem. Record your answer or state briefly how you solved the problem. When you have finished one problem and are ready to go on with the second, record the time to the nearest half-minute by means of the record being kept on the front board. Then proceed with the second and then the third, and record time when each is finished. Work the problems in the order listed.

At the top of the set of problems given to each group of 4 individuals were the following instructions:

A chairman has been appointed to manipulate the necessary materials. Work together as a cooperative group to solve the three problems given below. Work them as quickly and accurately as possible. There is a correct solution to each problem. Record your solution or state briefly how the problem was solved. Each individual, including the chairman, should make his contributions to the group solution spontaneously as they occur to him. Indicate to the note-taker when you have finished one problem and are ready to proceed to the next; the note-taker does not participate in any way as a member of the group in solving the problem.

Every individual in the group was provided with a separate set of the problems, but only one set of the necessary materials was given to each group; this made it more essential that all cooperate to solve the problems. The first individual in each group of 4 was appointed chairman to manipulate the materials in order to obviate the confusion and delay which might result if each attempted to carry out his own ideas. The chairman was appointed rather than being elected by the group to prevent unnecessary delay in starting to work, and because in many cases the individuals had never before met except in the more formal classroom atmosphere. It was thought that any formal or parliamentary organization of the group might tend to restrict spontaneity and cooperation and thus perhaps limit the possibilities of getting the best results.

The note-taker, referred to in the group instructions above, was for the purpose of securing more qualitative and quantitative facts concerning the group activity than the time of solving and answers to the problems would provide. In the first half of the experiment the note-taker was given the following instructions:

You are to act as note-taker and time recorder for a group of persons solving three problems. You are to take absolutely no part in the group activity. Do not indicate by any means your approval or disapproval of their activities. Record the final solution of the group on each problem. Record the time required to solve each problem. Record as many of the detailed suggestions made by any member of the group as it is possible for you to get.

In the second half it was thought that the following plan might afford more quantitative data concerning the activity of the groups.

Tally separately every suggestion made by any member of the group so that a record can be made up of the complete number of suggestions made in any one group. Get as much as is possible of each suggestion made. Record this in your notes. If the suggestion is rejected check the tally. Note whether it is rejected by the person who proposed it or by another member of the group. If the suggestion is accepted underscore the tally.

There were 10 sets of notes taken and in only 3 cases did the note-taker have any knowledge either of the problem or of its correct solution. Thus the knowledge of whether a rejected suggestion was in reality an erroneous or a correct suggestion could have but little effect on

the notes taken, and can be determined by E only from these same notes.

Equalization of the Groups. In order to equate the groups, that is, to be reasonably sure that no one group was made up of four superior individuals and that those who worked in groups were on the whole neither inferior to nor superior to those working as separate individuals, shifts were made so that the composition of the groups differed in the two halves of the experiment. Individuals making up the first group were chosen from the class roll by placing every other man and woman in a group. Certain deviations had to be made from this general procedure in the case of absence from class, since the aim was to keep the total number of men working in groups and as separate individuals approximately equal for the total experiment; the same being true for the women. Every group was composed of 4 individuals because it was thought that a group of this size would cooperate to better advantage than a very much larger or smaller one. Also the limited number of available Ss made it impossible to increase the number much and still have enough single groups to make the comparisons meaningful. Limited room accommodations also limited the number of groups.

Table 1 below shows the accomplishments of every S as he worked alone in the first half of the experiment. Table 2 shows the accomplishment of the groups in the second half of the experiment. Group A' in the second half of the experiment was composed of individuals Y, G, I, and R of the first half of the experiment; Group B' of K, U, W, and an individual not before present; Group C' of M, J, A, F; Group D' of Q, L, R, C; and Group E' of H, T, X, B. It will be seen that each group contained only one person who had solved a problem correctly in the first half of the experiment. Since the groups in the first half were chosen at random it was necessary to check the individuals in the second half

TABLE 1

SHOWING FOR EVERY INDIVIDUAL S AND FOR EVERY GROUP OF Ss THE TIME IN
MINUTES REQUIRED FOR A SOLUTION AND THE NATURE OF THE SOLUTIONS
OF THE PROBLEMS OF THE FIRST HALF OF THE EXPERIMENT

		Problem 1		Problem 2		Problem 3	
		Time	Solution	Time	Solution	Time	Solution
Individuals	D	6.5	Incorrect	29.0	Incorrect	6.0	Incorrect
	F	4.5	"	17.5	"	13.5	"
	G	3.5	"	6.0	"	20.5	"
	H	1.0	"	3.5	"	10.0	"
	K	2.0	"	4.5	"	18.0	"
	L	1.5	"	2.5	"	9.5	"
	N	1.0	"	2.5	"	15.0	"
	P	7.0	"	5.5	"	15.5	"
	R	1.5	"	3.0	"	19.0	"
	A	6.0	"	15.0	"	14.5	Unsolved
	C	4.5	"	5.5	"	14.0	"
	W	6.0	"	18.0	"	14.0	"
	J	4.5	"	6.5	"	5.5	"
	X	4.0	"	12.5	"	13.0	"
	Y	4.5	"	10.0	"	15.5	"
	T	10.5	"	20.0	"	15.0	"
	B	3.0	"	8.5	"	60.0	Correct
	I	4.5	"	8.5	"	21.0	"
	M	5.0	Correct	8.0	"	5.0	Incorrect
	Q	9.5	"	9.5	"	5.5	"
	U	4.0	"	12.5	"	16.0	Unsolved
	Av.	4.5		9.9		15.5	
	S.D.	2.5		6.7		11.0	
Groups	A	5.0	Incorrect	7.5	Incorrect	4.5	Incorrect
	B	4.5	Correct	34.0	Correct	17.0	Correct
	C	5.0	"	12.0	"	37.0	Unsolved
	D	16.0	"	27.0	"	29.0	Correct
	E	2.0	Incorrect	4.0	Incorrect	4.0	Incorrect
	Av.	6.5		16.9		18.3	
	S.D.	4.97		11.6		13.1	

to see that no group in the first half had been superior. From Table 2 can be seen the accomplishments of the individual Ss in the second half. Group A was made up of individuals A', J', N', and an S not used in the second half; Group B of H', F', M', and P'; Group C of B', C', X', and an S not used in the second half; Group D of E', K', L', and Q'; and Group E of D', G', I', and an S not used in the second half. Thus it seems probable that no group was composed of 4 superior individuals. In neither half of the experiment did a group contain more than one individual who had solved a problem correctly in the other half of the experiment, and no single individual ever correctly solved more than one problem.

RESULTS

Table 1 summarizes the time (in minutes) required for and the nature of every solution presented by a group or by the individual Ss in the first half of the experiment. It will be seen that only 5 correct solutions out of a possible 63 were returned by the different Ss. There were 8 correct solutions out of a possible 15 for the groups. That is, 7.9 percent of the solutions turned in by individual Ss were correct, while 53 percent of the solutions turned in by groups were correct. It was found that the false solutions to the problems could be divided into several different types. In Problem 1 two types of false solution, handed in by 13 different individuals, made an error in the first move, 4 made an error in the third move and 1 made an error in the fifth. It took 7 single moves to solve the problem correctly. No group erred on the first move; one erred on the third and one on the fourth. Group activity would seem to insure not only a larger proportion of correct solutions, but also that even in erroneous solutions the error is not made so early in the solution.

The solution to Problem 2 shows the same. It takes 13 single moves to arrive at a correct solution. Among the individual Ss, 3 erred on the first move, 4 on the second, 6 on the third, 2 on the fifth, 2 on the sixth, 1 on the seventh, and 2 on the eighth. The last 3 who erred on the seventh and eighth did not consider their solutions completed as all the cannibals and missionaries had not been transferred to the B-side of the river. It is interesting to note that no group got as near as this to a correct solution of this problem and then failed to reach it. Three groups solved the problem correctly; both of the others erred on the fifth move.

Problem 3 cannot be classified so easily on the basis of the first false move, since in all cases, except in one group, once the method of transfer was hit upon success

was assured. In the case of 7 individual Ss no solution at all was recorded; it may be assumed that they were unable to reach one. Six individual Ss skipped circle B, the transfer station. Two spread the disks out in B until 4 had been transferred; then the disks were piled up and the fifth one either transferred through B to C or skipped over B to C. After this the others were again spread out and then transferred to C. Four individual Ss slipped the disks from underneath. One group skipped the transfer station; one spread the disks out as described above. No group slipped them from underneath; 2 groups contemplated this but abandoned it as being too simple; one group abandoned spreading them out as also being too simple. In Group C, Problem 3 has been recorded as unsolved, but this does not fairly represent the group. They had successfully transferred 4 disks into circle C and the fifth into circle B, but in manipulating to get the fifth disk into C they lost sight of their real aim and became confused. They quit work then, although saying that they "probably could figure it out if they stayed with it long enough." The instructions for this problem appear not to have been sufficiently clear in the prohibition of certain procedures. It was felt that too many instructions here might make the correct solution too obvious, although the bizarre plan of spreading the disks out in the circles was never anticipated. The problem had been previously tried out both on groups and separate individuals, and neither the plan of spreading out the disks nor that of slipping them from underneath had occurred. The instructions had, therefore, been assumed to be adequate. It is to be noted that several Ss indicated that they were aware of not having followed the directions exactly. For example, one individual who slipped them from underneath commented, "This seems too simple but I can't see how it can be solved without moving a covered disk."

TABLE 2

SHOWING FOR EVERY INDIVIDUAL *S* AND FOR EVERY GROUP OF *S*s THE TIME IN MINUTES REQUIRED FOR A SOLUTION AND THE NUMBER AND NATURE OF THE ERRORS MADE IN THE PROBLEMS OF THE SECOND HALF OF THE EXPERIMENT

		Problem 1		Problem 2		Problem 3		
		Time	Errors	Time	Solution	Time	Location	Excess
Individuals	*A′*	6.0	2	27.0	Unsolved	5.0	1.25	0.0
	B′	8.0	1	37.0	"	21.0	.125	.5
	C′	12.0	10	150.0	Incorrect	35.0	.25	.5
	D′	7.0	8	25.0	Unsolved	25.0	1.0	.5
	F′	8.0	1	16.0	Incorrect	16.0	1.25	.5
	G′	2.0	1	6.0	Unsolved	13.0	3.0	.5
	H′	14.0	1	20.0	"	15.0	.25	.5
	J′	6.0	1	85.0	Incorrect	30.0	6.0	1.75
	K′	9.0	2	35.0	Unsolved	12.0	4.0	1.75
	L′	7.5	1	20.0	"	24.0	6.0	1.75
	M′	11.0	7	42.0	Incorrect	18.0	1.25	1.25
	X′	12.0	3	39.0	Unsolved	14.0	4.0	2.0
	P′	8.5	9	17.0	"	12.0	1.25	.5
	Q′	5.0	1	31.0	Incorrect	10.0	4.0	2.25
	W′	6.5	0	29.0	Unsolved	18.0	Unsolved	
	I′	6.0	0	78.0	Incorrect	29.0	4.0	1.25
	N′	10.0	0	26.0	Unsolved	10.0	3.0	1.5
	Av.	8.2		40.2		18.0	2.5	1.06
	S.D.	2.9		33.8		7.9	1.9	
Groups	*A′*	3.0	0	28.0	Incorrect	3.0	.25	.5
	B′	12.0	0	45.0	"	10.0	4.0	2.25
	C′	6.0	1	69.0	"	00.0	Unsolved	
	D′	2.0	0	26.0	"	8.0	5.0	1.50
	E′	4.5	0	40.0	"	10.0	1.25	.75
	Av.	5.5		41.6		8.0	2.6	1.25
	S.D.	3.5		15.4		2.9		

Also, after the experiment, one individual *S* was overheard by *E* saying that "since the instructions did not say that the disks should not be slipped from underneath" she solved the problem that way because she "could not see how else to do it."

Table 2 gives the time and number of errors made by every individual *S*, and by every group of *S*s on the three problems given in the second half of the experiment. The seventh column, which is headed "location," gives the number of miles which the proposed location is from the best location. The eighth column gives the number of excess miles which the two buses travel, the shortest possible number of miles being 12.

It will be noted that here, as in Problem 1, a greater percentage of the groups obtained a correct solution than individual *S*s. Of the solutions reported by the different *S*s 5.7 percent were correct; and by the groups, 27 percent were correct.

The incorrect solutions in this half of the experiment also are interesting when analyzed. Among the groups there were 4 correct solutions on the first problem, the single error being the transposition of the words "time immemorial" to read "immemorial time." Only 3 Ss completed the sentence to read as it had in the original. By far the greatest number of errors lay in the placing of the single word "there," which could be put in 7 different places without disturbing the smoothness of the sentence. This error was made (often together with others) in 10 cases by individual Ss but by no group. Five Ss submitted solutions wherein the structure of the sentence was poor.

None of the individual Ss solved Problem 2 correctly; 11 stated that they could not solve it and presented no solution. The 6 other individual solutions varied in their degree of imperfection. One S simply composed a complete sentence to finish the sonnet. Three others had either 3 or 4 of the rhyme words, but an erroneous rhyme scheme. One person had the first line in accord with the original and one had the last line correct. Others made more or less serious errors here. The second and third lines were never correctly written by any individual. All groups turned in a solution. The rhyme scheme was correct in all cases; the first line was correct in 3 cases and the last one in 4. Group B had the two middle lines almost correct. The meaning was the same as that in the original, although several words were misplaced. In some group and some individual solutions the words had been so arranged as to convey a meaning almost opposite to that in the original.

Neither a group nor an individual arrived at a correct solution of the third problem. The average error in location and average excess number of miles traveled were about equivalent for the groups and individuals. In part, the absence of a correct solution may be due to the fact that it took a long time to solve the first and second problems. In many cases the completion of the third meant dismissal for the evening; thus perhaps any apparently suitable location was accepted. (On the other hand many persons took the problems home with them in order to complete the second and third. They kept time for themselves and returned the solutions the next week.) A comparison of Tables 3 and 4 shows that among the groups the total number of suggestions was by far the least in the third problem.

Reference to the notes kept by the note-takers will give more definite information regarding the activities within the groups. All those in a group do not participate equally in the group activity. Such remarks or tabulations as the following are found in the notes from three groups in all. (The note-takers numbered the Ss to facilitate taking notes.) "S 1 and S 3 were leaders in the solution." From the tabulation of suggestions given in the solution referred to it is found that S 1 made 7 suggestions and S 3 made 14 suggestions; while S 2 and S 4 made, respectively, 2 and 3 suggestions. Later in these same notes we find, "S 2 not contributing much." In another set of notes: "S 3 and S 4 offered no suggestions during the solution." In the next problem solved by this same group S 2 made 16 suggestions, S 1 made 12, S 4 made 8, and S 3 made 5. From yet another set: "S 1 and S 4 did most of the suggesting, S 2 and S 3 not working much." In solving Problem 2 in the first half of the experiment the note-taker remarks that "S 2 and S 3 draw their own diagrams and become absorbed in them: do almost no suggesting." In solving Problem 3 "S 3 made no comments at all, S 2 spoke only a few words." In one of the above groups an S who participated a great deal in group activity very soon assumed the task of manipulating the material in the place of the less active S who had been appointed

TABLE 3

SHOWING, FOR EVERY GROUP OF Ss, THE NUMBER OF CORRECT AND INCORRECT
SUGGESTIONS AND REJECTIONS, AND THE NUMBER OF REJECTIONS BY
THOSE MAKING THE SUGGESTIONS AND BY OTHERS OF THE GROUP

(Problem 1, Second Half of Experiment)

Groups	Suggestions			Rejections			
	No.	Correct	Incorrect	Correct	Incorrect	Maker	Others
A′	29	18	11	3	11	7	7
B′	24	18	6	1	6	1	6
C′	17	8	9	0	8	0	8
D′	20	11	9	2	9	2	9
E′	31	25	6	2	6	2	6
Totals . .	121	80	41	8	40	12	36

chairman. Possibly one could get interesting, meaningful, and perhaps quite different sets of results by using in one set of cases groups with a chairman either equal or superior to the group, and in another set groups having a chairman inferior to the group in ability.

In some groups quite the reverse situation is found, and all members cooperate splendidly. Such comments as the following are found in the notes from the three groups: "All contributing beautifully," and later, "all cooperating and making check suggestions." From another, "suggestions coming from all four about equally." Another records, "the four members cooperate well," and on another page, "splendid group work."

In the first half of the experiment Groups A and E solved all problems incorrectly. From notes kept there was apparently but little criticism of the work in Group E. The note-taker remarks, "All satisfied with the solution." The members of Group A, however, seemed to recognize that they were not taking all specifications of the problem into consideration, but rationalized their procedure and turned in solutions. At the end of the first problem the recorder notes that "they conclude that they have solved the problem, though perhaps not in the way the directions signify." This group is one of those referred to above in which the members do not participate equally in the group activity. In Problem 2 they finally agreed that the boat's contact with the shore would not constitute a case of outnumbering by the cannibals! In Problem 3 they failed to consider circle B always as a transfer station, but skipped it whenever it was convenient to do so.

In the other groups there is much more reference to the checking of errors and meeting the conditions of the problem. One group worked a solution through three times to be sure that they had met all specifications; in the last trial they discovered an error which would have made their solution wrong. The notes on these groups also mention numerous references to the stated problem to see that all qualifications were being taken into account.

Table 3 above deals with Problem 1 in the second half of the experiment. Column 2 shows the total number of suggestions made in each group. Columns 3 and 4 show respectively the number which were in reality correct and the number which were incorrect. Columns 5 and 6 indicate whether those suggestions which were rejected were respec-

TABLE 4

SHOWING, FOR EVERY GROUP OF Ss, THE NUMBER OF CORRECT AND INCORRECT
SUGGESTIONS AND REJECTIONS, AND THE NUMBER OF REJECTIONS BY
THOSE MAKING THE SUGGESTIONS AND BY OTHERS OF THE GROUP

(Problem 2, Second Half of Experiment)

Groups	Suggestions			Rejections			
	No.	Correct	Incorrect	Correct	Incorrect	Maker	Others
A′	71	32	39	10	35	18	27
B′	49	23	26	9	20	8	19
C′	76	35	41	9	29	7	31
D′	32	15	17	2	13	4	11
E′	37	17	20	2	14	3	13
Totals . .	265	122	143	32	111	40	101

tively correct or incorrect. Columns 7 and 8 show the number of suggestions which were rejected by the individual making the suggestion or by another member of the group.

It will be noted from Table 2 that there was only one error (a word transposition) in any group solution. In one case, Group A′, the suggestions rejected by the proposer or by another are exactly equal in number; in all other cases more were rejected by another member. Considering all groups together, three times as many suggestions were rejected by another member of the group as by the proposers of the suggestions. Five times as many incorrect as correct suggestions were rejected, whereas of the total number of suggestions made, twice as many were correct as incorrect. This fact may be considered in connection with the relative number of correct solutions among groups and among individuals. This quantitative check on rejections was not kept in the first half of the experiment, but from its results in the second half, together with the proportion of correct solutions in the first half, and the fact that notes on the groups presenting correct solutions emphasize the checking of erroneous moves, it seems as though group supremacy in the first half

might have been in part due to the rejection of incorrect suggestions or the checking of errors. Also it was found that no group was composed of four superior individuals. All this would seem to indicate that one point of group supremacy is the rejection of incorrect ideas that escape the notice of the individual when working alone. Perhaps this may be the greatest point of group supremacy.

It is impossible to say with any certainty whether the rejected correct suggestions were rejected oftener by the proposer or by another member of the group. Only 8 correct suggestions were rejected, and these were all later accepted, since the solutions were with but one exception absolutely correct. (In the solution where two words were transposed, the correct suggestion concerning their position was never made: this was a case of the acceptance and retention of an incorrect suggestion.) Five of the correct suggestions were rejected by the proposer and 3 by another, but with so small a total the difference is not significant.

Tables 4 and 5 summarize the data received on Problems 2 and 3. Since neither of these problems was correctly solved in any case, the value of the group checking does not appear so clearly. But a con-

TABLE 5

Showing, for Every Group of Ss, the Number of Correct and Incorrect Suggestions and Rejections, and the Number of Rejections by Those Making the Suggestions and by Others of the Group

(Problem 3, Second Half of Experiment)

Groups	Suggestions			Rejections			
	No.	Correct	Incorrect	Correct	Incorrect	Maker	Others
A'	17	6	11	3	7	4	6
B'	10	3	7	1	6	0	7
C'			(No solution attempted)				
D'	10	2	8	0	5	0	5
E'	13	5	8	2	4	1	5
Totals . .	50	16	34	6	22	5	23

sideration of these results, with an analysis of individual and group work on these two problems, brings out the same fact as above. For example, only 6, or 35%, of the individual Ss presented a solution to Problem 2, as compared with 5, or 100%, of the groups. But perhaps more important than this is the fact that only one individual solution presented the idea conveyed by the part of the sonnet quoted; the other presented an opposite situation. (That is, they had *Simple Simon* railing "at ill luck and unkind fate.") Three groups conveyed the correct idea, while only 2 reversed the conditions. That is, only $\frac{1}{6}$ of the individual Ss, as compared with $\frac{3}{5}$ of the groups, succeeded in grasping and presenting the proper situation. It seems not altogether improbable that this is a direct result of the rejection of incorrect ideas in the group; which, it should be noted again, is done largely by another member than the proposing one (2.52 times as many suggestions were rejected by another as by the proposer).

We find in the case of Problem 3, first, that all groups met the requirement as to the capacity of the buses, whereas 2 individual Ss placed more than 35 pupils in a bus (one placed 43 and the other 37 in one of the buses). Other than this, however,

no superiority either of group over individual or of individual over group is shown when the two are compared as a whole.

Summary

The purpose of the present study was to compare the ability of individuals and cooperating groups of 4 persons in solving complex problems. The problems involved a number of steps, all of which had to be correct before the right answer was obtained, but they are still far from the life-situations usually met. The groups were roughly equated so that no one group was composed of 4 superior individuals, but the students used were a highly selected group when compared with the population as a whole.

Upon the basis of the data and discussion presented in the foregoing pages the following conclusions seem justified:

(1) Groups seem assured of a much larger proportion of correct solutions than individuals do.

(2) This seems to be due to the rejection of incorrect suggestions and the checking of errors in the group.

(3) In groups of the size here used more incorrect suggestions are rejected by another member of the group than by

the individual who proposed the suggestion.

(4) All members do not cooperate or participate equally in the solution of the problems.

(5) In erroneous solutions (where it is possible to determine the exact point at which the first error was made), groups do not err so soon as the average individual does.

NONADAPTIVE GROUP BEHAVIOR   By Alexander Mintz

THEORETICAL CONSIDERATIONS

It is common knowledge that groups of people frequently behave in a way which leads to disastrous consequences not desired or anticipated by the members of the group. At theater fires, people often block the exits by pushing, so that individuals are burned or trampled. Since it normally takes only a few minutes for a theater to be emptied, the strikingly nonadaptive character of this behavior is obvious.

In the explanations for the occurrence of such behavior offered by social psychologists, intense emotional excitement resulting from mutual facilitation (or "contagion" or "suggestion") and leading to interference with thinking, adaptive behavior, and the operation of moral codes, has tended to be viewed as the decisive factor. Ultimately they stem from the theories of the nature of crowd behavior of Le Bon,[1] who has been an extremely influential figure in the thinking on social issues of the past fifty years.

Material will be presented in this paper suggesting that violent emotional excitement is not the decisive factor [2] in the nonadaptive behavior of people in panics and related situations. Instead, it appears to be possible to explain the nonadaptive character of such behavior in terms of [people's] perception of the situation and their expectation of what is likely to happen.

What are the reasonable expectations of people at a theater fire or in similar circumstances in which a panic is apt to develop? Situations of this type tend to have a characteristically unstable reward structure, which has been generally overlooked by social scientists as a factor in panics. Cooperative behavior is required for the common good but has very different consequences for the individual depending on the behavior of others. Thus at a theater fire, if everyone leaves in an orderly manner, everybody is safe, and an individual waiting for his turn is not sacrificing his interests. But, if the cooperative pattern of behavior is disturbed, the usual advice, "Keep your head, don't push, wait for your turn, and you will be safe," ceases to be valid. If the exits are blocked, the person following this advice is likely to be burned to death. In other words, if everybody cooperates, there is no conflict between the needs of the individual and those of the group. However, the situation changes completely as soon as a minority of people cease to cooperate. A conflict between the needs of the group and the selfish needs of the individual then arises. An individual who recognizes this state of things and who wants to benefit the group must sacrifice his own selfish needs.

From *The Journal of Abnormal and Social Psychology*, 1951, XLVI, 150–159. Reprinted by permission of the author and the American Psychological Association, Inc.

[1] G. Le Bon, *The Crowd* (London: Unwin, 1916)
[2] Its existence is not denied.

It is suggested here that it is chiefly the reward structure of the situations which is responsible for nonadaptive behavior of groups at theater fires and similar situations. People are likely to recognize the threats to themselves, as they appear, and behave accordingly. These situations may be compared to states of unstable equilibrium in mechanics; a cone balanced on its tip is not likely to remain in this position a long time because a slight initial displacement of its center of gravity allows the force of gravity to make it fall all the way. Similarly, cooperative behavior at a theater fire is likely to deteriorate progressively as soon as an initial disturbance occurs. If a few individuals begin to push, the others are apt to recognize that their interests are threatened; they can expect to win through to their individual rewards only by pressing their personal advantages at the group's expense. Many of them react accordingly, a vicious circle is set up, and the disturbance spreads. Competitive behavior (pushing and fighting) may result as, e.g., at theater fires, or the group may disperse as in military panics. There is another factor which makes for further disintegration. As the behavior of the group becomes increasingly disorderly, the amount of noise is apt to increase, and communication may then become so difficult that no plan for restoring order can emerge.

This interpretation is almost the reverse of the conventional ones which ascribe nonadaptive group behavior to emotional facilitation and to the supposed alterations of personality in group situations.

The existence of mutual emotional facilitation is not denied; its operation can be readily observed, e.g., in college students during final examinations, in audiences at sports events, etc. However, it is not believed that emotional excite-

ment as such is responsible for nonadaptive group behavior. There are many situations in which intense emotional excitement is the rule, and yet no nonadaptive group behavior appears. Thus it has been reported that intense fear is practically universally present in soldiers about to go into battle, and yet no panic need develop. Similarly, participants in an athletic contest are apt to be so emotionally excited that vomiting is common; no markedly nonadaptive group behavior appears to develop as a result of this kind of intense excitement.

The assumption of personality alterations of people due to crowd membership appears to be entirely unsubstantiated in the case of panics. On the contrary, the competitive behavior or dispersal occurring in panics suggests that group cohesion disappears and that people begin to behave purely as individuals in accordance with their selfish needs.[3] Rather similarly Freud has explained certain types of panics in terms of the disappearance of the libidinal ties between individuals.[4]

As a first step toward the verification of the proposed theory, a set of laboratory experiments was devised. It was thought that if the theory were correct, it should be possible to illustrate its functioning in the laboratory. If not substantiated by laboratory findings, the theory would have to be discarded.

EXPERIMENTAL DESIGN

The experiments were conducted with groups of people, 15 to 21 subjects in each group. The subjects had the task of pulling cones out of a glass bottle; each subject was given a piece of string to which a cone was attached. Cooperation on the part of the subjects was required if the cones were to come out; the physical setup made it easy for "traffic jams" of cones to appear at the bottle neck. Only one cone could come out at a time;

---

[3] I am indebted to Dr. M. Scheerer for pointing out this inference from the suggested theory.
[4] S. Freud, *Group Psychology and Analysis of the Ego* (London: Hogarth Press, 1910), pp. 45–48.

even a near tie between two cones at the bottle neck prevented both from coming out because the narrow apex of the second cone, wedged into the bottle neck, blocked the path for the wide base of the cone ahead of it. The cones had to arrive at the bottle neck in order, one at a time.

Experimental Situations. 1. One of the experimental setups was designed to show that it was possible to produce disorganized, uncooperative, nonadaptive group behavior resulting in "traffic jams" by duplicating the essential features of panic-producing situations, as explained in the theoretical section of this paper. The experimental situation was represented to the subjects as a game in which each participant could win or lose money. A subject could win or lose depending on how successful he was in pulling out his cone. Success was defined in terms of arbitrary time limits in some experiments. In other experiments water was made to flow into the bottle through a spout near the bottom, and the subject was successful if his cone came out of the bottle untouched by the water. Inasmuch as the rewards and fines were offered to individuals, depending on what would happen to their particular cones, it was thought that the cooperative pattern of behavior, required for group success, would be easily disrupted; a momentary "traffic jam" at the bottle neck would be perceived by some of the subjects as threatening them with loss in the game as a result of the anticipated failure of cooperative behavior. These subjects would be tempted to save themselves from the loss by pulling out of turn. Some of them would probably do so, and thus the situation could be expected rapidly to deteriorate after an initial disturbance occurred.

In order that subjects who recognized that full success was out of their reach should not stop trying, intermediate steps between full success and full failure were announced. The details and the amounts of rewards and fines are summarized in the table of results. The monetary rewards and fines were very small, the rewards for full success ranging from 10 to 25 cents, the fines for full failure from 1 to 10 cents. The very small fines were decided upon because it was intended to show that the characteristically inefficient, nonadaptive features of group behavior such as occurs in panics can be reproduced in a situation in which there was no opportunity for fear. It was not thought that the small rewards and fines were likely to constitute real financial incentives for college students. They were introduced to emphasize the nature of the experimental situation as a game in which individuals could win or lose.

2. In the contrasting experimental setups there were no individual rewards or fines, and there was no flow of water except for a few control experiments. The experiments were described as attempts to measure the ability of groups of people to behave cooperatively. Good performances of other groups were quoted. It was expected that under these conditions no "traffic jams" would develop. Subjects had no motivation to disregard any plan that might be devised by the group; the only incentive offered was membership in a group of people who were going to show their ability to cooperate effectively with each other.[5] Thus the reward structure was the principal experimental variable studied in these two experimental situations.

3. Another variable investigated was the excitement built up by mutual facilitation. In a number of "no-reward"

---

[5] The need to belong has been particularly emphasized as an important motive, among others, by E. Fromm in *Escape from Freedom* (New York: Farrar and Rinehart, 1941) and M. Sherif in *An Outline of Social Psychology* (New York: Harper, 1948). The important role which group membership plays in industry has been investigated particularly in the Hawthorne studies; *see*, for example, T. N. Whitehead, *The Industrial Worker* (Cambridge, Mass.: Harvard University Press, 1938), Vol. I.

experiments several subjects were asked to act as accomplices. They were secretly instructed, before the experiment began, to scream, behave excitedly, swear, and make as much noise as possible. To limit their influence to emotional facilitation they were asked not to give specific bad advice nor to disturb the workings of any plan the group might decide upon. It was expected that the added emotional excitement, which is the major factor in Le Bon's and similar theories of panics, would not have much effect on results.

4. In certain of the reward-and-fine experiments an attempt was made to minimize the opportunities for mutual emotional facilitation by largely preventing the subjects from seeing each other. This was accomplished by a circular screen with holes for eyes and arms and with vertical partitions on the outside, placed around the glass bottle. Each subject stood in an individual "stall" hiding him from his neighbors; he saw the bottle standing on the floor through the eye hole; only his arm and eyes could be seen by the other subjects, and the eyes were not likely to be seen because the subjects were mainly looking at the bottle tied to the floor. In order to prevent excited screams, the subjects were asked to remain silent after the experiment began, which request was largely complied with. It was expected that the results would be essentially the same as those in the other reward-and-fine experiments.

5. A third variable which was introduced in a few of the experiments was interference with the opportunity to arrive at a plan of action. In most of the experiments the subjects were not prevented from conducting preliminary discussions; in almost all instances either they started such a discussion immediately or asked for permission to do so, which was given. Only twice did a group fail to discuss and agree upon a plan when discussion was not explicitly forbidden.

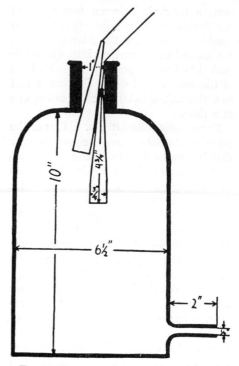

FIG. 1. Cross section of the glass bottle with two cones shown blocking the bottle neck. Main dimensions of the equipment are given.

On the other hand, in two of the reward-and-fine experiments conducted early in the study the subjects were forbidden to talk to each other both before and during the experiment; in one reward-and-fine experiment conducted immediately after three no-reward experiments with the same group, the subjects were prevented from having a preliminary discussion so that no plan could be agreed upon beforehand, but were allowed to talk during the experiment.

Apparatus and Procedure. Figure 1 gives the shapes and dimensions of the cones and of the bottle and shows where the pieces of string were attached. The cones were made of wood in the early experiments. Later, aluminum cones were substituted [6] because the wooden one tended to become tightly forced into

---

[6] Postwar shortages prevented the use of smooth plastic material, as had been intended.

the bottle neck and had to be loosened by hand (which was done promptly by the experimenter). In the experiments with the aluminum cones the glass bottle had too large an opening, which was remedied by the insertion of a cylinder with a 1-inch hole bored through it. This cylinder, made of aluminum, had rubber tape wound on the outside. It was forced tightly into the bottle neck and was tied down with wire. In addition to cutting down the opening of the bottle to the desired diameter, it also protected the glass from the impact of the aluminum cones. A sponge rubber pad was cemented to the bottom of the glass bottle. A rubber tube could be attached to the spout and lead either to a water faucet or to another similar bottle placed high up.

The screen was made of corrugated cardboard. Two strips 23.5 feet in length were cut off a 3-foot-wide roll and glued together, so that a strip 6 feet wide resulted. The ends of the strip could be brought together and the strip could be made to stand on edge in the shape of a cylinder around the bottle. Pieces of corrugated cardboard, 3 feet by 1 foot, were attached to the screen at intervals of 1 foot 3 inches, subdividing the space immediately around the screen into individual stalls. The rectangular eye holes cut in each stall were 1.5 inches high, 5 inches wide; their bottom was 4 feet 8 inches above the ground; the roughly circular arm holes were about 5 inches in diameter and 3 feet 1.5 inches from the ground, near the right-hand edges of the stalls. There were 18 stalls.

In putting the cones into the bottle, care was taken to prevent the tangling of strings; as an added precaution, the fishing line used as string was waxed in later experiments. In the early experiments the bottle was tied to the legs of a table on which it was placed. In the later experiments it was placed on the floor and tied to nails driven into the floor like tent stakes.

The instructions were not rigidly standardized. The rewards were always larger than the fines, ranging from 10 to 25 cents in different experiments. The fines ranged from 1 to 5 cents. Examples of the two main types of instructions and other details of the experiment follow:

1. *A reward-and-fine experiment.* "I need volunteers for an experiment which is set up as a game in which you can win up to a quarter or lose up to 2 cents [or 5 or 10 cents as the case may have been]." Then, after the volunteers (sometimes after some urging) assembled: "As I said, this is going to be like a game. Each of you will receive a cone with an attached piece of string. All cones will be placed into the bottle. The object of the game is to get your cone out before it gets wet. You may start pulling when I give the signal, 'ready-go!' but only one cone can come out at a time. If two get into the bottle neck, neither comes out (demonstration). Simultaneously, I shall start water flowing into the bottle. If your cone comes out dry you get a quarter. If less than a third of it is wet, you get nothing; if more than a third but less than two thirds of it gets wet, you pay a penny fine. If the cone is more than two-thirds wet, you pay a two-cent fine. The fines will be contributed to the Student Council." Then the students were asked to put their cones in the bottle. While they were doing it, a discussion of a plan of action generally started and was not interfered with by the experimenter.

The signal to begin was given after an agreement was reached by the subjects. When in doubt, the experimenter asked the group whether they were ready.

2. *A no-reward experiment.* "This is going to be an experiment in which your ability to cooperate with each other will be measured. I need volunteers." Then, after the subjects assembled around the bottle, the procedure continued exactly as in the reward-and-fine experiments except that no rewards were offered, the rubber tube was not attached, and no reference to water was made. Instead, after the possibility of "traffic jams" was

demonstrated, the experimenter said: "In spite of the smallness of the opening, a group of students from the University of Nevada succeeded in cooperating with each other so well that they got all their cones out in 10.5 seconds. See if you can do as well as the Westerners!"

RESULTS

Forty-two experiments with 26 groups of subjects were performed altogether, including some preliminary and control experiments conducted to investigate potential sources of error. One experiment (R_1) was conducted before the procedure was fully developed; there were no fines and only one reward level was announced. No "traffic jam" resulted.

There were 16 experiments with rewards and fines. In three of them (RF_1 to RF_3) discussion was interfered with before the experiment, so that the subjects had no opportunity to devise a plan of action. In all three experiments "traffic jams" developed. In only one of them did the subjects succeed in pulling *any* cones out of the bottle—two cones out of 19 in 40 seconds; these same subjects had successfully pulled out *all* cones in 18.6 seconds and 23 seconds in two immediately preceding trials in which they had had the opportunity to agree upon a plan of action.

In the other 13 reward-and-fine experiments (RF_4 to RF_{16}) discussion was not interfered with. In eight of these experiments (RF_4 to RF_6, RF_9, RF_{10}, RF_{12}, RF_{13}, and RF_{16}) there were serious "traffic jams," the large majority of the cones failing to be pulled out of the bottle within times ranging from 1 to approximately 2 minutes. In another experiment almost half of the cones were in the bottle after 1 minute (RF_{15}). In two of these experiments (RF_{15} and RF_{16}) the factor of mutual emotional facilitation was minimized by the use of the screen. The results were much the same as in most of the other reward-and-fine experiments, suggesting that this factor was not primarily responsible for the results.

In four of the reward-and-fine experiments (RF_7, RF_8, RF_{11}, RF_{14}) there were no serious "traffic jams"; all or almost all of the cones came out of the bottle in less than a minute. In three of these experiments the experimenter was unable to persuade the winners to take the rewards; apparently the subjects had failed to accept the situation as a game with winners and losers. In one of these experiments there was an additional factor which probably interfered with "traffic jams"; immediately before this experiment (RF_{14}) these subjects had participated in another (NR_5) in which no rewards had been offered and in which the fastest time of any group was achieved (10 seconds). The subjects knew the time of this trial; the time allowance for winning exceeded it by 5 seconds, so that the chances of losing must have been recognized as slight by the subjects.

In the remaining 25 experiments there were no rewards or fines. Twenty of these experiments were described to the subjects as measures of cooperation. These experiments fell into three groups. Experiments NR_1 to NR_5 were conducted with groups of subjects who had not been previously exposed to similar experiments, and under "natural" conditions, i.e., without the experimenter entering into a conspiracy with accomplices. Experiments NR_6 to NR_{12} were similar but were conducted immediately after experiments with accomplices. Experiments ANR_1 to ANR_8 were the experiments with accomplices who had been instructed to make noise and to stir up excitement in the group.

No serious "traffic jam" developed in any of these experiments, not in those with new subjects, nor in those with accomplices, nor in those preceded by experiments with accomplices. The times for taking *all* cones out of the bottle ranged in these three groups of experiments from 10 to 22 seconds, from 10.5 to 30 seconds, and from 13.4 to 59 seconds.

The experimenter's accomplices were generally able to stir up excitement, but this excitement failed to disrupt the co-operative behavior of the group to an extent comparable to that of the effect of the individual rewards and fines. In most of the reward-and-fine experiments the majority of the cones were still in the bottle after a minute or longer had elapsed.

Did the accomplices have any effect? The mean times of the two groups of the no-reward, no-accomplice experiments were 16.8 seconds (NR_1 to NR_5) and 19.6 seconds (NR_6 to NR_{12}); the mean time of the accomplice experiments was 34.4 seconds. The difference between the times of the two groups of experiments without accomplices is very small and not statistically significant. In the accomplice experiments the mean time was longer, significantly so at the .01 level of confidence, suggesting that the accomplices did have some disrupting effect. However, a closer examination of the data shows that the two longest times in the accomplice experiments were obtained when some of the accomplices had misunderstood the instructions and gave bad advice to the group. If the results of these two experiments (ANR_1 and ANR_8) are eliminated, the mean time drops to 26.4 seconds, and the critical ratio (Fisher's t for small, uncorrelated samples) indicates that the difference between this time and that of the no-accomplice experiments is too small to reach the conventional standards of statistical significance ($t = 1.82, d.f. = 16, P > .05$). Thus it was not established with certainty that the accomplices who made noise and stirred up excitement without giving bad advice had a disrupting effect on group cooperation. They may have had; the evidence was inconclusive. More experiments would have been needed to establish this point. The experiments with accomplices were designed merely to discover whether an additional opportunity for mutual emotional facilitation would seriously disrupt group cooperation. They served their purpose in showing that it did not.

There were several additional no-reward experiments (PC_1 to PC_5). One of these was described to the subjects as a preliminary trial conducted in order to determine the proper conditions for the next experiment in which rewards were to be offered. This was the only no-reward experiment in which a serious "traffic jam" developed; there was no organized plan for action in this group, probably because the subjects were not sufficiently motivated to devise one before the experiment began. The remaining four experiments were described to the subjects, who had previously participated in reward-and-fine experiments, as control experiments conducted in order to demonstrate to the group what were the effects of the rewards. In view of the common claim of the subjects that the flow of water was primarily responsible for the "traffic jams," water was made to flow in three of them. No serious "traffic jam" developed in any of the control experiments. On the other hand, three out of the four times were distinctly slow ones as compared to those in the other no-reward experiments. It is not clear whether this finding was due to fluctuations of random sampling ("chance"), whether the subjects were inadequately motivated in these "control" experiments, or whether the earlier reward-and-fine experiments had continued bad effects on the cooperative behavior of the subjects. The matter was not investigated at this time.

After each experiment or group of experiments the subjects were told by the experimenter about the true nature of the experiments and about the results obtained so far. The explanations were followed by discussions. In the groups which had failed to pull out the cones from the bottle, marked tendencies toward rationalization appeared during these discussions. Subjects tended to explain the bad results of their group in terms of supposedly tangled strings, effects of the water, or insufficient time for the formulation of a plan, disregarding the fact that these failed to produce "traffic jams" in no-reward experiments.

DISCUSSION

The experiments provide laboratory demonstrations for our hypothesis and partially verify the hypothesis. The behavior of the subjects did not tend toward inefficiency unless the reward structure of the situation provided them with incentives to behave uncooperatively after the cooperative pattern of group behavior was disturbed. There were no "traffic jams" in the no-reward experiments. Emotional excitement produced by the experimenter's accomplices interfered with the efficiency of group behavior only to a minor extent, if at all, compared to the effects of individual rewards and fines. On the other hand, there were inefficient behavior and "traffic jams" in more than half the reward-and-fine experiments, in which the subjects were confronted with the probability of individual failure as soon as the bottle neck was temporarily blocked. This result was obtained without any more serious threat to the individuals than the loss of 10 cents at most and probably a mild feeling of failure in a game. Thus intense fear was not found to be an essential condition of chaotic, nonadaptive group behavior analogous to that occurring in panics.

"Traffic jams" did not occur in all the reward-and-fine experiments and were not expected to. In an experiment with 15 to 20 subjects one cannot be certain that one or a few subjects will create a disturbance within the short time available. With larger groups the percentage of "traffic jams" should be larger; the more people there are, the more likely it becomes that one uncooperative individual will create the initial disturbance which leads to deterioration of the situation.

The theory presented here, if correct, appears to apply to many situations and to contribute to the understanding of a number of social and economic phenomena. Situations with reward structures resembling those of panics and the reward-and-fine experiments reported here seem to be numerous. Tendencies toward non-adaptive group behavior are clearly present in many such situations, regardless of the presence or absence of face-to-face contacts between people and opportunities for mutual emotional facilitation. There are situations in which the appearance of danger does not provide incentives for antisocial behavior, and no chaotic nonadaptive behavior of groups seems to occur in spite of the catastrophic nature of the danger and ample opportunity for face-to-face contacts. There seem to be no panics when people are so trapped that there can be no struggle for an exit, e.g., submarine and mine disasters.[7]

The experiments reported here belong also in a second theoretical context. In these experiments a system of individual rewards resulted in strikingly inefficient behavior, while the goal of demonstrating the ability of the group to cooperate produced much more orderly action. These findings may be compared with those of the type reported by Maller[8] and Sims,[9] who found that individual competition led to greater efficiency than group competition. It should be noted that the structure of the tasks in these earlier experiments and those reported here differed. In the former the subjects worked separately and could not interfere with each other as readily as in our experiments. Thus the experiments provide an additional illustration for the caution that any generalization pertaining to the effect of competition on behavior is limited not only by the prevalent social norms and personality characteristics but also by the nature of the task.

---

[7] Dying miners wrote notes to their families as deadly gas crept in on them in an Illinois pit. *New York Times*, March 31, 1947, p. 8.

[8] J. B. Maller, "Cooperation and Competition," *Teach. Coll. Contr. Educ.*, 1929, No. 384.

[9] V. M. Sims, "The Relative Influence of Two Types of Motivation on Improvement," *J. Educ. Psychol.*, 1928, XIX, 480–484.

GROUP FACTORS IN WORKER PRODUCTIVITY   *By*
George Caspar Homans

In April, 1927, six girls were selected from a large shop department of the Hawthorne works. They were chosen as average workers, neither inexperienced nor expert, and their work consisted of the assembling of telephone relays. A coil, armature, contact springs, and insulators were put together on a fixture and secured in position by means of four machine screws. The operation at that time was being completed at the rate of about five relays in six minutes. This particular operation was chosen for the experiment because the relays were being assembled often enough so that even slight changes in output rate would show themselves at once on the output record. Five of the girls were to do the actual assembly work; the duty of the sixth was to keep the others supplied with parts.

The test room itself was an area divided from the main department by a wooden partition eight feet high. The girls sat in a row on one side of a long workbench. The bench and assembly equipment were identical with those used in the regular department, except in one respect. At the right of each girl's place was a hole in the bench, and into this hole she dropped completed relays. It was the entrance to a chute, in which there was a flapper gate opened by the relay in its passage downward. The opening of the gate closed an electrical circuit which controlled a perforating device, and this in turn recorded the completion of the relay by punching a hole in a tape. The tape moved at the rate of one-quarter of an inch a minute and had space for a separate row of holes for each operator. When punched, it thus constituted a complete output record for each girl for each instant of the day. Such records were kept for five years.

In this experiment, then, as in the earlier illumination experiments, great emphasis was laid on the rate of output. A word of caution is needed here. The Western Electric Company was not immediately interested in increasing output. The experiments were not designed for that purpose. On the other hand, output is easily measured, i.e., it yields precise quantitative data, and experience suggested that it was sensitive to at least some of the conditions under which the employees worked. Output was treated as an index. In short, the nature of the experimental conditions made the emphasis on output inevitable.

From their experience in the illumination experiments, the investigators were well aware that factors other than those experimentally varied might affect the output rate. Therefore arrangements were made that a number of other records should be kept. Unsuitable parts supplied by the firm were noted down, as were assemblies rejected for any reason upon inspection. In this way the type of defect could be known and related to the time of day at which it occurred. Records were kept of weather conditions in general and of temperature and humidity in the test room. Every six weeks each operator was given a medical examination by the company doctor. Every day she was asked to tell how many hours she had spent in bed the night before and, during a part of the experiment,

From Chapter 4, "The Western Electric Researches," in *Fatigue of Workers: Its Relation to Industrial Production* by the Committee on Work in Industry of the National Research Council (New York: Reinhold Publishing Corp., 1941). Reprinted by permission of the author and the publisher.

what food she had eaten. Besides all these records, which concerned the physical condition of the operators, a log was kept in which were recorded the principal events in the test room hour by hour, including among the entries snatches of conversation between the workers. At first these entries related largely to the physical condition of the operators: how they felt as they worked. Later the ground they covered somewhat widened, and the log ultimately became one of the most important of the test room records. Finally, when the so-called Interviewing Program was instituted at Hawthorne, each of the operators was interviewed several times by an experienced interviewer.

The girls had no supervisor in the ordinary sense, such as they would have had in a regular shop department, but a "test room observer" was placed in the room, whose duty it was to maintain the records, arrange the work, and secure a cooperative spirit on the part of the girls. Later, when the complexity of his work increased, several assistants were assigned to help him.

When the arrangements had been made for the test room, the operators who had been chosen to take part were called in for an interview in the office of the superintendent of the Inspection Branch, who was in general charge of the experiment and of the researches which grew out of it. The superintendent described this interview as follows: "The nature of the test was carefully explained to these girls and they readily consented to take part in it, although they were very shy at the first conference. An invitation to six shop girls to come up to a superintendent's office was naturally rather startling. They were assured that the object of the test was to determine the effect of certain changes in working conditions, such as rest periods, midmorning lunches, and shorter working hours. They were expressly cautioned to work at a comfortable pace, and under no circumstances to try and make a race out of the test." This conference was only the first of many. Whenever any experimental change was planned, the girls were called in, the purpose of the change was explained to them, and their comments were requested. Certain suggested changes which did not meet with their approval were abandoned. They were repeatedly asked, as they were asked in the first interview, not to strain but to work "as they felt."

The experiment was now ready to begin. Put in its simplest terms, the idea of those directing the experiment was that if an output curve was studied for a long enough time under various changes in working conditions, it would be possible to determine which conditions were the most satisfactory. Accordingly, a number of so-called "experimental periods" were arranged. For two weeks before the operators were placed in the test room, a record was kept of the production of each one without her knowledge. In this way the investigators secured a measure of her productive ability while working in the regular department under the usual conditions. This constituted the first experimental period. And for five weeks after the girls entered the test room no change was made in working conditions. Hours remained what they had been before. The investigators felt that this period would be long enough to reveal any changes in output incidental merely to the transfer. This constituted the second experimental period.

The third period involved a change in the method of payment. In the regular department, the girls had been paid according to a scheme of group piecework, the group consisting of a hundred or more employees. Under these circumstances, variations in an individual's total output would not be immediately reflected in her pay, since such variations tended to cancel one another in such a large group. In the test room, the six operators were made a group by themselves. In this way each girl received an amount more nearly in proportion to her individual effort, and her interests became more closely centered on the experiment. Eight weeks later, the directly experimental changes began. An outline will reveal their general character: Period IV: two rest pauses, each five minutes in length, were established, one occurring in midmorning and the other in the early afternoon. Period V: these rest pauses were lengthened to ten minutes each. Period VI: six five-minute rests were established. Period VII: the company provided each member of the group with a light lunch in the midmorning and another in the midafternoon, accompanied by rest pauses. This arrangement became standard for subsequent Periods VIII through XI. Period VIII: work stopped a half-hour earlier every day—at 4 : 30 P.M. Period IX: work stopped at 4 P.M. Period X: conditions returned to what they were in Period VII. Period XI: a five-day work week was established. Each of these experimental periods lasted several weeks.

Period XI ran through the summer of 1928, a year after the beginning of the experiment. Already the results were not what had been expected. The output curve, which had risen on the whole slowly and steadily throughout the year, was obviously reflecting something other than the responses of the group to the imposed experimental conditions. Even when the total weekly output had fallen off, as it could hardly fail to do in such a period as Period XI, when the group was working only five days a week, daily output continued to rise. Therefore, in accordance with a sound experimental procedure, as a control on what had been done, it was agreed with the consent of the operators that in experimental Period XII a return should be made to the original conditions of work, with no rest pauses, no special lunches, and a full-length working week. This period lasted for twelve weeks. Both daily and weekly

output rose to a higher point than ever before: the working day and the working week were both longer. The hourly output rate declined somewhat but it did not approach the level of Period III, when similar conditions were in effect.

The conclusions reached after Period XII may be expressed in terms of another observation. Identical conditions of work were repeated in three different experimental periods: Periods VII, X, and XIII. If the assumptions on which the study was based had been correct, that is to say, if the output rate were directly related to the physical conditions of work, the expectation would be that in these three experimental periods there would be some similarity in output. Such was not the case. The only apparent uniformity was that in each experimental period output was higher than in the preceding one. In the Relay Assembly Test Room, as in the previous illumination experiments, something was happening which could not be explained by the experimentally controlled conditions of work.

The question remains:

With what facts, if any, can the changes in the output rate of the operators in the test room be correlated? Here the statements of the girls themselves are of the first importance. Each girl knew that she was producing more in the test room than she ever had in the regular department, and each said that the increase had come about without any conscious effort on her part. It seemed easier to produce at the faster rate in the test room than at the slower rate in the regular department. When questioned further, each girl stated her reasons in slightly different words, but there was uniformity in the answers in two respects. First, the girls liked to work in the test room; "it was fun." Secondly, the new supervisory relation or, as they put it, the absence of the old supervisory control, made it possible for them to work freely without anxiety.

For instance, there was the matter of conversation. In the regular department, conversation was in principle not allowed. In practice it was tolerated if it was carried on in a low tone and did not interfere with work. In the test room an effort was made in the beginning to discourage conversation, though it was soon abandoned. The observer in charge of the experiment was afraid of losing the cooperation of the girls if he insisted too strongly on this point. Talk became common and was often loud and general. Indeed, the conversation of the operators came to occupy an important place in the log. T. N. Whitehead has pointed out that the girls in the test room were far more thoroughly supervised than they ever had been in the regular department. They were watched by an observer of their own, an interested management, and outside experts. The point is that the character and purpose of the supervision were different and were felt to be so.

The operators knew that they were taking part in what was considered an important and interesting experiment. They knew that their work was expected to produce results—they were not sure what results—which would lead to the improvement of the working conditions of their fellow employees. They knew that the eyes of the company were upon them. Whitehead has further pointed out that although the experimental changes might turn out to have no physical significance, their social significance was always favorable. They showed that the management of the company was still interested, that the girls were still part of a valuable piece of research. In the regular department, the girls, like the other employees, were in the position of responding to changes the source and purpose of which were beyond their knowledge. In the test room, they had frequent interviews with the superintendent, a high officer of the company. The reasons for the contemplated experimental changes were explained to them. Their views were consulted and in some instances they were allowed to veto what had been proposed. Professor Mayo has argued that it is idle to speak of an experimental period like Period XII as being in any sense what it purported to be—a return to the original conditions of work. In the meantime, the entire industrial situation of the girls had been reconstructed.

Another factor in what occurred can only be spoken of as the social development of the group itself. When the girls went for the first time to be given a physical examination by the company doctor, someone suggested as a joke that ice cream and cake ought to be served. The company provided them at the next examination, and the custom was kept up for the duration of the experiment. When one of the girls had a birthday, each of the others would bring her a present, and she would respond by offering the group a box of chocolates. Often one of the girls would have some good reason for feeling tired. Then the others would "carry" her. That is, they would agree to work especially fast to make up for the low output expected from her. It is doubtful whether this "carrying" did have any effect, but the important point is the existence of the practice, not its effectiveness. The girls made friends in the test room and went together socially after hours. One of the interesting facts which has appeared from Whitehead's analysis of the output records is that there were times when variations in the output rates of two friends were correlated to a high degree. Their rates varied simultaneously and in the same direction—something, of course, which the girls were not aware of and could not have planned. Also, these correlations were destroyed by such apparently trivial events as a change in the order in which the girls sat at the workbench.

Finally, the group developed leadership and a common purpose. The leader, self-appointed, was an ambitious young Italian girl who entered the test room as a replacement after two of the original members had left. She saw in the experiment a chance for personal distinction and advancement. The common purpose was an increase in the output rate. The girls had been told in the beginning and repeatedly thereafter that they were to work without straining, without trying to make a race of the test, and all the evidence shows that they kept this rule. In fact, they felt that they were working under less pressure than in the regular department. Nevertheless, they knew that the output record was considered the most important of the records of the experiment and was always closely scrutinized. Before long they had committed themselves to a continuous increase in production. In the long run, of course, this ideal was an impossible one, and when the girls found out that it was, the realization was an important element of the change of tone which was noticeable in the second half of the experiment. But for a time they felt that they could achieve the impossible. In brief, the increase in the output rate of the girls in the Relay Assembly Test Room could not be related to any changes in their physical conditions of work, whether experimentally induced or not. It could, however, be related to what can only be spoken of as the development of an organized social group in a peculiar and effective relation with its supervisors.

Many of these conclusions were not worked out in detail until long after the investigators at Hawthorne had lost interest in the Relay Assembly Test Room, but the general meaning of the experiment was clear at least as early as Period XII. A continuous increase in productivity had taken place irrespective of changing physical conditions of work. In the words of a company report made in January 1931 on all the research which had been done up to that

date: "Upon analysis, only one thing seemed to show a continuous relationship with this improved output. This was the mental attitude of the operators. From their conversations with each other and their comments to the test observers, it was not only clear that their attitudes were improving but it was evident that this area of employee reactions and feelings was a fruitful field for industrial research."

At this point the attention of the investigators turned sharply from the test room to the regular shop department from which the girls had come. Why was the mental attitude of the girls different in the test room from what it had been in the department? In their conversations with one another and in their comments to the observers, the girls were full of comparisons between the test room and the department, very much to the disadvantage of the latter. They felt relief from some form of constraint, particularly the constraint of supervision. They were exceedingly disparaging about the supervisors in the department, although management felt that the department had particularly good supervisory personnel. These facts suggested that the management of the company really knew very little about the attitudes which employees took toward conditions in the plant and very little also about what constituted good supervisory methods. Such was the atmosphere in which the so-called Interviewing Program, the third phase of the work at Hawthorne, was planned. So far the interests of the investigators had been centered on the question of what were good physical conditions of work. Now they shifted definitely in the direction of a study of human relations.

Finally, the investigators discovered, in the course of the regular interviews, evidence here and there in the plant of a type of behavior which strongly suggested that the workers were banding together informally in order to protect themselves against practices which they interpreted as a menace to their welfare. This type of behavior manifested itself in (a) "straight-line" output, that is, the operators had adopted a standard of what they felt to be a proper day's work and none of them exceeded it by very much; (b) a resentment of the wage incentive system under which they worked —in most cases, some form of group piecework; (c) expressions which implied that group piecework as a wage incentive plan was not working satisfactorily; (d) informal practices by which persons who exceeded the accepted standard, that is, "rate killers," could be punished and "brought into line"; (e) informal leadership on the part of individuals who undertook to keep the working group together and enforce its rules; (f) feelings of futility with regard to promotions; and (g) extreme likes and dislikes toward immediate superiors, according to their attitude toward the behavior of the operators. The investigators felt that this complex of behavior deserved further study.

In view of these considerations, the decision was taken in May, 1931, to assign selected interviewers to particular groups of employees and allow them to interview the employees as often as they felt was necessary. The story of one of these groups is characteristic of the findings reached by this new form of interviewing. The work of the employees was the adjustment of small parts which went into the construction of telephone equipment. The management thought that the adjustment was a complicated piece of work. The interviewer found that it was really quite simple. He felt that anyone could learn it, but that the operators had conspired to put a fence around the job. They took pride in telling how apparatus which no one could make work properly was sent in from the field for adjustment. Then telephone engineers would come in to find out from the operators how the repairs were made.

The latter would fool around, doing all sorts of wrong things and taking about two hours to adjust the apparatus, and in this way prevented people on the outside from finding out what they really did. They delighted in telling the interviewer how they were pulling the wool over everybody's eyes. It followed that they were keeping the management in ignorance as to the amount of work they could do. The output of the group, when plotted, was practically a straight line.

Obviously this result could not have been gained without some informal organization, and such organization in fact there was. The group had developed leadership. Whenever an outsider—engineer, inspector, or supervisor—came into the room, one man always dealt with him. Whenever any technical question was raised about the work, this employee answered it. For other purposes, the group had developed a second leader. Whenever a new man came into the group, or a member of the group boosted output beyond what was considered the proper level, this second leader took charge of the situation. The group had, so to speak, one leader for dealing with foreign and one for dealing with domestic affairs. The different supervisors were largely aware of the situation which had developed, but they did not try to do anything about it because in fact they were powerless. Whenever necessary, they themselves dealt with the recognized leaders of the group.

Finally, the investigator found that the group was by no means happy about what it was doing. Its members felt a vague dissatisfaction or unrest, which showed itself in a demand for advancements and transfers or in complaints about their hard luck in being kept on the job. This experience of personal futility could be explained as the result of divided loyalties—divided between the group and the company.

In order to study this kind of problem further, to make a more detailed investigation of social relations in a working group, and to supplement interview material with direct observation of the behavior of employees, the Division of Industrial Research decided to set up a new test room. But the investigators remembered what happened in the former test room and tried to devise an experiment which would not be radically altered by the process of experimentation itself. They chose a group of men—nine wiremen, three soldermen, and two inspectors—engaged in the assembly of terminal banks for use in telephone exchanges, took them out of their regular department and placed them in a special room. Otherwise no change was made in their conditions of work, except that an investigator was installed in the room, whose duty was simply to observe the behavior of the men. In the Relay Assembly Test Room a log had been kept of the principal events of the test. At the beginning it consisted largely of comments made by the workers in answer to questions about their physical condition. Later it came to include a much wider range of entries, which were found to be extremely useful in interpreting the changes in the output rate of the different workers. The work of the observer in the new test room was in effect an expansion of the work of keeping the log in the old one. Finally, an interviewer was assigned to the test room; he was not, however, one of the population of the room but remained outside and interviewed the employees from time to time in the usual manner. No effort was made to get output records other than the ones ordinarily kept in the department from which the group came, since the investigators felt that such a procedure would introduce too large a change from a regular shop situation. In this way the experiment was set up which is referred to as the Bank Wiring Observation Room. It was in existence seven months, from November 1931 to May 1932.

The method of payment is the first aspect of this group which must be described. It was a complicated form of group piecework. The department of which the workers in the observation room were a part was credited with a fixed sum for every unit of equipment it assembled. The amount thus earned on paper by the department every week made up the sum out of which the wages of all the men in the department were paid. Each individual was then assigned an hourly rate of pay, and he was guaranteed this amount in case he did not make at least as much on a piecework basis. The rate was based on a number of factors, including the nature of the job a worker was doing, his efficiency, and his length of service with the company. Records of the output of every worker were kept, and every six months there was a rate revision, the purpose of which was to make the hourly rates of the different workers correspond to their relative efficiency.

The hourly rate of a given employee, multiplied by the number of hours worked by him during the week, was spoken of as the daywork value of the work done by the employee. The daywork values of the work done by all the employees in the department were then added together, and the total thus obtained was subtracted from the total earnings credited to the department for the number of units of equipment assembled. The surplus, divided by the total daywork value, was expressed as a percentage. Each individual's hourly rate was then increased by this percentage, and the resulting hourly earnings figure, multiplied by the number of hours worked, constituted that person's weekly earnings.

Another feature of the system should be mentioned here. Sometimes a stoppage which was beyond the control of the workers took place in the work. For such stoppages the workers were entitled to claim time out, being paid at their regular hourly rates for this time. This was called the "daywork allowance claim." The reason why the employees were paid their hourly rate for such time and not their average hourly wages was a simple one. The system was supposed to prevent stalling. The employees could earn more by working than they could by taking time out. As a matter of fact, there was no good definition of what constituted a stoppage which was beyond the control of the workers. All stoppages were more or less within their control. But this circumstance was supposed to make no difference in the working of the system, since the assumption was that in any case the workers, pursuing their economic interests, would be anxious to keep stoppages at a minimum.

This system of payment was a complicated one, but it is obvious that there was a good logical reason for every one of its features. An individual's earnings would be affected by changes in his rate or in his output and by changes in the output of the group as a whole. The only way in which the group as a whole could increase its earnings was by increasing its total output. It is obvious also that the experts who designed the system made certain implicit assumptions about the behavior of human beings, or at least the behavior of workers in a large American factory. They assumed that every employee would pursue his economic interest by trying to increase not only his own output but the output of every other person in the group. The group as a whole would act to prevent slacking by any of its members. One possibility, for instance, was that by a few weeks' hard work an employee could establish a high rate for himself. Then he could slack up and be paid out of all proportion with the amount he actually contributed to the wages of the group. Under these circumstances, the other employees were expected to bring pressure to bear to make him work harder.

Such was the way in which the wage incentive scheme ought to have worked. The next question is how it actually did work. At first the workers were naturally suspicious of the observer, but when they got used to him and found that nothing out of the ordinary happened as a result of his presence in the room, they came to take him for granted. The best evidence that the employees were not distrustful of the observer is that they were willing to talk freely to him about what they were doing, even when what they were doing was not strictly in accord with what the company expected. Conversation would die down when the group chief entered the room, and when the foreman or the assistant foreman entered everyone became serious. But no embarrassment was felt at the presence of the observer. To avoid misunderstanding, it is important to point out that the observer was in no sense a spy. The employees were deliberately and obviously separated from their regular department. The observer did not, and could not, pass himself off as one of them. And if only from the fact that a special interviewer was assigned to them, the members of the group knew they were under investigation.

The findings reached by the observer were more detailed but in general character the same as those which had emerged from the early interviews of other groups. Among the employees in the observation room there was a notion of a proper day's work. They felt that if they had wired two equipments a day they had done about the right amount. Most of the work was done in the morning. As soon as the employees felt sure of being able to finish what they considered enough for the day, they slacked off. This slacking off was naturally more marked among the faster than among the slower workmen.

As a result, the output graph from week to week tended to be a straight line. The employees resorted to two further practices in order to make sure that it should remain so. They reported more or less output than they performed and they claimed more daywork allowances than they were entitled to. At the end of the day, the observer would make an actual count of the number of connections wired—something which was not done by the supervisors—and he found that the men would report to the group chief sometimes more and sometimes less work than they actually had accomplished. At the end of the period of observation, two men had completed more than they ever had reported, but on the whole the error was in the opposite direction. The theory of the employees was that excess work produced on one day should be saved and applied to a deficiency on another day. The other way of keeping the output steady was to claim excessive daywork allowance. The employees saw that the more daywork they were allowed, the less output they would have to maintain in order to keep the average hourly output rate steady. The claims for daywork allowance were reported by the men to their group chief, and he, as will be seen, was in no position to make any check. These practices had two results. In the first place, the departmental efficiency records did not represent true efficiency, and therefore decisions as to grading were subject to errors of considerable importance. In the second place, the group chief was placed in a distinctly awkward position.

The findings of the observer were confirmed by tests which were made as a part of the investigation. Tests of intelligence, finger dexterity, and other skills were given to the workers in the room, and the results of the tests were studied in order to discover whether there was any correlation between output on the one hand and earnings, intelligence, or finger dexterity on the other. The studies showed that there was not. The output was apparently not reflecting the native intelligence or dexterity of the members of the group.

Obviously the wage incentive scheme was not working in the way it was expected to work. The next question is why it was not working. In this connection, the observer reported that the group had developed an informal social organization, such as had been revealed by earlier investigations. The foreman who selected the employees taking part in the Bank Wiring Observation Room was cooperative and had worked with the investigators before. They asked him to produce a normal group. The men he chose all came out of the same regular shop department, but they had not been closely associated in their work there. Nevertheless, as soon as they were thrown together in the observation room, friendships sprang up and soon two well-defined cliques were formed. The division into cliques showed itself in a number of ways: in mutual exclusiveness, in differences in the games played during off-hours, and so forth.

What is important here is not what divided the men in the observation room but what they had in common. They shared a common body of sentiments. A person should not turn out too much work. If he did, he was a "rate-buster." The theory was that if an excessive amount of work was turned out, the management would lower the piecework rate so that the employees would be in the position of doing more work for approximately the same pay. On the other hand, a person should not turn out too little work. If he did, he was a "chiseler"; that is, he was getting paid for work he did not do. A person should say nothing which would injure a fellow member of the group. If he did, he was a "squealer." Finally, no member of the group should act officiously.

The working group had also developed methods of enforcing respect for its attitudes. The experts who devised the wage incentive scheme assumed that the group would bring pressure to bear upon the slower workers to make them work faster and so increase the earnings of the group. In point of fact, something like the opposite occurred. The employees brought pressure to bear not upon the slower workers but upon the faster ones, the very ones who contributed most to the earnings of the group. The pressure was brought to bear in various ways. One of them was "binging." If one of the employees did something which was not considered quite proper, one of his fellow workers had the right to "bing" him. Binging consisted of hitting him a stiff blow on the upper arm. The person who was struck usually took the blow without protest and did not strike back. Obviously the virtue of binging as punishment did not lie in the physical hurt given to the worker but in the mental hurt that came from knowing that the group disapproved of what he had done. Other practices which naturally served the same end were sarcasm and the use of invectives. If a person turned out too much work, he was called names, such as "Speed King" or "The Slave."

It is worth while pointing out that the output of the group was not considered low. If it had been, some action might have been taken, but in point of fact it was perfectly satisfactory to the management. It was simply not so high as it would have been if fatigue and skill had been the only limiting factors.

In the matter of wage incentives, the actual situation was quite different from the assumptions made by the experts. Other activities were out of line in the same way. The wiremen and the soldermen did not stick to their jobs; they frequently traded them. This was forbidden, on the theory that each employee ought to do his own work because he was more skilled in that work. There was also much informal helping of one man by others. In fact, the observation of this practice was one means of determining the cliques into which the group was divided. A great many things, in short, were going on in the observation room which ought not to have been going on. For this reason it was important that no one should "squeal" on the men.

A group chief was in immediate charge of the employees. He had to see that they were supplied with parts and that they conformed to the rules and standards of the work. He could reprimand them for misbehavior or poor performance. He transmitted orders to the men and brought their requests before the proper authorities. He was also responsible for reporting to the foreman all facts which ought to come to his attention. The behavior of the employees put him in an awkward position. He was perfectly well aware of the devices by which they maintained their production at a constant level. But he was able to do very little to bring about a change. For instance, there was the matter of claims for daywork allowance. Such claims were supposed to be based on stoppages beyond the control of the workers, but there was no good definition of what constituted such stoppages. The men had a number of possible excuses for claiming daywork allowance: defective materials, poor and slow work on the part of other employees, and so forth. If the group chief checked up on one type of claim, the workers could shift to another. In order to decide whether or not a particular claim was justified, he would have to stand over the group all day with a stop watch. He did not have time to do that, and in any case refusal to honor the employees' claims would imply doubt of their integrity and would arouse their hostility. The group chief was a representative of management and was supposed to look after its interests. He ought to have put a stop to these practices and reported them to the foreman. But if he did so, he would, to use the words of a short account of the observation room by Roethlisberger and Dickson, "lose sympathetic control of his men, and his duties as supervisor would become much more difficult."[1] He had to associate with the employees from day to day and from hour to hour. His task would become impossible if he had to fight a running fight with them. Placed in this situation, he chose to side with the men and report unchanged their claims for daywork. In fact there was very little else he could do, even if he wished. Moreover he was in a position to protect himself in case of trouble. The employees always had to give him a reason for any daywork claims they might make, and he entered the claims in a private record book. If anyone ever asked why so much daywork was being claimed, he could throw the blame wherever he wished. He could assert that materials had been defective or he could blame the inspectors, who were members of an outside organization. In still another respect, then, the Bank Wiring Observation Room group was not behaving as the logic of management assumed that it would behave.

Restriction of output is a common phenomenon of industrial plants. It is usually explained as a highly logical reaction of the workers. They have increased their output, whereupon their wage rates for piecework have been reduced. They are doing more work for the same pay. They restrict their output in order to avoid a repetition of this experience. Perhaps this explanation holds good in some cases, but the findings of the Bank Wiring Observation Room suggest that it is too simple. The workers in the room were obsessed with the idea that they ought to hold their production level "even" from week to week, but they were vague as to what would happen if they did not. They said that "someone" would "get them." If they turned out an unusually high output one week, that record would be taken thereafter as an example of what they could do if they tried, and they would be "bawled out" if they did not keep up to it. As a matter of fact, none of the men in the room had ever experienced a reduction of wage rates. What is more, as Roethlisberger and Dickson point out, "changes in piece rates occur most frequently where there is a change in manufacturing process, and changes in manufacturing process are made by engineers whose chief function is to reduce unit cost wherever the saving will justify the change. In some instances, changes occur irrespective of direct labor cost. Moreover, where labor is a substantial element, reduction of output tends to increase unit costs and instead of warding off a change in the piece rate may actually induce one."

What happened in the observation room could not be described as a logical reaction of the employees to the experience of rate reduction. They had in fact had no such experience. On the other hand, the investigators found that it could be described as a conflict between the technical organization of the plant and its social organization. By technical organization the investigators meant the plan, written or unwritten, according to which the Hawthorne plant was supposed to operate, and the agencies which gave effect to that plan. The plan included explicit rules as to how the men were to be paid, how they were to do their work, what their relations with their supervisors ought to be. It included also implicit assumptions on which the rules were based, one of the assumptions being that men working in the plant would on the whole act so as to further their economic interests. It is worth while pointing out that this assumption was in fact implicit, that the experts who devised the technical organization acted

[1] F. J. Roethlisberger and W. J. Dickson, "Management and the Worker," *Business Research Studies, No.* 9 (Cambridge: Harvard Business School, Division of Research, 1939). (All quotations relating to the Western Electric researches are from this study as well as from the book of the same title by the same authors.)

upon the assumption without ever stating it in so many words.

There existed also an actual social situation within the plant: groups of men, who were associated with one another, held common sentiments and had certain relations with other groups and other men. To some extent this social organization was identical with the technical plan and to some extent it was not. For instance, the employees were paid according to group payment plans, but the groups concerned did not behave as the planners expected them to behave.

The investigators considered the relations between the technical organization and the social. A certain type of behavior is expected of the higher levels of management. Their success is dependent on their being able to devise and institute rapid changes. Roethlisberger and Dickson describe what happens in the following terms: "Management is constantly making mechanical improvements and instituting changes designed to reduce costs or improve the quality of the product. It is constantly seeking new ways and new combinations for increasing efficiency, whether in designing a new machine, instituting a new method of control, or logically organizing itself in a new way." The assumption has often been made that these changes are designed to force the employee to do more work for less money. As a matter of fact, many of them have just the opposite purpose: to improve the conditions of work and enable the employee to earn higher wages. The important point here, however, is not the purpose of the changes but the way in which they are carried out and accepted.

Once the responsible officer has decided that a certain change ought to be made, he gives an order, and this order is transmitted "down the line," appropriate action being taken at every level. The question in which the investigators were interested was this: What happens when the order reaches the men who are actually doing the manual work? Roethlisberger and Dickson made the following observations: "The worker occupies a unique position in the social organization. He is at the bottom of a highly stratified organization. He is always in the position of having to accommodate himself to changes which he does not originate. Although he participates least in the technical organization, he bears the brunt of most of its activities." It is he, more than anyone, who is affected by the decisions of management, yet in the nature of things he is unable to share management's preoccupations, and management does little to convince him that what he considers important is being treated as important at the top—a fact which is not surprising, since there is no adequate way of transmitting to management an understanding of the considerations which seem important at the work level. There is something like a failure of communication in both directions—upward and downward.

The worker is not only "asked to accommodate himself to changes which he does not initiate, but also many of the changes deprive him of those very things which give meaning and significance to his work." The modern industrial worker is not the handicraftsman of the medieval guild. Nevertheless, the two have much in common. The industrial worker develops his own ways of doing his job, his own traditions of skill, his own satisfactions in living up to his standards. The spirit in which he adopts his own innovations is quite different from that in which he adopts those of management. Furthermore, he does not do his work as an isolated human being, but always as a member of a group, united either through actual cooperation on the job or through association in friendship. One of the most important general findings of the Western Electric researches is the fact that such groups are continually being formed among industrial workers, and that the groups develop codes and loyalties which govern the relations of the members to one another. Though these codes can be quickly destroyed, they are not formed in a moment. They are the product of continued, routine interaction between men. "Constant interference with such codes is bound to lead to feelings of frustration, to an irrational exasperation with technical change in any form, and ultimately to the formation of a type of employee organization such as we have described— a system of practices and beliefs in opposition to the technical organization."

The Bank Wiring Observation Room seemed to show that action taken in accordance with the technical organization tended to break up, through continual change, the routines and human associations which gave work its value. The behavior of the employees could be described as an effort to protect themselves against such changes, to give management the least possible opportunity of interfering with them. When they said that if they increased their output, "something" was likely to happen, a process of this sort was going on in their minds. But the process was not a conscious one. It is important to point out that the protective function of informal organization was not a product of deliberate planning. It was more in the nature of an automatic response. The curious thing is that, as Professor Mayo pointed out to the Committee, these informal organizations much resembled formally organized labor unions, although the employees would not have recognized the fact.

Roethlisberger and Dickson summarize as follows the results of the intensive study of small groups of employees: "According to our analysis the uniformity of behavior manifested by these

groups was the outcome of a disparity in the rates of change possible in the technical organization, on the one hand, and in the social organization, on the other. The social sentiments and customs of work of the employees were unable to accommodate themselves to the rapid technical innovations introduced. The result was to incite a blind resistance to all innovations and to provoke the formation of a social organization at a lower level in opposition to the technical organization."

It is curious how, at all points, the Relay Assembly Test Room and the Bank Wiring Observation Room form a contrast. In the former, the girls said that they felt free from the pressure of supervision, although as a matter of fact they were far more thoroughly supervised than they ever had been in their regular department. In the latter, the men were afraid of supervision and acted so as to nullify it. The Bank Wiremen were in the position of having to respond to technical changes which they did not originate. The Relay Assemblers had periodic conferences with the superintendent. They were told what experimental changes were contemplated; their views were canvassed, and in some instances they were allowed to veto what had been proposed. They were part of an experiment which they felt was interesting and important. Both groups developed an informal social organization, but while the Bank Wiremen were organized in opposition to management, the Relay Assemblers were organized in cooperation with management in the pursuit of a common purpose. Finally, the responses of the two groups to their industrial situation were, on the one hand, restriction of output and, on the other, steady and welcome increase of output. These contrasts carry their own lesson.

13

Intergroup Tension, Prejudice

NEGRO INFANTRY PLATOONS IN WHITE COMPANIES
By Shirley A. Star, Robin M. Williams Jr., and Samuel A. Stouffer

During World War II, a number of all-Negro platoons were introduced into white infantry companies with white officers and white noncommissioned officers. Since many activities in the Army —mess, recreation, housing, for example —were on a company basis, this arrangement meant a limited amount of integration.

Shortly after VE Day, a survey was undertaken by the Research Branch (Information and Education Division, War Department) in Europe to evaluate this program. Seven of the 11 divisions containing Negro platoons were visited, and interviews were conducted with officers and enlisted men. The sample included three highly experienced divisions and four with less combat experience. Two of the divisions were predominantly Southern in background. The range of experience sampled was thought to be representative of what would have been found if all 11 divisions had been investigated.

At the outset, one must keep in mind the fact that the Negro platoons were *volunteers* for combat, and to say this is to imply a difference from the rank and file of Negroes in orientation and motivation, even though they came from the same service branches and the same sorts of relatively unskilled jobs as those who did not volunteer. No data on the atti-

tudes of these Negro volunteers exist, but it is safe to assume that they were motivated by convictions about the war, and by desires to prove the ability of their race and to make this "experiment in race relations succeed," as well as by the many individual motives which led men to choose combat. The Negro infantry volunteers were, like other volunteers, younger on the average than white infantrymen. More important, probably, for their subsequent relationships with white infantrymen, the Negro volunteers were somewhat better educated than Negro troops generally and had somewhat better Army General Classification Test (AGCT) scores. These differences, however, can easily be exaggerated; compared with the greater differences between white infantrymen and the Negro volunteers, they represent only minor fluctuations:

	Percentage who were high school graduates	Percentage with AGCT scores of I, II, or III
White riflemen in ETO *	41	71
Negro riflemen in white companies	22	29
All Negroes in ETO	18	17

* ETO refers to European Theater of Operations.

Excerpt from Ch. 10 in Samuel A. Stouffer and others, *The American Soldier*, Vol. I in *Studies in Social Psychology in World War II* (Princeton, N.J.: Princeton University Press, 1949).

TABLE 1

EVALUATION OF NEGRO INFANTRYMEN BY WHITE OFFICERS AND
ENLISTED MEN SERVING IN SAME COMPANIES WITH THEM

(Europe, June 1945)

	White company officers (percent)	White platoon sergeants and other enlisted men (percent)
Question: *How well did the colored soldiers in this company perform in combat?*		
Very well	84	81
Fairly well	16	17
Not so well	—	1
Not well at all	—	—
Undecided	—	1
Question: *With the same Army training and experience, how do you think colored troops compare with white troops as infantry soldiers?*		
Better than white troops	17	9
Just the same as white troops	69	83
Not as good as white troops	5	4
No answer	9	4
	(N = 60)	(N = 195)

In the companies in which Negro platoons served, the overwhelming majority of white officers and men gave approval to their performance in combat. This is shown in Table 1. As some of the respondents indicated in their comments, the Negro troops were fighting for a relatively short time during the closing, victorious stages of the war and did not have to meet the test of long, continued stalemate fighting with heavy casualties, but the same was true of some of the white troops with whom they fought and were compared. There was some indication in the data that the performance of Negro troops was rated highest by the officers and men in the companies in which the colored platoons had had the most severe fighting. The comments of their leaders indicated again and again, however, that in bestowing this praise, they were strongly aware that these men, as volunteers, were special cases. For example, as a company commander from Pennsylvania said: "Would do equally well with the best of the whites. Our men are good because they are volunteers, but an average of Negroes would probably do as well as the average of white soldiers." And a platoon sergeant from North Carolina commented: "I don't think you can say that about all of them. These are volunteers, and most colored men wouldn't be as willing to fight. These here are just the same as we are in combat."

As might be expected from these results, almost all the officers and enlisted men endorsed the idea of having Negroes used as infantry, sometimes with qualifications like "if they are volunteers" or "only while we're in combat, but not in garrison," a point which will be discussed more fully later. These men favored the organization they then had of separate Negro platoons within the same company as the best arrangement for the utilization of Negro infantrymen. These facts are shown in Table 2. It should be remembered, however, that not all the white support of using Negroes as infantrymen necessarily reflected "democratic" or "pro-Negro" attitudes. It could be simply a reflection of the desire of combat men to have their own burden lightened by letting others do part of the fighting; it might even conceal the most extreme attitudes of racial superiority leading to the reasoning that inferior Negro lives should be sacrificed before white lives. Moreover, the Negroes were still in separate platoons, which, to some Southern respondents, preserved at least the principle of segregation.

In fact, the reasons advanced for favoring the "separate-platoon, same-company" pattern of organization clearly show that there were at least two points of view involved. The five leading reasons, in order of their frequency, were:

1. *Competition-emulation* ("encourages friendly competition, each tries to make a good showing"; "gives them something to come up to").
2. *Avoidance of friction* ("saves any chance of trouble to have them in their own platoon," "because of the old feeling of boys from the South").
3. *Better discipline and control among the Negro soldiers* ("whites have a steadying influence on them"; "colored boys feel more secure in combat this way").
4. *Feeling of participation or nondiscrimination on part of the Negro soldiers* ("gives them the feeling of being with the white boys"; "avoids that feeling of being set apart and discriminated against").
5. *Improved interracial understanding* ("work close enough together so they can get to know the other better and see what they can do")

It may be seen here that some men accepted the platoon idea and assimilated it to usual white views by regarding it as a form of separation, as compared with mixing within the platoon, and justifying the interracial contacts it did bring in terms of the inferiority of the Negro and his need for white supervision. Other men, however, were in favor of it for opposite reasons: because it seemed to them to do away with enforced separation and encourage understanding.

But, though motives might vary, the white and Negro infantrymen did get along together amicably. Both white officers and fellow enlisted men reported that the white and Negro soldiers got along well together (93 percent of the officers and 60 percent of the enlisted men said "very well"; everyone else said "fairly well"), in spite of the fact that two thirds of each group had begun, according to their own retrospective reports, with relatively unfavorable attitudes toward serving in a mixed company. In a similar fashion, the bulk of both groups (77 percent) reported that their feeling had become more favorable since serving in the same unit with Negro soldiers. As a platoon sergeant from South Carolina said,

When I heard about it, I said I'd be damned if I'd wear the same shoulder patch they did. After that first day when we saw how they fought, I changed my mind. They're just like any of the other boys to us.

However, many took occasion to note that relationships were better in combat than they were in the garrison situation. Not that there was serious overt friction between Negro and white soldiers. Such instances were, as far as is known, confined to isolated cases and involved white soldiers from other units who did not know the combat record of the Negro men. There were, however, some tensions in companies stationed where friendly contact with liberated populations was possible, and there was some expression

TABLE 2

Attitudes of White Officers and Enlisted Men Serving in Same Companies
with Negro Platoons toward the Utilization of Negro Infantrymen
(Europe, June 1945)

	Officers (percent)	Enlisted men (percent)
Question: *On the whole, do you think it is a good idea or a poor idea to have colored soldiers used as infantry troops?*		
Good idea		
Unqualified statement	55	72
Qualified statement *		
"In combat, yes; but not in garrison"	25	26
"If volunteers," "If like the ones we have now"	15	—
Undecided	5	—
Poor idea	—	2
Question: *If colored soldiers are used as infantry, do you think they should be set up by platoons as they are here or would some other way be better?*		
In same platoon with white soldiers	7	1
In a platoon within the company	64	85
In separate companies	19	12
In separate battalions or larger organizations	10	2
	(N = 60)	(N = 195)

* These percentages represent the number of men who *volunteered* comments. If direct questions had been asked on these two qualifications, the percentages endorsing them might well have been considerably higher.

of preference for separation in garrison. Some typical comments were:

Company commander from Nevada: Relations are very good. They have their pictures taken together, go to church services, movies, play ball together. For a time there in combat our platoons got so small that we had to put a white squad in the colored platoon. You might think that wouldn't work well, but it did. The white squad didn't want to leave the platoon. I've never seen anything like it.

Company commander from Tennessee: Good cooperation in combat. They were treated as soldier to soldier. Now they play ball, joke, and box together. The colored go to company dances—we've had no trouble, but some of the white boys resent it. In garrison the strain on both parties is too great.

First sergeant from Georgia: Got along fine in combat. But we don't like to mix too much now and I think they should be pulled out if we're going to stay in garrison.

Platoon sergeant from Indiana: They fought and I think more of them for it, but I still don't want to soldier with them in garrison.

As some of these comments imply, relationships in combat could be regarded as working relationships rather than social relationships. More precisely, they could be confined more narrowly to a functionally specific basis than could the contacts involved in community living. In particular, the combat situation was exclusively masculine, and issues of social relationships between men and women did not appear as they did in

QUESTION: *Some Army divisions have companies which include Negro platoons and white platoons. How would you feel about it if your outfit was set up like that?*

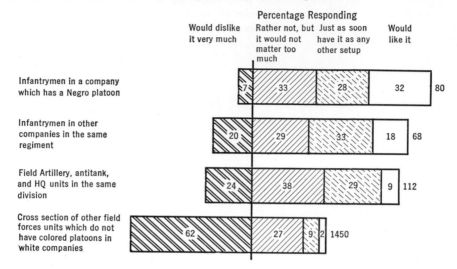

FIG. 1. Attitudes toward serving in a company containing Negro and white platoons among men who have done so and men who have not (Europe, June, 1945). The numbers following the bars are the number of cases on which percentages are based.

garrison. Far from being a "test case" in ordinary Negro-white relations, the combat setting may be regarded as a special case making for good relationships, for the sense of common danger and common obligation was high, the need for unity was at a maximum, and there was great consciousness of shared experience of an intensely emotional kind. In many respects the experience of fighting together is analogous to the kind of informal working together that results from any community crisis or disaster: fighting a forest fire or fighting a flood.

Relationships between white and Negro infantrymen turned out to be far better than their officers had expected: 96 percent of the officers questioned on this point reported themselves agreeably surprised. However, the comments made by the officers indicate that in some instances special precautions were taken. For example, one regimental commander said:

I'm from the South—most of us here are—and I was pretty dubious as to how it would

work out. But I'll have to admit we haven't had a bit of trouble. I selected the best company commander I had to put over them.

And a platoon commander from Texas said:

We all expected trouble. Haven't had any. One reason may be that we briefed the white boys in advance—told them these men were volunteers coming up here to fight, and that we wouldn't stand for any foolishness.

In other words, in at least some of these cases there was careful selection of officers and orientation of the white troops. In some instances, the white officers or noncoms who were later to lead the colored platoons went back to the replacement depots and trained the men for combat, thus getting to know and work with their men before they were thrust into combat.

In spite of the qualifications introduced—the volunteer character of the Negro platoons, the fact that the war was in its final successful stages, the peculiar nature of the combat situation, the special reasons for and the precautions taken to insure smooth functioning—there can be little question that these Negro troops performed well by the criteria applied to white troops. Nor can there be any doubt that, *under the conditions specified*, Negro-white relations were harmonious. Of more interest than this historical conclusion, however, is the question of how far, in the face of these limitations, one can generalize from these data

From this point of view, perhaps the most illuminating piece of data coming out of the study was the finding, shown in Figure 1, that the closer men approached to the mixed company organization, the less opposition there was to it. That is, men actually in a company containing a Negro platoon were most favorable toward it, men in larger units in which there were no mixed companies were least favorable, while men in all-white companies within a regiment or division containing mixed companies held intermediate opinions. When we note that the proportion of men having no experience with mixed companies who say "they would dislike the arrangement very much" is almost exactly the same (62 percent) as the two-thirds proportion

of white enlisted men in mixed companies who were previously noted as reporting retroactively that they were initially opposed to the idea, we can get some conception of the revolution in attitudes that took place among these men as a result of enforced contacts.

Though this still leaves unanswered the question of whether whites would ultimately adjust to and come to accept enforced interracial contacts under other circumstances, it does show that integration between Negro volunteers and whites could be achieved under the stress of combat. Extensions of this sort of experimentation [1] could show how successfully Negro troops in general could be integrated in white units in combat and how far such integration could be extended into noncombat situations.[2] The results of this experiment suggest that efforts at integration of white and colored troops into the same units may well be more successful when attention is focused on concrete tasks or goals requiring common effort than when it is focused on more abstract considerations of justice or of desirable policy which emphasize the "race issue" and arouse traditional prejudices.

---

[1] Another experiment in the integration of Negroes and whites into the same units is sympathetically reported in John Beecher's *All Brave Sailors: The Story of the S. S. Booker T. Washington* (New York: L. B. Fischer Corp., 1945), about a merchant marine ship with a Negro captain and racially mixed crew. Here the whites as well as the Negroes would appear to have volunteered specifically to demonstrate the feasibility of such interracial cooperation.

[2] At the time of this writing, racial integration in the United States armed forces had not yet been accomplished. (Ed.)

RACIAL IDENTIFICATION AND PREFERENCE IN NEGRO CHILDREN
By Kenneth B. Clark and Mamie P. Clark

PROBLEM

The specific problem of this study is an analysis of the genesis and development of racial identification as a function of ego development and self-awareness in Negro children.

Race awareness, in a primary sense, is defined as a consciousness of the self as belonging to a specific group which is differentiated from other observable groups by obvious physical characteristics which are generally accepted as being racial characteristics.

Because the problem of racial identification is so definitely related to the problem of the genesis of racial attitudes in children, it was thought practicable to attempt to determine the racial attitudes or preferences of these Negro children—and to define more precisely, as far as possible, the developmental pattern of this relationship.

PROCEDURE

This paper presents results from only one of several techniques devised and used by the authors to investigate the development of racial identification and preferences in Negro children.[1] Results presented here are from the Dolls Test.

Dolls Test. The subjects were presented with four dolls, identical in every respect save skin color. Two of these dolls were brown with black hair and two were white with yellow hair. In the experimental situation these dolls were un-clothed except for white diapers. The position of the head, hands, and legs on all the dolls was the same. For half of the subjects the dolls were presented in the order: white, colored, white, colored. For the other half the order of presentation was reversed. In the experimental situation the subjects were asked to respond to the following requests by choosing *one* of the dolls and giving it to the experimenter:

1. Give me the doll that you like to play with— (a) like best.
2. Give me the doll that is a nice doll.
3. Give me the doll that looks bad.
4. Give me the doll that is a nice color.
5. Give me the doll that looks like a white child.
6. Give me the doll that looks like a colored child.
7. Give me the doll that looks like a Negro child.
8. Give me the doll that looks like you.

Requests 1 through 4 were designed to reveal preferences; requests 5 through 7 to indicate a knowledge of "racial differences"; and request 8 to show self-identification.

It was found necessary to present the preference requests first in the experimental situation because in a preliminary investigation it was clear that the children who had already identified themselves with the colored doll had a marked tendency to indicate a preference for this doll and this was not necessarily a gen-

Condensed by the authors from an unpublished study made possible by a fellowship grant from the Julius Rosenwald Fund, 1940–1941.

[1] Other techniques presented in the larger study include: (1) a coloring test; (2) a questionnaire and (3) a modification of the Horowitz line drawing technique. (R. E. Horowitz, "Racial Aspects of Self-identification in Nursery School Children," *J. Psychol.*, 1939, VII, 91–99.)

uine expression of actual preference, but a reflection of ego involvement. This potential distortion of the data was con- trolled by merely asking the children to indicate their preferences first and then to make identifications with one of the dolls.

SUBJECTS

Two hundred fifty-three Negro chil- dren formed the subjects of this experi- ment. One hundred thirty four of these subjects (southern group) were tested in segregated nursery schools and public schools in Hot Springs, Pine Bluff, and Little Rock, Arkansas. These children had had no experience in racially mixed school situations. One hundred nineteen subjects (northern group) were tested in the racially mixed nursery and public schools of Springfield, Massachusetts.

Age distribution of subjects:

Age, years	North	South	Total
3	13	18	31
4	10	19	29
5	34	12	46
6	33	39	72
7	29	46	75
Total	119	134	253

Sex distribution of subjects:

Sex	North	South	Total
Male	53	63	116
Female	66	71	137

Skin color of subjects:

Skin color	North	South	Total
Light [a]	33	13	46
Medium [b] . . .	58	70	128
Dark [c]	28	51	79

[a] light (practically white)
[b] medium (light brown to dark brown)
[c] dark (dark brown to black)

All subjects were tested individually in a schoolroom or office especially pro- vided for this purpose. Except for a few children who showed generalized nega- tivism from the beginning of the experi- ment (results for these children are not included here), there was adequate rap- port between the experimenter and all subjects tested. In general, the children showed high interest in and enthusiasm for the test materials and testing situ- ation. The children, for the most part, considered the experiment somewhat of a game.

RESULTS

Racial Identification. Although the questions on knowledge of "racial dif- ferences" and self-identification followed those designed to determine racial pref- erence in the actual experimental situ- ation, it appears more meaningful to discuss the results in the following order: knowledge of "racial differences," racial self-identification, and finally racial pref- erences.

The results of the responses to requests 5, 6, and 7, which were asked to deter- mine the subjects' knowledge of racial differences, may be seen in Table 1. Ninety-four percent of these children chose the white doll when asked to give the experimenter the white doll; 93 per- cent of them chose the brown doll when asked to give the colored doll; and, 72 percent chose the brown doll when asked to give the Negro doll. These re- sults indicate a clearly established knowl- edge of a "racial difference" in these subjects—and some awareness of the relation between the physical character- istic of skin color and the racial concepts of "white" and "colored." Knowledge of the concept of "Negro" is not so well developed as the more concrete verbal concepts of "white" and "colored" as applied to racial differences.

The question arises as to whether choice of the brown doll or of the white doll, particularly in response to ques-

TABLE 1

CHOICES OF ALL SUBJECTS

Choice	Request 5 (for white)		Request 6 (for colored)		Request 7 (for Negro)		Request 8 (for you)	
	No.	Percent	No.	Percent	No.	Percent	No.	Percent
Colored doll	13	5	235	93	182	72	166	66
White doll	237	94	15	6	50	20	85	33
Don't know or no response	3	1	3	1	21	8	2	1

tions 5 and 6, really reveals a knowledge of "racial differences" or simply indicates a learned perceptual reaction to the concepts of "colored" and "white." Our evidence that the responses of these children *do* indicate a knowledge of "racial difference" comes from several sources: the results from other techniques used (i.e., a coloring test and a questionnaire) and from the qualitative data obtained (children's spontaneous remarks) strongly support a knowledge of "racial differences." Moreover, the consistency of results for requests 5 through 8 also tends to support the fact that these children are actually making identifications in a "racial" sense.

The responses to request 8, designed to determine racial self-identification follow the following pattern: 66 percent of the total group of children identified themselves with the colored doll, while 33 percent identified themselves with the white doll. The critical ratio of this difference is 7.6.[2]

Comparing the results of request 8 (racial self-identification) with those of requests 5, 6, and 7 (knowledge of racial difference) it is seen that the awareness of racial differences does not necessarily determine a socially accurate racial self-identification—since approximately nine out of ten of these children are aware of racial differences as indicated by their correct choice of a "white" and "colored" doll on request, and only a

little more than six out of ten make socially correct identifications with the colored doll.

Age Differences. Table 2 shows that, when the responses to requests 5 and 6 are observed together, these subjects at each age level have a well-developed knowledge of the concept of racial difference between "white" and "colored" as this is indicated by the characteristic of skin color. These data definitely indicate that a basic knowledge of "racial differences" exists as a part of the pattern of ideas of Negro children from the age of three through seven years in the northern and southern communities tested in this study—and that this knowledge develops more definitely from year to year to the point of absolute stability at the age of seven.

A comparison of the results of requests 5 and 6 with those of request 7, which required the child to indicate the doll which looks like a "Negro" child, shows that knowledge of a racial difference in terms of the word "Negro" does not exist with the same degree of definiteness as it does in terms of the more basic designations of "white" and "colored." It is significant, however, that knowledge of a difference in terms of the word "Negro" makes a sharp increase from the five- to the six-year level and a less accelerated one between the six- and seven-year levels. The fact that all of the six-year-olds used in this investi-

---

[2] These results are supported by similar ones from the Horowitz line drawing technique.

TABLE 2

CHOICES OF SUBJECTS AT EACH AGE LEVEL*

Choice	3 yr.		4 yr.		5 yr.		6 yr.		7 yr.	
	No.	Per-cent	No.	Per-cent	No.	Per-cent	No.	Per-cent	No.	Per-cent
Request 5 (for white)										
colored doll	4	13	4	14	3	7	2	3	0	
white doll	24	77	25	86	43	94	70	97	75	100
Request 6 (for colored)										
colored doll . . .	24	77	24	83	43	94	69	96	75	100
white doll	4	13	5	17	3	7	3	4	0	
Request 7 (for Negro)										
colored doll . . .	17	55	17	59	28	61	56	78	64	85
white doll	9	29	10	35	14	30	12	17	5	7
Request 8 (for you)										
colored doll . . .	11	36	19	66	22	48	49	68	65	87
white doll	19	61	9	31	24	52	23	32	10	13

*Individuals failing to make either choice not included, hence some percentages add to less than 100.

gation were enrolled in the public schools seems to be related to this spurt. Since it seems clear that the term "Negro" is a more verbalized designation of "racial differences," it is reasonable to assume that attendance at public schools facilitates the development of this verbalization of the race concept held by these children.

In response to request 8 there is a general and marked increase in the percent of subjects who identify with the colored doll with an increase in age— with the exception of the four- to five-year groups.[3] This deviation of the five-year-olds from the general trend is considered in detail in the larger, yet unpublished study.

Identification by Skin Color. Table 3

shows slight and statistically insignificant differences among the three skin-color groups in their responses which indicate a knowledge of the "racial difference" between the white and colored doll (requests 5 through 7).

It should be noted, however, that the dark group is consistently more accurate in its choice of the appropriate doll than either the light or the medium group on requests 5 through 7. This would seem to indicate that the dark group is slightly more definite in its knowledge of racial differences and that this definiteness extends even to the higher level of verbalization inherent in the use of the term "Negro" as a racial designation. In this regard it is seen that 75 percent of the dark children chose the colored doll

[3] These results are supported by those from the use of the Horowitz line drawing technique.

TABLE 3

CHOICES OF SUBJECTS IN LIGHT, MEDIUM, AND DARK GROUPS*

Choice	Light		Medium		Dark	
	No.	Percent	No.	Percent	No.	Percent
Request 5 (for white)						
colored doll . . .	2	5	8	6	3	4
white doll . . .	43	94	118	92	76	96
Request 6 (for colored)						
colored doll . . .	41	89	118	92	76	96
white doll . . .	4	9	8	6	3	4
Request 7 (for Negro)						
colored doll . . .	32	70	91	71	59	75
white doll . . .	9	20	27	21	14	18
Request 8 (for you)						
colored doll . . .	9	20	93	73	64	81
white doll . . .	37	80	33	26	15	19

*Individuals failing to make either choice not included, hence some percentages add to less than 100.

when asked for the doll which "looks like a Negro child" while only 70 percent of the light children and 71 percent of the medium children made this response. The trend of results for requests 5 and 6 remains substantially the same.

These results suggest further that correct racial identification of these Negro children at these ages is to a large extent determined by the concrete fact of their own skin color, and further that this racial identification is not necessarily dependent upon the expressed knowledge of a racial difference as indicated by the correct use of the words "white," "colored," or "Negro" when responding to white and colored dolls. This conclusion seems warranted in the light of the fact that those children who differed

in skin color from light through medium to dark were practically similar in the pattern of their responses which indicated awareness of racial differences but differed markedly in their racial identification (responses to request 8 for the doll "that looks like you") only 20 percent of the light children, while 73 percent of the medium children, and 81 percent of the dark children identified themselves with the colored doll.

It is seen that there is a consistent increase in choice of the colored doll from the light to the medium group; an increase from the medium group to the dark group; and, a striking increase in the choices of the colored doll by the dark group as compared to the light group.[4] All differences, except between

[footnote] These results substantiate and clearly focus the trend observed through the use of the Horowitz line drawing technique.

TABLE 4

Choices of Subjects in Northern (Mixed Schools) and Southern (Segregated Schools) Groups*

Choice	North, percent	South, percent
Request 5 (for white)		
colored doll	4	6
white doll	94	93
Request 6 (for colored)		
colored doll	92	94
white doll	7	5
Request 7 (for Negro)		
colored doll	74	70
white doll	20	19
Request 8 (for you)		
colored doll	61	69
white doll	39	29

*Individuals failing to make either choice not included, hence some percentages add to less than 100.

the medium and dark groups, are statistically significant.

Again, as in previous work,[5] it is shown that the percentage of the medium groups' identifications with the white or the colored representation resembles more that of the dark group and differs from the light group. Upon the basis of these results, therefore, one may assume that some of the factors and dynamics involved in racial identification are substantially the same for the dark and medium children, in contrast to dynamics for the light children.

North-South Differences. The results presented in Table 4 indicate that there are no significant quantitative differences between the northern and southern Negro children tested (children in mixed schools and children in segregated schools) in their knowledge of racial differences.

While none of these differences is statistically reliable, it is significant that northern children know as well as southern children which doll is supposed to represent a white child and which doll is supposed to represent a colored child. However, the northern children make fewer identifications with the colored doll and more identifications with the white doll than do the southern children. One factor accounting for this difference may be the fact that in this sample there are many more light colored children in the North (33) than there are in the South (13). Since this difference in self-identification is not statistically significant, it may be stated that the children in the northern mixed-school situation do not

[5] K. B. and M. P. Clark, "Skin Color as a Factor in Racial Identification of Negro Preschool Children," *J. Soc. Psychol.*, 1940, XI, 159–169; "Segregation as a Factor in the Racial Identification of Negro Preschool Children: a preliminary report," *J. Exper. Educ.*, 1939, IX, 161–163; "The Development of Consciousness of Self and the Emergence of Racial Identification in Negro Preschool Children," *J. Soc. Psychol.*, 1939, X, 591–599.

TABLE 5

CHOICES OF ALL SUBJECTS

Choice	Request 1 (play with)		Request 2 (nice doll)		Request 3 (looks bad)		Request 4 (nice color)	
	No.	Percent	No.	Percent	No.	Percent	No.	Percent
Colored doll	83	32	97	38	149	59	96	38
White doll	169	67	150	59	42	17	151	60
Don't know or no response . . .	1	1	6	3	62	24	6	2

differ from children in the southern segregated schools in either their knowledge of racial differences or their racial identification. A more qualitative analysis will be presented elsewhere.

Racial Preferences. It is clear from Table 5 that the majority of these Negro children prefer the *white* doll and reject the colored doll.

Approximately two thirds of the subjects indicated by their responses to requests 1 and 2 that they like the white doll "best," or that they would like to play with the white doll in preference to the colored doll, and that the white doll is a "nice doll."

Their responses to request 3 show that this preference for the white doll implies a concomitant negative attitude toward the brown doll. Fifty-nine percent of these children indicated that the colored doll "looks bad," while only 17 percent stated that the white doll "looks bad" (critical ratio 10.9). That this preference and negation in some way involve skin color is indicated by the results for request 4. Only 38 percent of the children thought that the brown doll was a "nice color," while 60 percent of them thought that the white doll was a "nice color" (critical ratio 5.0).

The importance of these results for an understanding of the origin and development of racial concepts and attitudes in Negro children cannot be minimized. Of equal significance are their implications, in the light of the results of racial identification already presented, for racial mental hygiene.

Age Differences. Table 6 shows that at each age from three through seven years the majority of these children prefer the white doll and reject the brown doll. This tendency to prefer the white doll is not as stable (not statistically reliable) in the three-year-olds as it is in the four- and five-year-olds. On the other hand, however, the tendency of the three-year-olds to negate the brown doll ("looks bad") is established as a statistically significant fact (critical ratio 4.5).

Analyzing the results of requests 1 and 2 together, it is seen that there is a marked *increase* in preference for the white doll from the three- to the four-year level; a more gradual *decrease* in this preference from the four- to the five-year level; a further decrease from the five- to the six-year level; and a continued decrease from the six- to the seven-year level. These results suggest that although the majority of Negro children at each age prefer the white doll to the brown doll, this preference decreases gradually from four through seven years.

Skin color preferences of these children follow a somewhat different pattern of development. The results of request 4 show that while the majority of children at each age below 7 years prefer the skin color of the white doll, this preference increases from three through five years and decreases from five through seven years. It is of interest to point out that

TABLE 6

Choices of Subjects at Each Age Level*

Choice	3 yr. No.	3 yr. Per-cent	4 yr. No.	4 yr. Per-cent	5 yr. No.	5 yr. Per-cent	6 yr. No.	6 yr. Per-cent	7 yr. No.	7 yr. Per-cent
Request 1 (play with)										
colored doll . . .	13	42	7	24	12	26	21	29	30	40
white doll	17	55	22	76	34	74	51	71	45	60
Request 2 (nice doll)										
colored doll . . .	11	36	7	24	13	28	33	46	33	44
white doll	18	58	22	76	33	72	38	53	39	52
Request 3 (looks bad)										
colored doll . . .	21	68	15	52	36	78	45	63	32	43
white doll	6	19	7	24	5	11	11	15	13	17
Request 4 (nice color)										
colored doll . . .	12	39	8	28	9	20	31	43	36	48
white doll	18	58	21	72	36	78	40	56	36	48

*Individuals failing to make either choice not included, hence some percentages add to less than 100.

TABLE 7

Choices of Subjects in Light, Medium, and Dark Groups*

Choice	Light No.	Light Percent	Medium No.	Medium Percent	Dark No.	Dark Percent
Request 1 (play with)						
colored doll	11	24	41	32	31	39
white doll	35	76	86	67	48	61
Request 2 (nice doll)						
colored doll	15	33	50	39	32	40
white doll	31	67	72	56	47	60
Request 3 (looks bad)						
colored doll	31	67	73	57	45	57
white doll	6	13	22	17	14	18
Request 4 (nice color)						
colored doll	13	28	56	44	27	34
white doll	32	70	68	53	51	65

*Individuals failing to make either choice not included, hence some percentages add to less than 100.

TABLE 8

CHOICES OF SUBJECTS IN NORTHERN (MIXED SCHOOLS) AND SOUTHERN (SEGREGATED SCHOOLS) GROUPS (REQUESTS 1 THROUGH 4)*

Choice	North, percent	South, percent
Request 1 (play with)		
colored doll	28	37
white doll	72	62
Request 2 (nice doll)		
colored doll	30	46
white doll	68	52
Request 3 (looks bad)		
colored doll	71	49
white doll	17	16
Request 4 (nice color)		
colored doll	37	40
white doll	63	57

*Individuals failing to make either choice not included, hence some percentages add to less than 100.

only at the seven-year level do the same number of children indicate a preference for the skin color of the colored doll as for that of the white doll.

The majority of these children at each age level indicate that the brown doll, rather than the white doll, "looks bad." This result shows positively the negation of the colored doll which was implicit in the expressed preference for the white doll discussed above.

The evaluative rejection of the brown doll is statistically significant, even at the three-year level, and is pronounced at the five-year level. The indicated preference for the white doll is statistically significant from the four-year level up to the seven-year level.

It seems justifiable to assume from these results that the crucial period in the formation and patterning of racial attitudes begins at around four and five years. At these ages these subjects appear to be reacting more uncritically in a definite structuring of attitudes which

conforms with the accepted racial values and mores of the larger environment.

Preferences and Skin Color. Results presented in Table 7 reveal that there is a tendency for the majority of these children, in spite of their own skin color, to prefer the white doll and to negate the brown doll. This tendency is most pronounced in the children of light skin color and least so in the dark children. A more intensive analysis of these results appears in a larger, yet unpublished study.

North-South Differences. From Table 8 it is clear that the southern children in segregated schools are less pronounced in their preference for the white doll, compared to the northern children's definite preference for this doll. Although still in a minority, a higher percentage of southern children, compared to northern, prefer to play with the colored doll or think that it is a "nice" doll. The critical ratio of this difference is not significant for request 1 but approaches significance for request 2 (2.75).

A significantly higher percentage (71) of the northern children, compared to southern children (49) think that the brown doll looks bad (critical ratio 3.68). Also a slightly higher percent of the southern children think that the brown doll has a "nice color," while more northern children think that the white doll has a "nice color."

In general, it may be stated that northern and southern children in these age groups tend to be similar in the degree of their preference for the white doll—with the northern children tending to be somewhat more favorable to the white doll than are the southern children. The southern children, however, in spite of their equal favorableness toward the white doll, are significantly less likely to reject the brown doll (evaluate it negatively), as compared to the strong tendency for the majority of the northern children to do so. That this difference is not primarily due to the larger number of light children found in the northern sample is indicated by more intensive analysis presented in the complete report.

Some Qualitative Data. Many of the children entered into the experimental situation with a freedom similar to that of play. They tended to verbalize freely and much of this unsolicited verbalization was relevant to the basic problems of this study.

On the whole, the rejection of the brown doll and the preference for the white doll, when explained at all, were explained in rather simple, concrete terms: for white-doll preference—" 'cause he's pretty" or " 'cause he's white"; for rejection of the brown doll—" 'cause he's ugly" or " 'cause it don't look pretty" or " 'cause him black" or "got black on him."

On the other hand, some of the children who were free and relaxed in the beginning of the experiment broke down and cried or became somewhat negativistic during the latter part when they were required to make self-identifications. Indeed, two children ran out of the testing room, unconsolable, convulsed in tears. This type of behavior, although not so extreme, was more prevalent in the North than in the South. The southern children who were disturbed by this aspect of the experiment generally indicated their disturbance by smiling or matter of factly attempting to escape their dilemma either by attempted humor or rationalization.

Rationalization of the rejection of the brown doll was found among both northern and southern children, however. A northern medium six-year-old justified his rejection of the brown doll by stating that "he looks bad 'cause he hasn't got a eyelash." A seven-year-old medium northern child justified his choice of the white doll as the doll with a "nice color" because "his feet, hands, ears, elbows, knees, and hair are clean."

A northern five-year-old dark child felt compelled to explain his identification with the brown doll by making the following unsolicited statement: "I burned my face and made it spoil." A seven-year-old northern light child went to great pains to explain that he is actually white but: "I look brown because I got a suntan in the summer."

THE EFFECT OF PUBLIC POLICY IN HOUSING PROJECTS UPON INTERRACIAL ATTITUDES
By Morton Deutsch and Mary Evans Collins

There have been very few studies which have centered about changing prejudices.[1] Not only have there been few such studies, but most of them have been limited to the investigation of influences (such as a college course, a motion picture, a visit to a Negro hospital) "which were probably relatively minor in relation to other influences in the subject's social milieu."[2] The often discouraging and inconclusive results of such investigations may well reflect the comparatively superficial nature of the influences being studied. The strength of the social and psychological barriers to democratic race relations as well as the pervasiveness of discrimination and prejudice suggests that a reduction in prejudices will require strong influences.

The social scientist is rarely in the position where he, himself, has the opportunity to create these influences. He has neither the political power nor the financial resources to produce of his own accord a major social experiment. Nevertheless, social "experiments" are going on all the time; or, perhaps more accurately, major attempts at producing social and psychological changes of one sort or another are a commonplace.

With the aid of scientific controls, the social scientist may occasionally be able to convert an attempt at social change into a social experiment. This is the purpose of our study. *We wish to investigate the effects upon prejudice of what is perhaps one of the most important "social experiments" in the area of race relations—the establishment of publicly supported non-segregated interracial housing projects.* Unfortunately, as in most "social experiments," social scientists did not participate in the design of the "experiment." The problem we face, then, is to convert, *ex post facto*, a "social change" into a scientific "social experiment."

The Significance of Interracial Housing. There are many reasons why residential segregation can be considered to be of central importance to intergroup relations in general. First of all, residential segregation brings with it, as a natural consequence, segregation in many other areas of living. If Negro and white people do not live near each other, "... they cannot—even if they otherwise would—associate with each other in the many activities founded on common neighborhood."[3] Segregated racial neighborhoods tend to bring with them segregation in schools, recreational centers, shopping districts, playgrounds, theaters, hospitals, leisure-time facilities, etc. Thus, one result of residential segregation is that prejudiced whites have little opportunity to see Negroes in social contexts which bring out the fundamental *condition humaine* of Negroes and whites. They do not see the Negroes, for example, as school children disliking homework, as

Adapted and condensed by Morton Deutsch from M. Deutsch and M. E. Collins, *Interracial Housing: A Psychological Evaluation of a Social Experiment* (Minneapolis: University of Minnesota Press, 1951). The study was supported by a grant from the Marshall Field Foundation.

[1] For a good summary of such studies, see A. Rose, *Studies in the Reduction of Prejudice* (Chicago: American Council on Race Relations, 1947).

[2] R. M. Williams, Jr., *The Reduction of Intergroup Tensions*, Social Science Research Council Bulletin No. 57 (New York: Social Science Research Council, 1947).

[3] G. Myrdal, *The American Dilemma* (New York: Harper & Bros., 1944).

expectant mothers in their first preg-nancy, as tenants complaining about their landlords, or as breadwinners facing a contracting labor market.

Residential segregation, in yet another way, is of central importance. Next to employment discrimination, segregation is probably the most significant way by which Negroes, as a group, are disadvantaged. Residential segregation for Negroes in the North has always resulted in increased competition for a limited number of dwelling units, with the consequence that Negroes have invariably paid higher rentals for poorer accommodations. With limited incomes, high rentals have resulted in severe overcrowding and rapid physical deterioration. The economic and psychological burdens resulting from these housing conditions have contributed notably to a high incidence of delinquency, broken homes, emotional instability, and the general brutalization of life. These characteristics of Negro ghettos also tend to support the rationales for prejudice, helping to perpetuate the vicious circle which Myrdal and others have fully documented.

With a few exceptions and apart from run-down neighborhoods or areas in a process of racial transition, the only major instances of a break with the traditional practices of residential segregation in the United States have occurred in public housing. However, even in public housing the common pattern is complete segregation; Negroes and whites live in separate housing projects. But there are important exceptions. These exceptions and the variations among them, in effect, provide a natural social experiment which permits those engaged in carefully controlled social research to gather valuable information about the conditions which affect interracial attitudes.

THE RESEARCH PROBLEM

To orient ourselves to the various factors which might influence race relations in public housing projects and to determine the social urgencies and vital issues, we interviewed officials with experience in interracial housing throughout the country. From our survey of expert opinion and from other social-science knowledge, it was apparent that one of the most crucial influences affecting race relations in housing communities is the *occupancy pattern*. To determine the impact of different occupancy patterns, we decided to do a comparative study of race relations in two types of housing projects: the *integrated interracial* project (families are assigned to apartments without consideration of race) and the *segregated bi-racial* project (Negro and white families live in the same project but are assigned to different buildings or to different parts of the project).

We obtained the cooperation of two large housing authorities [4] in neighboring cities, Newark and New York, which differ in policy with respect to the type of occupancy pattern in interracial public housing projects. In Newark, the projects, which house both Negro and white families, have a segregated occupancy pattern; in New York the pattern is integrated. In each city two projects were selected for study. Realizing that the ratio of Negro to white families might be an important influence on race relations, we selected projects in the two cities that had approximately the same ratios. In one project in each of the two cities, there are about 70 Negro families to 30 white families; in the other project in Newark the ratio is 50–50, while the second project in New York has 60 white to every 40 Negro families.

Of course, other factors in addition to

[4] We wish to express gratitude to both the Newark and New York Housing Authorities for their constructive cooperation throughout the study. Without their objectivity and their concern with the broadening of knowledge this study would not have been possible.

the ratio of Negro to white families may influence race relations. Fortunately the projects we were comparing are similar in many relevant respects: they all are low-income projects containing families who had to meet similar eligibility requirements in order to move in; they were all built at about the same time, just before World War II, the neighborhoods surrounding the various projects are much alike—all of them are predominantly Negro neighborhoods, and one of the projects in each city is located in a neighborhood that is considerably deteriorated and characterized by much delinquency; the staffs in each of the four projects include both Negro and white personnel; the project managers have all had considerable experience in interracial public housing projects; etc. The projects differ somewhat, as one would expect, e.g., one New York project is larger and the other smaller than the corresponding projects with similar racial ratios in Newark. Also, it should be indicated that population differences exist that act to enhance some of the results reported below. However, statistical analysis reveals that these population differences are by no means sufficient to "explain away" the differences we attribute to the effects of occupancy pattern.

The data for this study were collected primarily through systematic interviewing of white housewives. The home is, after all, largely the domain of the woman. She spends more time in it than anyone else; she is, by and large, the initiator of activities and contacts that develop directly out of the home. Whether or not she "wears the pants in the family," she is the key person in activities centered about the place of residence.

The funds at our disposal made it unfeasible to interview both Negro and white housewives in equal proportion.

We decided to interview more white housewives as a result of our conviction that prejudiced interracial attitudes are more socially crucial among whites than among Negroes, since the practices of segregation and discrimination are enforced by the white and not by the Negro segment of the population.

We interviewed approximately 100 white and 25 Negro housewives in each of the four projects. In addition, a total of 24 Negro and white adolescent boys and girls were interviewed in one project in each of the two cities. The interviewees were selected by a random procedure.

THE INTERVIEW

The interview was long and intensive; on the average, it lasted about one and a quarter hours. Some interviews ran over two hours. In the course of the interview, data were obtained about five major areas:

1. *The Attitudes of the Housewife toward Living in the Project:* What she liked most and least about the project; her feelings about public housing, the neighborhood, the apartment, etc.; the anticipations she had before moving into the project; her future plans; and her feeling toward people in the project.

2. *Attitudes toward Negroes:* [5] A series of questions attempted to uncover the attitudes of the housewife toward Negroes, her feelings about them, her "knowledge" and beliefs about them, and her feelings about living in an interracial project.

3. *The Amount and Intimacy of Contact with Other Women in the Project:* Questions were asked about neighborly contacts (such as visiting, shopping together, minding children, going to movies together), friendships, how one gets to know people, etc. Information was obtained about the types of contacts with Negro women.

---

[5] Essentially the same questions were asked of the Negro housewives but, of course, we asked them about white people.

4. *The Social Supports for Attitudes:* The housewife was asked, for example, to tell how her relatives, friends, people in the project, management staff, etc., would react to her being friendly with Negro people.

5. *The Characteristics of the Housewife:* A miscellaneous assortment of questions was asked about the housewife: her age, number of children, her activities, her education, her religion, her interests, etc., to obtain information about the comparability of the populations in the projects we were studying.

The interview, for the most part, encouraged the respondent to answer freely in her own words rather than restricting her to "yes" or "no" answers. Interviewing was done in the respondent's home.

RESEARCH RESULTS

In an *ex post facto* experiment such as we are here reporting, there is always need to be cautious in making causal inferences. One must inevitably face the critical question, "Which came first?" That is, did the attitudinal differences between the housewives in the integrated interracial and the segregated bi-racial projects exist prior to their residence in public housing and perhaps *cause* them to move into the one or the other type project? Or did the differences in attitudes *result* from their living in the different types of projects? In the book from which this article is adapted and condensed considerable indirect evidence is brought to bear upon these questions. This evidence, for which we do not have space here, leads us to believe that the differences primarily reflect the effects of the different occupancy patterns. The evidence is of several sorts: (1) an examination of the socio-psychological situation of prospective tenants; (2) an exam-

ination of refusal rates and voluntary move-outs; (3) an examination of the housewives' prior interracial experiences; (4) the reports of the housewives about their prior attitudes; (5) comparison of housewives who did or did not know about the nature of the occupancy pattern before they made their applications; (6) a comparison of housewives in the different projects who were equated for education, religion, and political beliefs. All these types of evidence give credence to the interpretation that the occupancy pattern had causal efficacy.

Getting to Know Each Other. As our knowledge about the development of prejudice has increased, it has become more and more evident that prejudice rarely originates in personal experiences with the members of a minority group. We know that many people who are extremely prejudiced against Negroes or Jews have never known a Negro or a Jew.

Further, we know that the nature of prejudice is such that it results in a reduction of intimate, equal-status contacts with the objects of prejudice. Prejudices combine with social custom to prevent the bigot from having the types of experiences, with Negro people, for example, which would destroy his prejudices. Hence, the main source of information about Negroes comes to be the "experiences," beliefs, and feelings of other prejudiced members of his own group. As a consequence, members of the prejudiced group, through contact with each other, tend mutually to confirm and support one another's prejudices. A vicious circle or a "socially shared autism"[6] is established whereby, without personal experience with members of a minority group, contact with the prevailing attitude toward them provides the "experience" to support a prejudice.

[6] Gardner Murphy has originated the term "socially shared autism" to refer to phenomena such as these in which members of a social group develop considerable confidence in their belief about something with which they no longer have contact, as a consequence of their mutual reinforcement of each other's beliefs. See his *Personality: A Biosocial Approach to Origin and Structure* (Harper & Bros., 1947).

TABLE 1

PERCENTAGES OF HOUSEWIVES INDICATING THEIR MOST LIKELY
CONTACTS WITH NEGRO PEOPLE

Meeting place	Integrated interracial projects		Segregated bi-racial projects	
	Koaltown *	Sacktown *	Bakerville *	Frankville *
As neighbors in the building	60	53	0	0
Through laundry facilities located in or near building	13	17	0	0
Outside on benches	46	64	7	21
In office, etc.	2	1	7	17
At tenant meetings	2	17	28	28
Shopping in stores, in the streets around project	12	13	81	60
Through the children's schools . . .	1	3	14	0
Total cases †	102	86	43	42

* The project names are pseudonyms.

† Only the people who responded "yes" or "uncertain" to the question of getting to know Negro people are included. The percentage figures add up to more than 100 because many people named more than one place.

Perhaps the first problem that faces the person who wishes to change the attitudes of a prejudiced individual is that of breaking through this vicious circle so as to bring to bear upon the bigoted the experiences necessary to a change in attitudes. Something must be done to "prevent" the prejudiced person from selectively avoiding the experiences which might disrupt his prejudices. One method of accomplishing this objective would be to "compel" him to get to know Negro people in equal-status contacts of a sufficiently intimate and extended nature to resist perceptual or memorial distortion. This latter qualification must be inserted because we know that attitudes tend to select and distort experiences so as to maintain themselves. However, persistent, intense experiences that are repeated are likely to survive

attitudinal distortion, if only because of the individual's need to accept the reality of his own senses and experiences.[7]

One of the basic hypotheses of the study is that *the greater physical and functional proximity of Negro and white families in the integrated interracial projects will result in more frequent and more intimate contacts between Negroes and whites in these projects as contrasted with the segregated bi-racial projects*. Let us consult the data.

In the interview, we asked the housewife to indicate whether she thought that a person who moved into the project would "be likely to get to know any colored people in the project." The differences in responses of the housewives in the two types of projects are striking. More than 95 percent of the women in each of the two integrated projects assert

[7] It is important to emphasize the strength of the motivation to accept as real one's perception and experiences. If they were not customarily accepted, the individual would be in a continuous state of insecurity and indecision.

TABLE 2

PERCENTAGE OF PERSONS KNOWN BEST WHO ARE NEGRO

Percentage of Negroes among people "known best"	Integrated interracial projects		Segregated bi-racial projects	
	Koaltown	Sacktown	Bakerville	Frankville
0	73	38	100	100
20–39	19	18	0	0
40–59	6	23	0	0
60 or over	2	21	0	0
Total cases	96	84	99	98

that a person will get to know some Negro people in the project; the few dissenters voice the opinion that "it depends upon you." In contrast, only a minority (30 percent in one and 21 percent in the other) of the housewives in the segregated bi-racial projects feel that there is any chance of getting to know Negro people; the majority are quite convinced that no such likelihood exists.

Clearly, then, the opportunity to get to know Negro people is considerably greater in the integrated than in the segregated project. Table 1 helps to explain why there is such a striking difference in this respect between the two types of projects. The most frequently mentioned places of contact with Negro people for white residents in the integrated projects are the buildings in which they live, laundry facilities located in or near their buildings, or outside on benches. (People in the projects, for the most part, during the warm season customarily sit on benches located near their buildings.) It seems evident that the major source of Negro–white contact— contacts that arise from living in the same building—is not available to residents of a segregated bi-racial project.

Several of our questions in the interview of the housewives had the purpose of finding how intimate the contacts were with Negro women in the two types of projects. Only 3 percent of the housewives in each of the two segregated projects report "knowing any Negro people in the project pretty well—well enough to call them by their first names"; in contrast 77 percent of the housewives in one and 49 percent in the other integrated project report having at least this degree of intimacy. The tenants were also asked to tell us the five people in the project they know best. Table 2 indicates the percentage of persons "known best" who are Negro. None of the women in the segregated projects include Negro people among those they know best in the project. In contrast, 27 percent of the women in Koaltown and 62 percent in Sacktown indicate that at least one of the women they know best is Negro.

Similar differences obtain in "neighborly" activities, such as *visiting back and forth; helping one another out*, for example, with shopping or taking care of the children or when somebody is sick; *informal club activities*, such as "card" clubs, sewing or ironing clubs; and going out together, such as going to the movies, shopping together, or going "downtown" together. Only a very small percentage (1 percent and 4 percent) of white housewives in the segregated projects engage in any such activities with Negro women; in the integrated projects many of the white women (39 percent and 72 percent in the two projects, respectively) engage in such activities with their Negro neighbors.

To sum up, the data we have presented so far have demonstrated that the likelihood of white tenants getting to know Negro people and of having intimate social relationships with them is considerably less in the segregated than in the integrated projects. Our interviews with Negro housewives and with children of both races give the same results. Further, when we compare people in the two types of projects of the same religion or of similar educational backgrounds, or with similar political attitudes (or people who are similar in all three respects—religion, education, and political attitudes) it is still strikingly clear that the occupancy pattern markedly affects interracial contact. . . . The integrated project is, thus, considerably more successful in stimulating unprejudiced behavior toward Negroes among the white people in the project. Many more white people in the integrated than in the segregated projects violate, in actual behavior, the social prejudices and social customs which have the consequence of preventing intimate, equal-status contacts between Negroes and whites. In effect, living in the integrated projects produces a *behavioral* change with respect to race relations for many of the white people.

Social Standards for Behavior with People of the Other Race. A housing project may be seen as composed of many informal groups organized around various types of goals. These groups are intricately connected through the overlapping memberships of individuals within each group. Within this complex network it is likely that group standards or social norms will develop with regard to issues which are collectively important to the interconnected groups. In a society where prejudice is commonplace and where interracial association is a possibility, race relations will be such an issue. It is our hypothesis that *the social norms in the integrated projects will be more favorable*

to friendly interracial relations than will the corresponding social norms in the segregated projects.

There are several reasons for advancing the foregoing hypothesis. First of all, it has long been recognized that people tend to behave as they are expected to behave. The expectations of others in a social situation, particularly if these others are important to the individual, help to define what is the appropriate behavior. There is little doubt that a public housing authority looms importantly in the life of residents in public housing projects, since it controls their only means of obtaining decent housing at a low rental. Thus, to the people who live in the projects, the action of a housing authority in establishing a policy of integration or of segregation is not likely to be without significance. Further, the policy of integration or segregation is an "official" decision implicitly carrying public sanction, and as such it may set up standards for what one "should" or "should not" do. The policy of segregation may be seen as implying the notion that Negroes and whites should be kept apart; the policy of integration, that race should *not* be a criterion for distinguishing among tenants.

In addition to the direct psychological impact of official policy decision in shaping social norms, the policy decision has indirect effects upon social norms through the physical environment that it creates for race relations. In the previous section, we have seen how interracial contact is promoted or hindered by the physical nature of the occupancy pattern. The differences in interracial behavior resulting from the different occupancy patterns are likely to have consequences for the social norms which emerge in the projects. Thus, a housewife in the integrated projects is more likely to have friendly relations with Negroes, as well as to see other housewives as having similar relations. These differences combined with the inclination to moralize one's own behavior (to rationalize the status quo) and with the tendency to conform to and to accept as "right" the behavior of one's peers would work in the direction of producing more favorable social norms in the integrated projects. Another factor working in the same direction would be the comparatively greater number of cooperative relationships between Negroes and whites in the integrated projects.

Several questions were designed to determine whether and to what extent the decision with respect to occupancy pattern by a public authority and the fact of occupancy pattern do establish a standard for interracial conduct. Such a standard, we felt, would be reflected in the housewife's description of how "the other people in the project would react if she were friendly with Negro people" and in her answer to questions about whether it would influence her reputation in the project if she had much to do with the colored people.

The evidence strongly indicates that the housewife in the integrated project expects more approval than disapproval from others in the project if she is friendly with the Negro people. She thinks it is better rather than not better for her "to have much to do with the colored people." In contrast, the housewife in the segregated project expects to be socially ostracized by the other white women if she is friendly with the Negro people, and asserts that it is better not to have much to do with them. Thus, one woman in a segregated project said: "They'd think you're crazy if you had a colored woman visit you in your home. They'd stare at you and there'd be a lot of talk." Another said, "I used to be good friends with a colored woman who worked with me at the factory before I moved here. She lives in the other side of the project but I never have her over to my side of the project—it just isn't done. Occasionally, I go over and visit her."

Perhaps the most striking evidence as to the effects of occupancy pattern in

creating guides for behavior comes from interviews with the children. The children in Bakerville (a segregated project) go to unsegregated elementary schools, where Negro and white children mix freely. As a consequence of meeting in the schools, they all have at least speaking acquaintances with members of the other race. Many of them play games together and belong to the same clubs. Yet in no single instance among the children interviewed in Bakerville do they engage in such activities with children of the other race in the project. The children in Bakerville implicitly understand that different standards with respect to interracial association exist in the school and in the housing project. In contrast, the children in Sacktown (an integrated project) play together at the project as well as in the school, visiting in each other's homes freely.

Some examples will illustrate the effects of social norms on children in Bakerville (a segregated bi-racial project):

One twelve-year-old white girl stated that she had made friends with a Negro girl at camp and she thought the girl was very nice. The girl lived in the project, but they never saw each other.

A Negro girl who feels that she is friendly with a number of white children stated, "I play with them at school and go to the movies with them. In the project, I have nothing to do with them."

Thus, it is clear that the occupancy pattern brings along with it a frame of reference which helps to establish expectations and values with respect to race relations within the project. Since this frame of reference is *shared* by other housewives with whom one is interacting, it can be said that a consequence of moving into one or another project is that the housewife becomes exposed to one rather than another social norm with respect to being friendly with the Negro people in the project. It is apparent that the social norm that one is exposed to as a result of moving into an integrated project is more likely to favor friendly interracial association than the norm of the segregated project; the latter is more likely to favor avoidance (with the more or less inevitable connotation in American society that interracial association brings trouble or that it is socially degrading).

The fact that the tenants in the various projects are exposed to "shared frames of reference," as Newcomb [8] calls them, rather than merely their isolated individual experiences, is a matter of some significance. Lewin and Grabbe have pointed out that "only by anchoring his own conduct in something as large, substantial, and superindividual as the culture of the group can the individual stabilize his new beliefs sufficiently to keep them immune from day-by-day fluctuations of moods and influences to which he, as an individual, is subject." [9] This is why attempts to change significant social attitudes must be directed not only at the individual but also at the social institutions and social norms which determine the individual's values and which help to induce the goals for which he strives.

The Effects upon Interracial Attitudes. So far, the results have indicated that the integrated occupancy pattern creates more opportunities for close contact with members from the other race, an atmosphere more favorable to friendly interracial associations, and friendlier interracial relations.

Let us now make the assumption that the tenants who moved into the two types of projects had, like most people of similar education and circumstance, rather prejudiced attitudes toward Negroes. If this were the case, one would expect many of the tenants in the integrated projects through their experiences and relationships with Negro neighbors, to shift their attitudes in a more favorable direction; few of the tenants in the segregated projects could be expected to change. That is to say, we hypothesize that *the differences between the two types of projects with respect to interracial contacts and social norms which have already been indicated would result in attitudinal differences between the residents in the two types of projects.* These attitudinal differences would be most directly reflected in attitudes toward the Negro people in the project; they might be generalized somewhat to include Negro people in general, and perhaps might even extend to other minority groups.

In our data we have many different indicators of attitudes toward the Negro people in the project; some of the measures of interracial association and interracial contact may be so considered. All give the same results: the attitudes of the housewives in the integrated projects are considerably less prejudiced than those of the women in the segregated bi-racial projects. Almost three times as many women in the segregated projects (36 percent and 31 percent as compared with 13 percent and 10 percent) in describing the Negro people spontaneously use words like "aggressive," "dangerous," "trouble-makers." There are approximately *two* housewives who want to be friendly *to every one* who wishes to avoid contact with Negroes in the integrated projects; in the segregated developments there is approximately only *one* who wishes to be friendly to *every ten* who wish to avoid relationships.

We also obtained many different indicators about attitudes toward *Negro people in general:* reactions to social-distance questions, acceptance of stereotypes about Negroes, interviewer ratings, reports of the housewives about their own attitudinal change, etc. Again, all provide the same result. The attitudes of the

---

[8] T. M. Newcomb, *Social Psychology* (New York: Dryden Press, 1950).

[9] K. Lewin and P. Grabbe, "Conduct, Knowledge, and the Acceptance of New Values," *Journal of Social Issues*, I (1945), 53–64.

housewives in the integrated projects are considerably more favorable than those of the women in the segregated developments. We can infer that the *changes* in attitudes toward Negroes in general among the women in the integrated projects have been considerable. In other words, many of the women in this type of development have not only come to respect and like the Negro people with whom they have associated, but they have also changed their notions about Negroes in general. Their experiences in the project with Negro people have become partially *generalized*, so that they now have more favorable attitudes toward Negroes as a group.

Perhaps the most striking data come from the reports of the housewives themselves about their own attitude changes toward Negroes in general.[10] We asked the housewives a series of questions which included: "Can you remember what you thought colored people were like before you moved into the project?" "How much have your ideas about colored people changed since you have lived in the project?" (If some change occurred) "In what ways have they changed?" And, "What do you think made you change your ideas?"

Results which cannot be presented in full here indicate that the *net gain* (percent of housewives reporting favorable changes minus percent reporting unfavorable changes) for the two integrated projects among housewives who indicated that they were initially highly prejudiced is 71 percent and 78 percent; for the housewives reporting moderate prejudice initially, it is 46 percent and 61 percent; for housewives reporting favorable initial attitudes it is 13 percent and 28 percent. In the two segregated projects, the corresponding net gains are much smaller: for those reporting much initial prejudice it is 26 percent and 19 percent; for those

indicating moderate initial prejudice, it is 18 percent and 2 percent; for those reporting that they were originally unprejudiced, there is a net gain of 15 percent in one and a *net loss* of 18 percent in the other segregated project.

The interview material provides dramatic illustration of the nature of the attitudinal changes that occurred among many of the housewives in the integrated projects. Thus one woman, when asked to tell how she felt about living in the project, said: "I started to cry when my husband told me we were coming to live here. I cried for three weeks. . . . I didn't want to come and live here where there are so many colored people. I didn't want to bring my children up with colored children, but we had to come; there was no place else to go. . . . Well, all that's changed. I've really come to like it. I see they're just as human as we are. They have nice apartments; they keep their children clean, and they're very friendly. I've come to like them a great deal. I'm no longer scared of them. . . . I'd just as soon live near a colored person as a white; it makes no difference to me."

Another woman put it quaintly: "I thought I was moving into the heart of Africa. . . . I had always heard things about how they were . . . they were dirty, drink a lot . . . were like savages. Living with them my ideas have changed altogether. They're just people . . . they're not any different."

Another one said: "I was prejudiced when I moved in here but not any more. . . . I find there is no such thing as 'my kind.' . . . I was under the impression that every colored man that looked at you wanted to rape you or was going to pull out a razor. . . . I don't feel that way any more. . . . I know the people. I have been in their homes . . . been to church with them. . . . I know they're not dirty,

---

[10] To be sure, such reports must always be evaluated with caution because of distorting effects in recall. We have examined the data to see if differential distortion between the two types of project has occurred and could find no such indications.

My doctor is colored . . . my dentist is colored. He's a surgeon and he's wonderful."

In contrast with the above, the following remarks express typical findings in the segregated projects: "I don't have anything to do with the colored people . . . they don't bother me . . . I don't mingle with them. I guess I don't like them because they're colored . . . the Bible says 'God created them equal' so I guess they're equal, but I don't like them. I don't like living so close to them. I think they ought to be in separate projects. Let them live their lives and let us live ours. . . . My ideas haven't changed any since I've lived here. . . . They're colored and I'm white. They don't like us and we don't like them."

CONCLUSIONS

Our results provide considerable evidence to discredit a notion that has characterized much of social-science thinking in the field of race relations: the notion originating with William S. Sumner that "stateways cannot change folkways." The implication of our study is that official policy, executed without equivocation, can result in large changes in behavior and attitudes despite initial resistance to that policy. Thus, it is clear from our data that, although most of the white housewives in the integrated projects we studied did not, upon moving into the projects, like the idea of living in the same buildings with Negro families (and certainly the community as a whole did not favor it), a considerable change has taken place in their beliefs and feelings as well as in their behavior. *It is evident that from the point of view of reducing prejudice and of creat-*

ing harmonious democratic intergroup relations, the net gain resulting from the integrated projects is considerable; from the same point of view, the gain created by the segregated bi-racial projects is slight.

Further, our results are consistent with the growing body of evidence about the effects of equal-status contacts, under certain conditions, upon prejudiced attitudes. Studies by Allport and Kramer,[11] by Brophy,[12] by the Information and Education Division of the U. S. War Department,[13] by Mackenzie,[14] among others, all support the notion that prejudices are likely to be diminished when prejudiced persons are brought into situations which compel contacts between them and the objects of prejudice, provided:

(*a*) that the behavior of the objects of prejudice is such as not to conform with the beliefs of the prejudiced. That is, the Negroes with whom the prejudiced person has contact are not "lazy," "ignorant," "delinquent," etc.

(*b*) that the intimacy and amount of contact with objects of prejudice not conforming to the stereotypes of the prejudiced are such as to result in experiences which are sufficiently compelling to resist marked perceptual and memorial distortion.

(*c*) that the contact takes place under conditions which make the nonconforming behavior seem relevant to the basis on which the objects of prejudice are grouped together. Thus, if a Negro attendant is seen to be clean and honest, there may be little effect on stereotypes if the perception of cleanliness and honesty is connected primarily with the requirements of the situation, with the

---

[11] G. W. Allport and B. M. Kramer, "Some Roots of Prejudice," *Journal of Psychology*, XXII (1946), 9–39.

[12] I. N. Brophy, "The Luxury of Anti-Negro Prejudice," *Public Opinion Quarterly*, IX (1946), 456–466.

[13] Information and Education Division, U.S. War Department, "Opinions about Negro Infantry Platoons in White Companies of Seven Divisions," pp. 502–506 in this book.

[14] B. K. Mackenzie, "The Importance of Contact in Determining Attitudes toward Negroes," *Journal of Abnormal and Social Psychology*, XLIII (1948), 417–441.

classification of the individual as an attendant rather than as a Negro or Negro attendant." [15]

(d) that the prejudiced person has values or is exposed to social influences (e.g., democratic values or the social influences emanating from a policy of an official, public body) which would strongly conflict with the unabashed retention of unrationalized prejudices.

In addition, if the contact situation is such that it encourages the development of new sentiments to replace prejudiced sentiments either as a result of the experience of cooperative activity with the objects of prejudice or as a result of the internalization of the social norms of an unprejudiced group, the reduction of prejudiced sentiments will be much facilitated.

INTERPERSONAL DYNAMICS IN RACIAL INTE-GRATION   By Marian Radke Yarrow, John D. Campbell, and Leon J. Yarrow

This is a study of social change, a study of racial integration at a time when this issue is of great importance in the American culture. When integration occurs, what are the experiences of the individual Negro and white children involved? What happens when attitudes built up over a lifetime dictate one course of action, while the new situation requires different behavior? This is a basic social psychological question posed by integration.

It was with this question in mind that we undertook to study the children in a racially integrated summer camp. We attempted to examine the *process* of integration by studying the actions, feelings, and perceptions of the campers from their first day in the integrated camp to the time of their departure. To provide a base line for evaluating the effects of interracial contact we also obtained comparable information from racially segregated camps. We assumed at the outset that two kinds of factors would be important in understanding how the children reacted to integration: the customs and attitudes in the homes and communities from which these children came, and the demands of the immediate situation in which they found themselves.

It is more than likely that, in their home environment, most children in the study had learned certain racial stereotypes and certain customary modes of interacting with members of the other race which were based on a policy of segregation. There were many indications of this learning in unsolicited comments. When such a background is brought into an in-

Prepared especially for this volume, this study is part of a larger project concerned with children's interpersonal relationships. The authors are indebted to John G. Theban, executive secretary of Family and Child Services of Washington, D.C., and George Greene, director of the Summer Outings Committee, for making this research possible in the camp setting. To the camp staff and counselors we are grateful for their generous cooperation.

[15] Just as there is likely to be little effect upon prejudiced beliefs if "good" behavior upon the part of the objects of prejudice is seen to result from the requirements of the situation rather than from the person or from the person's membership in a minority group, so too, one can expect a reduction in prejudice if "bad" behavior upon their part comes to be seen as emanating from their circumstances rather than from their personality or minority-group membership. This is why changes in theories of behavior (from a genetic to an environmental emphasis) may have a subtle influence even upon prejudice.

tegrated camp situation, it appears inevitable that integration initially will certainly present confusion, if not conflict, to the child. New face-to-face contacts will confront him with many uncertainties regarding his behavior and his expectations of others' behavior toward him. Not all children will have the same degree and kind of conflict, however. Quite possibly, there will be differences in the socialization pressures impinging on Negro and white children or on boys as compared with girls. Since we assume that early socialization experiences (particularly those related to the expression of aggression, nurturance, and dominance) influence how a child thinks and feels about, as well as behaves toward, others, it is possible that one race or one sex might be especially facilitated, or especially handicapped, in functioning in a racially mixed group.

The kind of situation in which racial contacts occur is known to be significant. To a marked degree the camp situation was well defined in advance. Integration was a *fait accompli*. The children were matter-of-factly assigned to racially mixed cabins; all activities were mixed; the authority of the counselors stood behind the "rules of the game," rules prescribing equal-status participation for white and Negro children.

RESEARCH DESIGN: SETTING AND SAMPLE

Only minor adjustments to the requirements of research were necessary to create a uniquely controlled situation out of a natural setting. Children from low-income families with Southern and border-state backgrounds were studied in two summer camps. Both camps were under the direction of the same agency and had essentially similar facilities and leadership. Children came to the camp for two-week sessions. For the first three sessions of the summer, the camps were racially segregated; the children in one camp were Negro, in the other, white. The last two sessions were racially integrated. The same Negro and white adult leaders served as counselors in both the segregated and the integrated sessions.

Thirty-two cabin groups and their adult counselors were studied. Children, aged eight to 13, who had had no prior acquaintance with one another were assigned to a cabin. Approximately eight were in each cabin. The groups were homogeneous in age and sex: 131 boys and girls in 16 segregated cabins and 136 in 16 racially integrated cabins. White and Negro children were in equal numbers in the integrated cabins.

We obtained information about each child from the following sources: (1) detailed behavior observations, (2) individual interviews with children, (3) interviews with counselors, (4) ratings of the children by their counselors, and (5) journal records by participant observers—members of the research staff living in the cabins.[1]

Children were interviewed in the first days of camp. Questions focused on the child's impressions and feelings about his cabin mates and his counselor. (Photographs of each child and the counselor permitted ready identification and helped to hold the respondent's interest.) Early in the interview each child was asked to choose one of his new acquaintances about whom he felt he knew the most. He was encouraged to tell all that he knew about him (as if he were telling a friend back home) and to tell how he learned what he had described. Since the aim was to capture the child's impressions in terms of the attributes that were salient to *him*, predetermined questions were not imposed at this point.

[1] The writers wish to acknowledge their indebtedness to the following persons who assisted in the various phases of data collection: Florence Christopher, Ruth Orcutt, Doris Linn, John Lucas, Gladys Morris, Frances Polen, and Olive W. Quinn.

Excerpts from the impressions of 11-year-old Rosemary show the nature of replies:

Betty is little. Children always blame her. When we clean, kids make her sweep the floor. She plays with me when I have no one to play with. She's scared of everyone in the cabin. . . . They pick on her. She was sitting at the supper table and kicked Rosy by mistake. Rosy said she's going to get her and Betty started crying. Doris told Betty, "You better not let people pick on you, or you will all your life. Fight back." . . . I'm scared too [like Betty, but] I know I can fight back.

Free descriptions were followed by "guess-who" questions, which asked the child to pick a cabin mate who best fitted a given description of behavior. Characteristics such as aggressiveness, submissiveness, leadership, and anxiety were tapped. To assess spontaneous racial stereotyping, the research worker clearly must not ask his questions in such a way as to impose, or imply, a stereotype. In our research, the child was never required to respond to abstract racial classifications. In his own description of another, the child was completely free to evaluate and appraise in the terms he found most relevant. On the "guess-who" questions, he could freely choose any one of his cabin mates (or himself) as best fitting behavior categories. Other questions in the interview explored friendship choices within the cabin, the child's views of his counselor, and his expectations about camp. At the end of the two-week session essentially the same interview was repeated.

Counselors were interviewed at the beginning and end of each session. Interviews dealt with (1) the counselor's appraisal of individual children and rela-tionships in the cabin, (2) his assessments of his own relationship to the group, and (3) his expectations and attitudes about serving as leader in a racially integrated group. Further, at the beginning and end of each session the counselor rated his children on aspects of behavior that paralleled the "guess-who" items in the children's interview.

Systematic observations of behavior were made in 20 cabins. Beginning on the first day, series of five-minute samples were taken at specified times during the two-week session. Observations were recorded in the form of detailed running accounts. In addition to these scheduled observations, the research member living in the cabin served as a participant observer, keeping a journal record of the counselor's functioning and characteristics of group interaction.[2]

INTERPERSONAL RELATIONS IN SEGREGATION

The first problem with which we are concerned is whether there are characteristic differences between Negro and white children in patterns of interaction with their peers in *segregated* situations. Do the children differ in ways that would lead one to anticipate that their standards of behavior would be incompatible when they are brought together and required to interact? To answer this question, observed behavior and children's descriptions of their cabin mates in segregated camps were analyzed in terms of categories such as nurturance, dominance, dependence, aggression, etc.

During the first days at camp, as the children became acquainted and established themselves among their peers,

[2] Personality factors are recognized as significant but are not included in this analysis. Similarly, specific racial attitudes held by the child or his parents are important. But for reasons which are apparent, the research did not specifically ask the children their attitudes toward Negroes and whites. Children in segregated and integrated groups were drawn from the same population and, it is assumed, held similar attitudes. Parents opposing integration, with the choice of an integrated camp or no camp for their child, more often chose the former, sometimes admonishing the child, as he departed for camp, not to play with children of the other race.

TABLE 1

CHILDREN'S BEHAVIOR IN SEGREGATED CABINS *

Behavior category	Initial phases (percent of behavior units)				Later phases (percent of behavior units)			
	Negro		White		Negro		White	
	Girls	Boys	Girls	Boys	Girls	Boys	Girls	Boys
Dominance, aggression, nonconformity	18	25	15	19	22	25	10	22
Fearful submission	5	2	3	0	3	1	3	2
Mild dependence	6	6	12	9	5	9	11	7
Conformity	2	3	5	3	5	2	3	5
Sociability	34	39	27	36	29	27	34	27
Affiliation and nurturance	24	11	21	21	16	15	19	16
Assertive leading	11	14	17	12	20	23	20	21

* This table summarizes peer-directed behavior. It excludes children's solitary actions and their behavior directed toward adults. The latter types constitute 41 percent of the 2,909 behavior units recorded in initial observations of children in segregated cabins and 35 percent of the 3,753 units in observations made during later phases of segregated camping.

similarities in the behavior of Negro and white children in segregated groups were more striking than differences. However, in culturally significant areas relating to control and expression of aggression and dominance-deference patterns, small but consistent subgroup differences appeared. As can be seen in Table 1, aggressive-dominant behavior occurred with highest frequency among the Negro boys (25 percent of their total behavior was coded in these categories); this occurred least frequently among white girls (15 percent and 10 percent at beginning and end of camp respectively), while white boys and Negro girls were in intermediate positions. Consistent with their high proportion of aggression, Negro boys showed the lowest proportion (11 percent) of nurturant and affiliative behavior toward their peers while Negro girls showed the highest proportion of such acts (24 percent).

These subgroup differences also appeared in the descriptions children gave of the cabin mate they felt they knew best. Negro boys, in addition to behaving more aggressively, were more alerted to dominance, aggression, and nonconformity. That is, they, more often than the other children, described their cabin mates in these terms. (Initially, Negro boys referred to aggression in 50 percent of the cases; the other subgroups, in approximately 12 percent. Girls of both races, more than boys, appraised other children in terms of their nurturant qualities (girls, 44 percent; boys, 32 percent).

Although race and sex groups did not differ profoundly from one another in either their behavior or their perceptual sensitivities in segregated settings, the areas in which differences did occur have psychological significance for integration. The expression of aggression, nurturance, dominance, and deference are critical areas in Negro-white relationships. Will these small differences make a difference in racially mixed groups? Possibly because they are "sensitive" areas in intergroup relations, they are likely to take on added meaning in a mixed setting by being interpreted "racially." If slightly more overt acting out of aggression occurs in Negro boys, will it be seized upon by white children as aggression along racial lines or as evidence supporting a stereotype they may hold of Negroes? Will slightly more overt nurturing behavior (such as expression of affection) in Negro girls be given a racial interpretation in interaction by the white girls? Will both white and Negro children behave in an integrated situation as they did when segregated?

INTERPERSONAL RELATIONS IN INTEGRATION

It would be difficult to grow up in our culture unaware of racial stereotyping and tensions. Such awareness is a part of the social learning brought by the children to interracial groups. A question of interest for our research is, then, to see to what extent stereotyping and tensions emerge in the Negro and white children's perceptions of one another in this face-to-face experience, and in their interactions with one another.

To answer this question we have compared segregated and integrated groups in the ways in which they develop a mode of living together, and the ways in which individuals judge one another and establish their own positions in the groups. Secondly, we have examined in integration the relationships among children of like race and of unlike race, and the self-analyses of children of each racial group.

Behavior in Segregated and Integrated Groups. The behavior of children in segregated and integrated groups was markedly similar within the first days of the groups' development and over the two-week period studied. A high rate of interaction was generally maintained or developed in integration, both within and across racial lines. Affiliative, submissive, fearful, and aggressive interactions occurred with similar frequencies in both settings. In segregation, 18 percent of the units of recorded interactions fell into categories of negative, nonconforming behavior; 55 percent in categories of friendly, supportive, social interactions. The comparable percentages in integration were 16 percent and 52 percent.

Within these similarities were also differences. Boys, particularly Negro boys, began integration with a somewhat lower amount of interaction with other boys than they showed in segregation. Among the Negro boys, the proportion of solitary activity and passive observation was 14 percent greater in integration than in segregation. Over time, however, the amount of interaction in the boys' groups increased and did not differ from that observed under segregation.

The Negro boys, who displayed slightly higher proportions of aggressive and disruptive behavior in segregation than did white boys, continued to do so when integrated (see Table 2). They directed these actions to white and Negro boys alike. The white boys' aggressive and nonconforming acts did not increase in frequency in integration nor was either race the preferred target. Friendly and supportive actions were as frequent in integration and segregation. They were initially directed across racial lines more often than toward members of a child's own race.

Girls' groups showed no differences between segregation and integration in amount of interaction with others and no gross alterations in frequencies of negative and positive forms of behavior. But, in integration, actions directed within and across racial lines differed.

In the boys' behavior, there appeared to be emerging a pattern of cautious but equal-status "give-and-take." The behavior of the girls suggested a status differential. White girls directed more of their aggressive and less of their friendly actions toward Negro than toward white girls. Negro girls followed the white pattern; that is, they directed more aggressive behavior toward girls of their own race and more friendly sociability toward white girls. In each instance the differences were small.

TABLE 2

CHILDREN'S BEHAVIOR IN INTEGRATED CABINS

A. Initial Phases of Camp (Percent of behavior units)

Behavior category	Actions by Negro girls		Actions by white girls		Actions by Negro boys		Actions by white boys	
	Directed toward		Directed toward		Directed toward		Directed toward	
	Negro	White	Negro	White	Negro	White	Negro	White
Dominance, aggression, nonconformity	15	13	19	12	27	25	20	21
Fearful submission	2	0	1	0	0	1	0	0
Mild dependence	11	8	13	7	12	14	7	13
Conformity	3	4	2	4	0	5	6	9
Sociability	32	34	29	36	28	17	22	18
Affiliation and nurturance	24	29	21	25	12	23	26	14
Assertive leading	13	12	15	16	21	15	19	25

B. Later Phases of Camp (Percent of behavior units)

Behavior category	Actions by Negro girls		Actions by white girls		Actions by Negro boys		Actions by white boys	
	Directed toward		Directed toward		Directed toward		Directed toward	
	Negro	White	Negro	White	Negro	White	Negro	White
Dominance, aggression, nonconformity	29	19	24	13	25	23	21	24
Fearful submission	1	1	1	1	1	1	0	2
Mild dependence	9	9	6	8	5	8	7	10
Conformity	5	3	3	5	8	6	7	6
Sociability	19	26	26	30	26	28	26	22
Affiliation and nurturance	20	22	19	25	9	15	17	14
Assertive leading	17	20	21	18	26	19	22	22

These assessments of the children's behavior were based on the samples of interaction recorded systematically on each cabin group at specified times. Other less quantifiable behavioral evidence of the children's adjustments to integration was provided by the journal records of the participant observers. For example, just how did the social groupings look in the camp at large—in the dining hall, at the council ring, on the playground? What behavioral evidences of anxiety appeared?

Throughout camp, the children of the two races intermingled in all activities. The amount of this intermingling varied, however. The factors of former acquaintance and kinship make it difficult to evaluate precisely the meaning of spontaneous mixing and separation. In activities for which the entire camp rather than the cabin group was the unit, some children quickly sought out precamp acquaintances, who were most often of the same race. Some instances of segregated grouping occurred at the camp fires, ball games, etc. However, this spontaneous segregation never included all the children, nor were camp issues clearly defined along racial lines.

Whether it be segregated or integrated, camp away from home is likely to bring out anxious behavior in children. The usual variety of overt signs was observed in both camp settings—attempts to "leave the field" physically or symbolically, fearful or withdrawn behavior, minor accidents and physical complaints, bed-wetting, and disruptive, overt acting-out behavior. Children whom observers noted as particularly anxious indulged in substitute behavior. For example, one boy tended to withdraw from the group and kept with him a small toad that he petted, cuddled, and talked to. It is difficult to determine the extent to which such anxious behavior is intensified in integration. There is evidence suggesting, however, that such anxiety indicators appear more frequently in integration. For example, one such symptom, "leaving the field," is most literally represented by those children who, for one reason or another, left camp prior to the scheduled ending of the session. Of the 267 children studied, only ten fell in this category and seven of these ten were children from integrated groups. The existence of such anxieties and the anticipation of underlying tensions also modify the way the adult leaders function in the integrated groups. (The leader's role is discussed later.)

Although the psychological environment was most certainly altered by integration for children without prior experience in racially mixed association, their overt behavior in camp continued to present a picture of overwhelming conformity to the requirements of the situation. The effectiveness of the setting in evoking conforming and compatible behavior in segregated and integrated groups alike would appear to stem from the newness of the situation (new peers and adults with whom to become acquainted, new living routines to learn) and from the explicit and implicit demands for equalitarian behavior. To throw further light on the psychological environment of the children, we turn to their perceptions of interpersonal relationships and associates in camp.

Perception in Segregated and Integrated Groups. The descriptive details that the child selects to relate about his peers almost always concern social relationships and behavior. These he gives as predictions or expectations, as much as observations of past performance. When he says that Jack is always causing trouble, he has the future as much in mind as the past. Seldom does he report characteristics such as appearance, skills, home background, and the like.

Rarely did the total descriptions of other children in integration sound like racial stereotypes (with a few children excepted). To this extent, the expression of the familiar racial stereotypes in face-to-face appraisals was rare. However, the indirect effects of these stereotypes were apparent in a perceptual sensitivity to those behaviors which cluster around domination and aggression. These effects were reflected both in the findings for segregation and integration and in differences in Negro and white children's perceptions of one another in integration.

A comparison of cabin-mate descriptions in segregated and integrated groups shows that both Negro and white children came to the integrated situation with a heightened concern about aggressive, disruptive behavior of their peers, but that the object of their concern differed. In white children, this increased sensitivity was seen chiefly in their as-

TABLE 3

Percent of Children in Integrated Cabins Selecting a Negro Child in "Guess-who" Responses

"Guess-who" items	Initial interview				Final interview			
	Girls		Boys		Girls		Boys	
	Negro	White	Negro	White	Negro	White	Negro	White
"Does what he is told"	28	53	49	58	57	46	64	32
"Helps, is kind"	34	43	62	61	47	50	72	44
"Good leader"	28	40	54	47	40	39	69	47
"Good at 'sizing up' others"	17	23	57	25	37	28	55	44
"Bosses others"	45	33	54	58	40	32	58	65
"Gets mad easily"	45	47	43	55	40	36	53	65
"Afraid, shy"	58	67	43	33	74	68	36	50
	(N=29)	(N=30)	(N=37)	(N=36)	(N=30)	(N=28)	(N=36)	(N=34)

sessments of Negro children. With the Negro children, concern was directed toward their own race. Aggression was important in the white children's descriptions of their peers in 12 percent of the cases in segregation and in 19 percent in integration, but in their evaluations of Negro children the frequency rose to 39 percent. Thirty-one percent of the segregated Negro children mentioned aggressiveness in their cabin-mate descriptions; in integration, 43 percent did so with regard to Negroes, 27 percent with regard to white peers. This suggests that Negro children were more anxious about control of aggression in their own group than about aggression from the white children.

An interesting comparison is provided by the children's answers to the "guess-who" questions. When asked to choose which child best fitted the description of a child who "gets mad easily," 25 percent of the segregated Negro girls and 16 percent of the segregated Negro boys chose themselves. In integration, none of the Negro girls and only 8 percent of the Negro boys viewed themselves in this light. Furthermore, in integration, 25 percent of the Negro children named themselves as the child who "helps others out," while in segration only 7 percent did so. Thus we see that as Negro children seem more concerned about aggression in *other* Negro children in the integrated situation, they are less likely to see this trait in themselves—a reaction which would be consistent with the interpretation that their anxiety over aggression from Negroes to whites has led to a denial of their own aggressive impulses.

In integration, power relationships are important for both the white and Negro children. Roughly half the white children interpreted peer behavior in terms of accomplished or attempted leadership or domination. These interpretations were introduced less frequently (30 percent) by the Negro children. On the other hand, Negro children (particularly the girls) were more concerned about the behavior in themselves that was complementary to leadership and dominance, namely, fearfulness and submission.

On "guess-who" questions, race-linked roles stressed similar components of behavior (see Table 3). Negro girls were seen by white and Negro cabin mates as fearful and anxious, as lacking leadership skills and social sensitivity. White girls were cast in a mold characterized by social competence and ascendance, again by both Negroes and whites. Negro boys were selected for descriptions emphasizing assertive and helpful behavior. The white boys were not clearly typed. (Statistical tests confirm the general patterns described.) The influence of sex in determining racial role typing is crucial. When sex groups were combined, the systematic picture of racial role assignments was obscured.

Since precamp background and the immediate camping situation were not congruent with respect to race relations, integration presented to both Negro and white children a situation in which there was greater ambiguity and greater conflict, initially, than in segregation. Evidences of this changed psychological environment were found in increased anxiety manifestations (discussed earlier) and also in an increased tendency for children to seek out cues to lessen ambiguity. Intensified cue-seeking, we suggest, should result in perceptions of other children which are more complex in integration than in segregation and which search out explanations and draw inferences about what is observed in the "other."

The less complex descriptions, those consisting of unrelated bits of behavior or global descriptions, were rated at the lower end of a seven-point scale. For example, a low rating was given the following: "She sleeps next to me. I know her name. She has kind of brown complexion. She's nice." Where there was a more thorough assessment of peer relationships and various aspects of behavior were interrelated and motivational inferences were made, as in the excerpt from Rosemary's interview (p. 625), a high rating was given. The ratings of children's impressions of their peers were higher in integration than in segregation. The median rating of initial descriptions in the segregated groups was 3.96, in the integrated, 4.58. One would expect that chance differences between the two groups of this magnitude would occur less than ten percent of the time.

Differences in complexity of interpersonal perceptions appeared in cross-race and in-race descriptions. White children made more searching appraisals of Negro than of white cabin mates. The other race, presenting the greater ambiguity in face-to-face interactions, called out the greater alertness to cues. Negro children, on the other hand, made fuller descriptions of members of their *own* race in the beginning of the camp session. That is in line with the findings presented earlier, which we have interpreted as pointing to the Negro children's initial hyperconcern regarding their own behavior in a racially mixed setting. However, at the end of camp, they, too, were attending more closely to the characteristics of children of the other race.

Interracial Friendship. So far we have discussed how campers actually behaved toward one another in the segregated and integrated settings and how they perceived each other's characteristics. Equally important is the question of affective relationships—how feelings of liking and disliking find expression in friendship groupings. Sociometric research and social distance questionnaires have repeatedly documented racial cleavage in children's groups. Our study provided a picture of the kinds of interpersonal attraction that develop when background factors such as neighborhood and family ties do not guide friendship pairing.

Each child was asked, after one day in camp, to rank his cabin mates on friendship potential, beginning with his choice of best friend and continuing in order of his preference. In addition, he was asked to choose the children whom he would like to have with him if he could set up a new cabin. When each child's average friendship ranking of white children was compared with his average ranking of his Negro peers, the evidence is abundantly clear that significantly higher friendship rankings were given to white than to Negro children (see Table 4). The underchoosing of Negro children was somewhat more pronounced among the Negro children themselves. Negro

TABLE 4

FRIENDSHIP PREFERENCES IN INTEGRATED CABINS

Average friendship appraisal	Initial interview (percent)				Final interview (percent)			
	Negro		White		Negro		White	
	Girls	Boys	Girls	Boys	Girls	Boys	Girls	Boys
Higher average ranking to Negro cabin mates	14	32	37	34	24	31	48	39
Same average ranking to Negro and white	10	18	7	6	21	11	7	12
Higher average ranking to white cabin mates	76	50	56	60	55	58	45	49
	(N=29)	(N=38)	(N=30)	(N=35)	(N=29)	(N=36)	(N=28)	(N=33)

girls stood as a group apart, markedly underchoosing members of their own race.

A similar pattern of racial preference appeared in the selection of children for hypothetical cabins. However, this opportunity to compose a new group seldom resulted in hypothetical segregated cabins. None of the Negro and only eight percent of the white campers set up such cabins. Quite the reverse composition, in which the chooser makes himself the only member of his race, occurred among 13 percent of the Negro and 14 percent of the white campers.

The underlying motivations for patterns of friendship and cabin-mate choice were doubtless varied. Clearly some of these children were consciously choosing on racial lines; thus, their selection of desired cabin mates may have represented an attempt at direct control of potential power relationships and subgrouping possibilities. This conscious choice was sometimes expressed: "There would be five whites in one room and five colored in the other. They could talk their way, and we could talk ours." For many others, race as a criterion for choice may have intruded more indirectly and unconsciously. In other instances, however, children showed an awareness of race, yet consciously rejected it as an adequate basis for selecting friends. Thus one girl,

in naming her best friend, stressed interests shared in common, "even though we are different colors and everything."

Race- and Sex-linked Patterns in Integration. The interactive effects of race and sex have appeared in each set of data examined thus far. The meaning of being white or Negro and the impact of integration are not the same for boys as they are for girls, nor are the relationships among behavior, attitudes, and perceptions identical for each race and sex group. As we have noted, status relationships and the expression and control of aggression are significant areas in Negro-white relations, and in these areas sex differences enter quite crucially. Social norms and socialization practices grant boys more freedom for expression of aggression than is the case for girls. The relevance of this difference became apparent in the adaptation of white and Negro boys to integration. They tested each other aggressively but without clearly patterning this behavior along racial lines. Their behavior suggested that they were able to act out interracial hostilities and apprehensions which they may have felt within the limits tolerated in the boys' culture of their particular social class.

The Negro boys were required to come to terms with two conflicting codes regarding aggression. As *boys*, aggression within limits is permitted, but, as *Negro boys,* they must learn control of hostility toward whites. Their initial concern about hostile acts was not only high, but it was especially focused on such behavior in their own race. At the end of two weeks, the Negro boys showed a decrease in awareness of aggression in their own race, with a corresponding increase in sensitivity to it in white children. This may have reflected a shift from a pervasive anxiety about control of their own aggressive impulses to a greater sensitivity to the behavior of others toward them.

White boys, we have noted, were more concerned about aggression in their Negro peers than in their own group. We have noted, too, some basis for their concern in the actual higher frequency of aggressive actions by Negro boys. In giving more prominence to aggression in their perceptions of Negro boys, the white boys, therefore, may have been perceiving "acurately" as well as out of stereotyped expectations regarding Negroes.

In each of the indices we have used, race has been different and probably more important in the thought-patterns and behavior of the girls than of the boys. Girls' groups, while generally conforming to the equality requirements of the situation, showed more frequent deviation in their behavior in temporary and partial cleavages. Further, concepts of the self and others and the meaning of the total situation were quite different for the girls of the two races.

Segregated white girls displayed least overt aggression toward their peers, which we have interpreted as being in line with cultural prescriptions of greater conformity for girls. When integrated, however, their aggressive actions toward Negro girls were much less inhibited. Their more hostile behavior was also echoed in their expressed negative feelings and opinions about the Negro girls and was further underscored by their preferential regard for other white girls.

What was the reality basis in the immediate situation for their reaction? What were the underlying dynamics? Negro girls did not counter aggression with aggression; in fact, they directed less aggression toward their white cabin mates than toward other Negro girls. They did not counter the white girls' expression of rejection. In other words, their reactions were not adequate to evoke the negative responses of their white peers. To the extent that behavior and feelings of the white girls were out of line with the approved model for girls and were in accord neither with the prescriptions of equality in the immediate situation nor with the general behavior of members of the other group, one would suppose that white girls had feelings of conflict and guilt.

The Negro girls came to integration with elements of self-rejection, with awareness of the favored position of the white girls, and with tightened control over their own behavior. In the integrated camp, they experienced at first hand equalitarian living with white children, which in a large measure was successful. But they experienced, too, the undercurrent of the white girls' resistance. What did these diverse aspects of the experience add up to for the Negro girls? The picture was not simple, but it pointed to evidence of change. By the end of camp there was lessened self-rejection among the Negro girls. Yet they did not, at the same time, harbor clearly developed negative stereotypes concerning white girls. The camp situation had provided sufficient supports to permit Negro girls to feel somewhat freer to express aggression at the end of the camp session, although such hostile acts were less characteristic of their relations with white girls than with Negro girls. The barrier of race remained, inhibiting and channeling patterns of action.

It might be noted that the nature of the sex differences in this study is in line with expectations regarding adult role relationships. Negro and white males from the lower socioeconomic status levels may find themselves side-by-side, engaged in the same type of work; the culturally imposed status differential does not preclude this relationship. For Negro women, the extent to which such nearly equal-status contact with white women is possible has been considerably more limited, at least in the past. To a noticeable degree contact between white and Negro women in occupational spheres would typically involve marked status differences, with the Negro a servant and the white woman her employer.

Changes in Intergroup Relations. Under conditions of intensive, equal-status contacts in an atmosphere supporting favorable interracial relations, it is relevant to ask whether changes occurred over the two-week period. The question ordinarily asked in "change experiments" is simply whether there has been a shift from unfavorable to favorable attitudes. Seldom is it known, when such a measured change is reported, whether or how the total constellation of the individual's beliefs and motivations and behavior is similarly altered. Yet only by knowing this are predictions regarding stability of change and consequences of change possible. Our study, of course, does not provide all the information that would be needed to approach this ideal; however, we can examine changes occurring in behavior and perception as well as in attitudes toward the opposite race.

In the two weeks of living in the integrated setting, radical shifts in long-standing interracial orientations did not occur. However, there was a rapid initial behavioral adjustment to the situation, a quick establishment of a behavioral equilibrium, which was overwhelming conformity to what was expected in the immediate situation but which also incorporated within the conformity varying degrees and manifestations of tension and resistance.

Small changes occurred over time with a slight drop in over-all social and friendly interactions and a slight rise in disruptive interactions. These shifts, however, are not greatly unlike time changes in segregated groups and cannot be assumed to have special significance in integration.

Concurrent with the behavioral adaptation that takes place in integrated groups, are there changes in friendship choices and perceptions? If the experience of integration is successful in reducing social distance between racial groups, one would expect that race as a criterion (conscious or unconscious) for assessing friendship should exert less influence at the end of the two weeks. The findings support this. Although the children still tended to prefer their white cabin mates as friends at the close of camp, there was a statistically significant drop in the extent to which they were the favored group.

The white children's shifts over time were primarily in friendship choices. The roles the white girls attributed to girls of both races remained relatively unchanged. The white boys, neither at the beginning nor at the end of the two weeks, made stereotyped role assignments.

The Negro children showed greater change effects than the white children on each of the levels of response. Initially, as we have seen, they tightened the reins of control over their behavior. With the passage of time they permitted themselves greater freedom of action. More often at the end of camp than initially they assigned socially valued roles to cabin mates of their own race. This suggests an altered evaluation of their own group. One should not lose sight of the fact, however, that the changes for the Negro girls did not result in a conflict-free situation. Although their self-regard by some indicators had improved, they nevertheless held the white girls as their models of persons they want to be like. The Negro girls' constellation of responses pointed to this subgroup as the one facing the greatest difficulties in resolving self-other attitudes in the integrated setting.

The specific measures of interracial behavior, perception, and attitudes that have been discussed in this paper cannot, by themselves, fully show the total impact on the individual participant of the two-week experience of around-the-clock integration. It would be important to know how this experience effects the acceptance of the *idea* of integration and the individual's anxious anticipations regarding intergroup relationships. Children coming to an interracial setting for the first time bring with them, as we have indicated, certain anxieties about coping with the new situation. If these anxieties are not supported by the actualities of subsequent experience, the participants may more fully accept the total situation. This increased acceptance may be necessary, in itself, to provide a climate in which attitude change can take place. In general, the experience of integrated camping was viewed favorably by the children. A significantly greater proportion of children in integrated than in segregated sessions indicated at the end that they would have liked to extend the camping period. Under integration, 76 percent wanted to "stretch it out"; 64 percent of those under segregation so signified. Thus, the two-week experience of integration should probably be viewed not as completing the process of change in intergroup relations but as providing the necessary first steps in a long-term process of reorganizing beliefs and feelings.

Influence Agents in Integration. Although many of the standards of home and school were carried over into the new camp setting, it is likely that, initially, patterns of approved and expected interracial behavior were not fully clear to the camper. In an ego-relevant ambiguous situation such as this, the participants seek clarification of appropriate behavior.

The ambiguities lend themselves to structuring by any influence agent. Our study points to the crucial role of the adult leader in this respect, both as a formal, institutionally accepted leader and as an individual participant whose motives, attitudes, and feelings have a subtle impact on the total atmosphere. While the present report is not intended as an analysis of the leader role, a number of leader influences may be mentioned.

The leaders directly influenced the children's responses to the experience of integration by: (1) defining equalitarian behavior, both explicitly and by example, as the behavior that is expected; (2) manipulating the situation to enforce equal status; and (3) directly controlling the degree of freedom of action permitted in the interracial situation. Leaders reflected increased anxiety and strong motivation for the success of integration by exhibiting tighter control over their groups than had been the case in segregation. Tighter control was evident by their more explicit definition of acceptable and unacceptable behavior and by their quick reactions to the slightest indication of interracial tension. (For example, in integration, 62 percent of the counselor interactions with the children were of a directive nature as compared to 46 percent in the segregated situation).

We found a strong tendency for the counselors to deny the existence of any interracial tensions among the children and, in fact, to be unaware of obvious tension signs. This probably stemmed partly from their desire for integration to succeed and partly from their anxiety. Preceding desegregation the counselors were freer to admit and express their uncertainties and anxieties than they were when they became involved in the new situation. For the leader who consciously wants to participate in a racially integrated setting, it is clear that his is a dual role; he is an influence agent with respect to the children and he is himself influenced by the situation.

CONCLUSIONS

Our study consistently points to the importance of the immediate situation in channeling behavior. We might hypothesize that new standards of behavior, such as those so quickly established in the camp, are more readily inculcated in a situation where new elements predominate over the familiar. The consistent expectation of equality, as conveyed by a racially integrated adult culture (counselors), enforced by the leader in his control techniques, and expressed in his behavior toward the children, were of overwhelming importance in setting the tone of the situation.

A short period of equalitarian contact is not sufficient to bring about marked and enduring alterations of attitudes or perceptions towards others and oneself. Yet, within a limited time span and with favorable situational supports, the beginnings of such changes have been noted. Should such a group experience be continued over a longer period of time, more pronounced and lasting changes might be anticipated. That these might prove to be limited solely to the situation experienced is possible. Yet the broad range of contact experienced in the supervised group living suggests the likelihood that more basic and enduring changes resulted than would be the case in more situation-specific experiences.

Adjustment of the individual child to membership in an integrated group and the nature of group functioning are conditioned by the social sex roles of the children of the minority and majority groups. Influences of significance in this respect probably stem from child-rearing differences for boys and girls in the expression and control of impulses and from the special racial roles of each subgroup (including not only their racial roles as children but also their anticipated adult roles). These sex-linked aspects of integration warrant more systematic study.

The effects of change in intergroup relations are most often conceived of in terms of changed responses toward the out-group. It was the minority child's changed self-evaluation which even the short period of integration appeared to influence most. Change in the evaluation of one's own membership group is an integral aspect of the integration process.

THE ANTIDEMOCRATIC PERSONALITY   *By Else Frenkel-Brunswik, Daniel J. Levinson, and R. Nevitt Sanford*

INTRODUCTION

The present research was guided by the conception of an individual whose thoughts about man and society form a pattern which is properly described as antidemocratic and which springs from his deepest emotional tendencies. Can it be shown that such a person really exists? If so, what precisely is he like? What goes to make up antidemocratic thought? What are the organizing forces within the person? If such a person exists, how commonly does he exist in

This paper is a report of research carried out jointly by the University of California Public Opinion Study and the Institute of Social Research, with the sponsorship of the Research Department of the American Jewish Committee. This research will be more fully reported in a forthcoming volume by T. W. Adorno, E. Frenkel-Brunswik, D. J. Levinson, and R. N. Sanford.

our society? And what have been the determinants and what the cause of his development?

Although the antidemocratic individual may be thought of as a totality, it is nevertheless possible to distinguish and to study separately (a) his ideology and (b) his underlying personality needs. Ideology refers to an organization of opinions, attitudes, and values. One may speak of an individual's total ideology or of his ideology with respect to different areas of social life: politics, economics, religion, minority groups, and so forth. Ideologies have an existence independent of any single individual, those existing at a particular time being results both of historical processes and of contemporary social events. These ideologies, or the more particular ideas within them, have for different individuals different degrees of appeal, a matter that depends upon the individual's needs and the degree to which these needs are being satisfied or frustrated. The pattern of ideas that the individual takes over and makes his own will in each case be found to have a function within his over-all adjustment.

Although ideological trends are usually expressed more or less openly in words, it is important to note that, in the case of such affect-laden questions as those concerning minority groups, the degree of openness with which a person speaks will depend upon his situation. At the present time, when antidemocratic sentiments are officially frowned upon in this country, one should expect an individual to express them openly only in a guarded way or to a limited extent. This most superficial level of expression would afford a poor basis for estimating the potential for fascism in America. We should know, in addition, what the individual will say when he feels safe from criticism, what he thinks but will

not say at all, what he thinks but will not admit to himself, and what he will be disposed to think when this or that appeal is made to him. In short, it is necessary to know the individual's *readiness* for antidemocratic thought and action, what it is that he will express when conditions change in such a way as to remove his inhibitions. Antidemocratic propaganda, though it makes some appeal to people's real interests, addresses itself in the main to emotional needs and irrational impulses, and its effectiveness will depend upon the susceptibility existing in the great mass of people.

To know that antidemocratic trends reside in the personality structure is to raise the further question of how this structure develops. According to the present theory, the major influences upon personality development arise in the course of child training as carried forward in a setting of family life. The determinants of personality, in other words, are mainly social; such factors as the economic situation of the parents, their social, ethnic, and religious group memberships, and the prevailing ideology concerning child training might be factors of crucial significance. This means that broad changes in social conditions and institutions will have a direct bearing upon the kinds of personalities that develop within a society. It does not mean, however, that such social changes would appreciably alter the personality structures that already exist.

It was necessary to devise techniques for surveying surface expression, for revealing ideological trends that were more or less inhibited, and for bringing to light unconscious personality forces.[1] Since the major concern was with *patterns* of dynamically related factors, it seemed that the proper approach was through intensive individual studies. In order to

[1] E. Frenkel-Brunswik and R. N. Sanford, "Some Personality Correlates of Antisemitism," *J. Psychol.*, 1945, XX, 271–291; D. J. Levinson and R. N. Sanford, "A Scale for the Measurement of Antisemitism," *ibid.*, 1944, XVII, 339–370.

gauge the significance and practical importance of such studies, however, it was necessary to study groups as well as individuals and to find ways and means for integrating the two approaches.

Individuals were studied by means of (*a*) intensive clinical interviews and (*b*) a modified Thematic Apperception Test; groups were studied by means of questionnaires. It was not hoped that the clinical studies would be as complete or profound as some which have already been performed, primarily by psychoanalysts, nor that the questionnaires would be more accurate than any now employed by social psychologists. It was hoped, however—indeed it was necessary to our purpose—that the clinical material could be conceptualized in such a way as to permit its being quantified and carried over into group studies, and that the questionnaires could be brought to bear upon areas of response ordinarily left to clinical study. The attempt was made, in other words, to bring methods of traditional social psychology into the service of theories and concepts from the newer dynamic theory of personality, and in so doing to make "depth psychological" phenomena more amenable to mass-statistical treatment, and to make quantitative surveys of attitudes and opinions more meaningful psychologically.

In order to study antidemocratic individuals, it was necessary first to identify them. Hence a start was made by constructing a questionnaire and having it filled out anonymously by a large group of people. This questionnaire contained, in addition to numerous questions of fact about the subject's past and present life, and a number of open-answer ("projective") questions, several opinion-attitude scales containing a variety of antidemocratic (anti-Semitic, ethnocentric, reactionary, profascist) statements with which the subjects were invited to agree or disagree. A number of individuals (identified by indirect means) who showed the greatest amount of agreement with these statements were then studied by means of clinical techniques, and contrasted with a number of individuals showing strong disagreement. On the basis of these individual studies, the questionnaire was revised, and the whole procedure repeated. The study began with college students as subjects, and then was expanded to include a variety of groups from the community at large. The findings are considered to hold fairly well for non-Jewish, white, native-born, middle-class Americans.

THE STUDY OF IDEOLOGY

Anti-Semitism was the first ideological area studied. Anti-Semitic ideology is regarded as a broad system of ideas including: *negative opinions* regarding Jews (e.g., that they are unscrupulous, dirty, clannish, power-seeking); *hostile attitudes* toward them (e.g., that they should be excluded, restricted, suppressed); and *moral values* which permeate the opinions and justify the attitudes.

In what senses, if any, can anti-Semitic ideology be considered irrational? What are the main attitudes in anti-Semitism—segregation, suppression, exclusion—for the solution of "the Jewish problem"? Do people with negative opinions generally have hostile attitudes as well? Do individuals have a general readiness to accept or oppose a broad pattern of anti-Semitic opinions and attitudes?

These questions led to and guided the construction of an opinion-attitude scale for the measurement of anti-Semitic ideology. This scale provided a basis for the selection of criterion groups of extreme high and low scorers, who could then be subjected to intensive clinical study. The source material for the scale included: the writings of virulent anti-Semites; technical, literary, and reportorial writings on anti-Semitism and fascism; and, most important, everyday American anti-Semitism as revealed in parlor discussion, in the discriminatory practices of many businesses and institutions, and in the literature of various Jewish "defense" groups trying vainly to counter numerous anti-Semitic accusations by means of rational argument. In an attempt to include as much as possible of this type of content in the scale, certain rules were followed in its construction.

Each item should be maximally rich in ideas, with a minimum of duplication in wording or essential content. In order to reflect the forms of anti-Semitism prevalent in America today, the statements should not be violently and openly antidemocratic; rather, they should be pseudodemocratic, in the sense that active hostility toward a group is somewhat tempered and disguised by means of a compromise with democratic ideals. Each statement should have a familiar ring, should sound as it had been heard many times in everyday discussions and intensive interviews.

The 52-item scale contained five subscales—not statistically pure dimensions but convenient and meaningful groupings of items—the correlations among which should provide partial answers to some of the questions raised above. (a) Subscale "Offensive" (12 items) deals with imagery (opinions) of Jews as personally unpleasant and disturbing. Stereotypy is most explicit in the item: "There may be a few exceptions, but in general Jews are pretty much alike." To agree with this statement is to have an image of "the Jew" as a stereotyped model of the entire group. (b) Subscale "Threatening" (10 items) describes the Jews as a dangerous, dominating group. In various items the Jews are regarded as rich and powerful, poor and dirty, unscrupulous, revolutionary, and so on. (c) Subscale "Attitudes" (16 items) refers to programs of action. The specific hostile attitudes vary in degree from simple avoidance to suppression and attack, with intermediate actions of exclusion, segregation, and

suppression. The social areas of discrimination covered include employment, residence, professions, marriage, and so on. (d) and (e) Subscales "Seclusive" and "Intrusive" deal with opposing stands on the issue of assimilation. The "Seclusive" subscale accuses the Jews of being too foreign and clannish; it implies that Jews can themselves eliminate anti-Semitism (a problem of their own making, so to speak) by greater assimilation and conformity to American ways. The "Intrusive" subscale, on the other hand, accuses the Jews of overassimilation, hiding of Jewishness, prying, seeking power and prestige. These items imply that Jews ought to keep more to themselves and to develop a culture, preferably even a nation of their own.

The total scale is intended to measure the individual's readiness to support or oppose anti-Semitic ideology as a whole. This ideology is conceived as involving stereotyped negative opinions describing Jews as threatening, immoral, and categorically different from non-Jews, and of hostile attitudes urging various forms of restriction. Anti-Semitism is conceived, then, not as a specific attitude (jealousy, blind hate, religious disapproval, or whatever) but rather as a general way of thinking and feeling about Jews and Jewish-Gentile relations.

For two groups, the reliabilities were at least .92 for the total A–S scale, and between .84 and .94 for all subscales ("Intrusive," second group only), except for "Seclusive," for which .71 was obtained (second group only). The correlations among the subscales "Offensive," "Threatening," and "Attitudes" are .83 to .85, while each of these correlates .92 to .94 with the total scale.

These correlations seem to reveal that each person has a rather general tendency to accept or reject anti-Semitic ideology as a whole. The correlations of subscale "Seclusive" with "Intrusive" (.74) and with "Attitudes" (also .74) reveal basic contradictions in anti-Semitic ideology.

(All the raw coefficients, if corrected for attenuation, would be over .90.) Most anti-Semites are, apparently, willing to criticize both Jewish assimilation and Jewish seclusion. This is further testimony to the irrationality of anti-Semitism. Also irrational is the stereotyped image of "the Jew" (the item about Jews being all alike was very discriminating), an image which is intrinsically self-contradictory, since one person cannot be simultaneously rich and poor, dirty and luxurious, capitalistic and radical.

The question then presents itself: Are the trends found in anti-Semitic ideology—its generality, stereotyped imagery, destructive irrationality, sense of threat, concern with power and immorality, and so on—also expressed in the individual's social thinking about group relations generally? Can it be that what was found in anti-Semitism is not specific to prejudice against Jews but rather is present in prejudice against all groups?

Considerations such as these led to the study of ethnocentrism, that is, ideology regarding in-groups (with which the individual identifies himself), out-groups (which are "different" and somehow antithetical to the in-group), and their interaction. A 34-item Ethnocentrism scale was constructed along lines similar to those employed for the A–S scale. There were three subscales: (a) A 12-item subscale deals with Negroes and Negro-white relations. The items refer to Negroes as lazy, good-natured, and ignorant; also aggressive, primitive, and rebellious, and so on. (b) Minorities. These 12 items deal with various groups (other than Jews and Negroes), including minority political parties and religious sects, foreigners, Oklahomans (in California), zoot-suiters, criminals, and so on. (c) "Patriotism." These 10 items deal with America as an in-group in relation to other nations or out-groups. The items express the attitude that foreign,

"inferior" nations should be subordinate; they include a value for obedience and a punitive attitude toward value-violators, and, finally, they express regarding permanent peace a cynicism which is rationalized by moralistic, hereditarian theories of aggressive, threatening out-group nations.

The reliabilities for the subscales ranged from .80 to .91; and for the total E scale .91. These figures, considered together with the correlations of .74 to .83 among the subscales, and the subscale-Total E scale correlations of .90 to .92, indicate a generality in ethnocentric ideology that is almost as great as and even more remarkable than that found in A–S.

The correlations of A–S with E complete the picture. The A–S scale correlates .80 with the E scale, and from .69 to .76 with the subscales. Through successive revisions there finally emerged a single E scale of 10 items (including 4 A–S items) which had reliabilities of .7 to .9 in different groups of subjects. It is clear that an attempt to understand prejudice psychologically must start with the total pattern of ethnocentric thinking, including both general out-group rejection and in-group submission-idealization.

Space does not permit a detailed discussion of the study of politics and religion. Ethnocentrism is related, though not very closely, to political conservatism ($r = .5$) and to support of the more conservative political groupings. In the responses of individuals scoring high on the conservatism scale, two patterns could be distinguished: a traditional, *laissez-faire* conservatism as opposed to "pseudoconservatism" in which a profession of belief in the tenets of traditional conservatism is combined with a readiness for violent change of a kind which would abolish the very institutions with which the individual appears to identify himself. The latter appeared to contribute more to the correlation between E and conservatism than did the former. The nonreligious are less ethnocentric on the average than the religious, although such sects as the Quakers and Unitarians made low E scale means (nonethnocentric).

THE STUDY OF PERSONALITY

The main variables underlying the various ideological areas above represent personality trends expressed in ideological form. A primary hypothesis in this research is that an individual is most receptive to those ideologies which afford the fullest expression to his over-all personality structure. Thus, a person clinically described as strongly authoritarian, projective, and destructive is likely to be receptive to an antidemocratic ideology such as ethnocentrism—ultimately fascism as the total social objectification of these trends—because it expresses his needs so well.

The attempt at a quantitative investigation of personality variables underlying ethnocentric ideology led to the construction of a personality scale. It was called, for convenience, the F scale because it was intended to measure some of the personality trends which seemed to express a predisposition or deep-lying receptivity to fascism. The items are statements of opinion and attitude in nonideological areas (not dealing with formal groups or social institutions) such as self, family, people in general, sex, personal values, and so on; they are not tied by official statement or surface meaning to items in the other scales. Any consistency in response to the F and E scales, as indicated by the correlation between them, must be due primarily to the fact that both scales express the same underlying trends, since their surface content is quite different. The main difference between the scales is that the F items are less openly ideological.

Ten main variables guided scale construction, each variable being repre-sented by a cluster of several items. The clusters were partially overlapping, since several items were intended to express more than a single variable. In three successive forms the scale contained 38, 34, then 30 items, but the 10 main variables were always represented.

The cluster variables were as follows: conventional values, authoritarian submission, authoritarian aggression, anti-intraception, superstition stereotypy, pseudotoughness, power, cynicism, projectivity, and sex.

Three of these clusters may be discussed to illustrate the general approach. "Authoritarian submission" refers to an inability seriously to criticize, reject, or actively rebel against one's main in-group (particularly the family) figures and values. There is a highly moralized and idealized conception of authority-representatives and a submissive relation to them. Examples: "No sane, normal, decent person could ever think of hurting a close friend or relative"; "Every person should have complete faith in some supernatural power whose decisions he obeys without question."

"Anti-intraception" involves opposition to a psychological, insightful view of people and oneself. This includes a rejection of emotion and of attempts to look into one's deeper motives and conflicts. Personal inquiries tend to be regarded as prying, and there is often an exaggerated idea of how much prying is going on. Work and keeping busy are emphasized as ways of "not thinking about yourself." Examples: "When a person has a problem or worry, it is best for him not to think about it but to keep busy with more cheerful things"; "Nowadays more and more people are prying into matters that should remain personal and private."

"Projectivity" refers to the disposition to imagine strange, evil, dangerous, destructive forces at work in the outer world; these imaginings have only the smallest basis in reality but can be understood as projections of the individual's deep-lying sexual and aggressive strivings. Examples: "Wars and social troubles may someday be ended by an earthquake or flood that will destroy the whole world"; "Nowadays when so many different kinds of people move around and mix together so much, a person has to protect himself especially carefully against catching an infection or disease from them"; "The wild sex life of the old Greeks and Romans was tame compared to some of the goings-on in this country, even in places where people might least expect it."

The successive forms of the F scale involved elimination, modification, and addition of items, based on both statistical considerations and on theoretical requirements of richness of ideas and over-all inclusiveness. The reliability of the scale increased from an average of .74 for the first form to .85 on the last. Each high quartile scorer is high on most items and clusters; on each item and cluster the difference between high scorers (total scale) and low scorers is statistically significant.

Correlations of F with A–S and E increased from an average of about .6 to about .75 in later forms, that is, higher than the correlation of .50 with the conservatism scale. This correlation, in conjunction with the clinical findings reported below, gives evidence of the functional role of personality trends in organizing and giving meaning to surface attitudes, values, and opinions.

Does ethnocentrism help the individual avoid conscious ambivalence toward his family by displacing the hostility onto out-groups (the morally "alien") and thus leave in consciousness exaggerated professions of love toward family and authority? Do high scorers on the F scale (who are usually also ethnocentric) have an underlying anticonventionalism, in-group- and family-directed hostility, a tendency to do the very things they rigidly and punitively oppose in others?

What impels an individual to feel, for example, that aggression against his family is unthinkable and yet to agree that "homosexuals should be severely punished" and (during the war) that the "Germans and Japs should be wiped out"? Such contradictions suggest that the deeper personality trends of high scorers are antithetical to their conscious values, opinions, and attitudes. The clinical studies reported below investigate further these and other questions.

The so-called "projective questions" are intermediate between the scales and the intensive clinical techniques. As part of the questionnaire they are used in group studies in order to determine how common in larger populations were the relationships discovered in clinical studies. They are open questions to be answered in a few words or lines; each question deals with events or experiences which are likely to have emotional significance for the individual. The original set of about 30 questions was gradually reduced to 8, which were both statistically differentiating and theoretically inclusive. These deal with "what moods are unpleasant," "what desires are hard to control," "what great people are admired," "what would drive a person nuts," "what are the worst crimes," "what moments are embarrassing," "how to spend your last six months," "what is most awe-inspiring."

The responses of the entire high and low quartiles on the A–S (later the total E) scale were contrasted. For each question "high" and "low" scoring categories were made; a "high" category expresses a personality trend which seems most characteristic of ethnocentrists and which can be expected significantly to differentiate the two groups. A scoring manual, giving the specific categories (usually two to six) for each item, was the basis on which two independent raters scored each response (not knowing the actual A–S or E score of the subjects). Each response was scored "high," "low," or "neutral"—the neutral category being used when the response was omitted, ambiguous, or when it contained "high" and "low" trends equally. Less than 10 percent of the responses received neutral scores.

The scoring agreement for the battery of items averaged 80 to 90 percent on a variety of groups (total, 200 to 300). The high quartiles received an average of 75–90 percent "high" scores, as compared with 20–40 percent "high" scores for the low quartiles. Almost never was an individual ethnocentrist given more than 50 percent low scores, and conversely for the anti-ethnocentrists. For each item the difference between the two groups was always significant at better than the 1 percent level.

The differences between the ethnocentric and anti-ethnocentric groups may be illustrated by the scoring of the item "What experiences would be most awe-inspiring for you?" The "low" categories are: (a) Values which refer to personal achievement (intellectual, esthetic, scientific), contribution to mankind, the realization of democratic goals by self and society, and so on. (b) "Power," as exemplified in man's material-technological achievements and in nature. (c) Intense nature experiences in which there are clear signs of esthetic, sensual-emotional involvement.

The "high" categories for this item, in contrast, are: (a) "Power" in the form of deference and submission toward powerful people; emphasis on a generally authoritarian and ritualized atmosphere (military, superficial religious, patriotic, etc.). (b) Personal power in self, with others playing a deferent role. (c) Destruction-harm of people (e.g., "death of a close relative"; no open hostility). (d) Values which refer to conventionalized sex, material security, ownership, vague sense of virtue, and so on. (e) Dilute nature experiences which differ from those of the low-scorers in that they are matter-of-fact, unspecific, surface descriptions with no indication of sensual-emotional involvement.

Some other general differences between these two groups were found. Deeplying trends such as hostility, dependency, sexuality, curiosity, and the like exist in both groups, but in the unprejudiced group they are more ego-integrated, in the sense of being more focal, more tied to other trends, more complex affectively, and with fewer defenses. This group is also more aware of inner conflicts, ambivalence, and tendencies to violate basic values. Their inner life is richer if more troubled; they tend to accuse themselves of faults, while the prejudiced group externalizes and engages more in idealization of self and family.

CLINICAL ANALYSIS OF INTERVIEW MATERIAL

As mentioned above, those scoring extremely high or extremely low on the overt ethnocentrism scale of the questionnaire were further subjected to clinical interviews and to projective tests.

The interviews covered the following major fields: vocation, income, religion, politics, minority groups, and clinical data. The directives given to the interviewer listed in each field both the kinds of things it was hoped to obtain from the subject and suggestions as to how these things might indirectly be ascertained by questioning. The former were the "underlying questions"; they had reference to the variables by means of which the subject was eventually to be characterized. The "manifest questions," those actually put to the subject, were framed in such a way as to conceal as much as possible the real purpose of the interview and yet elicit answers that were significant in terms of over-all hypotheses. The manifest questions used to obtain material bearing on a given underlying question were allowed to vary greatly from subject to subject, depending in each case on the subject's ideology, surface attitudes, and defenses. Nevertheless a number of manifest questions, based on general theory and experience, were formulated for each underlying question. Not all of them were asked each subject.

Examples of manifest questions, taken from the area of Income are: "What would you do with (expected or desired) income?" and "What would it mean to you?" The corresponding underlying issues are the subject's aspirations and phantasies as to social status, as to power as a means to manipulate others, as to (realistic or neurotic) striving for security, as to lavish and exciting living, the readiness really to take chances, and so forth.

It was the task of the interviewer subtly to direct the course of the interview in such a way that as much as possible would be learned about these underlying attitudes without giving away to the subject the real foci of the inquiry.

In attempting to achieve a crude quantification of the interview material, so that group trends might be ascertained, there was developed an extensive set of scoring categories, comprising approximately a hundred headings. An attempt was made to encompass as much as possible of the richness and intricacy of the material. The complexity of the categories introduced inferential and subjective elements, but, as it turned out, this did not prevent adequate inter-rater reliability and validity. The categories were arrived at on the basis of a preliminary study of the complete interviews and of all the other available material pertaining to the same subjects. These categories represent, in fact, the hypotheses as to which clinical characteristics go with presence or absence of prejudice.

In order to test all the categories, passages of the interview protocols referring directly to political or social issues and all other data that might indicate the subject's identity or ideological position were carefully removed before two clinically trained scorers undertook the evaluation of the protocols.

Interviews of 40 women were thus evaluated. (A later report will present results from a group of men.) Three kinds of judgments were used for each category: (1) whether the interview revealed attitudes tentatively classified as "high" or as "low"; (2) whether no decision could be reached; or, more often, (3) whether no material was available on the issue in question. A number of categories proved nondiscriminating either because "high" and "low" statements appeared with equal frequency in the interviews of those found "high" and of those found "low" on the questionnaire, or because of a large proportion of "neutral" responses.

Some of the most discriminating categories included the following. Of the fifteen interviewed women who were extremely low on ethnocentrism, 0 (none) displayed a conventional "idealization" of the parents, the variable previously assumed to be characteristic of ethnocentrism, whereas 12 showed an attitude of objective appraisal of the parents.[2] On the other hand, of the 25 women interviewees extremely high on ethnocentrism, 11 clearly displayed the "high" and only 6 the "low" variant (the remaining 8 being "neutral"). This distribution of attitudes toward parents is in line with the general glorification of and

---

[2] In view of the small number of cases (40) and the frequency of the neutral categories (about 30 percent), these differences between the high and low scorers must be regarded as tentative. However, there is additional evidence that these differences would be found in a large sample. (1) Even with this small number of cases the differences are very striking. (2) The data on men appear to reveal similar differences. This not only provides an independent confirmation, but it will provide a sample twice as large as the present one. (3) The variables considered here are similar to those found to be differentiating in the ideological material, the Thematic Apperception Test, and the projective questions.

submission to in-group authority, on the surface at least, by the high scorers on ethnocentrism. In fact, the corresponding figures on the category "submission to parental authority and values (respect based on fear)" vs. "principled independence" are 1 to 7 for the "low" subjects as against 9 to 0 for the "high" subjects.

The "high" women emphasize sex as a means for achieving status; they describe their conquests and—as they do in other fields as well—rationalize rather than admit failures and shortcomings, whereas the "lows" do not shrink from open admission of inadequacies in this respect (8 to 3 for "highs"; 1 to 8 for "lows"). In the same vein we find in "highs" underlying disrespect and resentment toward the opposite sex, typically combined with externalized, excessive and counteractive "pseudoadmiration," vs. "genuine respect and fondness for opposite sex" in the "lows" (11 to 4 for "highs"; 2 to 7 for "lows"). Similarly, the attitude toward the opposite sex in the "high" women is power-oriented, exploitative, manipulative, with an eye on concrete benefits hiding behind superficial submission as contrasted with a warm, affectionate and love-seeking attitude on the part of the "lows." Thus, the traits desired in men by "high" women are: hard-working, energetic, go-getting, moral, clean-cut, deferent, "thoughtful" toward the woman; the desiderata mentioned by the "low" women, on the other hand, are: companionship, common interests, warmth, sociability, sexual love, understanding, and liberal values. (For the entire pattern just described the figures are 14 to 4 for the "highs" and 2 to 10 for the "lows.")

As to attitudes toward people in general, the "highs" tend to assume an attitude of "moralistic condemnation" vs. the "permissiveness" shown toward individuals by the lows (14 to 3 for the "highs," 2 to 10 for the "lows"). Of special importance for the problem dis

cussed here is the "hierarchical conception of human relations" in the "highs" as compared with an "equalitarianism and mutuality" in the "lows" (13 to 2 in the "highs" and 1 to 10 in the "lows").

All through the material it was frequently observed that the difference between the high and low subjects does not lie so much in the presence or absence of a basic tendency but rather in the way of dealing with such tendencies. As an illustration from the field of interpersonal relationships, we may refer to the category of Dependence. Whereas the dependence of the high subjects tends to be diffuse, ego-alien, and linked to an infantile desire to be taken care of, the dependence of the lows is focal and love-seeking as can be expected in cases where a real object relationship has been established (11 to 1 in the highs; 1 to 7 in the lows). The traits desired in friends are in many ways similar to those desired in the opposite sex (see above); we find emphasis on status, good manners, and so forth in the highs as compared with intrinsic values in the lows (9 to 2 for highs, 0 to 10 for lows.)

In the high scorer's attitude toward the Self, we find self-glorification mixed with feelings of inferiority which are not faced as such, conventional moralism, the belief in a close correspondence between what one is and what one wishes to be, and the "denial of genuine causality" (e.g., an explanation of one's traits or symptoms in terms of hereditary or accidental factors), as contrasted to opposite attitudes in the lows, with figures generally as discriminatory or better than those mentioned above for the other fields.

In the case of more general categories pertaining to personality dynamics an unusually large proportion were found to be discriminating. This might be due to the fact that the scoring of these categories was based on the over-all impression of the subject rather than on a spe cific piece of information. High-scoring women tend to give particular evidence of "rigid-moralistic anal reaction-formations" as ends in themselves, e.g., totalitarian-moralistic conceptualization of two kinds of people—"clean and dirty"—and overemphasis on propriety and kindliness, often with underlying aggression. The women with low scores show more evidence of "oral character structure"; and when such values as cleanliness and kindliness are present they are of a more functional nature.

As far as aggression is concerned, the high-scoring women tend toward a diffuse, depersonalized, moralistic, and punitive type of aggression, whereas the aggression of the low-scoring women is more focal and personalized, and more often it seems to be elicited by violation of principles or as a response to rejection by a loved object.

Ambivalence, e.g., toward the parents, is not admitted into consciousness by the "high" subjects but is rather solved by thinking in terms of dichotomies and by displacement onto out-groups. The ambivalence of the "lows" is more often expressed against the original objects (e.g., parents) or representatives, in reality, of the original objects, e.g., real authority.

There is a strong tendency in the high-scoring women to display "femininity" exclusively, whereas the low-scoring women are more ready to accept and to sublimate their masculine traits.

Some of the categories scored under the tentative assumption of their relevance to prejudice did not prove discriminating. Among these are various "childhood events," e.g., death or divorce of parents, number of siblings, and order of birth. The conception of one's own childhood, e.g., image of father and mother, proved only slightly discriminating, mostly because of the great number of neutral scores due often to lack of information in these categories. The fact that some of the categories were not discriminating may be taken as evidence that the raters were at least partially successful in their attempt to eliminate halo effect.

As was mentioned above, the over-all contrast between the highly prejudiced and the tolerant women hinges less than originally expected on the existence or absence of "depth" factors such as latent homosexuality, but rather, as seen here again, on the way they are dealt with in the personality: by acceptance and sublimation in our tolerant extremes, by repression and defense measures in our prejudiced extremes.

It is because of their repressions, it may be supposed, that the high scorers are found to be outstanding on such formal characteristics as rigidity, anti-intraception, pseudoscientific thinking, and so forth.

The differences between high and low scorers revealed by the several independent techniques of the study reported here are consistent one with another and suggest a pattern which, embracing as it does both personality and ideology, may be termed the "antidemocratic personality."

RELIGION, VALUE ORIENTATIONS, AND INTER–GROUP CONFLICT   *By Robin M. Williams, Jr.*

Both research and social action dealing with intergroup relations in the United States have tended to conceive of interreligious relations in much the same way as interracial and interethnic relations. The grounds for doing this are rarely made explicit. Although there are important similarities among these concrete types of relations, it has not been adequately demonstrated that propositions which are valid in the case of ethnic or racial minorities will actually hold in the same way for relations among collectivities or groupings based on distinctive religious affiliations.

Indeed, there are persuasive theoretical reasons for expecting that interreligious relations will *not* be fully explicable in terms of the variables found, say, in interracial relations. For example, close personal contact between persons from different racial categories sometimes discloses an agreement upon basic values and goals, not previously recognized, that leads to modification of stereotypes and an increase in friendly feelings. In the case of persons having different religious orientations, on the other hand, the proximate result of interaction in which these differences are communicated may establish (or reinforce) outgroup stereotypes and lead to attitudes of estrangement, rejection, or active hostility.

This issue of the *Journal* thus provides an important opportunity for a reexamination of what we often loosely characterize as "religious conflict." Great importance is attached to the subject at this time by social scientists, political spokesmen, and large segments of American religious leadership, as well as by appreciable numbers of persons having

other effective commitments to organized religious groupings. The topical interest in and concern with "religion" and "religious conflict" are obvious, well publicized, and widely prevalent. What is not so obvious or commonly discussed is the problem, basic to social science and to social policy, of the sources and consequences of those human conflicts which are posed in terms of differences in religious beliefs, evaluations, rituals, and modes of organized social action.

Let us begin by noting that our present subject is not religious "prejudice." It is now increasingly recognized that religious conflict can and does occur in the absence of any trace of prejudice, properly speaking. Conflict, defined in religious terms, can emerge even if everyone involved is initially devoid of stereotypes, ignorance, standardized modes of scapegoating, or diffuse unfulfilled needs for aggression. Those elements of prejudice which do appear in the opposition and conflict of religious groupings often can be subsumed under the concepts and hypotheses developed in the study of other intergroup relations. But strictly religious conflict is not explicable in the terms which have served to illuminate interethnic and interracial relations.

If one conceives of "religious values" as those conceptions of the desirable that are "ultimate" for people who are committed to them, then, differences in these final and irrevocable values are *by definition* not subject to compromise or resolution. So defined, one could then visualize the reduction or elimination of religious tension and conflict only at the price of renouncing any ultimate commitments to values.

But such irreducible commitments

From the *Journal of Social Issues*, 1956, XII, 12–20. Reprinted by permission of the author and the publisher.

have their maximal impact on the social order only in the case of religions which claim exclusive validity and engage in active proselytizing along with active intervention in the social order. Save in such limiting cases, the "social absoluteness," so to say, of religious orientations is a matter of degree. A central empirical question, therefore, is just that of the conditions under which varying systems of beliefs and values allow for toleration, compromise, insulation, partial incorporation and the like, or else eventuate in conflict, domination, and persecution. Presumably there will always be some element of religious conflict in society so long as men have religious values and differ in respect to those values, but the tension of differences may be very mild or it may reach the ferocity of a holy war. Obviously, all religious differences do not have the same potency in producing conflict, and a given difference in value orientations is likely to have varying consequences in different social contexts. Hence, the problem for social science is that of specifying the variables that help to account for varying prevalence and intensity of conflict as a function of variations in religious value orientations.

We have come to be sharply aware of the dual social role of religion as either a focus of consensus, solidarity, and integration or as a source of societal cleavage and implacable opposition. As Nottingham summarizes this point:

Worship in common—the sharing of the symbols of religion—has united human groups in the closest ties known to man, yet religious differences have helped to account for some of the fiercest group antagonisms.[1]

The sharing of religiously significant symbols occurs within historically unique communities of believers, even though the doctrinal position may include the universal brotherhood of men. Ultimate focuses of values are thus localized in particular group associations. This embeddedness of religious experience and commitment within distinctive group contexts is associated both with ambivalence toward religious values on the part of the individual believer, and with in-group and out-group distinctions that sometimes become the basis for or symbol of fundamental social cleavages.

Presumably it is not essential here to try to elaborate further upon formal definitions of "religion" and "values." Such attempts at definition abound in the literature, and the great difficulty of arriving at precise and stable formulations is widely recognized. It will be enough, for the present purposes, to conceive of values as consequentially important conceptions (standards) of desirability which influence behavior and to which conduct is referred for judgments of goodness, appropriateness, and the like. Within the enormous and diverse universe of values are some values which have a specifically religious character by reason of some direct connection with a nonempirical, usually transcendent, view of life and the cosmos. In one formulation, religious values are a special class of values, distinguishable from the wider range of values by their "ultimate," "sacred" reference. In another view, all values may have a religious aspect or dimension, being interpreted by the believer as so many varying manifestations, guises, or expressions of an underlying ultimate reality. In any case, one confronts in religious collectivities grouping based on sharing of a "faithful commitment to a reality transcending the historical situation," in the words of Kenneth Underwood. Identification by persons of themselves as members of a specific religious "communion" which constitutes a supreme center of loyalties is the mark by which we locate our object of study.

---

[1] Elizabeth K. Nottingham, *Religion and Society* (Garden City, N.Y.: Doubleday & Co., 1954), p. 2.

Now, many observers of the current American scene have commented recently upon what appears to be a substantial increase in interreligious tension. As Don Hager has pointed out in his introduction, the relationship between an allegedly heightened religiosity and increased religious strife has not been adequately explored. Certainly, the conditions that make for the peaceable coexistence of collectivities that are characterized by different religious values are not well understood. Historical examples of mutual respect and of cooperation in secular affairs show that even quite marked differences in beliefs, values, rituals, and social organization of the respective religious "communities" do not necessarily lead to a high level of tension or conflict. Other examples can be adduced to show that doctrinal and ritual differences that appear quite minor to the external observer can be defined as instigations to total conflict. To account in any measure for such radically opposing outcomes is a task requiring a research effort far beyond any so far exerted.

Some clues do exist. The most obvious, perhaps, is that not all conflict in the name of organized religion is actually "religious." It is more usual than unusual that strictly religious differences are compounded with other systematic differences: power position, economic roles and relations, typical modes of family life and courtship behavior, and a wide variety of other social patterns, important in the secular world but not directly derived from religious orientations. That the early immigrants to America from Ireland were Catholics was surely important, but it is also certain that their Catholicism was not the sole occasion for the reactions their presence evoked.

Communal conflict of Hindu and Muslim in India had its religious aspects, but the strictly religious differences were neither necessary nor sufficient causes for the mass violence that accompanied the appearance of India and Pakistan as new nations. If we wish to analyze the place of religious beliefs and values in social conflict, we must seek research opportunities that will permit us to disentangle religious factors from these other elements in the causation of conflict.

A second complex of factors centers around the degree of involved commitment actually at work in nominal religious affiliations. The fact of relatively slight interreligious tension in the United States in recent decades often has been interpreted as an outcome, in part, of low intensity of conviction, i.e., organized religion as "religion at a low temperature." To the extent that it "did not really matter," religious differences could be ignored, passed over, or accepted as matters of slight consequence.[2] To the extent that what is popularly called religion thus passes over into the zone of matters of taste, one may well say that intrinsic religion has moved elsewhere. The trivialization of religious allegiance is assuredly one mode by which conflict can be reduced.

Short of this kind of extreme attenuation of commitment to specifically religious values, it is possible to conceive of a sufficiently large and important core of common values running through otherwise different religious positions to render interfaith relations relatively easy and smooth. Very little is known as to specifically what must be shared in what ways to bring about this outcome. It is certain that the answer is not simple. For one thing, "family quarrels" among religious groups are often intense—the just-no-

---

[2] "Whenever there is active theological construction there is a strengthening of the walls between religions, for however universal the themes of theology may be, each system has its peculiar idioms and is part of a particular faith." Herbert W. Schneider, *Religion in Twentieth Century America* (Cambridge, Mass., Harvard University Press, 1952), p. 137

ticeable differences seem to evoke especially strong reactions under some conditions. A further complication appears in the very definition of the problem: To the extent that religious values are distinguished from secular values, religious differences may be minimized by the sharing of a large fund of nonreligious values. Something like this has occurred in the United States.[3] But if a particular faith does not make this religious-secular distinction, or claims to permeate and sanction all important values, it is likely, insofar as it is religiously distinctive at all, to be regarded by members of other faiths as challenging or encroaching upon their own distinctive religious commitments. To put it another way, the more compartmentalized and restricted are the claims of a particular faith to define and regulate value orientations, the less likely it is that religious-group membership will be a divisive factor.

The terms of religious conflict are no longer publicly those of theology and bigotry but rather church-state relations, on the one hand, and questions of religious liberty on the other:

Contemporary religious controversy does not have the flavor of past struggles—of theological strife and religious bigotry. This is not a conflict born of nativism, cries of "Popery" and the infamous Protocols of Zion. Violence is rare. The head-on clash is generally averted or postponed. It most commonly takes the form of quiet pressure, of unyielding resolve to express competing religious views on matters of public and social policy.[4]

As conceived here, value orientations contain both existential (beliefs, ideas) and evaluational elements. It is a familiar fact that there are radical divergences among the major value orientations distinctive of the various organized faith groupings in the United States. A partial list of the more important of such divergences that may become involved in interreligious opposition or strife includes:

1. Whether there is a sharp distinction between a religious and a secular realm.

2. Whether religion is regarded as one among many of the interests of men or as something which pervades or dominates all aspects of behavior and experience.

3. Whether all religions are considered to have some validity, e.g., as "ways" or "paths" toward an ultimate reality, or whether only one specific religion is true and all others are in error or positively sinful.

4. Whether authentic, valid religious status can be established solely through individual experience or only through the medium of a divinely established organization.

5. Orientations toward both secular and religious authority; evaluation of discipline.

6. Whether major stress is placed upon the religious organization ("Church") as a community of individual believers, or as a disciplinary agency, or as a sacramental order.

7. Whether the individual's particular religious orientation and affiliation are accepted as a matter of choice or election or as given.

8. The evaluation of individual religious questioning and speculation.

9. Whether social morality is deemed impossible without commitment to organized religion or without faith in the Deity.

10. Whether the existing social order is to be attacked as evil, shunned, tolerated, supported, or reformed; whether organized religion should seek to influence "secular" social action, and if so, how.

11. Estimation and evaluation of the scope, quality, and potentialities of human intelligence and rationality.

[3] C. Will Herberg, *Protestant, Catholic, Jew* (Garden City, N. Y.: Doubleday & Co., 1955)
[4] Don J. Hager, "Introduction: Religious Conflict," *J. Soc. Issues*, 1956, XII, 4.

12. The evaluation of science.

13. Whether human nature is considered to be basically evil, good, mixed, or neutral.

14. Estimation and evaluation of the possibilities of human improvement; the perfectibility of man versus the conception of man as a creature inherently weak, fallible, and prone to error and evil.

15. The scope and quality of personal responsibility for conduct; e.g., total culpability versus environmental extenuation.

16. Whether asceticism is positively or negatively valued.

17. Orientation toward suffering and punishment.

18. Orientation to religion as a means of "therapy" or "adjustment"; religious commitment as a solution for personal difficulties or for social, economic, and political problems.

19. Estimation and evaluation of the possibilities and means of resolving conflicts arising from differing religious views.

20. Evaluation of religious heterogeneity, religious "liberty," and "toleration"; e.g., approval of sectarian diversity versus ecumenical movements.

This listing could be extended to include such important additional matters as conflicts of religious and secular assumptions concerning value priorities and hierarchies, or the use of religion to promote and obtain nonreligious goals.[5] Even this limited inventory is enough, however, to suggest in a fairly specific way that divergent value orientations,

associated with particular faith groupings, contribute directly to interreligious dissension in matters of public social policy and personal social conduct. Note again that this implies that interreligious conflict is not merely a matter of "prejudice." We are here confronted with real differences in the values to which people are, or may be, deeply committed. A further implication is that religious conflict is not traceable to the sheer fact of different affiliations and the struggles for social and political influence and power among the resulting groupings. That is, our assumption here is that the explanation of conflict requires taking into account the actual content of beliefs and values; it is not enough simply to note that Protestants, Jews, and Catholics are culturally defined as "different" and that real social groupings develop on the basis of that definition.[6]

If we are thus able to see religious conflict as a problem of divergent value—abstracting both from "prejudice" and from *group* allegiance as such—we secure some clues as to what we may need to do to advance our knowledge of the contemporary problem of interreligious relations in the United States. We need data on intensity of convictions, on the extent and nature of individual participation in religious-group activities, on the actual value commitments of adherents of the various faiths (as over against theological or "official" pronouncements) on similar affective conceptions of desirability that are shared by adherents of different religious groupings. It is necessary, further, to analyze the specific

---

[5] For several suggestions of significant points to include in the above enumeration, I am indebted to Don Hager.

[6] However, it remains important to take into account the values that inhere in group affiliation and participation, apart from the specific values espoused by the group. Having established his credentials of belief, commitment, and participation, the member of a religious grouping secures many rewards in sociability, security of belongingness, reinforcement of norms, emotional support, structure for behavior, and the like. Positive affect toward, and personal need for, the particular religious community can thus emerge from participation as such rather than as purely an outcome of internalization of the religious values peculiar to that community. Presumably it is in this sense that we can appreciate the meaning of the quip that fox hunting was once a part of Anglican religion in England.

modes by which differences in value orientations affect interreligious relations.

Such differences may, in the first place, serve to limit, restrict, or distort communication among religious groups themselves and between religious and nonreligious groups. Restriction of communication favors the emergence of stereotypes, which can serve as vehicles for diverse fears and hostilities. Restriction of communication may have the effect, on the other hand, of averting direct clashes of value positions. The frequently observed tendency to avoid discussion of religiously controversial matters in ordinary social interaction in our society deserves penetrating empirical study. If we ask what are the grounds upon which individuals forego such discussion, dissent, argument, and debate, even a preliminary inspection of the problem reveals considerable complexity. For example: (1) Controversy may be avoided because of relatively low involvement with a specific religious position. The desire for social harmony—to avoid "unpleasantness"—can then take priority over differences in religious beliefs and values. (2) Discussion may be avoided, *per contra*, because one's religious faith is intensely held as indispensably valid and essential, to the point at which discussion with those of other religious allegiances is regarded as profaning, or at least inappropriate or undignified on religious grounds. (3) Each of several religious positions may be regarded as worthy of respect in its own right, and thus, out of religious considerations, inviolate to hostile attack or skeptical discussion by persons of a differing allegiance. (4) Controversial discussion may be eschewed because the believing adherent to a particular faith group is, out of firm conviction, so assured of the triumph of his own position as to regard controversy as irrelevant. This obviously is a difficult position to maintain but is approached by some militant sects and

orders. (5) In some rare instances, there is lack of motivation to talk about or otherwise manifest overt concern for religious questions because of an inward, mystical orientation which transcends religious particularity and leads to quietistic withdrawal. It is fairly certain that these five orientations do not exhaust the possibilities.

On the other hand, when there is firmness of faith in a religious system that imposes on the believer an obligation to actively defend the faith and to seek new converts to it, there is certainly no lack of effort to communicate, but "distortions" of communication are frequent because of the resistance of persons of different faith groupings.

In addition to these consequences with regard to communication, differences in value orientations and the axiomatic beliefs that represent effective religious commitments set some limits, however broad, to the range of alternatives for definition or solution of "problematic" social situations. For instance, one may not, by reason of religious commitment, be able even to consider ways of dealing with social problems that may appear entirely proper and reasonable to those who approach the situation from different evaluational premises.

Differences in those value orientations having a specifically religious (sacred, nonempirical) reference may define the significance of a collectivity or group to its members in such a way as to hinder or completely prevent compromise or negotiation with regard to the social consequences of these differences. Tendencies toward unyielding finality are given special force by the particular characteristics of the value orientations we must recognize as religious. Beliefs and value orientations regarding the nature of man, the problem of evil, the final ends of life—all the primordial questions—are not subject to immediate, pragmatic demonstration in any sense. Yet they stand between the believer—the committed participant—and the agony, chaos, meaninglessness of an incomprehensible world. And, more positively, they define avenues of meaning, security, and fulfillment in an ordered life, transcending the "bare surface of things." Thus, what are from a nonreligious point of view essentially unprovable, "arbitrary" beliefs, values, and symbols are at the same time the essential base of life itself to the religiously devout. So conceived, we see again how differences that are defined as religious can come to have a peculiar acuteness and poignancy. The fact that similar stances and effective intensities can be generated by group differences that are popularly considered to be nonreligious, e.g., nationalism, is worthy of note. But this does not remove the necessity for investigating the possibility that adherence to religious values has distinctive social consequences, even while we recognize that such value-belief complexes as nationalism may contain "transcendental" elements.[7]

In still another way, value orientations may influence interreligious relations through their effects upon the organization and functioning of the religious body itself. The degree of central control and direction and the degree of development of an ecclesiastical hierarchy are only two of the more obvious illustrations. It is not only that such different modes of organization represent, in part, differences in underlying value assumptions, but also that the modes of organization can have a tangibly direct influence upon interreligious interaction, e.g., the extent to which corporate commitments govern the extent of interreligious cooperation in the local community, or the extent to which individuals from different faith groups meet as "representatives" or "ambassadors" from a constituency to which they feel responsible. Although very little precise knowledge is available concerning such differences or the mechanism by which they affect interreligious relations, their possible importance would seem to be great enough to warrant intensive research explorations.

It is necessary to note, also, the possibility that interreligious relations in some instances may be affected by strains and tensions with regard to value orientations *within* a given religious grouping. The highly complicated processes set in motion by internal divergence in values constitute still another largely unexplored area that awaits scientific understanding.

This article has limited itself to a broad exploration of a few salient problems. It has not attempted a formal codification, either of variables and hypotheses or of established empirical findings. Its main objectives have been two: (1) to point to the direct significance of value orientations in interreligious relations;[8] (2) to suggest some of the specific differences in values that may turn out to be important and some of the particular ways by which these differences may affect interreligious conflict and cooperation. It is hoped that the considerations reviewed here will stimulate the basic thinking and research so urgently needed in a little-understood field of great importance to men in society.

---

[7] When communism is referred to as a "secular religion" this is already implied. See Talcott Parsons, *The Social System* (Glencoe, Ill.: Free Press, 1951), Ch. VIII, especially pp. 372–373.

[8] The views expressed on this matter have been influenced, in particular, by Talcott Parsons, *Religious Perspectives of College Teaching in Sociology and Social Psychology* (New Haven, Conn.: Edward W. Harzen Foundation, 1951).

Index